HISTORY OF THE WORLD

THE FACT OF PROGRESS
IS WRITTEN PLAIN AND
LARGE ON THE PAGE OF
HISTORY; BUT PROGRESS
IS NOT A LAW OF NATURE.
THE GROUND GAINED BY
ONE GENERATION CAN
BE LOST BY THE NEXT.

H. A. L. FISHER.

HISTORY
OF THE WORLD

SECOND EDITION

Planned and Edited by

W. N. WEECH, M.A., F.S.A.

HERODOTUS
THE FATHER OF HISTORY

ODHAMS PRESS LIMITED · LONG ACRE · LONDON

CONTENTS

General Editor:

W. N. WEECH, M.A., F.S.A.

SYNOPSIS OF CHAPTERS

5

PREFACE TO THE SECOND EDITION

THE first edition of this History, which appeared during the war, took the record down to the day when Germany attacked Poland. The present edition adds the story of the last twelve troubled years.

Nowadays everyone wants to know something about the diverse peoples of the world and to appreciate their traditions and their hopes. This book tries to tell their stories as simply and accurately as possible, without laying undue stress on political, military or constitutional affairs. The authors have described how ordinary men and women have lived and thought, and how their lives have been influenced by the great figures who have passed over the stage of recorded history.

In the earlier parts the story moves from region to region of the Eastern Hemisphere, as civilization grows and dwindles in its various centres, and the nomad tribes find new homes. Islam and Christendom begin to draw the scattered strands together, and the Age of Discovery brings the Western Hemisphere into the pattern. The later parts deal with the different epochs of world history as a whole. Comparatively few dates have been inserted in the text. The book is designed for the ordinary man or woman, and an effort has been made to give the latter some share in the record of mankind's development.

I am most grateful to the authors who have collaborated with me and to the many readers who have sent me helpful criticisms and suggestions. I also owe a debt of gratitude to my publishers for bringing out this second edition, in spite of the disastrous shortage of paper and skilled labour, and to the individual members of their staff, who have worked cheerfully with me in a difficult task. I have found a great deal of pleasure in planning, writing and editing the History. I hope that some part of that pleasure will be shared by those who read it.

W. N. WEECH.

Cheltenham,
Lammas, 1951.

9

INDEX TO THE MAPS

PROLOGUE

THE story of mankind forms only a small fragment of the earth's long life, and little of that fragment has been set down in written history. Yet even in the period which men have recorded in monumental inscriptions and annals and histories, the face of the globe has been altered profoundly by natural agencies. Our own country comes late into the main stream of history; but already it can show inland cities which were once famous ports, and can tell of other harbours that, with the crumbling of the coast, have long sunk beneath the surface of the sea. New islands have been formed by the submergence of the peninsulas which joined them to the mainland; others have sunk downwards, to become shoals or quicksands.

If we look beyond our own shores and our comparatively brief history, we are conscious of more striking changes. Volcanoes have flung their blankets of lava and ashes over fertile countrysides and busy market-towns. The drifting sands of the desert have choked the water-channels, which for centuries gave life to prosperous cornfields and nourished teeming multitudes of farmers and artisans. The jungle has spread its green rankness over abandoned cities.

SHIFTING BOUNDARIES OF LAND AND SEA

But these things are as nothing to the vast changes which shifted the boundaries of land and sea, during the ages when man had not yet begun his long struggle with the forces of nature. A generation whose childhood has been educated on neat maps and the solid facts of modern geography may find it hard to picture the many alterations which the earth's surface has undergone. Air-views of what geologists call the Primary and the Secondary epochs of the world would show little similarity to the familiar outlines traced on the globes which stand in modern classrooms.

The two epochs were separated by enormous changes, which spread the waters of ocean over vast stretches of land surface; other parts, where during uncounted time the slow deposit of matter had formed the sedimentary rocks, were thrust upward from the sea-bed to become broad tablelands; others again were twisted by the conflict of immeasurable and antagonistic forces into mountain ranges. In the Secondary epoch, a huge oblong of land stretched from the neighbourhood of what is now the west coast of South America through South Africa to Australia. North of this oblong, almost all the present continent of Europe and the western half of Asia were covered by a sea whose shrunken remnants survive as the Mediterranean, the Black Sea and the Caspian. Later, the old southern continent broke up. While it was being split into three parts by the steady encroachment of the waters, another continent came slowly into existence, and this had the effect of uniting New Zealand with Siberia.

11

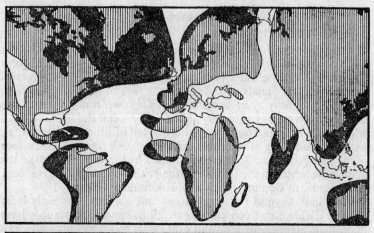

GROWTH OF THE LAND MASSES—I

These maps show the evolution of the land masses (contemporaneous with the early evolution of animal life). The Eocene period (*top*) gave way to the Oligocene (*bottom*).   Black parts of the ancient continents are now under the sea.

The Tertiary epoch saw changes almost as vast. The earth's crust was still too weak to withstand the strains and stresses of subterranean and submarine forces. While these transformed the globe on a grand scale, frost and rainfall and wind carried on a smaller, gradual but ceaseless work of change. Rivers scored their courses over the face of the land, and brought down their deposits of sediment to form new coastal plains. Alterations in climate periodically took place, and with the climate the distribution of vegetation in the various land-masses underwent a slow, corresponding alteration.

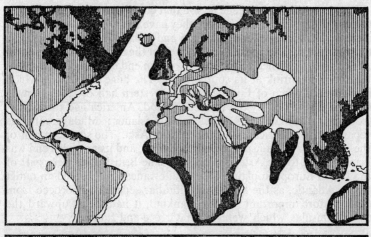

GROWTH OF THE LAND MASSES—II

With the coming of the Miocene period (*top*), North and South America became joined, and with the Pliocene (*bottom*) the world as we know it to-day had almost taken shape. In all four maps the seas and oceans are shown in white.

The accompanying maps show, in broad outline, how land and sea have shifted since the beginning of the Tertiary epoch. During the Eocene and the Oligocene periods, there was very little to suggest the world that we study in our modern atlases. The British Isles were still attached to the northern half of the American continent, which was divided by a broad stretch of water from the southern land-mass of the western hemisphere. India formed part of a huge island to the south of the Asiatic coastline. Europe had not yet extended her eastern plains, but was cut off from Asia by a broad shallow sea.

It was not till the Miocene period that continents and oceans began to assume shapes similar to those they have now. The North Atlantic increased its area, and made Britain and Ireland one large island. A narrow neck of land arose to bind together the two halves of America. Africa was still joined to the south-western end of Europe, but it was beginning to shrink at its southern tip. The huge inland sea, which had covered much of Europe and the western half of Asia, showed signs of drying up. By the Pliocene period, America had thrown off from her mainland the West Indian islands; Madagascar was separated from Africa, and Borneo from Asia. The southern half of the Indian island had sunk below the waves, and its northern end was firmly joined to the Asiatic mainland. The British Isles were part of the North European plain. The Mediterranean had forced an outlet to the Atlantic, as the Straits of Gibraltar separated Morocco from Spain. More important still for mankind, it had thrust upward the two peninsulas which were to be Greece and Italy.

THE BEGINNING OF LIFE

It is impossible to say how long these changes in the earth's surface took to effect. Scientists have made various careful computations from time to time; the figures they set before us tend to grow larger. A million looks neatly intelligible in print; but few of us have a clear mental picture of what it is. When the tale of years passes into thousands of millions, the figures cease to have a meaning for the average individual. We cannot say how old the earth is; nor can we say when life first appeared on the planet. The oldest rock-formations, which are the earliest part of the earth's present crust, show no sign of life. We must remember that the small organisms, which first brought life to the inanimate world, probably left no trace behind. It was not till these organisms had armed themselves with a protective covering, or acquired the power of moving from place to place, that their records were imprinted in the earth's crust, so that modern scientists can study their fossilized bodies and follow the paths they made in distant ages.

Only a thin upper layer of the globe has yet been scratched in the effort to discover how life developed. The conclusions which have been reached to-day may have to be modified profoundly, as more facts are discovered. But it seems probable that some form of vegetable life began, not on land, but in warm stretches of shallow water, when the earth was what may be called "middle-aged". In other words, our planet has been without life for the longer part of its journey through space. And even where there were living things in the waters, it took countless years before life climbed on to land or rose into the air. The earliest forms had been "sunk without a trace"; but their successors left their mark in sand, mud and limestone. Geologists can trace the sequence of living organisms with a fair degree of certainty, though there are gaps in the record.

Naturally, we are chiefly interested in the animal, rather than the vegetable, world. Yet the course of modern history was being determined in part by other changes in the distant past. Great forests were formed, whose giant trees overshadowed a dense, ferny growth. As the earth's crust was cracked and shivered into fresh shapes, or sank down slowly under the waters and their load of silt, these forests were covered and pressed down beneath new layers of earth. With the passage of time, they were changed into the coal-deposits which form the basis of industry and wealth in many parts of the modern world. As one country owes its pre-eminence in manufacturing to its coal-mines, another may hold beneath its surface vast stores of crude oil, on which a great part of the efficiency of modern transport ultimately depends. Through a third, run veins of the heavy metals which are the raw material of most of our conveniences to-day. A fourth may be rich in precious stones and metals. All these were formed in the body of the earth by the slow processes of nature, numberless centuries ago.

The early development of mankind was not influenced by the unguessed existence of these subterranean treasures. But even in that far-off, long-drawn struggle, the shaping of the world's surface played its part. Grassland, forest, mountain, swamp and coastal plain had each its different effect on the human beings who dwelt on them or journeyed over them. In some districts, berries, nuts and edible roots provided a necessary alternative, easily acquired, for those whose main food was the flesh of slain animals. In others, the soil bore grain, which seemed of little value to the passer-by; yet when it was cultivated, its crops were capable of supporting far greater numbers than the grasslands or the forests. Clay, flint, obsidian and other stones lay ready to the hand of man in his widely scattered habitations; and their use twisted his method of life to a new pattern. Where animals abounded, he could find many uses for their bodies, after he had satisfied the primary need for food; sinews, teeth, pelts, furs, bones and horns were all there, for experiment and experience to turn to good account in his everyday life.

THE DEVELOPMENT OF ANIMAL FUNCTIONS

But life had to pass through many stages before man came to use the gifts which nature had moulded for him on the earth and beneath its surface. Our museums show us the relics of what seem, as yet, the earliest memorials of animal existence. Most of us find it hard to concentrate our attention on the primitive forms; unless indeed some kindly biologist explains to us the splendid structure of the eye of the trilobite, a three-lobed marine creature resembling a wood-louse, who seems to have been the first creature to develop the organ of sight; life in the deep waters led later to the disuse of this eye. Usually our interest is not aroused till trilobites, sea-worms and shell-fish have given place to real fishes. It is true that their predecessors possessed the qualities which separate the animate from the inanimate; they absorbed nourishment, they grew, they moved from place to place, they reproduced their kind, and they died. But it was the fish that first had a backbone; and life without backbone is hardly worth consideration. With the fish, there also appear teeth and a well-defined breathing system. All the essentials of a full life under water were there, and the race multiplied itself by spawning eggs so easily and frequently that it has survived to the present day, outlasting hundreds of animal types that came into existence later on dry land, but failed to adapt themselves to changing conditions.

It is not easy to understand how animal life accomplished the great change from water to earth and air. Breathing, food, sight, methods of movement and reproduction had all to undergo radical alteration. Creatures which we call amphibia, because they live both on land and in the water, slowly developed the necessities of land existence through long ages. The gill, through which the fish breathes, gradually gave place to the lung. Earth supplied the creature with food, which it had previously found in the sea. The eye, that had needed the contact of water, adapted itself to the air. Fins and tail had given guidance in sea or lake; legs and feet were needed on the hard earth, and though the tail survives, it no longer serves as a means of progression. In the air, there were other requisites, beak, claw, wing and feathers. More important than these, the egg, which contained the next generation, no longer needed water to cover it. Later came the mammal, the animal that bears its young in its own body and suckles it after birth. The task of carrying on the race had become far more arduous than it had been with the earlier, simpler forms; yet in that very fact lay progress; danger and difficulty could be met only by co-operation and the subjection of the primary instinct of self-preservation to a wider aim. Though its origin was humble and its early existence precarious, the mammal gradually developed until it outstripped by far other forms of life which still survived.

FANTASTIC CREATURES ROAM THE EARTH

But many forms of life held the stage before the mammals became dominant. If mere size were the criterion, the palm must go to those huge reptiles or saurians whose remains have been unearthed and reconstructed for display in our museums. They were larger than any land creature we know to-day; their fantastic appearance added to the terror they inspired by their bulk; the very names that have been given them are shattering—stegosaurus, diplodocus, brontosaurus, gigantosaurus. Most of them moved on land; but some seem fitted for an existence mainly spent in the waters. Some maintained their monstrous bodies on a vegetarian diet, if we may trust the evidence of their teeth. But others, by preying on their ill-protected, unwieldy fellows, earned a right to the poet's description of "dragons of the prime That tare each other in their slime."

It is possible not only to reconstruct the saurians' skeletons from their remains which have been dug up, but also, as it were, to clothe the dry bones with flesh. Walt Disney has drawn us pictorial nightmares of their old-world battles, showing serrated jaws, snake-like necks, and scaly carapaces garnished with hideous bony protuberances. Their cousins, who shared the air with the insects, were equally repulsive; the pterodactyl, with its strong beak and its leathery, featherless wing, was a fit companion for the monsters of the earth. Apart from their bulk and their ugliness, the great reptiles are mainly noticeable for combining a vast cubic capacity for food with very small brain-cases. Both these attributes may have led to their disappearance. Their nourishment demanded almost unlimited supplies of vegetable or animal matter, which were forthcoming only in a warm moist climate. When the climate changed, they failed to adapt themselves to new circumstances, and their different tribes disappeared from the face of the earth.

ANCESTORS OF THE MAMMAL

Contemporary with the great creatures of saurian times, there were tiny animals whose descendants were destined, after many thousands of years, to develop into the mammals. Probably the two stages were separated by a long period of widespread change in the formation and the climate of the globe. The evidence of science leaves little doubt that there have been frequent and violent fluctuations in the earth's temperature. Our planet's fortunes are dependent inevitably on the sun, and as yet astronomers can tell us little of the sun's past. It seems improbable that its heat has increased or diminished to any appreciable extent in the thousands of millions of years during which our globe has spun round it. Some of the violent changes, which have shattered repeatedly the continuity of life on our planet, seem due to changes in the path it follows on its journey through space and the angle at which it rotates. These variations in the earth's orbit and axis, combined with periods of increasing sea-surface and prevalent moist winds, would produce colder conditions over great parts of the earth's surface; such conditions were dangerous to the huge animals whose survival depended on continuous warmth and almost limitless food.

Before the Secondary epoch had closed, the great saurians had disappeared, and when, after the laying down of the chalk, the Eocene period brought in another age of warmth, the mammals had taken their place. The British Isles had a sweltering temperature, and provided sustenance to animals whose descendants we now find south of the Mediterranean. Many of the mammals were large, though they did not reach the size of the largest of their reptile predecessors; but it was the smaller animals whose types were destined to survive and to develop into the horses, camels, pigs and monkeys that we know to-day. They had wide spaces over which to roam, and plenty of grass and nuts and other provender to eat. As the climate grew cooler, and the great mountain ranges were built up by the rending and twisting of the earth's crust in the Miocene period, some types died out; others adapted themselves to the new conditions, under their covering of fur. By the Pliocene period, the distribution of land and water was roughly as it is to-day, and the stage was set for the coming of man. But the scenery was violently distorted when the ice-cap round the North Pole expanded and ground its relentless way southward over mountain and plain.

NEAR-MAN AND MAN

Fragments of skulls and bones found in different parts of the globe seem to show that creatures which were nearly human existed about half a million years ago. It must be remembered that the evidence is still scanty. However skilfully a whole skull is reconstructed from a splintered part, or a body from a few broken bones, we cannot yet accept as fully established facts the theories based on these reconstructions. But it seems almost certain that many districts widely separated from each other supported near-human beings, who moved generally on their feet and could use their hands with considerable effect. They appear to have lacked many human characteristics; forehead and jaw were unlike ours; the neck was barely noticeable; their feet and their legs did not produce a human gait.

From the fact that their fossilized remains are found in Palestine, central Europe, southern Africa and China, it seems probable that the near-humans were widely spread. Present evidence seems also to show that they appeared first in the eastern hemisphere. The best known of the near-human type is called Neanderthal, from the German valley where its remains were discovered. Its skull suggests a comparatively small brain, and possibly, although it could make animal noises, it was incapable of real speech. Like the other mammals, it cared for its young and had taken the first steps in cooperation with its fellows. Its most important human characteristic was that it made good use of its hands and arms. Its reach was widened by the grip of stick or club; it worked stones which it handled for various purposes. But, like the other near-humans which had preceded it, the Neanderthal type failed in the struggle against nature. Articulate speech and a better brain might have enabled it to work with its fellows and overcome the dangers which threatened from climate and its animal neighbours. Perhaps it was swept out of existence by disease. Whatever the cause of its failure, the Neanderthal race, like other near-humans, died out and left no descendant on the earth.

Nature treated humans and near-humans alike with a rigour which civilized man might find almost unendurable, for all his many inventions. Only an amazing will to survive could have carried early man through his troubles. He was the creature of his surroundings, but he was not their slave. Though he did not have to face the tyrannosaurus or the other terrific saurians of an earlier age, he was far feebler in body than much of the surrounding animal creation. He fought with beasts many times his size, armed with teeth and claw that could rend his softer limbs to ribbons. Worse still, he never knew whether nature would blow hot or cold. He was exposed alike to the shock of bitter frost and tropical heat, and the constant struggle to find the bare means of existence for himself and his family. His ability to survive was amazing indeed.

Four times the ice-cap came down from the Pole over the northern land-masses of the two hemispheres; at least three times, it flowed outward from the twisted mountain-ranges of central and southern Europe, the Caucasus, and central Asia. Vegetation was altered by the descent of the ice and its retreat before fresh periods of heat. Fruitful land was turned to desert, as the rain-bearing winds changed their courses. Great stretches of forest fell away before the onset of drought, first to scrubland of evergreens and then to grassland plains. Many animal types disappeared, but others survived by moving south or north, east or west, as the climates of their old habitations changed. Man saved himself sometimes by a similar flight. In other cases, his stubborn determination to hold his ground forced him to find means of adapting his body and his habits to new surroundings; he refused to yield to nature's onslaught, and his powers of reasoning enabled him to conform to fresh conditions, which changed his old way of living, but which his intelligence enabled him to exploit.

TEMPERATE AND INHOSPITABLE ZONES

The two great land-masses of the world, and the islands that lay near them, gave mankind widely differing kinds of climate and surface conditions to test his powers. The ice-field round the South Pole, and the shrunken remnant of the old ice-cap in the north, denied everything necessary to human existence. The lands on either side of the equator were almost as inhospitable. Their hot steamy atmosphere favoured the growth of forests, whose tall, almost branchless, trees built up a nearly impenetrable canopy of foliage and shut out sunshine from the ground below. In their damp shade, there was no animal life which could be of service to man, and the soil was unfit to afford him nourishment. The vegetation was too rankly vigorous to yield to the efforts of the small family groups of the primitive forest-peoples. Except along the river banks, there was little chance for man in the equatorial forests of the Amazon and the Congo basins. It was between the three regions of excessive heat and cold that human life had its chance. Of the two temperate zones the northern was far the more important in the development of mankind, although it must not be forgotten that one great human stock was able to live and thrive in the southern half of Africa and in those countries and islands that lay beyond its eastern coastline.

Two parts of the land-mass of the eastern hemisphere were particularly favourable to human life: the first centres round that narrowed remnant of the old Eocene sea which we call the Mediterranean: the second stretches south of the Caspian, from the eastern shores of the Mediterranean to the Persian Gulf and the Indian Ocean. On both sides of the Mediterranean run mountain ranges, roughly from west to east. On the north, the Pyrenees, the Alps, the Dinaric Alps of Yugoslavia, and the Balkans just fail to make connection with the Caucasus and the mountains of Asia Minor; in the south, the great sweep of the Atlas links across the Straits of Gibraltar with the Sierras of Spain, and through Sicily with the Apennines, to ring the western half of the Inland Sea. The high tableland of Asia Minor forms the junction between the second region and the first. The two parallel ranges which flank this tableland run eastward till they meet the mountains of Armenia and Kurdistan. The line then turns south-eastward, sweeping its two loops round the uplands of Persia through Afghanistan, and joining them in "the Pamir Knot" near the Hindu Kush. The Himalayas, the earth's highest mountains, carry on the line south-eastward. This great mountain-barrier defended the countries that lay to the south of it from the bleak winds of central Asia. From its lofty gorges flowed great rivers—Euphrates, Tigris, Indus, Ganges and Brahmaputra—that carried down loads of precious silt with their waters, and steadily pushed the boundaries of their fertile plains into the sea.

These two regions—the European, Asiatic and African lands that centre round the two halves of the Mediterranean, and the plains and uplands that lie south of the high mountain-rampart of Asia—are of primary importance for the story of man's development. Far away to the east, stretch the river valleys of the Yangtze Kiang and the Hwang Ho, where man made a home and built up a way of life as interesting as those which arose beside Indus, Euphrates and Nile. However, the long history of China stands apart from that of the Mediterranean and the Near East.

THE NORTHERN FLATLAND

Between them stretched a fourth region, which, in the slow process of time, affected its neighbours to east, south and west. This was the great Northern Flatland, which sweeps westward from the neighbourhood of the Yellow Sea, down towards Hindu Kush and the Caspian Sea, and thence across Europe to the Baltic and the Atlantic. There are many differences of level, climate and vegetation in the huge plain. On its western edge, it receives the moisture of the Atlantic winds; in its eastern half, the winter gales spread from it, north to the Arctic circle and south to the mountain-ranges which protect southern Asia. During the winter months, the temperature falls below freezing-point over its whole extent. Much of the Asiatic part of the plain is too far from the sea-coast for the rain-bearing

winds to reach it during the summer. This has made great stretches
of it desert; but, as the climate has altered, the desert areas have
shifted through the ages.

The fifth region that is of special importance for human progress is
Arabia, which, like the great northern plain, affected the Mediterranean and Near East. This "great quadrangular slab" had been
broken off from the African lands in the convulsions of the early
world; its western edge was tilted upwards, from the waters of the
Red Sea, to form a mountain-mass, from which the rest of the tableland slopes down to the Persian Gulf. Though a great part of the
eastern half is now desert, there is evidence of ancient fertility in many
districts. Northward, its sands thrust a broad wedge of waste between
Palestine and Syria on the west and the plains of Euphrates and Tigris
on the east. Round the top of this Syrian desert, there was communication between the coast-lands and Mesopotamia, but the
barren plains forced Palestine to look south towards Egypt and west
to the Mediterranean.

The Arabs call their country an island, and it has water on three
sides. But with the right transport, the man who lives in the Arabian
quadrangle can move west and north and east into richer lands than
his own. There are large oases in the very heart of Arabia; but a
third of the country is sheer desert, and over nine-tenths of it life is
poor and difficult. Only along the western edge do the mountains
draw down rain from the sea-winds in sufficient quantity to yield
fertile crops. Most of the good country lies in the south-east corner
of the quadrangle. In Arabia, as in the Northern Flatland, men were
scattered in the early days into small groups, which seem to have been
contented with a simple unchanging form of life. But, when some
new force came to upset the balance, they moved out into neighbouring lands, and the results of their migrations were far-reaching.

THE FIVE LANDS

The leading parts in the earlier history of man were played by the
inhabitants of the five regions—Near Eastern, Mediterranean, China,
the Northern Flatland and Arabia. To a great extent, the development of these lands was controlled by climate and the facts of
geography. The rich soils of well-watered plains gave an easy livelihood to those who discovered how to cultivate good crops in ever-
increasing quantity. Quiet waters and slow-moving rivers made a
kindly nursery for the first sailors. Men of the grass-land naturally
find themselves driven to tame and use grass-land animals, if
they are to feed themselves, their mates and their young; once this
problem was solved, there was little need for further progress, unless
some violent stimulus shattered the old way of life. The forest
naturally breeds the hunter, whose erect carriage needs widespread
cover if he is to approach his prey successfully; he naturally tends to
range far afield, while his mate creates and cares for the home.

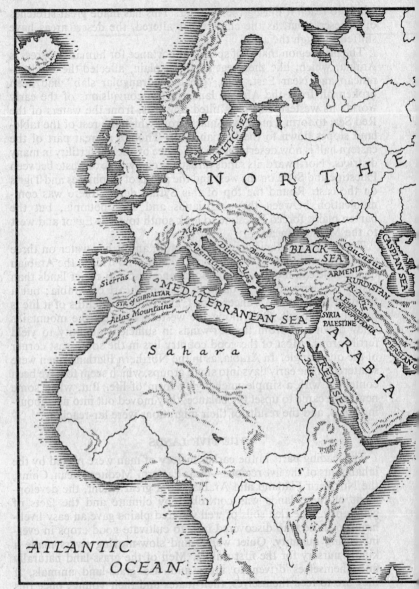

THE NORTHERN

An important part in the earlier history of man was played by the people of the Northern Flatland, the great Plain which extends from the Yellow Sea to the Baltic and Atlantic. The Ural Mountains divide the Asiatic from the European portion, and the Aryans and Mongols formed two corresponding racial groups.

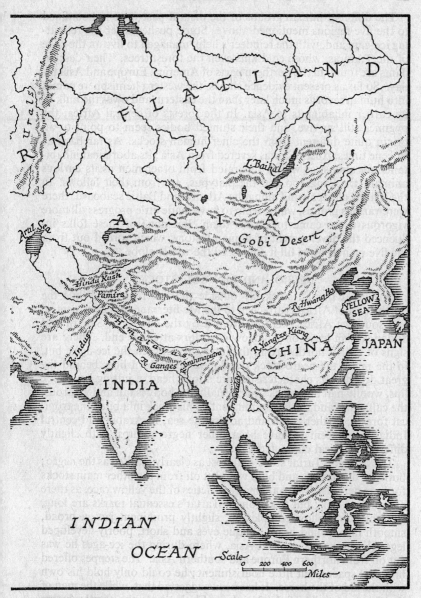

FLATLAND

The inhabitants of the Flatland reared horses and the Mongols became especially dependent upon them, as they had to cover great distances in their search for a scanty and precarious subsistence.   The Aryans represented various white strains, but a distinct stock, taller than others, predominated amongst them.

The different human groups of the distant past were not confined to the five regions mentioned above. Some pushed after the retreating ice-cap, and, with the reindeer's help, managed to live on the edge of the Tundras, whose cold kills even the forest trees. Their descendants are found in the northern parts of America, Europe and Asia to-day. So far as present evidence shows, the western hemisphere comes into human records much later than the eastern, and owes the bulk of its earlier inhabitants to Asia. In the forests of central Africa, the pygmies still survive, and their stunted bodies seem to point to an origin quite different from the chief human stocks. As far back as Eocene times, Australia was severed from Asia; its aboriginal inhabitants are almost as widely separated from other men as its curious animals, the kangaroo and the platypus, are from their fellows. In the islands of Japan and along the Atlantic and Baltic seaboard, there were various groups, which seem to have made little progress till more vigorous tribes came to absorb them. But none of these folks influenced the development of human history, which spread out from the five main centres till it embraced the whole globe.

NEGRO AND MONGOL STOCKS

One great human stock lay outside the five regions. While the north coast of Africa is attached to the Mediterranean region, central and southern Africa is cut off from it by the deserts of Sahara and Sudan, which leave only narrow corridors at either end. There are signs of a drift northward in the intervals between the ice-ages, but, in the main, the negro stock developed on its own lines behind the great deserts. Its characteristics are a long head, a jutting jaw, thick lips, woolly hair and black skin; usually the body is tall and vigorous, the calf small and the heel prominent. This stock inhabited the tropical forests; farther south and across the sea, in Arabia and central India, there seem to have been other negro groups, with slightly different physical characteristics.

The Mongol–Tartar stock is almost as clearly marked as the negro; both are distinctive, and both were cut off from the other main stocks for long periods. There are many varieties of the yellow race, as there are of the black; but the Mongol–Tartar's essential marks are long, straight hair, yellow complexion, slightly prominent jaw, a broad, smooth face, round head, oblique eyes and short, poorly-developed legs. His home was central Asia, where during the ice-ages he was cut off from northern Europe and southern Asia. The steppes offered him vast spaces, but little nourishment; he could only hold his own with the aid of the horse. It has been suggested that, while the men of the European part of the Northern Flatland ate the small, shaggy quadruped, the Mongol–Tartar became its parasite; he lived on mares' milk and moved on horseback over his unfertile grass-lands. As time passed, the yellow men moved north-east and became hunters, or eastward down the great river-basins of Yangtze Kiang and Hoang

Ho, where they learnt the art of agriculture. The western gates that led from the steppes were still barred to the main Mongol stock. But it seems probable that, long before the great migration which created China, some Mongol groups had established themselves in north-east Asia, whence they crossed to Alaska and turned southward into the forests and the grass-lands of North America. They were horse-less, and so they lacked many Mongol characteristics. Their yellow skin deepened till it became copper-red, but the long, straight hair persisted. Perhaps they were joined later in central America by a darker race, which came across the Pacific from south-eastern Asia.

THE ILLUSION OF RACIAL PURITY

It is far harder to define the so-called white races than the yellow or the black, or the tribes that wandered over the Arabian quadrangle. These last developed on well-marked lines; they had small bones and slight wiry bodies; constant exposure to the sun deepened their sallow complexions to a shade of brown; they had brown eyes and aquiline noses.

With the white races, the usual distinctions are confused; skulls may be long or broad or medium; eyes blue, green, hazel, brown or grey: hair wavy or curled, and of any shade from platinum blonde to deep black. Complexions may be pink, dull white, sallow or bronzed, and bodies tall or short, slim or bulky. From the medley that exists to-day, it is difficult to sort out the original racial strains. Such terms as Nordic, Mediterranean and Alpine serve as a rough grouping, but each covers many different strains, which have become fused by the passing of the years. From implements and refuse extracted from deposits of different periods, archaeologists find evidence of a surprising amount of migration in the earliest times. What seems clear is that the Mediterranean and Near Eastern regions soon lost any purity of race and blood they may once have possessed; the same may have happened in the European part of the Northern Flatland.

The idea of a white stock whose blood is free from any admixture of black and yellow, has no foundation in the records of the past. There are Mongol strains spread over Europe to-day, and the caves along the Mediterranean hold many remnants of men who clearly possessed the chief characteristics of the negro. In many secluded spots, cut off from the paths commonly traversed by the bigger tribes, there were small pockets of folk who represented, and still represent, the survival of dwindling races. But apart from these, it seems clear that there were three main stocks round the Mediter-ranean and in the lands north of the long mountain-barrier. The European, African and Asiatic coasts of the Inland Sea were the home of a dark-white race of rather short stature, with small clever hands and sallow or bronzed complexions. In different districts, they inter-mingled early with other stocks, notably in the narrow Nile valley, into which men drifted both from the Arabian quadrangle and from the negro south. Farther along the north coast of Africa, a more robust type prevailed among the Berber tribes, who were akin to the men of southern Spain. The Mediterranean stock spread northwards across the Pyrenees, and the memorials of its expansion were distributed in France and reached as far as the British Isles.

THE ALPINE–ARMENOID STOCKS

The second white stock had its original dwelling in the great mountain-ranges, which guard the three Mediterranean peninsulas. It is usually called Alpine, but its eastern members have slightly different characteristics, and for them the term Armenoid is used. The Alpine tribes spread northwards to western Russia, Denmark, the Low Countries and eastern Britain. The Armenoids inhabited the tableland of Asia Minor, the highlands of Armenia and the long mountain-zone that stretches eastwards to the Pamirs. There were marked differences between various divisions of the Alpine–Armenoid stock; some were tall, others short; their complexions were various shades of lightish brown. Their bodies were sturdier than the Mediterranean men, and they had broad heads.

FOLK OF THE EUROPEAN FLATLAND

North and east of the Alpine folk, lay the European portion of the Northern Flatland. The ebb and flow of the ice-cap caused great changes in its soil and its vegetation; these, in their turn, affected the animal and the human life that ranged its surface, and with grim determination, forced itself to survive the constantly-changing conditions of its unkindly surroundings. Men of Alpine, Armenoid and other types drifted down from their old homes to the broad plain, and mingled their strains with the men and women they found already in possession. But the bulk of the inhabitants of the European Flatland were of a distinct stock. They were taller than either of the two other white stocks; both skin and hair were lighter, and their eyes were often grey, blue or green. Unlike the tribes that roamed the spaces east of the Urals, they did not become parasites of the horse, and their bodies were large and well-proportioned. This Flatland stock is usually called Nordic. Though the name has lately been used for political purposes, to convey a false idea of lordship over other races, it will be necessary to talk of Nordics in our story of the development and the clash of the great stocks who fashioned the history of mankind.

PART I

CIVILIZATIONS OF THE NEAR EAST

CHAPTER I

THE SHAPING OF HUMAN LIFE

WE have seen, in broad outline, how the structure of our globe was slowly developed; how the surface of land and sea was changed widely through the ages; how life came in the waters and on the earth and in the air. We have watched the emergence of near-man and man from the rest of the animals, and the failure of near-man to hold his own against the forces of nature; we have recognized the main stocks into which the children of men are grouped. Man had a vast field for his endeavours, and our eyes cannot survey the whole of it. History confines itself to a few parts of our world, disregarding those lands whose inhabitants were content to accept a bare livelihood from the earth without feeling any urge to improve their lot.

THE STRUGGLE TO SURVIVE

Human records begin in that small group of lands which have been described briefly in the Prologue. We must turn to the Near East and the Mediterranean regions, and see how they were affected by their neighbours in Arabia and the Northern Flatland, before we look at the stories of Persia and India and watch the different tribes of Tartars and Mongols moving into their Turkish and Chinese homes. We must ignore the other lands, "where fragments of forgotten people dwelt" and human life early reached a stage of apathy, where some kind of living could be won from nature by familiar means and there was no desire to change old habits. These lands are said to "have no history", till restless men come to them from beyond the horizon and bring a new method of living. But prehistory comes before history. We must try to understand some of the unrecorded ways in which man struggled upwards from the other animals and "became a living soul". He has left odd, and sometimes ugly, memorials of that long effort, not only in the five regions we have marked as the real cradles of history, but over all the face of the earth. Every year adds to the knowledge which science accumulates, so that we may understand dimly how our remote ancestors shaped their lives.

The earliest men and women lived and died in the open, and so they left no traces; their bodies decayed, or were eaten by the beasts. Probably their implements were mainly fashioned from wood, and vanished as completely as their owners. Consequently there is little to show us how man made the first vital discoveries which were to give him in due time the lordship of the earth—the use of tools, the

27

idea of clothing his body, and the great miracle of fire, which warmed him, frightened off wild animals, and helped him to make the most of his weapons and utensils. Perhaps his reason taught him to make fire, when he had seen a forest blaze started by lightning. More probably the amazing discovery came by accident, when some industrious worker, intent on improving his wooden tool, produced the spark that kindled into warmth and service.

Early man may have made fire in the fashion of the Australian bushmen, who whirl a sharp-pointed stick in a hollow trunk until sparks ignite dry moss and leaves heaped in the hollow. When fire had been discovered it was carefully guarded; if there was a settled camp, the spark was probably never allowed to go out. Men lived in family groups, sleeping round their fire at night and cooking food on it by day, after they had found, again probably by accident, that cooked flesh tasted better than raw. Wooden weapons lasted longer, and their points were harder, if burnt in the fire. When man had the secret of making and controlling fire, he was, once and for all, on a higher plane than the animals which he hunted to obtain food.

WHAT STONE AGE REMAINS TELL US

There have been no remains of men found dating from the second Warm period, although implements have been discovered. The earliest that have survived were made of stone, and from the differences in them archaeologists have divided early mankind into three great divisions: the Old Stone Age, Middle Stone Age and New Stone Age. These are not strictly divisions of time, for man progressed more quickly in some parts of the world than in others; the Old Stone Age might still be in existence in one part of the earth while more advanced men elsewhere had reached the Middle Stone Age. Even in the last two hundred years, peoples have been discovered who had not progressed beyond the Stone Ages. When the English reached Tasmania, though the inhabitants had wooden weapons, tipped with stone, they could not even build a roofed hut; they had no sort of pottery, and did not use bows and arrows, or know how to fish.

The first widely-distributed objects that have been found dating from the Stone Age are hatchets. These were pear-shaped stones, with the edge, or edges, sharpened. Archaeologists can tell to which of the Stone Ages the implement belongs by the method of sharpening employed on it. The first hatchets were improved by little bits being knocked off the edge by sharp blows: this was in the Old Stone Age. At its close, the edges were flaked away by pressure, and by the time of the New Stone Age, grinding had been discovered as a method of making stone better suited to the purposes required of it.

The colder conditions brought by the descent of the ice seem to have killed off near-man. True man, with his better brain, managed to adapt himself, and from the skins of animals he killed with his stone weapons, he made himself clothes, which were probably laced together with leather thongs. He took to living in caves, which he decorated with drawings of beasts he knew. He used bone and ivory for more delicate weapons, and he made needles. The reindeer, driven south by the ice, served for food as well as clothing, and their horns made useful tools, such as picks, which men used when they wanted to enlarge their caves; later, they learned to mine for flint. A skeleton of a Stone-Age miner has been found in Belgium; he had been killed by a fall of rock, and lay as he had fallen, with his deer-horn pick in his hand. Coloured pictures painted in the caves at Altamira in Spain are perhaps thirty-five thousand years old; they show a remarkable artistic skill, being vivid and lifelike, and the animal portraits are far better than most of the efforts of their descendants.

The fourth ice-period was comparatively short. Man managed to survive it, though many of the great animals perished, as well as the near-human species. When the ice had retreated, Europe was covered with a dense forest that only gave way to grass-land in a few places. Through the forests roamed herds of elephants, wolves, lions and bears. Formerly, the climate had specially favoured the Sahara and the regions lying south of the Mediterranean and stretching eastward from it to the rivers Oxus and Indus. Early man had flourished there; but when the ice-field shrank northward, the winds and the rainfall altered, and the Sahara became the desert it is now. All round the two halves of the Mediterranean were strips of fertile land. At its south-east corner, well-watered districts fringed the coast, curving round to link up with the basins of Euphrates and Tigris and form the area which is often called the Fertile Crescent. On poorer lands, wandering people, such as the upland Berbers of North Africa, led a nomad life as huntsmen. In richer districts, this life gave place to that of the herdsman; man had learnt that, instead of merely capturing and killing animals, it was easier and more profitable to tame them, feed them and breed from them.

KITCHEN MIDDEN FOLK

In northern Europe, all the interior was either forest or swamp, and man was forced to live along the sea-coast, where his lot was desperate. In Denmark, there are huge ridges running parallel to the shore, for miles on end; these were originally made by the refuse thrown out by hundreds of generations of early men, who are consequently known as the Kitchen Midden folk. The ridges consist mostly of shells of the fish that was their most common food, stone weapons, and bits of the earliest known pottery. It is highly probable that these were the first people who utilized the dog as a domesticated and companionable animal.

The Middle Stone Age went on in Europe for perhaps forty thousand years; so slow was the improvement of man. Skeletons have been found, varying in type; they are named as a rule after the place of their discovery. Thus, though some types of Aurignacian man, so called after the district of France where their remains were found, are very nearly as small as the Neanderthal near-man of a much earlier period, some, notably the variety known as Cro-Magnon, were over six feet in height; their direct descendants still exist in Wales, France, Spain and North Africa. This Middle Stone Age people had a larger brain-case than their predecessors, and we find left crude drawings and carvings which give an idea of their habits and appearance. The men, it seems, were hairy, and the women very fat, and they already decked themselves with ornaments. Family life had by now given way to tribal life, and men seem to have hunted, or tended their flocks, in an organized fashion under leaders. Their dead—or at any rate, some of them—were buried, usually in the cave where the family lived. Perhaps dreams of some departed chieftain or friend produced the first ideas of a future life.

The Middle Stone Age gradually merged into the New Stone Age. More remains have been found belonging to this period than to either of the previous Stone Ages. This is not only because it is nearer our own times, but also because there were many more things in use. Grinding was improved till stone weapons became very effective, and a great stride forward was made when man learned to fix his stone axe to a handle. The handle was usually of wood or bone; holes were drilled in the stone, and the head was tied on. Bows and arrows, the latter tipped with stone, were invented, and there were almost as many tools as a modern carpenter possesses. Though otherwise much in advance of the Middle Stone Age men, artistically the New Stone Age people lagged far behind their predecessors. Their drawings were not only of animals: they included circles and the beginnings of geometric designs. An interest in form and mass was awakening, and the heavenly bodies were reproduced in rough drawings.

POTTERY AND AGRICULTURE

During the transition from Middle to New Stone Age, came the invention of pottery: perhaps more than anything else, this has helped archaeologists to discover the habits of early peoples. Probably pottery came into being in different parts of the world independently, and only after great efforts to make a water-tight vessel. Men dabbed clay on whatever vessel they already had, and probably the accidental hardening by fire of one of these mud-covered objects showed them that baked clay could be put to many uses. Western people first plastered mud over a basket foundation; their early pots show the impression left by the reeds. In the east, they were probably moulded on gourds. Pottery was cheap to make, and easily broken; so there are plentiful remains to be found in and around early settlements. Since it was made by women we can discern whether the invaders married the women of the conquered race, or whether they brought their own women with them, the result of this latter course being a sudden alteration in the style of pottery. The potter's wheel was not invented for long ages—but so skilled did potters become that, before the introduction of the potter's wheel into Egypt, round jars were made whose circumferences were true to within one-thousandth part of an inch.

It was in the development of the human hand, especially the thumb, that man gained his advantage over animals. Without it, the holding and manipulating necessary for the making of tools and other objects would have been impossible. This gain did not go unbalanced; undoubtedly other parts of the body lost their gifts as the hand gained. The sense of smell, for instance, which must once have been a great help to primitive man, has almost entirely vanished, except for discriminating between the more obvious odours and as far as it is linked with the complementary sense of taste.

Agriculture began in the New Stone Age. For centuries, the women of the tribe had collected and crushed the seeds of the wild grasses; then it was discovered that these could be planted to produce a crop. It is not known where corn was first cultivated. Possibly it was in Switzerland; possibly in Mesopotamia or the Indus valley. The earliest grains to be sown were barley and wheat; maize came first in America. Instead of roaming as a hunter, or moving along with his herds to seek for fresh pastures, man settled down, at any rate for short periods, so as to be near the crops he had sown. At the start, the work was done by the women, and the ground was hoed; but soon a rude plough was invented, and man had to undertake the heavy work entailed in order to produce a regular crop.

FISHERMEN, LAKE DWELLERS AND TEMPLE BUILDERS

During the past century, an unusual shallowness in one of the big Swiss lakes disclosed hundreds of piles driven into the bottom. On investigation, these proved to be the remains left by a New Stone Age community. Their homes were built of wood, on platforms which rested on piles driven into the bed of the lake; bridges, which could be removed at night for safety, joined them to each other and to the mainland. Like other men of the times, they kept domestic animals. They got a great part of their food by fishing with line and hook, through trapdoors in the floors of their houses. They had what may have been the first boats ever invented—which consisted of long, hollowed tree-trunks—and they paddled over the lake, setting large fishing-nets, very similar to those used to-day. They sowed corn on the shore near their homes, and also cultivated flax. This meant a great step forward, and clothes were now made of woven material, as well as from the skins of animals.

There seems to have been a leader to each community, and the work was often organized labour. Their pots were shaped like the leather vessels, consisting of whole skins of small animals, which they

had previously used to hold liquid. Though their most noted relics
have been found in Switzerland, it is certain that lake-dwellers existed
in many other parts of the world. Scotland, as well as England, had
them: remains of their dwellings and their wooden boats can be seen
to-day at Glastonbury. Other New Stone Age remains can also be
seen in England—the enormous stone tombs they erected to some of
their dead, and the great temples, such as that at Stonehenge. The
size of the stones is immense, and it is obvious that the builders must
have been organized on efficient lines, in order to move and set up
the colossal blocks. At Carnac, in Brittany, for miles across the
country, stretch parallel lines of enormous stones, spaced at intervals.
These stone avenues may have been used for religious processions
and also for some kind of chariot races; for the New Stone Age
people used the horse for hauling and riding.

Probably the first vehicles were sledges, and it must have been an
enormous improvement when someone invented the wheel. The
horse came originally from the great Northern Flatland of Asia. Before its advent in the west and south, the donkey was chiefly used
for transport. For long ages, harnessing was very badly managed,
and the animal's breathing was hampered. He was not able to use
his full strength, and it was many centuries before he was shod.

WANDERINGS AND WARS

When quarrels occurred between tribes and they set out to fight
each other under their tribal leaders, everyone killed as many opponents as possible. Then the conquerors discovered that it was a
great saving of trouble if, instead of killing men, they made them
prisoners and took them home to work as servants. In this way
began slavery, which has lasted down to modern times.

As will be seen in later chapters, nearly all the advances in civilization were made in the east and spread slowly westward. The Stone
Age method of life persisted in Europe, especially in the western
parts, for centuries after the peoples of the Near East were using
metals and enjoying a high level of comfort. Even the domestic
animals of Europe came from distant lands; the cattle kept by the
Lake Dwellers of Switzerland were of an eastern type, very different
from those that roamed wild in the forests of the Northern Flatland.
Before they learned to settle in communities, nomadic tribes in
regions possessed of suitable pasturage owned herds of cattle which
represented the acquisition of wealth.   The males were used for
draught work, and the milk from the females provided an invaluable
source of food.   Needless to say, the beasts possessed by these wanderers differed vastly in appearance from modern dairy cattle.

It is known that near-man did not survive the last descent of the
northern ice-cap, and probably many human types also succumbed
in the long struggle with adverse climate and hostile beasts. No one
has yet been able to decide with certainty on which portions of the

globe man first appeared. His few early remains are widespread; but immense and continued changes of temperature in the different lands greatly influenced the growth or the decay of the different groups. Some tribes dwindled into impotence. Others were cut off from their fellows—for example, the Australians by the waste of waters, and the negroes of Africa by the great Sahara barrier. Others again multiplied their numbers in favourable surroundings, and spread their surplus members over distant countries. The dark-whites of the Mediterranean race reached northward to Britain and Ireland. The tall fair Nordics seem to have moved incessantly over the European part of the Northern Flatland, and from time to time groups of Alpine–Armenoid and Mongol stock mingled with them.

ARYAN AND SEMITIC TONGUES

These European nomads must have lived together long enough to use a common tongue, and to reach a fair level of life, before they separated to their later dwelling-places. After this dispersion, each language developed on individual lines; but they kept much the same sounds for words indicating things they had owned in the life they had shared in common. Many of these terms, which now are used from the Atlantic to the Indian Ocean, prove that, in their earlier days together, they had learnt the rudiments of farming. Their common tongue, with its many widespread variants, is known as Aryan. It is important to remember that "Aryan" denotes the primary language, from which many different ancient and modern languages are descended. It does not mean a common racial stock. The men and women of the different tribes who used the Aryan speech lived for many centuries in constant communication with one another, as they roamed the steppes north of the Black Sea and the Caspian; but they were of different blood.

Among the most interesting of the Aryan-speaking peoples were the Kelts; they penetrated into Gaul and Britain, and overcame the Mediterranean tribes who had preceded them into western Europe. Later on, other groups, somewhat like them in appearance and speech, settled in Germany and Scandinavia; their womenfolk took an active part in the life of the community. Tribes, later known as Slavs, drifted towards the Danube and Black Sea lands. South-eastward, the Aryan-speaking groups marched into the Iranian tableland, and some filtered slowly across the Himalayas, to settle in northern India. In the Indus valley and the Punjab, there had already been a civilization, whose remains have been unearthed at Mohenjo-Daro and elsewhere. The invaders passed on to the Ganges country, where they made an easy conquest, but they did not intermarry with the conquered; in the south of India, the original inhabitants were left undisturbed and are known as Dravidian.

The second primary language was Semitic. The languages which developed from it include Hebrew, Arabic, Abyssinian and many

B   (H.W.)

others. The early tribes which spoke it were tall people of a dark-white complexion; they lived in the fertile parts of Arabia, or wandered about in the high tableland of the country, and in times of drought always overflowed into other districts.

The negro type seems early to have passed across from Africa to south India, and thence down into Malaya, Australia, and Tasmania. From there, they may have worked their way through Polynesia to Central America; for remains found in all these parts show traces of a similar negroid race.

THE YELLOW-SKINNED PEOPLES

While the negroes went south over the land-masses, and the Semitic tribes wandered round Arabia, and the Aryan peoples occupied most of northern Europe, another great group spread over Asia. These were the short, squat, yellow-skinned stock which is called Mongol or Tartar. They travelled ever farther eastward, menacing the early people of China. Some of their bands had crossed the Behring Straits, and travelled down through the American continent, as well as across to Greenland. Like other early people of the Northern Flatlands, they lived on horse-flesh, and existed by following the herds of wild horses that roamed over northern and central Asia. Then they learned to ride, and seldom moved on their own feet, being on horseback all the time, except when they were asleep. The shape of the face and skull varied in different types of men, according to the different uses to which the muscles were put—that is, according to whether the man lived on fruit and berries, or was a flesh-eater, or a milk-drinker. It is thought probable that the Mongols got their broad flattened faces and oblique eyes from their habit of sucking milk from the mare's udder. The Pamirs and the dense forests about the region of the Ural Mountains, prevented them having much intercourse with the tribes of Europe; but the Aryan peoples learned the use of the horse from them. Most Mongols were not creative, their one passion being for a life of movement and violence. Urban civilization meant nothing to them, and they were not interested in progress, except in such matters as improving harness or bettering their fighting weapons. To this day, their descendants, riding over central Asia, lead much the same lives as their early ancestors.

THE NOMAD AND THE FARMER

The great and all-important difference between the early peoples was that between the nomad and the farmer. When wanderers came to exceptionally fertile lands, they settled down, and instead of merely hunting or herding animals, they domesticated them. Then they began to grow corn and flax, and work methodically under leaders for the good of the community. Instead of using portable tents, they took to fixed abodes. But the tribes who still wandered, either on horseback or on foot, had no respect for their settled neighbours. When they came upon a civilized community, they attacked it, if they were strong enough, and either looted all they could, or else settled themselves as conquerors and became farmers in their turn. Throughout history occur the struggles between the nomad and the citizen; invasions of fertile land by the peoples of the desert were always happening; they were sometimes caused by famine, sometimes by increase of population, or by the rising of a leader with a lust for power.

It is noticeable that religion was not a great force among nomad peoples, but as soon as they settled into civilized communities, it grew stronger. Whether early men got their idea of God from the powerful personality of some leader, or from the power they associated with natural forces, the gods soon developed definite personalities. Those worshipped by the wanderers were single deities, whereas the gods of the settled communities were married. This was natural, as the importance of a large family, and consequently of marriage, was not so great among the nomads, whose food was usually scarce, and who thus looked upon children as a mixed blessing. Population increased much more quickly among the settled tribes; with the necessaries of life in abundance, people had time to use their brains. With the growth of religion, there grew up a new class, that of the priesthood, who did much to develop the processes of thought.

While the Western peoples, whether sedentary or migratory, retained the old rough life, civilization grew, as the ensuing chapters show, in the lands we now call the Near East. Away in the Far East, men slowly built up another civilization whose story is told in Part VII. The western hemisphere and Australasia came late into the stream of human progress, and their comparatively uneventful stories can be briefly outlined in later pages when we read how the vigorous sailors of Europe came to their distant shores.

CHAPTER 2

EGYPT

EGYPT, as Herodotus said, is the gift of the Nile. The great river cut the narrow valley out of the barren rock, brought down fertile soil which settled on its banks, and finally, by its yearly floods, provided a perfect natural means of irrigation, ensuring a comfortably easy existence to any inhabitants of the land.

The country consists of two well-defined parts: a long narrow strip of soil on either side of the gently winding river, and a fan-shaped delta, formed by the many mouths of the stream running into the Mediterranean. On either side of the valley, the rocks rise in sheer cliffs. Beyond them, stretches the desert—to the east, between the

Nile and the Red Sea, only a narrow strip, but on the west, continuing unbroken for hundreds of miles. The headwaters of the river rise far to the south in the Nubian mountains, and its smooth course is interrupted by six cataracts. Nearly five hundred miles of the river, from the sea up to the First Cataract, are easily navigable.

The history of Egypt is less broken, and the blood of her peoples less mixed, than those of other nations, owing to the shut-in nature of the country. There are only three narrow approaches—from the south, by the Nile; from the west, along the coastal border of the Mediterranean; from the north-east, by the narrow peninsula of Sinai. The climate is delightful; there is perpetual sunshine, a low rainfall, and a dry and bracing air. Consequently, relics of ancient times, especially the graves covered in warm sand, are wonderfully preserved, and we can look to-day on objects which have scarcely altered since being buried over six thousand years ago.

Historians divide the records of Egypt into different dynasties, each consisting of the reigns of several kings, and they speak of an even earlier age, known as the Predynastic period. This period is also prehistoric—that is to say, it precedes all written records, and knowledge of it has been obtained from the discovery of its burials. It is not certain where these first Egyptians came from, but it is thought possible that they moved from the east, via Aden and down the Nile, probably as early as 5000 B.C. They were short, slenderly built but very strong, with long narrow skulls, pointed chins and flat noses. Their hair was very dark and they were usually clean-shaven, though some had moustaches and a small pointed beard. (Even to-day this early type of Egyptian survives in some villages of the country.) They spread down the valley, and when the marshes of the north became what is now the land of the Delta, they realized its fertility and settled there also. For over a thousand years, they remained undisturbed by invasion and in this rich and fertile region made rapid strides in civilization.

THE EARLY EGYPTIANS

These Egyptians lived in a great number of small independent tribes, each having an animal as its totem or badge: this it came to look upon as the god of the tribe, and at that stage the animal was treated as a sacred beast. The people had a firm belief in life after death, and throughout the ages, the Egyptians retained a great horror of physical death, refusing to admit that a man could really die. So when they buried their dead, they thought of them as still needing all the things they used on earth. In the earliest graves that have been found, the body is always lying on its left side, with the arms bent and the knees drawn up to the chin. The graves were parallel with the course of the river.

All round the body were grouped jars containing supposed necessaries for the future life; corn was there, drink also, and the men had their favourite weapons with them. These were made of stone, which was worked so skilfully that it was used even after the discovery of copper in Sinai. The Egyptians had early learned to attach a stone head to a handle of ivory or wood, and the sharpness of the weapons is amazing as an example of primitive craftsmanship.

In order to beautify themselves in the next world, the women had in their graves small pots of rouge, also malachite for making up the eyes, together with the little palette used for grinding it. These earliest discovered jars were beautifully made. Although the potter's wheel was then unknown and they were modelled entirely by hand, they are symmetrical and show great artistic merit. The colour was bright red, sometimes with a black rim made by drying the jar upside down in the ashes. Often they had simple patterns in white, and were highly polished with a bone polisher. Examples of this work may be seen in our principal museums.

AGRICULTURE AND THE CALENDAR

These men were skilled agriculturalists, understanding irrigation and quick to take advantage of the flood seasons of the Nile. They invented the device called the *shaduf*, which is used by the Egyptian peasants to this day, to carry the waters of the Nile to the canals which were dug on a level several feet above the surface of the river. It consists of a seesaw arrangement, with a bucket at one end and a weight at the other. The worker lifts the weight: down goes the bucket into the water. When he lets the weight go, its descent raises the bucket to the higher level, from which it is quickly tipped into the canal. Where the river is especially low, several of these *shadufs* are used, one above the other. The chief crops grown were split wheat, barley and flax. In the graves, mouldering fragments of linen clothes are yet to be seen, and the fineness of the linen weave is still perceptible.

From the advanced state of writing in the earliest dynastic times, it is certain that the predynastic peoples possessed a kind of writing of their own, of which, however, no traces have been found. It must originally have consisted of pictures, with signs for different syllables, but by the first dynasty, an alphabet had already developed, although the syllable signs were often used along with it. The first dated event in all history is the setting up of the calendar in 4241 B.C. The Egyptians divided the year into twelve months of thirty days each, and the five days remaining were kept as a holiday at the end of the year. Centuries later, the Romans adopted this arrangement; so the European calendar is directly descended from that originated and habitually used by the Egyptians.

Throughout this remote period, quarrels frequently occurred among the tribes in the Nile valley, and as some grew more skilled at the making of weapons, they gradually gained ascendancy over their neighbours. When one tribe conquered another, the defeated were forced to acknowledge the conqueror's totem as their supreme god; their own would still be worshipped, but had to take a subordinate place. So for ages, in inscriptions and pictures, we find Thoth the ibis-god, Sebek the crocodile, Anubis the jackal and Pasht the cat. About the year 4300 B.C. two tribes had absorbed all the rest, and the valley was divided into two kingdoms. The northern lands of the Delta were ruled by the tribe whose totem was the uraeus serpent. The narrow land of the south acknowledged the sway of Horus the falcon-god, and took the symbol of the vulture-goddess, Nekhebet.

THE OLD KINGDOM, c. 3500–2700 B.C.

Eventually the kingdoms of Upper and Lower Egypt became one. Legend says that Menes was the first king of the joint kingdom. The south conquered the north, but the Delta was never in subjection; the country remained as two kingdoms under one ruler. Thus, if at any time, through war or the reign of a weak monarch, there was unrest and dissension, the country split into the two kingdoms as of old. The king, known as Pharaoh (which means "the Great House"), wore a double crown, composed of the white one of the south fitted inside the red of the north, and he was adorned with the symbols of the two kingdoms—the vulture and the serpent.

There was fairly frequent intercourse between Egypt, Syria and other lands, and some Armenoids from the north settled in Egypt, intermarried with the natives and produced a livelier, big-boned type, with a larger brain capacity than had the first inhabitants. Foreign trade began, and Egypt exchanged her surplus wheat for wine and timber, which she lacked.

At the Court there was a very high standard of living. Class-divisions were clearly defined: there were the royal family, the nobility, the priests, scribes, skilled workers and peasantry. The scribes dealt with all records of business, government and religion. An excellent writing material was ready to hand; this was papyrus, which grows along the banks of the Nile in great quantities. The Egyptians pasted the leaves together, with the edges overlapping, thus forming a thin sheet. For the finished product, two sheets were pasted back to back with the grain going opposite ways. The papyrus plant is now extinct in Lower Egypt, but is found in the regions of the Upper Nile and also in Abyssinia.

The houses of the nobles were extremely comfortable. They were built of brick and stood in handsome gardens, with palm trees and ornamental lakes. The roofs were flat, and usually had an awning made of cleverly worked tapestry. Carpenters were extremely skilful; houses were beautifully furnished and the walls tastefully painted. Statues were coloured, and had eyes of rock crystal, which gave them a natural look. Gold was used plentifully for decoration in the houses of the rich, and the nobles were entertained by skilful dancers and by musicians playing on the harp.

The animal-gods that had developed from the tribal totems were still worshipped, especially by the peasants, to whom they seemed old-fashioned, friendly gods. But the religion of the state had been changing, and Re, god of the sun, who, together with the Nile, was regarded as producer of Egypt's fertility, was worshipped as supreme over all. There was a strong tendency to harmonize this sun-cult with the earlier totem-worship. Thus Horus was identified with the sun, and the sun represented as a falcon flying across the sky. The wish to combine the two ideas led to amazingly contradictory legends, so that Horus is also regarded as great-grandson of the sun.

There are many versions of the story of Osiris and Isis, the parents of Horus. They were brother and sister, as well as husband and wife, and were grandchildren of the Sun-god. Their brother Set hated Osiris, and managed to kill him, casting his coffin into the sea. It was carried to a foreign land, where a tree grew up and enclosed it. Isis wandered in search of the body for many weary years; at length she found it and brought it home to Egypt. Her son Horus, in endeavouring to avenge his father, had many fierce encounters with Set. The cult of Isis grew in importance during later Egyptian history. Osiris was associated with the Nile and the spring rebirth of Nature. He was regarded as patron of the dead and his worship spread all over the land. Naturally he was important to this people who believed firmly in an after-life, and the prosperous nobility took great care to make their tombs really comfortable abodes for the departed spirit. The climax was reached in the second dynasty, when the more lavishly furnished tombs were even equipped with lavatories for the use of the departed.

The outside of the tomb began to be considered. During the second dynasty, copper being then in use, men were able to quarry huge limestone blocks, which were regarded as too precious for ordinary houses, or even for palaces, and were kept exclusively for tombs; those of the kings became more and more magnificent.

PROGRESS IN ARCHITECTURE

The first architect in stone was Imhotep, chief counsellor to the Pharaoh Zoser. During the lifetime of his patron, Imhotep designed and built for him at Sakkara a burial-place of pyramid shape. This still stands, and is known as the Step Pyramid. The shape was adopted by succeeding kings, and each, in his own lifetime, had one of these vast monuments erected; several of them remain to-day, outwardly much the same as when they were built, to make us marvel when we think of the labour required for their construction. The Great Pyramid, built at Gizeh for the Pharaoh Khufu, covers thirteen acres, and is solid, save for the various burial-chambers and their connecting passages. It is obvious how absolute was the power of the rulers of those days, and how hard-working were the lower classes. For the horse was then unknown in Egypt, and a hundred thousand men are said to have worked for twenty years on the building of the Great Pyramid. Some were slaves, but the majority were probably procured by means of a forced levy of the population.

At the death of a Pharaoh, his body was carefully preserved; the entrails, heart and brain were removed and placed in sealed urns beside the body, in its richly decorated coffin. In order that the king should not lack service, various personal attendants were—during the first few dynasties, at any rate—put to death and buried with him. Smaller pyramids stood all round that of the monarch; these belonged to the nobles, who thus rested near their master and could attend him still beyond the grave. These elaborate tombs were, however, liable to plundering and looting by marauders.

THE RULE OF PHARAOH

Pharaoh was all-powerful. So much above the people, even the nobles, was he that, in the course of time, he was regarded as being the son of the chief of the gods. Very often a dynasty was named after its family god, and every Pharaoh had a throne-name added to his own at accession. It was partly owing to this attribute of divinity that the king and heir-presumptive always married within the royal family. The other reason was that descent and succession to property went through the female; so it greatly strengthened the claim of a prince to his father's throne if he married his sister, half-sister, aunt, or even his stepmother. This excessive inbreeding naturally weakened the royal stock.

Next in rank to the Pharaoh came the hereditary princes, who each owned almost as much land as the king himself. They were very powerful, often holding important government posts. The Pharaoh was head of a very efficient organization, with a complicated system of taxes and a clearly defined code of laws. As yet there was no money; goods were bartered and all taxes were paid in kind. So in order to store his dues, which consisted of quantities of wheat, flax, cattle, timber or wine, the Pharaoh needed vast storehouses and a competent staff to run them.

Trade was carried on both by sea and land. For long ages, the people had been accustomed to travel on the Nile. They used boats with both sails and oars, though probably the first of all, which may have been made of bark, were paddled, not rowed. The large square sails were set high up the mast, so as to catch the breeze above the high banks of the river. Then they ventured down through the delta into the Mediterranean. It is unlikely that, during the time of the Old Kingdom, cargo-boats crossed the easterly end of that sea. Goods were brought by land through Sinai, whence came copper; the chief import from the north was rare wood, much valued for its use in beautifying furniture. Traders sailed far to the south down the Nile, and donkey caravans also travelled into Nubia, bringing back ivory, gold, fragrant gums and ostrich feathers.

Among the famous monuments which remain standing, though somewhat defaced, is the Sphinx. This creature has the body of a lion, but the head was a portrait of the Pharaoh Khafre, who built the second of the three pyramids at Gizeh. The Sphinx lies a little distance away, guarding the huge tomb. Several statues of the Pharaohs of the first dynasties have been discovered. But Egyptian art was conventional. After the formative period of the first three dynasties, it settled into a style which persisted for centuries; the features are slightly conventionalized, the dress entirely so. For three thousand years afterwards, the Pharaohs were always shown in the clothes of the fourth dynasty. Pepi I built many splendid temples for the gods, using red granite as a building material; successive Pharaohs followed his example.

A little while before his reign, there lived a wise man named Ptahotep, who wrote a book of maxims. These were used in schools for many years afterwards, so doubtless several generations of Egyptians were brought up on them. His advice was extremely practical: he recommended respect towards one's betters, lest they ill-treat one, and respect towards inferiors, lest the gods be angered. The *nouveau riche* was warned not to put on airs, and the wisest man was held to be he who keeps his mouth shut. Ptahotep gave advice on various points of etiquette, and concerning the management of a wife, said: "Give her food in abundance, and raiment for her back; anoint her with unguents. Be not harsh in thy house, for she will be more easily moved by persuasion than violence."

Towards the end of the sixth dynasty, Pepi II ruled. He enjoys the distinction of having the longest reign in history; he lived to be a hundred, reigning for ninety-four years. This was fatal to the country; the old man became incapable of keeping a firm control of the government. The great feudal nobles had gained tremendous power, and when the Pharaoh died, chaos resulted. There were quarrels about the succession, and negro tribes invaded the land from the south. Men neglected to pay their taxes; they rallied round different claimants to the throne; they fought spasmodically against the invading negroes; the Delta broke away from Upper Egypt. In this manner the Old Kingdom came to an end.

THE MIDDLE KINGDOM, c. 2400–1800 B.C.

For several hundred years after Pepi II's death there was no real king in the land. Leaders sprang up in different parts of the country, and often several persons were calling themselves Pharaoh at the same time. After this period of anarchy one race, stronger than the others, gained the ascendancy, and settled themselves fairly firmly on the ancient throne of Egypt.

From the remains of these kings, it appears that they had a strain of negro blood in them, which may account for the new energetic spirit that entered the government. In order to make the succession surer, these Pharaohs hit upon the idea of naming their son as successor and proclaiming him as co-regent. In this way, the people and officials were already accustomed to the rule of the new king before his accession. Unlike most of their predecessors, these new rulers really had a conception of their duty to their subjects; the chief boast on their memorial tablets is of the plenty and happiness of their reign.

At the beginning of the twentieth century B.C. Senusret III managed to conquer and hold the land as far as the Second Cataract, and he bequeathed to his son a united and peaceful kingdom. This son, Amenemhet III, saw to the governing of his kingdom in person. He appointed governors over different provinces, but made frequent tours through the kingdom, travelling mainly on the Nile. He was a great trader and sent his fleet far afield in search of goods. Trade flourished with the peoples of Crete, Syria and Babylon, as well as the less civilized tribes of the south. The king took an active interest in farming, and reorganized the irrigation system of the Nile. There was already a canal connecting the river with the Red Sea. An efficient army was built up, and this was retained as a permanent part of the state's organization.

EGYPTIAN RELIGION

But in spite of political changes, social and religious life was very much the same as during the Old Kingdom. The upper classes of Egypt lived in great luxury, and the poor very much as they still do to-day. The former prided themselves greatly on personal cleanliness; they shaved their heads and faces and wore wigs. Their religion was really unchanged, although Amon had come to be regarded as the same deity as Re, and was worshipped by the name of Amon-Re as chief of the gods. The habit of burying slaves with their masters to serve them in the next world had died out; instead of this, they had little statues representing slaves, and they made models of ships as symbols of the possessions which the dead man would have in the next world. Rolls of papyrus, inscribed with spells, were also buried in the tombs; these were designed to prevent the body from telling of its earthly misdeeds when it was being judged by the gods. They were sealed in jars, and sometimes, as well as spells, there would be a whole library of different works—tales of adventure, travel and magic, songs and poetry—all of which were designed for the entertainment of the body in its new life.

Though the Egyptians were a gifted people and loved luxury, they cared little for thought or contemplation. They never liked discarding anything, so in spite of new ideas, fashions or beliefs, the old usually persisted. Consequently we find what seem to us extremely contradictory beliefs. Despite the proclamation of Amon-Re as the all-powerful god, the Egyptians continued to worship all those who had previously been considered great, even their oldest totemic animal-gods. In the same way, they stated that a virtuous life on earth would avail nothing after death; its sole advantage was that, on the whole, it paid to behave decently when alive. At the same time, they believed that after death the gods gave judgment, after enquiring into earthly actions. Mental laziness prevented the people, with one notable exception, from evolving a worth-while religion.

THE SHEPHERD KINGS

During the dynasty of the Sebek Pharaohs, whose patron was the crocodile-god, the land was invaded by a race called the Hyksos, who came from the north-east through Syria. In their army they had horses, which were previously unknown in Egypt and gave the invaders an easy victory. Some of their weapons may have been made of iron; all were vastly superior to those of the Egyptians. They set up their own chief as Pharaoh, and ruled the land, as the Shepherd Kings, for several centuries. They were a barbaric horde, which cared nothing for civilization. Rich towns were plundered and temples and palaces destroyed. The Shepherd Kings failed to gain the adherence of the whole country; patriot nobles never acknowledged them as Pharaohs. The people of Egypt remembered the looting and despoiling of the land by the Hyksos rulers, and they never forgave it. It spurred them on to become a fighting nation, whereas in earlier times, though well-disciplined and militarily efficient, they had never been enthusiastic in their soldiering.

THE EMPIRE, c. 1600–1000 B.C.

After various risings against the usurpers, at last Ahmose, a descendant of the old royal line from Thebes, managed to drive out the Shepherd Kings. He also had to fight other claimants when he attained to the throne, and in doing so, he killed most of the hereditary princes. The confiscation of their land strengthened the throne considerably.

Ahmose's first concern was his army. It was well organized, and had horse-drawn chariots, with broad wheels and solid leather tyres. The traditional indifference to soldiering disappeared, and not only the lower classes, but the nobles also, eagerly took up a military career. The generals of Ahmose were the first military tacticians who are recorded in history; in the accounts of their battles against the western invaders from Libya and of the expeditions into Asia, we read of the army being in divisions, with a centre and wings, and of well-thought-out attacks, which included the use of flanking movements. Records were kept of all expeditions and wars, as well as of every kind of business transaction.

Ahmose's son, Amenhotep I, was another great soldier, and went far into Asia, winning great campaigns. He ruled an Empire which stretched from Nubia to the Euphrates. Tutmose I succeeded him: his chief claim to the throne being that his wife was a descendant of the old royal line. He completed the conquest of Nubia begun by Amenhotep, and spent a long while in his conquered dominions, building forts which he left garrisoned, and seeing personally to the organization of the country. He also attacked Asia, since the tribute which Egypt exacted from conquered peoples was not coming in as regularly as it should have done. By the middle of his reign, affairs were so settled that he was able to devote himself entirely to the internal business of Egypt, and he began to rebuild and re-endow those wonderful temples that had suffered heavily at Hyksos hands.

Religion was becoming more and more associated with the royal family: the king acted as high priest; the queen and royal princesses were priestesses of Amon. The priests grew richer and more powerful; they did a flourishing secondary trade in written scrolls and charms, which were intended to preserve the body from evil in the next world. The ritual became more and more elaborate, and apart from the royal family, the priesthood was the most powerful class in the land. Even the governors of the districts into which the country was divided, and the officials who would correspond to our modern mayors, held less power than the local head priests.

Though there was no actual law of succession, it was generally hereditary. Tutmose had no son by his queen, and when she died, the question of the succession became a problem. At this time, it was customary for the Pharaoh to have a harem, but only his chief wife bore the title of queen. The partisans of the old dynasties, fearing lest a son of one of the lesser wives should become king, persuaded Tutmose to settle the throne upon his daughter.

THE FIRST GREAT WOMAN RULER

Her name was Hatshepsut, and she is the first great woman ruler in history. Her half-brother, later known as Tutmose III, who until then had been an obscure priest of Amon, made a great effort to secure the throne; he married Hatshepsut, confidently expecting to be hailed as Pharaoh. But the powerful backers of the lady insisted that she alone should rule, and Tutmose III occupied an inferior position as consort. All court etiquette had to be altered to suit a woman sovereign. Even the temple-worship needed adjustment; the god Osiris was given a part-feminine nature, in order that the queen might be associated with him.

Hatshepsut inherited her father's love of building, and she decorated the land with vaster and more splendid temples than it had ever known. She was a busy trader, and sent her fleets far and wide to collect materials for beautifying her new buildings and gardens. We have an account of a journey to Punt, far down south on the coast of the Red Sea, whence the ships came back laden with myrrh, ivory, ebony, gold, incense, precious eye-cosmetic, baboons, dogs, monkeys, leopard-skins and natives. So notable an achievement was this expedition that, on their return, the captains of the boats organized a procession from the river up to the palace, to the great excitement of the large gathering of the Egyptian people, who had never before seen such curious—and perhaps alarming—beasts.

Owing to the plundering of the rich royal tombs by the Hyksos, the Pharaohs of the time abandoned the custom of burial in pyramids, and had caves hollowed out of the cliff wall in the Valley of the Kings near Thebes. Only a chosen few were allowed to know their resting-place. The thought of all their treasures, and more especially their protective spells, being stolen, thus leaving them powerless and comfortless in the life after death, was horrible to them. Hatshepsut had two tombs constructed, so that there should always be a doubt as to which of them was the one she actually occupied.

PROSPERITY AND PEACE

The queen was extremely proud of her prosperous and peaceful reign. For her fifteenth jubilee celebrations, she had two obelisks erected. They were nearly a hundred feet high, weighed three hundred and fifty tons each, and were brought by boat down the Nile to be erected at the end of the temple of Amon begun by her father. The obelisks were quarried, each in a single block, brought down the Nile, put up and finished in less than six months. Their coating was of electrum, and the precious metal was actually measured out by the peck. One authority avers that he piled up twelve bushels of the material in the festal hall. Hatshepsut had the outstanding events of her reign engraved on the obelisks, her chief pride being the temples that she had restored and built.

Great ruler though she was, her peaceful reign was not altogether a blessing. The Asiatic provinces had not been properly subdued, and they gradually ceased payment of regular tribute. When she died, Tutmose III went to much trouble to erase her name from the glorious monuments she had erected. He had the famous obelisks covered with an outside coating, bearing the records of his own and his father's prowess. Centuries later, his covering crumbled away, and now Hatshepsut's obelisks once more declare her achievements.

TUTMOSE III: SOLDIER AND ADMINISTRATOR

Fortunately for Egypt, Tutmose III was a warrior. His first task as Pharaoh was to suppress an Asiatic rising. He led his army, probably about twenty thousand strong, against the rebels, and the story of their encounter, at the battle of Megiddo, in Palestine, shows his impulsive nature. Hearing that the enemy was drawn up in front of Megiddo, Tutmose called a council of his generals. There were three routes through the mountains; one leading directly to the gates of the city. The generals tried to dissuade the king from this route; as the pass was narrow the army had to march through it slowly. But the Pharaoh swore an oath that he would himself lead the army by the shortest way, and, if his generals were afraid, they need not follow. So he swept his troops through the narrow way—the same by which Allenby attacked the Turks in 1918—and at the first charge the Asiatics fled. The gates of the city had been closed and heavily barred; the inhabitants tied clothes together, let them down from the top of the walls, and so hauled up their fleeing friends. Had the Egyptian discipline been perfect, many more would have been killed, but the soldiers could not resist the rich booty in the enemy camp outside the walls, and they stopped to plunder. Tutmose was determined to take the city, and settled down to besiege it; eventually it capitulated, and so ended the first battle of Megiddo. Many fights have taken place on this same plain, and its later name of Armageddon has become a synonym for decisive battle.

Over the conquered lands, Tutmose appointed governors whose loyalty he considered unquestionable. He took their sons back to Thebes with him, and they were brought up in luxury as Egyptians. They succeeded to the governorships on their fathers' deaths; by this means, Tutmose kept his governors closely bound to the mother country by ties of education and friendship. So great was the power of Egypt that even far countries sent the Pharaoh gifts which were regarded complacently as tribute. He obtained complete supremacy over the eastern Mediterranean, and the ports of Phoenicia were obliged to keep supplies in readiness, so that he could at any time start a lightning raid from any one of them.

Until over seventy years of age, Tutmose went on a campaign every spring. He was a man of terrific energy and versatility; besides building many temples, he designed exquisite vases and decorated instruments. His all-seeing eye watched every detail of government; he himself commanded his army, navy and civil service. His personal heroism was well known throughout the civilized lands, and he was the first empire-builder.

The succeeding Pharaohs continued to be great princes. They started a policy of intermarriage with foreign princesses, and so kept the Empire stable by alliance as well as by force. Conditions in Egypt among the upper classes were extremely luxurious. In fact, too much luxury was sapping the morale of the nobles, who, instead of having wide lands to control as of old, merely lived at court, trying to find new ways of spending money. The many slaves captured in battle made building even easier. Houses were richly decorated with gold and silver; clothes were very complicated, always of spotless white, with plaited and pleated skirts, elaborate wigs over shaven heads and sandals with exaggeratedly curled tips. Hunting was a favourite sport; the nobles chased lions and wild cattle. Women came much more into public affairs, following the fashion started by Queen Tiy, wife of Amenhotep III. It seems that she was of humble birth, and the marriage was consequently against all precedent.

AKHNATON THE RELIGIOUS REFORMER

This Pharaoh began his rule (c. 1375 B.C.) at a very early age, and soon effected a revolution in the religion of the country. The cult of the god Aton had been practised in his father's reign, and the new king adopted it. Aton was a name of the sun; the king identified it with the power of the sun rather than its material form. Amon also was a sun-god, but he represented only the sun of Egypt, while the founder of the new religion conceived of Aton as the beneficent power of the sun which lights the whole world. He set up, as its emblem, the disk of the sun with rays issuing from it, each one terminating in a hand; this symbolized the protective hand of God stretching to all parts of the world. Not content with bringing Aton's worship to the fore, the Pharaoh decreed that the worship of all other gods should cease, since Aton was the only God. The entire suppression of the country's gods had never before been attempted; the feelings of the powerful priesthoods can be imagined, and it says much for the young king's strength of personality that they were unable to set a rival on his throne. He had all the priesthoods disendowed, and on every monument the name of Amon was erased. Even his father's name, compounded of that of the god, was everywhere suppressed. He changed his own name to Akhnaton, deserted the royal city of Thebes and built a new one which was entirely dedicated to Aton.

Akhnaton's conception of godhead does not seem very strange to us, but to his people it was heretical, and almost beyond their under-standing. He taught that Aton was the god of all peoples and also of all creatures; and that he was a beneficent god. These characteristics had previously been regarded as very far from divine. The beautiful hymns written by Akhnaton survive to give us his idea of Aton as the creator of all things; Psalm civ, which we still sing, is a fairly close copy of one of them, and the following portion of another is remin-iscent of some of our religious chants to-day:

> "How manifold are thy works!
> They are hidden from before us,
> O sole God, whose power no other possesseth.
> Thou didst create the earth according to thy heart
> While thou wast alone:
> Men, all cattle, large and small,
> All that are upon the earth,
> That go about upon their feet;
> All that are on high,
> That fly with their wings.
> The foreign countries, Syria and Kush,
> The land of Egypt;
> Thou settest every man into his place,
> Thou suppliest their necessities.
> Everyone has his possessions,
> And his days are reckoned."

The king's private life was open; he delighted to take part in public affairs with his beautiful wife and four daughters. He was frequently painted with his family, and insisted on doing away with the artistic conventions. Since the days of the earliest dynasties, this is the only period in Egyptian history when art was entirely naturalistic, and we see men and women faithfully portrayed. The king's dislike of the old conventional style was so great that the portraits of himself often show his physical faults so plainly as to be almost caricatures. There are many pictures showing him taking part with his family in the worship of Aton, but the new religion never reached the common people. They could not begin to understand it, and they pined for their old friendly animal-gods.

So earnestly did Akhnaton carry out his conception of Aton as a god of peace, that he even refused to send military assistance to his garrisons in Asia. The frantic letters of the captains of these outposts, begging for aid against the ever-increasing resistance of the Asiatics, can still be read. Like the priests, the soldiers turned against him; yet nothing shook him in his faith. He died, possibly of the epilepsy to which he was subject, before he was thirty, after a reign of eighteen years; the throne passed to a son-in-law, since he had no son.

From all the early history of mankind, Akhnaton stands out as a real person, the world's first idealist, monotheist and prophet of internationalism. His followers had prayed that his teaching would endure "till the swan be black and the raven white, till the mountains rise up and move away, and the waters flow uphill". But his son-in-law, Tutankhamen, was forced to restore the worship of Amon.

LUXURY AND DEGENERATION

Anarchy reigned during the lifetime of several Pharaohs, though they managed to regain part of the lost provinces in Asia. By now, the Hittites were armed with iron, and so they were too strong for the Egyptians. During the reigns of the many Rameses, there was a state of luxury still, but the greatness of the Empire was crumbling. The priesthood of Amon was so powerful that in reality it controlled the kingdom. Little tribute came in, owing to the loss of rich parts of the empire, and the upkeep of the temples became a serious problem. The priests usurped both the land and the mines; as for the poor, they no longer had any part in the state religion; this worship was only possible for the rich. So the poor made gods of anything they could: trees, gates, stones, or the great departed Pharaohs of old.

Rameses II was very vain and fond of luxury. He had an enormous harem, more than a hundred sons and perhaps as many daughters. In some of his portraits he is shown with a pet lion running alongside his carriage. He and his successors lived in comfort, though the people were very short of food, since all the corn was in the temple granaries; the priests were the real rulers of the land, and the army consisted entirely of foreign mercenaries.

Considering the progress made in the art of living comfortably in the great days of the empire, it is surprising how little the Egyptians advanced in the sciences. They used extremely complicated measurements, and accomplished difficult building, such as the Pyramids, and so they had to study mathematics. In spite of this, they never managed to multiply or divide by any number larger than two. If they wished to multiply by seventeen, they had to multiply by two eight times, and then add in their original sum. In the same way, despite the cutting up of bodies when preserving them after death, they knew very little about anatomy and still less of diagnosis, while their medicine, though practical in an elementary way, was mixed up with every kind of magic and spells. This was largely because books were venerated on account of their antiquity, and so a medical treatise that had been handed down for hundreds of years appeared far more valuable than an up-to-date one. They regarded illness as being the habitation of the body by a demon, and thought that the quickest cure must necessarily be the driving out of the demon by emetics, a strong purge or really nasty medicine. Their surgery was slightly more advanced; but the law which enacted strong punishments against anyone whose patient died after an operation, prevented the more difficult cases from being attempted. Their astronomical observations were accurate; they mapped the stars and knew five of the planets. The new year was fixed by the rising of Sirius the Dog Star; they could foretell eclipses of the sun, and measured time by shadow clocks during the day and by water clocks at night.

And so we pass to the story of other lands, and leave Egypt dozing comfortably in the sun—the nobles forgetful of the heroic past; the merchants handling the goods of many lands; the peasants drawing wealth from the rich soil for their masters; and over all, the shadow of the priest. The fighting spirit of the race died away; the Pharaohs were content to hold a weaker kingdom with the help of foreign mercenaries. There was beauty and comfort in the lives of the upper and middle classes and splendour in the temple ritual. But Egypt herself became a "bruised reed", and her people were content to pass under the dominion of a series of foreign conquerors—the great empires of the world, of which Egypt was the forerunner.

●

CHAPTER 3

MESOPOTAMIA. SUMER AND AKKAD

THE land of the two great rivers, Tigris and Euphrates, we call Mesopotamia. In the Old Stone Age, the head of the Persian Gulf was at a point slightly north of modern Baghdad. The silt brought down by the two rivers, whose mouths faced each other lower down the gulf, soon built a bar; the water between this and the mainland became first a lagoon, then a marshland, and finally a rich alluvial plain, called by the early inhabitants the Plain of Shinar. On the west was

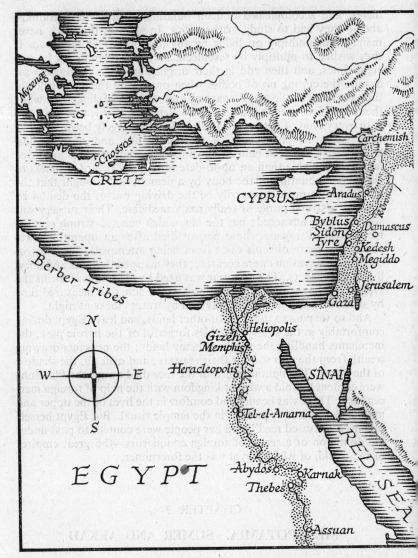

KINGDOMS OF THE NILE

The influence of geography upon civilization is well instanced by the communities which grew up in the regions irrigated by the three great rivers, Nile, Euphrates and Tigris. The fertility of the soil enabled the peoples who settled in the Nile Valley and around the Delta of the river, and the wanderers who made their home between the Mediterranean and the Persian Gulf, to make rapid strides in culture. Their civilization was based upon irrigation systems.

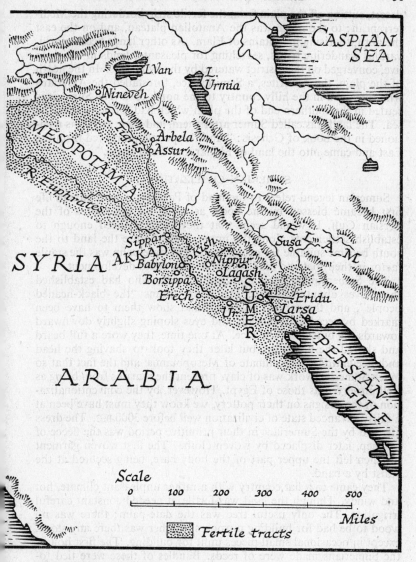

Scale
0   100   200   300   400   500
Miles

Fertile tracts

AND THE EUPHRATES

The cities which sprang up and flourished are known to us principally through
the painstaking work of archaeologists, but such as Ur and Babylon, Memphis
and Thebes, once represented the mightiest achievements of mankind in the
west. The courses of the rivers, which have been drawn in their modern form,
have changed considerably in the passage of centuries, as has the character and
mode of life of the people through the continual influx of invading races.

desert, cutting off the plain from the fertile strip bordering the Mediterranean; to the north was the Anatolian plateau, and on the east the abruptly rising mountains of Elam. As other lands became arid, various wandering tribes, searching for pleasanter lands in which to live, converged on the district watered by the two rivers. In the north of the plain, the Amorites, a Semitic race, forestalled the Assyrians who remained in the hilly country to the north-east. The Sumerians settled in the southern end of the plain which had formerly been the sea. The land was called Sumer after them, and their arrival is mentioned in the book of Genesis: "And the people journeyed from the East and came into the land of Shinar and dwelt there."

SUMERIAN CIVILIZATION

Sumerian legend refers to the land of Paradise, where human life first became blessed by the gods, as being on the shores of the Persian Gulf. It would seem that they were civilized enough to establish settlements along the upper Tigris before the land to the south became suitable for occupation. The date-palm was the staple factor in their diet and made possible their rapid development.

The Sumerians were a non-Semitic race, who had established themselves about 5000 B.C. The name means "the black-headed people", and the earliest statues found show them to have been marked by receding foreheads and eyes sloping slightly downward towards the outside of the face. At one time, they wore a full beard and shaved the upper lip, but later they took to shaving the head and face entirely. The climate of Mesopotamia, and the fact that so much Sumerian work was of clay, prevent the remains from being as well preserved as those of Egypt. However, by the conventionalization of the designs on their pottery, we know they must have been at a fairly advanced state of civilization well before 3000 B.C. The dress affected by the Sumerians in their primitive period was the fleece of a sheep, later displaced by woven cloth. The first woven garment for men left the upper part of the body bare, being secured at the waist by a band.

They came to a flat country with a rather unpleasant climate, hot and windy. Though the land was fertile, it needed constant careful irrigation. The only useful tree was the date-palm; there was no wood to be had for building purposes; neither was there any stone, except in occasional small pieces unfit for building. The first houses the Sumerians made were of reeds. Bundles of these were tied together to form long columns; then they were rammed into the ground and bent over to meet each other in the form of an arch—the forerunner, in all probability, of all the arches which have been used in building. Several arches would be erected; the space between was filled with woven reed mats, and the whole structure was plastered with mud. The doors were made of reeds, on a framework, and pivoted on a small stone. Later Sumerian huts were made of clay; at first, the bricks were dried in the sun, but after a while ovens were used, very much as is done to-day. As in the reed huts, the arch was employed: there was not sufficient wood to make a flat roof. Their earliest remains, such as those found at Susa, represent the late stone and the early copper ages, with art represented by primitive sculptures in stone.

As the land rose higher above the marsh, the Sumerians started cultivating cereals. The first sickles discovered are of stone, shaped like the jaw-bones of animals, which perhaps had actually been used for the purpose by primitive man. Fish were caught, both with hook and line and in nets; flocks of sheep and cattle were kept, and donkeys were used for transport. The sledge was used for carrying goods, and as far as we can tell, the Sumerians were the earliest people to use the wheel. When they came into the land, they wore sheepskin clothes, with the leather next to the skin; very soon they learned the art of weaving, and for a long time, their garments were adorned with loops of wool, hanging in rows, in imitation of their former fleecy clothes. Bone spindles and needles have been discovered, and it is thought that both men and women were often tattooed.

Owing to the lack of other material, clay was used for every possible purpose; even nails were made from it, and these were a pleasing decoration, since the heads were often formed in the shape of a flower. The Sumerians had elegantly decorated pottery for every kind of utensil, and wrote on clay tablets. At a very early date, they invented a form of writing, called cuneiform. A wedge-shaped stylus was used for this, to impress marks on a damp clay tablet. Though started as a picture-writing, the signs soon became unpictorial. Each sign represented a syllable, not a letter, and as early as 3000 B.C., there were about four hundred of them. For the children struggling to learn all these, the clay tablet must have been very convenient; a rub with the thumb would erase bad work, while a fair copy could be preserved by baking it. The Sumerians were not so skilful with their calendar as the Egyptians: months were measured by the moon, but as they counted only twelve to the year, they were frequently out of reckoning with the solar year. The calendar was adjusted from time to time by different kings, but no permanent correction was made. The Jews and the Mohammedans adopted it in an altered form. The chief numeral unit was sixty, and from this we get our present-day division of the hour, the minute, and the circle.

THE SUMERIAN CITY-STATES

A number of city-states grew up in the land. Each consisted of a city and a considerable amount of land round it, governed by a king; each had a powerful high priest called a *patesi*. Sometimes perhaps the king and the *patesi* were the same person, and occasionally the *patesi* was the king's son; in later times the power of the office gradually declined, and it became only a temporary governorship.

The town lay by a canal or river, in front of a forest of date-palms, among which grew pomegranates, figs and grapes. Beyond, were fields of wheat and barley, and beyond again, the pasturage for the flocks. The whole country was a network of canals, and the irrigation system would have done credit to a modern engineer. The river-beds were constantly rising owing to the silt brought down; the banks had to be built up; the danger of floods was ever present and figured largely in the earliest legends of Sumer. Each city had complicated water-laws and regulations; heavy fines were imposed on landlords who neglected their property, and those who brought new land under cultivation were exempted from taxes.

The city-states were perpetually quarrelling among themselves, generally over the water question; there was nothing easier than tapping the main canal of your nearest neighbour, and diverting his water supply for your own use. Consequently the cities were frequently destroyed, some twice in a generation. Each time, they were rebuilt on the same site, so that gradually each was situated on the top of a mound which was composed of its own ruins. All over Mesopotamia to-day can be seen these "tells", some vast and some tiny, rising abruptly from the surrounding flat plain.

SUMERIAN RELIGION

Religion played a great part in the everyday life of the Sumerians. Among the earliest gods they worshipped were Enlil, the earth-god, and Enki, god of the waters. Gradually others were added to these, and by the time the city-states were flourishing, each had its own presiding deity. In every city was a temple, built in the shape of a tall tower called a *ziggurat*, which rose above the rest of the buildings and could be seen many miles away. Since Enlil was a mountain-god of Elam, his followers felt that he must be worshipped on a high place; so his shrine was placed at the top of the *ziggurat* and a wide ramp led up to it. When the worship of other gods arose, each city built its temples in the same *ziggurat* form.

At no time were the Sumerian gods supposed to have any power over the future life. The people prayed to them for material blessings and for a long life, but they regarded the life after death as, at best, one of dull grey shadows. If a corpse was not buried, they supposed that it roamed the streets, scavenging food. The fear of being haunted by the dead was ever present with the living, and consequently the greatest care was taken with their funerals. People were buried under the floor of the house, so that their spirits should not feel neglected, and should be present at the worship of the little family gods. The body was usually placed on its side, with the knees drawn up. Jars of food were put with the dead, also fish-hooks and weapons for the men, and for the women, mirrors of polished copper.

Among the objects frequently found in these graves, the most characteristic is the cylinder seal. The business man, who wished to record a transaction, stamped it with his own seal, a tiny cylindrical object, worn on a string round the neck. The carving on these seals reached a very high artistic level, figures of gods, goddesses and animals being wonderfully represented. They are useful to us in showing, by their changes through the centuries, the development of the people's ideas about their oft-represented deities. They also show that the Sumerians must have had some intercourse with the early peoples of India, for some of the seals depict Indian animals. Amongst the finds at Mohenjo-Daro, in Sind, have been objects of Sumerian origin, which suggest that there was trade between the two countries.

There were also burials of a different kind. Recent excavations have disclosed, at Ur, several enormous tombs, now known as the Royal Tombs, dating possibly from about 3000 B.C. The king and the queen have each a separate chamber, and they lie surrounded by a quantity of beautiful and useful objects including exquisitely worked gold and silver ornaments, musical instruments and utensils of every kind. In addition to these inanimate objects, large numbers of royal attendants were slain and buried with the king. A servant holds a cup to the lips of each of the royal pair, who are clothed in rich garments and laden with jewels. The ladies and gentlemen of the Court repose in an adjoining chamber. There was one girl who was evidently late for the ceremony. All the other ladies were carefully dressed, each wearing a silver headband, but hers was still coiled up in a neat roll, inside a sort of pocket-bag that must have been attached to her dress.

It seems certain that this human sacrifice took place only at a royal burial. In other tombs, some of the bodies have been buried with even more valuable personal objects than those in the royal tombs, but so far, the only attendants found have been with royalty. We do not, of course, know how the ceremony took place, but from the arrangement of the bodies, it seems certain that they did not die a violent death. They probably entered the tomb-chamber, took up their prescribed positions and died as the result of some drug. In the tombs were also oxen, donkeys and chariots with grooms, and among the harness was found a beautifully modelled silver donkey-mascot. Sledges, tools and statues were among the many articles buried with them; the queen had a chest of clothes, and there were also gaming-boards and other beautifully inlaid objects.

THE SUMERIAN ARMY

The Sumerians were the first of the early peoples to be great in the arts of war, although they were probably the most humane also, having a genius for religious speculation and lacking genuine warlike ambition. They fought in solid phalanx, shoulder to shoulder, armed with spear and shield, and wearing helmets of leather. In the intervals of squabbling among themselves, they joined to fight the nomad

tribes that perpetually raided the fertile plain and provided a source
of danger to Sumerian civilization. Not only with these wanderers
did they have trouble, but with the Semitic people who settled in
Akkad, the name given to the northern part of the plain of Shinar.
The Semites fought in open order, using the bow, and for centuries
were no match for the Sumerians, whose kings were often overlords
of many Akkadian cities as well.

SARGON'S EMPIRE

Probably about 2750 B.C., a Semitic chieftain called Sargon
ruled in Akkad, and he was a truly great soldier. There were many
legends about his birth and his rise to power: some said he was the
son of one of the temple prostitutes; others that he had been exposed
in a basket of reeds—like the infant Moses, centuries later; another
version was that he had been cup-bearer to the king, whose throne he
usurped. Whatever his origin, he made himself master over all Akkad
and her cities, and then marched to battle against the Sumerians.
He defeated them in one fight after another, and became king over
the land. He then went on to gain other conquests over the wandering people known as Amorites.

At this time, the prosperity and trade of Sumer were considerable,
and to ensure them, it was imperative that the trade-routes should be
well policed and safe for travellers. Continuous warfare would have
been fatal to trade. So the Sumerians, after a show of resistance,
settled down happily under the rule of a Semite.

Sargon continued to expand his kingdom: after conquering the
Amorites, he overran Elam. Eventually he was ruler of an empire
which stretched from Elam on the east across to the Mediterranean,
and reached far up the two rivers. He sailed to Cyprus, but it is unlikely that he conquered it. His empire was divided into districts,
each under a governor, some of these being of Sumerian birth and
others being Semites.

This widespread Semitic kingdom meant that various nomad tribes,
who had never before settled in any district, had to learn a new mode
of life. They discarded their tents and built brick houses, and they
began to write their own tongue, using cuneiform writing. They
learned the Sumerian methods of government, and quickly absorbed
their culture, soon outstripping them in the arts. The two races lived
peaceably together, the Sumerians still with their shaven heads, the
Semites with heavy beards and moustaches, and long, dark hair
flowing over their shoulders, or done up into a "bun" for active
occasions, such as going into battle.

In religion, the Sumerians refused to allow any infusion of Semitic
thought. The worship of their gods went on side by side with the
Akkadian. On the carved seals, we first see the gods portrayed as
feasting and making merry; then the reliefs show men in prayer to
them. Sargon's rule was so great that the divinations made for him

in the temples were copied and handed down, for future generations to profit from the wise courses they indicated. The Semites did not always remain in power; the rulers came sometimes from the one land, sometimes from the other. The two peoples lived peaceably together under a central government, both countries being regarded as equal, and the king was called King of Sumer and Akkad.

While Sumerians and Semites lived together, the latter became more and more the dominant race politically. This was probably because they were constantly being replenished by small tribes or families that came from the desert and settled down, whereas it seems there was never a second influx of Sumerians. The scribes continued to write the old language, but the Semitic tongue of Akkad was in general use, Sumerian being used only on ceremonial occasions. The trade of the country was considerable. Overland, the caravans travelled into far countries, to India, to Egypt, while the rivers provided an easy route to the northern countries. The Sumerians were not great travellers themselves, but they sold their wares to the wandering peoples of the desert, who acted as middlemen and established trading-routes throughout the plain. The stuffs of Mesopotamia were more famous and much more advanced than those of their contemporaries. Many varieties were made and brilliant dyes were used: lists have been found, showing many names and a wide difference in prices. Through trade, other details of Sumerian culture were spread abroad, and often their gods were worshipped by the inhabitants of distant lands.

LITERATURE AND TRADITIONS

A good deal of early Sumerian literature has survived. The legend of Etana is the first story of flying. Etana was a shepherd who wished to find a certain herb that would make his sheep more prolific. Failing to find it on earth, he mounted an eagle and flew to the skies, but was hurled down to earth and killed. The legend of Adapa told how eternal life was lost for ever to mankind. Adapa was a king, who, when fishing, was thrown from his boat into the sea by the violence of the south wind. In a rage, he broke the wings of the wind, and was summoned to the gate of heaven for punishment. Two of the gods interceded for him, but a third was jealous and warned him not to partake of any food offered to him. The chief of the gods, on hearing that he was the wisest of men and needed only immortality to make him a god, asked him to eat, offering him the bread and water of life. But mindful of the advice he had received, Adapa refused, so he and all his people remained for ever mortal.

The only human being to obtain everlasting life was Uta-Napishtim, who, like Noah, was the hero of a great flood. Being loved of the gods, he was warned of its approach, so he took his house of reeds to pieces and made it into a raft-like boat. He and his family alone survived the deluge, and later he became immortal. Actual proof of a flood of great magnitude has been found in Mesopotamia during recent excavations. The silt left by it has a depth of eight feet, an entire civilization appears to have been overlaid by it. From these first written tales, derived from a period before writing was in use in the land of the two rivers, we see that the belief in the immortality of the gods was held at a very early epoch.

THE EARLY DAYS OF BABYLON

About the year 2200 B.C., the Semitic Amorites came down the Euphrates and settled round the village of Babylon. They became powerful, and in the days when Senusret III ruled Egypt one of their kings, named Hammurabi, determined to conquer the neighbouring cities and make an empire as strong as that of Sargon. He was young and vigorous, and he started to wage war with the cities of the south. The full story of Elam, which lay, a perpetual menace, on the flank of Mesopotamia, is told in later chapters; like the Amorites, its warlike people were searching for fresh territories, and for thirty years Hammurabi fought them. He was content to conquer gradually. Every city taken was at once fortified and garrisoned, till at last Babylon was supreme in the land.

For the rest of his life Hammurabi proved that he could be an even greater ruler in time of peace than in war. A great many of his letters have been discovered, and these give some idea of the huge machine of government that he organized. These letters were written on soft clay with a stylus, by the king's secretary; the tablet of clay was then sanded over to prevent it from sticking to the envelope, which consisted of another piece of clay wrapped round the first. The name and address was then written on the outer covering, and the whole was baked. The person who received it had merely to break off the outer roll in order to be able to read his letter.

HAMMURABI'S RULE

Being descended from nomad forefathers, Hammurabi was much interested in the rearing of his people's flocks, as well as in the corn-growing that had long been the chief occupation in the country. He built a huge new canal, and reorganized and improved the management of the irrigation system. Flocks of sheep and goats were kept, and oxen and camels were used for transport in trade. There were also farmyard fowls, and many game-birds, such as partridges. A formidable list of vegetables grown by the king's gardener includes garlic, onions, beans, mint, cardamoms, leeks, lettuce, saffron, turnips, mangolds, thyme and radishes. Travel was speedy, it being possible to cover a hundred miles in two days and nights by water. The boats were sailed, and also poled along. Travel by land was more dangerous, owing to the lions, jackals, wild asses and wild boars.

The king is chiefly famous for the list of laws known as Hammurabi's Code. In this, he collected and codified the old laws of the country, besides publishing his own edicts. The punishments in the

Code are severe; probably they were not always enforced. The priestess who entered a wineshop was liable to be executed; so, too, was a very extravagant wife, as well as more serious offenders. There was a judicial system which included magistrates' courts, judges' courts, and also a court of appeal. A final appeal could be made to the king, and from the tablets found, this seems frequently to have occurred. The parties concerned in a lawsuit could agree together what day to appear before the court within a certain time, but in criminal cases the accused were allowed six months in which to produce witnesses. Such cases were rare, probably because the Code laid down that "If a man accuses another of death and cannot prove him guilty, he himself is liable to death". Widows, orphans and poor people were assured of justice, but it was of the "eye for an eye" variety; for instance, should a brick fall from a newly built house and kill the owner's eldest son, then the eldest son of the builder was to be put to death. The Code also specified the fees for every kind of work: surgeons, veterinary surgeons, tailors, builders, boatmen and labourers are all mentioned.

SOCIAL AND BUSINESS CUSTOMS

Society was divided into three main classes. First were the *amelu*, or aristocrats, then the *mushkinu* or middle-class, and lastly the slaves. Slavery existed in Mesopotamia from an early date, but it had not the stigma that we now attach to it. Slaves could marry free people, and on the slave parent's death, the children would be free. They had stated privileges and could appeal to the law, but they had no part in the state. Any offences against aristocrats were doubly punished, but to balance this the aristocrats had to pay double for all services rendered them. The *mushkinu* were free in all ways, and need never serve in the army, unless danger from invasion was imminent.

There was no religious ceremony at a wedding. We do not know whether the husband and wife made their own choice, or whether the marriage was arranged. It was the custom for the bridegroom to take the bride's father a present, which was probably the outcome of the earlier buying of a wife. The bride brought with her a dowry and trousseau. We have the record of one of these—the lady had a furnished house and a garden, a slave girl, gold for bracelets and earrings, dresses, leather girdles, grinding-stones for corn, copper spoons, seven chairs and a parasol. If she or her father broke off the engagement, the man was entitled to keep part of the dowry; if he put an end to it, he could not take back the present made to her father. There was a legal ceremony, and the wife was obliged to have her marriage-lines. In case of a wife's lasting illness, the man could remarry, but was bound to provide for the invalid. Very often children were adopted into families in order to provide for the parents in their old age. It is noteworthy that it was the custom for sons to inherit equally, the eldest being entitled to no special rights.

Woman was very far from being a chattel; she was recognized as an individual and a citizen. She retained control over her own money and could go to law independently of her husband. She had a legal share in the estate of her husband and her father, and could possess her own business and slaves. If she ran her husband's business during his absence, she was entitled to one-third of the profits. On the other hand, a debtor could make his wife a slave to his creditor, but only for a period of three years.

The towns, each situated on its mound, were rather grim-looking, being all made of brick with flat-topped houses having few windows. Over them, in each town, towered the *ziggurat* of the presiding deity. The streets were several feet above the level of the doors, owing to the habit of throwing refuse on to them, but the insides of the houses were large and comfortable. The rooms were built round a central hall, in the middle of which was a drain, for the washing of feet took place on entering. Each house had its own small chapel, in which were housed the household gods, and under which reposed the household dead. In the palaces and large houses, bathrooms and toilets were plentiful, and the drainage systems were well planned, with inspection-points for the main drain, which was large enough for a small boy to pass through. In the royal palaces, there were even bathrooms for the slaves, and in the ladies' rooms have been discovered a variety of aids to beauty—iron oxide for rouge, pots of ointment, eye-black, manicure implements, and tweezers for eyebrow-plucking. A favourite occupation of ladies of the time was to do very fine inlay-work with snippets of mother of pearl. As in some modern towns, several large houses were given over to business interests, and were altered accordingly, perhaps to serve as banks or eating-houses.

AGRICULTURE AND COMMERCE

Country life was very much as it is to-day in Mesopotamia, though food was far more plentiful. The products of the country were chiefly agricultural, and in addition to corn and flocks, the date-palm was greatly cultivated. It was used as fruit, and for cakes, honey and vinegar; the stones were made into charcoal or cattle fodder. Inferior trees were cut down and the wood was used for bridges, while the tender top part of the trunk was eaten. At harvest time slaves and children were hired out to the landowners. Corn was all ground by hand, and bread was leavened and baked inside a small brick oven. It was made in a flat cake and was thrown against the inside oven wall, where it stuck while cooking; this method is still used in Mesopotamia to-day. The clothes in common use were made from wool and leather.

The temples were the centres of business, as well as of the religion of the country. They acted as banks, though there was no coinage—merely silver lumps, valued by weight, often in standard shapes. Gold was used, but only in small quantities; it was worth fifteen times as much as silver. The fixed rate of interest on a loan was 20%, and all governmental taxes were paid to the temple. As they were paid in kind, enormous storehouses were necessary, and the outbuildings and enclosures for the flocks were extremely large.

THE LIFE OF THE TEMPLES

The temples were also responsible for the schools, in which the children learned the numerous signs for writing. Each temple had to possess enormous staffs to deal with their many departments. Besides secretaries, they included shepherds and fishermen, as well as the household servants of the priests and their families. The temple was regarded as the connecting-link between God and man; indeed, the name "Babel", which the Hebrews erroneously translated "confusion", meant in reality "the gate of God". Both national and private prayers were made there; the services were accompanied by musicians who played on "lyres, drums, tambourines, reed pipes, cymbals and bagpipes", while the choir kept up a mournful chanting. Perhaps owing to the perpetual struggle with encroaching desert and the rather unpleasant climate, Babylon was never a cheerful land. The singing would have seemed most unpleasant to a western ear, for it is thought that the singers intoned through their noses, making a sound rather like bagpipes.

In addition to the large staff of priests, there were also priestesses, and the position of high priestess was a very important one; the kings often bestowed it on their daughters. The high priestess was regarded as chief bride of the god, and the priestesses represented his harem of greater and lesser wives. In addition, there was a group of temple prostitutes. Their calling was apparently regarded as quite respectable for females of the lower classes; besides their usual duties, they were employed to nurse the children of wealthy ladies in society. Attached to the temple were also seers, who divined the future. Usually they based their utterances on marks on the livers of sacrificial animals; they also poured oil on water, and foretold happenings of national importance from the shapes it took.

HOUSEHOLD AND OTHER GODS

Enlil was chief god at one time, but when the rule of Hammurabi began, Marduk of Babylon took his place. Besides the chief gods, who were in early days patrons of their cities, there were lesser deities. Some of these had many shrines, and were responsible for the minor comforts and niceties of life, such as good health, safe travelling, and so on. In order to represent himself as always in prayer before the god, a man would leave a small clay figure of himself in the shrine. Rows of such figures have been found, usually in a room adjoining the one where the statue of the god or goddess stood. There were also the household gods, who were supposed to be intimately connected with the spirits of the departed, and were responsible for the fortunes of the family. In the religious attitude of the times, we can find no trace of affection and little of respect for the gods. They were feared, and had to be propitiated, but all that was prayed for was long life, prosperity, material comforts and the preservation of the family. Life after death was still regarded as only a cold, grey, shadowy existence.

SEALS AND SCULPTURE

Artistically, the inhabitants of Mesopotamia never surpassed the level reached before the age of Sargon. The later seals and pottery were not so good, nor was there any improvement upon the early worked metals. Unlike the Egyptians, these people never reached a high standard of sculpture; this is not surprising when we remember that stone was so rare, that it was unheard-of to use a block just for practice. The sculptor was always hampered by the fear of spoiling his costly material, and experimenting was consequently difficult. In many cases, it seems that the figure has been dictated by the shape of the block, as received from the merchant. The great progress of the early people of Mesopotamia in the arts of civilization is remarkable, when the lack of material is considered. Unlike Egypt, the land had no plentiful supplies of stone, and all metals had to be obtained from other countries. The material prosperity of Mesopotamia was built up solely as the result of her abundant agricultural produce, her copious supplies of clay, and the invaluable date-palm which served so many useful purposes in the life of the people.

HITTITE RAIDS FROM THE HILLS

Although commerce flourished in the age of Hammurabi, Mesopotamian civilization was on the downward track. Perhaps the people neglected the arts of war, in spite of the constantly repeated lesson of the invading nomads and Elamites. The Hittites launched raids from the north-west, and made alliances with a tribe called the Kassites, who came from the east, somewhere about the year 2070 B.C. The latter brought with them the horse, and the inhabitants of the plain viewed with wonder the "ass from the mountains", which was to cause such a change in the progress of humanity. With its advent, correspondence was speeded up, and intercourse between the people of Mesopotamia and their neighbours in Syria and to the north was greatly increased. Some of the Kassites merely returned to their mountain homes with their booty; but others remained, and largely destroyed the civilization of the plain. The canals, as soon as central control was lost, silted up and flooded the districts near the rivers, and in consequence the whole country stagnated. For five or six centuries, the invading Kassites ruled over the land which they had helped to impoverish; but they and their allies had brought by their depredations the first age of the Two Rivers to an end.

CHAPTER 4

HITTITES, SYRIANS AND PHOENICIANS

THE Anatolian plateau, which now forms the core of the Turkish dominions, is a land of rugged mountains, rising abruptly from the seas, which surround it on three sides; it contains many fertile valleys whose rivers drain into the salt lakes of the interior. It is known to have been inhabited from very early days, but it did not produce a civilization so early as did the valleys of the Nile and Mesopotamia. Excavations during the last thirty years have unearthed records from which the annals of the country have been deciphered. Events were recorded both in cuneiform and hieroglyphic writing, the lines reading alternately from left to right and vice versa.

The peoples who inhabited the country between 3000 and 2000 B.C. built their settlements in the open, without defences of any kind. Each small community had its own ruler, who, if he was especially powerful, was called the Great King. This title frequently fell to the king of Hatti, a district in the centre of the northern half of the plateau. The little kingdoms traded with other countries, especially Sumeria and Assyria; they were influenced by their southern neighbours, and worshipped some of their gods. Records tell of Semitic merchants journeying to Sumer to implore Sargon's aid against an oppressive king of Hatti. Sargon's counsellors demanded a description of the Anatolian country, and strongly opposed the long and difficult expedition; but after learning of the riches of the country, the king led a small army northward and defeated the tyrant, forcing him to acknowledge Sumerian overlordship. After settling trade grievances, Sargon led his merchants home in triumph, bringing with him tribute, which included various kinds of strange trees and ornamental shrubs for his royal garden. It was the mineral riches of the plateau that gave it peculiar interest, and legend points to the inhabitants of the southern coast of the Black Sea as having been pioneers in the working of iron.

THE HITTITE EMPIRE

Upon the civilization which Anatolia had gained from Mesopotamia another one was superimposed. Some time before 2000 B.C., Hatti was invaded by an Aryan race who spread over the entire land, bringing with them customs very different from those of the old inhabitants and their neighbours. They built up a powerful empire, and though we have little idea of where their actual frontiers were, we know that they waged war successfully against their neighbours, and were overlords of many places. Unlike the Assyrians, they never boasted of useless cruelty to those they conquered, but seem to have been among the more humane early powers. When they captured a city, they took the entire population into slavery, and brought flocks,

63

herds and all portable goods back to their own land. The town itself they destroyed utterly; and the king solemnly cursed any man who should attempt to rebuild it: then the desolation was sown with a small, extremely prickly shrub. A large proportion of the wealth gained in their successful expeditions went to build and endow temples, especially those dedicated to the storm-god, whose worship was wide-spread throughout Hatti.

GOVERNMENT ON FEUDAL LINES

The empire was governed on feudal lines. At the head was the Great King, and under him lesser kings, who were often men of his own family. There were also warlike nobles, each ruling his own lands and leading his men to battle. In contrast with all other monarchs of early days, the Great King was not an autocrat, though he was head of the government; any private quarrel or personal matter had to come before a supreme court, consisting of the members of the royal family. The king could choose his own successor, but his choice had to be approved by the family assembly. Records have been found of a dispute on this matter which arose in the reign of King Hattousil, who had appointed one of his sons as successor, and later found it expedient to disinherit him in favour of one of his brothers. He proscribed his queen Hastajar, whom he upbraided before the family council, calling her a viper, because she had intrigued on behalf of the dispossessed son. At the end of his reign, there was a revolution in Hatti; the inhabitants rose against their governors and put them to death, seizing their goods. Despite many royal assassinations and struggles for possession of the throne, the Hittites kept their empire intact, and continued to enlarge it. Their expeditions went farther and farther afield; they devastated Babylon and took its spoils back to Hatti. However, in spite of these successes, they did not settle in Sumer, or colonize it in any way, this being due to its distance from their own country.

DOWNFALL AND RECOVERY

Some time during the seventeenth century B.C., this old empire of the Hittites crumbled. Unfortunately no records have been found of this period, probably because, during the days of the New Empire, they were suppressed as discreditable. So we do not know who caused the downfall; possibly it was the people known to the Egyptians as Hyksos. For when the Egyptians managed to defeat their Hyksos conquerors, the Hittites once more appear on the scene, and build up another powerful empire, which lasts for over two centuries. The greatest king of this epoch was Shubbiluliuma. He fought the nomad tribes to the east and the Mitanni near the headwaters of the Euphrates, and was powerful enough to exact tribute from many vassal kings. He remained on friendly terms with Egypt, congratulated Akhnaton on his accession, and sent him presents.

Statues of Teshub and Hepet, Hittite deities (*left*), found in the temple of Tell Halaf and (*right*) bust of an inhabitant of Mohenjo-Daro discovered in the Indus Valley.

Representation of Sumerian home and field life, found in a temple at Ur, showing the early kilted dress of Sumerians in the fourth millennium B.C.

This stele, recently excavated at Nimrud (the ancient Calah) and reproduced by permission of the British School of Archaeology in Iraq which holds the copyright, represents Ashur-nasir-pal II, who extended the Assyrian Empire in the ninth century B.C. The cuneiform inscription gives a detailed list of the thousands of guests invited to his banquet. The list made a useful summary of manpower available for military duties and public work.

The first thirty years of the reign of Assur-Bani-Pal, who is seen here at dinner with his queen, were the golden age of Assyria but before the end of his reign bad times came and he was forced to lament: "Misery of mind and flesh bow me down; with cries of woe I bring my days to an end."

A letter has been found which gives a vivid picture of the political relations between the two countries. At the death of Tutankhamen, his widow, one of Akhnaton's daughters, wrote to Shubbiluliuma and begged him to send her one of his sons as a husband, in order to maintain her own royal line upon the throne of Egypt. The king was suspicious and sent messengers to enquire into the genuineness of the princess' request. On their return with another letter, half reproachful, half frantic, from the young widow, a Hittite prince was dispatched to Egypt. He died as soon as he got there, probably murdered by the usurping Pharaoh, who, however, declared that it was a natural death. Great was the grief of Shubbiluliuma. He declared war, and marched down into the Delta, where he gained many victories and collected great spoils. On the return of the army to Hatti, an epidemic broke out, which ravaged the country for twenty years. An oracle declared this to be a punishment for liberating some Semitic prisoners in Egypt, in violation of an oath made to the storm-god. Shubbiluliuma died at a great age, and his son, who followed him, died of the pestilence soon afterwards.

The succeeding kings continued their successful campaigning, greatly enriching the country with the booty they captured. War with Egypt went on intermittently, a really great battle being fought at Kadesh, during the reign of Rameses II. Though the Egyptians recorded this as a national triumph, it was in reality a drawn battle, which gave the Hittite king an opportunity to incite all Canaan to revolt against Egypt.

THE HITTITE ROYAL FAMILY

The office of the Great King called for extreme energy and varied talents. He was responsible for the welfare of his subjects, seeing that none lacked, and that justice was done to the poorest as well as the richest of his people. He was commander-in-chief of the army, and generally led it in person. Finally, he was responsible for the attitude of the gods to his people, and had to take the chief part in all great religious ceremonies, and pay attention to the many and complicated rites and feast days. Some of the ceremonies could not take place without the king's presence, in which case he had to forego his annual campaign and leave it to his generals to conduct. If absent, he was represented in the ceremonies by a loaf of bread, over which he had made a certain gesture. He was the supreme judge over all courts, and made and proclaimed the laws. The Great King was not regarded as being in any way divine during his lifetime, but he was numbered among the gods when he died. The Hittites did not say "when the king died", but "when the king became a god".

Queens could never rule; if the king had no son, he appointed as heir his daughter's husband. A queen could act as regent during the absence of her husband or the minority of her son; she also took an active part in religious ceremonies. Besides the chief queen, there was a royal harem consisting of three different ranks. If the queen had no sons, the heir was chosen from one of the sons of the first rank in the harem, but no child of a lesser wife was eligible as ruler. Unlike the Egyptians, the Hittites never married near relations; the laws against this were very strict. Often the heir presumptive was appointed as one of the lesser kings; sometimes he was a priest. There were three holy cities in the country, which were governed entirely by the priests.

MILITARY SERVICE AND SOCIAL CUSTOMS

The great lords each had a following of warriors, who served under them in the king's army. Each lord took an oath of allegiance to the king, and many of them had command of bands of chariots—each chariot requiring a driver, a shield-bearer and a warrior armed with lance and bow—as well as infantry; he received a definite proportion of the spoils, and every common soldier had his portion. The army consisted entirely of feudal levies and foreign mercenary troops, chiefly from nomad tribes. They had competent engineers, and their weapons were of iron, which gave them a great advantage over their enemies. They fought only in summer, and camped in enemy territory in winter. Treaties were engraved with much care on gold, silver or iron tablets.

The workers, farmers and artisans were called by the Sumerian name of *mushkinu*. There were many slaves, mainly of foreign origin, and the system of taxes was much the same as in Mesopotamia.

Marriage took place between different social grades, and was usually arranged in the same way as in the land of the Two Rivers; if a man carried off a bride, he had to pay the usual marriage-present to her father, or if she was engaged, to the bereaved fiancé. A married woman could live either in her husband's house or in her father's. Adultery was punishable by death, but divorce was common. A widow had to marry her late husband's father or brother.

For committing a murder, the criminal had to deliver a body in return, though this need not necessarily be his own. If the murder was premeditated, the penalty was four bodies. When the murderer was unknown, the town was responsible for the tally of bodies (a practice which resembles the group responsibility of the early English); but if the murder was done in open country, there was no redress. For any injury, the culprit had to replace the workman, give the injured man an indemnity, and also pay the doctor's expenses. The indemnity varied according to the part of the body injured. Deportation was frequently imposed as a punishment, especially for offences of a violent kind.

The Hittites had, literally, hundreds of gods: their own, their neighbours', and those of the people whom they conquered. The chief divinity was the sun-goddess, who was wife of the storm-god. In addition to this goddess, there were several sun-gods, and the storm-god was often a different one for each city. The bull was regarded as a sacred beast, as it was by those Aryans who had conquered India; the disc of the sun often appears in the temples, and the two-headed eagle of Babylon was used as a heraldic emblem on the round flat seals.

One of the earliest legends concerns a god who had a quarrel with a great serpent, and enlisted the aid of a man to help him in the struggle. He got the man to give a great feast and invite the serpent, which duly arrived, with its children. They ate so much that they were unable to get back into their holes, and so the god was able to kill them. Another story concerns a god who was lost, the famine which resulted over the whole earth in consequence, the search made for him by other gods, and his final reappearance, which ensured prosperity and plenty.

There were small chapels and large temples, often standing in a sacred wood. Sacrifices were made, and worshippers had to undergo strict purifying rites. Foreigners were regarded as unclean and were never allowed to join in the national religious ceremonies. The gods were thought of as having the same needs as human beings; their statues were every day washed and dressed by the priests, and small meals were set before them. There were two kinds of prayer, those which made requests and those which expressed penitence. The Hittites prayed for long life, health and prosperity, and thought that their prayers would be more readily answered if the petitioner entered the temple in a state of holiness. The gods made known their will by visions, and the future was foretold by seers, who read signs in the entrails of sacrifices, as the Sumerians did. There were also priests who looked after the sacred birds attached to some of the temples, and prophesied future happenings from their movements.

Some of the towns were built on mounds, like those of Mesopotamia, but the capital, Hattous, the modern Boghaz Keui, was a mountain town and a fortress with immense double walls. The gates had stone arches and were decorated with sculpture. The Hittites were the first users of the porch, which they decorated with guardian animals. The Assyrians adopted their ideas in sculpture, and improved greatly upon their chisel work. The Hittite god of war was portrayed with a pointed helmet, adorned with horns, and cheek-guards. The people are always shown wearing high head-dresses, and their salute was to extend the hand with the fist closed.

THE END OF THE HITTITES

The empire was finally destroyed by an influx of the "people of the seas" and nomads who attacked it from inland. A few tribes remained intact in the interior of the country for five hundred years, but they were then overwhelmed by Sargon II of Assyria, and the Hittites were heard of no more. Yet they had left their mark on the history of the Near East. They had kept the eastern nomads at bay, and so helped the civilizations of Syria and Mesopotamia. By their military skill, they had checked the expansion of Egypt and destroyed much of the empire which Tutmose had established. Their control of the iron mines greatly influenced the military and economic development of their southern neighbours. Their stone buildings served as a model to the Assyrians who conquered them, and their policy of keeping an empire at peace by deporting rebellious populations set an example of ruthless efficiency which was to be copied by other nations in subsequent years.

THE EARLY CITIES OF SYRIA

South of Hatti, west of Mesopotamia and north-east of Egypt lay Syria. All intercourse between the three powers, either for trade or war, led them across this small and difficult country. Syria is four hundred miles long, and less than a hundred miles wide. The whole district is cut up by rugged mountain-ranges which merge into desert on the east and south. The fertile strip along the north-west coast, called Phoenicia, is entirely cut off by the mountain-barrier from the fruitful valleys of the interior. Palestine, the southern part of the country, consists of bare hills on either side of the deep valley of the Jordan, and has an almost harbourless coastline. Its geographical features made the formation of a strong and centralized government difficult, but this political weakness did not interfere with economic progress. Recent digging, at Jericho and elsewhere, has given ample proof that seven thousand years ago the Syrian communities had advanced far on the road of civilization.

Syria seems to have been inhabited from earliest times. Its first people probably belonged to a great dark-white stock that was spread round the shores of the Mediterranean, and reached as far as France and Britain. But ever since the tribes began to move about, Syria had endured one influx after another. In times of drought, Semites from Arabia migrated into its low fertile valleys, rich in grain and fruit. In addition to the peoples of the three great civilized nations, Syria was open on the west to the traders and pirates of the Mediterranean, and sometimes to invasions of barbarian tribes from the north-east.

It is not surprising that the Syrians became the chief traders of early times. Their markets flourished; in their bazaars, the glass and beautiful handiwork of Egypt could be exchanged for the brilliantly coloured stuffs of Mesopotamia, and the metals of the Hittites for carvings of strange Indian beasts. As early as 4000 B.C., the Syrians had access to copper, but that of Cyprus was more in demand by the other nations who needed to buy it. After 2000 B.C., horse-breeding became important in the country, and later still the iron mined near the Black Sea gave a further impetus to trade.

About 1400 B.C., there was a fresh desert invasion, by tribes called Aramean. Under the influence of Egypt on the one hand and the Hittites on the other, they built powerful royal cities. Perhaps the greatest of these, owing to its position at the intersection of important trade-routes, was Damascus. For a long time, the power of this city blocked the Assyrian empire's route to the sea, and protected the little Hebrew tribes to the south. The Arameans raised Syrian trading reputation to a great height. Their language, Aramaic, was the language spoken by Jesus—not, as might be expected, Hebrew. The Syrians spread the use of the alphabet, which they had taken from the Phoenicians, to the east, where it was adopted by the Persians, and by even more distant peoples. Ever-increasing trade encouraged the practice of lending securities, and the first banks, apart from the temples, grew up.

Palestine, the southern part of Syria, took its name from the Philistines, a fierce people who probably came from Crete. They were civilized and well-armed when they reached their new country, and wore body-armour and feathered head-dresses. Their cities fought perpetually against the Hebrews, who dreaded them, till David and Solomon managed to shake off their domination.

PHOENICIA AND THE UNCHARTED SEAS

The northern coastland, called Phoenicia, was inhabited by the people who are called Canaanites in the Bible. Probably they came from the shores of the Red Sea, somewhere about 2800 B.C.; the Greeks nicknamed them the Phoenicians or Red Men. They were very independent, building strongly fortified cities, sometimes on islands. The chief of these were Tyre, Sidon, Byblus and Aradus; each was ruled by a king, and there was much rivalry between them, especially between Tyre and Sidon. A stubborn taciturn race, leaving few records behind them, the Phoenicians are chiefly interesting to us today as having been the inventors of the alphabet and the real forerunners of the sea-going peoples.

The first sea ventures were probably made in search of food. Those who lived on a coast with poor soil soon found that a catch of fat fish was a better meal than a half-starved animal. The Mediterranean is the home of the tunny, a monster capable of supplying several large families with many adequate meals. It has been used as food for thousands of years. The earliest boats were probably rafts and wooden canoes, made by laboriously cutting down a tree with a stone axe, and hollowing out the inside, often by fire. They were propelled and steered by a paddle; it was a real advance when someone first thought of fixing his paddle to thole or rowlock and using it as an oar. Quite soon a small sail was in use, made of oxhide, papyrus, hemp or flax. These primitive boats were used only for short coastal journeys.

When the Phoenicians arrived on the Syrian coast, they quickly showed themselves extremely competent mariners. They had only the narrow seaboard as their territory, and so were forced to make a living by trade, instead of by production. The abundant supplies of wood from the forest of Lebanon were ideal for building ships and making pine oars. Lack of good harbours forced the Phoenicians to go further afield, and they soon discovered helpful currents that made it a simple matter to journey from Tyre to Cyprus, south to Egypt, and then home. Their boats, with anything up to thirty rowers, had one movable mast amidships, with a single square sail, and were steered by two paddles in the stern. There was no cabin-space, and no anchor. If possible, they tied up the ship to the shore, otherwise stones, attached to ropes, were thrown overboard.

When the power of Egypt declined, the people of Crete, who had dominated in the maritime world, were overwhelmed in a great disaster. The carrying trade that had been Crete's passed entirely into Phoenician hands. Very soon their ships became known in many lands, and their sailors were famed for skill and daring. They carried cargoes of Cypriote copper, and Egyptian glass and porcelain; they also sailed to the head of the Adriatic to fetch tin and amber. Once tin had been discovered, the voyages westward became imperative, and the Phoenicians were always willing to take a risk if they thought the profit would be worth while. And very full of risk must those early voyages have been. There was no compass and no maps, and each ship kept lookouts, who, on coastal voyages, stood at the prow, sounding with long poles. Unlike a sailing ship, which may be driven helplessly on to rocks, these early ships, with their many oars, could back water and so save themselves. At an early date, the Phoenicians learned to steer by the stars, and so could sail all night, instead of having to stay in harbour till daylight.

PHOENICIAN COLONIZATION

As they became accustomed to voyaging the length of the Mediterranean, some of the Phoenicians settled at different places along the coast. Perhaps these early colonies began with just a few people, staying in a small community of strangers, in order to collect such goods as were suitable for barter when next a ship arrived. Soon the Phoenician element increased; emigration was an excellent way to dispose of the surplus population, and the settlements became recognized trading-centres, useful to the sailors as friendly harbours. They grew up all along the north coast of Africa, in Sicily, on the southeast coast of France and even as far off as Spain. Most of them prospered exceedingly and continued their founders' mercantile and marine tradition, long after the fall of Tyre. Phoenicians are said to have sailed to Cornwall and traded there for tin, but it is more probable that the tin was transported by the straits of Dover and then sent overland; it would have been almost impossible to get a heavily freighted boat of that time safely across the Bay of Biscay. The return journey from a mining country must always have been perilous; having no headsail, the boats were difficult to manage with a heavy cargo, and they could not be rowed against a strong gale.

There is a pitiful record of the adventures of an Egyptian envoy, named Wenamon, who was sent by Rameses XII to Byblus, to procure cedar wood for the priesthood of Amon. As their wealth had greatly declined, he was provided with only a small quantity of silver and gold. He took passage on a Phoenician ship from the Delta, and, when it stopped at Dor, on the way to Byblus, he was robbed of all he had. He complained to the prince of the city, who refused to grant him compensation; however, he managed to obtain a bag of silver. When he arrived at Byblus, a city which sixty years previously trembled at the might of Egypt, the king refused to give him an audience. After some weeks of waiting, Wenamon was about to return to Egypt in despair, when he obtained his audience by a stroke of luck. One of the young priests went into a religious frenzy, and in a fit of prophetic ecstasy, declared that the king should receive the envoy.

Wenamon wrote of this interview: "I found him sitting in his upper chamber, leaning his back against a window, while the waves of the great Syrian Sea were beating against the shore behind him." Wenamon asked for the cedar wood, and the king demanded payment for it. Wenamon argued with him, but, while fully admitting the debt of culture that his country owed to Egypt, the king remained adamant. A messenger was sent back to Egypt, and, apart from a small quantity of heavy wood, sent in advance as a proof of good faith, the logs were not cut until he returned with some gold and silver vessels, bales of cord, and rolls of papyrus. The king told Wenamon of the last Egyptian envoy, who waited so many years that he never returned to his own country, and then, with grim humour, offered to show him the tombs of the city. The unfortunate envoy must have been thankful to start his homeward voyage, but his trials were not yet at an end. He was shipwrecked on the way back, and barely managed to escape with his life. The story provides an interesting example of the profound change that had occurred in the relative military strengths of Egypt and Syria.

THE GENIUS OF PHOENICIA

Herodotus wrote that the Phoenicians were reported to have sailed the whole way round Africa, about 600 B.C., on behalf of the Pharaoh Necho. The report said that it took them two years, during which time they laid up the ships twice, sowed corn and waited for it to ripen. It is not certain if this is true, but it is at all events quite probable. There had long been a belief that Africa was circumnavigable, and the coastline was not particularly difficult. The Phoenicians' report as to the different position of the sun after the Cape had been rounded, and the fact that they took the easy way, in which any boat is helped by currents, make the tale credible. Men who had long been accustomed to sail through the Red Sea to the land of Punt, would certainly be capable of enduring the extremes of African climate.

During the centuries when the Phoenicians had the monopoly of the Mediterranean carrying trade, they became very good workmen. But not one object which has survived shows any trace of originality; they borrowed all their designs and ideas from other people. A landslide in 1922 disclosed the tomb of a prince who had ruled about the year 2000 B.C. There were wonderful gold and silver objects in the grave, but all reproduced Egyptian designs. The Phoenicians became expert with metal, casting, hammering and engraving it perfectly. They learned the art of making glass, again from the Egyptians, and they became renowned for their stuffs, which were dyed with the famous Tyrian purple; this was obtained from a small shell fish, called murex, which was very plentiful on that coast. The civilization of the west was also greatly influenced by the oriental designs passed on by the Phoenicians. The lotus flower, the sphinx and various winged monsters were all made familiar to western eyes by Phoenician craftsmen. Styles of dress were taken from one land to another as the result of trade.

Perhaps most important was the spread of the alphabet to the west. This invention had been developed from Egyptian hieroglyphics, and had twenty-two signs, all consonants. The Phoenicians adopted it, imported papyrus from Egypt and arranged the letters in a fixed list. Each was called by an everyday word that began with it; from the words representing a and b, the Greeks took their alpha, beta, from which we get our present word alphabet. All western alphabets are descended from the one arranged by the Phoenicians. They themselves seem to have used it for solely material purposes; the only literature they have left us is in the form of business transactions, religious records and a treatise on farming.

The Phoenician religion was a sensual and cruel form of polytheism. Baal, the supreme god, was associated with the sun; Taanit, the moon goddess, Astarte, or Ashtoreth, goddess of fertility, and many lesser divinities were also worshipped. Their rites were performed with extreme licentiousness, and there is evidence that they included child-sacrifice.

Phoenician workmen were in demand in many countries; they were frequently employed by the Assyrians to make furniture; Solomon used them for the building of the temple at Jerusalem. He also purchased much of his material from Hiram, king of Tyre, who sent the cedars and pines down by sea, tied together into rafts.

But although, during the reign of Solomon, there was friendship between the people of Tyre and the Jews, and later between Ahab and Sidon, as a rule there was no love lost between them. For the Phoenicians were pirates as well as traders, and were especially addicted to stealing women and selling them as slaves. It may be the intense distrust that the Hebrews had for their seafaring neighbours that gave them that perpetual horror of the sea which is noticeable throughout the Bible, from Genesis to Revelation.

The Phoenicians were unpopular with other races. They were known as the biggest liars of their age, and doubtless the wish to keep their all-important trade-routes and objectives to themselves, made them adepts at fabricating legends designed to scare other people away. They are credited with the invention of the tale, so horrifying to ancient mariners, of the perils of Scylla and Charybdis. The prophet Jeremiah was indignant with the people of Jerusalem for buying fish from the men of Tyre on the Sabbath day, and the hatred of the Jews for the cities of Tyre and Sidon was heartily expressed by Ezekiel, who prophesied the abasement of their excessive pride by the powerful armies of Nebuchadnezzar. Though Tyre, when the time came, managed to defy this king for thirteen years from her rocky island, Phoenicia was constantly menaced by Babylon.

Even the stout hearts of the Asiatic Phoenicians could not save their ancient cities from the armies of Persia and Macedonia; and their history becomes merged in the great empires which absorbed them. But the colonies they had planted in Africa kept their independence, and in later centuries, Carthage was destined to dispute the rule of the western Mediterranean with Rome. Though Syria lost her freedom, her people played a great part in the intellectual life of the world, and her story is the true connecting-link between East and West, and between ancient and medieval history.

CHAPTER 5

ASSYRIA AND CHALDEA

THE hilly country to the north-east is very different from the plain of the Two Rivers. It has a good climate, and does not need the careful irrigation of Mesopotamia, as it has a regular rainfall and is well watered by the Tigris and its tributaries. Among the well-wooded hills are fertile valleys and red undulating ploughland, similar to that of the west of England. There are plenty of varieties of stone for quarrying, and many trees, but the date-palm is not among them.

ASSYRIA'S EARLY STRUGGLES

This high land, formerly known as Assur, and later as Assyria, has no natural frontiers, and it is uncertain who first inhabited it. Some of the earliest relics appear to be of Eastern origin, but by 3000 B.C. a Semitic tribe had settled at Assur, where they founded a city-state. They spoke a dialect akin to that of their neighbours of the plain, and were in constant intercourse with the Sumerians. For hundreds of years they were ruled by other nations. During the reign of Hammurabi, picked Babylonian troops occupied Assur; sometimes it was under Hittite domination, sometimes under that of the warlike Mitanni to the west, or of northern tribes. Assyria adopted many customs from these countries: she used the cuneiform writing of Babylon, and copied the Hittite artists, decorating buildings, which were of brick on a stone foundation, with carved stone animals and reliefs. Babylonian gods were worshipped, but the chief divinities of the land were Assur, or Ashur, god of war and thunder, who was represented by the sun, and Ishtar, goddess of war and fertility.

Fifteen hundred years of war toughened them, and the use of the horse strengthened them. The struggle to the south-west, between Egypt and her Syrian dependencies, left Assyria free to expand. A record of a present of gold, sent from the Pharaoh Amenhotep III, shows that Assyria was regarded as a potential power. About 1250 B.C., an army went down the Tigris and captured Babylon, which was still under its Kassite rulers. The Assyrians held the city, and their king, Shalmaneser I, then marched against the Hittites, drove them back from the Euphrates and invaded their country. He narrowly escaped defeat from a king who managed to cut off the entire water supply of the Assyrian army, but the invading soldiers, accustomed to hilly country, made successful attacks on the villages and small towns, wiping them out piecemeal.

THE SOLDIERS OF ASSYRIA

About 150 years later, Tiglath Pileser I increased the boundaries of the kingdom, conquering more Hittite land, and exacting tribute from Sidon and Byblus. He was a mighty hunter, slaying elephants and wild bulls on the plains of the river Khabur, as well as lions, of which he claimed a bag of eight hundred from his chariot and a hundred and twenty on foot. He rebuilt many palaces and temples, adorning the gardens and parks with foreign shrubs and fruit trees brought back from his campaigns. He increased the prosperity of the country by repairing the water-machines and accumulating stores of grain. From every conquered town or village, his soldiers drove away the herds of sheep and cattle to increase the property of the monarch. His collection of animals was well known, and it was enriched by the present of a crocodile from the Pharaoh of Egypt.

The successors of Tiglath Pileser lost his western possessions, and the Assyrians were once again reduced to a small community, living round the cities of Assur and Nineveh. For two hundred years, they endured many hardships from invaders; the fiercest were the Scythians who swept down from the northern steppes, wearing coats and long trousers of leather, which must have appeared strange to the eyes of a people accustomed to robes. But the Assyrians were loyal to their kings, and they were the most stubborn fighters of their time. They recovered the road to the mines of Cappadocia, and once more their troops were fully armed with iron; they launched an attack on the tribes of Chaldeans and Elamites in the south with great success, and began laying the foundations of the greatest empire that the world had known up to that time.

The Assyrian Empire was essentially a product of the Iron Age. Doubtless its rulers were inspired by the past greatness of Egyptians, Hittites and Akkadians, but their empire far surpassed these predecessors. Geographically their advantages for expansion were few, but from the very beginning they seem to have been a nation, and not the usual collection of semi-independent city-states. Assyria was a military state with a deliberate policy of expansion, the persistence of which was remarkable. She was the first great oriental monarchy, and fell only before an empire that had learned from her the arts of war and government.

THE ASSYRIAN TERROR

Assyria began her policy of expansion by attacking and plundering wealthy cities. Ruthless punishment, such as mutilation, crucifixion or blinding, was meted out to the governors and prominent men of these conquered cities, and whole sections of the population were deported, in the fashion adopted from the Hittites. These captives were useful as labourers and craftsmen, and, in addition, they acted as hostages to guarantee the good behaviour of the conquered province. The terror inspired by the relentless Assyrian troops in other nations was phenomenal. Isaiah speaks of their irresistible onslaught: "They shall come with speed swiftly. None shall be weary nor stumble among them; none shall slumber nor sleep; whose arrows are sharp and all their bows bent, their horses' hoofs shall be counted like flint, and their wheels like a whirlwind; their roaring shall be like a lion; yea, they shall roar, and lay hold of the prey, and shall carry it away safe, and none shall deliver it."

Ashur-nasir-pal III began a series of successful campaigns, consisting of hill-fighting in the north. He succeeded in conquering many cities; a great many submitted peaceably to him, perhaps because he invariably had anyone who caused him much trouble flayed alive. An efficient if unamiable ruler, of a cautious nature, he never undertook any really difficult venture, but contented himself with campaigns the success of which was a virtual certainty.

His successors continued to fortify their towns, which were encircled by a double wall and a moat, and they used their prisoners of war to reclaim and cultivate waste land. The rulers were usually men of cultured taste, who encouraged building and the arts. Their palaces were built of brick and faced with stone, and were decorated with alabaster and glazed tiles, as well as wonderful friezes showing everyday scenes of a religious or warlike description. The human figure in these reliefs was still very stiff and unnatural, but dress and decoration were extremely detailed and animals were portrayed in vivid lifelike style. At one period, the empire was ruled for three years by the queen-mother, who for this period acted as regent for her young son. This in itself is an indication of the high standard of disciplined and orderly development which had been reached.

The monarch was absolute, and appointed all the provincial governors, who were always Assyrian by birth, and were all-powerful in their several districts, owing allegiance only to the king. The chief factor in the success of this method in Assyria was that the governors could always rely on support from the central government in time of need. They were responsible for their own troops and for the material prosperity of their districts. A letter has been found from one governor to his king, reporting that bee-keeping has been started in his province and appears to be flourishing and profitable; he adds proudly that he himself understands the whole process.

THE DYNASTY OF SARGON

The succession was hereditary, but about 725 B.C. a usurper obtained the throne. He took the already famous name of Sargon, and is the only king to whom Assyrian records refer with a numeral attached to his name. He founded a great dynasty and built up an empire which lasted for over a century. He had to face opposition from the ever-worrying tribes of the north, from Syria, Egypt, Elam and Chaldea. These two last, hereditary enemies, formed an alliance in order to fight Assyria, but the Chaldeans, rather typically, arrived late for the first encounter, which resulted in a drawn battle. Sargon II retreated and waited for the propitious moment when the alliance broke up. He then routed the Chaldeans and gained a decisive victory over the Elamites.

Sargon's son, Sennacherib, had taken an active part in the government before he came to the throne. He turned his attention to enlarging the empire, conquered the Chaldeans, who had been trying to combine Egypt and Syria against him, and imposed his suzerainty on the Jews. Afterwards, he sacked Babylon and made his son supreme governor of the south. The prosperity of the empire was now considerable; trade was much increased and Nineveh was adorned with rich buildings. The king formed a system of couriers, which might be considered as the first postal service, so that he could receive regularly the reports from the governors of the provinces, which were about sixty in number. It is unfortunate that so little is known of the actual characters of the Assyrian kings, for they would prove an interesting study. Sennacherib paid little attention to the religious duties that were obligatory for the reigning monarch. He was greatly interested in engineering; he had the streets of Nineveh relaid, making them very much wider than previously, and he improved its water supply by erecting an aqueduct from the hills. Cotton-plants had been imported from India, and the king started the growing of cotton as a subsidized industry, setting aside various tracts of land and using prisoners of war for its cultivation.

Sennacherib's son, Esar-haddon, extended the boundaries of his dominions still further, for he conquered the greater part of Egypt, which had for years been inciting the western provinces of Assyria to revolt, and he held Cyprus. He ruled over the greatest empire yet formed, stretching from the Mediterranean to the Persian Gulf, and from Ararat to Egyptian Thebes.

The first thirty years of the reign of Ashur-bani-pal were the golden age of Assyria. Nineveh, his capital, was the most important city of the day—a cosmopolitan city, in whose flourishing and colourful bazaars many languages could be heard. Trade was brisk in her markets, banks grew up, and a coinage, consisting of metal lumps of standard weight, first of lead and later of silver, was used. There was a vast class of slaves, who were distinguished by their shaven heads and pierced ears; they were humanely treated, and could acquire property. The freemen were divided into three classes: the nobles, who were priests, governors and generals, were a comparatively small section of the community (occasionally a lady of high birth was appointed as governor); the commoners, who consisted largely of soldiers; and craftsmen, who were divided into guilds which included bakers, traders, scribes, potters, carpenters and masons. Each calling was usually hereditary, and was strengthened by the system of apprenticeship which was applied in a comprehensive fashion.

ASSYRIAN EMPIRE UNDER ASHUR-BANI-PAL

Ashur-bani-pal himself was well educated in the science and letters of his age, and boasted his proficiency in the art of tablet-writing and literary composition. He collected a great library: over twenty-two thousand clay tablets have been discovered in it. In this were gathered the religious and scientific writings of his own times, as well as those of earlier date. It is thanks to them that we are familiar with the early legends and epics of Mesopotamia. The scribes of Ashur-bani-pal searched far afield for material for the book-loving monarch; many of the works in his library were in foreign languages; all military records were kept, and in addition the details of consultations of the priestly oracles.

ASSYRIAN RELIGION AND LAW

These oracles supplied the only means possessed by the nobles of swaying the all-powerful king, for the priests who controlled the oracles were drawn from the nobility. The Assyrians never started a campaign without being assured of the support of Ishtar. In addition to Assur and Ishtar, sixty other "great gods" were worshipped. There was a prevalent belief in magic and the power of demons; protective charms were always worn. An impressive ritual existed for the expiation of sins.

The Assyrians were gloomy and fanatical in their beliefs. They had little deductive reasoning power, and always imagined that, of two succeeding events, the first was the cause of the second. In order to profit from such results, they made lists of every possible happening. Their love of collecting data was of great use to later nations; Greek progress in astronomy was facilitated by the carefully arranged mass of observations made by the Assyrians for purposes of astrology. Their science, which was entirely derived from the Babylonians, was all carefully recorded for the benefit of posterity, and they had a certain medical skill.

The system of law in Assyria seems to have sprung from an entirely different source from that used in Babylon. The Code of Hammurabi must have been far too mild for this fierce fighting people, who were constantly coming into contact with the ferocious northern tribes, which, then as now, perpetually attempted to invade the country. Punishments were severe: among the mildest were slitting of ears and noses, whipping with from twenty to a hundred lashes, and imprisonment with hard labour. There were comprehensive laws for the management of the empire, including state benefits for widows. If a married man was taken prisoner of war, his wife was kept by the state for two years, after which she was entitled to marry again. Should her first husband return later, she went back to him, the second husband keeping any children of the second marriage.

The state was organized on extremely efficient military lines. The army consisted of chariotry, light cavalry, heavy and light infantry, and sappers. The troops received a definite part of the spoils of battle, thus having an incentive to fight. Their strategy and tactics were far in advance of those of any other previous or contemporary power; they excelled especially in the besieging of cities. Enormous battering-rams were used effectively against the walls of brick towns; for stronger defences, there were scaling-machines, protected by arrow-proof covers; and the defending walls could be undermined.

THE REVOLT OF BABYLONIA

At the start of Ashur-bani-pal's reign, it seemed as though the empire's greatness would continue. The king suppressed a revolt in Egypt; later, he allowed a native to reascend the throne, and made an alliance with him. The growing dissatisfaction of neighbouring countries with the relentless Assyrian policy of aggrandisement urged Babylonia to revolt, under the leadership of the governor of the south, who was the king's brother. He made a secret alliance with Elam against Ashur-bani-pal, but the latter defeated them and suppressed the rebellion. Despite the siege machinery of the Assyrian army, Babylon itself held out for two years, and then succumbed only to famine. The governor set his palace alight and perished in the flames. The reign continued prosperously, until the last twelve years, when bad times came. The aged Ashur-bani-pal lamented the troubles that had overtaken him: "The rules for making offerings to the dead and libations to the ghosts of the kings my fathers, which had not been practised, I reintroduced. I did well unto god and man, to dead and living. Why have sickness, ill health, misery and misfortune befallen me? I cannot away with the strife in my country, and the dissensions in my family. Disturbing scandals oppress me always. Misery of mind and flesh bow me down; with cries of woe I bring my days to an end."

THE SUDDEN COLLAPSE OF ASSYRIAN POWER

There were quarrels about the succession, and at Ashur-bani-pal's death the kingdom was in great disorder, and the provinces broke away from the central power. Other nations seized their chance to destroy the hated Assyrian domination. In the north, the Medes and Persians advanced; from the south, came the Chaldeans, who took Babylonia and then, assisted by the Medes, attacked Nineveh, which fell amid universal rejoicings. Nahum the prophet gives a vivid picture of the last carnage: "The valiant men are in scarlet; the chariots flash with steel . . . and the spears are shaken terribly. . . . The noise of the whip and the noise of the rattling of the wheels; and prancing horses and jumping chariots; the horsemen mounting and the flashing sword and the glittering spear, and a multitude of slain and a great heap of carcases; and there is none end of the corpses." So thoroughly was the hated city laid waste, that Xenophon, two hundred years later, marched over its site unaware that he trod the ruins of one of the greatest cities the world has ever known. Not until twenty-five centuries later was it rediscovered. The Medes carried off most of the craftsmen into captivity; a handful of Assyrians survived for a few years in the fortress of Harran, after which the people seem to have been absorbed into other communities; even their language was no longer spoken.

The fall of the Assyrian Empire is even more astonishing than its rise to power. The great military machine destroyed itself, for the constant replenishment of the army took the peasants out of the fields, which consequently lay fallow. The loss of man-power was always a pressing problem, for the Assyrians were never a prolific race; even in the lower classes, there were rarely more than two or three sons to a family. It is significant that the most severely punished crime in the Assyrian penal code was that of abortion. The great dominions needed many men for their defence; the lack of them, and the dwindling prosperity resulting from the neglect of the country's natural resources, caused the fall of the empire.

Assyria showed to later powers, such as Persia and Macedonia, the possibilities of a big oriental empire dependent on soldiers. The Assyrians also perfected the earliest Asiatic architecture, and preserved in their libraries records of their own history and achievements, as well as those of others. Perhaps the most lasting influence they had on subsequent history, was that their military régime created the situation which, through the teaching and counsel of the great prophets, gave rise to the Jewish conception of God.

THE CHALDEAN EMPIRE

Nabopolassar, who, following the old tradition of hatred of the Assyrian yoke, had led the Chaldean tribes to the sack of Nineveh, was proclaimed king of Babylonia in 625 B.C., and founded a dynasty that saw the last great age of Mesopotamia. The country took the name Chaldea from Kaldi, the old name of the new ruling tribe, who appear to have come originally from the head of the Persian Gulf. The power of the king depended largely on the backing of the priests; the lack of hereditary right to the throne had to be made up by a favourable opinion from the oracles. Consequently the Chaldean kings of Babylon showed a rather nauseating piety: Nabopolassar, when rebuilding the great temple of Marduk, made his two young sons work as common labourers on the building, in order to do honour to the gods.

One of these sons, named Nebuchadnezzar, succeeded to the throne, and under him the country rose to great power and splendour. His reign was troubled by constant wars; he protected his northern frontier by an alliance with the Medes, who, like the Persians, were of Aryan origin; their story is told in Part IV. Nebuchadnezzar married a Median princess, and so was free to turn his attention to the little countries in the west, who were backed by Egypt. He was a really great soldier. His first important victory was at Carchemish, where he completely routed the Egyptian troops. He then conquered the Phoenician cities, with the exception of Tyre, which, after a siege lasting thirteen years, remained unsubdued. Afterwards he besieged Jerusalem, sacked it, and carried away thousands of the inhabitants into captivity in Babylon. Eventually he controlled all the Euphrates valley and the whole of Syria and Palestine, as far as the borders of the revived Egyptian kingdom.

THE SPLENDOUR OF BABYLON

In spite of perpetual warfare, Nebuchadnezzar found time to beautify Babylon, whose splendours soon became world-renowned. He appears to have had no affection for literature, but he was a very great architect, and showed a masterly genius for producing marvellous buildings from the clay that was still the only local material. He continued work on the temple of Marduk, and constructed a festal avenue, which passed through the beautiful gate dedicated to Ishtar; he connected the temple with the royal palace, a tiered building, overlooking the river and the whole city. On the terraces he laid out luxurious gardens, filled with rare plants and beautiful trees. The fame of these Hanging Gardens of Babylon spread far and wide; they were one of the Seven Wonders of the world. Nebuchadnezzar also had a bridge built across the Euphrates, which is, as far as we know, the earliest bridge ever to have been constructed.

Once again there was true prosperity in the land, and trade flourished as in the days of Hammurabi. The Chaldeans seem to have absorbed the culture of their predecessors in the country, for under them art and science made good progress. Their most important science was astrology, and through its study they gained much astronomical knowledge. The equator was divided into three hundred and sixty degrees, and the twelve signs of the zodiac were mapped out. They had a strong belief in the influence of the stars on the lives of men; observatories were set up all over the country, and popular books on the subject were much sought after by the common people. Many superstitions still in vogue are inherited from the Chaldeans, as well as such expressions as "a lucky star" or "an ill-starred venture".

They were further advanced than any of their contemporaries in the study of medicine, at least five hundred and fifty different kinds of drug being in general use. The doctors used instruments of bronze, and cloth or leather was recommended for poultices.

THE END OF MESOPOTAMIAN RULE

Nebuchadnezzar's heirs lacked his mental and physical strength, as well as his fine statesmanship. After his death, the kingdom was weakened by struggles between the nobles, and quarrels about the succession. Eventually the priests elected Nabonidus, a retiring, scholarly man, to the throne. He was interested only in the glories of the past, and lived quietly in a town of northern Arabia during most of his reign. Though the great power of Lydia kept the Medes busy in the north, the kingdom of Babylonia dwindled rapidly as other rising nations encroached on it. When Cyrus of Persia marched into the plain, the cities opened their gates to him in peaceable surrender, and Mesopotamia finally resigned her independence. But Babylon's fate was very different from that of Nineveh. She remained the market of many nations, a source of wealth to her Persian conquerors. The caravan-routes from India and the north still converged on her, and the power of her priesthood continued. And when, two hundred years later, a greater conqueror than Cyrus received her submission, he planned to make the great city into the capital of an empire which should have the power to link Asia with Europe.

CHAPTER 6

THE JEWS

FROM the point of view of religion, the Hebrews are the most important people of antiquity. Their country, Palestine, is the southern part of the bridge of fertile land joining Africa and Asia, a narrow strip between the desert and the sea. In times of drought, nomad tribes from the desert have always overflowed into it; it lay between the great empires of Egypt, Hatti and Assyria, and their armies constantly crossed it. The land consists of arid limestone hills, with extremely fertile valleys in the north, cut off from each other by barren ridges. These valleys are rich in wheat, rye, barley, figs and vines; sheep and goats pasture on the hills, and there are few industries. The country was too poor to develop into a political power, and the isolation of each fertile centre made it extremely difficult to rule the land as a whole. The Hebrews had practically no access to the sea, as all the harbours, which are in the north, were held by the Phoenicians, and the Philistines lived along the coast to the south.

It is the importance of the Jews in the world's religious history that makes it necessary to tell at some length the political history of a people who only for half a century achieved political importance among their more powerful neighbours.

The Hebrews were originally men of the Arabian desert, leading a wandering life with their flocks and herds. Babylonian chronicles, as well as letters written to Akhnaton, describe a tribe called the Habiru as plundering both Mesopotamia and Palestine. It is thought that the Habiru were the ancestors of the Hebrews. They moved into Palestine somewhere between 1400 and 1200 B.C., settling wherever possible, and always trying to oust the people they found already there. They intermarried with other inhabitants, including the Hittites, who dwelt there in great numbers; it is even thought that the prominent nose associated with the Hebrews is really of Hittite origin. Another group of tribes had settled in Egypt. Probably they wandered there during the rule of the Hyksos, who, being Semites like themselves, would give them a good reception. Joseph, one of their number, rose to high rank as governor of Egypt, second only to the Pharaoh.

But when the Hyksos domination ended, the new Pharaohs were not so kind. The condition of the Hebrew tribes grew worse till it became no better than slavery. At last, a leader named Moses arose and led the tribes out of Egypt. Besides being an organizer and sanitary expert, he was their chief law-giver, and most of their code was originated by him. For a long while, they returned to their nomad existence, wandering about with their flocks, living in tents and moving on when they needed fresh pasturage. When they reached Palestine, they attempted to conquer it, but were not altogether successful. They were unable to oust the Canaanites; after a while they settled in such parts of the country as were available, finding many friendly tribes of the same extraction as themselves. The Hebrews from Egypt did not attempt the conquest of Palestine as a united people. They were divided into tribes, and each fought its own battles, only rarely combining.

Though the Hebrew tribes were racially similar, they were mixed through constant intermarriage, and the only union between them was the bond of religion. Like the Arabs, they claimed descent from Abraham, who had lived beyond the Euphrates and had migrated from Ur to Palestine by way of Harran. They worshipped Yahweh as the god of Abraham, though the fathers of Abraham had held to other deities. It is possible that Yahweh, who was regarded by the invading Hebrews, first and foremost, as a god of battle, and developed eventually into the god of the New Testament, was originally one of Abraham's household gods at Ur, worshipped as a tiny stone figure belonging to the third and least important class of deity. Abraham, having left his own land and its gods, came to regard the god that was always with him as his special benefactor and protector, and worshipped "the God of Abraham" instead of the gods of the different lands in which he sojourned.

HEBREW SETTLEMENT IN PALESTINE

So the Hebrews settled in Palestine, bringing with them their god Yahweh or Jehovah, and his house, in which were kept the stone tablets engraved with their law. This habitation was called the Ark; it was carried on poles and kept in a special tent in the camp. In the north, the invaders became a settled people, and abandoning their tents, copied their Canaanite neighbours by building dwelling-places. In the poorer south, the wandering shepherd life still continued. Though they worshipped Jehovah, they regarded him as but one god among many; each Canaanite community had its own Baal or lord, who was supposed to give fertility to his own district. There must have been grave doubts in the Hebrew mind as to whether Jehovah, being a wandering god, would prove as efficacious in an agricultural community as the long-settled Baal. Frequently the worship of both Baal and Jehovah was carried on side by side, and but little difference was made in the ritual. We know from the story of Jephthah's daughter that human sacrifice did occasionally take place among the Hebrews as among some of their neighbours, and Jehovah was not regarded as having any more influence on life after death than had any other local god. In reading the Bible, it is easy to lose sight of this, as great emphasis is always laid on the worship of Jehovah. It must be remembered that the books of the Old Testament were compiled from many sources. They were not written in their present form until about 350 B.C., at least eight hundred years after the Hebrews had settled in Palestine, and they are not always, especially in the accounts of the times before the kings, in accord with contemporary records. The Book of Judges, which contains the Song of Deborah, the oldest document in the Bible, tried to show the prosperity of the country when the people adhered strictly to the worship of Jehovah. In point of fact, the Judges did not succeed each other as rulers; they were local magistrates, each governing his own district only, and many of them were contemporary.

SAUL AND DAVID KINGS OF ISRAEL

Though there were often raids and battles against the Canaanites, the real menace to the Hebrews were the Philistines. They served a valuable purpose in uniting the tribes, who, for the first time, felt the lack of a military leader. At the end of the eleventh century the Hebrews united to face the enemy; a southerner named Saul became their first king and led them to victory. Saul had a difficult task. It needed a strong ruler to keep the scattered and intensely individual tribes united, and to stir them up to fight when it was not their own piece of territory that was threatened. The prophet Samuel, whose power as a religious leader was considerable, disliked Saul and was jealous of his influence. During the rare times of peace, Saul was troubled by his rival David, who had a large following, including Samuel. After an eventful reign, during which he moulded Israel into a nation, Saul died by his own hand, having suffered a heavy defeat and the slaying of his son Jonathan by the Philistines.

He was succeeded by his son-in-law, David, who little by little regained the cities conquered by the Philistines. He gained the support of the south and took Jerusalem. This conquest of Jerusalem was a great military feat, for the city is situated high on the rocks, and was strongly fortified. Its capture encouraged the north to rally round David, and he began a long and prosperous reign which ranks as the most successful in the annals of the Jews, and which laid the foundations of his successors' power.

The exploits of David, who was a great soldier and a great poet, were re-told from generation to generation; he was the most popular and well beloved of the Hebrew heroes. Before he became king, his career had been full of excitement: Saul, who feared him as a rival for the throne, exiled him; many daring men joined him, and he became leader of a powerful band of outlaws who took toll of the neighbouring districts. David had an organization whereby all neighbouring landowners paid him a protection levy, in return for which the outlaws saw that no harm came to them and their lands. If the money was not forthcoming from one of them, the unfortunate man's goods were seized and he himself was driven away.

When Ishbosheth, Saul's son, and Abner, his chief captain, were slain, David had no rivals for the throne. He wisely made Jerusalem the capital; being on neutral ground, it favoured neither the north nor the south. The ark was installed there, and plans were made to build a temple. The king's religion was sincere; he worshipped Jehovah and had a great respect for both priest and prophet. He was an excellent soldier and diplomatist, and built up the military strength of the nation. His reign of about forty years lasted till approximately 970 B.C.; his declining years were rendered troubled by the rebellion and death of his son Absalom.

Solomon succeeded to the throne amid many political assassinations. The number of wives kept by the kings of Israel always gave rise to trouble and competition among their sons when the king died. Whoever wanted the throne must be prepared to remove several near relatives from his path before he himself could be secure. Solomon, once firmly settled on the throne, pursued a policy of peace, making many alliances, and building up a great trade. He shared a fleet with Hiram, king of Tyre, and did business with Egypt as well as with the countries of the east. To strengthen the ties with other nations, he married foreign wives, and the size of his harem became proverbial. This policy was horrible to the prophets and religious leaders of the people, for altars were built, so that foreigners visiting Jerusalem, as well as the ladies themselves, could worship their own gods. Solomon himself seems to have regarded these places of worship as mere international courtesies—Jehovah remained his god, and shared the glory of his prosperous people.

THE GLORY OF SOLOMON

The king had a great love of show and display, and was especially interested in building. He fortified many provincial towns, and set out to make Jerusalem as splendid as any other capital. His father's plans for building a temple were carried out, and the portable tent that had hitherto housed the ark was discarded. The temple was small in comparison with the royal palace, on which far more money and care were spent. Solomon had a reputation for wisdom, and he undoubtedly gave Israel a remarkably high place among the

nations. But his building caused heavy taxation, money and workmen being raised by forced levies in the different districts, and by
the end of his reign, there was widespread discontent in the land.
When his long reign ended, the northern tribes seized the opportunity
to separate from the south, and Israel finished its short career as a
united kingdom.

Solomon's son, Rehoboam, ruled the southern kingdom of Judah,
while the rebel tribes elected Jeroboam as their king in the north,
which retained the name of Israel. The latter was by far the more
important, being more wealthy, civilized and vigorous than Judah,
which consisted largely of a shepherd population, and had only one
large town, Jerusalem. The southerners always felt that the other ten
tribes were cut off from the true worship of Jehovah; they took
pride in their temple at Jerusalem. The Old Testament was compiled by supporters of Judah; consequently many of the wisest rulers
of the northern kingdom are dismissed with the curt statement that
they made Israel to sin. Judah was sometimes a foe, sometimes an
ally, and more often a vassal of the more powerful Israel.

THE OVERTHROW OF THE TWO HEBREW KINGDOMS

After the death of Elijah, his successor, Elisha, anointed Jehu, an
army officer, as king. Jehu slew Jehoram and also the king of Judah,
who was staying with him, and entered in triumph into Jezreel. The
queen mother, Jezebel, hearing of the triumph of her enemy, decked
herself bravely in royal attire, and greeted the conqueror from a window with the taunt: "Had Zimri peace who slew his master?" The
sting of the remark lay in the fact that Zimri, who had murdered a
former king and usurped his throne, reigned only seven days. At
Jehu's command, the attendants threw her from the window, and she
was killed. The new king then had all the remaining sons of Ahab
slaughtered. To strengthen his position on the throne, he revived the
worship of Jehovah, casting down all the altars of the various Baals
worshipped in the district, and killing their priests and prophets.

The might of the Assyrian empire had been steadily growing, and
soon after the reign of Jehu, Tiglath Pileser I overwhelmed Israel,
carrying many of the inhabitants away as captives. The northern
kingdom became a mere province of Assyria, after an independent
existence of only two centuries.

For a little while longer, the southern kingdom remained, though
it came under the Assyrian domination for a short time. The feeling
of the people, after the fall of the northern kingdom, was that perhaps
the gods of Assyria were stronger than Jehovah, and it needed all the
eloquence of the prophets to keep them to their faith. When the inhabitants of Jerusalem trembled at the approach of Sennacherib,
Isaiah exhorted them to stand fast in the faith of Jehovah, declaring
that he was all-powerful, and that Assyria was the scourge with
which he punished his disobedient people. When the enemy was at

the gates of the city, he prophesied the plague that destroyed their army. The rejoicings over the retreat of Sennacherib, and later over the fall of the hated Nineveh, were short-lived. The new power of Babylon threatened Judah. In 597 B.C. an army, with Nebuchadnezzar at its head, was at the gates of Jerusalem. There was a siege of three months, and the king, his harem, and nearly all the wealthy people and skilled craftsmen, were deported to Babylon, along with the valuables from the palace and the temple.

Nebuchadnezzar set up Zedekiah as vassal king, exacting an oath of obedience from him. But Zedekiah began to plot with the rulers of Egypt and Tyre and Sidon against the might of Babylon. Soon another army was besieging Jerusalem, which, after a year and half, surrendered. The prophet Jeremiah was a prominent member of the pro-Babylonian party, and during the siege, constantly advocated surrender. Eventually it was taken, and Zedekiah was captured at Jericho. His sons were slain before his eyes, and he himself was blinded, before setting forth as a captive on the long hopeless journey to Babylon, where he ended his days. A second group of the inhabitants of Jerusalem was taken prisoner, all the chief buildings were systematically destroyed, and the city walls were broken down. There was a brief attempt to continue the government with a Jewish noble acting for Babylon as governor at Mizpah. He was murdered, and the few remaining great families fled to Egypt.

JEWISH WORSHIP SPREADS

It looked as if the Israelite nation had gone the same way as the hundreds of other Oriental peoples, who had enjoyed a brief prosperity and then been absorbed into one or other of the great empires. Its tribes had known little political ability, and except under David and Solomon, had been of less importance than their neighbours in Phœnicia, Philistia and Damascus. The bulk of the poorer classes had been left in their mother country; but the men of substance and learning were exiles in Mesopotamia and Egypt, the two centres of ancient civilization. It would have been natural for the exiles from Palestine to fall under the spell of richly endowed religions that were older than Abraham, and to sacrifice their old customs for the rewards of busy commerce and material comfort. But this did not happen. The dispersion of the Jews, which Nebuchadnezzar began, stopped the old temple-worship of Jehovah, but carried the worship of Jehovah over a wider area. The faith was kept alive by the prophets and their devout followers by the waters of Babylon and Nile. In both countries, though some of the captives fell away, most remained true to their god, without being oppressed by their new rulers. The Persian conquest left them free to return to the old country, where, after a short attempt to restore the monarchy, government was organized on a religious basis, with the High Priest at its head. Many remained in Mesopotamia and Egypt, to be the forerunners of that Dispersion of the Jews throughout the civilized world which has lasted to this day and influenced many nations.

It is a question of supreme importance how the Hebrews, originally a wandering people and never—even when they had become settled agriculturalists—very powerful, created their high ideal of God, in spite of the outside influences to which they were continually subjected. Their early view of Jehovah differed little from their conception of Marduk, Assur or any other god. The forms of worship were similar; many seem to have been inherited from older inhabitants of the land. The Hebrews regarded certain stones and trees as the dwelling-places of a god, and hence as being sacred; and in early times, water was revered as a creator of life. The idea of existence after death was that it happened in a dark place underground. By all the peoples who inhabited Palestine, burial was regarded as essential, and there was a great horror of the Babylonian magic.

The essential difference between the early and late Hebrew religions, was that the latter was a definite monotheism. Jehovah came to be regarded as the one god, and as a moral deity, whereas no other god had ever been regarded as free from human faults and foibles. This view of God was formulated and constantly impressed upon the people by the prophets of Israel.

THE LAW OF MOSES

Tradition associates the beginnings of Jehovah-worship with Moses. He was a great law-giver, and, if he is the originator of the Decalogue, he was certainly a great religious leader also. Though the word Yahweh is older than Moses, names made up with it do not appear among the Hebrews until his time, and we are told in Exodus: "I am Yahweh, and I appeared unto Abraham, unto Isaac and unto Jacob, but by my name Yahweh was I not known to them." The idea of monotheism had appeared in the world once before—it is probable that Moses, living in Egypt, knew the details of the faith of Akhnaton, and may have been influenced by it. Despite the teaching of their leader, the main body of the Hebrews often found it easier to worship the gods of the country in which they were settled. Even when the Baal-worship of a district was changed to that of Jehovah, it usually went on with no alteration in the ritual. The religious feasts took place on dates of festivals of an agricultural nature that were already celebrated in the land. There was consequently the danger of people beginning to believe that, like the different Baals, the Jehovah worshipped in each village was a different god. The strictest view of Jehovah worship was kept alive by a band of fanatical devotees, named the Rechabites, who drank no wine, refused to cultivate the soil or build houses, and led austere lives as shepherds. Self-seeking kings, such as Jehu, who caused a revival in the national worship for their own ends, deeply religious men, such as the prophet Elijah, and fanatics like the Rechabites, all had a purifying effect on the people's religion. The essential difference between the Hebrew worship of Jehovah, and that of their neighbours for their own gods, was that whereas the Baals were regarded as being akin each to its own tribe, Jehovah was not akin to the Hebrews, but had deliberately chosen them as his people and had elected to be their special protector. A covenant or treaty had been made between the people and their god; he would guide and guard them only if they kept their part of the bargain, and would not, like other deities, protect them whether their behaviour was right or wrong. This difference gave the prophets a starting-point for the teaching that was to raise Jehovah high above all other gods.

THE EARLY PROPHETS

Prophets were not peculiar to the Hebrews. Other peoples' gods had them in their service; many of them were possessed of the gift of second-sight. Most of them were subject to fits of ecstasy; they frequently made use of music or some form of hypnotism to assist them into a state of trance. A state of frenzy is extremely infectious—often whole groups of men would be found, all acting as if they were possessed. There were many of these lesser prophets in Israel, but great men, such as Elijah, sometimes rose among them and wielded political as well as religious influence. A prophet did not set himself up to be a foreteller of the future, but an interpreter of the commands of God. If he did foretell, it was certainly only for his own generation, and concerning the events of the near future. The Hebrew prophets were much addicted to the use of symbolic actions, which were regarded as extremely potent. They were far from pandering to public opinion, frequently taking very unpopular courses of action. There are many points of difference between the great Hebrew prophets who have left their words in writing, but their conception of God was fundamentally the same. Attempts have been made to show that some of them gained ideas from external sources, but no true parallel has been found, and they stand unique among the religious teachers of the world.

Earliest of the writing prophets was Amos, who, although a southerner, preached in the northern kingdom in the eighth century B.C. He was a countryman, and is the first known social reformer in western Asia, condemning the life in towns and the exploitation of the poor by the rich. He warns the wealthy who are battening on their less fortunate brethren, that the day is at hand when Jehovah will send the Assyrians to punish them; their luxurious habitations will be destroyed, and they themselves carried away captive. Amos taught that God is pre-eminently righteous, and that his people must become so too. Exile was the punishment foretold for the neglect of their duty. He wrote little of theological interest, but passionately denounced the crime of inhumanity.

Hosea, who succeeded Amos in the northern kingdom, was possibly of much the same social station, being a smallholder. He was, however, a native of Israel, and the shortcomings of the land made a more personal appeal to him. He lived through its most troublous times, and contemptuously denounced the vacillating policies of the kings. Though not indifferent to the social evils of the day, Hosea is more concerned with the wrong attitude of the people towards Jehovah. Amos's god was a god of justice, Hosea's is essentially a god of mercy. The prophet reproaches the people for their falling away from the worship of Jehovah; he pours contempt on the practice of sacrifice, and urges that, above all things, man must love God.

ISAIAH, JEREMIAH AND EZEKIEL

Isaiah, who, later in the eighth century B.C., wrote the first part of the composite book of that name, was a native of Jerusalem, a member of the upper classes, possibly even of royal blood. He started his career as a prophet by the vision which is told in the sixth chapter of his book, and foretold the coalition of Syria with the northern kingdom, the fall of Samaria, and the invasion of Sennacherib. More than any other prophet, he held that Jehovah was the ruler of the entire universe; all nations were but as tools in His hands and He used one to chastise the other. Isaiah counselled an implicit faith in Jehovah, instead of reliance on alliances with other nations. Though concerned more with kingdoms than individuals, he attacked social wrongs. The first known prophet to predict the coming of a Messiah to the Jews, Isaiah was given to ecstatic experiences and was a great worker of wonders, and a healer. Above all things, he persistently preached the majesty, holiness and trustworthiness of God.

The prophet Jeremiah was possibly a descendant of Moses. He was a man of culture, well versed in tradition and greatly influenced by the work of Hosea. Unlike the earlier prophets, who bewailed the evils and dangers of national sin, Jeremiah held that the worst sins were individual sins. He preached that religion was a matter of the heart more than of outward observance, and that it should rest entirely between the individual and God. Like Isaiah, he advocated trust in God, rather than in foreign allies; during the siege of Jerusalem he preached a doctrine of passiveness, and held the unpopular opinion that it would be better to give in to the Babylonians. When the city was captured, he was taken prisoner, but was liberated, in order, presumably, to act as a good influence on the people who were not deported. When the headlong flight to Egypt took place, the people forcibly took Jeremiah with them, but no more is known of the fate of the tenderest and most peaceable of the prophets.

Ezekiel was a priest who was deported to Babylon after the first surrender of Jerusalem. He seems to have been given a great deal of freedom, and many people resorted to him as an oracle when they wanted predictions of the future. His gloomy prophecies do not seem to have been taken seriously until the destruction of Jerusalem, which he predicted, actually came to pass. More than the other prophets,

Ezekiel was gifted with second-sight, and he frequently fell into trances or was possessed by ecstasy. He represents the change from the old Yahwehism to the Judaism of later days, and preached an especially individual religion. He denounced the ancient idea that the sins of the fathers were visited on the children, maintaining that each received treatment according to his own merits. Though predicting the fall of Jerusalem, Ezekiel foretold that a new, purified people would be drawn from the remnant, who would rise to be a great nation. He laid emphasis on the ritual of worship, and preached of a judgment day to come. The birth of a shepherd was foretold, who would be descended from David, and become king of the Jews. Ezekiel was firm in his faith that the influence of Jehovah would give a great earthly triumph to the Jewish nation in the future. He was always kindly disposed towards the northern kingdom, which was included in the rosy future he predicted.

Most of the second part of the book of Isaiah was written by an unknown prophet who gave fresh heart to the despondent Jewish captives in Babylon. He clearly expresses the great idea of absolute monotheism, and prophesies that other nations, seeing its triumph in the future, would emulate the Jews in their worship.

GREATNESS OF THE HEBREW FAITH

The change in belief from a local to a universal god is entirely the work of the great prophets. As a small example of the change of view, the Temple, hitherto regarded by the Jews as the most wonderful building on earth, they declared not worth rebuilding, as it was unable to house the greatness of God. For the same reason, they proclaimed the uselessness of sacrifice.

Certainly the religion of the Hebrews owes something to other great civilizations. The book of Psalms, attributed to David, consists of a number of chants written throughout the ages. Some of them, notably Psalm 104, which is almost identical with a chant written by Akhnaton, were of Egyptian origin; many were written as ritual psalms, such as those concerned with the ceremonial employed with regard to the ark. Psalm 45 was obviously written by a court poet to celebrate the nuptials of a king. Some have to do with ritual, others are prophetical, and they express many contradictory doctrines. But their survival, and the use of them in modern life, is the best proof of their being a collection of the finest expressions of inner religious life in literature. From other religions, Israel borrowed mainly matters of ritual; had it been more than that, the resulting hotch-potch would hardly have survived and spread as it has done. The noble doctrine of one great deity—a god of mercy, righteousness and love—is a vital religion. The best elements of the Hebrew faith are still carried on to-day in Judaism, Mohammedanism and Christianity. No parallel to the teaching of the prophets has been found; no foreign source existed from which they could have drawn their beliefs. Its conception and survival indeed possess all the attributes of divine revelation.

CHAPTER 7

CIVILIZATION'S DEBT TO THE NEAR EAST

BEFORE we go on to the story of the great empires of Persia, Macedon and Rome, it would be well to consider what debt these civilizations and those following them owed to the countries of the Near East.

Outside the Fertile Crescent wandered prowling nomad hordes; they lived in tents, and while a few of these were comparatively luxurious, on the whole their furnishings were extremely simple, as was their manner of living. The nomads counted their wealth mainly in the flocks and herds they possessed; these forced them to be constantly on the move in search of fresh pasturage. For this reason, during normal conditions they seldom formed large communities; often a family would maintain only occasional intercourse with its neighbours. Families were seldom large, for in bad seasons it was a handicap to have many mouths to feed. The children took their part in the care of the flocks from a very early age, and education was entirely of a practical nature. Bad seasons forced them to go further afield in search of food for the flocks, and in times of famine they would band together to attack the cities of the dwellers in the fertile lands, whose early history has been described in the past chapters. These people, in every way a striking contrast to the wandering tribes of herdsmen, had passed from the domestication of animals to the complete control and understanding of agriculture, the discovery of metal, of writing and the arts, before they fell under the rule of the great Aryan empires.

CULTURE IN THE RIVER VALLEYS

The fertile valleys ensured good crops to their inhabitants, who produced the first organized form of government when they developed the city-state. This consisted of the city itself, and its surrounding area of cultivated land, and beyond that, pasturage. Often the nomads were independent, leading a self-contained existence under the rule of the local priest or prince. Sometimes there were quarrels between neighbouring states, or an unusually ambitious prince set out to increase his possessions; then for some time one of the cities would be the head of several others, and its prince would be overlord of the conquered rulers. But whether independent or under the government of a neighbour, these states quickly developed a very high degree of civilization. As soon as an efficient system of irrigation was organized, the necessities of life came so easily to the people that they had plenty of time to think about comfort, and to experiment with ways of enhancing it. From the Near East came the first highly developed practical arts: metal-working, weaving, glass-blowing, paper-making and many others. It is not generally realized that an amazing degree of comfort and luxury was enjoyed by the upper classes of civilized peoples several thousand years before Christ. In the homes of the rich, well staffed with slaves, living was probably just as comfortable as it is to-day. Hygiene was considered extremely important, and great care was taken about personal cleanliness. Furniture was both beautiful and comfortable, houses were elegantly decorated, and interest was taken in the varying fashions of clothing, hair-dressing and personal adornment.

THE GIFTS OF COMMERCE

Travel was easy in the river-valleys, either by land or by water, and the trader helped the worker by taking his goods to the next town or village for exchange. Markets grew up, people travelled to them, sometimes from great distances, with their handiwork; tales of adventure, rumours and general information, were exchanged, as well as goods; credit became general, and business agreements were stamped with personal seals. The Lydians were the first to invent a genuine coinage; after that, money began to pass from hand to hand. In order to transport their goods, the people of the Near East built the earliest roads, bridges and ships. They were the first to move heavy weights, and to create buildings that were large even by modern standards. Present-day architecture is much indebted to these early builders, for they made use of the first colonnades, arches and towers. Sculpture, too, was very far advanced: decorative work was finely done, and figures were cleverly portrayed, both in the cutting of enormous statues, such as those of the Pharaohs of Egypt, and in the tiny engravings which adorned the cylinder seals.

Shipbuilding had reached an efficient standard, and by the sixth century B.C., the waters of the Black Sea, Red Sea and Persian Gulf were well known to mariners, and they had even ventured into the Indian Ocean, and beyond the straits of Gibraltar. There were many adventurous sailors willing to set out for uncharted seas, although piracy was frequently the object of these early mariners. Often trade and piracy went hand in hand, and many seafarers turned to trade only when a strong power had curbed their marauding. None of the early great kingdoms or empires maintained their sea supremacy for long; generally, if possible, they made use of the navies of conquered subjects or of their own allies. Crete and Phoenicia are possibly the only two nations to have a lasting effect on maritime affairs before the advent of the Greek sailors, who are described in the next part of this book. Nevertheless, the Mediterranean was busy with shipping throughout the summer months, and the spirit of adventure and discovery, which later animated the great sailing peoples of the north-west, had in this region already come into being.

Writing was one of the most important inventions of the Near East, which also produced the alphabet we use to-day. The modern world is indebted to Egypt, and still more to Assyria, for the libraries which preserved so much of interest—prose, verse, history, social discussions, and even drama. The calendar was worked out, and a start was made in the study of medicine, astronomy and mathematics. But there was a lack of freedom of the mind among these early peoples, so that they made little enquiry into the natural causes of things. Consequently, sciences did not make the same progress as arts, but there was, at any rate, a concrete beginning, which served materially to assist the researches of the Greeks who were at a later period in history to carry the methodical study of these things to a pinnacle of development which had no parallel in previous ages.

GOVERNMENT AND SLAVERY

From early days in Egypt and Sumer, there had been an administrative form of government, with salaried officials, and civil servants, definite scales of payment for them, taxation, and state relief for the needy. There had also been a movement towards the building up of large kingdoms, in which tribute and obedience were paid to the conquering leader. The Assyrians developed the idea of the Empire, with colonies and dependencies governed by officials from the mother country, with whose profit and welfare the subordinate land was intimately connected. In the founding of these kingdoms and empires, organized warfare was brought to a fine art; arms and methods of fighting became more and more efficient, and discipline was instilled into the troops. Wars produced hordes of slaves, and when the fashion for wholesale deportation came in, these were of many different classes. Some worked at trades, such as pottery, weaving or metal-working; others were kept as entertainers— singers, dancers, musicians or acrobats—but the great majority either worked on the land, or were set to the hard labour of transport, road-building or mining. They were often ill-treated, especially in Egypt and Mesopotamia; for the slave population increased so enormously that it was a matter of no importance to the wealthy master how soon they became worn out. Farm workers were better off, and so were domestic servants; but even in the empires where laws were most favourable to slaves, there was always the knowledge of a complete lack of freedom that in all probability must pass on to their children also. It was, in fact, man's steadily increasing dependence on slave-labour, that eventually proved to be the essential weakness of the ancient civilizations and empires.

DESPOTISM OF THE ORIENTAL RULERS

Oriental monarchs were absolute rulers, with no obligation whatsoever to render account for their actions to their subjects. The king might be swayed by priests, or advised by officials and generals, but there was no idea of the people having a voice in the government, no notion in any mind of such a thing as democracy. Consequently, the people as a whole lacked the stimulating responsibilities that produced the great men of Greece and Rome. The kings often took their names from the gods of their countries; like the gods, they could do no wrong, and in many cases they were regarded as divine or semi-divine by their subjects. Sometimes the king was associated with the chief god of the land, regarded as being the personification of the deity, and worshipped by the people accordingly. At other times, he was thought to be the son of a god or goddess, and in some districts he was thought to attain divinity only on his death.

EARLY RELIGIOUS IDEAS

It was in matters of religion that the Near East made perhaps the greatest progress. Though we still have superstitions that have been handed down from the Babylonians, and even from the earlier days of nature-worship, yet from the same lands came the earliest belief in a sole god, which has endured till to-day. The importance of the sixth century B.C. in the religious history of the world cannot be over-emphasized. Before this time, among the cult of, at worst, blood-thirsty, at best, worldly, gods, Akhnaton was the one solitary religious reformer, and his work was soon lost.

It is, of course, impossible to surmise what were the very earliest ideas about the gods. It is noticeable that religion did not play nearly so large a part in the lives of the nomads as in those of the city-dwellers. It was probably when man turned from his flocks to become a grower of corn that he first began to associate divine power with nature. He noticed the different positions of the stars at the various seasons, and saw the corn seemed to flourish when planted under the auspices of some particular stars, and not when others were in the ascendant. The influence of sun and rain and storms on the crops struck the imagination of the early agriculturalists, and increased the tendency to worship, and try to propitiate, various manifestations of nature. From earliest times, some form of sacrifice seems to have been associated with burials, and the idea of a divine death and re-birth was originally connected with the yearly rites inspired by the planting of seed and the spring-growing.

THE POWER OF THE PRIESTS

For the most part, especially as their cult spread eastwards, the nature gods were regarded with fear, and their rites were usually cruel and licentious. With the conception of gods and goddesses as being very much like human-persons, came the idea that, like people, they needed a house to live in and servants to tend them. Thus came into being the temple, and, of far greater importance, the priesthood. The tremendous influence exercised by the priests on all classes and kinds of civilized people cannot be over-estimated, and they were largely responsible for the encouraging and developing of the powers of thought. But throughout all early religions, there was a deep-seated pessimism—the gods were regarded with genuine fear—and men's chief thought was of how to placate them in order to gain material benefits when on earth. There were only vague, unformed ideas about any form of future life; men's minds lacked true powers of reasoning; fear of the gods and a belief that events were foreordained by Fate, make the religions of the early civilized peoples unhappy.

THE GREAT SIXTH CENTURY

But during the sixth century B.C., there was a sudden stirring of religious feeling that stretched from the lands of the Mediterranean, right across to China—an impulse towards a better idea of God. The conception of a god of mercy, righteousness, truth and kindness was evolved by the Jewish prophets; and the dispersal of the Jews, after they had adopted their new idea of a universal god, was paramount in spreading this new cult. Their fanatical hatred of images, which had long been a matter of supreme importance to their religious leaders, became widely known. The tremendous change from the state where the priest, with his ritual and sacrifice, was all-important, to that directed by the prophet, with his moral teaching, differentiation between collective and individual sin, and his idea of a god of mercy, justice and love, was the product of the sixth century in the Near East, and one which represented a great step forward in the whole evolution of the human race.

INFLUENCE ON WESTERN CULTURE

In this cradle of our own civilization dwelt the rich agricultural and manufacturing peoples, whose wealth continually attracted raiders from the desert. Some were merely destructive, or only improved on methods of warfare, but others remained, adopting the life of the conquered civilized communities, and bringing fresh blood and new energy into these lands. The mixed population resulting in the Near East set an example, both to the rising civilizations on either side of it, and to the later ones of Europe—most of which was still in a state of complete barbarism—of the building of empires, of trade, travel, seamanship, architecture, decoration, literature, organized warfare, art, music, science and high religious fervour. It was the culture which first grew up in the lands of Egypt, Mesopotamia and Syria that permanently influenced the development and spread of civilization throughout the Western World.

An Assyrian stele showing tribute sent by King Jehu of Israel to Nineveh.

A portion of one of the bronze bands decorating the gates of the Palace of Shalmaneser III, King of Assyria, 860–825 B.C. In the upper panel are seen Assyrian infantry and chariots at the storming of a fortress, and, in the lower panel, chariots advancing from an Assyrian camp.

Statue, found at Gizeh, of King Kephren of Egypt, builder of the Second Pyramid.

This Minoan figure of carved ivory and gold represents the Snake-goddess of Crete.

Tutankhamen, Pharaoh of Egypt (*left*), fourteenth century B.C., abolished the Aton heresy and restored the traditional worship of Amon. The colonnade of Amenophis III (*right*) is part of the Temple of Luxor near Thebes.

PART II

THE GLORY OF GREECE

CHAPTER 8

GREEK HISTORY TO 500 B.C.

THE wonderful and distinctive history of ancient Greece is wrapped up with its peculiar geography and climate. Greece is a Mediterranean country, half-way between the cold North and the tropical South, cut off from the great Northern Flatland by the Balkans, a land of sharp outlines and strong vivid colours, of mountains everywhere rising steeply and suddenly from inlets of the sea, their bare peaks and ridges dominating little plains below in an atmosphere of unique clarity.

The striking beauty of this land has lured men in all ages to come from the North to live in it, and the extraordinary clearness of the air had its effect on generations of Greek artists and thinkers: clear vision and clear thought both came naturally to the majority of Greeks, and for this, as for much else, they could thank their climate and the surroundings in which they were born and bred. Mountains and sea both breed among men the love of independence and freedom, and very few Greeks lived out of reach of either. The whole country consists of mountain chains interrupted again and again by deep depressions, so that, like Palestine, Greece is divided into a great number of separate compartments by mountain-barriers, ideally suited for the growth of small communities of settlers, but making unity extremely difficult. Only rough tracks crossed the ranges between valley and valley, and if it had not been for the sea, communication would have been almost impossible. Fortunately for the Greeks, the sea was as universal as the mountains.

GREEK DEPENDENCE UPON THE SEA

The fantastically irregular coastline is scarred and cut by innumerable gulfs and inlets: very few communities lacked some sea-board, and none was more than forty miles distant from the coast. Most Greeks felt a hearty contempt for land-lubbers: they depended on the sea for travel and trade, and yet they were cautious in their use of it. Though more placid than the oceans of the world, the Mediterranean is often whipped to fury by sudden winds, called "snatchers" by the Greeks, and in the winter months was much too treacherous for navigation in small ships: the Greek had to sail without either map or compass, and knew little of the currents and reefs in waters far from his home. But in summer, there was constant traffic between the many harbours on the mainland and the countless small islands of the Aegean, which form stepping-stones for timid sailors up and down the length of Greek waters; and the Greek states which won power were those Sea Lords who forced a passage for their ships into every harbour. Greek history without the mountains would have been very different: without the sea the Greek feats of intellect and the foundation of prosperous colonies and sea routes in the Mediterranean, Aegean and Black Seas would have proved impossible, and the subsequent history of mankind impoverished.

Climate, too, had a profound influence on life in Greek lands. The Greeks themselves believed their own to be by far the best-tempered climate in the world, with its sharp division between winter and summer, its regular seasonal rainfall, and equable trade-winds. Occasional snow is quite common, even on the plains, in winter months, but the cold was not extreme enough to prevent the Greeks from living that open-air life which in the long summers was the most delightful and natural thing in the world for them. Between the regular torrential rainfall of spring and autumn, there were at least five perfectly dry months, with a steady North wind and a clear sky, when the torrents from the mountains dried up in their rocky beds, and the sea smiled with the countless laughter of rippling waves, and it was pleasant to lie out on the warm stones, and no man wanted a roof over his head.

The harvest came in May and early June, but this was no big affair. Very little of the total area of the country is cultivable. On the little plains, corn, wine and oil were produced, and the lower slopes of the mountains supported sheep and goats on their rough scrub, while bees sucked honey from myriad wild flowers, but it was never long before the rocky unproductive land intervened. The geography of Greece and the spirit of her people was summed up by the earliest and greatest of Greek poets, "Rough, but a fine mother of men, and the sweetest land that I can ever see."

THE AEGEAN SEA LORDS

Such was the geographical nursery of the Greek race. But for the beginning of Greek history, we must turn not to the mainland but to the island which lies like a great bulwark across the southern end of the Aegean Sea. By 2000 B.C. Crete was already the home of a remarkable civilization. This reached its zenith soon after 1600 B.C., and then endured for some four centuries more. Known as Minoan, after a legendary King Minos of Crete, this imperial culture ranks with the early civilizations of the Euphrates valley and the Nile delta as one of the great sources of human progress. The men of Crete were the first Sea Lords of the Aegean; their whole power rested on a strong navy and an enterprising overseas trade. They exported copper and purple dye, but the foundation of their greatness was rather their brilliant seafaring skill and the native quickness of their intellect than any natural product of their island. They were middlemen, trading between the Greek islands and the Nile delta and Syria; their art and way of life owed much to Egyptian influence.

Crete at this time was thickly populated by a busy and prosperous people, engaged in farming, industry and trade, leading an elaborate social and political life, and enjoying the elements of a literary education. The capital of the island was the city of Cnossos, where the king had his gorgeous palace, though Phaestos was important.

THE CULTURE OF MINOAN CRETE

Cnossos may well be called the first great city of European history. Its population in 1500 B.C. was 80,000, and they lived for the most part in houses that would stand comparison for cleanliness and comfort with those of any modern city. The town was laid out in streets, in which the houses were often of two or more stories. A group of rooms was built round one central court, through which came light and air, and among these rooms, a bathroom was often included. The royal palace at Cnossos was divided into two main suites, one official and the other private, with a magnificent staircase of five flights, a series of sumptuous halls and chambers, bathrooms, lavatories and workshops. The official suite included a throne-room, storage-magazines for weapons and food, and a shrine for the worship of the Cretan nature-goddess. The entrances to the palace were narrow and tortuous, probably for purposes of defence, though the city as a whole had no fortifications: so little did man fear invasion.

The artistic achievement of these people was wonderful in its refinement, delicacy and power. Their palaces were adorned with frescoes of women and animals against a country landscape, with paintings of stately cupbearers and dancing-girls and bull-baiting sports watched by fashionably dressed lords and ladies.

The Cretans were experts in gem-cutting, ivory-carving and pottery: they have also left behind them examples of metal-work and exquisite statuettes in ivory and gold. The costumes were interesting, and sometimes elaborate. Men were satisfied with a loin-cloth covered with a kilt, with overcoats for wintry weather, but the ladies favoured coloured bodices, small waists, long flounced skirts and high head-dresses. Both sexes wore jewellery, necklaces, earrings and engraved seals. In the long prosperous centuries of Cretan power, while the kings of Cnossos were extending their influence among the Greek islands and even on the mainland in the Peloponnese, life in the capital, for the nobles and the merchant classes, must have been a splendid, colourful thing.

THE KINGS OF MYCENAE

There were two cities in the Greek world whose power could be compared with Cnossos—Mycenae in the north-east corner of the Peloponnese, and Troy, which controlled the Hellespont, or straits of the Dardanelles. As early as 1600 B.C. Mycenae was the seat of kings, marvellously rich in gold, ruling a strong community with arts and crafts modelled on those of Crete. Cretan civilization had taken a firm hold on the Greek mainland, and when Cnossos was sacked with fire by sea-raiders at the beginning of the fourteenth century, Mycenae, "the golden city", supplanted it as the chief centre of culture and dominion in the Aegean. Under the rule of a great unknown king, who built a mighty fortified palace and a huge domed tomb of hewn stone, which survives to-day to be one of the wonders of the world, the people of Mycenae made their influence felt through the length and breadth of Greece. They were known as Achaeans: they spoke the Greek tongue, one of the forms of the Aryan language, and this name soon was used for the inhabitants of Greece as a whole. (The name "Greeks" was actually given to Achaeans, or Hellenes— as they were also called—by the Italians when they settled in the western Mediterranean.)

By the beginning of the twelfth century, all the peoples of Greece were united in a loose federation under the leadership of the Mycenaean kings, who were of the family of Atreus. Theirs was no strictly ruled empire; the other princes of Greek peoples acknowledged their eminence, and the most famous of them, Agamemnon, styled himself "King of kings". It was he who led the host of Greek chieftains and their peoples in the famous war against Troy.

"THE WIDE-WAYED CITY" OF TROY

For many centuries, men had lived on the site of Troy by the river Scamander, but it was not until 1600 B.C. that a powerful fortress was built, from which Trojan princes ruled the country far and wide. Their palace was surrounded by a huge wall, fifteen feet thick, with high gates and strong square towers and a rampart of brick, inside which a broad terrace ran, giving to Troy the name of "the wide-wayed city". All men spoke of it as rich in gold and rich in bronze: its great wealth came partly from trade and tolls exacted from ships passing through the straits, partly from the tribute of its subjects and the spoils of piratical raids. A clash of arms between Troy and Mycenae was probable, since they were the chief rival powers of the Aegean. The pretext for the Trojan war is enshrined in the old story which tells how Paris, son of King Priam of Troy, visited Sparta in the Peloponnese, seduced queen Helen, the wife of Agamemnon's brother Menelaus, and carried her off to Troy: to avenge the wrong, all the Achaean princes followed in the train of Agamemnon to do battle with the Trojans, and after a siege of ten years, Troy was taken and laid waste.

The Greeks themselves always thought of the Trojan war as the first important event in their history, the glorious achievement of their heroic ancestors. The minstrels who were kept at the courts of the Achaean princes composed many lays about the great deeds of their masters in war and adventure, and gradually from these lays arose a large body of poetic myths gathering round the names of the heroes who fought in the Trojan war. Some three centuries later than the war, a poet of genius, called Homer, made of these myths two great epics, long poetic tales, which are still read and acknowledged to be among the greatest poetry in the world. They are the *Iliad* and the *Odyssey*. From them, we derive our knowledge of these great Achaeans and of their way of life, and though the people themselves perished utterly when hordes of invaders entered Greece from the north, their name and their achievement live for ever in the poetry of Homer as well as much concerning their social life and customs.

HOW THE HOMERIC PRINCES LIVED

The Achaeans now had no strong military power to challenge them in the Aegean, and were free to found a series of settlements in the Asiatic region which Troy had formerly ruled. Of these, Lesbos was the most important. The Achaean princes lived in houses simply planned but lavishly adorned with gold, silver, bronze and finely-wrought handiwork. The living-room was a large hall, with a hearth in the middle and an opening in the roof, through which the smoke escaped. Round the courtyard were bedrooms and storehouses, and a bathroom was usually included. The women of the house had their own quarters, but they often mixed freely with men, and in Homer's poems there are many feminine characters of striking beauty, strength and charm. Perhaps because of this, the Achaeans were remarkable for the delicacy of their good manners: they were extremely courteous to the elderly, to women and to strangers.

They took joy in many amusements, notably singing, dancing and vigorous athletic sports. "The perfect pleasure for a man," says a Homeric hero, "is to sit among the banqueters in a palace and listen to a goodly minstrel, when the tables are laden with bread and meat, and the cupbearer draws wine from the mixing-bowl and pours it into goblets." They were great eaters, great tellers of tales and great adventurers. Homer tells us often how a chieftain would collect a company of his men and how they would launch a swift dark ship with bright vermilion prow and, sitting in due order on the thwarts, smite the grey water with their oars as they journeyed far over the wine-dark sea in search of gold or slaves, or simply for the love of seeing new lands and daring strange things.

Hunting was one of their favourite pastimes—lions and wild boars, deer and hares—and fighting was part of the stuff of life. Their chief weapon was the spear; for armour, they had bronze helmets with waving horse-hair plumes, a cuirass of metal or leather, bronze greaves for the legs, and huge enveloping shields of ox-hide stretched taut on wooden struts and strengthened with bronze. The chieftains rode into battle in small chariots, driven by a squire, and then, dismounting, engaged an enemy in single combat with the spear. Battle was mainly an affair of such single combats between chieftains: the common people were but lightly armed, mere stubble before the ravening flame of some great warrior's armed onset.

ACHAEAN GREECE

It was indeed an age of princes, beside whom the common people counted for little in peace or war. The princes were hailed as "fosterlings of God", ruling by divine right, and even in their agriculture, of which Homer gives us some delightful pictures, the Achaeans laboured in all things for their chiefs and not for themselves. We see men at work ploughing in a rich tillage field, with helpers handing them sweet wine as they come to the furrow's end; reapers cutting corn with sickles, while the boys of the village carry armfuls to three binders; lads and lasses dancing to the music of a boy's sweet instrument along the path to the vineyard, stripping the vines of the black grapes and bringing them home in plaited baskets; shepherds watching peacefully over a great pasture of white sheep; herdsmen with their dogs, driving their cattle from byre to pasture and facing the sudden excitement of an attack by two lions upon the herd; a gathering of the folk in the market-place, with the elders giving judgement in a dispute about the shedding of blood; a marriage-feast, with a throng leading the bride through the streets from her chamber, beneath the blaze of torches, to the sound of the bridal song. This picture of happy country life we may set against all the tales of grim fighting and sudden death which were depicted in the legend and tradition which had Achaean history as their source.

Religion played a large part in the life of the Achaeans—a religion very different from the savage and degrading cults of most other peoples at that time; in many essentials it was to undergo little change through all the centuries of Greek history. They worshipped many gods and goddesses, each clearly defined with name and attributes, and each with specially appointed function. These divinities were believed to be in the fashion of men and women but immortal, with human minds and passions but more than human power, divine beings conceived in the glorified image of man. They dwelt on the quiet snow-capped heights of Mount Olympus, whose peak rises serene and sparkling above the clouds in northern Greece, and formed one great divine family, under one supreme God, Zeus, "the father of gods and men". Besides this High God Zeus, who was lord of thunder and lightning and tempest, and at the shaking of whose locks the heavens and earth trembled, there were also Poseidon of the dark-blue locks, lord of the sea and god of horses; Apollo of the golden hair, who carried a lyre as patron of all music and god of healing; Ares, the swift terrible one, god of war; Athena of the grey flashing eyes, goddess of all craftsmanship and skill; golden Aphrodite, lover of laughter, goddess of love; Artemis the swift huntress— virgin mistress of the chase.

The Achaeans believed that these gods, though jealous of any slights to themselves, were, on the whole, on the side of justice and mercy. They are angry only with those who despise prayer and worship and who, in cruel pride, hurt the innocent and the weak: they do not wantonly bring evil upon men: the cause of all evil is in the wickedness of men's own hearts. In their ritual, the Achaeans had outgrown the old customs of magic and human sacrifice: the centre of their worship was the splendid sacrifice of oxen and sheep, a solemn and beautiful burnt-offering accompanied by priestly prayer and hymn and dance. These sacrifices were not usually bribes to the deity, but rather a friendly and intimate communion in which, by the sharing of meat and drink, men could draw near to their god, and contrast favourably with most primitive religious rites.

THE DORIAN INVASIONS

Troy fell to the Achaeans about 1180 B.C. Only two generations later, the Achaeans themselves and all their settled ordered life began to go down into darkness, swept away by invading hosts entering Greece from the north. Chief among these was another Aryan-speaking folk, the Dorians, who, now as single spies, now in battalions, for several generations came marching steadily south to possess themselves of Greece. The Achaeans, effete and degenerate in their turn as the Cretans had been before them, were pushed into corners of the land or overseas. The great Achaean strongholds of Mycenae and Tiryns were burnt; the invaders made themselves masters of the whole Peloponnese except the central block of Arcadia; throughout central Greece the old peoples of the heroic world were dispossessed by these virile invaders.

DECAY OF THE ACHAEAN ORDER

Only in Attica did they remain undisturbed; where, centuries later, was to spring a flower of brilliant genius, finer far than any of the intrusive Dorian race. Many of the old Achaean peoples found refuge in Attica, and from Attica swarmed across the Aegean to occupy the islands and the coast of Asia Minor opposite. Among these were the people called the Ionians, who were to give their name to those parts for the next thousand years and more. The northern corner of the Asia Minor coast was occupied by other fugitives known as Aeolians, while those Dorians who could find no room in the Peloponnese spread over Crete—now exhausted after her centuries of glorious power—Rhodes, and the south-west of Asia Minor.

Thus, amid the Dorian conquest and the great migrations of the Greek peoples, the old Achaean order of things crumbled away. A dark age follows, through which no gleam of light shines till the eighth century. The Dorians, who, though Greek-speaking, were backward compared with the Achaeans, brought a fresh robust strength to Greece, but for many generations after their first conquest of the land, there was no culture worthy of the name in Greece. In later ages, the Greeks looked back, for the origin of their genius, beyond the Dorians to the heroic age of Mycenae, rich in gold.

THE GREEK CITY-STATES

For long years after the great migrations, the Greeks lived, as they had settled, in scattered villages; but gradually the people of each valley or plain leagued themselves together to form a single political community for worshipping the gods, for buying and selling, for common defence and common government. The centre of the community was usually some commanding rocky height in the middle of the plain—the shape of many Greek valleys is like an inverted saucer—which was a fortress and a capital. Such a community was called in Greek a *polis*, or city-state, and the central fortress an acropolis—a word which means literally the upper part of a town. The most famous acropolis is, of course, at Athens.

There grew up a vast number of these city-states, each diminutive and distinct from its neighbour over the mountain-range. States numbering millions, like those of the great kingdoms of the East, were impossible in Greece: the mountains prevented that. The citizens of a city-state lived so close to the centre of government that they felt it only natural that they should all have a share in it. One after another, the local kings and chieftains were deposed, and the

Greeks entered upon the biggest political experiment in human history, the experiment of governing themselves. They took a fierce pride in their freedom, and for their own particular *polis* they felt a love and adoration so passionate and intense that what we call patriotism pales in comparison. To a Greek, life outside a *polis* was hardly worth living. In the frequent wars between one city-state and another, the citizens cheerfully died for their city. But they did more than that; in all their thoughts and acts, they lived for her, from the cradle to the grave.

At first not all the inhabitants of a city-state enjoyed a direct share in the government. In the eighth and seventh centuries it was the large landowners who had the power, and the majority worked as agricultural labourers in their employment without much say in affairs. The invention of coinage, which spread to Greece from Lydia, aggravated the condition of the smallholders and peasants. They knew neither how to get nor to manage this strange money, and so fell an easy prey to the grasping ambition of the big landowners, until many of them found themselves dispossessed of their parcels of land and little better than serfs.

GREEK COLONIZATION

Thus, in almost every city-state, there arose a large class of landless men. The oligarchs, as the wealthy few who ruled a state were called, were faced with the dangerous discontent of an increasing number of paupers. Greece itself was not fertile enough to support this growing population, and in order to avoid a division of their own estates among the citizens, the rulers, like the Phoenician kings, hit upon the expedient of sending out colonies to foreign lands. Overpopulation and political discontent, caused by the concentration of wealth in the hands of a few, were responsible for that great colonizing movement which, in a few generations, changed the entire face of the Mediterranean world.

A Greek colony was no haphazard affair. A company of men and women was sent overseas to occupy some carefully-chosen site, under the command of a prominent citizen as "founder" of the colony, and the whole enterprise was organized by the state. The colony founded by them was intended as a replica of the mother city, and though politically independent, remained bound to its parent by strong ties of sentiment and religion. The Greek colonies, unlike most of the Phoenician, were not merely trading-stations, but commercial intercourse between a city-state and its colonies flourished. Thus, for trade purposes, and because communication could only be by sea, a good harbour was the first essential in the site for a Greek colony: trees, too, there must be for ships' timber, good spring-water for drinking, virgin land for cultivation, pasture for flocks, and a friendly people in the hinterland with whom they could establish a peaceful relationship.

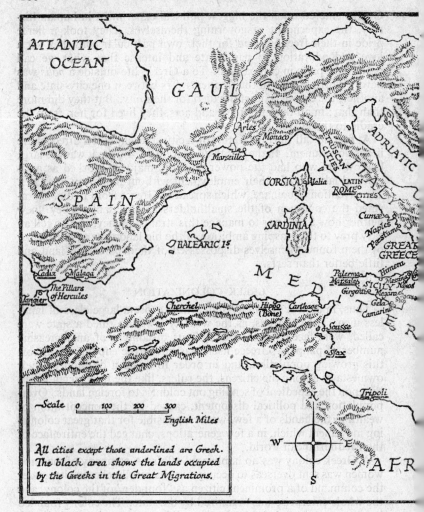

Scale 0 100 200 300
English Miles

All cities except those underlined are Greek.
The black area shows the lands occupied
by the Greeks in the Great Migrations.

THE EXTENT OF

Owing to the comparative poverty of Greek soil and the monopoly of large
landowners, the rulers of Greece encouraged organized colonization, thus following the example of the Phoenician kings. These planned migrations were at their
height from the middle of the Eighth Century B.C. to the middle of the Sixth
Century B.C. and served not only to establish thriving new cities, but to spread
Greek thought and customs. A good harbour, water for drinking and fertile land
were the essentials looked for by the Greeks in their search for suitable sites.

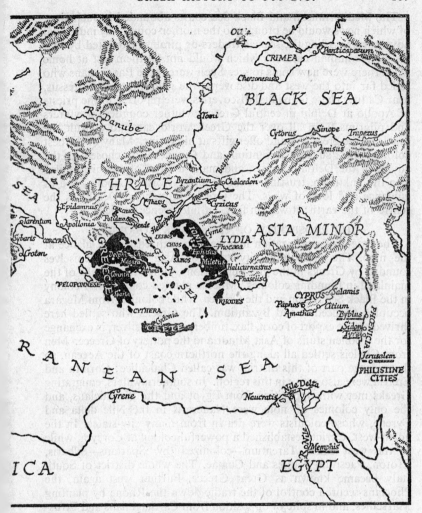

GREEK COLONIZATION

Greek settlements were established in the islands of Sicily, Cyprus and Corsica, and along the coastlines of the Mediterranean, Aegean and Black seas. Greek colonies were politically independent from the first, though exceptions did exist, particularly during the age of Athenian imperial supremacy. The Greeks intermarried with the native inhabitants of the regions colonized, and this had no evil results, many famous figures in Greek history having mixed blood. No barrier existed in practice between the Greek citizen and the hellenized native.

The Mediterranean and Black Sea coasts abounded in such sites, of which news would be brought to the mother-country by individual adventurers, sailing the seas as traders or pirates, prompted by that instinctive human curiosity which would not let them rest at home when there were new lands to see. Such were those Phoenicians who sailed far into the west and discovered the gold-mines of Tartessus, near Cadiz. These individual discoveries were reported to the priests of Apollo at Delphi in central Greece, whither countless wayfarers and pilgrims from all over the Greek world came to consult the oracle of the great god and offer gifts at his shrine. Many of the best colonial sites, such as Byzantium and Cyrene, were chosen on the advice of the Delphic priests, and many a band of colonists sailed into the unknown, trusting in the oracular word of Apollo, god of guidance and lord of ways. The Greeks thought of Delphi as the centre of the earth: it was, in fact, an intelligence service.

THE PROSPERITY OF THE GREEK COLONIES

The extent of colonization may best be realized from a glance at the map. The flourishing city-states of Asia Minor, themselves founded by Greeks in the great migrations, joined the Greeks of the mainland in founding colonies. Miletus planted colony after colony in the Black Sea region and the Crimea, while colonists from Megara occupied Chalcedon and Byzantium. The Greeks who settled here thrived on the export of corn, flax, timber, iron and silver, in exchange for the woollen stuffs of Asia Minor and the pottery of Greece. Men from Chalcis settled all along the northern coast of the Aegean, so that a large part of this district was called Chalcidice: Corinth and Eretria were also active in this region. In southern waters, emigrating Greeks met with opposition from Egypt and the Phoenicians, and the only colonies of note were Naucratis in the Nile delta and Cyrene, whose colonists were drawn from many city-states. In the north-west, Corinth established a powerful colony at Corcyra, while in the west came Tarentum—colonized by Spartans—Sybaris, Croton, Paestum, Naples and Cumae. The whole district of South Italy became known as Great Greece. Further west again, the Phocians secured control of the traffic down the Rhône by planting Marseilles, and in spite of opposition from Carthaginians and Etruscans, Sicily was girded with a ring of Greek colonies—Syracuse, Camarina, Girgenti, Messina, Naxos. Thus the amazing vitality of the Greek city-states in propagating themselves turned the Mediterranean, in two centuries, into something like a Greek sea.

Unfortunately, the rivalry between city and city in Greece spread also to their colonies, and so the Greeks never established a single indivisible supremacy in the Mediterranean. Only Rome, with her greater genius for organization, could achieve that. But it was through the hundreds of colonies that the leaven of Greek influence worked among other nations and the legacy of Greece was transmitted to posterity.

Of all the invading Dorians, the strongest were those who settled in the lovely valley of Lacedaemon, with Sparta for their capital. They enslaved the original inhabitants on both sides of Mount Taygetus and lived among a sullen, hostile population of these serfs, called helots, who outnumbered them by twenty to one. In the seventh century, these helots rebelled, and it was only by a desperate effort that the Spartans at last quelled them. Henceforward the Spartans lived in perpetual fear of another such crisis, and to meet the danger they suddenly changed their whole Greek way of life and government. They bade farewell to music and poetry and art, and imposed upon themselves and their children an iron discipline designed to weld them into an efficient garrison to suppress the serfs. In this way their city became a permanent barracks.

THE SPARTAN LIFE

Men underwent a continuous military training from birth, when any weakly infants were mercilessly killed: women were taught that their sole function was to produce soldiers for the state of pure Spartan blood, and, unlike other Greek women, received vigorous physical training with the men to make them strong mothers. Boys, from seven upwards, lived in barracks under the superintendence of older citizens and young Spartans with the sinister name of "Floggers". There they learnt to endure physical pain without a murmur, to make their bodies strong by constant gymnastics and drill, to develop pugnacity by particularly brutal games, in which loss of life was not unusual, and to increase resourcefulness by stealing food from their neighbours: the only shame in theft was in being caught. The toughness and brutality of these lads can be imagined. They were completely illiterate, though the people as a whole acquired a reputation for dry pungent wit. Manhood brought compulsory service in the secret police, and then, at thirty, came the even sterner discipline of a communal military life. No Spartan was allowed to trade or farm land: this was left to helots, and money was forbidden to citizens.

There was no beauty in Spartan life, and no softness either. Notorious for the filthiness of their personal habits and the nastiness of their food, the Spartans were the best fighters and the worst rulers in Greece. Their physical courage has never been surpassed, but so stern was their discipline that they could not learn personal responsibility, so constant the restraint imposed upon them that they never learnt to restrain themselves. Even the two kings who led them in battle were watched by government spies. The result was that, when a Spartan went abroad beyond the authority of his government, he usually indulged in drunkenness, greed and gross physical excess. The unique Spartan system, in which no change was allowed, taught men courage and unquestioning obedience, but it made them cruel, unimaginative and stubborn. Their methods of training had the result of endowing them with magnificent bodies and brutalized minds.

The Spartans knew only one master, their own law. Elsewhere in the seventh and sixth centuries B.C., there arose men who became sole masters of their city-state. In spite of the safety-valve of emigration, discontent and poverty were rife, and the small farmer, trader and artisan, who had not the time nor money to rule themselves, but resented the selfish rule of the nobles, sometimes found a champion who asserted their interests by force of arms and made himself "tyrant" of the state. These tyrants were often cruel and arbitrary in their rule, but they were men of great ability and energy, who encouraged trade and industry and added to the wealth and beauty of their cities by great public works, thus helping to solve the unemployment problem of their day. Some exercised influence far and wide in the Greek world. Such were Cleisthenes of Sicyon, who championed the old pre-Dorian population against the Dorian ruling class; Periander of Corinth, whose brilliant colonial and foreign policy made Corinthian trade and naval power the greatest of his day; his friend and ally, Thrasybulus of Miletus; Polycrates of Samos, Theagenes of Megara, Peisistratus of Athens.

But in spite of their political achievements and the encouragement which they gave to literature, religion and the arts, the tyrants and their successors never kept power or popularity for very long. Quite apart from any cruelty of which they may have been guilty, the inquisitive Greek disliked a form of government which, however beneficent, allowed the man in the street no political importance. For the Greek, government was everybody's business: he loved to discuss political problems in the market-place with his fellow-citizens, and to feel that he was, in some way, personally responsible for his city's fortunes and welfare. But the tyrant made politics his own preserve, suppressed the criticism of the market-place, and was responsible to no man. Under a tyrant's rule, the Greek citizen could not be free.

AGRARIAN REFORMS IN ATTICA

At the beginning of the sixth century B.C., Attica and its capital, Athens, depended on agriculture: the land was suitable for olives and vines, but its corn crop was poor. Bad harvests and the greedy oppression of the great landowners had made life almost insupportable for the small farmers, who were rapidly losing their lands, and even their persons, to their creditors: slavery and starvation stared them in the face. Reform was essential, and Solon was elected chief magistrate to carry it out. By his law known as "The Shaking off of Burdens", he cancelled all debts incurred on land, thereby declaring the farmers bankrupt and discharging them, and he forbade the bartering of personal freedom in payment of debt. To cheapen food, he prohibited the export of corn and encouraged olive-growing. He fostered trade by reforming the currency, making it possible for Athenians to trade with Corinth and her many colonies, and tried to make Athens a manufacturing centre by inviting skilled craftsmen from other states to settle in Attica, where they would receive Athenian citizenship. He reformed the constitution by admitting all citizens to the National Assembly and to the list of jurymen, who had power to try the magistrates after their year of office.

In spite of Solon, discontent remained, and thirty years later, in 560 B.C., Peisistratus seized power as tyrant. He exiled many of the great nobles and divided their estates among the peasants, but he ruled constitutionally, and under him Athens flourished. He employed the idle populace in building an aqueduct and temples on the Acropolis. He promoted the importation of corn from the Black Sea district, for which the products of the increasing pottery industry were exported in exchange. He extended Athenian influence by sending Miltiades to govern the Thracian Chersonese, and by alliances with Thessaly, Macedon, Argos, Eretria and Thebes. His wealth and power attracted a brilliant circle of poets, scholars and religious teachers to his court. Above all, he welded the people of Attica together into a unity.

Peisistratus' son, Hippias, was not so successful a ruler as his father, and he was expelled with Spartan help in 510 B.C. The Spartans tried to impose an oligarchy on the Athenians, but the latter were as tired of the old quarrelsome government of the nobles as they were of tyranny, and responded eagerly when, in 507 B.C., Cleisthenes, a member of the powerful family of the Alcmaeonidae, offered to revolutionize politics by establishing a complete democracy. He gave the government to the people. He abolished the old clan-groups, and divided the people instead into ten tribes whose organization was based on the deme, or parish; the qualification for citizenship became residence in a certain locality, not membership of a family, a change which weakened the influence of the old noble families. The ten tribes elected ten generals annually, to lead the people in peace and war. There was a Council of Five Hundred, chosen annually by lot from the ten tribes, and a National Assembly, whose meetings every citizen was entitled to attend, discussed proposals put before it by the Council. The Athenian people were now masters of their own fate, and the effect of this peaceful revolution was electric. The old listlessness vanished; in its place a fierce restless energy, born of freedom, inspired them to achievements unequalled in Greek history.

THE POWER OF SPARTA

Meanwhile, Sparta had won the position of the leading Greek state. By 600 B.C., Messenia was already under her heel, and in the two generations following, her invincible soldiers forced the whole Peloponnese, except Argos and Achaea, to acknowledge her leadership and to enter a Peloponnesian League, whose members were bound to send troops to serve under Spartan command in any joint enterprise of war. Argos, Sparta's ancient enemy, was crushed in 545 B.C., and remained in sullen impotence for the next fifty years.

It was the Spartan's policy to oppose tyrants in other city-states, and their influence was felt and feared far and wide. But their dread of a helot rebellion at home prevented any attempt to extend their League north of the Isthmus of Corinth, although after 520 B.C. the great Spartan king, Cleomenes I, who had vision and imagination far beyond his fellows, interfered actively in Athenian affairs and encouraged an expedition to North Africa, where Phoenicians were threatening the Greek settlements. The timid Spartan government hated the ambitious genius of Cleomenes, thwarted him at every turn, and, thus, for fear of a monarchy, it forfeited an empire. The sixth century closes with Sparta undisputed head of the Peloponnese, the new democracy of Athens asserting its strength in central Greece, and, on the eastern horizon, a threatening cloud gathering that was to overshadow all rivalries between city and city and imperil the very existence of the Greeks as a people free from alien domination.

CHAPTER 9

THE FIFTH CENTURY B.C.

IN the drama of the fifth century B.C. the curtain rises in Asia Minor. There the Ionian Greeks could already look back upon brilliant achievements in science, commerce and art. The founders of western philosophy and science—Thales, Heraclitus, Pythagoras, Hecataeus —were all Ionians. These thinkers were the first to ask themselves questions about the mysterious universe in which man moves and has his being, and to be satisfied only with answers which their reason could accept. They rejected superstition and sought to discover natural laws: they believed that the world was no blind plaything of chance, but worked on an orderly rational system, which the mind of man might hope to understand. At Samos and Ephesus were temples which were a new revelation of beauty in stone, and in Lesbos lyric poetry had been born with Alcaeus and Sappho. Sappho has won immortal fame by her lovely lyrics of passionate tenderness and joy, so rare in beauty and perfect in expression that nothing can be added or taken away.

The great natural resources of Ionia had been increased by industry; the fine woollen textiles of Miletus, with the metal-work and pottery of many other cities, went along the main trade-routes of the East and through innumerable ports overseas, in exchange for the goods of Asia, the Black Sea, Egypt and the western lands. But fatal disunion cost the Ionians their political independence. The rich kings of their neighbour, Lydia, absorbed them in their empire: they were humiliated by the payment of taxes, and from their overlords they learnt a new luxury of living which brought effeminacy and softness in its train.

When, in 546 B.C., King Croesus of Lydia lost his kingdom to the all-conquering Cyrus, founder and ruler of the great Persian empire, whose story is told in a later chapter, the Ionian Greeks fell easy victims to the attack of this second eastern conqueror. The Persians set up puppet tyrants in the Greek cities to rule in their interest, and proved far harsher masters than the Lydians. Soon after the Persian King Darius had returned from an unsuccessful expedition into Scythia, the Ionians revolted and appealed to mainland Greece for help against Persia. Sparta, cautious as usual, refused, but Athens and Eretria sent troops, and at the beginning of the fifth century there began the first round in a conflict of East and West, which was to do more than any other of the wars waged by the ancients to determine the course of future history.

THE PERSIAN ATTACK ON GREECE

Once Cyrus's empire had reached the Aegean, a Persian attempt to conquer mainland Greece was inevitable. Only on its western frontier was further expansion possible, and the traditions of the Persian people demanded continuous expansion, if the empire was to remain a harmonious unity. Darius knew the Greeks as valuable subjects and restless neighbours, and with their ill-organized levies, they might be expected to fall an easy prey to the greatest military machine the world had yet seen. The first round went to Persia. The Ionians were again hampered by disunion in their ranks, the Athenians abandoned their cause, and after the Ionian defeat at the sea-battle of Lade in 494 B.C., the revolt collapsed. But the Ionian fiasco had a brighter side in that it served to teach the European Greeks the two essentials for success in the attack that they could now expect—control of the seas and unity of command.

In 490 B.C., a Persian expedition, some forty thousand strong, crossed the Aegean to punish Athens and Eretria for their share in the Ionian revolt. With it came Hippias to recover his lost tyranny, and the Persians hoped that partisans of the former tyrant in Athens would betray the city into their hands. Eretria was captured, and the Athenians were petrified with terror. But the democracy stood the test. Miltiades rallied them and led the full Athenian forces to the plain of Marathon, where the Persians had landed. There, helped by the absence of the Persian cavalry, who had been sent to attack Athens itself, the Athenian heavy-armed soldiers won a crushing victory, and then marched back to defend the city. The Persian commanders decided that the enterprise was hopeless, and with feelings of immense relief, the Athenians watched the sails of their ships sinking below the eastern horizon.

This astounding victory gave the Athenians what they most needed, confidence against their "barbarian" foe. The Persians were no longer invincible, and the day of Marathon remained the chief pride and glory of their national annals for generations. On the advice of their new leader Themistocles, the money from a rich silver mine just discovered in Attica was devoted to building a powerful navy and providing Athens with a strong harbour at Piraeus. In a few years, she had a fleet of two hundred triremes, which established her superiority over her maritime rival Aegina, and was soon to prove the salvation of all Greece.

Darius's son, Xerxes, decided to carry out his father's policy by an invasion of Greece on a vast scale. In 480 B.C. he led a host numbering hundreds of thousands across the Hellespont, which he bridged by a line of anchored ships, into Thrace, and thence into northern Greece. Parallel with the army, there advanced his fleet of some twelve hundred Phoenician and Egyptian vessels, so that the Greeks might be overwhelmed on land and sea simultaneously. As news reached the Greeks of how the invading hordes which had gathered from all the lands of the East were drinking the rivers dry in their advance, so terrified were they that, for the first time, they decided to unite in defence of their freedom against the common enemy. The leadership of all the Greek forces fell to Sparta, who had proved herself the greatest military power in the land.

THE TRIUMPH OF UNITED GREECE

But the genius behind all the plans and action of the Greeks was Themistocles, an inspired opportunist and the cleverest Greek of his day. Argos and Thebes remained aloof from the national cause, and the priests of Delphi betrayed their god in proclaiming through his oracles the certain doom of the Greeks. But the majority stood firm. Themistocles induced the reluctant Peloponnesians to come north of the Isthmus to hold the northern passes with the army, while the fleet attacked the Phoenician ships. The Greek forces had no hope of defeating the full Persian army in a pitched battle on land; but a victory on sea would force the Persians to retreat by threatening their long line of communications. Leonidas, King of Sparta, advanced with a small picked body and occupied the narrow pass of Thermopylae, the Gates of Greece, while the fleets engaged at Artemisium close by. To the eternal glory of the Spartan name, Leonidas and his men held their ground for days, until they were surrounded and, fighting to the bitter end, were overwhelmed by thousands of the enemy. Xerxes himself was amazed at the cool cheerful courage of Spartans in the face of certain death.

Dismayed by the defeat and death of a Spartan king, since the fleet had failed to make full use of the opportunity given to it by Leonidas's stand, the Greeks retreated and abandoned all Greece north of the Isthmus to the enemy. The Athenian women and children were hurried to Salamis and Aegina, while Themistocles kept his fleet in the narrows between Salamis and Attica. Here the decisive naval engagement of the war was fought. The hearts of the Greeks sank when they looked across the water to where the glare of the blazing homes and temples of Athens showed fiercely red against the dark background of the encircling hills. But when the Persian ships had been induced to attack them in the narrows, Greek superior seamanship told. They fought with magnificent courage and skill all the day and their victory was complete: only darkness saved the poor remnant of the Persian fleet. Xerxes, fearing that the victorious Greek sailors might cut his line of retreat at the Hellespont bridge, immediately withdrew with the bulk of his army. He left his general Mardonius with one hundred thousand men, to conquer the remaining portion of mainland Greece.

Mardonius attempted to bribe the Athenians to desert their fellow-countrymen, but was met with the reply: "So long as the sun moves in its course, the Athenians will never make terms with Xerxes." Athens commanded the sea, and the campaign that followed was therefore on land. Not until the following spring did Pausanias lead the army of the Peloponnesian League north of the Isthmus, to find the Persians encamped in a strong position near Plataea, in Boeotia. There, in a stubborn battle, the foot soldiers of Greece broke the barbarian lines and massacred them in their thousands. This "crowning mercy", by which Greece was delivered from all danger, was a triumph of Spartan military discipline, inspired by Leonidas's faithfulness unto death, and of Athenian determination to avenge their ravaged homes and desecrated shrines. This great victory was finally clinched by the simultaneous naval success which was gained by the Athenians at Mycale, near Samos, and which freed the Ionian cities from Persian rule.

THE MENACE OF CARTHAGE

In the same year that Xerxes invaded Greece, the Greek cities of Sicily were exposed to a like peril from Carthage, the great Phoenician colony in north Africa: it was a concerted attempt by the oriental races to overwhelm the Greeks in both East and West together. The Sicilian Greeks at this time were ruled by tyrants and were well equipped to withstand the invasion. The huge Carthaginian army was routed at the battle of Himera by Gelon and Theron, tyrants of Syracuse and Girgenti, and Sicily was saved. Six years later the other important rivals of the western Greeks, the Etruscans, were defeated at sea by Gelon's brother, Hieron. Thus the third and decisive round in the conflict between East and West ended in the complete triumph of the Greeks. They offered up thanksgivings in every temple for the great deliverance from the deluge of oriental barbarism, which would have engulfed their culture and broken their spirit.

The end of the Persian peril meant the end also of Greek unity under Spartan leadership. The cautious and conservative Spartans did not wish to extend their interests beyond mainland Greece; they had still to guard themselves against the ever-present danger of a rebellion among their subject helots and the possibility of an attack from Argos and Arcadia. Aggressive schemes further afield were in their eyes both unnecessary and accompanied by far too many risks.

THE LEADERSHIP OF ATHENS

Very different was the position and the policy of Athens. The magnificent navy founded by Themistocles, proved to be the salvation of Greece at Salamis and Mycale, lay ready to her hand. The eager confident throngs in the streets of Athens and Piraeus were resolved to use it to free all the Greeks of Asia Minor from Persian rule, to carry the war into the enemy's country, and to make the influence of their triumphant democracy felt through the whole of the Greek world. When a Greek force was besieging Byzantium in 478 B.C., the unbridled arrogance of the Spartan commander Pausanias provided the pretext for the change in leadership. Pausanias was dismissed, and the Greek allies turned to the Athenians as their natural leaders. They were willing and able to fight Persia, and they were considered to be "kinsmen" of the Ionians. Claims of kinship, which dated as far back as the great migrations, were a strong force in Greek history. And so Greek unity vanished, and a dual leadership took its place. The Spartans withdrew, seeking only to maintain their position as the chief land power in Greece, and leaving to the Athenians the unquestioned leadership of a league of the maritime Greek states. This league is known as the Confederacy of Delos.

The old alliance under Sparta had been essentially defensive, but the Athenians and their allies pledged themselves to aggressive action against Persia. For this purpose they required a navy, a revenue for the navy's upkeep, and some kind of committee to direct activities. The allies promised to provide ships or a certain quota of money instead. This "tribute" was paid to Athenian officials, and the fund so formed was to be spent by the Athenians on equipping triremes. The treasury of the Confederacy was at Delos, the Holy Isle which was the traditional centre of Ionian culture. Here for centuries the Ionians had met to worship Apollo with music and dance and song, and here, in Apollo's temple, the representative council of the allies met annually under Athenian chairmanship.

The Confederacy included most Greek cities of the Ionian seaboard and the Hellespont region, and nearly all the islands of the Aegean. Athens alone was more powerful than the rest of the members. Her navy far outnumbered the ships contributed by any other state, and from the beginning, the control of the treasury was virtually in Athenian hands. Most members preferred to pay tribute rather than supply ships. The manufacturers, traders and farmers of Ionia had little time or inclination for fighting: the quotas of tribute, assessed by the Athenian Aristides, were not heavy; it was less trouble to find the money than to man the ships. The Athenians themselves contributed no fixed quota of either ships or money, but were responsible for the maintenance of a fleet strong enough to deal with Persian sea-power: this fleet was always commanded by an Athenian. It was left for future occasion to decide whether any state had the right to withdraw from the Confederacy at pleasure, and this ambiguity proved fatal to the independence of Athens' allies.

A few years after the Persian invasion, Themistocles was exiled through political intrigue, and the command of the Confederacy's fleet was given to the richest and most influential Athenian of the day. Cimon, son of Miltiades, the victor of Marathon, proved himself one of Athens' greatest military geniuses. Under his command, the Athenians and their allies brilliantly justified the Confederacy. The Persians were forced to give up their hold on the main trade-route that ran from the Black Sea past Byzantium and Sestos to the Aegean, and were then driven from the towns which they were still holding on the Thracian sea-board. Cimon's capture of Scyros, the rocky island-home of pirates, helped to strengthen this trade-route, and to emphasize Athens' role as policeman of the Aegean.

Then, in 467 B.C. the Athenians decided to deal the final blow to the authority of the Great King in the Aegean. Cimon led a large allied fleet to south-western Asia Minor, and as he sailed past Caria and Lycia, city after city joined the Confederacy. He met a big Persian force near the river Eurymedon, and won a crushing victory on sea and land in a single day. The moral effect of this spectacular success was enormous. The chief object of the Confederacy had been fulfilled; every Greek town on the shores of the Aegean had been freed, and Greek waters had been cleared of Persian ships. The ships' crews brought home magnificent spoils, and the Athenian market was glutted with oriental slaves.

THE ATHENIAN EMPIRE

The spell of Athenian victories was broken ten years later by a terrible disaster in Egypt. A large allied force had been sent to rob Persia of the rich Nile delta: after some early successes, the Greeks were blockaded and forced to capitulate. They lost 200 ships and 30,000 men, and of these, 6000 were Athenians. It was the worst blow Athens had suffered in her history, and it was fortunate indeed for Greece that Athenian prestige was restored by victory over a Persian fleet near Cyprus. When Athens had thus shown that she was still mistress of the seas, there was little object in continuing the war with Persia, especially since Cimon was dead. About 448 B.C., an agreement became observed between Athens and the Great King, by which the Greek right to Aegean waters and the coast of Asia Minor was acknowledged, on condition that no further attack was made on the Persian empire elsewhere. It remains a matter of conflicting evidence whether a formal agreement between the two countries was ever concluded, or whether it was merely a tacit understanding due to a mutual need for peace.

Meanwhile, Athens, from being the mere president of a voluntary League, was becoming the undisguised mistress of a subject Greek Empire. After the Athenian defeat in Egypt, the treasury of the Confederacy was transferred from Delos to Athens, there to be at the complete disposal of the Athenian government for purely Athenian purposes. Only three of the original members still contributed ships: the rest paid tribute. The money went to Athens, and with money went power. The subject allies paid the piper, but they could not call the tune. Moreover, Athens with her great navy compelled several Greek states to join the League, and forcibly denied to original members the right to secede. This compulsion made the pretence of a "voluntary confederacy" impossible: Athenian leadership had become Athenian domination. The peace with Persia destroyed the original reason for the existence of the Confederacy: but the Empire remained. In itself, it is the outstanding fact of the fifth century: in its consequences, it is the outstanding fact of all Greek history. Imperial Athens, brilliant, progressive, cultured, belligerent, bestrides the Greek world like a Colossus. But there was, nevertheless, a price for this grandeur, and it was one which fell upon the subject-allies with an increasing degree of heaviness.

THE ATHENIAN EMPIRE

The Athenian Empire was the first attempt at imperialism on a basis of democracy. The source of Athenian power was the control of the Aegean Sea.

The subjects of Athens bitterly resented her rule. They did her will, not through affection, but through fear. "We became their allies", they said, "to free the Greeks from Persia, not to enslave ourselves to Athens." For they regarded themselves as indeed her slaves, and the Athenians admitted that Athens was a "tyrant city", ruling through force and fear. The Empire conflicted with the vital Greek conception of the city-state as a free, self-governing community. This freedom was the dearest thing in life to a Greek of the fifth century, and Athens had taken it away from her subject states.

The outward and visible sign of their subjection was the hated tribute. This was not really excessive: it was the very fact of payment that was resented. And when the allies saw Athens spending the tribute on making herself beautiful with splendid temples, "like a vulgar woman decking herself with jewellery", and then boasting of her artistic achievement, they felt that she was adding insult to injury. They had other grievances; many of them were compelled to receive Athenian colonists, who farmed their land and acted as a garrison in their midst. Their constitutions were frequently dictated by Athens, who suppressed governments in the hands of the privileged few, and established democracies on her own model. All the allies had to resort to Athens for the hearing of any serious litigation in which they might be involved, and were put to much expense by the journey and the long period of waiting before their case was heard. The Athenians insisted on this because it saved them the trouble of travelling round the Aegean, it flattered the Athenian juries, and it greatly increased the profits of the city's hotel-keepers.

BENEFITS OF ATHENIAN SUPREMACY

Athens was confident that her empire was justified by its results. She argued that, as long as she kept Persia out of the Aegean, she was entitled to the contributions of other cities, who, thanks to Athenian sea-power, needed no ships of their own and so saved themselves great expense; they had therefore no right to question how the tribute was spent. It was certainly true that, the moment Athenian sea-power vanished, Persia would pounce again upon the Greek cities of Asia Minor. This sea-power brought the allies further advantages: pirates had been wiped out of the Aegean, commerce flourished, and money had become cheaper. Athenian judicial procedure was often slow, but it was usually just: the allies, who disliked receiving Athenian colonists, should remember that they themselves, in return, were welcomed in Athens, and were given generous opportunities, not only for trade, but for the enjoyment of a culture which was the pride and glory of the Greek world. Above all, the allies had only themselves to blame if they had become subjects; they had been too lazy to fight and had preferred to pay tribute. First the Spartans, and then the members of the Confederacy, "caught by the bait of their own idleness", let the empire of the Aegean go by default.

The Spartans regarded the rapid growth of Athenian power with jealous suspicion. As early as 478 B.C., they tried unsuccessfully to prevent the fortification of Athens and Piraeus, which, twenty years later, was completed by "Long Walls" between the two fortified towns, making Athens open to the sea and impregnable by land. But Sparta was kept busy with serious trouble nearer home, in Arcadia, Elis, and Argos. As soon as she had crushed opposition there, her subject helots revolted. At Sparta's own urgent request, an Athenian force came to help in quelling this dangerous rebellion, but was soon dismissed with that rudeness to which the Spartans were always prone. The Athenians were naturally furious and decided that friendship with Sparta was impossible: from this point (461 B.C.) the two go each their own way. Athens openly attacked the allies of Sparta: she conquered the great Dorian island of Aegina and, by establishing control of the sea on both sides of the Isthmus of Corinth, she ruined Corinthian trade.

THE DEVELOPMENT OF ATHENIAN DEMOCRACY

The manifold vitality of Athens at this time is amazing. A famous war memorial tablet of one Athenian tribe for the year 458 B.C. tells us that "The following men died in war in Cyprus, in Egypt, in Phoenicia, at Halieis, in Aegina, in Megara, in the same year". For a state whose adult male population of citizens was barely 60,000, it is an astonishing record of widespread activity. By 445 B.C., failure to control Boeotia for more than a brief ten years, and a Spartan invasion of Attica, taught the Athenians that they must forego a land empire, as long, at least, as Sparta and her allies retained their strength. Peace was made with Sparta, but the rivalry for the unchallenged leadership of the Greeks remained unsettled.

The fifty years after the Persian war saw many social and economic changes which profoundly affected Athenian politics. With the growth of Athenian sea-power, and the increase in the urban population which greater commerce meant, the government became more democratic. The majority of citizens still lived in the country, and, like most countrymen, they were conservative in outlook. But the people who controlled the popular Assembly, and with it the whole state, were the men on the spot, the men of Athens and the Piraeus, who depended for their living on trade and, above all, on service in the warships' crews. These poor but vigorously intelligent citizens were responsible for radical changes in political life.

The old conservative Council of the Areopagus was robbed of its powers: they were transferred to the Council of Five Hundred and the popular courts of law, which became more and more powerful with every year of the Empire. Service on the juries of these courts was open to every citizen, and provided a magnificent political education for the masses. A jury numbered several hundred, and every citizen was liable to jury service, especially after the system of pay for jurors was introduced by Pericles. Mainly elderly men sat on juries, and the pay served as a sort of Old Age Pension. Pericles also introduced state pay for the members of the Council, and for all magistrates except the Generals. State pay was henceforth a characteristic of Athenian democracy.

The one important principle which underlies that democracy is *government by the amateur*: not the expert, but the man in the street, appointed by the chance of the lot, must govern the state. This is what the Athenians meant by the Sovereignty of the People. Now if such government is to be possible, public service must be paid. The Athenians sought to abolish a governing class by making the practice of government an economic proposition for every citizen. Only the office of General remained, for a time, practically the preserve of the noble families. The ten Generals, who alone of the magistrates were still appointed by direct vote and not by lot, were the Cabinet of Athens. Most of the great Generals, such as Cimon and Pericles, were also great nobles, and it was they who led the people. But in time, even this supreme office was claimed by popular demagogues, as the People demanded that they should be led by elected representatives from their own class, and could enforce their claim.

The rise of these demagogues in the last quarter of the fifth century was fatal to the political well-being of Athens. This was the first office invaded by the people which they proved themselves incompetent to fill, and their incompetence led to their city's downfall. The demagogues exercised an enormous influence over the Sovereign People in Assembly, without holding any office whatever. Any man could speak there and propose a motion; a popular demagogue could be sure of seeing his motion carried, though his legal position was no more powerful than that of any other citizen. Holding power without any official status, the demagogue could claim credit for success and avoid responsibility for failure.

ATHENIAN MASTERY AT SEA

In the fifth century, few used the rough tracks from one Greek valley to the next, except occasional travellers, pilgrims on their way to the great festivals, and armies on the march. But by sea, communication was regular and frequent, and the prosperity of many cities depended largely on the extent of their sea-born commerce. The chief commercial state was Athens, with Corinth second in importance and Aegina third. Athens made full use of her magnificent fortified harbours at Piraeus and of her unchallenged naval supremacy, founded at the battle of Salamis and confirmed by her masterful leadership of the Confederacy of Delos. Pericles claimed that "Because of the greatness of our city, the fruits of the whole earth flow in upon us, so that we enjoy the goods of other countries as freely as of our own". And the claim was true: corn and dried fish from the Black Sea region, dates and figs from Asia Minor, special cheeses from Sicily, fine wines from the Aegean islands, all these, and more, combined with home produce to form the diet of an Athenian. Muslins, fine linen, costly clothes and furniture were also imported from the Near East cities, and in return, Athens exported her unrivalled pottery.

All this was made possible by efficient policing of the seas and by remarkable progress in navigation. The Greeks had learned much from their Phoenician rival, sailors became bolder in traversing the open sea, and ships were made larger and faster. Some were of 250 tons burden, and a trireme covered 120 nautical miles in a day with the help of its oars, an average rate of about 8 knots; a merchantman, depending on sails alone, often averaged 5 knots. Freights and fares for passengers by sea were both very low. Never before had the Aegean been so crowded with the busy traffic of goods and men. At Piraeus, among the throng of porters loading and unloading fresh cargoes, and the ceaseless beat of shipwrights' hammers, travellers and traders from all over the Mediterranean world met and discussed their business and bargained as only a Greek can.

PERICLEAN DEMOCRACY

For more than thirty years in the middle of the fifth century, so outstanding was one single man in Athens that this, the greatest, age in Greek history bears, and must always bear, his name. The man was Pericles. Of him, the contemporary historian Thucydides wrote:

> In time of peace, he governed with prudent moderation. He kept Athens safe from all dangers, and under his guidance Athens reached the heights of her greatness. And when war came, he showed that here, too, he had correctly anticipated Athenian power.

Pericles' blood was the noblest in Athens. On his mother's side he belonged to the family of the Alcmaeonidae, and his father was Xanthippus, commander of the Athenian fleet at Mycale. With high birth, he combined a steadfast strength of character, rare among the volatile Athenians, and an intellect whose brilliance was remarkable among a brilliantly intelligent people. He was a tall commanding figure, with a face dignified and reserved. He hated cheap publicity and avoided mixing with his fellow-citizens in the streets or at private festivities. His domestic life was one of strict economy, and he jealously preserved its privacy. The Athenians, who often felt strong love or hate for their leaders but hardly ever respect, nicknamed him "the Almighty".

For the whole of his career, Pericles showed himself a sincere believer in democracy carried to its logical extreme; government not only for the people, but by the people also. Such government is only possible in a small community, and Pericles accordingly made the citizen body smaller by restricting citizenship to those of pure

Athenian birth on both sides. This restriction, to the Greek mind, was not undemocratic. The society which Pericles did so much to create was one in which all were sure of equal justice before the law, where merit, not wealth, was the road to promotion in the public service, and where individual freedom existed, side by side with reverent respect for the laws and the unwritten code of morality: an ordered society, poised triumphantly on the razor edge between despotism and anarchy. And yet Pericles was also an autocrat. No other word does justice to his supreme authority over the Athenian people, which he won and maintained by his unrivalled eloquence. "His power", said Thucydides, "rested on acknowledged worth and wisdom. A man of transparent financial integrity, he controlled the multitude without being a tyrant: he led them, rather than was led by them. So strong was his character that he dared to anger them by opposition. The government of Athens, though nominally a democracy, was in fact the rule of her first citizen."

PERICLES'S ENCOURAGEMENT OF SCIENCE AND ART

Pericles successfully realized his ideals in science and philosophy, in art, and in politics. Himself a close friend of the philosopher Anaxagoras, and deeply interested in the scientific pursuit of knowledge, he made Athens, in his own words, "the school of Greece", by attracting thither the best scholars and teachers of the Greek world. He gave to the artistic genius of the Athenians the opportunity for glorious expression by promoting the building of great temples, on which architect and sculptor and painter lavished their skill, so that Athens became a city of marvellous beauty, inspiring her citizens with a heroic spirit of passionate devotion. Teaching them that courage is freedom and freedom is happiness, he made the Athenians happy in freedom and in power. Under his wise statesmanship, they held fast to their great Empire: under his inspiration they forced every land and every sea to lie open to their daring, and everywhere left abiding memorials of their friendship and their enmity. Pericles was ambitious for wisdom, beauty, and power; he found or created them all in the Athens which he loved. Yet he did not so worship the city that he forgot the citizens, and with his dying breath, he could claim that "No Athenian ever put on mourning because of me". Pericles was noted in his personal life for his calm and dignified manner. Indeed, he was often compared with the god Zeus, a comparison which, even when flattery is discounted, indicates the impression which he produced upon his fellow-countrymen. One can gain an idea of the nobility and strong character of his features from the well-known bronze bust by Cresilas, a copy of which is to be seen in the British Museum.

Sparta was bitterly jealous of Athens. For long years the Spartans had kept quiet in their own Peloponnese, sulky and resentful, while Athens went proudly on from strength to strength. Corinth, too, was angry because she was beaten in the race for trading supremacy in the Mediterranean. In 431 B.C., the smouldering enmity between Athens and these Peloponnesian states flared up, and the Peloponnesian War began. Pericles had foreseen this challenge to the empire of Athens, and had made adequate financial preparation for it. The Athenians were no match for their enemies on land, where they had to contend with the professional soldiers of Sparta and the excellent troops of Thebes, but they were supreme on sea, and had far greater resources of wealth. Pericles therefore persuaded the Athenians to sacrifice the land of Attica to the annual invasions of the Peloponnesians, concentrating their own forces behind the Long Walls and using their sea-power for purposes of retaliation. In addition to this advice, he urged them to keep a firm hold on their empire, but, at all costs, to attempt no addition to it, until the war was over.

THE CAUSES OF ATHENIAN COLLAPSE

With this policy of masterly and watchful inaction, he was confident that Athens would win a war of exhaustion. But a frightful plague broke out in the overcrowded city, and went far to ruin Athenian man-power and morale. Pericles himself fell a victim to it in 429 B.C., and the politicians who succeeded him in the control of the Assembly—small traders and artisans, for the most part— lacked his ability. They abandoned his policy, and involved Athens in madcap schemes in Boeotia and north-west Greece. Cleon the tanner, an energetic but ignorant demagogue, notorious for his ostentatious vulgarity and brutal methods, was the leader of the war-party in Athens for some years. He was killed in trying to recover Amphipolis, and, since nobles and farmers longed to return to their life and livelihood in Attica, his death removed the chief obstacle to an armistice. The lucky capture of a few hundred Spartans, some years before, enabled the Athenians to bargain successfully, and after ten years of bitter but inconclusive fighting, a peace between Athens and Sparta was patched up, which left the rivalry between them unsettled. Thebes and Corinth refused to accept it.

ATHENIAN DISASTER IN SICILY

The war demoralized the Athenians, who reasserted their shaken power over their subjects with a bloodthirsty brutality quite foreign to them, and began to entertain wild schemes of distant conquest such as Pericles had expressly warned them to avoid. Alcibiades, cousin of Pericles, caught the imagination of young Athenians with his proposal to lead a great armada against Sicily and Great Greece, and then to attack and subdue Carthage. He hoped, on his return, to find the Greek world at the feet of Athens. Accordingly, a huge armada was sent, in 415 B.C. to the west, the greatest force that had ever left a Greek city-state; with it, went all the hopes and prayers of the Athenian people. Alcibiades was in command, but, though brilliant and captivating, he was completely unreliable, and the Athenians never really trusted him. He was recalled before operations in Sicily began, and fled into exile. His recall left only incompetent half-hearted generals in charge, and the enterprise was doomed to failure. The resistance to the invasion centred in Syracuse, which the Athenians besieged. In time, the Syracusans won a crushing victory on land and sea, and hardly a man of all the great Sicilian expedition returned to Athens to tell the tale of this disaster, the most serious and spectacular ever suffered by a city-state.

THE DOWNFALL OF ATHENS

Athens was beaten to her knees. She had lost nearly all her ships and the flower of her men; the members of her empire at once revolted; her old Peloponnesian enemies leaped to attack her; she was torn by civil strife between democrats and oligarchs. And yet she struggled on against overwhelming odds, building another navy, beating the clumsy Spartan fleets again and again. But Persia stepped in, eager to avenge Salamis and the Eurymedon, and offered Lysander, the Spartan admiral, an unlimited supply of money. No Spartan could resist such a bribe, and the end of the great war between Athens and Sparta, once partners in the fight for freedom from Persia, saw the one accepting Persian gold to destroy the other. The end came in 405 B.C., when the last Athenian fleet was defeated at Aegospotami near the Hellespont. Lysander sailed south and compelled the proud city to surrender. Corinth and Thebes, implacable in their hatred, wished to raze Athens to the ground and enslave her people, but Sparta refused "to put out the eye of Greece". The Long Walls were demolished to the music of flute girls, and men said that that day was the beginning of freedom for Greece.

Athens had lost her empire, for good and all, and she had lost it more through her own folly than through her opponents' strength. The people had listened to selfish politicians who had set their private interest above the good of the state, and had ruined policy at home and abroad by pandering to every whim of the Assembly. "A democracy", said Cleon, "is incapable of governing an Empire." A complete democracy, with every citizen sharing directly in government, is impossible if the number of citizens is too large; Athens therefore could not afford to grant the gift of her citizenship to her subjects and make them partners in empire instead of servants. Only that gift could have assured to her the love of her subjects, instead of their hatred and fear, and have remedied her fatal weakness as a governing state —lack of manpower. Such an extension of privilege was impossible for the Greek city-state. Athens failed because she was a democracy, but she failed gloriously. Her experiment in empire had lasted long enough for the age of Pericles to achieve heights of greatness which man has never touched before or since and to provide valuable lessons for the guidance of posterity.

CHAPTER 10

THE AGE OF PERICLES

ONE of the glories of the Periclean age is the tragic drama. Tragedy had sprung from the crude mimes of early ages, in which Greek villagers dressed themselves like goats to worship with dance and choric song the wine-god Dionysus, whose religion had come to Greece in the eighth century. Gradually the religious song to Dionysus became a stately choric hymn with music and gesture, a dramatic cantata in which the chorus leader acted the part of some legendary hero.

THE ATTIC THEATRE: TRAGEDY AND COMEDY

Attic tragedy began at the great spring festival of Dionysus in 535 B.C., when Thespis with his chorus of "tragoedoi", or goat-singers, presented an elementary drama with only a single actor. Attic tragedy never lost sight of these simple beginnings. It remained closely associated with Dionysus; a tragic performance was not so much an entertainment as a religious service. Its character is nearly always serious, its themes the eternal issues of life and death and the relation of man to God. The actors on the stage at one time never numbered more than three, but a chorus was always present, whose lyrics, chanted to music, divided the action of the play at regular intervals. These lyrical songs were used by the dramatic poets to express their deepest meditations on morality and religion : the chorus leader also took part in the dialogue of the actors. All the dialogue and speeches were written in unrhymed verse. The plots were nearly always taken from legends well known to the audience, and were suited to a solemn occasion. The Greeks did not think it seemly to represent violent and fearful action on the stage, but preferred their poets to describe it to the audience through the lips of a messenger; most tragedies included such a messenger's speech. This Attic tragedy, with its stately set speeches, its conversations where the actors speak in complete alternate lines, its long choral songs, its deep religious atmosphere, differs widely from modern drama, but its sublime poetry and lofty thought give it a universal appeal, far beyond its own place and time.

The surviving Greek tragedies are the work of the three tragedians whom the Greeks considered the greatest; Aeschylus (525–456 B.C.), Sophocles (495–406 B.C.) and Euripides (480–406 B.C.). Aeschylus, it was said, portrayed men on the level of gods, Sophocles men as they ought to be, and Euripides, the realist, took men as they are. Aeschylus created tragedy in its enduring form by making the spoken element more important than the sung. He was a great religious thinker, whose mind moved in the same awful and sublime world as the Hebrew prophets. The majestic figures of his plays are vivid images of dramatic art, but they are also mouthpieces of a seer who saw deep into the mysteries of human and divine suffering, and who had pondered deeply on human destiny and on the wisdom and the power of God. Aeschylus belonged to the generation which had humbled Persian power and pride, and in his plays he is preoccupied with the divine punishment meted out to men made insolent by prosperity. His greatest plays are the "Prometheus Bound" and the "Agamemnon"; supreme poetry and religious revelation combine to make "the greatest spiritual work of man".

Sophocles, a gentle and beloved figure, wrote tragic masterpieces whose first concern is with the effect of suffering on great and noble natures. He aimed at justifying the ways of God by showing that character can be ennobled by suffering, and that an end to the most terrible passions comes at last in perfect peace. In the "Antigone", he describes, with a power of vivid characterization, the conflict between the law and order of a man-made society and "the unwritten eternal laws of heaven"; in all his plays, the root of the tragedy lies in the conflict between man and circumstance, and the triumph of human nature, even in defeat. In two famous choral lyrics, he hymned the praise of "Love, unconquerable in battle", and of "Man, of all wonders the most wonderful". He loved and sang the natural beauty of his native Attica, but knew also the vanity of things which underlies beauty and the sorrow of this transitory life:

> "Old age and death leave God alone untouched:
> Time conquers all, and brings all else to dust.
> The earth's strength dies, and dies the body's might."

Sophocles was a great poet who "saw life steadily and saw it whole".

To Euripides, a brilliant genius, the drama was a means of bringing his ideas to a wide audience, in an age when there were no newspapers and no books. The Olympian gods he hated, and treated them in his plays as evil and destructive powers of nature. He was not interested, like Aeschylus, in the ordered march of Providence, nor, like Sophocles, in the trials of noble natures: for his characters, he went to the despised and scorned classes of his day, the poor, the enslaved, women. He shocked and delighted his audiences with his amazing studies in womanhood, by which he made the old legends new, and pleaded woman's cause, as in his "Medea", where a woman tells men that she "would rather face the battle of the spears five times than childbirth once". He was an acute psychologist, who probed human nature with sympathy, pity and insight; a superb poet, unequalled in glittering diction and choral lyrics of weird, unearthly beauty; a radical thinker, who dared to criticize openly his countrymen's conduct of a war, and challenged all their accepted standards of life. Because he attempted to teach no moral lesson, but was content with the sheer tragedy of suffering and anguish, he was rightly known as "the most tragic of the poets".

Another form of literature flourished at the festivals of Dionysus. Attic comedy likewise had its roots in religion, and never lost its associations with the age-old cult of the reproductive powers of nature. This was responsible for coarseness and licence, but in the hands of Aristophanes—a dramatist of genius, several of whose plays have come down to us—comedy had other qualities. He ranges from broad buffoonery to sparkling wit, from ingenious juggling with words to pure poetry of charm and beauty, from amazingly frank and furious outbursts of scurrilous abuse against contemporary politicians and artists to the expression of as deep and true a patriotism as Pericles' own. His characterization is often sheer caricature, but he could draw subtle portraits if he chose; he delighted especially in introducing homely country folk, reeking of garlic and broad common sense. He attacked the corrupt deceitful demagogues and the "highbrow" young gentlemen of the day, who, with logic-chopping and hair-splitting, spent their time in making the worse argument appear the better. Aristophanes understood the people better than most politicians did, but he was a conservative in the best sense, mourning the loss of the old simplicity of life and deploring the fatal demoralization that overtook his beloved Athens in the Peloponnesian War—"the gleaming, violet-crowned city of song, the bulwark of Greece, Athens the glorious, the strong city of the gods". Beneath his exuberant humour and fantastic foolery, we find eloquent evidence of a rare and generous spirit.

THE GREEK HISTORIANS

The Periclean age saw the creation of another great literary form, in the work of the historians Herodotus and Thucydides. Herodotus, deservedly known as "the father of history", was born at Halicarnassus, but travelled the known world and spent much of his time at Athens. He wrote a history, in nine books, of the great Persian invasion of Greece, but he is delightfully diffuse and his inimitable story-telling covers a much wider field—the odd customs of Egypt, the strange animals and stranger people of North Africa, early stories of Berbers, Assyrians, Medes and Persians, burial rites of wild Scythian kings, Phoenicians who sailed round Africa, Indians who ate their parents. Herodotus never invented anything, and nearly all his vividly picturesque tales are founded on fact. He was not a critical historian, but he was genuinely interested in the times of which he wrote. He saw the Persian wars as the culmination of the age-old rivalry between East and West, and found in the defeat of Persia the great lesson of his faith—that God is jealous of human prosperity and punishes pride. Herodotus's work is of priceless value to history and science, but the man himself is memorable, with his beautiful artistic style, his sense of humour, his broad humanity and tolerance, his racy enthusiasm—above all, his insatiable curiosity. In his enormous work, there is not one dull page.

Thucydides, whose work is a history of the Peloponnesian War, offers a deliberate contrast to Herodotus. He set out to write a calm, dispassionate record of the facts, without fairy tales or digressions. With Herodotus a woman had been at the bottom of most of the troubles in history, and his two mottoes might well have been "Find the woman" and "Forget not God"; in the history of Thucydides, women and gods are conspicuous only by their absence. Thucydides hated all sentimentalism and superstitious piety, and was determined to be rational at all costs. His was a brilliant and fearless intellect: the long speeches which he puts into the mouth of historical personages show that he possessed an acute grasp of mob psychology, and in them he reveals what is even more important than an accurate record of fact—men's motives, and the moral and spiritual issues at stake in any situation. He was a supreme artist in style, and underneath his cold calm words, there burned a passionate love of all that was good in Periclean Athens, and a fiery indignation at the crimes of cruel men. "My work", he wrote, "is not a prize competition for the public of a passing day, but an everlasting possession." Time has proved the claim of Thucydides to be true.

ARCHITECTURE AT ITS ZENITH

Nowhere was the achievement of the Greeks greater than in art and architecture, and both were at their best in Periclean Athens. For Pericles believed that the ideals of Athens could best be expressed by building beautiful temples for the gods. Under the direction of the architect Ictinus, the Parthenon, or "Temple of the Virgin", was built on the Acropolis, of Attic marble from Mount Pentelicus. With its perfectly shaped columns, combined with frieze and pediments to form a symphony in stone, this temple is famous as "the supreme effort of genius in pursuit of beauty". Even in ruins, it retains its perfect balance and form. Within was placed a colossal statue of the Virgin Athena, wrought by the sculptor Pheidias in ivory and gold, majestic and smiling, with helmet, shield and golden robe, keeping watch over her city and her people. On the pediments, Pheidias carved solemn and tremendous scenes, the birth of the Virgin and the coming of gods to earth in glory and power; on the frieze running round the wall of the temple, he represented the people of Athens in their joyous procession to the Acropolis, men, boys, maidens and horses, marching in ordered beauty to worship their gods.

Another gigantic statue of Athena, in bronze, stood on the western cliff of the Acropolis, looking out to Piraeus and the sea, a landmark to returning sailors: in addition, two smaller temples, the Erechtheum and the temple of the goddess Victory, were built near the Parthenon, and a splendid marble approach, or Propylaea, formed a triumphant entrance to the whole Acropolis. Every day as he walked through the streets or talked in the market-place, the citizen of Athens had the opportunity to look up and feast his eyes on buildings and

E   (H.W.)

statues whose perfect beauty gleamed and shone in the clear Attic air. Pheidias, the sculptor of gods, and Polyclitus, the sculptor of men, were only the two most famous among a host who wrought the graceful statues of the market-place and theatre, and the lovely memorial figures for tombstones, with their faces of unruffled peace, so vividly and yet calmly busy with their work or play that here in stone the dead seem to live again. On the vases, too, for which Athens was renowned, artists painted small graceful figures of mothers and their children, weddings and funerals, maidens playing and dressing and making music. The normal characteristics of all this great art are an intense interest in the human figure, moderation, simplicity, idealism, and a sweetness which goes hand in hand with strength. People sought beauty because they loved it.

SUPERSTITION AND MYSTIC RITES

Art was closely connected with religion. Both city and citizens still worshipped the many gods and goddesses of the Achaeans, and religion thus required of art not only the building of temples, but the fashioning of countless images of these divine beings. All the old stately worship of sacrifice and burnt-offering and prayer was still familiar to the Athenians, besides the immemorial rites of the countryside linked with rivers and streams and all the forces of nature. Science and philosophy were not yet widespread enough to destroy the crude religious faith of the ordinary man and woman, which was indeed more alive in the fifth century than before.

With so many deities whom it was only too easy to anger, superstition was naturally rife. When a man found himself in trouble, he would cry "What bad omen did I encounter as I left home this morning?", and the superstition of the masses sometimes affected important affairs of state: the refusal of a pious Athenian general to move during an eclipse of the moon brought death and disaster on the entire Athenian expedition to Sicily. One of the most common superstitions was the belief in oracles, which purported to give divine counsel; that at Delphi was the most famous. But in spite of these superstitions and the tremendous influence of the mystic rites at Eleusis in Attica, the fifth-century Athenian was not the victim of any religious tyranny. He did not grovel to his gods, but prayed, standing erect, in a clear, bold voice. His religion was, on the whole, a cheerful open-air worship, rooted in all the glorious life and beauty of the world about him.

SOPHISTS AND PHILOSOPHERS

Among the monied class, there was arising a steady demand for higher education in astronomy, geography, mathematics, physics, history, philosophy. This demand was met by Sophists, men of wide if sometimes shallow learning, who travelled from city to city and offered to teach any subject under the sun to pupils willing to pay.

Some of them, like Protagoras, won an enormous reputation and great wealth by their teaching. Although they were accused of self-advertisement, and of degrading wisdom by accepting fees, the sophists stimulated the intelligent world of their day to a more rational approach to the problems of life. They taught men to take little or nothing for granted, to criticize and question all conventional ideas and institutions, whether social or political, and to probe and analyse human nature.

The Ionian philosophers of the previous century had been mainly interested in asking questions about the physical world, but in the fifth century the centre of interest is man himself. "Man is the measure of all things" was a popular doctrine. What kind of society is best for man? What ought man to do and what leave undone, and why? Is it possible for man to have knowledge? These were the questions to which the sophists turned attention for the first time. There was one Athenian who asked and answered them in such a way that his life and death are among the most notable in human history.

THE LIFE AND DEATH OF SOCRATES

Socrates lived through the time of Pericles's ascendancy and of the Peloponnesian War, in which he served. He was a man of strong physique and unusual habits, and his flat, snub nose and prominent eyes made him conspicuously ugly. He was subject to trances of meditation, and, when thus rapt in thought, he would stand for hours, unconscious of intense heat or cold or of anything that went on around him. From his childhood, he used often to hear the warning of an inner voice, restraining him from doing wrong. He fulfilled the public duties of a citizen with careful respect for the laws and with remarkable moral and physical courage. He was no ascetic, and took part in convivial drinking-parties; but his head was strong, and he was known for his temperance and sobriety. Though Socrates always insisted that he did not possess knowledge, he taught the many young men who were his constant companions as no one had taught in the world before. Among them were all who in the next generation were to be the great philosophical thinkers of Greece.

The Socratic method of instruction was indirect, and included the constant asking of questions. Socrates walked and talked every day in the market-place, ready to cross-examine any who wished to argue with him as to the nature of goodness, or beauty, or wisdom; he was content if he could shake men from their ignorant self-satisfaction and impress upon them how little they really knew about these questions. Alcibiades, the gifted young noble who planned the Sicilian expedition, tells us of his stimulating and commanding power in conversation: "When I listen to Socrates," he says, "his talk makes my heart beat wildly and the tears stream from my eyes. When I used to listen to great orators like Pericles, I felt nothing like this: my soul was not stirred to its depths, nor was I tormented by the realization of my own degraded condition. But Socrates has often made me feel this, and has convinced me that my present life is not worth living."

Like all great teachers, Socrates brought home to men the sense of sin, of their own utter inadequacy compared with the absolute and perfect goodness of God. He felt always that his work was a divine mission, and that the cause of truth and beauty and goodness was God's cause. His deep religious faith brought him into conflict with the official state religion; he rejected everything in the traditional stories that was inconsistent with God's goodness. In 399 B.C. he was prosecuted for impiety, and for corrupting the minds of the young by upsetting their traditional morality: the Athenian people, demoralized by a generation of bitter war, committed the greatest crime in its history by condemning him to death on these charges.

His last hours in his cell were passed in a discussion with his intimate friends on the survival of the human soul after death: as recorded by the greatest of his disciples, Plato, it is incomparably the finest work on immortality in the world's literature. Socrates died as he had lived, in the quiet confidence that his soul was returning to God from whom it came, and that he was about to see the indescribable light of God's perfect goodness, no longer darkly through the mirror of the body's senses, but face to face. Having described the last calm moments of his master, Plato wrote: "Such was the end of our friend, whom I may truly call the wisest, the justest and the best of all the men I have ever known."

POLITICAL LIFE AT ATHENS

Politics was the foremost interest of the Periclean Athenian. A citizen who showed no interest in public affairs was not tolerated as harmless or congratulated as care-free: he was condemned as useless. The regular meetings of the Assembly took place soon after dawn, in the open air, on a sloping hill-side near the Acropolis, and began with prayers and sacrifice. Here any citizen who wished to express his opinion on the matter under debate spoke from a platform of rock. His speech might well influence a momentous decision in home or foreign policy. Nor was this all: the public-spirited citizen would stand for election to the state Council of Five Hundred, which carried on the routine business of the state and performed most of the functions of a modern civil service. A committee of this Council, appointed by monthly rotation, presided over the business of the Assembly, one councillor acting as chairman for the day. Thus it was the regular Athenian practice for any man to find himself, once in his life, presiding over his city's parliament as first servant of the state, with the keys of the Treasury in his keeping.

The Athenians felt a deep mistrust of paid officials in politics: government was the job, not of professional experts, but of disinterested amateurs. Many other posts, such as that of archon, the annually elected president of religious ceremonial, and the inspectorships of harbours and markets were filled by citizens; wealthy Athenians were expected to finance the equipment of warships and the presentation of plays at the dramatic festivals of Dionysus. Such "liturgies" were a substitute for taxation, and in the Periclean age, citizens took a pride in fulfilling them. The preservation of public order was entrusted to a paid corps of barbarian archers, for no one citizen was allowed a policeman's authority over his fellows.

There was no public prosecutor in Athens: the initial step, in bringing any criminal to book, was always left to the individual, who would summon the offender in the presence of witnesses. The first hearing was before a magistrate, who had power to take evidence, and the trial proper took place before a large jury of citizens. Much of a citizen's time was spent in serving on these public juries, which were empanelled in the court itself only on the morning of the trial. After hearing long speeches from each party—no professional pleaders were allowed—the jury voted "guilty" or "not guilty" by ballot, and conviction was followed by a second vote on the penalty. The whole trial was thoroughly amateurish. All kinds of irrelevant arguments were tolerated, personal abuse was the order of the day, and strong emotional appeals were made to the jury. But in law, as in politics, native wit saved the Athenian amateur from catastrophe, and the Athenian courts were renowned for their high standard of justice.

MILITARY SERVICE

Military service was a normal part of Athenian life. From eighteen to twenty, the young men underwent their training; the second year they spent in the frontier-forts of Attica. From twenty to sixty, the citizen was liable to service. Any day, the Assembly might decide on war against an unpopular neighbour: mobilization orders would be posted in the market-place, and men would hurriedly take their sword and shield, draw their rations of salt fish and garlic, and join the citizen army. All must be ready to march at a moment's notice: the safety of the city could wait on no man's trade or calling. When it came to fighting, the citizen soldiers with their heavy armour formed a battle-line, shield touching shield, which advanced ponderously against the exactly similar line of the enemy. Standing well behind the wall of shields and thrusting with their long spears, they strove to heave the enemy back: once the shield-line broke, casualties were likely to be heavy: the runaway would throw aside his heavy shield, and leave the lower part of the body exposed. Flat ground was essential for this type of fighting, to which the Greeks clung as to the rules of a game. The "season" normally lasted only through April and May, for the soldier-citizens were impatient to get home to their reaping. This habit explains Sparta's vast superiority; she alone had a standing army of professional soldiers.

But at sea, the Athenians were supreme. Their triremes, or warships, with three banks of oars and a mainsail, were manned by the poorest citizens as rowers, who were highly trained for complicated manoeuvres. Perfect precision was needed for the ramming of enemy ships in choppy water and time was given by a coxswain, helped by a piper. A few marines might be carried on board, but it was the rowers of Piraeus whose unrivalled skill and endurance gave Athens her long naval supremacy, and with it her Empire.

OPEN-AIR SOCIAL LIFE

Climate and character alike made the Athenians satisfied with extreme simplicity in their physical comforts. They could rely on the weather at the various times of year, and they preferred to use their quick wits in devising experiments in politics and art, rather than in inventing material luxuries, in which Rome was later to excel. Their normal dress consisted of two oblong pieces of woollen stuff; an under-garment, or tunic, doubled round the body and pinned over the shoulder, with a girdle at the waist; and a cloak, to be wrapped tightly round the body in wintry cold, and in summer carried loosely or not at all. Men wore the tunic to the knee, women to the ankle. The feet were covered only by sandals, and hats were rarely worn. Men often unpinned the tunic so as to leave the right shoulder bare, and for any strenuous exercise, stripped completely. The Greeks were too much interested in the human body as a work of art to feel any shame at nakedness.

Houses were a collection of rooms opening off a central court, through which came light and air; there were no windows in the outside walls of bare unbaked brick, whose monotony was broken only by the front-door. The floors were of beaten earth with no carpets: furniture was often beautiful, but never luxurious. There was no drainage system whatever: the street was the place for all refuse. The Greek used his home for eating and sleeping, but only rarely for social pleasures. The real centres of his life were the busy sociable market-place and the gymnasium, where one did not stand on ceremony with strangers or greet them with sour looks, and where among that race of superb happy talkers conversation never flagged.

The ordinary man could count on a fair amount of leisure in his day, and it is significant that the only Greek word for "business" was "lack-of-leisure". After breaking his fast with bread and wine, a well-to-do Athenian would go out to the barber's shop, then, as always, the recognized place for gossip, where he would have his hair trimmed and perhaps be treated for ophthalmia. Next would come any necessary shopping, with an attendant slave to carry home the goods; men, and not women, did the household shopping in Greek cities. After talk in the market-place and a light lunch, there would come exercise and more talk in one of the many public gymnasia, where even the elderly and the middle-aged trained daily to keep themselves fit. Then came the daily bath—a generous use of oil to remove the dirt, with a cold douche to follow: soap was unknown, and warm baths were despised. The main meal of the day was taken in the cool of the evening, when men dined with their friends: but even this was frugal enough. The Greeks were not heavy meat-eaters: eggs, fish, cheese, and all manner of vegetables were the normal diet, garlic and onions being universal; most dishes were drenched in olive-oil, and honey was used for sweetening. Fingers did duty for knives and forks, and the diners reclined at full length while they ate. After dinner, dessert was served as an accompaniment to the rich wines, which were drunk diluted with water, and the carousal might last late into the night; there was singing to the lyre, riddles were asked, games were played, and often there was witty and intellectual talk. The Greeks were different from the grosser Romans. They continued to use their minds, even when satisfying their bodies.

"A nation of noblemen is a luxury for whom someone has to pay." The pleasant leisure of Athenian life was made possible partly by tribute from the subject-allies, but far more by the constant work of two large classes in the state—women and slaves. For Athenian women, life extended very little beyond the home. They never shared the social pleasures of the men. Even in her own home, a woman never dined with the men if there was company. When they only walked in the streets, they were accompanied by an attendant, unless they were going to one of those religious festivals from which males were excluded.

THE WOMAN'S WORLD

Girls were brought up in strict seclusion, learning household duties from their mother, in the certain expectation of marriage. They were married at about the age of sixteen to a man whom their parents considered suitable, and so passed from the legal guardianship of one man to that of another. A woman had no alternative to marriage; legal independence was never allowed her. The wedding-day was the great festival of a girl's life; she brought her playthings to the goddess Artemis, the watcher of childhood, and went from her parents' house to a life of quiet serious work and self-denial. In her new home, she would superintend the household slaves, give her time to spinning and sewing, and remember to use her jewelry, and her rouge too, to give pleasure to her husband, who was her master.

In the later years of the fifth century, Athenian women showed signs of discontent with this narrow life. While the citizens were happy in their unlimited opportunities for glorious self-expression, their wives sometimes felt uneasy at their own lack of opportunities. As can be seen from the comedies of Aristophanes, who laughed at Athenian "suffragettes", and from many a play of Euripides, the position of women was being widely questioned. Their seclusion was the more noticeable because there also lived in Athens large numbers of foreign-born women, who mixed freely with men, earned their own living, and contributed gaiety and wit to the society of the day.

These "companions" often bore children to citizens, and though inferior in status to Athenian women, their position was recognized by law. "The greatest glory of woman", said Pericles, "is that her name, whether for good or ill, should be as little as possible on the lips of men." Yet Pericles himself was the constant companion of Aspasia, the most famous and popular "companion" in Athens. Such inconsistency made the lot of pure-born Athenian women hard. But in spite of it the vast majority of them were reasonably happy and contented. They were far more than mere domestic drudges.

The Athenians never had a low opinion of womanhood. They were determined to guard their wives and daughters, as their most precious possessions, from the dangerous masculine world outside the home. In their supreme service of bearing sons for Athens, the women were ready to show the same unselfish devotion and courage as the men who faced battle. "It is men who make a city," wrote Thucydides, "not walls or ships empty of men." Athens valued and honoured her wives and mothers for their creation and care of men, the true source of her greatness. The women portrayed on tombstones and vases are grave and gracious figures, happy and tranquil amid the scenes of their daily life. They often found love in marriage. One husband inscribed on his wife's tombstone the mournful question: "What is there except sorrow for the husband alone on earth when his wife has gone?" A woman called Callirhoë dedicated garlands, a tress of her hair and her girdle to her patron goddesses, "because she found a wooer to her heart, was given a stainless prime, and bore male children". There have been less worthy ideals for woman than this.

THE SYSTEM OF SLAVERY

Slaves were everywhere in Athens and in every Greek city of any size. Most of them came from "barbarian" countries—Thrace, Scythia and the Levant. The enslavement of Greeks by Greeks was condemned by popular sentiment, and occurred on a large scale only in bitter wars; but the slave labour of these barbarians was accepted as an essential part of daily life. The slave, as always, was his master's chattel, and a bad master might inflict brutal punishment on an unsatisfactory or runaway slave. But though a slave's evidence in a trial was always obtained by torture, the Athenian law in other ways safeguarded him. Unprovoked assault on a slave was punishable, and the death penalty could be inflicted only by a court of law. Slaves in Athens were free from the frightful oppression common elsewhere. They were not cringing creatures: they often dressed as well as citizens: they carried their heads high in the streets: they were allowed to earn wages which they could save in the hope of ultimately buying back their freedom. Ex-slaves sometimes grew very prosperous: one became a great banker. Household slaves—and most houses kept a slave or two for the domestic work—were often treated as members of the family; hundreds of others were employed, along with freemen, in the workshops of potters, stone-masons and sculptors, where their artistic and creative skill was given scope. Since their work was not mechanical, it was bad policy to treat them like machines. Only in the state silver-mines of Attica, where the most savage type was employed on a very large scale, were the conditions of labour frightful in their cruelty. The organized misery of these thousands of human beings is the worst disgrace of Periclean Athens, a terrible reminder of how the social conscience, when dulled by custom, can condone an unthinkable wrong.

EDUCATION AND ATHLETICS

In the schools of Athens, run by private enterprise, all boys were taught to read, write and count, and to learn long passages by heart from Homer's poetry. Most, too, went to music-schools to become skilful on the lyre and to sing; for the wealthy there were the schools of sophists and rhetoricians. Oratory was naturally in great demand in a democratic state, and not many schools were like the one of which a wit wrote: "Greetings to seven pupils of Aristides the rhetorician, four walls and three benches". Above all, training in athletics was a regular part of every boy's education, and the running, wrestling, javelin-throwing and boxing, which the Greek had learnt as a boy in the wrestling-school, remained one of the passions and pastimes of his life. Every four years, a famous athletic contest, open to all Greeks, was held at Olympia in the western Peloponnese, and the victor in the Olympic games was hailed by his fellow-citizens as one who brought great glory and honour to their city. A public gymnasium was as necessary a part of a Greek city as the town-hall, and athletics were the most regular form of recreation for men. Athletic contests were an integral part of Greek life, and for this reason the gymnasium was important.

RELIGION AND DRAMA

Recreation of a different type was provided in the many religious festivals, when, for many days together, the entire city would keep holiday. The most interesting was the spring Festival of Dionysus, the wine-god, at Athens, when dramatic competitions were held in the open-air theatre near the Acropolis. The tiers of stone seats were ranged round the circular dancing-floor or "orchestra", where the chorus in the play sang and danced in rhythmic movement: beyond it rose a shallow stage, for the tragic actors, who wore weird masks, sweeping robes, and big boots to increase their stature. Ritual, not realism, was the rule on the Athenian stage. There was no curtain and no lime-light; actors and audience alike looked across the Attic plain to Piraeus and the blue sea lapping the mountains of Salamis and Aegina.

Here, on three successive days, an eager holiday crowd would come, from early dawn, to fill the great semicircle of stone seats, there to sit attentively for hours together; three linked tragedies, by a single poet, and one comedy, formed the day's programme. The greatness of the drama made up for the discomfort of the hard narrow seats in the hot sun, and the lively critical audience of Athenian men and women enjoyed the intellectual fare set before them, as very few modern audiences would be able to do. On the last day, the verdict between the rival dramatists would be given by special judges chosen from the citizen body, and the audience would disperse, arguing with excited gestures about the respective merits of the new plays by Sophocles and Euripides, or roaring with laughter as they remembered Aristophanes' abuse of politicians and parody of a poet.

The drama was a magnificent education in taste, and one of the most powerful of the spiritual forces which moulded the Athenian spirit. The true pride and glory of Athens lay in her drama and her handicrafts—pottery, sculpture, carving, building. Through them and in them all, the Athenians deserved the description of them by Pericles: "We are lovers of beauty, yet simple in our tastes, and lovers of wisdom, yet strong of heart."

FIFTH-CENTURY GREECE

CHAPTER 11

THE FOURTH CENTURY AND MACEDON

THE end of the great war between Athens and the Peloponnesian states marks a turning-point in Greek history. With the fall of the Athenian Empire came the end of the first resolute attempt to solve the key problem of Greek politics, the binding of the many Greek city-states into a United States of Greece. The failure of Athens, which was the failure of democracy, and the exhaustion of most of the leading cities encouraged the disruptive forces arising from the long war. The beginning of the fourth century ushers in a period of political decay and post-war disillusionment. The youthful buoyancy of the years of the great deliverance from Persia, when all things had seemed possible to the triumphant Greeks, had vanished beyond recall. Great achievements in art, literature and philosophy still lay ahead, but they are the work more of individuals than of communities. The community spirit had been fatally weakened by the war, which had brought with it a restless criticism of old ideals and a rude snapping of the old ties in the fellowship of the city-state.

CLASS ANTAGONISMS AND SPARTA'S TYRANNY

The fourth century is an age of conflict: conflict abroad, where the citizen spearmen fought again and again in the senseless suicidal strife of city against city; conflict within the minds of men, as they felt new ideas fighting their old faith, and the foundation of their lives slipping away from them; conflict within the city walls, where democrat and oligarch struggled mercilessly for the prizes of human power. Of all the fatal legacies of the war, this bitter class antagonism was the most widespread and the worst. Thucydides has described it:

> "The ties of party were stronger than the ties of blood: revenge was dearer than safety: the seal of good faith was not the moral law, but fellowship in transgressing it. Treacherous antagonism everywhere prevailed: for there was no word binding enough, no oath terrible enough, to reconcile enemies. The leaders of either party used specious names, but all they really wanted was power. They were carried away by senseless rage into the extremes of merciless cruelty, and committed the most frightful crimes. Neither justice nor the public interest could set any limit to their revenges. The father slew the son, and the suppliants were dragged from the temples and slain."

Thus raging faction helped the decline and fall of the Greek city-state in the fourth century. Though an interesting period, and in some ways a great one, there was a feeling in Greece that the spring had gone out of the year, and that the first, fine flush of greatness had given place to something smaller and less inspiring.

139

In 404 B.C., as after the defeat of the Persian invasion, Sparta had greatness thrust upon her. Athens lost the leadership of the Greeks, and her mantle fell upon Sparta's shoulders. The Spartans had several advantages for their new task. Their military prestige was immense, and it was said that "a Spartan could now do as he liked in any Greek town": they had a unique reputation for stability in their own character and national institutions; they already had valuable experience in leading the Peloponnesian League. But they fell far below the average level of Greek culture; they suffered from the besetting sins of cruelty and rapacity; their citizen man-power was severely limited; their past experience had been confined to the Peloponnese, and they had not the imagination to understand Greeks with a mentality different from their own.

From the very moment of Lysander's triumph over Athens, they showed themselves incapable of ruling, except by force and fraud. They repaid Persia for her help in destroying Athens by surrendering to her tender mercies many of the Greek cities of Asia Minor. In the other cities of the Athenian Empire, they established Spartan military governors who supported the oppressive rule of the local nobles. Athens itself they handed over to bloodthirsty oligarchs, whose government was such a nightmare of brutality that they were called the Thirty Tyrants. They treated the members of the Peloponnesian League with shameful ingratitude, refusing them all share in the spoils of the war they had helped to win. They attacked Elis, they destroyed Mantinea, they went to war with Corinth and Argos, they captured Thebes by treachery. Sparta in a few years became hated as Athens had never been.

THE TEN THOUSAND

The long fighting and revolution in Greece had created a large class of homeless men, whose only desire was to live not by work, but by war. Thousands of these men turned mercenaries, ready to sell their swords to the highest bidder, to go anywhere and do anything as long as they were paid. Ten thousand of them enlisted with the Persian prince, Cyrus, who attempted to wrest the Persian Empire from his brother by armed rebellion. They marched from Asia Minor into the heart of the empire, and at the battle of Cunaxa, in Babylonia, the Greek spearmen routed the oriental hosts of the Great King, but the Persians made shrewd use of their cavalry. Cyrus, deficient in cavalry, fought bravely, cutting his way through the ranks of the enemy until overwhelmed and killed. With nothing left to fight for, the Greeks withdrew. Their forces were left three months' march from home, in the middle of a hostile kingdom. Even when their generals had been treacherously massacred, they steadfastly refused to consider the solution of surrender.

With no maps or guides, and with no bond of union except their common language and their contempt for barbarians, they determined to force their way back. They elected an Athenian volunteer, called Xenophon, to be their general, and thanks to his tact and common sense, they obeyed him, until their courage and discipline had carried them through to the Black Sea. Xenophon himself wrote a book on the "going-up" (Anabasis) of the Ten Thousand into Asia, in which he tells us how on the return march, the Greeks fought a rearguard action with Persians, stormed rocky heights held by fierce Kurdish mountaineers, and fought their way through ambushed passes into the plateau of Armenia: how they had to endure blinding blizzards of hail and snow, were misled by false guides, and suffered from sudden night attacks, frost-bite and starvation; how, at last, in a mountain pass, hearing a commotion in the van, Xenophon dashed forward thinking that there was another attack, and found that it was his men crying aloud "The Sea, The Sea!" After all those weary months among deserts and mountains, the sea meant salvation at last. Not only men, but hundreds of women, "companions" and slaves, had survived this feat of heroic endurance. The Going-up of the Ten Thousand fired the imagination of Greeks everywhere, and proved that a Greek army could go where it liked in the empire of the Great King.

Encouraged by Xenophon's success, the Spartans felt bold enough to quarrel with their Persian paymasters in Asia Minor. They won some land victories, but the Persian fleet, led by an Athenian admiral, Conon, defeated the Spartans, and Persia began to stir up trouble for Sparta in mainland Greece. Athens had broken free from the tyranny of the Thirty, and Persian gold now enabled the Athenians to rebuild their Long Walls, recover some of their old allies and join the enemies of Sparta. The Theban Pelopidas freed his city from its Spartan overlords; Thebes joined hands with Athens, and helped her to found a second maritime confederacy. Sparta's attempt at empire was failing miserably. In 386 B.C. all the Greek states accepted the humiliating King's Peace, which acknowledged the Persian right to the unhappy Greek cities of Asia Minor, and Sparta's chance of empire in the east vanished. Athenian fleets again began to lord it over the Aegean, as in the great days of Pericles. Worse still, the Spartan soldiers were being defeated by the new tactics of lightly armed mercenaries led by Iphicrates and by the infantry of Thebes. Although her enemies were not strong enough "to go and burn the wasps out in their nest", the days of Sparta's supremacy were numbered. The seesaw of political power next inclined to Thebes.

SPARTA YIELDS TO THEBES

For centuries, Thebes had been the main city in Boeotia, and from time to time had exercised authority over the other Boeotians. The Thebans were known as stubborn fighters, keen hunters and good eaters, but were proverbially the most stupid of the Greeks. Their political past was an unattractive record of complete selfishness, and with the exception of the great lyric poet Pindar, who celebrated the victories of fifth-century athletes in the national Games, Thebes had no claim to culture. Her brief period of supremacy was due to the military brilliance and personal magnetism of two of her citizens, Epaminondas and Pelopidas. These leaders trained the Theban hoplites to fight in an entirely new formation, by which the army's main force was concentrated on one wing, fifty men deep, and cavalry and light-armed troops co-operated with hoplites.

At the battle of Leuctra in 371 B.C., the steam-roller tactics of the Thebans completely defeated the flower of the Spartan army, and the spell of Sparta's military invincibility, unbroken for centuries, was smashed. All the Peloponnesian states were in turmoil at the collapse of Spartan power. Epaminondas formed Arcadia into a free federal state, and robbed Sparta of the whole of Messenia, from which her serfs were drawn. Messene, a magnificently fortified city, was built as its capital. Though Sparta herself resisted capture, she no longer controlled any territory outside Laconia. Epaminondas also established Theban influence in Thessaly and Macedonia, and the Macedonian prince, Philip, was brought to Thebes as a hostage. But, though an empire-breaker, Thebes was no better an empire-maker than Sparta. The Thebans made the same fatal mistake of accepting Persian gold, to build a fleet with which to break the naval power of Athens and rob her of the Black Sea trade. If they had summoned the Greeks to a joint attack on Persia to reverse the disgrace of the King's Peace, they might have brought some unity into the divided counsels of the city-states and great glory to Thebes. But they lacked vision : their only policy was a haphazard military intervention with their rivals. When Epaminondas and Pelopidas fell in battle, the power of Thebes waned. By the standards of the day the number of troops engaged at Leuctra—about 10,000—was not large, but the methods employed by the Thebans were new in military history up to that time.

Greece was in a state of frightful chaos. The command of affairs had been wrested from Athens by Sparta, only to be lost to Thebans too stupid to retain it. The experiments in empire of the city-states had all failed. Greece was torn by the perpetual local rivalries and petty ambitions of communities who were still passionately jealous of the political independence which they no longer did anything to justify. Unable to rule one another, the cities were also failing to rule themselves. One after another was infected with the plague of civil faction. Only in Athens was the memory of the Thirty Tyrants so vivid that no attempt to overthrow the restored democracy had any hope of success.

Athens recovered well from her defeat in 404 B.C.: the land was again cultivated intensively, Pentelic marble was greatly in demand, the carrying trade of Greek waters again came into her hands, and the rise of big banking made her the financial centre of the Aegean.

But she no longer had a steady income from any subjects, and her second attempt at a maritime empire failed miserably, because the strain ruined the exchequer. Politically Athens was as degenerate as the other cities. Fortunately Persia was too weak and distracted at the time to take advantage of the political discord in Greece. Just when it seemed that the slate of Greek achievement was about to be wiped clean, Fate wrote upon it again with a vengeance. The glory of the independent city-state had gone beyond recall, but under the guidance of a Power from the north, its unique spirit went forth to strange and undreamt-of conquests.

In the fourth century, Athens was more than ever "the school of Greece". Although the city was no longer wealthy or vigorous enough to finance and inspire artistic activity, individual artists and thinkers produced work of imperishable greatness. In architecture a new style, called the Corinthian, became popular: it involved more graceful ornament than the severely simple style of the Parthenon. Vase-painting declined, but in sculpture the great Praxiteles and many lesser men were creating statues, less majestic and exalted than the figures of Pheidias with their serene, unapproachable beauty, but none the less wonderful in lovely grace and lively charm. Praxiteles allowed human feeling and experience to show in his sculpture of gods, bringing them by his art nearer to men. Painting on wooden tablets and on house-walls became fashionable, and was enriched by the discovery of how to paint light and shadow and perspective.

CHANGES IN LITERARY EXPRESSION

The tragic drama was declining, and there was no great successor to Euripides. Comedy was no longer the splendid humorous criticism of contemporary life, but was degenerating into the ingenious invention of cynical trivialities. But though poetry was neglected, the Athenians were busy perfecting prose. As the demand for set speeches in law-courts and the Assembly grew, oratory reached its greatest heights in the work of Isocrates and Demosthenes. Isocrates was a great teacher of literary style, and his political theories, expressed in beautifully lucid essays, struck a new note in Greek thought. He appealed to all Greeks to bury their petty differences and to transfer their energies from a local patriotism to a united crusade against the decaying Persian Empire. But this prophet was without honour in his own country. The citizens of the various states admired his style, applauded his sentiments, and then turned again to thoughts of how best to score off their neighbours. Not the pen of an essayist, however polished, but the sword of a strong king, was needed to end the strife of the city-states.

The greatest triumphs of the fourth century were in philosophy. Plato was the most gifted of the companions of Socrates, and he gave his life to the pursuit of philosophy by the method of question and answer which his master had invented. Plato was mystic and mathematician, moralist and artist, all in one: in him, the characters of poet, prophet and thinker were all blended. He expressed his thought in dramatic dialogues, in which Socrates is represented as taking the chief part. At first, he busied himself with those questions of conduct which had been the chief interest of Socrates, but later went on to embrace the whole range of human knowledge. The old question of the Ionian thinkers, "What is it all really?", again comes to the forefront. But the question meant more to Plato than it had done to them. He sought to explain not only the world of matter, but the inner world of mind and spirit also, and his conclusions and method stand supreme in the realm of thought.

PLATO'S TEACHING

As Plato pondered on what is really meant by justice, truth, beauty, goodness and the like, he came to believe that we never find them in their absolute perfection in our human experience. Things which we call true or beautiful fall short in some way or other of perfect truth and beauty. These are ideas which lie behind and beyond us in the realm of spirit. All the things of this world are constantly changing, shifting, unreliable—mere "appearances", as Plato called them. But quite distinct from this world, there exists another world of changeless eternal realities, which our spirits can come to know, and which are alone really true. Plato believed that before our birth our spirits dwelt in this spiritual world, and that we lose sight of it when we are imprisoned in our material bodies. Space and time, which is "the moving image of eternity", blind us to the splendid vision of the truth which once we had, and only a long course of careful education can enable men to recapture it in their lives. The centre and sum of the spiritual world, Plato believed, was perfect goodness—that is, God, who in beauty and truth and righteousness is the same for ever and ever. The aim of men and women must be to obtain knowledge of this perfect goodness, and to live their lives after its pattern.

In his greatest work, the *Republic*, Plato sketched his ideal human society, in which men and women could live lives of complete satisfaction and happiness. Education is all-important, for nothing else can give the vision of God, without which life is meaningless and the people perish. The aim of education must be to turn the mind away from thoughts of this world and its passing pleasures to the contemplation of the world of eternal Ideas. Only those who are able to profit by the educational course of thirty-five years in literary studies, gymnastics, music, mathematics and philosophy, are fit to govern their fellows.

Plato was born about 428–427 B.C. and died about 348–347 B.C. at the age of over eighty years. He came from one of the most distinguished of the Athenian families, his mother's family being related to Solon. Although originally inspired by political ambition, the condemnation of Socrates convinced him that he had no place in the political world of his day, and about 387 B.C. he founded the Academy, over which he presided, for the systematic advance of philosophy and science.

He believed that perfect happiness was only possible in a society where philosophers were kings. For the sole purpose of society should be the creation of good men and women, and only those who have won the knowledge of true goodness can be trusted to make their neighbours good. As a boy, he had seen the failure of Athenian democracy to govern well, and all his life he profoundly mistrusted government by the amateur. Government was an art needing the highest skill and wisdom, and it was absurd to entrust it to ignorant men. In some of his political ideas Plato was far ahead of his time, notably in his conviction that women deserved just as big a part in public service of all kinds as men. More clearly than any other Greek, he perceived the two main principles of statesmanship: first, that society can be built aright only on a spiritual foundation, and second, that the main business of the state is the education of its citizens. True happiness depends on the vision of divine reality, which can be won only by long laborious effort, and only when people of spiritual insight govern the nations will that City Beautiful be realized on earth, the city of which, now and for ever, "a pattern is laid up in Heaven for him who desires to behold, and as he beholds, to become a dweller therein".

He towers head and shoulders above all other philosophers of the western world. Most of the great thinkers of succeeding ages have owed much to his teaching: none has been able to ignore it. He is the fountain-head whence idealists have constantly drawn their inspiration, the guide to whom men have returned again and again in perplexity of mind, when weary of the passing pageant of the material world and eager to discover the unchanging reality of God.

ARISTOTLE'S SCIENTIFIC MODE OF THOUGHT

Hardly less great has been the influence of his pupil Aristotle, also an Athenian (384–322 B.C.), whose philosophical works, so far as they were known, were accepted by the medieval Christian Church for centuries as the basis of her learning. Aristotle was no visionary: his feet were planted firmly on the earth. He had a passion for facts, and for reducing facts to an orderly system with definite terms. He is the first example in history of the modern scientific spirit in the search for truth; the first who tried to establish laws of general application, by basing them on the observed facts of nature, duly collected and tabulated. He had none of Plato's literary graces, but he arranged his thoughts in lucid order. His chief scientific interest was in biology, but we have works of his on literary criticism, politics, physics, morality, logic. His activity was enormous, his intellect gigantic. He said never a foolish thing, and many a wise one. Although he was preoccupied with the material world and his method of enquiry was most matter-of-fact and exact, he reached conclusions very like Plato's on the great questions of philosophy, the importance of education, the divinity of the human soul, the nature of eternal God. Aristotle will always remain, as he was called in the Middle Ages, "the master of those that know".

THE RISE OF MACEDON

While in Greece city squabbled with city, a great power was being born in the northern mountains of the Balkan Peninsula. Beyond Thessaly there stretched the ancient kingdom of Macedonia, where hardy peasants lived a life scarcely touched by Greek civilization. Their kings, who depended for their power on the loyalty of noble chieftains, had welcomed Greek poets and artists to their court at Pella and had interfered from time to time in Greek politics, but the Greeks always looked down on Macedonians, as being more than half barbarians. In 359 B.C., in one of the family feuds which were common at Pella, Philip made himself king of Macedon. From the beginning he planned to win control of the whole disunited Greek world. He himself had enjoyed a Greek education: he had studied the speeches of Isocrates, with their plea for a united Greek front against Persia, and while a hostage at Thebes, he had learnt invaluable lessons in the art of war from Epaminondas. Philip was to show himself the strongest man in Greek politics since Pericles. He combined resolute energy with cool and calculating craft. His remarkable courage, his gaiety and love of good-fellowship, his genuine appreciation of culture, his genius for friendship, all won the loyalty of his close companions. His peculiar power of divining other people's intentions made him a master of intrigue and deception. He saw clearly what he wanted, and he displayed an amazing patience and an entire lack of moral scruple in obtaining it.

PHILIP'S MILITARY SKILL AND POLICY

Philip knew that the first essential for success was military strength. He created a standing army of professional soldiers from the Macedonian peasantry, and trained them after the Theban fashion. But he surpassed the skill of Epaminondas, massing his men in even deeper formation and arming them with longer spears. This Macedonian phalanx proved irresistible in battle, when combined with large squadrons of disciplined cavalry on its wings. The army went into action on an oblique front, cavalry and infantry working together on a strictly pre-arranged plan, the whole forming a military machine such as had not been seen in the world before. With this new model army, Philip first conquered the wild tribes between Macedonia and the Danube, in a series of expeditions which gave his troops the experience they needed and provided a new reservoir of man-power, on which he drew for fierce light-armed fighters. His progress in the north brought him into conflict with all Greek cities which were interested in the gold-mines of Thrace and the trade-route from the Black Sea through the Dardanelles.

Philip was faced with a delicate situation. His veteran army might well overcome the city-states, but his ultimate aim was to gain recognition as the champion of Greek civilization against Persia; force would not suit his purpose so well as diplomacy. The Greeks were suspicious of his motives and afraid of his rising power. At Athens, Isocrates urged all Greeks to accept Philip's offer of friendship and welcome him as the saviour who alone could unite Greece, but there was a vigorous anti-Macedonian party, led by the orator Demosthenes, which regarded him as a barbarian tyrant who threatened to enslave the free cities. Although Philip was most careful to conciliate Athens by his respect for her culture and deference to her leaders, Demosthenes swayed the Assembly by his marvellous eloquence, unsurpassed and unsurpassable in its vivid passion and tremendous power.

But the Athenians were not the men they used to be. They voted patriotic resolutions but were too listless to carry them out. They were loath to fight themselves, and no citizen army could have stood before the trained veterans of Philip. Demosthenes' policy of uncompromising hostility to Macedon was doomed to failure, but he gains our respect, as he gained Philip's, by his magnificent fight for a great ideal, the freedom of the city-state. He was struggling to preserve the conditions in which the Greek spirit had soared to heights of greatness far above any that the future held in store. But these conditions belonged to the past: the Greeks no longer deserved to be free. Little by little, Philip won the victory. By a masterly policy of diplomacy and force, he got control of the northern Aegean, and then slipped past Thermopylae to establish his supremacy in central Greece by smashing the resistance of the Phocians.

The end came at the battle of Chaeronea in 338 B.C., when the Macedonian phalanx and cavalry routed the full forces of Athens and Thebes. The day of the city-states was over. A Macedonian king was lord of Greece. All the cities, except Sparta, sent representatives to meet Philip at Corinth, where he outlined his plans for leading a united Greece against the Persian Empire. Everything was ready, when a palace plot was hatched by the fierce Macedonian Queen, Olympias, and in the midst of his daughter's wedding festivities, Philip was assassinated.

ALEXANDER'S CAREER OF VICTORY LAUNCHED

In 336 B.C., at the age of twenty, Alexander succeeded to his father's throne. From his mother Olympias, he inherited a nature proud, emotional, terribly passionate: from his father Philip, a practical mind, with a capacity for politics and a genius for war. At the age of thirteen, he had been placed by his father under the tutorship of the philosopher Aristotle. The boy profited from his education.

He studied Homer, and took as his hero the splendid Achaean warrior Achilles, who in Homer's story went with Agamemnon against Troy. He acquired an interest in philosophy, science, and medicine, so that, later in his life, he took great care of his army's health and insisted that his military expeditions should also contribute to knowledge by the collection of scientific evidence from the ends of the earth. He learnt that moderation and compromise were necessary both for the individual and the state; the whole of his great career was influenced by his constant effort to impose his will upon his rebellious passions. At the age of eighteen, he had commanded his father's cavalry in the charge that shattered the picked soldiers of Thebes at Chaeronea, and at his accession, he was already worshipped by the Macedonian army, as a dashing cavalry leader of splendid courage and masterful charm. He was generous, loyal to friends, and ambitious: in appearance, fair-skinned and clean-shaven, with soft upturned eyes and head inclined slightly to the left: he had an old head on his young shoulders, but the flaming enthusiasm of youth was in his heart. Alexander was born great. He was also to achieve greatness, such as no man in the world before him had ever conceived.

In Greece misguided men believed that Philip's power had died with him. While Alexander was subduing the fierce tribes in the Danube basin, Demosthenes was stirring up Athens and the other cities to revolt. The young king decided to teach the Greeks such a lesson that there should be no further fear of their giving trouble while he was away in the East. He swept southwards, and captured and destroyed Thebes utterly, sparing only the house of the poet Pindar and the temples. Greece was cowed. Alexander treated Athens with courtesy, and contemptuously pardoned Demosthenes. Like Philip, he was proclaimed Captain-General of the Greeks at Corinth, and all the cities except Sparta sent troops to increase his army for the invasion of Persia.

Leaving garrisons at the key points of Greece, in 334 B.C. he crossed the Dardanelles to join his general Parmenio. Alexander had inherited the plan of an invasion of Persia, and he never stopped to wonder if it was advisable. He had learnt from Aristotle the common Greek view that the "barbarians" of the East were an inferior race and that it was naturally right for Greeks to seize any opportunity of attacking them. The expedition did not seem glorious robbery, but a championship of civilization against a decadent barbarism, of light against darkness. In spite of the enormous size and wealth of the Great King's empire and the millions of fighting men on whom he could call, in spite of its powerful fleet, strong roads and fortresses, and immense prestige, the Macedonians had a good chance of success. The Going-up of the Ten Thousand had revealed serious weaknesses in Persia, and the Macedonians were the men to make the most of them. They had shown that they possessed extraordinary skill, endurance and bravery in war: they were inspired by a fierce national spirit: they had wonderful generals in men such as Parmenio, Ptolemy, Antigonus, Seleucus, and Nearchus: above all they had their young king. With his beauty, his frank charm, his fantastic courage, Alexander was the idol of his men. His inspiring personality made them eager to follow wherever he led, his resolute will refused to be baffled by any obstacle of man or nature, his military genius rose superior to any sudden crisis of war. Compared with the weak and vacillating King of Persia, Alexander seemed like some hero of legend, dauntless and invincible.

THE CONQUEST OF THE EAST

In the campaign that followed, Alexander carried all before him by the furious speed of his attack. Sweeping away the resistance of the Persian generals, he freed all western Asia Minor from Persia, and led his army by the route of the Ten Thousand, through the pass known as the Cilician Gates, down into fertile Syria. Here, at the Gulf of Issus, he met the vastly superior army of the Great King in a strong defensive position. The charge of the Macedonian cavalry, led by Alexander himself, broke the enemy line, King Darius fled, and his huge host scattered. Darius offered to make peace, surrendering all Asia west of the Euphrates to Alexander. Parmenio and the older Macedonian generals advised acceptance; but the imperious young king, with a vision of world-conquest before him, rejected the policy of caution and marched on.

By a brilliant use of the new siege-engines invented in Sicily, Alexander captured all the naval bases of the Phoenician fleet in the eastern Mediterranean, though the strong city of Tyre held out for seven months. Then Egypt, restless under Persian rule, fell an easy prey, thus robbing the Persians of all possible harbours for their fleet. With a brilliant eye for a site, the conqueror founded the city of Alexandria to be a centre of Greek commerce and civilization. After reorganizing the government of Egypt, he returned to Asia, crossed the Tigris near the site of Nineveh, and in 333 B.C. routed the last great army of Darius at Gaugamela. Darius fled and was killed, and the Persian Empire lay at Alexander's feet.

As he lay at ease in the palace of the King of Kings in Babylon, Alexander could reflect that, for the first time, he had established a European power in possession of two great cradles of human civilization, the valleys of Nile and Euphrates. But it was not enough. On he marched to Susa to seize the enormous treasury of the Persian royalty, and thence to Persepolis, where with his own hand he fired the magnificent palaces, as once the Persians had fired the holy Acropolis of Athens. Some of the Macedonian nobles began to murmur at the favours shown to conquered Persians of ability, and plots were discovered, which led to the execution of the old general Parmenio and his son Philotas. But the army remained devoted to its king, and followed him with absolute trust, as he moved eastward into lands unknown to Greek geography. From 330 to 324 B.C., Alexander led the Macedonians through perils of mountain and desert, snow and flood, fighting their irresistible way past every kind of foe, thousands of miles into the heart of Asia, eastwards into Bactria, northwards across the Oxus and Jaxartes rivers into Turkestan, southwards across the Indus into the Punjab. But when he would have gone yet further, his soldiers at last called a halt.

ALEXANDER'S EMPIRE

The king who had never known defeat at the hands of his enemies, accepted defeat from his own men. The Macedonians hated the strange climate of India, and after ten years of continuous campaigning, they were hungry for their far-distant homeland. Alexander turned his face back towards Babylon. His westward march took him through dreadful deserts along the shores of the Indian Ocean, while the fleet, built on the Indus, sailed round into the Persian Gulf to the mouth of the Tigris and Euphrates. The feat of the admiral Nearchus in bringing his ships through the strange terrors of those unknown seas, to rejoin his king, is perhaps the most amazing of all the exploits of those amazing years. Seven years after he had left it, Alexander, tired but triumphant, entered the capital city of Babylon. There, a few months later, while planning still further schemes of conquest over Arabia, Carthage, Italy, and the western Mediterranean he fell sick of a fever, and died. He was only thirty-three.

Alexander the Great was fortunate in his death. His fame and his power were already unquestionably the greatest upon earth. He had made war as no man in the world had made it before, but, if he had lived, he would have had the more difficult task of preserving peace. It was easier to conquer the world than to use the conquest aright. Yet Alexander might have been equal to the task; even in his short lifetime, he had begun to put into practice his supreme plan of blending Europe with Asia on a basis of common Greek culture. For this end he encouraged a vast scheme of Greek colonization in Asia, differing from the older colonization in that many of the cities were not on the sea and the settlers were a mixed crowd from many Greek towns.

Alexander was the greatest city-builder of all time. From Egypt to Afghanistan he founded city after city—often called, after himself, Alexandria—and settled them with Greek mercenaries and traders, natives of the country, and a few Macedonians. These cities gave Greeks control of the great trade-routes of central Asia and helped to spread Greek influence. But as the settlers intermarried with native women, the mixed population often became more Asiatic than Greek; for nationality depends chiefly on the mother. There were simply not enough Greeks in the world to Hellenize all Asia. Moreover, Alexander was aiming at a joint commonwealth of Europeans and Asiatics, and intended that the Greek race should fuse with the

Persian by intermarriage. He himself married a Persian princess, and celebrated with great pomp the marriages of his chief captains with Persian ladies. He did all in his power to persuade his Macedonian troops to take Persian wives. This courageous attempt to break down racial barriers failed, because the idea of nationality was too strong to be overcome even by Alexander. But the policy did succeed in giving to large parts of Asia community of culture with Greece, and Greek influence in art and thought penetrated even as far as India, where it had a marked effect on the future of the Indian kingdoms.

THE GREAT SOLDIER AND VISIONARY

The greatest difficulty of all was in keeping the vast empire together as a harmonious whole. It included countless different races of men, with different customs and manifold religious beliefs. Alexander was ready to tolerate them all, but something more active than toleration was needed to preserve unity. He allowed men to worship himself as a god, so that they might all serve under one divine ruler. But, except in Greece, the notion of the divine king had little political effect. There was no common idea or common ideal running through the whole empire to bind it together. Nothing could have given it cohesion except the personality of Alexander himself, if he had lived. Far greater than all possible measures for the organization and government of the conquered peoples, was the personality of the man. In his character was destiny.

He was the greatest general of the ancient world, supreme in strategy, tactics and organization, swift and sure to strike, understanding absolutely how to keep his men's affection and trust, possessing such immense driving power and sheer force of character that his generals, themselves soon to be the rulers of great empires, faded into pygmies in his presence. But he was much more: a romantic dreamer, who saw great visions and had the tremendous energy of body and mind to fulfil them: a mystic and yet intensely practical and terribly alive: a man who felt himself separated from other men, as an instrument of God, and yet knew that it was more kingly to conquer himself than others. He left his mark upon Asia for many centuries, and even to-day there can be found traces in distant lands of the legends that gathered in hosts about that terrible name.

HIS INFLUENCE ON HISTORY

Alexander started a new epoch of civilization. He replaced the narrow limits and restraints of the city-state by the new idea of "the inhabited world", the common possession of civilized men, with a common culture and common speech. It was the Hellenistic world created by Alexander which transmitted to Rome the message of Greece, and when at last Christianity came, to make possible the spiritual unity for which men were seeking, it was able to grow and spread so quickly only because it was in the midst of this common

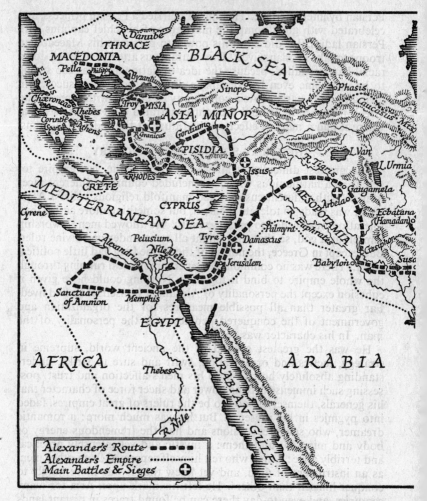

Map legend:
Alexander's Route ━ ━ ━ ━
Alexander's Empire ·············
Main Battles & Sieges ✚

THE CONQUESTS OF

Alexander the Great, although he died in 323 B.C. at the age of 33, stands out as one of the supreme military geniuses of any age. His victorious progress through Asia Minor by way of Egypt, Mesopotamia, Media and Parthia, followed by equally successful marches through Afghanistan into Turkestan and back viâ the Indus Valley, was all the more remarkable because much of the territory traversed was up to that time unknown, or only vaguely known, to the ancients. After Gaugamela, Alexander faced the responsibility of leading his men into an uncharted world. By the winter of 329 B.C. they had reached the Kabul Valley.

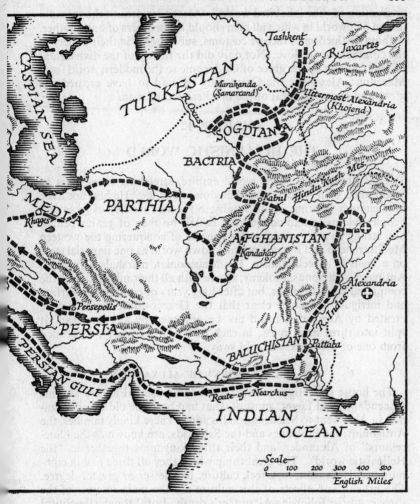

ALEXANDER THE GREAT

The year 328 B.C. saw Alexander cross into Bactria and Sogdiana (Bokhara), and the following year he retraced his path through the Hindu Kush on his way to India, where he pushed deeply into the valleys. In 326 B.C. his troops made their way across the Indus into the Punjab. After defeating King Porus, who afterwards became an ally, the home-sick invaders proceeded down the Indus Valley, reaching Pattala in 325 B.C. Nearchus successfully sailed in search of a sea-route from the River Indus to the Persian Gulf, Alexander and his remaining forces marching through coastal Baluchistan, and reaching Babylon in 323 B.C.

civilization of "the inhabited world". Alexander dreamt the splendid dream of a world in which all men should be members of one another, without distinction of race or customs, subject only in their society to the common law of love. Not only did the theory of the divine right of kings, ruling by the grace of God, come to the modern world from Macedon: Alexander the Great may be said to have created the great and enduring ideal of the brotherhood of man.

CHAPTER 12

THE HELLENISTIC WORLD

THE possibility of a single world empire, stretching from India to Spain, died with Alexander at Babylon in 323 B.C. He had not lived long enough to bring any real unity to the vast medley of races and peoples whom he had conquered; he left no man of genius behind him strong enough to realize his dreams of conquering the western Mediterranean and organizing the known world as one imperial state on a basis of Greek culture. His Macedonian marshals, Perdiccas, Antipater, Antigonus, Ptolemy, strove with all their might to hold the conquered lands together, but after long years of continuous warfare and intrigue, it became clear that the Graeco-Macedonian world, created by Alexander, could not be governed by any one man. It split into three main parts, in each of which a dynasty, descended from one of the marshals, held sway.

THE "SUCCESSORS" OF ALEXANDER

The house of Antigonus ruled Macedonia itself; Ptolemy and his descendants held Egypt; most of what had been the old Persian Empire in Asia went to Seleucus and his sons. These kingly families, the Antigonids, the Ptolemies and the Seleucids, are known as the "Successors" of Alexander, and their three kingdoms together as "the Hellenistic world". The great thing which they all three had in common was Hellenism, or Greek culture, to a lesser or greater degree. The growth and effects of this culture are the main interest of the three centuries following Alexander's death. For through all political changes and wars, the civilization of the Mediterranean world remained Greek. Even when Rome interfered in the eastern Mediterranean in the second century B.C., and ultimately destroyed all the kingdoms of the Successors, it was the same Greek culture which impressed itself upon the conquering race and fixed the development of Roman life and thought.

Men and women found that the Greek world was a very different place after Alexander the Great's brief life. Aristotle had summed up the Greek life of former centuries when he said: "Man is a creature whose natural environment is the city". Now, although city life remained universal for Greeks, their horizon was no longer limited by the city. Greeks came to feel that their natural environment was the whole civilized world. The old barriers separating them from one another and from "barbarians" had been broken down. The Greek language, known as "the common speech", could carry a man from the Caspian to the Cataracts of the Nile, from Spain to the Hindu Kush. Wherever he went, he would find men trained in a common education, with Greek gymnasia and Greek magistrates interested in a common literature and music and philosophy. The immense widening of men's horizon altered the whole of life. Some felt lost and frightened in this vast new world; others rejoiced in the greater scope allowed to a "citizen of the world" for the expression of his personality.

In the fifth century, Greeks had lived and died, not so much as individuals, but as members of the city-state. In the Hellenistic world, a man came to feel that he had an individual importance: he was able to think freely, more freely than for centuries afterwards; he worshipped what gods he pleased; he gave his whole time and attention to any particular work he cared to choose. Periclean Athens had been the place for the amateur in all things: the Hellenistic world was the place for the professional specialist, in craftsmanship, in science, and even in government.

Nor was this the only way in which the Hellenistic world resembled our own very closely. In economics, there were similar disputes about prices and wages, strikes, the ideas of Socialism and Communism. There was a growing belief in the ideals of humanity and brotherhood in the midst of a warring world, amazing developments in science and learning in the midst of ignorance and superstition, the spread of popular education and of political propaganda, the emancipation of women and the restriction of the population. But there were also great differences, notably the absence of machines, and the presence of slaves. In the latter part of the last three centuries B.C., the numbers of the pure Greek, "the racial aristocrat of the Aegean", decreased, and under the military domination of Rome, the Greek spirit certainly lost something of its old energy and vigour. But the race retained enough vitality to make this period in the world's history of permanent importance and interest to mankind.

THE REVOLT OF THE CITY-STATES

Macedonia was the smallest of the Successor Kingdoms, and its kings had the difficult task of controlling the turbulent Greek cities. The Greeks of the homeland were still apt to insist on being masters each in their own city, forgetting that Alexander had given them the chance of being masters of the world. After Alexander's death, the city-states again fought for their freedom, and were again humiliated by a defeat sustained at the hands of a Macedonian army. Demosthenes, when it became apparent that all hope of independence for Athens had been lost, committed suicide, and the Greeks submitted to Macedonian control.

Other troubles disturbed the peace of Macedonia; in 280 B.C., hordes of barbarian Gauls broke through the northern mountains, and wasted the country as far south as Delphi; another group burst into Asia Minor and ultimately settled in the region called after them Galatia. Antigonus II of Macedonia defeated the invaders and drove them north again in 277 B.C., but this flood of Celtic barbarians deeply impressed the Greeks. Antigonus went on to establish Macedonian sea-power in the Aegean, where for the last generation Egyptian fleets had ruled the waves, and his kingdom regained some of the power which it had had under Philip and Alexander.

Later in the third century, the Greek cities made another effort to throw off Macedonian overlordship. Too weak now to defend themselves separately, they combined into leagues for mutual protection. Unfortunately, the two main leagues, the Achaean on the south side of the Gulf of Corinth and the Aetolian on the north, were hostile, and Macedonia was able to play one off against the other. Thus the Greek experiment in federation came too late in their history for it to succeed against more powerful neighbours.

The Spartans had fallen on evil days, but they recovered some of their old strength under King Cleomenes III, who reorganized Spartan society and defeated the forces of the Achaean League. The Macedonians intervened and crushed Cleomenes in 222 B.C., and for the first time in her history, the town of Sparta was taken by a foreign foe. The Aetolian League remained independent, until it courted subjection by inviting Rome to intervene in Greek affairs at the end of the third century, and the island of Rhodes secured the mastery of the Aegean for a time; but the Greeks of the homeland never won real political freedom again. Athens was recognized by all the powers of the Hellenistic world as a neutral, and her fame as a brilliant University town endured. Kings came to solicit her honours as the hallmark of Greek culture.

THE RULE OF ANTIGONIDS AND SELEUCIDS

The other Greek cities under Macedonian rule were prosperous on the whole. Low wages caused periodic social unrest, but the rich gave generously to public causes. Great progress was made in legal procedure by the use of professional arbitrators instead of large popular juries. A movement was set on foot for the liberation of many slaves. Women could now have all the freedom they pleased in education and in social life, but still endured the terrible wrong of seeing the children they bore killed at birth if times were hard. Infanticide was a crude method of limiting the population where food was scarce. All over Greece, families were restricted in this way to one or two living children. The steady decrease in the population, and the admixture of oriental blood by the intermarriage of Greeks and freed slaves, did much to lower the standard of Greek achievement in the homeland under Macedonian and Roman rule.

The Seleucids, lords of an Asiatic empire, were the chief heirs of Alexander. Though their realm fluctuated in size and they never acquired such wealth from their possessions as did the rulers of Egypt, they attempted, with extraordinary success, to carry on Alexander's policy of establishing Greek culture in Asia through Greek cities and settlements. The early Seleucid kings ruled an empire stretching from the Aegean to Afghanistan, but in the last quarter of the third century, the lands east of Media were seized by the Parthians. This race of fierce nomad horsemen established a kingdom, under the rule of Arsaces, which lasted for five centuries; at the same time the independent kingdom of Pergamum seized control of all Asia Minor north of the Taurus mountains. But the Seleucid Antiochus III took southern Syria and Judaea from Egypt in 198 B.C., and for the rest of the second century the Seleucid dynasty ruled.

ACHIEVEMENTS OF THE SELEUCIDS

Their revenue was derived from a tithe of the harvest in their dominions and from many commercial taxes, levied on the innumerable kinds of merchandise which flowed through Seleucid territory from Arabia, India and China to the Mediterranean world. The bulk of the population was the native peasant class, farming the king's land, with which they were bought and sold as serfs. Although the Seleucids did not free these serfs as a class, they alleviated their lot by appointing special judges to protect them before the law, and allowed some of them to gain their freedom by making them citizens of one of the many new cities with which the empire was dotted.

We have no complete list of the cities founded, but the vastness of this colonization is one of the most amazing things in history. The chief cities were Seleucia, on the river Tigris, which contolled the rich land of Mesopotamia and guarded the eastern provinces, and Antioch, in Syria, on the navigable river Orontes. Antioch was a great trade emporium, rivalling even Alexandria, and the most notorious pleasure-city of the ancient world: the Syrian Greeks of Antioch were proverbial for their luxury and indulgence. The whole of northern Syria became a second Macedonia, full of cities and fortresses occupied by Macedonian veterans and Greek traders and craftsmen. These, and the countless other Greek settlements up and down the empire, not only secured the great trade routes and military points of vantage: they were also the nerve-centres from which Hellenism radiated through Asia to endure through centuries of Roman and Parthian rule.

The citizens of the new cities paid taxes to the king, but they enjoyed municipal self-government and all the Greek institutions for corporate life: to Greeks, a collection of houses, however large, without these distinguishing features was not a city, but a village. The cities, like all the rest of the empire, worshipped the king as a god, who could be obeyed without offence to their susceptibilities. Though the Seleucid kings fought the power of the numerous priests who ruled petty states and villages in many parts of Asia, and took from them their revenues and government, they respected the varied religious beliefs of their subjects. The faith of the Asiatic peoples was rooted in the worship of fertility-gods and goddesses, almost as old as the human race itself. Conquerors could come and go, but the ancient religions of Babylon and Phoenicia and Persia endured.

EGYPT UNDER THE PTOLEMIES

In Egypt, the third of the great Successor kingdoms, Alexander's marshal Ptolemy founded a long line of rulers known by his name. Egypt differed in many ways from the other Hellenistic kingdoms. For untold centuries, its peasant population of some nine millions had laboured for the harvest of corn in the rich mud fields of the Nile, ruled now by one dynasty and now by another, but always oppressed and never ruling themselves; illiterate and poor, strong only in their age-old religion. The Ptolemies made no attempt to raise this native population to a higher level of culture. There were many Greeks in the country; the king needed them as mercenaries to guard and extend the empire and as officials to carry on the government. The rule of the Ptolemies rested on Greeks. They remained strangers among the mass of the natives, and there was no effective mixture of races and cultures, as in Asia under the Seleucids. The whole country was regarded as the king's estate, and the sole object of the Ptolemies was so to organize the government, by their Greek agents, that the estate might be farmed to the best profit and the royal treasury filled. They were indeed unworthy rulers compared with the Macedonian monarchs—who at least protected Greece from the northern barbarians—or with the Seleucids, who were busy civilizing half a continent. The Ptolemies treated Egypt as a vast money-making machine, and all their efforts were directed to their own enrichment rather than to the prosperity of their subjects.

Egypt and its empire was ruled from Alexandria, the greatest port in the Mediterranean and the most magnificent city in the ancient world, except imperial Rome. Large numbers of Greeks lived here, but it was much too large to be a city in the Greek sense. Here was the gorgeous Palace of the Ptolemies, with a great Museum and Library hard by, wonderful harbours, the buildings which housed the huge Civil Service and the royal store for corn and oil, and a canal bringing water to the million inhabitants, with their shops and bazaars, along all the busy thoroughfares. The country was controlled by a vast organization of local government officials, but all the threads of this network ran to Alexandria. Ptolemy was an absolute king, claiming the right to do as he pleased with his subjects, as the Pharaohs of Egypt had done for thousands of years before; the whole produce of the country was directed through innumerable official channels to his royal capital.

Everything in Egypt, except the affairs of the Greeks, was run by the state: banking was nationalized; textiles and oil, two of the staple products, were royal monopolies, in which production, fabrication and distribution were state-controlled: all corn-land—and that was most of Egypt—paid a heavy tax in corn direct to the king. Bad harvests might ruin the peasants, but Ptolemy always demanded his full quota. Millions of bushels poured into Alexandria, making the Ptolemies the greatest corn-merchants the world had seen. Everything taxable was heavily taxed; death duties, taxes on sales, slaves and cattle, poll-tax, import and export dues at the harbours, all helped to make the dynasty of the Ptolemies the richest power in the world. An elaborate system of registration was necessary to run the state on these lines, and the compilation of statistics kept an army of officials busy in Alexandria.

Little attention was paid to the personal welfare of the ultimate source of all the king's wealth, the peasants. They were compelled to work each in his own village, and when, as often, things became desperate, they would leave "their own place" and strike, not for better conditions—for these were inconceivable in Egypt—but as a passive protest. If they could take refuge in one of the numerous native temples, the king's officials could not touch them: many temples had possessed the right of asylum from time immemorial, and though the Ptolemies were themselves worshipped as gods and did much to break the power of the Egyptian priestly caste, they did not interfere with the religious rights and beliefs of the natives. There is little to admire in the régime of the Ptolemies, but it was an interesting experiment in thorough-going nationalization, and it supplied a model of bureaucratic government which Rome was later to copy and develop with characteristic efficiency for the exploitation of her vast and wealthy empire.

THE JEWISH WAY OF LIFE

There was one race in the Hellenistic world which was strong enough to resist the influence of Greek culture. The Jews formed a world apart. The descendants of those who had returned from the captivity still lived in Judaea, under the government of Jehovah's High Priest. They had brought back from Babylonia two great institutions, the Torah and the Synagogue. The Torah was the Law, which they attributed to Moses, who had led them out of Egypt; its precepts formed the basis of all Jewish life and conduct. It enforced circumcision on the male infant; established the Sabbath, the last day of the week, as a day of rest; fixed the national festivals; laid down strict rules of diet; and enjoined piety and charity. The Synagogue was the meeting-place, to which the exiles had gone for prayer, when they were separated from their ruined Temple. It was adopted both by those who returned to Palestine and by their kinsfolk, who remained in Mesopotamia and Egypt. There was no sacrifice in the

Synagogue, which was devoted to prayer and the reading of the holy writings: in many ways, it is the predecessor of the Moslem mosque and the Christian church.

In the third century, the Ptolemies had been overlords of the Jewish homeland; but in 198 B.C., the Seleucids seized all this part of Syria. Although some of the educated classes in Jerusalem favoured the Greek way of life, the masses hated the attempts of the Seleucids to force Hellenism upon them. When Antiochus "the Illustrious" resolved that the Jews must be brought into line with the rest of his subjects, in order that his empire might present a united front against the threat of Rome, the people rebelled under Judas Maccabaeus "the Hammer". The rebels, under Judas and the other Maccabees, fought fanatically for their religious freedom and the Hammer shattered the Illustrious. The effort to hellenize Judaea went down in a welter of destruction and bloodshed.

Elsewhere, the Jews of the Dispersion, who had followed in the wake of Alexander's victories to every corner of the Hellenistic world, came into happier contact with Greek culture. They did not practise infanticide, and their numbers grew rapidly. Their two chief centres were still Mesopotamia and Egypt, but many of them settled in the big cities of Asia Minor and in the Greek islands, while some, encouraged by the friendship of Rome for the Maccabees, took their trading and financial skill to Italy. Most of the Hellenistic kings welcomed them, and in Egypt, many thousands settled in Alexandria, where they were often employed as tax-collectors by the Ptolemies. Many of the Dispersion learnt to speak Greek and took Greek names, examples of these being Theophilus (God's Friend) and Dorothea (God's Gift).

JEWISH LITERATURE AND THOUGHT

Their synagogue services were conducted in Greek, and at Alexandria, in the third and second centuries, Jewish scholars translated the Old Testament into Greek. This translation, known as the Septuagint, spread knowledge of the Hebrew religion, and for centuries was the most common form in which the Old Testament was read.

Some Jewish literature was influenced by Hellenism, in more than outward form. The author of "Ecclesiastes" expressed an attitude to life found in the most popular philosophies of the Greeks at this time, "Let us eat and drink, for to-morrow we die". The writer of the "Wisdom of Solomon" had probably read Plato, who inspired his belief that "the souls of the righteous are in the hand of God". But for the most part, while influenced by many of the outward forms of Hellenism, the Jews learnt very little of the Greek spirit.

The Law of Moses proved stronger than any pressure from Greek civilization. To the Jew, as to the Persian, the Greeks were idolaters, bowing down to senseless sticks and stones, not to the true God of whom no graven image can be made. The Greeks wanted to be free

The Erechtheum, Athens temple dating from 400 B.C. and dedicated to King Erechtheus. The ordinary pillars are replaced by figures of caryatid priestesses.

Pericles, who ruled the Athenian Empire firmly, made Athens the centre of Greek art and literature. This bust is in the Vatican.

The theatre in the precincts of the temple of Delphi, at the foot of Mount Parnassus. The Delphic Oracle played a large part in directing Greek colonization.

A Roman statue of Socrates, the Athenian philosopher who was born about 470 B.C.

Alexander the Great, King of Macedon and conqueror of Persia and Egypt.

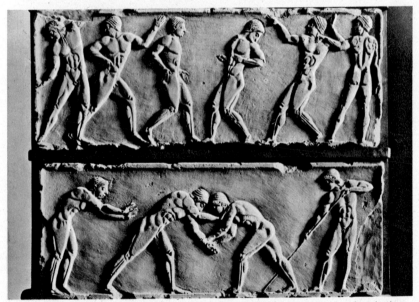

Reliefs from the base of a statue of about 500 B.C. in Athens showing (*top*) youths playing ball, and (*bottom*) runners, wrestlers and javelin throwers.

for freedom's sake, the Jews only in order that there might be no interference with their traditional devotion to a divine Law. Jew and Greek alike praised wisdom, but to the Greek wisdom was a thing to be attained by the exact investigation of reality, while to the Jew, it was the fear of the Lord, in whom is no shadow of turning, a fear handed down from father to son from generation to generation. The ideals of Jew and Greek were fundamentally different and, since both were of value to the world, it was fortunate that this tough race withstood the Greek thought that was overrunning the East and provided the cultural background of the Roman Empire.

WEALTH OF THE ANCIENT WORLD

The conquests of Alexander threw the riches of the East open for the first time to the Mediterranean peoples. The Periclean Athenian had enjoyed the goods of "the whole world": but the world for Greeks had been enormously enlarged since his day, and the trade of the Hellenistic world was on a bigger scale than anything in history before. State-aided exploration discovered new trade-routes by sea and land. The riches of China and India came to Seleucia through the Persian Gulf up the river Tigris, and by the caravan-route from Candahar; Alexandria had her share of the Indian and Arabian trade, by way of the Red Sea. The distribution of merchandise was helped by the increased size of ships and by the new habit of sailing the high seas instead of coasting, as well as by the growing amount of money in circulation. With the hundreds of new cities and the rising standard of living of the upper classes everywhere, demand normally outran supply, and merchants could be sure of a good profit on their wares.

The greatest part of international trade was concerned with oriental produce, and trade activity shifted from Greece to Egypt and Asia. The richest cities of the Hellenistic world were not manufacturing centres, except Alexandria, but were fed by transit trade: such were Seleucia, Syrian Antioch, Ephesus, Rhodes, Cyzicus on the Black Sea, and Corinth. Their merchants grew rich by dealing in precious metals from Spain, tin from Cornwall and Brittany, corn from Egypt and the Crimea, wine from northern Syria and the Ionian islands. The fashionable rich in Alexandria demanded Ionian vintages as London demands champagne, whatever the price. Alexandria supplied the world with fine linen, paper and glass: the best wool came from Miletus, oil and honey from Athens, silks for king's courtiers from China. The frankincense which priests burnt on their altars came from Arabia and Somaliland to Alexandria. Many of these commodities were out of reach of ordinary citizens, whose income went in buying corn, fish, wine and the oil so necessary for light and fat. But the thriving trade carried on by Greeks, Phoenicians and Carthaginians certainly brought increased happiness and prosperity to the Mediterranean world as a whole.

F   (H.W.)

There is only one blot on the record—the vast slave-trade. Slaves were still employed in domestic service and in agriculture, while in every factory they did duty for the modern machine. In the African gold-mines of the Ptolemies, they suffered the most frightful tortures. But the greatest demand was for slaves to work the new plantations in Italy and Sicily. Cilician pirates made it their business to capture hundreds of Greeks and Asiatics in systematic slave-raids, and the chief market and clearing-house for the foul traffic was the tiny Aegean island of Delos, once the Holy Isle of the Ionian Greeks. The traders of Delos boasted that they could easily handle over 10,000 slaves a day. It was a sad sign of the times that, while slaves were being freed at Apollo's shrine at Delphi, Apollo's island was, year after year, made the disgraceful scene of human misery and greed by Greeks, Orientals and Romans, who flocked thither from the ends of the earth.

Civilized life in the Hellenistic world was more comfortable than it had ever been before. Private houses were now usually built of stone masonry, and their central courts were surrounded by colonnades. The living-room might be floored with brightly coloured mosaics, and the walls decorated with paintings, as in Crete fifteen hundred years earlier, or panelled with marble. Great attention was paid to a town's water supply, and in a few great cities, like Alexandria, every house had water laid on. Baths became more common, and the main streets were provided with drainage channels or pipes; but proper sewerage was unknown before Roman times, and there was never any system of street lighting in the ancient world.

HOW HELLENISTIC CITIES WERE PLANNED

A Hellenistic city, whether in Macedonia or in furthest Asia, was laid out on a careful plan like a chess-board, with straight streets some thirty to forty feet wide, running at right angles, and the buildings in rectangular blocks. The town-planning of a tiny place like Priene in Asia Minor, which had a population of only four thousand, would put to shame most modern cities a hundred times the size. In the middle of the city there was always the market-place, surrounded by long colonnades, and near by, the town-hall, assembly-room, theatre, gymnasium, and at least one temple, the whole forming an artistic group. The Greek still counted these public buildings of his city as more important than his private house, and though the standard of the Parthenon at Athens was never attained, the old Greek sense of beauty insisted on excellent design and workmanship in the city's architecture. The countless new cities which sprang up after Alexander's conquests gave architects and town-planners a unique opportunity, which they used to the full, although much work was unenterprising. The conquests of Alexander had familiarized the Greeks with the burnt bricks used in Mesopotamia, but brickwork did not appear in Greece until Roman times.

Artists, too, found employment readily in the Hellenistic world. Every city set up hundreds of statues in honour of notable people; princes and kings rivalled one another in encouraging artists and collecting masterpieces. Sculptors and painters both made remarkable progress in portraiture, though in many ways the art of this age is inferior to that of the fifth and fourth centuries. Wall-painters executed graceful little scenes of flowers and landscape, but the lovely art of vase-painting had perished.

ARTISTIC AND LITERARY TENDENCIES

Sculpture was the chief artistic achievement of the age, and though Hellenistic sculptors have given us some works of famous beauty, such as the Aphrodite of Melos (Venus of Milo) and the Victory of Samothrace, their art shows only too clearly the restlessness and striving for theatrical effect which flourished everywhere under the absolute monarchies of the Hellenistic world. The best-known sculpture of the time is from the altar of Zeus at Pergamum, in northern Asia Minor. It depicts with tremendous power the old subject of a battle between gods and giants, but whereas earlier sculptors had treated even this violent subject with figures of calm impassive beauty, at Pergamum the onlooker received the realistic impression of terrible struggle and tumult going on before his eyes. The artist had been inspired by the memory of the Celtic invaders who had swept into Asia Minor in the third century: he captured their ferocity in stone, and left a monument eloquent of the conflict between civilization and barbarism.

In literature, new forces were at work. Elementary and higher education was now more widespread than ever before, and had given to thousands the desire to express themselves publicly, to millions the desire to read. This demand was met by the large-scale supply of specialist and popular literature; the world's paper manufacture was now entirely in Greek hands in Egypt, and educated slaves were employed in copying books. The rulers of the new kingdoms honoured learning, and entertained poets, historians and scholars at their courts. Above all, they established libraries in their capitals, at Syrian Antioch, at Pergamum, and, greatest of all, at Alexandria. Besides the Museum, which was the centre of scientific research, the Ptolemies founded a State Library, where books brought from all over the world were collected and catalogued by an official librarian and a trained staff. Here famous men of learning studied the writings of earlier Greek poets and historians, writing notes on difficult passages, making dictionaries of obscure words, and compiling Greek grammars to help their own generation in understanding the great works of the past. Estimates of the number of volumes in the two Alexandrian libraries vary between 42,800 and 400,000, but it must be remembered that the contents of the ancient roll or volume were less than that which is contained in modern books.

THE DIVISION OF

Although the Empire of Alexander the Great disintegrated after his death for want of any one man capable of taking his place, hellenistic influence and civilization continued to spread. International trade, stimulated by the knowledge of new trade routes to the Orient, grew enormously, and cities such as Alexandria achieved prosperity on a scale hitherto unknown. In Egypt, Ptolemy, possibly the shrewdest of Alexander's generals, founded a dynasty that was to last until Queen Cleopatra and the reduction of Egypt to a Roman province.

THE HELLENISTIC WORLD

The Antigonids and the Seleucids established their own spheres of influence. The early Seleucid kings ruled an empire which stretched from the Aegean Sea to Afghanistan. Seleucia, situated on the River Tigris, served to control the great wealth of Mesopotamia, while Antioch rivalled Alexandria as a great trading centre and was noted for its luxury. The Antigonids ruled Macedonia itself, and tried to exercise control over the turbulent Greek states. The spread of civilization in this period helped prepare the way for the Roman Empire.

No effort was made to write original works to rival those of the supreme names in Greek literature, Sappho, the tragedians, Thucydides, Demosthenes. Learned men, like Callimachus, wrote polished verses and clever epigrams on love and friendship, life and art. But the scholarly poets of the Hellenistic age are as inferior in real genius to the men of the fifth and fourth centuries as the English writers of the eighteenth century, like Pope, are to Shakespeare and his fellow Elizabethan poets. The trouble was that they never let themselves go in their writing: they were out of touch with genuine human feelings, living and working in their marvellous library, "like fatted fowls in a hen-coop", as one unkind critic of their day described them.

The only great poet of this age was Theocritus, who wrote charming little "idylls" about country life in Sicily: he returned to Nature for inspiration, and has left us word-pictures of singing matches between Sicilian shepherds, of a forsaken girl trying to charm back her lover, of grasshoppers and yellow bees and the sweet things of the countryside, pictures which are still vivid after two thousand years, inspiring countless imitations among poets of the western world in many ages.

A modern kind of comedy was still written and produced at Athens, witty and elegant, but superficial. The best of such comedies were the work of Menander, some of whose lines have become English proverbs, "He, whom the gods love, dies young", "Evil communications corrupt good manners". There were serious historians, the greatest being Polybius, who described the expansion of Rome's power over the Mediterranean world. Innumerable prose works on scientific subjects were produced for the educated public; for the great mass of the half-educated, there were popular books on history, biographies, collections of anecdotes, and crude sketches from daily life, acted or sung on the stage and known as mimes. The output of literature was far greater than it had ever been in the world before, but royal patronage was no proper substitute for freedom. The genuine inspiration of Greek literature had died with the political liberties of the city-state.

SCIENTIFIC RESEARCH ADVANCES

Science was the one thing in which the Hellenistic age of Greek history far excelled all its predecessors. In the Museum at Alexandria, scientists, paid by the Ptolemies, conducted their researches and delivered lectures to students eager to keep abreast of the advancing thought of their day. Alexander's expeditions through Asia had thrown new realms of knowledge open to the Greeks, and had greatly stimulated scientific enquiry. Greek astronomers now made use of the observations and discoveries made long ago at Babylon: they learned to calculate the measurements of the earth, and some even worked out the revolutionary theory that the earth moves round the sun. The great geographer Eratosthenes (275–200 B.C.) was the first to teach the truth about the oceans of the world and originated scientific map-making by his use of the lines of longitude and latitude. Little advance was made in zoology, botany or physics, and chemistry was unknown, but the third century saw remarkable progress in medicine and surgery. By the vivisection of animals and dissection of corpses, doctors discovered the function of the nerves and of the brain, previously unknown, and they were able to establish how the blood circulated through the body.

GEOMETRY, ENGINEERING AND PHILOSOPHY

But the greatest achievement lay in mathematics. Geometry, which had reached an advanced stage in Plato's school at Athens, was perfected at Alexandria. Euclid wrote a textbook of geometrical proofs which has remained in use from 300 B.C. down to the twentieth century. Greatest of all Hellenistic scientists was Archimedes of Syracuse. He applied his brilliant theoretical discoveries to practical uses in mechanics and engineering. Many stories were told of him: how his arrangement of pulleys and levers enabled the king to launch a great ship by turning a light crank: how he boasted "Give me a place to stand on and I will move the earth", and people believed him: how he discovered specific gravity by suddenly noticing the water he displaced in his bath, and ran through the streets naked, crying "Eureka" ("I have found it"): how, through the long siege of Syracuse, his engineering devices kept all the might of Rome at bay. Other scientists invented practical appliances: notable were the world's first lighthouse, the great Pharos at Alexandria harbour: slot-machines for dispensing holy-water at the doors of temples; mechanical marionette shows in city theatres; presses for olive-oil worked by the principle of the endless screw.

But daily life was not full of scientific inventions as it is in the modern world. The Greeks never possessed reliable scientific instruments: except in surgery, they did not use the method of experiment: they had no natural gift or inclination for mechanical devices, and, until debased by Roman influence, vastly preferred the individual work of a craftsman to the imitation article of mass-production: finally, the universal institution of slave labour saved them from the necessity of using machines in their factories.

In philosophy, Hellenistic Athens was the school not only of Greece, but of the world. The chief interest of philosophers had shifted again, from speculations as to the nature of truth to the field of human conduct. Now that man felt himself, above all, an individual, he needed practical guidance for the conduct of life. Thus philosophy aimed at the individual's happiness and laid down rules for conduct. At Athens, the successors of Plato and Aristotle carried on their masters' principles at the Academy and Lyceum, but they were overshadowed for a time by two new schools of philosophy.

The first was founded by Epicurus, who taught that happiness was to be found in escape from all worry, in the pure pleasure that comes from absence of passions and desires and pain. His disciples renounced the ordinary effort and pleasures of the world, living simply and quietly together in friendship. This philosophy never influenced the masses, but for centuries it appealed to a few in every age; it failed because it really meant a running away from the world, a shirking of life's duties.

ZENO AND THE STOICS

More influential was the other new school, founded by a Phoenician called Zeno, a man of noble simplicity like Socrates. He taught in the Stoa, or Porch, at Athens, and his followers are known as Stoics. Zeno held that the world is one great state, in which all men are brothers, ruled by one supreme Providence, all-wise and all-good, who has made the laws of nature and fixed the course of history for ever. Man will only be happy if he tries always to live according to the divine will: that is the only true wisdom. It means accepting whatever comes with perfect calm, content with little or much of the world's goods, equally indifferent to pleasure or pain. If a man will listen to his conscience and do his duty by resigning himself to God's will, then he will have virtue. Virtue is essential. Virtue alone enables a man to rise superior to all the changes and chances of life, to be, as Zeno put it, "self-sufficient", the master of his fate and the captain of his soul. In the depths of a man's own soul is a fortress which not all the kings in the world can capture. If the poor slave in the African gold-mines possesses Stoic virtue, then he is the equal of King Ptolemy with all his fine raiment and gorgeous palaces. This philosophy appealed to strong, self-reliant natures, and was particularly suited to the Roman character at its best. But it left the masses untouched, chiefly because it took little account of the frailty of human nature and left no room for the emotions. The Stoic did not love his neighbour as himself. Stoicism attacked the worship of sacred shrines and images, whilst acknowledging and upholding the truth of polytheism. One result of its insistence upon the existence of rational explanations for all things was the increase of scientific research into archaeology and jurisprudence; while it influenced strongly such men as Cato, Seneca, and the emperor Marcus Aurelius.

THE SPREAD OF EASTERN RELIGIONS

While the few found their consolation in philosophy, most men everywhere turned to religion: not to the old Greek worship of the Olympian deities, for that had been wrapped up with the corporate life of the city-state and no longer had any message of comfort, but to the multitude of strange faiths that came flooding into the Greek world from the East. Greece gave to Asia science and philosophy and city-life, but in religion Asia was far stronger than her conquerors.

The age-old worship of sun and moon and stars came from Babylon, with its terrible belief in a pitiless, overmastering Fate. Thousands went in fear of the stars, believing that the secrets of their lives were locked in the movements of the seven planets in heaven, oppressed by the faith that they were mere puppets of a blind and awful Power. Such a faith could offer little to those in search of hope or consolation, and bred a spirit of hopelessness.

In rebellion against such hopeless doctrines, they took refuge in other oriental faiths that seemed to offer some escape from the clutches of Fate or Fortune, in the ancient practices of magicians who claimed to alter the stars in their courses and the mystery religions of Asia and Egypt which promised salvation to the chosen few who should be "initiated" into their secrets. At the root of all these mystery cults was the idea of salvation for the faithful; chief among them was the worship of the goddess Isis, which spread from Egypt all over the known world. Isis was worshipped as the divine wife and mother, and her religion made an enormous appeal to women. The old Olympian worship, in spite of its goddesses, had nothing really feminine about it, and brought women little comfort. But Isis had loved as women love, had suffered as women suffer: she was their friend who understood. Therefore her worship swept the Mediterranean world and spread to Rome in spite of being periodically viewed with suspicion by the emperors. Worship of Isis lingered in Europe until the sixth century A.D., when the last remaining shrine was closed.

THE END OF THE HELLENISTIC WORLD

Between the upper stone of these eastern creeds and the nether stone of Rome's irresistible might the Greek spirit was being crushed. Although, in time, "captive Greece led her fierce conqueror captive" in culture and thought, in the last century B.C. Rome seemed to have destroyed all that Greece stood for. One by one the successor kingdoms had gone down before her. First Macedon and Greece itself, then Asia yielded to the Roman soldier and suffered from the greed of the Roman tax-gatherer. The end of the Hellenistic world came in 31 B.C., when Cleopatra, last of a long line of Egyptian Queens and more beautiful than them all, lost her kingdom to the Roman Augustus, and rather than yield herself, clasped the poisonous snake to her breast, and cheated her conqueror by death, triumphant in defeat. Distracted by generations of warfare, the Greek world turned to Rome for the gift of peace. But Rome could not meet the other supreme need of that time, a saving faith which should give to all men what the philosophies and mystery religions had failed to give— a sure hope of immortality and mutual love between man and man. Weary and heavy-laden, the world was waiting for a light to lighten the Gentiles, and it came from Bethlehem.

CHAPTER 13

THE GREEK GENIUS

IT is a far cry from Crete to Cleopatra, from little Mycenae to vast cosmopolitan Alexandria. Yet throughout Greek history, there are certain characteristics in which the genius of the race found expression. First comes the principle of "Nothing too much"—sober moderation in all things. For the Greeks, this did not mean an attitude of cold calm or dull stagnation, but an exacting effort to hit the mean between two extremes; not living in a rut, but balancing delicately and dangerously on a razor edge. It was hard for them to avoid excess. They had no long traditions of civilized life behind them: beneath the surface was primitive wildness, the natural instincts of the savage, which had constantly to be curbed. They were lively, excitable and passionate like all southerners, using eager gestures as they talked in the market-place, giving full play to their emotions in the law-courts, quick to sense the drama of a political situation. Yet the chief characteristic of their genius is a balanced moderation, a highly developed sense of order, at which they aimed in all their activities. The Greeks did not speak of "a bull in a china-shop": their corresponding proverb referred to "a bull in a city".

LOVERS OF MODERATION

The city-state was a community founded on law, maintained in due order not by force, but by consent. When King Xerxes asked who was the lord and master of the Greeks, he was told, truly, that "they had no master save one, the law". This self-restraint and sense of order appeared also in their daily life. They hated excess in eating and drinking. The professional who carried athletics too far was despised no less than the man who neglected them altogether. A decent and dignified worship of the gods was preferred to hysterical excitement or self-abasement. There is the same moderation in Greek architecture, where not a stone too many or too few was used, and in Greek literature, which says neither too little nor too much. Architects and sculptors were content to achieve beauty within the ordered framework of the temple's traditional pediment and frieze, just as the tragic poets accepted the restraint of the ancient traditions of tragedy. Above all, in the realm of thought, they kept the mean between anarchy and blind obedience to authority. They liked to think out problems for themselves, in an orderly rational way. They accepted reason as the guide to life.

"You Greeks are always children", said a shrewd Egyptian to the Athenian Solon. They were indeed childish in many ways, in their constant bickering between city and city, in their superstitions, in their fear of the unknown, in their fixed custom of treating war as a game with well-recognized rules and conventions. They took a childish pleasure in scoring off a neighbour, especially when bargaining in the market-place, called by a truth-loving Persian "the place in the middle of a Greek city, where men meet to talk and tell lies and cheat one another". They often indulged in a harmless vanity, as when the poll was taken to decide the cleverest Athenian, and Themistocles was declared elected because every good citizen put himself first and Themistocles second.

Like children, too, they were consumed with curiosity—the wondering desire for knowledge, which, Plato said, is the beginning of all philosophy. They had the child's gift of seeing objects as they are, neither ignoring them nor adding to them, which made simplicity the keynote of their art; the child's habit of unhesitating, direct expression, which enabled them to create a great literature; the child's natural love of fellowship, which made them the most sociable beings in the world, convinced that life outside a community was not worth living. Like children, they found happiness in giving themselves absolutely to the work in hand, whatever it might be. They were so intensely interested in their life upon earth that they rarely bothered to speculate concerning life after death.

The Greeks loved beauty and were quick to appreciate it, as no other people has done. Natural beauty was part of their heritage; they found keen delight in the fine things in the world—"dawn, the rosy-fingered", sunset over the mountains, the grey shimmer of olive-groves seen from rocky heights, the violet light at evening creeping up from the sea to the city on its hill, the sight of a ship coming safely home to port, of a field of corn waving in the wind, of a mother and her child. But more than these was the beauty created by their own hands and minds, the beauty of marble temples, sculptured images, delicately painted vases and wonderful plays.

BEAUTY THROUGH SIMPLICITY

Yet with this beauty, which was common to all and not merely the preserve of a privileged few, went an extreme simplicity. There was nothing extravagant or exaggerated in their works of art or in their daily life. Just as their temples and sculpture were free from any unnecessary ornament and from anything complicated or ostentatious, so their daily life was severely simple. Their requirements for physical comfort were few: a little plain food and wine, two pieces of woollen stuff for clothes, some shelter for sleep, and a healthy open-air life for most of the day. They laughed at a man of extravagant dress and habits as a "barbarian", or despised him as vulgar and uneducated. They were not intent on amassing treasure which moth and rust can corrupt, and where thieves could dig under the walls of unbaked brick and steal. They raised magnificent buildings for the city and the city's gods, but they were content in their personal lives with the plainest and simplest of houses. The Athenians created and enjoyed the world's greatest drama; but they were capable of achieving their happiness without drains.

The most noticeable thing about the Greeks was their extraordinary vitality of mind. They attacked the problems of life with clear logical thought; they tried to solve difficulties by reason, not by appealing to authority; they argued, and were ready to follow the argument fearlessly to its conclusion. By dint of hard thinking, they worked out the ideas of freedom, equality and justice, and put their ideas into practice. They were passionately interested in the things of the mind and in the search for truth, not because they hoped to make their lives safer or more comfortable, but because they believed this to be the noblest activity of man. But they were never unpractical, and they cultivated the mind without neglecting the body. Pericles was one of the most intellectual men of his day; but he found time to govern a state. Socrates himself was a stonemason, and performed all the public duties of a citizen. Plato was an accomplished gymnast and the counsellor of a king.

THE BALANCE BETWEEN BODY AND MIND

Love of learning did not soften the Greeks. They lived a hardy life; they were brave soldiers; they showed more interest and care in physical training than any other people. They saw the human body as a thing of beauty, which must be kept lithe and supple and fit by gymnastics. Every Greek city had at least one public gymnasium, and so keen was the national interest in all kinds of athletics that once every four years a Sacred Truce between all Greeks was declared, while in the Games at Olympia, the flower of Greek athletes from every city ran and leapt and wrestled together. An athletic festival was the only thing serious enough to call a halt in the wars. Greek philosophers and historians have proved that the Greeks had splendid minds: their artists, who went to the gymnasium for their models, have shown us that they had splendid bodies.

"Man, know thyself!" ran the inscription over the portal of Apollo's temple at Delphi. And the Greeks' chief interest was the knowledge of man, his mind and body, his powers and weaknesses, his triumphs and disasters. For the knowledge of God, posterity has turned to the Jews, but in the science of man the Greeks are supreme.

In other fields, Greece has left a unique legacy to the world. Nearly all the great achievements of western civilization, in politics and philosophy, in art and architecture, in literature and science, have either drawn their inspiration from ancient Greece or at least owed much to her example. The Greeks were "a race accustomed to take little and give much". They have given a treasure to the world that is not exhausted. "Children" the Egyptian called them: with the confidence, hope and exhilaration of inspired children, they carried human nature almost to the limit of its glorious power. Their call to the eternal ideals of Truth and Beauty, Political Freedom and Justice still echoes clearly down the centuries from that distant time when the world still seemed lit with morning glory.

PART III

THE ROMAN WORLD

CHAPTER 14

THE GROWTH OF THE CITY AND THE CONQUEST OF ITALY

WHEN, about 1200 B.C., the Empire of Crete fell, the peoples went wandering about the Eastern Mediterranean, sacking and founding cities in Greece and Asia Minor, fighting their little wars and singing great songs about them. One of these peoples made its way into the central part of the sea, and worked up along the west coast of Italy. These were the Etruscans, a mysterious and rather sinister race, the visible fragments of whose civilization lie still upon the soil they occupied. A few survivals of their institutions into later times give us a hint of what they were like. The treasures unearthed from their tombs show that they were luxurious and pleasure-loving; the gladiatorial combats which they bequeathed to their successors give us an idea of the grimness of their public entertainments; the cruel and superstitious nature of their religion is shown by their elaborate methods of divination, and by the paintings of horrors which have been found in their tombs.

EARLY ITALIAN PEOPLES

The Etruscans occupied the northern part of Italy, which included the rich valley of the Po. To the north were the Alps, a formidable barrier to an invader. To the south, running down the great peninsula, was the long range of the Apennines, on either side of which were rich coastal lands. Here lived simpler and more primitive peoples. Some of them had been there from time immemorial; others were recent immigrants, related to the Aryan-speaking tribes who were making their way down into Greece. They lived in open villages, which formed themselves into small cantons; and groups of cantons leagued themselves together for purposes of defence, forming the tribes of which we hear a great deal; they were purely military groups, and the unit of government was the canton.

These, the genuine Italian peoples, were agriculturalists, and their religion was a religion of the cultivation of the land. Their gods were the Aryan gods of rain, sun, fire, growth, and all powers that the farmer must court or propitiate. In a country where land is hardly won, a country of rugged hills and soggy marshes, the farmer must be prepared to defend himself; and the occupation of the best land in Italy by the Etruscans must have made the earlier inhabitants more careful of what was left to them, and increased their warlike qualities.

After the Etruscans came the Greeks. From the eighth century onwards, a line of Greek colonies was planted in Sicily and South Italy; some, like Syracuse and Naples, survive today. Unlike the Etruscans, they were not aggressive; by teaching the natives how to cultivate the vine and the olive and to use the alphabet, they had their effect on the everyday life of the peninsula, but little directly on its politics. The Greeks, careful not to encroach on the Etruscan preserves, colonized only the coastlands in the South, and did much to develop the regions in which they lived.

The southern boundary of the Etruscan power was, roughly speaking, the river Tiber, which flows down from the Apennines, through a fertile plain, into the sea. This plain is naturally subject to floods, but at about fifteen miles from the river's mouth there is, on the southern bank, a collection of small hills, which are free from flooding and command what is, in normal weather, the lowest convenient crossing of the river. This was the natural outpost of the Latins, the Italian tribe which was the southern neighbour of the Etruscans, and the separate communities which inhabited these hills early formed themselves into a league to resist the encroachments of their formidable Etruscan neighbours. Thus came into being the city of Rome, a joint foundation of people from more than one tribe. Probably the Romans were not far wrong in saying that this happened in 753 B.C.

ROME UNDER THE KINGS

When, in after years, Rome became the capital of the Western world, legends told of her foundation, connecting it with the ancient heroes of Troy and the gods of Mount Olympus. But divine intervention was not needed to account for her phenomenal growth from such small beginnings. Her geographical position was favourable. She was half-way on the main road from the South to the North, and she lay on the Tiber, whose estuary formed the best harbour on the west coast. Thus she held the key to Italy; and when the Mediterranean world became one, Italy was its natural centre. But in early years, these advantages were only potential; Rome was a confederation of villages perched on a few little hills, from which the country-folk might look out any day across the river and see an army of fierce-looking, highly-armed Etruscans massing for attack. The need for perpetual preparation against attack had a permanent influence on their character; the Romans were an essentially military people, and all their institutions reflect a warlike habit of mind, while their inventive genius had its fullest expression in military works.

At first, they were ruled by a king, who as high priest, general and law-giver regulated their dealings with the gods, with foreigners and with each other. The people under him were by no means equal in rank. There was a privileged class of nobility, known as Patricians; the remainder of the people, the Plebeians, worked for them and hoped to enjoy their protection. The Patricians provided the King with his Senate, or advisory body of old and experienced men; this Senate had the right of recommending the appointment of the new King when the old one died, and the people, as a whole, would approve its choice by a shout.

For some time, this system served the state well. From a mass of unreliable tradition one fact emerges: Rome was almost continually at war, and the Kings proved adequate leaders. That her small army, consisting of all citizens who could afford to buy themselves armour, could do much against the Etruscans is unlikely; but against other Latins, the Romans proved formidable fighters, and established a sort of pre-eminence among them.

About the beginning of the sixth century, Rome came under the control of the Etruscans, or at any rate of Etruscan kings. These Tarquins, as they were called, were regarded by the later Romans as cruel tyrants, but in actual fact they did a great deal for Rome. It was they who first enclosed all the communities with a single wall; thus they can be regarded as the founders of the city. They gave it a drainage system, and beautified it with a magnificent temple. They reorganized the army, enlarging it and dividing up the citizens into classes according to their wealth, which, since the soldiers had to pay for their own equipment, was a very necessary contribution to efficiency. But though they were efficient rulers, they were none the less aliens, and their rule lasted less than a hundred years. For Rome, like other Latin towns which had to submit to Etruscan rule, rose and drove out her alien lords.

Tradition always referred to this revolution as the Expulsion of the Kings; and for centuries afterwards, the very idea of monarchy was abhorrent to Rome. Even five hundred years later, when force of circumstance compelled the establishment of personal sovereignty, the name of King had to be avoided, so deeply ingrained was the hateful memory of the last of the Kings, Tarquin the Proud.

INSTITUTION OF REPUBLICAN GOVERNMENT

Freed from their bondage, the Romans set up a republican form of government, in which every precaution was taken to stop too much power from getting into the hands of one man. The priestly functions of the old Kings were continued in a religious officer, who held the title of King of Sacred Things; but he had no political powers whatsoever. The power of the Kings was vested in two Consuls, who were equally heads of the state; but they only held office for one year, and therefore could never become too powerful. Later, other magistrates were established, and the functions of the consuls became confined mainly to affairs of war; the general tendency was for power to be divided up among more and more people, so that none could become supreme. Every magistrate had at least one colleague to share his powers. Greater importance attached to the Assembly of the people, who elected the magistrates, and to the Senate, who advised them.

As power became more widely spread, the importance of the division between Patricians and Plebeians, which had existed from earliest times, increased. For two hundred years, the struggle to retain privilege on the one hand, and to break it down on the other, dominated the internal politics of the city. The Patricians started with everything in their favour. They alone had the right to become magistrates. Though far less numerous than the Plebeians, they controlled the Assembly; for its organization was that of the reformed army of the period of the Kings, and they comprised the three highest of the five property-classes into which it was divided, thus having a permanent majority. They alone could sit in the Senate. All the priestly offices were in their hands, and they could always say that a proposal they disliked was against the will of the gods. Most important of all, they alone had knowledge of the law; there was no written code of laws, nothing to which a Plebeian could appeal.

PATRICIANS AND PLEBEIANS

Against this mass of privilege, the Plebeians had only one advantage. They had immense and ever-increasing numerical superiority; and the Patricians depended on their loyalty in wartime and their work in peace. This made possible the weapon of the Strike. When they wanted to go to extremities, the Plebeians used to leave Rome and establish themselves in some stronghold a few miles away; and the Patricians would be bound to compromise. The Plebeians are said to have used this weapon on five occasions, and no doubt they threatened it on many others. In course of time, they won more and more liberty. Their first success was the institution of tribunes, officers whose sole duty was to protect them against the consuls; these had the right of vetoing any act of a Patrician magistrate which they regarded as damaging the interests of the Plebeians. As time went on, the tribunes used their veto more freely, and gradually established a large degree of control over the whole life of the city. Another of their functions was to organize the Plebeians. Side by side with the official Assembly of the People, which was controlled by the Patricians, arose the Council of the Plebeians, which, at first unofficial, in the course of two centuries won legal recognition.

But before this happened, there were other reforms to be carried against the stubborn resistance of the Patricians. In the first century of the republic, the greatest concession to the liberty of the individual was wrested from them; they were compelled to make out and publish a code of laws. A commission of ten Patricians was set up, and after a year's work, they produced the Twelve Tables, a document inscribed on stone, containing laws covering the greater part of the life of the citizens. The Plebeians were disappointed; the Twelve Tables made no new law, but merely reaffirmed previously unwritten law. They were suspicious of the Commissioners, who, seeking re-election after their work was done, looked like trying to establish a new and unconstitutional form of government. A strike brought the Patricians to their senses; the hard-won rights of the Plebeians were confirmed; and in time they came to realize what a step forward the publication of the Twelve Tables had been. For they knew now what their rights were, and the tribunes were on firm ground in asserting them. The Twelve Tables were never repealed, though they were brought up to date on several occasions; they outlasted the city of Rome, and the Empire itself; they are the ultimate source of much of the law of Europe to this day.

The next advance was the abolition of the social exclusiveness of the Patricians. Marriage between them and the Plebeians was legally recognized, and family relationships began to cut right across political divisions; the resistance of the Patricians became less whole-hearted. Further, many of the Plebeians had become rich, and the social barrier was no longer fortified by the barrier of wealth. But this took some time to be fully realized; it was several generations before the fusion of the classes by marriage became effective. Rome was greatly occupied with the wars which will be described in the following pages, and Patrician and Plebeian often lost sight of their quarrel. But when other affairs allowed them, the Plebeians pressed hard for the chief prize that still eluded their grasp, the right to fill important magistracies. Attempts by the Patricians to reach a compromise over the consulship only put off the inevitable surrender; in the first half of the fourth century, they gave way completely, and it was enacted that, of the two consuls for each year, one must be a Plebeian. This opened the way for the Plebeians to all other offices, except some of the religious ones; and more important still, it automatically admitted them to the Senate, which had become, in the course of time, a gathering of ex-magistrates. And when, early in the third century, the resolutions of the Council of the Plebeians became officially recognized as having the force of law, the long struggle was over. Only the dim vestiges of social prestige remained to the Patricians; before the law, all Roman citizens were equal.

THE ETRUSCAN WARS

Along with the struggle for supremacy between the two classes of the Roman people, had gone a struggle for the very existence of the city in which the two classes had fought side by side. When Rome drove out her Etruscan kings, she had to face continual warfare with the other Etruscans across the river; for the first hundred years of the Republic this was her main foreign preoccupation. That she survived the attacks of this formidable people was due to three things. In the first place, the Etruscan dynasty had given her good fortifications and an efficient army; secondly, the Etruscan power was decaying; and thirdly, by astute diplomacy the Romans secured an alliance with the other Latin tribes, who formed a bulwark for her against the assaults of the highland tribes of the Apennines, destined to give her much trouble in years to come. This alliance did not mean that Rome was free from attacks from the South and East; often during this period she had to fight hard to repel them; but the loyal assistance of her Latin kinsmen turned the scale, and successive victories allowed her to concentrate on the war against the Etruscans. Her chief Etruscan enemy was the powerful city of Veii, which stood about twelve miles from Rome, on a rock with a deep moat on three sides. When the Romans finally captured it, it was only after a long siege, during which it proved necessary actually to drain the moat.

For Rome, the capture of Veii was a landmark in her history; for the Etruscans, it was only a small part of a much greater disaster. Here we must leave the wars of Rome for a moment, and turn to the adventures of one of the most important of the great divisions of the Aryan-speaking race, the Kelts.

THE COMING OF THE GAULS

Hard upon the heels of the tribes who pressed down into the Mediterranean and peopled Greece and Italy, came their cousins the Kelts, whose speech was derived from the same parent-language as their own. From the upper waters of the Danube, they moved first into Germany; and then turned westwards. Between 1000 and 500 B.C., they reached France, Spain and South Britain. Meeting apparently with weak resistance from the natives—they were armed with iron weapons, and the natives were still in the Bronze Age—they prospered in their new homes, and their numbers increased. In the fifth century B.C., some of them turned southwards, one branch invading the Balkans from the Danube, and the other, known to the Romans as Gauls, crossing the Alps into the Etruscans lands. The North was where the Etruscans least expected invasion—long security had made them careless, and they had little organization with which to defend themselves. The Gauls easily took possession of the north of Italy, which became known even to the Romans as "Gaul this side of the Alps" (Cisalpine Gaul); "Gaul the other side" (Transalpine Gaul) meant modern France and Belgium. On neither side of the Alps did the Gauls exterminate the old inhabitants; they ruled them, and no doubt exchanged ideas and ways of life with them, in the manner of a conquering aristocracy.

This was the end of Etruscan power in Italy. The Gauls had defeated them in the north, the Romans to the south; their sea-power had fallen into the hands of the Greeks of Sicily, and their possessions in the south of Italy into the hands of the hill-tribes. But they remained on the land, and many of their cities kept their independence; to a great extent, they were absorbed by their conquerors.

The final stages of the Gallic occupation of Etruria brought them into contact with the Romans, who, proud of their capture of Veii, underestimated the strength of the new invaders, calmly warning them to come no further. The reply of the Gauls was swift and devastating. They advanced on Rome in 390 B.C. and easily over-whelmed the army that was sent to stop them, for the Roman soldier, once he had discharged his javelin, had only a short thrusting sword with which to parry the long cutting sword of the Gaul. The enemy laid siege to the city, and though the Romans held out desperately in their citadel, they had in the end to buy off the Gauls by paying a large ransom after most of the city had been sacked.

Had the Gauls been more far-seeing, Rome would have ceased to be; as it was, they had no definite plan of conquest, and having exacted their price they were prepared to leave the Romans to themselves. Their invasion shattered Roman prestige among the tribes further south. The hill tribes saw in the sack of Rome their opportunity; the Latin allies were less enthusiastic in helping a city in which they had lost confidence. The next fifty years were critical. Now was displayed, more than ever before, the traditional Roman courage in the face of disaster. The fortifications of the city were re-built and increased. The army was reorganized and re-equipped to cope with the unfamiliar tactics of the Gauls. The main body of the troops was equipped with long swords, as well as javelins, and its flanks were protected by light-armed slingers and javelin-throwers. The legions, the regiments of Rome which at this time consisted of about 3000 men apiece, were split up internally, so as to allow more rapid manoeuvring; the soldiers could now fight in close ranks or in loose separate bodies, according to the way in which the enemy were attacking them.

These reforms, designed to meet any fresh Gallic attacks, were, in practice, of the greatest possible advantage in resisting the attacks of the tribesmen to the South and East, who, fortunately for Rome, had little tendency to combine; she was usually able to deal with them separately, and always successfully. But more than once in these years, she had to abandon her constitutional principles, and appoint, instead of two consuls, a single dictator with supreme powers. Her chief leader was the conqueror of Veii, Camillus, who suffered the penalty of greatness by being exiled; but after the Gallic invasion, the Romans saw that they could not get on without him. He was recalled, and was responsible probably for the army reforms, and certainly for many of the victories which they made possible.

THE STRUGGLE WITH THE SAMNITES

By the middle of the fourth century, Rome had re-established her ascendancy over her former allies, and extended her dominions up to the foothills of the Apennines. Across the river, she held much of the old territory of the Etruscans; and the Gauls seemed disposed to leave her alone. It was in the southern parts of the Apennines that the next danger arose. The chief tribe of this district was the Samnites. Some of them had settled in the plain of Campania, and become civilized; they were on good terms with Rome, but those that had remained in the hills were barbaric. They were half drovers, half brigands, who terrorized the more advanced peoples of the plains. They were superb fighters, much sought after as mercenaries by the Greek cities of Sicily and South Italy.

Three separate wars against the Samnites, spread over fifty years, are recorded in the annals of Rome. In the course of them, Rome suffered more than one tremendous disaster, and had to face another rebellion of her Latin allies. But the latter were completely crushed; many were actually incorporated in the Roman state, and the rest, though still called allies, were put in a position of servile dependence. Eventually the Samnites, too, were overcome; in the final battle at the beginning of the third century, they had the assistance of the

EARLY ROMAN ITALY

The strength of Rome sprang from small beginnings, aided by her strategic position on the Tiber, astride the line of communications from North to South.

Gauls and the Etruscan remnant; but, desperate though their resistance was, they could not withstand the army of Rome. The last of the warrior peoples of Italy had to submit. There was now no genuine Italian people which was not in some way subordinate to Rome.

The policy of the Romans towards the other Italians was to rule them by dividing them. Most of them were allowed self-government in internal affairs; but their relations with each other were jealously supervised, to see that they did not combine. In military matters, they were completely subordinate; their troops were always under the command of a Roman consul, and the Romans decreed how many soldiers each state should have. Apart from this, there was little uniformity in their treatment. The most favoured were the Latins, who had nearly the same rights as the citizens of Rome itself; below them, there was a large variety of status, depending partly on degrees of civilization and partly on past history; a city which had welcomed the Roman advance, or soon abandoned resistance, received its reward in the shape of favourable treatment. Thus, instead of chafing under the yoke of a conqueror, many of them valued the privileges they had been granted; the growth of loyalty to Rome among her former enemies was surprisingly quick. Another force for Romanization was the planting of Roman colonies in Italy, especially on the West Coast. As we shall see in the next chapter, when a foreign invader came to Italy, the support he expected to get from the Italians was not generally forthcoming; most of them were well content with the rule of Rome.

THE ROMAN SENATE

The uniting of Italy under the rule of one city was accompanied by a new unity within the city itself. The final conquest of the Samnites took place at the same time as the end of the struggle of Patricians and Plebeians. In appearance, the latter was a triumph of democracy; the will of the people was henceforth law. But, in practice, the government was aristocratic, though the aristocracy was not one of Patricians but of the Senate, which now consisted of Patricians and Plebeians alike. Membership was officially open to all comers; ex-magistrates entered it almost automatically, and the election of magistrates was in the hands of the Assembly of the People. But the people preferred usually to elect men of influential families, and thus brought into being a new nobility, a governing class.

The power of the Senate arose from three causes. In the emergencies of the third century, and still more in those of the second, quick decisions were needed; the popular assemblies were too large and unwieldy to be able to make them. Usually they were ready to take the advice of the compact body of experienced ex-magistrates who formed the Senate. Secondly, the system of having a number of magistrates with equal power was bound to lead to their authority clashing; the natural arbitrator in such cases was the Senate. From this arose a custom by which magistrates continually consulted the Senate; eventually its advice was given and followed by magistrates as a matter of course. Thirdly, long tradition had given the Senate control of finance; as the Roman dominion grew larger and money matters became more complicated, this control increased in importance. When policy depends on money, its direction falls into the hands of those who hold the purse-strings.

ECONOMICS AND RELIGION

But, though finance was beginning to play its part, it must not be thought that the economic condition of Rome was far advanced. The city itself had few stone buildings, beyond its temples; the poor lived in mud-huts and the rich in wooden houses with stone foundations. But no one was really wealthy; the nobles were small landlords or even simple farmers, who did much of their own work; things had altered little since the day when a consul was summoned hastily from the handles of his plough to lead Rome's forces to battle. Foreign trade scarcely existed; even coinage was an innovation in Rome at the beginning of the third century. In spite of their recent conquests, the Romans had few slaves; the custom of doing one's own work died hard. In art, they lagged far behind some of the peoples of Italy; they did not care to imitate the Etruscans, and they had as yet learnt little of the arts of peace from the Greeks of the south; even the Samnites of Campania were ahead of them in this. From Campania, they were just beginning to import some sort of drama. Inscriptions on tombstones, public records and a few ballads were all the literature there was. For the Roman farmer-soldier had no time for what he regarded as the graces of life.

On the other hand, over anything that had an obviously useful purpose, he was ready to spend infinite pains. The race that afterwards provided its dominions with magnificent highways, many of which are still in use to-day, began early the practice of roadmaking as the surest way of pacifying a conquered country. Another speciality of the Romans was the aqueduct; they had not the skill nor the amount of lead required for making the vast waterproof pipes with which water is nowadays brought down from the hills; to ensure an adequate supply of water for their growing city, they began to build vast stone aqueducts which provided a slight but regular slope downwards all the way. Thus, primitive though their private buildings remained, the Romans were developing a talent for architecture; and the practice they obtained in building arches for their aqueducts enabled them to outstrip in size, if not in beauty, the buildings of the Greek civilization.

In one department of life, the Romans were quick to learn from foreign peoples. The early simplicity of their religion soon vanished. Their agricultural gods seemed inadequate to deal with the troublous times through which the early republic passed. Though they did not give them up, they were always ready, so as to be on the safe side, to adopt the gods of their neighbours. Their own gods were not jealous gods, and it seemed no dishonour to them to import the worship of new gods. Often these innovations were made with a particular purpose; a plague in Rome caused the introduction of the worship of the Greek god of healing. In many cases, the Romans identified one of their own gods with a Greek god who had similar functions; thus the stories that were told about the Greek goddess of love, Aphrodite, were applied to the Roman Venus, and new methods of worshipping her were introduced. The ruling class kept a careful watch, and suppressed anything that they thought immoral or hysterical; otherwise they made no attempt to keep out new gods or new forms of ritual.

It was all the easier for the Romans to adopt these gods because for them religion was still entirely a matter of the feelings. Gods were mysterious beings whom they feared. They did not think about them. They had no theology; still less had they any philosophy. At a time when Plato and Aristotle and their followers were speculating on the mysteries of the mind and of the universe, the Romans were still occupied entirely with practical affairs. Thought for its own sake would have been incomprehensible to them; thinking was a thing they did before they built a road or elected a consul or laid an ambush. Their character and achievements were those of men of action.

CHAPTER 15

ROME BECOMES A WORLD POWER

VICTORIOUS from the River Po to the Sicilian straits, Rome was supreme over all the Italian tribes. But extension of power brought with it new contacts; the young military state had to enter into dealings with older and more civilized peoples—the Greeks of South Italy, Sicily and the mainland of Greece, and the Carthaginians across the sea.

Naturally, the first contact was made in South Italy. Here many Greek states welcomed the advance of Rome as a security against the bandits from the hills. But the rich and strong city of Tarentum felt able to look after itself, and regarded the Romans as a menace to its independence. It took an early opportunity to provoke war with Rome, and called for assistance to its ally, Pyrrhus, king of Epirus across the Adriatic. Pyrrhus was one of the ablest of all Greek generals. He had a large well-trained army, which he was eager to use, and he had a supply of elephants, the ancient equivalent of the modern tank, formidable beasts in themselves, and additionally terrible to the Romans because they had never faced them before. But Pyrrhus found that, though he could win battles, he could not win campaigns; the Romans had more to lose in Italy than he had, and were ready to make greater sacrifices. After eight years he gave it up, surrendering Tarentum and the other Greek cities whom he had induced to join him. Rome was mistress of all Italy south of the Po; and further, she knew that she could beat the Greeks.

A yet more formidable enemy had now to be faced. While Pyrrhus was fighting, the Carthaginians still remained friendly towards Rome, but his withdrawal left the field clear for a gigantic war. There was plenty of material for a quarrel. The expansion of Rome had been due to the desire for security and the military genius of her people; that of Carthage to the desire for trade. The Carthaginians had the commercial ability of their Semitic ancestors, and the nautical skill of the early Phoenician explorers; all round the western Mediterranean, and up and down the Atlantic seaboard from the mouth of the Niger to the coast of Cornwall, their merchantmen fared, bartering their purple woollens for gold and ivory and tin. With this commercial activity went colonization; Corsica and Sardinia were Carthaginian possessions, and the western half of Sicily was in their hands. They understood the arts of peace, and developed city life not only in their own part of Africa but in their trading-stations, particularly at Cadiz and New Carthage in Spain. In their own country they showed that they were skilful farmers, and in later times, the agricultural textbooks of the Romans showed how great a debt was owed to the estate management of the Carthaginians.

THE FIRST PUNIC WAR

The Carthaginians did not enjoy fighting as the Romans did; but they were always ready to fight if their interests demanded it, and they were well able to do so. Unlike the Romans, they had no citizen army; the business of the citizen was to trade, and they were rich enough to pay foreigners to fight for them, if necessary. The generals were citizens, but they were also professional soldiers, who held their commands for years in succession; the lower ranks were mostly mercenaries from the Berber tribes of Africa and the coasts of the Mediterranean. Thus there was no patriotic sentiment in the Carthaginian armies; the soldiers were simply out for what they could get.

But though the Carthaginians did not go to war unless it seemed absolutely necessary, their efficient government of nobles kept a sharp look-out for possible encroachments on their spheres of commercial interests; when the Romans had conquered the whole of Italy and began to interest themselves in the affairs of Sicily, Carthage became alarmed. Unless some diplomatic arrangement could be reached, war was inevitable; and events moved too swiftly for diplomacy. In 264 B.C., a comparatively minor incident set Rome and Carthage in direct opposition; neither side would withdraw, and in consequence Rome embarked on her first overseas war.

For this, it was necessary to build a fleet; and, thanks largely to the expert advice of Greek mariners, she was able to do so at a great speed. The original object of the Romans was to drive the Carthaginians out of Sicily, a policy which met with considerable support from the Greek cities; but when, in spite of victories by land and sea, they seemed no nearer to success, they decided to strike at Carthage itself. A naval victory enabled them to land in Africa; and the army immediately proved so successful that the Carthaginians sued for peace. But the Roman terms were harsh, and Carthage, in a typically business-like way, hired a general from Sparta, and prepared a new army. This was the undoing of the Romans; the invading army was practically destroyed, and its general captured. Peace was now impossible; the Carthaginians were too elated by their victory, and the Romans were too stubborn to ask for terms. So the war dragged on, both sides resting slightly after their labours. But Rome was more in earnest, and rebuilt her fleet while the Carthaginians let theirs dwindle; and in the twentieth year of the war they made a final effort. A great naval victory made another invasion of Africa possible; the Carthaginians felt that the Romans would not repeat their mistakes, and asked for peace once more. This time it was granted, on condition that they should leave Sicily and pay a large sum of money in the nature of an indemnity.

These twenty years of warfare cost both sides dear, Rome in man-power and Carthage in money. It was plain that the peace that followed was only a truce; each side was suspicious of the other; though the Sicilian question was solved in favour of Rome, there were other places where a clash was likely. So the next twenty years were occupied in undisguised preparations for war. Rome seized Sardinia and Corsica, while Carthage was too weak to object; she then proceeded to conquer and organize the northern part of Italy, which was still inhabited by independent Gaulish tribes; finally she established a completely Roman system of government in Sicily. But Carthage was not idle; writing off Sicily, Sardinia and Corsica as dead losses, she decided to seek compensation in Spain. The Spanish natives, without adequate leadership, were no match for the trained mercenaries of Carthage, under the command of leaders of real genius. For Carthage had produced a family of soldiers which supplied leaders for the army; Hamilcar began the conquest of Spain, and his eldest son Hannibal completed it. It was now only a matter of waiting for an incident to start another war.

HANNIBAL'S WAR ON ROME

Hannibal had been brought up to regard Rome as a natural enemy, and the conquest of Spain as merely an incident in an everlasting struggle. It gave him the two things he most needed—a foothold in Europe and an army—for the Spaniards, when properly led, formed some of the best fighting material in the world. In the previous war, Carthage had laboured under two disadvantages: she had lost command of the sea, and she had no leader of genius. Now the former did not matter, as she already had a large force in Spain, and the latter was no longer true; Hannibal was one of the great military geniuses of all time. Never before had Rome had to face so formidable an enemy; never before had anyone hated her so much.

Hannibal had all his plans laid. His motley army consisted of men gathered from many places—Berber horsemen; Greek adventurers; mercenaries from the Eastern Mediterranean; and fierce fighters from Spanish tribes, who had been admirably trained in mountain warfare. Thus he felt confident that he could force his way over the Pyrenees and then over the Alps, and reach Italy before the Romans were ready for him. This was a feat which sounded impossible in ancient times, and the Romans could not possibly anticipate it. That was all the more reason for attempting it.

THE TERROR OF CARTHAGE IN ITALY

Accordingly, when the time seemed ripe, he provoked war by attacking the city of Saguntum in Spain, an ally of Rome, whose independence he had promised to respect. This served two purposes: it committed his reluctant government to war, and it drew a large force of Romans to Spain. But Saguntum fell before the Senate made any move. Hannibal was across the Pyrenees and had fought his way over the river Rhone, before the Roman expedition had got half-way along the south coast of Gaul. Then an astonished messenger brought the Roman commander news of Hannibal's advance, and the expeditionary force retired into Italy to wait for the Carthaginians. Hannibal's march over the Alps was successful, but very expensive; the resistance both of nature and of the Alpine tribes cost him dearly; but he was prepared for sacrifices, and counted himself fortunate in reaching Italy with 26,000 men, and receiving welcome recruits from the discontented Gauls of the north.

The Romans faced the invader as soon as they could. But, elated by their successful invasion, and brilliantly led, the Carthaginians cut to pieces two Roman armies in the first two years of war. This was good, but not good enough. Hannibal's victories cost men; the Romans had command of the sea, and he could be reinforced only from Spain. The forces ultimately available to Rome were nearly thirty times as many as his. The only ways to complete victory were the capture of Rome, or the stirring up of general rebellion in Italy. To capture Rome was impossible. The city was well fortified, and the speed of Hannibal's march and the route he had taken had prevented him from bringing any siege engines. It was, therefore, on a general rebellion that he counted. Rome had not yet been mistress of the whole of Italy for a hundred years; surely her subjects would look upon the Carthaginians as deliverers.

There was rebellion in the south; but the tribes of central Italy were, by now, thoroughly Romanized, and not one of them went over to the invader. Hannibal's only hope was to win more victories, with the aim of impressing the Italians and bringing about a rising. Rome's obvious strategy was to avoid pitched battles, and let the Carthaginians wear themselves out. Once only, in 216 B.C., they let themselves be tempted from this policy, and Hannibal's military genius was allowed full play. But the battle of Cannae, though a signal disaster, benefited the Romans ultimately. For it taught them the lesson that they must not oppose Hannibal in the field; and it rallied all the forces of Rome under the rule of the Senate. Hannibal was secure in the south of Italy, but he was no nearer to conquering Rome; for nine more years, he stayed there, while the Romans made isolated attacks on the southern cities that had gone over to him. With his small forces, Hannibal could not defend them all; and the Romans took care to avoid pitched battles. And though, after Cannae, Hannibal secured the alliance of King Philip of Macedon, Roman sea-power effectively prevented any help reaching him from that quarter.

Weary of this indecisive warfare, the Carthaginian government decided to reinforce Hannibal. His brother Hasdrubal took all the forces he could raise in Spain and Gaul and made another crossing of the Alps. Unopposed by the Alpine tribes, he managed to get his army intact into the north of Italy; but Hannibal was in the south, and the Romans were determined to prevent their joining. For once, the Romans were better led than the Carthaginians; Hasdrubal was no Hannibal, and in Gaius Claudius Nero the Romans had found a general. At the battle of the river Metaurus, they cut the enemy to pieces. Hannibal was waiting in the south, when one morning the gory head of Hasdrubal was tossed into his camp.

SCIPIO STRIKES AT AFRICA

The Romans could now afford to take the initiative. Hannibal might safely be left to his own devices in the south of Italy; the Romans decided to invade Africa. A young man named Scipio had already distinguished himself by expelling the Carthaginians from Spain. He came of a well-known military family, and combined, with the usual virtues of the Roman soldier, powers of imagination which were uncommon in Romans of that day. He saw infallibly what ought to be done, was confident that he could do it, and persuaded other people that it must be done. His eloquence won over a reluctant Senate and a war-weary people to his enterprise; neither volunteers nor contributions of money were lacking; and his force set sail for Africa.

The early successes of the expedition nearly brought the Carthaginians to their knees; but Rome had still to reckon with Hannibal. In his city's extremity, he returned to Africa, to face Scipio in the field. The dice were loaded against Carthage; many of her vassals had rebelled; many Berbers—on whom she relied for cavalry—had joined the Romans; much of her infantry was of indifferent quality and doubtful loyalty. She had in fact, to pay the penalty for her mercenary system. Her only assets were her corps of elephants and the genius of Hannibal. Scipio was a worthy opponent, and he had adapted his tactics to make the elephants useless. At the battle of Zama in 202 B.C., the Romans won a complete victory; a mere handful of men escaped from the field with Hannibal, who returned home to advise that immediate peace should be sought. Scipio, like most men of imagination, was a generous conqueror. Carthage had to give up all claim to overseas possessions, pay a large indemnity, and break up her fleet; but she suffered no loss of territory in Africa, and though she was forbidden to wage war without the consent of Rome, she was not left utterly defenceless against the Berber tribes.

CARTHAGE DESTROYED

But there were many in Rome who shook their heads at Scipio's clemency. The depredations of Hannibal in Italy had made a lasting impression on their minds, and they looked for revenge. When, in course of time, Carthage became rich again, her enemies in Rome increased in influence, and, though Hannibal was dead, it was easy to raise the alarm. It was equally easy to persuade the Berbers to attack her, and when she defended herself, to protest that she was breaking the treaty. Time after time, Cato, the chief of Rome's die-hards, called for her destruction; and finally, half a century after Zama, the Senate decided to take his advice.

The Carthaginians put up a desperate and heroic resistance; for four years, the traditional stubbornness of the Semite held the vastly superior Roman forces at bay. But however long delayed, the result was never in doubt. When the survivors of the siege finally surrendered, no mercy was shown; they were sold into slavery, the city was utterly destroyed, and a curse was laid upon the site. The African territories of Carthage became a Roman province.

ROME ABSORBS THE GREEK KINGDOMS

The Carthaginians had been a Semitic people, and had had nothing in common with the Romans, and when they came to blows, it had to be war to the end. The story of the dealings of Rome with the Greeks is a happier one. Wars there were, but not about the question of sheer existence. The Greek had a healthy respect for the military qualities of the Roman, and the Roman recognized in the Greek the possessor of a valuable civilization. The Greek, indeed, thought the Roman a "barbarian", and the Roman thought the Greek soft; but neither wished to destroy the other. In fact, the Roman conquest of Greece, shortly after the defeat of Hannibal, could be plausibly represented as the liberation of the Greek cities from the "successor" kings who had divided the Empire of Alexander.

Besides Macedon, Syria and Egypt, there were a number of smaller kingdoms, notably that of Pergamum, in the north-west of Asia

Minor; rightly suspicious of the designs of her larger neighbours, she sought and obtained the alliance of Rome at the first possible opportunity. The Romans were prepared to grant it because of the alliance which Philip V of Macedon had made with Hannibal.

When Philip entered into a compact with Antiochus of Syria, to make a joint attack on Egypt and despoil her of her more northerly possessions, the Romans, who had no desire for further conquests, but a very pressing fear of anyone else becoming too powerful, decided to intervene. Only two years after Zama, she sent a powerful expeditionary force against Philip, while Antiochus was engaged in attacking Egypt; many of Philip's Greek subjects joined the Romans, and in a single campaign he was utterly defeated. He was left with his kingdom; Rome had no desire to rule it; but she hoped that he would never be a menace again.

Antiochus of Syria was the next enemy. When he returned from his war against Egypt, he found Philip already defeated, and prepared to seize some of the Macedonian territories which the Romans had declared free. Reluctant though they were to fight any more wars at present, the Romans could not overlook this; and when he crossed into Greece, they drove him out. This was not enough; he must be defeated in his own country, and Scipio and his brother were sent to do this. Rome was victorious at Magnesia, and Antiochus' power was reduced, so as to make him harmless. Many of his subject-cities were declared free, and became the favoured allies of Rome.

The third of the succession states to the Empire of Alexander, Egypt, was careful not to provoke war with Rome, whom she welcomed as a protector; before long, she acknowledged the suzerainty of Rome without fighting. The whole of the Mediterranean was now under Roman influence.

But it was not under Roman government. All these wars had been fought for security, and not for extension of dominions. Rome had not the machinery for ruling vast domains, nor any desire to develop it. She wanted peace and a breathing-space after the exertions of the war with Hannibal; she welcomed the continued rule of Philip and Antiochus, if only they did not menace her security. But the kings were not ready to play the part allotted to them. First, Philip's son and successor was discovered to be planning war against them; they attacked, deposed him, and divided his kingdom into four small states. Antiochus kept quiet, but the Romans evidently suspected the loyalty of their ally, the King of Pergamum, for they did all they could to weaken him. Gradually the impression grew at Rome that the protectorate system was insecure and unsatisfactory and that a better system must be devised.

At last they decided on a complete change of policy. For over fifty years, they had administered Sicily, Sardinia, Corsica and Spain directly; now they proposed to do the same with the territories they had subdued more recently. In the same year in which Carthage was destroyed and the Roman province of Africa established, Macedonia and Greece (under the name of Achaea) were also formed into provinces. Thirteen years later, Pergamum was bequeathed by its last king to the Roman people, and became the province of Asia. Thereafter, more and more territory came under the direct rule of Rome; for though, time and again, she tried the protectorate system, it nearly always failed. Within the next hundred years, the whole of Western Europe, most of Asia Minor, and Syria were organized into provinces, and administered directly by Roman governors.

ROME'S PROVINCIAL SYSTEM

As Roman conquests had been made to obtain security, the administration of these provinces was not at first enlightened. The business of a governor was simply to see that his subjects did not disturb the Roman Peace, and in early days, their interests were hardly considered. The idea of trusteeship was slow to develop; in many cases, the subject races were by no means "backward" in the arts of peace; it was simply the lack of ability to get on with their neighbours that had caused them to come beneath the yoke of Rome. So Rome had little to teach them, and all she tried to do was to stop them from fighting, for purely selfish reasons.

With nothing more than this negative policy to guide them, the Romans paid little thought to the problems which the government of the world presented; but eventually experience taught them that the system of annual magistracies, which had been invented in the earliest days of the Republic to prevent the possibility of tyranny, did not make for efficiency in the administration of a distant province. A governor of a province who was there for a year only could hardly begin to understand its needs, before he had to leave. Unless he were an exceptionally able and enlightened man, he would think mainly about his subsequent career and his purse. When, owing more to a lack of suitable men than to any desire for the better government of the provinces, the Romans took to extending the period of governorship to three years, little improvement came. The attitude that regarded a province as a gold-mine was now too well established, and the extension of service was regarded by most governors as simply a further opportunity for personal gain.

It was the easiest thing in the world for a governor to enrich himself. In the richer provinces, the Romans were only too willing to accept payment of tribute, in money or in corn, instead of military services; it made their subjects more docile, and themselves richer. The system of taxation varied from province to province; where there was an efficient method of collecting money already in use, there was no point in changing it. But whatever the system, it was under the control of the governor, and he could always manage to get a share of the money for himself. In Asia, for instance, the taxes were farmed out; companies of business men in Rome bought from the government the right to levy taxes in particular districts; the government was spared the trouble and expense of collecting its dues, and the tax-farmers, or publicans, made a profit. The size of the profit depended on what support they could get from the provincial governor; and he usually expected to be paid for his support. He had other, and more direct, methods of making money. His unlimited power of quartering troops on the provincials was an obvious source of gain; his control of the law-courts in which the ever-increasing tribe of money-lenders prosecuted their unfortunate victims was another; and compulsory presents from insincerely grateful provincial communities became a regular and highly profitable institution.

The provincials had no means of defence, and no real means of retribution. For, though there was a special court at Rome to deal with corruption of this sort, it was a very expensive matter to send representatives to it; the governor could easily afford to bribe the jury from his ill-gotten gains. The most infamous of all Roman governors declared that the profits of his first year he would keep for himself; those of the second would go to the friends who had got him the post; and those of the third to the jury. In his case, this did not work; his offence was so rank that no jury could have acquitted him; but condemnation was the exception rather than the rule.

BENEFITS OF ROMAN RULE

Yet there was a brighter side to the rule of Rome. It was effective in securing peace. The small cities of Greece no longer wasted their manhood in squabbling with each other, or forming desperate leagues against the King of Macedon. The fierce tribes of Spain renounced their feuds, and with their keen intelligence rapidly became a centre of the new civilization. If the Roman governor was often a brigand, he did, at any rate, try to secure a monopoly of brigandage for himself, his staff, the tax-collectors and the money-lenders; the more commonplace brigands who lived in the hills and had only fitfully been kept in check by former governments were largely exterminated by the soldiers of Rome. The pirates who for centuries caused untold damage to Mediterranean trade, had been hardly affected by the sporadic attacks of the rulers who were occasionally goaded to action by their outrages; when the whole sea was the preserve of a single power, it was possible to begin effective measures against them. Action was slow in coming; but when it did come it was final.

Again, although the power of the governor was absolute, many of the provincial cities had treaty rights which were only occasionally infringed. Provided that he could enrich himself, the governor would be content to leave the administration of the cities to themselves. The old Greek city-state continued much as before, except that its foreign relations ceased to be under its own control. It had its magistrates and its law-courts, retained its own individuality and valued its old traditions. Readers of the New Testament will remember Ephesus as the centre of a cult of Diana, and Athens as the city of learning, the University of the Ancient World. Even in the backward provinces, in the north of Gaul and subsequently in Britain, the Romans used existing organizations where they were suitable; here the unit of self-government was the tribe; its old market-town became the centre of administration for the district, and the son of the old warrior chief became a magistrate, dispensing justice and ensuring that his belli-cose followers kept the Roman Peace.

Thus, although the objects of Roman provincial government origin-ally were purely selfish and its instruments corrupt, there were features in it that gave good ground for hope. After all, the Roman conquests had been largely a chapter of accidents; there had been no great plan to conquer the world, and it was not to be expected that there would be a ready-made plan for governing it. The Senatorial government inevitably failed to appreciate provincial grievances; it was only when they began to affect the well-being of Italy that notice was taken of them. But, by then, Rome was in the midst of other prob-lems, and reform was slow in coming. It was not until the radical change of government in Rome, which will form the subject of the next chapter, was complete, that the essential change of attitude took place. Until then, the policy of the Roman senators was to get rich quickly; and the source of their riches was the provinces, which they called "the estates of the Roman people".

CHAPTER 16

THE PASSING OF OLD ROME AND THE
TRIUMPH OF GREECE

ROMAN arms had triumphed. Rome's writ ran from one end of the Mediterranean to the other. Spain, Sicily, the most important part of North Africa, Greece, Macedonia and a rich territory in Asia Minor had all been formed into provinces; many countries bordering on these were under Roman protection; it was only a matter of years before the south of Gaul and the rest of North Africa and Asia Minor should be brought under direct Roman control. The question of who should rule in the Mediterranean had been settled for years to come; it remained to be seen what form that rule would take.

The conquests of the Roman Senate and the Roman soldier affected not only the conquered peoples; directly and indirectly, they brought about a profound change in the conquerors themselves. The Romans had conquered, because the Roman state was admirably fitted for conquering. The citizen army, led by men of genius, worked well under officers drawn from a class with a tradition.

These African mosaics show: (*above*) gladiators fighting in an amphitheatre; on the left are band and ambulance; and (*bottom, left*) sending a condemned man to death by delivering him to a tethered wild beast. The statue (*bottom, right*) shows Augustus as the unchallenged ruler of the Roman Empire.

This second-century Roman terracotta mural relief shows a chariot race at a
circus. The charioteer, with reins encircling his waist is about to round the
turning point.

Ruins of the Forum, Pompeii. The city was partly destroyed by earthquake in
A.D. 63; sixteen years later it was overwhelmed by an eruption of Vesuvius.

That the consuls changed every year mattered little; they all had much the same ideas of leading an army; they fitted like parts into a machine; if there was a breakdown, a spare part could always be found, and the machine would be set going and do its work in the end. Except in rare instances, individuals did not amass great power.

The army itself was made up of citizens of the same race. General and private soldier alike were farmers in time of peace; they and their labourers tended their flocks and herds and tilled their fields and vineyards, and sallied forth to defend them when an enemy approached. Their interests were the same; they felt the blessings of peace and the curse of war alike. The Senators were better off than the rest and better educated; but the standards of wealth and education were low, and the gap was small. The Senators were content to live quite simply and the ordinary people very simply.

GRAECO-ROMAN CIVILIZATION

The conquest of the world, and of the Greek and Oriental world in particular, widened the gap by raising the standards of the senators. They brought into their homes a host of Greek slaves. The mistress of the house had a maid to dress her; the master had a valet to shave off his beard, the symbol of old Rome's rugged simplicity. The mistress deserted her kitchen and gave it over to a *chef* who knew all the mysteries of Sicilian cookery. Meals were now served on pottery imported from the East, or on silver plate looted from Greece. The Roman noble became a collector of antiques. Theatre-going was a popular amusement, Greek comedies being presented in a Latin dress. Most important of all, the care of the children was handed over to Greeks; they were either sent to schools, kept by Greeks who had come to Rome to earn a living, or else they were brought up at home by Greek slave-tutors. Thus the civilization that was an exciting novelty to the older generation, became part of the normal outlook of the younger. Girls, as well as boys, were brought up in the new way; the Roman lady became a fashionable hostess instead of a housewife. The meeting-place of wit and elegance, in the second century, was the drawing-room of Cornelia, the daughter of the great Scipio. Scipio's rival, Cato, raised an almost solitary voice against the increase of luxury and the fashion of imitating the Greeks. Even he, in his old age, found that he could not get on without learning Greek; he came to recognize with regret that, as the poet Horace put it a century later, "captive Greece had led captive her fierce conqueror".

Thus the governing class at Rome adopted a new civilization as fast as it could. Humbler folk could not keep pace with it, as the gap in wealth also increased, for a number of reasons. Hannibal's invasion had done untold harm to the land-system in Italy. His army had had no supplies of its own, but had lived entirely on the country. Reconstruction was bound in any case to take a long time; and in-

G   (H.W.)

stead of being allowed to get to work, the citizen-farmer was called upon to fight in overseas wars. This told most heavily upon the small farmers, who could not afford bailiffs and farm servants; many of them sold their farms when they came back from the wars, and retired to the city to live on their capital as long as it lasted. They became unemployed city-dwellers, content to exist on the cheap corn that flowed in from the newly-conquered provinces.

This imported corn harmed Roman agriculture. Mass-produced in the provinces, it could, even with a long sea-journey, be sold more cheaply than corn produced within a few miles of Rome. So the farmer in central and south Italy had to turn to grazing; and the nature of the country made the small holding useless for this purpose; for only on the large ranch, which had cool highland pastures for the summer and warm coast-land for the winter, could sheep and cattle thrive. So the small farmers gave up hope, and sold their land to the large farmers, who joined holding to holding and built up vast estates, which they worked by means of the slaves whom the Roman conquests had made cheap and plentiful.

The gap between rich and poor widened. Senators and People had all been farmers before, and their interests had been the same. Now the Senators were big landowners, the People were urban unemployed, and their interests were opposed. While the robust stock from which Rome's soldiers had been drawn was deteriorating in the slums of the capital, the land they once had tilled now harboured thousands of ill-treated, sullen, rebellious slaves. In the light of after-events, it is easy to see the dangers of the situation; but the governing class as a whole proved to be blind to everything except its new-found wealth. The first attempt that was made to set things right ushered in a century of strife and weakening internecine warfare.

REFORMS OF THE GRACCHI

The fight was begun by two brothers of noble birth, Tiberius and Gaius Gracchus. Their father, a distinguished general, had died when they were children. Their mother was Cornelia, Scipio's daughter, and they had been brought up according to her ideas. Their wits had been sharpened by their Greek education, and they could see the problems of Rome better than others; in face of the interests of their own class, they made a bold attempt to strike at the evil of large estates, and restore the yeoman farmer, whom they rightly regarded as the backbone of Rome.

The land which the Romans had seized during their conquest of Italy was still officially public land; but long occupation, rent-free, had caused it to be treated as private property, to be bought and sold by private individuals. Much of it was swallowed up in the large estates by now; but Tiberius Gracchus, when he became tribune in 133 B.C., proposed to reclaim this land for the state without compensation, and distribute it among small-holders. This was a direct attack on the interests of the Senate, who put up another tribune to oppose it with his veto. Tiberius thereupon got the people to depose this tribune, thus committing the first definite breach of the law. The bill was passed; but if it was to be worked successfully, Tiberius must remain in power to manage it. The Senate, with the law and a good deal of justice on its side, opposed any idea of Tiberius being re-elected; but when they saw that it was likely to happen, they resorted to violence; the result was that Tiberius Gracchus, together with three hundred of his followers, was murdered.

Ten years later, Gaius Gracchus was elected tribune, and at once revived his brother's scheme. But he saw that, with the economic problem, there was bound up a political problem. Against the unyielding Senate he must gather together all the support that he could. So he brought forward a comprehensive democratic programme. To the Italian allies he offered enfranchisement; to the city unemployed a system of corn-doles; to the people in general he offered a number of colonies, including one at Carthage. A business class, called the Knights, had grown with Rome's conquest. Their wealth was increased by the tradition that forbade the Senators to engage in trade, and their influence was becoming greater in proportion to their wealth. To the Knights he gave the right of collecting taxes in the new province of Asia, together with the control of the court that dealt with corruption, which, in other hands, might have checked their policy of getting rich quickly at the expense of the provincials. Thus he created a large number of interests in opposition to the Senate. Again the Senate had no reply but violence. Gaius Gracchus was murdered.

The schemes of the two brothers made little difference to the economic situation; but they profoundly changed the political outlook. The power of the Senate had been shaken; the people had been taught to act against it; the Knights had been raised to greater wealth and influence. Most important of all, the example of violence had been set; blood had flowed in the streets of Rome. Henceforth, there was war between the Senate and the people; the actual grounds of the quarrel shifted, but the quarrel itself remained, and grew more bitter and bloody with the passing of every year.

MARIUS AND THE SENATE

The next issue arose, ten years later, out of foreign politics. Popular outcry had forced the Senate to declare war on Jugurtha, a North African king who was an obstreperous vassal of Rome. A Senatorial general had been shamefully defeated; and the people insisted on the appointment of Marius, a man of middle-class birth and popular sympathies. Marius proved himself a superb general, and easily overcame Jugurtha. He returned in triumph to Rome, only to find that a new menace had arisen in the north. Keltic tribes were advancing on Italy; the Senatorial generals had failed to check them.

Marius was reappointed; the enemy was annihilated. Here at last was a great popular leader who could win battles. The common people had good cause to rejoice; the Senate quaked with fear.

Marius' successes had been won only at a price that the Senate was reluctant to pay. He had been elected consul for six years in succession. The old system of yearly generals, which left the real direction of affairs to the Senate, had broken down; in an overseas campaign prolonged over several years, it was essential to have a continuous policy directed by a single brain. The professional general had come to stay; and with him came the professional soldier. Marius abolished the old citizen army, and organized a system of voluntary recruiting. Service in the legions was made attractive, and there was no lack of recruits; but they took the oath of allegiance not to the Senate or even to the people, but to their general, the man on whom they relied to protect their interests when they came to retire from active service. This made for an efficient war machine; but it was a machine which could be used with equal efficiency against the other citizens of Rome as against the tribes of Africa or Gaul.

ROME AND HER ITALIAN ALLIES

Unfortunately, Marius was a general and nothing more. He could win a war and create an army; but he was no statesman, and took no interest in the internal problems of Italy. While he had been fighting, these problems had increased. The Italian "allies" had for long been chafing at their inferior status. They rightly regarded themselves as just as civilized as Roman citizens; they had suffered no less from Hannibal's invasion, a hundred years before; they had reaped few of the rewards of victory. For a long time, they had kept quiet, impressed with the might and efficiency of their overlords; but now they began to question that might and that efficiency. Gaius Gracchus had raised their hopes; the Senate had dashed them. Now they decided to use force; they got together and rebelled.

The rebellion was formidable. Fortunately for the Romans, the north of Italy and the country round Rome itself remained loyal; but all along the east coast, and in the Apennines, the Italians rose. The original object was the attainment of Roman citizenship; but, once war had started, the Samnites were eager to break away from Rome and form a new Italian confederate state. The course of the war, however, showed the difficulty of collaboration between the different tribes; despite victories in the field, they could not risk an attack on Rome itself, and they could not trust their allies. When the Romans offered citizenship to those who submitted, the league began to break up, and the Romans began to win battles. The final victories of the Romans in this war brought to the fore a young and brilliant Senatorial general named Sulla, who had won the devotion of his troops by his conduct during the campaign. He further advanced his popularity with the citizens by lavish expenditure, and an exhibition of lions.

Citizenship did not matter very much, but Sulla did. The war with the allies had given him an opportunity of raising an army of the new Marian type for his own purposes. An occasion soon arose. On the southern shores of the Black Sea lay the small but wealthy kingdom of Pontus. Some ten years before, there had ascended the throne a young and energetic king named Mithridates, who combined in himself the blood and the characteristics of Greece and Persia. Early in his reign he had established an overlordship of most of the Black Sea, thereby gaining enormously in wealth and power. Now he turned his attention southwards, to the Roman dominions in Asia Minor. The Senate was prepared neither to be conciliatory nor to oppose him with sufficient force. So he swept down on the province of Asia, and massacred eighty thousand Romans; then he crossed over into Greece.

Plainly the Senate had to take strong measures. A dispute immediately arose as to whether the command should be given to Marius or to Sulla. Sulla settled the question by advancing on Rome with his legions and overawing the people by a display of force. Marius and his friends fled; Sulla arranged things in the city, and then went to the East to fight Mithridates. He defeated him both in Greece and Asia, driving him back to his own kingdom. After four years he returned to find a new situation in Rome. The popular

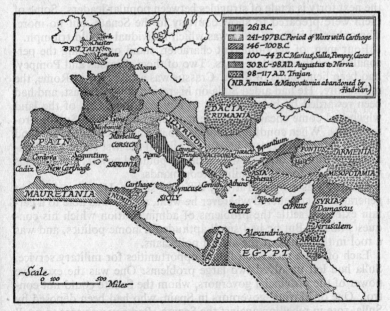

261 B.C.
241–197 B.C. Period of Wars with Carthage
146–100 B.C.
100–44 B.C. Marius, Sulla, Pompey, Cæsar
30 B.C–98 A.D. Augustus to Nerva
98–117 A.D. Trajan
(N.B. Armenia & Mesopotamia abandoned by Hadrian)

THE GROWTH OF THE ROMAN EMPIRE

The search for safe and easily defended frontiers caused the boundaries of the Empire to be pushed forward in the successive stages shown in the map above.

leaders had triumphed, recalled Marius and practically suppressed the Senate. But after Marius's death they had no great general to resist Sulla. His seasoned troops easily defeated the popular forces, and he was able to enter Rome at the point of the sword.

SULLA, POMPEY AND CRASSUS

Sulla still believed in the Senatorial machine. He saw that it had broken down, but he thought that all it needed was a good cleaning and the strengthening of some of its parts. The cleaning took the form of "proscribing" nearly five thousand of his opponents—that is to say, outlawing them, confiscating their property, and giving rewards to anyone who cared to murder them. This example was to be followed only too readily in the years to come. The machine was strengthened by making into law the ascendancy of the Senate which had arisen purely out of usage. For instance, it was made illegal for a man to hold the consulship more than once in ten years; and everything possible was done to prevent an individual from attaining supreme power within the law. When Sulla retired, he left the constitution to work itself. Although the Senate had the law entirely on its side, it had no force to maintain the law, and was at the mercy of the first successful general who should be prepared to act illegally. Sulla's system lasted for nine years, and then faded out; the tale of the next forty is a tale of struggles between popular leaders. Some of them were prepared to show courtesy to the Senate, but no more. The only real issue at stake was which individual should triumph.

Four men, of very different character, stand out among the personalities of the next few years. Two of them, Crassus and Pompey, had been lieutenants of Sulla. Crassus was a new type in Rome, the millionaire. He had aided Sulla on his return from the East, and had been rewarded by being allowed to buy vast quantities of the land which had come cheaply into the market as a result of Sulla's proscriptions. When conditions returned to normal, the value of the land had gone up; and Crassus had found himself the first Roman millionaire. In an age of bribery, wealth meant political power; and Crassus was thus able to obtain military commands.

Pompey was a man of a very different stamp. He was a brilliant general, who conquered wherever he went, and he was able to a certain extent to settle the problems of administration which his conquests raised. But he had small aptitude for home politics, and was a tool in the hands of the skilled politicians.

Each of these men soon found opportunities for military service. Sulla had left unsolved two large problems. One was the excessive power of the provincial governors, whom the Senate could not control. One of Marius' governors in Spain, who had been deposed by Sulla, rose in rebellion against the Senate. Pompey was sent to quell him, and took eight years over it. He returned with a trained army. The second problem was that of the slaves in Italy. Many of these wretched creatures worked in chain-gangs on the vast estates which the Gracchus brothers had failed to abolish. They were treated like inferior animals; as a result, they were ready to behave like animals. Death seemed to them the only possible release from their sufferings. Little more fortunate were the slaves whose duty it was to look after the herds; they had more freedom, but nothing was done for their welfare. However, they were dangerous, as they carried arms to safeguard their herds. It can only have been a despairing feeling of their own inferiority to the lords of the world that kept them peaceful for long periods. When they found a leader, they could do much harm, as had been seen when the slaves of Sicily revolted, in the time of Tiberius Gracchus. Now, under the leadership of an escaped gladiator, the slaves of South Italy rebelled in force. It needed Crassus and an army of forty thousand men to crush them. Crushed they were; and of the survivors the Roman government made a horrible example, crucifying six thousand slaves by the roadside.

Crassus returned, like Pompey, with a victorious army; and as his interests were in some ways opposed to Pompey's, another civil war seemed possible; but they found common cause in disliking certain provisions of Sulla's constitution, and joined forces to amend it. The Senate was forced to give way, and henceforth it ceased to have any more than the pretence of power.

Pompey, however, was not interested in politics, and soon obtained other military commands. He spent the next few years out of Rome, clearing the Mediterranean of pirates in a single whirlwind campaign, and finally settling the problem of Mithridates, who had broken out again. Five years' campaigning achieved his objects, and brought immense glory to him. Then he returned, a victorious hero, and everyone in Rome wondered how he would use his power.

CICERO AND THE SENATE

During his absence, two new figures had risen to prominence. In the days of Sulla a completely unknown man named Cicero had come from the same small Italian town as Marius, to seek his fortune at the Roman bar. He was a man of wide education and astonishing eloquence, and having both courage and push, he soon made his mark in the courts. Entering politics, he became consul shortly before Pompey's return, and increased his reputation by a display of firmness in crushing a dangerous conspiracy against the state. Henceforth, though despised as "a new man" by many of the Senate, he was one of its staunchest champions. He believed that Rome could still be governed constitutionally, if the forces of all good men could be combined. The only hope, to his mind, was that the prestige of the Senate and the wealth and influence of the Knights should be enlisted to this end; to this already formidable combination, he proposed to add the military power which was possessed by Pompey. He thus thought to preserve the power of the Senate.

The man who was destined to prevent this combination was Gaius Julius Caesar. Of the four great figures of the time, Caesar was the greatest. He had not Cicero's eloquence, but he was a man of wide culture, and a master of written language. He had not Crassus' wealth; but he was clever enough to dominate Crassus and use him. As a soldier he was, at least, Pompey's equal; and, unlike Pompey, he was quite at home in the political intrigues of the day. He had a genius for inspiring personal devotion in his troops; his aristocratic connections on his father's side made it impossible for the Senate to despise him; and, being a nephew by marriage of Marius, he was an obvious choice for the position of popular leader. A man of vision, he saw that the Senate was incapable of ruling the Empire through a system of annual magistracies; he knew that Cicero's ideal was impracticable, though he could respect it and did respect Cicero. The trend of the times was in the direction of dictatorship, and Caesar was determined that he should direct the affairs of the state.

CAESAR WINS SUPREME POWER

When Pompey returned from the East, he found himself courted on all sides. Cicero, the champion of the middle classes, talked to him of the coalition of the orders and the hope of constitutional government. Pompey, the soldier, was bored. Caesar came forward with concrete proposals for the benefit of Pompey's troops. Pompey accepted. So Caesar, Pompey and Crassus combined against the Senate; and in a few years, they came to an arrangement which gave each of them a province and an army. Caesar went off to Gaul, and spent the next nine years in conquering it and organizing it into provinces. Crassus went to the East, to fight against the rising power of the Parthians, with whom Pompey's successes had brought the Romans in contact. Pompey received Spain as his province, but ruled it by deputy, himself remaining in Rome.

Then came three changes in the situation. The first was the defeat and death of Crassus at the hands of the Parthians. The second was Caesar's conquest of Gaul. The third was the reconciliation of Pompey and the Senate, owing to their fear and dislike of Caesar. All these made for civil war. With Crassus out of the way, Pompey felt strong enough to support the Senate against the absent Caesar; Caesar and his troops had tasted victory in Gaul, and felt ready to meet all comers. In 49 B.C., Caesar, exasperated by political attacks, led his forces into Italy, and advanced, like Sulla before him, on the city. Pompey was unprepared, and fled to Greece with most of the Senatorial party, collecting his scattered troops; Caesar followed and defeated him at the battle of Pharsalus. A year or two was spent in clearing up the remains of Pompey's army in various parts of the world; and then Caesar returned to Rome, undisputed master of the Roman Empire. For the first time, the government of Rome was in the hands of a single man who really understood her problems.

Crassus was dead; Pompey was dead, treacherously murdered in Egypt; Cicero remained in sullen submission. There was one old-fashioned senator for whom submission was unthinkable. Cato, the great-grandson of Scipio's old enemy, who had resisted the invasion of Greek civilization, had as little liking for new ways as his ancestor. For him, Rome was not Rome if the Senate did not rule; rather than submit to the detested power of a dictatorship, he committed suicide.

JULIUS CAESAR'S VAST REFORMS

Caesar's behaviour after his victory was in the strongest contrast to Sulla's. He showed the utmost clemency to individuals, and supreme contempt for institutions. For he faced the problems of empire in a realistic way; he saw that the old form of government was incapable of dealing with them, and that he must get the support of all good men in dealing with them in a new way. As it happened, he had no more than two years left to work in; but in that time, he got through an amazing amount of reform, and pointed the way to that general reorganization of the Empire which was to come.

The economic problem was perhaps the most urgent; and Caesar acted vigorously. In Italy, a vast scheme of public works, including a town-planning scheme for Rome and land drainage in the country, was designed to relieve unemployment; and at the same time, a drastic reform of the corn-dole went far to solve the financial problem. Emigration to decaying towns in Italy and to new colonies abroad, relieved the over-populated quarters of the city. The provinces were strengthened by the new colonies, and by improved systems of taxation.

Caesar fully realized the need for political stability. Individual rule was now essential, but it must be the rule of one individual; there must be no civil wars arising out of the rivalry of several. So he abolished independent commands in the more important provinces, and ruled them through "legates" who owed allegiance to himself. While thus reducing the importance of the provincial governors, he raised the status of the provincials themselves, by lavish grants of citizenship outside Italy. By admitting Gauls to the Senate, he complimented the provincials, at the price of insulting the old nobility. Four hundred years later, a Latin poet wrote a poem to Rome, in which he said, "Thou hast made into a city what was once a world". The originator of this policy was Julius Caesar, and it was that followed by his successors.

Equally significant was his treatment of the towns throughout Italy. He paid much attention to local government, decreeing a more or less uniform system for all towns, and giving them magistrates and senates after the Roman model. As the Senate and people of Rome were ceasing to have any real power outside the city itself, the result of this was to put the previously despised inhabitant of the small Italian town on a political level with the citizen of Rome itself.

There were other things of the same kind in Caesar's programme, and they were nearly all brought to completion in the years that followed. But in many ways Caesar was ahead of his time; other men did not see the needs of the state so clearly, and were still obsessed with the ideas of the old republic. Caesar, who was so good usually at facing facts, had one blind spot. He did not realize the strength of the opposition to his policy. He felt that the good he was doing was sufficient safeguard for his person, and he went about without a bodyguard. He was wrong. In 44 B.C., he was treacherously murdered by a band of disgruntled conspirators. He died with his work half done, but the seeds of reform were sown and were to be brought to fruition by Augustus.

It is almost impossible to over-estimate the importance of Julius Caesar in world history. Two facts, unimportant in themselves, serve to show the permanence of his influence. His reform of the Calendar lasted, without modification, in the whole of Europe until 1582, in Great Britain until 1752, and in Russia until 1917. It is interesting to note that the three Emperors who lost their thrones in the World War of 1914–18, the Kaisers of Germany and Austria and the Czar of Russia, all derived their titles from Caesar the dictator.

AUGUSTUS TAKES OVER CAESAR'S TASK

The murder of Caesar was no more than an interruption in the work of reform. The conspirators had no programme, and no ideas beyond a hatred of the dictator and all his works. The only result of their act was that the world had to suffer another thirteen dreary years of bloodshed, in which the conspirators were cleared off the face of the earth, and their conquerors disputed the supremacy. The final struggle was between the most brilliant of Caesar's lieutenants, Mark Antony, who fancied himself a second Alexander, and a young man named Octavian. Antony had immense advantages—military genius, social prestige, eloquence and experience; Octavian was young and untried. But he was the great-nephew of Julius, and bore the name of Caesar; and it is that, more than his stout heart or his astute brain, that accounts for his ultimate triumph over Antony and Queen Cleopatra of Egypt at the naval battle of Actium in 31 B.C. He returned to Rome, to rule the world under the title of the Emperor Augustus.

This chapter has been a record of bloodshed and civil war, of the defeat of the old Roman government by the new ideal of personal sovereignty. But men's minds had not been all intent on slaughter. In the midst of carnage, they talked philosophy and history, and wrote poetry. Cicero's life was spent in the heat of the political arena; and many of his speeches have survived to show us his greatness as an orator. But he had moments of retirement, in which he wrote about religion and philosophy and literature; he dabbled in poetry; and his letters to his friends depict him as a man of culture and charm, whose friendship was valued by men of all parties. And there were others, such as Catullus, the love-poet; Lucretius, the poet of science, who wrote with white-hot passion about the atomic theory, seeking to show that all things are matter, body and soul alike, and therefore, in death, body and soul are both dissolved, and man need not fear the pains of hell; Varro the scholar, who took the whole of life for his province; and others of lesser importance, who took no part in the great events that were going on around them. But, in their own way, they, too, were taking part in a revolution. When Greek ideas first came to Rome, the Romans simply imitated them; the imitation was somewhat crude, and the ideas sounded odd in a language that was not built to express them. But, in these years of revolution, the language changed, and the ideas became part of it; the literary men of Rome became creators instead of imitators.

When peace came at last, men turned once more to the glories of old Rome. Livy, the most brilliant of Roman historians, told the story of the city's rise to greatness. Horace, the poet of love and wine, celebrated, in the metres of Greece but with the authentic tongue of Rome, the old virtues that had conquered the Carthaginians. Virgil, the greatest of them all, won the friendship of the Emperor by his poems of Italian country life, and crowned it with the noblest achievement of Latin literature, the *Aeneid*, in which he sang of the old legends of the founding of the city. Half-way through the poem he told, as if in a prophecy, of the glories that were to come; and here he summed up the contrast between the Greek artist and the Roman ruler, a contrast that, in spite of all appearances, was bound to remain; however much he might imitate the Greek, the Roman was still a Roman, and his abilities lay in a different field.

"Others shall mould with grace the breathing bronze,
And charm, methinks, from marble the live face,
Plead with more power in courts, trace with their rods
The paths of heaven and tell the rising stars:
Know thyself, Roman, ruler of mankind—
That is thy art—impose the law of peace,
Bear with the humble and beat down the proud."

CHAPTER 17

THE GLORY OF THE EMPIRE

AUGUSTUS was a very different man from his great-uncle. He had neither the supreme military genius of Julius Caesar nor his amazing personal charm; but he had other qualities which peculiarly fitted him for his task. On his father's side, he was descended, not from a long line of senatorial nobles, but from a respectable family in a small Italian town; he had all the virtues of the class which it represented—

common sense, thrift, perseverance and simple habits. But his supreme qualification was tact; he never showed his contempt for contemptible people, and he could respect prejudices and traditions for which in point of fact, he was unable to feel any genuine sympathy.

AUGUSTUS, THE SENATE AND THE ARMY

The inability to suffer fools gladly had been the chief cause of Julius Caesar's murder. He had almost entirely ignored the forms and traditions of the Republic; the Senate had shown itself incapable of governing, and he saw no sense in pretending that it could. Augustus was wiser; so long as it was deprived of the power of doing serious harm, he was ready to leave it with great prestige, and even a certain amount of administrative power. He reserved to himself everything important; but he governed, as far as possible, through powers belonging to republican magistracies; his unique position was obtained, not by creating any new office, but by concentrating in himself the powers of many existing offices. Thus, though he held the consulship only for comparatively few years, he obtained from the Senate and People permanent powers by which he could override the authority of any magistrate. He also had granted to him for life the powers of a tribune, and by the use of these he could veto the acts of other magistrates, and in addition those of the Senate itself.

In a military state, the army is of the first importance; Augustus was sole commander of the army, and the legions took their oath of allegiance to him alone. The name Emperor, which in Republican times had been applied to successful generals, and had had no suggestion of royalty in it, became his most distinctive title, and has come, in the modern world, to imply a sort of super-royalty. But, though these and other powers gave him complete control over the whole of the Empire, no single power violated the constitution of the Republic; among a people who set great store by legal forms, this was a matter of vital importance. Augustus actually claimed to have restored the Republic; and this did not seem to his subjects to be a piece of hypocrisy. But the real strength of his position was that the Imperial system provided the stable government that the Senate for the last hundred years had failed to provide. On one or two occasions in later years, a few people, disgusted with the vices or the savagery of a particular Emperor, talked about returning to Senatorial government; but, outside their own clique, they were never taken seriously, and in time the idea became unthinkable. The problem of what form the government of the Empire should take had been solved by Augustus, once and for all.

There was another problem which gave him much thought, but which neither he nor his successors solved. Who, on the death of one Emperor, should become the next? The most obviously convenient method by which the Empire should pass was the hereditary one; for by this the transition from one Emperor to another was automatic.

and no dispute could arise. Though Augustus had no son, he numbered among his family circle several men of distinct promise. But he had very bad luck. Early in his long reign of forty-odd years, his favourite nephew, who had married his only daughter, died; then her children by a second marriage; and finally Augustus had to appoint as his heir his daughter's third husband, his step-son Tiberius, whom he cordially disliked. To create a family dynasty, Augustus made his relations intermarry in such a way that the evil effects of this inbreeding can be seen in the personalities of his successors. The first, Tiberius, degenerated from an efficient, though unpopular, ruler into a morose and cruel tyrant; the second was mad; the next, Claudius, the conqueror of Britain, was a well-meaning pedant, who had the wit to leave the government largely to his advisers, but could inspire neither respect nor affection in the minds of his subjects; and the next, the last of his line, was the megalomaniac Nero, who, after an auspicious start, threw over his able advisers, murdered his mother, drained the treasury by his private extravagances, shocked all Rome by appearing as a performer on a public stage, and put an end to the dynasty by killing off any of his relations who might be regarded as possible rivals to him. His reign speedily became intolerable.

THE PROBLEM OF THE IMPERIAL SUCCESSION

A series of conspiracies and rebellions brought about Nero's end in A.D. 69. Upon his committing suicide, the hereditary principle lapsed for want of an heir, and another method of appointing Emperors, proclamation by the army, came into force. Unfortunately, the armies of Rome were not agreed. First, the Spanish troops put forward their candidate; then the Praetorian Guard, the garrison of Rome; then the Rhine armies; and finally the army of the East. Within a single year, there were four new Emperors, each of whom got rid of the last by battle or murder; and when finally Vespasian, who was the nominee of the Eastern army, emerged triumphant, it was at the conclusion of a civil war which had done untold harm to the economic life of the Empire.

Vespasian was the first of the Roman Emperors who had no aristocratic connections; he had come from a small Italian hill-town, and made his way in politics and war by sheer ability. In ten years he restored much of the prosperity of the Empire, and so impressed his subjects with his solid worth that, in spite of their previous unfortunate experience with the hereditary system, they were ready to accept his sons as his heirs without question. After all, the only alternative seemed to be civil war. His elder son, however, died after two years, and the younger, Domitian, though an efficient ruler, was in many ways like Nero. Power went to his head, and he executed everyone whom he had any cause to suspect of objecting to his tyranny. In the end, the Emperor was murdered by a freedman; and all Rome rejoiced in the final downfall of the second Imperial dynasty.

On this occasion, the Romans, tired of bloodshed, left the choice of a new Emperor to the Senate; and it chose well. Its nominee was an old man who lasted only two years; but in them he established a new method for the succession, that of adoption. Having no children of his own, he adopted as his son, Trajan, the commander of one of the Rhine armies. This precedent provided the Empire with a succession of good rulers for the next eighty years. They were men of very different types—Trajan, the Spanish soldier, who thought to rival Alexander the Great in the extent of his Eastern conquests; Hadrian the administrator, also a Spaniard, who made a tour of his Empire, strengthening its weak places; Antoninus the Good, who did nothing in particular and did it very well; and Marcus Aurelius the philosopher, who showed that a man of books could also be a man of affairs. Most unfortunately, Marcus Aurelius had a son to succeed him; the hereditary principle was revived, with disastrous results. For the son was like Nero in many ways; and the sequel to his reign was like the sequel to Nero's. His immediate successor was a capable man, who tried to abolish the corruption that had been allowed to grow up; but he was murdered by the Praetorian Guard, who had most to lose by this reform. There followed another spell of civil war between the nominees of various armies.

RIVAL CANDIDATES FOR THE THRONE

Of the candidates for the throne, Septimius Severus, the governor of the Danube army, was far the cleverest. He disposed of his rivals in a succession of speedy campaigns. Septimius was an African by birth, the tradition that the Emperor must be a native of Italy having long vanished. But he was no barbarian, and he provided the Roman world with twenty years of good government, and restored security on the frontiers. He, too, established a family dynasty of a sort, but most of his relations proved incurably corrupt and inefficient. The last of them, Alexander Severus, was better than the rest, and was fortunate in having as his mother a woman of great ability, and wise in deferring continually to her judgment. Under her guidance, Alexander ruled well for thirteen years; but his troops chafed at his strict discipline and finally murdered him. With the end of the Severus dynasty, stable government vanished from the Empire for half a century; there followed a bewildering succession of pretenders to the throne, soldiers from all parts of the Empire, some of them men of ability, but few of any strength of character. They mostly ascended the throne by violence; none of them felt secure upon it. If the army could make an Emperor, it could also unmake him.

Thus the tale of the succession to the Empire is chequered and melancholy. The hereditary principle ended in disaster or sterility. Election by the Senate never established itself as the rule. Adoption gave the best results, but was applied only when the hereditary system could not be applied. Appointment by the soldiers, which almost always involved the Empire in civil war, became the regular thing; yet this was just what Augustus had striven to avoid. It is to his credit that, from the first, he saw the importance of the problem; but neither he nor his successors ever devised a permanent solution.

The next problem that faced Augustus and his successors was how to provide for the defence and administration of the vast territories which the generals and soldiers of the later Republic had brought beneath the rule of Rome. The Roman conquests had been made without any central plan; new lands had been subdued simply to prevent encroachments by their inhabitants on older Roman possessions. Occasionally, too, an ambitious general had undertaken the conquest of a country in order to train his troops or strengthen his own position at home, as when Julius Caesar conquered Gaul. Augustus, therefore, was faced with the task of providing a planned administration for an Empire which had come into being by a series of accidents. On the whole he faced it with remarkable success.

THE DEFENCE OF THE FRONTIERS

The first need was to provide for the defence of the frontiers. Augustus saw clearly that the Empire could not go on expanding indefinitely, as it had tended to do in the past. His object, therefore, was to push the boundaries of the Empire forward until it had reached its natural frontiers, and then stop; and he regarded water as the best frontier in most places.

For part of the Empire, the Atlantic Ocean provided a boundary that needed no defence. Augustus himself seems to have regarded the English Channel in the same way, for he made no attempt to invade Britain, as his great-uncle had done. But the Keltic tribes across the Channel were related to the Belgians of North Gaul, and even now that Gaul was part of the Roman Empire, they had close intercourse with them. The Romans had treaty relations with some of the British tribes, among whom Roman customs were beginning to spread; but they never felt happy about North Gaul while Britain remained unconquered. Augustus' successors realized that the Channel was less of a barrier than a waterway; thirty years after his death, Claudius resolved on action. The invasion was successful, and though in the first seventy years of Roman rule there were fierce rebellions, the country was ultimately Romanized; it never became rich, but it was one of the happiest and most peaceful parts of the Empire. For purposes of easy defence the frontier was fixed on the line between the Solway Firth and the Tyne, and this was marked by the Emperor Hadrian with a great wall, much of which can be seen to-day.

The next part of the frontier, as Augustus found it, was the line of the river Rhine; after the Rhine the natural boundary was obviously the Danube. Early in his reign, Augustus established this line by conquering the Swiss Alps, and by A.D. 6, the Danube was the official boundary of the Empire. But this meant that the German tribes beyond the rivers jutted out into the Roman domains in an awkward way, giving the Romans a long northern frontier to defend. Augustus determined to abolish this salient by conquering Germany as far as the Elbe and taking in Bohemia, thereby shortening the frontier by 300 miles, and by straightening the line, enormously reducing the number of troops required to man it. In the first half of his reign, he gradually penetrated into Germany and accustomed the natives to Roman ways. But Germany was not Gaul. Instead of vineyards and farm lands, there were huge stretches of forest and swamp; instead of Kelts with some idea of civilization—though not Roman civilization—the inhabitants were largely ferocious savages, to whom civilization meant nothing. There were no roads, no towns; the progress of the Roman legions depended on the information of native guides.

THE CHECK TO ROMAN EXPANSION

So long as the Romans went slowly, building their own roads, and not getting too far away from them, all was well. But towards the end of his reign, Augustus made one of his rare mistakes; he sent out, as governor, a man who knew nothing about Germany and did not trouble to learn its problems. This Varus treated the half-conquered territory as if it were an old and civilized province; he introduced Roman courts and Roman taxation, without considering native feeling; and he took no proper precautions against insurrection. The natives found a leader, Hermann, who became a national hero. Varus marched against them with 20,000 men, and became lost in a dense forest; the Germans descended on his army and wiped it out. Varus committed suicide; only a few stragglers found their way back to Gaul, to tell of a disaster "somewhere in Germany".

This was the end of the project of an Elbe frontier. In later years, there were one or two expeditions to prevent possible attacks by the tribes across the Rhine. In the time of Vespasian and his sons, the angle between the Rhine and the Danube was cut off by the annexation of the Black Forest, and a line of fortifications was established. But there was no further attempt to conquer the whole of Germany; so the Romans continued to have difficulty in making communications between their armies on the Rhine and the Danube; also, they lost the opportunity of ruling one of the best sources of recruits in Europe.

Across the Danube, the Romans made one permanent conquest. The tribes north of the lower reaches of the river were always giving trouble, and early in the second century A.D., the Emperor Trajan decided that Augustus' water-frontier was not so good as a mountain-frontier would be. He therefore crossed the river with 120,000 men, and, after a series of arduous campaigns, annexed the country, peopled it with colonists, and Romanized it thoroughly. To this day, it retains the name of Rumania, the Roman land across the Danube. Seventy years later, Marcus Aurelius tried to continue the mountain-frontier westwards by annexing Bohemia, but the attempt was cut short by his death. In spite of repeated efforts the northern frontier never became satisfactory, and the expanses of central Europe remained a breeding-place for the barbarians who were eventually to overwhelm completely the power of the Roman empire in the West.

SETTLEMENT OF THE PARTHIAN FRONTIER

The next stretch of frontier was the Black Sea, which was well policed by a Roman fleet and gave no trouble. Not so the land-frontier in Asia Minor. Here the Romans were faced, not with disunited barbarian tribes, but with the great power of Parthia. The Parthians had descended from the steppes of central Asia about fifty years after Alexander's death; and, being magnificent fighters, they had met with little effective resistance. When the Romans won Asia Minor, there lay between them and the Parthians the kingdom of Armenia, whose king they both distrusted; both Sulla and Pompey were glad of their help against him. But Pompey, who had promised them Armenia, broke faith as soon as it was conquered, preferring a weak buffer-state to the neighbourhood of a formidable Empire. Hence arose a perennial quarrel.

The Parthian Empire was organized on the feudal system. At the head was a king, and beneath him great nobles, who owed allegiance to him, but were largely independent. His armies consisted of the troops that the nobles led. They fought as knights in armour; their dependants also fought on horse-back, using a peculiar type of tactic; they would lead an enemy on by pretending to flee, and then, turning suddenly, would pour in a volley of arrows. Thus they were a novel type of enemy for the Romans, and it was only their poor internal organization, and the nobles' lack of loyalty to the king, that prevented their following up their numerous victories and overrunning all Asia Minor.

After Pompey's breach of faith, both sides were on the look-out for a quarrel, and there was a long succession of wars and threats of war. The Parthian cavalry won the first round at Carrhae where Crassus was killed; but they did not follow up their victory. Julius Caesar intended to conquer them outright, and trained an army especially to do so; but he was murdered when on the point of setting out. Mark Antony proposed to carry out his patron's plans, but precious time had been lost, the Parthians had got wind of the Roman plans, and seized the initiative themselves by invading Syria. They were beaten off, and the Roman invasion took place; but the element of surprise was lost, and though Antony penetrated far into Parthian territory, he achieved little. Augustus was unwilling to spend his resources on a war with Parthia, and was content to let Armenia play the part of a buffer-state; his only care was that there should be a reasonably pro-Roman King of Armenia, and until the reign of Nero, this compromise was to remain the future policy of the Roman emperors. Nero's government took strong measures to ensure that henceforth the King of Armenia should be a nominee of Rome; though the country was not annexed, the Eastern boundary of Armenia became, for all practical purposes, the frontier of the Roman Empire. Both Rome and Parthia seemed satisfied with this for half a century; the Parthians knew that the Romans had learnt all about their methods of warfare, and were bound to win if provoked to decisive action; the Romans were occupied with rectifying their northern frontier, and had little desire for war in the East. But when Trajan came to the throne, he revived the plans of Julius Caesar, and cast himself for the part of Alexander the Great. In three years, he conquered the Parthian Empire; and though he left some of it independent, he created the provinces of Armenia, Mesopotamia and Assyria.

THE ARMY AND THE FRONTIERS

This was the moment at which the Empire reached its greatest extent; and the Eastern Question seemed to be settled. Hadrian, Trajan's successor, felt that it was no settlement, but an extension of the frontier which he could not afford to defend; almost his first act as Emperor was to abandon Armenia and the lands beyond, returning to the policy of Nero. This was unsatisfactory; Armenia became once more a storm-centre. Marcus Aurelius, Septimius Severus and Alexander Severus all had to fight against the Parthians and annex territory, in the effort to find a satisfactory frontier. Even the fall of the Parthian dynasty, towards the middle of the third century B.C., did not solve the problem; for a new Kingdom of Persia arose, fanatically attached to the old religion of their country, and Rome was never able to feel easy about her Eastern Frontier.

From Spain to the Euphrates, the frontier of Rome was a water-frontier in the main, a line of sea and river, helped out in Britain and in South Germany by land fortifications. Beyond that, the frontier was altogether different, and far easier to defend. It was desert. The peoples of the Syrian desert are nomad tribes, whose wars are among themselves; they quarrel over the possession of wells, and raid each other's flocks and herds; but they have no fixed abode, and if they meet with a stronger tribe, they move on to the next oasis where they can dispossess a weaker one. They are fierce fighters, and brave, but, living in small communities, they are not formidable to a great power; it needs something very extraordinary to induce them to combine. The strongest inducement they can have is religious enthusiasm, which, in the heyday of the Roman Empire, did not exist among them; the Romans had to keep a number of troops on the border of the desert, but these had an easy time.

To defend these frontiers, behind which about eighty million people enjoyed security and a measure of prosperity, the Romans maintained an army of only 300,000 men. About half of these were in the legions, the crack troops of the Roman army. The legionaries made a permanent profession of soldiering; they served for twenty years before qualifying for a pension, and even after that, they were often kept on. Originally, it had been the prevailing custom for them to receive a grant of land upon their discharge, but later they received a large money payment, the equivalent of a dozen years' wages.

COMPONENTS OF THE ARMED FORCES

A legion consisted of 6000 men, of whom only 120 were cavalry; they were commanded by nobles, but the subordinate officers, who were the real backbone of the Roman army, were the centurions; sixty served with each legion, and these were all drawn from the ranks. Legionary soldiers had to be Roman citizens, and therefore, at first, were mainly Italians; as the franchise became extended, other recruiting-grounds were found, and the legions were filled with men from the country round their stations. In many cases service in a particular legion became a family tradition; and, as men naturally married women from places near their station, the personnel of the legions became largely identified with the people amongst whom they were serving. These troops, who served far longer, and were therefore far more highly trained than those of any modern army, were very precious. Varus' loss of three legions in Germany was a devastating blow. It became the practice of Roman commanders to avoid using the legions in the field, wherever possible; although they were used freely in engineering works, and in building fortifications and roads, in battle they were often held in reserve. Their permanent quarters were never on the actual frontier, but a discreet distance behind, where their man-power would not be frittered away.

For minor skirmishes, the Romans preferred to use auxiliary troops, who made up the other half of the army. These were not Roman citizens, though they were usually granted citizenship on discharge; they were organized into cohorts of infantry or squadrons of cavalry, each cohort or squadron containing about 500 men. They were named after the tribe from which they were originally recruited, but when they were sent to another country, natives of that country joined them; thus we find Germans serving in African squadrons, and men from the Danube in Spanish cohorts. Whereas the legionaries were all armed in the same way, the auxiliaries provided forces of varying kinds—cavalry, archers, slingers and javelin-throwers. It was they who manned the forts on Hadrian's Wall in Britain and along the great roads near the frontiers; the legionaries were concentrated in much larger fortresses behind the line. The command of the auxiliaries was entrusted not to the nobility, but either to the Knights, or to Centurions seconded from the legions, or else to chiefs of the tribes from which they were recruited. It must not be thought that, because they were called auxiliaries, they were, in any sense, irregular troops. They were professional soldiers, serving for twenty-five years, but their lives were regarded as less precious than those of the legionaries because they were not Roman citizens and so there were more

Map labels:

Hadrians Wall
BRITAIN
York
Chester LEAD
Cærleon WOOL CORN
Bath LEAD
TIN IRON *London* OYSTERS
Boulogne CORN
Trèves WINE
GLASS
GERMANY
GAUL
BRASS POTTERY
PITCH TIMBER WINE CORN
Lyons
R. Rhone
OIL
Arles *Marseilles*
Narbonne *Fréjus*
WINE
R. Ebro
SPAIN
SILVER COPPER IRON TIN LEAD
CORN OIL LINEN
New Carthage
CORSICA
Ravenna
ITALY
POTTERY
Rome
Brindisi
SARDINIA CORN
Cherchel
CORN ANIMALS FOR SPORT
Hippo (Bône)
Carthage PURPLE
WOOL CORN
MARBLE NUMIDIA
CORN OIL WINE
ILLYRICUM
TIMBER
IRON
HIDES
Sabrata *Tripoli* CORN
Leptis Magna

Scale
100 200 300 400 500
Miles
⚓ --------- Naval Base

ECONOMIC RESOURCES OF

Under the Empire the Roman provinces possessed every incentive to export their products, and cities grew up which based their prosperity upon trade. Some specialized in the production of certain goods, such as Tyre, famous for a purple dye made from a shellfish. Others owed their importance to a favourable site on one of the important trade routes, as, for instance, Lyons on the River Rhone.

THE ROMAN EMPIRE

Most active in the sphere of trade were Gaul, Germany west of the River Rhine, Syria and Egypt. Britain, noted for its oysters, occupied a comparatively unimportant position in the Roman world. The tentacles of trade reached out towards the riches of the Orient, Arab traders bringing their caravans of ivory, silk and spices to the cities of Palmyra and Petra, both of which achieved great wealth.

to draw from. Distinct from them were the irregular detachments used on the frontiers, troops commanded by native leaders, who, when they could be trusted, were very useful men; for they knew the lie of the land and the ways of the people beyond the frontier.

The only other soldiers of the Empire were the 9000 men of the Praetorian Guard, the official bodyguard of the Emperor. These were the pampered troops of Rome. Their conditions of service were lighter, they qualified for a pension sooner, and they were better paid. They lived in barracks in Rome, and were called upon to fight only when the Emperor went to war in person. As the only troops in Italy, they often dominated the situation on the death of an Emperor; the new Emperor had to give them a present to gain their support, and on one occasion they actually held what amounted to an auction of the Empire, selling it to the highest bidder.

The Roman fleet played little part in history after the defeat of Carthage and the suppression of piracy, for there was no naval power to oppose it. Its work was mainly confined to police operations; it kept the Mediterranean free of pirates, and patrolled the Black Sea and the English Channel. In later times the Channel fleet, based on Boulogne, had plenty of work to do in defending the British and Gallic coasts against the tribes of Germany and of Ireland; but in the first two or three centuries of the Empire, there was little naval warfare of any kind.

The distribution of the military forces of the Empire naturally varied from time to time, and any emergency in a particular quarter would call for a special concentration of troops. The normal arrangement, in the reign of Tiberius, was to have three legions in Spain, eight on the Rhine, seven on the Danube, four in Syria, two in Egypt and one in Africa. Four legions were transferred for the conquest of Britain; by that time, Spain could safely be left to one legion, and the Romans felt able to reduce the Rhine and Danube garrisons as well. There were other modifications later, but the general scheme of distribution remained the same. Auxiliaries were allotted to the frontier provinces in about the same proportions as the legions; thus the total number of troops stationed in any given province amounted to about twice the number of legionaries on service there.

THE ROMAN PEACE

Except for the Praetorian Guard, all the troops were concentrated in frontier provinces; the rest of the Empire was completely ungarrisoned. A police force, organized on military lines at Lyons, was the nearest approach to a garrison that was to be found in Gaul. There were no troops of any kind in Greece or in Asia Minor. Behind the frontiers, the Roman Peace was firmly established.

The frontier-provinces were governed by nobles who were soldiers directly responsible to the Emperor. The unfortified provinces behind them were governed by men of the same class, responsible to the Senate. This made little difference, as the Senate was under the thumb of the Emperor; but it emphasized their unmilitary character. In practice, the Emperor ruled both, through the medium of his civil service, which, oddly enough, was composed in early times of freedmen who had been slaves of his household. These were mainly very highly educated Greeks, confidential private secretaries of the Emperor, who by sheer ability turned themselves from secretaries into advisers and then into ministers of state. Vespasian, who valued character more than brains, gave more of these posts to the soldier class of the Knights; ultimately, most of the administration of the Empire was in the hands of the upper middle-class. They became responsible for the office work of the central government, the collection of taxes in the provinces, poor-law administration and distribution of relief, and a certain amount of legal jurisdiction. In addition, the Knights were entrusted with the entire government of Egypt, which was not an ordinary province, but the private property of the Caesars, as it had once been of the Ptolemies; the bureaucracy which the latter had established was carried on by the Knights, and no Senator was allowed any place in the administration of the country.

PROSPEROUS CITIES OF THE EMPIRE

Although the Empire was organized into provinces, it was only for purposes of administration. Local patriotism was directed not to the Province, but towards the City. For the provinces were new, but the cities were many of them very old. In the East, some of them dated back to the days of Sumer and Akkad and the great Oriental Empires, whose heirs the Romans were. In Africa, there were the foundations of the Phoenician mariners; even Carthage had been refounded by Augustus. In the West, many of the cities had grown out of the old market-towns of the tribes, and a few, such as Marseilles, could claim a Greek ancestry. And, for all their insignificance in world politics, the ancient Greek cities of Sicily and Greece itself kept alive the memory of a glorious past. The same feeling of pride existed in the new cities which the Romans established, planning them by the art which they had learnt from the Greeks. At peace with each other, all these cities enjoyed a prosperity hitherto unknown. They had aqueducts to bring them pure water from the hills; scientific sanitary arrangements; large markets; well-paved streets and covered footways; elaborate public baths; gymnasiums and wrestling-grounds; public buildings of all sorts, libraries, council-chambers, municipal offices, law-courts, theatres, sculpture-galleries, lecture-rooms and, in the larger cities, huge amphitheatres for large-scale entertainments, such as gladiatorial shows and wild-beast hunts. That the cities were prosperous is shown by the scale upon which these things were provided; payment for these amenities came partly from the public funds and partly from the generous gifts which were made by the wealthier inhabitants of the cities as a manifestation of their civic pride.

Some cities were manufacturing centres, producing the articles for which their province was most renowned; from the cities of the East came all kinds of textiles, leather goods, paper and parchment, glass and jewellery. From Gaul came vast quantities of pottery and bronze articles. Other provinces had other specialities. In most cases, the factory was in the city, and brought wealth to it. Transport was easy, both along the waterways and the network of magnificent roads which the Romans never tired of building; there were no tariff restrictions to hinder trade; all duties were for purely revenue purposes and were kept low. Every city had a certain amount of land attached to it; in the less fertile provinces this land provided the necessities of life; in the more fertile provinces, it produced corn, wine and olive oil for export. Some cities were neither industrial nor agricultural, but purely commercial; Trèves on the Moselle grew wealthy as the city through which supplies passed, on their way from Gaul to the army on the Rhine. One or two of the cities of Greece and Egypt existed on tourist traffic; Athens had long lost her old commercial prosperity, but she remained a university town, and even the unlearned were glad of the opportunity to visit her and spend money there in order to see the sights and the glories of a world that had passed away.

LANDOWNERS AND PEASANTS

All of the land in the provinces did not belong to the cities. Much of it formed the estates of the Emperor, and was an important source of income to him. The methods by which he farmed them varied; in some places slave labour was still used, though all the earlier Emperors realized that this system was not profitable in the long run. Accordingly, they preferred, where possible, to let their lands to tenant farmers, many of whom sub-let much of their holding to smaller tenants. Besides the Imperial estates, there were lands belonging to companies and private people in the cities, large landowners who let their land, like the Emperor; these men spent part of their time on their estates, in their villas, large country houses which were scattered all over the Empire. Often the villa was a sort of home farm; sometimes it was the centre of a rural industry. Many of them, particularly in Italy and Gaul, were very luxurious; the chief rooms had elaborate mosaic floors, and particular attention was paid to the bathrooms, which were arranged on the Turkish-bath principle. Central heating was another very general feature. The really large villas even had their own amphitheatres. Living in the country was made by the Romans exceedingly comfortable.

This was for the rich landowners. However, the great majority of the inhabitants of the country were not landowners but peasants, small tenant-farmers and hired labourers. These lived not in the cities, but either in tiny farms or in villages; they thus remained largely in the state in which they existed before the coming of the Romans. They were little affected by the brilliant civilization of the nearby cities;

they looked upon them with a mixture of awe and jealousy. Not for them the excitements and the amusement of the town; when their rent was paid (in kind more often than in money) they had little to spend on luxuries. Their only way of escape from their conditions was to join the army; from the time of Marcus Aurelius onwards the peasant population was the chief source of recruiting. This division of the population into the people of the cities who had the wealth and the people of the country who had the arms was to have grave results in days to come. But until the last years of Marcus Aurelius, all seemed well; the whole of the Roman world was enjoying unexampled prosperity, and subsequent generations looked back upon this time as having been the golden age of Roman history.

SEEDS OF IMPERIAL DECAY

Thus two centuries of government by Emperors had produced order out of chaos and prosperity out of bankruptcy. Augustus had built well. But if Cato could have foreseen what was to happen during those 200 years, he would have been not so much impressed by the glories of imperial civilization as shocked by the thought of those who had created them and those who now enjoyed them. For the old senatorial aristocracy had been swamped. Many noble families had been killed off by jealous and suspicious Emperors, like Nero and Domitian; those that remained had to rub shoulders in the Senate-house with upstarts from all over the world. Not that the Senate counted for much; occasionally it had a voice in the appointment of a new Emperor, and it still carried out a certain amount of administration, under the Emperor; but it was rapidly approaching the position it ultimately filled, that of the town council of the city of Rome. And the city was losing much of its importance. It was still the capital of the Empire, the seat of the central government; it was continually being embellished by the Emperors with huge and sometimes beautiful buildings. Augustus built himself a great palace, which Domitian enlarged; Vespasian made the large amphitheatre called the Colosseum; Hadrian built a lovely temple to the gods of the seven planets. Trajan cut away a large part of a hill in order to construct a really commodious market-place; and other Emperors enriched the city with quantities of statues and columns and triumphal arches and public baths.

But for all this, Rome was slipping backwards. To be a native of Rome, or even of Italy, was no longer a qualification for a great public career. In practice, few of the distinguished men of the Empire were Italians. In the first century, Spain was the hothouse of talent of all descriptions, and in the second, it had the distinction of providing the first non-Italian Emperors, Trajan and Hadrian. Their successors, Antoninus the Good and Marcus Aurelius, came from Gaul. In the second century, Africa became prominent, particularly in the realm of literature, and at the end of it she, too, produced an Emperor, Septimius Severus, and an imperial dynasty. Later came the turn of the Balkans, and other provinces played their part. The Romans had conquered the Mediterranean world and then failed to rule it; but they enabled it to rule itself.

The problems of Empire were partly solved, partly aggravated by the military assistants of the Emperors. Agrippa, who helped to put Augustus on the throne, and fought his wars for him at sea and in the East, was a loyal subordinate; although, had he survived him, he, and not Tiberius, would have been Augustus' successor, he was never suspected of desiring the Emperor's death. Others, like Germanicus, who did yeoman service in restoring Roman prestige in Germany during the reign of Tiberius, and Corbulo, the terror of the Parthians in the early years of Nero, were not above suspicion. The strength of the early Emperors lay in the ability of the generals they chose to serve them, their weakness in their natural fear of outstandingly successful soldiers as possible rivals for the imperial throne.

CHAPTER 18

CHRISTIANITY AND ITS RIVALS

THE Empire was a collection of peoples of very different descent, speaking different languages, with only one thing in common—their allegiance to Rome. By the third century, there was no real distinction of status left between the inhabitant of the city of Rome and the inhabitant of Cadiz or Damascus or York; there was no political inferiority, no feeling that the Romans were an oppressor race. When Caracalla, Septimius Severus' son, gave Roman citizenship to all free men in the Empire, he did little more than give the force of law to an existing situation. The Roman Empire was a thing taken for granted in the Western world, to which all civilized people belonged. There was no nationalism within the Empire; there could be no cry of "Gaul for the Gauls" or "Britain for the Britons", because there never had been a united Gaul or a united Britain, but only collections of tribes, vaguely related, who happened to live in Gaul or Britain. Nor was language more of a tie than race; for whatever their native tongue, the inhabitants of the Empire could mostly speak Latin in the West and Greek in the East; to speak two languages fluently is not a difficult thing, but simply a matter of habit and opportunity.

The one thing that could rival their loyalty to Rome in the minds of Roman citizens was religion. In the days of the Republic, this would have been inconceivable; for then religion was simply a part of the state. In Greece and Italy alike, the old Aryan gods had grown up with the city; they looked after it in peace and war, and they received payment by sacrifices and building of temples. Greek ideas spread into Rome; a great many tales, which really belonged to the gods of Greece, came to be told about the gods of Rome; when

Greek philosophy came to Rome, these tales were regarded as legends. The educated Roman of Cicero's day had really no religion; he went through the form of worshipping the gods, because they were part of the state system. He might even be a priest, and he would use his priesthood as a means of ornamenting his social position; if he could fake a few oracles, it might be useful to him politically. Except among simple people in country places, the Aryan gods, whether of Greek or Roman origin, were dead. Such morality as can be derived from religion, the educated citizen of Rome usually derived from the teachings of the great Greek philosophers.

At no stage of the world's history has mankind found it possible to live for long without religion. The decay of the Western gods proved the opportunity for the triumph of the religions of the East. From the end of the second century B.C. onwards, there was a constant succession of new faiths coming in from the Eastern lands, from Egypt, from Palestine and later on from Persia.

From Egypt there came, about 100 B.C., the worship of Isis, the mother goddess. This religion appealed to women especially. Worshippers committed a voluntary act, taking part in an emotional and rather noisy ceremony. The goddess shared in their joy and their suffering; instead of cold formality, there was a feeling of personal contact. Isis taught few lessons of morality, much of her ritual was immoral in tone, but stress was laid on the importance of the individual, and thus, in some degree, prepared the way for the higher religions that were to come.

The cult of Isis and of other oriental gods was not altogether welcomed by the ruling classes in Rome. They did not themselves believe in the state gods, but they found them useful; anything that tended to make the masses disbelieve in them was a threat to their own political ascendancy. Those nobles who were philosophers and had high moral ideas derived from their philosophy, looked upon the new religions as merely being in the nature of degrading superstitions, and feared that they would destroy the old Roman austerity.

INAUGURATION OF EMPEROR WORSHIP

It was not surprising, therefore, that part of Augustus' programme of reconstruction was a religious revival, an attempt to infuse new life into the dead gods of Rome. After Julius Caesar's murder, a temple in honour of Isis had been decreed in a moment of weakness; Augustus suspended this, and tried to turn men back to Jupiter and Diana and the rest of the old gods. The attempt was vain. The people enjoyed the pageantry that Augustus gave them; it was a sign of renewed peace and prosperity. The poet Horace was called in to write a hymn; he produced some polished verses, but his heart was not in it. It was not Jupiter who had made them prosperous, it was Augustus. They were prepared to worship him.

The worship of a man was an idea entirely new to the people of Rome itself. In the Eastern parts of the Empire, it was not at all new. The earliest Greek legends told of heroes who had become gods after their death; in the Eastern lands, potentates had been worshipped, Alexander the Great and his successors no less than Hammurabi, Sargon and the Pharaohs. When the Romans conquered the East, their victorious generals were surprised to find that, in the eyes of many, they were regarded as gods. In the East, then, the idea was familiar; in the West, it was novel and meant a great deal. The method of the worship differed in different places; but throughout the Empire Augustus received divine honours of some sort or other. The movement started spontaneously; Augustus seems to have been even a little shocked when it came to Italy, and tried vainly to stop it. He saw that what had begun as an expression of enthusiastic gratitude might be made politically profitable. A common object of worship would help to bind the Empire together. Further, the assemblies of people who came together to worship him made it possible for him to have direct communication with them instead of through his governors. Once he realized the advantages to be obtained from this new cult, Augustus did his best to spread it; in Gaul and Germany, he ruthlessly imposed it on his subjects, and they had to worship him as a god whether they liked it or not.

RELIGIOUS CULTS FROM THE EAST

But the religious value of Emperor-worship died quickly. When the horrors of the civil war had faded from men's minds, and a generation had grown up for which the imperial system was a matter of course, the enthusiasm that had proclaimed the Emperor a god faded, too. The worship continued; all Emperors who were not conspicuous failures became deified, at any rate when they died, but Emperor-worship became as formal and lifeless as the worship of the old gods of Rome. Something more personal was needed to satisfy the unexpressed desires of the masses throughout the Empire. The educated nobility sought satisfaction and consolation for the mysterious unhappiness of the lot of man in philosophy; simpler people looked elsewhere. Increasing numbers adopted the worship of Isis, which Augustus had failed to discourage permanently; others turned to similar mystery religions from the East, cults whose chief feature was a rather unhealthy excitement. A few, even in the first century, embraced the new faith of Christianity, which educated Romans looked upon as a rather obscure offshoot of the religion of one of the most troublesome races in the Empire, the Jews.

Rome first met the Jews as a friend, when she saved them from Antiochus the Illustrious. Later, they incurred the wrath of Pompey, who besieged and conquered Jerusalem. National prosperity and religious energy had increased under the Maccabee princes; they held a territory larger than Solomon's, and they converted many of its Gentile inhabitants. There were probably four million Jews in Palestine under Augustus. He formed the southern part of the country into the province of Judaea; Galilee and Transjordania he left to client kings, called Herod, while the Chief Priest and his Council, the Sanhedrin, exercised certain powers in Jerusalem.

The Torah, or law of Moses, was the centre of Jewish life. Rabbis, or teachers, explained its difficulties, and their teaching eventually formed the Talmud. The synagogues of Palestine fostered religious fervour. Jehovah remained "a jealous God", and the Rabbis kept his worship free from foreign influence.

The Roman governor in Jerusalem rarely interfered with Jewish susceptibilities, making concessions which were granted to no other religion. Outside Palestine the Jew, who had long ceased to be a farmer, practised the lessons of commerce and finance he had learned from his Phoenician cousins. His success aroused the same jealousy which Tyre had once stirred in the Hebrew prophets; occasionally the Italian Jews were expelled, but they soon returned to do business as usual. In spite of their unpopularity, the purity of their religion impressed their neighbours and they won converts over wide areas, particularly in Asia Minor. But the Torah seemed too narrow to win the allegiance of the Gentile world. Some Jews were beginning to find it insufficient for their needs and blamed its strictest adherents, the Pharisees, for burying the object of their worship under a mass of wearisome details. Though the Roman world longed for a religion which would heal its wounds, the Torah of the Jews could not satisfy its needs.

THE TEACHING OF JESUS CHRIST

Yet it was among the Jews that such a religion arose. Late in the reign of Tiberius a young carpenter, named Jesus, left His home at Nazareth in Galilee, which Herod ruled, and went about the country teaching the people and healing the sick. His closest friends were Peter, James, John and nine other apostles; they went with Him in His journeys through Palestine and learned His teaching of a new way of life. He also sent out a band of seventy followers "two and two before His face" with the message "the Kingdom of God is come nigh to you". He and His companions spent much of their time with the sick and the suffering, women as well as men.

Everywhere Jesus attracted large crowds, who were fascinated by His teaching and believed Peter's cry: "Thou hast the words of eternal life." While rejecting the formalism of the Pharisees, He built upon the old faith of the Jews. He told men to centre their lives on the One God who was their Father and to pray that the Father's will should be done on earth. But He swept away the narrow nationalism of the old religion and put in its place a gospel of meekness and love. "Love your enemies," He cried, "bless them that curse you, do good to them that hate you and pray for them that despitefully use you and persecute you." To a world ruled by power and wealth He brought His new message of pity. His blessing went not to the statesman or the warrior but to the poor in spirit, the pure in heart, the merciful and the peacemaker. In place of the wisdom of Hellene or Hebrew He set the virtues of the child: "except ye become as one of these little ones ye cannot enter into the Kingdom of Heaven."

Teaching such as this first irritated and then alarmed the Jewish leaders; "for the people heard Him gladly." An orderly society resented brilliant criticism of its established values. The exhortation: "Sell whatsoever thou hast and give to the poor," seemed to lead straight to social anarchy. Jesus was fearlessly outspoken and never shrank from denouncing the leaders in front of the people. For three years He carried out His work of teaching and healing. Then the authorities decided that He must be stopped. On one of His visits to Jerusalem to celebrate the Passover, after He had taken His Last Supper with His twelve Apostles, He was seized and brought before the High Priest, Caiaphas. To the charge of blasphemy against the Jewish law was added that of treason against the rule of Rome. The governor, Pilate, tried to pass the responsibility to King Herod of Galilee, but was forced, against his better judgment, to put Jesus to death. So on the hill called Calvary outside Jerusalem Jesus of Nazareth was crucified between two thieves.

Pilate thought it was all over. But this was not the end. From every point of view the Crucifixion of Jesus set the seal on His ministry. As a Roman, Pilate had blundered badly by giving unnecessary advertisement to a troublesome section of a troublesome people. To the followers of Jesus, who believed that He was the Messiah, the Christ, the Anointed One, the Son of the Living God, the Crucifixion and the Resurrection which followed it became the central facts of their religion. John and Peter and the rest had shown cowardice when their Master was arrested; after His death they were filled with a new Spirit, which defied Rome and Jerusalem alike.

Early Christianity seemed merely a heresy directed against orthodox Judaism. But the Jews were spread over much of the Roman world and the heresy was likely to reach their scattered communities. The Apostles were simple men; but their burning faith in Jesus and their steady loyalty to Him revolutionized the minds of those to whom they preached Christ Crucified. They travelled among the Jews of the Dispersion, and made converts among men and women who felt the need of something more than the orthodox religion.

PAUL AND THE SPREAD OF CHRISTIANITY

The man who saw that the message of Jesus Christ was universal was Saul of Tarsus. He believed that the gospel of love was meant for all mankind and that Christianity could carry to the whole world the great Jewish doctrine that there is one God only. Saul was a strict Jew, a highly educated man, and a Roman citizen. His early training in Asia Minor and Jerusalem had made him one of the fiercest opponents of Christianity; his conversion on the Damascus road caused consternation among his old companions. For Paul, as he now became known, was not one for half measures; he threw over the details of the Mosaic law; he attacked both those who wanted to destroy Christianity and those who wanted to keep it as a part of Judaism. Being Paul, he had his way.

Paul was the ideal missionary for the Roman world. True, he was not much to look at, a stumpy little man suffering from some disease of the eyes which made him peer about in a curious way. But constitutionally, he was amazingly tough; he suffered constant hardship and ill-treatment without permanent ill-effect. Mentally, he was perfectly equipped. He had the serious attitude of the Jew towards religion; his Greek education had made him alert, and able to meet anyone on level terms in argument; and he had the self-confidence that only Roman citizenship could give in the Roman world. Thus endowed, he set out to convert mankind; throughout Asia Minor and Greece, he founded churches, communities of the faithful, and he ended his career a prisoner, but still a missionary, in Rome itself.

THE EARLY CHRISTIAN CHURCH

Paul had his disciples and imitators, and throughout the first century the gospel spread. In Nero's reign, there were enough Christians in Rome for them to be accused of causing the Great Fire. It was not until the second century that the Roman Government began to regard them as a problem. There was still no general persecution; but there were occasional outbreaks of animosity, and a Christian, when once accused, stood little chance in a court of law. Unlike the Jews, they were not exempted from the worship of the Emperor; yet to take any part in it was to betray their own faith.

Still, in the first two centuries, the Christians were mostly let alone, and they quietly built up the Christian Church. At first, there was no central organization; there were assemblies of Christians in most important towns, which met to worship God and perform the sacraments. At times, they were visited by one of the great missionaries, or received letters from them; many of these letters, especially those of Paul, were treasured as a storehouse of doctrine, and are read in Christian churches to-day.

As the generation that had seen Jesus Christ grew old and died, it became necessary to have written records of His life and teaching; four of these records survive to-day, and are called the Gospels. The fourth, the Gospel of St. John, is less simple than the others; it tells the story of Jesus' life in a way that would appeal to those who were steeped in Greek philosophy. The need for this Gospel to be written showed how far Paul's work had succeeded; Christianity was a religion not for the Jews alone, but for the world that derived its civilization from the Greeks. All this literature, with other literature now lost, was read aloud in the Churches, and ensured a common tradition of belief and ritual; in time, regular communication between the churches was established, and early in the third century, it became the practice for the Bishops, who were overseers elected by the laity of each church, to meet at the chief town of their province. From this, it was but a step to the World Councils, which began in the fourth century and undertook to settle controversial questions.

ROME AND THE JEWS

If the Roman Government was, on the whole, tolerant of the Christians in the first two centuries, it was because they were, as a rule, inoffensive. Not so the orthodox Jews. For them, God's kingdom was of this world; the presence of a Roman governor in Jerusalem was a perpetual challenge to Jehovah. Judaea was always alive with nationalist feeling, which the more prudent of the Jewish leaders could only keep in check when the Romans were tactful. In Nero's reign, mistakes on both sides led to war, which only ended when Vespasian had become emperor; his son, Titus, captured Jerusalem after a six months' siege. The Jews still nursed their grievances, and there was a second outbreak during the reign of Trajan, who planted a Roman colony in Jerusalem. When, in Hadrian's time, there was another rebellion, it was the last. The temple was destroyed, a great part of the population was exterminated, and henceforth the Jews had no national home until our own day.

The loss of Palestine and the temple had two far-reaching results: Judaism ceased to be a religion which demanded the ritual of sacrifice; the Jew was cut adrift from his eastern home and became, in the main, a man of the west. There was no more blood and smoke in the desolate temple courts. In their stead, the Jew of the Dispersion had the Synagogue, the Scriptures, the Torah and the beginnings of the Talmud. The latter grew rapidly, fostered by a wise system of education. The Sanhedrin ceased to consist of politicians and was recruited from the ranks of the learned. The Jewish community in Palestine still had a ruler in the Patriarch, who was recognized by the Roman Government. The Rabbis went wherever their fellow-countrymen were scattered. Some of them found refuge in the east, where the old Babylonian community remained prosperous under the rule of the Prince of the Captivity; in later centuries persecution came to them also, and the Dispersion spread to Persia, India and farther eastward.

The majority went to the west, to Italy, North Africa, Spain, Gaul and even western Germany. Many of them were captives, sold in the slave-markets, which flourished on the triumphs of the legions. The Jew made an unsatisfactory slave; his attachment to the sabbath and his special food made him an awkward chattel in the home and the workshop. The Torah and the Talmud kept him aloof from his Gentile neighbours. Under the peaceful rule of Antoninus the Good memories of the fighting round Jerusalem died down, and the Jew was accepted as a useful member of the Empire. His education helped him to excel in commerce and science, and the free Jew was generous in ransoming his slave cousin from servitude. His way of life seemed odd to the Gentile, but though there were a few instances of local persecution, he preserved his religion and his own customs.

THE PATHWAY TO CIVIL WAR

If, then, we look at the state of the Roman world towards the end of the second century, we find a curiously confusing picture. At the head of it, there was a philosopher Emperor, Marcus Aurelius, who lived an austere life, according to the highest traditions of the Stoics, counting it virtue to be above all human emotions. Officially, the State religion went on, together with the worship of previous Emperors, but Marcus Aurelius refused to be worshipped himself. Of the nobility many were frankly irreligious; some were Stoics after the manner of the Emperor; more found some sort of satisfaction in the cults of the East. In the poorer classes, the worship of Isis and of other such deities was widespread; an ever-increasing number were becoming Christians; and another religion, the worship of Mithras, was gaining popularity, especially in the army. Mithras was originally a Persian sun-god; on his journey westward, he accumulated various properties from other sources. The distinctive outward feature of Mithraism was baptism in the blood of bulls, but it was a purer and higher religion than this would suggest. It promised immortality, and this had to be bought by the observance of a high standard of conduct, which had much in common with the Christian law of love. Not being a "jealous" religion like Christianity, it met with no official opposition, and spread rapidly.

In curious contrast with this spiritual ferment was the apparent political stability of the Empire. But in the last years of Marcus Aurelius, there were signs that all was not so well as it seemed. Things were beginning to happen beyond the northern frontier; the plan of Marcus Aurelius to annex Bohemia was intended as a counter-attack upon tribes who had crossed the Danube and penetrated almost as far as the border of Italy. The vicious silliness of Aurelius' son did not improve the situation; during his reign and the civil wars that followed it, the frontier defences were neglected. Much of Septimius Severus' life was spent in repelling the Parthians in the East and the fierce tribes of Scotland in the North. The other Emperors of his dynasty kept the frontiers secure; but on the murder of the last of them in A.D. 234, the storm broke.

The history of the next half-century is a tale of almost constant civil war within the Empire, resulting in weakness which was an opportunity for the powers and the tribes outside to invade and plunder it. Nineteen men wore the Imperial purple during those fifty years; many others made a bid for the throne. The causes of this anarchy were various. The most obvious was the lack of a satisfactory solution to the problem of the succession; the return of Marcus Aurelius

H   (H.W.)

and Septimius Severus to the hereditary system had proved fatal, because of the unsuitability of their descendants. In these disastrous years, force became the only road to the throne; during the confusion after Alexander Severus' death, the Senate, for the last time, played an important part in history by nominating Emperors, but they were soon superseded by candidates of one or other of the armies. Practically all the Emperors of this time died violent deaths, most of them at the hands of their own armies. It seemed as if the soldiers actually enjoyed civil war; for even successful Emperors who led them to victory against the barbarians were murdered by them.

The bulk of the army was now recruited from the peasantry, who had no part in the prosperous life of the cities, and had long hated their inhabitants. Now their opportunity had come. Each new outbreak of civil war gave the soldiers a fresh chance of looting the cities; even Septimius Severus had not restrained his men from destroying Lyons, and such cities as Byzantium, Antioch and Alexandria all suffered at the hands of Roman soldiers. The civil wars, nominally fought to put first one and then another pretender on the throne, were in reality wars between a peasant soldiery and an urban bourgeoisie. Some of the Emperors tried to save the civilization of the cities; but they were powerless in the hands of their troops, who were always ready to murder them if they were not granted full liberty of plunder. The soldiers were bound to win; the cities had no force at their disposal; the anarchy came to an end, after fifty years, only because the wealth of the cities was exhausted and the possessing class stripped of most of its power. Only Britain and Africa, which were far from the centre of civil war, remained prosperous.

PERSIANS AND GOTHS THREATEN ROME

Thus occupied in pillaging the territory it was paid to defend, the Roman army had little time to repel foreign invaders. Two new and formidable enemies had arisen. After the fall of the Parthian Empire, its place had been taken by a native Persian dynasty, which aimed at reviving the old glories of the Empire of Darius; and across the Danube had come into being the power of the Goths. This people of German stock had become powerful in South Russia in the second century, and were now moving westwards. They had first come into contact with the Roman Empire shortly after the death of Septimius Severus, but had been beaten off. They kept their eye, however, on Rumania and the lands south of the Danube, and bided their time.

When the civil wars began to occupy the attention of the Roman armies, the Goths struck. Their first attack took them far into the Balkan peninsula, before they were driven back. The second attack was more successful because it was only one of many which the Empire had to face at the same time. There was a new spirit abroad in Germany; the small tribes were joining together, and their union made them formidable. The Gothic land-forces swept down upon

Greece from the north; their fleets skirted the shores of the Black Sea, and passed through the Dardanelles to join the pirates of the Aegean, who had raised their heads again. Meanwhile, to the West, other German tribes were crossing the Upper Danube; the Franks and the Alemans were raiding Gaul by way of the Rhine; while the Alemans ravaged the Rhone valley, the Franks penetrated to Spain, and crossed the Straits into Africa. Farther north, another combination of German tribes, known as the Saxons, were attacking the coast of Britain and the shipping of the Channel. In the East, the new power of the Persians overran Syria, and one of their armies made its way through the whole length of Asia Minor.

INDEPENDENT DEFENCE OF THE PROVINCES

At first, the central Government was powerless to meet the crisis, and the provinces had to look to themselves for defence. In the East, the rallying-point was Palmyra, one of the ancient cities of the Arabian desert. It had grown rich in the centuries before, because it lay in an oasis through which the caravans from Arabia passed on their way to Palestine and Syria. In the reign of Augustus it admitted the suzerainty of Rome, and was treated with special favour by later Emperors. It became more and more like a Greek city of the Roman world; but it was distinguished from the rest in being allowed and encouraged to have its own armed forces; the archers of Palmyra were famous all over the world. The triumphant progress of the Persians was a blow to the prosperity of Palmyra that its citizens could not afford to overlook. Seeing that no help was coming from the official Roman forces, they took action themselves, invading Mesopotamia and defeating the Persian army. Their leader assumed the title of King, with the assent of the Roman Emperor, who was only too glad to be relieved of the responsibility of defending his eastern frontier. Upon the King's death, his widow, Zenobia, took over the reins of government. She was a woman of great learning and culture; in her court, Greek civilization seemed to flower again. She also possessed great practical ability, and boundless ambition; it was with justice that she regarded herself as a more worthy heir of Augustus than the rough soldiers who were being elevated for brief spells to the imperial throne by the armies of the West. The cities of the East welcomed her forces, which, unlike the official armies of Rome, came to preserve their civilization and not to destroy it; in a very short space of time, the rule of Palmyra was acknowledged from the Bosphorus to the Nile. It was only when Zenobia showed signs of coming to terms with Persia that the Roman Emperor was stung to action.

In the West, a somewhat similar situation arose. The raids of the Franks met with little resistance from the central Government; a soldier named Postumus, who set up a government on his own in Gaul, managed to drive them out. He did not claim to be the Emperor of Rome; he founded, as it were, a new Empire of Gaul, in which Spain and Britain joined. This was not a national Empire; it carried on the traditions of Rome; all that happened was that part of the Roman Empire, suffering severely from barbarian invasions, decided to put its own house in order. In other provinces, other independent rulers arose, but none of them had the success or the importance of Postumus or Zenobia. In Africa and in the Danube provinces, the central Government retained control; the former was vital, for it was the granary of the Empire; in the latter, one of the abler Emperors of the time decided to deal faithfully with the Goths who were for ever swarming over the frontier, and were now trying to make Greece their permanent home. Both by land and sea, he decisively defeated them, killing many and capturing more. After A.D. 270 we hear nothing further of the Goths for about a century.

AURELIAN RESTORES THE FRONTIERS

This success showed that the Roman Empire was still capable of great things, and the next Emperor, Aurelian, set about the work of restoration. Aurelian, like all the Emperors of the time, was a soldier; he was a native of one of the Danube provinces, who, by sheer ability, had carved out for himself a distinguished military career. He was immensely popular in the army, and troops would follow him anywhere. Unlike many of his predecessors, he was not interested solely in his own enrichment and prestige; he thought much of the glories of the Empire that seemed to be vanishing. In particular, he regretted the establishment of independent kingdoms and tyrannies, and the threatened break-up of the Roman world. His first act on coming to the throne was to restore the Danube frontier; he abandoned Rumania as too difficult to hold; but any German who ventured south of the Danube had short shrift from him. He then went to the East to conquer Zenobia; he swept her forces out of Asia Minor while one of his lieutenants recaptured Egypt; then, after reconquering Syria, he besieged and captured Palmyra itself. Zenobia was deposed, and her city, the glory of northern Arabia, was utterly destroyed. Aurelian then turned back to Europe. In Gaul, Postumus was dead, but his Empire continued under a civilian; Aurelian made short work of him, and when he celebrated his triumph in Rome, he could claim to have reunited the Empire. He was rightly hailed on all sides as the man who had restored the world. A year later, he suffered the usual fate of Emperors in his time: he was murdered by men of his own army. The Empire again reverted to civil war, but its frontiers were relatively secure. The cities of the Empire remained free from foreign marauders; plunder became the monopoly of the soldiers of Rome. Even they grew tired of fighting each other; when, in 284, Diocletian came to the throne, he was to enjoy twenty years of practically unchallenged power in which to carry out the necessary reforms which had been made necessary by the long process of disintegration in the administration of the Empire.

The progress of the Christian Church was a strong contrast to the aimless confusion of public affairs. As the Empire lapsed deeper into anarchy, the organization of the Christian community improved. As the power of the Government became less and less a thing that men could respect, so they turned more and more to the religion that could engross them and arouse their enthusiasm. Increase of numbers did not necessarily mean increase of religious fervour; even in the second century, there had been a party in the Church which had counselled compromise, or at any rate flight, in the face of persecution. Tertullian, the clever lawyer from Carthage who had been turned to Christianity by the sight of men facing the most horrible kinds of death for the sake of their religion, would have none of this half-heartedness. He openly proclaimed that Christianity was waging a war upon the old institutions of the Empire. He saw that the ordinary life of a Roman citizen implied acceptance of the pagan gods; the metal-worker would be called upon to make a heathen image; the house-decorator would be told to repair the temple of Jupiter; by long custom, the schoolmaster had to dedicate part of his fees to Minerva, the patron goddess of his profession, and he took his holidays on festivals of heathen gods. Tertullian's answer to these difficulties was quite simple; the Christian must not recognize the heathen gods in any way at all. This was to set the Church in direct opposition to the state. His writings, for all their violence and occasional bitterness, proved an inspiration to those who came after him, giving courage and strength to the victims of the persecutions that were becoming more frequent and more cruel than ever before.

CHRISTIANITY'S ANSWER TO PERSECUTION

In his own time, these persecutions were not general, nor were they part of the Imperial policy. Christianity offended against the law in many respects, and Christians were often prosecuted for these offences and called upon to renounce the religion that made them commit them; when they refused, they suffered death on the cross, or were burnt, or torn to pieces by wild beasts in the public amphitheatres. It was not until the period of anarchy, however, that any Emperor tried to stamp out Christianity by a general persecution. In 250, a general edict was issued against it, on the ground that it was responsible for much of the lawlessness of a terribly lawless age. Many Christians renounced their faith; many suffered martyrdom rather than do so. All over the Empire, the worship of Christ continued, in secret if not openly. In Rome itself they held their services unmolested in the Catacombs, the subterranean burial-places that their ancestors had dug near the city.

Though it was easy to blame the Christians for the parlous state of the world, it was more difficult to stamp them out; by this time, they were numerous and influential, and had public opinion to a great extent on their side. After ten years, the Government gave it up; the

Christians remained free from persecution until the reign of Diocletian. Then came their sharpest trial, mass executions on a scale not
known before. But it was the darkest hour before the dawn. The
Christians remained firm, the Government weakened; the Emperor
might condemn, but his officials hesitated to carry out his orders.
When Diocletian retired, the decrees against the Christians were withdrawn; his great successor Constantine became a Christian, and in
323, proclaimed Christianity to be the official religion of the Empire.

THE POLITICAL TRIUMPH OF CHRISTIANITY

This was a great act of statesmanship; henceforth the loyalty of
Christians towards the State was assured; but its effect on the Church
was another matter. When Christianity had been a persecuted religion, membership of the Church had entailed personal sacrifice; no
one would become a Christian unless he believed in the faith from his
heart. Now it seemed to be the road to favour and high office; there
must have been many insincere professions of faith. Before Constantine, in spite of disagreements among themselves, Christians had
faced together a hostile world; now that the world smiled upon them,
controversy ran riot. Much of it bore rich fruit; the Councils of the
Church worked out a theology, without which a Catholic or universal
religion cannot stand for long. The chief point at issue was the relation of Jesus Christ, the Son of God, to God the Father and to the
Holy Spirit; the solution reached at the Council of Nicaea in Constantine's reign, that there are Three Persons in One God, did not
win universal acceptance. Quarrels arose between Catholics, who
accepted this, and Arians, who rejected it; and in arguing about the
nature of Jesus of Nazareth, both tended to forget His teachings.

CHAPTER 19

THE FALL OF THE EMPIRE IN THE WEST

THE official recognition of Christianity was the culmination of a
policy designed to put the Roman Empire on its feet again. Constantine was the successor of the man who originated the policy. The
fifty years of anarchy, in the third century were brought to a close by
the Illyrian Emperor Diocletian, who in 285 was raised to the throne
by a victory over a rival candidate. Diocletian must rank with Augustus himself, Vespasian and Septimius Severus as a restorer of stable
government; and in some respects his task was more difficult than
theirs, because of the devastating effect of the civil war that preceded
it. The fair civilization of the cities was in great part ruined. The
soldier-peasants who now had the power knew little of urban civilization; Government officials took little interest in good administration,
because, with civil war always imminent, they had no security of
tenure. There was no stability in anything, and for those who did not

find peace in the contemplation of a future life, nothing seemed worth while, except to make money by force or fraud, and spend it while the going was good.

Diocletian, who was more of an organizer than a soldier, faced these problems realistically. The first thing to be done was to prevent the recurrence of civil war; peace was the first condition of prosperity. Accordingly he revived the principle of adoption, which had done so much to secure peaceful successions in the second century; but he extended it by providing himself with three colleagues, and dividing the Empire into four military districts which he shared out with them. His own gifts as an administrator commanded their respect, and none of his colleagues disputed his supreme authority; each of them had his own frontier to defend, and his opportunity of military glory. Diocletian was thus free to carry out his reforms in peace.

RULE BY DIVINE RIGHT

He could not hope to restore the conditions of the second century; he had to make the best he could of the third. The world he had to rule had lost all sense of Augustus's subtle tradition; the idea of the Emperor being several Republican magistrates rolled into one no longer had any meaning. Diocletian therefore abandoned all pretence of being anything else than a complete despot. He ruled by virtue of divine right, and was more like one of the old kings of the East than a Roman. His court was modelled on that of Persia. His position was hedged round with pomp and ceremony; men admitted into his presence found him clothed in all the trappings of royalty, and had to make elaborate obeisance to him. From his time, date many of the titles of courtesy that exist in Europe to-day; Dukes and Counts and Serene Highnesses were inventions of Diocletian. It must not be thought that Diocletian used all this ceremonial because he liked it particularly. He was really a man of simple tastes who looked forward to retiring into private life, but he saw that the people he had to rule no longer felt reverence for old Roman customs and ideas, yet could easily be impressed by ostentatious display and outward magnificence.

Together with this external glorification of the position of the Emperor went the final disappearance of the administrative power of the Senate. The rank of Senator was still honourable; but, outside Rome itself, the Senate had no powers and no duties. It became simply a town council. All the provinces were now directly administered by the Emperor, through an ever-increasing host of civil servants, and the administration was far wider than before, owing to the decay of local self-government during the civil wars.

Had these civil servants been a body of incorruptible men, concerned only with restoring the Roman Peace and the prosperity of the Empire, all might have been well. As it was, they too often regarded their position as an opportunity for personal enrichment, and the Emperor, in his desire to check their extortions, had to institute a sort of spy system, a secret police who spied upon his own servants. But these men were no less corruptible than the rest; and they bred an atmosphere of suspicion throughout the Empire.

The necessity for this extraordinary institution, and its failure, show the poorness of the material with which Diocletian and Constantine had to deal. This, more than any defect of their own intelligence, accounts for the crude simplicity of their financial reforms. The financial situation that they had to face was serious. In the years of anarchy, the rival Emperors and pretenders and their troops had plundered where they could, and had allowed regular systems of taxation to lapse. The subtle methods by which the early Emperors had raised money, largely through various devices of indirect taxation, had completely gone by the board; Diocletian possessed neither time nor sufficiently able ministers to restore them effectively.

TAXATION AND SERFDOM

Yet he had somehow to raise more money than the early Emperors had dreamed of. For the situation on the frontiers was far more menacing. A repetition of the invasions of the third century must be avoided at all costs; for this, a complete military reorganization was necessary. The army, which had been gradually increasing from the 300,000 of the second century, was now raised to over half a million; this made possible the creation of a large general reserve, which could be rushed, in whole or in part, to any place on any frontier where hostilities had broken out. Thus, for the first time, the Roman Empire had a second line of defence. This was admirable from a military point of view; but it cost money, which the Empire could afford far less in these latter days.

To raise the money, Diocletian had to invent a totally new form of taxation. Not having a body of trained economists at his disposal, he could not be certain how much money indirect taxation, customs duties and the like would bring in; so he decided to raise his revenue by direct taxation, on a scale dictated by his own needs, without regard to the taxpayer's capacity to pay. For this purpose, he adopted the simplest possible system, irrespective of fairness or ultimate effect upon the community.

The people of the country were taxed according to the land they occupied. Each peasant or farmer was required to declare the amount of land which he held; he and his heirs were then bound, for all time, to pay a yearly tax on that land; he could not get out of it by leaving his land, because, in the official register, he was recorded as its occupant, and must provide the tax.

Thus began the institution of serfdom all over the Empire; a system which, in a more equitable form, had existed for centuries in Egypt, was made to apply in the crudest possible way to the whole Roman world. The cities were treated similarly. Here a list was made of citizens who were eligible to hold office, the qualification being the possession of quite a small amount of property; from them, too, a fixed sum was exacted every year; and they were no more at liberty than the peasant-serfs to leave their place of abode to escape burdens. Further, a system was gaining ground by which everyone who engaged in trade was compelled to join a commercial guild, from which he was not allowed to resign, and in which he had to enter his children. The carpenter's son had to be a carpenter, the cobbler's a cobbler. Thus, in every branch of life, an hereditary caste-system like that of India to-day came into force; the Emperor got his taxes fairly regularly, but at the cost of debasing the status of the population, taking away its freedom and crushing enterprise.

The only comparatively prosperous people, besides the Imperial officials, were the large landlords, who let out their land to the serfs who were bound to continue as their tenants. Even they enjoyed only a precarious prosperity; for the system of serfdom led naturally to discontent among the peasants; when opportunity occurred, many fled from the horrors of civilization across the frontiers to the freedom of barbarism. Now that the foreign conquests of Rome had ceased, fresh slaves were unobtainable; all that the landowner could do to make his estate prosperous was to keep a watchful eye on his serfs, to see that they did not run away. It was not his fault that the system was oppressive; he merely made the best of a bad world. And he must be given credit for keeping the torch of culture burning in a community that was preoccupied with earning a scanty living. Civilization, which had gradually become forgotten in the towns, found a refuge in the life of the country gentry.

DIOCLETIAN'S TEMPORARY SUCCESS

Although Diocletian did not put new life into the Empire, he did at least succeed in temporarily arresting its process of mortality. The twenty years of his reign were a time of peace within its borders, except for an abortive attempt by a Roman general to set up an Empire by himself in Britain. On the frontiers, Roman arms were in the ascendant, and a notable victory was gained over the Persians. On the military side, Diocletian's system was so successful that he felt himself justified at last in retiring into private life and watching his successors carry on the good work.

Unfortunately, the system broke down at once. The colleagues whom he had appointed squabbled, and a new series of civil wars began; from them, emerged triumphant the son of one of Diocletian's old colleagues, Constantine, one of the greatest of all the Emperors of Rome. Constantine faced much the same problems as Diocletian before him, but he profited from his predecessor's mistakes. The Christians had been persecuted as a menace to the state; Constantine took the far wiser course of accepting Christianity and allying it with the state. Diocletian had met the problem of frontier defence by appointing colleagues responsible for different parts of the frontier;

Constantine saw that this was the road to civil war, and therefore kept the whole Empire under his own control, providing for efficient defence in a far more prudent, though revolutionary way. He saw that the city of Rome was no longer the right capital for the Empire. Recent Emperors had deserted her for towns in the north of Italy, where they could be nearer to the scenes of military operations; but it needed the genius and bold imagination of Constantine to make a sharp official break with the tradition of a thousand years.

THE GREATNESS OF CONSTANTINE

He decided to move the capital from Rome to Byzantium, the strategic centre of the whole Empire. Here he could himself direct operations either against the tribes of Germany or the armies of Persia; the new reserve force could be sent rapidly along the great military highways to any point where danger threatened. The new capital was almost impregnable, and its superb harbour afforded a base for the fleet, which could prevent any repetition of the Gothic sea-raid of the third century. Constantine had chosen well; long after old Rome had fallen into the hands of barbarians, the new capital remained secure; for over a thousand years it lasted as an Imperial city. It was fitting that the place he chose and fortified and adorned with all the trappings of Roman civilization should be called Constantinople, the city of Constantine.

Constantine was undoubtedly one of the greatest figures of the ancient world. His two immense feats of statecraft, the recognition of Christianity and the foundation of Constantinople, mark him out as the wisest man of the fourth century; and if those who named him "the equal of the Apostles", a title by which the Greek Church still commemorates him, attributed to him a saintliness which he was far from possessing, those who defamed his memory after his death were equally wide of the mark. Charges of barbarous cruelty are recorded against him by pagan writers who were supporting a dying cause; and it is certain that he was guilty of the judicial murder of some of his own family. Whatever the truth may be, Constantine deserved well of the Empire and of civilization. For, by his acts, he secured a centre of civilization which remained unaffected by the barbarians who were so soon to overrun the Empire in the West.

RENEWED DIVISIONS IN THE EMPIRE

But where Constantine failed was where his predecessors had failed, in the matter of the succession. At his death in 337, he divided his Empire among his three sons, and this meant further civil wars which the Empire could afford less than ever. The situation on the frontiers, which had been comparatively quiet since the accession of Diocletian, soon became dangerous again. In the middle of the century a serious invasion of Gaul had to be checked by vigorous action on the part of a great soldier, Julian, who subsequently became Emperor, and obtained fame from his vain attempt to reintroduce Paganism at the expense of Christianity. But his campaign against the Persians, a better organized and therefore more formidable enemy than the German invaders, was less successful; he died before his elaborate plans were completed, and his successor signed a treaty with Persia that gave away all he had won. In the next year, A.D. 364, the inevitable return to the system of a dual Empire was made; one man could no longer face the enemies of Rome on all her frontiers. Two brothers divided the Empire, and for a dozen years, kept it free from invasion. Then the crisis came.

The immediate trouble was with the Goths, the East German people who had wrought havoc in the previous century. They had been kept at bay by Diocletian, and, in the reign of Constantine, when they had attempted to cross the Danube, they had been severely defeated, and had been glad to accept terms of peace. They were on friendly terms with Constantine's successors; and gradually became more civilized. For some time Christianity had been spreading among them. About 340, the missionary Ulfila translated the Bible into Gothic, and spread the Gospel throughout their lands; but unluckily for the peace

BARBARIAN INVASIONS OF THE WEST

The Roman Empire gradually succumbed to attacks launched by the various barbarian tribes. The dates indicate the chronology of the principal invasions.

of the world, the form of Ulfila's Christianity was that of the Arian heresy, which had been rejected by the Church within the Empire at the Council of Nicaea in the reign of Constantine. The difference between Arian and Orthodox Christianity turned on the relation of Christ and the Father. It must have been hopelessly obscure to the barbarian mind; but the fact that a Council held under the auspices of Constantine had decided against the Arians gave it a vast political importance; to be an Arian was often regarded as a challenge to the authority of the Empire. Thus the Christianity of the Goths, which might have linked them to the Empire, formed instead a barrier.

HUNS AND GOTHS

A new enemy pressed on from central Asia. The Huns were a Mongolian people, who had no fixed homes, but wandered about during the summer, looking for somewhere to settle down for the winter. They carried all their property in horse-drawn carts. Never staying in one place for two years at a time, they had no ideas about the value of land or immovable property; whatever they found on their wanderings, they used up at once by the first method that occurred to them. People of other races they regarded as obstacles to be pushed out of the way; and they usually succeeded. For there was a terrifying ferocity about these sallow devilish creatures who dug their spurs into their horses and swept down like a hurricane upon the foe, and in the eyes of the milder peoples of the West, they seemed almost irresistible. They observed no rules of war; they never dreamed of entering into friendly relations with other peoples; they either killed them or made them slaves. Thus their progress westwards was one of simple murder and pillaging. Of all the peoples with whom the Romans came into contact during their long history, the Huns alone never showed any sign of knowing the meaning of mercy.

But, at present, the Romans were not to suffer in person. The Huns moved slowly. At the beginning of the third century, they had been harassing the moribund Parthian Empire; it was not until after the middle of the fourth that they began to trouble the Goths of Rumania. When they did come, they proved irresistible; after a rather half-hearted resistance, the Goths fled in terror before the ferocious hordes, and massed on the Danube bank to ask for shelter within the Roman Empire. The Eastern Emperor, Valens, admitted them, rightly thinking that to do so would save him from having to face the Huns; the Goths could be excluded only by a war which would weaken the Roman power and make the Empire an easy prey when next the Huns should advance. So huge tribes of Goths were ferried across the Danube, to settle down, they hoped, to a peaceful and civilized life.

Unfortunately, the people of the Empire, and especially the Imperial officials, did not see the matter in the same light as their guests. The latter were barbarians, they thought, and must be treated as such.

It took only two years for war to break out; the Romans were unprepared, and suffered a tremendous defeat in 378, at the battle of Adrianople, where Valens and two-thirds of his army were killed. It was the mailed Gothic cavalry that won this victory; and from now on, until the invention of gunpowder, the knight in armour was supreme upon the battlefields of Europe. It looked as if there were nothing but the walls of Constantinople to prevent the Goths from overrunning the whole of the Eastern Empire.

As had happened before in Roman history, the hour brought forth the man; a Spanish soldier, descended from the family that had formerly produced a great soldier-emperor in the person of Trajan, was proclaimed Emperor of the East by the western Emperor; and this Theodosius knew not only the arts of war, but the art of keeping peace. A series of campaigns took the fighting spirit out of the Goths. Tactful treatment of them after this had been accomplished, and firm control of the officials who had to come in contact with them, turned them for a time from a menace into a firm bulwark of Empire.

THEODOSIUS COMPLETES THE WORK OF CONSTANTINE

Having saved the Empire in the East from dissolution, Theodosius now did his best to put it in good order. He completed the work of Constantine in religious matters. If his methods with Arians and other heretics were at times unduly forceful, it was because he wished to put an end to the religious controversies that were turning men's minds away from the service of the State and from the practice of true religion alike. If old-fashioned people regretted his abolition of ancient institutions such as the Olympic Games, he was none the less justified in seeing in them a continuation of paganism which a Christian state could no longer countenance. In civil matters, he showed great wisdom; economy was his watchword, and never had it been more necessary. He set an example by reducing the expenses of his court; and many of his laws were directed to reducing those of his subjects, particularly by checking the extortions of the civil service. By his prudent policy, he was able to give peace and a measure of recovery to the East, and at the same time, much-needed assistance to his colleagues in the West, where a fresh series of pretenders was threatening to break up the Empire. But in 395, at a moment when the legitimate Emperor of the West had been murdered, and Theodosius had defeated and executed his murderer, Theodosius himself died. Both thrones were vacant, and were given to the two sons of Theodosius, aged seventeen and eleven. The elder bore nominal rule in the East, but the real power was in the hands of a Greek official, the Chamberlain of the Palace; the younger was placed under the guardianship of a barbarian soldier, the Vandal Stilicho.

This was a very significant fact. Without any large-scale military invasion, the barbarians had established themselves in great numbers within the Empire during the fourth century. Valens's admission of the Goths from across the Danube had been typical; similar settlements took place across the Rhine. The enlistment of many Germans, to fill the gaps in the legions, aided the process of peaceful penetration. Theodosius had made the best of a tendency that he could not arrest, and used the invaders to defend his territory. For the West German was a more civilized being than the East German, and it was better to welcome him than to have to face his more alarming cousin. But if Theodosius attempted to educate and Romanize his protéges, he failed; instead of the barbarians becoming Romanized, the Romans became barbarized. So there seemed nothing shocking in the fact that the real ruler of the Western Empire was a Vandal, a member of one of the East German tribes. Stilicho was a very efficient ruler, and proved himself to be a staunch defender of the Empire against his own kinsmen. He had need to be.

ALARIC'S SACK OF ROME

The Goths, whom Theodosius had conquered and pacified, saw in his death an opportunity for plunder, and descended again on Constantinople. Their king, Alaric the Bold, had no desire to break up the Empire; he only wanted to do the best that he could for himself and his people within it. Accordingly, he accepted a bribe from the government at Constantinople to go away and ravage some other place, and after plundering Greece for a few years, turned his attention to Italy. There he was opposed by Stilicho, who kept him at bay for some years. But when the young Emperor of the West reached manhood he grew tired of his great adviser. His execution of Stilicho made possible the triumph of Alaric; the Emperor had neither the vigour to oppose the Goths nor the sense to grant their demands. In 410, Alaric besieged and captured Rome, and gave it over to his troops to sack. It was no longer a seat of government; the Western capital was at Ravenna, on the east coast of Italy. But Rome was still the most famous city of the world, and it had not been captured by a foreign enemy for eight hundred years. The news caused consternation all over the world, though it created no new political situation; the damage had been wrought before. The city recovered; Alaric's troops had done less harm than might have been the case; but the Western Empire was never to recover from the ravages that he had inflicted all over it for the last ten years.

The stout resistance that Stilicho had put up had been at the expense of the frontier defences of the north. To oppose Alaric, he had denuded the garrison on the Rhine, and a host of German tribes, Vandals and others, had swarmed over the undefended frontiers into Gaul, and through Gaul to Spain. In the far north, the legions had been withdrawn from Britain, which, a generation later, suffered practically unchecked invasions of heathen barbarians—Picts from Scotland, Scots from Ireland, and Saxons from across the North Sea. Alaric's death and the withdrawal of his forces from Italy did not enable the Imperial government to recover control of its northerly dominions. The situation was accepted, and the Goths were used against more barbaric peoples, just as Theodosius had once used them in the East. Gaul became divided into three kingdoms: that of the West Goths in the south-west, the Burgundians in the south-east, and the Franks in the north. These all recognized the Western Emperor as their overlord, but it cannot be said that they allowed him to control them in any way, though they were ready to fight for him when their own interests demanded it.

The Vandals had gone into Spain, where they met with weak resistance from the Imperial troops; eventually they made peace with the Emperor, very much on their own terms, though they acknowledged his authority in theory. Spain was not rich enough to last these barbarians for long; though they liked living on the land, they had no desire to work it for a living, and they cast longing eyes on the smiling fields of the province of Africa, the richest part of the Roman world. So, after twenty years in Spain, their king Gaiseric led them across the Mediterranean, and overran the country. But however formidable they were in the field, they knew nothing about siege-craft, and the walled cities of Africa held out for a long time. What he could not achieve by force of arms, Gaiseric resolved to do by treachery. He made peace with the Empire, and lulled the Romans into a false sense of security; then suddenly, without any declaration of war, he attacked and captured Carthage, the capital, and sacked it. With this great seaport in his hands, Gaiseric could dictate terms; the Emperor had to recognize him as an independent monarch, ruler of the better part of North Africa; the large fleet which he built made him the controller of the Western Mediterranean. The Vandals methodically consolidated their power in Africa by dispossessing the former landlords, assiduously demolishing the fortifications of the towns, and killing or sometimes enslaving the Catholic clergy.

ATTILA AND THE HUNS

Meanwhile, a yet more terrible enemy had appeared in the north. The Huns, who had driven the Goths across the Danube, had been the main reason for the recent German migrations. For twenty years, they had extended their dominion over practically the whole of Germany; a leader, Attila, had arisen among them, and given their scattered tribes some sort of unity, which made them much more formidable than they had been. Such German tribes as had not fled before them were pressed into their service; the Eastern Empire was thankful to avoid invasion by paying them tribute. The Western Empire at first tried to live on as friendly terms as it could with this power that was the enemy of all mankind, and even used it as an ally in crushing the Burgundians of South-East Gaul. Eventually both parts of the Empire grew tired of trying in vain to satisfy demands which continued to grow more and more pressing.

When war broke out in 451 Attila determined to break the Western Empire first, and from the central camp on the plain of Hungary half a million men set out to conquer Gaul. Roman and Goth stood side by side to meet them; where the Huns were concerned, the Western Empire was still a reality. At Châlons, near the spot where in the summer of 1918 the last German offensive was broken by the Allied forces of France, Britain and America, the Romans and the Goths defeated the power of the Huns. Attila withdrew from Gaul; and though he invaded Italy in the next year, he did not stay. Why he withdrew from Italy is an unsolved problem; perhaps his army was getting out of hand; at any rate, after his death, which occurred two years later, his vast dominion broke up. His German subjects revolted, and there was no great personality who could enforce their obedience. The danger to Christendom was at an end.

VANDALS, WEST GOTHS AND ARIANISM

But the troubles of the Western Empire continued. No sooner had the Huns departed than the Vandals again made themselves felt. Gaiseric held an immensely strong position in the Mediterranean; on one occasion, he actually invaded Italy and took Rome, subjecting it to a fortnight's plundering. For twenty years after this, the Western Empire was at his mercy. Even the Eastern Empire was not free from the attacks of his squadrons, and its Emperor was glad to come to terms. When Gaiseric died, full of years, in 477, he held the whole of North Africa, and all the islands of the Western Mediterranean, except Sicily, which he sold back to the Western Empire. But after his death, the Vandal kingdom became less powerful; it depended too much on his own personality, as that of the Huns had depended on Attila's; and apart from that, it began to suffer from raids by the Berbers from the mountains to the south.

After the repulse of Attila, the happiest part of the Western Empire was that ruled by the West Goths. They had expanded into Spain and repaired some of the damage done by the Vandals; but the seat of their rule was at Toulouse, in Gaul, and it was in Gaul that comparative civilization mainly flourished. Within limits, the old Roman landowners and landholders were allowed to continue in possession, at any rate of part of their land; on the whole, the relations between the old and the new inhabitants were amicable. The Goths had some appreciation of Roman culture; many of them learned Latin, and the court of the Gothic king became one of the last refuges of Latin literature. But there was one important fact which prevented the fusion of the two peoples: the Goths were Arians, the Romans were Catholics.

At first there was mutual tolerance; the Catholic Church continued undisturbed. Most of its Bishops were men of high birth, social distinction and considerable wealth; in the intervals of their religious duties, they spent a pleasant cultured life, reading and discussing

Latin literature with each other in country houses, writing letters, sending little poems to each other, as if nothing had happened in the last hundred years to alter the face of the world. They had, too, a social conscience, and spent a good deal of their wealth on the relief of distress among the poorer classes. So long as the clergy did not engage in politics, the Catholic and the Arian Churches existed side by side without much quarrelling; but when, towards the close of the century, the Catholics began to interfere in administration, the Arian resistance was naturally supported by the Gothic government, and a bitter persecution followed which effectively prevented the gradual fusion of the two races and the growth of a strong and enduring state in the South of Gaul.

If Gaul was comparatively happy during the second half of the fifth century, Italy was supremely miserable. From the double humiliation of Attila's invasion and the Vandal sack of Rome, the Western Empire never recovered. As in the third century, Emperor succeeded Emperor with distressing rapidity; but they were mere puppets, and the real power was in the hands of barbarian leaders who cast themselves for the part of Stilicho, without having Stilicho's ability. The last Emperor of the West was the son of one of these upstarts, a boy named, inappropriately enough, Romulus Augustulus; when his father was defeated and killed by a leader of barbarian mercenaries named Odovacar, the young Emperor was deposed, for Odovacar saw no point in keeping up what had by this time become a farcical pretence of the Emperor's personal authority.

THE BARBARIAN KINGS

So the long line of Emperors in the West came to an end, and Italy passed under the rule of a barbarian king. There was no formal break with tradition; Odovacar recognized the Eastern Emperor at Constantinople as his overlord, and the Eastern Emperor recognized him as the ruler of Italy within the Roman Empire. This was mere theory, but a time was to come when an Eastern Emperor tried to turn the theory into a reality. Whatever the exact position of their rulers, the people in Italy suffered; it made no difference to them whether their nominal Emperor was an insignificant boy at Ravenna or a remote potentate at Constantinople; it was on the policy of a barbarian chieftain that they depended for the safe convoy of their food-supplies, and for a barbarian chieftain that they had somehow to raise the money to provide the sinews of war.

With eastern Britain passing under the rule of heathen Saxon tribes, Gaul divided up into the Frankish and Gothic kingdoms, Spain under the rule of the West Goths, Africa and the islands in the hands of the Vandals, and Italy in those of a barbarian soldier, it seemed that, in the West, nothing remained of the Empire to which, less than a hundred years before, the vigour and statecraft of the Emperor Theodosius had looked like giving a new lease of life.

Actually two things did remain. Throughout all the subsequent history of Europe, the ideal of unity can be traced; it has never been fully realized, but it has been at the back of the minds of many of the great figures of history. In the fifth century, the Empire in the West broke up, because its rulers were incapable of carrying it on in face of successive difficulties and disasters. There was no repudiation of the idea of the Empire, and, in a vague sort of way, men have been trying to restore it ever since.

Secondly, there remained the Christian Church. When Alaric sacked Rome in 410, there were those who thought that the end of the world had come. Some of them went further, and said that it was all the fault of the Christians. To them an answer was provided by one of the great books of the ancient world, " The City of God ", by St. Augustine of Hippo in North Africa. St. Augustine was an elderly man when Alaric sacked Rome; he had been born before the Goths were admitted to the Empire by Valens, when the Roman world still seemed secure. In his autobiography, he tells of the wildness of his youth and his delight in the sensual pleasures which the Roman province of Africa provided; on a visit to Milan, he was converted, and returned to Africa to become priest and bishop, and to defend the Catholic Church against the attacks of the heretics.

TEACHINGS OF ST. AUGUSTINE

His writings were voluminous and sometimes confusing, but from them one doctrine stands out clear, the supremacy of God and the helplessness of man, who can achieve nothing without divine grace. There were, no doubt, defects in his teachings; if taken literally, they led to the conclusion that salvation belonged only to the fortunate who were chosen by God, and that the rest of mankind were condemned for no fault of their own. But the problem of free-will has never been solved by anyone, and Augustine cannot be blamed for failing where everyone else has failed.

The important thing is that he kept his head in the midst of disaster. He saw that, while the old dominion of the city of Rome was crashing about him, there remained another city, the City of God, whose citizens were joined together by no material ties, but by the recognition, in their life and thought, of eternal truths that no Goth or Vandal could affect. The pagan Roman Empire, he wrote, founded upon bloodshed and injustice, could not be expected to last for ever; the City of God, to be embodied in the Roman Church, was founded upon love and justice, and could not pass away. Thus, though he did not despair of the possibility that the Empire might become Christian in spirit as well as in name, he was not unduly perturbed when it began to look as if it was soon to come to an end. He was prepared to help to defend it against the Vandals, who were heretics, and actually met his death as an old man during the siege of his own city of Hippo; but the impression he gave was that it did not really much matter what happened to men in this life. Such an attitude might lead to despair, but courage can be born of despair; and it was due to the influence of such men as Augustine that, in the centuries of darkness and of violence that followed, the Gospel continued to be read, and men continued, in however imperfect a way, to worship Christ. The city of the Caesars had fallen; the true City of God could be seen only by the eye of faith; but there remained, for all to see, something that was called Christendom, the City of God upon earth.

CHAPTER 20

THE THREAT OF ISLAM TO DISUNITED CHRISTENDOM

EXCEPT for the Church, there was nothing stable left in the West. A barbarian general ruled in Italy, Vandals in Africa, Goths in South Gaul and Spain, Franks in North Gaul. Neither Odovacar's kingdom in Italy nor the West Gothic dominion was destined to last; there was nothing in common between them and the peoples they had conquered. They used their subjects not only to farm the land, but to administer the civil government; the subjects had no feeling of loyalty, and were prepared to tolerate, or even to welcome, a change of master. Permanence and stability were only to be found in the East, where there was still a Roman Emperor.

THE STRUGGLE BETWEEN CATHOLIC AND ARIAN

The first sign of weakening in the West Gothic kingdom was when the Burgundians, who, after their sufferings at Attila's hands, had been confined to the hill-country of Savoy, moved down into the Rhone valley. The West Goths came to terms with them, for they had a more formidable enemy to face. The Franks in the North were Catholics, and thus appeared to many of the subjects of the West Goths in the guise of deliverers; for though their conversion to Christianity was very recent, and their ideas of it crude, they were infinitely preferable to the Arian Goths, who were no longer tolerant of Catholics. The Frankish King, Clovis, was an able soldier and statesman, who prepared the way for his victories by astute diplomacy. He took his enemies one by one, and made them in turn his subjects or allies. When, in 507, the West Goths had to face him on the field of Poitiers, they had no allies; his victory was complete. Except for a corner in the North-West, where Keltic refugees from Britain had settled in the country that came to be known as Brittany, and in the extreme South, Clovis was supreme in Gaul.

For the men of Clovis's day, this ensured the triumph of the Catholic over the Arian faith. Even in Gothic Spain Arianism lingered on for less than a century. Henceforth there was only one religion in the West. But except in matters of faith, the Franks were farther from Roman civilization than the West Goths had been; they did not value the culture of Roman Gaul. Even the name of the country was changed; Gaul ceased to be, and was known, from this time on, as France, the land of the Franks. The victory of Clovis marked the end of the old civilization and the triumph of the Church of Rome. The creation of Augustus was dead; but men stumbled forward in the light of the vision which had been given to Augustine.

DIETRICH AND THE WEST GOTHS

In spite of many vicissitudes, the kingdom of Clovis, founded in alliance with the Catholic Church, lasted for 1200 years. Shortly before this, a new kingdom had arisen in Italy that was to have a life of only sixty years. Dietrich or Theodoric, was a chieftain of the East Goths or Ostrogoths, a tribe related to the West Goths, or Visigoths, of Gaul. Although, like all Goths, he was an Arian, he was invited by the Eastern Emperor to invade Italy and overthrow Odovacar, whose independent attitude was irksome to the court at Constantinople. Five years' fighting established the East Goths as masters of Italy; Dietrich set up his court at Ravenna, and ruled with undisputed sway from Sicily to north of the Alps. This new kingdom was very different from that of the Franks. In religion, it was Arian, but in its early stages it was tolerant of the Catholics. In other respects it was as Roman as Dietrich could make it. He himself was a rough Gothic soldier, as illiterate as most of his type; but, unlike Clovis, he recognized the superiority of the civilization which his military conquests had put under his control, and he respected and fostered everything Roman within his dominions. Once again, literature and art flourished in Italy; Dietrich had no understanding of them, but he encouraged those who had. The past greatness of Rome appealed to him; he had visions of restoring the Western Empire. The Goths in Spain recognized him as their overlord, and his alliance with the Vandals of Africa aimed at restoring unity in the Western Mediterranean. The South of Gaul he snatched from the Franks. But his ambitions were frustrated by the religious barrier; Catholic and Arian could not live at peace for long. A persecution of Arians in the Eastern Empire led to retaliation in Italy, and the unity of the new kingdom was broken. The future of the Western Empire was destined to lie with the Catholic Franks.

THE SPREAD OF MONASTIC LIFE

Dietrich was an unusual figure in this age of warfare. Most of the warrior heroes cared nothing for the arts of peace; it seemed as if literature and art might vanish off the face of the earth, or survive only behind the walls of Constantinople. But, while the ceaseless tramp of barbarian soldiers resounded up and down the roads that the Romans had made, there existed havens of peace and comparative security where men might retire from the world.

Christianity attracted men who felt the need of withdrawing from the temptations of the world and living in poverty and seclusion, to think about God and worship Him undisturbed. The practice, long prevalent among the Buddhists of the East, spread to the Christians of Egypt in the early fourth century. Numbers of men left the rich valley of the Nile to seek solitude in the desert, where each lived in his lonely cell, and saw his companions only when they met on Saturdays and Sundays for congregational worship. For the rest of the week, they meditated and prayed alone, doing just enough work at basket-making or linen-weaving to earn their scanty keep.

To some, the life of these hermits seemed useless, however pious their motives; they thought it valuable to withdraw from the world, but better to do so in company with other religiously minded men. These were the founders of the first Christian monasteries, in which men congregated to live the religious life. In these, more work was done; the settlements were organized to be self-supporting, and the day was divided into a strict routine of religious service, Bible study and manual labour. These two forms of monasticism continued to exist side by side; they both aimed at subduing the bodily desires; both enjoined plain living and abstention from marriage; but the hermits went farther in self-denial, even torturing themselves for the glory of God. It was in the monasteries, however, that the Christian virtue of charity was practised, and there can be little doubt that the life led there was more in accordance with the teaching of Christ.

Both forms spread rapidly round the Roman world, varying in popularity from country to country. In the East, the hermit's life found more favour, especially in Syria; there were many monasteries in Asia Minor, but their inmates tended more and more to give up works of charity and study, and to devote themselves, like the hermits, to continual prayer and meditation. In the West, the hermit's life had a great vogue, especially in Gaul; but there were monasteries as well, and it was in Italy that the idea arose of priests joining together to live the monastic life. In a monastery of this type, Augustine, while visiting Italy, first turned to religion; and it was this type of monasticism that he took back with him to Africa.

It was found in time that community life was more suitable than the hermit's for the West; but it was not until the beginning of the sixth century that a great man, who had tried both, came forward and boldly stated that community life was better in all respects. St. Benedict lived as a hermit in a cave, about forty miles from Rome; his fame spread, and disciples flocked to him to share his life. In time, he founded about a dozen monasteries, for which he established a uniform Rule of Life, which became the practice of nearly all the monasteries of Western Europe. He divided the day into periods of worship, work and study; he made much of charity; he enjoined self-denial, but not to the point of injury to health; and he laid great emphasis on obedience to the Abbot, the ruler of the monastery.

This element of discipline, utterly lacking in the life of the hermit, was of supreme importance; in the chaos that was spreading over the Western world, the monasteries served not only as storehouses of learning, but as models of the orderly conduct of life. In these early days, the monasteries were comparatively free from the attacks of barbarian soldiers, who could find nothing in them to loot; so they were a far more secure repository of civilization than the cities had been in the third century. Late in the sixth century, Benedict's own monastery was sacked by barbarians who happened to be Arians. The Benedictine monks found a refuge behind the walls of Rome, and from Rome, the centre of the Catholic faith, the Benedictine rule spread rapidly.

Women, as well as men, felt the urge to the monastic life. They came together in nunneries to keep the rule of Benedict. Vowing themselves to perpetual virginity, they spent their lives in worship and works of charity. The world owes them a great debt; it was only through them that the idea was kept alive that women can be educated. The schools for girls which were attached to the convents or the nunneries at least secured that the wives of the warrior rulers of the West should not all be completely illiterate.

THE BEGINNING OF THE PAPACY

The walls of Rome did more than shield fugitive Benedictines. With the breakdown of the Empire in the West, and the practical separation of Western from Eastern Europe, travel in Mediterranean lands became more difficult and dangerous. This raised grave problems in the government of the Church. The councils that had met, in the last two centuries, to settle problems of doctrine and administration, could no longer meet so easily. To resolve their difficulties, churchmen began to look for an authority which they could all accept. For many reasons, this position of authority was claimed by the Bishop of Rome. Rome had been the centre of the world and of that civilization of which the Church was the sole heir in the West. It had been the scene of the martyrdoms of St. Peter and St. Paul, and it began to proclaim itself the centre of Christianity. Christ had said: " Thou art Peter and upon this rock (*petra*) I will build my church". The Bishops of Rome held that St. Peter was the first of their line, and from him they claimed to derive the right to rule the Church. In the West the claim came to be acknowledged. In the East the Patriarchs of Constantinople refused allegiance to the Bishops, or Popes of Rome, as they began to be called. So commenced the drift apart that was to culminate in an open breach between the two.

At first, the Popes claimed only spiritual dominion; but at the beginning of the seventh century a new phase began. Gregory the Great was a son of one of the old noble families of Rome; he had great wealth and still greater ability. While still a young man he had reached the highest civil office in the city; he was an acknowledged leader of society. Yet the same instinct which prompted his mother to go into a nunnery on her husband's death, made Gregory himself give up his career in the world; he turned his palace into a monastery, living according to the Benedictine rule. The Church had need of his statesmanlike qualities; he was called to be the right-hand man of the Pope, and then became Pope himself. His position was unique. He was Bishop of Rome; the churches of the West owned his supremacy. He was a Benedictine; everywhere Benedictines respected him, and were proud of him. By planting Benedictine monasteries he started the great missionary movement that was to convert the barbarians of the North. He was a Roman noble; the citizens of Rome looked to him as a leader; he was thus able to build up a Papal state which claimed and exercised the government of the country round Rome and acquired a special importance.

JUSTINIAN AT CONSTANTINOPLE

The Papal state was important for the independence of the Church. For, by now, the tolerant and inoffensive government of the East Goths was over. They had had one fault: they were Arians; as their cousins in Gaul had fallen before the Catholic Franks, they fell before the power of the Orthodox Empire of the East.

The Emperors at Constantinople had long been preoccupied with their own affairs, and quite incapable of coping with the advance of the barbarians in the West. They had had to face the Persian menace, guard the Danube frontier, and preserve order in their own noisy capital. In the West they played off one set of barbarians against another; it was at their invitation that the East Goths first came to Italy. But, in 527, there came to the throne a man named Justinian, who dreamed of reviving the old glories of the Roman Empire; and he was aided and inspired by his wife Theodora, who proved herself in social grace, in wisdom, and, most important of all, in courage, to be vastly superior to the other women of her time.

THE CONQUESTS OF BELISARIUS

Besides a great consort, Justinian had a great lieutenant. Belisarius was a military genius. He started his career as a general with successes against the Persians; conquest of them was impossible, but he did enough to force them to an agreed peace and enable the armies of the Empire to be sent to the West. The Vandals of Africa were his first victims; Belisarius was completely successful, and the Vandals disappeared from history, leaving as their sole memorial the name of a Spanish province through which they had passed more than a century before—Andalusia. Then came the turn of the East Goths. Belisarius captured Sicily and the South of Italy; but the Goths counter-attacked, and there followed a Thirty Years' War. The Catholics of Italy supported the invaders. The struggle took on the usual features of civil war, in which each side tried to exterminate the other; the most appalling atrocities were committed: the population of Italy was cut down: the countryside was ruined: and the East Goths disappeared. The South of Gaul fell into the hands of the Franks. But Africa and Italy had both been restored to the Roman Emperor.

It was a hollow victory. Africa was held, but was subject to continual attacks from the Berbers of the interior and Moors of the West. Belisarius had to build a great chain of protecting fortresses, and the defence of Africa was a constant drain on the exchequer of the Empire. Italy was lost almost at once. A fierce barbarian people, called the Lombards, swept down from Germany and settled in the country; they, too, were Arians, and remained so for another seventy years; and they were not so tolerant as the East Goths had been. But neither were they so well organized, and under the leadership of the Church, various cities remained fairly secure. The Imperial government was powerless; each city had to fend for itself. So Italy became divided up into little principalities and dukedoms, which were not reunited until nearly 1300 years had passed. In fact, the only power that still was able to command some sort of respect outside its own borders was that of the Roman Church under the Papal authority.

JUSTINIAN'S TRANSITORY AND PERMANENT ACHIEVEMENTS

Justinian's policy ended in complete failure in Italy, and gained only partial success in Africa and in Spain, where he had won the South-Eastern corner from the West Goths. But the chief criticism of him is not that he failed to conquer the West completely and permanently, but that he ever tried. His forces were needed elsewhere. Constantinople itself was in a state of ferment. The centre of its quarrels was the great Circus of the city, where passions rose high over the chariot-races that absorbed the minds of a people which remained unmoved by the fortunes of the imperial armies in the West. Rival factions—the Blues and the Greens—yelled themselves hoarse in support of their favourite charioteers, like crowds at a modern Cup-tie; but unlike the latter, they carried this rivalry of sport into every branch of life. Even in the religious discussions which were the chief interest of the theologically-minded East, the Blues and the Greens took sides; serious men who were genuinely concerned to reach a right opinion about the nature of God must often have been appalled at the violence of their supporters, who decided these questions for themselves in the light of their views on racing. The lunatic attitude of the population on one occasion nearly drove Justinian to leave his capital; it was the courage of Theodora that persuaded him to stay and quell the rioters.

On the frontiers, too, Justinian had his troubles. The peace that he signed with Persia, before embarking on his Western adventures, did not last for long; at the height of the struggle with the East Goths, he had to face a large-scale invasion of Asia Minor, and in the end to buy the Persians off with an annual tribute. From the North came new enemies. The Slavs, who moved gradually into the lands north of the Danube, were a comparatively minor nuisance; the Mongolian tribes who came after them, and conquered and enslaved them, were the real menace. Far away in Asia, the Mongolian Turks were expanding, pushing ahead of them other Mongolians, Huns and Avars and Bulgarians; both Persia and the Eastern Empire suffered from the raids of these fugitives, who on occasion swept up to the very walls of Constantinople. Justinian, with his chief forces engaged in the West, could not hope to defeat the invaders in the field; he relied partly on diplomacy, which consisted mainly in buying them off, and partly on a chain of fortresses, like that in Africa, which, by their lack of siege-craft, they could not take. But the fortresses could not prevent untold damage being done to the countryside, and the money payments exhausted the exchequer. Only the growing importance of Constantinople itself saved the Empire from bankruptcy.

Yet, for all his unwisdom in foreign policy, Justinian has left an honoured name behind him. It is true that the sensible laws which he passed to check the corruption of his officials failed in their purpose; it is true that he could not settle the religious dissensions that were always bringing his people to blows. But he has two achievements to his credit. He built the lovely Cathedral of Santa Sophia at Constantinople, and, using the lesser work of his predecessors, he collected into one great system all the laws and legal precedents that had grown up with the Roman state. The days were at hand when the world was to have little use for law; Justinian secured that it should not be altogether lost, and that, when men should grow tired of the rule of force, they should find in his book the record of a better way. The Empire of Justinian has long passed away; yet St. Sophia still stands, though it is no longer a Christian church; and study of the text-books that were compiled in the reign of the Emperor Justinian still forms part of the training of every lawyer in Europe.

FRESH RELIGIOUS CONTROVERSIES

Under Justinian's successors the religious quarrels which he had tried to check began to break up the Empire. The Council of Nicaea in Constantine's reign had pronounced against the Arians; henceforth, the Catholic faith contained the definite belief that Christ was divine. But a new question had arisen; if Christ was divine, was there any element of humanity in Him at all? All Justinian's efforts failed to settle the question; it divided faction against faction, province against province. Constantinople and Asia Minor pronounced for the Dual Nature of Christ; Egypt and Syria for the Single Nature. The divisions of the Empire proved the opportunity of its enemies; its rulers after Justinian were unable to deal with the situation. Barbarians attacked in the North, the Persians in the East; the one thing that kept the Empire in existence was its sea-power, which prevented its enemies from joining hands across the Bosphorus. When, in 610, Heraclius, the son of the Imperial ruler of Africa, seized the throne, he had to spend ten years in reorganizing the forces of the Empire; by the time he was ready, the Persians had conquered Syria and Egypt, and the barbarians from the North were encamped beneath the still-impregnable walls of the capital.

Heraclius did well. In his reign, the barbarians gave up hope and retired; the Persians were driven back and their own country invaded; Syria and Egypt were recovered by the Imperial armies. But reconquest did not mean restoration of loyalty; Heraclius failed in his frantic attempts to settle the religious controversy by an ingenious compromise; Egypt and Syria had no more love for the Emperor than they had had for the King of Persia. With the Pope in the West claiming supreme authority over the Church, the Emperor in the East doing the same, and Egypt and Syria repudiating him, the ranks of Christendom were fatally divided. Yet it was just at this moment that they had need to be closed. For a new and mighty power of the Spirit was about to arise out of Arabia.

THE ARABIAN WORLD

This land of sandy deserts and green oases had long supplied fighting men for the countries to the north of it. From there, in immemorial times, had come men of Semitic speech, to be absorbed by the civilizations of Mesopotamia, Syria and Palestine. More recently it had become a closed country; Alexander's army had passed by it on the north; an adventurous Roman of the days of Augustus, who had penetrated some way along one of its trade-routes, had been glad to get away in safety, without learning much about it.

The south-west of Arabia was a green fertile land, known to the ancient world as Arabia the Blessed; but in the north and centre there were miles and miles of desert sand and rock, broken only at intervals by oases. The country is over 1200 miles long; a few miles inland from a point about midway on its Red Sea coast, was the city of Mecca, from which two great trade-routes ran northwards, to reach the Roman border at Palmyra, Zenobia's city, and at Petra in Southern Palestine, a city whose rose-red ruins are one of the wonders of the world. To these places the merchants travelled on their camels, going in companies for safety's sake.

In the extreme north, Christianity had filtered through in a very debased form; and the Jewish faith was also known. To the south, Christian missionaries had been sent from Constantinople, in the fourth century, and had made some headway; in the time of Justinian, there had been a persecution of Christians by the Jews, and the Christian Emperor of Abyssinia had established a short-lived dominion over the country. But in the seventh century, Arabia was nominally under the rule of Persia; in reality, it was under no rule at all. Fierce warrior tribes inhabited the interior, living a hand-to-mouth existence, frequently fighting with each other, and caring nothing for Persian or Christian or Jew. Their own religion was a low form of idolatry; it did not perhaps satisfy them, but there was nothing in it which did not square with their ideas. Chief among the objects of their worship was the famous black stone of Mecca contained in the Kaaba, to which men flocked every year.

MOHAMMED'S TEACHING

Mecca became famous for something much more wonderful than the Kaaba. For there was born, in 570, Mohammed. Mohammed started his career as an agent in a business belonging to a rich widow; as other young men have done, he married his employer. The marriage was happy, the business prospered; but Mohammed was no ordinary business man. To the surprise of some of his friends, and the scandal of others, he began to see visions; gradually there came to him the conviction that the truth about God and the world was being revealed to him through the archangel Gabriel. He could not read or write; but when he went into a trance, he used to dictate what he saw to his friends, who wrote it down on the first thing that came to hand, whether it was a palm-leaf or a stone or a shoulder-bone of mutton or an odd scrap of leather. These records were carefully preserved in a box by one of the prophet's wives, and the collection became known as the Koran; the central doctrine of the Koran was this: "There is one God (Allah), and Mohammed is his prophet."

To the fanatical idolaters of Arabia, this was subversive doctrine, and Mohammed's followers suffered persecution and ridicule. He himself was left alone at first; riches and social position were an excuse for madness. As his influence increased, he found himself growing more and more unpopular, and in 622 he fled along the Petra road to Medina, some 250 miles north of Mecca. Here the atmosphere was more favourable; the people were less conservative, and knew something of other religions than idol-worship; there was a Jewish colony, and Christianity had been heard of. Medina was racked with internal strife; everybody was heartily tired of it, and wanted a leader to end it. They welcomed Mohammed and his ideas; the Jews were glad to find an Arab who believed in one God; the Arabs were glad to find a man who could unite them.

The flight to Medina—the Hejira—was the turning-point of Mohammed's career. He stayed there for nine years, elaborating the details of his religion. The Koran grew apace; revelation followed revelation. He built the first mosque, or house of prayer, after the fashion of the Jewish synagogue; five times a day, at stated hours, his followers were to offer prayers, wherever they were and whatever they were doing. But whatever the outcome, they must submit themselves to the will of Allah; this submission was called Islam, which became the title of the new religion. Rules of conduct were laid down. Strong drink was forbidden, a command which was not without its influence on the efficiency of Mohammedan armies in later years. Men were commanded to have several wives; this may have had the effect of increasing the numbers of Islam, but it certainly served to debase the status of women. In the Christian world, the wife was the honoured consort of her husband; in the Mohammedan, she was one of a number who competed for his favours, and could be divorced by a single word from him. This, if nothing else, made any union between Christendom and Islam impossible. But if Mohammed rejected Christianity, he did not reject Jesus of Nazareth. He accepted the truth of the Jewish scriptures and the necessity of Jewish practices, such as circumcision and abstinence from pork, maintaining that his own religion was really that of Abraham.

FIRST MILITARY SUCCESS OF ISLAM

Those nine years at Medina were a time of intense excitement. At any moment, a new revelation might be forthcoming; the people of the city were wild with desire to spread the new truths that had been vouchsafed to them through the mouth of the prophet. And he was not only a prophet; he was a leader in war, and Mecca was their enemy. The struggle between the two cities was long and bitter, but in the end, religious zeal gave Medina the victory. In 630, Mohammed captured Mecca; Islam enjoyed the first of many military triumphs. One concession only to the old idolatry did Mohammed make: the Kaaba was admitted into the faith as an object of veneration, and Mecca became the holy city of Islam. Mohammed, though he continued to live at Medina, went to Mecca every year on pilgrimage, and enjoined his followers to do the same. Few Mohammedans today can do this; but it is an inspiration with all of them, and all over the Moslem world, at the hours of prayer, the faces of the faithful are turned towards Mecca and the Kaaba.

Mohammed did not live to see the great triumphs of the forces which he had let loose. When he died, at the age of 62, Islam had only just made contact with the Empire; an embassy which he had sent to Heraclius had been treated with amused contempt, and an affray on the Palestine frontier had resulted in the triumph of the Imperial troops. But Mohammed had laid his plans, and his successors were swift to execute them.

The first Caliph, or Representative of the Prophet, was his father-in-law, who rode forth to battle at the head of a host, united in its desire to spread the faith, and wildly excited at the prospect of easy plunder. One year sufficed to complete the conquest of Arabia; then they turned north to invade Palestine. The shock to the Empire and to Persia was intense; from the land whence merchants used to bring the luxuries of the East, there suddenly appeared fierce and ruthless warriors, who cared only for their outlandish religion. They were utterly unexpected, and, before any resistance could be organized, they were in possession of Syria, had dealt a death-blow to

Persia, and were pouring into Egypt. When Heraclius died in 642, his Empire, so hardly restored, was gradually crumbling once again.

Of all its losses, Alexandria was the most serious. It was the second city of the Empire, a centre of civilization, the home of a famous library, and a most important seaport. In the hands of the Emperors, it could serve as a base of operations for the recovery of the coast-towns of Syria; in the hands of the Moslems, it might become a base for an attack by sea on Constantinople itself. So it was at Alexandria that the first counter-attack was delivered. Unfortunately for the Empire, all loyalty had vanished in Egypt; the population preferred the Arabs as the lesser known of two evils. Although one of Heraclius' successors recovered Alexandria, he could not hold it; the Arabs fastened their grip upon Egypt, and rode onwards to win the province of Africa. Here resistance was stronger; the Berbers as well as the Imperial forces had to be encountered; the city of Carthage proved a hard nut to crack. The Arab advance could only be delayed, it could not yet be stopped; by the end of the century the work of conquest of North Africa was complete.

THE ARAB PLAN OF CONQUEST

The Arabs had a definite plan of conquest. With all its weaknesses, the Empire was the chief bulwark of Christendom, the chief barrier in the way of the spread of Islam. So Constantinople must be captured. The rulers of Syria, who were in the vanguard of the attack, naturally claimed the government of the Moslem world; the rulers at Mecca opposed them with the force of tradition. This dispute saved Christendom. It took two civil wars to establish the supremacy of Damascus; by then, the Empire had had a breathing-space in which to reorganize. The Emperors who succeeded Heraclius were not men of genius, but, when they had the chance, they were vigorous; and they were assisted by a piece of good fortune. A Syrian scientist discovered a new weapon, which he called Greek fire; it seems to have been a kind of inflammable liquid which could be thrown into enemy ships and made to ignite there.

By the end of the seventh century, the rift in the Moslem world was closed. The southern part of the old Empire of Rome was in the hands of Mohammedans, determined to destroy what remained in the north. At either end of the Mediterranan, at the Straits of Gibraltar and in Asia Minor, they faced their Christian foes. There was no unity in Christendom. East and West were drifting farther and farther apart. The Empire was forgetting its connection with the Latin world. Its inhabitants spoke Greek, its laws were in Greek; its capital, Constantinople, was beginning to be spoken of again by its old Greek name Byzantium. In the West was a new world altogether; the Latin Church was the chief survival of the Roman Empire; apart from that, there were the separate " succession states", the West Goths of Spain—now good Catholics, the mightier power of the Franks in France, and the Lombard and other petty states of Italy. All these acknowledged the Church of Rome; but they were more barbarian than Roman in their manner of life.

CHAPTER 21

THE ACHIEVEMENT OF ROME

So the Empire of Augustus became a thing of the past. The unity of the Mediterranean world was gone. The seaways that Pompey had cleared were once again the hunting-ground of pirates; the roads that the legions had built passed over the frontiers of a disunited world. The spread of Christianity had owed much to the ability of men like St. Paul to travel in safety from land to land, and to the fact that everyone in the Empire could speak Latin or Greek. Now all that was changed; in the Eastern Empire, Greek still held its own, but in the West, Latin was becoming merely the language of lawyers, priests and monks. Ordinary people were beginning to use the dialects derived from Latin, which have become, in modern times, the Romance languages, Italian and Spanish, Portuguese, Provençal and French. In Brittany, Cornwall and Wales, where the Saxon invaders did not penetrate, the old Keltic tongues continued to be used; they survive to-day as Breton and Welsh, together with their sister-languages of the unconquered regions, the Gaelic of the Scottish Highlands and the Erse of Ireland. To the east of the River Rhine were spoken Teutonic languages, and the Saxon invaders brought this form of speech with them when they settled in Britain.

SERIOUSNESS OF THE ROMAN CHARACTER

What was the secret of Rome's greatness, and of her fall? Her own literature provides the answer. The great period of Roman letters begins at the time of the conquest of Greece, when there was an awakening of the mind among the Roman people. Greek literature served as a model; but something genuinely Roman was produced. Horace copied the metres of the Greek lyric poets, and though he missed some of their fire, he added a neatness that they had not possessed; the Roman love of order shaped his work. Virgil took his cue from Homer, but he showed in his epic a serious purpose, a majestic pessimism about the lot of mankind, combined with a superb confidence in the destiny of Rome, which sprang from the national qualities that defeated Hannibal. There was lightness, even frivolity, in some of Latin literature, but the dominant note was seriousness. Even Satire, the one branch of literature that the Romans invented, in which amusement was the original object, was turned into an instrument of castigation for the follies of the age.

For it was character, not cleverness, that brought the early Romans through their ordeals. They conquered Italy because they refused to say die. Veii was impregnable because of its moat; they drained the moat. The Gauls sacked Rome; the Romans rebuilt it, and saw to it that the Gauls should not get there again. Hannibal beat three armies in the field; they raised new armies, and wore him out by waiting. No sooner was this peril over than a crisis arose in the East; they did not hesitate to meet the danger half-way. Even the civil wars of the last century B.C. gave the enemies of Rome no respite; nearly all the rival leaders—Marius, Sulla, Pompey and Caesar—added something to her dominion. Then came the great work of Augustus, who recalled the Romans from civil strife to a sense of their destiny; under his leadership, they consolidated what they had won.

DISCIPLINE AND LOYALTY

The seriousness of purpose which achieved the ordered government of the first two centuries A.D., the Romans called "gravity". The writers of the early Empire complained that it had been undermined by the influx of other races. To some extent this was true; much of Nero's silliness, for instance, can be traced to an indiscriminate admiration for all things Greek. But to us it is more remarkable how far the Romans succeeded in passing on their tradition to their partners in the Empire. The spirit that succeeded in preserving the Republic after the disastrous Battle of Cannae was manifested to the full by the Spaniards Trajan and Hadrian, the African Septimius Severus, the Illyrian Aurelian and the Spaniard Theodosius.

Allied with this "gravity" was another virtue called "piety". This meant not so much care for religious observances, though it often included that, but loyalty to the family and to the state (regarded as a large family). In early Rome, the father of the family was an unchallenged despot; he had power of life and death over his children, and where the honour of the family was concerned, he did not hesitate to use it. The stern discipline of his childhood did much to mould the character of the Roman; it might repress his imagination, but it made for courage and perseverance.

After the reign of Marcus Aurelius, these qualities began to fail. With its man-power reduced by the burden of taxation and the ravages of plague and civil war, the Empire had to admit barbarians to fill its ranks more quickly than it could civilize them. There was no sudden change, but a gradual debasement of the Roman virtues. There were men of serious purpose still, and happy families, but they were fewer; there was less that seemed worth preserving, and less will to preserve it.

Yet much remained of the work of Rome. The city itself still stood, ruled over by the Popes. Nor was it the only visible memorial of past greatness. The architects of the cities of the Empire had built well. Italians still worship in churches of the fourth century; the cities of the South of France are adorned by the triumphal arches of Roman Emperors; the vast palace of Diocletian contains within it a large part of the Yugo-Slavian town of Split. Except where a fanatically anti-Roman power, like that of Islam, occupied the country, city life continued, though at a lower level. In the course of ages, many buildings decayed or were pulled down, and later inhabitants often abandoned the Roman lay-out of the streets; but the town was still a town, with a Roman or even earlier lineage.

WHAT WE OWE TO ROME

We owe more to the Roman architect than mere buildings: we owe an architectural tradition. When the Romans adopted the arch from the Etruscans, they opened up possibilities of which the Greeks had never dreamed. They were incapable of the chaste beauty and the exquisite decoration of the temples of Athens; but they could span wider gaps and therefore build larger buildings than the Greeks; and the vault and the dome, the companions of the arch, enabled them to roof-in vast spaces. The cost of building would have confined their skill, had it not been for their own invention of concrete, which they faced with stone, and their use of brick. With these advantages, they were able to proceed to the great works of Imperial times, the Colosseum, the Pantheon, the great aqueducts and the public baths. These were an example of magnificence to the architects of later ages; a more continuous tradition is to be seen in the development of the churches of Christendom. The typical basilica, or law-court, of a Roman city consisted of a long, narrow building, rounded at one end and with slight projections from the sides near that end, where stood the platform from which the barristers could speak; in these features can be seen the origin of the nave, the apse and the transepts of a Christian church as known to us to-day.

Although the fortress and the castle superseded the pleasant villa of the Romans, it was not without its influence on architecture; the courtyard house survived in the monastery cloisters. In the towns a less obvious legacy can be observed. In Roman times streets consisted of rows of houses, several stories high, carried in front on a succession of arches; the front wall of the ground floor was set back, and thus an arcade was formed to serve as a shaded path for pedestrians. This design, still common in Italy, and found in England at Chester, has been modified in most places by the filling in of the arches with glass to make shop-windows.

But Rome did more than teach Europe the use of bricks and mortar. She created the conditions that made possible the missionary effort of the early Church. She bequeathed to the world a system of law. She not only created a literature from which, nearly a thousand years later, the great revival of the intellect was to take its inspiration; she preserved the still greater literature of Greece. Most important of all, she left behind her the memory of a united world.

PART IV
THE STORY OF PERSIA

CHAPTER 22

FROM OLD ELAM TO ALEXANDER THE GREAT

THE tale of man's development has led us westward from the river valleys of Euphrates and Nile, first to the little cities of Greece, and then to the empire of Rome. We have seen how the achievement of the East influenced the life of the West. The Greek proclaimed reason as the guide of life, but he built many of his scientific triumphs on the knowledge stored up by the Egyptian and the Chaldean. His commerce followed the routes made before him by Cretan, Babylonian, Assyrian and Phoenician. The bright gods of Olympus, the rustic gods of Italy, and the state deities of Rome lost their hold on the Western world, just as the old nature-gods ceased to satisfy the East. But it was from the Semitic-speaking lands that the new religions came to take the place of outworn faiths that had already lost their fervour and ability to hold converts.

In them lay the gift of proselytizing, and their teachers were eager to win converts. We have read how two great creeds came from the tiny land of Palestine, and a third from the desert wastes of Arabia. Even in government and administration, first Macedon and then Rome felt the influence of the East. Both in Greece and Italy, as the republican tradition gradually lost its power, men accepted the unchecked rule of an emperor, whom they worshipped with semi-divine honours, just as men had done in Egypt, Sumer, Akkad, Babylon, Assyria and Persia for unremembered centuries.

THE LAND OF IRAN

Before we follow the struggle between Islam and Christendom, we must turn to Asia and the records of Persia, India, the countries of the Turks and the Chinese, and the Islands of Japan, to see the different modes of life men made for themselves there. Since the Stone Ages all of them had had some sort of connection with their Western neighbours. Sumeria was closely linked in its earliest records to the peoples who inhabited the south-west end of the Iranian tableland, and the two countries may have formed part of an early civilization which stretched across the width of Turkestan to China. But their fortunes were very different. Existence came easily in the broad plains of Mesopotamia, as long as its water system was kept in being. The highlander who dwelt on the eastern boundary faced conditions of climate and geography which had the result of turning his life away from the flourishing cities of the plain.

The Iranian tableland lies south of the Caucasus and the Caspian Sea, and is nearly encircled by two long mountain ranges, which branch outward from the heights of Armenia. The Elburz range at its eastward end presents a formidable barrier to any advance from the north along the shores of the Caspian; when it dwindles down into foothills, barren steppes carry on the line to the outposts of Hindu Kush. The Zagros range sweeps in a south-easterly direction towards the Persian Gulf, splitting into numerous parallel folds along the eastern frontier of Babylonia; at its southern end it loses height, and gradually falls away into the marshes that lie between the sea and the alluvial plain. But at this south-west corner, where its mountain barrier fails, Iran is protected by the vile climate of the coastland. On the south-east stretch the equally horrible wastes of Baluchistan, with the mountains of Afghanistan as a further obstacle.

Much of the eastern part of the tableland is salt desert, which holds few places fit for human habitation. The whole country is poorly supplied with rivers. Most of western Iran is more suitable for grazing than for ploughing; but there are stretches of fertile cornland, and the climate produces excellent fruit crops. Its mountains furnished supplies of gold, silver, copper and lead, besides much-prized stones, such as obsidian and diorite.

The circle of mountain and desert sets the country apart from its neighbours, and gives continuity to its history. But Iran has never been entirely isolated. There have always been well-marked lines of communication between the Zagros valleys and the Caucasus, and between Hamadan and the Baghdad district. Traders and invaders have used these paths from the earliest days, and the tableland has been the connecting link between Mesopotamia and the Far East. Conquerors have come to it from east, north and west; but it has preserved its identity, and probably many of its inhabitants to-day are descended from races which won their livelihood from its soil during the Stone Ages.

ELAM AND MESOPOTAMIA

The inhabitants of the Iranian tableland seem to have learnt the use of copper at an early date; they wore it for ornament, even while stone tools served them for all ordinary purposes. They were clever potters, and the *tell* or mound which covers the ancient city of Susa under 120 feet of earth and rubbish has provided many examples of delicate, painted ware. The craftsmen who made paint and used the potter's wheel with such skill seven thousand years ago seem to have been of a mixed stock. The evidence of their skulls, some round and others long, and of their language, points to the conclusion that they were connected with the inhabitants of the Caucasus, as well as with the Dravidian tribes of India, of whom we shall read in a later section of this book. They grew corn, and tended their flocks of sheep and herds of long-horned cattle.

As time went on, city-states grew up in the south-west part of Iran, which was called Elam. The strongest city was Awan, though Susa was important for commerce and industry. The rich countries of the alluvial plain on the west proved an irresistible lure to the men of the mountain. The Elamites raided the Sumerians, and the annals of Lagash and other Sumerian cities tell of their soldiers marching victoriously into the Zagros valleys. But this warfare did not seriously interfere with the trade between the highlanders and the dwellers in the plain. Records have been found of Elamite commerce, in which women took their part; in fact, they seem to have enjoyed as much freedom as the Assyrian women did in later centuries. They owned property and went to law, and succession to the throne was largely through the female line. Although the chiefs of their many gods were male, the most popular deity seems to have been the mother-goddess, who brought fertility to the land.

After many centuries of struggle, the cities of Elam were beaten decisively by the great Akkadian conquerors, Sargon and Naram-Sin. Their soldiers carried back stores of metal from the Elamite mines and blocks of diorite to be set up in honour of the divine kings. The men of Susa and their neighbours began to adopt the Semitic speech, which they retained after hard-fighting Iranian tribes from the centre of the Zagros range had overwhelmed both Akkad and Susa itself. Elam recovered her prosperity, and carried on the old struggle with the plain, whose chief city had become Ur, with which we dealt in Part I.

But a fresh danger began to threaten from the north. Invaders came down from the Caucasus, bringing with them the horse from its home in the great Northern Flatland. It took two centuries for these Kassites to establish their power in north-west Iran. Their chieftains may have been part of the great movement of Aryan-speaking races which were drifting southward from their old grazing-grounds in the centuries round 2000 B.C.; some of these northern nomads went south-east to India, while others journeyed with the Hyksos hordes to plunder the Nile valley. Elam had passed under the rule of Hammurabi of Babylon; but, when the great law-giver was dead, neither Babylon nor Elam could stand against the new power of cavalry. The Kassites established their government in Hammurabi's capital, and held most of Mesopotamia for five centuries, during which they seem to have been overlords of Elam.

When the rise of Assyria and their own weakness sapped the rule of the Kassites, the Elamites again asserted themselves. At the beginning of the twelfth century B.C., an Elamite prince was placed on the throne of Babylon, and the stone recording Hammurabi's code was carried off as booty to the highlands. Towards the middle of the century the power of Susa reached its zenith in the reign of Shilhak-Inshushinak, the greatest of all the kings of Elam. He fought successfully both on Tigris and Euphrates, subdued the central Zagros, held the country down to the Persian Gulf and Persepolis, and fully earned his title of "Expander of Empire," by which he became known. He was a great builder, and used 'the riches, which commerce brought to Susa from all parts of his dominions, to raise temples to his country's gods. In particular, he honoured the local god of the capital, Inshushinak, whose temple was built of brick, set in bitumen, and was adorned with statues and trophies of Elamite victories. A bronze relief shows the soldiers who won those victories—bearded men, armed with bow and quiver, curved swords and maces, and wearing helmets with pointed visors, to protect the face. But with the death of Shilhak-Inshushinak the glory departed from Elam for three centuries. When its kings began to take a vigorous share in the struggle between the Assyrians and rebel Babylon, a new and dangerous enemy had already become dominant in north Iran.

THE COMING OF THE ARYANS

While the main body of northern, Aryan-speaking invaders, who swept down from Turkestan into Iran about 2000 B.C., pressed on to the Himalayas, smaller tribes settled in the west of the tableland. For many centuries they remained in separate groups, under the rule of petty chieftains. Gradually two races emerged from the ruck, and won leadership over the rest. They are known to us as Medes and Persians. They were good fighting horsemen, who moved swiftly and struck unexpectedly at the scattered cities of the older races. Gradually they became the strongest power in western Iran, the Medes holding the north and the centre, and the Persians passing southward, after leaving their name to districts east of Nineveh and Susa.

As the Aryan-speaking groups spread westward into the Zagros valleys, they learnt many of the customs and adopted many of the conveniences of the Elamite civilization. Some of their chieftains made themselves rulers of the old cities; but the majority went on living in villages. They did not accept the language or the gods of Elam. They kept their Aryan speech, and they continued to worship the gods of the open sky, as their ancestors had done when they roamed over the vast empty spaces of the Northern Flatland.

LIFE AND CUSTOMS OF THE MEDES

It was a long time before the Medes learnt that union under a strong central authority was necessary if they were to set up an enduring government over the Iranian tableland. By the middle of the ninth century B.C., they were in conflict with Assyria; but, good natural fighters as they were, they proved no match for the better discipline and equipment of the soldiers of Nineveh, as long as they maintained their life in tribes and villages. Eventually they built a capital, on the site of modern Hamadan, in a country admirably fitted for horse-breeding. Their main wealth still lay in their transport animals; Assyrian records tell of tribute of horses, mules and camels won from the Median kings, whose soldiers are shown wearing sheepskin cloaks and high boots and equipped with spears and wicker shields.

The Medes were hammered into a strong nation on the anvil of war. Not only had they to fight the older rulers of the Zagros cities and Assyrian kings, bent on raiding the plain of Hamadan for war-horses; they were faced by a barbarian enemy, who followed the path their ancestors had ridden twelve centuries before. The invasion of the wild hordes, who are known as Scythians and Cimmerians, constituted a threat to the peoples of Assyria, Iran and Syria.

CYAXARES AND CYRUS THE GREAT

When the storm-cloud from the north was finally scattered, they felt strong enough to resume the struggle with Nineveh. Assyrian man-power had been wasted by widely scattered campaigns in defence of their sprawling empire. For a time the Median effort failed. Ashur-bani-pal made Egypt his ally instead of his subject, raided western Media, defeated the Scythians, crushed the Babylonian rebels and exterminated the last native kings of Elam. But his successors were unequal to the struggle against Cyaxares, who united the Medes into a formidable nation. He rid himself of the Scythian danger, though we need not believe that his success was entirely due to making the barbarian chieftains drunk, as Herodotus suggests. He allied himself with Babylon, who had again asserted her independence, and married his granddaughter to the Babylonian prince, Nebuchad-nezzar. The Persians, who had gradually overrun most of Elam and spread south-eastward to the country round Persepolis, acknow-ledged his suzerainty. In 612 B.C. Nineveh fell before the armies of Media and Babylonia.

Cyaxares and Nebuchadnezzar had made themselves the greatest kings of the Near East; only Egypt and Lydia could pretend to dis-pute their claims. Twenty years after the capture of Babylon, Cyaxares conquered Armenia and seized the eastern half of Asia Minor. After some fighting with the Lydians, he acknowledged the river Halys as his western boundary. On the north, he pushed his dominions to the Elburz range. On the east, the wandering horse-men of Parthia accepted his claim of overlordship. In Elam and the south, the Persian princes were his vassals.

When Cyaxares died, it looked as if Media were destined to succeed Assyria as the great empire of western Asia. But his son, Astyages, proved unequal to his inheritance. During his long and peaceful reign, his grandson, the Persian prince Kyrash of Anshan, whom we know as Cyrus the Great, built up a formidable army from the southern Iranian tribes, who acknowledged his rule. Cyrus allied himself with the amiable archaeologist, Nabonidus, who ruled a dis-united Babylonia, and began to build a royal city at Pasargadae. His leadership attracted the Median generals, and, when his grandfather faced him in the field, many of them deserted to Cyrus. Medes and

Persians joined forces under a warrior, who could lead them to victory against any foe, and Cyrus the Achaemenid set forth on his amazing career of conquest.

The sixth century before Christ is one of the most important in history. It saw the final extinction of the ancient Mesopotamian kingdoms, the swift expansion of the Persian empire, the first contacts between Persians and Greeks, and the beginnings of the Roman republic. Commerce grew rapidly, as communications developed under the first three Persian rulers. Racial differences still continued, but thought passed more easily from land to land. There was a religious stirring in many countries far distant from one another. In China, Confucius and Lao Tse taught their different codes; Buddhism and Jainism began in India; Jeremiah proclaimed the doctrine of individual responsibility to the stricken nation of the Jews; and Zoroastrianism guided the thoughts of Persia's kings and princes.

CREED OF ZOROASTER

Whether Zoroaster himself lived in the sixth century we do not know. But there is no doubt of the influence of his teaching on the men who were bringing the old kingdoms under the sway of Iranian highlanders. Zoroaster believed in a supreme, impersonal god, Ahura Mazda or Ormuzd, the Lord of Great Knowledge, the Creator of the World. Opposed to Ahura Mazda was Ahriman, the spirit of Evil, the Lie. All men had a choice between true knowledge and the Lie, and as they chose, so would be their reward; "in perpetuity shall be the torment of the liars". Ahura Mazda is the spirit behind earth, sun, moon, stars, wind and rain, and his followers turn away from the idols of these, which men have made to worship. Zoroastrianism was soon linked with the ritual of the Magi, who became its priests, and taught that men's corpses should be exposed to the air and not buried. The old nature-religions also attached themselves to it; the name of Ahura Mazda was joined with Mithra, the unconquered Sun, whom the Aryan nomads had worshipped in their northern homes, and with Anaitis, who represented the ancient Elamite goddess of fertility.

The Persian kings, who followed Zoroaster's teachings, were necessarily opposed to idolatry. But in the early years of their conquests they did not allow this to make them intolerant. The rapidity of their success was largely due to their calling themselves the instruments of the older gods, whose cities they attacked. Their country of Parsa had few natural resources to account for their triumphs. Its cities had little farming land round them. Its fetid harbourless coast was no training ground for sailors. There were fertile valleys in the highlands, where the climate made for vigour and physical health; but Parsa itself could never support a big population. The Persian advance was due to the great fighting qualities of its Aryan-speaking horsemen and infantry, the leadership of its nobles, and, above all, the military genius of its earlier kings.

Cyrus claimed descent from Achaemenes, who seems to have reigned in Anshan or southern Elam, possibly as a vassal of the Medes. His fighting powers were joined to great diplomatic skill. In twelve years he conquered and annexed Media, Lydia, Babylonia, and Syria, and created the largest empire that had yet existed west of China. After the fall of Astyages, the Lydian king, Croesus, recognized the Persian menace, and formed a defensive alliance with Egypt, Babylonia and the Greek city-states along his coasts. Cyrus boldly forestalled the allies' attack, crossed the Halys, and captured the Lydian capital, Sardis, in 546 B.C. He left to his generals the task of making the Greek cities of Asia his subjects or his allies. Then he turned his attention to his former supporter, Nabonidus, whose archaeological interests had led him to interfere with the religious practices of his subjects. After a short campaign, Nabonidus was "weighed in the balance and found wanting", many of his subjects deserted him, and his kingdom was "divided and given to the Medes and Persians".

The fall of Babylon was ascribed by Cyrus to the Babylonian god, Marduk, who "delivered Nabonidus into his hand". The Persian king was tolerant of the religions of his new subjects, and even supported them from the royal revenues. He allowed the Jews of the Dispersion to go back to Palestine and rebuild the temple of Jehovah. Though he placed Persian nobles in office over conquered territories, he aimed at making his rule acceptable to the conquered.

THE PERSIAN EMPIRE

Egypt remained Cyrus's last formidable rival. But he had another urgent duty to perform, and he left the organization of the army, which was to attack the Pharaoh, to his son, Cambyses, whom he had made king of Babylon. Cyrus took up the inherited task of defending Iran and Mesopotamia from the northern nomads. He met his death in battle against these barbarians, and was buried at Pasargadae, where his tomb stands to-day.

Cambyses carried on the task of extending his empire. After killing his younger brother, whom he feared as a rival, he led his army against Egypt. The Pharaoh's allies deserted him, and his troops were completely routed by the Persians at Pelusium in 525. Cambyses had himself recognized as Pharaoh, and took a throne-name, which bound him to the Egyptian sun-god, Re. He pushed on into Ethiopia, but, after conquering the north, he was forced to retreat by difficulties of supply and news of rebellion in Iran. On his return from Ethiopia he seems to have reversed his policy of religious toleration and shown his contempt for Egyptian idolatry.

At Cambyses' death, the Persian empire had absorbed Egypt, Syria, Asia Minor, Mesopotamia and Iran; its boundaries stretched from Elephantine on the Nile and the Persian Gulf to the Black Sea and the Caspian on the north, and from the Mediterranean to the deserts round the Oxus. But rebellion at the centre threatened to destroy the work of Cyrus and Cambyses. Fortunately another descendant of Achaemenes, Darayavaush or Darius, was equal to the situation. He crushed the rebels after hard fighting. Neither Egypt nor Lydia wavered in their new allegiance, and, after restoring order with vigorous brutality, Darius turned northward to deal with the nomad menace. It was probably to attack the Scythians in their homeland that he led the first Persian inroad into Europe. The Greeks of the Asiatic coast towns helped him with their ships, and it was largely through them that he and his army were not cut off on the steppes north of the Danube. The campaign led to no tangible result, except the annexation of Thrace. Darius was more successful at the other end of his empire, where he imposed his rule on large parts of Sind and the Punjab.

DARIUS THE ORGANIZER

The Persians had shown no animosity against their Greek subjects on the coast of Asia Minor. Cyrus seems to have felt towards them the warrior's mild contempt for the trader. Darius found both Greeks and Phoenicians useful in supplying naval forces, which were outside the experience of his countrymen. He ruled his Greek subjects through tyrants, and was entirely unconscious that the Greeks had a longing for liberty and resented the decline of their trade, which they attributed to Persian domination. He was surprised when they revolted in 499 B.C., irritated by their attack on Sardis, and outraged by the help which Athens sent to the rebels. When he had duly punished the Asiatic Greeks, he decided to invade Europe again, restore to Athens its tyrant, who was in attendance at his court, and show once more the invincibility of Persian arms.

His brother, Artaphernes, led the expedition, which won some successes in the Aegean islands and Euboea. Then Marathon proved not only the fighting spirit of Athens, but also the efficient equipment of the Greek hoplite. Artaphernes took his booty and his captives home, and reported the check to his brother. There was little wealth in Greece to tempt invaders, but Darius knew that his prestige had suffered. He set to work to organize an overwhelming force. Fortunately for Greece, the Egyptians revolted and turned Persian thoughts from the Aegean to the Nile. In 486 B.C. Darius died, leaving to his son, Xerxes, the task of avenging the great defeat on the plain of Marathon.

Darius was not as great a soldier as Cyrus, but he was an even better organizer. In his reign, as the accompanying map shows, the Persian empire reached its greatest extent. That it lasted for more than two centuries after the overthrow of Lydia and Babylon was largely due to the form of government inaugurated by Cyrus and perfected by Darius. Both rulers believed that the basis of their power must be the Iranian highlanders—the Persians in the first place, and then the Medes. On his tomb Darius proclaimed himself "a Persian,

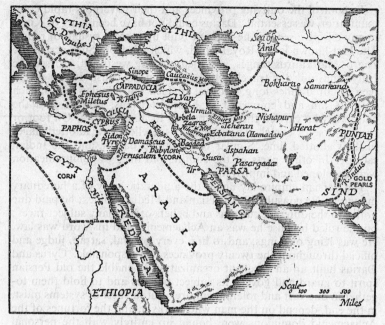

THE PERSIAN EMPIRE UNDER DARIUS I

Darius I (521 B.C. to 486 B.C.) consolidated the Persian hold on Egypt, Syria, Asia Minor, Mesopotamia, Iran and the Punjab, as is shown by the dotted lines.

the son of a Persian, an Aryan of Aryan stock". The youthful Persian noble was trained at the court in the old traditions of his race; he learnt the religion and the history of his country, he was trained in riding, shooting, hunting, and he was taught the virtues of a simple life. By these means the Achaemenids hoped to have to their hands governors and generals who would prove superior to the luxurious life of the east, which had sapped the fibre of earlier empires and in the course of time led to their decay.

The Persian dominions were divided into twenty provinces or satrapies, and had four capital cities, Babylon, Susa, Pasargadae and Hamadan. Among the provinces, Parsa, Media and Elam took precedence, and with Parthia, Armenia and Cappadocia provided the best troops; the wealthiest were Babylonia, Egypt and India. The satraps, who governed the twenty provinces, were almost entirely either Persians or Medes. They had command of the local militia, and were responsible for law and order; they seem to have administered justice without undue oppression. The satraps were also responsible for raising taxes from their subjects. In order to secure loyalty and good government a high official, who was given the title of the King's Eye, inspected their work from time to time.

To control the outlying provinces and their governors rapid communication was essential. Darius could not have been King of Kings in any effective sense if he had not built up a great system of roads. The best known is the Royal Road, which ran from Susa across the Zagros and Taurus ranges, and then, turning westward, crossed the Halys and took the traveller to Sardis and the coast. It was seventeen hundred miles long, and was divided into regular stages, each with its inn and courtyard to house caravans, traders, and the couriers, who carried the royal post to local governors. On foot or riding horse or camel, the messengers travelled their allotted stages in their allotted time. Similar roads ran to Bactria and the Indian satrapy. In other parts of the empire, old lines of communication were developed and improved.

The Persian empire lay under the autocratic sway of a hereditary monarch. He consulted his Persian and Median nobles; he paid due notice to the different customs and beliefs of his many subject-races; but he ruled because he was an Achaemenid, and his word was law. He was King of Kings, and to him every general, satrap, judge and official throughout the twenty provinces was responsible. Cyrus and Darius built up an excellent organization to enable the old Persian spirit to guard and govern its subject peoples and to hold them together in one vast and tolerant empire. But the best of systems must, in the end, depend on the man who works it, and the fortunes of the Achaemenid dominions were bound up entirely with the personal character, whether strong or weak, of their monarchs.

DECLINE OF THE ACHAEMENIDS

When he had defeated his Egyptian rebels, Xerxes took up his inherited task of chastising the insolence of the Greeks. As son of Darius and grandson of Cyrus, he enjoyed great prestige, but he did not possess the genius of his forbears. His preparations for the campaign were methodical, and the assembly of army and fleet was a triumph of Persian organization. Herodotus and other Greeks exaggerated the numbers for patriotic motives, and the five and a quarter million soldiers, who were said to have crossed the Dardanelles, must represent not the expeditionary force, but the whole fighting strength of the empire. Numbers were overwhelmingly on the side of Xerxes, but probably less than two hundred thousand men accompanied him into Greece, supported by a fleet of about seven hundred and fifty men-of-war, with many transport and supply vessels. The core of the Navy was the Phoenician squadrons, of the army the Persian cavalry and the infantry division, which was called the Immortals. Persian generals commanded the various corps, which were composed of six divisions, each division containing ten battalions of a thousand men.

We have read in previous chapters how the Greeks smashed the invaders at Salamis and Plataea, and then carried the war into the enemy's country. The Hoplite had beaten the Immortal, and the Athenian sailor his Phoenician rival. Had Salamis and Plataea gone the other way, Persia must have become the unchallenged master of the western world, and the history of Europe would have taken an entirely different course.

But the Persian empire was far from ended, though her military prestige had suffered, and her Phoenician subjects had to acknowledge the naval superiority of Athens. For another century and a half, her organization and her wealth made her supreme in western Asia and often the decisive factor in Greek and Egyptian affairs. But the character of her rulers was changing. The courts of the King of Kings and his satraps grew more luxurious, and the practice of polygamy destroyed the unity of the Achaemenid house. The old Elamite tradition, by which the crown passed through the female, began to revive, and royal ladies intrigued for the succession of their children and favourites.

Xerxes was assassinated in a palace conspiracy, his heir was also murdered, and a child took the throne of Cyrus and Darius. The satraps became almost independent of Susa, particularly in the more distant provinces, and many tried to make their governorships hereditary in their own families. The quarrels of the Greek cities prevented Athens from making any advance in Asia Minor, and the money of the King of Kings subsidized the opponents of whichever state was most powerful. Persian wealth equipped the fleet of the Spartan, Lycurgus; when the Long Walls of Athens were destroyed, the court of Susa could feel that it had bought revenge for the destruction of their ships and men at Salamis.

But the Achaemenids missed their chance. Palace intrigues and a quarrel in the royal house allowed the Greeks to learn the military weakness of Persia. When the Ten Thousand, whose story is told by Xenophon, marched to Cunaxa in 401 B.C. and marched safely back to the Black Sea, the weakness and the disunion of Persia were made plain. Just before the end came, Artaxerxes III revived the fine traditions of his house; he recovered many districts, which had broken away, and restored Persian rule in Egypt. But again conspiracy placed a weakling on the Achaemenid throne, and the weakling had to face Alexander of Macedon.

ACHIEVEMENT OF THE FIRST PERSIAN EMPIRE

With the death of Darius III in 330, the first Persian empire ended. For all its outward strength, it collapsed as suddenly as the Assyrian and the Babylonian had before it. Yet it left behind permanent results. It contributed nothing original to literature or architecture. The Persians borrowed cuneiform writing from the Babylonians and adopted the Semitic language, called Aramaic, for inscriptions. Their great buildings at Pasargadae and Persepolis show the influence of Babylon, Egypt and perhaps Greece. But the old Elamite tradition of good craftsmanship persisted, and the fluted Persian column with its richly ornamented bases and capitals is more graceful than the Greek or the Egyptian. The two centuries of Achaemenid rule left an enduring tradition of stubborn national pride, which survived the shocks of foreign conquest.

The better type of Persian noble stirred the admiration of many Greeks; "ride straight, shoot straight, and speak straight" was a simple and attractive code of conduct; it is still the aspiration of many a sportsman, whose summer diversion, polo, was invented by later Persians and celebrated by their poet, Firdousi. The religion of Zoroaster is now represented by a small group of Parsee families; but its teachings left with the inhabitants of Iran a belief in one god and a deeply rooted hatred of idols. Persian methods of government were largely adopted by Alexander in organizing his eastern conquests, and he employed Persian nobles alongside Macedonians and Greeks as generals and officials. The rich ceremonial of the Achaemenid court appealed to him and his successors, and, in later centuries, to the Roman emperors. The road system of Cyrus and Darius served as an example to the Europeans, who conquered western Asia, and eventually formed part of the vast network of communications which the Roman legions made in their progress.

CHAPTER 23

PERSIA'S DUEL WITH ROME

ALEXANDER'S conquest of Darius's empire left Persian religion, language and government very much as they had been for the two previous centuries. Some of the great nobles were influenced by the Greek way of life; but in the uplands the peasants carried on their business as shepherds and farmers, just as they had under their national kings. When the Successors parcelled out Alexander's dominions, the men of Parsa fell to the share of Seleucus, whose wife was a Persian lady of rank. Though Seleucus made his capital in Mesopotamia, his descendants transferred it to Syria, and southern Iran was left unmolested to live its own traditional pastoral life.

RULE OF THE PARTHIANS

The eastern provinces of Bactria and Parthia soon broke away from their Macedonian rulers, who failed to grasp the old lesson that Iran is vulnerable on its eastern frontier. Gradually the Parthian horsemen developed into a formidable army. The Successors were weakened by their quarrels with one another and by the rising power of Rome; in 249 B.C. Arsaces revolted from the Seleucid king and led his Parthians into Iran.

Arsaces and his immediate successors on the Parthian throne showed themselves vigorous leaders. They extended their power over

the centre and south of Iran, and their overlordship was acknowledged by the inhabitants of Parsa. Mithridates I pushed eastward
to the Indus valley and westward to the Euphrates. The Arsacids
had to struggle in their turn with savage nomads who tried to follow
their path south-west of the Oxus; two of their kings were killed, like
Cyrus the Great, in resisting Scythian tribes. The Parthians spoke a
language not unlike Persian, and had certain ties of blood with their
Iranian subjects; but for two centuries they seem to have regarded
themselves as the heirs of Alexander rather than of Darius. They
employed Greek as the language of the court and the government,
they enjoyed Greek plays, and they carried on the traditions of Seleucus, as their coinage shows. They held far less of the Iranian tableland and the Mesopotamian plain than the Achaemenids, and the
unity of their dominions was threatened frequently by the domestic
struggles which broke out among members of their royal house.

INDECISIVE WARS WITH ROME

In 70 B.C. Phraates II recovered the whole of the Parthian realm.
The weakly descendants of Seleucus had vanished before the attacks
of republican Rome. Phraates claimed Armenia and northern Mesopotamia as part of his dominions, and was forced to defend them
against the eastward thrust of the legions. The decisive clash came at
Carrhae in 56 B.C. The financier-politician, Crassus, proved himself
a poor leader in the sandy wastes of Mesopotamia. His cavalry was
no match for the heavily armoured Parthian horsemen, and, though
the legionaries fought their usual dour fight, they were shot to pieces
at long range by the mounted bowmen of Phraates.

The Arsacids held their own with Mark Antony when he came to
the east. Later they made peace with Augustus, retaining their conquests and satisfying Roman pride by restoring the trophies won at
Carrhae. Neither power was anxious for a fight to a finish. Armenia
remained the chief bone of contention; a curious solution was found
by allowing Parthia to nominate a king who undertook to acknowledge himself the vassal of Rome, and thus preserved either side from
any loss of prestige.

The compromise worked well for many years; but there was a good
deal of fighting, and the western empire often supported Arsacid
princes, who led discontented provinces against the king ruling at
Ctesiphon on the Tigris. Parthia's worst disaster came when the
great soldier, Trajan, conquered Assyria and Babylonia and led his
legions to the Persian Gulf. But Trajan's successor abandoned the
dream of recovering Alexander's empire, and restored Mesopotamia
to the Arsacids. The struggle weakened both powers, whose wealthy
cities were threatened by the hordes who roamed the Northern Flatland. Rome needed her legions to guard her European frontiers;
Parthia was seldom free from the nomad menace beyond the Oxus.
But her northern dominions were worth fighting for; they were still

rich, and they gave her the control of the silk trade with China; as middleman she could extort heavy profits from the luxury, for which the demand of Roman ladies seemed inexhaustible. The silkworm had not yet been introduced into Italy.

The chief grievance of the Persians of southern Iran against their Parthian rulers was that the latter were lukewarm in their worship of Ahura Mazda. To Darius and Xerxes it was Ahura Mazda that created the world and gave the Achaemenid house dominion over the nations. But the Arsacids seem to have set greater store by Mithra, the unconquered Sun, and embodied the name of their god in their throne-names, such as the rulers of Elam, Mesopotamia and Egypt had used since the dawn of history.

Their Greek inheritance made them tolerant in religious affairs, though in the latter part of their rule they inclined more to Zoro-astrianism and favoured the Magian priesthood. The worshippers of Christ and Jehovah lived almost unmolested by the side of those who followed Ahura Mazda and Mithra. It was a time when men's thoughts turned more and more keenly towards spiritual things, and political frontiers formed no bar to the exchange of ideas. As Nestorian Christianity pressed eastward into Parthia and founded many bishoprics, so Mithraism went to the West and became in time the most popular religion of the legions, particularly as the Roman hold on Asia grew tighter. The cult also drew many converts from the ranks of the slave population.

THE ARSACIDS DISPLACED BY THE SASSANIANS

It was not Roman rivalry, but the strong nationalist feeling of the highlands of Parsa that eventually ended Arsacid rule. For nearly four centuries the Parthians had shown themselves a hard-fighting race; but, like the later Turks, with whom they have been compared, they had little real art or culture of their own, and their political ability was small. The organization of their government was bor-rowed from their Seleucid predecessors. They failed to produce unity among the different races they had conquered, or to control the half-independent princes who ruled the fringes of their realm. Often the Parthian kings were mere figureheads in the hands of army chieftains, who had led their savage horsemen from the frontiers to overawe the capital. It was easy to collect these hordes in the hope of quick and plentiful loot; it was impossible to keep such a force together for any length of time. So when Ardashir raised the flag of revolt in Parsa, the Arsacid power crumbled. The highlanders had kept alive their pride in the old Persian tradition for five centuries, and, since Ardashir claimed descent from the Achaemenids, they rallied to him, as their forefathers had rallied to Cyrus. In A.D. 212 he defeated the last Parthian ruler, captured the city of Ctesiphon, which was the headquarters of the Arsacids, and was thus able to proclaim himself King of Kings of the Iranians.

The new rulers of Iran had a firm hold on the loyalty of their subjects, and they took up the struggle with Rome with ferocity and success. Hitherto the western power had held the advantage of union and central control, while her Parthian rivals were frequently distracted by domestic quarrels. Now the rôles were reversed. With the end of the Septimian House, the Roman Empire fell a prey to disunion and the rivalries of ambitious generals. Ardashir reduced to submission the half-independent chiefs, who had controlled the Parthian provinces, united the various subject races, and led his armies into Cappadocia and Syria. His seventeen years of rule produced a strong empire, nationalist in spirit, and made possible the brilliant successes of his son, Shapur I. The new King of Kings overran Armenia completely and then captured and looted Antioch on the Orontes. The old emperor, Valerian, crossed the Euphrates to avenge the sack of his city; but Shapur captured him and sent him to end his days in prison. Shapur II ravaged the lands which Rome held in Mesopotamia, and was only withheld from repeating the foray into Syria by the threat to the eastern frontiers of Iran.

For most of the second half of the third century Persia had the better of her duel with Rome, and the Sassanian kings are still numbered among the heroes of Iranian romance. The two armies were well matched, except for the weakness of the Romans in cavalry. As the century drew to its close, the Western power recovered unity and strength under a line of vigorous Balkan soldiers. Religious hatred added fuel to the flames of racial dislike. The fighting grew more bitter, but the Sassanians had to give ground.

ZOROASTRIANISM AND CHRISTIANITY

Immediately on his accession Ardashir had made it clear that he was a devoted believer in Zoroastrianism. He gave power again to the Magian priesthood and turned his back on the tolerance of the Arsacids. As a Zoroastrian, he felt the same contempt for Roman idols that Xerxes had shown for the statues that stood in Athens seven centuries earlier. Fanaticism sharpened the temper of the Persian soldier, when he attacked the cities and villages, which bowed down to Jupiter or the Great Mother, or burnt incense to the stones that represented Apollo or a "Divine" Roman emperor. The same spirit guided the Sassanians on the field of battle and at home. For men and women who did not worship Ahura Mazda, life began to be less comfortable than it had been under the Parthian kings.

When the Roman empire became Christian, the ferocity of the descendants of Ardashir seemed to increase. The old idols had gone; but the Christians adorned their churches with images of Christ and His saints, and to the sincere Zoroastrian these were as repulsive as Apollo and Jupiter had been. The conversion of Armenia to Christianity in the days of Shapur II and Constantine the Great increased the anger of the Sassanians. They made many efforts to win their old subjects back from their new faith; but the Armenians clung to Christianity and have maintained it to the present day in spite of all the persecutions they have undergone.

Perhaps it would be wrong to label the Sassanians as the first religious persecutors. The Taoists had suffered centuries before their day in distant China, and the priests of Amon had extirpated the worship of Aton efficiently. The old city-states of Elam and Mesopotamia had looted one another's gods. Elijah gave short shrift to the prophets of Baal. The Egyptians had bitter memories of Cambyses. But the Sassanians certainly seem to have been the first kings who carried on a deliberate policy of religious persecution through several centuries. Under their pressure the Christian bishoprics began to dwindle, and many Christians went back to the West. Bahram, "that great hunter" whose name is familiar to many English singers and sportsmen, made a treaty with Rome in A.D. 422, which gave back to his Christian subjects a certain freedom of worship; but two generations afterwards they adopted the Nestorian heresy, and were no longer of interest either to the Emperor at Constantinople or the Pope at Rome. Sassanian policy had beaten Persian Christianity.

It dealt equally harshly with the curious religion which Mani had founded in the early days of Sassanian rule. Manicheism took over some of the teaching of Christianity; like Zoroastrianism, it taught that the world was based on two spirits, one good and the other evil, and that life was a conflict between light and darkness. But the blend was unacceptable to the followers of both the older religions. After thirty years of teaching, Mani was executed by the Sassanian king, and his followers were persecuted. Yet the creed spread widely, in spite of many of the Manichees being martyred. Centuries later in Europe the Christian Church added to the numbers of those who perished because they clung to the teachings of Mani.

HOW THE JEWS FARED

An older religious community than either Christian or Manichee also suffered from Sassanian intolerance. The Jews of the Dispersion had been in Mesopotamia when Cyrus the Great founded the first Persian empire. For eight centuries they had remained loyal to Jehovah. Their recognized head was the Prince of the Captivity, who was reckoned a lineal descendant of David. Some of them took part in the commercial life of the cities, but most of them were prosperous agriculturists. The Dispersion had a keen spiritual and intellectual life, and won converts in northern Mesopotamia. The Rabbis worked hard at extending and explaining the beliefs of their forefathers. The Talmud grew in importance, and its pages contained the actual discussions which took place in the Jewish schools in Persia. Scraps of scientific knowledge and many fascinating tales were stored up together with rules governing logical thought. "Even a voice from heaven cannot override logic."

Shapur I was kind to his Jewish subjects, but, as time went on, they shared the persecution which attacked their Christian enemies. Possibly this was due to the spread of their doctrines into Persia itself, where there was a flourishing community at Ispahan. Under Yezdegerd II in the fifth century, they were accused of murdering two Magi, and were hunted remorselessly from their homes. Some fled into India and formed a settlement on the Malabar coast, which still exists. Later their leader, the Prince of the Captivity, led them in a seven years' revolt, which ended with his capture and crucifixion. Yet the work of the Rabbis was not lost. The Talmud survived, to serve the Jew of the Middle Ages as "a fatherland which he could carry about with him, when his own land was lost." It is the Talmud which has enabled the Jew to maintain his identity and achieve one of the greatest miracles in history.

THE EXHAUSTION OF THE SASSANIANS

The fifth century saw the addition of another enemy to the ranks of those with whom the Sassanian princes struggled. The eastern border was threatened by the White Huns, who poured out of Chinese Turkestan into the country south of the Oxus. Khusrau or Chosroes I, who, as Anushirvan the Just, is one of the greatest heroes of Persian tales, had to struggle with them and the armies of Justinian. He welcomed to his court the pagan philosophers who were expelled by the Christian emperor. Against the White Huns he made alliance with the Turks, a hitherto unknown race, who were following the previous invaders to the south-west. The allies shepherded the Huns safely into India, and fixed the Oxus as the boundary between their dominions. Later, Chosroes entered Arabia to support its inhabitants against the Christians of Abyssinia, and added to his dominions the overlordship of southern Arabia during the boyhood of Mohammed.

The Sassanian power reached its zenith under Chosroes I. He held the land from the Black Sea to the south of Arabia and from the Roman empire to the Oxus wastes. Manufacture and commerce flourished, and writers flocked to his sumptuous court, where they could translate the books which Chosroes had brought from India or watch his courtiers playing the new Indian game of chess.

Chosroes II seized the opportunity of Roman weakness to push Sassanian power to the west. Like Shapur I, he captured Antioch, and then went on to snatch the holy city of Jerusalem from Christian hands and to carry off from it the Holy Cross itself. The conquest of Egypt seemed to promise the complete overthrow of the rival empire at Constantinople. But it rallied under Heraclius, who led his troops in A.D. 624 into the heart of Iran. Chosroes was deposed and executed by his own subjects, and Heraclius recovered the Cross.

The two great powers had fought one another to a standstill. Neither had won any tangible results from four centuries of war. Both had been fatally weakened in man-power, and this weakness gave a new enemy the opportunity of attacking both. Heraclius's eastern armies collapsed before the onset of the desert warriors, who poured out of Arabia, proclaiming that Allah is God and Mohammed His prophet. But the walls and the wealth of Constantinople gave the Christians time to rally their forces. Persia had no such refuge. The Arabs captured Ctesiphon and looted its treasures. In 641 the last remnants of the Persian forces were scattered at Nihavand.

CHAPTER 24

MOSLEM PERSIA

THE Arabs broke the old Sassanian government to pieces, but they had nothing to put in its place. Their life in the desert had left them ignorant of the government of cities or provinces. They were eager to enjoy the riches and the comforts, which their new subjects had amassed through many generations of civilized life; but they could hold their dominions together only by employing Persians, Greeks and Romans to carry on the work of government. Many parts of the Iranian tableland became almost independent states; the others acknowledged the rule of the Caliphs, or successors of the Prophet. The capital was first fixed at Dasmascus. About a century after the battle of Nihavand, the Abbasid Caliphs, who were descended from Abbas, the uncle of Mohammed, founded Baghdad near the site of the old capital Ctesiphon. Many of their chief ministers were Persians. Their dress and their way of life followed the old Iranian models. Only in religion and language were they different.

THE INFLUENCE OF ISLAM

Mohammed had been in touch with Jewish and Christian teaching, and he recognized Abraham, Moses and Jesus as teachers. His early followers did not force Islam upon the conquered; the true Moslem was free from taxation, which was paid by the unbeliever. But Mohammed had set his face against idols, and the Christian communities were treated as infidels by his followers. At first the Zoroastrians were tolerated, as they too were haters of idols. But, in spite of this similarity, there were many differences between the religions of Iran and Arabia. Before the burning earnestness of the Moslems, Zoroastrianism lost ground quickly, and Allah took the place of Ahura Mazda as the supreme object of Persian worship.

Zoroaster had taught the existence of two great spirits and the continual conflict of Good and Evil. Mohammed insisted that there was only one god. Allah ruled the world, and he had no rival. He had declared his commandments to his Prophet through the mouth of the archangel Gabriel; these messages were duly set down in the Koran, the holy book, which contains not only the religious laws of

Islam, but a complete civil code, still scrupulously observed by Moslems to-day. After Mohammed's death, traditional acts and words of himself and his friends were collected to form the Hadith, and the Koran and the Hadith are the basis of Islamic religious and civil law. Prayer was the means by which the Moslem must approach Allah; the law laid it down that the true believer should turn to the holy city of Mecca and offer prayer five times a day. Wine weakened man's reason and strength; it was forbidden to the Moslem, whose duty demanded physical fitness, so that he might carry Islam through the world by the sword. Islamic law taught that all Moslems were equal, and encouraged charity and brotherhood among them. The Christian practice of allowing a man only one wife was repudiated; Islam continued the practice of polygamy, ordered that woman should go veiled, but did something to raise her position in the East.

Most of these practices were accepted readily by the Persians, but some proved difficult. They did not give up the winecup as easily as the inhabitants of the Arabian wastes. Their traditions of government had never been democratic, and they believed in son following father on the throne. They disliked the democratic idea of equality and election, and this led them to accept a line of successors to the Caliphate, whose claims cut the Persians off from the rest of the Moslem world, and keep them separate to-day.

The three Caliphs who followed Mohammed held office by right of election and not by right of blood. The fourth Caliph was Ali, Mohammed's cousin and son-in-law. To his sons, Hassan and Hussayn, the Persians gave their loyalty; the traditions of centuries led them to hold the claims of the Prophet's grandsons superior to those of more distant connections, no matter what election had taken place. From this point of view, the Abbasids and the various other dynasties who ruled Moslem lands were usurpers; the only true Caliphs were Ali, Hassan, Hussayn and their nine successors. Those who held this theory were called Shiahs, or the sect of The Twelve. The great mass of Iranians accepted this belief against that of most of their rulers, who were Sunnis and approved the orthodox line of succession by election. But many centuries were to pass before the official religion of Persia at length became Shiah instead of the old orthodoxy.

WEAKNESS OF THE ABBASID CALIPHATE

For five centuries the Abbasids remained the nominal rulers of Persia. The best known of them is Harun-al-Rashid, the contemporary of Charlemagne. The Caliphs' court at Baghdad was a centre of Persian art and literature; but, after Harun's death, they lost control of their Persian subjects and became mere puppets, reverenced only for their kinship with the Prophet of Islam. Local chieftains became nearly independent, and struck coins bearing their names and titles, while Persian officials controlled the central government at Baghdad. The most vigorous of the provinces was Khorasan, with its great cities of Herat and Naishapur. Its rulers used Turkish soldiers to fight their wars and appointed Turkish governors, the most important of whom held his court at Ghazni in Afghanistan. The greatest of these, Mahmud, who reigned in A.D. 1000, beat off other Turkish invaders, held most of the dominions of the Abbasids, and made his court a centre of Persian poetry.

THE LANGUAGE AND LITERATURE OF PERSIA

Islam brought to Iran not only a religion and a Civil Law, but also a language. The sacred books of the Zoroastrians had been written in an Aryan tongue, and commentaries on them were composed in Pahlavi, a later development of Iranian speech, which lasted down to the end of the Sassanians. The Koran was written in Arabic and, wherever the Moslem conqueror went, Arabic became the medium of religious ceremonial. The educated Persians welcomed the Arabic alphabet in place of the cumbersome Pahlavi. Many of them became bilingual and wrote both in Arabic and Persian. Semitic words were introduced into the Iranian vocabulary. In most Islamic countries Arabic drove out the older tongues. As the language of religion it was accepted in Persia, and it was also employed for poetry and scientific works. In spite of these influences the old Persian speech survived, and it became richer through its borrowings from the language of the invaders.

The greatest poet at the court of Mahmud of Ghazni was Firdousi. He preserved in his works the legends of the early Iranian heroes, and his themes were so popular that they inspired painters to illustrate them with charming miniatures. The chief forms which Persian poetry took were the narrative poem in rhymed couplets, the ode and the quatrain. The latter was employed by Omar Khayyam, when he wrote the *Rubaiyat* in the eleventh century. Though Firdousi, Nizami and Hafiz may perhaps rank as greater poets to Persians, Omar is the most familiar to English readers, because his quatrains, brilliantly translated, convey a view of life easily intelligible to Western minds.

The descendants of Mahmud of Ghazna were overthrown by other Turks, who overran the cities of Khorasan and then marched westward to Mesopotamia under the leadership of Togrul Beg. They captured Baghdad in 1055, but left the Abbasid Caliph on his dim throne. These Turks, who are called Seljuks, took up the Persian tradition even more keenly than their predecessors. They employed Persians in the government of their widespread empire, and they encouraged native art and literature at their court in northern Iran. They carried their empire to the Mediterranean, and their capture of Jerusalem led to the Crusades. Omar Khayyam wrote his famous quatrains and his forgotten scientific books under their rule. When the main Seljukian empire broke up, their princes continued to govern provinces in the Iranian tableland.

The opening years of the thirteenth century mark a new and dramatic phase in the history of Iran, of which there are, indeed, few parallels in world history. The story of the Mongol hordes who roamed the steppes north of the Gobi desert and south of Lake Baikal is told in the next chapter. They had recently united into a formidable fighting force under Chenghiz Khan, and now poured into north-east Persia, leaving death and devastation in their wake. Whole cities were wiped out, and some of them—including Rhages, the capital—survive in ruins to our own day as a memorial of the desolation caused by the passage of the Mongol horsemen. Some ancient Persian historians have deliberately left this period out of their stories, merely saying that the catastrophe was too terrible to record.

THE RULE OF THE ILKHANS AND TAMERLANE

The same tradition of ruthless brutality continued under Hulagu Khan, the grandson of Chenghiz. His followers were still nomad horsemen, who took their movable encampments through western Asia and blazed a trail of ruin over the once-civilized lands. In 1258 Hulagu descended on the capital where the phantom heir of the Abbasid Caliphs still kept up a faint semblance of his famous predecessor, Harun-al-Rashid. Hulagu murdered the Caliph in his palace and sacked Baghdad. He and his successors were unchallenged masters of Persia and Mesopotamia, which they ruled for three generations under the title of Ilkhans. In the fourteenth century the Ilkhans gave up the savage traditions of Chenghiz and Hulagu and became patrons of arts and letters. Their architects built stately mosques, and their painters laid the foundations of the Persian miniatures, which were used to ornament the verses of the poets. Once again Iranian culture tamed the invader from the east.

When the Ilkhans became less warlike, their power declined. They were not suited to govern settled communities, and many of the officials they employed were Christians or Jews. As in the days of the Seljuks, minor princes began to assert their independence, and once again the splitting up of the provinces drew a new wave of invasion from the north-east under a leader of the blood of Chenghiz Khan.

The exploits of Tamerlane, or Timur the Lame, belong to Asiatic rather than to Persian history. His amazing campaigns between 1360 and 1405 ranged from the Chinese frontier to Moscow and Ankara in the west and to India in the south. He conquered Persia and Mesopotamia, and governed his huge empire from Samarcand. The buildings he has left there are among the best examples of Persian architecture which exist, with their splendid arches, domes and minarets; the ornamentation was carried out by faïence mosaics and glazed tiles, which lent colour to the mass. But Timur was never the unchallenged ruler of the countries he overran, and constant risings took place. Yet his reign benefited Persian art. The workshops of Ispahan sent out beautiful examples of faïence work. Miniatures reached their finest stage of development, and the subjects chosen show the influence of the Chinese part of Timur's dominions.

When Timur died at the age of seventy, most of Iran remained loyal to his successors. They were unable to deal with the constant menace of the Mongolian-speaking tribes on their northern frontier, as the great conqueror had done. There were always petty rulers in the Iranian tableland who owed little or no allegiance to Samarcand. By the middle of the fifteenth century the house of Timur had ended its rule, and Persia had lost her bond of union. Much of the north was under the control of tribes who held the country east of the Caspian. But the national spirit had outlasted the four centuries, during which their monarchs had been of central Asiatic stock. It had tamed their desert ferocity and taught them the graces of Persian literature and art. The capture of Constantinople by the Ottomans had shifted the balance of Turkish power into Europe, and left the way clear for a greater revival of Persian nationalism than had occurred when the Sassanians had replaced the Arsacids.

THE NATIONAL REVIVAL

The period of disunion which followed the extinction of Timur's descendants was ended by Ismail, who was proclaimed Shah of Persia at Tabriz in 1499. Founder of the Safavi dynasty, which held power for two and a half centuries, he championed the Shiah religion and made it the national faith of Persia. Ismail claimed descent from Hussayn, the son of Ali. His ancestry also connected him with the Sassanian dynasty, who traced their blood to the Achaemenids. Ismail represented all that was essentially Persian. He held the veneration of his Shiah subjects on religious grounds, and he could appeal to their patriotic feelings as the heir of Cyrus and Darius, of Shapur and Chosroes.

Ismail defeated the Caspian nomads and brought the whole of Persia under his rule, pushing down to the Euphrates, the Persian Gulf and Afghanistan. As ruler of the Shiahs, he aroused the anger of the Ottoman Sultan, Selim, who led his Turks out of Europe to crush the Moslem heretics. The hatred between the Shiahs and the orthodox Sunnis was deep-rooted and bitter. Selim was possibly the greatest warrior of his house; he defeated Ismail's army and annexed the north-western provinces of the new Persian kingdom. Religious persecution followed, and four thousand Shiahs are said to have been massacred. This was the prelude to hostilities between the two Moslem powers which lasted for three centuries.

But Ismail and his descendants retained most of their possessions and preserved Persian nationalism. The greatest of the Safavi house was Shah Abbas I, who reigned from 1587 to 1629 and was a contemporary of Elizabeth of England, Philip II of Spain and Akbar of India. He was the first Persian ruler to make contact with Englishmen, who followed the route taken by the Portuguese sailors nearly a century earlier. Shah Abbas was not only a fine soldier, who recovered his north-western provinces from the Turks. He won a great reputation as an administrator, and he covered Persia with a network of roads, bridges and caravanserais, just as Darius had done before him. He put down brigandage with a firm hand and encouraged trade and industry. Some of the great palaces which he built at Ispahan still survive to show the skill of his architects.

His reign seems to represent the most flourishing period of Persian art. The carpets woven on his looms cannot be equalled for texture and design. Some of them are made of silk, others of velvet blended with cloth of gold. They contain numbers of the small scenes which the miniature-painters of the period designed with great skill; many of the borders are filled with flowers, animals, and intricate geometrical designs. The better carpets took many years in the making. The same devoted and elaborate work was shown in the production of books, illustrated by attractive miniatures and written in beautiful handwriting.

The later years of the Safavi Shahs is a story of decline, such as seems inevitable in oriental dynasties, whose unity is affected by luxurious living and the intrigues of court ladies. The Sultans of Turkey kept alive the feud between Sunni and Shiah, and their troops captured Baghdad, Hamadan and Tabriz; the south-eastern provinces were wrenched away by invaders from Afghanistan and India, who looted Ispahan. Yet the descendants of Ismail continued to enjoy the same religious veneration which had been given to the founder of the dynasty, and, in spite of their incapacity, they commanded the loyalty of their Shiah subjects into the eighteenth century. It was not till 1732 that the last Safavi was deposed. With the growth of British power in India and the advance of Russia to the east and the south, old problems of defence gave place to new, and Persia was drawn into the main current of world history. She had to submit to foreign rulers; the Shiah religion was forcibly replaced by the Sunni; she was weakened by wars and grinding taxation. But the old national spirit recovered, and the Shiahs freely practised their faith when another Persian soldier, Reza Khan, seized the throne in the twentieth century.

IRAN'S INFLUENCE ON HER CONQUERORS

Iran has a longer continuous history than most parts of the globe. She has been invaded many times; but she has usually tamed her conqueror, as Greece tamed Rome, and taught him the arts of peace. Love of beautiful things has marked the work of her craftsmen from the early days. It may be fanciful to trace the skill of her carpet-makers and her miniaturists back to the Elamite potters of prehistoric days; but there seems no break in continuity from the Achaemenids to the Safavis. The same tenacity appears in her religious history. Iran has been a hater of idols since the Aryan-speaking Medes and

Persians conquered the Elamite cities. The Zoroastrian and the Moslem were alike in this, and the Shiah Persian has an honourable record of loyalty to his faith in spite of conquest and persecution. Nowadays we are apt to think of Persia in terms of miniatures, carpets and the verses of Omar Khayyam, and to forget the outstanding part she has played as the link between eastern and western civilization. For centuries her warriors held the pass against the fierce nomads who assaulted the north-east frontier of the Iranian plateau. Under Cyrus and Darius she was the greatest power west of China, and her military strength nearly overwhelmed the young civilization of Europe. Under the Arsacids she withstood the Roman Empire in its heyday. Under the Sassanians she inflicted wounds which crippled that empire beyond recovery and paved the way for the early expansion of Islam. Iranian art, literature and luxury made the courts of the early Abbasids and Timur famous throughout the eastern and much of the western world. Iran's real weakness has always been the lack of a good sea-coast. It is impossible to guess what her influence would have been on the history of the world, if she had had sailors to supplement the energies of her soldiers, her traders and her craftsmen.

PART V

MONGOLS, TARTARS AND TURKS

CHAPTER 25

THE MONGOL–TARTAR HORDES

THE stories of Egypt, Mesopotamia, Greece and Rome have shown us something of the struggle waged on the townsman and the farmer by the wandering warrior of the desert and the steppe. In the records of Persia, the nomad invader plays an even more frequent part. When we turn south to India and east to China, we shall find the same struggle acted again. The Wanderings of the Peoples extend over more than three thousand years of human history, and in them, tribes of widely different stock and speech played their parts. Most of the Aryan-speaking and the Semitic-speaking races adopted or adapted the civilizations which they attacked. The nomad of Mongolian speech did not mingle so easily with the conquered.

THE NOMAD AND THE CITIZEN

From one angle, it is possible to view history, down to the fifteenth century, as a long-drawn struggle between the nomad and the citizen. The life of the wandering herdsman does not produce written histories. A few traditions of his past may become embedded in the lays or stories told and sung round his camp-fires; but the records of his victorious forays are found mainly in the writings of his victims, to whom they appear as unmitigated disasters. It is hard to assess the amount of human suffering caused by the great waves of barbarian invasion; still harder to compare them with the slow and silent misery of the slaves, on whose constant labour rested the graces and the decencies of the civilization which the nomads attacked and looted. But clearly the great invasions played an outstanding part in what has been called "the Martyrdom of Man".

Lately, it has become fashionable to paint the invaders in brighter colours, against a dark background of decaying civilization. The life of the free warrior and his womenfolk is contrasted favourably with the squalor and servility of the towns they plundered. There can be no doubt of the vigour of the Arabs, who carried the teaching of Mohammed into three continents; as the records of Persia have shown, they breathed a new spirit into art and literature. Later, we shall see how the Teutonic invaders refashioned the ruins they had made in the Roman Empire, and how they rebuilt the Christendom which they had nearly destroyed. But it is less easy to trace this process of regeneration in the doings of the hordes of Mongolian-speaking tribes, who rode out of the waste spaces of central Asia.

The Goth and the Vandal chose the losing form of Christianity, and were pilloried as symbols of coarse and stupid destructiveness. But Attila made the Hun a name for sheer terror and annihilation. The Seljuks learnt the graces and the science of the Moslems, who became their subjects and taught them the faith of Islam; their greater leaders are tinged with the romance of chivalry. Mahmud of Ghazni and Saladin lent lustre to the Turkish name both as rulers and as soldiers. After them, came a fresh swarming time of the Asiatic nomads. Destruction tipped down the scales once more. The Mongol and the Ottoman Turk improved on the military skill of their forerunners, and they used their new powers ruthlessly.

DESERT LIFE OF THE NOMADS

So vast was the area over which their armies ranged that much of their story spreads into the records of Persia, India, China and the duel between Islam and Christendom. The Mongol hordes overflowed the ancient frontiers, and swamped people after people. Neither man's valour nor the obstacles of nature deflected their course. They made their way across deserts and mountain ranges, and, as their columns passed west, south and east, they left desolation in their wake. Europe suffered from their fury; but her sufferings were small compared to those of Asia. How the nomad rulers grew slowly milder, when they settled in the old centres of civilization, is told elsewhere; here an effort must be made to survey briefly their general history and its influence upon other civilizations.

The early home of the Mongols was in the eastern part of central Asia, near Lake Baikal and the head-waters of the Amur river. They are mentioned in Chinese annals as early as the seventh century, but it was not till the beginning of the thirteenth that they became of importance to the civilized world. There was little to mark them out from the other Mongolian-speaking tribes west of China as the future conquerors of half the world. Tartars, Naimans, Kirghiz, Karaits, Uighurs and Kipchaks stretched from China across the great Northern Flatland into south-eastern Europe. Some of them had modified their old wandering life, and trade-routes linked their cities.

The Mongols lived the primitive life of Asiatic nomads, riding their wiry horses from pasture to pasture, sleeping in tents, hunting for the pot, and raiding other wandering herdsmen under their chieftains. The different groups were not always at enmity with one another; sometimes there was a loose alliance, as one leader became powerful and attracted the weaker tribes to his standard. Courage, loyalty and endurance were the essential requisites for a tribe which aimed at leadership. The country south of Lake Baikal bred a hardy race, which tolerated weakness neither in its members nor its enemies. Food was scarce, especially in winter, when mares and cows supplied little milk and there were few deer for the hunter. Boiled millet was a poor substitute for game, and fermented milk from leather sacks made the Mongol sigh for the coming of spring. Then he could take down his dome-shaped tent of felt from its wooden framework, pack it on his ox-drawn waggon, and ride off to fresh pastures. When the tribe was at rest, the women and girls looked after the tent or *yurt*, cooked the meals in a huge pot over the stone hearth, and tended the carpets and the silks, which had been looted from another band. The whole community gorged itself to repletion, for the streams yielded abundant fish, and sheep and game were plentiful; in the starved winter months, the best went to the men, while the women and the children lived on the scraps.

The Mongol was trained in boyhood to fish and hunt, to guard the herds of horses, to round up lost animals, and to act as scout against possible enemies. He rode for days on end with little or no food. He endured snow and the bitter north wind without a fire. When he returned to the *yurt*, he strengthened himself by wrestling with his friends or practising with the bow. He knew nothing about books; but his mind had been sharpened to read the face of nature and to guard against surprise. As he grew up, he handled spear and mace, protected his body with a leather or metal breastplate, and took his place among the soldiers, on whose skill and endurance the life of the whole tribe frequently depended in times of crisis.

CHENGHIZ KHAN

Kabul Khan began the victorious career of the Mongols in the eleventh century by throwing off the Chinese yoke; his followers boasted that he had "pulled the Emperor of Cathay by the beard". But the nomads could not be a formidable power so long as they remained disunited. Kabul's grandson, Chenghiz, found many of his subjects in revolt when he succeeded his murdered father at the age of thirteen. His earlier successes were due to the courage of his mother, Houlum. She kept together a faithful few, and helped him to maintain his hold on part of his ancestral pastureland. But it was only after many years of desperate and bitter fighting that Chenghiz succeeded in reasserting the sway which his father had established over his Tartar neighbours and in uniting all the Mongol tribes.

He had a stern struggle with the Karaits, whose chieftain, Wang Khan, is supposed to have been Prester John, the "Christian" king of Crusaders' tales. But Chenghiz was learning his trade as a general; Wang Khan was defeated and killed, leaving his capital of Karakorum to the Mongols. By 1203, Chenghiz had prospered so greatly that he held a general convention or *Kuriltai* of the many tribes who followed his standard of the Nine Yak Tails. This date is generally considered to have marked the beginning of the great Mongol empire, though in fact it was not until the year 1206 that Chenghiz assumed the title of Khan and as such issued his *Yassa* or code of laws.

The first objective of the new military power was the rich territory behind the Great Wall of China. At this time the ancient empire was divided between a Northern dynasty, whose capital was near Pekin, and the Sung who still held the South. The latter resented the loss of their northern territories, and Chenghiz secured a working agreement with them. He sent forward his spies to secure information, won over some of the guardians of the Wall, and then, protected by a strong advance-guard, led a hundred thousand men against his enemies. In eight years, he had conquered northern China, overrunning the countryside with his cavalry columns, driving stragglers into the overcrowded towns, learning siegecraft, and winning discontented soldiers to his side.

THE MILITARY MACHINE OF THE MONGOLS

Chenghiz had built up a superb military machine. Eleven Orkhons, or Marshals, of whom the best known were Subotai and Muhuli, divided the higher command, in strict subordination to the Great Khan himself. The cavalry were organized in units, running from ten to ten thousand. Nomad tradition enforced the strictest loyalty in the groups; no member of the ten might leave his comrades, and none might abandon a disabled comrade. Arsenals were created for the storage and care of the heavy armour, shields and lances. The importance of recreational training was recognized, and the troops were turned out to hunt between campaigns. The Mongol expected little mercy from his enemy; he showed none. The inhabitants of many Chinese cities were massacred to the last infant. All captives taken west of the Wall, except artisans and learned men, were slain in cold blood. The army won much by fighting, and perhaps even more by the terror it inspired.

Chinese arts and literature had no attraction for Chenghiz or his Mongols; the latter would have been content to turn the whole country into grazing ground for their horses. Leaving the Orkhon Muhuli to govern in his name, the Great Khan established his court at Karakorum, the old capital of Prester John. There he ruled his Mongols by the *Yassa* and trained his four sons, Juchi, Chitagai, Ogotai and Tuli, while Subotai added Korea to his dominions and Muhuli completed the conquest of northern China.

Though Chenghiz based his rule on the old Mongol tradition, he did not remain a mere warrior. He saw that he could use his Chinese subjects to extend and govern his empire. Yeliu Chutsai was the most distinguished of the officials who served the new Yuan dynasty. He was a man of courage, integrity and wise statesmanship, and by his advice, he saved many cities and captives from Chenghiz's ruthlessness. He organized the tribute of the growing empire on a clear and reasonable scale. To train the Mongols to administer the countries they conquered, he established schools; an empire could be won from the saddle, but not governed from it. He was right-hand man to Chenghiz, and to Ogotai after him; it was largely through his statesmanship that the Mongol empire lasted as long as it did. Other Chinese assisted him as secretaries, financiers and administrators. The Great Khan needed them for the work of civil government. It seems improbable that Yeliu Chutsai had anything to do with army organization, though it has been suggested that Chenghiz employed the Chinese discovery of gunpowder, as a weapon to strengthen his unrivalled cavalry.

But mobility, not gunpowder, was the secret of the Mongol victories. When Chenghiz turned his eyes to the west, he relied on the extraordinary speed, the paralyzing savagery of his horsemen, and the leadership and loyalty of his Orkhons. A new power had sprung up in central Asia, under the Naimans and western Turks, who oppressed the Uighurs. Chenghiz sent Subotai to deal with them. The Mongols moved swiftly, manoeuvred the enemy out of favourable positions and followed up victory with a shattering pursuit. Many of the Turks joined the conqueror, and the Horde was swelled by excellent fighting material. Chenghiz's realm stretched from the Aral to the China Sea, and in all that vast expanse, there was peace and disciplined order.

Chenghiz was now a man of about sixty, and might well have been expected to content himself with an empire which covered fifty degrees of latitude. His sons had been trained as leaders; his Orkhons could hold down his conquests with their divisions of veteran horsemen; Yeliu Chutsai and his Chinese assistants kept the treasury full, without stirring discontent; the stern and simple commands of the *Yassa* were accepted and obeyed. The roads were open to the merchants' caravans, as had never been achieved since the great days when the Han dynasty ruled China.

Religious toleration was the rule. Many Mongols still clung to the pagan witchcraft of Shamanism which their fathers had reverenced. The Nestorian form of Christianity was popular among the Karaits and other tribes. In the eastern parts of Chenghiz's realm Buddhism flourished; in the west Islam had won many converts. But under the iron hand of the Great Khan, any attempt at religious warfare was crushed; a man could think as he wished about God, as long as he obeyed the *Yassa*, which forbade fighting between Mongols. Though Chenghiz had certainly turned many a city into desert, he had given his surviving subjects more than a nominal peace.

THE VAST DOMAINS OF CHENGHIZ

His restless spirit still hankered for victory. "To crush your enemies, to see them fall at your feet, that is best." Moslem traders told him of the rich kingdom that Mohammed of Kharesmia ruled, beyond the high mountain-barrier of mid-Asia. The trading-cities of Khorasan and Persia gave him a full treasury, and he had an army of nearly half a million men, well armed and supported by elephants.

Against this, Chenghiz had his quarter of a million horsemen and two thousand miles of formidable country to traverse. Yet, when an insult to his envoys gave him an excuse for war, he set out on the greatest march in all history.

As usual, his intelligence service was excellent and his widely separated corps worked together with amazing precision. The terrible mountain-ranges, which stretched from north of Tibet, past the Pamirs, down to Khorasan, gave no protection to the Kharesmian army. The Mongol horde, carrying a light but sufficient kit, overcame all the difficulties presented by ice, snow, tempest, sand, floods, precipices and parching heat, and eclipsed the great marches of Hannibal and Alexander of Macedon. Chenghiz's strategy and Mongol ferocity smashed the best Turkish troops. The Kharesmians were outgeneralled and outfought; Bokhara, Balkh, Merv, Samarcand, Naishapur, Tashkent and countless other cities were captured and mercilessly looted. At Herat, more than a million and a half corpses are said to have marked Chenghiz's vengeance. Huge pyramids of skulls warned surviving enemies of the uselessness of resistance to one who earned the title of the Scourge of God more thoroughly than Attila. Mohammed died a hunted fugitive, and his son's attempt to carry on the struggle drew the Mongols into India.

While Chenghiz was annexing Khorasan, Persia and north-west India, Subotai reached the Caspian in pursuit of Mohammed. He led his twenty thousand horsemen round the south coast of that sea, forced the barrier of the Caucasus, and scattered the Kipchaks who opposed his raid. In 1222, the Mongol host entered Europe, attracted by the fertile soil of south Russia. The Duke of Kiev led an army of Russians and Kipchaks into the Dnieper valley; Subotai defeated and captured him before raiding the Crimea, beating a Bulgarian army and marching two thousand miles to rejoin the Great Khan.

GROWTH OF THE MONGOL POWER

Chenghiz died in 1227, before he could lead his men eastward against the Sung rulers of China. It is hard to deny him the title of the greatest warrior in history. No army, between the Yellow River and the Dnieper, and between Lake Baikal and the Indus, ever withstood the Nine-Tailed standard: there is no reason to think that Egypt, Morocco or Europe could have produced forces to conquer him. With the help of Yeliu Chutsai and his officials, he governed his vast empire with great ability. He encouraged learned men, though he cared nothing for art or music. His system of couriers held his dominions together. Trade flowed unchecked over the great land-routes. An elementary system of education was established. Doctors were held in honour. The *Yassa* kept Mongols loyal, physically fit, and free from religious bigotry and the grosser vices—gluttony and drunkenness always excepted. The eighteen million massacred in China were part of the price which Chenghiz exacted.

Juchi had died before his father, and the *Kuriltai* which met in 1229, chose Ogotai to succeed. With loyal co-operation between its leaders, Mongol power grew still greater. In the east, Ogotai and Tuli first completed Muhuli's work by exterminating the northern dynasty of China and making the Korean king their vassal, and then began to eat into the Sung empire. Trouble threatened in Kharesmia; but Ogotai sent an Orkhon, who, by fighting and terrorism, won back the rebellious provinces and added Armenia, Georgia and Mesopotamia to Mongol rule. Subotai accompanied Juchi's son, Batu, on another raid into Europe. The same tale of speed and massacre showed that the Russian and the Danubian peoples could not hold the Mongols. Poland and Hungary were invaded and pillaged. The battle of Liegnitz in 1241 delivered Silesia to the invaders. Christian Europe was too intent on its own jealousies to combine against the Mongols, who captured Pest and crossed the Danube. Europe was saved because Ogotai drank himself to death, and Batu and Subotai were summoned back to Karakorum, to the *Kuriltai*, which settled the succession. Batu subsequently returned to Russia, to be the first Khan of "the Golden Horde" of Mongols, Kipchaks and Tartars.

CHENGHIZ'S SUCCESSORS

Quarrels between the families of Ogotai and Chitagai threatened to break up Chenghiz's dominions, but after ten years' disunion, Mangu, son of Tuli, grandson of Chenghiz and great-grandson of the indomitable Houlum, was chosen Great Khan. Another period of internal prosperity and foreign conquest followed. Mangu's brothers Hulagu and Kublai, pushed the frontiers forward east and west. Hulagu followed the old policy of ferocity, when he captured Baghdad; the last of the Abbasid Caliphs was tortured to death, together with three-quarters of a million of his Moslem subjects. Damascus and Antioch fell, and Hulagu advanced to within a week's march of Constantinople. Mesopotamia had been one of the world's granaries since the earliest days; he ravaged it so utterly that it remained nearly a desert for six and a half centuries. Egypt and eastern Europe were saved only by the bravery of the Mameluks and by Hulagu's return to attend the *Kuriltai* which followed Mangu's death in China. Hulagu afterwards established his family as Ilkhans of Persia, acknowledging the overlordship of the Great Khan.

His brother, Kublai, who succeeded in 1259 and reigned for thirty-five years, pursued a different policy in his eastern warfare. He took no pleasure in bloodshed for its own sake. He won territory from the Sung with little loss of life. Naturally, this brought him into disfavour, while Mangu was on the throne, but he persisted in his policy of conciliation, and when he became the Great Khan proved its superiority to mere massacre. But he was no weakling; he sent fleets to attack Java and Japan, and pushed his armies southward to Malaya and Burma. The last Sung emperor was drowned in a naval battle. The whole of China was at Kublai's feet, but his maritime enterprises failed; neither Japan nor Java was destined to become Mongol.

As we shall see in later chapters, China exercised her spell over her conquerors once again. The Mongol rulers of the Yuan dynasty settled down to be educated by their subjects. Kublai had a deep love of Chinese art, literature and religion. He had become a Buddhist, while his western brother, Hulagu, was being converted to Islam. The old capital of Karakorum was abandoned and slowly sank beneath the blanket of encroaching sand. In its place, Kublai built the great city of Cambaluk, or Peking. Its glories were celebrated by travellers, like the Venetian Marco Polo; men reckoned it the greatest city in the world, its only possible rival being Constantinople. To it came the riches of more than half the world. Eastern Europe, North Africa and Asia Minor were torn with warfare; but in all the dominions of the Great Khan there was peace and prosperity. Marco Polo's story leaves a vivid impression of thriving cities scattered over a fertile countryside, and of men skilled in painting, architecture, music and the making of beautiful things.

In spite of the splendour of Kublai's throne and the gradual softening of the Ilkhan descendants of Hulagu, it is hard to avoid looking on the Mongols as mainly a grim weapon of destruction. But it is a mistake to ignore the positive results of their raids. Chenghiz's conquest of the Kharesmian realm and Hulagu's destruction of Baghdad shifted the centre of gravity of Islam. The allegiance of Moslems was divided between the rulers of Spain, North Africa, Egypt, Asia Minor and Persia. This disunion in the thirteenth century saved Christendom, itself rent by the quarrels of Emperor and Pope, kings and nobles. Meanwhile, the destruction of centres of learning and civilization scattered artists and men of letters into other lands. Europe became conscious of the age-long civilization of the Far East, and its life was enriched from Chinese sources. Chinese trade became of high importance. When the Mongol empire broke up and the land-routes again became dangerous, it was the steady determination to find a way by sea that led to the great discoveries and opened the western hemisphere to the men of Europe.

DISINTEGRATION OF THE MONGOL EMPIRE

After Kublai's golden age, the empire of Chenghiz Khan began to break up. Tuli's descendants continued to rule in China and Persia, Chitagai's in central Asia and Juchi's in Russia. The arts of government and transport were not sufficiently developed for a single monarch to rule from Poland and Hungary to the China Sea. In the centre of the mass, the old barbaric life persisted with little change. The house of Chitagai, ruling at Kashgar and favouring the ancient ways, blocked all possible co-operation between Juchi's family, who governed the Golden Horde as Russian kings, the Moslem Ilkhans of

Persia, and Kublai's Buddhist descendants in the Far East. In the fourteenth century, Mongol unity was utterly lost. It was from an obscure Tartar tribe, nominally subject to the rulers of Kashgar, that the next nomad wave of destruction threatened.

The Barlas Tartars inhabited the hilly country south of Samarcand, and acknowledged Tugluk Khan, the hard-fighting descendant of Chitagai, as their distant overlord. Samarcand was the great desert junction of the trade-routes that crossed Persia and Afghanistan and went on to the markets of China, northward through Amalyk or south through Tugluk's city of Kashgar. It was a prosperous and pleasant place, but its civilization had little influence on the free life of the Barlas clan. Unlike many of the northern tribes, who still practised Shamanism and the witchcraft of their ancestors, the Barlas men were Moslems. One of their chieftains, who was deeply interested in the new faith, gave up his military ambitions and retired into a religious community, in order to pursue the life of contemplation. It was his son, Timur, who became the last great and successful leader of the Mongol–Tartar hordes.

TIMUR THE LAME

Timur, who was born in 1336, just before the outbreak of the Hundred Years' War between France and England, had many points of likeness to Chenghiz. In his early career of shifting clan-warfare, he passed through the hazards of merciless hand-to-hand fighting, and the hunger and thirst of desert wanderings; in his many dangers, he owed much to the courage and the loyalty of his womenfolk; he built up his power over the jealous Tartar and Mongol tribes with an iron will, which refused to admit defeat, and justified his name of Timur or Iron. Like Chenghiz, he loved fighting for fighting's sake, and yet possessed a cool brain, which learnt the weaknesses of distant enemies and dovetailed the movements of huge forces over vast spaces. But, unlike Chenghiz, Timur was well educated and he was a sincere Moslem. Although he did not spare any followers of Islam who withstood his ambition, he ended the old tolerance, which allowed Christians to spread their teaching in central Asia.

By 1369, Timur had been crowned at Balkh and had established his authority at Samarcand. Ten years of warfare and intrigue had killed off family rivals, won the allegiance of rival clans, and over-thrown the irresolute rule of Tugluk Khan. They also brought him an arrow-wound in the foot, which left him limping for the rest of his days, so that he became Timur the Lame; Timur-i-leng became a name of abuse to his Asiatic enemies, and Tamerlane a name of limitless terror to European ears. As lord of Samarcand and the Hordes, he had a wide choice of conquest; the rich lands of Persia and India were a tempting bait; when he had succeeded in winning their wealth, he could go eastward, in an attempt to regain Kublai's throne in China, or else westward against Russia and the Balkans.

K   (H.W.)

To achieve these wide conquests, he had a superb military machine. Unlike the European leaders of his day, he had a well-organized group of spies, scouts and traders, who gave him accurate information about the routes he was to traverse and the lands he was to attack. His horsemen could cover great distances on their small, wiry mounts. For attack they had a variety of weapons—short or long bows, two-edged scimitars, maces, and light and heavy lances; they also spread terror by their use of naphtha and gunpowder. They were protected against their enemies by pointed helmets and finely meshed armour, strengthened by plates of mail at the shoulders. Quarrelsome as they were by nature, the Tartar–Mongol horsemen submitted to the stern discipline imposed by Timur. In the early years, he won their obedience by his reckless personal leadership; later on, they came to recognize that he moved their masses over mountain and plain with the same unruffled skill with which he moved knight or pawn over the chessboard. Asia and Europe had been devastated by the terrible ravages of the Black Death; cities and armies were weakened, and the survivors were often leaderless. Timur had at his hand a splendid force for conquest.

The Mongol and kindred tribes which had once formed great kingdoms under the houses of Tuli and Chitagai gave the ruler of Samarcand little trouble. But, north and west, Juchi's descendants still ruled the Golden Horde in barbaric splendour. The different tribes that served them—Mongols, Kipchaks, Kirghiz, Turks and Russians—had not grown weak, like the Mongols who had followed Kublai to China or Hulagu to Persia. On horseback or in their *yurts*, they still roamed the steppes, and their Khans, who ruled from Sarai and Astrakhan, had formidable armies.

TIMUR'S CAMPAIGN AGAINST THE GOLDEN HORDE

Quarrels in the royal house gave Timur his first chance. He helped the prince Toktamish, who came to his court as a refugee. But when the latter reunited all the tribes of the Golden Horde under his leadership, Timur was faced by numbers greater than his own. The old loyalty to the blood of Chenghiz Khan still survived. Tribes which had been recently conquered were drawn away from the man who had once been only the ruler of the Barlas clan. Timur's genius for attack prevailed against numbers, disloyalty and the dangers of the desert. Toktamish's raiders swept down to Bokhara; but the Tartars' speed saved Samarcand, and when his enemies retreated to their grazing-grounds in the distant northern steppes, Timur led his men across barren wastes, pushed his enemies, first north and then west, across the Urals, and brought them to battle, after a march of eighteen hundred miles. The two greatest cavalry forces in the world fought out their fight with equal courage. Timur's generalship prevailed, and Toktamish fled. Timur led his men down the Volga, laden with booty from the Russian towns, which had paid tribute to the Khan of the

Golden Horde. Three years later, Toktamish again met him in battle and, for a moment, came near to capturing his enemy. It was his last effort. The tribes that had followed him scattered, Sarai and Astrakhan were destroyed, the Kipchaks joined forces with their conquerors, and the power of the great Mongol house was broken.

Fortunately for Europe, Timur turned back from the Don to win the richer booty that lay in Asia. Actually, by breaking up the Golden Horde into the tribes that composed it, he gave the princes of Moscow their opportunity to build up a new Russia; just as later, by defeating the Ottoman Turks, he relieved the hopeless position of Constantinople and allowed its rulers another half-century of comparative freedom. Toktamish had sacked Moscow in 1382, and its Christian defenders had no hope if Timur pressed on. But the Tartar cavalry withdrew south and east to win the lands which Chenghiz had once overrun. Much grim fighting lay ahead of them; yet Timur's greatest exploit remained the scattering of the Golden Horde.

THE MILITARY SUPREMACY OF TIMUR

In 1386 the Tartar armies captured Ispahan and overran Persia. Baghdad surrendered, and Timur pushed detachments down to the Persian Gulf, and to Kandahar and Kabul. His victories alarmed the Moslem rulers to the west of his growing empire; the Mameluk of Egypt and the Ottoman Sultan united to push the Tartars back eastward, while their main forces were engaged in India. They recovered Baghdad; but later Timur returned, stormed the city and destroyed everything in it, except the mosques and religious houses.

Into the last seven years of his life fell the fighting which made Tamerlane's name a portent to the men of Europe. His cavalry remained unrivalled; many of his veteran leaders still survived; his siegecraft had improved, and it was useless for his enemies to trust in walled towns. He used the utmost savagery to make his progress easy. When resistance exasperated him, he buried his prisoners alive. Pyramids of skulls were built for him, as they had been for Chenghiz Khan. When rebellious Baghdad fell, each of the ninety thousand men who had shared in the assault was ordered to bring in an enemy head. This policy of terrorism drove many to submit; but it only nerved the greater princes to more stubborn resistance. When, in 1398, he passed down the Khyber Pass, he had to storm Multan and Meerut. In the plains, he was confronted, like Alexander of Macedon, with the problem of the elephant as an engine of war. Timur lured the ruler of Delhi into the open, scattered his troops, and used the captured elephants to carry back the riches of northern India to Samarcand. Then he went west to face the dangerous alliance of the Egyptian Mameluks and the Ottoman Turks. He beat the Mameluks at Aleppo before capturing and burning Damascus; legend says that the holy city of Jerusalem, whose recovery the Crusaders had long abandoned as hopeless, was saved by a plague of locusts. Next he turned against the Turk, threatening his flank with forces massed on the Don river and near the Sea of Azov. He captured the Ottoman capital of Brusa, pushed down to the sea, and drove the Christian Knights of Rhodes from Smyrna. The Turkish Sultan, Bayazid the Thunderbolt was at the height of his fame as a soldier. But on the field of Angora, in 1402, the Iron Tartar withstood the Thunderbolt, and Timur stood at the south-east gate of Europe.

But again he turned back to Samarcand, and Christendom was saved. He exacted tribute from the wandering Emperor of Constantinople, received a mission from the King of Castile, and took his fabulous booty east to the capital city he loved. From his earliest years of conquest, he had built palaces and mosques amid the grooves and orchards of the old Tartar city, where Alexander had rested his troops and murdered his foster-brother. He brought in craftsmen from Persia and the conquered lands, but he moulded their architecture to his own sombre taste. The great square he built is still reckoned among the memorable sights of the world, and he honoured his dead with magnificent tombs. He copied the swelling dome of the Damascus mosque, which he burnt, for two of his greatest buildings. Samarcand was the centre to which came his warriors and rulers, but he did not set up an organized system of government. There was no *Yassa*, such as bound the Mongol empire under a single code of law. Everything depended on Timur himself, and when he died in 1405, on his way to attack China, the power of the Tartars broke up rapidly. One able son, Shah Rukh, ruled a prosperous kingdom in Khorasan, and India was to feel the attack of the warrior descendants of Timur.

By the end of the fifteenth century, the various principalities ruled by men of his race had disappeared, and the Uzbeg Mongols took their place. China was safe beyond her Wall. The Ottomans had conquered south-eastern Europe. The men of the west had found a new world. The victorious horsemen of central Asia were led by lesser men, and ceased to be a terror to the rest of mankind.

CHAPTER 26

THE OTTOMAN TURKS

Subotai and Timur had threatened the eastern frontiers of European Christendom, but they did not lead their troops across Germany into France and Italy, as Attila had led his Huns in the fifth century. Mongols and Tartars alike preferred the riches of Persia, India and China to the comparative poverty of the western lands in the thirteenth and fourteenth centuries. Neither Chenghiz nor Timur made any direct or permanent impression on the history of Europe.

The Turks, however, had begun to make their mark on the Mediterranean world in the eleventh century, when a branch, called the Seljuks, showed how the nomads who came out of central Asia could fight. It was another branch of the Turkish stock, at one time followers and dependants of the Seljuks, who were destined to effect a permanent settlement in Europe, where Mongol and Tartar had left only a fleeting name of terror.

These were the Ottomans, so called after their third Caliph Osman, who, in 1300, laid the foundations of the great Ottoman dynasty, which was brought to an end only in 1922. The name Osman was probably Turkish, but it came to be written in Arabic characters as Othman; this did not affect the pronunciation, since the Turks pronounce the Arabic "th" as "s". Ottoman is a European corruption of this Arabic form. Subjects of the Sultan were called, in Turkish, Osmanli, as was, too, the form of Turkish spoken in Turkey. The name Turkey is derived from *Turkiya*, and has never been applied to any other of the many lands peopled by Turks. Turkestan was the name given to the country east of the Oxus; in our own day, there is a Soviet Republic called Turkmenistan. The Turks of Turkey in Asia and Constantinople to-day speak of themselves as *Türk*, and the word *Osmanli* applies only to past history.

EARLY WANDERINGS OF THE TURKS

The original home of the Turks was the vast expanse of country lying between the Gobi Desert, Siberia and Turkestan. The nomad Turks moved about, in larger or smaller groups, with their herds and flocks, according to the season and the local resources. They lived in huge felt tents, which were carried on two-wheeled carts— the *yurts* of the Mongols. Like the Huns and the Mongols, they felt an urge to overrun the richer lands to west and south.

Among the Turks, of whom we first hear in the Chinese Annals of the sixth century, there were some who had taken to urban life, notably the Uighurs. These established themselves in the north of the Tien Shan mountains, with their capital at Turfan, and in the eighth century, they rose to a very high degree of civilization and culture. After their conversion to Islam—which made them familiar, through the Koran, with many Biblical stories—they traced their descent from Japhet, the son of Noah. Many of their tribes in central Asia had been converted to Nestorian Christianity; others professed Buddhism or Manicheism. But they also had their own legendary history, and one of the most important tribes, the Oghuz, took its name from their earliest national hero.

In the tenth century, the Oghuz (also called Ghuzz or Uzes) began to move from central Asia towards the south and the west, penetrating into Iran, Mesopotamia, Syria, Armenia, Anatolia, the Caucasus, Southern Russia and the Balkans. It was these Oghuz who aided the advance of the Seljuk Turks in the Eleventh Century.

The Seljuks took their name from the grandfather of Tughsil Bey, the founder of the dynasty. The Ottomans, who claimed descent from Qay, one of the sons of Oghuz, took their name from Osman, the actual founder of the Ottoman dynasty.

The group of Oghuz to which Osman belonged were among the large bands of Turks and Iranians, who, after the first westward movement of the hordes of Chenghiz Khan, in 1219, had been continuously filtering into Asia Minor in search of new pastures.

At the beginning of the thirteenth century, it was no longer easy for them to find vacant pasturage along the beaten tracks. Thus it came about that their chieftain Ertoghrul wandered as far as the north-eastern corner of Anatolia, almost within sight of the Bosphorus, before he was able to find a home. Osman, his son, was born in Bithynia in 1258, the year in which the Mongols destroyed Baghdad.

THE SELJUKS IN ASIA MINOR

The last country through which Ertoghrul and his people had journeyed was nominally under the rule of a branch of the Seljuks, who were known as the Seljuks of Rum (*i.e.* Asia Minor or Anatolia); since 1243, those Seljuks had been vassals of the Mongols. In order to understand the sudden rise to power of Osman and his immediate successors in the fourteenth century, we must have some idea of what had been passing in Asia Minor since it was invaded by the Great Seljuks, towards the end of the eleventh century.

In 1064, the Seljuk Sultan Alp Arslan, successor of Tughril Bey, sent an army into Armenia. After protracted warfare with the Byzantine Emperor, the Sultan, in 1071, himself took the field, and at the battle of Manzikert, near Lake Van, defeated the Emperor and took him prisoner. Alp Arslan proved magnanimous in the hour of victory; after concluding a pact of friendship, he allowed the Emperor to withdraw with his army.

This battle gave the Seljuks their first strong foothold in Anatolia. In the following year, Alp Arslan died, and his son and successor Melih (or Malik) Shah, in order to maintain the prestige of the Seljuks, appointed a close relative, Salayman ibn Qutalmish, to continue the campaign in Anatolia. Salayman readily accepted this post, and began at once to form ambitious plans for his own future. In the short space of six years, he drove the Byzantine armies out of the country, across the Bosphorus, and established himself as "Sultan of Rum" in Nicaea, the chief city of Bithynia, which he made his capital. But his real aim was the Moslem East, and it was during an attack on Aleppo, in 1086, that he died. His son, Kilij Arslan, finding that the throne had been seized by a usurper, fled to Ispahan, where he remained till 1092, when he returned to Nicaea as Sultan.

The Byzantines could not regain their Asiatic provinces unaided. It was Geoffroy de Bouillon and the other knights of the First Crusade who, in 1097, drove the Seljuk Sultan out of Nicaea. Kilij

Arslan withdrew to Konia, which now became the Seljuk capital. It was thus through no military merit of their own that the Greek Emperors again became holders of a corner of their Asiatic possessions. How Constantinople fell victim to the forces she had summoned from the West against the Seljuks is told in a later chapter.

During the Crusades, the Seljuks of Rum had established themselves in Konia as an independent dynasty, and ruled over most of Anatolia. In 1243, however, the Mongols captured Erzurum, at the battle of Kösedagh, inflicted a crushing defeat on the Seljuks, who thenceforward became their vassals, possessing only the title of Sultan, without authority or power. The Mongol Governors met with no opposition, and the Friday prayers were read and coins were struck in the name of the descendants of Chenghiz Khan.

There now sprang up all over the country independent groups of Turkish emirs, or chieftains, who paid homage to the Mongols, in order to secure possession of the States they had usurped. The Seljuks had, by conversion and assimilation, turned the inhabitants of Asia Minor into something like a nation, and the liberation of slaves had made the Seljuk Moslems better masters than the Byzantine Christians. With the downfall of the Seljuks of Rum, national sentiments disappeared, and each emir was for himself and against his neighbour. These emirs were for the most part descendants of Turkoman chiefs who had acted as *uch-begs* or frontier guards to the Seljuks of Rum, and it was probably as an *uch-beg* that Ertoghrul was permitted to establish himself and his following near Angora.

CHANGES IN THE MOSLEM WORLD

The Latin occupation of Constantinople and the defeat of the Seljuks of Rum were events of far-reaching importance. Before the Byzantines regained their ancient capital, another event took place which brought to an end the rule of the Caliphs and changed the centre of gravity in the Moslem world. This was the destruction of Baghdad by the Mongols under Hulagu.

Thus, when Osman appeared on the scene of action, in the year 1300, it was as if the Fates had prepared the way for him and his successors to crush and replace the Byzantines, and to make themselves the strongest rulers in Islam, and play the rôle of the early Caliphs of Baghdad. Osman himself only lived to make a beginning: his main efforts, as a *Ghazi*, or fighter for the Moslem Faith, were always directed against his Christian neighbours.

Apart from the great cataclysms which left the way clear for the foundation of a new state, certain features of social life in Anatolia were ready to hand, if properly used, for the organization of a national unity. These were the *Akhiyas*, or Brotherhoods, which still existed in 1335, and were then described by the great traveller Ibn Battuta: "Now in all the lands inhabited by the Turkmens in Anatolia, in every district, town and village, there are to be found members of the organization known as the *Akhíya* or Young Brotherhood. Nowhere in the world will you find men so eager to welcome strangers, so prompt to serve food and to satisfy the wants of others, and so ready to suppress injustice and to kill (tyrannical) agents of police and the miscreants who join with them. A Young Brother, or *Akhí* in their language, is one who is chosen by all the members of his trade (guild), or by other young unmarried men, or those who live in ascetic retreat, to be their leader. This organization is known as the *Futúwa*, or Order of Youth. The leader builds a hospice and furnishes it with rugs, lamps, and other necessary appliances. The members of his community work during the day to gain their livelihood, and bring him what they have earned in the late afternoon. With this, they buy fruit, food and the other things which the hospice requires for their use. If a traveller come to town that day, they lodge him in their hospice; these provisions serve for his entertainment as their guest, and he stays with them until he goes away. If there are no travellers, they themselves assemble to partake of the food, and having eaten it, they sing and dance. On the morrow, they return to their occupations and bring their earnings to their leader in the late afternoon. The members are called *Fityan* (youths) and their leader, as we have said, is the *Akhí*."

THE OTTOMANS AND THE JANISSARIES

These *Akhíyas* gave the young Ottoman power far greater unity than existed in the neighbouring states. They were particularly valuable in the earlier days, when the army was a loosely bound collection of families. Later on, a stronger weapon of victory was forged in the New Troops of Janissaries; Osman's successor may have found the model for these famous troops in the Mameluks of Egypt. The Turks did not forcibly convert all the Christians they conquered; they allowed them the privilege of paying taxes, and they offered attractive terms of military service to their young men ready to join as members of a fighting brotherhood and spend their lives as soldiers. Later, the Janissaries accepted the faith of Islam, and they were recruited, on a regular system, from the Christian population. They were subjected to an iron discipline, and made a splendid corps of infantry, which combined with the Turkish cavalry to give the Ottoman leaders a brilliant army for their wars.

It should be realized that the vassal Seljuks were unable to prevent the *uch-begs* from attacking the Byzantines, and further that, since the Byzantines had regained possession of Constantinople, they had relaxed their vigilance on the frontiers of the Nicaean Empire. Although the Emirate of Osman was among the least important, its position—a few hours march from Nicaea and not a hundred miles from Constantinople—was ideal for an energetic and ambitious chief inspired with the true *Ghazi* spirit.

Osman won his first victory near Nicaea in 1130, and became the recognized "lord of the lands near Nicaea". His reign is thus summarized by Gibbon:

"The annals of the twenty-seven years of his reign would exhibit a repetition of the same inroads; and his hereditary troops were multiplied in each campaign by the accession of captives and volunteers. Instead of retreating into the hills, he maintained the most useful and defensible posts, fortified the towns and castles which he had first pillaged; and renounced the pastoral life for the baths and palaces of his infant capitals."

"HOLY" WAR AGAINST CHRISTENDOM

Osman himself did not achieve the capture of the most important cities, but as he lay dying in 1326, he had the satisfaction of learning that Brusa had fallen to his son Orkhan, who made it the capital of the Ottoman Empire. The aggressive policy of "holy war" against the Christians was continued with such success that by 1338 very few towns in Asia remained in the hands of the Byzantines. Nicomedia fell in the same year as Brusa. In the mosque at Brusa there is an inscription in which Orkhan describes himself as "Sultan, son of the Sultan of the *Ghazis*, son of a *Ghazi*".

In 1329, a last attempt to save Bithynia was made by the Emperor, Andronicus III. In the hope of relieving beleaguered Nicaea, he crossed the Bosphorus, only to be defeated on landing, near the modern Haydar Pasha, from which he escaped, wounded, in a *caïque*. Thus ended the rule of the Caesars in Asia.

The Ottomans were now the most powerful of the maritime emirs. Orkhan realized, however, that he could have no lasting success in Asia unless he could obtain a foothold in Europe such as would give him command of the seas and a prestige enjoyed by none of his rival emirs. As in earlier days Byzantine princes had sought aid from the Court of Konia, so, in 1347, John VI Cantacuzene succeeded to the possession of Constantinople with the aid of Orkhan, to whom he gave his daughter Theodora in marriage. A few years later, Orkhan's troops set foot on European soil, no longer as mercenaries in the pay of a pretender to the Byzantine throne, but as the soldiers of the powerful Ottoman army.

The last years of Orkhan's life were mainly occupied in attacks on Macedonia and Thrace. He was fortunate in having, in his brother Ala-ud-Din, a capable minister and adviser who helped him to organize his troops and raised the first standing army of modern times. Hitherto, the Ottoman army had been composed solely of irregular cavalry. Orkhan now introduced paid regiments of infantry known as *Yaya*, recruited only from Turks. In addition to this, regiments were recruited from among the Christian youths who had been captured in the wars, and these, in 1328, formed the famous corps of Janissaries, to which reference had already been made.

Orkhan's second son and successor, Murad I (known to Europeans as Amurath), continuing his father's policy of European aggression, had by 1361 taken Philippopolis and Adrianople; Macedonia and Thrace now became Ottoman provinces. Three years later, at Maritza, near Adrianople, his general, Lala Shehin, defeated the combined forces of Louis I, King of Hungary and Poland, and the princes of Bosnia, Serbia and Wallachia; thus the Ottomans obtained about one-quarter of what ultimately became Turkey in Europe. In 1367, the capital was changed from Brusa to Adrianople. In the meanwhile, Murad had been successful in obtaining, by purchase or by his army, a title to several of the smaller emirates.

THE TURKS IN EUROPE

In 1389, King Lazarus of Serbia, who had collected an army of 100,000 Serbs, Hungarians, Wallachians and others, revolted against Murad, and on the plains of Kossovo a decisive battle was fought in which the Allies were totally routed and the Serbian king was taken prisoner. By this victory, the Northern Serbs and the Western Bulgars were finally crushed; the Eastern Bulgars had already been overcome at the battle of Maritza. The whole of Thrace was now Turkish, and the principal provinces of the Ottoman state lay on European soil. During the battle, Murad himself was murdered by a Serb, who had obtained admission to the royal tent by false pretences. Within his reign of thirty years he had greatly extended the area of Ottoman territory, both in Europe and in Asia: and his armed force, now disciplined and well equipped, had been constantly receiving large reinforcements from the recruitment of prisoners taken in newly acquired territories.

Towards the end of Murad's reign, hordes of Turks began to pour into Asia Minor before the invincible troops of Timur, who was now advancing across Northern Persia, just as similar hordes had fled, in Seljuk times, before the armies of the Mongols; and new comers were quick to realize that service under the Ottomans held out promises of better rewards than the service of any of the other emirs.

BAYAZID'S VICTORIES

Bayazid I was proclaimed on the field of Kossovo in 1389, and the first act of his reign was to put to death his brother and his son. The murder of their brothers was henceforward to be the principle of Ottoman succession. Having satisfied himself that for the present no further trouble was to be repeated in Europe, Bayazid crossed to Asia and devoted his energies to the destruction of the Turkish Emirates.

In 1391, the Byzantine prince Manuel, who had been serving in the Ottoman army, fled to Constantinople on the death of his father and ascended the Byzantine throne. Bayazid promptly began to besiege Constantinople. An army was sent into Macedonia, and Salonika and Larissa were captured. Bayazid is said to have declared that, after he had conquered Hungary, he would ride in triumph into the city of Rome and feed his horses with oats upon the altar of St. Peter's.

The siege of Constantinople was interrupted by the advance of a crusading army which, crossing the Danube, invested Nicopolis. Sigismund of Hungary, having persuaded the Pope to proclaim a crusade against the Turks, had invited the chivalry of Europe to meet him in Buda in the spring of 1396. Among the knights who responded to his call were representatives of the nobility of France, England, Scotland, Flanders, Lombardy, Savoy, Bohemia and all parts of Germany and Austria. The French contingent, numbering some 8,000, collected at Dijon under Jean de Nevers, eldest son of Duke Philip of Burgundy, then aged twenty-two; their baggage contained all the luxuries to which they were accustomed at home, and they had women and wine in plenty. The total force numbered between 100,000 and 120,000 men. The Serbians, faithful to their treaty with Murad, refused to join the Christian army; though they offered no opposition to its passage they were subjected to pillage and murder by the Hungarians, who marched across their country. The Emperor Manuel did not join them.

Before Nicopolis, whose capture by the Ottomans had marked the end of Bulgarian independence, Sigismund encamped for two weeks without giving assault. On the arrival of Bayazid, a battle ensued which lasted barely three hours. It was lost mainly on account of the impetuosity of the French. Sigismund in vain begged them to ascertain the exact disposition of the Ottoman army before attacking, but they rushed upon Bayazid's front line, which, according to custom, was composed of untrained levies (*uzbegs*) intended to exhaust the enemy's strength. The best Turkish troops were intact after this charge, and Bayazid's bowmen unhorsed the proud knights, who had imagined, after piercing two lines, that the day was won.

Bayazid's great victory was marred by his subsequent cruelty. He ordered a general massacre of all prisoners. Only twenty-four knights were spared, the chief among them being the Comte de Nevers, for whom the Sultan expected a great ransom from the King of France; they were obliged to witness the execution of their companions.

BAYAZID AND TIMUR

Bayazid was now free to resume his siege of Constantinople. He called upon Manuel to surrender, declaring "I must have Istanbul; you must evacuate the city." In reply, the Emperor offered to pay a yearly tribute of 10,000 gold pieces; to set a special quarter aside for Moslems; to build a mosque; and to appoint a Gazi or Judge. This was agreed, but when news came of Timur's invasion of Anatolia, the Christians burnt the mosque and drove the Moslems out of the city. Bayazid afterwards conquered Thessaly.

We must now turn to the Eastern frontier of the Ottoman Empire, which was threatened by the ever-victorious Timur. The lord of

Samarcand, who had already broken the Golden Horde, overrun Persia and sacked Delhi, had spent the winter of 1399–1400 on the Araxes. His first move was against Georgia; but, after capturing Erzurum, Erzinjan and Sivas, he was delayed by a quarrel with Nazir Faraj, the Sultan of Egypt, and operations against the Syrians and the Persians. Flushed with his Balkan victories, Bayazid sent threatening letters to Timur, and the latter replied with similar insults. At length, in 1402, Turk and Tartar met. The decisive battle was fought at Angora, where both sides employed elephants. The Ottoman army was completely defeated, and Bayazid himself was taken prisoner. The well-known story that Bayazid was carried about in an iron cage by his conquerors is without foundation; it seems probable that Timur sent his own doctor to attend Bayazid, who was a sick man and eventually took his own life.

Timur spent that winter in Aidin and sent a detachment of soldiers to Brusa, where they tethered their horses in the great mosque. He had no intention of incorporating Anatolia into his kingdom. Perhaps his sole motive was to re-establish the emirates which had been absorbed by Bayazid, but the fact remains that the surviving Ottoman possessions were left untouched.

From 1402 to 1413, the Ottoman Empire was in a state of disruption. Asia Minor was practically lost, and the four sons of Bayazid fought each other for supremacy in Europe. Yet the Christian powers were able to make no effort to take advantage of this state of affairs. In 1413, Mohammed, Bayazid's youngest son, became sole ruler, and in his short reign of eight years he managed to revive the Ottoman power by friendly treaties in Europe and a firm hand in Asia. On his death, he was succeeded by his son Murad II, whose thirty years' reign was divided between fighting in Europe and Asia and sporadic attempts to continue the siege of Constantinople.

FAILURE OF THE CHRISTIAN POWERS

In 1430, after protracted negotiations with the Pope, the Greek Orthodox Emperor obtained Catholic aid against the Turks; but the terms of the compact were bitterly resented by the Orthodox Church. The supremacy of Rome was acknowledged, and the Emperor himself agreed to change his creed. When war broke out again, John Corvinus, surnamed Hunyadi, was the leading figure among the Christians. At the head of a Bulgarian army, he inflicted two crushing defeats on the Turks, and in 1444 secured the independence of Serbia by the treaty of Szegedin. But the treaty was broken within three weeks, to the lasting disgrace of the Cardinal Legate, Cesarini; he attacked the Turks, declaring that any oath with infidels might be broken. The mercenaries from central Europe had already gone home; the Serbians were unwilling to take part in the war; Hunyadi opposed the renewal of hostilities. After a desperate struggle the Christians were badly beaten at the battle of Varna. Though Sikan-

dar Beg led a successful revolt in Albania, the general supremacy of
the Ottomans remained uninjured, and in 1448 they defeated a strong
Hungarian army, led by Hunyadi, at the second battle of Kossovo.
In spite of his early failures against Hungary, Murad II completed
the re-establishment of the Empire. Even before Constantinople fell,
the Balkan peoples regarded the Ottomans no longer as Asiatic conquerors, but as the heirs of the Byzantines. By the middle of the
fifteenth century, the Greek Emperors had been shorn of almost all
their power and influence. Constantinople was still regarded by the
Turks as the capital of the Christian world. But the supreme triumph
of its capture did not fall to Murad II, who died in 1451, and was
succeeded by his son, Mohammed II, who became known as Al-
Fatih, or the Conqueror.

MOHAMMED II CAPTURES CONSTANTINOPLE

Before attempting the great task, which had baffled his ancestors,
Mohammed, who secured the throne at the age of twenty-one,
decided to free himself from the menace of other enemies. Remem-
bering that his father had been hampered by the rebellious Emir of
Karamania, he crossed to Asia to conclude a peace with that prince;
then he returned to Europe and made a three years' peace with Hunyadi. He built a strong fortress at Rumeli Hisar, to secure command
of both sides of the Bosphorus and to seize tribute from ships passing
through its waters. Armed with this strong base for the final assault,
Mohammed answered the protests of the Emperor, Constantine XI,
by declaring war. With an army of more than a quarter of a million
men at his back, he demanded the surrender of the city. Though
Constantine had no more than 8000 fighting men, he refused. Perhaps he felt that the keystone of Europe, which had defied so many
assaults of the Umayyad Caliphs, would break the Ottoman Sultan,
and took comfort from the Moslem belief that Stamboul (as they
called it) could only be conquered by the promised Mahdi at the end
of the world.

To understand the details of the famous siege that followed, we
must picture Constantinople and the surrounding water and land.
The city forms a rough triangle, with land on the west and water on
two sides—on the north the Golden Horn, on the south and east the
Sea of Marmora. The narrows of the Bosphorus, separating Europe
and Asia, begin where the Golden Horn ends. Opposite Stamboul,
across the Golden Horn at the extreme south-east are Pera and
Galata. The latter was a walled city, under the Duke of Milan's protection and occupied chiefly by Genoese; it was not attacked during
the siege. (The Genoese were no more anxious than other Christians
to risk war with Mohammed in defence of Constantinople.) The
whole length of the walls surrounding the capital was about thirteen
miles. The land walls were triple, the innermost being about forty
feet high, and were exceptionally strong near the Golden Horn. The

sea walls were less strongly built. Not only was the fleet of the Emperor vastly inferior to that of the enemy, but his artillery also.

The Emperor received a few Christian volunteers, prominent among whom was Giustiniani of Genoa, before the siege began with a simultaneous attack by land and sea. While Mohammed's fleet tried to force an entry into the Golden Horn, his heavy artillery damaged the landward walls severely. The Sultan felt that he could reduce the city only by a simultaneous attack on the two elements. But the sea attack was foiled by a boom, composed of a chain fixed upon beams and guarded by vessels. This failure caused Mohammed to undertake the amazing enterprise of transporting a fleet of ships overland from the Bosphorus to a point in the Golden Horn outside the walls of Galata; possibly he was inspired by the memory of how the Ottomans had once captured Nicomedia by a similar stratagem. He constructed a roadway over a mile long, surfaced with heavy planks, and running from a point on the Bosphorus above Galata over a hill of 270 feet to the narrows of the Golden Horn. When the road had been made smooth by the application of animal fats, Mohammed transported over it in one night nearly eighty good-sized vessels. Men drew the ships with sails spread and a pilot on duty at the bow and helm of each. The sudden sight of this "overland fleet" filled the Christian defenders with consternation.

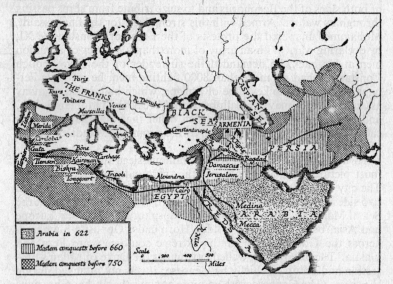

FIRST PHASE OF MOSLEM EXPANSION

After the death of its founder, Mohammed, in 632, the creed of Islam continued to advance as it gained new converts. This expansion, shown in its successive stages until the Eighth Century in the above map, paved the way for the powerful Seljuk and Ottoman Empires (see map of Ottoman Empire, pages 304 and 305).

Though the attack came now from the Golden Horn as well as from the land, the siege dragged on for seven weeks without any decisive result. The Sultan's advisers were for abandoning the struggle, as Hunyadi was reported to be marching to the rescue. But Mohammed determined on a final effort. Holding his 12,000 Janissaries in reserve, he hurled the rest of his land forces against the scantily manned walls, while the fleet attacked once more from the Golden Horn. Giustiniani, who commanded the Emperor's troops, repulsed the ferocious onslaught. Mohammed flung the Janissaries into the struggle. Giustiniani was wounded; Constantine took his place, at the head of his thinning ranks. Mohammed, shouting "The Wall is undefended; the city is ours already!" led the final assault, and thousands of Turks poured into the doomed city. Constantine, the last of the Roman Emperors, fell, fighting heroically to the last. Constantinople, the Rome of the East, had ended her long reign, and after repeated efforts for a hundred and fifty years the Ottomans had won their coveted prize.

Sultan Mohammed's great victory left the Turks settled firmly astride the straits between Europe and Asia Minor. In later chapters, we shall see how they pushed forward their boundaries under the fighting Sultans of the Ottoman house. The path of war led them into Egypt, Syria, Mesopotamia and Persia, up the Danube, and across the Mediterranean. Christendom, in her hour of weakness, had had the good fortune to escape the perils of the Mongol and Tartar hordes. But the fifteenth century drove the Turkish wedge solidly into south-east Europe, and in the sixteenth, the Christian nations had to face the constant threat of Moslem expansion to the north and west. Under the leadership of renegade Christians the striking power of Islam was to be built up along the whole North African coast; for more than a century after the fall of Constantinople the Inland Sea threatened to become a Turkish lake.

OTTOMAN RULE IN EUROPE

In Europe, the Ottomans remained a people set apart from their neighbours. They were not a separate race. Five centuries of contact with the lands once ruled by Romans and Persians had diluted the Turkish blood and mingled it with many other stocks. When they overran the Balkans they conquered men with much the same mixed blood in their veins. The great bar was religion. There could be no compromise between the Moslem and the Christian, though there were renegades on both sides. Except on the battlefield, the two ways of life lay apart. The Turk had forgotten the free life of the past, when the *yurts* carried mothers and wives and sisters to share the dangers of their menfolk. Once they were settled in Asia Minor and the Balkan peninsula, the Turkish women were shut into the harem; outside their homes they were veiled, and whatever fashions they might adopt in privacy, they all looked alike in public. The harem

THE OTTOMAN

The dissolution of the empire ruled by the Seljuks, brought about by the campaigns of the Mongols, enabled the vigorous Ottoman Turks to become the dominant power in Asia Minor and to extend their possessions into eastern Europe. The successes of Islam were aided by disunity within the Christian world.

Ottoman Empire before 1451

Conquered by Mohammed II
1451-81

Selim I
1512-20

Solyman the
Magnificent 1520-66

dependent states

MOLD-
AVIA   JEDISAN   CRIMTARTARY

SEA of
AZOV

CHIA   CRIMEA

RIA   BLACK SEA   CAUCASUS   DAGHISTAN   CASPIAN SEA

GEORGIA

Kastamuni   TREBI-
ZOND   ARMENIA

Angora   Sivas

Smyrna   A N A T O L I A   KURDISTAN   *Land disputed with Persia*

CARAMANIA

RHODES   MESOPOTAMIA   PERSIA

CYPRUS   Aleppo

SEA   Damascus

Jerusalem   PERSIAN GULF

EGYPT

EMPIRE

The Ottoman Turks were fortunate in possessing shrewd and capable leaders
endowed with great military skill, and in spite of periodic dissensions within,
their empire continued to expand until it reached its zenith, under Solyman the
Magnificent, with the capture of part of the kingdom of Hungary as shown above.

and the veil were symbols of a policy that had its inevitable result on the early training of the young.

The dangers of Constantinople scattered Greek books and scholars, and stirred new life and thought in Europe. Moslem teachers had no share in this upheaval. For them, the Koran contained all truth. The Turkish boy, when he came from the ignorance of the harem, learnt little outside the verses of the sacred book. Science played no part in the studies of orthodox Islam. Some few men and women of the upper classes received a good education and had a knowledge of European languages. But most were content, in a changing world, to cling to the ideals of those who followed Mohammed into Constantinople. Some were corrupted by the life of the court, with its abuses and indulgences. More often, the Ottoman made a gallant soldier, who loved sport and physical exercise, at least in youth and early manhood. Though sometimes subject to sudden outbursts of cruelty, the Turkish rulers did not share the ferocity of the men who had served Chenghiz and Timur. They held the Christian unbeliever in contempt, but they rarely persecuted him with the studied cruelty which Christian sects displayed towards one another; many a follower of the Cross was content to accept the rule of the Crescent, so that he might escape from Christian persecution. The Turk remained a warrior, and cheerfully left agriculture and commerce to the Christian peasant and trader. Constantinople remained one of the world's great capitals, where men of the conquered religion still prospered as merchants and craftsmen. But they felt that life was maimed for them. Many centuries were to pass before Serb, Wallachian, Bulgarian and Greek escaped from the dull weight of the Ottoman yoke.

PART VI

THE PEOPLES AND RELIGIONS OF INDIA

CHAPTER 27

THE FOUNDATIONS OF HINDU LIFE

No stories can offer a sharper contrast than those of the Mongolian-speaking tribes and the men and women of India. Immense mountains and deserts kept the fighting nomads of central Asia at bay; even when these had been passed, the barrier of Hindu Kush, the Pamirs and the Himalayas made invasion difficult, except through the rugged passes of Afghanistan. To-day the old home of Mongols, Turks and Tartars is almost unknown to the Western world. It is nearly impossible for the European to understand or imagine the Turkoman's way of life, or to enter into his motives and feelings.

Yet in modern India the old East and the new West confront each other. Air-liners fly from Karachi to Delhi and Calcutta, to Bombay and Madras, over a land where primitive hand-ploughs and bullock-carts are still in constant use. Education is broadcast by wireless to a population which is still for the most part illiterate.

India's civilization, like China's, is very old, and it is continuous. Verses of the *Rigveda* are still recited by Hindus at their morning and evening prayers and at their marriage ceremonies, as they were three thousand years ago. The foundations of their legal and social systems were laid before the foundation of Rome. There were Indian philosophers before Socrates was born. Universities flourished and great buildings arose in India before the British Isles emerged from a state of barbarism.

GEOGRAPHY AND RACIAL CHARACTERISTICS

The physical features and climate of a country largely determine the occupations, character and outlook of its inhabitants. But it is impossible to apply this law safely to India. It is as large as the whole of Europe without Russia, and has an amazing variety of climates and geographical features, deserts, swamps, jungles, fertile plains, barren hills, snow-covered mountains. Yet three things can be said of India as a whole which help to explain the history of the country and the character of its inhabitants.

First, it is geographically more self-contained than other countries of its size. It has the shape of a great, four-sided figure, with ocean on two sides and mountain-ranges on the other two. Until the science of navigation was well advanced, it was difficult of access by sea. By land, the Himalayas form a sure barrier on the north-east; the Khyber, the Bolan and other passes make natural gateways on the north-west, but they are not easily penetrated. From very early days, there was some intercourse with the outside world through these passes, and by small ships from the Persian Gulf and from Burma. At various times, culture, commerce and war gave India contacts with Mesopotamia, Persia, central Asia, Burma, China, Sumatra, Java, Greece and Rome. Yet the land has always tended to "keep itself to itself", comparatively uninfluenced by outside events, and, except for its one great gift of Buddhism, it has contributed remarkably little to the development of the outside world.

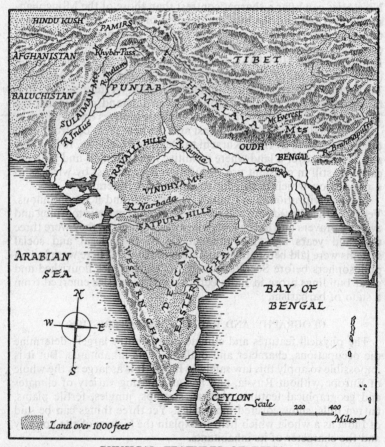

PHYSICAL FEATURES OF INDIA

Geographically self-contained, India is bounded by ocean on two sides and by mountain ranges on the other two. Most of her land is over 1000 feet high.

Secondly, apart from its snow-covered northern fringe, India is a very hot country. In the South the heat, though not excessive, is continuous throughout the year. The night-frosts that visit the northern plains in winter are more than balanced by the fierce day-time sun and the sultry nights of spring and summer. This constant exposure to high temperatures has naturally affected the temperament of the population of India and their material advancement to a considerable degree. No profitable generalization can, however, be made in the case of so vast a country, and the Indians as a whole are by no means deficient in energy and initiative.

The third physical fact is that, in India, nature works on a vast scale and man is dwarfed. Flood, storm, earthquake, the teeming life of the jungle, with its elephants, tigers and snakes, the majestic sweep of the Himalayas, all have their compelling effect upon the mind; man is not the master of nature, but an insignificant part of it. This feeling shows itself in the art and the literature of every period. With it are bound up the two most distinctive threads of Indian thought—the conviction that the individual life is of relatively little importance, and that the animals are not man's servants, but something like his equals.

Two other points may be noticed. The passage from the valley of the Indus to the Ganges–Jumna valley is comparatively narrow, because the desert runs far north from Rajputana, and the Aravalli hills stretch from the desert almost to the Jumna. Hence more battles have been fought in the land between Delhi and the Himalayas than in any other part of India. Once past this country, invaders had a clear run over the fertile plains of the north-east. The other line of division cuts off northern from southern, or peninsular, India by the Narbada river and the Satpura and Vindhya mountains. Broadly speaking, the great uplands of the Deccan and the country stretching down to Cape Comorin developed on their own lines, and their life was very different from that of the north.

THE FORGOTTEN CIVILIZATION OF THE INDUS

As we have already seen, rivers, such as the Nile, the Euphrates and the Tigris, were the cradles of ancient civilization. It was only on the plains fertilized by their waters that the land could be made first to support a settled population, and then to augment their numbers and increase their comforts. Indian rivers develop unbridled strength during "the rains"; their courses have been changed widely during historic and probably prehistoric times. But they played the same part in enabling man to change from the pastoral to the agricultural life. In the ill-watered steppes of Asia, with their frightening changes of climate, the ancestors of Mongols, Tartars and Turks have left few traces of their presence. In the valley of the River Indus, on the other hand, the forgotten inhabitants have bequeathed to us interesting memorials of the life they lived fifty centuries ago.

Recent discoveries have shown that the great river, which gives its name to India as well as to the Hindu people and the province of Sind, was the scene of a civilization which may rival those of Egypt, Sumeria and China in its antiquity. Until twenty years ago, we had few records of human life in India older than the days of the Aryan-speaking invaders apart from a handful of scattered relics of the Stone Ages. Now excavation has shown that great towns flourished as long ago as 3000 B.C. The chief of those which have been excavated was on the banks of the Indus, at Mohenjo-Daro in Sind. It covered nearly a square mile of ground, and its streets were laid out at right angles. The houses were stoutly built of brick, and nearly every house had its bathroom; a large public bath has also been discovered. Mohenjo-Daro cared for sanitation, and there was an elaborate drainage system.

The men used razors, and the women beautified themselves with the aid of mirrors and cosmetics. There was gambling with dice, and they played a game something like the "halma" of Victorian England. For the amusement of their children, they made toys, such as carts of pottery. From the bones and pots and metal-work, the drawings and the carvings, which the inhabitants have left behind them, it is possible to learn a great deal about their habits. They cultivated wheat and barley, and spun cotton for their clothes. They had gold and silver ornaments, and had discovered the use of the potter's wheel. There was no iron near Mohenjo-Daro, but copper was worked. The people were meat-eaters, and kept cattle, sheep, pigs and poultry; they probably had dogs to help them with their flocks and herds. No trace of the horse has been found, and it needed invaders from the north to bring that servant of mankind into India. The tiger, the rhinoceros and the monkey were familiar, and animals occasionally seem to have been worshipped; but the chief deity was a Nature God-dess or Divine Mother. There are signs also that they adored the male organ of fertility, which, under the name of *linga*, was afterwards associated with the great Hindu god, Siva. Another link between Mohenjo-Daro and Siva, "Lord of Beasts", is a seal-amulet, repre-senting a three-faced, long-horned god, with an elephant and other animals grouped round him. All this is in sharp contrast with the Vedic religion of the later Aryan invaders.

These early inhabitants of the Indus valley knew the art of writing. Hundreds of inscribed seals and amulets have been found, but no one has yet managed to decipher them. We do not know the origin of these people, or their connection with other ancient races, or the extent of their territory. They have no place in the Aryan records. But we know that there was trading between India and Mesopotamia at a very early date; seals inscribed with the mysterious Indus script have been found in Sumeria, and Sumerian writing was detected recently on a pot found in Sind. We know, too, that this culture lasted for centuries and covered a great area. Mohenjo-Daro is the best-known site, but four hundred miles to the north, there was another large town, at Harappa in the Punjab; and there are traces of a similar civilization which have been discovered in Baluchistan, and in the extreme north near Simla.

The Indus, which fed Mohenjo-Daro, had also a share in its downfall. The town was flooded more than once, and changes in the course of the river, combined with a deteriorating climate, probably made the site uninhabitable. What became of its people, we cannot say; but India possessed no town-planning of any sort, no baths and no drains for many centuries after they had disappeared.

THE ARYAN MIGRATIONS

We cannot be sure when the civilization of Mohenjo-Daro ceased in the valley of the Indus; and we can only date approximately the arrival of their successors. We have seen how mounted invaders came down from south Russia and Turkestan about 2000 B.C. and overcame the cities of the Iranian tableland. Some of these tribes, which spoke different varieties of the Aryan tongue, pressed on towards Hindu Kush and the Western Himalayas in their search for new pasture-lands. They advanced as a people, not as an army, the men on horseback and the women and children in the carts which were their movable homes. They streamed down through the Khyber Pass and other gates in the great mountain-barrier, driving their herds and flocks towards the upper waters and northern tributaries of the Indus. For a long time after their arrival in India, they were in many ways less civilized than the citizens of Mohenjo-Daro had been. They built no towns; their agriculture was primitive; the art of writing was unknown to them. They were still in the pastoral and tribal stage of society, and their wealth was cattle and sheep and goats.

Yet no other invaders have left so deep a mark on India. They shaped the whole course of its history; their language and the culture that grew up with it prevailed, and still prevail; the origin of most of the features of Hindu law and religion may be traced to them. Later invaders, Persians and Greeks, Huns and Mongols, were all in turn absorbed into the Indian population, and had little enduring influence. One reason for this is that these men came south merely as soldiers, and they had to intermarry with the people of the country, whereas the Aryans, who brought their wives with them, were able to keep their race and their customs comparatively unchanged for many generations. To this day, the people of the northwest frontier and the Punjab are taller and have fairer skins and finer features than other Indians; this seems to show that the Aryans lived long enough in these districts to establish a racial type. With their advance southward, towards the Satpura mountains, and eastward, through the corridor of Delhi, they gradually became merged in the shorter darker population by intermarriage. Another reason for the domination of the Aryans was their character. They were a vigorous, life-loving race, hardy and inured to both heat and cold in their old homes, and they had a firm belief in their own superiority. The name *Arya* by which they called themselves means "noble", and this spirit of pride made them despise the older, dark-skinned population.

ARYAN WORSHIP AND TRIBAL CUSTOMS

The great collection of poems, called *Rigveda*, which was handed down by word of mouth for centuries, tells us much about their life and customs. The foundation of their society was the family, and the tribe was their political unit. Each tribe was ruled by a chieftain or *raja*, usually hereditary, but sometimes elected. He received, not fixed taxes, but tribute, for protecting his people; he led them in war and conducted their religious worship. The Aryans worshipped nature-gods, personifications of the sun and fire, the dawn and the thunder-storm, whom they fed with prayers, milk, melted butter and intoxicating soma-juice. They prayed for victory, sustenance for themselves and their cattle and "an abundance of strong sons". But their prayers had other themes as well—"Lead us from darkness into light, give us vision to discern the truth, show us the path of righteousness." Their outlook was positive and optimistic. They had great confidence in their gods' power and generosity, and looked forward after death to a heaven similar to this world, but without its imperfections. All family relationships were sacred; the father's authority was supreme, and the begetting of sons was a religious duty. Monogamy was the rule, and widows were allowed to marry again. There is no trace of the later customs of suttee, *purdah* and child-marriage.

THE DRAVIDIANS AND THEIR CONQUERORS

It took many centuries for Aryan-speaking tribes to spread south and east from their first conquests in Kashmir and the Punjab. From a study of the medley of physical types in modern India, it is difficult to be certain of the peoples whom they conquered and dispossessed. But it seems clear that there were two main groups. The south was inhabited by Dravidians, small-boned, snub-nosed and dark-skinned —possibly connected in the dim past with eastern Africa and the Australasian lands. They spoke different varieties of the Telugu and Tamil language-groups, which still cover wide areas and have produced considerable literatures. In the north-east quarter were men who had moved down into the Ganges basin from Tibet and the lands beyond, men with thick-set bodies, flattish features and slanting eyes. The best representatives of the stock to-day are the Gurkhas of Nepal and the Burmese across the Bay of Bengal. The type is much less widely spread now than it was thirty centuries ago, when the Aryan-speaking bands moved down the Ganges. Its speech was allied to the Mongolian languages, which were spoken all over central Asia.

Some section of the Dravidian folk may have been overrun by the Aryans in their advance to Sind and to the middle Ganges. But the

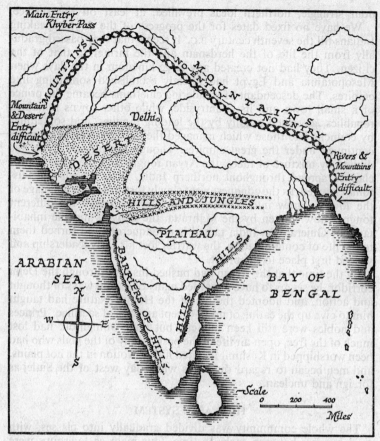

NATURAL BARRIERS OF INDIA

Peninsular India is guarded by dense forests and high mountains in the North, which make an invasion by land a matter of great difficulty. These barriers have the effect also of limiting communication overland with other countries.

bulk of the Dravidians were protected from northern invaders by the natural obstacles which guard peninsular India. Behind the dense forest- and mountain-barrier, the Dravidians developed their lives, almost untouched by northern influence. Their land had been old when there were no fertile river-plains south of the Himalayas, but only sea and swamp. It gave them rich supplies of cotton and pepper, gold and pearls, and they seem to have traded both to the west and the east in early days. It was not till the Aryan settler had become the Hindu, that the different lives of north and south made contact. Then the Hindu brought his teaching and his gods into the hot and prosperous lands, which still worshipped demons. After a dour struggle, northern ideas prevailed, at least on the surface.

We have no fixed dates for the progress of the Aryan-speaking Indians till the seventh century B.C. It seems that they passed gradually from the life of the herdsman and the farmer to that of the citizen. They had not created any large kingdom in the days when Mesopotamia and Egypt had already established something like empires. The descendant of wandering chieftains became the prince of a small town and its countryside, while other towns remained republics, governed usually by the leading families, and sometimes by councils like those which managed the villages. Village councils continued under the great empires. Though the physical type was diluted by mixture of races, the Aryan tongue and the ideas it proclaimed spread throughout northern India. Both speech and customs changed, as the conquest went slowly forward. The language of the *Rigveda* grew into Sanskrit, and later on began the different tongues now spoken by the Mahratta, the Bengali and the inhabitants of Gujerat. As India tamed her conquerors and turned them to the life of contemplation, the warrior lost his early leadership and yielded first place to the priest.

By the time that the Aryan had pushed his way through the Delhi corridor, he seems to have discarded many of his old ways of thought and action, and adopted the life of the Hindu. Nature had taught him to give up the eating of meat, except at times of sacrifice. Princes and nobles were still keen hunters, but their womenfolk had lost much of the free, open-air life of the past. Many of the gods who had been worshipped in Kashmir inspired little devotion in the hot plains, and men began to regard the lands which lay west of the Sutlej as foreign and unclean.

THE CASTE SYSTEM

The whole community was divided gradually into classes, with rigid barriers between each. In time, four main caste-groups were recognized. First stood the Brahman, the learned man or priest; next was the Kshatriya or warrior; below these came the Vaisya, who were farmers or traders, and the Sudras, the labourers who did the hard and unpleasant work of the world. Under all, were the men without caste, the Pariahs. Each caste was bound together to carry out with careful thoroughness the customs appropriate to its own way of life. These customs were particularly important in all matters concerned with marriage and food. The fourfold division into Brahman, Kshatriya, Vaisya and Sudra is a convenient simplification of the many castes of India, which number about three thousand at the present day. Kshatriya and Vaisya hardly appear in the Dravidian south, into which the system slowly spread as Hindu power expanded.

The pivot of the whole caste-system was the Brahman. All other men were bound to reverence him; he knew the wisdom of his forerunners, studied the will of heaven, made the ritual prayers, and kept himself undefiled from the pollution of his inferiors. Some Brahmans were no longer satisfied with the cheerful nature-worship of the *Rigveda*, with its promises of a heaven after death. They probed deeply into the great problems of the meaning of life, and their thoughts were embodied in the *Upanishads*, some of which go back to the eighth century B.C. These books form the foundation of all Indian philosophy, and some of their doctrines are to be found embedded in the teachings of Buddhism.

INFLUENCE OF BRAHMAN TEACHING

This Brahman speculation produced two new ideas, which have dominated the mind of India to this day. They taught that our life on earth is only one of a series of lives; after death we are born again, not in heaven but in this world; the state into which we are reborn depends entirely on our previous actions in this life. This is the doctrine of *Karma*; the word means not "fate", but "action", "deed". Animals are included in the series of human rebirths; an evil man may be reborn a jackal; the Buddha, or Enlightened One, may have been an elephant or a deer in a previous existence. This explains, or perhaps arises from, the specially Indian feeling towards animals, which constantly shows itself in literature and art; animals are "poor relations", not a distinct race created for man's enjoyment. The second great doctrine of the older *Upanishads* is that existence is an evil, and that the aim of life is to shake off the chain of repeated births. The means to this end are self-discipline, study, and a realization of the supreme truth that the world is one and the human self is one with it. The whole teaching of the *Upanishads* made the caste system stronger —as a necessity, not merely for to-day's life on earth, but for eternity.

Most men and women were concerned less with these deep speculations than with the worship of the many gods who found their way into the Hindu heaven. Siva the Destroyer and Vishnu the Preserver were joined by Parvati and Ganesa and by gods and goddesses of the river and forest. In spite of *Upanishad* teaching, cruel animal-sacrifices were still practised; in the busy towns, innumerable idols were worshipped, and courtesans and dancing girls gave their earnings to the upkeep of the temples. The ordinary soldier, merchant or artisan was content to obey the Brahman, who carried out religious ceremonies and knew the right method of prayer to the many gods. When he passed south of the Narbada river, he despised the Dravidian races of peninsular India, as beings outside the protection of caste, and he saw that they revered the Brahman and accepted his teaching.

Ordinary life, in the cities and fields of the northern plains, was stable. Warfare was on a small scale and did little to change the habits of farmers, traders, potters, smiths, carpenters and the rest. This stability made for the growth of the caste-system, and in its turn, caste kept life stable. To it is due the triumph of Hindu ideas over the mixed multitudes of non-Aryan stocks. The Hindu valued his place in the society which the Brahman dominated, and caste bound all Hindus together against the rest of the world. Other customs and faiths invaded India; but none of them has destroyed the hold which Hinduism fastened on the land. To western minds, caste seems an irrational barrier, blocking useful co-operation between the Asiatic and the European, the rich and the poor. Many reformers denounce parts of Brahman teaching as the chief obstacle to legal and hygienic reform. But that must not blind us to the overwhelming influence that caste and Brahmanism have had on the whole social development of India for three thousand years.

CHAPTER 28

THE GREAT HINDU EMPIRES

INDIA had been kept safe from invasion by her mountain-barrier for many generations; but at the end of the sixth century B.C., Darius of Persia sent his sailors into the Indian Ocean, while his soldiers conquered most of the valley of the Indus and part of the Punjab from the small rajas who ruled the native states. The new satrapy was rich in gold, and paid nearly the highest tribute to the Persian treasury.

The most powerful native kingdom of the time lay to the east, in Bihar, where the rajas of Magadha grew in power, pushing westward towards the Indus frontier of the Persian empire and north-east against the Mongolian tribes on the southern slopes of the Himalayas. Bimbisara was the first powerful ruler of this dynasty. He seems to have been a contemporary of the two great teachers, Mahavira and Gautama, and to have distinguished himself both as a soldier and a founder of towns. His descendants had lost their kingdom to the low-caste Nanda dynasty when Alexander of Macedon crossed the Indus in 326 B.C. Puru, whom the Greeks called Poros, gathered a strong force of infantry, cavalry, chariots and elephants, but he was defeated on the Jhelum. Northern India was saved, not by its military strength, but by the refusal of the war-weary invaders to advance farther into the unknown.

LINKS WITH OTHER LANDS

Alexander left small mark on India, though rulers of Greek blood played their part for the next two centuries. Neither Persian nor Greek ideas took root in the conquered districts, but the invasions increased trade with the Mediterranean lands, both by sea and by land, through Baluchistan and Kabul. In the north-east there was already a steady flow of trade from the markets of China. The merchant was beginning to link all India together; a rough coinage came into use, squares and circles of silver and copper being punched with crude designs. The north supplied elephants, horses and skins, and textiles came from China. The southern exports were more valuable; gold, pearls and precious stones were bought eagerly by the rajas, great or small, and by the nobles of the little republics, which still survived in the Punjab and on the Ganges in the days of Alexander's great march to the East.

The general growth of the royal power in the states of the north had not proved favourable to the claims of Brahmanism. Many of the fighting rajas were upstarts, like the Nandas of Magadha. Such men often looked on the Brahman as inferior to the Kshatriya. But, quite apart from political changes, there was considerable discontent with the extravagant ceremonial and wearisome ritual of Hindu religion. The sixth century B.C. saw a great uprising of thought and spiritual speculation in Persia, Greece and China. There was the same ferment of ideas in India, and many strange doctrines were preached in revolt against the worldliness of the orthodox worship. Most of these died out after the first enthusiasm had evaporated, but the teaching of Mahavira and Gautama nevertheless survived.

MAHAVIRA AND THE JAINS

Mahavira was a native of the Magadha state, and probably a cousin of Bimbisara. He rejected the sacrifices of orthodox Hinduism and the old laws of the *Rigveda*. After sharing the life of one of the communities which practised self-denial with intense earnestness, he began his teaching career at the age of forty. Though he accepted the greater Hindu gods, he did not believe that the Universe had a supreme governor. He taught that man has a double nature, spiritual and physical, and he recognized the beginnings of a soul in the animal, and even the vegetable, creation. The central point of Mahavira's teaching was that no hurt should be done to any kind of life. But he admitted that duty and obedience must govern the state; the soldier and the executioner ought to carry out his raja's orders and slay the enemy or the convict. Though his doctrines were extended to approve suicide by starvation, there is no doubt that Mahavira's was a merciful creed.

His followers, who were called Jains, opposed cruelty and bloody sacrifices, but they still recognized the Brahman as the priest whose ministrations and prayers were needed in the hours of birth and death. Jainism was, in fact, a reformed Hinduism, and for that reason it did not spread outside India. When Mahavira died, about the age of seventy, he had won more than ten thousand followers, among whom was probably his relative, Bimbisara. Many powerful rajas became converts, as wandering disciples, men and women, spread the Jain doctrines over the northern plains and carried them south to the Deccan and Mysore. The founder of the Maurya dynasty, who is said to have starved himself slowly to death, is reckoned to have been a Jain by a distinguished authority on Indian history. There are several points of similarity between Jainism and the Buddhist faith, which was taught by Gautama. Both acknowledged the reign of Indra and his fellow gods in heaven; both denounced animal sacrifice. But Gautama founded a religion which was bound to break away from the Hinduism in which his earlier years were spent.

GAUTAMA BUDDHA

As a young prince, he enjoyed the usual amusements of his class in the country near the great city of Benares. He hunted, played games, feasted, married and begat a son. But he grew discontented with his pleasant and comfortable existence. He renounced his inheritance, and sought enlightenment from Brahman sages, who made the ascetic life the only path to knowledge. He lived in a cave with other hermits, and shared their continual discussions. But mere theories did not content him; he felt compassion for his fellow man, and this compassion must be practised as well as taught. He rejected the hermit life and went back to Benares. There he had his famous vision under the fig-tree, the Bo Tree of Buddhist legend; an offshoot has been venerated in Ceylon for two thousand years.

THE SPREAD OF BUDDHISM

Gautama had the gift of winning intense personal devotion. His five original disciples, who had been shocked when he abandoned the ascetic life, hailed him as the Buddha, the Enlightened One, in whom wisdom was incarnate. Together they taught in the Deer Park near Benares, living in simple huts. Gradually the *Sangha*, or order of travelling preachers, was formed, and the Buddha's words were spread from Benares through the Ganges valley and beyond. Women helped in the work of the *Sangha*, but they had to be content with a lower position than the men.

Buddhist teaching steered a course between pleasure and extreme asceticism. Selfishness was the root-evil, and the Buddha taught men to destroy their desires for material prosperity, sensual delights and personal immortality. He laid down the Eightfold Path for his disciples to follow. The most important things in this so-called Aryan Path were right thought, right desire, right words and right conduct. The real Buddhist accepted a life of purity; he kept himself from killing, lying, adultery and theft; he gave alms, and he made knowledge and virtue his aims. In parts of his teaching, Gautama followed the ideas of the *Upanishads*. He acknowledged the doctrine of *Karma*, and he bade the true follower of the Aryan Path to aim at Nirvana or the soul's peace; man should desire to be absorbed into the Universal Spirit, and not to continue his own individual existence, with its personal longings and petty satisfactions.

In the teaching known as *Hinayana* or "Lesser Way of Salvation", Gautama remains an inspired man; but in the *Mahayana* or "Greater

Way", he was recognized as a god. In later ages he was worshipped as divine in many places, while Vishnu and other old Hindu gods received prayers as his assistants. But the links between Hinduism and Buddhism soon grew thin. Gautama's teaching was spread over large parts of India by the third Gupta monarch, and the *Sangha* passed from the simple poverty of its earlier years to great wealth. As rich and poor disciples alike obeyed the duty of almsgiving, the frugal huts of the Deer Park were replaced by prosperous monasteries. Their tonsured, yellow-clad rulers became worldly-wise as they learnt the duties and the rewards of managing big estates.

Unlike Hinduism, Buddhism became a great proselytizing religion. By the beginning of the third century B.C., it had passed into southern India and Ceylon. At one time, it looked like winning the bulk of the population from Hinduism. But tradition and caste proved too strong, and it was outside India that the greatest victories of Buddhism were gained. Gautama's lovely teaching of a pure and merciful mode of life appealed to many men in distant lands, while his opening of the Aryan Path to outcast as freely as to Brahman offended those who clung to the caste system as the foundation of conduct. So, while Buddhism declined in India, it won great numbers of converts in other lands. Ceylon, Burma, Siam amd Tibet became strongholds of the faith, under the well-organized missions of the *Sangha*. We shall see, in a later chapter, the part it played in the development of China. Many of its doctrines and practices were carried into the Mediterranean world, and it can hardly be doubted that they influenced the growth of Christianity. To-day Buddhism has probably more followers than any other religion except Christianity, although statistics are an unreliable guide.

CHANDRAGUPTA FOUNDS THE MAURYA POWER

Magadha, the birthplace of Buddhism and Jainism, had extended its territories, under Bimbisara's descendants and the Nanda kings, till, at the time of Alexander's invasion, it was the chief power in northern India. From about 326 B.C., two figures dominated the scene. Chandragupta Maurya, the future emperor, had as friend a crafty Brahman statesman, whose nickname, Kautilya, means crookedness. The two conspired against the Nanda king of Magadha. The plot failed, and Chandragupta fled: while in exile, he is said to have met Alexander. A few years later, Chandragupta was at the head of a well-trained army, first destroying the Macedonian garrisons in the Punjab, then back in Magadha, driving out the king and seizing the throne, with the crafty help of Kautilya. Further conquests followed, and when Seleucus, the heir of Alexander's eastern empire, tried to regain control over the rich Indus valley, he was met by such united resistance as India has never since been able to offer to an invader. Seleucus abandoned, at a price, not only the Indus province, but much of Afghanistan. Chandragupta ruled from the region of the Hindu Kush to the lower Ganges, and his power was unchallenged southward as far as the hills of central India.

The mainstay of the Maurya power was a standing army of 700,000 men, with a War Office of six departments, and an elaborate Secret Service which used cipher codes and carrier-pigeons. The civil administration included a Board of Trade, an Office of Works, Wages Boards, and a Registry of births, deaths and incomes. The capital, Pataliputra (later Patna), a city nine miles by two, was divided into six wards and had an elaborate municipal organization. The machinery of government was wonderfully efficient, but it was a machine without a soul. The peasants were heavily taxed, and the town-dwellers were harassed by a host of officials, inspectors and informers. Even for petty theft, death—preceded usually by torture—was the penalty. The only real check on the ruler's tyranny was the threat of assassination; Chandragupta, we are told, took the precaution of sleeping in a different room every night.

ASOKA THE HUMANE MONARCH

Such and greater—for Chandragupta's son brought part of the Deccan under his control—was the empire to which Asoka, third of the line, succeeded in 273 B.C. Asoka is unique among Eastern monarchs for his combination of high ideals with practical achievement. The new spirit of humanity which he brought into kingship was the product of Buddhism acting on a sensitive and unselfish nature. Early in his reign, he invaded Orissa, and the sufferings of the inhabitants moved him publicly to renounce war as an aggressive weapon. Thereafter, he set himself to show the right use of power and wealth, for the relief of suffering and the wide extension of Gautama's peaceful teachings. The record of his work remains to this day in the famous Edicts, engraved by his command on the great rocks and polished sandstone pillars throughout India, from Afghanistan to Mysore, and as far eastward as the Bay of Bengal.

These edicts have a high human interest. Some set forth the Buddhist moral code: obedience to father and mother, respect for all living creatures, self-control and truthful speech. In others, Asoka enjoins justice and mercy on governors and officials, or records his visit to Gautama's birthplace, or forbids the killing of animals for the royal kitchens. We read, too, how he provided rest-houses, wells and trees for the comfort of travellers, and built hospitals for men and beasts. "All men are my children." "I must work for the welfare of all folk." "His Majesty desires that all beings should have security, peace of mind and joy." The words are Asoka's, and no one has ever doubted their sincerity. His enthusiasm found a practical outlet in the missionary zeal which carried the Buddhist teaching far beyond the land of its birth. His preachers were able to convert Ceylon to the faith it still holds to-day. The movement continued to gather strength, and influenced profoundly the thought, religion, art and culture of countries so far apart as Burma, Siam, Tibet, China and Japan.

A copper statue in late Pellara style of
the ninth century from southern India,
showing Siva, the god of destruction.

A fifth-century image of Buddha from
Mattara. The ornament on the head
is a symbol of his enlightenment.

Interior of the great mosque at Mecca showing the Kaaba. Owing to the modern
transport introduced by King Ibn Saud the journey to Mecca is now much easier.

A painting of the Mogul Period (early seventeenth century) on fine bamboo-pulp paper showing Akbar, the greatest Indian monarch since Asoka, receiving visitors in a palace garden.

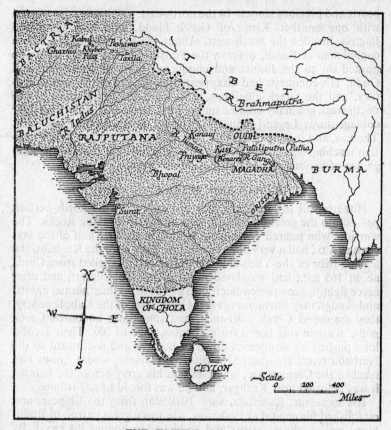

THE EMPIRE OF ASOKA

After his armies had extended the boundaries of the Mauryan Empire as far
as Madras, Asoka renounced all warfare and reigned on Buddhist principles.

Missionary, humanitarian and moralist as he was, Asoka was also
a strong ruler for most of his reign of forty years. Three generations,
however, seem to have exhausted the strain of genius in the Maurya
family. Fifty years after Asoka's death in 232 B.C. the dwindling
empire had passed finally out of the hands of his weakly successors.

For the next five centuries, India lost the political unity which the
Mauryas had given her. While the Arsacids revived the great days
of Persia, and Rome ruled an empire stretching from Armenia to the
Atlantic, India remained a prey to disunion. The strongest kingdom
lay in the south; there the Andhras, who favoured Brahmanism and
the caste system, broke away from the rule of Asoka's descendants
and the faith of Buddha. The Roman Peace encouraged sea-borne
trade, and the Andhra kings grew rich from the export of pepper,

L   (H.W.)

pearls and precious stones. In the north-east, ambitious rajas warred with one another. Kings of Greek blood, who had conquered Bactria, invaded the north-west. About 155 B.C., Menander, whose capital was at Kabul, overran the Punjab and the Indus delta; he pushed on to the Jumna and conquered parts of Rajputana and Oudh. His conquests had disappeared by the end of the second century, and the Greek chieftains, who ruled the small states of the north-west, gradually became Indian rajas, as the inscriptions on their coinage show. Legend connects the last of them with the name of St. Thomas, and it seems probable that, in the first century A.D., Christian teaching was added to the many religions that claimed the allegiance of various sections of the Indian peoples.

KUSHAN AND TAMIL KINGDOMS

Hitherto, all the invaders who came through the north-western passes into the great plains had been of Aryan-speaking stocks. The warriors who poured down from Kabul, in the first half of the first century A.D., had a very different origin. They were the Kushans, the leading tribe of the Yueh-chi, who, after being expelled from China about 165 B.C., had wandered north of the Gobi desert, and after fierce fighting, conquered Bactria. They gave up their nomad habits, and though they drove out the last Greek rajas of the Kabul country, they employed Greek craftsmen, and sometimes honoured Greek gods. Kushan rule lasted from about A.D. 50 to 300. Their second king pushed his dominions down to Benares and southward to the Narbada river. He quarrelled with the Chinese, whose troops had reached the Caspian sea; when he sent his army across the Pamirs, it was defeated near Kashgar, and he was forced to pay tribute.

His successor, Kanishka, won Turkestan from the Chinese, and established his capital at Peshawar. He was a great patron of Buddhism, and employed artists and architects to honour his creed. By this time, the "Greater Way of Salvation" had won general acceptance; Buddha was looked upon as the Saviour, and, while writers told legends of his earthly life and explained his teaching, sculptors began those images of him which have spread over the East. After Kanishka's death, about A.D. 162, the Kushan monarchy gradually split up into small principalities. The Tamil and Telugu states in the south, especially those on the coasts of Travancore and Madras, were rich and prosperous, and Tamil poets flourished. Their sailors took their cargoes of cotton to the Ganges and the Irrawaddy. But their soldiers were never formidable, and, though boundaries shifted, no southern ruler ever looked like uniting India.

Suddenly, after nearly five centuries of political confusion, a second great empire rose on the banks of the Ganges and brought unity again to northern India. Its capital was at Pataliputra, and its founder bore the honoured name of Chandragupta. He was a raja of Magadha who threw off his allegiance to the Kushans about A.D. 320. The rule of the foreigner was ended, and the people rallied to the growing power of the line of native kings. Samudragupta, who ruled from about 330 to 375, was a soldier of the first rank, and has been called "the Indian Napoleon". He extended his empire westward to the Indus, and southward far into the Deccan. His dominions were smaller than Asoka's had been, but his rule was more firmly established. His successors held the empire for more than a century, in spite of Hun attacks from the north-west.

THE GLORY OF THE GUPTAS

Though military power was the unifying force behind the Gupta, as it had been behind the Maurya empire, there was a great spiritual difference between the two. There was no repetition of the ruthless spirit which marked the first Maurya ruler. Fa-Hsien, the Buddhist pilgrim from China who visited India about A.D. 400, wrote enthusiastically about the prosperity of the country, the rarity of crime, and the absence of oppression. It may be that, like other foreign visitors, he was shown only the things which the authorities wished him to see. But Indian writers confirm his story, and the wealth of literature and works of art that the age produced show a free and vigorous spirit, which reflected a general feeling of security.

The Gupta kings were keen patrons of the arts. They gathered round them a body of poets, architects, painters, sculptors and scientists, who combined to make their age for India what the days of Pericles had been for Athens and the reign of Augustus for Rome. By far the greatest name is that of Kalidasa. He had the power of depicting every shade of human emotion, and his radiant imagination and mastery of the Sanskrit language have won him a supreme place among Indian poets; he stands high among the writers of all nations. It is harder to judge the works of architects, metal-workers and sculptors, as these were destroyed deliberately by the Moslem invaders. The temples, pillars and bas-reliefs that survive point to a high degree of artistic composition and technical skill, and the Ajanta frescoes are unequalled in antiquity. In the judgment of an able critic, "In the fifth century, Hindu art was at its best."

While the nobles and the court enjoyed the art, the literature and the science of the day, Gupta rule gave the mass of the people peace and prosperity. Trade built up busy markets in the towns, and charity provided almshouses and hospitals. Travelling was easy, with many inns on the roads and large Buddhist monasteries at frequent intervals. The natural fertility of the great plains yielded good crops to the farmer. The government did not interfere in the lives of men, except to check crime, and there was no religious persecution. Capital punishment was rare; most offences involved fines, excepting brigandage, for which the penalty was mutilation. India was in contact with the great powers of China, Persia and Rome. Merchants were able to exchange their wares and teachers their ideas.

But the four great powers were all threatened by a common enemy, whose hordes poured out from central Asia. The Chinese called them Hiung-nu; to the Romans they were Huns. Their armies killed a Persian king in A.D. 484, and the Guptas were at war with them as early as 455. The tribes who moved down from the Oxus valley towards Kabul were called the White Huns, and, though the Gupta kings were victorious at first, the pressure of the nomads prevailed after they had overrun the Iranian lands. Once more Indian unity was lost, though Harsha's reign of forty years, at the beginning of the seventh century, brought back something of the old prosperity. His kingdom stretched from the Ganges valley across Bhopal to the west coast north of Surat. Harsha favoured Buddhism in his later years, but many Hindu temples were built in his reign, as well as Buddhist monasteries. His rule was largely personal, and his death, in A.D. 648, was the signal for a long period of disunion, during which the descendants of the White Huns and other invaders were slowly absorbed by intermarriage into the mass of the Hindu population. In many respects the succeeding centuries were not unlike the Dark Ages of Europe. They had the effect of breaking the continuity of civilization and good government, and thus shut off the Golden Age of the Guptas from the next great epoch of Indian history.

CHAPTER 29

THE MOSLEM INVADERS

BETWEEN the seventh and the eleventh centuries, there were many states whose rajas possessed rich courts, and many dynasties whose doings are told in Indian literature. There were constant wars and palace intrigues, and the territories of the different rulers were continually shifting. The Palas of Bengal lasted for more than four hundred years, but they were an exception to the usual instability of the royal power. No other form of political institution came into existence. There were no more republics, in spite of the ineffectiveness of the many monarchies. The religious allegiance of the Indian peoples shifted almost as often as the political. There were many divisions among both Hindus and Buddhists, and some of these sank to degenerate forms of worship. Jainism lost influence in a world of warfare, especially in the east. Learned men still wrote in Sanskrit; but the ordinary tongues of to-day, such as Bengali, were beginning to form themselves for common use.

Much of the fighting was carried out by the Rajputs. These were warlike clans formed from groups of different races in the course of years. Many of them were White Huns or similar invaders who settled down to the faiths and the languages of their new home. Their name means "King's sons", and they conquered many of the smaller states that had once formed part of Samudragupta's empire.

They played a leading part in northern India, many of whose native rajas proved effeminate cowards. The rulers of Tibet, after annexing Nepal, conquered the conspirators who had seized Harsha's throne. China still exercised her suzerainty over Kashmir in the eighth century. Rajput generals carved out small principalities for themselves; but there was no state strong enough to bind the north together against the foreigner, or even against attacks from the south. Twice the Pala kingdom was invaded by Chola rulers of peninsular India, whose soldiers forced their way to the Ganges.

Islam's penetration of India was slow, in comparison with its rapid growth in Syria, North Africa, Persia and central Asia, Harsha was still reigning at Kanauj when Mohammed died, and a few Arabs settled on the coast of Baluchistan in his last years. In 712, a larger force invaded and conquered Sind; but their rule had no political effect on the rest of India. The Arabs were more important as traders than as conquerors. The old land-routes between India and Christendom had been broken by the solid wedge of Moslem conquests in the north, and the Arabs on either side of the Indian Ocean grew rich as middlemen, controlling the sea-borne traffic.

THE MOSLEM IMPACT ON NORTHERN INDIA

It was down the well-worn path of invasion from the north-west that Islam came at the beginning of the eleventh century. It brought an entirely new spirit into the religious life of India. In the eyes of its followers, the land was full of idols; the various sects of Brahmanism, Buddhism and Jainism were equally abominable to the worshippers of Allah, the One God. The fanatical Moslem preferred to kill the infidel in battle or butcher him in the subsequent pursuit; for the survivors there were two alternatives—acceptance of the teachings of the Koran, or payment of crushing taxation. Such a fanatic was Mahmud of Ghazni, whom we have seen controlling Persia from his Afghan court. His father had raided southward, defeated a strong confederacy of native rajas, and occupied Peshawar. Mahmud increased the pressure. His first expedition was in 1001, and he is said to have made sixteen others before his death in 1030. He had the weight of numbers against him; but his soldiers, drawn from Iranian, Turkish and other stocks, were better men than their opponents. He fought in the cold season, when his highlanders were not affected by the Indian sun. Like Alexander before him, Mahmud was faced with the problem of the fighting elephants; but his cavalry outflanked the enemy, charged his rear, and showed that the slow-moving beasts were a greater danger to their masters than to the invaders in the face of a resourceful general.

After defeating the Punjab rajas in his early campaigns, Mahmud crossed the Jumna, sacked Kanauj, and burnt all the great buildings of the capital, after its king had fled. Later, he conquered the Jats of Multan, overran Gujarat, and found his richest booty in the holy city of Somnath where a huge stone linga was worshipped in the temple of Siva. From his many raids, he took back pearls, rubies, emeralds, gold and silver to enrich his court at Ghazni. But he was only gathering spoil for another Afghan warrior; a century later, his capital was looted and burnt, and he left no permanent mark on the political map of India, except for his annexation of the Punjab.

Mahmud maintained a rich and cultured court. He admired Persian literature, and encouraged scholars and scientists. But, to India, Mahmud was an unmitigated disaster. With him begins the long enmity between Moslem and Hindu which has lasted to the present day. He broke idols and burned temples with the deliberate ferocity of the religious fanatic. He converted his enemies on the field of battle to the faith of Islam, sometimes in whole armies. The old inhabitants of the land became objects of contempt to their Moslem conquerors; taxation made the rich poor, and the poor beggars. Even food became a line of division between men. The big-boned meat-eating soldiers from the north-west despised those whom a thousand years of merciful teaching had taught to spare animal life.

Mahmud's successors failed to hold his empire together. In the north, they were threatened by the Seljuk Turks, who overran most of the Iranian plateau. They quarrelled with the Afghans, who ruled near Herat. Ghazni was captured by Mohammed of Ghor in 1150, and its ruler fled south to become raja of Lahore. With the ending of Mahmud's house, the policy of raids ended and conquest began.

THE MOSLEM CONQUESTS

Mohammed of Ghor was the first conqueror to extend the permanent rule of Islam beyond the frontier provinces of Sind and the Punjab. He was checked in his attack on Gujarat, and was defeated at Tarnaim by the allied armies, led by Prithiraj, the Rajput general, who ruled Ajmer and Delhi. Prithiraj was a gallant soldier, and he is still the hero of countless songs and popular legends. But he was handicapped by the obsolete tactics taught in the Hindu books of war, and by the caste-system, which prevented the different troops of the huge native armies from working together. Mohammed's cavalry proved too good for Prithiraj's numbers at the second battle of Tarnaim in 1192. The Rajput chief was captured and executed, and Mohammed pushed on to plunder Benares. The battle proved decisively the military superiority of the Moslem invaders over the Hindu masses.

When Mohammed went back to Khorasan, he handed over the Indian command to his general, Kutbuddin, who had entered his services as a slave from Turkestan. The old kingdom of Kanauj was annexed, and Kutbuddin overran Bihar, massacred the Buddhist monks, destroyed their libraries, and burnt their sanctuaries and idols. Some of the survivors fled to Nepal, others to Tibet, where Lhasa had grown into a great centre of the persecuted faith; the Buddhism of northern India never recovered from the disaster.

Bengal was overrun with amazing ease and rapidity; it remained under Moslem rule for nearly six centuries. The Hindus suffered all the furies of a Holy War, and, when peace came, they saw mosques and minarets arising in the great cities, to mark the permanence of the new faith.

Kutbuddin succeeded to the Indian provinces when Mohammed was assassinated in 1206. He ruled them as Sultan of Delhi, using the services of generals who had been slaves like himself. The line he founded is called the Slave dynasty; its records consist largely of parricide, debauchery, waste, and some good fighting. Like Mahmud of Ghazni and Mohammed of Ghor, Kutbuddin was a ferocious warrior whose personal pleasure and religious duty demanded the shedding of infidel blood. He pulled down old temples to build mosques and palaces, and the sultans of the Slave dynasty followed his example in war and peace. Their rule lasted till 1290, and, except in the north-west, they managed to hold the Delhi empire together.

The two dynasties which followed them enjoyed the same kind of savage prosperity, building on a sumptuous scale, encouraging Moslem writers and teachers, and grinding the faces of their Hindu subjects. Delhi's chief military weakness was its inability to hold the gateway of the north-west. Chenghiz Khan led his Mongol horsemen southwards in 1221, and during the thirteenth century there was constant danger from the kingdom founded by his son, Chitagai. Some of the Mongols settled at Lahore, and raided up to the walls of the capital itself.

The tide of Moslem conquest flowed onwards till 1340. The rulers of Delhi did not confine their ambitions to India; they made unsuccessful attacks on Tibet and Turkestan, and planned a wild campaign against China, sending their cavalry through the mountains of Nepal. Apart from these schemes, they achieved solid successes by over-running Gujarat and capturing Chitor from the Rajputs. Their armies crossed the Narbada and wrested much of the Deccan uplands from the Hindus. In the Madras country, the ancient kingdom of the Cholas still preserved its independence; Siva was worshipped with immemorial rites, and the villages governed themselves by the old customs which they had enjoyed for a thousand years. There were two other powerful Hindu kingdoms in the south and Ceylon remained loyal to Buddhism.

Islam was weakened in India, as in Persia, by the quarrel between the Sunnis and the Shiahs. Most of the ruling houses favoured the former creed, and persecuted Shiahs almost as ferociously as Hindus or devil-worshippers. But it was political, rather than religious, disunion that caused the Moslem tide to ebb. Ambitious chieftains of Afghan or Arab blood threw off their allegiance to Delhi. The successful revolt of Bengal in 1340 gave the signal to other provinces of the unwieldy empire. The Bahmani dynasty established its independence south of the Narbada, and misruled the territories of the

Deccan, which had enjoyed centuries of prosperity under Hindu monarchs. Kashmir broke away, and later the fertile and prosperous lands of Gujarat rejected the overlordship of the Delhi sultans. The final blow to their power was struck in 1398, when Timur led his incomparable cavalry down the Khyber, scattered all opposition and sacked Delhi itself. Though the invader contented himself with massacre and loot, and returned to Samarcand, Moslem power had been weakened and renewed Hindu resistance made possible.

HINDUS RALLY IN VIJAYANAGAR

In the south the Hindus rallied, and checked the further progress of Islam. The ancient Chola kingdom disappeared, but the foundation of Vijayanagar in 1336 gave the Hindus a bulwark, which lasted for more than two centuries. In the north, Moslem chiefs and sultans still ground their infidel subjects with bitter taxation, ordered their ministers to draw up codes to oppress them, and used their soldiers as slave-raiders. But south of the line running from Goa to the mouth of the river Krishna, there was a refuge in the empire of Vijayanagar.

The constant task of the Hindu kings was war with the Bahmani sultans of the Deccan. From small beginnings in the days of the five exiled brothers, who are said to have founded Vijayanagar, their armies grew till their numbers were estimated at over thirty thousand horsemen and nearly a million infantry, besides the usual mass of elephants. But the troops were not well organized; their success was largely due to the vigour and personal courage of their kings.

Gradually the Hindus gained the upper hand. Their capital was considered the richest in India, and their dominions covered most of the territories of Madras and Mysore. Travellers tell us that Vijayanagar was sixty miles in circumference, and its huge temples and populous bazaars were protected by seven concentric rings of fortifications. Religious wealth owed much to the earnings of the temple prostitutes, who were recognized by law.

There was no return to the mild rule of Asoka and the Gupta kings. Continuous warfare with the Moslem made physical courage the outstanding virtue, and duelling with swords was allowed. Savage punishments were inflicted on evil-doers; men were hooked up by the chin, and left to hang till they died. The most prosperous age of Vijayanagar began in 1480, when the Deccan split up into the five sultanates of Bijapur, Golconda, Ahmanagar, Berar and Bidar. Krishna Raya, who ruled from 1509 to 1529, was famous as a great warrior and a merciful prince. He showed rare magnanimity after his crushing victory over the army of Bijapur. Foreign travellers describe him as the greatest king in all India.

For a time after Krishna Raya's reign, Vijayanagar continued to draw trade and wealth through Mangalore, Calicut and other southern ports. It then allied itself with Moslem sultans to attack first Bijapur and then Ahmadnagar. This policy proved its ruin.

Although Berar remained aloof, the other four sultans combined against the great Hindu capital, and won a decisive victory at the battle of Talikota in 1565. The conquerors showed no mercy to the rich and helpless populace. Vijayanagar was levelled to the ground with ruthless efficiency; its rulers fled southwards, and were merged gradually with the small chieftains, who still maintained the Hindu cause beyond the reach of the Moslem.

The long Arab monopoly of the sea-borne trade of Western India was ended in 1498, when Vasco da Gama sailed into the harbour of Calicut. The Portuguese were the best organized seamen of the age; their ships and their guns gave them a big advantage over their Moslem rivals. Recent Turkish conquests had blocked the usual routes through the Mediterranean and the Balkans, and da Gama saw that a rich harvest could be reaped by opening up trade with India and the Spice Islands. This was also the view of the first Portuguese viceroy, who advised his king to maintain command of the sea and content himself on land with fortified harbours. But it was a time of intense ambition at the court of Lisbon, and Albuquerque, who became viceroy in 1509, aimed at establishing an eastern empire. This was to be done by building fortresses inland, and marrying Europeans to natives to create a loyal population.

ALBUQUERQUE AND BABER

Albuquerque occupied and fortified Goa, and drew up a scheme of government. Native customs of administration were adopted, and Hindu soldiers were enrolled. Malacca was seized, to control the Malayan Straits and the route to the Spice Islands and China. Albuquerque failed in his attempt on Aden, which would have given him command of the Red Sea trade; but his capture of Ormuz made him powerful in the Persian Gulf.

By the middle of the sixteenth century, the Portuguese possessed a string of strong trading-posts from the coast of Gujarat through Bombay to Goa. No European rivals had broken their monopoly, and rich cargoes poured into the warehouses of Lisbon. The Portuguese were bitterly hostile to their Moslem neighbours, and, when the Inquisition was introduced, their Hindu subjects suffered also. Religious persecution sapped their power, which was further weakened by the accession of Philip II of Spain to the throne of Portugal. Other European sailors began to follow the route round the Cape of Good Hope, and early in the seventeenth century, England, Holland and Denmark had established trading-stations on the Indian coast. But it was many years before the men from the west counted for much in the eyes of the new Moslem power.

Fifteen years after Albuquerque's capture of Goa, another invader entered India from the north-west. Baber of Samarcand came down to the great plains at the invitation of the Afghan rajas, who felt themselves oppressed by their overlord at Delhi. The blood of

Chenghiz and Timur ran in his veins; like those great soldiers, he had proved his personal courage and his powers of leadership in the hardships and perils of an adventurous youth. Fired by Timur's old conquest of the Punjab, he invaded that province with 12,000 men. He had with him artillery, which had improved since Timur's day. After overrunning the Punjab, in 1526, he beat the Sultan's army of 100,000 men and 100 elephants at Panipat, which commands the Delhi corridor. Next year, he defeated the Rajputs, and later, he crushed the Afghan rulers of Bihar and Bengal. Five years' hard fighting gave him military control of the north, and paved the way for the empire of his grandson, Akbar. But gifted as he undoubtedly was, Baber did not enjoy the necessary time to organize his new dominions.

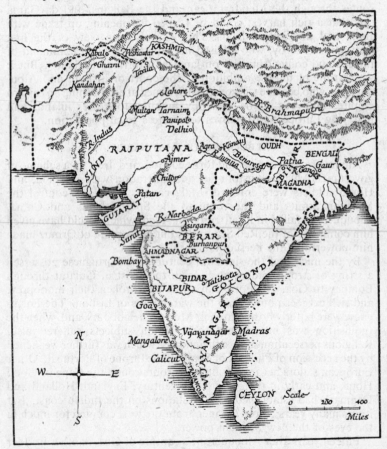

THE EMPIRE OF AKBAR

As is shown by the dotted lines in the map above, the Mogul emperor Akbar extended Moslem rule over the greater portion of India between 1556 and 1605.

Akbar inherited many of the qualities of the first Mogul ruler. Though he was no poet and did not write fluently both in Persian and Turkish like Baber, he had the same love of art and music and the same fiery ambition. His father had reigned for twenty-five years; but fifteen of them had been spent in exile, while an Afghan ruler of Bihar had rebuilt Delhi and ruled the north with firmness and success. Akbar was proclaimed sovereign in 1556 at the age of thirteen, and for the next six years gave little sign of future greatness. Then at the second battle of Panipat, his generals defeated Henñu, a Hindu tradesman who had risen to the control of the chief army of Delhi, and in spite of the corruption of his court, Akbar's cause prospered. When he was twenty-one, he got rid of the last of the bloodthirsty ruffians who had been given high office through the intrigues of his womenfolk. Thenceforth, till his death in 1605, he was the richest and most powerful monarch in the world. He conquered the greater part of India, and restored the unity which it enjoyed in Asoka's day.

There was some bitter fighting with the Rajputs, who showed their traditional courage; their princesses went to the funeral pyre rather than fall into Moslem hands. After securing Rajputana, Akbar conquered Gujarat; this brought him down to the sea, and into contact with the Portuguese; the trade of Surat added very greatly to the imperial revenue. Bengal was won in 1572. Though his hold on the Punjab was weak, he ruled all India between the Himalayas and the Narbada river, except for Sind, which was subdued later, together with Baluchistan, Kashmir and Orissa.

AKBAR'S TOLERANT RULE

Akbar tried to gain the allegiance of the southern rulers by diplomacy. When this failed, he sent his generals against them, and in 1599 he crossed the Narbada. After annexing three provinces, he pushed his south-western frontier down to the neighbourhood of Bombay. His last great victory was the capture of the almost impregnable fortress of Asirgarh, which was gallantly defended by Portuguese artillerymen. This took place in 1600, the year which saw his astute contemporary, Elizabeth of England, give a charter to the East India Company.

Akbar was the first Moslem conqueror to see that, in a united India, life must be made tolerable for the mass of Hindus. If the Great Moguls were to be Lords Paramount of Hindustan, they must be able to rest their power on all the many races and religions of their dominions. Akbar's Mongol and Tartar ancestors had become fanatical champions of Islam; but Akbar, in the great hall he built near Agra, was willing to hear all creeds, whether they were rival Moslem sects or Hindu or even Christian.

From 1581 onwards, he ceased to be a Moslem, for all practical purposes. He proclaimed a Divine Religion of his own, which rejected Mohammed's claims to be the Prophet of God and combined the teachings of Hindu, Jain, Parsee and Christian. Only a man of overwhelming personality could have attacked the cherished ideas of Islam, and yet kept the bulk of his Moslem warriors as loyal as the conquered Rajputs.

MOSLEM AND HINDU

Akbar's successors returned to the faith of their forefathers. The rift between Moslem and Hindu remained, though it was not so deep as it had been in the days of Timur and Baber. Apart from the Rajputs and other fighting races, most Hindu leaders were still largely devoted to the speculative life, while their enemies were the men of action. The rigid, clear-cut creed of Islam contrasted sharply with the fluid tolerant practice of the Brahmans with their many gods. In one important respect, the Moslems influenced the practice of their subjects. For many centuries, Hindu women had been confined mainly to domestic duties. The coming of the Moslem harem made this into a rigid custom for both creeds. The shutting off of women behind the veil in *purdah* had a profound result on Indian life.

CULTURAL LEGACIES OF INDIA

In art and architecture, both religions have left a noble legacy. The one has given us the sculptures of Sanchi and Gandhara, the great rock-cut shrines of Ellora, and the richly-worked temples of Southern India. To the other, we owe the mosques and minarets of the North, with the Taj Mahal at Agra as perhaps the supreme expression of the spirit embodied in stone. In literature, the best work was done by Hindus, most of it long before the Moslem came. Every conceivable subject found gifted writers to discuss it, and nearly every literary form was attempted. In grammar, the most famous work was Panini's, which dates from about 300 B.C., and fixed the Sanskrit language for ever. The principles of philosophy and law, medicine and mathematics, engaged the energies of able writers. The great epic *Mahabharata*, the book of animal fables called *Hitopadesa*, and the story of Rama are still recited in India, and read in translation in most countries of the world. Prose style reached a high degree of excellence in the romances of Bana, written in the seventh century A.D. Lyrical poetry touched perfection with Kalidasa, two centuries earlier. Sanskrit drama has a particularly distinguished history; again Kalidasa is the master, and the *Sakuntala* his masterpiece. In all these works, characteristics of the Indian mind are visible. Greater attention is given to detail than to construction. Fancy counts far more than imagination. Love of exaggeration and deep sympathy with Nature constantly show themselves. Through all Indian literature, as through all Indian art, run the twisted strands of sensuality and deep spiritual longing.

PART VII

CHINA AND JAPAN

CHAPTER 30

ANCIENT CHINA

BEFORE the name of Rome had any meaning, before Greece or Persia came into being, before Abraham set out on his momentous journey, the Chinese were living in China. If there was ever a time when the Chinese had not yet entered their home, it was so long ago that when history dawns they are already established in the flat rich land through which the Yellow River churns its way—yellow because, on its way through the rich soil, it takes the colour of that soil. With land like that, there was no need to wander about in search of livelihood; the Chinese "grew up" as dwellers in houses, not as nomads in tents. "Farmers of forty centuries" they have been called, and the number of centuries might be extended without exaggeration.

It is hardly probable that good ground like that was lying unnoticed except by the Chinese; there are still whole tribes of non-Chinese people, especially in the remote mountain-districts of south-west China, who are the descendants of those who at one time were to be found throughout the country. The displacement of these neighbours by the Chinese was very gradual; at first, the Chinese tribes were only a group of little embryo-states by the Yellow River, or Hwang-Ho, in what is now North China.

When the expansion was completed in the first century B.C., the territory of the Chinese was shaped like a great fan half-opened—the sea-board running along the curved edge, one of the straight edges lying east-and-west, the other north-and-south; their convergent point, the handle of the fan, lying where China proper merges into central Asia. Above the top, or east–west, rib, lie the deserts of Mongolia and the steppes of Siberia, wide and windswept. Behind the lower, or north–south, edge, lie the formidable mountains of Tibet and Burma, the eastern end of the Himalayas. No wonder the Chinese called their country the "Middle Kingdom"—sea on two sides, mountain and desert on the other two, and in the midst, China, with its rivers and vegetation.

CHINA'S INTRACTABLE WATERWAYS

The two greatest rivers, the Yellow River and the Yangtse, stretch their wandering length laterally across the top half of the fan. This top half was, for a long time, the whole of Chinese territory; during this period, their demesne would be better represented by a fan one-quarter opened, the topmost rib east–west, the lowest running north-west–south-east. And the fan must be pictured as ragged, for the water-courses were—and still are, on occasion—unstable and shifting, so that masses of water flowed this way and that.

An account of this problem of the rivers, and the engineering feat by which it was met, is to be found in the ancient "Book of History". From that record, we learn that, in the twenty-third century B.C., there was a great flood, so that many miles of country lay under water, and those people who survived drowning were threatened with starvation. The king entrusted the task of dealing with the flood to a man named Kun, who started to build walls and dams to hold in the terrible waters, which simply rose in their strength and pushed aside his work. Then the task was given to Kun's son Yü. Yü was a true engineer. He understood the nature of that which he was to handle; he worked with the water, not against it, deepening the channels of the rivers by dredging, as well as building up their banks, and providing a system of connecting channels to carry off the water, rather than attempting to hem it in. Yü had the spirit necessary for such a task. It is said of him that "he remained away from his home eight years; three times he passed his door but did not enter". "He restricted his clothing and his food, while he displayed an extreme piety towards the divine powers; he had only a humble dwelling, but he expended largely on ditches and canals." "He conducted the Jo-shui as far as Ho-li, the residue of the stream entering into Liu-sha; the To and Ch'ien waters having been led away, the Yung and Mung lands were rendered cultivable, though the soil was still muddy." The Chinese still have a saying about him: "We would have been fish but for Yü."

Thus the Chinese contemporaries of the ancient Egyptians were, at the other end of the world, learning, like them, to handle flowing water. But the Nile was tractable and of regular habits: not so the waterways of China; for them the dragon is the right and vivid symbol. It may even be that the deciding factor in the expansion of the Chinese and the shrinking of their neighbours was not conquest by arms but their broad realization of this problem of the water, and their resolve to cope with it by co-ordinated effort.

EARLY CHINESE SONGS

By the sixth century B.C., there was in existence a book of songs, some of them already centuries old, that tell us incidentally a great deal about the things in use, the things made, and the landscape familiar in those days.

Many of them are love-songs:

> "You came, a simple lad,
> In dark blue cotton clad,
> To barter serge for silken wear;
> But not for silk you dallied there.
> Ah! Was it not for me? . . ."

Blue dye from the indigo tree, madder and quite a number of strong colours were in general use for clothes. Patterned clothes were for special occasions or for great people.

In one song a man at whose village the sovereign is stopping to confer with the local subordinate rulers, is thinking of the levy his village must raise for its guests:

> "They gather the beans, gather the beans,
>   In their baskets square and round;
> The princes all are coming to town,
>   And where shall their gifts be found?
> The coaches of state and their teams go by—
>   What more for my lords have I?
> Dark-coloured robes with a dragon fine,
>   And silken skirts with the hatchet sign."

Beans were used as rations on journeys or while fighting or working out of reach of home; ordinarily, when the men were in the fields, the women would bring them meals made of a variety of foods, with cereals, chiefly millet and rice, as their basis. Cucumbers and pumpkins were much grown, as were peaches, apricots, cherries, chestnuts and plums; for flavouring, they had onions and mustard, besides a number of herbs unfamiliar to us.

DOMESTIC LIFE

Not only did the men remain in the fields for their meals, but they built themselves little huts and slept there until the precious crops were safely harvested. Barbarian tribes were always raiding from their lairs in the still-uncleared swamp land, so that the cultivators had to live much like the crew of a ship at sea, isolated and always vigilant. Thus came about that segregation of men and women which remained a feature of Chinese life after its cause had ceased. With the men away for the greater part of the year, it was natural that, with the exception of growing crops and paying the labour-tax, practically every sort of work should fall to the women; it was they who developed the technique of textile-production—hemp cloth, linen and, above all, silk. As woven stuffs were the chief medium of exchange, this was an important function.

The seed for next year, too, was in their keeping, carefully stored in the dark corner where the mother spread her sleeping-mat. Indeed, a man thought of his wife and his seeds together, both removed from him by their mysterious capacity for bringing life into being; the house was their domain, and he entered it as an outsider rather than with a feeling of homecoming, and was soon away again to the fields. These houses were of one room, with a fire in the centre and an outlet above it for the smoke. The thatched roof was cupped towards this hole, so that the rainwater should run in and be caught for use.

Houses were never isolated; the lonely cottage or farmhouse of the European countryside did not exist. The little mud houses were built in compact groups, each village set round with a wall or a prickly hedge to keep it safe from barbarian raiders, and placed on the highest ground of its district, so that it should be out of reach of floods and the fields could be overlooked from it. The most precious crops were grown near the village, where they were safest. This arrangement was good in several ways, for the land farthest off, the most recently won from swamp and jungle, was suitable for rice and other grain; rice does not mind swampy ground, whereas mulberry-trees refuse to grow on it. These were set higher up; their leaves were essential to the silkworms, and so to the production of silk, the most valuable in the scale of commodities. Besides, the womenfolk needed to have the mulberry-trees near, for silkworms must be fed on fresh-gathered leaves, and many journeys must be made to keep up the supply.

These islands of cultivation and ordered life represented toil as heavy as that of any Canadian settlers. No wonder that the heroes to whom the Chinese looked back in their ballads and legends were not warriors but teachers, leaders who had helped them win their land. Shen Nung taught them the uses of fire and made the first plough and hoe; Huang Ti showed them how to work metal and to make the boats which played a great part in Chinese life.

THE MAIN PHYSICAL FEATURES OF CHINA

With Huang Ti, whose traditional date is 2704 B.C., the mists of antiquity clear somewhat, and the Chinese emerge as a number of independent clans unified, for the first time, under one ruler, who thus became the Lord (Ti) of the Yellow (Huang) Earth. From this time onwards, the nation has had, as its characteristic structure, that of the complex whole—a number of component parts welded together, sometimes closely, under a strong government, sometimes loosely, when rival governments split the country with civil war. But even so, cultural and racial ties would hold, and the oneness reappear. At first, however, the component parts were individually governed, each belonging to a local prince. This hindered their people from mixing, for just as a farmer does not let his sheep and cattle stray from his fields to join another farmer's animals, so the prince would expect his human "stock" to remain on his land.

On the time-map of the world's great cultures, at first sight, the slow-growing culture of China appears at a disadvantage beside those of Mesopotamia, in whose great cities, built layer on layer, each on the ruins of the last, writing was accepted as a normal part of life. The Chinese cities were small, with no *ziggurats* or pyramids; there was a way of writing, but the knowledge of it was, in early times, confined to a small circle of "wise men", and was akin to magic.

EARLIEST CHINESE WRITINGS

The originals of the earliest books are long since lost; the earliest extant Chinese inscriptions are on comparatively small objects, such as bells and the flat shoulder-bones of sheep, and all they usually say is: "This bell was cast in honour of So-and-so. Afterwards it belonged to So-and-so". Or: "King So-and-so inquired if the omens were favourable to his going hunting on such a date. They were, and he went." Yet the formation of the words shows a system that had already reached a certain degree of perfection.

And if China's civilization was in its childhood when others were fully grown, it is equally true that when they had grown old and faded into the museum-world of the antique, Chinese culture was still young. Similarly, the languages of those races can now be reconstructed, and their records read, only by dint of painstaking deductions and deciphering on the part of scholars, whereas big daily papers are printed in Chinese, as are school-books and novels.

The first Chinese device for conveying ideas without using sound was that of tying certain knots in a cord; finding it too limited, they thought out a system of cutting small pictures on a smooth surface, such as bone or flat strips of bamboo. Each word had its picture, and the pictures were placed, one below the other, on the narrow surface. That plan worked, and was developed into the Chinese script as it is written to-day—and it is still, with the exception of the few books which are produced in Western style, written in columns downwards, as in the days when a "book" comprised a bundle of bamboo strips.

To make a complete picture for each word was, of course, a long process, so, as time went on, as few marks as possible were used. Since the writing crystallized into its present form, each word had had a definite number of strokes, and each stroke its position, but that did not come about until, in the third century B.C., a brush made from hair came into use for writing. Previously, the pictures, if they were not cut with a graving-tool, had been drawn with a bamboo pen and lacquer ink, made from tree-sap; the style was that of the line-drawing, and each word was rendered as the writer thought best, so that the variations were almost limitless. This use of the brush brought in its wake a gradual standardizing that resulted in easier reading, and a technique of firm individual strokes that formed symbols rather than pictures.

The writing did not lose its pictorial character. The Chinese consider the art of calligraphy one with that of painting; the same brush will be used by the artist for his writing and his painting, and the strokes will be as carefully placed in the one as in the other. A modern Chinese will, when in a hurry, use a fountain-pen for writing; but when he is enjoying the act of writing—and it is an enjoyment, as great as any game or sport—he pauses a moment, with brush poised over the paper, to visualize the pattern he is about to place there.

Soon after brush-writing had taken the place of the old style, the term for "writing-materials", or "stationery", changes from "bamboo-and-wood" (i.e., a bamboo pen to write with and strips of wood to write on) to "bamboo-and-silk". The word for "a chapter" is the one used for "a roll"—i.e., silk is now the material for writing. Only a few years ago, there were found, in an ancient watch-tower of the Great Wall, letters on wood and on silk written somewhere about the year A.D. 150. There were also eight letters on paper. This is the oldest paper in the world; the accepted date of the invention is A.D. 105—less than fifty years previously. Papyrus had been known all round the Mediterranean for some time, but its use had never, apparently, spread as far as China.

INVENTION OF PAPER

The Chinese invention was different. The tendency of papyrus to split and fray away at the end is absent from even the earliest specimens of Chinese paper. For, in the Chinese process, it was not reeds that were used, but rags and old fish-nets, pounded in a mortar.

Thus rag paper, which, until 1885, was thought to have been invented by German or Italian craftsmen in the fifteenth century, and then attributed to the Arabs of the eighth century, is now known to have been made by the Chinese in the second. Chinese prisoners of war had taught their Arab captors the craft, at Samarcand, in central Asia. In the intervening six hundred years, the process had been improved, surfacing introduced for easier writing, and the range of papers widened. The Arabs made few modifications; when the Spaniards and Italians learnt from them in the thirteenth century, it was still the Chinese invention, though not recognized as such. The Chinese evolved their writing-brush in the third century B.C., and paper in the second century A.D.; but the deep, live, satisfying black ink of China did not come before the fourth or fifth century. Someone took lampblack and mixed it with gum. This solution, left to harden in a mould, produced the ink-"stick". By rubbing one of the flat ends on a smooth stone with a little water, the stick is ground, and so the ink appears. It is used rather thicker than European ink, and only enough for one occasion is ground at a time. The making of inksticks has been brought to a fine art, and an outstandingly good one is treated as a work of art in itself; some are many years old and still in use. The grinding releases a faint fragrance, and this is sometimes helped by the admixture of some flower perfume: the writer's own inkstick, however, gives a smell of leaf-mould and damp logs— very pleasant, and very natural too, for it is a pine-smoke stick. Some are made from oil-smoke; the degree of blackness is not the same, and painters make use of this variation by employing oil-smoke ink for delicate work and for rain-washed and misty scenes.

CAPACITY FOR ABSTRACT THOUGHT

The Chinese had equipped themselves with writing, that essential tool of thought. Moreover, while their material civilization was still simple, the range of words in use shows a high level of thought. It was not limited to the concrete things of rustic life—earth, metal, wood, and so on—but included abstract terms, such as loyalty, unselfishness and righteousness. If the Chinese did not leave behind them the elaborate monuments that make happy hunting for the archaeologist, it was because they used their mental equipment for entirely different purposes.

They were apparently struck by the quality of pattern in the universe and moved to express their thoughts about this; for they made a series of patterns, arrangements of straight lines in threes and sixes, each line either whole or broken by a space in the middle. These patterns were to represent the build of the universe as they perceived it. For example, the arrangement ☰ stood for heaven, sky, and the qualities of hardness, brightness and maleness. The arrangement ☷ stood for earth, and for the qualities of softness (that is, receptiveness), darkness and femaleness. There were also ☲ for fire, ☵ for water, and so on. Every three-line pattern having been combined with every other, sixty-four arrangements were arrived at. By experimenting with these variations, the patterns could be used as a guide to the future, for if the things and forces of the universe and their natures could be studied under one's eye in the form of written symbols, the problem of what was going to happen could be worked out. In this manner are quantities symbolized, and the problems regarding them worked out, by methods of algebraic thinking.

Since life became separated into compartments, each with its label, philosophy and divination have been pigeon-holed at a distance from one another. But since the "Book of Changes" comes to us from a time before the pigeon-holing habit had set in, it might be true to say that the patterns are an attempt to understand the universe, and as such, a philosophical work; and that from this springs their use for divination—on the assumption that, if you know how a thing works, you can find out what it is going to do next.

At some periods in its long history, this book of the patterns was used exclusively for divination, so that it became a magician's handbook. Country sayings, like our "Red sky at night is the shepherd's delight", and omens of good and bad luck, were mixed in. At other times, it would be, as it were, snatched out of the magician's hand and replaced on an intellectual pinnacle by some scholar who had seen its philosophical aspect. In fact, people are still puzzling over the problems of the Book of Changes, just as they are still puzzling over the problems of the universe.

THE CHINESE PATTERN OF LIFE

The title "Book of Changes" itself illustrates Chinese thinking. Seeing the swing of the seasons, of light and dark, of growth and decay, the ancient Chinese felt that the art of living must be that of conforming to this movement, being in step with this rhythm. The things that humans make and do, they seem to have reasoned, ought surely to be cast in the mould of the natural things, e.g., a wheel should have the pattern of a month, a spoke for every day, the rim for the moon's cycle. The idea of conforming to the make of the universe, of going with the grain and not against it, has remained with the Chinese, marking out their thought from both primitive and modern scientific nations. The "savage" expects his magicians, by means of magic formulae, to harness the unseen powers, in order to make them do what he wants. The modern European expects his scientists by their formulae, passed on to technicians, to bend the circumstances of his life into the shape he has in mind. But the Chinese have sought to conform to rather than to master. This attitude has led them to accept change as always present, and to feel that to try to obstruct it would be a mistake. Such an outlook is obviously different from the European; philosophers and ordinary people alike, we tend rather to treat change as an intruder.

The Chinese, like other races, interpreted their sense of the unseen as the animation of everything by spirits—dwelling in the earth which mothered them and all things, and in the mountains and rivers and woods, and even in the doorway of their houses—and they sought to maintain relationship with these by sacrifice. Often this was human sacrifice. Each village had its "grove", sometimes the scene of ritual dances and of harmless offerings, but also figuring in the old writings as a threat to transgressors of what awaited them.

Over all other spirits and forces was the "sovereign on high" (or "supreme ancestor"); and the sovereign on earth must mediate between him and the people. At the turn of the year, the ruler, representing all his people, faced north towards the remoteness in which dwelt the Sovereign on High, and offered sacrifice, making request for the nation's need in the new year, asking forgiveness for things amiss and taking the blame himself. Once when there had been a drought for seven years, the sovereign known as T'ang the Completer planned to offer himself as expiation, that the misery might be lifted from his people. Until 1912, every year, except during very troubled times, grain, wine and a bullock have been offered by the Emperor in the age-old ceremony. From Heaven the earthly sovereign held his mandate to rule, and when a ruling house had become incapable of ruling well, it was considered to have forfeited the mandate; rebellion against it was considered quite legitimate.

No one but the sovereign might approach the Sovereign on High. He was remote from the individual, and indeed individual approach to any of the unseen powers was practically non-existent. It would almost be true to say that the individual was non-existent as yet; in everything, the unit was a group—family, clan, village—and independence of thought or action was unknown. Only as the primitive order began to break up did the individual emerge, in the form of thinkers who put forward suggestions to meet the needs of the times.

CHAPTER 31

CONFUCIUS AND OTHER TEACHERS

BY the sixth century B.C., cracks had appeared in the social and political structure of Ancient China. The sovereign lost his place of authority among the princes, and the federation of Chinese states broke into separate units, each trampling on or being trampled by the other, as the rulers strove each to be strongest and richest. It was an age of insecurity, and this being so, technical sciences and arbitrary government came to the fore, since they showed results.

UPHEAVALS IN SOCIAL LIFE

Armaments developed, changing the technique of fighting. Bureaucracy developed; in one state the government took two industries, iron and salt, out of private hands, establishing a monopoly in them, and with these two in its hands was able to make a strong position for itself among its neighbours. Political killings, too, though not on the scale of the modern "purge", came to be an accepted feature of official life; power was misused so habitually that its misuse passed into currency as its use. People were ceasing to expect goodness, to remember that they had ever had standards of rightness.

There was, of course, the need to make some reply to their out-raged sense of values. The one nearest to hand was, as always, fatalism; the Chinese form was slightly different from our modern determinism, in that they lacked our elaborate terminology. Tech-nics, dialectics, economics; economic stress, economic laws, the economic man, and so forth—with these words we have built our-selves an elaborate shelter; they made the word for "a decree", or "that which is decreed", serve to cover the muddle and suffering of their day.

Fatalism was not, however, the only reaction to the times. There arose thinkers who set themselves to devise ways of getting out of the muddle, and as nowadays, this involved them in a rethinking of what they really wanted life and the community to be like. These men gathered followers, and moved from one state to another, offering their advice and services to any ruler who would have them. The princes usually received them well, for the gathering of such scholars around him added to a ruler's prestige, and debating was a fashion-able hobby. All this naturally invited glib-tongued spongers, yet sincere people were there also, and, in this environment, Chinese philosophy took shape.

BASIS OF CONFUCIAN PHILOSOPHY

Best known of these philosophers is Confucius—indeed to many, his is the only name associated with Chinese thought. We find him easy to admire, since his mind worked along very English lines; for he wrote much of personal qualities, such as good faith and good manners, he dearly loved tidiness, he respected the decencies and amenities of life, had a keen sense of duty, and disliked extremes. Even in his limitations he was very English, as, for example, in his self-consciousness.

His attention to what are apparently mere forms of politeness needs understanding. "When the Master saw a person wearing mourning, or anyone with the cap and garments of full dress, or a blind person, on observing them approach, though they were younger than himself, he would rise up. . . ." "When a friend sent him a present, though it might be a carriage and horses, he did not bow. The only present for which he bowed was that of the flesh of sacrifice." This gift had in itself a value not to be confused with that of ordinary presents, how-ever handsome. This value must receive acknowledgment if people were to be taught a sense of values.

Seeking to bring back the quality of coherent pattern into the life of his day, he appealed to the days when it had had that quality and urged men to revive them. Undoubtedly, this appeal to the "good old days" led him to idealize them, but he was trying to set some definite standards before his hearers, for any usurper, having seized the power, could use a title to which he had no real right, and get himself accepted. Names must be given back their value, said Confucius; while a usurper was called "Duke" and an organization incapable of governing was called a government, the common people of the land possessed "nowhere to put their hands and feet".

Confucius also stood out against arbitrary government. He put the personal influence of the ruler, transmitted through his officials, before laws and penalties. "The Master said, 'If the people be led by laws, and uniformity sought to be given them by punishments, they will try to avoid the punishment, but have no sense of shame. If they be led by virtue, and uniformity sought to be given them by rules of behaviour, they will have the sense of shame, and moreover will become good.' " All the same, he did not think of treating "the people" as individuals like himself: "The Master said, 'The people may be made to follow a path of action, but they may not be made to understand it'."

It is nevertheless true that the individual had found a place in Chinese thought. But that place was a small one, and mostly reserved for officials; collectivism still occupied the foreground, though individualism was standing in the background: "From the sovereign down to the mass of the people, each must make the nurture of his mind and character his first consideration."

As with all the great Chinese teachers, it is not the events of Confucius' life that are most important, but his words, "The Master said . . ." is the phrase characteristic of Chinese teaching. Not that his actions belied his words, but that they were secondary, the outcome of his spoken teaching. This seems to be part of the reason why the comparison with Christ as a teacher, usually made by comparing the sayings of each, has to be forced. In Christ's teaching, what is said fills the secondary place; its use is to illustrate, to throw light on what is done, for in these acts lives the essence of the teaching. Confucius' teaching, on the other hand, is in his words, and his actions are those to which his words committed him.

THE LIFE OF CONFUCIUS

Confucius was born in 551 B.C., of a family that belonged to the ruling class, though his father did not hold a high position, being a subordinate official in the state of Lu, part of what is now Shantung. He was the child of his father's old age, and was left fatherless at the age of three. It is suggested that the emphasis he laid in his teaching on the obedience and care a son should give his father, and the solidarity there should be in the relationship, was due to his thoughts dwelling on his dead father, missing him, idealizing him. It may equally well have been because his own son had turned out a disappointment that he thought so much about this relationship.

He entered government service as a young man, and as each department entrusted to him prospered, he was steadily promoted. Soon he was Chief Justice. But the Duke of Lu was far from having a free hand in his own domain, and although Confucius could and did give service that came up to his principles, such a state of affairs gave him no scope for putting his administrative ideas into practice. When, therefore, the Duke received a present of dancing-girls from a neighbouring ruler and was so fascinated that for three days he neglected all state affairs, Confucius left his service.

By then, he was about fifty-three. The next fourteen years he spent wandering from state to state, seeking a ruler who would let him try out his theories. He failed to find one, and at the age of sixty-seven, returned to his native Lu, though not to official life. By now, he had formed a school—in all, he taught about three thousand people—of students of political philosophy. Their textbooks were the ancient writings, including the songs and the Book of Changes mentioned above. Confucius spent the last five or six years of his life studying these books, and adding his own explanations. He died in 479 B.C., at the age of seventy-two, in his last recorded words expressing his disappointment that he had never had the chance to apply his ideas in the sphere of government.

LAO TSE, THE PROPHET OF TAOISM

Another, and very widespread, reaction to the times was that of withdrawal. Instead of attempting to check the corruption of public life, many men turned away. The feeling that, in essence, things and people are good, that originally they were good, is deep-seated in the Chinese mind; as to how to bring out this essential good, we have seen that the Confucian type sought to do this by training and discipline. The other type wanted to let everything and everyone alone, so that artificiality might fall away, and the world go back to what it originally was before man started adding lists of regulations to the great quiet smooth-running natural laws.

Thus, while Confucius was, in effect, calling to people "Brace yourselves!—and you will bring back order as in the days of the great kings", the other type of mind was finding expression in Lao Tse, who said in effect "Relax yourselves—slip back to the days before there were any kings".

"Horses have hoofs to carry them over frost and snow, hair to protect them from wind and cold. They eat grass and drink water, and fling up their heels over the champaign. Such is the real nature of horses. . . .

"One day Poh Loh appeared, saying, 'I understand the management of horses'.

"So he branded them, and clipped them, and pared their hoofs, and put halters on them, tying them up by the head and shackling them by the feet . . . with the result that two or three in every ten died. Then he kept them hungry and thirsty, trotting them and galloping them, and grooming, and trimming . . . until more than half of them were dead. . . . Those who govern . . . make the same mistake."

"In the days of Ho Hsu" (*i.e.*, far away in the olden days) "the people did nothing in particular when at rest, and went nowhere in particular when they moved. Having food they rejoiced; having full bellies they strolled about. . . . But when the Sages came to worry them . . ."—in brief, once the wise men started teaching knowledge and duties, the troubles which beset mankind.

SAYINGS OF LAO TSE

The passages just quoted come from the book of Chuang-tse, who was perhaps the greatest exponent of Lao Tse's school of thought. Lao Tse's own sayings lie scattered through a book, partly verse, partly prose, in which the teaching of his school of thought is set out for the benefit of would-be followers.

Little is known of him—his very existence has been questioned—but it is said that he was Keeper of the Archives of the State of Chou. So it is possible that, in reading the books there, he came across the idea that became the centre of his thoughts—that of the Way. To express the idea, he used the word for a road, "tao", but made use of other comparisons, such as water, there being no single word to render adequately the result of a search for the source and heart and life-pulse of the universe. The poetical character and the general obscurity of its writing make it difficult to define what is meant by the "tao."

"The nature of the Way, how obscure . . . yet in its midst there is an image. . . ." The Way, though itself not to be thought of in terms of shape or place, held within it the image, the likeness, of the myriad things of the world. These things came into being as the Way put forth its power. This power operated in two forces, each necessary to the other, showing themselves as light and darkness, male and female, sun and moon, sky and earth, Summer and Winter, and all the opposites which, fitting into their places, complete each other and, in fact, "make the world go round".

The wise man, confronted with the task of governing, studied the nature of the Way: "the highest good is like that of water. The goodness of water is that it benefits the myriad creatures; yet itself does not scramble, but is content with the places that all men disdain. It is this that makes water so near to the Way."

"The Way is like a boat that drifts;
It can go this way, it can go that.
The ten thousand creatures owe their existence to it and it does not disown them;
Yet having produced them it does not take possession of them."

One who understood the Way, the Law of the Universe, would work along the same lines in the world of humans. In governing the people:

"Rear them then, feed them,
Rear them but do not lay claim to them,
Control them, but never lean upon them."

The Sage was as unconcerned about himself as natural things about themselves.

"Heaven is eternal, the Earth is everlasting.
How come they to be so? It is because they do not foster their own lives;
That is why they live so long.
Therefore the Sage
Puts himself in the background; but is always to the fore.
Remains outside; but is always there.
Is it not just because he does not strive for any personal end
That all his personal ends are fulfilled?"

"He does not strive"—here we have the keynote of Taoist teaching. Do not strive to alter things. In governing, action is merely interference. If only I keep from meddling, the poor stupid ordinary people will get on all right; stirring them up, with laws and teaching, only wrenches them out of their simplicity. "Govern a great nation as you would cook a small fish"—*i.e.*, don't overdo it.

It must not be imagined, however, that the Taoist saw himself loving his people, or even thinking of them as live individuals; he was to be remote and impersonal as the Way itself. Standing, in thought, so far away from them that they were all blurred into one whole, and no one stood out distinctly enough to be thought of as a person, he was to bear in mind that:

"Heaven and Earth are not ruthful;
To them the Ten Thousand Things are but as straw dogs.
The Sage, too, is not ruthful;
To him the people are but as straw dogs."

Straw shapes of dogs were used at funerals; modelled with care, carried in procession . . . and then burnt. Perhaps this idea, in later times, led to what seems an inhuman and ungrateful habit of "scrapping" the man who had given his service, his years and his brains, to the Empire, once that service, like the usefulness of the straw dog, had been accomplished.

TAOIST DISDAIN OF WORLDLY THINGS

Disdain of the world and withdrawal from all share in its doings and feelings were obviously not a teaching for the ordinary run of men; nor had its exponents ever wanted it to be so. Moreover, Taoism gave ideas, as such, so large a place that no room was left for action, even viewed as the fruit of thought. Confucianism, on the other hand, was full of instructions with regard to action, prescribing in detail, without providing any deeper root than the thought of a well-ordered community. This was noticed by a man named Mo Tse, who had studied the teachings of both schools.

For ourselves, the Taoist mind is not so easy to understand as the Confucian, which is not far from that of the type of Englishman who "doesn't go in for religion; live a decent life and do a good turn here and there—that's his religion". This twofold confusion of thought gives a clue to the Confucian attitude. First, there is the confusing of ethics, a code of conduct involving such things as decency and kindness, with religion, a relationship, the very name meaning a binding-together. Secondly, there is the surprising assumption that effect produces itself independently of cause, the cart goes on without the horse; that the kind of behaviour he appreciates, through having been born into a tradition coloured with religion, can be kept going without it. "Behaviour springs from belief", Mo Tse said in effect (and there he would have modern psychology with him): "we shall get nowhere while we put philosophy, our own theories and systems, in the place of our responsibility to Heaven, over us all, and the spirits, present unseen among us all. We want to get back to good times? It was because, in the days of old, people feared and honoured the unseen world, and lived accordingly, that well-being came about."

MO TSE'S REJECTION OF FATALISM

Mo Tse, in standing out against the Confucian putting of the cart of behaviour before the horse of thought-background, was in line with the Taoists, who, even if they were all horse and no cart, did put first the idea of the Tao and the understanding of it. But in his conception of Heaven as having a will for men—and moreover for their good—Mo Tse diverges sharply from that of the impersonal uncaring Way.

"Heaven, the Lord of the World . . . sees everything that happens —in the woods, in the valleys, in hidden places where no human sight penetrates. . . . Now Heaven intends good and abhors evil, loves justice and hates injustice. . . . Heaven wishes the ruler to benefit his people, and that all men should love each other, because Heaven loves all men. . . . No, the ultimate motive for conduct is not the pleasing of a prince or of the Sovereign (i.e., not human respect), it is the Will of Heaven."

Mo Tse soon had a large following; these people he was very anxious to keep out of the rut of ingenious argument and manipulation of words that had become as much a curse, in its way, as fatalism. To this end, he wrote a treatise on logic, on the process of thinking, and keeping one's thinking related to actuality, which is both the first and the finest of its kind in Chinese literature.

Fatalism, he pointed out, was a tool ready to the hand of unscrupulous rulers, and made oppression easy. Oppression and greed, as shown in the wars of self-aggrandisement, were against the sovereign will of Heaven: "Heaven abominates the oppression or the killing of an innocent man. What then of those conquering princes who crush the weak? . . . crops trampled . . . beasts killed . . . women widowed and children orphaned. . . . Those who go against their human king can sometimes save themselves by flight, but where will the culprit hide who has gone against the Heavenly King?"

The Taoists too held that violence could not establish itself, brought no enduring result. They too said it must perish because it was contrary to the nature of the Way. But Taoism was too far-away and too negative to help a tormented world; when, however, Mo Tse said "The man of Ch'u is my brother"—Ch'u being a rival state—people caught a glimpse of an attitude of mind that was positive, one in which the men of one state really mattered to those of another. To embody this idea of having feeling for others, distant as well as near, Mo Tse used a term which is translated "universal love".

In the face of this expression, it is puzzling to find, included among the Mohist books, writings on scaling-ladders for sieges and other military devices. But the word rendered "universal" is really "wide-spread". Perhaps the Mohists did not spread their fellow-feeling so widely as to include the barbarian tribesmen. "The man of Ch'u is my brother"—but a man from another state was, after all, a Chinese; the barbarian tribes of the north were a different matter, and it may be that the Mohist inventions were part of the preparations made to keep them at bay.

What is certain from the Mohist and other writings is that there was at that time a scientific spirit, an interest in things as well as in sociology and philosophy in the narrower sense. The characteristics of things and how they worked began to be investigated. Experiments were made, e.g., with convex and concave mirrors, and the foundations laid for physics, mechanics, etc. Confucius said that one who wished to govern must first develop a fine personality; this he could not have unless he thought sincerely, and how could his thoughts be true unless he had a wide range of knowledge? For this, he must "investigate things". Later, however, this phrase no longer stood for study of the nature of things outside oneself, but was used subjectively, with a sense of clearing from one's mind all that hinders its capacity for intuitive knowing. This change is an illustration of what happened to Chinese thought: the experimental approach, that had been opening up new fields of knowledge, was never explored very far; the field of things within the human mind was explored instead. There were no more great philosophers for fifteen hundred years, and the two that then appeared occupied themselves with the nature of knowledge and of humankind, still subjective.

SCIENTIFIC THOUGHT STIFLED

Of these three schools of thought, that of Mo Tse perished in less than two hundred years. It had a large, organized following, and its exponents were honoured even by those who disagreed with them. The cause of its disappearance has not been traced; but opposition was heavy, especially from the Confucianists, with their vested interests in the political world. Its disappearance may go towards accounting for the strangulation of the scientific spirit in China, for when, after the torrent of condemnation to which Mohism was subjected, the ban was lifted, it appeared that the thread of experimental study had been lost.

Confucianism became the code of official life; government service, in any branch, could be entered only by passing an examination in the Confucian classical books; and so it was until 1905. Other books and other subjects naturally suffered neglect; education tended to be narrowed down to preparation for a Civil Service examination. The emphasis on the past, too, ingrained conservatism even more deeply into the Chinese character. But the Confucian emphasis on good manners gave life a quality of fineness, raising it above materialism and vulgarity. Confucianism's greatest benefit, however, was probably the maintaining of an aristocracy which was not based primarily upon birth, or even the possession of money, but upon brains.

CHAPTER 32

DEVELOPMENT OF IMPERIAL RULE

BY the third century B.C., the philosophers' voices were drowned in the noise of ceaseless wars. The states had lost all trace of federation, and the wonderful racial and cultural solidarity of the Chinese—the sense of being bound together by their language and literature, by the art and tastes and way of life that were different from any other race's—had not yet appeared. Each little state had its own customs and ceremonies, its own system of weights and measures—and its own axle-gauge. This last actually mattered a great deal: the soft roads soon wore into ruts, and drivers had to use the established track or get stuck. Therefore travel between different parts of the country involved constant change of cart or refitting of axles.

All this was changed by one man, Ch'in Shih Hwang-ti—Ch'in dynasty, First (shih) Emperor (Hwang-ti). He found the country a patchwork, worked it into a coherent pattern and left it a nation—whole, if somewhat stunned. The Ch'in First Emperor gave himself that title because he wished to found a dynasty of a quite different stamp from any former ruling house. Though he did not, in the end, found a dynastic line, he was truly the first Emperor; succeeding rulers took over his pattern of administration—there were no more feudal sovereigns and separate vassal states.

He came from Ch'in, the state at the western end of Chinese territory (near the handle of our fan), so that he had more than a dash of Tartar blood. This is significant. Of practically every great leader —ruler, general or both—through the centuries of China's history, could the same be said. He fought in the Tartar manner, using mobile cavalry, terribly effective against the Chinese infantry grouped round war-chariots. The Chinese princes tried to satisfy him by offers of territory; but he continued to advance step by step, each step another state annexed. After ten years had passed, all the territory possessed by the Chinese had been taken under his direct control.

One night, he was walking incognito in the streets of his capital, with only four soldiers for escort, when he was set on by bandits, the product of the past years of chaos and beggary. Following this experience, he had their straggling bands collected, drilled them into soldiers and sent them off to frontier wars. One such ex-bandit army added an extensive piece of land in the south-east to his territory, bringing it nearly as far as the coast. So began the use of criminals for soldiers, characteristic of the Chinese attitude to war.

If this immense territory was to be under the direct control of one man, an efficient system of communications must replace the existing absence of system. The Emperor built a spider-web of military roads and canals. These roads were provided with wheel-ruts of one unvarying gauge, axles being likewise standardized. So, too, were weights and measures, and the writing-pictures; within a few years, the diversity of Ancient China had been hammered flat.

THE GREAT WALL AND THE BURNING OF THE BOOKS

The Emperor was to be the pivot of his people's life in every way. For this, he must have divine prestige as well as human. The sovereigns of ancient days, turning towards the south, had received their vassal princes as the representative of the Sovereign Above; but the First Emperor wanted to be more than a representative. He established Emperor-worship, and supplemented it by surrounding his person and movements with mystery. The rooms of his palace were connected by underground passages, so that no one knew in which one they would find him. Even the evil spirits, he hoped, would be baffled. He made his untiring tours of personal inspection up and down the country incognito, so that the people never knew if the Emperor was near, hearing all they said. This was a good imitation of the divine quality of unexpected nearness, and his capacity for reading despatches and reports (a hundred and twenty pounds weight of bamboo-slips a day) gave him an uncanny omniscience.

As soon as the Empire was a going concern, the Emperor took in hand the matter of the Tartar invasions. All along the northern bank of the Yellow River run mountains, and behind these lie the bleak deserts, where duststorms sweep over miles of shelterless treeless land; formerly, there was more water, and therefore more vegetation and more people. These people spent most of their time in the saddle, riding small, sturdy, clever horses; and they would vary their usual occupation of clan warfare by raiding the Chinese. Local effort had lessened the damage of the small raids by closing the gaps with fortifications, even building lengths of wall over the hills, so that, although the raiders still got through, they could not drive back large droves of domestic animals.

But the menace of the large-scale invasion remained. The tribes were always on the move, impossible to catch, impossible to conquer. So the Emperor decided to keep them out. To this end, about 228–

210 B.C., he built the wall for which he is famous, linking existing fortifications to make one long wall over hill and valley, mile after mile, with watch-towers commanding every foot of it. In its present form, the Wall covers about two thousand two hundred and fifty miles; though partly in ruins, long stretches remain intact, from 15 to 20 feet high. The twenty thousand towers are each planned for a garrison of one hundred men, and there are ten thousand lesser watch-towers.

The Wall is similar in principle to the Roman *limes* (or frontier line), but on a much bigger scale. Hadrian's wall from Tyne to Solway spanned an eighty-mile stretch; this is fractional compared with the span of the China wall, which had to twist its difficult way up hill and down dale in arid, inhospitable country. It was a great achievement, carried through by forced labour—like all the First Emperor's achievements, scarred with the lash.

With so much accomplished (within a life of only fifty years), it seems strange that the Chinese have not remembered his name with gratitude. The answer may be sought in the phrase "The Burning of the Books". Cutting right across all the old ideas as he did, he roused deep resentment among the scholar class, since he rejected all their antiquated statecraft; and they managed to hinder him considerably. The simplest remedy was to destroy both them and the books on which they based their ideas. In 213 B.C., he had more than four hundred troublesome scholars put to death, and books on history and philosophy were burnt, if they had any bearing on politics. However, copies were preserved in the Imperial library, so that the books might not be lost altogether, but merely kept out of the hands of argumentative people. Unfortunately, this library was destroyed soon after the Emperor's death—an event for which he cannot be blamed; and to the Chinese, he has always stood for the "Burning of the Books", the violating of their intellectual heritage.

THE HAN DYNASTY

The First Emperor's successor was a puppet in the hands of greedy advisers, and the people rose in revolt. In less than four years, their leader was on the throne; the year 206 B.C. saw the Han dynasty established. The great contribution of the Ch'in emperor, that of a unified nation with a central government, survived the change of rulers, though the Han drew the cords less tightly than their predecessors. The new ruler lightened forced labour, and substituted for the cruelly heavy penalties of the Ch'in laws the simple code: "He who kills shall die. He who wounds shall be wounded in the same fashion. He who steals shall forfeit according to the value stolen."

The chief necessity that pressed upon the new Emperor was that of satisfying those who had helped him to power. By the time he had bestowed titles and lands on everyone of whom he was afraid, China was again perilously near to her old decentralized, divided state.

Actual fighting was avoided, but not bloodshed, for the new Emperor resorted to the weapon of the trumped-up charge, followed by political execution. The first Han emperor was quite unlettered; his undoubted ability therefore lacked the moral standards that the Confucian books might have given it, and he built a tradition of false dealing into the relations between sovereign and minister. This lack of trust has countless times resulted in sanguinary rebellion, many an official, hearing from a friend that he is out of favour at court, and knowing he will not be given a fair hearing, has decided to strike first; though there have also been reigns in which this vicious circle was broken, and a Confucian relationship realized.

The founder of the Han employed a second means to preserve the authority of the crown; though he gave away the title of certain lands, he kept the administration in the hands of government officials appointed from the capital, so that these titles in fact conferred more prestige than power.

WIDENING OF MENTAL AND PHYSICAL HORIZONS

The other tradition inherited from the Ch'in, that of territorial expansion, was carried further; out beyond China and into far countries went the expeditions of the Han. But it was not only frontiers that expanded during the four hundred years (from 206 B.C. to A.D. 220) of this dynasty. The mental horizon widened; there was much more to think about; most of those things that, for better or worse, divide civilized from primitive life made their appearance in this period. By the Chinese themselves, the dynasty is looked upon as one of the two most glorious in their history; the Han gave to the Chinese the term "Sons of Han", by which the majority of them speak of their race when they feel patriotic.

Chinese rule was soon extended to include those stretches of land in South China that had remained in the hands of independent non-Chinese tribes, bringing the frontier down to meet the coast-line; and making complete our "fan". At the time, though, the tribes only half submitted; the Canton district was not really Chinese until the T'ang dynasty, and the Cantonese do not speak of themselves as "Sons of Han", but as "Men of T'ang", when they are thinking of their Chinese heritage.

Northward and westward, expansion was really a means of defence, for the single line of the Wall was constantly being broken through by the most powerful of the barbarian peoples, the Huns. The first two or three emperors had to buy off the barbarians with presents. Meanwhile the country was gaining strength, and then came Wu Ti, the "Martial Emperor". Using the magnificent military road that the Ch'in First Emperor had driven northward through the mountains, he organized a system of supplies equal to maintaining a really large force of cavalry, and threw this force more than once right into the Huns' country.

The Great Wall of China at the Nankow Pass which gives access into Mongolia.

An early-nineteenth-century Chinese painting, by an unknown artist, showing an empress surrounded by the ladies of her court.

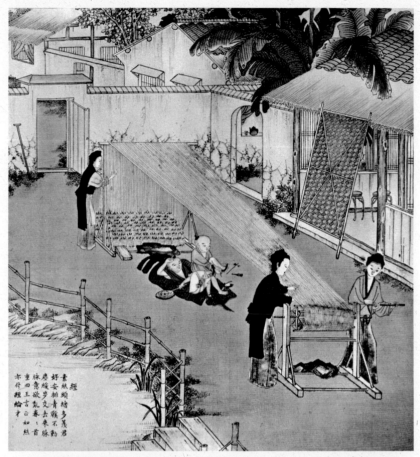

An original water-colour drawing showing weaving—the preparation of the warp —in the time of Emperor K'ang H'si (1662–1722). This drawing from the Victoria and Albert Museum, was prepared to illustrate "Silk Culture and Manufacture."

Meanwhile, he sent a man named Chang Ch'ien north-westward on a precarious journey, to find and negotiate with a people that had been driven out of their homelands by the Huns. These people would naturally be resentful, and ready to ally with the Chinese against the mutual foe.

So Chang Ch'ien set out on his long journey—farther than any Chinese had ever been before. He must indeed have felt lost in the vastness of mountain and silence and endless journeying. The Huns took him prisoner. Years went by, and he was still captive. He married a local woman. The Huns came to think of him as one of themselves, and took it for granted that the Emperor, too, had forgotten about him. Then one day Chang Ch'ien slipped away, taking his wife with him, straight on westward, ignoring his ten-year captivity as an incident on the road. In 128 B.C., he found the tribe he sought, but, after all, he found that they were unwilling to fight the Huns again.

The value of his journey, as it turned out, was to lie in the tremendous widening which it effected in the mental horizon of the Chinese. No Chinese had ever thought of such a thing as there being other civilizations comparable with his own, beyond the barrier of barbarian tribes. "There are cities, houses and mansions as in China", was an astonishing report. So far as is known, Alexander the Great had never been heard of in China, but now Chang Ch'ien came across two Seleucid kingdoms that bore the impress of the Macedonian empire. Other places introduced him to Persian civilization, and he heard, though he did not set foot there, of a great empire at the furthest end of the world—Rome.

THE SILK TRADE

Chang Ch'ien's report caused the thoughts of the Chinese government to turn westward. Embassies were sent to the more important central Asian nations and diplomatic and commercial relations with them were set afoot.

When the Han emperors sent out an embassy, the ambassadors would carry with them magnificent presents, in order that the foreigners might be impressed with the might, glory and prestige of China. And the presents consisted largely of rolls of silk.

One of the chief recipients of such presents was Parthia, situated east of the last outpost of the Roman Empire; it was not long before the Parthians realized that in Rome they had an eager customer. The Romans were both fascinated and mystified by the beautiful new textile which achieved rapid popularity.

So there came into being that most romantic chapter of commerce, "the silk trade". Loaded on to grunting camels, on to mules and thick-set pack-asses, carried across deserts and over mountains, taxed at strange city-gates; unloaded and re-loaded; sometimes defended in hand-to-hand encounters; guarded on lonely road and

M   (H.W.)

in crowded inn-yards—so the bales of silk went westward in their caravans. The Chinese merchants never saw the end of the journey; Parthian or Persian or other middlemen bought the silk and took it down to Syria, to be dyed at Tyre and elsewhere before being shipped to the wealthy centres of Roman civilization.

The Romans apparently did not care for figured Chinese silks, beautiful as they were; silk found its best market among them if it was taken only half-finished to the manufacturing towns of Egypt and Syria, and there unwoven, and either mixed with wool or linen, or re-woven as fine shimmering gauze, dyed in the popular colours. The middlemen were very careful not to let the Chinese merchants obtain direct access to their Roman customers; the Romans were even more anxious than the Chinese to cut out the middlemen, for Rome, and later Byzantium, was pouring currency into the East, unable either to redress the balance of trade by exports (since the East produced everything) or to restrain its craving for silk clothes.

This was the position when Justinian received an offer which, if he were willing to pay a suitable reward, would make him independent of imported silk—an offer to smuggle silk-moth eggs out of China. The offer was accepted, the eggs were brought through, hidden in a hollow cane, and in course of time China lost her Mediterranean customers. The trade could not have lasted so long if the secret of the process of silk-production had not been most carefully guarded. The Romans had no idea how it was made or from what.

In China, silk was an accepted part of everyday life, and had been cultivated in ordinary village homes since early times. This is still so, the racks holding the trays of silkworms sometimes standing in the corners of the living-room, though nowadays a room is usually set apart, in order to have temperature and atmosphere always right. The trays must have fresh air, though cold or draught would be fatal. When the sun shines, they must be lifted out.

In the course of his thirty-five or -six day career, the grub changes his skin four times, grows from a little black thing $\frac{1}{16}$ inch long to a fat, soft sausage-shape of about $1\frac{1}{2}$ inches, and consumes an enormous amount of mulberry-leaves and human energy. He then rolls himself up in yards of floss-silk of his own spinning, and waits until he has become a moth strong enough to break his way out. But before that can happen he is taken and killed by the application of heat. Afterwards the silk is reeled off, ready for the textile processes. Meanwhile, the trays are filled with a second crop of grubs, and when these have spun their silk, with a third.

IMPERIALIST EXPANSION

Following Chang Ch'ien's mission, the first century B.C. saw regular commercial and diplomatic intercourse established with those nations between China and the Caspian Sea. In the early years of the next century, internal troubles diverted China's attention, but as soon as they were settled, one of the ablest generals China ever had, Pan Ch'ao, put before the Emperor a bold plan. It was no less than the subjugating of those nations, but not with a vast army sent and maintained from China at great expense; the Emperor would never have consented to such a plan, for a strong party among his advisers were against further operations in the West, as being futile and costly. Pan Ch'ao only wanted a small force of picked Chinese troops with their officers, and he undertook to raise the army he needed from among the friendly nations, train them under his Chinese, and use them against the hostile nations. The Emperor consented, and Pan Ch'ao departed. Seventeen years later, in A.D. 97, he arrived on the shores of the Caspian at the head of seventy thousand men. Behind him, the entire length of central Asia with its many peoples lay under Chinese sovereignty. Chinese power stretched almost to the Roman frontier; this point in her history is China's high-water mark territorially. In other things, such as art and poetry and philosophy, the Han times were surpassed, but never again was Chinese rule carried quite so far.

When the first Han Emperor wanted a team of horses to draw his carriage, the entire country could not produce four of a colour, such was its poverty. Under lighter rule, the country revived rapidly, but the garrisoning of the wall drained off men and money, and when the Martial Emperor came to the throne with his large ideas, the problem demanded something different from the usual extra squeeze in taxes. The community had outgrown the government's view of it, and now the business of providing money raised the whole problem of the structure of society and means of obtaining livelihood.

RISE OF A COMMERCIAL CLASS

There were, broadly speaking, two factors in the Han economic problem. In the first place, there was not enough currency for the increasing population and its multiplying needs. But this, and the fact that more and more people lived in the towns and life was much more town-centred, were only surface-indications of the great social change that had taken place. Briefly, the business man had arrived. He it was whose circulation of the money had outstripped the supply of it, he it was who focused life in the town, and it was he, the merchant, the trader, to whom the governments so far had refused a place in the community. This second factor was the vital one.

The government came to realize that a great part of the country's wealth was flowing along channels which they had neither tapped for revenue nor regulated for the good of the community. While they were collecting taxes on farm produce, fortunes were being amassed in iron (then just coming into general use), in salt, and also in hoarding, profiteering and speculating. For the new commercial class had that lack of a sense of responsibility which is characteristic of people denied their privileges—they took all they could get while they could get it. Nevertheless, the Emperor, against his advisers' wish, turned to these very people to ask their counsel and help, and ultimately this step justified itself. As a result, the iron and salt industries were taken over by the state, but their operation was left in the hands of those who had formerly owned them under the supervision of the state.

Meanwhile, however, the opposing party prevailed on the Emperor to issue a decree that every trader must declare the total of his assets, for a capital levy. Attempts at concealment were punished by confiscation of all possessions and a year's forced labour on the frontier; men were encouraged to denounce each other by the promise of half the confiscated fortune. Chaos promptly resulted. All thrift and sober trading disappeared, giving way to a hand-to-mouth getting and squandering; the ruin of the commercial class had thrown the whole country's life out of gear; it began to be understood that the business man was an indispensable part of the community.

SOCIAL AND EDUCATIONAL CHANGES

We have seen through what great changes Chinese life was passing; in politics, with the coming of centralized government; in economics, with the recognition of commerce; in social life, with the arrival of a commercial class. The social structure was now very different; the old nobility had been destroyed by the First Emperor, but the scholar class had survived him, and so also had something of the old learning, in spite of the famous "Burning of the Books". To these people, the rank and file now looked with the respect formerly given to the old hereditary nobility, and not to those in power—uncultured men whose "push" had brought them to the fore. This applied to the new Emperor himself. The founder of the Han had, as he himself put it, "obtained the Empire on horseback". But a great nation cannot be administered from the saddle, and boors do not control indefinitely their intellectual superiors. The contempt and opposition of the scholars were a factor that had to be taken into account. The Martial Emperor faced this reckoning; he reinstated the scholars, although the school which had best survived was the Confucian, and Confucianism had, as its background, the very state of life and politics which the new rulers had been at such pains to destroy.

So far the scholars' only employment had been the piecing together of all that could be collected of the ancient literature, but it was work that disciplined their minds, for it involved the patient sorting of genuine from spurious, the critical outlook and the ideal of accuracy. They were thus fitted for administrative work when they were at last allowed to return to it.

The absorption of the scholar class into the Han national scheme was made easier by the distance which now separated them from the days of the philosophers they studied. The structure of society that Confucius knew had become dim and hazy. This haziness made easy the adaptation of his teaching to fit the monarchical state. As his discussions of political theories did not include the form of government that now prevailed, there was no passage that expressly condemned it. The Han commentators merely wrote their views beside the text, and the thing was done. To do them justice, however, they and all Chinese commentators on ancient writings have been most careful not to tamper with the text itself.

The examination of books which, it was claimed, had been kept safely hidden in walls at the time of the Burning, and the work of resurrecting the ancient literature, bred in the Han scholars a taste for historical research. Annals had been kept at the courts of the various princes and rulers for a long time, but now that there was a desire to see the past in a coherent form, the historian appeared on the scene.

The first half of the Han period produced the Herodotus of Chinese history—Ssu-ma Ch'ien. He wrote the history of China from remotest antiquity to his own day (first century B.C.), and his book has served as model for the histories of each subsequent dynasty. Having access to the ancient documents in the Imperial library, he used these as the bricks, and his own original writing as the mortar, to build his history. He did not summarize or quote, but copied his sources whole into his book, so preserving for us many documents that would otherwise have been lost.

Dictionaries also made their appearance during the Han; three, in all, were produced at this time. The Chinese have always based their dictionaries, not on an alphabet—since they use picture-writing instead—but on the number of strokes in a word. They evolved their system long before we had thought of ours.

It might be said of the whole Han period that it was the one in which, not only on the map but in every way, China took on her characteristic shape; Chinese life was developing those features which were to remain with it and give it its character. Not that the Han represents Chinese life at its best; in some ways, it shows it at its worst. This is especially true of the Han court.

THE CHINESE COURT

If one were to make a diagram of Chinese history, it would not be a single curve ascending to greatness and then dropping down again, but a series of waves, each corresponding to a great dynasty, each rising sharply on the impetus of the founder of the dynasty and his immediate successors, who carry the nation to great heights, not only of well-being, but of art and poetry and letters generally. Then the crest passes, sliding down a long slope into a trough of civil war, Tartar invasions, and upstart kinglets who between them dismember the country. The slope down which the people are carried is always that of the rottenness of the court; the Han court may be said to typify the enervating and highly artificial environment that slowly undermined each of the successive Imperial families.

THE EXTENT

Founded in 202 B.C., the Han Empire endured until A.D. 220, being for a time
contemporary with the Roman Empire in the West. The boundaries shown by
the dotted lines on the above map are necessarily approximate. The power of the
dynasty fluctuated, and with it the degree of its control over the subject states.

OF THE HAN EMPIRE

As the Han emperors controlled the caravan routes through central Asia, it was possible to open up trade with the Roman Empire, Chinese silk being the principal article of export. Contacts with other lands during this period influenced Chinese thought, as for example did the introduction of Buddhism from India.

While China was still a federation of small states, the marriage of rulers had been largely a matter of concluding an alliance with another state by marrying a daughter of its head, in the European manner. But now that there was only one state, the Emperor must marry among his subjects. This meant that the Empress and her family wielded supreme power, without training, and without thought of country and people or of anything but self-interest. Knowing that, once the young Emperor came to the throne, their family's brief blaze would be quenched, they would seek to prolong their spell of power. One child would be made successor to another who had conveniently died; if the nominee was a weakling or a baby, so much the better—one Emperor was one hundred days old at his accession, and his "reign" was one year. The alternative method of retaining power was a palace revolution; the throne might change hands before resistance could be organized. These attempts were frequent, but rarely successful; the father's family saw to that.

If we look at the upbringing of the fine Confucian Emperor who, in the first century A.D., gave the Han its second crest of greatness, and then at that of his spineless successors, the contrast will be explained. He had not been brought up in Palace courtyards, for a usurper was in possession of them at that time. His boyhood, if unsettled, was spent in the good company of ordinary Chinese people. These others, on the other hand, spent their early years in the company of feud-ridden, whispering Palace women, and the lying, scheming eunuchs who had charge of them. In an atmosphere of furtive evil, the young heir would grow up. Even when he was transferred from the women's quarters of the Palace, the eunuchs were still around, tossing the ball of power this way and that.

THE DISCOVERY OF TEA

Only second to the eunuchs as a curse, were the magicians. They are not much encountered during the later periods, but in Han times their power was enormous. Again in the T'ang, the next great dynasty, they found credulous Emperors eager for the elixir of life which should defy death. Four T'ang Emperors actually died of an overdose of "elixir of life". It is said, however, that it was while searching among the mountains for herbs to brew the elixir that men accidentally discovered tea, now the world's most widely spread drink. Tea is first mentioned in Han times; Europe had to wait till, at the beginning of the eighteenth century, English merchant ships were equal to making the voyage to "Cathay" a regular thing. Even then it had to remain a luxury until Indian tea-growing had reached the mass-production scale. But in China, except in the north, where the weather was too cold, it could be grown, along with the other crops, on the ordinary man's little plot of ground. It endeared itself to the Chinese by its fragrance as well as its taste, and by its social qualities of refreshment and welcome.

CHAPTER 33

THE SPREAD OF BUDDHISM

TAOISM was a very different thing in Han times from what it had been in the days of Lao Tse and Chuang-tse. Not that the original Taoism had ever died out,—the Chinese love of quietness and of nature was too great to allow that; but obviously the life of the hermit-sage is impossible to most people. On the other hand, it was a first-class commercial asset to have acquaintance with hidden learning and with potent medicines brewed from herbs found far away in the mountains, and there soon sprang up a numerous class of pseudo-sages. Where the original Taoist writers had spoken of riding the wind and not fearing the tiger's claw, thus symbolizing the mind of the man who understood the Tao, these quacks expounded such speech as literal, and represented themselves as holding the key to these powers. Primitive beliefs and fears fitted naturally into such a framework, and the ancient lore of spells and magic, rejected by the Confucianists, was taken up by the Taoists. Even as understood by educated people, Taoism had lost its spirituality; the idea of the sage not fostering his life, but resting like the sky and the earth in the unfailing operation of the Tao, had given place to a system of nursing one's physical powers by special breathing and special postures, and the non-striving attitude of mind had become a selfish indifference; by avoiding all strain and wearing-out of oneself, life might thereby be prolonged and ill-health avoided.

Thus, no advance had been made in the things of the mind since the days of the great philosophers. Certain barbarous customs had been dropped: human sacrifice at the village "grove" was no longer made; a king's servants were no longer buried with him at his funeral—clay figures were now put in his tomb instead. This may have been due to economy rather than humanity; there is no indication of the setting of a higher value on life. The discontinuing of such customs does not mark a step forward in the sense that, for example, Abraham's decision that the killing and offering of his son is not what is wanted marks such a step. Moreover, the life of the mind badly needed new soil. This it was soon to find.

INSPIRATION FROM CENTRAL ASIA

Now that the Chinese had made acquaintance with the central Asian peoples, they found that these nations possessed pictures of a rare beauty and a style quite new to them.

Sculpture, too, had been developed, thanks to Greek contacts. In itself, it was a new idea to the Chinese. When they used stone as a medium, they either cut words into it or they made pictures on it by

361

chipping away the background and letting the figures and other objects portrayed stand out as a pattern left by the chisel. Details, such as faces, clothes, horses' harness, were obtained by cutting fine lines, almost like our pencil strokes, across the raised part. This was not so near to sculpture proper as our bas-relief carving; it did not aim at giving a flattened version of the form; it was not concerned with rounded forms at all.

CHINA'S DEBT TO INDIA

It is true that, just before the Chinese saw the Buddhist statues, they had begun to carve in the round. But on the whole, sculpture in China goes with Buddhism. The Chinese did not make it an art of their own, it remained associated in their minds with Buddhism and they did not feel any desire to extend it to other subjects. Almost the only non-Buddhist sculpture is that of the half-fantastic stone animals that are sometimes placed in an avenue up to the entrance of a great tomb. The Chinese are not minded towards representation in the round, or to form as distinct from line; even their Buddhist statues are conceived from the point of view of someone standing in front to look at them. The figures have the lines of a picture, to be seen against a background.

The Chinese began to purchase pictures and statues in central Asia and take them back to China. The source of these things, as of the ideas that inspired them, was India, which became for them the wonderland in the west, rich in beauty and wisdom. They longed to possess more of the intellectual life hidden in Indian books and expressed in golden statues. Immense distances separated them; language separated them—not one word of the Indian books was like any of their own; yet in A.D. 61 or 62, the Emperor dispatched the first mission to India, which, following Ch'ien's route, made its way the length of the Himalayas and down into India proper.

In A.D. 67, they returned, bringing manuscripts and images, and also two Indian monks, who gave the rest of their lives to the work of translating into Chinese the "sutras"—the canonical books.

So Buddhism came to China. But for nearly two and a half centuries, it was largely held back from the mass of the people by a government decree that no Chinese might become a monk. Knowledge of its scriptures being virtually confined to those who had their whole time to give to the study, the Chinese again had to depend on the interpretation of people from the border countries.

Meanwhile, the work of translating the sutras went on—helped by learned Indian Buddhists who had heard of China's hunger for the Law—right up to the seventh century, and it was the motive of a number of journeys to India by keen Chinese Buddhists. The two best known of these travellers are Fa Hsien and Yuan Chuang; their writings enable us to look at the India of their days as it was seen through Chinese eyes.

Fa Hsien left China in A.D. 399, with eight companions; he was then twenty-five years old, and had been five years a monk. The little company trusted to find lodging at monasteries on their way, and food and help at the hands of devout laymen. One man saw them through a seventeen-day journey across a desert "in which there are many evil demons and hot winds . . . the only mark and indication [of the way] being the dry bones of the dead." This trek brought them to Shen-Shen, a central Asian kingdom that had owned China's sovereignty in the days of the Han empire. Its Buddhist king received them well. Fa Hsien notes that Buddhism was studied there in the original Sanskrit. The perils of rivers and mountains were the only ones they encountered, for everywhere was monastic hospitality: "When stranger monks arrive, the old residents meet and receive them, carry for them their clothes and alms-bowl, give them water to wash their feet, oil with which to anoint them, and the liquid food permitted out of the regular hours."

He traversed North India without succeeding in his quest for books, for there the teaching was transmitted orally. It was not until he had reached central India that he found what he wanted. There, in a monastery of the Mahayana school of thought, he settled down for three years to study Sanskrit and copy out the books.

THE MAHAYANA MISSIONARIES

Buddhism came to China in its Mahayana form. In India the two forms existed at that time side by side—Mahayana, the "Great Vehicle" (Maha = great), and the older school, called in contradistinction Hinayana, the "Small Vehicle". The terms "Northern" and "Southern" Buddhism are also used, lest "Hinayana" be taken to imply inferiority. Broadly speaking, the difference is between an exclusive and an inclusive attitude of mind. Hinayana has aimed at excluding inferior ideas, however attractive; the Mahayana has been inclusive rather than critical, which has resulted in a varied collection of ideas, some magnificently great, some disappointingly small.

Hinayana had not established contact with any other thought than that covered by the name Hindu. Mahayana, on the other hand, had acquired a wider circle of acquaintance. The recognition that absolute truth cannot be arrived at by reasoning or collecting information, but only by intuitive knowing, that once it is expressed in symbols it is inadequately rendered and can be no more than relative—since truth is infinite and human brains only finite—is a view by no means confined to Buddhism. But emphasis on this view shaped Buddhist history, for the Mahayanists were ready to enlarge their circle of knowledge from any source they came upon, and of course the more they travelled the more they found.

It is known that a number went to Syria, and to Bactria in central Asia. In these places, as well as at Alexandria and in South India, they came into contact with Christianity in some of its forms,

notably Nestorianism. In recent times, some scholars have emphasized the points of resemblance between the two religions. Others
have brought forward dates and arguments in opposition, denying
Christian influence on Mahayana thought. Whichever view is right,
these contacts must be mentioned.

These Buddhists were missionary-hearted; they wanted the whole
world to know the things they knew. To pass on one's knowledge was
a duty Gautama Buddha had set before his disciples in giving them
the ideal of Nirvana. This Nirvana, the understanding of the real
nature of things which of itself sets one free from them and from the
bundle of sensations and desires which go to make the illusion of
personality, is a state to be attained, and the knowledge of the way
to it a thing to be shared. But as time passed, the obligation to teach
others was eclipsed by the idea of escaping oneself from the wheel of
life with its cycle of re-births, never again to have to undergo the
process of living.

THE BUDDHIST IDEAL OF ENLIGHTENMENT

Many Buddhists, however, felt this ideal to be too selfish, and the
Bodhisattva became the Mahayana ideal. The Bodhisattva is one
who, having attained enlightenment, refuses the bliss of Nirvana that
he may remain within reach of humans, to serve them, teach them,
save them. "I shall not enter into final Nirvana before all beings
have been liberated." There is an exquisite Buddhist poem in which
a Bodhisattva expresses his desire to help: "May I be a protector of
the helpless! May I be the guide of wayfarers! May I be like a boat,
a bridge and a causeway for all who wish to cross! May I be a lamp
for all who need a lamp! May I be a bed for all who lack a bed! . . ."
". . . I have devoted this body to the welfare of all creatures. They
may revile me all the time or bespatter me with mud; they may play
with my body and mock me and make sport of me; yea, they may
even slay me . . . those persons who revile me, or do me harm, or
scoff at me, may they all attain Enlightenment!"

Who could help responding with loving devotion to such a one—
who could help turning to him, longing to find him? The Buddhists
did not speak of historical Bodhisattvas, but personified the idea,
giving such names as Maitreya, Manjusri and Avalokitesvara, and
placing these Bodhisattvas in one of the heavens where they were
invisible but not unapproachable. Thus the Bodhisattva idea brought
the quality of devotion into Buddhism.

The Mahayanists did not abandon the idea that Gautama had
held so firmly, that there is no such thing as a single entity, a permanent "this"—that both people and things are complex and always-
changing groupings of their components; but in practice they trans-
cended it; moreover, they counteracted its tendency to depreciate
the value of human personality by their teaching that the supreme
dignity of Buddhahood was open to all.

Thus it came about that the philosophy which of all had probably the most negative attitude towards the individual, and that automatically cut out worship, developed into the religion which met the two great needs of the Chinese man-in-the-street—his need for a value as an individual, and his need to find an outlet for the worship-instinct. The old philosophies of China had been chiefly concerned with the state. Since they grew out of political theories designed to remedy national ills, they were, from the start, collectivist; the value of the individual was only that of his contribution to the whole.

The religion-side of the Chinese mind was starved; it had had no food since the classical period, when Mohism had taken people's ideas about the relationship between the human and unseen worlds, and given those ideas philosophic form and literary expression. After Han times, there was only the recognition of a crowded pantheon, always receiving additions of capricious and rather stupid gods and demons, to be tricked or placated as the occasion indicated. Ancestor-worship, for all its dignity and naturalness, could not supply the lack; it merely continued after death the honour and service due to the senior members of a family. Name-tablets were set up to symbolize the people who had borne those names, and the family assembled in front of them and made symbolic acts of service, such as bringing bowls of food to set before them, that the ancestors might not suffer hunger in the next world. And when the living members had made their bows of homage, their respects had been paid. Thus when Buddhism offered itself, a religion of individual approach, it fed a twofold hunger.

TEMPLES, MONASTERIES AND PERSECUTION

Of the various difficulties that stood between the Chinese and their new religion, government distrust was the greatest; it gave Chinese Buddhism time to grow deep roots of patience and keenness. By the time Fa Hsien was born, the Han Empire was no more, the country was torn by competing rulers, and in North China several Tartar chieftains had set up small kingdoms. Here Buddhist temples and monasteries flourished, but this was hardly a recommendation of Buddhism to the authorities in the still Chinese-owned land further south. Taoist interests also lay in the direction of making things unpleasant for Buddhism.

Nevertheless, by the time China was re-united under Chinese rule, in A.D. 589, Buddhism was firmly established. Its position was enormously strengthened by the fact that women had a place in it. The "Lotus of the Good Law", one of the most revered sutras of Chinese Buddhism, tells of a woman becoming a Buddha. The passage envisages a scene in which Gautama Buddha sits in state, surrounded by Bodhisattvas. "Is there any being who . . . can attain speedily to Buddhahood?" asks one; "There is the daughter of the Dragon-king Sagara," replies another, ". . . wise and keen of faculties." The other Bodhisattvas are very sceptical; "How . . . could a woman's body so speedily become a Buddha?" Nevertheless, they see her transformed into a Buddha before their eyes. No wonder Buddhism had the women on its side.

From time to time, its popularity has drawn down on it government disapproval, not so much because it commanded the people's allegiance as because it drew so many away from production and military service to a monastic life. Sometimes this disapproval would amount to definite persecution, mostly in the form of the confiscation of monasteries and convents, and the driving back into secular life of the monks and nuns. The last and worst of these persecutions took place in A.D. 845, towards the end of the T'ang dynasty; but the faith sprang up again immediately, and there were no more attempts to crush it by violence. During the reigns of Buddhist emperors, the officials naturally could not take action against it, but the general tone of the administration was always Confucianist. Its attitude can be gauged from an edict issued in the eighteenth century, under a Confucianist emperor:

"If you seek no happiness that does not pertain to your lot in life, nor meddle with matters that do not concern you, but simply mind your own business, you will enjoy the blessing of the gods accordingly. Let the farmer just look after his farming, and the soldier go on his rounds at the guard station . . . and the Empire will be at peace. . . ."

The four troubled centuries between the Han and the T'ang saw progress and growth as well as violence; in fact, the wonderful blossoming of art and letters and knowledge, and indeed, the splendour of life in general that accompanied the T'ang dynasty was probably made possible only by this growth.

REPRODUCTION OF BUDDHIST SUTRAS AND SYMBOLS

Mention has been made of the need, soon felt by Chinese Buddhists, of a popular literature. The rapid expansion of Buddhism meant that not only the sutras, but simplified explanations of their teachings, were so greatly in demand that a duplicating process was badly needed.

It had long been the custom to take rubbings of inscriptions on stone, by which process the words were left white on a black background. But rubbings would not show detail of the smallness of words on a page.

Seals, too, had long been in use. The first use to which Buddhists put the seal-impression was that of reproducing quickly small pictures of Buddha. To make, or to buy, likenesses of Buddha was a means of accumulating merit as much as the repetition of the name of Buddha; this largely accounts for the immense number of representations, carved, like those cut in the living rock of the Tun-huang caves, painted on silk and on paper, and impressed from a seal.

Words, as well as Buddha-pictures, were carved on to seals, and the seal became bigger, to offer a larger surface for carving; it was no longer a little thing with a handle, but a square block. Then came the idea of laying the inked block flat, placing the paper over it (instead of putting the paper down first and the block on it), and brushing the paper with a dry brush, so that an even contact was made with the inked ridges of the carved words. This was practically the same technique as that for taking rubbings, except that, on the block, the words stood out, with the spaces between strokes cut away, instead of being cut in and the spaces left high.

THE INVENTION OF PRINTING

So from the seal and the "rubbing", there emerged the block print. It probably came into being during the reign of Ming Huang of the T'ang (A.D. 712–756); the oldest printed book extant is a copy of the *Diamond Sutra*, printed in A.D. 868. This was discovered in the Chinese province of Kansu in 1900.

The book is in the form of a continuous roll; another form was that of the long strip folded concertina fashion. This is still used in Buddhist literature, but in the tenth or eleventh century a more convenient mode was found—perhaps imported from the West. This, in an adapted form, has been for centuries the standard for Chinese books. Two consecutive pages are printed side by side on a sheet of paper, the sheet folded in the middle and bound in at the double edge. Each leaf of the book is therefore double, one side only being printed. The fine silky paper is too thin not to let the ink through, so that it does not stand printing on both sides, but even doubled, the leaves are thinner than those of most European books.

In a book dating from the Sung dynasty (10th to 13th centuries), there is on one page a word lying sideways. That means that movable type was being used. When, in the fifteenth century, printing came to Europe (whether invented independently or derived from the East it is impossible to say), block printing there gave way to movable type from the moment the latter appeared. In China, the survival of the block is probably traceable to the different character of the script. There the unit is the word; with us it is the letter, so that the preparation of a page for printing involves using a small number of units over and over again in different arrangements to make different words. But the Chinese page needs a very large range of units, and except where the same word occurs again, each one varies.

The wooden block, carved for two pages, is in fact typical of Chinese printing just as the press is of European. Nowadays the linotype machine has been successfully adapted for the Chinese script, but the word used for "to print"—"yin-shua"—remains the same. It means literally to press (with one's hand, as a seal) and brush; *i.e.*, the two actions of blockprinting, laying on the paper and carefully brushing it until it makes an even contact with the block.

The T'ang dynasty (A.D. 618–907) saw Buddhism in China grow into Chinese Buddhism. Many ideas deeply rooted in the Chinese mind were also in the Indian mind at the time of the conception of Buddhism, so that when Buddhism came to be grafted on to Chinese thought, the sap mingled readily. The Buddhist sought the state of mind in which he thought of himself as a temporary grouping of matter and energy that was part of the Whole; the state of mind which should make him free, detached. The Taoist philosopher sought to understand the Tao and share in its ways, and so give himself the freedom of impersonal detachment. Both held the ideas of release and of withdrawal, and both gave personality a secondary place.

BUDDHIST SCHOOLS OF THOUGHT

As regards the outside world, both held that change was at the very foundation of everything. Buddhism was derived from an Indian philosophy that held this view, and we have seen how, in the earliest times, China coined the word that stands as title in the "Book of Changes". Where Taoist and Mohist thinkers taught the quietening down of desires, Buddhists went further and taught the extinction of them. Where Confucian statesmen based their scheme of human relationships on the assumption that human nature was good in itself and proper training would bring out the good, Buddhist teachers proclaimed that everyone had, within himself or herself, the Buddha-seed, which each must nurture.

Later Confucianism, as we have seen, cultivated intuitive rather than experimental knowledge; Taoism had done so from the first, but Buddhism brought the cultivation to a fine art, especially in the Meditation school, a form of Buddhism brought to China in the sixth century by an Indian named Bodhidharma.

Of the several schools that Chinese Buddhism developed, that of Meditation is the one that has shown most intellectual life; there was another, based on the Indian "Mantra" sect (mantra, a spell), which revealed its teachings only to an inner circle of initiates, and made its words and terms carry hidden meanings. For the mass of simple folk there was the teaching of the Pure Land school. One worshipped Amitabha, the Universal Buddha, and sought rebirth in His paradise, the Pure Land. The Chinese felt the difficulty of conflicting teachings, so they devised a "Heaven-wide" school to embrace all the others. For a time, this school had a great vogue, but as it was designed to exclude no one, it never achieved much.

The triumph of Buddhism was a source of considerable anxiety to the Taoists. They met its competition with bare-faced imitation, and tried to counter its popular literature with a mass of stories of the uncanny powers possessed by Taoist magicians, and the marvels performed by them. Some of the Buddhists joined in this cheap scramble for popularity, with the result that the mass of the Chinese people was not offered the best in Buddhism.

CHAPTER 34

THE T'ANG DYNASTY

JUST as the Ch'in dynasty unified China, without producing a line of real rulers, and had that work taken out of its hands by the Han, so at the end of the sixth century the Sui dynasty re-united China, but failed to hold the country's allegiance and was superseded by the T'ang.

When the Sui restored order, the governorship of one province in the north-west corner of China was given to a family named Li, as Dukes of T'ang. Life near the frontier was an unremitting parrying of Tartar thrusts, and much depended upon the Governor's vigilance and energy. But such qualities were far from the Duke, who loved ease and hated making decisions. This being so, the officers of the frontier garrisons could not expect much backing from headquarters; but on the spot, they had the second of his three sons, Li Shih-min, a lad still in his 'teens and, naturally, without military experience.

A SCHOLARLY WARRIOR

That tough experienced soldiers should take orders from such a child sounds incredible; but the violence of the times had broken down the idea of deference to seniority, and emergencies were handled by whoever could do so. Besides, Tartar ideas had filtered in during the long domination of North China by those peoples, and to their thinking, a boy was a man at fourteen, provided he could ride and shoot to the satisfaction of his elders. That Shih-min could certainly do. His archery was such that he had few equals in this, the supreme art of the Tartars; and to be a dead shot from the saddle of a moving horse, with a bow of which the tension is affected by the weather, is marksmanship of a high order.

Not that Shih-min grew up a barbarian; his father gave him a sound Chinese classical education, and he became as good at calligraphy as at archery. Specimens of his handwriting were engraved on stone by copyists, and rubbings from these are still sold as models for students. In him the characteristic excellences of both races met.

When Shih-min was fifteen, the Emperor, tearing himself away for a while from the elaborate palaces and parks he had pressed his impoverished people into building for him, made a tour of the north-west, passing through the Duke of T'ang's province. One day, he ventured beyond the safety of the Wall. Down swooped the Turks. The Emperor, with his suite and escort, just managed to reach the shelter of a small fortress, which was promptly besieged. The Chinese standing army was miles away, and the muster of local troops quite inadequate. The Duke of T'ang called a council. The advice of his young son Shih-min was recognized as the best; he pointed out that, just as the Turks would not have attacked if they had not known that the available troops were unequal to their force, so if they thought that the main Chinese army was arriving, they would not stay to face it. Therefore, if the Chinese troops marched by day in open formation along miles of road, kicking up so much dust as to appear an immense force, and lighting camp-fires by night over a wide stretch of ground, the Turkish scouts would be deceived as to the strength of the relieving force. This did in fact happen, and the Emperor walked out unscathed.

While he had been cooped up in hourly fear, the Emperor had tried to stimulate action on his behalf by promising to abandon a burdensome and unsuccessful war which he was prosecuting in Korea. But no sooner was he out of his scrape than he re-started the war. Exasperated, the people were ready to follow anyone who promised better things. Within a few months, pretenders had sprung up all over the country, and civil war was again tearing apart the newly re-made unity of China.

The Emperor called on all loyal officials to stamp out the rebellions, and Shih-min's father was among those who received this charge. But Shih-min had been thinking. "Do you suppose you could possibly carry out these orders and suppress the rebels?" he said, in effect, to his father. "And if you did, your services would be beyond recompense, and the Emperor would take your life. In any case the dynasty is no longer worthy of support. Break away and raise our own standard." The Duke was still vacillating when the Emperor unconsciously gave the jerk that ended his inaction—a summons to appear at court on a charge of failing to suppress the rebels. The Duke knew that he would never return if once he obeyed. So in the early summer of the year A.D. 617, he assembled his willing officers and declared himself in open opposition to the dynasty.

LI SHIH-MIN'S STRATEGY

Shih-min was obviously the commander for the little compact body of men who set out on the almost fantastic task of defeating not only the Imperial army, but the forces of no less than eleven other would-be Emperors. Anyone but Li Shih-min would have failed.

His army was well received by the civil population, as it soon acquired a name for good discipline and for paying its way rather than "commandeering" what it wanted. Volunteers came in "like folk going to market". Once, in the teeth of reverses, when his prestige might be expected to be at low ebb, Shih-min arrived before one of the fortresses recently fallen into enemy hands. Settling his men in an entrenched camp, he waited. He waited for sixty days, although winter was setting in, and by then deserters had left the enemy side to join his in enough strength to ensure that the engagement, when it did come, issued in his favour.

As time went on and victories began to bring prisoners into his power, Li Shih-min showed a quality quite new and strange to the tormented Chinese people—they had no word for it, even. He showed mercy. Time and again, a man of real ability would fall into his hands, and awaiting death, would find himself pardoned and taken into Shih-min's service. Some of his closest friends, utterly trusted advisers, came to him that way, and his knack of collecting round him the right people and then trusting them, gave his rule a quality and stability far beyond that of the individualist dictator, however efficient the personal rule of the latter might be.

RIVAL CANDIDATES FOR THE THRONE

The most difficult decision of his military career came when he had eliminated all but two of his rivals and was within a short distance of the capital itself, working eastward. All the country behind him acknowledged T'ang rule; but his two remaining enemies were powerful, and one had his army north-east of the T'ang and the other east of it. The T'ang troops were advancing as a dividing wedge to prevent the two armies from combining.

Of these two rivals, one, calling himself the First Emperor of the Cheng dynasty, had managed to seize the capital, then at Lo-yang, and install himself therein, putting the Sui Emperor to death. But, by misrule, he had alienated his followers and lost territory, until his command scarcely held good outside the city itself, which was kept in a state of semi-siege by long-distance raiding carried on by a brilliant young general of Shih-min's.

This "Cheng Emperor", then, was not, by himself, very formidable. But the other, who called himself by the dynastic title of Hsia, was a different matter. He had something of the Prince of T'ang's own quality of chivalry, and his land and following in eastern China were comparable with those of the T'ang in the west. If he should come to the other's aid, or if the other should break out of the capital and join him, all the toil and effort of those three years of accomplishment would be lost in defeat.

Li Shih-min laid close siege to the capital. The winter wore on; the great walls remained firm and the defenders confident. The spirits of the T'ang men began to droop, and the cold to tell on them. Then came the news that the Hsia Emperor was moving towards them in force. In council, they surveyed the position.

The Emperor of the Hsia had an army estimated at over three hundred thousand men, well equipped. The army inside the capital was also considerable, and the extent of the walls meant that the investment of the city alone took most of the T'ang men. They could not stay where they were and be caught in that scissor-grip. Neither could they get T'ang reinforcements up, for the Turks were busy on the northern frontier, absorbing troops that might otherwise have been available. Yet to retire and concentrate on defending the west would mean giving up hope of uniting China. On the other hand, if they went out to meet the Hsia force annihilation was almost certain. "Retire and defend the west", urged the council, but the Prince decided to risk all and meet the Hsia force. The whole T'ang army was less than the Hsia one, and yet men must be left round the walls of Lo-yang; the Cheng officers must see no diminution of the investing force or they would be encouraged to break through, for their "Emperor" was getting desperate.

Shih-min took only three thousand five hundred men with him— but every man was picked—and without any noticeable thinning of the besieging force, he followed the eastward road until he came to a place where it dipped and ran across a flat-bottomed valley bounded by low cliffs. Here it crossed a stream, and at the crossing was a little town called Ssu Shui. This was the place he had chosen. The first Hsia attack failing to reduce Ssu Shui, the immense army encamped, blocked by Shih-min. The days went by, and the upkeep of such an army became more and more of a strain to its commander. His officers advised him to give up direct attack on Ssu Shui and the immediate plan of relieving Lo-yang, and invade T'ang territory elsewhere. The T'ang prince would then have to hurry off to defend his land and the stalemate would come to an end. But the Hsia leader felt himself in honour bound to stay and relieve Lo-yang next, for he had promised the Cheng leader that he would raise the siege. His wife urged him to draw the T'ang troops out into the open, where he could deal with them easily, and then pass on to Lo-yang. "Women don't understand these things," he replied.

LI SHIH-MIN REUNITES CHINA

So he planned an attack on a grand scale. This suited Shih-min, who would have been ruined if he had had to come out on to the open plain. The attack failed, the great army was scattered and never re-formed. The Hsia leader was taken prisoner and brought to the foot of the Lo-yang walls, there to inform his brother (and rival) Emperor, standing on the ramparts, that all was lost.

Thus Shih-min's most desperate decision had worked out as he had planned it; thenceforward till 624 it was only a matter of "mopping-up".

Like the First Emperor of the Ch'in, the T'ang prince had worked eastwards in his conquest, from the north-western point of China. Like him, too, Shih-min had Tartar blood in him. And like him, this soldier had plans for the country ready when the work of unifying had given place to the next stage. The parallel is a close one, except in personal character, where Shih-min is infinitely superior.

China had peace once more; peace within her borders, that is, but from outside, her peace was heavily menaced, this time not by the Huns but the Turks. So Shih-min and his generals set out once more. But this time they went with a backing of infinite prestige. Tribes and nations came to meet them glad to accept Chinese suzerainty, which only amounted in fact to abstention from acts hostile to China, and help for the Chinese and allied arms when called on. The name and prestige of China spread far and wide, as at the crest of the Han dynasty.

Li Shih-min, now Emperor, known to history as T'ang T'ai Tsung —the Founder of the T'ang—turned his attention next to rebuilding the administrative structure. The people had lost the sense of law as a reasonable ruling, because the Sui Emperor's laws had been so unreasonable. The T'ang Emperor lightened the penalties whole-sale, re-cast the laws so that they could be kept, and re-formed the schools. The examination syllabus, based on the Confucian classics, was finally fixed at this time.

THE PROSPERITY OF THE T'ANG DYNASTY

T'ang T'ai Tsung died in the year 650. He was only forty-eight, but already his wonderful circle of friends and advisers had been broken by several deaths. Among them was Wei Cheng, who had begun as his enemy, gained his respect by a blunt fearlessness when a prisoner, and kept that refreshing bluntness even when his master had become Emperor. T'ai Tsung felt his friend's death very keenly. He said, "In my life I used three mirrors. One of bronze to adjust my dress; the records of history to correct the mistaken policies of the present; and Wei Cheng, who served to reveal the faults of my character. Now I have lost the best of my mirrors." His beloved wife, too, was dead, and his sons were more or less disappointing. Nevertheless, to the best of them he gave his vast responsibilities, and so accomplished the last act of a commander, the handing on of his command and powers.

The Founder of the T'ang was more than a great general; he found his country flaming with war, and the result of his fighting was that the fire was put out. Alexander the Great possibly covered more ground—but his Empire broke up at his death. The T'ang remained.

So well and truly were the foundations of the T'ang rule laid that the nation's affairs "ran on greased wheels", and went on running even after the usual degeneration had robbed the throne of its driving-power. The T'ang dynasty lasted three hundred years, from A.D. 618 to 907, and it is quite impossible here to do more than glance at some aspects of the activity in the realms of culture and material achievement of which it was the setting.

It was, first of all, the golden age of poetry; the great poets of the T'ang receive more honour in China than those of any other period. Below is a translation of a poem by Tu Fu, who shares with his great friend Li Po the position of highest honour. The translation of poetry is admittedly apt in many cases to fall very short of adequacy, and Chinese poetry with its economy of words is especially difficult to render in another language in a form which preserves the original beauty.

Tu Fu, an old man now, breaks one of his many weary journeys to stand awhile at the place where a battle had been fought years ago:

"I dismounted from horse on old battlefield,
Looked in four directions: naught but vague immensity.
Before melancholy wind billowing clouds drift;
At my feet yellow leaves fall.
Mole-crickets, ants, make nests in rotting bones;
They lie wrapped in creeping vines.
With heavy sighs I, old man, move on;
Men of to-day still strive to widen frontiers."

The keen sense of landscape is characteristic of Chinese poetry; the note of melancholy is characteristic too. Chinese melancholy does not draw on love between man and woman as a theme; the lover "sighing like a furnace, with a woeful ballad made to his mistress' eyebrow" is rare among Chinese poets. With them it is separation, by distance, by death, that makes them see in their minds the loved scenes and old friends, and so be driven to express their thoughts. The T'ang men were great travellers—but not usually outside Chinese territory, and not usually from choice. Journeys were the result either of being appointed to a post in a distant part of the Empire or being banished from court. In both cases, the traveller's thoughts were turned towards home.

THE T'ANG POETS

It must not be imagined, however, that Chinese poetry could only be mournful or wistful. Li Po revels in the happy carefree state of drunkenness, in which one does not remember which season of the year it is, or care if the Emperor himself is calling. But to other poets, some of them less famous individually, belongs the gift of satire which is one of the happiest things in Chinese poetry. Po Chu-i once received the present of an Annamese cockatoo. He listened to it talking, and a thought struck him:

"Sent as a present from Annam—
A red cockatoo.
Coloured like the peach-tree blossom,
Speaking with the speech of men.
And they did to it what is always done
To the learned and eloquent.
They took a cage with stout bars
And shut it up inside."

Po Chu-i was Governor of Hangchow, and later of Soochow, and various other places. In fact, he was both a Government official and a great poet. The same applies to Tu Fu; these men and their kind were not dilettante poets. Poems were written by salaried people, *i.e.*, Government officials, Government service being the one recognized profession; sometimes, as in the case of Li Po, sinecure positions at court were given them. Therefore the picture of the poet starving in a garret is not familiar in China. Some Chinese poets did know poverty; but it was due either to failure to get into official life, or failure to keep their posts through political upheavals.

The everyday life of those days is brought vividly before us in the T'ang grave-figures. The primitive practice of killing and burying a man's slaves—and wives—at his death, to accompany him to the world of the dead, was discontinued and instead clay figures were made to represent them. As the dead man would lack in the next world any person or thing not represented in his tomb, every effort was made to make the list complete. There are horses ready saddled, camels, men-at-arms; dancing-girls with long graceful sleeves and supple wrists; sorcerers, foreign servants, farm animals. Racial types from as far away as central Asia and Africa are portrayed, and it is certain that the life of the T'ang was much more cosmopolitan, much wider in its range of contacts and sources of knowledge, than China had ever known in the preceding stages of her history.

FOREIGN RELIGIONS IN CHINA

Europe was at that time in the Dark Ages, the Near East in the throes of the Islamic campaigns; nowhere in the world was there a civilization or an Empire to compare with China. Foreigners were welcomed in the capital, and many foreign religions were represented in the China of those days—not only Buddhism but Islam, Manicheism from India, Mazdaism from Persia, and Nestorian Christianity, which had travelled the length of Asia.

Although there were, and still are, a number of Mohammedan communities in China, Islam did not come as a missionary religion. Moslem soldiers were brought in to help the Emperor quell a rebellion and they settled down, taking Chinese wives. But there seems to have been little or no attempt to present Islam to the Chinese. Its place in the country's life has remained small, and the Moslem communities are still foreign in Chinese eyes.

Zoroastrians, too, had temples in certain cities under the T'ang, but they were apparently only for the benefit of foreign residents and travellers who held that faith. Manicheism on the other hand did teach and collect a small following of Chinese. The same applies to Tantrism, another Indian religion, an offshoot from Buddhism. The only new religion, besides Buddhism, to give itself seriously to teaching was Nestorianism, which undoubtedly attracted a considerable following in China. It is recorded that there were churches in all the important towns.

In the latter part of the dynasty, a wave of fear about the spread of foreign ideas swept over the then Emperor, and he ordered a general persecution of all foreign faiths. This of course included Buddhism. The Emperor died the next year, and his successor lifted the ban; the persecution had been short but very sharp. Buddhism recovered, but religions with small followings, or but recently arrived, failed. A century later, an Arab writer tells how he met in Baghdad a Nestorian monk who had been sent to inquire into the condition of the Nestorian Christian faith in China, and had found the churches in ruins and no trace of their people.

This disappearance has puzzled historians. One suggestion is that it was not the full Christian faith and therefore did not endure. The Nestorians taught, in effect, that Christ on earth had been only using a human appearance. His real self was not involved. Someone who does not really feel or really suffer stops being real. And when immediate realities become sharp, as in times of opposition, trouble and death, the unreal has a way of fading. No attempt seems to have been made to revive Nestorianism in China, perhaps because it was fading elsewhere as well.

By the time the ninth century turned into the tenth, the T'ang had ceased to control the country, and in 907 the dynasty petered out. Division ensued once more, but this time only for fifty-odd years. It has been pointed out that before the T'ang, China was more often divided than united, but after it, the years of division are very much fewer than the years in which unity prevails throughout the land.

CHAPTER 35

THE SUNG RULERS AND THEIR SUCCESSORS

THE proportion in which the land was divided, during these fifty years following the fall of the T'ang, was roughly half and half, the northern half consisting of one unit passing every few years into the hands of a new general-become-king, the southern half made up of seven small states. But by now the people living in different parts of China knew they were one in reality, and by consent they re-united. Actually the initiative came from the north, but the south, even in districts where there were opposition-armies, soon joined in, and the year 960 saw a new dynasty established.

This period is characterized by an absence of rebellions, which bespeaks content. For the Sung rulers were not harsh. They loved the finer things of life, and did not hanker after military conquest. Thus it came about that, notwithstanding a restricted territory, the Sung population increased until it was soon bigger than that of Han or even T'ang times.

On the intellectual side, political science was free to breathe, as it had not been since the great days of philosophy; painting scaled great heights of perfection, and Confucianism was re-interpreted. There was a desire to get out of range of the shadow of examinations and re-read the Classics in the light of the ideas Buddhism had brought. Study circles were formed in the country; printing had made books easily available, and Chinese bindings are light to carry; little groups betook themselves to woodlands and sat beside streams to read and ruminate on the new intellectual problems which had arisen.

HOW THE CHINESE ARTIST WORKS

It is interesting to see how a Chinese artist goes about his painting and writing. The brush's point is minutely fine; yet at the root it is thick and bushy; this gives it great springiness and versatility. It is a straight piece of bamboo, thick enough to give a firm hold; the tension of the whole arm does not mean a crabbed action, but a free and yet controlled swing from the shoulder. Moreover, since the brush is held perpendicularly there is no unwilling drag, due to angle, to limit the directions in which it can be moved; hand and brush may move outwards and away from the artist, just as well as inwards and towards him in the characteristic Western action. The tenseness of hold and action gives an astonishing sense of exhilaration; fingers grip the brush with a feeling of excitement and responsibility; it might be the tiller of a racing yacht. A Western artist will say that he, too, feels exhilaration when he approaches a blank canvas with his different brush. But the sloping position of the European brush and canvas or paper has not the same feel as the poise of a Chinese brush held still and vertical over the paper.

Obviously the Chinese technique makes possible a rich variety of strokes: smooth flowing ones; wandering ones where the brush dips sideways and recovers itself, its track revealing a snow-laden branch; or rumpled rugged ones, dry and yet alive, like the bark of a tree. The painter can make an orchid's long grass-like leaf, twisting in the wind, with a single outward sweep of the brush—or he can show a bird's feathers by a vast number of tiny strokes carefully arranged.

The variety of stroke is practically infinite, but its enjoyment is disciplined by the fact that in any one picture there must be a defined range of strokes, a "key" in which the picture is set. The writer once watched a Chinese artist paint a spray of flowers. First he placed on the paper the leaves, using a bold sideways-twisting stroke; then the flowers, each petal a pair of fine curved lines; then the stamens, another action; and the stems that joined flowers, leaves, and so on, in their turn had their stroke. A range of five or six strokes was employed, and roughly speaking, each completed its contribution before the next was brought into play. This gives some insight into the mental discipline of the Chinese artist, for with this technique, the whole picture would have to be in his mind before he started to work.

Chinese painting calls for a high degree of decision as well as of visualization. The paper, or special silk prepared for painting, is very absorbent, almost like blotting-paper; this means that not only must the direction and character of a stroke be decided on beforehand, but also the speed at which it is to be made—a slow action giving time for the drinking-in of more ink; a stroke, growing swifter as it moves, yielding a tapering line, hesitation leaving a tell-tale bulge.

Let us look at what Chinese painters choose for their subjects. Going back over their history, in ancient times we find no fine art as yet, only applied art, albeit of a high standard—jade and bronze objects wrought into animal shapes or with patterns upon them. Then, with the establishment of the Empire and its more complex civilization, there appears figure-painting. Walls are decorated with frescoes portraying great men—philosophers, rulers, statesmen— not always portraits in our sense of likenesses, but representations in paint of the subjects' characters and attributes. The arrival of Buddhism gives both a new conception of personality and a new range of motifs, with the further newness of Indian influence.

After the Han dynasty, portraits of great men cease to be foremost, and figure-painting is thereafter confined almost exclusively to the illustration of incidents in the lives of poets and writers, incidents that have struck artists as paintable, and to Buddhist religious subjects, where the human figure is used to embody an idea or quality. The real focus of interest in Chinese art is not the human figure but landscape, which became prominent under the T'ang dynasty.

Mountains, conveying more of the majesty of truth than could ever be put into words; rivers and rocks; snow and lonely places—a range of subjects was established in which each stood for an idea, or group of ideas, so that a pictorial language came into being, not in competition with that of literature, but filling places the latter could not reach. This co-operation between the two mind-outlets, the two forms of language, issued in the practice of designing a picture with space for some writing which makes its meaning clearer. By this, pictures can be given a much richer content.

RELATED METHODS OF PAINTING AND WRITING

With the Sung dynasty, a third type of subject finds place, that of the single object, a type known to the Chinese generically as "bird and flower painting". This is something different from our "still life"; it deals with natural things in their own surroundings—a wind-hammered pine tree, a branch of plum in flower while the snow is still on the ground, a bird in song or watching for food with the utter intentness of the wild thing—the Sung artists strove to put not only the beauty but the meaning of these things on to their silk and paper.

All three types of subject find very fine exposition during this dynasty, indeed, it is regarded by many as the peak of Chinese art, but it would be too much to say that all later work is decadent—far from it; there developed, among other things, a boldness of both pattern and touch that is very stimulating.

With the Chinese, painting, like poetry, is an expression but not a profession. In China, the only art belonging to the professional is that of the theatre—the others find their exponents, even the greatest, among people who draw their livelihood from another source. The names of many such people stand high in the aristocracy of China, not because they entered by birth into a ruling caste, but because they entered by intellectual qualifications.

A painting of a bamboo plume may be simply a masterly arrangement of two sorts of strokes—one for the leaves, one for the stalks. That these strokes take years to master does not diminish the attraction of the brush-game; as any golf or bowls enthusiast will understand. But amenability to brush and ink supplies only half—the shallow half—of the answer to the question of choice of subject.

THE PHILOSOPHY OF CHINESE ART

The answer, at the deeper level, must be sought in the meaning which has accumulated round those particular things. Thus, in a spray of plum gallantly blossoming in spite of bitter weather, a Chinese sees the virtue of endurance, the courage that endures in the teeth of privation and calamity; in a pine tree, he sees an old age that has known storms and out-lived them; the lotus grows clear and beautiful out of the muddiest water—unsullied, raising its clean dignity unconcerned out of the dirt. And the bamboo: for "this gentleman"—"tz'u chün"—he keeps a very special, loving respect. He admires its power of recovery, springing back to normal directly its load of snow slides to the ground: its never-ending usefulness in the making of almost anything from houses and junks to furniture and small objects of household use. The hollow space in the centre of the cane signifies to him the open mind, readiness to learn; the straight uprightness of growth, integrity of character; and the shaking, waving leaves have a welcoming look, for in China one waves towards a guest to welcome him. Thus the Chinese artist chooses his subjects because they render the thoughts he likes to dwell on. His philosophy finds expression in them as well as in written books.

Chinese art is closer than Western to both philosophy and literature; it concerns itself with quietness and being, whereas Western art loves movement and action; it does not focus its attention or base its forms on the human figure, as European art with its Greek ancestry does; colour, also, has not with it the same priority as in Europe. Not only is the Chinese colour-sense very subtle, so that it finds its satisfaction in restrained colour-chords, but the very use of colour became suspect on the ground that it covered defects in brushwork; the man who could really draw could convey his ideas by the use of ink only. Many of the finest pictures are drawn in ink. Included in the term "Chinese painting" are those works not produced by laying on coloured paint at all, but by drawing with ink at strengths varying from deep lustrous black to cloud greys.

An Occidental, when painting a portrait, will look from his sitter to his work and back again; so will a student working from a model, and the length of time the latter takes on each look will probably be shorter and the frequency of his looking greater, for he takes in less, and hardly knows as yet how to use what he has noticed. A Chinese, on the other hand, divides the process of looking—absorbing and divining what it is he wishes to express—from that of expressing it, not starting painting till he has finished looking.

Beneath this divergence, however, there is oneness. The Occidental, too, holds that a work of art is an expression of thought and feeling and not a photographic record; he strives to find out what he wants to say before he starts speaking with his brush or pencil. However, in the West, the record-idea persists alongside, and sometimes gets in the way of, the expression-idea; as in many art schools, where measured accuracy and flowing decorative line are two qualities demanded in the same drawing.

Further differences between Chinese and Western painting lie in their respective handling of atmosphere and light; for instance, there are no shadows in Chinese pictures, and no reflected light. Perhaps one may put it that line occupies in their mind the place we give to light. There is now in China a school that is striving to weave into the fabric of Chinese art ideas gained from study in Europe of Western art. Possibly the chief offering the West can make here is in the handling of light; and the Chinese can show us, among other things, a new control of the brush—a mastery by brain and arm—and behind this, and through all their art, the quality of discipline which strictly governs their creative effort.

THE REFORMS OF WANG AN-SHIH

The peaceful Sung dynasty allowed political science to manifest itself in a new way. Two political parties appeared. They are usually called in English "Conservatives" and "Innovators"; as might be expected in China, ultimate victory went to the Conservatives, but the Innovators under Wang An-shih had eighteen years of power, and another short spell soon afterwards.

The eleventh century saw one of the finest Sung Emperors on the throne; free from vice, a great worker, open-minded and a judge of men. He saw that he had in Wang An-shih a man with ideas worth putting into practice. Therefore, in spite of the fact that this Wang was not a likeable man, and in spite of the unflagging and bitter opposition of the Conservative scholar-officials, he gave him the necessary power to put his ideas into practice.

Wang An-shih has been called a pioneer Socialist, and his reforms may be viewed as experiments in Socialism. But the label is misleading unless we remember that he had no such idea as dictatorship of the proletariat, no intention of exalting the workers. He started a system on the lines of one successful in the Han time, by which the grain-tax was paid in each province instead of being laboriously transported to the capital—the grain being sold locally by the Government, which kept the profits as tax-money. Exchange between provinces of commodities paid into the Government stores as taxes was also arranged, and famine relief was provided.

The peasants were always in debt to moneylenders and their goods were usually at the pawnbroker's. Wang An-shih made the state the poor man's banker instead. Loans were made to the farmers in the Spring, to be repaid at harvest. State pawn-shops were set up, and standard rates and conditions were introduced.

All these reforms sound simple and obvious, but their application was far from being so. They disturbed vested interests, which joined forces with the solidly Conservative official class to hinder their working. The Civil Service did not fit its members for such positive work; their view of administration was far more negative, and was confined to seeing that the peace was not broken and that the taxes did not fall into arrears. Yet it looks as though the reforms justified themselves, for those years show an increase of population, coupled with an absence of risings and rebellions. The peasant revolt being the only means of expression available to the inarticulate mass of the people, its absence is as good as a mark of approbation.

It would be doing Wang An-shih less than justice not to mention his way of tackling the problem of horse supply. China has never been a horse-breeding country, the usual lay-out of the land consisting of small highly-cultivated holdings, each representing a family's livelihood; big grass fields are simply not there, and where the land is not tilled, it is mountainous and unsuitable for horses. Horses have, therefore, never been part of the country's agricultural life, their work being done on a Chinese farm by buffaloes and oxen, or sometimes by means of mules. But the need for horses existed.

THE THREAT BEYOND THE WALL

It may be asked: "What then was the need for horses?" The answer is: "War". This meant war with the Tartars, who were invariably mounted. The breeding-ground for horses was precisely the Tartar country—the steppe lands. China's disadvantage is obvious, but while she had possessions in central Asia and dependencies which could pay their tribute in horses, the supply problem did not press. Under the Sung, however, the Chinese owned no supply-ground in the steppe lands, so Wang An-shih started a plan whereby households were entrusted with a horse, perhaps two, which they had to forage and keep in condition against the need arising of cavalry remounts. This was the first attempt to deal at all radically with the problem, and after Wang's day it was allowed to lapse, as, in the end, were all his reforms.

Unnoticed by the Sung, big things were taking shape beyond the Wall. The climate in those lands was changing, and the best weather was now in the extreme east, north-east of China. The nomad peoples followed the weather, turning this end of their land into a reservoir of manpower, which soon overflowed into China. In 1127, North

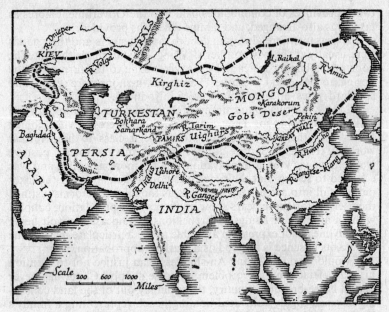

THE MONGOL EMPIRE UNDER CHENGHIZ KHAN

China fell to a Tartar king, but south of the line where the soft rice-fields began, his horsemen were no good, and the Sung dynasty continued in South China for another hundred and fifty-two years.

This Tartar nation, as was often the case with "barbarians", loved Chinese ways and books, and was soon all but Chinese itself; further north, however, untouched by the higher civilization, the Mongols were gathering strength. When, in their turn, they swept southwards, they engulfed both North and South, killing something like half the entire population. Meanwhile, another Mongol force had pushed westward as far as eastern Europe and the Islamic countries, and the Mongol leader, Chenghiz Khan, established his Orkhon, Muhuli, near where Pekin was built later, and continued to rule his immense empire from Karakorum. Most of his nomad warriors still preferred *yurts* to live in, but they hung them with stuffs as gorgeous as any palace could show. They styled their régime the Yüan Dynasty.

So it came about that after a lapse of some centuries contact was again established between China and Europe. "The road you travel from Tana"—a port on the Black Sea—"to Cathay (China) is perfectly safe, whether by day or by night, according to what the merchants say who have used it", says a handbook for merchants written about the year 1340 by an Italian. It is a gigantic statement, made possible by the firm and comparatively peaceful rule of Chenghiz's grandson, Kublai Khan.

Europeans began to take advantage of this unprecedented chance to know more of the mysterious East. Chinese silk came once more along the old caravan route; and this time patterned silks found acceptance on the European market. The readiness of the medieval West to appreciate Eastern patterns, where the classical world had rejected them, may be a small thing in itself, but it illustrates a changed outlook—less self-satisfied than the Graeco-Roman, keen to observe and know, not merely to buy. Kublai Khan and the European leaders were both eager to maintain and improve contact. The Europeans sent embassies to the Khan because they wanted help against the Saracen menace.

Kublai Khan's problem was administrative. The Khan's own people were not civilized enough to take on the task of governing China, yet to give the high positions back to Chinese would have been to court rebellion. So he imported men of brains from every possible source. Two Venetian merchants, brothers named Maffeo and Nicolo Polo, had been in China, trading. When they were to start on their second trip, Nicolo's young son Marco decided to come with them, and later rose high in the Khan's service. Some years later, there went also John of Montecorvino, a Franciscan, who was the first missionary of European Christianity to set foot on Chinese soil.

CHAPTER 36

MONGOL, MING AND MANCHU

MARCO POLO'S account of his seventeen years in China enables us to look at the country for the first time through European eyes, opened wide in amazement, although Polo's native Venice was as great and as highly cultured a city as any in the West. He says of Hangchow: "I will tell you all its nobleness, for without doubt it is the largest city in the world. . . . The merchants are so numerous and so rich, that their wealth can neither be told nor believed. . . . On each of the . . . bridges ten men keep guard day and night, so that no one may dare to raise a disturbance, or commit theft or homicide. . . . All the streets are paved with stones and bricks; and so are the high roads of Manji (South China) . . . the riches and profit which the Khan derives from the province of Manji is so great that no man could dare to mention it."

MARCO POLO'S DESCRIPTION OF THE MONGOL COURT

Polo was right in expecting incredulity when he talked of forty or fifty thousand people assembling in the market squares of Hangchow every market-day, of stone bridges over the canals so high that ships could pass beneath without dipping their masts, of a courier system involving two hundred thousand horses and over ten thousand posting-houses, besides innumerable foot-runners. It is said that when he and his father and uncle returned to Venice, their relatives did not recognize them in their strange Tartar clothes, shabby from the three-year journey. It was the same with the knowledge he brought; not until fifty years after his death was his information incorporated in the map of Asia.

"When this mighty monarch (Kublai) comes to one of his places . . . he causes his tents to be pitched, with those of his sons and barons. . . . That in which he keeps his court is so large that 1,000 knights can dwell in it; this is for his nobles and other attendants. He himself resides in another . . . where those to whom he wishes to speak are introduced; while there is an interior chamber in which he sleeps. The inside is lined with skins of ermine and zibelline, of the highest value . . . the whole hall is covered with them, worked most delicately in intaglio. . . ." The Khan's splendour was not drawn from China only. He and his court could wear sable and ermine brought from the far north of Russia and tread on carpets carried from cities of the Near East; Marco Polo's account implies a well-being that was not the lot of the individual Chinese, living as he did in a country just recovering from devastation. This first European contact with China thus sounds the note which later becomes dominant—that of misunderstanding.

If the Mongols took much from China and gave little, at least they did not come quite empty-handed. They brought with them a musical instrument, a "hu-ch'in" or Mongol lute—stringed and played with a bow, on the principle of a violin—which the Chinese adopted, adding it to their existing range of instruments, such as the flute made from their much-loved bamboo. With bamboos growing freely in the countryside, the reed only waiting a few skilful cuts to bring the flute inherent in it into being, it is natural that flute music should have come to be part of the stuff of Chinese life.

MUSIC AND SONG

The Yüan dynasty brought a second contribution to Chinese music—a new song rhythm, made possible by the changes that had been wrought in the language by repeated Northern infusions, and bringing a new kind of song into being. A song and a lute, small things certainly, strange from such a source, but pleasant after so much grimness.

Chinese singing had received the sort of impetus that a state opera house provides in Europe when one of the T'ang emperors founded, in A.D. 720, the Pear Garden College in an orchard in his palace grounds, where several hundred young students were given training.

It may fairly be claimed that this college laid the foundations of Chinese stage-training. The emperor who founded it became a kind of patron saint of Chinese actors, and they still keep little statues of him in the green-room behind the stage. The training he had in mind was more that of a singer than an actor; we must think of the Chinese stage as an operatic one; our word "play" does not render the idea of the Chinese stage performance nearly so well as the word "opera". Not only are the songs as important a part of the whole as the arias of our opera, but like the great Italian arias, they, or dialogue passages, are often sung apart from the rest of the work, the assumption being that the listeners know the plot and setting perfectly.

THE RISE OF CHINESE DRAMA

Dialogue is sung in recitative, or, to put it another way, spoken on given tones. Dialogue and stage action did not develop until the Yüan dynasty, which saw both the rise and the shaping of Chinese drama. The Mongols, since they could not well give high official posts to Chinese, left many active brains idle. There was little outlet for the classical learning and the classical language which had been necessary for the Civil Service examinations. Now, writing for the stage meant of necessity using the everyday language, and therefore had hitherto been beneath the dignity of scholars, but the new régime brought conditions that turned towards it abilities which would normally have been used elsewhere. This state of affairs only lasted for eighty-odd years, yet it was long enough to yield a great number of plays, and many of these are still performed in modern China.

SATIRE AND COMEDY

The tradition these authors had to work on was triple; there was the musical side; there were posturing and dancing, also tumbling and acrobatics, as in every nation; and there was another side, that of topical satire, where types of people with their characteristic failings were portrayed, relying almost entirely on extemporization and topical interest. The Yüan Dynasty also saw the development of the novel, and some of the productions of this period reached a high standard, although not at first regarded as literature proper.

"You'll be whipped for taxation one of these days," says Celia to the jester Touchstone in "As You Like It", and taxation, in the sense of taxing people—especially people too august to be criticized by any-one except a jester—with their foibles and comicalities, has always been the function of the court fool. In China, the fool's green cap, Chinese equivalent of the cap-and-bells, descended almost imper-ceptibly to the actor, so natural was the transference. From the Sung period, there comes to us the story of how a troupe of actor-jesters were in fact "whipped for taxation". They dressed up as famous philosophers—including Confucius—and using the great men's very words, as recorded in the classics, managed to introduce adroit admonition to the reigning Emperor on the subject of some unjust land-division he had recently imposed. The home-thrust was a little too sharp, and as a result the Emperor was "not amused".

N   (H.W.)

These rudimentary comedies contained the germ both of dialogue and stage action. The musical tradition contributed narrative, and neither music nor narrative has ever lost its place in Chinese drama; characters still announce themselves with a sketch of their lives, thoughts and occupations on their first entry—fundamentally the same device as the Greek chorus.

> "I am Sun, the Flying Tiger. At present the Empire is in a state of disorder. My Commander-in-Chief, Ting Wen-ya, has been discharging his duties in an irregular manner. I have been given a separate command of five thousand soldiers, including cavalry, to guard Ho-Ch'iao. I have ascertained that Ying-ying, the daughter of the late Prime Minister, Ts'ui Chueh, has black eyebrows with a winning expression, a face as beautiful as the lotus in spring, and is of such overwhelming charm as makes her the peer of the most famous beauties of old."

It is after this fashion that he outlines his romantic plans.

THE SYMBOLISM OF THE CHINESE STAGE

To render types—recognized, even conventionalized, types—with skill and fire and grace has been the aim of Chinese acting. In the early days, the range of types portrayed was very limited, and may be compared to the harlequinade group that has come down to us from the early days of the European stage. The villain wears a white patch on his nose; a reddened face indicates a great-and-good character. Devils have green faces, gods and goddesses golden-yellow ones, possibly to recall golden statues of Buddhas and Bodhisattvas to the audience's mind.

The clothes are as brilliant and elaborate as they can possibly be made, but it is a controlled exuberance—controlled by the type of character for which they are to be worn. Every garment has its meaning and tells the audience something about the character; in the same way, every action has its symbol-value. A man carrying a whip in his right hand is mounting a horse; if the whip is in his left hand, he is dismounting. A man making his way round the stage, feeling to left and right, is in the dark. The hands close together in front, then widening—a step forward—hands brought together again behind the back indicates that an invisible door has been opened, entered and its panels slid together again. But the door is not invisible to a Chinese audience, which uses its imagination as a matter of course, does not expect scenery, and sees the soft fall of snow in a few pieces of white paper shaken out of a red flag by a coolie who has walked on to the stage for that purpose.

The Mongol dynasty of Chenghiz Khan held China for only 87 years; in 1368 the Ming dynasty was established. The new ruling house had no great personal qualities to recommend it, but it was Chinese, and the country accepted it.

For the Mongols, China had been only a colonial possession; they had ruled it from a capital placed so as to have strategic value with regard to the rest of their possessions; the spot chosen was at the extreme north-east of China and south-east of their native Mongolia. But as soon as the Ming obtained possession, they made Nanking the capital; it is half-way down China, reckoning from north to south, and near the coast, so that it was roughly equidistant from all frontiers, and in the heart of the territory. Moreover, it had the Yangtse to connect it with western China.

PEKING—"THE NORTHERN CAPITAL"

When Yung Lo, the third and ablest Ming emperor, came to the throne, he shifted his capital back north, near to the old Yüan site. In so doing, he was putting strategic value before accessibility. He was moving near to the likeliest source of trouble, which, in his day, was the north-east. So it was that Peking ("Northern Capital") came to be built. Yung Lo's action was in tune with Chinese experience; the T'ang founder, in the seventh century, had had his capital, Ch'ang An, in the west, for in his day the focus of Tartar activity was to the north-west. Previously, the Han had, for the first half of the dynasty, made their capital Ch'ang An, but during its later years, the dynasty had retreated eastward to Lo-yang.

This east–west swing of the capital went noticeably with the ebb and flow of the nation's fortunes; the pendulum-swing continues to this day, but after T'ang, it is north–south instead of east–west. Thus the Sung put its capital in the centre of North China, at K'ai-feng-fu, a city with excellent communications. But these communications also served the invaders, who now for the first time came down from the north-east instead of the north-west. When the Sung government had to retreat, it went south instead of east, and placed its capital in Southern China, at Hangchow.

Peking was completed in 1421, and remained the capital until the Republic shifted it back to Nanking ("Southern Capital"). Its career survived a change in dynasty; 1644 saw China again conquered by a Tartar race. But the Manchus who established the Ch'ing dynasty were a very different type of people from the Mongols, although they came from the same quarter. Both races had their origin in the land north of the eastern end of the Wall, but the Manchus being only just the other side of the Wall, had adopted Chinese civilization. They made excellent rulers; K'ang Hsi was probably one of the finest administrative brains the world has ever known; his reign lasted 60 years, from 1662 to 1722. After him came Yung Cheng, also a great worker; then Ch'ien Lung, 1736–1796.

These three reigns mark another crest-period in Chinese history. The Ming started on their downward slope almost from the start, but for a century and a half, under the Ch'ing, China had well-being and greatness. It was not a creative period, but a high polish was put on all that had already been shaped. Among arts and crafts, porcelain manufacture and decoration was perfected and elaborated to an almost unbelievable pitch, as we can see from the examples now in museums and private collections. It was porcelain that caught the eye of Europeans. The English factories tried hard to guess the secrets of clay and colour from the china brought over by the English merchantmen with chests of tea, and the imports stimulated home production enormously.

During the K'ang Hsi–Ch'ien Lung period, jade and other hard stones were carved most exquisitely and elaborately; specimens dating from this period represent the peak of craftsmanship, though carvings made earlier (and jade has been carved in China from ancient times) may have as great a beauty with a simpler shape. Jade has been to the Chinese what jewels have been to the West. Its beauty is not only a matter of subtle colour, of translucent depth, at once solid and limpid; these are a matter of sight, and jewels, too, appeal to the sight. But jade has a quality of touch as well; it is beautiful to feel and has an appeal that sharp-cornered cut jewels can never have.

ECONOMICS OF CHINESE LIFE

It is often asked whether slavery is an institution in China. In Han times, we read of its being temporarily abolished. It was then, and for a long time afterwards, a usual thing for retainers to be owned, bought and sold, but in later times, the number of people of this status declined considerably, and was practically confined to household servants—mostly girls sold by their parents because poverty pressed hard. These children—victims of famine, very often—would probably have died of starvation if they had not been sold. When they grew up, they might be taken into the family as concubines, or married to men of humbler station. In the latter case, they are given a marriage-dinner and presents, and a farewell from the household in which they have grown up; they are not compelled to remain with their owners all their lives. The stigma of slavery has never been a matter of bitterness, nor is it associated with racial exploitation; it is merely an economic expedient.

Chinese shipping and ship design can only be touched on here. There are indications that in the days of the last Chaldean king, shipping linked up China, India, Chaldea and East Africa. Coins of T'ang date and fragments of Sung porcelain have been found at various places on the East African coast, such as Zanzibar. The Chinese of those days certainly had their own names for all these and many other far-away places, and possessed a certain amount of information about them.

Possibly the balance of trade was against the Chinese, and they imported more than they exported; quantities of Chinese coins have been discovered in East Africa, but the evidence is, on the whole, hazy. It is, however, definitely known that, in the Sung dynasty, a great deal of Chinese sea-trade was, in fact, not in Chinese hands at all, but in those of Arabs operating from Chinese ports. It is noteworthy that the Chinese and Burmese junks and the Ancient Egyptian ships possess many points of similarity, and it is suggested that the design of both originated in Babylonia. Certainly the Chinese build is very ancient. Everything Chinese was developed, as far as it was going to be developed, at so early a time, that there has been a tendency to ascribe the origin of nearly everything to the Chinese, and the compass has been attributed to them. But like the Babylonian origin of their junks, this can neither be proved nor disproved. It does seem, however, that the Chinese hit on the idea of bulkheads, in their construction of ocean-going craft, long before anyone else.

CHINA AND EUROPEAN TRADERS

Under the Ming, foreign contacts ceased to come mainly from the north and west and began to come overseas instead of overland, from the south and east. They continued to be of two kinds, raiding and trading. The new raiders were the Japanese, whose pirate vessels plagued the shipping and coastal cities; the traders were mostly Arabs. But at the beginning of the sixteenth century, the Portuguese appeared. At first, they were classed with the other merchants and given trading facilities, as was customary; but soon it was borne in on the Chinese authorities that they belonged to the first rather than to the second class of foreigner.

The Portuguese, and the Spaniards who shortly afterwards arrived also, had a kill-or-be-killed mentality—utterly alien to the Chinese—which they had acquired in the course of their long struggle with Islam. The Portuguese, Spanish, and soon the Dutch also, rapidly earned a reputation for murders and massacres ashore and piracy afloat. The authorities had two courses open to them; they could drive the Europeans away and shut the country to them (as the Japanese did later), which would have meant the loss of a lucrative trade; or they could, by rigorous control, prevent their getting sufficient foothold to be a danger. It was decided to take the latter course; the Portuguese were forbidden to land anywhere except at Macao, a small island off Canton; their merchants were permitted to come into Canton only on certain days. The Spaniards obtained no nearer foothold than the Philippine Islands. The Dutch, first known to the Chinese through their killing some Chinese merchants and pillaging their ships off the coast of Fukien province, settled in Formosa, outside Chinese jurisdiction.

Now the population of Manila, the Spaniards' city in the Philippines, was predominantly Chinese. Not wishing to be swamped by their Chinese neighbours, the Spaniards there adopted the simple expedient of massacre, first in 1603 and again in 1639. No wonder that the Chinese attitude in negotiating with foreigners was cautious. When, therefore, three English ships arrived in 1639, under John

Weddel, the Chinese multiplied delays before allowing them near the city. Weddel lost patience and sent out some boats to take soundings; fighting ensued; in the end, Weddel and his men were allowed to go by the Chinese authorities, on condition that they never attempted to go back.

By the eighteenth century, however, trade was being carried on with most of the European nations, and with Britain more and more. It was hedged by every conceivable restriction, it was confined to one port only, Canton, but whatever the conditions, they were accepted. As time went on, it became obvious that the balance of trade tipped heavily on to the Chinese side. There was nothing the Europeans could offer that the Chinese did not produce for themselves; the Europeans had to pay in silver and, as was in earlier times the case with the Roman Empire, the constant drain of precious metal to the East became an increasing source of annoyance.

THE OPIUM TRADE

Then it occurred to the English merchants to pick up cargoes of opium in India and trade with that. Opium was already being smoked in China on a small scale; when the English vessels began to bring it in quantity, the consumption increased. The amount of silver brought to China, of course, decreased correspondingly. This led the Chinese government to make the smoking and importation of opium illegal, and edicts were issued against it from time to time, not so much because of its harm to the people as to the exchequer. In any case, efforts to check it were ineffectual, and its hold increased upon certain classes of Chinese life.

In time, the Chinese authorities became alarmed. A fierce resentment took hold of them, against the people who persisted in bringing the stuff to their country; the British, on their side, were maddened by the persistent refusal to treat them as equals, by countless rebuffs and an attitude of contempt that prevented negotiations from ever being satisfactory. The quarrel blazed up in 1839, in the so-called Opium War, which forced from China the first of a long series of concessions to the western powers.

Japan, faced with the problem of the Europeans, first opened the door courteously, as the Chinese did. Then she shut it firmly, excluding them absolutely. When eventually she opened it again, it was because she had decided to meet the West. China, on the other hand, left the door ajar. Wider she would not open it, and when it was prised open, she was bitterly humiliated at her weakness.

For it so happened that Europe, Great Britain in particular, was briskly in the ascendant just when China was going down into the bad time that comes at the end of a dynasty. People talked glibly of "the break-up of China". But China was only in the process of shedding yet another outworn and feeble dynasty, as the silkworm sheds his outgrown skin.

CHAPTER 37

JAPANESE THOUGHT AND CUSTOMS

IT is a sharp contrast to turn from China—old, huge, self-sufficient—to Japan; young, small, quick to learn from other races. Japan being a string of islands, her people are sea-faring and water-wise. Even though one of the islands is much bigger than the others, the ratio of coastline to land area is, over the whole group of islands, higher than either Greece or Norway can show. If we add to this picture of bays and headlands, harbours and islets, the thought of mountains and of forests, of tumbling streams harnessed at the foot of the slopes to run into lush ricefields, of Shinto shrines built of cedar-wood that grew as a tree close to the spot where it now stands, blending into the landscape as naturally as when it drew sap—the beauty of Japan and the love of beauty in her people become as self-explanatory as their attitude to the sea. "If we open our hearts to the beauty of heaven and earth, and the ten thousand created things, they will yield us pleasure without limit, pleasure always before our eyes, night and morning, full and overflowing."

AINU INFLUENCE ON THE JAPANESE

When in China the Han dynasty was ruling an already complex civilization, the Japanese (a mixed group of immigrants, it is thought, from various points on the mainland of Asia) were still striving to maintain an existence made uncomfortable by the native tribesmen. Not until the end of the tenth century were these driven off the main island on to Hokkaido, to the north; and even now they preserve their own folklore and language. It is suggested that the primitive religion of the Japanese, "Shinto", the "Way of the Gods", took ideas from this Ainu people. Here is a translation of an Ainu's instructions for avoiding harm when in bear-infested country: "[Speak] . . . thus to the place where any tree stands—'O Sender down of the tree-genius, make great haste and hide me'; if he so say and hug the tree, even though the bear comes to attack him he will only come as far as the tree, and not seeing him, will return. Again, should one flee from a fierce bear and climb a tree, it will follow after. Then this is said to the tree trunk: 'O precious divinity of the rough bark, send Thou me help'. And what one should say to forks of trees is this: 'O divine and brave tree-crown, save me'; if this be said, no bear, however fierce he may be, will follow after one."

In the Shinto of the Japanese, there is the same animation of everything by spirits as is found in the Ainu stories; a pantheon conceived not merely as large in number, but as indefinite. Moreover, the islands themselves, trees, farm animals and countless other things are all born of the gods. So are further gods, and the founders of certain guilds, and the royal family. It is small wonder that the Japanese habitually speak of their country as "Land of the Gods". A Shinto priest was once asked how he could seriously elevate a sword, a mirror, a piece of stone, an old cap or the like, to a position of godhead. Said he, "Anything that has served a man's use, especially when he treasured or liked it, partakes of his spirit; for love is life and power. We use an implement or other object, and our virtue goes out into it."

SHINTO TABOOS AND MYTHS

Shinto kept its naïveté; it never developed a philosophy or a code of ethics. But it always had a keen sense of taboo, of ritual uncleanness, as the two earliest Japanese books, written in the eighth century A.D., show. "Uncleanness could be contracted . . . by contact with blood, diseases and corpses, and by incest and bestiality. . . . At the present day the common word for wound is *kega,* that is to say, defilement." It is to this agelong insistence on the necessity for bodily purification that the Japanese nation owes its ingrained habit of personal cleanliness.

The two eighth-century books were intended as records, but the minds of their authors had not yet outgrown the stage where legends and myths, facts and dates blend quite happily. "Curious and numerous gods and goddesses are seen. After the birth of a series of divinities whom we need not notice, the islands themselves and various gods representing the forces of nature come into existence as offspring of a divine pair, Izanagi and his wife Izanami. Izanami dies, and Izanagi goes to the underworld to seek her. He finds her, but angers her, and returns without her to the upper world. He finds himself contaminated by contact with the dead, and among other divinities, there are born, from the pollution which he washes off, the Goddess of the Sun (Amaterasu), the God of the Moon and the God of Force." This last god, Susa-no-wo, was always wailing and lashing around; ricefields and mountainsides were wantonly damaged by him—he is certainly the storm-god. On one occasion, he offended his sister, the sun-goddess, so that she hid in a cave and refused to come out. The earth was dark in her absence, and the gods held a consultation as to how to persuade her. They told her that a greater goddess than herself had been found, holding before her a mirror so that she saw her own brightness reflected. She was tempted out, and the god Stronghand seized the door so that she could not shut it again. Now the grandson of the sun-goddess was sent to earth (*i.e.,* Japan) to rule it. And he was the first Mikado. To this day the threefold insignia of the Emperor of Japan are a chaplet of jewels, a sword—and the mirror that tempted his divine ancestress out of her cave. This represents another aspect of Shinto—it is bound up with national feeling, and has therefore always been a very powerful political factor in Japanese life.

It seems strange that the Japanese should not have accumulated stories of the gods round their experience of earthquakes. With earthquakes making almost a running accompaniment to their daily lives, and with their quick imagination, it is somewhat surprising that, in the words of Dr. Nitobe: "Popular myth attributes these earth spasms to the wriggling of a huge catfish, living underground. But nobody thinks of fearing or worshipping this creature. It is treated as an object at which to poke fun." But of the effect on architecture, he says: "Recent accurate observations have confirmed the agelong popular belief that, were it not for the fires which ensue, wooden houses withstand the shocks better than stone or brick structures. . . . It is a remarkable fact that the tall five-storied pagoda has never been upset by a seismic disturbance. This is due to its construction being based on the principle of the wooden instrument known as the duplex pendulum seismograph. It consists of an inverted pendulum, which in the case of the pagoda is the outer frame of the tower, and an inner pendulum, the equivalent of which in the pagoda is the central suspended column, which does not touch the ground." Apart from pagodas, and Buddhist temples of Chinese design, it almost seems that the Japanese did not want permanence in their buildings; they would abandon a house when a death occurred in it, and the great Shinto shrine at Isé has been pulled down and rebuilt every twenty years. Their conception of architecture, in terms of timber, shingle roofs and temporariness, was altogether less solid than ours, different also from that of China.

CHINESE CULTURAL INFLUENCES

The Japanese people having the quick open mind of the child, with its eager admiration for the clever grown-up who can do so many things, Chinese civilization was the natural object of this admiration. Chinese knowledge and craftsmanship came into their ken through their trading contacts with Korea, for the peninsula was almost midway between themselves and China proper. During the Han period, it belonged to China, and after the Han broke up, it continued to be indebted to her for its arts and learning.

Among the Chinese immigrants were professional scribes, and the Japanese were introduced to the idea of writing. So far, what history they possessed was stored in the memories of professional reciters. But for a long time, they made little or no attempt to learn to write for themselves; writing meant the Chinese script, and though it fitted the Chinese language, it was quite unsuitable for the Japanese. In course of time various attempts were made to get over the difficulty, and two adaptations were worked out; these two are used concurrently, thus multiplying the natural complexity of the script.

Chinese books had, of course, come over with the other things, and a knowledge of the Chinese classics soon had the same place in Japanese education as Latin and Greek classics in ours. Just as we have largely been content to regard the Greeks as having originated philosophy, so the Japanese were content with Chinese thought.

The Shinto list of "sins"—or rather, taboos—classes together "breaking down of divisions between ricefields, filling up irrigation channels, removing waterpipes", with "calamities through the gods on high" and leprosy. The ritual impurity that puts the shedder of blood under a taboo applies even to the man who operates on an abscess. Not only is there no distinction between moral and non-moral matters, but no distinction is made between intentional and inadvertent offences. The Chinese classics introduced the subject of ethics; and then came Buddhism. The Japanese began to think out their values. Buddhism presented to them a field of thought in which they had never been exercised. When, in the middle of the sixth century, they decided to accept it, they exercised themselves so well that Japanese Buddhism came to stand alone. It has been influenced by Japanese political conditions and social customs.

TEA-DRINKING AS A RITUAL

Tea came to mean even more to the Japanese that it did to the Chinese. In the words of Okakura-Kakuso in *The Book of Tea*: "The fifteenth century saw Japan ennoble it [*i.e.*, tea] into a religion of aestheticism . . . a cult founded on the adoration of the beautiful among the sordid facts of everyday existence. . . . Under the patronage of the Shogun Ashikaga-Yoshimasa, the tea ceremony is fully constituted and made into an independent and secular performance. . . . Tea with us became more than an idealism of the form of drinking; it is a religion of the art of life." "The tea-room does not pretend to be other than a mere cottage—a straw hut, as we call it. . . . It is smaller than the smallest of Japanese houses, while the materials used in its construction are intended to give the suggestion of refined poverty. Yet . . . the details have been worked out with care perhaps even greater than that expended on . . . palaces and temples. . . . The garden path which leads . . . to the tea-room . . . was intended to break connection with the outside world. . . . One who has trodden this garden path cannot fail to remember how his spirit, as he walked in the twilight of evergreens over the regular irregularities of the stepping-stones, beneath which lay dried pine needles, and beside the moss-covered granite lanterns, became uplifted above ordinary thought. . . . Thus prepared, the guest will silently approach the sanctuary, and, if a samurai, will leave his sword on the rack beneath the eaves, the tea-room being pre-eminently the house of peace. Then he will bend low and creep into the room through a small door not more than three feet in height. This proceeding was incumbent on all guests—high and low alike—and was intended to inculcate humility. . . . The guests, one by one, will enter noiselessly and take their seats, first making obeisance to the picture or flower arrangement on the tokonoma (a slightly raised recess). The host will not enter the room until all the guests have seated themselves and quiet reigns, with nothing to break the silence save the note of the boiling water in the iron kettle. The kettle sings well, for pieces of iron are so arranged in the bottom as to produce a peculiar melody in which one may hear the echoes of a cataract muffled by clouds, of a distant sea breaking among rocks, of a rainstorm sweeping through a bamboo forest, or of the soughing of pines on some far-away hill. ... Everything is sober in tint ... the guests themselves have carefully chosen garments of unobtrusive colours. ... Not a particle of dust will be found in the darkest corner. ... One of the first requisites of a tea-master is the knowledge of how to sweep, clean and wash, for there is an art in cleaning and dusting."

Tea was first brought into Japan during the T'ang period, when everything Chinese was "the rage"—clothes, manners, habits; painting, verse-making, turns of speech. A new capital was built, copied minutely from the T'ang capital, C'hang-an. An attempt was also made to re-model the whole administration on Chinese lines; but the laws were unsuitable to Japanese life and were never applied.

After the T'ang there was less contact with China, and fewer Japanese went to the Chinese capital to study. They now had plenty of material for their thoughts to work upon, and could satisfy their own cultural needs without recourse to copying.

PORTUGUESE LAND IN JAPAN

Six hundred years passed, and then, in 1542 or thereabouts, a Chinese junk bound for Macao was blown off her course and made one of the Japanese islands instead. Aboard her were three Portuguese passengers.

These first Europeans to land in Japan were armed with arquebuses; the idea of firearms appealed tremendously to the military-minded Japanese, and they started immediately to make them for themselves. Firearms did not displace swords, which continued to be the standard weapon, carried by all who had the privilege of bearing arms, but they changed the character of fortifications; a technique of massive stonework was developed.

One of these Portuguese later went to Goa, taking two Japanese with him, of whom one, called Anjiro or Yajiro, there met St. Francis Xavier, and became a Christian. This first Japanese Christian persuaded the pioneer Jesuit to come to Japan, in 1549. Christianity soon made headway. The Japanese took kindly to it; indeed, many of them thought at first that it was simply a new sect of Buddhism. Those in power were anxious to foster good relations with Europeans for trade reasons. Commerce with the foreigners was going to be enormously worth while, they felt, and they noticed that the Jesuits were treated with respect by their merchant compatriots.

But it was not long before the Japanese began to feel that their welcome was not merited by the Europeans. They noticed that when

one of their own feudal families became Christian, it often persecuted Buddhist monks within its fief; they heard that in Europe
different sorts of Christians massacred and tortured each other, as
opportunity occurred; in Japan Franciscans, Dominicans and Augus-
tinians schemed against each other and the Jesuits. It was the same
with commercial as with missionary rights. The Portuguese wanted
to keep Spanish vessels out of Japanese ports, and both Portuguese
and Spanish hated the sight of the pertinacious Dutch.

In the first years of the seventeenth century, a vessel blown out of
her course entered Japanese waters. She had on board the pilot-
major of her squadron, an Englishman named Will Adams. Adams'
letters home are quaint and interesting; after voyaging for several
years over both the Atlantic and the Pacific, Adams and the remnant
of his exhausted crew found themselves at Japan. Adams was
brought before Ieyasu, virtual head of the state, who "shewed vs
great friendship. For he gaue vs an house a lande, where we landed
our sicke men, and had all refreshing that was needfull. . . . He
demaunded of me, of what countrey we were. . . . He demaunded
also as concerning the warres betweene the Spaniard or Portingall
and our countrey, and the reasons; the which I gave him to vnder-
stand of all things, which he was glad to heare, as it seemed to me.",

RELATIONS WITH HOLLAND AND ENGLAND

As a result of these conversations, Ieyasu decided to throw over
the South European states and encourage Holland and England. In
a letter to a member of one of the London Worshipful Companies,
Will Adams, now some years resident in Japan, says: ". . . And what-
soeuer the wourshipfull company shall have need in Japan, it shalbe
accomplished. This I dare insver: for the emperour and the kinge
(*i.e.*, Ieyasu) hath mad me such promis." Hitherto Japan had found
it impossible to get the foreigners' trade without admitting their
influence, for traders and missionaries were compatriots.

There was henceforth a cooling-off on the part of the authorities
towards the missionaries, though native Christians, and foreigners
who did not draw official attention to themselves, were left in peace.
In time, the sentiment of the government changed to crushing persecution. Anyone who did not register at a Buddhist or Shinto
temple was considered guilty of Christianity and was liable to the
death penalty.

On the commercial and political side, this policy took the form of
the forbidding of any foreign vessel, other than Dutch, to enter a
Japanese port. Japanese were forbidden to build a ship big enough
for an ocean passage. Any Japanese who did leave the country dared
not return. Thus was Japan guarded against the outside world, and
thus she remained sealed up for over two centuries, until 1853.

Considering the horror felt by the Japanese at the mere idea of
their beloved country coming under foreign domination, they held

their hand for a long time before adopting an anti-foreign policy. Only once had they experienced actual invasion, three hundred years before the Europeans came, when Kublai Khan had made two big efforts, without success, to conquer Japan. The whole nation had to forget its local allegiances in the bigger single loyalty to country, and the crisis made a lasting impression on their consciousness.

EMPERORS AND SHOGUNS

This national consciousness was a mixture of loyalty to the nation and enthusiastic allegiance to a number of feudal lords, between whom the country was divided. Japan's political structure was in origin that of a number of independent clans, in which the chieftainship and other positions, and even the right of livelihood, were all determined by heredity. Such a system does not lend itself to centralized government, which must involve obedience to people of other clans; and when, probably in the first century B.C.—though the old-time Japanese historians put the date six hundred years earlier—one clan began to dominate others until its chiefs could call themselves the Emperors of Japan, the political outlook of the Japanese changed very little.

The overlordship of the Emperors could hardly have lasted through the endless contending of the great families, had it not been for the habit of mind by which hereditary rights remained unquestioned. Rivals rent the country with civil war as they strove for power, but made no attempt to take the title of Emperor from its hereditary holder. Supreme political power was nearly always in the hands of one or other noble family; the periods of Japanese history are even spoken of by the name of the clan in power. After 1192, the men who ruled thus from behind the throne were called "Shogun", or General. In the early eighteenth century a bold Japanese lamented: "The sovereign, while occupying so high a place, has nevertheless been degraded to the intellectual level of a woman. The real power has passed into the hands of servants who, though they have never actually claimed the title, yet are sovereigns in fact. . . ." He blames the foreign Chinese customs; but feudalism always means the rivalry of powerful families, and this, being held back from open usurpation of the throne, found its outlet in becoming the power behind the throne. Actually the habit extended beyond the single stage of shogun-behind-emperor, and sometimes the Shogun would be a minor, another man having the power as his "regent". At one point, the "regents" were themselves puppets.

In the middle of the last century, when Japan opened herself to Western influence, the Shogunate was, by common consent, abolished. But the habit of mind engendered by it served a purpose; it helped Japanese to grasp the Western idea of the constitutional monarch ruling through ministers. There are, indeed, a number of factors that make it easier for Japan than China to handle modern Western things and ideas. Like ourselves, the Japanese live on islands, off the coast of a great continent to which they are indebted for all they possess; they are accustomed to taking things from abroad and adapting. But the Chinese are themselves the authors of their civilization, and are not so ready to import.

Feudalism was also abolished when Japan decided on Westernization, and in 1869, all castles had to be surrendered to the central government, which now preserves them as national treasures. They mostly date from the first half of the seventeenth century, when the then Shogun (Ieyasu, Will Adams' patron) decreed that each lord might only have one castle, all outlying ones to be destroyed. This brought into being magnificent buildings, for now they had to be spacious enough to house the garrisons and stores brought in from the demolished forts, and formidable, seeing their owner relied entirely on the one fortress. The civilian population looked respectfully at the splendour of great walls, rising from water, and upturned gables against the sky—and they set up shop at the gates. Thus urbanization followed, people settled round the new castles and made their living supplying the wants of the arms-bearing caste, the samurai, who now no longer worked in the fields, but stayed close to their master.

These samurai were both a glory and a danger. Their loyalty was to their lord, not to the nation. On the other hand, their code of honour, "Bushido", the "Way of knights", gave expression to the immense capacity of the Japanese for devotion; by applying Japanese courtesy to warfare, it produced chivalry. The samurai were given to vendettas, duels and brawls; but the maintenance in their lives of a balanced duality—thought and action—as from the mental work of Buddhist meditation they passed to fencing exercises and archery, was truly Japanese.

DUALITY OF JAPANESE CHARACTER

This two-sidedness of the Japanese character is very difficult for Europeans to understand. The same people who brought swordmaking to a fine art keep a general holiday when the cherry-blossom comes out; the people who have lavished thought and study on the refinements of landscape gardening have developed cheap mass production on a huge scale and utilized all the armaments of modern warfare for an industrial and territorial expansion unrelated to the old culture. The latest developments of Western science are welcomed with an enthusiasm which does nothing to abate the devout reverence paid to the divine origin of the Mikado. General, admiral, millionaire, peasant and mechanic alike hold fast to the national worship of the descendant of Jimmu, grandson of the Sun-Goddess, Amaterasu, who was sent down from heaven to govern mankind.

PART VIII

ISLAM AND CHRISTENDOM

CHAPTER 38

THE SPLENDOUR OF ISLAM

OUR study of the great Eastern nations has taken us far afield, and their stories have outrun the records of the West. Greece and Rome alike had felt the influence of Persia. Alexander had led the Macedonian spearmen and the Greek trader into the Punjab, and contact between India and the Graeco-Roman world was not broken till Mohammed kindled Arabia with his doctrine and his warriors went out to attack the Christian and Hindu worlds. Turks and Tartars became the militant disciples of the Arabian prophet, and bore his teachings into the older civilizations that lay west of them. But China lived her life apart. Nomads from beyond the Wall attacked her; preachers came from India to bring men to the Way of Gautama Buddha; but the continuity of Chinese life was unbroken by these foreign influences. So of necessity her story has been traced down to the days when the long sea-routes were opened and the sailors of Europe and North America reached the coast of China and made their contact with the island-harbours of isolated Japan.

THE DUEL OF EAST AND WEST

We must now go back to the beginning of the eighth century and take up the records of the Mediterranean lands and their neighbours in western Asia. The five earliest parts of our history have illustrated the persistent clash between the two groups from the days when Egypt struggled with Hyksos and Assyrians down to the fatal triumph of Heraclius over the Kingdom of Persia. The same great theme dominates the medieval scene; but now the spirit of the East and that of the West are represented by two rival faiths—Islam, the product of Arabia, and Christianity, which despite its Syrian origin was, in the details of its development, purely European. The history of the period which stretches from the victories of Mohammed's earliest successors to the middle of the thirteenth century, is predominantly concerned with the clash between the two faiths and the cultures to which they gave rise. They reacted continuously upon one another, and struggled ceaselessly for the control of western Asia, northern Africa and Europe. In this direction or in that, attack and counter-attack succeeded one another with hardly a pause throughout the period.

At the close of the seventh century, Islam was on the aggressive, and it was still uncertain whether the civilized society so painfully built up by the Greeks and Romans, and so deeply undermined by the infiltration of barbarians from the north, would not fall into irremediable ruin before its first onrush. Already many times in human history the fierce populations of Arabia, condemned to misery and poverty so long as they remained in the arid wastes that covered so much of their vast country, had been tempted by the fertility and accumulated wealth of happier lands. When Syria, Egypt and Mesopotamia were controlled by peoples capable of vigorous defence, the Arabs were kept within their bounds; but with a weakening of the barriers, there would follow an outpouring similar to those which had overthrown great civilizations in earlier ages. Mohammed gave the Arabian tribes the political unity necessary to make them formidable just at a time when the Empires of Byzantium and Persia had exhausted one another. His religion, the keynote of which was *Islam*, personal surrender to the will of God, provided them with a rallying cry and with just the discipline and capacity for co-operation that the wild tribes needed for success in war.

ARAB CONQUEST IN THE WEST

Under the able leadership of Mohammed's successors the Arab raiders gave up plundering forays, and established themselves as ruling aristocracies in the valleys of the Nile and the Euphrates, in Syria, and along the south coast of the Mediterranean. In every case their success was made possible by the feebleness of the resistance. Without fanaticism, they offered a religion far simpler and more easily intelligible than the form of Christianity taught by the Greeks; since adherence to it was rewarded by immunity from taxation and the promise of participation in future loot, converts became numerous— so numerous indeed as to cause some embarrassment to the tax-collectors. By 700 the Arabs ruled from the Tigris to the Atlantic. It remained for them to extend their rule to the European mainland.

In 711, a great host of the Berber inhabitants of Africa, under leaders of Arab origin, crossed from Ceuta into Spain, over the strait which still takes its name from Tarik, their first leader. They won an easy triumph. The ruling classes in Spain, descended from the West Gothic invaders of the fifth century, were divided amongst themselves and out of sympathy with the native population. There was little or no organized government. Roderick, the nominal king, was defeated and slain, and a single year sufficed to put the southern half of Spain at the conquerors' feet. Even the towns offered little resistance, for the numerous Jews in them preferred the tolerant rule of Moslems to the persecution which they sometimes suffered under the Christians. By 717 the invaders had penetrated the north-east and had reached the Pyrenees, but as the mountain valleys of the north and north-west contained nothing to attract, no systematic attempt was made then or later to conquer them. Christian rulers there retained their independence, and gradually grew in strength, until, centuries later, they emerged as the fighting princes of Aragon and Navarre, and eventually recovered all that had been lost.

Meanwhile a still more threatening advance was being made in the East. As we have seen, the outlying dependencies of the Greek Empire had quickly fallen before the raiders. After the capture of Egypt, the Arabs took to the sea and ravaged the islands of the eastern Mediterranean almost without hindrance. In Asia Minor attacks and counter-attacks continued with little pause for a hundred years. Upon the Greek mainland of Europe, the real danger-point, the Moslems could as yet make no impression.

CONSTANTINOPLE PROTECTS THE CHRISTIAN FAITH

The firmly rooted nationality of the Greeks constituted an impregnable fortress, with Constantinople as its citadel. After a series of preliminary attacks, the really formidable onslaught was made by sea and land in 717. Defended by the soldier-emperor Leo, the bulwark held, and the attack was not seriously renewed. Only the imagination can conjecture what might have followed if Constantinople had fallen at this time. Behind it the whole of eastern Europe lay without organization or defence, and only faintly tinctured here and there with Christianity. The Moslem faith might well have been spread through the Balkans to Hungary and Russia as rapidly and as easily as it had consumed North Africa and Spain. As it was, the east of Europe was given seven centuries of respite.

By this time the original impulse which had driven the Arabs so far afield had lost much of its force. Not only were there feuds between rival Arab leaders, but also between Arabs and the races whom they had enlisted in their cause. The further its successes took it from Arabia, the less exclusively Arab the movement became. Ardently Mohammedan it remained, but the characteristics which it assumed tended increasingly to be those of the country occupied. The conquests in the latter part of the seventh century had been conducted by the Umayyad dynasty, descended from the ruling caste of Mecca. These called themselves by the title of Caliph, or successor of Mohammed, and ruled from Damascus. The rival house of the Abbasids, however, representing the actual family of Mohammed, in their struggle with the Umayyads for supremacy, won the Persians to their side. In 750, with this assistance, they destroyed their rivals and seized the Caliphate. The Abbasid victory was in effect a victory of Persians over Arabs. Baghdad replaced Damascus as the capital, and it was from the Persians, the better educated and more cultivated race, rather than from the Arabs, that Islam in the East took its prevailing hue. Similarly Egypt soon fell away from the rest under the rule of the Fatimites, who claimed descent from Mohammed's son-in-law Ali and who also called themselves Caliphs. Spain remained under Umayyad rule for many centuries, and became more Berber or Moorish than Arab. Though out of sympathy with the Caliph of Baghdad, and often hostile to him, the Spanish Umayyads did not claim the title of Caliph until the tenth century; long before then, Islam as an attacking force had lost all cohesion. Within a century of the Prophet's death, the various provinces had become practically separate political units.

Thus when the time came for an advance from Spain into Gaul, the movement was no longer supported or controlled from the East, and Spain itself was very far from being subdued. In Gaul, however, there were rich convents and churches to loot, and in the south at any rate little organized resistance to overcome. The Gothic Duke of Aquitaine was overthrown in 732, and the Moors, now reinforced by recruits from Spain, advanced to the vicinity of Tours. Here, however, as at Constantinople, they encountered a really vigorous defence. The Franks were not so firmly rooted a nation as the Greeks, but under Charles Martel they proved strong enough to beat back the weakening Moslem attack in a great battle near Poitiers. The raiding impulse gradually faded out, and after 750, in the West as in the East, a halt was called. Except for raids from Africa upon Sicily and the south of Italy, which continued for three centuries more, Islam and Christendom settled down into comparative stability behind roughly drawn frontiers, each to develop on its own lines. Before the contest was renewed, Europe had recovered largely from the anarchic state in which the first Moslem onslaught had found it, while in Spain, in North Africa and in Persia, Islam used the respite to develop a brilliant culture.

Although Islam was quickly divided into two, and subsequently into three, Caliphates, each of which naturally tended to take colour from the subject races which it contained, the types of civilization developed in the three continued for centuries to show many features in common. This was, no doubt, due in part to the habit, general throughout Islam, of making pilgrimages to the sacred shrine of Mecca, where men of high and low estate regularly mingled.

MOSLEM TRADE AND SEA-POWER

There were, however, other means of contact. The first period of Arab conquest had been destructive, especially in Egypt, but the conquerors everywhere restored peace during the eighth century. They assimilated the knowledge of the conquered people with remarkable rapidity and began the work of reconstruction. Everywhere they were glad to preserve the Christian population and, in return for tribute, granted it complete religious freedom. The Christians steadily diminished in numbers. Yet, as late as 1100, there were still forty-seven Christian bishops in North Africa. A hundred years later, when Cordova was reconquered by the Christians from the north of Spain, the churches were found to be still in use and undespoiled. This contemptuous tolerance, and the complete absence of prejudice against intermarriage between the newcomers and the older inhabitants, made for the rapid fusion of the races and a general restoration of the arts of peace.

During the eighth and ninth centuries, commerce sprang up on an extensive scale, for the Arabs took to the sea much more readily than the early Teutonic invaders of the Roman Empire had done. Barbarian Europe had to await the infusion of Norse blood before resuming commercial life on any considerable scale. In 650 the western Mediterranean was a silent lake, only the Greeks in the East continuing the old commercial tradition. By 800 it was again becoming a great highway, keeping the two halves of Islam in contact nothwithstanding the political separation. Cotton and cloth from Egypt, silk from the East, and gold and ivory from the interior of Africa were exchanged in Spain for figs, wine and oil, timber, copper and iron, just as they had been in Roman days. Commerce sprang up with Christian states as well, for relations with them were not always hostile. With the Greek merchants of Constantinople and Amalfi much trade was done, and even with those of Pisa and Narbonne, where Jews sometimes acted as intermediaries. After 850, when the Norse adventurers appeared in the Mediterranean, they found piracy easy to combine with commerce, selling in Tunis or Tripoli the booty and captives seized on the banks of Seine or Trent. The bulk of Mediterranean shipping, however, remained for three centuries in Moslem hands.

MOSLEM CENTRES OF LEARNING

The recovery of commerce served to maintain some degree of uniformity in the Moslem world, but it had other reactions of equal consequence. Upon it was based a highly developed industry, and on that in turn a degree of wealth that enabled Baghdad, Cairo and Cordova to become centres of elegance and learning at a time when western Europe was only just emerging from barbaric degradation. From the Greeks in Egypt and Syria, the Moslems absorbed much of the Greek tradition of systematic thinking and logical reasoning. Though rejecting parts of the teaching of Plato, they were particularly attracted by the works of Aristotle, in which he sought to discover laws of general application by the close study of nature. These works and others they translated into Arabic, and learning his method, they made considerable advances in such sciences as chemistry, physics and medicine.

Two Moslem thinkers must be mentioned. Avicenna of Baghdad, who died in 1037 and who is said to have written over a hundred treatises, may be called the founder of modern medical science and of the practical treatment of disease. Some of his works, mainly valuable because based on his own clinical observations, were translated later into Latin by Spanish Jews and in 1650 were still in use as University textbooks in north Europe. The influence of Averroes of Cordova in the twelfth century was to prove still greater. It was his commentaries on Aristotle, introduced into France, also by Jews, in the thirteenth century, which called the attention of the West to the value of logical thought on Greek lines, and but for that discovery no foundations could have been laid for the edifice of modern scientific thought and experiment.

Geometry also was taken over by the Moslems from the Greeks and to it they added their own invention of Algebra, the basis of so many mathematical processes. The so-called Arabic numerals they borrowed from the East, but by the invention of the nought they made possible the decimal system, thus enormously simplifying all arithmetical calculation. From the Greeks also came their astronomy; in this field as well they made innumerable discoveries, later to be transmitted to Europe. In the details of daily life the Greek influence on them was profound. We talk of Turkish baths. They were the normal baths of the Roman Empire, which were still commonly used in the Greek world, though long since abandoned in the barbarian West. The Arabs learnt their use, preserved it and transmitted it to the Turk, from whom we borrowed it. Turkish carpets are those originally woven in Constantinople and in Persia, and copied throughout the Moslem world at a time when our ancestors were content with rushes laid on bare earth.

ARCHITECTURE AND DECORATION

For their mosques, the Moslems began by taking over and converting the existing Christian churches. Soon, however, they began to build imitations of them, taking columns and capitals from ruins, joining them with round arches and ornamenting them with marble tablets. Later they built pointed and horse-shoe arches, the latter borrowed from the Goths of Spain but ultimately carried through Africa to the East as far as India. The dome, a feature of Persian origin, common in Greece since the time of Justinian, was also frequently used. The mosques were often approached through a courtyard surrounded by a colonnade and containing the water-basins in which the faithful could perform their ablutions in preparation for the hour of prayer.

The Moslems invented no new structural style in their architecture, but in the brilliance of the decoration which they applied they have never been surpassed. For ornament, since the representation of the human form had been forbidden by Mohammed (as a safeguard against the idolatry rampant among the Christians), they used geometrical designs carried out in Byzantine glass or marble mosaic, and elaborate honeycombed plaster work, derived from Persia but still called Arabesque, often with texts from the Koran impressed with stencils on the plaster. In this style they obtained brilliant effects by the free use of contrasting colours in the cells of the honeycomb. Brightly coloured tiles were often used for roofing. Such buildings as the great mosques at Cordova and Cairo rank among the most impressive monuments in the world. Some of their domestic buildings, similar in style, were equally elaborate and as opulently decorated. They contained luxurious pavilions and halls of audience, arranged round courts, and bathrooms and gardens were provided on an equally lavish scale.

Their arts were similarly a fusion of Greek, Persian and Egyptian influences, subject here too in early days to a dislike of portraying the human face or form, even in secular buildings. Painting and sculpture therefore did not develop far, but in the making of porcelain, glass-ware, book-bindings and jewellery they reached great heights. Their weapons obtained early fame. In Damascus and Toledo, steel sword-blades were produced of a quality unequalled until the nineteenth century, and inlaid with gold and silver "arabesques". Such articles as these, together with brocades and rugs, ivories and bronzes, armour and leather-work, gradually found their way from Spain and Egypt into France and north Italy during the tenth and eleventh centuries. They were eagerly sought after by the wealthy, and as far as possible imitated. The later growth of similar arts in Europe owed as much to this source as it did to the development of direct traffic with the Greeks of Constantinople.

The immense luxury of the lives of the well-to-do gave scope to innumerable industries, such as the manufacture of silk, cotton and woollen cloth, carpets, cushions, curtains and furniture, and, in addition, paper, as yet unknown in Europe outside Spain, but of great importance to the growth of learning. In Cordova alone there were at one time thirteen thousand weavers. A city of two hundred thousand houses, it was the home of all kinds of leather-workers, hence called cord-wainers in England.

AGRICULTURE AND EDUCATION

Their agriculture, like that of their predecessors in inadequately watered countries, was based on large-scale irrigation. This science, learned in Mesopotamia, Egypt and other parts of North Africa, was introduced into Spain, or at least widely extended there. For its practice, law-abiding and peaceful conditions of life are necessary; few things more easily perish from misuse or neglect than dams and canals. For centuries, these conditions prevailed, and a huge peasant population became dependent upon the irrigation works. The vine was widely cultivated, in spite of Mohammed's veto on the use of wine; cotton, rice and sugar were also grown in Africa and Spain. When settled order vanished, so also did the prosperity, and as the irrigation works decayed, much of the population also disappeared from once thickly populated districts in Mesopotamia, in North Africa and in large areas of southern Spain.

Education was widely diffused. Flourishing universities existed in Baghdad and Cairo in the tenth century, and at Cordova before the end of the eleventh; in the twelfth, most Spaniards could read and write, a contrast with England or France at the time. Poetry was the most popular branch of general culture, and a copious ballad literature of the time, treating of love and war, has survived. There was also some poetry of a grave and reflective type; one masterpiece, the *Rubáiyát* of Omar Khayyám, a Persian work of the eleventh century, has won lasting fame. History and geography were widely studied, and the short story cultivated, as readers of the Arabian Nights will know, though they were Persian rather than Arabian. The demand for books was wide, and as paper was cheap, it could be plentifully supplied. In the ninth and tenth centuries, students, copyists and book-dealers flocked to the Baghdad of Haroun-al-Raschid and the Cordova of Abderrahman III. At the latter, besides private collections, the Caliph's library is said to have contained four hundred thousand volumes, all catalogued and richly bound. Book-collecting was a normal hobby of the well-to-do. In each locality the speech of everyday life was a mixture of Arabic with the tongue of the conquered race—in Spain the debased Latin of late Roman days. The official language, however, was everywhere the Arabic of the Koran. In this, East and West communicated and all important books were written. Hence, when new knowledge or fresh products were introduced into Europe from the Moslem world, Arabic words were used to designate them, such as algebra and zero, coffee and cotton, sofa and tariff.

An effort of the imagination is required for us to realize the wealth and density of population which had grown up so rapidly in districts such as Persia, Mesopotamia, North Africa and southern Spain—known to us to-day as sparsely-inhabited and in part desert—and still more to grasp the contrast between their civilized and ordered life and the conditions then prevailing in the western parts of Christian Europe. Between the cultured gentleman of Baghdad or Cordova and the ruthless barbarian of tenth-century France or Germany, little comparison is possible. The Arabian conquerors had accomplished much of what Alexander the Great had aimed at. They had fused East and West, in culture if not in politics, and had combined the long heritage of both in an imposing edifice. Their empire was as wide as that of Rome had been. The East at long last seemed to have won the final victory. Was it to dominate the future of mankind?

FUNDAMENTAL WEAKNESSES OF ISLAM

Looking back even at its greatest days, we can detect more than one fundamental weakness in the structure of Islam. The discipline which Mohammed imposed upon his followers, and the institution of polygamy, both assets to a fighting race, were of less value in an age of peace. The one brought out none of that self-reliance and love of individual enterprise which were among the main contributions of the races of Germany and Scandinavia to the common stock of Europe. The other, in sharp contrast with the ascetic ideal which pervaded Christian monasticism—and indeed Christianity in general—implied large families for the ablest and most vigorous men, but implanted none of that capacity for self-regulation and self-restraint which prevents races from falling into physical and mental decline.

Islam, moreover, left all women in a position of servile subjection to their men. No positions of responsibility were open to them. It was a condition of respectability that they should nowhere appear in public. None of that idealism attached to them which has always been implied in the Christian attitude. Throughout Christendom the respect and worship paid to the Virgin Mother were reflected in a general reverence for her sex. In the eyes of the Church as a whole, they were the equals of men, and in all ages were granted equal religious rights. Some rose to positions of great influence as the consorts of important rulers, as owners of property in their own right, or as abbesses of large nunneries; and what had always been the attitude of the Church was later reinforced by the teachings of Chivalry. In Islam, on the other hand, women remained mere chattels; and where that attitude prevailed, the possibilities of a culture to which women could, as in the West, make their own special contribution were very limited.

SUPERIORITY OF CHRISTIAN TEACHING

Islam, moreover, tended inevitably towards autocracy. The Caliphs, claiming to rule in the name of God, could brook no limitations to their power. They must be absolute, or fall. Such a system allowed no scope for the doctrine that civil rulers were responsible to their subjects or that they had duties as well as rights. In the religion of Mohammed there was no encouragement of work as a wise discipline, nor any teaching of the value of human personality as such, leading gradually, as Christian teaching did, to the ultimate extinction of slavery. Yet if drudgery is the lot of slaves, it becomes undignified for freemen to labour, and no work is undertaken except for the remuneration and independence which it brings. In such a system the slave-owning class may well have wealth and leisure, and may thus produce a brilliant culture, but it carries in it the seeds of inevitable decay. Above all, in the absence of any ideal of self-sacrifice or self-restraint, there was no feeling that obligations lay on those who were possessed of wealth, and no check to the reckless indulgence of luxury.

On the other hand, however hideously debased it may have been in barbarian Europe, Christianity had embedded in it ideals that are probably necessary to the foundations of an enduring civilization—those of sacrifice and restraint. It was capable at its best of inspiring its adherents for the service of their fellows and of bringing the highest motives to bear on mundane affairs. Granted that its loftiest principles have never yet been put into very general application, they have nevertheless from time to time come far enough to the front to exert an influence on social and industrial life very different from that of its rival, and to that extent they supply the reason why Christian culture survived when that of Islam fell. A civilization founded on such principles was slower to develop than that of Islam, but it rested on a surer base, as was to be proved in the next few centuries.

By the beginning of the eleventh century, Islam seemed rapidly to be falling into decay. In the East the decline was checked, but not in the West. In Spain the wealthy classes ceased to be warriors. Even fighting was left to slaves. Racial discord between Berbers and Arabs there had always been. Now class-feeling was added. A slave revolt marked the beginning of the end. The Western Caliphate broke up in 1031 into a number of petty kingdoms which constantly fought amongst themselves, and with settled order there vanished the irrigation system upon which prosperity depended. The local kingdoms were attacked by the Christian states of the northern mountains, which had never been altogether suppressed, and the eleventh and twelfth centuries saw a steady sequence of Christian victories. Though Spain never shook itself entirely free from oriental influences, by 1250 Islam was in full retreat.

THE COMING OF THE SELJUKS

In the East, signs of a similar decline were visible. Here, however, the process of disintegration was arrested by the coming of the Seljuks in the eleventh century. We have already watched the advance of this race of fighting leaders. At first they seemed to threaten the Islamic culture with complete ruin. Though less susceptible than the Arabs had been to civilizing influences, they soon absorbed something of their subjects' learning. The provinces were administered by Persian viziers, such as Nizam-ul-Mulk, the friend of Omar; under them literature and science continued for a time to flourish. Their real contribution to Islam was that at a critical moment they re-united in a single realm a vast area stretching from Afghanistan to the Mediterranean, and renewed in it the military ardour which had marked the earlier ages of their faith. The defeat of Diogenes Romanus at Manzikert in 1071 meant the permanent loss to Christendom of Asia Minor, and opened once more the way to Constantinople itself.

CHAPTER 39

THE GREAT ANARCHY

IT was to the Franks, and in an even greater degree to the Greeks, that Europe owed her respite. Of all the barbarian chieftains who had established themselves among the débris of the Roman Empire, none but Clovis managed to found an enduring state. The Merovingian kings, as his successors were called, maintained the Frankish domain for nearly three centuries. This success they owed to no merit of their own. Each king followed the Teutonic tradition of dividing the inheritance among his sons, who fought each other for the spoils. In character, and even in physique, they went from bad to worse, until at the beginning of the eighth century they had ceased to wield power, and had become no more than crowned figure-heads, mere symbols of royal authority. "Nothing was left to the king", says a chronicler, "except the name. He sat on his throne, gave audience to envoys, and dismissed them with the answers which he had been schooled to give. He had nothing to call his own but one small residence and a not numerous retinue." Yet an aura of sanctity clung round the kingly office. Its holders commanded the loyalty and obedience of the Frankish warriors by right of descent. No usurper dared claim to oust the revered family so firmly established.

THE FOUNDATION OF A GREAT FRANKISH DYNASTY

The wielding of the kingly power, the right to make decisions and to lead in the king's name, fell into the hands of the chief of the king's household, the Mayor of the Palace; and this office was held in turn by four members of a remarkable family. Its founder, Pippin, who became Mayor of the Palace in 622, married his daughter to one for whom it was claimed that he was descended from a Roman senatorial family. His grandson, Pippin II, also Mayor, was the father of Charles Martel, who led the Franks against the Moors in 732, and the great-grandfather of Charlemagne. It was the vigorous leadership and unfailing resource of this family that ensured the permanence of the Frankish realm amongst so much that was transient. Teutonic by language and sentiment, but claiming also the prestige that attached to Roman ancestry, they were well fitted to take the lead in that fusion of barbarian and Roman culture which fostered the growth of a new civilization upon the ruins of the old. They were in truth neither Frank nor Roman, neither Teutonic nor Gallic, but the pioneers of a new Europe, which was to be the product of both.

The Mayors of the Palace maintained and strengthened the tradition, founded by Clovis, of close alliance with the Roman Church. Most of the other barbarian tribes, as for example, the Lombards and the West Goths, had learnt their Christianity from Arian teachers. They were slow to abandon the heresy, and were accordingly debarred from friendly relations with the Catholic population. The Franks on the other hand were regarded by the Christian bishops and their flocks not as heretics, but as friendly defenders. Intermarriage with their subjects became possible, and with it the rise of a new stock, derived, like the house of Pippin, from barbarian and Roman.

But both the Church and Carolingians, as Pippin's descendants were called, gained more immediate advantages from their alliance. The Lombard invaders of North Italy, from the moment of their arrival, had taken up an attitude towards the Church exactly contrary to that of the Franks. In 700 the Bishops of Rome were already in the position of being the political rulers of central Italy. That position, however, would soon be lost if the Lombards became the masters of the whole peninsula. The Greek Emperors were far away, and were themselves no friends of the Papacy; and it was to the Franks that the Popes appealed. After Charles Martel had defeated the Moors at Poitiers, Gregory III sent the keys of St. Peter's tomb to the conqueror, with the request that he would defend him from the Lombards. Charles refused—he had too much else on hand—but the alliance was maintained. A few years later Pippin III, who had succeeded Charles, propounded to Pope Zacharias the momentous question—who should be king, he who had the title but no power, or he who had the power without the title? Zacharias returned the required answer, and accordingly in 751 the last of the Merovings was deposed, and in the Cathedral of Soissons Pippin was formally anointed King of the Franks. Much turned on that anointing. The sacrosanct position of King came to Pippin not by right of descent, but by the "Grace of God", and of that Grace the Pope might, and afterwards did, claim to be the mouthpiece.

But this was not all. In 753, after a fresh Lombard advance, a memorable bargain was struck. The Pope bestowed on Pippin the Roman title of Patrician, and required the Frankish nobles to take an oath never to choose their ruler from any other house. In return for this final consecration of the family to the kingship, Pippin undertook to invade Italy, to recover from the Lombards the territory which they had annexed, and to restore it not to the Greek Emperor, from whose viceroy it had been taken, but to the Bishop of Rome. Finally, after Charlemagne had succeeded his father Pippin, Pope Hadrian appealed once more to the Franks against the hated Lombards. Again the Frankish host crossed the Alps. The Lombard kingdom was this time extinguished, and Charlemagne solemnly confirmed the Pope as the political ruler of central Italy. To the claim of being the head of western Christendom, the successor of St. Peter now added that of being a territorial sovereign. Thus, out of the curious alliance between the barbarian and Rome, there sprang not only an immense accession of strength to the Franks, and the right of the Church to alter the succession of barbarian kings, but also that peculiar feature of European history, the Papal state. The Frankish leaders earned the title, Protector of the Church.

THE BREACH BETWEEN EASTERN AND WESTERN CHRISTENDOM
Meanwhile, the Graeco-Roman Emperors, seemed no longer able to maintain their rights in Italy. Although most of western Europe had long since ceased to have direct political connection with Constantinople, the Roman Empire had up to this time been always regarded as a unity, temporarily weakened but still capable of restoration. Italians, Spaniards and even the inhabitants of Gaul were legally subject to the Emperor, however rarely he might remind them of his existence. Similarly, although the churches of East and West had had many differences, most of these had been merely doctrinal.

There now occurred a momentous controversy between East and West, which rent Christendom in twain. The seventh century had been a period of moral and spiritual decay everywhere except in England and Ireland. The reverence paid to images was carried to such lengths as to constitute, along with magic and miracle-mongering, the main religion of the people. Pure idolatry was fast superseding a spiritual religion. The symbol was replacing the reality. In 726, the Emperor Leo III, who nine years before had brought the main onslaught of Islam to a standstill before Constantinople, commanded the destruction throughout his dominions of all sacred pictures and images, known as *Icons*. In Asia he was obeyed. Elsewhere he was defied. The monks and the populace rose everywhere in defence of their beloved images. In Greece it meant a civil war. In Italy the Emperor's viceroy was murdered and the last trace of his authority was erased. Pope Gregory III, supported by the Italian bishops in council, declared the *Iconoclasts*, or image-breakers, to be heretics and blasphemers.

The consequences were momentous. It was not merely a question of schism between the churches. As the Emperor was himself a declared blasphemer, the Christians of the West felt themselves freed from all allegiance. The Empire, it was held, was in suspense, vacant and awaiting a more worthy claimant; it was to the Bishop of Rome and to the Franks that men looked henceforth for leadership. Just when Christendom should have been uniting all its forces to face the challenge of Islam, such unity as it had was finally destroyed. Between Constantinople and Rome there remained an enduring legacy of jealousy and suspicion, and although from time to time the urgent need for common action against Islam raised the question of reunion, popular feeling proved too strong. The division was permanent. In the times of its greatest need, as we shall see, Constantinople, after a first betrayal, was finally abandoned to its fate.

THE STRENGTH AND VISION OF CHARLEMAGNE

To western Europe it seemed that there was no valid Emperor. Yet now there had arisen in the West a man in whom all the imperial attributes seemed to be combined. In 768 Pippin III was succeeded by his son Charles, known later as Charlemagne—Carolus Magnus— who for forty-three years dominated Europe as no one had done for many centuries. He was a big man, well over six feet in height, commanding in presence and outstanding in personal strength. To a vast appetite for enjoyment he joined wide vision, strong common sense, an immense capacity for detail and an unbending will. To his warriors he seemed the ideal leader, "iron his helm, iron his weapons, iron-hued his war-horse, his gaze that of a lion". A Frank in speech, he loved the war-songs of his race and wore its traditional costume, a belted linen tunic, a long mantle of blue, and scarlet hose. Yet if to his followers he seemed wholly a Frank, in all matters of culture and religion he revealed himself a true son of Rome. To extend the Church and the influence of its priests was always his first object. Within his inherited dominions, he ruled with a discipline that was Roman in its severity as well as in its justice.

His career was one of almost ceaseless warfare. During the first thirty years of his reign he is said to have personally conducted twenty-six campaigns. In Italy, as we have seen, he overpowered the Lombards and annexed their kingdom. Later he added the region round the northern shore of the Adriatic between Venice and Trieste, and also the island of Corsica. He brought the whole of Gaul into obedience, and cleared from it the last of the Moors; and although a venture into Spain was less fortunate—it ended in disaster at the pass of Roncesvalles—he established the Pyrenees as a frontier that has endured to this day. But the hardest and most continuous of his wars were waged to the east and north, especially against the Saxons. As under his predecessors, missionary work and conquest went hand in hand. Down the Danube he established Christianity throughout Bavaria, with an outpost as far forward as Vienna. The Saxons, the last German race to resist, were subdued after years of bitter fighting, in which many thousands were slaughtered. Beyond the Elbe the Slavs, and beyond them again the Avars, both races that hitherto had had no contact with the West, were forced into obedience. The Avars disappeared from history, but the Balkan Slavs retained their racial characteristics under the yoke of their northern conquerors.

SYSTEM OF LOCAL GOVERNMENT

For carrying on the government of his vast territory, inhabited by such diverse peoples, Charles had to combine old methods with others devised to meet the circumstances. It was necessary to provide some form of local government and at the same time to keep all local leaders in regular touch with the centre. The whole realm was divided into counties, each with its Count, or Graf, who was responsible in his district for justice and order, and for raising troops for the royal army. These men, usually chosen from the local landowners, were supposed to hold office for life. They could be removed, and at death could be replaced by the monarch. Everywhere, however, there appeared a tendency for them to make their positions hereditary and to look upon their offices as personal possessions. If unchecked, this tendency would in time have rent the realm into semi-independent districts, as in fact occurred as soon as the great leader's hand was removed. To control them, therefore, and to supervise their work, Charles sent round specially chosen officials, called *missi dominici*, king's agents, on regular tours of inspection, to hold special courts of justice and to make reports on what they found. At the same time, Charles encouraged trade by allowing Jewish merchants to settle in his territories, and prosperous Jewish communities grew up at Lyons, Augsburg and Worms.

On Charles in person fell the task of giving some degree of unity to the whole edifice of government. As a capital, where central business could be conducted, he chose Aachen, and here a great palace was built. But he was rarely in residence. He constantly moved from one end of his dominions to another, campaigning, redressing grievances, issuing edicts, arbitrating, inquiring, reconciling, and supervising. In a word, government was not yet a matter of institutions or any kind of permanent machine. From first to last all depended on the personality of the monarch. Given an active leader, respected and feared, the vast realm could be held together. Its size was superficially impressive, but before the days of rapid communication no empire stretching from the Elbe to the Pyrenees, and containing such diversity of races, could long endure.

THE REVIVAL OF SCHOLARSHIP

But if his political achievement was short-lived, his work for education had permanent effects. In the intervals between his campaigns he made it his principal task to promote an intellectual revival throughout his illiterate domain. He surrounded himself with the best scholars of the day, drawn from every part of Europe where civilization still survived, the chief among them being Alcuin of York. The work of the scholar was confined to copying and expounding to his pupils what had been known and written in the Roman past. Though this copyist age produced no new knowledge and little literature of its own, it recovered much of what had been forgotten, and preserved it at a time when there was real danger of its being lost for ever. In the future, when the old had been grafted into the new, though the barbarian North would always retain some impress of its virile and passionate ancestry, the lines of men's thought and expression, the level of their knowledge and culture, would at least in part be those of the Latin past. Above all, though Charles did not Latinize Germany as Caesar had Latinized Gaul, he had done enough to make central Europe safe for the Roman Church.

It is not surprising that to Charles and his scholarly courtiers, with their knowledge of what the old Roman Empire had been, should have occurred the notion of restoring it. He who already wielded imperial power deserved also the lustre and prestige which attached to the title. The Greek Emperors were held of no account. It was true that the iconoclastic decrees had been withdrawn, but the Byzantine throne was actually occupied by a woman, Irene, who had won her way there by blinding and deposing her own son. A woman could hardly be recognized as even the titular ruler of the world, nor could such a criminal be regarded as the protector of the Church. Yet if Charles was to be Emperor, it would be well to avoid the charge of usurpation. Accordingly, towards the close of the century he opened negotiations with Constantinople with a view to obtaining recognition for himself as the legitimate Emperor of the West.

TERRITORIES RULED BY

Greatest of the Frankish kings, Charles the Great embarked upon a career
of almost ceaseless warfare from 768, with the object of restoring the authority
of the Western Roman Empire. His acquisitions of land and power resulted in
his being crowned Emperor by Pope Leo III in Rome on Christmas Day, 800.

THE EMPEROR CHARLEMAGNE

Charles succeeded in bringing the German lands under one ruler, annexing Bavaria and ruthlessly subduing the heathen Saxons. He smashed the power exercised by the Lombards in Italy, and won back the Spanish March from the Saracens. In the East he set up provinces against the Slavonic tribes.

Just at this juncture there occurred a revolt in Rome against the Pope, Leo III. Accused of evil-living and perjury, he was maltreated and driven from the city. He appealed across the Alps for justice; and Charles, as protector of the Church, agreed to try the issue. Late in the autumn of 800, he descended upon Italy and entered Rome. On December 23rd, in the church of St. Peter, Leo swore to his innocence on the Gospels and was reinstated in his office. Two days later, as Charles was kneeling at the Christmas Mass, the Pope placed on his head the Imperial crown, while all present, clergy, Franks and Romans, shouted their approval, hailing him as Augustus and the chosen of God. Once more Frank and Pope had done one another good service, though the service was more apparent than real.

EMPEROR AND POPE

Charles is said to have been taken by surprise and even annoyed by the manner of his coronation. No Emperor had ever received his crown from a Pope, and of course, negotiations with the East were at once broken off. His instinct proved ultimately to be right. In years long after, Popes claimed that, as one of them had granted Charles the crown, that crown was in their gift, to be awarded or withheld at pleasure. The immediate importance of the coronation, however, lay not in the manner but in the fact. It brought Charles no fresh territory or authority; he was just as much the master of the clergy, including the Pope, before 800 as after. The significance is that it was the response to an instinctive call for the unity of Europe.

Rome had been prosperous and strong because it had been one. The Empire had fallen, and ruin and chaos had supervened. Someone there must be to restore and to symbolize that unity. There must once more be an Emperor in the West under whom church and state might prosper. That instinctive call has been preserved through the centuries. It inspired the later Popes and Emperors, though they struggled with one another for the privilege of obeying it. Silenced for the time by the rise in Europe of warring nations, it was revived by Charles V and again by Napoleon.

CHARLEMAGNE'S SUCCESSORS AND THE NORTHMEN

The great Emperor died in 814, and was buried in the church that he had built at Aachen. Of his immediate successors little need be said. His sons, and after them his grandsons, divided the inheritance in the Frankish manner, and fought each other over the division. Their power steadily declined, and as it did so, the counts, abbots and other landowners built up for themselves little local centres of government and authority. It seemed as if the unity for which the Carolingian house had struggled had given place to just such anarchy as had preceded it. But it was not so. The ideal of strong, civilized government remained firmly rooted, and men said that the great Charles slept and would awake.

In 800, Charles was promising Europe imperial unity and prosperity. By 950, a fresh series of barbarian invasions had filled it with ruins, and the growth of feudalism was rending it to pieces; before 1100, the Papacy was claiming to supplant the Empire. There is no generally accepted reason why the heathen inhabitants of Denmark, Norway and Sweden should suddenly have launched themselves upon their Christian neighbours; but once their raids had begun they were continuous, no part of Europe being safe from them. The Northmen sailed in fleets of oaken ships of some seventy to one hundred and twenty feet long, propelled by oars and sails, built strongly enough to face the open ocean and yet not too broad to pass easily up the rivers. Fearless navigators, they did not limit themselves to coasting voyages as most shipping—Greek, Carthaginian, Roman or Arab—had done until their day, but boldly struck across the open sea, first to the Hebrides and Ireland, and later to Spain, Iceland, Greenland, and even North America. Their tactics were to land suddenly and destroy mercilessly. From strong resistance they recoiled, to re-embark and vanish. Sometimes after sailing up a river, they seized horses from neighbouring farms and spread destruction far and wide. It was along the river valleys of the Neva and the Dnieper that Rurik led his Swedish host in 862. Kiev and Novgorod fell to these fighting merchants, who were called Rus and gave their name to the broad plains of the Slavs.

CONQUESTS OF THE NORTHMEN

England was first attacked in 787. Before long, the Seine, the Loire and the Garonne had been raided, Rouen and Bordeaux being destroyed, as well as Antwerp and even Aachen. In 860, penetrating the Mediterranean, the Northmen plundered Pisa and many old Roman cities of Provence. By this time, however, the character of the attacks was changing. Raiding passed into conquest and permanent settlement. This process was at first no less destructive. The brilliant art and culture of Ireland and of Northumbrian England was extinguished. The growing towns were depopulated, the trade-routes abandoned; if the raiders showed no mercy, their victims relapsed from their new-found peaceful ways into equal savagery. All over Europe, the slow civilizing process of the last two centuries was un-done in a little more than a lifetime.

The attempts of the Northmen to conquer England, though destructive, were thwarted by the rise of the house of Wessex. In France, however, the invaders made themselves independent rulers. By 910, the whole valley of the lower Seine had been united under a Norse leader named Rolf, whose descendants were formally recognized as Dukes of Normandy, "the place of the Northmen", with Rouen as their capital. In practice the subjects of the King of France, they made Normandy an independent state for nearly three centuries, during which time they won for themselves the throne of England.

O   (H.W.)

From Normandy, there emerged another remarkable band of adventurers. Southern Italy and Sicily were still nominally in the possession of the Greek Empire. Arabs and Berbers, however, had occupied all Sicily, whence they made continual raids upon the mainland, and threatened the Papal State. In the ceaseless fighting there was opportunity for bold soldiers of fortune, and from 1020 onwards, we hear of many Normans making their way through France to south Italy and offering their services to the highest bidder. Three sons of one Tancred took service with the Greeks and were rewarded by grants of land. They soon repudiated their Greek paymasters and established themselves as independent princes. Their vigour and their ruthless efficiency in war made them the admiration and the terror of the motley population of south Italy, a jumble of Greek, Arab, Berber, Italian and Jew. In thirty years, this remarkable band of brothers, with the backing of a hundred or so of their own race, made themselves masters of south Italy, and before the century ended, had wrested Sicily from the Arabs.

Pope Leo IX was greatly alarmed at their encroachments. Their frontier was too near Rome for comfort. He tried to eject them, but was defeated. A later pope, Nicholas II, showed more foresight. In 1059 he struck a bargain with them, and taking convenient authority from his claim to be the ruler of all Italy, he appointed one of the brothers, Robert, nicknamed Guiscard, or Wizard, to be Duke of Apulia. He thereby gained a formidable ally, both against the Greeks, whose territory he was giving away, and against the Roman Emperor, with whom the Papacy was by this time at odds. In 1101 Robert's nephew, Roger, united the whole of southern Italy, with the island itself, into a single realm, and took the title of King of Sicily. In eighty years the adventurers had already made a remarkable contribution to history. They had won a crown, had built up a solid and prosperous state, had finally ousted the Byzantines from the West, and had safeguarded Italy against Islam.

RESULTS OF THE INVASIONS

In the course of two centuries, these fierce northern warriors had swept into every part of Europe. So far except in Russia their activities had been for the most part destructive. The distinctive culture of Ireland never recovered from their depredations, and northern England was thrown back for many centuries. Yet, in the long run, there were compensations. Amongst whatever race they settled, they infused into it their own love of enterprise and bold adventure. After the first age of destruction was past, they showed themselves just as eager as the Arabs to acquire the arts and culture of their former victims, and far more able to inspire them with a new spirit of vigorous originality. Both Arab and Norman built anew among the ruins which they had made. The Arab edifice was short-lived. That of the Norman endures, for it was better founded. For reasons of expediency, as the Franks had done, they everywhere exchanged their native paganism for the Christianity of the new home, and though the cultivation of the Christian virtues was as slow a process with them as with other northern races, they soon produced many faithful sons of the Church. They excelled as builders, taking what was left of Carolingian or Byzantine architecture and developing it into such noble monuments as the cathedrals of Caen or Durham, or the Monreale at Palermo.

Equally important was the Northmen's contribution to the art of government. The need of the day, as the very success of the Norse raids had shown, was the development of some form of strong central government. Even Charlemagne had created nothing permanent, and since his death the unity which he had promised seemed as far off as ever. It was the Normans in Sicily and England who first showed western Europe how to organize and administer such a government, and this was the only antidote to the disintegrating influence of feudalism.

THE NATURE OF FEUDALISM

Feudalism is a form of society which tends to appear wherever, owing to the collapse of central government, men come to group themselves, for purposes of local defence, round others who are stronger than they. Something like it has been found in countries as far apart as Sweden and Japan, as well as those which had been subject to Rome. For its first origins in the West, we should have to look back to the downfall of the Roman Empire, when it was evolved as the unconscious response to meet an urgent need. It can be traced to the fifth century or earlier; to a time when the central government had abandoned all attempt to provide defence or to guarantee security for life and property. But with its origin we are not here concerned, for Charlemagne by his own activity and by his provision of Counts and *missi* had checked its growth and minimized its evils. After the break-up of his empire, however, the same need for local direction was felt as before, and the same kind of response was evoked. During the anarchy of the ninth century there was no central authority in France or Germany competent to impose order, to chastise evil-doers, to protect the weak from the strong or to organize defence. Yet there was no district upon which the raiding Northmen might not suddenly descend. Who then should perform the work of government? Feudalism was a crude attempt to find an answer, a groping after a system of local government.

Its essence lay in the two ideas that every man had certain rights over his social inferiors and certain duties towards his superiors, and that those rights and duties were determined in every case by his position on the land. The king, however far off, incompetent or powerless, was conceived to be the sole landowner and to be ultimately responsible for justice and defence. From him all land was held by tenants, on definite conditions. The vassal was bound to his suzerain by an oath of fidelity. He was under obligation, when required to do so, to follow his lord in war with a prescribed force of horse or foot and for a prescribed period, and upon him was imposed the duty of maintaining justice and order within the area of land so held. In return, this being the essential point, his suzerain promised him justice and protection against all external force. Each oath of fidelity taken and each duty imposed was symbolized in concrete form by some prescribed act of homage, such as kneeling bare-headed before the suzerain, or by some ceremony, known as Investiture, such as the presentation of a sword. The process was continued to the bottom of the social scale. There the serf, tied as in late Roman times to the estate on which he was born, owed specified duties, often onerous, to its master, in return for which he too was promised protection. Otherwise he was free, and he was responsible for no one. Each tenant, whether of high degree or low, raised his own army, built his own fortified castle for defence, issued his own decrees and presided in his own court of law, before which his tenants might be summoned and to which they could refer their disputes.

Wherever feudalism spread, it substituted local law, the decrees of the local magnate, for the laws of the land, and without a national system of law, and regular institutions for enforcing it, neither prosperity nor progress is possible. The barbarian invasions had destroyed Roman institutions, and feudalism completed the resulting legal anarchy, leaving the Greek Empire the only area of Europe where civilized law, enforced by central institutions, still existed.

THE UNHAPPY POSITION OF THE SERFS

The age was therefore one of general anarchy, in the midst of which the portion of the common people was for the most part rude, monotonous and miserable. Clustered in small villages, they lived a life not far removed from savagery, ignorant of all but the simplest arts of life, and practising a husbandry of the most primitive type. Whatever the theory, the peasant was in fact dependent upon the caprice of his landlord, and was often treated with gross inhumanity. His inability to cope with the powers of nature made him the victim of bad seasons, floods and epidemic diseases. He was at the mercy of the wild beasts which roamed the forests—wolves being specially dreaded, owing to their numbers and their savage depredations. Cattle were puny compared with ours, and were rarely eaten. Pigs, pastured in the forests, supplied the staple meat. Communications were generally so difficult that when one place enjoyed abundance the next village might be starving.

Nominally Christians, but in practice worshippers of some local saint who could still the storm, send the needed rain or stay the pestilence, the people regarded God as a dim far-off being, like the king, worthy of far less respect than the local potentate. They looked to the next world for their only hope of secure happiness, and to the Church for the betterment of their material lot on earth. The best of the churchmen did what they could to mitigate the misery of the age, both materially and morally. On the whole, the higher clergy and the monasteries were better landlords than the lay nobility. At least, they were less prone to private war. They did something to keep in order such roads and bridges as survived from the Roman or Carolingian ages. They made some effort to provide the elements of education, and they encouraged the arts, particularly that of architecture.

THE CHURCH RULES MEN'S LIVES

Yet in an age when the general level of morality was low, the higher clergy were mainly concerned with their wealth and position as landed magnates, while the parish priests, few of whom could translate the services which they recited, were little ahead of their flocks in mentality or conduct. The daily lives of the people, from birth and baptism, through the confessional, marriage, the absolution of sins and extreme unction, to death and burial, were wholly in their hands; but in spite of the constant exhortations of the enlightened few there was little that was spiritual in the popular religion. Miraculous interventions in the order of nature were its main objective. Wonder-working images and relics were frankly worshipped. The church services, culminating in the Mystery of the Mass, were regarded as magical incantations ensuring the passage of the worshippers to heavenly bliss, if not also their material good fortune then and there. Of Christianity, in any sense which the founder would have recognized, there was little enough. The most that can be said is that the centralized organization of the Church still kept alive the idea of European unity, that many a parish priest, however far removed his ideals from those of earlier Christian ages, still did his duty as he saw it, and that in a barbarous age, when every branch of human activity and culture was subject to degrading influences, a few devoted leaders still handed on the torch of piety and learning, from which, when social conditions improved, real spirituality could be rekindled.

During the early years of the tenth century, the state of the Christian West was in marked contrast with that of Mohammedan Spain. Germany and France were divided into numberless provinces —duchies, counties and marches—whose dukes, counts and margraves fought each other and were in practice subject to no law. Yet at the darkest hour there arose a leader in whom men thought they saw the great Emperor's promised successor. Just as in England the necessity for organized defence had brought into eminence an efficient dynasty of monarchs, the House of Wessex, so in central Germany the incursions of the Magyars had a similar result.

The Magyars were a race of Mongol origin who had migrated from Asia into the plain now known as Hungary, and had thus divided, as their descendants still do, the northern Slavs from those of the south.

Like their descendants to-day, they were great horse-breeders, and during the ninth century, they made rapid plundering raids through south Germany, piercing even to Italy and France. Their movements were so swift that no ordinary defence could check them. The Duke of Saxony, however, won fame by his method of dealing with them. Across the line of their advance, he established a number of well garrisoned fortresses. He encouraged the population, who had hitherto lived for the most part in scattered straggling villages, to gather round them—to live in peace-time as they would have to do in war. The next Magyar raids were held in check by the new defence, and in 919, the last descendant of Charlemagne being dead, the Duke, Henry by name, was recognized by the feudal nobility of Saxony and Franconia as King of the Germans. He was succeeded by his more famous son Otto, afterwards styled The Great.

GERMAN RECOVERY UNDER OTTO THE GREAT

Otto possessed many of the qualities required for the task of restoring the unity of Germany, or at least of staying the process of disintegration. He was a natural leader, fearless, active, and of splendid presence. But for the distractions which led him to abandon the task before it was well begun, he might have had success. The new German kingship was very different from that of the Franks. The power of the feudal nobility was firmly rooted and the independence of each in his own territory not to be directly questioned. Further, though Otto had been chosen to succeed his father, his position was elective rather than hereditary, a matter more of convenience and utility than of sacred right. Neither at this time nor later, was any dynasty allowed in Germany to take deep root.

Otto's success was such as to suggest that, if he could have founded a lasting hereditary dynasty, like that which was soon to emerge in France, and if he and his successors had devoted their whole energies to the task of building up the central control, Germany might have defied feudalism and have become a united state six centuries before the time of Bismarck. In France and England the same conflict, that of central control against feudal separation, broke out later, and in both countries the royal power ultimately prevailed. Hereditary monarchy replaced election, and the countries were firmly held together. Before the battle in Germany had been fairly joined, however, Otto succumbed to a lure more brilliant than that of German sovereignty. He shouldered fresh responsibilities, and bequeathed to his successors a legacy which to Germany was disastrous.

In Italy, as elsewhere, the times were evil. In the absence of any central government, anarchy prevailed. The Papacy had fallen into utter disrepute. The throne of St. Peter was the prize for which rival noble families contended. Between 896 and 904 there were eight Popes, three of whom were removed by acts of violence. Later, John XI, a notorious evil-liver, became the head of western Christendom at the age of twenty, and soon after, a boy of sixteen was appointed. This monstrous state of things produced, at long last, a reaction. To save himself, the boy, John XII, invited Otto from across the Alps. The bait was of course the Imperial title.

In 961, Otto descended upon Italy, and early the following year was crowned Emperor in Rome. It was agreed that no Pope thereafter should be consecrated until he had first taken an oath of allegiance to the Emperor. In return, Otto confirmed John both in his position as Bishop of Rome and in his rights as ruler of the Papal State. Four years later, the Pope had further trouble with the Roman nobility. Otto returned and remained in Rome for some time, ruling both the city and the Papal State as absolute master. He could well claim to be the protector of the Church. Like Charles, he wished his new position to be recognized at Constantinople. He received this and more, for upon his son was bestowed a Greek princess in marriage. He believed that by his coronation he had restored the empire of his great predecessor, and many wrote and spoke as if it were so. All the West still lived in the idea that there could be no welfare for Europe without such an empire. And as now re-founded it was to last, under the title of the Holy Roman Empire, for many centuries with varying significance.

Yet there were important differences between Otto's empire and that of Charles. It was far less extensive. There was now no claim to France or Spain. Otto held only Germany and northern Italy, and even there he was not secure. In Italy, since 800, enough racial feeling had arisen for him to be hated as a foreigner. In Germany, feudalism was untamed. It was not on such foundations that the unity of Europe could be erected. His real legacy was that henceforth, whenever German kings were men of energy and vision, they disappeared over the Alps to claim their imperial inheritance, and in trying to rule Italy, they governed Germany badly or not at all. Moreover, in claiming Italy the Emperors were soon to be drawn into a struggle with the Church which led to even greater disaster.

THE PAPACY AND THE CLUNIACS

During the tenth century, the Christian Church lay in just such anarchy as had enveloped the political world. We have seen the depths to which the Papacy had been debased. There were many bishoprics and abbeys of which a similar tale could be told. With a few exceptions, the higher clergy were, at best, mere feudal lords, and many of the lower, morally debased, ignorant and illiterate, had degenerated into dealers in spells and incantations, the meaning of which they did not profess to understand. The age of ideals, moral leadership or spiritual zeal might seem wholly to have passed.

Yet even in these dark times there were some monasteries where the Benedictine ideal of chastity, piety and learning was still cultivated. In one of these, that of Cluny, in Burgundy, there began in

910 a campaign for the renewal of faith and practice. The fame of this house soon spread, and the wide response that was given to its teachings showed that the time for reform was at hand. New monasteries arose, all subject to the Abbot of Cluny, and preachers trained there travelled all over the West, recalling men to spiritual zeal of the most earnest type. Before the end of the century, the movement had gradually widened out into a comprehensive programme of church reform, not confined to the monastic houses. The teachings of Christ, it was held, would never penetrate the world at large until the clergy themselves had been subjected to strict discipline, and the highest standard of morals and spirituality demanded of them. Next, the Church must be extricated from the savage beastliness of feudal society. The Papacy itself must be reformed, freed from the influence of German kings and Italian nobles, and placed in a position to lead the world. Lay rulers must be reduced to a subordinate position. There must be an independent Church, and at its head an omnipotent Pope, owing allegiance to no human sovereign and ruling Christendom through his clergy. Here, indeed, was a new basis upon which to found the unity of Europe.

POLITICAL AIMS OF THE PAPACY

The first step towards putting the programme into practice was taken in 1048, when a Cluniac, Leo IX, was appointed by the Emperor Henry III to the Papacy. His first step was to declare that it was the right of Popes alone to invest all bishops with the emblems symbolizing their office. To prevent the appointment of unworthy men, the Pope himself must select and control them. They were in no respect to be the servants of any layman, but of the Pope alone. Even the Emperor was not to require an oath of allegiance from them. Such a claim cut at the root of feudal land-tenure. If, under these new conditions, bishops and abbots retained the lands and palaces with which they had been endowed in Germany, and almost to an equal degree in France, political rulers everywhere would lose control of the very districts which hitherto had been most subject to them.

In 1073, a new Pope, Gregory VII, was elected, who deliberately provoked the struggle which was to dominate the history of Europe for the next two centuries, the struggle to create a Papal sovereignty co-terminous with Christendom. He decreed that the lay investiture of priests should cease forthwith. The fully developed Cluniac programme was now revealed. Popes were already recognized to have a threefold capacity: they were Bishops of Rome, they were the political rulers of central Italy, they were the spiritual leaders of the whole Church. They must now add a fourth, namely that of universal, omnipotent and infallible despots. Gregory was not personally ambitious. His single aim was the purification of the Church. In that cause he was a passionate idealist, and, like many such, fervent, implacable, and so deeply convinced of his own righteousness as to be careless of the means employed. He pictured himself leading an army of disciplined clergy to evangelize the world, and for that end he claimed universal supremacy. "Human pride", he wrote, "has created the power of kings. God's mercy has created the power of bishops. The Pope is master of emperors." And he went on specifically to claim the right in God's name and as the successor of St. Peter, to depose emperors and kings as he thought fit and to be above all human jurisdiction in so doing. Lay rulers were to be his servants, wielding their authority as his viceroys and at his pleasure.

THE DUEL BETWEEN HENRY IV AND GREGORY VII

The Emperor Henry IV had succeeded when too young to rule. Recently declared of age, he was an inexperienced and headstrong young man who had no inkling of the impending storm. He was unpopular in Germany and was threatened with serious feudal revolts. He saw no further than that, if he yielded to the Pope, he would be deprived of the support of the wealthy clergy just when he most needed it. To Gregory's decree, he returned an angry and defiant answer. He was then summoned to Rome to explain his disobedience, and as he refused to appear, Gregory forthwith declared him excommunicate and deposed.

Henry was now in a difficult position. The best of his subjects were on the side of reform, many others were ready for revolt, and others would rather desert him than incur the ban of the Church. The sentence of excommunication was a formidable weapon. It outlawed its victim and absolved all his subjects and dependents from their oaths of loyalty to him. Since it deprived him of the sacraments which were regarded as necessary to salvation, it consigned his soul to hell. So long as men generally believed in the Pope's right to wield it, it outweighed the power of armies. So it proved now. Henry was bluntly told by his German followers that unless he made his peace with Gregory his throne was forfeit. He had no course but to make a show of submission. Though it was mid-winter he hurried across the Alps, practically alone, and threw himself upon his enemy's mercy. He found him at Canossa, a fortress in the northern Apennines. For three days he was kept waiting in the snow outside the gate, fasting and clad in the robe of a penitent. On the fourth day he was admitted, but before receiving absolution, he was made to promise to appear for judgment before a court presided over by the Pope in person. If acquitted, he might resume his crown.

The news of this dramatic event re-echoed through Europe. It could never be forgotten that an Emperor had knelt before a Pope. The struggle seemed over, while in reality it had hardly been begun. Henry had accomplished his purpose. He had been deeply humiliated, but he had freed himself from excommunication, and had thereby deprived his rebellious subjects of the show of legality. He returned to Germany to deal with them. Moreover, the Pope had overshot the mark. Men thought him arrogant and unforgiving. Thus the Emperor was able to raise large forces to his side, and beat down the rebels in Germany. In 1083 he came again to Italy, this time at the head of an army. In the north, he was welcomed, for the tide of reaction against Gregory was running strongly. Rome itself was besieged. In despair, the Pope called upon his Norman allies from the south. They drove off the Germans, but once in Rome they seem to have forgotten in whose service they had come. Their old plundering instincts came to the surface and they sacked the sacred city. The Romans were so enraged that when the Normans retired, Gregory thought it unsafe to remain. He therefore withdrew with them to Salerno, where he died.

The issue which had provoked the struggle remained unsettled for another forty years. In 1122, however, Emperor and Pope came to terms. It was agreed that the lay prince should renounce investiture by ring and staff, which were the symbols of a bishop's spiritual authority, but that he might require homage for lands and other possessions held in feudal tenure—a compromise reached sixteen years earlier in England, where a similar struggle had been waged between king and archbishop. Each side claimed the victory, but in reality nothing was settled. It still remained an unanswered question, whose servant was the bishop and at whose disposal was his land. In any case the Investiture question, important in itself, especially in Germany, was a minor matter in comparison with the main issue of which it was an offshoot. Nothing had been done to decide who should wield final authority in the European commonwealth, the Roman bishop or the princes of this world.

Suddenly Gregory's successor found a fresh opening. In 1095 Urban II assumed the definite leadership of the Christian world by proclaiming a Holy War against Islam. There could be no better climax to the campaign for Cluniac ideals than a crusade to recover the grave of Christ for the sake of Christendom.

CHAPTER 40

THE CHRISTIAN COUNTER-ATTACK

AFTER repelling the first attacks of Islam, the Greek Empire, as we have seen, was for a time seriously weakened by the *iconoclastic* controversy. When this died down, however, it recovered much of the strength and solidity of its greatest days. It was threatened during the tenth century by the incursion of the Bulgarians from Russia into southern Europe, but the power of these had been broken, and the process of converting and civilizing them was well in hand by the early years of the eleventh. At that time the Empire seemed, more than ever, to be the one impenetrable fortress, where the faith and the traditions of the past were safe. The loss of its non-Greek possessions in the East, in Africa and in Italy had proved a gain in solidity; what was left was mainly Greek in speech and Graeco-Roman in tradition, and its strong sense of nationality, unique in Europe at that date, its pride in itself and its history, and its conviction of being the natural centre of the world, were sources of tremendous strength.

THE POWER OF THE GREEKS

There were other foundations for its power and splendour. It had a permanent and disciplined army, kept at great strength and maintaining the fighting traditions of a thousand years. This force was elaborately organized. Both horse and foot were divided into heavy and light armed regiments, and there were separate medical and engineering corps, the whole being largely recruited from the sturdy peasantry of Asia Minor and officered by the landowning class of the same districts. The navy was less formidable, but it could draw upon a large population of experienced seamen, and it had developed an elaborate fighting technique in which much use was made of "Greek Fire", a substance whose composition was for centuries a carefully guarded secret and puzzles experts even to-day. Rome's great legacy to posterity, the imperial law, enforced uniformly throughout the empire, was an invaluable basis for social order and prosperity, and enough by itself to distinguish the land where it was preserved from the rest of the world. Administration was conducted by a permanent, trained civil service, a costly but effective governmental machine such as existed nowhere else until the thirteenth century. Control was always centred in the capital. The Emperor's will was obeyed throughout his dominions to a degree unknown in the West and never approached in Islam.

The financial system was based on a stable gold coinage. The *byzant* was never depreciated and was accepted the world over as the standard of value. Taxation was levied in money; and for eight hundred years the government remained solvent. It could finance its army and pay its generals in coin instead of granting them land, thus retaining central control and avoiding one of the principal causes which had plunged the West into feudal anarchy. Its diplomatic service kept the emperors well posted with information of the events of the barbarian world outside. Potential enemies were dealt with in all sorts of ways. Some were won to friendship by gifts and pensions and high-sounding titles, or, like Otto, drawn into alliance by the timely bestowal of a princess in marriage. Others found themselves embarrassed by internal strife quietly fomented by Greek agents. To one barbarian chief an Emperor wrote, "I sent you a token of my esteem because I judged you to be the most important prince in your district. One of your rivals has appropriated it on the ground that he has more right to it than you. It is open to you to show him that he is wrong. If you do not, it will be clear that it is he upon whom we ought in future to bestow our favours." It was the normal imperial policy to throw the Germans and the Lombards upon the Papacy, Venice against the Sicilian Normans, the Slavs and the Magyars upon the Germans, and all, if need be, upon Islam. Once the iconoclastic reforms had been abandoned, the Church made no such difficulties for the civil rulers as were rending Germany and Italy. The Emperor was himself the sacred chief—high priest as well as king—patriarchs and bishops being no more than his spiritual advisers.

Commerce and manufactures, helped by the universal currency of the byzant, were conducted on a scale comparable with that of Rome in the second and third centuries. The geographical position of the capital and its splendid harbours made it the natural focus of all trade routes, north and south as well as east and west. There were exchanged the furs and amber, the salt and caviare of Russia, the flax, wines and metals of the West, the pepper and aloes, the perfumes and raw silk of India and the farthest East, the grain of Egypt, the glass and embroideries of Syria, the sapphires and pearls of Ceylon, the cattle and gold of Africa, and slaves from everywhere. No wars interrupted this commerce for long. There was as much trade with Alexandria and Baghdad in the eighth and ninth centuries as in the sixth. There also were made silk cloth, carpets, brocades, jewellery and fine glass, the secrets of which were later discovered by the Venetians and are still exploited in Venice. It was from tolls on this far-reaching commerce that the government took the bulk of its revenue and derived much of its stability.

THE MAGNIFICENCE OF CONSTANTINOPLE

Above all, the Empire had in Constantinople not only a centre of trade unequalled in the world, but also a formidable fortress, and a museum of art treasures which gloriously symbolized its history. Its miles of ramparts and towers remained unstormed for seven centuries. They still stand for the most part intact and provide a spectacle of unsurpassed grandeur. In it had been assembled much of the best statuary of classical Greece. There were columns commemorating great emperors of the past, immense public buildings, senate-house, law-courts, and a host of churches, besides Justinian's splendid cathedral of Santa Sophia, the Holy Wisdom; the Imperial Palace, embellished or enlarged by almost every emperor since Constantine, was a town in itself, with gardens, baths, libraries and barracks, its halls hung with gold brocade and glittering with marble and glass mosaics. To the university came students from all parts, from the Moslem world as well as the Greek, and in it, although little new knowledge was amassed and little literature created, medicine, mathematics and music were assiduously studied, and the works of the classical Greek writers, poets, historians and philosophers, were in constant use. There was a flourishing art, which gave noble expression to the Christian faith.

It was no wonder that every visitor who found his way there from western Europe was staggered by its magnificence and wealth, all in such utter contrast to the primitive poverty at home. The varied riches of the markets, the fortifications, the crowded shipping, the thronged streets, the halls rich with embroidered hangings and mosaic, the white uniforms of the palace guards, the interminable splendour and elaborate etiquette of the Imperial court, even the square miles of slums, were all things to astound. He returned home torn between two emotions, awe and reverence for the city which contained such marvels, and the lust to loot it.

The Greek Empire was a survival from the past. It enshrined a civilization continuous with that of Greece and Rome, for it had as yet suffered no such tragedy as had overwhelmed the western world. There still in working condition were the Roman order and law, the Roman conception of the sovereign state, at a time when in the West all authority was being decentralized by feudalism, and the Church was only beginning to obtain control over savage tribal custom. Here, too, were the Greek love of beauty and intellectual intensity.

THE SELJUKS ATTACK THE GREEKS

Yet, like Islam at the same date, it also had elements of weakness. The office of Emperor was sacred, but not the person of its holder. There was no such reverence as prevailed in the West for the sanctity of royal blood. Anyone might aspire to the throne, and military conspiracies and usurpations were frequent. The population of Constantinople, fickle and hysterical, was apt to rise in sudden and violent riot and to destroy the persons of its rulers, though never the system. If the emperors were despots, their rule was often cut short by the assassin's knife, and defeat in war was usually followed by such outbreaks. Above all, though it had inherited two great traditions and had fused them into one with Christianity, it had, no doubt, in its determination to preserve the legacy intact, made it rigid and utterly unprogressive. Looking always to the past, the Greeks, like the bees in a hive, destroyed without pity all that did not conform to the type. The state, the art and the religion were so conservative as to be unalterable. Moreover, in Constantinople as in Islam, a civilization based on absolutism had reached its farthest limit, and since the human spirit will not always be constrained into inherited moulds, the future lay with lands where there was room for individual freedom and where traditions could be leavened with vitality. The contribution of the Greek Empire to ourselves was that in it the old traditions were preserved intact, until such time as the barbarians of the West should be civilized enough to receive them and to warm them back to life.

Such was the empire upon which Islam opened its second attack. In 1071, after the battle of Manzikert, three emperors in quick succession were dethroned, and during this period of disorder the

Seljuks overran Asia Minor right up to the Sea of Marmora. Ten years later, however, an intelligent soldier named Alexius Comnenus was raised to power. The situation was threatening. The Empire was at war with the Sicilian Normans, who, after absorbing Greek territory in Italy, had landed in Dalmatia under Robert Guiscard, his army including a contingent of Sicilian Moslems. More serious still was the loss of Asia Minor, the principal recruiting ground of the army. To recover it was vital, for without it the army would be permanently weakened. Alexius appealed to the West to help him in this task. The first requests were not effective, but in 1095 he addressed himself to Pope Urban II, as the only person commanding general recognition in the West. It seemed an adroit piece of diplomacy. If the Pope swallowed the bait, reinforcements would be available for a campaign in Asia Minor, and the Normans, the close allies of the Papacy, would be disarmed.

POPE URBAN CALLS FOR A CRUSADE

The appeal fell on willing ears. Urban and his predecessors, as we have seen, had been trying to substantiate their claim to be the leaders of the West, and he was flattered by this timely recognition. What more effective way to establish his position as against the German Emperor than to lead the West in arms? Might not the outcome be to unite under Rome the Churches of East and West, so long at bitter enmity? One of the predecessors of Alexius, with characteristic Byzantine diplomacy, had already dangled that prospect as the price of help. As the best place to raise the army that would be required, Urban went to France, his native country, where spiritual fervour was still at a high level. At Clermont, in the Auvergne, and elsewhere, he delivered a series of orations, calling on all who could bear arms to join in a Holy War.

He turned another circumstance to advantage. At the time of their occupation of Asia Minor, the Seljuk Turks were also at war with the rival Fatimite Caliphate of Egypt. Syria, the ancient battle-ground of Asia and Africa, had consequently fallen upon troubled times. Jerusalem itself had been captured by the Seljuks. Though not intolerant, the Seljuks were a rougher race than the Arabs; in the wars the native Christians of Syria suffered, and western pilgrims to the Holy Places, more numerous than ever before owing to the Cluniac revival, found their way difficult. There had been many previous complaints to the West, both from the Christian Patriarch of Jerusalem and from others, but they had fallen on deaf ears.

Urban was therefore able to add rhetorical point to his appeal by referring to the hardships of the pilgrims, which did not grow less in the telling, and to the occupation of the Holy Places by unbelievers, though that occupation had already lasted for four centuries. He mentioned indeed the needs of the Christian Greeks, but the whole emphasis was upon Jerusalem. His hearers were immediately inflamed. Thousands swore to devote themselves to the cause and went off to organize their forces. By one of the tragic accidents of history, it was to recover the Holy Sepulchre that they swore, not to defend the Greek Empire. On the contrary, Greek Christendom was generally looked on as a rival, heretical Church, to be suppressed rather than assisted, as the Normans, with their eyes on the wealth of Constantinople, had already proposed. Thus the movement which might have united the forces of Europe against the East took a disastrous direction from the start. Whatever immediate assistance Alexius obtained as the result of his appeal, the movement which he started not only perpetuated the fatal division of Christendom, but also was gradually warped into a force that betrayed and ruined his empire. The eastern bulwark of Christendom was destroyed, and the path to the West laid open to Islam. The false strategy of making Jerusalem the main objective and of sacrificing Constantinople meant five centuries of Turkish rule in Europe.

That Urban's appeal obtained a ready response was in part due to a newer ideal, which for a century had been rapidly permeating the West. Chivalry, like Papal ambition, was in its origin an offshoot of the Cluniac revival. The Church in France had long been trying to curb the fighting instincts of the feudal aristocracy—to educate the military caste out of their brutalizing routine of war and pillage. If such instincts could not be eradicated, they must be disciplined and consecrated to noble purposes. Under the influence of the reformed clergy, a code of conduct and honour had come into being, to which the knight, the mounted warrior, was expected to conform. He was to succour the weak and to protect the Church.

STRENGTH AND WEAKNESS OF CHIVALRY

This code, the special privilege of the horse-soldier—hence the use of the words Chivalry and Knighthood to denote it—was symbolized by an elaborate ceremonial of initiation. To prove his control of his worldly desires, the candidate for knighthood fasted for twenty-four hours. He made confession of his sins. He spent a whole night in prayer before an altar and took a cere-monial bath to symbolize his purity. He swore to fight only in causes which the Church had blessed.

In later, gentler days, when it had done its work, the institution of chivalry, as has happened to many a noble ideal, was elaborately organized, in an attempt to perpetuate its spirit by expressing it in rules and regulations. It then degenerated into a mere social code, a means of distinguishing the fighting aristocracy from their inferiors. If no enemy offered, the knights kept themselves prepared by cere-monially fighting one another, using only such weapons and tactics as the rules prescribed. Thus, when war followed, they fell easy victims before ignoble tactics and weapons to which their code gave them no reply. In the meantime the movement developed its own

THE NEAR EAST
IN 1100

||||| The Byzantine Empire

⋮⋮⋮ The Latin Kingdom of
Jerusalem

-●- { Routes of the early
Crusades

-●- { Sea Routes of the
later Crusades

Scale

100   200   300

Miles

THE PATH OF

The Holy City of Jerusalem was captured by the Moslems in A.D. 673 and its
recovery became a cherished ambition of the Christian Church. At the end of
the Eleventh Century, the Pope, Urban II, successfully appealed for a crusade.

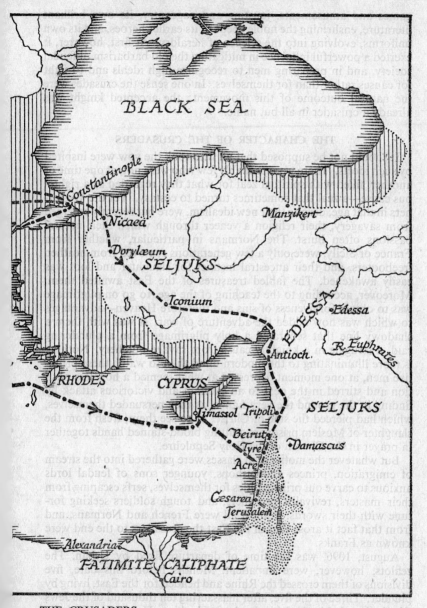

THE CRUSADERS

Aroused by religious fervour, the first crusaders made eventful journeys across Europe to their rallying-point at Constantinople, where their strength was probably 150,000. Later crusaders journeyed mainly by sea routes to Cyprus.

games and amusements, jousting and pageantry, its own brilliant literature, enshrining the noble deeds of its earlier heroes, and its own uniforms, evolving into the science of heraldry. At first, however, it exerted a powerful influence in mitigating the old barbarism of feudal society, and in preparing men to recognize high ideals and to fight for causes rather than for themselves. In one sense the crusades were the natural outcome of this movement; the accepted knight was already a crusader in all but name.

THE CHARACTER OF THE CRUSADERS

It should not be supposed that all who took the vow were inspired by such ideals. There were probably few who were not, at one time or another, filled with spiritual zeal for what they regarded as a righteous cause—a zeal that sometimes turned to ecstasy. Yet the Westerners in that age, despite their new idealism, were but recently emerged from savagery, their religion a veneer through which their natural passions often burst. The Normans in particular, whether from France or Sicily, were only a few generations removed from heathen freebooters, and their ancestral instinct for slaughter and loot was easily awakened. The fabled treasures of the East awaited them. Moreover, according to the teaching of the age, to go on pilgrimage was to obtain forgiveness of sins and therefore Heaven—advantages to which was now added the adventure of war. It was with them a shadowy line that separated a holy pilgrimage from a plundering raid, a struggle in a knightly cause from savage butchery. Nothing is more illuminating to the modern mind than to watch these primitive men, at one moment depressed at what seemed a hopeless position and stirred in the next to an exultant and victorious attack by finding in the ground the very Lance, as they persuaded themselves, which had pierced the side of Christ; or to see them, fresh from the slaughter of Moslem prisoners, putting blood-stained hands together in prayer in the Church of the Holy Sepulchre.

But whatever the motives, all classes were gathered into the stream of emigration, princes and bishops, younger sons of feudal lords anxious to carve out principalities for themselves, serfs escaping from their masters, revivalist preachers, and tough soldiers seeking fortune with their swords. Almost all were French and Normans, and from that fact it arose that in the East the crusaders to the end were known as Franks.

August, 1096, was the time of departure fixed by Urban. The zealots, however, were impatient. Months before this date, five divisions of them crossed the Rhine and headed for the East, living by plunder. Three of the five, after massacring ten thousand of the Jews who had settled in the Rhineland, marched into Hungary, only to be destroyed there in revenge for their excesses. The others reached Constantinople in July. Such men were obviously useless to Alexius. After feeding them for a time, he shipped them across the Bosphorus, and in, October they were annihilated by the Turks. The organized fighting men, some one hundred and fifty thousand in all, marched later, and reached Constantinople in December. They followed three routes, the northern French through south Germany and down the Danube, the southern French by way of Italy and Trieste, and the Normans, after crossing by sea from Sicily to Dalmatia, due east by the old Roman road. These last, led by Bohemund, the son of Robert Guiscard, and his nephew Tancred, were destined to play a leading part in the campaign. They were old enemies of the Greeks, and their arrival in the capital raised misgivings in the Emperor's heart.

THE LIBERATION OF JERUSALEM

Alexius has been likened by a modern writer to a magician who summons a ministering spirit and is instantly surrounded by a legion of demons. Byzantine diplomacy had for once overreached itself. His daughter Anna, a literary lady who kept a diary, has recorded the impression made by the uncouth western leaders on the elegant Greeks. Their gluttony, their uncleanly personal habits and their insolence caused horror, and their obvious hostility was also noted. It was an effort to be cordial to such savages. Yet the effort was necessary. Alexius was anxious for his lost provinces. The danger was that whatever the crusaders won they would keep. After long delays he induced them to do him homage, so that what they conquered they would hold as his vassals. It was a formality, but they would yield no more. Co-operation was impossible. In May, 1097, in order to be rid of them, he shifted them, too, across the strait.

The Seljuks also were divided. They had no great leader living. Their armies, under separate generals, jealous of each other, were widely scattered. They were still at war with Egypt, and in Asia Minor and Syria their position was that of a military garrison in a hostile country. The crusading leaders, who were actually in touch with the Egyptian Fatimites, knew of the Moslem dissensions and profited by them. Indeed, it was to such divisions that the Christian successes of the next fifty years were due. Once across the Bosphorus, they advanced quickly and captured Nicaea, Alexius making some show of assistance in order to ensure that it should not be put to sack. A Turkish army was defeated at Dorylaeum in July, and Antioch was besieged. Here there was a long check, but with the assistance of the Genoese, who had arrived by sea, the town was taken in June, 1098. The Christians were then in turn besieged by a fresh Moslem army, and were near abandoning the enterprise. The timely discovery of the Holy Lance revived their spirits and enabled them to win a decisive victory. The southward march was then resumed. Their forces were much depleted, not only by desertion, disease and losses in battle, but also by the fact that as each town was captured, the leader to whom it was allotted insisted on staying there with his forces, in order to make it a principality for himself. In

July, 1099, a handful reached Jerusalem. They stormed the Holy City and in a frenzy of religious ecstasy they massacred the inhabitants, Moslem and Jew alike.

The conquered territory was now organized on the only system of government which the conquerors knew—that of feudalism. At the head was placed Baldwin, Count of Flanders, with the title of King of Jerusalem; three other leaders, each in his own principality, took their places as his vassals, at Antioch, which fell to Bohemund, in Syrian Tripoli and in Edessa. The new rulers reigned as absolute monarchs, and leased out their land on feudal lines to their followers as sub-tenants. For serfs they had the native Syrian peasantry, who seem to have been left undisturbed in their villages as tillers of the soil. The crusaders, great and small, built themselves formidable castles, and in building them evolved a new science of fortification, partly based on that of the Greeks. Some of these huge fortresses still dominate the Syrian landscape, as do those built later in Cyprus and Rhodes. Copies of them were afterwards erected in Europe by returning crusaders, for example at Carnarvon and at Château Gaillard in Normandy.

Alexius, meanwhile, following in the wake of the conquerors, recovered some of the coast of Asia Minor, though not his main recruiting grounds in the interior. He claimed Antioch as his own, and when Bohemund repudiated the claim he washed his hands of the enterprise. He and his successors were henceforth hostile to the whole crusading movement, and at times actively supported the Moslems. In return, Bohemund, who returned to Sicily in 1104, leaving Tancred in Antioch, waged open war upon the Greeks until the time of his death.

SOCIAL EFFECTS OF THE CRUSADES

The crusading movement has sometimes been divided into numbered expeditions, but this practice conceals its real character. For two centuries, there was scarcely a year when new bands of armed pilgrims did not arrive at one point or other of the Frankish kingdom, led by kings or humble preachers, and there was as constant a return flow of deserters, whether satiated with their gains or disappointed at their failure. Such newcomers seldom added strength to the Christian states, for they were looked on with jealous suspicion by the original conquerors and their descendants; but their ceaseless ebb and flow served to familiarize the West with the East, and accelerated, if it did not inaugurate, a social revolution in Europe, as we shall see. It rapidly disillusioned the West, at least to the extent of producing a sophisticated class amongst whom the magic and wonder of the early adventure soon evaporated. Increasingly, as time went on, the new arrivals were men whose coming was the result of a calculation of profit and loss. Enthusiasm was slow to die, but it was soon left for the most part to the simple-minded.

Among the pilgrims of the new style came at an early date the merchants of Genoa, Pisa and Venice, anxious to buy eastern products, however acquired, and offering provisions in exchange. They did good business in warlike material, such as timber for siege-engines, which they offered impartially to Moslem amd Christian. As early as 1100, there was a fleet of 200 Venetian ships at Jaffa. The following year the Genoese struck a regular bargain. They promised armed assistance in return for freedom from tolls, a third of all booty and a trading monopoly in any town captured; and it was with this aid that Caesarea and Acre were taken. Venice followed suit, and on the same terms helped to capture Tyre. In 1110, there arrived a fleet of adventurers from Norway, open to any similar offer. In this way there grew up during the twelfth century a trade between these ports and the West, far larger than that which the Moslems themselves had carried on, and supplementing that which Venetians and Genoese had been developing in previous centuries.

THE SHORT-LIVED KINGDOM OF JERUSALEM

The Latin Kingdom of Jerusalem, as it came to be called, held its own until 1144, but from its foundation the new kingdom existed on sufferance. Many causes were at work to weaken it. The only standing military forces were provided by the two institutions, half monastic orders and half warrior fraternities, of the Hospitallers and the Knights Templars. These orders, vowed like monks to poverty, chastity and obedience, and pledged to perpetual war in defence of the Holy City, sent regular drafts from their recruiting stations in France and England. Subject only to the orders of the Pope, they held many of the strongest fortresses in Syria and drew vast revenues from the estates in Europe with which their well-wishers endowed them. The knights, however, suffered in physique and energy from the unaccustomed climate, and in their morals from the sudden atmosphere of extreme luxury into which they had been transplanted; partly as a result of their wealth, they soon lost the zeal that had at first inspired them. The four states, true to their feudal tradition, did not co-operate either with each other or with the Templars and Hospitallers, who were an independent command. Each state was divided into local units, jealous of each other. The ruling class was far too small for the work it had to do. The princes tried to safeguard themselves by establishing friendly relations and even commercial treaties with the Moslems to the east and south. Some of the lesser barons, however, who retained their energy, owned no law and did not abandon their habits of freebooting adventure. They swooped down from their castles to plunder caravans or to seize captives for ransom. The Moslems might have tolerated them as infidels, but could hardly leave such brigands in permanent possession. Re-united, Islam would sweep the newcomers into the sea, despite anything that a divided Europe could do in the way of opposition.

By 1140 Syria and Mesopotamia had been brought together under a vigorous leader, and the counter-attack began. Four years later, Edessa, the eastern outpost of the Latin Kingdom, was captured and the Christians put to the sword. The news shocked Europe. Two sovereigns, the German Emperor Conrad and Louis VII of France, raised armies. Unfortunately they made the mistake of going out by land. The old difficulties with the Greek Emperor recurred, and as the leaders co-operated neither with him nor with each other, both armies were destroyed before reaching Syria. The Asiatic Moslems next attacked Egypt, and it was here that the fate of the Latin Kingdom was decided. Egypt was quickly conquered and the Fatimite Caliphate extinguished. Saladin, under whose brilliant leadership the conquest of Egypt was completed, and who was now at the head of a vast empire, declared in his turn a Holy War upon the Christians. In July, 1187, the scanty army of the Latin Kingdom was destroyed by overwhelming force, and Jerusalem fell.

Again the shock brought kings into the field, the Emperor Frederick I, Philip Augustus of France and Richard Coeur de Lion of England. They raised large armies, but for all their efforts they effected little. The German expedition went by land and suffered exactly the same fate as that of Conrad. The Emperor was accidentally drowned in Asia Minor, and his force evaporated. The others sailed to Palestine, but their own dissensions, and still more the open strife between their subordinates, prevented any real success. Saladin's strength was unshakeable. The leaders realized this, and it is some evidence of the changing spirit of the times that they discussed terms of peace with him, relations for a time being almost friendly. Saladin was courteous but firm. The most that could be obtained was a truce and a safe-conduct for pilgrims to Jerusalem from the coast. Philip returned home in 1191 and Richard the following year. For all the latter's zeal and feats of arms, his one achievement was the seizure of Cyprus, a possession of the Greek Empire, which he fortified and made his base of operations. He afterwards sold it to the nominal, but now homeless, King of Jerusalem, in whose successor's hands it remained until the Venetians acquired it three centuries later. Here lived the Latin Kings. On the mainland nothing remained to them but a strip of coast-line, and that only by reason of Saladin's forbearance.

DISILLUSIONMENT AMONG THE CRUSADERS

The surge to the East was not over, but its character had changed. The leadership had been transferred from Pope to lay princes, with whom the taking of the vow had become a matter of calculation and policy rather than of passion or faith. In them, as in their followers and in others during the succeeding century, the religious motive was still present, though to most men it now meant the mere fulfilment of a duty rather than the passionate pursuit of adventure. The truth was that the crusades had already consumed their own impulse. They had so far civilized the wealthier classes of western Europe as to produce in them an atmosphere of calculation and disillusionment, and in such an atmosphere the torch of faith burnt low. Among the simple-minded, the old passion could still be awakened, but to the leaders the game was plainly not worth the expense; and they were finding more urgent business at home. By taking the vow, lesser men could still win freedom from taxes, absolution from their sins and even release from prison, but inducements of that kind did not attract men of the quality required to face a reinvigorated Islam. Even the freebooting impulse had lost its force to send men to the Holy Land, for it had been found more profitable to trade with the Moslem than to fight him. The age was past when chivalry implied an exalted ideal of fighting in a holy cause.

AMBITIONS OF POPE INNOCENT III

Yet in the new century one further attempt was made to bring the movement back to its religious basis and under Papal direction. In 1198 there was elected to the Papacy a man who represents the last and highest stage of its development. In the forefront of his policy Innocent III placed three ambitions: to recover the Holy Land, to purge the Greek Church of heresy and to re-unite it to the Church of the West. The conjunction of these ideals in his mind involved Europe in disaster. Although there was civil war in Germany between a Papal and an anti-Papal party, and bitter strife between Philip II of France and John of England, his first act as Pope was to send letters of appeal far and wide. There was no response from any sovereign, and little of any sort. A second appeal was made two years later, and by special promises of forgiveness of sins and of money for expenses, to be raised by taxes on the clergy, an army of thirty thousand was somehow raised, mainly composed of French and Norman soldiers of fortune.

Innocent's plan was to attack the Moslems in Egypt, now the seat of their power. This involved a sea-passage. For transport, application was made to Venice. The Venetians had no sort of interest in a crusade as such, least of all to Egypt, with which they already did a profitable trade, but they were willing to take part in any enterprise which might gain for them fresh commercial monopolies in the East. They drove a hard bargain. They would transport the army in return for a cash payment in advance of eighty-five thousand silver marks and the half of all territory won. In 1202, the army assembled in Venice. It was then found that the total cash which could be raised was less than two-thirds of what had been promised. There was a deadlock, the future of the expedition lying with the Venetians.

In the meantime a conspiracy had been hatched between Boniface of Montferrat, who had been appointed to command the expedition, and Duke Philip of Swabia, the head of the German anti-Papal party, who was also in close touch with the Sicilian Normans. At a conference held in Germany during the closing days of 1201, it was decided to divert the expedition. The attack on Egypt was a papal scheme. The German princes, fearing the power which the success of his plan might bring to Innocent, were determined to wreck it. The past crusading failures were generally ascribed to Greek treachery and obstruction. Now was the time for the West to take revenge. The Normans nursed an ancient feud with the Greek Empire, and rejoiced at the chance of recovering the territory in Asia Minor of which they said the Greeks had robbed them. For the rank and file of the crusaders, the fabled wealth of Constantinople would be sufficient lure. Even an excuse was not lacking. The Emperor Isaac Comnenus had recently been deposed by a usurper. His son Alexius, who had been touring Europe in search of aid, was summoned to the conference, and in return for help in restoring his father to the throne wildly promised to provide ten thousand soldiers and vast sums of money for the re-conquest of Palestine.

Nothing remained but to win the co-operation of Venice. For the Greek Empire the Venetians had no love. They had once enjoyed a privileged commercial position at Constantinople, with a special suburb of the city for their trade. Recently, however, the Venetian quarter had been destroyed in a riot, and they had been compelled to share their monopoly with the Pisans. They therefore came quickly to terms with the conspirators. On condition that their monopoly should be restored, they would transport the expedition to Constantinople instead of to Egypt, would assist in the occupation of the Greek Empire and the restoration of Isaac, and would waive the debt owing to them.

The secret leaked out and reached Innocent's ears. He was horrified and prohibited the plan. His protest, however, was ignored, and the expedition sailed. In July, 1203, Constantinople was reached. The usurper, who was himself unpopular, fled, and Isaac was restored; but when the time came for Alexius to fulfil his promises, he asked for a year's delay while he raised the money. The crusaders waited, but in the interval the population of the city, resenting the presence of the insolent and hated Latins, rose in rebellion against an emperor who owed his throne to them. In March, 1204, tired of waiting, the crusaders decided to occupy Constantinople and to divide the Greek Empire among themselves.

LOOTING OF CONSTANTINOPLE

The moment had arrived of which their ancestors had dreamed. The wealthiest city in the world lay defenceless before them. They stormed and sacked it, venting upon it all the worst passions that can animate armed men. The palaces were burnt. The accumulated treasures of antiquity were recklessly looted and destroyed. The richest monuments went into the melting-pot for the value of their metal—the statue of Hercules by Lysippus, that of Augustus commemorating Actium, the Roman bronze of the Wolf suckling Romulus and Remus, the Jewish Ark of the Covenant, saved by Titus from the sack of Jerusalem. The twined serpents, placed at Delphi in 479 B.C. as a thankoffering for Plataea, to-day stand headless, just as the crusaders left them after hacking off the heads with axes for the sake of the rubies in the eyes. The libraries, containing the assembled literature of the classical and early Christian ages, went up in flames. Sacred tombs were rifled and the churches despoiled of their relics. The high altar of Santa Sophia, a heretic shrine, was publicly desecrated. No such disaster had ever befallen European culture—a calamity even greater than the destruction of the great libraries of Alexandria and Cordova had taken place.

CRUMBLING OF THE GREEK EMPIRE

No more was heard of the project of a crusade. One of the adventurers was placed on the throne of the Caesars, and he and his successors ruled the remains of the city for sixty years. The Empire, so long the bulwark of Christendom, fell to pieces immediately, the position of the Latin emperors being perilous and futile. They were faced by the implacable hatred of the population of the city, and by Greek states both on the mainland of Europe and in Asia Minor. They were enabled to maintain their position only by the support of the Venetians and by an alliance with the Moslems against the Greeks. In 1261, the last of them was replaced by a native ruler, whose descendants sat there for two centuries, awaiting the next Moslem advance.

To the Venetians went the substantial gains. Such loot as they were able to secure they preserved, using some of it to decorate their home cathedral of St. Mark, itself modelled on the church of the Holy Apostles at Constantinople. They obtained three-eighths of the city to govern for themselves and established a complete monopoly of its trade. They seized and afterwards fortified most of the important Greek islands, including Crete and Rhodes, and all other strategic points commanding the trade routes, to the Crimea in the north and to Egypt in the south. The result was to transform the mercantile republic into a haughty colonial empire. A Venetian too was appointed Patriarch of the Greek Church. Under an armed guard he celebrated Mass with the Latin ritual in Santa Sophia, and declared the Eastern and Western churches to be re-united.

Innocent made the best of the calamitous issue of his venture. At first, he threatened the leaders with excommunication, but when asked to ratify the union which had been declared between the Churches, he acquiesced and gave public approval to what had been done, boasting that he had become Pope of a new world. He even thought that he saw in the Latin Empire of the East an advanced base from which fresh crusades might emerge. For, in spite of the fiascoes in which all recent expeditions had ended, no one suggested or imagined discontinuing them, least of all the Pope. Expeditions, large and small, continued throughout the thirteenth century, some of them, notably those of Louis IX of France, led by men with the profoundest sense of religious duty. None of these, however, affected the current of history. Only that of Frederick II, in 1229, accomplished anything, and this one, as we shall see, was conducted on anything but spiritual lines. The old spirit of ecstatic faith in the Holy War did burst occasionally from its embers, but only among children and lowly men, like St. Francis. In 1212, a French shepherd boy induced thousands of children to follow him, promising to lead them dry-shod to the East. They reached the coast near Marseilles and sat down to wait. The real characteristic of the thirteenth century, how-ever, was not the faith that brought these children there, but the commercial enterprise which recognized them as valuable mer-chandise. They did reach Egypt, but only through being kidnapped, and sold there as slaves.

By 1300, the last Latin stronghold in Asia had fallen and the Holy War was over. It failed because during two critical centuries no leader emerged who was capable, as Charlemagne had been, of impos-ing the nobility of his character upon the selfishness of unruly men. It had revealed in close contact and in sharpest contrast the highest ideals of which men are capable and the lowest depths of short-sightedness, treachery and greed to which they can descend. As often happens, enthusiasm undirected by genius merely gave openings for the basest instincts. Under a Charlemagne, a united Christendom must surely have succeeded. As it was, Islam easily beat off the counter-attack, and was soon to resume its advance. Nothing remained in the East as a reminder of the Christian effort but the grim relics of greed: the commercial empire of Venice, the ruins of despoiled Constantinople and the feudal castle walls of Syria.

CHAPTER 41

EUROPE LOOKS FORWARD

EVEN in the worst days of anarchy, the mental vigour and enterprise of the European races never died. Beneath the surface of a society apparently reduced to primitive savagery, there was always a vital current flowing, ready to burst into commercial, spiritual, artistic and intellectual life as soon as conditions allowed. The Carolingian renaissance of learning, architecture and trade, the high level of culture in eighth-century England, and the Cluniac movement are not the only evidence. Nor did the Church and the monasteries pro-vide the only centres from which, after each catastrophe, the elements of civilization were radiated. Western Europe as a whole was certainly reduced to the purely agricultural level of society, in which small rural communities were all but entirely self-sufficing, growing their own food and making their own clothes and what simple instruments they needed. Roads were always bad, and in large districts non-existent. Tolls were exacted on the borders of every feudal fief, and were almost as harassing to trade as other less legal forms of highway robbery. Standards of value, and weights and measures were always uncertain. In twelfth century France there were a dozen or more different coinages in use, for each of the greater landowners minted his own. Until uniform systems of law and properly organized central governments were established, there could be no widespread recovery of trade and prosperity among European nations.

CITIES EMERGE FROM ANARCHY

Yet the cry was always: "How long, O Lord?" Wherever there was a government capable of taming the wilder spirits into some semblance of orderly life, traders and pilgrims—the two could not always be distinguished—got to work as far as the difficulties of transport permitted. With the growth of the wealth which comes from the interchange of goods, mental and artistic activity soon followed, as for example in Italy under Otto I and III and in Sicily under the Normans. Many of the cities founded in Roman days, such as Milan, Naples, Paris, Orleans, Lyons, Marseilles, Cologne and perhaps London and York, though reduced to the extremes of poverty, had never lost their civic tradition nor ceased to be refuges for the elements of secular learning; even schools survived, and the simpler crafts were still practised. To them was soon added Venice, founded by refugees from the earlier barbarian invaders of Italy, and never violated or sacked until 1797. Others followed, such as Amalfi, Salerno and Ancona, largely Byzantine in culture, and in close contact with Greek and Moslem Mediterranean trade, as were Pisa and Genoa. Their regular contact with the civilization of southern Spain and the East always maintained a higher level of economic and social life in Italy than elsewhere, especially in the Lombard plain. By the end of the tenth century such cities as Milan, Bologna, Parma and Florence, together with numbers of lesser towns, had achieved some degree of prosperity, either as markets or by working up imported raw material—Florence, for example, specializing in weaving and dyeing; and where there was prosperity, the arts and architecture always sprang to life.

Such progress was later, and less marked, north of the Alps. Yet we have noticed the early rise of towns in Germany as cities of refuge. Others, such as Aachen and Munich, sprang into importance as capital cities or centres of authority; at the crossing places of rivers, like Basel and Oxford; as ports like Bruges, Southampton and Bordeaux; or like Tours and Canterbury, round monasteries or the seats of bishops. Such towns fortified themselves against attack and began to develop other industries than the traditional one of agriculture.

Nor were men's minds asleep. Life in the cities, punctuated by starvation and pestilence, was short, but it was intense; there were always some whose wits were sharpened by close contact with one another and who were at least conscious of their ignorance. The knowledge of the ancients had for the most part died, and there was no conception yet of what could be learned by investigating nature. Yet, within these limits, highly comprehensive systems of thought were erected upon the authority of the Scriptures and of such scraps of knowledge and scanty principles of Greek philosophy as filtered through from Moorish Spain or the East. Before 1100, for example, Anselm of Aosta, who was sent from Italy to Canterbury as Archbishop, had worked out the philosophic arguments for the existence of God by processes of pure reason, and these have never been superseded.

Some lines of thought alien and even hostile to the Church were developed. At a time when religion was outwardly dominated by the ideals of the Cluniac reformers, Berengar of Tours was denying any change of nature in the sacred Elements of the Mass. Abélard of Paris was teaching that "we must believe a doctrine only if our reason convinces us of its truth", and his pupil, Arnold of Brescia, was soon to go to Rome, where he preached the sovereignty of the people and raised the populace against the Pope in the name of the Roman republic. The Patarini, "rag-pickers", of Milan were demanding that the princes of the Church should be replaced by men of Apostolic poverty and brotherly humility, and the Cathari, the "Pure", of Toulouse were whispering the monstrous heresy that the power of the clergy to save men's souls depended not upon their official position but upon their worth and character. Such mental stirrings were easily kept under control as yet, but they were never suppressed.

THE REVIVAL OF TRADE AND TRANSPORT

These developments made the Crusades possible, and were in turn much stimulated by them. During the twelfth century regular intercourse with the East was re-established, and the shipping needed for the transport of the armed expeditions made possible also an immense increase in sea-borne trade. The West was made acquainted with innumerable articles of use or luxury, such as glass-ware, furniture, carpets, hangings and rich cloths, clocks and lamps, some new to the West and others hardly known for many centuries. New desires and needs sprang up, in satisfying which regular trading routes were established, and the commercial cities which lay along them amassed considerable wealth.

In finding a market in Europe for their immense imports, the Venetians had a decided advantage, quite apart from the immunity of their island-city from land attack. Pisa fed the rising manufacturing town of Florence, and Genoa served Milan and other towns of the Lombard plain; but to the north of Venice lies the Brenner Pass, which until the nineteenth century was the only route through the Alps open to trade throughout the year. This route, leading to the upper Danube and thence to Strassburg and down the Rhine to the North Sea, soon became a long line of municipal development. Market towns grew at important river crossings and wherever the route debouched from mountains into populous plains. Verona, Innsbrück, Munich, Ulm, Nuremberg, Augsburg and Bruges are some of the towns that owed to it their prosperity, if not their foundation. In all of them, the merchant class achieved a wealth that enabled them in time to defy and ignore the local feudal landowners.

Venice itself, feeding also the cities of the Lombard plain, and even sending regular fleets to England and the Netherlands, laid foundations upon which in the thirteenth century was erected a formidable empire. Genoa also prospered, and the other Italian cities, though to a less degree. From the French Mediterranean ports, similar routes took the new commerce to Toulouse and Limoges, and up the Rhône valley to Lyons and so on to Dijon, Orleans and Paris. In districts of France and Germany where the trade was insufficient to support regular markets, commerce centred about the great fairs, which were held at fixed seasons. These ancient institutions were revived to provide meeting-places where goods brought from the ports in caravans could be passed on to pedlars from smaller places, at which in turn fairs were held. Such fairs were of far-reaching importance, for at them were exchanged not only goods but also ideas brought from far and near. They have had a continuous existence ever since. Their significance in modern times has vanished, though the custom still survives of showing at them collections of strange beasts, just as was done in the twelfth century.

In North Germany also, trading towns grew up, such as Lübeck and Hamburg. As there was here no central government of any kind, the German towns formed themselves into leagues for mutual protection and to safeguard their caravans against feudal and other robbers. The most influential was the Hanseatic League, whose merchants brought southwards the raw materials of the Baltic lands, even from Novgorod in Russia and Bergen in Norway.

WIDENING HORIZONS OF KNOWLEDGE

The effects of this extension of commerce can scarcely be overestimated. It widened the horizons of every kind of knowledge, and brought men into contact far closer than before with new ways of life and new modes of thought. Little communities hitherto living their own lives in isolation from the outside world, except for the activities of the Church, came into regular touch with one another wherever political conditions allowed. As the means of communication improved, travellers began to make their way far afield, at first in pursuit of profit, but soon for other reasons, until at the end of the thirteenth century we find Marco Polo, a Venetian, crossing Asia and

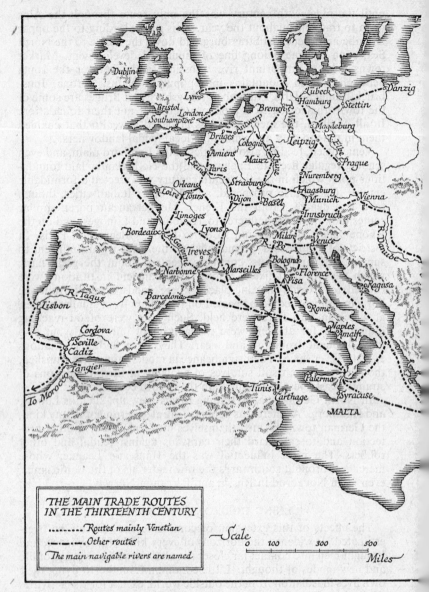

THE MAIN TRADE ROUTES
IN THE THIRTEENTH CENTURY
.... *Routes mainly Venetian*
.—.—.— *Other routes*
The main navigable rivers are named

Scale

0   100   300   500
                                        Miles

TRADE ROUTES IN

It was the newly growing desire for imported articles of use or luxury which stimulated trade in this period. By sea, trading fleets from Venice made regular journeys to England and the Netherlands; while Naples and lesser cities also achieved prosperity. North European ports rapidly became famous and wealthy.

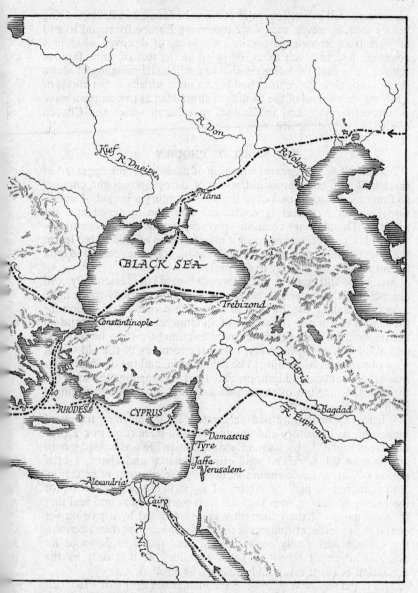

THE THIRTEENTH CENTURY

Thriving towns grew up along the overland trade routes. From the French Mediterranean ports merchants took their goods along the Rhone Valley to Lyons, Dijon, Paris and other towns; the Brenner Pass afforded the only passage through the Alps from Italy to the Upper Danube and to the North Sea.

returning to tell marvellous tales of life as he found it in Peking. Long before then, however, men were traversing Europe from end to end in pursuit of knowledge for its own sake, to discover what new countries had to teach them, or to sit at the feet of some famous scholar. The exchange of goods led to a wholesale mingling of ideas. What in the eleventh century had been a mere stirring in the minds of a few was by the end of the twelfth so stimulated as to become a wave of mental ferment and intellectual speculation which the Church controlled with difficulty.

THE SPIRIT OF ENQUIRY

As a result of this general widening of horizons, signs appeared of three well-marked changes in the cast of European thought, changes so fundamental as to make the thirteenth century a period of transition between two sharply contrasted eras, the medieval and the modern. The material creation—physical nature and its beauties—were at last appreciated as being a manifestation of God. Men learnt the essential value of human life and personality. They ceased to look for inspiration exclusively to the past.

Medieval Christianity had always taught the essentially evil character of the material creation. Just as a man's body was a mere temporary habitat for the soul, to be kept in perpetual subjection for the reason that it was the source of all temptation, so nature and all her phenomena were the direct manifestation of evil, to be shunned and abhorred. Now, however, began the recovery of the old Greek view of nature as something to be delighted in, and the discovery was made that beauty could be appreciated not only through the soul, but through the medium of the senses, and that physical nature might itself be God's creation.

Wherever Christianity had penetrated, it had led men to regard human life as transitory and unimportant—a mere stage in preparation for eternity. In barbarian Europe, human life was indeed a hard and narrow thing, racked with crime, violence and chaos, a brief period of horror made endurable only by the prospect of salvation. And as there was little possibility of joy in living or any feeling for the beauty of nature, men kept the next world so near and real that the very nature of their thought was impregnated by a passion for eternity. Since this attitude gave the clergy power over men's actions, the Church had gladly encouraged it, and had laid down as an essential article of Christian belief the doctrine that only by the mediation of its priests could salvation be ensured.

This belief was now passing. Such men as the Emperor Frederick II and those who learnt from him were recovering the old Greek attitude towards life. Men of high and low degree were awakening to a consciousness of their powers here and now, and to a new confidence in themselves. Life was itself an aim—a thing to be enjoyed and made the most of, for its own sake. Eternity began to seem un-

Scene from the Bayeux Tapestry representing the Battle of Hastings.

Winchester Cathedral, begun in 1079 by Bishop Walkelin, was built on the site of a Saxon church. It is the longest cathedral in England.

Robert of Normandy, the Crusader, son of William the Conqueror, portrayed in oak in Gloucester Cathedral.

A specimen of Byzantine ecclesiastical architecture of the Orthodox Church at Dafni, Athens.

Twelfth-century mosaic in the cathedral at Cefalu, Sicily depicting Jesus Christ.

real and far off; and with the growth of such ideas—quite apart from intellectual scepticism, of which there was soon to be plenty—the Church lost what had hitherto been its chief lever to affect the lives of common men. It was even whispered that just as Frederick claimed to be king without clerical mediation, so the common man might make his own approach to the throne of God—a heresy fatal to the priestly claims. Far and wide, individual development replaced salvation as the goal of human effort, and Europeans began to recover the open-minded outlook.

In the realm of thought, men's gaze had been wholly on the glorious past. In philosophy and science, as well as in religion, all knowledge was assumed to have existed in ancient days and to have been lost. From such ancient writings as remained, from Aristotle and Plato, from the Scriptures, St. Augustine, Jerome and the other Fathers, all truth, so men supposed, could be recovered. What had been written by such authority or could be deduced from the revered text, whether in matters of medicine, philosophy or the Christian religion, was to be believed, and since there was no other valid source, there was begotten that blind worship of authority which we call faith. The typical medieval had neither room nor desire for original or speculative thought, any more than for the testing of belief by observation of nature or experiment; the Faith—all truth indeed— had been delivered once and for all. In the thirteenth century came the urgent striving for new methods. From the point of view of Roger Bacon and his like, knowledge was seen to be in the future rather than in the past. With the steady growth of the spirit of open-minded critical inquiry, the Age of Faith was clearly beginning to wane in spite of all efforts to maintain the old beliefs.

APPEARANCE OF NATIONAL LITERATURE

These fundamental changes took innumerable forms, some inside the Church, and some in defiance of it, the latter often provoking fierce reaction. One early sign was the growth in Provence and in France of a literature written in the vernacular languages for the amusement of the well-to-do. Semi-epic songs appeared, relating to the deeds of King Arthur, Charlemagne and other heroes of the past, and much exquisite lyric poetry, especially in Provence and at the court of the Count of Toulouse, dealing with chivalric love, and otherwise glorifying purely human relationships. These were spread by minstrels, and often by the authors themselves, who were known by the name of troubadours, and who wandered from castle to castle, making their poems widely known.

The movement was eagerly taken up in Spain and Germany, and in each country there followed an outpouring of literature, the national language in every case replacing the Latin, which had previously been almost the only vehicle of literary expression. In Germany the heroes sung were Tristan, Parsival and the figures of ancient

P (H.W.)

German folk-lore, such as Siegfried. Here, too, there was much lyric poetry, and also a good deal of ribald verse of a popular and satiric character, in which both Church and churchmen were unsparingly lampooned. In the Kingdom of Sicily, the lyrics of Provence were known and imitated, and there, too, arose a vernacular literature, the first known use of Italian as a literary language.

The popularity of lyric love-poetry is significant of the remarkable change coming over the position of women. In previous centuries, the tendency in Christian countries, as well as in the Moslem world, had been to keep them in a subordinate position. Among the poor they were merely toiling slaves, and in the castle, whatever the Church might teach, they were hardly more than the chattels of their owners. Though to the monks they were lovely snares, chivalry began putting them on pedestals as objects of romantic adoration—a practice which was to endure until the twentieth century. They were also welcomed in the service of the Church. Those of them who adopted the celibate life in nunneries were highly honoured, the abbesses of some of the larger houses taking rank as high ecclesiastical dignitaries, a state of affairs unthinkable in Islam or in the Christian East.

POEMS IN STONE

The thirteenth century also witnessed the development of architecture and its allied arts to a level of achievement never surpassed. Here northern France led the way. The massive structures of the eleventh century gave way to mystical halls of beauty, imaginative poems in stone which symbolize the aspiring energy of their creators, lofty beyond previous imagination, and sustaining their roofs on a maze of graceful buttresses. Glass painters demanded scope in vast windows, and sculptors in elaborate porches, where they, too, in colour and statuary could glorify God and symbolize their tumultuous dreams and fears. Cities such as Chartres and Bourges, Rheims and Amiens, vied with one another in their cathedrals, King Louis IX set an example in his Sainte Chapelle in Paris which Henry III of England equalled, or perhaps surpassed, in his abbey church of Westminster. English churches did not soar to such heights, but in the choir of Lincoln and the sculpture of Wells, and in a host of lesser churches, we have ample evidence of the same exalted spirit. In Germany and Italy, political conditions were not such as to allow much building, but Venice in her isolation completed St. Mark's and vowed the spoil of Constantinople to its decoration. The palace of Monreale at Palermo was adorned with brilliant pictures in glass mosaic after Byzantine models, and the Germans began the magnificent cathedral of Cologne.

In the field of religion the muttered questionings of the eleventh century developed into widespread discontent which in some districts for a time defied clerical control. Among the artizans of Milan and other Italian cities and the peasants of Provence and southern France, there was open revolt from a Church whose leaders seemed given up to the pursuit of power and wealth. The study of the Gospels taught men the contrast between such a Church and the pure morality and poverty of Jesus and his disciples. Wandering preachers, under the leadership of Peter Valdes of Lyons, from whom they took the name Waldenses, or Poor Men of Lyons, travelled from village to village, declaring that the authority of the Bible was superior to that of the Church and trying with their followers to live lives of Apostolic simplicity. Their teaching, followed by that of St. Francis, laid emphasis on the equality before God of all human souls, and did much to promote the social upheavals of later centuries. The recognition of equality before God was necessarily followed by the demand for social rights. In spite of condemnation by the Pope and bishops, the Waldensians appointed ministers and built churches of their own, in which the dogmas of the Church were declared to be contrary to primitive Christianity and were openly derided.

A still more fundamental departure from orthodox Christianity was that of the Cathari, who were known as the Albigenses, from one of their headquarters, the southern French town of Albi. Here and in other towns, notably Toulouse, a doctrine of oriental and pre-Christian origin was revived. There were two deities, it was taught: one an evil being who created the material world and all belonging to it, and the other the author of things spiritual. Thus, all that involved matter was necessarily evil, including human life, marriage, flesh-eating and even the Christian sacraments. To save men's souls, no priestly aid could avail, but only their purification from the taint of matter by the extremes of self-denial and self-mortification. Such doctrines, only to be paralleled by those of some Buddhist and Hindu sects, were frankly revolutionary and threatened the whole order of existing society. They were intolerable to a Church which believed itself to be the sole repository of the Faith, given by Christ to his Apostles and by them transmitted to their successors. The Truth, once and for all revealed to the Church, was not to be found elsewhere than in its traditions. It was necessary to the welfare of mankind, and must therefore at all costs be vindicated.

CATHOLIC ATTEMPTS TO EXTERMINATE HERESY

To combat Waldensian and Albigensian doctrines, the Popes at first tried teaching and persuasion, but when these failed, Innocent III determined that it was necessary to protect mankind by using force. In 1208, he declared a crusade against them and authorized Philip II of France to stamp them out. Philip, for motives of his own, took up the task with enthusiasm. The heretics' cause was supported by the local nobility, headed by the Count of Toulouse, partly out of dislike of the Church and partly to maintain their independence against the King. There followed thirty years of desperate warfare, during which, though it was still called a crusade, the original causes were forgotten. By the end of the struggle, the whole culture of Provence and southern France had been ruthlessly obliterated, even the Provençal language all but disappearing. The Kings of France, vindicating their authority, inherited a desert. The heresies were suppressed, that of the Albigenses for ever, except in so far as those who recognize Satan as an independent power for evil can be called its heirs. Waldensianism, however, was only driven into concealment in the mountain valleys of Provence and Savoy. Here and elsewhere its doctrines never died. They were revived by Wycliffe a century later, and again by Luther and Calvin.

THE INQUISITION : DOMINICANS AND FRANCISCANS

During the struggle, special Church courts, afterwards known as the Holy Inquisition, were established by Innocent III to search out heretical beliefs and to extirpate their teachers. They were so successful that later on they were introduced into Spain and elsewhere for similar purposes. Granted an infallible Church, whose business it is to save mankind, those who disagree with it are by axiom wrong and dangerous, and to suppress them is logically defensible. It was probably well for mankind that Albigensian teaching was suppressed. The Inquisition, however, was used later for far more doubtful purposes. It became the main bulwark of the Church against free thought of every kind, and remained so for many centuries.

In dealing with the Albigenses, Innocent III did not rely on force alone. "Heresy can only be destroyed by solid instruction." A Spaniard, named Dominic, took part in a mission sent to France for this purpose. It was a complete failure, and the Spaniard concluded that to be successful such missioners must have two qualifications. They must be well enough educated in the foundations of their own faith to be able to meet the heretics in disputation, and they must live the same lives of poverty and self-denial as their opponents. St. Dominic devoted the rest of his life to educating and training missioners on these lines, to preserve the purity of the unchanging faith. His disciples were organized on monastic lines to be, in the first instance, highly educated preachers, and many monasteries were founded where theologians and scholars of high repute were trained and from which a literary warfare was waged on behalf of orthodoxy. They did not, however, neglect their main duty, which was to visit disaffected districts, to live there in complete poverty and to preach without ceasing.

The Dominicans, as they were called—(*Domini canes*, "God's watchdogs")—were essentially intellectual. They were unlovable, austere and often harsh. They wished to meet the new rebellious spirit on its own ground, but when persuasion failed, they were ready to use the most brutal means in exterminating the obstinate. In time they numbered in their ranks the most famous scholars of the age, including St. Thomas Aquinas himself, and since they were regarded as the supreme authorities on all questions of orthodox belief, the conduct of the Inquisition Courts was handed over to them. They became the surest henchmen of the Popes.

Meanwhile, there appeared in Italy another religious order which resembled that of the Dominicans in its devotion to the ideal of poverty, if in nothing else. In the career and teaching of Francis Bernadone are summed up many of the leading characteristics of the age. A well-to-do merchant of Assisi, he had made close contact in the course of travel with the brilliant culture of Provence, the spirit of whose romantic poetry he absorbed to a remarkable degree, and with the Waldenses, whose teaching profoundly impressed him. Returning to his native district, St. Francis developed in the soft Umbrian landscape an intense love of nature and its beauty, and learnt therefrom the exact converse of the Albigensian doctrine, for in the material creation he came to see the manifestation of God. To him the true spirit of religion meant the complete subordination of self to the love of his fellow men and of all nature, its highest aim the union not only of all souls but of all creation in the praise of God. He renounced his worldly position and lived thenceforth as a penniless beggar, "God's Troubadour", preaching the simplest elements of primitive Christianity with lyric rapture and unequalled force. By word and deed he awoke a like spirit in countless hearers, for his ideal exactly satisfied the inarticulate yearnings of the age. Before long, all Italy was ringing with his fame, and his disciples were penetrating France, Germany and England.

THE ENDURING INFLUENCE OF ST. FRANCIS

By the Church, to whom the new movement seemed to smack dangerously of Waldensianism, St. Francis was at first regarded as a heretic; but since his followers grew too numerous to be suppressed and Francis himself protested his utter obedience and devotion to the Faith, Innocent III decided to take the movement under his own protection and to harness it in the service of the Church. The next two Popes, Honorius III and Gregory IX—against the expressed wish of St. Francis, who knew the deadening effect of rules and regulations —organized his followers, like those of Dominic, into a regular order. Unlike monks in that they mixed freely with the world, but bound together in a disciplined body by monastic vows, the Franciscans, thus organized, continued for centuries, and still continue, to keep alive something of the essential spirit of Christianity. Unlike the Dominicans, their impulse was love not orthodoxy, simplicity not learning, for their founder especially warned them against the pride that comes from too much knowledge.

St. Francis died in 1226. Unfortunately only a few years passed before the same fate befell his movement as has usually caused the degeneration of great spiritual outbursts. His disciples found that the easiest way to impress their founder's transcendent greatness upon superstitious people was to write accounts of his career in which it was enveloped in sensational miracles. In creating the Franciscan legend, they probably persuaded themselves, as men will, that such interruptions in the normal course of nature had actually happened, but strictly contemporary accounts of his life suggest no such portents. On the contrary, they show that his real greatness owed as little to sensationalism as did that of Jesus or Mohammed. It was characteristic of the thirteenth century that to prevent their neighbours, the Perugians, from stealing so valuable a relic, the citizens of Assisi buried St. Francis in the centre of an immense cube of masonry. It is characteristic of the twentieth century that the Italians have tunnelled the masonry, and installed a tasteful system of concealed lighting so as to encourage not only Catholic pilgrims but tourists also to view the remains of this great man.

NATURALISM IN ITALIAN PAINTING

The spirit of St. Francis was perhaps best perpetuated not in the Franciscan movement, but in Italian pictorial art, the early inspiration of which was certainly derived from him. Until the thirteenth century the mosaics and frescoes produced in the West, like those of Byzantium, had been mainly concerned not to represent actual people and things, but to symbolize religious ideas and doctrines, such as the Majesty of God, the fear of Hell, or the Incarnation. A Byzantine mosaic of Christ or of the Virgin and Child was not intended to be human, but to express and to fix in the memories of its beholders an idea. It was essentially symbolic, not realistic. During the thirteenth century, however, a race of artists arose who, though still in the main devoted to the service of the Church, and ostensibly depicting the same religious subjects as before, found their chief interests in the representation of real men, of things as they are, and of the beauty of nature. Natural grace replaced conventional attitudes in the human figures. Landscape, birds and flowers were used first as a mere decorative background, but were soon so lovingly depicted as to show where the artists' real passion lay. To them, as to Francis, nature was a clearer clue to God's goodness than the dogmas of the Church, and they glorified it in their art as he had done in his life and poetry.

By the end of the century Duccio of Siena, Cimabue of Florence and his pupil Giotto, who painted at Assisi and elsewhere innumerable scenes from the life of Francis in the new manner, had firmly established the art of realist painting, based on nature study, and on their foundations the glorious art of Renaissance Italy was subsequently developed. The old symbolic art faded out all over Europe, only to be revived in our day, to the bewilderment of those who expect painting and sculpture to represent things as they are. No doubt to old-fashioned people of the thirteenth century, the new realism seemed just as shocking as the works of Epstein do to some people to-day.

Throughout these centuries, students of every class, but most of all the poor, were flocking from every quarter of Europe to the old cathedral and monastery schools in search of knowledge. In some cases, the teachers formed themselves into associations to direct the studies of their swarming pupils. In others, the students themselves formed the associations to hire the services of teachers. To the schools of both types, the name of University was applied, for the reason that it was then a regular term used to denote any kind of association or guild. On the former basis, the University of Paris, whose cathedral school had long enjoyed a great prestige, was one of the earliest to be organized, with rules and regulations to control the behaviour of the students and separate colleges for their residence. In imitation of it, a similar institution grew up at Oxford, of which the University of Cambridge was in turn a later offshoot. In these and others, the Church retained the control, and the studies were in the main those which served its purposes, theology and philosophy, though law and medicine were later added. The lines of thought were still for the most part those of pure logic. The facts available were limited, and were derived from the statements of great writers of the past, of whom Aristotle was the most deeply revered, and from the Bible. Upon these statements, regarded as infallible authorities, was built a vast edifice of logical conclusions, so contrived as always to be in agreement with the traditional teachings of the Church.

SCHOLASTICISM AND THE UNIVERSITIES

Thus arose the comprehensive, almost awe-inspiring, system of thought known as Scholastic Philosophy, a prodigious effort to square Christian dogma with pure reason. The greatest thirteenth-century exponent was the Dominican Thomas Aquinas, a member of a Norman-Sicilian noble family. His most famous work, the *Summa Totius Theologiae*, the completed expression of a mode of thought strange to us, is none the less one of the most monumental of human intellectual achievements, which still provides the intellectual basis of Roman Catholic doctrine. Of using observation and experiment to test the links in their chains of reasoning the Scholastics had no notion, nor did it occur to them to doubt the authorities upon whose statements the whole edifice was based.

On the other hand, the Italian University of Bologna was a type of those founded by the students themselves and independent of the Church. Here also the tendency was to regard the past as the source of all learning, but the special subject of study was law rather than theology. Roman law, as codified by Justinian, was taken as the sacred text and the necessary basis of all civilized conduct. The study of it consisted in explaining its meaning and applying it to real or imaginary cases. It did indeed present a picture of a state of unified and disciplined society from which Europe had much to learn. The Universities of Bologna and Ravenna between them in the twelfth and thirteenth centuries trained innumerable students, whose subsequent teaching in their own countries was of enormous assistance to the advance of civilization. Notably in France they did much to prepare the way for absolute monarchy, for in Imperial Rome the Emperor had been regarded as the source of all authority. Other schools, particularly at Salerno, whose university dates from the eleventh century, drew upon Greek and Arabic sources for medical and surgical knowledge. It cannot be said that even these free universities in their early days did much for the advancement of real learning. Nevertheless, the movement as a whole assembled what knowledge there was, and thus did essential work in preparation for the time when the critical spirit should be emancipated.

ROGER BACON : PIONEER OF SCIENCE

While the Dominicans and the Scholastics, for mankind's welfare as they saw it, were busy restraining the spirit of free enquiry, some of their despised rivals, the Franciscans, ignoring their founder's warning against learning, became its leaders. The most modern of medieval thinkers outside Italy was the Englishman Roger Bacon, one of a small group of Franciscans settled in Oxford. He scornfully rejected the whole system of reasoning which the Scholastics had built up, for he saw the essential weakness of its foundation. Reasoning based on past authorities was worth just as much or as little as those authorities themselves. Before there could be valid reasoning at all, old facts must be verified and new ones collected by the observation of natural phenomena and by experiment. He himself did much experimental work in physics and optics, and his speculations on future progress are said to have included forecasts of motor cars and aeroplanes. What was of real consequence, however, was his total lack of reverence for authority, his bold rejection of the past. He pointed out that in any case it was useless to rely on Aristotle, for only fragments of his works were known and even these were probably mis-translated. It is this attitude which ranks him alongside his predecessor in the same field, the Emperor Frederick II, with whom he shares the credit of being the pioneer in experimental science and in reasoning on modern lines.

In his own day few listened to him. A small group continued his work in Oxford for a time, but he himself spent the later part of his life in prison as a suspected wizard, and he died obscurely. The time was not yet for the ideas of the few to capture the world. More than three centuries elapsed before the edifice of systematic thought was ordered by his namesake, Francis Bacon, into a shape which we can recognize as scientific. Meanwhile, whatever ferments lay beneath the surface, the higher clergy and the Universities, reinforced by Scholasticism under Dominican leadership and by the Inquisition, held their own. The Church retained its grasp on education in France until 1791, in Italy until 1866, and in Spain until 1935.

CHAPTER 42

THE BEGINNINGS OF NATIONAL CONSCIOUSNESS

Up to the middle of the eleventh century, the course of events in France and England ran on roughly similar lines. Both had been occupied and brought into the main current of European culture in the early days of the Roman Empire. Both had been swept from end to end in the fifth and sixth centuries by Teutonic invaders. Both were slowly shepherded back by the Church into contact with civilization, and both were then tormented and devastated by the Northmen. Some contrasts, however, can be noted which were of permanent importance. Whatever the reason, whether the Roman culture in England was more superficial and more easily uprooted than in Gaul, or whether the Saxon invaders, untouched by Roman influences in their northern homes, were more savage destroyers than the Franks or Goths, the England of the sixth century was largely a pagan and Teutonic land. Though there was no doubt some mixture of blood, all living trace of Roman culture, even the language, was obliterated in the Eastern half. In France, on the other hand, the speech, the religion, even the towns and some of the institutions, though mutilated, managed to survive and in the course of time to be adopted and cherished by the newcomers as their own.

THE UNITING OF ENGLAND

In both countries the Norse raiders, as soon as the settlement stage was reached, accepted the language and culture of their new homes, becoming Latin in France and English in England. But whereas in France their coming hastened the break-up of Charlemagne's empire into semi-independent feudal duchies, of which their own principality of Normandy was one, in England the effort to resist them tended to unite the country instead of disintegrating it. The House of Egbert, at the opening of the struggle Kings of Wessex only, by 950 ruled from the Channel to the Clyde, the Northmen themselves being incorporated in the single realm. The sense of solidarity thus achieved was never lost. The conquest by Canute the Dane left England still a unity, and although in the eleventh century the disintegrating tendencies of feudalism were visible in the rise of four rival earldoms, which if unchecked might have rent the country asunder, the conquest by William of Normandy saved the situation. His powerful rule so strongly welded the whole country into one that, except for disputed successions and a brief period in the reign of Stephen, England had never to endure the feudal anarchy which permanently divided Germany and threatened France with similar disruption.

Before the Conquest, there was a possibility that England, in which Latin culture had almost entirely disappeared, might have drifted into isolation from the southern centres of learning in spite of the efforts

457

of the Church, and have been left behind, as Ireland was, and for a time Scotland and Wales. It was because of allegations of illiteracy and lethargy against the English clergy that Gregory VII had authorized William's expedition. As it was, the coming of the Normans recalled England to the Latin world.

The language of the ruling class, law-court and battlefield, became French, and remained so for three centuries. From France and indirectly from Rome, England drew her inspiration in theology, political organization, literature and the arts. One of the first results was to bring two Italians, Lanfranc of Pavia and Anselm of Aosta, in succession to the Archbishopric of Canterbury; these men quickly restored the standard of clerical piety, learning and discipline to that which the Cluniac reformers had established in France. Raised to symbolize the new idealism, the great cathedrals, such as Durham and Canterbury, were French in style. Chivalry, a fresh impetus of monastic zeal, and the university movement, as well as new methods of fighting and cooking and a new elegance of manners, were all importations without which England would have remained in barbarous isolation. As it was, there were no frontiers between France and England until the closing years of the thirteenth century. William himself and his successors for two centuries were also dukes in France. The English did not hesitate to invite Louis VIII to wear their crown, nor to adopt Simon de Montfort as their national leader.

Yet there were also marked differences. If William paid his followers for their services at the battle of Hastings by distributing to them a great part of the land of England in feudal tenure, they were prevented from building up independent duchies, like those of France, by the fact that the estates granted them were widely scattered. In return they owed him military service, but they were never allowed to monopolize the work of government. The older Saxon institutions were taken over and kept in use where they served the king's purpose. The old obligation of all freemen to follow the king in war was still maintained, as a counter-weight to the feudal landowners, and in his name the sheriffs still administered justice, according to the time-honoured traditions of Saxon law and customs, in the shire-ocurts.

FOUNDATIONS OF ENGLISH COMMON LAW

Thus the old laws of England, Teutonic in origin, never died out and were never superseded. They were altered and adjusted from time to time to suit altering circumstances, but their underlying notions still persisted, to become in time the foundation of the "Common Law" of England. Under William's successors the king's household or "court", the *Curia Regis*, became a regular organ of central government, its members serving as finance ministers, judges and secretaries as occasion required, and going on regular circuit to represent the power of the king and to keep every district constantly in touch with headquarters, to the discomfiture of would-be independent local landowners. By the time of Henry II the court had been divided into departments, each with its separate functions, such as the headquarters court, known as the Court of King's Bench, the Circuit or Assize judges, and the Exchequer court, all of which to this day bear their ancient names. By these means, while preserving much of what they found, the Angevin and Plantagenet kings kept England a single centralized state, thus saving it from the curse of feudalism.

LIMITATIONS OF ROYAL POWER

Yet the centralization of the government under the king did not in England mean dictatorship. Feudal estates were too small to give their individual owners such authority as the French or German dukes wielded, but they were numerous, and on occasion the baronage could assert the rights that ancient English custom gave them against the crown. From early times, it seems to have been vaguely understood that "a King of England cannot, at his pleasure, make any alteration in the laws of the land. He is appointed to protect his subjects in their lives, properties and laws; for this very end he has the delegation of power from the people, and he has no just claim to any power but this." No doubt great military leaders and powerful personalities like William I and Henry II could and did impose their will upon the nation, but Roman law, with its doctrine that the king's will was the source of all authority, was not much studied in England until the thirteenth century, and by that time the Saxon principle was well established.

Thus, when John and Henry III, by their mistakes, earned the hostility of the whole country, they had to buy support by admitting their subjects' ancient rights against them. In the Great Charter (*Magna Carta*) of 1215, John agreed that the landowners' consent was necessary before he could levy more feudal dues upon them than were sanctioned by ancient custom; he thus conceded a principle which was later extended to apply to all taxation. The landowners, led by Simon de Montfort—a foreigner brought up in a country where the baronage had enjoyed full feudal freedom—compelled Henry III to submit his government to their control. Edward I, to unite the whole nation, summoned to his court not only officials and landowners, but clergy, and even the wealthier townsmen, thus laying the foundation of what is still called the High Court of Parliament. It was not long before this body insisted that their consent to new taxation should be conditional upon the reform of certain abuses, which they specified, thus laying down a momentous precedent for the future.

No regular method was discovered of registering or enforcing the general will until much later; the rank and file of the populace, though they benefited from the clause in the Great Charter which guaranteed them legal trial before punishment for crime, had to wait several centuries before being admitted to any political rights. Yet by the thirteenth century a rough compromise had been reached between the landowners, including the higher clergy, and the king and his officials. Government was to be based neither on feudal land-tenure nor on centralized authority, the one leading to disintegration and the other to royal despotism, but on the partnership of all con-cerned and on the Common Law of England.

Meanwhile, as the Norman conquerors, who cannot have num-bered more than a few thousand, intermarried with their subjects, the weight of numbers told. Just as Norman blood became a tinge in the whole rather than a separate colour, so French ceased to be a spoken language, though enough words of Latin origin remained embedded in the older Saxon speech to remind us that the English language, like the race, is the result of a fusion. In the same way English culture and modes of thought and life, at first based largely on those of France, and never to this day altogether out of touch with them, began to develop on divergent national lines. Imported architectural styles such as those of Durham and Canterbury gave way to purely English creations like those of Salisbury and Lincoln. French and Latin yielded to English as the literary medium. Even chivalry and methods of fighting took on peculiarly English forms.

The same process can be seen in ecclesiastical affairs. The Norman conquest brought the English Church into close relation with the papal ideals, and the clergy promptly demanded their independence from the state. Anselm fought the same battle with Henry I on the subject of Investitures as had divided popes and emperors. In defiance of Henry II, Becket, as Archbishop of Canterbury, insisted that the clergy were his subjects, not the king's. He denied the right of laymen to judge or try them, and, though he died a martyr to the cause, he established his point. John and Henry III both held their crowns in feudal tenure from the Pope. Yet the national spirit which later rallied the English behind King Henry VIII in his struggle with the Papacy was already visible in the thirteenth century. The sub-servience of Henry III to Rome provoked a general rebellion. The clergy themselves were becoming more national than Roman. In 1250 the Bishop of Lincoln publicly defied Pope Innocent IV, and a few years later Edward I needed to use little pressure to win the support of the Church against Boniface VIII.

THE HOUSE OF CAPET IN FRANCE

France also grew to nationhood, but on very different lines. There the great fact of the times was feudalism. On the death of the last Carolingian in 987, the influence of the Archbishop of Rheims secured the throne of France for Hugh Capet, Duke of Paris, a nephew of the Odo who had won fame for his House by his defence of Paris against the Northmen. The dynasty thus founded ruled France, with only two seriously disputed successions, for eight hundred years. Its assets were the strong strategic position of the Capetian personal possessions, the remarkable number of really able men which the family produced, and the old Frankish tradition of close alliance between King and Church. To the French, in a degree never known in England or Germany, the sovereign, the anointed of God, was sacred, the Eldest Son of the Church, and the Most Christian King. As he had no claims which conflicted with those of the Papal State, the Popes had no reason to fear him as they did the Germans. They refrained from pressing their pretensions in France, with the result that for three centuries the problem of the rights of the Church against the State did not arise. During this time the French clergy were usually strong supporters of the king and eagerly preached the sanctity of his position, until royalty became a religion.

The Duchy of Paris, though small, lay astride the Seine and the Loire, the two main arteries of communication and trade in northern France, and its two cities, Paris and Orleans, both eminently defensible, were soon to be sources of wealth as well as of strength. Almost without exception the early Capetians were active able men, for ever on the move to keep their own domain in order. Above all, inspired by no very lofty ideals, they concentrated their efforts on what was practicable. Until 1100 they added little to the territory under their direct rule, and at a time when English unity was already secure, they were content to allow the great feudal fiefs, such as Burgundy, Flanders, Normandy (whose dukes after 1066 were also Kings of England), Brittany, Aquitaine, Gascony and Champagne—most of them larger than the Duchy of Paris—to be in practice independent states over which they could exercise little control.

THE WORK OF PHILIP AUGUSTUS

The reign of Louis VII, however, brought France to a crisis. He married Eleanor, the heiress of Aquitaine and other fiefs in the south, but after fifteen years divorced her. She was immediately re-married, this time to Henry Plantagenet, Count of Anjou, whose father had built up a compact territory in the valley of the Loire. According to feudal custom her own possessions were now transferred to the control of her second husband. When Henry, who through his mother was a great-grandson of William the Conqueror, succeeded to the Duchy of Normandy and the throne of England, the King of France was confronted by a nominal vassal many times as powerful as himself, who ruled from the Pyrenees to the Channel, with the resources of England at his disposal as well. It seemed as though France must be permanently cleft in twain.

The crisis produced the man, Philip II, known later as Augustus, "the increaser". In his long reign, this astute and unscrupulous ruler, probably the ablest of his line, laid firm foundations for national unity. He turned to advantage the rebellions of Henry's sons, Richard and John, against their father, and then played the two against each other. He went on crusade with Richard, mainly in order to prevent his rival from securing the prestige which would accrue from any victory in the East. As soon as he saw that no victory was likely, he hurried home to take advantage of Richard's absence. Each of these steps won some small reward. His real chance, however, came when John succeeded Richard and quarrelled with his subjects in both France and England. All the north and much of the centre of John's French possessions fell into Philip's hands. John allied himself with the Emperor Otto IV, in an endeavour to retrieve his position, but in 1214, Philip, with the active support of Pope Innocent III, won the great battle of Bouvines, which not only decided the fate of France, but also put John at the mercy of his English subjects and Otto at that of the Pope. Philip's position was established beyond doubt.

PROVENCE MERGED IN THE ROYAL DOMAIN

Meanwhile, Philip had been equally successful in other directions. At Innocent's behest, he took the Cross for a second time, and fell upon the Albigensian heretics of the south of France. The onslaught, conducted with horrible brutality and met with the fiercest determination, extinguished the strange and delicate civilization of Provence, the home of the lyric poetry of the Troubadours and probably at that date the centre of the highest culture in Europe. But since it brought a great part of the country, hitherto almost a foreign state, to Philip's feet, it resulted in an immense accession of strength to the monarchy. By the end of his reign, Philip had increased the royal domain three-fold and had destroyed its principal enemies.

To safeguard the regained royal rights for the future, Philip began the creation of a centralized system of government resembling that of Henry II in England and the more elaborate administrative edifice which Frederick II was raising in southern Italy. Choosing men of humble birth, so that they should owe all authority to himself and not to their position in the feudal scheme, he sent them with the title of baillis to the various districts of the kingdom. These agents were to represent the crown in every respect, to enforce the king's decrees, to superintend local administration, and to act as permanent links between every locality and Paris. Under his grandson, Louis IX, the new system encroached still further upon the local rights of feudal landowners, the baillis being authorized to hold courts of justice in the king's name, to which appeals could be made from the local feudal courts. The great vassals protested, but were compelled to accept the situation, their independence being correspondingly weakened. Further, as in England, the *Curia Regis*, the assembly of the king's officials, which hitherto had advised the king in all affairs of state, was divided into specialized groups so as to form the embryo of great government departments. The group dealing with judicial business heard appeals from all local courts, feudal as well as royal, and to it, as well as the courts of the baillis, Louis appointed men specially trained in the law.

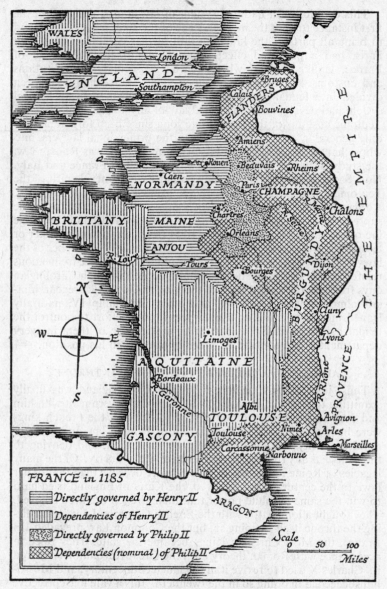

WEAKNESS OF FRANCE IN 1185

King Philip II of France succeeded to a throne weakened by the power of his feudal vassals, one of whom was Henry II of England, who had inherited the great Duchy of Normandy from his mother. Dissension among the English after Henry's death enabled Philip to lay the foundations of national unity.

This creation of a national system of law-courts, designed in the first instance to limit the independence of the great feudal vassals and to bring all parts of the kingdom into regular communication with Paris, had a profound effect upon the political development of France. Unlike England, where, as we have seen, Saxon institutions and customs had never been superseded, France had long been divided into feudal duchies, in each of which a separate judicial system had developed; no national law of any sort existed. The old Teutonic customs of the Franks had long since been forgotten. The only general system of law known to the professional lawyers, into whose hands public affairs of all sorts now passed, was Roman law, the study of which was being ardently pursued in France and Italy. Now Saxon customs, representing perhaps the primeval spirit of the Teutonic race, gave subjects rights against the royal authority. Roman law did not. In it the sovereign was considered to be the supreme and only source of law and justice, and indeed of the whole life of the state. He alone had the right to legislate, to administer or to tax. His will was supreme and his decree final. The influence of the lawyers, trained in the very spirit of absolutism, came as a tremendous reinforcement to the mystical notion, inherited through Carolingian days from the far distant past, of the king as God's vice-regent, himself almost divine. Louis IX, and after him Philip IV, naturally leaned more and more on the lawyers in their effort to control the feudal baronage, Philip in particular making use of them in every department of government in order to strengthen his position.

ABSOLUTE AUTHORITY OF THE FRENCH THRONE

Thus, just at the time when Edward I in England was finally admitting the right of his subjects to share the government with him and even to withhold taxation if they so decided, the French kings were busy erecting on the foundation of Roman law an edifice of royal authority unassailable except by revolution, and denying to their subjects any rights whatever, even of life or liberty. Of the many legacies of Rome to France, none was more decisive than that of her law. In the centuries that followed, the Kings of England tried hard to win the same absolute power that their French brethren enjoyed. They fought a long battle with the English Common Law, jeopardizing the throne itself in doing so, but the Common Law prevailed. In France, the Most Christian Kings became the state. They ruled in accordance with Roman theory until the Great Revolution shattered it. Charles X tried to revive it in the nineteenth century, and Mussolini succeeded in doing so in the twentieth. It is a valuable corrective to disintegration, but recent English sovereigns have been so fortunate as not to need it.

Philip II laid firm foundations for the unity of France. His successors each contributed something towards making the kingdom a nation-wide monarchy like that of England. Louis IX further undermined the independence of the feudal fiefs by allotting several of them which fell vacant to members of the royal house, a policy immediately profitable but the cause of difficulties later. The monarchy also gained much authority from the perfection of his character. A true son of the Church, he fulfilled in every respect the ideal of chivalry. He appealed to the imagination and won the hearts of the whole nation by the high standard of piety, justice and knightly courtesy which he maintained. His strong sense of duty took him on two crusading expeditions, in which something was recaptured of the old fervency and high Christian motive of the ideal crusader. They accomplished nothing practical. That of 1248 was defeated in Egypt, Louis himself being captured and held to ransom. On the second, which he led to Tunis in 1270, he died. Nevertheless, his pure idealism added lustre to the crown, and made him a revered symbol of the growing sentiment of nationalism, in the face of which not even the stress of the Hundred Years' War could divide France permanently, and to which Joan of Arc triumphantly appealed.

THE DISINTEGRATION OF GERMANY

We have watched the growth of two proud self-conscious peoples, each bent on pursuing its own affairs, even at the expense of wider considerations. The same centuries witnessed the last struggle of a German king to recover the imperial position. By the middle of the twelfth century, subdivision in Germany had been carried further than it ever was in France. A host of small principalities had been so long, for all practical purposes, independent, that no one could dream of re-establishing a central government. The kingship, lacking the sanctity which surrounded that of France, was further weakened by being strictly elective. Although a son might be chosen to succeed his father, the first principle followed by the princes, in whose hands the election lay, was to choose as their figure-head a man who would be unlikely to threaten their own independence. On this principle, in 1130, they elected Conrad, the head of the Swabian family of Hohenstaufen, and on his death in 1152, his nephew Frederick, nicknamed Barbarossa, the Red-bearded. The Hohenstaufen family had extensive estates both in Swabia and in Franconia, and from the moment of his election, Conrad based his position in Germany not on royal rights but on his personal possessions. The princes might go their own way, while to his private resources Conrad added what he could by bartering away further relics of royal power, a policy in which he was followed by most of his successors for three hundred years.

No shred existed of central institutions like those which were being consolidated in France and England. Thus, when Frederick, a man of great ability, energy and ambition, was elected, he found his outlet not in building up a national government but in securing for himself and his family a position outside Germany, reviving for this purpose the old imperial claims. Like Otto, two centuries before, he allowed his imagination to be captured by the romantic glamour of Rome. He also pressed into his service the students of Roman Law, and from them acquired the conviction that it was his right to be a new Justinian, the absolute monarch of the world, and his duty forthwith to enforce his rule on Italy. Just when central control was finally abandoned in Germany, in Italy we find Frederick determined to impose it. He had hardly obtained the German crown when he crossed the Alps to be crowned Emperor in Rome and to assert the rights he claimed to Italian dominion.

THE INDEPENDENCE OF THE ITALIAN CITIES

Since the last attempt to revive imperial rule, a new and formidable force had arisen—the Italian cities. In the north, these were now even more independent than princes of Germany. They were wealthy self-governing republics. Each of them had absorbed into itself the small nobility of the surrounding country-side. They were fiercely individual, proud of their own position, jealous and utterly independent of one another. They might admit the vague suzerainty of a distant emperor, but they had every reason to resist any attempt at direct control. Their main interests were commercial, and these would certainly be taxed and regulated, and perhaps sacrificed, if imperial officers were thrust on them. Moreover, though the notion of Italian political unity existed only in the minds of a few dreamers, national consciousness was already strong; the Germans were foreigners, who had no business south of the Alps.

In Rome, peculiar conditions prevailed. The Roman Republic, set up by Arnold of Brescia, though repudiating Papal rule, welcomed the restoration of the Empire. True to his dreams of ancient Rome, however, Arnold imagined an emperor whose power should emanate from the senate and people of Rome rather than a dictator after the model of Justinian. In 1154, the Pope, Adrian IV, the only Englishman to reach that dignity, was entrenched in the Vatican, all but a prisoner there. When Frederick appeared in Italy, he was invited by both Pope and republic to come to Rome as mediator. His intervention was decisive. He was crowned by Adrian. He quickly disposed of the claim of the Roman people to be the source of his authority. He attacked and captured the city. Arnold was seized and handed over to the Pope, who straightway burnt him as a heretic.

The coronation revived the old controversy as to whether Pope or Emperor was the final authority. The unsolved question, however, was now couched in the language of feudalism. Did the Emperor hold office as the Pope's vassal? Had not the spiritual power the right to homage from the material? It was their way of asking whether right or might should prevail. On this momentous topic a bitter correspondence followed between Emperor and Pope. Each could quote precedents in his favour. If the Emperor cited Otto, Adrian reminded him of Canossa. To each it was a matter of the highest principle, and

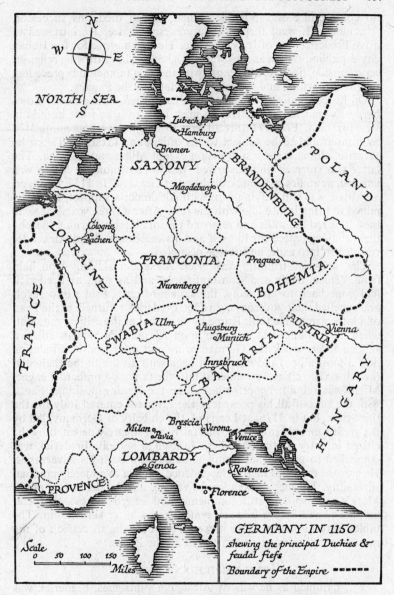

NORTH SEA

Lübeck
Hamburg
Bremen

SAXONY

Magdeburg

BRANDENBURG

POLAND

LORRAINE

Cologne
Aachen

FRANCONIA

Prague

Nuremberg

BOHEMIA

FRANCE

SWABIA *Ulm*

Augsburg
Munich

AUSTRIA *Vienna*

Innsbruck

BAVARIA

HUNGARY

Brescia
Milan *Verona*
Pavia *Venice*

LOMBARDY
Genoa *Ravenna*

PROVENCE

Florence

Scale
0   50   100   150
Miles

GERMANY IN 1150
shewing the principal Duchies &
feudal fiefs
Boundary of the Empire ------

DIVISIONS WITHIN GERMANY, 1150

Ravaged by bitter quarrels between the princes, Germany in 1150 was characterized by wide-spread unrest and the failure of attempts to build a strong central power. After returning from crusade in 1149 King Conrad was unable to restore order, and this task was left to his nephew, Fredrick I, known as Barbarossa.

no compromise was possible. When Adrian died, his successor, Alexander III, went further than correspondence. He intrigued to drive Frederick out of Italy by force. He had no love for the Italian city-republics, ridden as they were with heresy; but throwing religious scruple aside, he joined his cause with theirs, a momentous precedent for his successors, and one ultimately fatal to the Papacy.

On his coronation visit, Frederick had ordered the cities of Lombardy to send representatives to meet him, to hear what he had in view for them. For the future all were to accept governors nominated by himself and to be subject to his orders and taxation. Taken by surprise, all made their submission except Milan and Tortona. The latter was stormed and destroyed, but for the moment Milan was ignored, as affairs in Rome called Frederick away. In 1159, however, as Milan was still defying him with Alexander's support, he determined to bring it into line with the rest. After a three years' siege he took it, razed the walls and removed the inhabitants, earning thereby their undying hatred for himself and his successors. Pope Alexander was driven into exile, and Rome occupied.

The imperial triumph was brief. Alexander skilfully won help from Venice, Sicily and Constantinople, and as soon as Frederick had gone back to Germany, the Lombard cities broke into revolt and expelled their governors. In 1166 Frederick returned, at the head of a large army. He took Rome by siege, but at the critical moment, when he was about to advance upon Alexander's Sicilian allies, a sudden fever struck the German army and destroyed it. Frederick fled, almost alone, and barely got back with his life to the shelter of the Alps. The cities now entered into the famous Lombard League. Milan was rebuilt, henceforth to take the leading position. Faced with the ruin of all his prospects, the Emperor entered Italy for the third time, but in 1176, at Legnano, the chivalry of Germany, led by the great Emperor in person, was fairly and squarely defeated by the citizen infantry of the republics—in itself a portent. Frederick was compelled to make what terms he could with both his adversaries. He granted the cities their independence, subject to a merely nominal suzerainty. He met Alexander in Venice, and in the porch of St. Mark's—the spot is still commemorated in red marble—he ceremonially knelt before him, to symbolize his utter submission. The tables were turned, and the way was open for the succession of the most imperial minded and astute of all the Popes.

THE EMPIRE AND SICILY

Yet, humbled as he was by Alexander's intrigues, Frederick was able, before his fatal journey to the East in 1188, to engineer a diplomatic master-stroke, which had far-reaching results. The Norman Kingdom of Sicily, the best governed realm in Europe, with a full treasury and a well-trained army largely recruited from Moslems, had been for a century the staunch supporter of the Papacy. In 1186

Frederick married his son, soon to be Henry VI, to Constance, the heiress of the Sicilian crown. A son of that marriage might well combine the imperial claim, the German kingship, and the solid strength of southern Italy. Before such force the insurgent republics of Lombardy must yield, and the Popes, between two fires and deprived of their most powerful ally, would surely be reduced to the position of mere bishops. The marriage was a declaration of war to the death. It proved as destructive to the Empire as to the Papacy. Frederick, the heir on whom so much turned, was born in 1194.

Almost a generation passed before the final storm burst. It was, however, foreseen by both parties, and the time was spent by each in preparation. Henry VI, as ambitious as his father, followed his father's policy. He ruled Sicily and south Italy through his wife as if it were his own. He bought the support of the German princes by further concessions. He almost induced them to make the kingship hereditary in his house. If he had succeeded in this, he might, even at that late date, have altered the whole course of German history; but the elective principle was too strong for him. He overawed the Italian cities and even recovered control of the Papacy, for Alexander's immediate successors were feebler men. He actually planned to extinguish the Papal State altogether and to rule in Rome as Emperor. He might perhaps have permanently united Italy. Certainly he was more nearly an absolute ruler there than any of his predecessors. In 1197, however, he suddenly died, leaving his task to a boy of three. The scheme to unite Germany and Sicily fell into the background; Sicily, a hereditary kingdom, passed to the child at once, Constance acting as regent, but in Germany all was thrown into anarchy, owing to a contested election. At the height of the confusion, there was elected to the Papacy a man well fitted to put the situation to profit, an aristocrat by birth and trained to the law, young, able and resolute in decisions, and determined to restore Papal authority.

RIVAL CLAIMANTS TO THE GERMAN THRONE

We have watched the crusading zeal of Innocent III and his efforts to combat heresy. We must now follow him while he put into practice the theory, so long preached, that the Pope, as God's representative on earth, must control all earthly rulers. Sicily, which an earlier Pope had granted to the Normans, he claimed to be his to bestow. When Constance died, he assumed the regency himself on the boy Frederick's behalf, hoping by this means to keep the kingdom out of German hands, or at least so to train his ward as to make him duly subservient to the Church. The rival candidates for the German kingship, Otto, the head of the House of Guelf, and Philip of Swabia, the late Emperor's brother, both appealed to him for support. After a long delay, during which he made a show of investigating their fitness, he decided in favour of Otto, who had sworn to protect all possessions of the Papacy, including Sicily, and ultimately

PAPACY AND EMPIRE, 1209

Conflict between Pope and Emperor gave Italy an unhappy history in the thirteenth century. By 1209 the ability and ambition of Pope Innocent III had strengthened the influence of the Papal State, aided by the minority of the future Emperor, Frederick II, an orphan who was under Papal protection.

secured him the election. He organized his own party in Germany as well as in Italy to support the Guelf as Emperor, thereby, as we have seen, giving Philip cause to wreck the Pope's crusading project.

He forced the strongest European sovereigns to obey him. When Philip Augustus of France repudiated his wife and married again, Innocent declared the first to be his only legal wife and ordered him, in the interests of morality, to take her back. On Philip's refusal, Innocent excommunicated him, and in six months compelled him to yield. Later, it was Innocent who wielded the same weapon of excommunication against John of England, and then, when John surrendered to him, set aside the Great Charter and excommunicated the barons who were supporting it. To demonstrate his power, he assembled in council the bishops and abbots of all Europe, together with representatives of all European sovereigns, to consider his proposals for a comprehensive scheme of world reform, including, for example, the means of preventing war and the humanizing of criminal law, as well as matters of church discipline and doctrine.

TRIUMPH OF THE PAPACY

There was no country in Europe, not even Portugal, Sweden and Hungary, in which Innocent did not make good his claims, at least in part. When excommunication was defied, he declared a crusade against the offender and called upon some civil ruler to lead it. In this way, he destroyed the Albigensians in southern France, and compelled John to surrender England to him and to receive it back in feudal tenure. What he thought to be his final triumph came when Otto turned against him. He made the experiment of sending his ward Frederick, still a boy, to Germany to undermine Otto's position. It was brilliantly successful; Frederick's charm of manner, his striking appearance and above all the memories which he awakened of his father and grandfather, won all hearts. In 1215, after Otto had been disposed of by Philip Augustus—the Papal champion—at Bouvines, Innocent, relying on having trained his protégé to support the Papal cause, put him forward as a candidate for the German crown, and secured his election. He was indeed the dictator of Europe, his one great failure being the crusade of 1203. Apart from his spiritual position, for ten years he wielded political power more vigorously and over a greater area than any emperor had done.

Yet his success was more apparent than real and in any case could hardly last; as soon as any race reached conscious nationhood, it would cease to tolerate the interference of a foreign despot in its internal affairs. There was also one fatal weakness in the Papacy itself. The Cluniac reformers had claimed political power in order to use it for spiritual ends. All the great Popes before Alexander III had kept the spiritual welfare of Europe before them and had wielded their power for that end. Alexander, however, and after him Innocent, went dangerously near subordinating spiritual to political ambitions; they made the maintenance of the Papal State against the Hohenstaufen their principal objective. Their immediate successors went further on the path. The end was forgotten, the Papacy became primarily a political machine, and moral scruple was thrown aside. When that happened, the Popes lost the respect of earnest Christians, and with it, all semblance of authority. Even excommunication lost its force, for when it came to be used as a regular political weapon, it was universally ignored, even by the clergy. The Popes forgot that the authority of the Christian Church, like that of any other institution, must ultimately depend upon the spiritual character and integrity of its officers.

It is noteworthy that the most brilliant of the Holy Roman Emperors, Henry VI, was immediately followed by the most imperial of the Popes, and that the careers of both were scarcely ended when the struggle opened which destroyed both Papacy and Empire as world-powers, and for the ideal of Christian unity substituted free competition in every sphere of activity between the rival nations.

CHAPTER 43

THE DEATH STRUGGLE OF THE EMPIRE AND PAPACY

THE great Innocent died in 1216, just as his ward's reign began in earnest. Frederick II was elected King of the Germans in 1215, and was crowned Emperor in Aachen, taking, as was his duty, the crusading vow. Five years later, he was again crowned in Rome, by Innocent's successor, and once more took the Cross, undertaking this time to proceed to the Holy Land in the following year. The new Emperor—though he achieved little that was permanent and revealed in his character features utterly unintelligible to most of his contemporaries, and not a few startling contradictions—nevertheless reached a point of dazzling eminence. In one sense he was the last great figure of the Middle Ages, exemplifying in his career both its ideals and its limitations; in another he was a daring pioneer, summing up in himself the mental ferment with which, as we have seen, Europe was by this time seething—cynical, clear-sighted, tilting ruthlessly against the prejudices and opinions of his age, and foreshadowing the intellectual and political revolution of which the modern world is the outcome.

Frederick's ancestry was German and Norman. Brought up in close contact with the Arabs and the Jews of Sicily and with the Greeks of southern Italy, he was entirely free from racial or religious prejudice, and learnt to appreciate all that was best in the culture of each. He spoke nine languages and wrote in six. He never shook off some of the superstitions common to his time, such as a blind belief in astrology and magic, and like his predecessors, he was obsessed throughout his life by the ideal of dominating Europe—the legacy of the Holy Roman Empire so fatal to the development of Germany and Italy. Yet his motive was primarily political rather than religious, and in that sense it may be classified as modern.

FREDERICK II'S IDEALS

He aimed at justice and order in this world rather than at salvation in the next. He was a leader in every branch of knowledge and culture, but his interests were in secular learning, not in that of the Church. He was himself a poet and surrounded himself with poets and scholars. The University of Naples, which he founded, was to produce intelligent laymen, not priests, to be a nursery of imperial administrators independent of the clergy. The subjects taught, law, science, mathematics and medicine, were those required by laymen who wished to be the intellectual equals of the churchmen, hitherto the monopolists of learning. The scholars, of whom he himself was the foremost, worked in the spirit of Aristotle, Avicenna and Averroes rather than in that of Anselm or the Scholastics. They were trained to use their eyes, to see things as they are, and not to rely on the authorities of the past. Teachers were imported from the East and from Spain, and with them a new spirit of enquiry which, as it spread, shook to their foundations the doctrines of the Faith.

This pursuit of knowledge for its own sake knew no limits. Nothing was worthy of belief unless it was acceptable to reason, and based upon observed facts. The Emperor's own passion for enquiry led him to investigate the causes of the winds, the origin of volcanoes, the qualities of drugs, the properties of the magnetic needle. To observation he added scientific experiment, an idea abhorrent to the age. Which of two men digested his meal the better, the one who rested or the one who took exercise? He cut them open to see. Which was the original language? He isolated a number of babies in order to discover what tongue they would first use. Unfortunately, they died before speaking. He saw no exclusive merit in Christianity. Neither he nor his intimates were orthodox believers. The freedom of their thought ranged to the length of openly questioning many dogmas then taken to be essential to Christianity—for example, the Virgin Birth and the Resurrection—and he was generally believed to be the author of the famous remark: "The world has been misled by three deceivers, Jesus, Moses and Mohammed, of whom two died in honour." Given his way, Frederick would have rationalized the Christian faith, and shorn the Church of all her worldly property.

Equally striking was his interest in natural history. He collected innumerable anecdotes on the behaviour of animals. To ascertain how long they lived, he ringed and released fish. A carp thus dated is said to have been caught two centuries after his death. To study the development of the chicken in the egg he built incubators. He proved by experiment that birds of prey detect their quarry by sight and not by smell. He kept menageries and animal reserves in many places, with special breeding-stations for hounds, camels, horses and pigeons. He was a mighty hunter, but hawking was his favourite sport, for from it "a man may learn more of the secret workings of nature than from any other pursuit".

Frederick's great work, *The Art of Hunting with Birds*, was a first-class piece of original research, covering every branch of ornithology—a survey of all species of birds and their habits, migration and the mechanics of flight, as well as methods of training and using birds of prey. He collected observations from far and wide, from Iceland and from India and used them to set forth "things as they are", venturing even to correct and contradict the revered Aristotle. This work, magnificently illustrated, in part, at any rate, by the Emperor's own hand, became widely known in the succeeding centuries and was the model of all subsequent research in its own and in other fields of learning. Its significance, however, lies not in its being the first great product of a new scientific spirit—Frederick owns his debt to Arabic essays on the same lines—but in the fact that the ideal of seeing things as they are came to fruition in the work not of some obscure scholar like Roger Bacon, but of the Roman Emperor himself. Whatever disappointment befell the imperial scientist, he had at least pointed out the way to a new world.

FREDERICK'S "MODERN" STATE

Something of the same spirit can be seen in Frederick's political achievement, the erection of a state on modern lines. To recover the control of Germany was beyond his powers. He was content to leave the princes in possession of their local rights so long as they recognized him as their feudal suzerain, and for the greater part of his reign, his name and fame were enough to prevent the rise of rivals. In Italy, however, he was determined to rule, and especially in the Sicilian inheritance which was always the centre and source of his power. Sicily meant to him the kingdom which included the southern half of the Italian peninsula. The island itself he rarely visited. During his minority the strong state built up by his grandfather Roger had been shattered, and in 1220 the usual feudal chaos reigned. After his coronation in Rome, Frederick set himself at once to recover all the crown property which had been seized, and to root out all the little nests of local power which had been established, each with its local fortress. In two active years, by turning first the lesser nobility against the greater and then the remainder against each other, he reduced them all to subservience.

So far Henry II of England had gone, but Frederick went further. In the course of the next twenty years, the loosely-knit framework of a feudal kingdom, held together by land-tenure, was succeeded by the firm architecture of a state in which all power and authority, everything that made for law, order and justice, emanated from him alone. All castles and fortresses were made into national strongholds, and the right to build them was rigidly reserved to the crown. The mere possession of land was to give its owner neither weight nor authority. In place of feudal dominions, the whole country was divided into ten provinces, each to be governed by a Justiciar, all hereditary offices being abolished. Over these ten were two Master Justiciars, and beneath them a host of judges, clerks, and constables, a complete official caste, all trained at Naples to conduct the business of government, military, judicial, financial and administrative, and to enforce in the minutest detail the imperial will. All officials were appointed by the Emperor and they performed their tasks under his immediate supervision.

The system was carefully safeguarded against the gradual growth of abuses such as had brought to nothing the efforts of earlier reformers. The governing class were forbidden to own land or any property in their official districts. They held their positions for a single year only, at the end of which they had to give an account of their stewardship. They had no permanent headquarters, for their principal duty was to tour their districts, holding daily courts of justice and enquiry. Nevertheless every decision made by the official class, together with a detailed report on every enquiry and all expenses and receipts, had to be recorded on parchment and submitted to the Emperor at stated intervals for his approval.

COMMERCIAL ORGANIZATION

Such a system of government, much of it, of course, borrowed from the Greek Empire, was far in advance of anything as yet practised in the West. It brought the whole kingdom under one uniform system of law and administration to a degree unparalleled for many centuries except in England, though, as we have seen, Louis IX, himself copying Frederick, went some way towards it in France. The deliberate intention was to override all local interests for the good of the state—a wholesale denial of liberty to the individual for the advantage of the whole.

Nor did Frederick confine his centralization to the political sphere. During the years of feudal anarchy, the foreign trading-states of Amalfi, Pisa, Genoa and Venice had established themselves in all the harbours of the kingdom and had obtained special privileges, such as freedom from duties and tolls. These privileges were now withdrawn. All imports and exports were to be regulated by officials appointed by the Justiciars for the purpose. Import and export taxes became a regular source of revenue to the crown, and in some articles, in wheat for example, a state monopoly of foreign trade was established, as in modern Russia, the royal government providing fleets of ships for the purpose. Commercial treaties were negotiated with Moslem states in Africa and Syria, guaranteeing a fixed rate of customs duties and mutual protection to each other's merchants. In internal commerce, we see the same process. The sale of salt, and the manufacture of iron, dyes and silk cloth were all royal monopolies. State inns were established for travelling merchants, and also state baths, slaughter-houses, sugar refineries, coinage and weights and measures. On the crown lands, experiments were made with new crops, such as henna and indigo, and with new methods of agriculture. State looms and workshops supplied the needs of the court, clothing for the army, weapons, armour and machines of war. For soldiers, Frederick was at first dependent upon feudal levies, but by the end, these had become subsidiary to a regular professional force, partly Sicilian Moslems, partly mercenary knights drawn from every quarter of the Empire, recruited and paid by the government.

This complex and highly centralized state, modern in form and spirit, put into Frederick's hands power and wealth beyond that of any monarch in the West since Charlemagne. Yet, for all its modernity, he used it to further the same ancient ideals that had inspired his ancestors, and in so using it, he wrecked it. It was his duty as Emperor to go on crusades, though in no spirit of religious exaltation. Like Barbarossa, he must impose his rule on north Italy, with the difference that Germany was no longer the base of operations. It was for these tasks that Frederick steadily prepared himself.

GREGORY IX'S EXTREME DEMANDS

The growth of his despotic power was watched with alarm both by the cities of Lombardy, the very homes of republican self-government, and by the Popes, who feared the encirclement of their principality. In the time of Innocent's successor Honorius, a gentle and cautious statesman, friendly relations were maintained; but in 1227, Honorius was succeeded by Gregory IX, an implacable and passionate supporter of the extremest Papal claims, who from the first moment of his power set before himself one aim—the humiliation, if not the annihilation, of his Imperial rival. In that year, after many delays, Frederick was preparing to fulfil his crusading vow and had actually sworn to embark in August. An outbreak of plague decimated his army, but in September he sailed. After a few days, developing the disease himself, he put back.

This was Gregory's opportunity. Refusing to listen to the reason, he excommunicated the Emperor as an oath-breaking apostate. Though Frederick sailed again as soon as he was well enough, he repeated the ban on the ground that he had not waited to receive the pardon of the Church for his first offence. As soon as the crusade was well on its way, Gregory released Frederick's subjects from their oath of fealty, invaded the kingdom of Sicily with his own army, fighting under the banner of St. Peter, and ordered the Christians in

Palestine to have no dealings with the heretic and excommunicated Emperor. It was strange to see the Head of the Christian Church doing everything possible to ensure the failure of a crusade and treacherously attacking the leader in his absence. Yet there is a certain truth in the justification which Gregory put forward: "To preserve the Christian Faith, it is necessary to drive this tyrant from his throne."

FREDERICK'S TREATY WITH THE SULTAN

Arrived in Palestine at the head of hardly more than a thousand knights—the plague had slain many times that number—and finding the Christian population primed by Gregory to hinder and obstruct him, Frederick decided that warlike action was impossible. Probably he had always intended to barter rather than to fight. With cynical realism, in sharpest contrast with the blind fanaticism of earlier crusaders, he saw that East and West had everything to gain from friendly co-operation. Jerusalem was a sacred city to Moslem, Jew and Christian. How they might all visit it without friction was obviously a matter for agreement between gentlemen. He was already in negotiation on the subject with the Sultan of Egypt, with whom he had much more in common than with Christians of the type of Gregory. The Sultan, a nephew of Saladin, was himself a poet, a cultivated scholar and an admirable administrator, who naturally held Frederick in great respect. He now sent a suitable envoy to discuss the situation. Frederick was a master of Arabic, and amid refreshing discourse on logic, poetry and mathematics, compared with which the fate of Jerusalem must have seemed of secondary importance, an agreement was quickly reached. Though at the moment the Pope was publicly execrating Frederick for treating with the infidel and secretly exhorting the Sultan on no account to hand over Jerusalem, a treaty was signed early in 1229, by which the Christians were granted free access from the coast to Jerusalem and Nazareth, and a truce of ten years was proclaimed.

In full imperial state, the banned and excommunicated Emperor then made a formal entry into the Holy City. Before the altar of the church of the Holy Sepulchre, proud and unabashed, he crowned himself King of Jerusalem, thus forestalling Napoleon by six centuries in ceremonially claiming that he held his kingship from God without the mediation of Pope or any priest. Without bloodshed, he had accomplished more than fifty years of futile warfare. Yet the manner of his victory, and still more the revolutionary impiety of his coronation, struck the orthodox with horror. Under threat of excommunication, Christians were forbidden by Gregory to profit by the "infamous treaty". Between such a monster of daring iniquity and the Christian Church, there could henceforth be no real peace. In order to destroy the intellectual free-thinker all the available forces on the side of fanatical reaction must combine.

On returning to his kingdom, Frederick easily chased the Papal army over the frontier, and the Pope, biding his time, agreed to withdraw the sentence of excommunication. Before the opening of the final struggle, there was an uneasy truce of seven years, during which each side manoeuvred for position. In 1236, however, the Lombard cities, under the leadership of Milan, then as always the focus of opposition to the Emperor, were discovered to be tampering with the loyalty of Frederick's eldest son, Henry, who had been left in charge in Germany. Henry was caught in the act of rebellion. He was deposed and condemned to lifelong imprisonment, to escape which he committed suicide. Frederick next turned upon the cities. Prophetically, he saw in the free democratic republics the germ of a principle utterly incompatible with centralized dictatorship such as he had imposed upon his own kingdom. Claiming to be fighting in God's name the battle of unity and discipline against "the head of all dissensions in Italy", he fell upon the Milanese and their allies, and decisively defeated them at Cortenuova. It remained to destroy their independence for ever.

In this struggle between sovereignty and liberty, between order and anarchy, he demanded that the Papacy, itself the most monarchical of dictatorships, should support him. Gregory's choice was difficult. With the northern republics, hotbeds of anti-clerical free-thinking, the Papacy had little enough in common. Moreover, their cause seemed lost. Of all the Lombard League, only five cities remained faithful to Milan after Cortenuova. Yet to support Frederick in his present temper would mean abandoning not only the whole of the Papal pretensions to world-power but even the political control of Rome. Flushed with his victory, and in a mood of mystical exaltation, Frederick announced that the time had come for him to be Caesar in fact as well as in name. The political sovereign, not the religious, should rule the world. The Church, Papacy and all, must be included in a true and final Roman Empire. He himself was to be in Rome what he had already declared himself to be in Jerusalem, Emperor by the direct Grace of God.

GUELF AND GHIBELLINE

In defence of the rights of the Papacy, any ally was better than none. Gregory determined to follow the policy of Alexander III and to join the rebels. Working at first in secret, he sent his agents into every city in Italy, where they organized and united all who for any reason were hostile to the Empire, of whatever rank or status, patrician or plebeian, heretic or orthodox. In each city that had hitherto been loyal there arose, under the name of Guelf, a determined party. Even Venice and Genoa were induced to lay aside their rivalry and join the League. Before long there was no town, hardly even a family, upon whose loyalty Frederick could rely. All were rent asunder by the warring ideals of Papacy and Empire. The

Emperor lashed this way and that, but the cities were well fortified
and none could be taken without a lengthy siege. Once united and
organized as they now were, the citizens proved a force too strong
to be trodden under foot. There was nothing to be done but to
organize counter-parties in each city. Under the name of Ghibelline,
an Italian version of the old race-name of the Hohenstaufen, Frederick's agents enrolled their own supporters, and between Guelf and
Ghibelline began an interminable and confused war, inside each
city as well as between them. All this, however, did little to advance
the Emperor's cause or to promote the disciplined order of which he
had dreamed.

Finally, in 1239, Gregory came into the open. Once more he
excommunicated Frederick and called upon all Christians to join in
a Holy War against the heretic who had likened Jesus to Mohammed
and had maintained that "no man should believe aught but what may
be proved by the power and reason of nature". A year later, he
followed up this attack by summoning to Rome a general council
of the Church for the purpose of passing public sentence upon
the enemy of Christendom. The council never met. The French,
Spanish and north Italian bishops assembled in Genoa, to sail
thence to Rome. The ships in which they travelled were captured by
the imperial fleet, and over a hundred high dignitaries of the Church
were sent to Sicily, where they were rigorously imprisoned.

FREDERICK MAKES OPEN WAR ON ROME

Unable to end the matter in any other way, Frederick was determined to use open force against the Pope himself. Announcing to
the world that he was attacking not the Church but only its unworthy
head, he advanced with his whole forces against Rome. His Moslem
cavalry were already under its walls, and he was about to strike the
final blow when the news came that there was nothing to attack.
Gregory had won his last great victory for the Papacy by dying.

For two years Frederick enjoyed an empty triumph. By bringing
violent pressure to bear on the cardinals, he even secured the election
of a new Pope whom he thought to be his friend, an intellectual
politician in place of a fanatic priest. Yet Innocent IV was to prove
a subtler and even deadlier and less scrupulous enemy than Gregory.
Whatever his previous attitude, his duty as Pope was to carry on the
war, even if at first he wore a friendly mask. Only later did Frederick
discover that "No Pope can be a Ghibelline". In 1244, Innocent
fled from Rome to the independent city of Lyons, far from the
Emperor's reach. From this retreat, until Frederick's death, he
directed the Holy War, offering to all who attacked Frederick the
same spiritual rewards as had been promised to earlier crusaders.
Not content with stimulating the resistance of the Italian cities, he
carried the war to Germany, where wandering Dominicans and
Franciscans, under the Pope's orders, preached general rebellion,

and collected money from all quarters to be used in carrying on the struggle. Every kind of political, social and religious discontent was fostered and exploited by the distribution of lavish bribes and promises without limit. Even in towns where Ghibellines held the upper hand there was no certainty of loyalty. Treachery and disaffection were rife, and on at least two occasions the Emperor's life was attempted on Innocent's direct instigation. No semblance of discipline or control could be maintained without extreme severity; this in turn soon degenerated on both sides into savage and inhuman cruelty, including the free use of torture. In 1249, Enzio, the Emperor's favourite son, was captured in a skirmish by the Bolognese, and was condemned to perpetual imprisonment. He was released only by his death, twenty-three years later. At the end of 1250, in the midst of the chaos, Frederick suddenly died while visiting southern Italy.

FREDERICK'S POLICY ENDS IN FAILURE

The last and greatest of the medieval emperors achieved nothing. He struggled for unity and discipline, and he left an empire in chaotic ruin; for the reform of the Church, and there was Innocent, triumphant at his death; for reasoned progress, and he left the forces of fanatical reaction in the field; for the prosperity of Italy, and after him it remained for centuries in the grip of merciless civil war. Was he Caesar re-incarnate, the lay Messiah, or the Anti-Christ? His own age had no certain answer to the question. To them he was a staggering mystery, an insoluble contradiction—*Stupor Mundi*—though Dante consigns him, alone of all the Roman Emperors, to Hell. Yet his career was a significant portent of things to come. The absolutist governments of Henry VIII and Louis XIV owe to him their precedent and inspiration, for they, too, claimed their authority to be divine. Not until his system was revived in Italy did that country again discover a sense of its unity. "It was upon poverty and simplicity", wrote Frederick, "that the primitive Church was built when she was the mother of saints. No one should presume to lay other foundations than those appointed by the Lord Jesus." In their demand for a return to primitive Christianity, neither Luther nor Bunyan could have said more. His clear-sighted reason and his insistence upon observation founded the tradition followed later by Bacon, Voltaire and Faraday and by nearly every leader of modern scientific thought.

Frederick failed for three reasons. Like his ancestors he was under the fatal spell of the imperial inheritance. If he had limited himself to the reconstruction of the Kingdom of Sicily, he might have built up there a prosperous and enduring state, comparable to those at that moment developing in France and England, and capable in time of absorbing Italy. Even his keen vision failed when it came to distinguishing between the ideal and the practical. Secondly, he encountered a spirit as indomitable as his own, and one more vital to

This fifteenth-century illustration from Froissart's Chronicles represents John of Gaunt in a hand-to-hand fight outside the town of Brest.

Now in the British Museum, this illustration from the fifteenth-century Harleian manuscript shows mummers performing with musicians in the gallery.

Vincent de Beauvais in the scriptorium of a monastic library at the end of the fifteenth century.

Wood-chopping in the fifteenth century. An illumination from a Flemish Book of Hours in the British Museum.

The great medieval fortress of Carcassonne was unsuccessfully attacked by the Black Prince. Its present appearance is due to restoration by Viollet le Duc.

the next stage of European progress, the passionate devotion of the Italian cities to their independence. But for that obstacle, he would surely have swept aside a spiritually bankrupt Papacy and might well have anticipated the Reformation by two centuries. Thirdly, he was one of that illustrious band of intellectuals who are so far in advance of their age as to be beyond its comprehension. No one leads the world who starts by staggering it, and no policy can have early success that antagonizes the commonly held beliefs of the people.

DOWNFALL OF THE EMPIRE

The Emperor's death hardly interrupted the struggle, for it was continued by his generals and by his sons, Conrad and Manfred. There was no one, however, to co-ordinate their efforts. Innocent was determined to extirpate the whole Hohenstaufen brood. At his instigation the German princes deserted Conrad and chose an Emperor of another family. Conrad was driven out and died in 1254, but Manfred held his own in the south. Finally, after two Papal armies, financed by English money, had failed, the Pope turned to France for help. He offered the crown of Sicily to Charles of Anjou, a brother of Louis IX, on condition that he could win it. Charles invaded Sicily, and in 1266 won a decisive victory at Benevento. Manfred's troops, bought by the Pope, deserted him in the battle and he himself was slain. His wife and children were imprisoned, and died in their chains. Finally, two years later, Frederick's grandson Conradino, a boy of fifteen, who was the last survivor of Frederick's family except for the miserable Enzio, was captured and publicly beheaded in Naples.

No one profited by the struggle. The Empire was destroyed beyond recall. The title remained, but henceforth its holder was a German princelet, with hardly a shadow of authority outside his own estates. For six centuries Germany was to have no political unity and to become the battleground of Europe. In northern Italy the cities retained their independence, but at a terrible cost. During the incessant warfare, the necessities of defence drove one after another of them into the control of military despots, for the most part cruel self-seekers. They and their successors, ruling as tyrants in the larger cities and dragging the smaller in their wake, waged perpetual warfare upon one another under the party-labels of Guelf and Ghibelline, for a century or more. Only Venice and Florence retained their old republican forms. In the others, though they remained free cities, and though the tyrants were often distinguished for an enlightened patronage of literature and the arts, individual liberty vanished, and the dream of racial unity was everywhere forgotten and submerged beneath the rivalries of the separate states.

The Papacy, outwardly triumphant, was left without a rival. The Popes could now declare that they were Emperors as well. Not a jot of their pretensions had been abated. "We declare", wrote Boniface

Q   (H.W.)

VIII, in 1294, "that it is altogether necessary to salvation for every human creature to be in all things subject to the Roman pontiff." Yet the Papacy had forfeited for the time its spiritual character, and with it much of its moral influence. Moreover, as we have seen, a new force had arisen, of which the Popes seemed as yet to be oblivious. Nations were forming themselves which would no longer endure the interference of a foreign despot in their internal affairs, and with their rise, the Papal claims seemed out of date.

The thirteenth century looked forward and back. Men's minds were the battleground between free thought and authority, between the scholastic learning and the growing appreciation and study of physical nature, between the enjoyment of this life and preparation for the next. The close of the century was adorned by one whose writings mirror both attitudes. Dante was born in Florence in 1264, at a time when Guelf and Ghibelline antagonisms were at their highest and when the last of the Hohenstaufens were being hounded to their end. During his youth, he watched the apparent triumph of the Papacy, but he lived to see its overthrow and the beginning of its captivity at Avignon. Florence itself was torn with dissension, the party to which he belonged was thrown from power, and from 1301, until his death in 1321, he lived in exile. Aloof from active politics, he devoted himself to reflection and writing, making his home in a number of places in Lombardy, Tuscany and the Romagna, where he lived under the protection of various friendly lords. Eventually he retired to Ravenna under the patronage of Guido da Polenta.

DANTE MIRRORS HIS AGE

His greatest work, the *Divina Commedia*, is cast in the form of a journey to the future life to find answers to the questions: What is Good? What is Evil? Who deserves eternal punishment or reward, and why? Dante's guide is Vergil, the representative ancient authority on such subjects. Yet the nature of the questions, and still more the free and independent judgment shown in the answers, are utterly unmedieval. They give us a complete review of the personalities of the age and the best summary of its beliefs.

Dante's learning, much of his method of reasoning, and his theology are purely medieval. Yet in many respects he is the very herald of the future. Full of appreciation of individual human character and achievement, he taught that what men are—not their place in society or the Church nor the efforts of clergy on their behalf—determines their relation to God and the conduct of their lives, both here and hereafter; he places several Popes in Hell and mentions only one in Paradise. His poetry, written in the language which Frederick and his courtiers had been the first to use as a means of literary expression, is full of studies painted straight from nature, and especially of scenes from Italian country life. If Francis was the first who experienced life and nature as a mystical emotion and Frederick the first to trace in them an eternal and unvarying law, Dante was both in one. However orthodox his beliefs, he demanded a thorough-going puritan reformation of religion, and dreamed of a Church divested of wealth and power, ruling the world by moral force alone. His standpoint was that of a detached aristocratic observer of life, but his writing is nowhere more moving than in the passage where he recounts the life of Francis and his devotion to the service of his brother men.

DANTE'S STUDY OF AN IDEAL STATE

The same contrasts appear in his political views. His sympathies were Ghibelline. In a second great work, the *De Monarchia*, a study of the ideal state, he sketched out just such a form of government for Italy as Frederick had tried to erect. The best hope for the peace and prosperity of mankind lay in royal authority. Like any medieval, Dante preached the essential unity of Europe. He looked back to the Roman Empire and proclaimed that its revival was the only means of stilling the tempest of anarchy in which he saw his beloved Italy engulfed. Yet, believing, like Frederick, the Waldenses, Joan of Arc, and the Protestant reformers later on, that all men were individually responsible to God and capable of direct access to Him without priestly mediation, he claimed that the Emperor should be in no way subject to the Papacy, since his title and authority were themselves divine. It is characteristic of the age that Dante should have exalted Frederick's own ideals of government, but none the less should have condemned Frederick himself to Hell as a heretic, and that the Church should have placed the *De Monarchia*, a reactionary work, on the Index of Forbidden Books, where it remained until 1897. Although the reputation of Dante as a writer was widespread among Italian scholars in the years immediately following his death, it underwent something of an eclipse in succeeding generations. Now, however, Dante has long been acclaimed for the greatness of his poetic genius and the profundity of his thought.

THE FRUIT OF THE MIDDLE AGES

During six centuries, the history of Europe had been dominated by the instinct to restore in one form or another the unity which Rome had first implanted. From that instinct, Charlemagne, the barbarian chieftain, Otto and Barbarossa, the German knights, Gregory VII and Innocent III, the successors of St. Peter, Frederick and Dante struggling for secular theocracy, had one and all received their inspiration, as from a flaming beacon. The golden age of prosperity and peace was to them, as all knowledge was to the scholars, something to be recovered and restored. They failed, and Dante's *De Monarchia* was their epitaph. The beacon died down. The whole notion of a European unity was forgotten for the next five centuries. In the meantime, apart from theorists, the field was to be occupied by lesser men with narrower aims, looking to the development of their several national units rather than to any kind of world-wide federation. By 1300, national languages, literatures and cultures, national prejudices, ambitions and self-consciousness, were already in being, England and France showing the way. The Hundred Years' War, the first of those great struggles between nations which were to become so characteristic of the next stage of human development, was already brewing between France and England.

The age which had aimed at the restoration and recovery of the glorious past was yielding to one which set progress towards an unknown but doubtless golden future as its ideal. The Middle Age had done its work. To the enfeebled Roman civilization had been added the youthful vigour of the northern barbarians, together with something of the brilliant culture of the Moslem world, and into the new fusion there had infiltered, directly from Byzantium and also through Venice and Sicily, some little of the Greek learning and tradition. These elements, heterogeneous and often hostile, needed time before they settled into a unified European culture—they have not yet succeeded in so doing—but all the materials were there whose gradual fusion has produced the modern world as we know it.

THE DISAPPEARANCE OF EUROPEAN UNITY

Finally, with the disappearance of all sense of European unity and the substitution for it of national rivalries growing ever more bitter, the feeling of essential conflict between Christendom and Islam grew rapidly weaker. If Moslems harried Mediterranean shipping, or overran what had been Greece, or even threatened Germany, they might be punished as pirates or welcomed as allies, as the political or economic situation suggested. The modes of thought which had dictated the earlier crusades were gone for ever. In the next age, the characteristic motive-force was to be not unity but patriotism, with frenzied national animosities and individual self-seeking beneath its cloak. Human beings have a strange aptitude for hiding their barbaric and short-sighted passions behind fine-sounding phrases. The age of reason is not yet, although our ancestors proclaimed it complacently two centuries ago.

PART IX

THE END OF THE MIDDLE AGES

CHAPTER 44

THE DECLINE OF THE FEUDAL SYSTEM

WE have seen how the implacable rivalry of Papacy and Empire shattered the ideal of the unity of Christendom. The crusades had promised the union of all Christians to rescue the Holy Places from Moslem rule. But, after a brief triumph, the soldiers of the Cross had been repulsed, and had turned their arms against one another. The rift between eastern and western Europe had been deepened by the sack of Constantinople. The Pope's claim to universal spiritual authority was baulked by the existence of a rival Christian Church, ruled by the Orthodox Patriarch. In spite of the victories won by the two Innocents over the lay rulers of western Europe, there was a stirring in men's minds against the limitless claims of the Papacy, and as the thirteenth century waned, Christendom moved steadily away from the medieval idea of unity.

The deaths of Frederick II and his sons brought the Hohenstaufen dynasty crashing to disaster with dramatic swiftness; but there was no sudden break in the European tradition. The development of institutions and culture was not vitally disturbed by political events, but it ceased to be controlled by Empire and Papacy. The feudal system itself, the basis of all social and military life, became distorted. As time went on, it was destroyed by the rise of new classes and interests, which burst the limitations of the old system of land-tenure. Though outward forms remained intact, feudal institutions lost their universal character, and the ideals they embodied slowly decayed.

OLD FEUDS RENEWED IN ITALY

For fifty years after Innocent IV had cried "Let the heavens rejoice and the earth be glad", because *Stupor Mundi* was no more, the Popes seemed stronger than ever. Disregarding the imperial ideal of a united Italy, they set themselves to secure their own territorial power by ending German rule in the south once and for all. But when Charles of Anjou had triumphed over the last Hohenstaufen at Benevento and won the kingdom of Sicily, the old animosities reappeared. In the towns of northern Italy the feud of Guelf and Ghibelline flared out with all the old bitterness and was used to cloak what really amounted to trade-wars between the rival city-states such as Florence, Siena, Pisa and Genoa; and in the south there arose an increasingly bitter hatred directed against oppressive French rule.

The hatred felt by the Sicilians for their French masters was in the end responsible for bringing yet another alien power into Italy. On Easter Monday, 1282, the peasants of Sicily fell upon the garrisons as they were on their way to mass and massacred almost every French man, woman and child on the island. The French at Naples at once prepared to revenge these "Sicilian Vespers", as they were called; and to save themselves the Sicilians called for Spanish help. The King of Aragon was not able to establish any very real authority over this new kingdom offered him by the Sicilians. But he established the first Spanish foothold on the Italian peninsula, and so began that long rivalry between Spain and France for the possession of Italy which ultimately ruined the country.

Meanwhile, while one line of Emperors perished in the attempt to unite Italy, there were other rivals fighting for the imperial crown in Germany. The Popes, in their determination to ruin the Hohenstaufen, appointed one anti-king after another, most of them foreigners, to raise factions against them in Germany. William of Holland, who died in 1266, almost succeeded in uniting the country under his rule. But his successors, Richard of Cornwall, brother of Henry III of England, and Alfonso of Castile, both of whom claimed the allegiance of a faction of the German princes, never established any real authority; Alfonso, indeed, earned his title of "the Wise" by never going to Germany. Imperial rule in Germany practically ceased to exist; and although this "Great Interregnum" was ended by the undisputed election of Rudolph of Habsburg in 1273 to all the titles and pretensions of the Holy Roman Empire, he had been chosen because he was far less powerful than the Hohenstaufen had been and was never likely to recover the real authority of his predecessors.

THE TEUTONIC ORDER

In Germany, as in Italy, the collapse of the imperial government ushered in a long period of anarchy and civil war. City fought against city, prince against prince. There was no central power strong enough to keep the peace or to restrain the lawlessness of the Knights, whose castles dominated roads and bridges and who lived largely by plundering or taxing the merchandise of the great trade-routes. The Kings of France took advantage of this confusion to extend their frontiers to the north-east, and by the end of the century Namur, Liège, and most of Flanders had fallen into their hands. Germany, however, was amply compensated for this loss of territory in the west by a period of great expansion on her eastern frontier. This she owed mainly to the work of the Teutonic Order.

The Teutonic Order of St. Mary was one of the many orders of chivalry, such as the Templars, which had been formed to carry on a permanent fight against the infidel. It was not only in Palestine and Asia Minor that Christendom was threatened. The front stretched from Spain and Africa to the Baltic. Slavs had encroached on the eastern frontiers of Germany, and the House of Chenghiz Khan had devastated eastern and central Europe throughout the thirteenth century. In the north the Teutonic Knights took the offensive. By 1283 they had cleared the whole of Prussia and most of Silesia, and the reconquered lands had been settled by German peasants. It is calculated that over 1500 new villages were founded by German colonists between 1150 and 1300; and farther south, in Hungary and Poland, the same process was at work, though on a smaller scale. Mongol raids had laid large areas of both these countries waste. They were only driven back after a long struggle which, like the crusades, was something of an international effort on the part of Christendom. The English poet Chaucer, writing in the fourteenth century, gives us, as one of the characters he found riding on a pilgrimage to the shrine of St. Thomas at Canterbury, a knight who had seen service on the German frontier: in Prussia, Lithuania and Russia. At the very end of the century the Earl of Hereford, later King Henry IV of England, wiled away part of an exile by joining the Teutonic Knights and fighting against the Slavs.

POLAND, BOHEMIA AND HUNGARY

These Slav and Mongol raiders resembled, in race and character, the Huns rather than the Goths. They were incapable of assimilating the culture or civilization of the people they conquered, and devastated the land and slaughtered the population. When they were driven back there were large districts in Hungary, Bohemia and Poland which were left entirely depopulated; and here again German peasants poured in as colonists. The result of this was to create in all these three countries German minorities which remained a fruitful source of international trouble, although for the moment Germany was too distracted to pursue a very aggressive policy outside her immediate frontiers. The immediate effect of this colonization was merely to complicate the bitter rivalries of Hungary, Bohemia and Poland for control of south-eastern Europe.

In all these countries, the central government was weak and the nobles of the provinces led a factious, semi-independent life of plunder and civil war. Occasionally, in one of them, a strong ruler would achieve some order and stability; Wenceslas II, who died in 1305, even gained control both of Hungary and Poland. But no one man ever succeeded in holding all three kingdoms together for long, and the death of each king meant a fresh outbreak of wars and of attempts to subdivide his inheritance. Eventually, in all three kingdoms the great nobles—the Magnates—became strong and independent enough to prevent any single family from holding the throne by hereditary right. They established, instead, elective monarchies, reserving to themselves the right to elect their king, so that they further weakened the central government and served to prolong the anarchy of the thirteenth century for another three hundred years.

Meanwhile one family in south-eastern Europe had already set itself to unite these various elements into a single empire. By successful wars, but above all by clever marriages, the Habsburgs had gained control of most of the German-speaking parts of the old East Mark—Carinthia, Carniola, the Tyrol and Austria. Their success in the marriage market became proverbial: "Let others", so ran the old Latin tag, "make wars, but do you, happy Austria, make marriages."

THE EMPIRE AND THE ELECTORS

They had originally come from further west, having been the Swiss landlords of Habsburg—the Hawk's Castle—near Lake Lucerne; the election of Rudolph of Habsburg to the Empire in 1273 was to turn their interests back once more to the west. But through all their German difficulties they never lost sight of their designs on the thrones of Hungary and Bohemia. After a long series of treaties, intrigues, wars and dynastic marriages, they were at last successful, though not until 1526, when more than half of Hungary had fallen into the hands of Moslem invaders. This elective principle, which ruined the monarchies of eastern Europe, was soon established firmly in Germany, and destroyed the last vestiges of imperial authority. The Habsburgs, though they gradually established themselves as the only family powerful enough to hold the Empire, never achieved the position enjoyed by the Hohenstaufen. They had to compete with the rival houses of Wittelsbach and Luxemburg, and they slowly lost all hold over the greater princes within the Empire. The Golden Bull of 1356 finally established the system of election to the Empire and vested the right of election in seven of the great princes, the Archbishops of Mainz, Trier and Cologne, the King of Bohemia, the Count Palatine of the Rhine, the Duke of Saxony and the Margrave of Brandenburg.

These princes were always in a position to extract concessions in advance from any candidate for the imperial throne. Before long it became necessary for candidates to expend vast sums in bribing the Electors; and the expenses attached to the imperial crown steadily increased as its real power diminished. It soon ceased to be anything but a purely German institution. The Pope no longer troubled to interfere in the choice of an Emperor who, even in Germany, enjoyed little but the prestige derived from an ancient and glorious tradition. It seemed that all those parts of Europe north of the Danube and east of the Rhine, which had never come under the effective rule of the old Roman Empire, were incapable of developing the instinct for strong, central organization which was one of Rome's greatest legacies to her western provinces.

Feudalism had been based on the assumption that every man and woman had a place to which they belonged; the serf enjoyed certain rights and privileges, but only on condition that he remained on the land to which he was attached; and in return for such rights and privileges, a man must perform certain duties. The feudal system provided an elementary, but on the whole effective, defence in time of war and the necessary framework for the preservation of law and order. It was not, however, sufficiently flexible to be adapted to a growing society whose needs were becoming more complex and which was no longer content to remain essentially static. As the peasant began to want to leave the land to which he was tied and the towns-man found the scope of his trading activities depending more and more on travel, the feudal system began to break down and to reveal certain fundamental defects.

The greatest and most obvious danger to feudal monarchy was its dependence on the character of the king. The whole organization was based on the overlord's efficiency. If he failed to enforce the obligations due from his tenants-in-chief, they rapidly got out of hand. The reign of Stephen in England had already shown how quickly the whole system of government would crumble into confusion when there was a weak man on the throne; and this was the primary cause of the chaotic conditions which prevailed in Germany and in all south-eastern Europe save the Byzantine Empire, from the thirteenth century onwards. The Emperors, largely owing to the long struggle with the Papacy, had failed to maintain their position at the head of their vassals. In the West, in France, and in England, the feudal monarchies held their power longer; but in the end both were to fall victims to a disputed succession and a weak king.

GRADUAL DECLINE OF THE CAPETIANS

The Capetian monarchy in France reached the zenith of its power in the second half of the thirteenth century. Louis IX had been the perfect pattern of a medieval king. He had combined a great zeal for the welfare of Christendom with a careful stewardship of his own kingdom of France, and had proved himself both a saint and an efficient administrator. His grandson, Philip the Fair, who reigned until 1314, was a less striking figure. We do not hear of him sitting, as St. Louis had done, under an oak at Vincennes, dealing out a fatherly justice to his people, yet he continued to enforce royal justice by methods which were less picturesque, but certainly more efficient, sending judges round the kingdom, as Henry II had used Assize judges in England, to hold courts of enquiry into the conduct of the local authorities responsible for the maintenance of law and order. He did not go on crusade, as his grandfather had done; and one of his most important achievements was to limit the power of the Papacy over the French Church by a concordat, or treaty, with the Pope. He cared less for the unity of Christendom than for the prosperity of France, but he was a fine example of medieval kingship.

One new thing Philip introduced into France which might have saved the monarchy from the many dangers of over-centralized power. He called together representatives of the nobles, the clergy and the townspeople to form the Estates General of the realm, which could be consulted on matters of policy and taxation, and so share some of the responsibilities of government with the king. Had they developed into a responsible representative institution similar to the English Parliament or to the Spanish Cortes, the Estates General might have saved France from some of the disasters of the coming collapse, and might even have prevented the French monarchy from growing into the irresponsible autocracy which was to provoke the French Revolution four centuries later.

Under Philip's successors, however, the Estates General failed to develop the independent existence which was necessary. It remained a body which was called together only occasionally and at times of crisis, dependent on the king's will and pleasure, to be consulted by him if he wished but having no right to make laws. Meanwhile, under a series of weak kings, the power of the monarchy began to decline. It could not raise the taxes needed to maintain the new system of justice and administration. The greater vassals began to reassert their independence; and, when the direct male line of the Capetians failed, the power of the crown was further weakened by a doubtful succession. Edward III of England put forward a claim to the throne and went to war to enforce it in 1337. Before long, the war with the English became also a civil war; and it was more than a hundred years before France was reunited under a single sovereign.

In England, the collapse of the monarchy was postponed, in spite of several earlier crises, until the fifteenth century, largely because the kings were able to unite the nation behind them in a successful war against France. The struggle between the barons and the Crown had been prolonged throughout the reign of Henry III and it was probably only the accession of the able and powerful Edward I in 1272 which saved the country from further civil war and anarchy.

FIRST ENGLISH EXPERIMENTS IN DEMOCRACY

Edward I, like his contemporary, Philip the Fair, set himself to strengthen the position of his own country rather than to further the aims of a united Christendom. In his youth he had accompanied Louis IX on crusade to the East, but all his fighting, after he came to the throne, was on the English frontiers. He carried out a final conquest of Wales, and by the end of his reign, in spite of the heroic resistance of William Wallace, had almost subdued Scotland. Like Philip, too, he set himself to limit the power of the Church, and recovered from the Papacy some of the ground lost by his grandfather, King John; and he, too, tried with greater success than the French kings to organize a representative assembly to share the responsibilities of the Crown in government and taxation.

The first experiments in associating representatives of the people with the government in England had been made by Simon de Montfort, the leader of the baronial party against Henry III, whose family fortune had been made out of the Albigensian Crusade. Simon tried to make allies among the smaller landowners in the country and the citizens of the towns by calling together two knights from every shire and two burgessesfrom every borough to sharewith the Great Council of the barons the duty of advising the king and voting taxes. Edward I continued the experiment, seeing that the Crown would be far less dependent on the greater barons if it could win the co-operation of the other tax-paying classes. He formulated the maxim that "what touches all should be decided by all"; and in the Model Parliament of 1295, set up a regular precedent for calling together in council representatives of the towns and counties, as well as the barons and higher clergy.

Unlike the French Estates General, this Parliament survived in England to take an increasingly important part in national affairs. For the first hundred years its existence was precarious. It bore little resemblance to a modern Parliament; the Commons sat with the barons and clergy in one "House", and its meetings were infrequent and irregular. Burgesses and knights disliked the expense of long journeys to Westminster and often tried to evade the duty of attendance. A strong king could always ignore the wishes of Parliament. But gradually the lower clergy withdrew altogether, and the Commons separated themselves from the barons, bishops and abbots, and began to claim special rights in the voting of taxes. Already, in 1376, we find them seeking some control over the conduct of government, and impeaching, or bringing to trial, an unpopular minister. They proved, even in the early stages of their development, useful in forcing the king to take more account of popular wishes; and in the end they were to be invaluable allies to the Crown in its final struggle with the baronage.

The weak and effeminate Edward II lost much of the ground gained by his father. The conquest of Wales held; and in time the Principality was completely united with England. But the Scots rallied under Robert Bruce, and at Bannockburn defeated the English and preserved their national independence. The old quarrels with the barons flared out again, accentuated by Edward's preference for low-born favourites; in the end the queen helped the baronial party to depose her husband and place his son, the third Edward, on the throne. Within a few years, the new king had directed English energies abroad; and for the next century, the destinies of both England and France were bound up with the long and useless struggle known as the Hundred Years' War, which drained the strength of both.

THE HUNDRED YEARS' WAR

In different ways, the Hundred Years' War was responsible for the end of the feudal monarchies, both in England and France. It did not last continuously for a hundred years. There was a period at first when the English gradually gained ground, thanks largely to the generalship of the Black Prince and the use of new tactics. At Crécy and Poitiers the English and Welsh archers showed themselves more than a match for the heavy mail-clad feudal cavalry of the French; and henceforth, until it became possible to use gunpowder in small arms, the long-bow was to dominate the battle-fields of western Europe. It would be true to say that the destruction of the power of the feudal nobility was begun by the archer and completed by the musketeer. This first phase of the war ended with the treaty of Bretigny in 1360, when the English had occupied half France and devastated her fairest provinces. Then the English were distracted by troubles at home. Richard II, son of the Black Prince, alienated the most powerful barons, much as Edward II had done, by relying over-much on unworthy favourites, and was in his turn deposed and murdered. His successor, Henry IV, was too busy securing his inheritance to be concerned with foreign quarrels. But Henry V, largely in order to divert the energies of the English baronage from plots and treason, renewed the war, quickly recovered the ground lost since Bretigny, and added Agincourt to the list of triumphs of the English long-bow. He died before he could complete the conquest of France; but his infant son, Henry VI, was actually crowned as King of France in Paris.

The French monarchy almost collapsed under the strain of this constant warfare. The Black Prince has survived in history as a pattern of chivalry, but he allowed every man, woman and child in Limoges to be massacred, and under his leadership great tracts of the French countryside were laid waste. The farms were burnt, crops destroyed, and cattle driven off; such peasants as escaped the English usually died of starvation. The military system of feudalism failed in its first duty of protection; indeed, before long, the greater feudal lords added to the miseries of France by private quarrels. The great houses of Burgundy and Armagnac fought for control over weak kings, and English successes after Agincourt were largely due to an alliance that had been concluded with the Dukes of Burgundy.

JOAN OF ARC

France's salvation came not from the feudal nobility, but from a peasant girl, Joan of Arc, from Domrémy in Lorraine. She believed that she heard in the church bells, as they sounded across the fields where she watched her father's cattle, the voices of saints urging her to save France. Though she was only eighteen and entirely un-lettered, she got to the French court to rouse the army leaders with her vision of St. Michael. Some believed her; others saw that her pious simplicity might at last inspire their disheartened troops to victory. Under the leadership of the "Maid", riding in armour at the head of the army, the English were, in fact, driven back and a new King of France, Charles VII, was crowned at Rheims. And though she was later captured by the English and Burgundians and burnt by them on a trumped-up charge of heresy and witchcraft, her work was finished within twenty years of her death. By 1453 the English held only Calais to remind them of the provinces they had ruled beyond the Channel. The French monarchy had recovered its dominions, but it had been in spite of the feudal nobility. The national revival inspired by Joan of Arc brought to birth new ambitions and ideas which could hardly be harmonized with medieval ideals and by the end of the Hundred Years' War France was entering on what was to be the last phase of her transition from a medieval to a modern nation with a strong central government.

THE END OF FEUDALISM IN ENGLAND

In a totally different way, the war altered the whole nature of feudal England. From the purely military standpoint, the old feudal levy, designed only for defence, was inadequate for long campaigns across the Channel. The king could not lead his vassals and their tenants on such an expedition; he needed professional soldiers. The better-known leaders, nobles or knights, would engage to furnish a given number of men and would recruit them independently. It soon became the practice for any great noble to retain a force of professional soldiers, men who slept under his roof, ate his food and wore his badge. Such retainers knew no other master than the man who paid them; they made the baron a far greater danger, both to the Crown and to his neighbours; when they were not actively engaged abroad, they were a permanent menace to the civil peace at home. The unemployed soldier who was not retained by some great man was equally a nuisance. He rarely settled back to a peaceful but dull life on the land or in trade, but roamed the country as a vagabond and a thief. These evils intensified during the long minority of Henry VI, and he was too feeble a ruler to deal firmly with them. The barons were a far greater menace to the Crown in the fifteenth century than ever before and, when Richard of York, the King's uncle, claimed the throne, the general discontent flared out in a series of civil wars known as the Wars of the Roses.

This long struggle, which marked the end of feudal England, did not greatly affect the lives of ordinary men and women. There are letters and records preserved which show that men of business, lawyers, merchants and farmers continued about their affairs without bothering overmuch about the fortunes of Lancaster or York. It was essentially a struggle between two great factions of the nobility; and although occasionally a retreating army, such as the Lancastrian before the battle of Towton in 1461, might lay waste the country through which it passed, there was no general devastation. The lack of a strong central government did, however, mean that highway robbery and piracy flourished unchecked. In Cornwall the whole countryside lived by piracy, the magistrates and landowners holding shares in the ventures and arranging the sale of captured goods, so that the London merchants, in particular, were prepared to support any man who would restore a strong and stable administration. It was this exasperated public opinion which was to be the main support of Henry VII when he set about reorganizing the government after the final defeat of the Yorkists at Bosworth in 1485.

In the great days of the Middle Ages, the Church had tried to make the nobility feel that they, too, were servants of God, entrusted with powers, duties and responsibilities for which they would be called to account. The ceremonies which attended the dubbing of a young knight had been meant to symbolize his enrolment as a soldier of Christ; and though there had always been men who would not accept the responsibilities implied by the laws of chivalry, kings and nobles had, on the whole, believed that they owed certain duties of protection and care in return for their power. During the thirteenth and fourteenth centuries, this ideal disappeared almost entirely. Nobles and knights who fought the Hundred Years' War regarded fighting partly as a sport, partly as a trade. They became more and more interested in capturing rich prisoners who could pay a handsome ransom for their release. It was possible to make a fortune out of a successful war, and the laws of chivalry degenerated into a complicated system of rules governing the new game. When the Black Prince took King John of France prisoner at Poitiers, he was careful to treat him with exquisite courtesy, even waiting on him at dinner; but to the weak and helpless, he was a scourge and a terror. Chivalry was restricted to the court and the castle, and its laws applied only to the fine ladies who watched their squires fight in their honour.

ISLAM IN EASTERN AND WESTERN EUROPE

Though many of those who went to the Holy Land were rogues, robbers, adventurers and fortune-hunters, the crusades could only have been possible while western Europe as a whole believed in the ideals of the medieval Church. The decay of these ideals, accompanied by the political chaos of the later Middle Ages, meant the end of any organized attempt to stem the main advance of Islam. The Eastern Empire held out bravely against a new enemy, the Ottoman Turks, who had begun to attack their frontier by the beginning of the fourteenth century. Constantinople was given a short respite while the Turks were engaged on their eastern front with the Mongol advance which wrought such havoc in Poland and Hungary; but the Emperors were distracted by the rebellions of Serbs and Bulgarians in their rear. When the Turks, under their most famous Sultan, Mohammed II, delivered their final assault, they met with little resistance. Western Christendom, divided against itself, could offer no help. By 1358 the Turks had already established themselves on European soil. A century later, as we have seen, Constantinople itself fell into their hands in 1453, and the whole of the Balkan peninsula lay at their mercy.

The other wing of the Mohammedan advance, once checked at Tours, was never again able to penetrate beyond the Pyrenees. But Europe made no concerted attempt to drive back the successive waves of the Moslem attack, and the Spaniards were left to reconquer their own land as best they might. After a long and heroic struggle, they were at length successful, though the last Moorish stronghold, the Kingdom of Granada, did not fall until 1492.

SPAIN AND PORTUGAL

This century-long struggle, in which the cities, such as Toledo and Saragossa, co-operated with the kings and nobles in the task of clearing the country of the infidel, bred in the Spaniards a proud tradition of isolation and independence. A few individual adventurers from elsewhere helped them, among them Simon de Montfort's father. But, on the whole, foreigners were a hindrance rather than a help; and the Black Prince even diverted his energies from French warfare for a time in order to invade northern Spain. In consequence Spain developed constitutionally more slowly than England or France. But even there, representative institutions, similar to the French Estates General, had been evolved by the fourteenth century. It is even possible that de Montfort first got his idea of calling the Commons into Parliament from the custom which prevailed in Spain of summoning two delegates from each city to assist the Crown by means of advice and subsidies.

The country, however, remained divided, even after the Moors had been driven back, into a number of kingdoms, such as Castile, Aragon, Valencia and Catalonia. Navarre, which lay across the Pyrenees, half in Spain and half in France, maintained its independence until the sixteenth century. Even when one man was strong enough to unite all the kingdoms under his rule, they still retained their separate Cortes, or Parliaments, and their own customs and administration. Portugal, in particular, worked out her own salvation. Her kings were able to drive back the Moors and to found a strong and prosperous state when the rest of Spain was fighting for mere survival. Thus Portugal was a far more civilized country at the end of the fourteenth century than any of her neighbours. Her flourishing ports enabled her to take the lead in maritime trade and exploration, and she was to become, for a time, the most prosperous nation in Europe.

By the middle of the fifteenth century, the feudal organization of western Europe had completely broken down. This was very largely due to political events, to the Hundred Years' War and the Wars of the Roses. But these political developments were only a part of a more fundamental change in the whole fabric of society. The decline of the Papacy was to follow the collapse of the Empire; and behind the collapse of those two great medieval institutions there were social and economic forces at work which were to make a new world.

CHAPTER 45

THE DECLINE OF THE ROMAN CHURCH

THE Papacy never really recovered from the long struggle with the Empire. It was only by bringing the French to Naples that the Popes had been able to defeat the Hohenstaufen; and they were to find their new allies as great a danger to Papal independence as the Germans had been. Moreover, the strongest spiritual weapons had been mis-used and were becoming discredited. Innocent III had been able to break King John of England by interdict and excommunication; the people, terrified by the closed churches, had turned against their king and supported the Pope. But very soon public opinion began to swing the other way, and men began to look to the king to protect them from the exaggerated claims of the court of Rome. Excom-munication had been made to look ridiculous when it was employed three times against Frederick II during one crusade. When Boniface VIII at the end of the thirteenth century made a last great attempt to assert the old Papal claims against the Kings of France and England, he found that his authority over their subjects had been sadly shaken and that Rome had lost much of its political power.

SECULAR THOUGHT AND THE CHURCH

There were other causes at work to undermine the prestige of the Church among ordinary men and women. Under kings like Edward I and Philip the Fair, England and France achieved a much higher degree of orderliness and prosperity. The Church was no longer the only civilizing influence in men's lives; peace was to be found outside the walls of monasteries and nunneries. The monarchies felt them-selves strong enough to take over the full responsibility for maintain-ing order and justice which they had hitherto shared with the Church; and even learning began to spread to laymen, and especially to the lawyers, on whom the Kings of France were relying more and more for government and administration. The result was that people began to question the rights and privileges enjoyed by churchmen every-where. The old quarrels over "criminous clerks" flared out afresh; and the freedom of Church lands from ordinary taxation was increasingly resented. Thus Parliament in England and the Estates General in France were both prepared to back their kings in a financial struggle against the Papacy.

The question of taxing Church lands came to a head in 1296, when the expense of his Scottish wars forced Edward I to demand a fifth of all the personal property of the clergy in England. Pope Boniface VIII retorted with the famous Bull, *Clericis laicos*, which forbade the clergy to pay any taxes whatever to secular governments and threa-tened any prince who demanded such taxes with excommunication.

This challenge was at once taken up by Philip the Fair, who forbade the export of gold or silver from France, and so cut off one of the main sources of Papal income. This forced Boniface to give way, and from then on, the clergy both in England and France were regularly taxed by the state. But before long, there were fresh quarrels between the French King and the Pope. Boniface was an arrogant bad-tempered old man, determined to become, in fact as well as in theory, the head of western Christendom; Philip, with the people of France, represented in the Estates General, behind him, was determined to stand out for what he believed to be his rights, and was prepared, if necessary, to have resort to force in order to obtain them.

THE TRAGEDY OF BONIFACE VIII

Boniface was able, before he surrendered, to give one last splendid demonstration of the power and magnificence of Rome and of the prestige which the Pope could still enjoy throughout western Europe. He celebrated in 1300 a great Jubilee to mark the beginning of a new century, and two million pilgrims flocked to Rome to pay homage at the shrine of St. Peter and leave money at his tomb. It was one of the largest gatherings of people the medieval world had ever seen. Though the streets of old Rome had been specially widened for the processions, hundreds of spectators were crushed to death. The amount of money which flowed into the coffers of the Papal Court was enormous; at the Tomb of St. Peter two men were kept continuously busy collecting with rakes the offerings of the faithful.

The Pope was encouraged to push his claims even further and to attempt to interfere in the internal affairs of France. His pretensions were firmly rejected by King and Estates General alike; and they brought down upon him an insult from which he never recovered. Nogaret, one of the French King's legal advisers, led a small band of soldiers to the Pope's palace at Anagni. There, where earlier Popes had solemnly excommunicated two Emperors, Boniface received them in full pontifical state, robed and crowned and surrounded by his Cardinals. Frenchmen, however, refused to be overawed by this display of spiritual authority. They heaped abuse on the raging, powerless old man and finally set on him and shamefully beat him. The townspeople of Anagni rose in his favour the next day and expelled Nogaret and his troops. But the Pope had been seriously injured and bitterly humiliated; he returned to Rome only to die, possibly as a result of those injuries.

Philip did not rest content with this partial and temporary victory. He wished to have some permanent security against the revival of such claims and pretensions on the part of the Papacy, and he was in a position to bring pressure to bear by force on the College of Cardinals. He compelled them to meet at Lyons on French territory and elect a French Archbishop as Boniface's successor. The new Pope remained for the rest of his life in France, living as the guest of each of the rich abbeys in turn; and he gave way to Philip on every point which had been disputed by Boniface. It was obviously very profitable to the French kings to have the Papacy thus under their control, and they finally established the Papal court at Avignon, on the southern frontiers of France, in a nominally independent principality which was in reality a French protectorate. There the Papacy remained, cut off from Rome, for the next seventy years.

THE LUXURIOUS CAPTIVITY OF THE CHURCH

There were many evil results of this "Babylonish Captivity of the Church", as it was called. In the first place, the Popes lost the prestige which they had derived from their historic association with the city of Rome, so long the centre of the western world. It was, moreover, essential that the Papacy, if it was to lead and represent a united Christendom, should enjoy an international independence, and its subservience to France from 1305 till 1377 naturally undermined its authority with the rest of Europe. Finally, the Papal court at Avignon became much more splendid and luxurious. A magnificent new palace was built and decorated by the best artists and craftsmen to be found in Europe. There, surrounded by rich and pleasure-loving cardinals who were hardly distinguishable from worldly nobles and performed few of their ecclesiastical functions, the Popes lived the lives of great princes. But all this magnificence was developed at a time when they had lost the revenues from the estates around Rome which had previously helped very largely to support the expenses incurred by their court.

They were forced, therefore, to develop a new system of Church taxation to maintain their new splendour. They began to demand the first year's income from every newly appointed bishop or abbot. All fees for lawsuits heard at the Papal court were raised and the cost of dispensations increased. High charges were made for confirming the appointments of bishops and archbishops, and certain benefices in every country were claimed as the special property of the Papacy and reserved for Papal favourites, who enjoyed their revenues but seldom troubled to take up their duties.

Thanks to their control over Avignon, the French kings were able to protect themselves from the worst results of these abuses; they even won further concessions from the Papacy, and were given leave to suppress the order of the Templars and appropriate the lands and revenues accumulated by the knights. Nothing shows, perhaps, so clearly the decline of the Popes from their proud position as leaders of Christianity against the infidel as this sacrifice of a military order of the Church. But elsewhere in Europe, the new financial policy of the Papacy roused universal resentment. In Germany, there was no central government strong enough to resist, and the country continued for two centuries to be exploited by Papal tax-collectors, who left behind them a discontent which was to play an important part in the history of the Reformation. In England, King and Parliament combined to prevent the worst abuses of the new system; the Statute of Provisors was passed to prevent the granting in advance of English benefices to foreigners, and that of Praemunire to limit and control the number of expensive appeals to the Papal court. But even these measures failed to stop the steady drain of money out of the country, and Parliament declared in 1376 that the Pope raised (in England) five times as much money in taxes as the King.

It was plain that the authority and prestige of the Papacy could be restored only by a return to Rome and independence. But the first attempt to bring this about only made the situation worse. In 1378, Pope Urban VI took up his residence in Rome and began a much-needed reform of the Church "in head and members". He failed, however, to carry with him a powerful party among the cardinals, who claimed that they had been terrified into electing him by fear of the Roman mob. Rome had fallen into a sad state of disrepair during the absence of the Papal court, and her ruined churches and palaces seemed gloomy and uncomfortable after the splendour and luxury of Avignon. The rebellious cardinals therefore retired once more to Avignon, and there set up a rival Pope, Clement VII, who was at once recognized by the King of France. This was not a case of a puppet anti-pope, such as had been set up before by the Emperors. The Roman mob had, in fact, brought pressure to bear on the cardinals at the election of Urban.

THE GREAT SCHISM

Italy naturally supported Urban; and England's hostility to France put her in the same camp. Scotland, perpetually at war with England, supported Clement. Thus there followed for forty years "the Great Schism"; for when these two men died, each college of cardinals elected a successor. There continued to be two Popes, each claiming the allegiance of all Christendom, and the confusion spread into every country in western Europe. Both Popes appointed successors to vacant benefices, so that there were rival claimants to every important office in the Church.

In Germany, France and England the rulers had, since the tenth century, fairly consistently opposed all Papal claims and pretensions which threatened their authority or their financial interests. They had been helped to resist Boniface VIII by the new class of lawyers, the richer merchants and the smaller gentry who made up the Third Estate in France and the Commons in the English Parliament. Now, however, there appeared, especially in England, as a result of the Babylonish Captivity and the Great Schism, a new type of opposition which was genuinely popular. There had long been a general discontent with the riches and privileges possessed by the monks and higher clergy, and this tendency had been clearly voiced in poems such as Langland's *Piers Plowman* and Chaucer's *Canterbury Tales*.

Langland expressed the grievances of a downtrodden class which looked in vain for relief to wealthy bishops and a corrupt priesthood. He was no revolutionary and he loved the Church. But he found all classes among the clergy ready to deceive the people for their own profit. Bishops allowed their seals to be used on "Pardons", which were sold to ignorant men who thought they could buy forgiveness of their sins, so that:

> "The parish priest and the pardoner part the silver
> That the poor of the parish should have, but for them."

And though he admired the ideal of poverty which had originally inspired St. Francis, he found now everywhere friars who "preached to the people for their own profit". This was the dissatisfaction which was to drive the peasants to revolt both in England and France before the end of the century.

MORAL DECLINE OF CHURCH AND COURT

Chaucer, writing at the same time, gives a similar picture, though from a different standpoint. Chaucer was more of a satirist, a polished court-poet who did not clamour for reform, but was content to depict for his readers the types into which church men and women were degenerating—the monk with a passion for hunting, the pardoner who sold pig's bones as holy relics, the silly affected abbess with her worldly ways and her lap-dogs, and finally, as the only lovable cleric, the poor parson:

> "Christe's law and his apostles twelve
> He taught, but first he followed it himself."

Both in the court and in the country, men had already noted a steady decay in the morals and standards of the Church everywhere. The last and most dangerous attack came from the University of Oxford, when the scandals of Avignon drove John Wycliffe into open revolt.

Wycliffe was a much more learned man than either Langland or Chaucer and, unlike them, he had the courage to propose a thorough and basic reform of the Church. The abuses of which he complained were the same: "Our priests are so busy about worldly occupations that they seem better bailiffs or reeves than ghostly priests of Jesus Christ." But his attack was more open. He began by challenging the right of the Pope to levy any money at all in England, and was gradually drawn into a whole series of disputes with the Papacy. His writings and teachings were condemned by the Church, but he had powerful protectors at court, and his pamphlets were widely read among the educated upper classes in England. The University of Oxford, where he was a popular lecturer and teacher, supported him almost to a man, in his attacks on the worldliness and slackness of the clergy and on the excesses of outward observances, such as pilgrimages and indulgences. Indeed, as long as Wycliffe confined himself to pleading for a simpler and more pious religion, he had the majority of well-informed public opinion behind him. In the end, however, he went too far. He attacked the Papacy itself and re-developed the old Waldensian doctrines about the mass and the position of the priesthood, which the Church condemned as heretical.

TEACHINGS OF WYCLIFFE AND HUSS

One of Wycliffe's great sources of strength had been the fact that he wrote in English, instead of the more scholarly Latin or French, and so appealed directly to the ordinary people. He and the group of learned friends who surrounded him at Oxford had also under-taken the translation of the Bible into English, a magnificent piece of work which laid the foundation of modern English prose; and he had established an order of "simple priests", poor folk who went about expounding the scriptures from the new Bible and striving to teach the value of true piety unencumbered by outward forms and cere-monies. Wycliffe and his priests were accused of stirring up unrest and disorder, and their teaching was said to have been one of the indirect causes of the Peasants' Revolt. In face of this accusation, and of the fact that he had clearly become a heretic as regards doctrine, his powerful friends could no longer protect him. Under pressure from the government and the Papacy, the University was forced to condemn one of its most able and popular teachers and to burn all his published books in a great bonfire in Carfax square, at the centre of the city. He himself was allowed to retire to a country parish and to die there in peace, though his body was later dug up and burnt. The movement which he had started continued for a time to flourish. In the end, Parliament and King turned against these "Lollards", as they were called, and started a severe persecution which appears to have been successful. There are few traces of Lollardy to be found in England in the later fifteenth century, though it is probable that some of the teachings of Wycliffe survived in the memories of ordinary folk to make England an easy convert to the Protestant Reformation a century later.

The immediate effect of Wycliffe's teaching in England was not very great. But Richard II of England had married a Bohemian queen, and the close connection established between the two countries for a time enabled the Lollard doctrines to spread to Bohemia. There, too, they found a home in Prague University, where John Huss showed himself even more of a revolutionary and a puritan than Wycliffe. Huss was one of the first great nationalist leaders, as well as a religious reformer, and his strong opposition to the penetration of his country by German immigrants had already won him a large following among the Czech natives. He attacked the Church from the same standpoint as the Lollards, denouncing the excessive ceremonies and pointing out that no authority could be found in the New Testament for the great wealth, privileges and immunities enjoyed by the clergy.

Huss pushed his attack on the priesthood even farther than Wycliffe had done, and announced the doctrine that people ought not to be forced to obey the spiritual authority of those who were themselves living in mortal sin: that is to say, that the teachings of a wicked and loose-living priest should not be regarded, since the teacher himself was certain of damnation. And this he finally pushed even farther to its logical conclusion, denying the authority of secular rulers, kings or ministers who did not live according to the Law of Christ. Such a doctrine obviously undermined all law and order, whether civil or ecclesiastical, and defied every organized institution both of Church and State. It roused the immediate opposition of the whole Church and of the Emperor; and the Hussite movement, which spread rapidly throughout Bohemia, became another of the crying scandals which threatened to undermine the unity and prestige of the Church.

It was clear that the ordinary machinery of the Church for preventing heresy and controlling the clergy had broken down completely. The Papacy, divided against itself, could not lead a crusade against the Hussites as it had against the Albigensians and Waldensians. The Inquisition, set up under the Dominicans by Innocent III as a special tribunal for discovering and dealing with heretics, clearly could not serve two masters, one at Avignon and one at Rome. The Friars themselves had forsaken the old rules of poverty and simplicity laid down by Francis and Dominic; they had begun to accumulate wealth and to live in houses, instead of wandering as beggars among the people. Monks and nuns were often allowed to leave their cloisters on purely worldly business, and many of them lived lives which were no better than those of ordinary laymen. There were bishops who lived openly in luxury and sin, and the complaints voiced by Langland, Wycliffe and Huss were clearly only the echo of a widespread discontent among laymen in general. In a time of great misery, when thousands were dying from plague and the Hundred Years' War was exhausting England and devastating France, the Pope had become, in the words of King Edward III, the shearer rather than the shepherd of his flock.

AN AGE OF MYSTIC SAINTS

This corruption within the Church did not undermine the religious outlook of people in general; the enthusiasm roused by the preaching of Huss and Wycliffe shows how anxious men were for reform and unity. The rich still gave money for the building of churches and the endowment of chantries where masses could be said for the souls of the departed; and it was an age of great mystic saints. In a small house at Siena, which can still be seen, St. Catherine showed that a life of religious contemplation could be lived in the midst of a family, maintaining intercourse with the world, and by her writings and example she inspired others to seek salvation. It was her influence which was chiefly responsible for persuading Pope Urban to make his residence in Rome. In Germany and the Low Countries, during the fifteenth century, there grew up a whole school of mystic Christianity which sought to return direct to the simple truths taught by Christ; its greatest representative was Thomas à Kempis, whose *Imitation of Christ* has been an inspiration to Christian men and women ever since. But more was needed than religious feeling, however sincere and widespread, if the Church, as an institution embodying the unity of Christendom, was to be saved from the effects of corruption and disorganization which assailed it.

ATTEMPTS TO HEAL THE GREAT SCHISM

Nothing perhaps shows so clearly the strength of the medieval sense of the unity of Christendom as the way in which western Europe banded together to put an end to the scandals of the Great Schism. The Papacy was divided against itself; the Empire had ceased to have any real claim to universal sovereignty; Germany and Italy were torn by internal feuds and wars; France and England were absorbed in the long struggle of the Hundred Years' War. Despite all these disruptive tendencies, the Church was able to unite Europe for the common purpose of saving the unity of the Catholic faith.

There had, of course, been other influences at work to make it easier to bring Europe together than it had been in the time of the crusades: men were no longer tied to a single patch of land; there were large trading cities and improved roads, and a steadily increasing number of universities. The political unity of Christendom had depended, in the early Middle Ages, on the goodwill of a few powerful individuals, Popes and bishops, emperors and kings. Now it rested on a surer and wider foundation. The movement to put an end to the worst abuses within the Church by a co-operative effort was supported as strongly by laymen, lawyers and merchants as by the rank and file of Churchmen. It was the University of Paris which first, in 1381, put forward the idea of a General Council of the Church to decide between the rival Popes and restore unity and order.

In the days of the later Roman Empire, the General Council had been the supreme authority in the Christian Church. The bishops gathered together at Nicaea in the reign of Constantine had formulated the Creed. During the next five centuries, there had been many such gatherings for the purpose of re-defining Christian doctrine and suppressing heresy. Men had believed these Councils to be inspired by the Holy Spirit and had recognized their decrees as binding, even on Popes and Patriarchs. Since the division of the Eastern and Western Churches, there had been other Councils in the West, but these had been called by the Pope, presided over by him or his representatives, and had been treated by him as consultative assemblies, whose decrees were valueless unless confirmed and published by him. The Pope's claim to be above all earthly judges, the sole authority in spiritual matters, was naturally weakened by the schism. Men began to seek for some higher power which would better represent the will and conscience of an undivided Church. Already Wycliffe and Huss had refused to accept the pretensions of the Papacy, since they could find no justification for them in Holy Scripture; by the beginning of the fifteenth century many loyal and sincere churchmen wanted to return to the historic practice of the early Church.

There were cardinals both at Avignon and Rome who desired the end of the schism, and they at last, in 1409, decided to put themselves at the head of this growing body of public opinion, and summoned a General Council of the Church to meet at Pisa. The reforming cardinals, bishops from all over Europe and representatives of many of the kings met there, and with solemn ceremony called upon both Popes to appear at the doors of the cathedral, that the Council might judge their claims. Neither of them appeared, and the Council, rather rashly and hastily, declared them both automatically deposed for not answering the summons, and elected yet a third person to take their place. The result was confusion worse confounded. There were now three men who claimed to be Pope, since neither of the two original Popes would recognize the right of the Council to discuss the matter. The new Pope elected by the Council, John XXIII, was a man of doubtful character, with a shady past as a soldier of fortune: no real attempt had yet been made to decide between the rival claims of Rome and Avignon to be the headquarters of the Church.

LEADERS OF THE CHURCH MEET AT CONSTANCE

The increased scandal, however, provoked Europe to a further attempt at remedy, and within five years, another and greater Council met at Constance. John XXIII himself was persuaded to summon it and preside over it. The Emperor Sigismund, who had taken the lead in the preliminary negotiations, was present, and with him, twenty-three cardinals, thirty-three archbishops and bishops, one hundred and fifty abbots and many hundreds of laymen, nobles, lawyers and scholars. It was one of the most imposing gatherings the western world had ever seen; it made a genuine effort to solve the problems of Christendom, and it was, on the whole, successful. It very quickly settled the main scandal of the Church by deposing all three Popes and inducing them to accept its decision and submit to the authority of its own new Pope, Martin V. But on the wider questions of general reform and the suppression of heresy, it was less successful.

One of the motives which had inspired Sigismund to support the idea of a Council had been the desire to strengthen his hands against the Hussites, who were not only heretics, but rebels against the authority of a German Emperor. Under his leadership, the Council of Constance had at once summoned Huss himself to appear before it under safe-conduct and answer the charges of heresy; and Huss, trusting the good faith of the safe-conduct, and convinced, in any case, that he could convert the Council to his views, came with several of his more important disciples to argue his case. He was wrong on both points. The Council decided, as soon as he arrived, that the safe-conduct, which had been issued by the Emperor, could not be respected in the case of a heretic. There was no possibility of reconciling the views of Huss, which in their extreme form amounted to a denial of all regularly constituted authority, whether spiritual or temporal, with those of a Council called to re-establish the authority of a united Catholic Church. The Council had little difficulty in establishing the fact that Huss was a heretic, and after a vain series of attempts to get him to retract his doctrines, handed him over to the secular authorities, who, without any further enquiry, burnt him along with one of his disciples before the gates of Constance, and threw his ashes into the Rhine so that later generations should not recover and worship them.

The Council had boldly claimed the right to reform even the Papacy. But it proved incapable of carrying out the thorough reform of the Church which had been desired. The abuses were clearly recognized by the more earnest churchmen, but it was difficult to find a method of remedying them. The Council was too large and cumbrous a body to deal effectively with such a problem, which could only be solved by the Papacy, working through the ordinary machinery of the Church government. After three years of fruitless debate, the Council broke up, without having done anything important towards a general reform. It was obviously impossible, in days when even a short journey was a slow, expensive and dangerous undertaking, for such a body to assemble regularly and often enough to manage the ordinary government of the Church; nor could it very profitably discuss details of reform. But there was some justice in its claim that the worst abuses had crept in because no general councils had been called to settle disputed points of doctrine and limit the activities and pretensions of the Papacy. For a short time, indeed, the doctrine that a General Council was superior to the Pope was maintained; and before 1450, two more Councils were called to complete the work which had been commenced at Constance.

THE COUNCILS OF BASEL AND FLORENCE

It had been left to the Emperor to stamp out the Hussite heresy, since the Council had no force which it could employ. The Germans did, in fact, undertake a series of crusades against the Bohemians, but without any success. The Hussites fought desperately, with all the enthusiasm inspired by religion and by the new feeling of nationalism which Huss had preached among them. The crusaders were decisively defeated; and at the conclusion of twelve years of fighting, it was felt that it would be better to preserve the unity of the Church by finding some suitable compromise through which the Hussites might be reconciled to the Roman Church.

The Council of Basel, which Martin V called in 1431, succeeded in making an agreement with the more moderate of the Bohemians which put an end to the war. But apart from that, it achieved nothing. It wasted eighteen years in futile debates on reform without reaching any decision, and in quarrelling with the Pope. Meanwhile the Pope had summoned another Council to Florence to attempt to reunite the whole of Christendom. The Eastern Emperors were being hard pressed by the Turks, and they turned in desperation to the West for help, hoping that another crusade might come, not to recover the Holy Land, but to save Constantinople itself from capture. It was in support of this policy that the Patriarch of Constantinople came to the Council of Florence to seek a reconciliation with the Western Church. Such an agreement was in fact patched up, though the Patriarch was immediately denounced by the Eastern bishops on his return for having accepted, even though in a very vague formula, the headship of the Pope.

The general reform of the whole Church which had been expected from the conciliar movement was never carried out. The outward unity of the Church under a single head was restored; but the abuses which had resulted from the Babylonish Captivity and the Schism remained practically untouched. There were still voices, both within the Church and without, which clamoured for reform, but the restored Papacy did not put itself at the head of such a movement. The Popes of the fifteenth century were more interested in re-establishing their own authority. They felt, and they were largely right, that many of the evils of the past hundred years had been due to the fact that the Papacy had not been able to remain independent of political rulers. They believed that they could not preserve their position as impartial rulers of the Church if, at any moment, the Emperor, the King of Naples, or the King of France, could bring pressure to bear on them by force. To prevent this they devoted all their energies to building up round Rome a principality strong enough to resist any attempt to bully them or to dictate their course of action.

CHAPTER 46

THE NEW SOCIETY AND THE NEW STATE

THE decay of the great institutions which had embodied the ideals of medieval civilization was only the first stage in a general process of disintegration. The break-up of the feudal system destroyed the very framework of the Middle Ages. It was inevitable that, as the control exercised by Church and State relaxed, the administrative organization which made both function and privilege dependent on land-tenure should also perish. There was one external factor, in particular, which hastened this process.

In the middle of the fourteenth century, a plague from the East had swept across Europe with devastating effects. It is calculated that in England this "Black Death" killed between a third and a half of the population, causing a very serious shortage of labour. Landlords who no longer had serfs enough to till their fields were inevitably tempted to offer wages which would attract men from elsewhere; serfs were naturally eager to better themselves by leaving the thatched hovels to which they had been tied. Hitherto it had been almost impossible for them to escape. There was a maxim that "Town air makes free". The serf who could reach a town and remain hidden there for a year and a day gained his freedom; it was sometimes possible for him to take minor orders in the Church. But now there were greater opportunities for the common people.

SERFDOM DISAPPEARS FROM ENGLAND

Kings and Parliament combined to try to prevent the peasant from thus taking advantage of his increased value in the labour market; but the harsh laws passed for the purpose only succeeded in provoking the Peasants' Revolt of 1381. The miseries caused by the Black Death itself and by the oppressions of landlords produced a movement which was almost communist in outlook. The teaching of Wycliffe and his poor priests had already prepared the ground, and the country people were easily roused to fury by the slogan of a renegade preaching friar named John Ball:

> "When Adam delved and Eve span,
> Who was then the gentleman?"

Under leaders such as Wat the Tyler and Jack Cade, the peasants marched on London to enforce their claims to economic freedom. The revolt was, in the end, crushed by the government. But it proved impossible to keep the old laws in force; and serfdom or villeinage rapidly disappeared from England.

This process, whereby the villeins became paid labourers, or tenant-farmers who paid their rent in money instead of in service, began the break-up of the manorial system. Landlords were no longer able to find labour enough to till large areas of arable land and, to save themselves from ruin, began to put it down to grass and use it for sheep. Before long, the already flourishing wool trade had grown into the staple and most prosperous industry of the country. Landlords were tempted to extend their farms at the expense of the old common lands of the villagers, which they fenced off for their own use; the villeins, though they had gained the freedom to move from one place to another, to marry as they pleased and to serve whom they would, often found themselves deprived of the lands on which they had depended for a living. But this was an indirect and accidental result of what was, in fact, the final liberation of that class which had in actual fact been little better off than slaves.

In this respect, England was far ahead of the rest of Europe. In France, in the middle of the fourteenth century, the peasants had been driven by the oppressions of their landlords and by famine, plague, and miseries caused by the Hundred Years' War, into revolts known as the *Jacquerie*. These risings, however, were suppressed as ruthlessly as in England, and did not have such immediate economic and social results, though the same process was beginning. The feudal lords were strong enough, however, to maintain the old system for much longer, and the disappearance of serfdom in most parts of France was long delayed. Elsewhere in Europe, in Spain and Italy, in Germany and Austria, and in parts of Scandinavia, it survived until the eighteenth century. The nobles clung to their rights with obstinate tenacity; King Christian II of Denmark was to lose his throne in 1535 for trying to liberate the serfs; and in Russia, serfdom was not abolished until 1861. This early development of a strong and independent class of yeoman farmers was of incalculable benefit to England; more than anything else, it made the English constitution and government in later ages much more stable than those of other European nations.

HOW THE GUILD SYSTEM WORKED

There were important social changes taking place in the towns as well as in the country; and these were not peculiar to any one part of Europe, but were similar almost everywhere. Trade and industry had depended in the early Middle Ages entirely on the Craft Guilds. Every town worker had to be apprenticed to a master and learn his trade. Once qualified, he might work as a journeyman, and if he was thrifty and hard-working, he might hope in time to become a master himself, with an establishment of his own and journeymen working for him. This entailed both privileges and responsibilities.

The whole Guild system was a mass of careful regulations and restrictions. It was the medieval attempt to organize town life and industry on the same principle as that which underlay the feudal organization on the land. Property and the exercise of rights were to be dependent on the performance of valuable functions. Every man must have a place in society and do his duty there without infringing his neighbour's rights or exploiting the public. The apprentice rules were there to ensure that every man was competent to produce good work. There were restrictions on prices so that no man should charge too much or attempt to undercut his rivals by putting cheap and shoddy goods on the market. The master craftsman, moreover, must keep a shop as well as a workshop and sell his own goods direct to the public. For medieval society had no use for a middleman who took a profit without actually producing anything in return, since there was little trade between towns and men produced everything they used locally. By this means it was hoped to create and maintain a contented and prosperous social system.

The growth of inter-city and international trade, due largely to contact with the East in the period of the Crusades, had played havoc with all these restrictions and rules. The merchant was essentially a middleman; and the Merchant Guilds, Grocers, Mercers, Fishmongers and the rest, obviously could not for long be fitted into the organization which had been found suitable for Tailors, Carpenters and Wheelwrights. The merchant naturally sought to break through the close barriers which every city had set up against foreign trade; and his success in so doing had brought to the towns of northern Europe a steady increase in wealth and prosperity from the thirteenth century onwards. But this wealth tended to be concentrated in the hands of a few men. The merchant was a man who needed capital; for he might have to wait months for the delivery of a cargo before he could realize his profit on it. This was only possible for a few.

NEW CLASS DISTINCTIONS BASED ON WEALTH

The result was a fundamental change in the whole constitution of town life. Hitherto the Guilds had all shared equally in the freedom of their cities and in the election of officers and delegates. Now the richer merchants began to make themselves into a privileged class. Families accumulated wealth and formed a city aristocracy, patricians who did all they could to keep the government of the city in their own hands and to pass their privileges on to their children. At Lübeck, for example, there was one guild containing all the richer merchants, the Zirkelbrüder—Brothers of the Belt. These men gradually ousted the smaller guilds and gathered all municipal government and election into their own hands. This development in the Hanseatic cities was soon to be found everywhere. In Venice, government fell into the hands of a Doge and a Council of Ten. It might still be possible in London for a Dick Whittington to rise from the humblest origin to be Lord Mayor; but, on the whole, power tended to fall into the hands of the Mercers, who controlled the wool trade with Flanders, or of the Goldsmiths, who, by the very nature of their craft, became some of the earliest capitalists and the first bankers and lenders of money.

It was not long before such men began to wield more power than some of the feudal nobility. Their wealth was more productive and more easily realizable than that of a landowner, and their support, in the long run, more valuable to a government than that of the nobility. They could provide the means whereby a king could pay an army of mercenaries which would be far more efficient than a feudal levy. In some countries, this reality was recognized early. In England, it soon became the practice to knight the Lord Mayor of London. Rich merchants would invest their savings in country estates, and their families within a few generations were indistinguishable from the old aristocracy; the country gained immensely by this steady recruiting of the ruling class from among the most able of the city merchants.

In Germany the nobles fought hard to preserve the privileges of hereditary rank; and though a knight might gratefully marry the well-dowered daughter of a mayor, very few of the great merchant families of the German cities were ennobled until long after the fifteenth century had ended.

In Italy, the process was reversed. Elsewhere there was a tendency for the nobles to remain proudly aloof on the land and to despise the merchant as low born, though they might covet his wealth. So it was in Germany, where the Free Imperial Cities became almost a separate community with a separate civilization. But in Italy the nobles tended from the beginning to concentrate in the towns, to build their palaces there and to share in the city government. Merchant and noble met on common ground. Ceaseless faction fights gave any able man, whatever his origin, the chance of power. Thus the Visconti, having climbed to wealth and influence by Church preferment, seized power in Milan and ruled there as tyrants for two hundred years; they were succeeded by a professional soldier, Francesco Sforza, whom the city had got in to help against Venice and then could not get out again. The Medici, one of many banking families of Florence, rose first to the government of the city-republic and finally to equality with the oldest royal houses. Popes Leo X and Clement VII were both Medicis; and two of the Medici women married Kings of France in the sixteenth century.

RISE OF THE CAPITALIST CLASS

It is impossible to describe in detail the rise of the merchant class to power in the cities of Europe. As prosperity spread along the trade routes which radiated from Venice, there was much the same result everywhere. The Craft Guilds lost their influence and the journeymen became mere paid artizans who no longer owned their tools or took any share in city administration. Power and wealth were alike concentrated in the hands of rich burghers. At Augsburg and along the Rhine, in the Hanseatic cities, in Paris and London, Antwerp and Ghent, and as far afield as Copenhagen and Malmö, the process was the same; and it produced far-reaching results. For it substituted a society based on money and material wealth for one which had depended on land service, and it made the banker a far more important person than the Marcher Earl.

The rise of the banking industry depended directly on the decline of the influence of the Church; medieval theologians had taught that usury, the lending of money for interest, was contrary to Christian belief, and for a long time the Church was strong enough to enforce her views. Jews, however, were obviously not subject to any such restriction. The crusades and the Guilds had broken their position as traders, but their wide dispersal and their linguistic skill helped them to make money-lending a Jewish monopoly. This privilege was largely responsible for the early unpopularity of the Jews: men naturally resented such a monopoly, particularly when they themselves happened to be in debt; and it became a popular move for any government which was in difficulties to turn on the Jews. Their race was therefore subject to constant and brutal persecution. In every city they were made to live in special quarters, known as ghettos, and to wear a distinctive dress, sometimes marked by a yellow streak. Pious Christians spat on them as they passed in the street, and princes in financial difficulties would imprison and torture them to extort their secret hoards of wealth. Money-lending was thus a dangerous occupation, as is shown by the fact that the standard rate of interest in the Middle Ages was 40%; and the combination of religious hatred with financial jealousy has persisted to this day.

INTERNATIONAL BANKING : THE MEDICI AND THE FUGGERS

The richer merchants of northern Italy soon rebelled against the Church's restrictions. In Lombardy, international banking had already been developed on a large scale by the fourteenth century. Lombard Street in London still commemorates the fact that Edward III borrowed much of the money for his campaigns in France from Italy—so much, in fact, that many Lombard firms were ruined when he went bankrupt at the end of his reign. Venice and Genoa both had banks of their own, which later put up big sums of money for voyages of discovery; but it was in Florence that the greatest of the Italian banking houses, that of the Medici, grew up. Early banking was indistinguishable from pawnbroking, since kings were usually the largest borrowers, and the best security they had to offer was their crown jewels. Pawnshops still remind us of the hold which Florence maintained over international banking in the fourteenth and fifteenth centuries by using as their sign the three golden balls which were the Medici coat-of-arms.

In the fifteenth century, the centres of European prosperity began to shift northwards as the advance of the Turks cut off portions of the Venetian trade and gave northern and western trade-routes a new importance. The merchants of Augsburg, the great distributing centre for all the merchandise which came over the Brenner Pass, had early developed a wealth and influence which rivalled that of the Italians. They were in a better position than the Medici to establish branches in the cities of the Netherlands, and the control of European banking passed from Florence to the greatest of the Augsburg families, the Fuggers. At the beginning of the sixteenth century, the Fuggers were probably the most powerful family in Europe. Even the Habsburgs were dependent on them. "It is well known", old Jacob Fugger wrote to the Emperor Charles V in 1523, "that Your Imperial Majesty could never have won the Roman Crown without my help." By 1550, the Fuggers and their great rivals, the Welsers of Hamburg, had control of more than half the revenues of Spain and Austria. They were partially ruined by Habsburg bankruptcy later in the century, but they remained for a long time a power in the European banking world, and were forerunners of the Rothschilds.

These new trends naturally affected women as well as men. In the early Middle Ages the wives of common men had been regarded and treated as chattels, unpaid domestic drudges. Very often peasants compelled their women-folk to do the heavy work in the fields, a practice which survives in some districts to this day. Even among the ruling class, a woman was allowed but little freedom of action or of thought.

Unmarried, she was perhaps a useful pawn in negotiations; if she were well-dowered, she was a valuable acquisition to a man with a landed estate. Once married, her duty was to make a submissive house-wife and to produce an heir; if she could not find a husband, she was expected to disappear into a nunnery. The age of chivalry had improved her status; she became an object of romantic worship, the disposer of favours in the tournament-yard and the recipient of courtly admiration in verse. But though chivalry taught the service of all who were weak and defenceless, the benefits of its lesson were confined, on the whole, to well-born ladies. The wife of the farmer or tradesman did not share in the new romantic attitude. Nevertheless, women were naturally among the first to benefit from the introduction of new luxuries and comforts into the home. The merchant's wife had silks and satins quite as costly as those of the court lady.

The wife of the emancipated serf became a farmer's wife, with activities about the farmyard and in the farmhouse kitchen very similar to those practised there to-day.

It would, in fact, be a mistake to think that the position of women has become very startlingly changed and emancipated in modern times. The wife of Bath whom Chaucer put into his *Canterbury Tales* was probably quite a good example of her kind, though she may have been fatter and possessed of a coarser sense of humour than most. She contrived to ride away on pilgrimage quite unaccompanied; there was nothing dependent or submissive about her.

COMMERCE AND THE ROYAL POWER

Such far-reaching social and economic changes inevitably produced political changes as well. It was no longer sufficient if town walls protected the citizens themselves. They needed efficient policing of the great highways of trade everywhere, prompt and even-handed justice, and the preservation of order and peace, such as could not be provided by local authorities. So there was a universal demand among the commercial classes during the fifteenth century for efficient centralized government which would prevent private wars among the feudal nobility and curb the thieving traditions of a class such as the Knights of Germany. Kings found a new and powerful ally in their struggle with refractory barons; and a more absolutist

An illumination from the title page of a grammar, printed in 1516 in York, showing a Renaissance schoolmaster.

An illustration showing a printing press of the kind in use in 1520. Each page was "pulled" by hand.

The great basilica of St. Peter's, Rome. The indulgences issued in connexion with its rebuilding led to Luther's attack on Roman Catholicism and the beginning of Protestantism.

Bronze statue of Perseus with the Medusa's head by the Italian Renaissance artist Benvenuto Cellini.

Virgin and Child by Leonardo da Vinci, the most universal genius of the Renaissance.

Bacchus and Ariadne by Titian the great sixteenth-century Venetian master. It is now in the National Gallery, London.

type of state was evolved to meet the need; for the merchant did not, as a rule, care if the form of government was that of tyranny so long as it proved itself able to keep the peace and foster trade.

The French monarchy, under Louis XI, was one of the first to respond to this need. Louis had little of the glamour which was attached to a great medieval king. He was crafty, mean and suspicious, and quite unscrupulous in his methods. He set himself to perform one great task, the establishment of royal authority throughout France, and he did not care how he did it. His shabbily dressed, unimposing figure was often to be seen at the dinner-tables of the rich merchants of Tours, whom he delighted to favour; but among the nobles he was feared and hated. He found France still disordered after the Hundred Years' War. He left her comparatively at peace, with royal justice re-established throughout the land, and with all the great feudatories, save the Dukes of Burgundy and Brittany, brought into subjection under the Crown. His successor married Anne, the heiress to Brittany; and the end of the century saw France a compact and powerful nation-state, more prosperous than ever before in her turbulent history and relatively free from internal disputes.

PROGRESS OF CENTRALIZED GOVERNMENT IN EUROPE

In England, the same function was performed by the Tudors, the new dynasty which emerged triumphant from the Wars of the Roses at the battle of Bosworth in 1485. Henry VII was also mean and crafty, and quite ruthless in his dealings with the few great nobles who had survived the butchery of the civil wars. He was often tyrannical, and had no hesitation in attacking privilege and immunity, however well sanctioned they might be by law. In this he found enthusiastic support from the House of Commons, which expressed the opinion of merchants and lawyers. His councillors he drew from this same class, men of undistinguished birth who owed everything to him: they would have been denounced as favourites by the barons in earlier days, but they embodied the spirit of the new age. Elsewhere in northern Europe this nationalist and centralizing tendency was not so well marked. Scotland remained backward and disunited, and in the Scandinavian countries the attempts to restore law and order were defeated by internal jealousies and rivalries between the three lands, Norway, Sweden and Denmark, which had been united under the rule of one family by the Union of Kalmar in the fourteenth century.

In the Netherlands, however, there was a serious attempt to re-create the old central Rhine kingdom which had existed for a short time after the death of Charlemagne. The Dukes of Burgundy, who had been a thorn in the flesh of the French monarchy during the war, had accumulated a large number of Duchies and Counties by marriage and purchase, until they ruled over the whole of the area known as the Netherlands and as far south as the Alps, with only a small gap

R   (H.W.)

in Lorraine. Duke Philip the Good tried to weld this diverse inheritance into a solid nation. By sound finance and peaceful foreign policy, he built up the most prosperous state in Europe, with a court of unrivalled magnificence. But his son, Charles the Bold, ruined much of his work by a lifetime of wars. He tried to join up his lands in north and south by annexing Lorraine, a policy that involved him in war with the Swiss, in which he was defeated and killed. The Netherlands did not go to pieces after his death, though Louis XI seized the opportunity of recovering the old Duchy of Burgundy. But they were very soon involved in the Habsburg web of matrimonial intrigue, and were ultimately to be attached to Spain, with disastrous consequences to their prosperity.

Central and eastern Europe once again failed to achieve the efficient centralized governments which they needed. The Emperor Maximilian was too wayward a genius and too keen a huntsman; he had not the patience to do for Germany what Louis XI had done for France. Sometimes princes or local leagues of cities kept order over a limited area. One such league, which had sprung from a rebellion against the tyrannical overlordship of the Habsburgs, was establishing itself as the independent federation of Switzerland, controlling the central Alps between Italy and Germany; it was organized on sturdy republican lines which made it possible to hold together in one community the French-, German- and Italian-speaking peoples of that area. Save when she was attacked by Charles the Bold, Switzerland fought no wars; but her soldiers became the best in Europe, and were regularly enrolled as mercenaries for fighting elsewhere, especially by the French and by the Pope, who still keeps a Swiss guard of honour. On the whole, however, the Empire, Hungary, Poland and Bohemia remained as confused and anarchical as ever. Far to the East, in Novgorod, Ivan the Great held a barbarous state together in a continuous war against the Mongol Golden Horde; but though Russia was to inherit, along with a daughter of the Greek imperial family of Constantinople, what still remained of the culture and traditions of eastern Christianity, her day was not yet.

ITALIAN DISUNITY

In spite of her prosperity, Italy inherited from the Holy Roman Empire the same legacy of disorder as Germany. She suffered above all from too many unscrupulous despots. In every city, tyrants arose and were overthrown with bewildering rapidity. City republics, such as Florence and Siena, changed their governments as restlessly as those of ancient Greece. They fought wars with each other, hiring bands of professional soldiers—*condottieri*—for the purpose, and often were incapable of controlling their troops in the moment of victory. The Papacy, especially in the time of Alexander VI and Julius II, concentrated all its energies on extending its frontiers, by fair means or foul. Alexander's "nephew," Cesare Borgia, became one of the most able of the professional soldiers, whose restless ambition might have succeeded in uniting all northern Italy under the Pope, but for his premature death. For life in fifteenth-century Italy was glorious but uncertain. Assassination was regarded as a legitimate political weapon, and, since poison was the easiest and least detectable method, it was the golden age of the poisoner. All the Borgias gained an unenviable reputation for ruthless efficiency in this branch of statecraft, even Alexander's "niece," Lucrezia, one of the loveliest, but most dangerous, women of her age. So Italy remained disunited; and at the end of the century her problem was further complicated by a series of French invasions under Charles VIII and Louis XII. The Spaniards were established in Naples, the French in Milan, and Italy became the unhappy battle-ground between the two rival powers.

EXPANSION OF SPANISH POWER

A similar history might have been expected in Spain, where there were six kingdoms to dispute the sovereignty of the peninsula. But Spain was more fortunate. Though Portugal continued independent, Ferdinand of Aragon, Catalonia and Valencia married Isabella the Catholic of Castile, and so united the Spanish into a nation. Together they conquered the last fragment of the Moorish empire, the Kingdom of Granada, in 1492; and Ferdinand annexed the Spanish half of Navarre in 1512. These two rulers were able to do for Spain much of what Henry VII and Louis XI did for England and France. The nobles were tamed, finance and justice reorganized, and communications were improved. Spain was about to enter on the most glorious period of her history, when she would dominate the world for almost a century; much of the credit for her triumph must go to the solid work of Ferdinand and Isabella. But the foreign glories came too soon. Isabella's Catholic sympathies led her to expel all the Jews, though many had held high office in the past, and to begin the persecution of the Moors who had remained in the country. Both these steps seriously weakened the nation economically, since agriculture depended largely on the Moors and trade on the Jews.

Attempts were made to stimulate industry, and steps were taken to encourage the development of herds of merino sheep; in another sphere ship-owners were expected to build merchant vessels of what was then a very large size. In trade itself fixed prices and rigid regulations prevailed under the authority of an army of government officials who were in many cases corrupt. None of these practices produced the controlled prosperity desired from them and they gradually undermined the economic life of the country. But the effects of them were not visible for a long time. To all appearances Spain in the sixteenth century entered on her era of vast expansion united, and with all the pronounced national pride and the national institutions which were the distinguishing characteristics of that particular period in the history of western Europe.

CHAPTER 47

THE RENAISSANCE

THE Renaissance, or rebirth of learning and art, was not a sudden event in European history. In the early Middle Ages, as we have seen, there had been scholars and artists at work preparing the way for a revival of the thought and culture of Greece and Rome; and although, once contact had been re-established with the ancient civilizations, the movement developed with startling speed, the actual change was gradual. It has often been said that the capture of Constantinople by the Ottoman Turks in 1453 was responsible for the revival of learning and the re-discovery of Greek literature, because it sent many Greek scholars flying with their precious ancient manuscripts to the West. But, although this undoubtedly did stimulate vigour of thought, the interest was already there. The essential change was in men's outlook. It was a movement which began at the moment when the ideals and ideas of medieval civilization first began to lose their hold on thinkers and artists.

The great schoolmen of the Middle Ages had taught that man was of no importance in himself save as a soul to be saved—as one member of a great Christian community, whose duty it was to try to perfect the world in accordance with the teachings of Christ. Decay of the old unities—disappointment of the hopes placed in the idea of a universal empire, and loss of faith in the universal Church—made men think of themselves more as individuals with important lives of their own. It was here that they made contact with the Greek outlook, which had concentrated so completely on the wonderful possibilities of man's mind and body and taken an exquisite pleasure in his achievements. They began to acquire knowledge after the fashion of Frederick II, to look at nature with different eyes, and were no longer content humbly to wonder at the world as a miraculous creation of God, but considered it in an enquiring spirit, conscious more and more that they were capable of discovering how it worked.

NEW SPIRIT OF ENQUIRY

Such a change of outlook affected every department of life. It led to a more careful study of ancient documents, and especially to a scientific examination of early texts of the Bible. It produced, naturally, a new preoccupation with the problems of education, to develop all the potential qualities in children. Artists ceased to be content with flat lifeless drawings of human beings. They perfected a new technique in order to give an impression of perspective and depth; and they studied anatomy and natural history in order to represent nature more faithfully. Scholars realized the importance of beauty and style in the presentation of their work, and took as their

516

models the classics of Greece and Rome. It is important to remember that all these developments were part of the same thing—a revival of man's interest in all the varied activities of man—although the historian is obliged to divide them up and to consider each separately.

The movement began in Italy, stimulated by contact with the remains of Roman civilization and by the connection maintained through Venice with the Greek Empire of Constantinople. As early as the thirteenth century, the poet Dante had shown that the promise of a new development was already to be found in medieval Europe. Dante had been one of the greatest of the propagandists on the side of the Emperor against the Pope. But although in that he was essentially a medieval figure, there was much about his work which foretold coming changes. He made Vergil his guide through heaven and hell in his great poem, the *Inferno*; and he was as interested in the fate of the ancient pagans as in the more modern Christians. He wrote, moreover, in Italian, and did perhaps more than any other man to form that language as a literary medium.

RENEWAL OF GREEK AND LATIN STUDIES

The lead thus given was soon followed up in the fourteenth century by men like Petrarch and Boccaccio. Both wrote their most famous works in Italian. But Petrarch modelled a whole series of Latin letters on the style and language of Cicero; and Boccaccio, though the amusing tales of his *Decameron* were in Italian, was a fine Latin scholar who did more than merely imitate classical writers. It was not long before the interest in the history and literature of Rome inspired by such men led to a new interest in Greek language and thought. Before the end of the century a Greek scholar from Constantinople, Manuel Chrysoloras, had settled at Florence to teach his language to eager Italian students; and there were three famous teachers of Greek at the University of Padua between 1420 and 1430. In 1438 the Greek Emperor came over to the Council of Florence, which was endeavouring to reunite the Orthodox Greek Church to that of Rome, and one of the most learned men who accompanied him, Bessarion, stayed behind to become a Cardinal and to leave his great library to the Church of St. Mark at Venice. This meant that the new learning had invaded the Church; and the election of a famous Greek scholar as Pope Nicholas V in 1447 made secure the alliance between the Papacy and the new studies. Henceforth the Popes were some of the greatest patrons of learning and letters, notably Aeneas Silvius Piccolomini, who became Pope Pius II, Alexander VI, the greatest of the Borgias, and Leo X, the most splendid of the Medici Popes.

Thus the Church, instead of opposing the new learning, which was bound at first to weaken the ideas and beliefs underlying her authority, became its greatest ally. Many scholars directed their labours to the study of the original Greek texts of the New Testament, discovering and correcting mistakes in the Latin Bible of the Middle Ages—the Vulgate. One of the greatest of them, Pico della Mirandola, who was reputed to know nineteen languages before he was twenty-one, set himself to translate the whole Bible into Italian. But their main effort was directed towards a revival of secular learning and literature, not by copying, but by recapturing, the spirit of the Romans and Greeks. Petrarch's tales and Boccaccio's *Decameron* were not written to express religious convictions. They were designed to please and to amuse the cultured public, which had grown up in the rich background of Italian city life, just as the Troubadours had set themselves to please the nobles and courtiers of Provence.

Many of the works of the greatest Greek and Roman authors had disappeared entirely since the Dark Ages, and it was the work of the new scholarship to re-discover, decipher and translate them. Fresh treasures constantly came to light in old monastery libraries, in cellars and store rooms, like the famous manuscript of Quintilian which the Italian, Poggio Bracciolini, found in a German abbey, "lying in a most foul and obscure dungeon at the bottom of a tower". Scribes were continuously at work transcribing the newly discovered books for the libraries of men like Bessarion and Pius II or Lorenzo de Medici. Before long, it became the fashion for a great nobleman to surround himself with scholars and artists who lived at his expense, and whom he employed to build houses and to fill them with pictures, statues and books. Often the scholar would be employed as tutor to the children of some noble or prince; and this in turn led to a fresh study of the theory and practice of education, which produced such books as *The Courtier*, written by Castiglione, tutor to the family of the Duke of Urbino. For it was expected of a gentleman in fifteenth-century Italy, as it had been in Ancient Greece, that he should acquire all the arts and graces of a classical education and should develop his mind and body alike to the greatest possible pitch of perfection; and a great lady was permitted to emerge from the somewhat cloistered seclusion imposed on women by medieval ideas, and to share with her brothers the advantages of the new education.

THE NEW HUMANISM

It was inevitable that the new spirit of enquiry and speculation should spread beyond the realms of purely classical and literary activity. Dante had pointed the way to a revival of political thought by his treatise in favour of imperial authority—the *De Monarchia*. The art of government had been a favourite study among the Ancient Greeks, and a renewed interest in Plato, and the changed approach to the works of Aristotle, naturally led to a fresh examination of the political and social conditions of the day. The most famous of the political thinkers of the Renaissance was the Florentine, Machiavelli. He was secretary to the Council of Florence, and passed his whole life in the confused background of petty Italian politics. But he also

studied Latin and Greek thought and ancient history; his most celebrated book, *The Prince*, was not only a close study of the political
problems and customs of his own day, but also an attempt to lay
down rules as to how people should be governed. The principles
which he formulated were widely used by the politicians and princes
who were building up the new nation-states for fifteenth- and
sixteenth-century Europe, and later came into their own again in
Fascist Italy.

The new learning touched, indeed, every department of life. A
renewed acquaintance with Euclid and Pythagoras stimulated fresh
mathematical studies. Men began, once again, to apply scientific
methods of investigation to the problems of the universe. Medicine
escaped from the superstition which had clung to its medieval
practitioners, and became once more the science of Hippocrates and
Galen; doctors no longer sought to cure men by placing lead weights
on their chests at certain phases of the moon, but based their treatment on a knowledge of anatomy gained by dissecting human bodies.
Historians saw the need for a more careful sifting of truth and error
and a more attractive presentation of facts than the bald recitals of
the chroniclers of the Middle Ages. A new interest in contemporary
events led Benvenuto Cellini, the celebrated goldsmith, to write one
of the most outspoken and exciting autobiographies of all time, and
Vasari to leave a priceless record of his times in his *Lives of the Italian
Painters*. It was this many-sided interest in the potentialities and
achievements of mankind which suggested the word "Humanism"
to describe all its varied activities.

ITALIAN ART AND ARCHITECTURE

It is, perhaps, for its achievements in painting, sculpture and
architecture that the Italian Renaissance is chiefly remembered; and
it was in these spheres that the city republics of Florence and Venice
made their greatest contributions to Renaissance civilization. The
practice of the arts was not, of course, confined to these two cities.
Sienese artists had been employed to decorate the Palace of the Popes
at Avignon, and the Sienese, Duccio, was one of the greatest of the
early Renaissance painters. Every city produced her great artists;
every Italian prince wished also to become a patron; Visconti
tyrants summoned artists to beautify Milan, and the Popes employed
the greatest of them all to build and adorn a new Rome. But it was
in Florence, with her large leisured class whose wealth was derived
from banking, that the greatest artists congregated. The heads of
the great Florentine banking firms, the Strozzi and the Medici, were
the most generous patrons of artists and men of letters in Europe.
Men like Lorenzo de Medici, the Magnificent, made fifteenth-century
Florence resemble Athens in the days of Pericles. There was the same
zest and excitement of intellectual life, the same breathless appreciation of all artistic achievement and the same political restlessness.

It was only very gradually that the new movement freed itself from the control which the medieval Church had exercised over all the arts. Already, at the beginning of the fourteenth century, Cimabue and his still greater pupil, Giotto, the shepherd boy whom he had found drawing on a stone and brought to his workshop to train, had broken away from the flat Byzantine style of painting. Giotto visited Rome in 1300 to design mosaics for the old church of St. Peter's; and while he was there, he absorbed a new spirit from the ruins of ancient Rome, learnt the value of design in a picture and the possibility of producing the illusion of solidity on a flat canvas or panel. But in his choice of subjects, Giotto, like the Florentine painters who followed him throughout the fourteenth century, had remained the servant of the Church. They painted pictures almost entirely of religious scenes, of the Madonna and Christ, of the Crucifixion and the Adoration of the Three Wise Men.

This atmosphere of quiet piety and the development of medieval ideas and technique remained typical of the Umbrian school of painting almost to the end. The Sienese cult of the Virgin kept all the greatest of her artists, such as Duccio and Simone Martini, working within the framework of religious ideas; and the next great development of Italian art was also to come from Florence, at the beginning of the fifteenth century. It was due chiefly to the sculpture of three great men, Ghiberti, Brunelleschi and Donatello, and it took the form of a new naturalism—an attempt to show, in sculpture and in painting, bodies and forms of nature not only as they really looked, but as they worked and moved and grew. "I have always sought", said Ghiberti, "how nature worked in herself."

These three men were called to Florence in 1400 to compete in designing a pair of bronze doors for the Baptistery which the city was proposing to cast in gratitude for relief from the Plagues; from their influence sprang a new experimental school of Florentine art. Masaccio, though he died when he was only twenty-eight, showed the way with a new method of painting distant objects in perspective; and the movement towards naturalism and away from religion, began in this way, culminated in the classicism of Botticelli, who preferred painting Venus and nymphs rather than angels, and who developed a pure, serene and untroubled art whose only religion was beauty.

DA VINCI, MICHELANGELO AND RAPHAEL

The fifteenth century in Florence was a period of ceaseless experiment in every branch of art. It was also a period of intense intellectual activity; and it produced, in the end, two of the greatest figures of the Golden Age of Renaissance painting—Leonardo da Vinci and Michelangelo. Leonardo's life best illustrates the versatility and experimental passion of the period. He left behind him very few finished paintings—even his masterpiece, the "Mona Lisa", is unfinished—but hundreds of sketches and drawings. He studied music and anatomy, wrote a treatise on the flight of birds, designed a flying-machine, and occupied himself at every kind of scientific research. He could turn his theories to practical uses, as he showed by designing water-works, drains and fortifications for the city of Milan and engines of war for Cesare Borgia. For him, it was impossible to departmentalize knowledge. The artist could not know too much of nature; for all life was the province of art.

Michelangelo was a man of a different stamp. He concentrated above all on the portrayal of the human body as the finest revelation of the majesty and divinity of the God, who had made man in his own image; and in the great frescoes of Biblical scenes in the Sistine Chapel at Rome, he produced the most impressive work of all Renaissance Italy. Yet his life was an unhappy one. He was thrown always among men who could not understand or value him; and the despair which he felt in life infected all his work, so that the "Last Judgment" which completed his twenty years' work in the Sistine Chapel inspires awe and terror, but gives no sign of the mercy or of the love of God.

One other name must be set beside those of Leonardo and Michelangelo—that of their contemporary, Raphael. He combined all the gentleness and quiet skill of the Umbrian School with an intellectual understanding which rivalled that of the greatest of the Florentines. If much of his work was spoilt by an attempt to emulate the large-scale work of Michelangelo, beside whom he worked at Rome, his smaller paintings, and more particularly his Sistine Madonna, were as fine as anything Italy ever produced. There were other great Umbrian masters, notably Perugino, Raphael's teacher, and Piero della Francesca. But both Piero and Raphael owed much to other schools of painting, and it is impossible to divide the artists of the Renaissance very carefully into different schools. By the end of the fifteenth century, all the great artists were learning from one another; both the great schools of Italian painting played a part in helping to inspire the last great phase of the Italian Renaissance, the Venetian.

VENETIAN PAINTING

By the time that Raphael died, in 1520, the inspiration was going from the Italian Renaissance. The intellectual preoccupations and doubtings of Michelangelo already pointed the way to an age which was losing the joyous confidence and faith in man which had made such a movement as the Renaissance possible. Italy was passing into the period of the Reformation and Counter-Reformation when dogmatism and theology were to displace the ideal of beauty from men's minds. Only in Venice was there a splendid after-glow, lasting for another fifty years. Owing to the historic, political and commercial association with Byzantium, Venetian art during the fourteenth and fifteenth centuries had remained singularly untouched by the influences at work in the rest of Italy. Its inspiration came rather from the East, and when the great age came, it was a gorgeous richness of colour which chiefly distinguished it. Venice's great period which lasted roughly for a century—from 1475 to 1576—was one of splendid secular painting which was well-suited to a republic of rich merchants and patricians. Giorgione and Titian, Paolo Veronese and Tintoretto were all among the greatest masters of technique, and their ability to portray the richest colours and textures surpassed anything of the kind achieved elsewhere in Italy. It was perhaps at portraits that they most excelled; and it is noteworthy that the Emperor Charles V, having once seen some of Titian's work, refused ever to allow himself to be painted by other artists.

THE VERSATILITY OF RENAISSANCE ART

The Renaissance in Italy produced so many painters of the first rank that it is easy almost to forget its achievements in other branches of art, in sculpture and in architecture. But it is important to remember that all the greatest artists of the period aimed at the versatility which was seen at its best in Leonardo da Vinci. Leonardo himself designed a famous equestrian statue of Francesco Sforza at Milan, later destroyed by French invaders; some of the greatest works of Michelangelo were the marble statues of David and Moses and the figures of Day, Night, Twilight and Dawn which he carved for the Medici tombs in Florence; and Giotto showed—notably by the superb belfry of the Cathedral at Florence—that he was as great an architect as painter. Renaissance sculpture was at least as great as Renaissance painting, though most of the best of it was the work of men who were also great painters, with the notable exception, perhaps, of Luca della Robbia, who specialized in terracotta work. Other crafts were touched by the same spirit, and men like Benvenuto Cellini produced exquisite masterpieces of craftsmanship which have never been surpassed.

But on the whole the great names in all the arts were the same. Brunelleschi, whose design for the Baptistery doors at Florence was rejected, became responsible for the dome of the cathedral; and the designs for the great new church of St. Peter at Rome, originally made by Bramante, were modified both by Raphael and Michelangelo. Architecture was the field in which the classical tradition naturally had most scope. Everywhere in Italy there were the remains of ancient Roman buildings to serve as models and inspirations; and Italian Gothic, which had never wholly lost touch with the Byzantine tradition, was soon merged into a more purely classical, and especially Roman, style. Though the new architectural developments were responsible for many new churches and cathedrals, and notably for St. Peter's in Rome, they were applied, on the whole, more to secular than to ecclesiastical buildings. The great families of fifteenth- and sixteenth-century Italy demanded palaces and villas to take the place of the gloomy fortress-like dwellings of the Middle Ages. Renaissance architecture is typified best by the Medici palace, the Farnese Palace at Rome and the Villa Giuliana which Pope Julius III built as his summer residence. Here again, as with portraits, the wealthy ruling-class of Venice provided artists with their best markets; and men like the Lombardi and Sansovino, found in Venice the finest scope for their talents and filled her with their masterpieces.

THE RENAISSANCE NORTH OF THE ALPS

The classical tradition was never so strong north of the Alps as it had been in Italy. There was not the direct contact with a Roman past to stimulate northerners to so complete a break with the traditions of the Middle Ages; and although the Renaissance visited the remotest corners of Europe and fired Germans, Flemings, Portuguese, Dutchmen and Englishmen to splendid achievements in art and letters, it was only in France that the classical spirit of Italy really dominated the new movement.

Yet even in France, most of the work of the Renaissance was an imitation of earlier Italian models rather than an original and creative effort. In literature, the poet Ronsard inspired a whole new school of poetry—the Pleiad—which sought to give the French language a classical elegance and beauty to rival that of Italian and Latin; and Rabelais' great works, *Gargantua* and *Pantagruel*, show all the creative genius of the true Renaissance. But otherwise the French were content to borrow and to copy. The Italian expeditions of Charles VIII and Louis XII had familiarized them with a new type of architecture, and the French kings set themselves to build magnificent *châteaux*—country residences rather than castles—in the new classical style. But they mostly borrowed architects and craftsmen from Italy. Francis I even tempted Leonardo da Vinci into his service, and rewarded him with a country house near Amboise in which to end his days.

The new style in architecture appeared late in northern Europe. The Gothic tradition had decayed and lost itself in the fussy over-decoration of the *flamboyant* style long before classical ideas supplanted it. The first half of the sixteenth century saw the building of the great *châteaux* of the Loire in France; and early Tudor manor-houses in England show a definite Italian influence in shape and design. But the classical tradition did not establish itself fully in Spain until after the middle of the century and did not invade England in its purest form until the reign of Charles II, a hundred years later. In Germany, too, and in the Netherlands, the tradition which finally produced such masterpieces as the Town Hall of Antwerp and the Castle of Heidelberg was slower and more gradual. The portraits of Clouet show that France, too, could produce great painters. But, on the whole, the greatest achievements of the Renaissance in France were architectural and decorative, and these were, in reality, but an echo of the Italian triumphs; though they possessed much of the polish and grace of Italian classicism, they lacked the sincerity and originality of the revival of learning and art in Germany and the Netherlands. It has been said that the Renaissance in northern Europe never entirely lost the contact with religion which had been the keynote of medieval art and letters. The scholars of the north, men like Erasmus and Reuchlin, Sir Thomas More and Dean Colet, must be considered rather as forerunners of the Reformation than revivers of a classical tradition. They took pains to form their style and perfect their language: but fundamentally they were more interested in truth than in beauty, in what they had to say rather than how they said it. Most of them, and More in particular, were much more medieval in outlook and ideals than any Italian scholar; and although More's great book, *Utopia*, shows the same social and political interest as *The Prince*, it has none of Machiavelli's cynicism. For More pictured an ideal state whose foundations were largely the ideals of the Middle Ages.

There were, indeed, strong Italian influences to be traced in English literature. Chaucer, the greatest of the English poets before Shakespeare, the man who had first begun, in the fourteenth century, to form the English language as we know it now, had borrowed many of the stories told in his *Canterbury Tales* from Boccaccio and Petrarch. The poetry of Skelton, in the time of Henry VII, was strongly influenced by Italian verse-forms. But the great age of English literature was to come later in the sixteenth century, when the Renaissance was almost over elsewhere in Europe; and the development of German as a literary language was to come, not from a school of poetry, but from the translation of the Bible which was undertaken by Martin Luther in the early years of the Reformation.

GUTENBERG INVENTS THE PRINTING PRESS

Outside Italy, indeed, the revival of learning almost always assumed a practical, and very soon even a scientific, form. Perhaps the greatest contribution of Germany to the development of thought and literature was Gutenberg's invention of the printing-press in 1450. New paper, made from linen by methods used by the Arabs, displaced the old and very expensive parchment, and the laboriously copied manuscripts of the scribes were replaced by printed books which were cheaply and easily produced. In many ways, this was a loss, for the old manuscripts had often been things of great beauty with illuminated capitals, and decorated with exquisite pictures in miniature. But the gains were inestimable; the printing-press with its movable type was quick and efficient; the new learning could spread swiftly, and men no longer needed to spend years collecting even the smallest library. The earliest printers were also publishers and booksellers, and they helped literature and learning by their patronage of scholars and writers. In 1477, Caxton set up the first English printing-press, and the new invention spread rapidly. Perhaps the most famous of the early printers was Aldo Manuzio, who established his press in Venice and was responsible for the most beautiful of the early editions of the classics. Aldo was the friend and collaborator of almost all the great writers of his day; his house became a great literary centre, and when the great Dutch writer Erasmus came to Venice to publish a book with Aldo, he actually stayed with him as his guest for eight months.

THE REBIRTH OF SCIENCE

The new scientific approach to the problems of nature soon inspired fresh discoveries and inventions. Already, in the heyday of the Middle Ages, the English monk, Roger Bacon, had discovered how to make gunpowder, though it was a long time before man learnt how to use it effectively: cannon were still primitive and chancy things even at the end of the fifteenth century. The medieval alchemist, intent on discovering a method of changing base metals into gold, began to disappear. Chemistry became a science whose primary function was to assist the medical researches of men like Andreas Vesalius, Charles V's Flemish physician, who produced one of the first great books on anatomy, *On the Structure of the Human Body*, in 1543.

In the same year, there was also published a book which revolutionized the whole medieval conception of astronomy, *Concerning the Revolutions of the Celestial Bodies*, by a Pole named Copernicus. The thinkers of the Middle Ages had accepted without question the statement of the Greek geographer, Ptolemy, that the earth was the centre of the universe and that the sun and the planets revolved around it. Working without a telescope, Copernicus was able to establish the fact that the earth was but one of the planets revolving round the sun and that day and night were caused, not by the revolutions of the sun, but by the rotation of the earth on its own axis. The full implications of this discovery were left to be worked out by later scientists. It is important, however, to realize that the spirit of enquiry which had animated Leonardo da Vinci drove many scholars, especially in the north, to scientific researches, and that the great advances made in the sixteenth century in chemistry, physics, astronomy, mathematics and medicine were all aspects of the Renaissance. The revival of learning was not merely a mechanical return to the classics of Greece and Rome; it involved rather a fresh application of Greek methods of thought to the problems of the universe, combined with a new respect for scientific truth and accuracy.

THE RENAISSANCE IN GERMANY, NETHERLANDS AND ENGLAND

On the artistic side, the Renaissance in the north showed even less evidence of direct contact with classical ideas. Throughout the fourteenth and fifteenth centuries there was a steady Italian influence at work on the artists and craftsmen of south Germany. But Germany, as a whole, was poorer than Italy, and her communications were much worse. There were fewer rich patrons of art, and it was more difficult for artists and sculptors to travel, and so to gain the stimulation of new ideas. So, in Germany, the arts hardly broke away from the tradition of medieval religion until the end of the fifteenth century; and then, almost immediately, the Reformation came to turn all men's minds back into the channel of religion. There was much lovely work in bronze and wooden statuary done in fourteenth- and fifteenth-century Germany; and much of it showed a true Renaissance study of anatomy. But it was not until the end of the fifteenth century that Germany produced, in Lucas Cranach and Albrecht Dürer, two artists who could rank with the greatest Italian painters. In his large-scale paintings and in his woodcuts, etchings and water-colours, Dürer showed a supreme mastery of technique. But even he had the preoccupation of the German with religious ideas, and little of the sheer joy of beauty which characterized a painter like Botticelli.

The Netherlands were richer than Germany and enjoyed a fine civilization, based, like that of Italy, on the wealth of great merchant and industrial cities. There, though the Renaissance came much later, it produced as fine a school of painting as any of the Italian schools. There is still to be found, in the works of men like Memling and David, the strong pietistic influence of the Church on north European art, even at the end of the fifteenth century. But in Flanders, as in Venice, there were rich merchants who demanded portraits of themselves and their families, and so fostered a more secular school of painting which was later to take advantage of the rich, varied and picturesque life of the Netherland cities. The two Van Eycks, perhaps the greatest of the early Flemish school, had discovered how to preserve the brightest colours of an oil painting by the use of a transparent varnish. These and other technical discoveries gave the later Dutch and Flemish painters an opportunity which they exploited to the full and an inspiration which lasted long after the Italian Renaissance had degenerated into florid fussiness.

England produced no great native school of painting. Her Renaissance was essentially literary, musical and architectural, and the great English portraits of the time of Henry VIII were the work of a German, Hans Holbein the Younger, who spent the last years of his life in London. England was, paradoxically enough, both the most conservative and the most progressive European nation in the sixteenth century. She was one of the first to achieve political unity; but she preserved more of the medieval ideas and outlook than any other; the revival of learning, literature and the arts came later there than anywhere else and was a slower, more continuous and gradual process. In particular, there was one aspect of the new learning, of which she was very slow to take advantage. The study of other sciences had naturally produced a new interest in geography, and this in turn led to explorations and discoveries which gave the nations of the Atlantic seaboard a new opportunity and importance. England allowed Portugal and Spain to get ahead of her; and it was not until the second half of the sixteenth century that English seamen began seriously to interest themselves in American and Indian trade. The history of this is properly the history of yet another aspect of the Renaissance; but it played so vital a part in the break-up of the Midde Ages and the subsequent development of the modern world, that it becomes necessary to treat it as being a separate subject.

CHAPTER 48

THE DISCOVERY OF NEW WORLDS

THERE had been some attempt during the Middle Ages to explore and to exploit the land-routes to the Far East; we have seen how Marco Polo reached the court of Kublai Khan in the thirteenth century; the cities of northern Italy had steadily developed their commerce with Asia through Constantinople and Baghdad. In the fifteenth century, almost all luxury articles, spices, silks and jewels, still came from the East, and Venice had practically established a monopoly in this trade. But there was a growing shortage of such merchandise. The advance of the Ottoman Turks and Timur's raids had partially closed the great land-routes to the Far East; and traffic by sea was possible only during the intervals, increasingly rare, when Venice was at peace with the Turks. This had the natural effect of encouraging enterprise in other directions and of suggesting, in the first place to the Portuguese, that the Atlantic Ocean might be a waterway and not merely a limit to European expansion. The poorness of the soil of Portugal encouraged its inhabitants to seek an outlet abroad, and they naturally resented their dependence on the Mediterranean trade which supported Venice and Genoa.

PORTUGAL'S SEA POWER

Thanks to the comparatively early expulsion of the Moors, Portugal was in a far better position than any other nation to take the lead in discovering and exploiting new commercial outlets. While England and France were still engaged in apparently endless wars and civil wars, and the Spanish kingdoms were still fighting against the Moors or among themselves, the Portuguese had achieved political stability and comparative peace. Learning and the arts had begun to flourish; the spirit of Renaissance Italy had penetrated the country, to drive men to explore anything that was new or unknown; an era of peace had resulted in an increasing population, which, in a country not richly endowed with natural resources, inevitably produced the expressed desire for expansion overseas, just as it has, in more recent times in world history, driven other nations to demand for themselves colonies and "a place in the Sun".

Already, by the beginning of the fifteenth century, the Portuguese had become important traders on the North European sea-routes. But they had also begun to look south, had discovered and annexed the Canary Islands and had started a tentative exploration of the west coast of Africa. It is doubtful, however, if they would have achieved so spectacular a success at the end of the century, had it not been for the organizing genius of one man who, as a member of the royal family, was able to put government resources at the disposal of the merchant adventurers and to co-ordinate both their efforts and their results. Prince Henry, the Navigator, had fought in his youth as a crusader in North Africa; and it was he who first turned the main effort of the Portuguese in that direction, concentrating on finding a way round by sea to India and so establishing an alternative trade-route to the coveted riches which were found in the Far East.

CHARTING OF NEW SEA-ROUTES

He surrounded himself with a staff of expert geographers and map-makers, navigators and ship-designers, and with their help equipped almost annual expeditions to explore the west African coast. One of his first and most important achievements was the perfecting of a new type of ship for the purpose. The nations which had hitherto monopolized the most profitable maritime trade had become accustomed to think only in terms of the comparatively windless Mediterranean and to depend largely on galleys driven by oars. Constant naval warfare with the Turks and with the Barbary pirates of North Africa compelled Spaniards and Italians to stick to this type of vessel far into the sixteenth century; even when Spain acquired South American colonies her shipbuilders were so accustomed to old ideas that they designed clumsy fair-weather galleons, which were to prove no match for the more seaworthy craft perfected by the English and Dutch. Prince Henry saw that Portugal, with an entirely Atlantic seaboard, must think in terms of rough seas and long voyages. He devised for his expeditions the three-masted caravel of between fifty and two hundred tons, which proved admirably adapted to his purpose: it did not need to hug the coast, but could achieve safety in stormy weather by keeping well out to sea.

The expeditions thus equipped and financed by Prince Henry discovered the various groups of islands off the western coast of Africa, Madeira, the Azores and Cape Verde, all of which were to prove useful bases for further exploration both southwards and westwards. Before long, his captains had disproved the old legend that if men went farther south than Cape Bojador, they would turn black and die, and had penetrated to the Gulf of Guinea. Each successive piece of the coastline which they explored was carefully mapped; and the expeditions were made profitable, partly by trading for gold, partly by carrying off the natives and selling them as slaves. Prince Henry died in 1460, before his work was completed; and for a time, little further progress was made. King John II, however, resumed the work under a somewhat different system. The government farmed out the African trade to private merchants, granting them licences on condition that they explored and mapped another hundred miles of the coast every year.

In 1487, one of these, Bartholomew Diaz, was driven by storms much farther south than he had intended, and found himself able to round the Cape of Good Hope—which he himself christened the Cape of Storms—and strike northwards, towards India. His crew, however, mutinied and forced him to turn back almost immediately; and it was left to Vasco da Gama to complete his work some ten years later. Da Gama set out with four small ships provisioned for three years, with the deliberate intention of reaching India. Storms drove him out of his course, and it took him five months to round the Cape and nearly a year to reach Calicut on the west coast of India. He returned "Admiral of the Indian Ocean", his ships laden with a cargo worth a fortune, though with only a third of his men. His vast profits stimulated other merchants to follow his example; and the King of Portugal took for himself the title of "Lord of the Conquest, Navigation, and Commerce of Ethiopia, Persia and India".

VAST NEW SOURCES OF WEALTH

It has been a favourite maxim of imperialists that "trade follows the flag"; but more often in history, the flag has followed trade. The Portuguese had tapped a vast source of wealth in the East Indies, and their motive was almost purely commercial. But they had also infringed a Venetian and Arab monopoly, and their presence in the Indian Ocean roused the vested interests already there. It soon became clear that a fleet was necessary in Far Eastern waters to protect the new trade; and a fleet needed naval bases. The Portuguese were forced to acquire vast colonial possessions overseas.

Much of the wealth derived from the Eastern trade came from spices of the islands away to the south and east of India proper. But a great deal of the most valuable merchandise came from and through India itself, and even the produce of the islands was often shipped to Calicut for distribution. India, as a whole, was in a state of confusion. Though there had been no great invasion since Timur's sack of Delhi, sporadic fighting and feeble government weakened the country. This anarchy ended in the final wave of Moslem invasion which set up the Mogul Empire under Baber. Such constant disturbances naturally upset the caravan-routes and made land-borne trade risky and uncertain. Almost all the China trade tended to be diverted southwards, and an increasing proportion of the commerce between Asia and Europe passed across the Indian Ocean.

In this carrying trade, the Arabs had established a monopoly similar to that of Venice in the eastern Mediterranean. Both these profitable monopolies were now challenged by the Portuguese;

for though the voyage round Africa was long and dangerous, it was hardly less tedious than the long overland journeys across Arabia, and it eliminated many middlemen on the way. The result was a very powerful combination against the interlopers. The Sultan of Egypt and the Turks sent aid to the Arab merchants; and the Venetians not only prayed publicly in their churches for the success of the infidels, but actually equipped a squadron in the Indian Ocean.

PORTUGAL LEADS IN COLONIAL POSSESSIONS

Here, however, the Portuguese experience of deep-sea navigation stood them in good stead. Their ships were better built and better gunned, and they maintained a steady superiority. In 1509, their admiral, Almeida, won a great and decisive victory over the combined fleet of their enemies; and from then on, though there was constant fighting, the Portuguese established themselves as masters of the eastern trade—a position which they were to maintain for over a century, until they were superseded by the Dutch. Their commercial supremacy needed a political framework if it was to survive permanently; and this was provided by the work of one of Portugal's greatest men, Albuquerque, who was sent out as Viceroy to consolidate the scattered trading-stations into an overseas empire. Albuquerque established his government and capital at Goa, to the north of Calicut; he secured naval control of the Indian Ocean by capturing and fortifying Ormuz, at the mouth of the Persian Gulf, and finally established the Portuguese hold on the spice trade by setting up trading-posts farther east, in and beyond Malacca. The difficulty of commerce with China, through an India distracted with petty warfare, he solved by sending fleets to trade direct with the Chinese.

The greatness of Albuquerque and the solidity of the power which he had built up, frightened King Emmanuel into recalling him; but his work had been done, and the Portuguese Empire endured and continued to expand. It placed, however, an almost unendurable strain on the man-power of so small a nation. The steady drain of men to staff and protect so vast an empire inevitably began to impoverish the mother country, just as in Rome the quality of her citizens was sapped by their imperial responsibilities. Thus Brazil, though it was discovered by the Portuguese in 1500 and fell to Portugal's share when the Pope partitioned the New World into spheres of influence, was left undeveloped and unexploited for many years, though it was ultimately to become Portugal's largest colony. In the end, the effort was to prove too great and the eastern empire was to fall into the hands of the Dutch and the English. But in the sixteenth century, the Portuguese supremacy was unchallenged. Portuguese sailors were everywhere in the forefront, even taking part in some of the early explorations across the North Atlantic. "Had there been more of the world", boasted their greatest poet, Camoens, in the sixteenth century "they would have discovered it."

Such a period of excitement and discovery naturally reacted on the intellectual and artistic life of the nation. Contact with the East brought eastern ideas and eastern decoration into favour, and Indian art exercised, to some extent, the same influence and stimulation on the Portuguese which that of ancient Greece and Rome had exercised on the Italians. The result was, as it were, a separate and individual Portuguese Renaissance with a charm and beauty of its own—a peculiarly happy blending of eastern and western styles which left its mark on all the architecture and sculpture of the period. For a short time, Portugal led the world; and it is possible that she would have maintained her commercial and colonial supremacy for considerably longer, had she not, towards the end of the sixteenth century, first wasted her military strength in Morocco and then been annexed by Philip II of Spain. Her commerce was deliberately starved in order to divert the wealth and prosperity of Lisbon to Cadiz and Seville, and her particular contribution to European civilization was swallowed up in the larger greatness of the Spanish Empire.

THE ATLANTIC QUEST

The discovery of a sea-route to India did not seriously alter fifteenth-century ideas as to the shape and size of the world. Astronomers had already realized that the world was round, and an Italian named Toscanelli had discussed the possibility of reaching India by sailing westwards across the Atlantic. The geographers did not suspect the existence of the continent of America. Vikings had crossed the Atlantic in their long boats and had landed on the coast of the American mainland; but the memory of their discoveries had perished and maritime enterprises ever since had been concentrated in the Mediterranean and along the Atlantic coasts. The tales of Marco Polo and other travellers had left only the vaguest ideas as to the size of Asia, and it was the coast of Japan and China which the fifteenth-century explorers expected to find on the other side of the ocean. Apart from the revived interest in geography, due largely to the tales of early travellers, there had been a marked improvement in the instruments available for deep-sea navigation to encourage the enterprise of explorers. The compass had been in use since the thirteenth century; but since then the astrolabe had been invented, to make it possible for a navigator out of sight of land to estimate his latitude, and the quadrant for measuring altitudes.

It was the Genoese who chiefly exploited these new opportunities. They were prevented by the Venetians from participating largely in the Mediterranean trade, and very soon passed the Straits of Gibraltar in search of other commerce. The Portuguese were obsessed with the Far East, and their energy and interest were all directed to securing and exploiting the African trade-routes. Thus it was left to a Genoese sailor, Christopher Columbus, to work out the ideas of Toscanelli. He was convinced that Japan was but a few days' sail

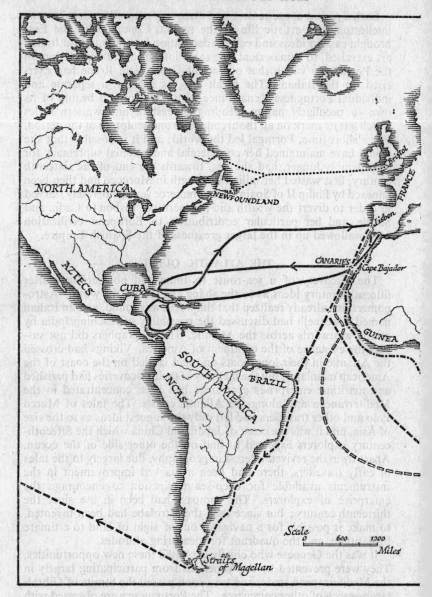

VOYAGES OF

The above map illustrates the discovery of the great sea-routes that profoundly influenced subsequent European and world history. Christopher
Columbus discovered the New World in the service of Spain, although he
believed he had landed in a part of Asia, and in all he made four voyages.

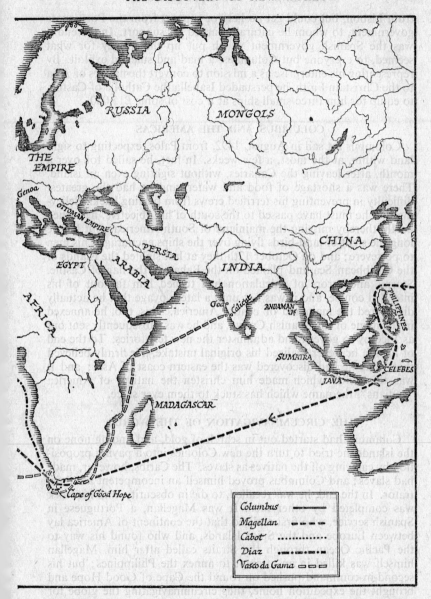

DISCOVERY

The expeditions of John Cabot, under the patronage of Henry VII of England, resulted in the discovery of Newfoundland, while other important feats were the circumnavigation of the world by the Portuguese Ferdinand Magellan and the discovery of the Cape of Good Hope by Vasco da Gama.

from Lisbon, but could get no help or support from the Portuguese government, to whom he naturally turned for support. In the end it was the Spanish government which put up the money for what seemed, to everyone but Columbus, a mad and suicidal exploit. By representing his enterprise as a mission to convert the natives of Asia to the Christain Faith, he persuaded Isabella the Catholic of Castile, to equip for him three small ships at a cost of some £15,000.

COLUMBUS AND THE AMERICAS

Columbus set sail in August, 1492, from Palos, expecting to sight land within, at the most, a few weeks. In fact, he sailed for over a month, after leaving the Canaries, without sighting even an island. There was a shortage of food and water, and he had the greatest difficulty in preventing his terrified crews from turning back. Believing that he must have passed to the south of his objective, he turned north, thereby missing the mainland of South America. But before long the sight of land-birds flying over the ships encouraged his men to persevere; and on October 12th they at last sighted the islands of the Caribbean Sea and planted on the Bahamas the flag of Castile. Storms and errors of calculation had turned him far out of his intended course, and it was not until a later voyage that he actually discovered the mainland of central America. This, too, he annexed in the name of the Spanish Crown, and he was subsequently sent out as Viceroy to govern and administer the new territories. To the end of his life he never realized his original mistake. He firmly believed that what he had discovered was the eastern coast of Asia; and it was this belief which made him christen the natives of America "Indians", the name which has stuck to them ever since.

THE CIRCUMNAVIGATION OF THE WORLD

Columbus had started out in search of gold, and finding none on the islands, he tried to turn the new Colonies into a paying proposition by carrying off the natives as slaves. The Caribs, however, made bad slaves; and Columbus proved himself an incompetent administrator. In the end, he was recalled, to die in obscurity, and his work was completed by other men. It was Magellan, a Portuguese in Spanish service, who first realized that the continent of America lay between Europe and the Spice Islands, and who found his way to the Pacific Ocean through the Straits called after him. Magellan himself was killed in an attempt to annex the Philippines; but his second-in-command pushed on round the Cape of Good Hope and brought the expedition home, thus circumnavigating the globe for the first time. Other Spanish expeditions explored the coastline of South America, and the continent was ultimately named after a merchant adventurer, Amerigo Vespucci, who accompanied one of these and wrote a book describing his experiences. There were voyages of discovery also to North America, notably that of the brothers Cabot, also Genoese, who sailed from Bristol in 1496 to Newfoundland. But the English could not see any way of turning North American discoveries to profit; most of their energies during the first half of the sixteenth century were devoted to the development of their European commerce, though French and English fishing-vessels found their way in increasing numbers to the rich fishing-grounds which were discovered off the coast of Newfoundland.

THE "INDIANS" OF AMERICA

It was some years before the Spaniards made any real attempt to penetrate the mainland of central and southern America. They were drawn there ultimately by legends and tales of the riches and splendour of the native civilizations of Mexico and Peru. Very little is known of the origins of the so-called "Indian" inhabitants of America. The first men had probably wandered into the continent from Mongolia and Siberia in the post-glacial age, though there is some possibility that the Polynesian races inhabiting the islands and coast of the Caribbean Sea were older inhabitants still. By the time of Columbus and Cabot, there was an infinite variety of races, languages, life and customs to be found in the American Continent. This was partly the result of differences between the successive waves of invasion from the north-west, partly of the variations of climate and country which they found. In the extreme north, the strange and primitive race of the Esquimaux developed a type of life adapted to a region of almost perpetual ice and snow, clothing themselves in furs, building round snow huts for the winter, and living exclusively on meat and fish.

The western part of North America, on the other hand, was an area of rolling prairies where roaming herds of wild bison were hunted by Indians of the Plains, who lived a wandering life, following the movements of their game. The eastern area was chiefly one of forests and great rivers where tribes of Iroquois and Algonkin Indians had settled in villages. These, too, hunted; but they also cultivated crops of maize, and some of them had learnt to use bark to build canoes and to cover their huts. None of these tribes attained any high degree of civilization; they lived on in the same way for centuries, warring with one another, hunting and fishing; and it was only in the south-west, in and around what is now California, that the "Pueblo" Indians developed some of the arts of civilization, making pottery, building in stone, and weaving cloth. But even they were primitive, compared with the great civilizations which were developed in central America, on the Mexican Plateau, and on the Pacific coast of South America.

The race responsible for this civilization was called Nahua and consisted of many different tribes. It is probable that they came originally from further north in several waves, since there were people called Chibchas in Colombia who had similar institutions and culture. Their main settlement, however, was on the Mexican Plateau, where a branch of them, known as the Mayas, constructed a civilization far more advanced than any other on the continent. Their temples and palaces still stand as monuments to their architectural skill, and were highly and elaborately decorated with carving and stucco, most of it distinguished by the peculiar twisted "serpent motive". They never fully learnt the art of smelting metals, and in consequence were never very effective warriors. But their government was well organized, they had an elaborate system of roads, grew large crops of maize and cotton, and showed astounding scientific ability. With a view to protecting their crops, they made a careful study of astronomy; their calendar was far more accurate than that which was in use in Europe in the Middle Ages, and they were accustomed to measure time by sundials. Only their religion remained gloomy and barbaric, though even this was far milder than that of the people who ultimately came in from the north, probably about A.D. 1000, and who were able to destroy their civilization and impose their own national customs.

AZTECS AND INCAS

These were the Aztecs, who, after centuries of wandering, settled in Mexico, subjugating the Mayas and appropriating most of their civilization. Their architecture, administrative system and agriculture were almost exactly the same as those of the Mayas. But their religion was far more fierce and bloodthirsty, depending as it did on the wholesale sacrifice of thousands of human beings every year. So it was that the Spaniards, when they arrived, were astonished at the mixture of mildness and ferocity which they found among the natives, the contrast between the civilization which had invented a kind of paper, formed an alphabet and developed the arts of reading and writing, and the religion which demanded human sacrifices to the god of war. When the Spanish conqueror, Cortez, first arrived in Mexico, he was entertained by the Aztec king, Montezuma, as an especial privilege, at a human sacrifice.

Further south, along the Pacific seaboard, another Indian race had built up an astonishing civilization. The Incas of Peru had neither the scientific ability nor the artistic skill of the Aztecs, though they, too, built cities, cultivated crops, developed the arts of spinning, weaving and pottery-making and evolved an elaborate social order. Their worship was centred on the sun, the chief of their gods, and their Prince, the Inca himself, was regarded as divine, the Child of the Sun. It was a land rich in gold and silver mines, all of which were the property of the Inca, who also owned all the flocks of llamas in the country and their wool. The Incas had only the most primitive tools, and the only metal with which they worked was bronze. Yet they contrived to fit great blocks of stone exactly together and build vast temples and palaces, the greatest of which was the Temple of the Sun in their capital of Cuzco. Their administration depended on an elaborate system of well-constructed roads; though they had not discovered how to make a wheel, and the horse was unknown in the

American continent, they had learnt to use the llama as a trained beast of burden. But this lack of horses was to be one of the deciding factors in the Spanish conquest. For, when the Spaniards appeared mounted and in armour, the Indians took them for new and terrible four-footed monsters and their troops were completely demoralized.

SPAIN INVADES AMERICA

When they first came in contact with American civilization, the Spaniards brought nothing but ruin and destruction. In 1494, the Spaniards and the Portuguese had signed a treaty, dividing the whole of the newly discovered worlds into two halves, so as to avoid perpetual disputes. Central and southern America, with the exception of Brazil, fell into the Spanish sphere of influence, and it was not long before the more adventurous of the colonists were tempted to leave the islands and explore the mainland. In 1518, Spanish explorers had first sighted Mexican villages inland; and a year later, Hernando Cortez sailed from Cuba to conquer the Aztec kingdom of Mexico. He landed at what later became the city of Vera Cruz, and having burnt his boats, so that there should be no chance of a retreat, advanced on the capital. Without gunpowder, horses or any of the harder metals, the natives were at the mercy of even a small force of European soldiers. By a mixture of treachery and courage, Cortez was able to conquer the whole kingdom within three years. King Montezuma, whose guest he had originally been, he made his prisoner and annexed a new and vast province for the Spanish Crown. "I gave you more provinces", Cortez once said to Charles V, "than your ancestors left you cities." More important still, from the point of view of an emperor who was constantly in need of money for his innumerable campaigns in Germany and North Africa, Mexico proved to be rich in gold and silver, of which large quantities were soon exported to Spain. But there was even greater wealth to be won farther south from the Incas of Peru.

Incredible legends of the wealth and splendour of the Incas reached the Spaniards through the natives of Mexico. It was even said that the streets of Cuzco were paved with gold; and it was not long before greed sent the Spaniards out on further conquests. Pizarro, the man who, with but a handful of soldiers, conquered the whole kingdom of Peru, had all the unpleasant qualities and few of the virtues of Cortez. He was recklessly brave and utterly ruthless and treacherous; but it is doubtful if anyone less unscrupulous could have achieved what he did. It took him seven years to penetrate the Inca kingdom and five more to conquer it; and even then there was a bitter civil war between the conquerors, in which Pizarro himself lost his life, before the kingdom was finally secured to Spain as the province of New Castile. There is nothing in the records of Cortez and Pizarro to suggest that their conquest of America was a triumph of civilization over barbarism. Pizarro invited the Inca king, Atahualpa, to a con-

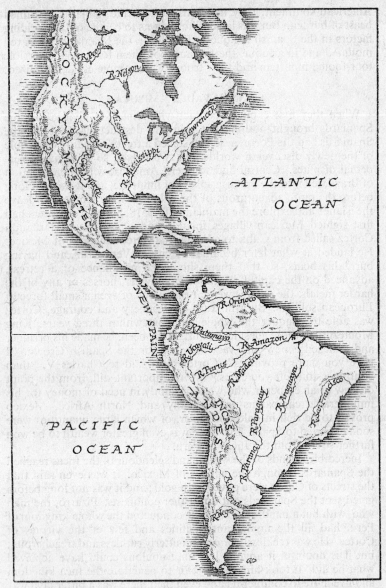

Labels on map: R.Peace, R.Nelson, ROCKY, R.Missouri, Colorado, R.Arkansas, Canadian, R.del Norte, R.Mississippi, S.Lawrence R., MTS, AZTECS, NEW SPAIN, ATLANTIC OCEAN, R.Orinoco, R.Putumayo, R.Ucayali, R.Amazon, R.Puris, R.Madeira, ANDES, R.Paraguay, INCAS, R.Parana, R.Paraguay, R.S.Francisco, PACIFIC OCEAN, R.Colorado, R.Negro

AMERICA AT THE TIME OF THE SPANISH CONQUEST

The two main indigenous civilizations of America were those of the Aztecs in Mexico and the Incas of Peru. Though both North and South comprised immense tracts of virgin territory the so-called "Indians" were scattered extensively over the present area of the U.S.A. and Canada, and the central and southern regions. The majority of Indians lived a primitive tribal life.

ference, made him prisoner, promised him his freedom in return for a roomful of gold, and after having been paid in full, put him to death. The whole history of the Spanish Conquest was marked by treacherous episodes of this kind. During the course of the next twenty years, the continent of South America was brought under European rule, and everywhere the Spaniards' progress was marked by bloodshed and violence. Even when the conquest was complete, matters scarcely improved, for the Spaniards proved themselves bad colonists, They desired only to extort from their new lands as much gold and silver as possible, and in so doing they reduced the natives from a condition of happy prosperity to misery, starvation and death. It was impossible to get enough immigrants from Spain to work the gold and silver mines, and the Spaniards therefore forced the Indians to dig for them. It was soon found that the health of the natives would not stand up to forced labour of this kind. Thousands of them died, and others were herded in to take their place. Sometimes whole villages of Indians would commit suicide together rather than face slavery in the Spanish mines. Soon such methods began to depopulate the country. In the end, the problem was solved by the importation of African negro slaves, who were better able to withstand the heavy labour and dangerous climate; but the prosperity and fertility of the new provinces had already been almost destroyed by excesses.

ASPECTS OF SPANISH COLONIZATION

The blame for this disastrous history cannot be laid entirely on the Spanish government. Charles V took an intense interest in his South American dominions, drew up an elaborate scheme of government and did everything in his power to protect the natives from exploitation. Thanks to his energy and interest and to the ability of Mendoza, the first Viceroy of New Spain, some remarkable progress was made. More than two hundred cities were established, with municipal governments organized on European lines. An elaborate system of law courts was set up. Mendoza himself was a wise governor who did his best to make Spanish government a beneficial and civilizing influence. The importation of European horses and cattle, of new crops, vegetables and fruits, and of European methods of agriculture and industry certainly made possible a fuller and richer life, in the material sense, than had existed before the Spanish Conquest. But the example of Mendoza was only too seldom followed by other Spanish Governors. It was impossible to control the colonies from Spain, and in spite of Charles V's efforts, there is no doubt that millions of the Indians perished as a direct result of Spanish methods of colonial administration. Many laws were passed for the protection of the natives, but there was no adequate machinery to enforce them.

The one great civilizing influence which the Spaniards brought with them to the New World was that of the Church. The conversion of heathen Asiatics had been one of Isabella's chief motives in subsidizing Columbus; and even Cortez felt himself to be something of a crusader and was careful to provide his expeditions with Catholic missionaries. Though the conquerors cared little enough for the bodily welfare of the Indians, they showed much zeal for their spiritual salvation; the Church, in fact, did a great deal to soften the hardships of Spanish rule. It was not only that the religious orders of Spain, and more especially the newly founded Jesuits, found a splendid field for missionary work. The Church made genuine efforts to prevent the enslavement of natives in the mines; a priest named Las Casas did most to bring home to the central government the disastrous conditions to which the Indians were being reduced. The American Church was very soon organized on European lines, and her monasteries became an important civilizing influence.

The explorers had suddenly increased the size of the known world and, in so doing, had put new and vast sources of wealth at the disposal of western Europe. The spices and fabrics, jewels and curiosities which flowed in from the East proved a great stimulant both to commerce and art, and made life suddenly fuller and richer. The gold and silver of South America were a more doubtful blessing to Spain, since they upset the economic organization of the kingdom, encouraged Spaniards to live idly on the profits of their colonies, and ultimately caused widespread misery by changing all price-levels. The Church, also, had gained a whole new world, but for her, too, there were dangerous results from the new discoveries. Her authority depended very largely on tradition, and on the acceptance of all the old ideas handed down from generation to generation. These ideas had now received yet another rude shock. Here were new worlds and whole civilizations undreamt of by the Schoolmen; and this shock to traditional ideas and doctrines came just at the moment when the Church needed, more than ever before, to use the weight of tradition and authority. For she was about to be attacked from within; and the allegiance of the new believers beyond the Atlantic was to be offset by the serious losses which she sustained in Europe.

CHAPTER 49

THE REFORMATION

THE belief that the Christian world ought to be united and indivisible had inspired the work of the greatest philosophers and writers of the Middle Ages, and had given its driving force to such international movements as the crusades. But the decay of the greatest medieval institutions, the Papacy and the Empire, had seriously weakened this ideal of the unity of Christendom, and both the Renaissance and the discoveries of explorers and scientists had loosened the hold of all the old ideas. Men had become more conscious of their own individual, local and national concerns, more ambitious and grasping, as the possibilities of power and wealth increased; they worried less about their responsibilities as members of the western civilization which was still fighting desperately against the danger of the gradually advancing power of the empire ruled by Ottoman Turks.

At the beginning of the sixteenth century, however, the outer forms of the old unity still survived. Between 1516 and 1521, Charles V inherited an Empire which included more than half Europe and the greater part of the newly discovered continent of South America. He held the title of Holy Roman Emperor, and actually united under his rule a greater proportion of the known world than any of his predecessors since Charlemagne. Thus the ideal of a united Empire of the West survived into a world which was fast changing from medieval to "modern" ideas. In the same way, the Church had still preserved all the appearance and outward forms of her power. The Pope was still spiritual head of Western Christendom, despite the weakening of his authority by the Babylonish Captivity and by the growing luxury and corruption of his court at Rome. So long as western civilization remained united in religion under the Papacy, there was a chance that the old ideals of unity and brotherhood might be saved from perishing in the perpetual rivalries and quarrels of the new nation-states.

It was the Reformation which finally destroyed the last vestiges of solidarity, completed the work of the Renaissance, and made the differences that had already appeared between the various parts of Europe fundamental and permanent. It completely broke up the old religious unity of western Europe, and, in so doing, ultimately made it impossible for Charles V to revive a real Empire in the West.

AIMS OF THE REFORMERS

Both these results of the Reformation were very largely accidental. For none of the leaders, in the early stages of the movement, intended to challenge the authority of the Pope or to set up churches in opposition to the Church of Rome. They aimed only at reforming the abuses and abolishing the corrupt practices which infested almost every department of the Church. Very often the lead was taken by great churchmen themselves, such as Colet, Dean of St. Paul's from 1504 to 1519, who saw that there was much truth in the complaints of men like Wycliffe and Huss, and denounced from the pulpit the vices, luxury and slackness of their fellow-clergy. Martin Luther himself, the man who first broke away from Rome and defied the authority of the Pope, was a distinguished theologian and a monk.

The aim of the reformers was, in fact, to reorganize and purify the old Church, not to establish a new one; and their work owed its impetus to a general discontent with the state of affairs which had been growing steadily for over a century. There were three main elements which combined to form this general discontent with the rule of the Church of Rome. In the first place, the man in the street had long been dissatisfied with a religion which had become too formal. There were more priests than ever, but less and less piety; more and more churches were being built, but the services held in them were increasingly mere matters of form, of hastily mumbled prayers with little meaning or reality in them. People flocked to buy indulgences or pardons for their sins, but bothered less and less about the sins themselves; and those who wanted a genuine religion, as an aid to leading a better life, turned away in disgust from this spectacle.

LAYMEN'S APPROACH TO CHRISTIANITY

The Lollard movement in England had sprung from a desire among ordinary men and women to get back to the simple truths of Holy Scripture, which were becoming overlaid with too much ceremony and formal prayer and fasting. Men desired to be good Christians, without having to shut themselves up in monasteries away from the temptations of the world; women sought a faith which would help them to be good wives, rather than one which required them to dedicate themselves as nuns. So, in Germany during the fifteenth century, the same feeling produced private societies among the tradespeople and ordinary folk in almost every town which met to pray together and discuss the Scriptures, without the need of a priest to mediate between them and God, or of formal service and ceremony.

This feeling among ordinary laymen in northern Europe was reflected among the scholars. The Italian Renaissance had never been much concerned with religion, though a few of the greatest humanists south of the Alps, notably Pico della Mirandola, perhaps the greatest of them all, had set themselves to reconcile the best of the ancient philosophers with the doctrines of Christianity. The one notable religious reformer of fifteenth-century Italy, the Florentine friar, Savonarola, was a strong opponent of Renaissance art and learning. His powerful sermons persuaded the people to burn whole stacks of priceless works of art as "frivolities". The Renaissance Papacy had no use for such a man, and he was burnt as a heretic. But in the north, in Germany, and the Netherlands, and in England, the great scholars and writers nearly all used their learning to expose the mistakes which had crept into the Church's teaching, to correct the faults in the translation of the Bible from Hebrew and Greek into Latin, and to ridicule and denounce the corruption and stupidity of the majority of the clergy. Such men as Reuchlin in Germany, Grocyn, who brought the study of Greek to Oxford, Linacre, and the great French scholar, Lefèbre, devoted their lives to a critical examination of the texts of Scripture on which Christian teaching must be based. All these men wanted to see the Church purified and regenerated, but not superseded; and Sir Thomas More, one of the greatest and most charming men of his age, though he bitterly criticized the corrupt and loose-living English clergy, preferred, in 1535, to be beheaded rather than deny the authority of the Pope.

By far the most distinguished of the scholars who attacked the moral degeneracy of Rome was Erasmus of Rotterdam. He very quickly gained a European reputation for learning and for the polished style of his writings; and in consequence, when he turned his pen against the corruptions of the Church, he found a large and sympathetic public ready to read and to applaud what he had to say. His most famous work of this kind, the *Praise of Folly*, published in 1511, did a great deal to lower the prestige of the Church and loosen her hold on men's minds, and he himself admitted that he "laid the egg" of the Reformation; but he went on to claim that "Luther hatched a bird of quite a different breed". For Erasmus remained a loyal son of the Church to the end, and bitterly attacked Luther for breaking away into heresy. He only wished to provoke the clergy to reform by satirizing their vices, but there is no doubt that his works did much to turn the minds of thinking men and women against the guidance of Rome.

There was one other important influence at work to undermine the power of the Papacy. The rise of the new nation-state and the increasingly nationalist outlook of most Europeans made people resent more than ever the spiritual authority of a foreigner in Rome. Above all, they hated having to contribute money towards the up-keep of the vastly expensive Papal court and towards the buildings with which the Popes were beautifying Rome. Kings, nobles, merchants and common people were, for once, agreed on this. The taxes levied on ecclesiastical revenues by the Pope and the profits from the sale of pardons and indulgences were grudged, especially in England and Germany, by hard-headed men who wanted money to stay in their own country; and the fact that the court for which they were paying was luxurious and corrupt made the burden yet more intolerable. In addition to this, the local clergy had become too wealthy and too powerful. The broad lands which had been left to monasteries and cathedral chapters were coveted by the rising middle class, who wanted land in which to invest the profits of trade; and kings and princes disliked the existence of a large and wealthy body of clergy who were largely exempt from taxation and in addition immune from the jurisdiction of the royal courts of justice.

MARTIN LUTHER

All these influences had been at work for more than a century, preparing men's minds for a change and weakening the hold of the Church, when, in October 1517, Martin Luther launched his attack on indulgences which was to provoke the Reformation. In Germany, in the Scandinavian countries and in England, there was already a discontented public opinion, inclined to dislike all things which were Latin or "Italianate", and only waiting for a leader and an opportunity to attack the Italianized Papacy, which seemed to care only about extracting money from the faithful followers of the Church.

Luther was a monk and a university lecturer at Wittenberg, the capital of the Elector of Saxony, and he was one of the many men who had long been dissatisfied with the apparent lack of religious feeling behind the ceremonies of the Church. He himself had become a monk on a sudden impulse, after a friend, walking with him through the forest, had been struck by lightning and killed. He had felt that he owed his life to God, but had no real vocation for the monastic life, and was for a long time very unhappy as a monk. He was tortured by an exaggerated sense of sin, from which he could not escape however harshly he starved and mortified his body, until his confessor sent him to the Epistles of St. Paul to discover the real meaning of that Grace of God which can relieve from the burden of their sins all who trust and have faith. From then on, Luther had been happy, and he had developed into one of the leaders of thought in the German Church, famous as a preacher and teacher, one of the star lecturers who attracted students to the newly founded University of Wittenberg. But he had begun to hold doctrines not wholly consistent with Roman theology. No good works of his had saved him from sin; it had been simply an act of faith on his part. He had believed in the love and mercy of God, and God's grace had done the rest. Thus he tended, on the basis of his own experience, to emphasize the importance of justification by faith and to minimize the other equally important Catholic doctrine of justification by good works.

The Epistles of St. Paul had also influenced Luther towards a more simple piety and a dislike of over-elaborate ritual and outward observances. St. Paul had been largely concerned with the problem of substituting the simple truths of Christianity for the more formalized religion of the Jews; Luther found much that was similar to formal Judaism in the Catholic Church of the sixteenth century. Luther's mind was already prepared for attack when a man named Tetzel set out on a tour of Germany in 1517 to sell indulgences to raise money for rebuilding the church of St. Peter's in Rome.

SCANDAL OF PAPAL INDULGENCES

Indulgences were precisely the type of abuse which Luther had learnt to hate most. They offered people a chance to buy remission of their sins, instead of showing a true repentance by leading better lives; and Tetzel was a gross, vulgar man who played on the superstitions of the people. When he found some of his own flock slipping away to buy indulgences, Luther felt that he must attack this practice; he nailed up on the church door at Wittenberg the famous Ninety-Five Theses denouncing the theory and practice of indulgences, which he was prepared to defend in argument with any theologian who cared to take the opposite view.

The effect in Germany was instantaneous. Every class felt that here, at last, was a man who had the courage to protest against all the things which they had hated for so long. Princes who were

A geographer of the fifteenth century pictured by Ian Stradanus. The revival of geographical science contributed to the discoveries of Columbus and da Gama.

This drawing is attributed to Columbus: it shows a Spanish Caravel, the type of ship in which his voyage to America was made.

Fernando de Magellan, 1470–1521, the great Portuguese navigator who rounded Cape Horn when in the service of the King of Spain.

Lucas Cramach's portrait of Martin Luther, 1482–1546, leader of German Protestantism and founder of the Evangelical Church.

John Calvin, 1509–64, the Frenchman who founded Presbyterianism. For over twenty years he preached his doctrine of predestination.

The Court of Lions at the Alhambra, in Granada, Spain, one of the best examples of Moorish architecture in Europe.

anxious to seize the lands of the clergy, knights who hoped to save themselves from extermination by the princes, merchants and townsfolk who grudged money to Rome, and peasants who suffered terrible hardship under the old system and expected any change to be for their good, all rallied to Luther's support. Tetzel was mobbed and forced to give up trying to sell indulgences, and in some towns the bishops and higher clergy were afraid to appear in clerical dress, so strong was the feeling against them. But the Papacy, fearful of losing a good market for indulgences, refused even to let the Theses be openly discussed. Luther was simply ordered to withdraw them, and on his refusal to do so, was promptly excommunicated.

MARTIN LUTHER QUESTIONS ROMAN AUTHORITY

The result of this short-sighted attitude of the Papal court was to inflame feeling in Germany and to drive Luther to question the whole authority of Rome. He began to publish a series of pamphlets and sermons, appealing to Holy Scripture against the Pope, and developing his idea that a man who believed in the teaching of the New Testament was sure of God's grace, without any need for the intercession of the Church or of any priest. These pamphlets were printed in thousands by the Wittenberg University Press and circulated throughout the length and breadth of Germany; the most famous, the *Appeal to the Christian Nobility of the German Nation*, published in 1520, was one of the best sellers of the century. The result was that when Luther was summoned by the Emperor Charles V to appear on a charge of heresy before the Diet of Worms in 1521, he had become a national hero, as Wycliffe and Huss had before him.

The young Emperor was forced by his very position to stand for the unity of Christendom, and was, moreover, a sincere Catholic who thought it his duty to support the Pope. He managed to get Luther proclaimed an outlaw by the Diet of Worms, and his firm stand for the Church rallied many wavering Catholics to her side. But the Emperor was never able to devote much time to Germany's problems. A French war, a big rebellion in Spain and the danger of the Turkish advance called him away almost immediately. Luther was snatched into safety by the Elector of Saxony, and hidden in the castle of the Wartburg. From there he continued to pour forth pamphlets rallying his followers, and finally issued what was perhaps his greatest work, his translation of the New Testament into German.

Luther's teachings had the effect of stirring up every class in Germany which felt oppressed or dissatisfied. The Knights, a class which lived largely by robbery and private warfare, tried to win some support for themselves by attacking the princes of the Church in the name of Luther, and thus provoked the so-called Knights' War. The peasants all over Germany rose in revolt in the belief that Luther's teaching meant the beginning of an era of equality and communism. Both these risings were crushed by a combination of the more power-

S   (H.W.)

ful princes, and both were condemned by Luther. He was essentially a conservative, and disliked all the extreme views which appeared as soon as men broke away from the old Church. So there arose a close alliance between Luther and those North German princes who sympathized with his religious beliefs; Lutheranism became an established church closely linked to the state and very conservative in outlook. The more extreme forms of Protestantism were found mostly in the towns, and were generally associated with a vague communism. The men who joined these movements were mostly Anabaptists—that is to say, they believed in a second, or adult, baptism—and whenever they appeared they were ruthlessly crushed by the princes, with the full approval of the majority of Lutheran leaders.

Thus, when Charles V was able to return to Germany, in 1530, there was already a large body of Lutherans in North Germany. Even then, the Emperor was unable to move against them, owing to a fresh invasion of Turks into Austria. The result was that a new "Protestant" church was able to develop complete independence, and gradually almost all the North German states joined the new religion. In South Germany, in Bavaria and in Austria, the old Church was able after a little to hold its own; later on, it was even able to recover some of the ground lost farther north. But it was not until 1544 that Charles got a more lasting peace with France and secured a truce with the Turks, which left his hands free to attempt to reunite the Church in Germany; and by then, the differences between Protestant and Catholic had become so great that it was impossible satisfactorily to reconcile the two. He could only hope to bring the Protestants back to the fold of Rome by means of force.

ZWINGLI AND CALVIN

Meanwhile, other men had been spreading the new doctrines outside Germany and developing beliefs which began to differ from those of Luther. The South German princes remained, on the whole, loyal to the Roman Church. But in the cities of the south and west, such as Constance and Strassburg, the new doctrines flourished; from there, they soon found their way over the frontier into Switzerland, where the Protestant headquarters at Zürich became almost as important as those at Wittenberg. At Zürich the leader of the new movement was Zwingli, a more kindly and tolerant man than Luther, but a more logical extremist in belief, without Luther's caution and conservatism. Unfortunately Zwingli linked religion too closely to politics, and so involved Zürich in war with the Catholic Forest Cantons, which feared an attempt to break up the Swiss Confederation. At the battle of Kappel in 1531, Zürich was defeated and Zwingli himself was killed. Although the Forest Cantons allowed their enemies to keep their new faith, Zürich lost her prestige, and the centre of Swiss Protestantism was gradually shifted to Geneva.

Differences of opinion between Lutherans and Zwinglians had already divided Protestantism into two camps. This division became permanent when Calvin arrived in Geneva in 1535 to organize the new religion there. Before long he became the acknowledged leader of the Swiss Protestants. Calvin found Geneva struggling to preserve her independence from the Prince Bishop whose rule she had just thrown off. The citizens had rejected the old religion when they first rose in revolt, but they had not found any real faith to take its place. In consequence, the city had become the scene of moral collapse, the home of every kind of loose living and debauchery, and likely to fall an easy victim to the forces of reaction unless some great leader could be found to restore her morals. Calvin proved himself to be the man they needed. He had just fled from Paris to escape arrest for heresy, and he brought to the organization of Church and State in Geneva the hard cold logic of a French lawyer. He had a difficult fight to persuade the city to accept the rigid and severe discipline which he believed to be necessary both for the service of God and the salvation of the city from the Prince Bishop. But in the end he triumphed, and succeeded in his efforts to establish in Geneva an independent government which was completely dominated by his Church.

THE SPREAD OF LUTHERANISM AND CALVINISM

Calvin could tolerate no faith which could not be proved to the satisfaction of his reason. He produced, therefore, a totally new system of belief, every detail of which was logically worked out, and which, unlike Lutheranism, was not linked by conservative tradition to the old Catholic theology. The central belief of the Calvinist system was that of predestination. Those whom God wished to save, the "elect", were granted faith and permitted to see the truth; the remainder, those who had not been arbitrarily chosen for salvation, were utterly and irrevocably damned, and could do nothing to save themselves from Hell. Moreover Calvin believed that the service of God must be more important than the service of man, and accordingly forced all civil magistrates into subordination under the ministers of the Church. No government has ever imposed a harsh moral code so rigidly. Until Calvin's death in 1564, the citizens of Geneva had to abandon worldly pleasures. Card-playing and all light amusements were forbidden; and a woman who showed vanity in her dress, or a man guilty of a thoughtless swear-word, was liable to severe punishment.

Though Luther must, of course, be regarded as the man responsible for starting all the different Protestant movements in Europe, his own doctrines, developed after the Diet of Worms in Saxony and Hesse, never spread far beyond Germany itself. Luther was, in outlook and temperament, a very typical German, and was able to understand and to satisfy the needs of Germans who felt as he did. His doctrinal system, too, was nicely adapted for the use of a ruler who wished above all to become the head of the Church as well as of the state within his own dominions. But it had none of the qualities of a fighting creed. Its essentials were too negative to enable it to stand any very serious persecution, and persecution, as a rule, tends to produce fanaticism. The fact, moreover, that it was so definitely German in its appeal made it difficult for Lutheranism to make converts outside Germany. It is true that it spread through the Hanseatic cities on the south coast of the Baltic into Denmark, Norway and Sweden; but here, again, there was no threat of serious persecution, since the rulers found the change of belief as convenient as the Princes of North Germany had found it. Elsewhere, particularly in France and the Netherlands, where there was persecution to be met, it was the harder, more logical creed of Calvin, which inspired the missionary zeal of Protestantism.

In the years after 1535, Geneva became the teaching-centre of the new faith. Men flocked to the university there from all over Europe, and a constant stream of preachers and teachers issued forth again to spread the Gospel. Already there were signs that the Catholic Church was preparing a great revival and setting her house in order, in an attempt to recover some of the lost ground. Where it had no political organization to fall back on, Lutheranism soon proved incapable of holding its own against a revitalized Catholicism. In Austria and South Germany the old religion regained the hold which at one time it had almost lost, and it is possible that, but for the effect of Calvin's teaching, Protestantism would have been suppressed.

PROTESTANTS PERSECUTED IN THE NETHERLANDS

The Netherlands had been quickly affected by the Lutheran movement in the neighbouring German states, more especially because they contained many great cities where there was a large and prosperous middle-class sufficiently educated to appreciate the need for reform. But in the Netherlands, Charles V was in a much stronger position than in Germany. There were no independent princes to take the new beliefs under their protection and use them for their own convenience, and the Government therefore felt itself strong enough to try to stamp out heresy by force. Here, again, Lutheranism showed itself ineffective against persecution, and though Protestantism continued to exist, it was only in its extreme and more fanatical forms, mainly Anabaptist. It is doubtful if even these fanatics would have survived the severe persecution which they suffered under Charles V and his son, Philip II, but for the sudden influx of Calvinist missionaries from Geneva. Their zeal at once stiffened the resistance of the Protestants, especially in the northern provinces, which were soon to be converted entirely to the new faith. But this reinforcement of Protestantism came later than elsewhere in Europe, and until his abdication in 1555, Charles V was able to maintain the hold of the Church of Rome over his dominions in the Netherlands.

For very similar reasons the development of Protestantism in France was also comparatively late. Francis I was an unscrupulous man who had no hesitation in allying with German Protestants, and even with Turks, when he needed their help against the Emperor. But when heresy appeared in France itself, he regarded it as a threat to his own political authority, and feared to see the expanding power of France crippled by internal religious quarrels. He persecuted Protestants in France even more ruthlessly than Charles V did in the Netherlands; and once more it needed the stiffening influence of Calvinist teachers to establish the new doctrines. They were able to build up a strong Protestant or "Huguenot" Church in France which proved itself capable of standing up to persecution. It rapidly increased in numbers and popularity until, in 1559, before the outbreak of the first of the French wars of religion, the Huguenots numbered perhaps a fifth of the total population of the country.

JOHN KNOX BRINGS CALVINISM TO SCOTLAND

The other great field for Calvinist preachers was in Scotland, where John Knox, who had studied under Calvin at Geneva, was able to convert rapidly more than half the population to the Calvinist creed, in the form which we have learnt to call Presbyterianism. Knox's system was a careful adaptation to Scottish needs of Calvin's idea of a theocracy—the rule of the Church over the State. Here again, the Reformation came late, and its progress was held up for a time by the loyalty of Mary, Queen of Scots, to her Catholic faith. But in the end, Mary was defeated and driven into exile, and in 1560 Knox issued the Confession of Faith which established the Kirk, the Presbyterian Church of Scotland, as the sovereign authority in the country, in all matters, secular as well as strictly ecclesiastical.

ENGLAND'S NATIONAL CHURCH

The beginnings of the Reformation in England had very little to do with any of the movements on the Continent, but were chiefly the result of a quarrel between King Henry VIII and the Pope. Henry wanted to be rid of his wife, Catherine of Aragon, and the Pope refused to grant him the necessary dispensation. There was already in England almost as much resentment at the financial and political pretensions of the Papacy as in Germany; and when the King, in order to get his way, decided to deny the authority of the Pope and take for himself the office of Supreme Head of the English Church, the nation wholeheartedly supported him. All the taxes levied by Rome were abolished by Act of Parliament, and between 1529 and 1536, the English Church was reorganized on a national basis. Before long, Henry went still farther. The monasteries in England were wealthy and powerful, but were filled largely with worldly men who made little attempt to lead godly lives. Henry made their laxity an excuse for suppressing them and distributing their lands among those

families who had most faithfully served the new Tudor dynasty. He
provoked some opposition, especially in the north, where there was
an armed insurrection known as the Pilgrimage of Grace; but, on the
whole, Englishmen felt that the monasteries had outlived their usefulness, and were glad to see them go.

Apart from his attack on the Papacy and the monasteries, Henry
VIII had no wish to make any changes in Catholic doctrine. By
writing a book against Luther, he had earned from the Pope the title
of Defender of the Faith; and during the last years of his reign, he
tried hard to enforce the old Catholic teaching and burnt Lutherans
and Anabaptists as ruthlessly as any Catholic. But the teaching of
Wycliffe had left its mark in England, and no amount of persecution
could prevent the spread of the new doctrines from Germany and
Switzerland. In 1535, Coverdale published the first printed Bible in
English; and under Henry's son, Edward VI, part of the nation was
converted to Protestantism. The extreme Protestant party con-

RELIGIONS OF EUROPE, 1550

The teaching of Calvin, Luther, and Knox caused the Protestant creed to super-
sede the Roman Church over most of Northern Europe. Portugal, Spain, Italy,
Austria, Hungary, Poland, and most of France and Ireland still clung to the old
beliefs. Russia and Greece observed the ritual of the Greek Orthodox Church.

trolled the Council and exercised a decisive influence over the young King. The Government went too fast for the people, and in the end, provoked a reaction under Edward's sister, Mary, in the next reign; but by 1553, there were certainly nearly as many followers of Protestant doctrines as Catholics in England.

Thus between 1520 and 1550, Reformed Churches superseded the Church of Rome over most of northern Europe, and for a time even threatened her supremacy farther south, in Austria and the Tyrol, and in Southern France. It was to be expected that such a movement would provoke an organized counter-attack; and in fact, the Emperor Charles V spent his life fighting the new faith and striving to reunite Christendom. The Counter-Reformation, as it was later called, was most active in the second half of the sixteenth century. But very soon after Luther's first defiance of the Pope, the Church of Rome began to set her house in order, to suppress the abuses which had given the reformers such a handle against her, to re-define her doctrines, and to forge the weapons with which to regain her lost dominions.

We have still to consider the political events of the first half of the sixteenth century, on which the Reformation exercised so decisive an influence, and the gradual stiffening of Catholic resistance to the reformed doctrines. There was a preliminary attempt to rally the Catholic forces and prevent the disaster before it was too late; this had failed before the Counter-Reformation really began. The failure, with all its manifold consequences, both political and religious, centres round the career of the Emperor Charles V.

CHAPTER 50

EMPIRE OF CHARLES V

THE last attempt to restore the unity of western Europe resulted from the too successful marriage policy of the Habsburg family. The Emperor Maximilian had, as we have seen, joined the Netherlands to his own lands by marrying Mary of Burgundy. This was sound policy. For the Netherlands were part of the Empire, and if the Habsburgs were to make a nation of Germany, they must steadily increase their private fortune and power there, until they were strong enough to dominate all the other princes. It was, however, a mistake to extend this matrimonial web outside Germany and to marry Philip the Fair of Burgundy, son and heir of Maximilian and Mary, to Joanna of Castile, daughter of Ferdinand and Isabella. For Joanna's brother and sister died and left her heiress to the whole of Spain, the New World discovered by Columbus, and the southern half of Italy which belonged to Aragon. Thus Philip's eldest son, Charles V, inherited an empire greater than that of Charlemagne, and so accidentally revived the idea of a united Western Christendom.

It was too big an empire for any one man to rule. Government had become a much more complicated affair since the days of Charlemagne and Frederick II, and as civilization advanced, the problems of the different parts of Europe became more varied. There was much work to be done before Spain was properly united and reduced to order; Germany and the Netherlands each required clever government for a long time, if they were to be saved from anarchy; and the ruler of a vast colonial empire could not spare enough time for the political difficulties of Germany. He had at the same time to meet a fresh advance of the Turkish invaders in the Balkans and along the Mediterranean coast of Africa, and to deal with the growing problem of heresy that beset the church in northern Europe.

DIFFICULTIES OF CHARLES V

Though he was conscientious and hard-working enough, Charles V was scarcely the man to deal with so complicated a problem. At the age of seventeen, he was still a shy, awkward, silent boy, with an impediment in his speech, who struck foreign ambassadors as being half-witted. He, who ruled over so many different races, never learnt any of their languages well, and so had the greatest difficulty in understanding their problems; and he was given no time to learn how to govern before he had to shoulder all his many burdens. For his father died when he was only six, and the shock sent his mother mad, so that Charles inherited directly from both his grandfathers, who died before he was nineteen. In consequence, he very nearly lost Spain through inexperience at the beginning of his reign, and never quite, throughout his life, caught up with the delays and mistakes of the first few years. But he did succeed in holding together all his scattered dominions; he did check the advance of the Turks; and he made a heroic effort to bring the German Lutherans back into the fold of the Catholic Church. He accomplished what he did by sheer hard work and an obstinate refusal to recognize defeat. His whole life was spent in ceaseless journeyings from end to end of his empire, often carried in a litter because his gout made it impossible for him to ride, until he was forced to retire, crippled and exhausted, to a Spanish monastery to die. The story of his life, in fact, sums up the history of Europe, and indeed of much of the world, between 1500 and 1558.

Through all his difficulties Charles had the added handicap of war with France. Save for Austria, each of his dominions had long-standing quarrels with the French. As ruler of the Netherlands, he inherited the old enmity of the Dukes of Burgundy for the French Crown; as King of Spain, he had to uphold the right of Castile to the kingdom of Navarre on the Pyrenees and to check Moslem sea-power in the Mediterranean; as suzerain of Milan, he had to prevent the French from establishing themselves in control of northern Italy; as German Emperor, he had to defend Imperial interests on the

Rhine. For France could not tolerate being hemmed in by the Habsburg dominions. Like Germany at a later date, she felt herself "encircled"; and Francis I of France, Charles's contemporary, spent his life trying to break this Habsburg ring. It was a very equal struggle. Charles had the greater resources; but Francis had the advantage of interior lines, and he could strike suddenly where he liked, while it took Charles a long time to concentrate his strength for a counter-stroke. Thus the internal problems of the lands over which Charles ruled were all gradually subordinated to three more general objectives—the defeat of the French, the defeat of the Turks and the conversion or subjugation of the Lutherans. He regarded his subjects as sources of money and men which he could use for these purposes, and taxed them ruthlessly in order to advance what he conceived to be the benefit of Christendom as a whole.

We cannot summarize in detail the internal history of Charles's dominions during the first half of the sixteenth century. In the Netherlands, he was lucky enough to find two very able women, his aunt Margaret and his sister Mary, to take over the burden of government for him. Habsburg women often had far more outstanding ability than the men, and the Archduchess Margaret was an excellent example. She had a masterful domineering personality, a factor which may have helped to make Charles himself so backward in early years, since he was under her care; and she was almost the only member of her family who ever understood anything of economics. She ruled the Netherlands tactfully, but very firmly, and did a great deal to preserve their wealth and prosperity. It was a difficult period, since the woollen manufactures of Flanders were being slowly destroyed by the competition of the new English weaving industry; but by carefully fostering the trade of the cities farther north which had an outlet to the sea, she was able to ensure that, as the prosperity of Ghent and Ypres declined, the commercial importance of Antwerp and Bruges steadily grew. Her niece, Mary, sometime Queen of Hungary, was something of a virago. She was said to be able to outride any of the men in her suite; and what she lacked in knowledge she made up in energy and strength of will. Under her rule, the various provinces were gradually welded into a more solid whole, in spite of perpetual warfare on the southern frontier; it was largely owing to her that the Netherlands were in the position to make large contributions of money and men to Charles's campaigns.

WAR AGAINST THE TURKS

In the Austrian lands, Charles was able to make use of yet another member of his family, his brother Ferdinand. He had not quite Mary's energy, and he was less single-minded and persevering than Charles. But, although educated in Spain, he adapted himself well to his new German subjects. By the death of his brother-in-law, Louis, in battle against the Turks, he later inherited also the kingdoms of Hungary and Bohemia. It thus fell to him to meet the main force of the Ottoman advance as it moved up through Serbia and Hungary; and it was he who had to act as deputy for the Emperor in Germany during Charles's long absences, to deal with the lawlessness of the knights and the factiousness of the princes. He performed his difficult task faithfully and, on the whole, successfully, and was rewarded in the end with the succession to the Empire on Charles's abdication from the throne in 1556.

But in spite of the use he made of the various members of his family to relieve him of his responsibilities, Charles was still too heavily burdened. In any major crisis, he had to be present himself. Mary had to summon him from Spain in 1540 to overawe the rebellious city of Ghent with an imposing display of Spanish and German troops. He had to take the field himself against the Turks in Hungary in 1532; and he had to be present in person whenever it was necessary to take active steps against the Lutheran Princes in Germany. He was personally responsible for maintaining order in a disunited Italy, perpetually at the mercy of a French invasion; and his personal presence was constantly required in Spain. As ruler of South Italy and Spain he was, moreover, directly responsible for the protection of the eastern Mediterranean from the Barbary pirates of North Africa, who were the advance-guard of the western wing of the Turkish attack. All these tasks had to be performed in the short intervals of peace allowed to him by the King of France.

THE RIVALRY OF CHARLES V AND FRANCIS I

The history of Europe, at the beginning of the sixteenth century, was largely determined by the rivalries between Charles and two other young rulers who succeeded at about the same time. Francis I of France had all the easy charm which Charles lacked, the courtly graces and the love of beauty which were to make the French court famous for its splendour and luxury. He succeeded to one of the strongest powers in Europe. The strength of France had not yet been seriously sapped by campaigns in Italy; the nobility had been subjugated, if only temporarily, by the Crown, and the people were rich and prosperous. Francis himself was largely responsible for the ruin of all this. The extravagance of his court and the expense of his mistresses threw a heavy burden of taxation on his subjects, which was further increased by a series of costly invasions of Italy. Though the lovely *châteaux* on the Loire, at Blois, Chambord and elsewhere, were some of the supreme achievements of the French Renaissance, their cost was enormous. But, above all, it was the long rivalry with Charles V which sapped the strength and prosperity of France.

This struggle was partly the inevitable result of youth and ambition: Charles set out for his first campaign with the remark, "Soon he will be a poor king or I shall be a sorry Emperor." This light-hearted spirit swiftly perished amid the realities of war. Francis could not trust Charles to refrain from aggression. Rightly or wrongly, he felt that he must break the threatening Habsburg ring round France and cut Austria off from Spain by occupying Milan. Charles was determined to leave to his son all the territories which he had inherited. The war dragged on, with intermittent truces that were preludes to further fighting, from 1517 until 1559.

Henry VIII of England was perhaps an even more striking figure

THE EMPIRE OF CHARLES V

than the other two. He was taller and stronger than most of his subjects, a fine athlete and a good soldier. He was also a shining product
of Renaissance education. He had been taught by Skelton and More,
and was able to exchange courtly letters in Latin with Erasmus. In
every way he typified and embodied the new national pride of England, and he was determined to demonstrate his power on foreign
battlefields. He had inherited from his father a tradition of alliance
with Spain and had married a Spanish princess; on the whole he kept
on the Spanish side throughout the war, save for a short time
after 1526 when by repudiating his Spanish wife he alienated
Charles V. But the situation in 1517 gave England a splendid chance
of increasing her power and prestige by selling her alliance as dearly
as possible. Henry's great Minister, Cardinal Wolsey, realized that
the English control of the Channel might be a valuable asset to either
side, since she could cut all communications by sea between Spain
and the Netherlands and provide useful diversions by invading either
Flanders or north-western France. So Wolsey was able to bargain
with a strong hand and to carry out for a short time a policy for which
England was to become famous in later centuries—the maintenance
of the Balance of Power. There was a splendid meeting between
Francis and Henry at the Field of the Cloth of Gold, where each
king tried to outdo the other in magnificence and extravagance of
his followers and equipment. But behind this luxurious demonstration of friendship, Charles V and Henry VIII met quietly at
Gravelines, and riding alone along the sand-dunes, arranged an
alliance much more to England's advantage. So, for the next forty
years, the continent of Europe remained roughly divided into two
armed camps, with England normally grouped on the side of the
Habsburgs.

FRANCE INVADES ITALY

The fighting between Charles V and Francis I was almost continuous, and quite indecisive. They signed five different peace treaties
in twenty-five years, each of which was supposed to be a permanent
settlement. But, in fact, there could be no peace until France was
too exhausted to send any more futile expeditions into Italy. The
climate, the difficulty of maintaining a long line of communications,
and shortage of food, always in the end brought the French invasions
of Italy to disaster; and when Charles, in his turn, took the offensive
and invaded southern France, he was defeated by just the same difficulties. There was a spectacular battle at Pavia in 1525, when the
desperate Imperialists turned on an apparently victorious French
army and destroyed it, actually taking Francis himself prisoner.
But, on the whole, the campaigns were monotonous. The armies on
both sides consisted largely of Swiss and German mercenaries, who
were quite prepared to change sides if offered better pay; neither side
produced a great general. The French could boast of the last great

figure of chivalry, the Chevalier Bayard, who was universally known and loved as "the Knight without fear and without reproach", and who threw away his life to save a retreating French army in a desperate rearguard action in 1524. And the Spaniards produced one heroic figure in Antonio de Leyva, who, though crippled with gout, had himself carried into action at Pavia in a chair. But apart from these men, none of the leaders possessed the heroic qualities necessary to inspire their troops.

When the war at last dragged to a temporary close at the Peace of Crespi in 1544, Francis I was a prematurely old man, worn out by disease and debauch, and Charles was already exhausted and crippled by ceaseless attacks of gout. Neither side had gained or lost anything. Only Charles might claim that, having lost nothing, he had won the war. For he fought always on the defensive, to keep and not to win. The only importance of this long struggle was that it prevented Charles V from concentrating his strength to preserve the unity of the Church and the integrity of Christian Europe. All that he accomplished against the Turks and against the Berber and Moorish pirates had to be done in the short intervals of campaigning against France; and his main effort against the German Protestants had to be postponed until the six years of peace with France and the Turks which followed the Peace of Crespi, when it was too late.

DISCONTENT IN SPAIN

It was fortunate for Charles that he was able to settle the main problems and difficulties of Spain before the French War began. The work of welding Spain into a united nation had been left incomplete by Ferdinand and Isabella. There was great jealousy between the kingdoms of Aragon and Castile; the Catalans longed for independence: there was considerable opposition between the townsmen, who made up the Third Estate in the Spanish Cortes, and the nobles. The Spanish grandees were proud, stubborn, intolerant and cruel. They hated and despised foreigners and they regarded Charles himself as a foreigner. The situation required great tact; but Charles was too young and inexperienced when he arrived in Spain to understand it. He brought with him a host of greedy Flemings from the Netherlands, to whom he gave all the profitable jobs at his disposal. He foolishly irritated the nobles and peoples of Castile by spending longer in Aragon than he had with them; and he made it clear that he regarded the Cortes as a mere machine for extorting money, most of which he spent on bribing the Electors to support the claims of the German Empire.

These mistakes very nearly cost Charles his Spanish kingdom. When he sailed in 1520 to take over the German Empire to which he had been elected, he left a country seething with discontent, which broke out within a few weeks into open rebellion in Castile and Valencia. There is no need to describe at length the course of the revolution. The rebels concentrated on the capture of Charles's mother, the mad queen Joanna, who had been shut up in the castle of Tordesillas, believing that they would find her a sane woman imprisoned merely in order to prevent her from sharing the government with her son. They succeeded in capturing her, only to find that she was, in fact, quite mad. From that moment, the rebellion lost heart. Charles was able to play off the nobles against the towns, and the jealousy of the Aragonese prevented them from supporting the rebellion. The only result in Castile was to strengthen the hand of the royal government. The Parliamentary system, which had given the representatives of the towns at least a share in the government, received a blow from which it never recovered. The administration of the country was concentrated more and more in the hands of a small Royal Council, which was directly under Charles's control, and so the way was paved for the Absolutist Government which was to be the ruin of Spain under Charles's son, Philip II.

CHARLES IN SPAIN AND ITALY

The revolt of Valencia had more far-reaching results. The rebels there turned against the Moors, who formed the bulk of the agricultural population, and forcibly baptized them. When the rebellion was over, these Moors naturally returned to the practice of their old religion, which Charles, by his coronation oath, had promised to allow. The fact that they had been baptized, however—even though forcibly—made them, in the eyes of the Inquisition, members of the Christian Church. The Moors were regarded as Christians who had lapsed into heresy, and in 1526 Charles, feeling that he ought to make some return to God for the miraculous victory of Pavia, secured a dispensation from the Pope absolving him from his coronation oath. The Inquisition was allowed to proceed against the Moors, who refused to submit, and were in consequence either exiled or massacred. Large numbers were rescued by their pirate brethren from North Africa, and the remainder perished. The persecution thus started was extended throughout southern Spain in the later years of Charles V and under Philip II; and as a result of this, the flourishing agriculture of those districts almost ceased to exist. There were no labourers left to till the fields; and Spain came to depend more and more for her wealth and power on gold and silver imported from America, while the real prosperity of the country itself steadily declined.

Charles treated Spain very largely as the paymaster of his vast Empire. The result, in the end, was to drain the country of men and money and to leave it ruined and exhausted. But the full effects of this were not realized until the following reign. For the time, Spain was the most powerful nation in Europe, and the strong national feeling which resulted from the glories of foreign victories enabled Charles to build up a strong, solid and united kingdom. The problem which he faced in Italy was a very different one.

The French wars had kept all the old intrigues and jealousies alive in Italy and had destroyed any hope there might have been of an immediate unification on a national basis. It is true that there was no longer the problem of the French occupation of Milan, since Charles, after ten years of fighting, had finally driven them out. But the Papal States remained a solid block across the centre of the country to prevent any union of north and south; the Pope, Clement VII, was as obstinately determined as his predecessors had been not to sacrifice his temporal independence to the needs of Italian nationalism, and the Papacy remained as suspicious as ever of an Emperor who was also ruler of Naples and Sicily.

When he first visited Italy in 1529, Charles had two main problems to solve. He had to find some sort of political framework which would hold the country together in face of future French invasions; and he had to settle the age-old question of his own relations with the Papacy. In the first, he was comparatively successful. He realized, quite rightly, that it was too soon to think of giving Italy any sort of national constitution, and aimed instead at welding the existing states into a more solid federation. His instinct was conservative; and he left the small states of North Italy intact, re-establishing the hold of the Medici on Florence, and leaving Milan as an independent duchy, though he insisted on maintaining an imperial garrison there. True to Habsburg tradition, he cemented the whole framework together by a number of family marriages; his niece, Christina, had to sacrifice her youth and beauty to the family interest and marry the elderly and diseased Duke of Milan; others of the Emperor's female relations were distributed among the important princes. The system established in 1530 was perhaps a ramshackle solution of Italy's needs. But it achieved its main object in keeping the French out for the next thirty years, and it had the merit of permanence—it lasted almost unchanged for nearly three hundred years.

PAPAL FEAR OF CHARLES V

The settlement with the Pope appeared equally successful, but left the main problems untouched. Clement VII's politics were dictated by fear. He had the old dread, inherited from the days of the Hohenstaufen, of any imperial power which dominated both northern and southern Italy, and so threatened his own states from both sides. He had a particular fear of Charles because in 1526, after the battle of Pavia, the starving and unpaid imperial army had suddenly turned against the Papacy, regarding it as a traitor to Italy and an ally of the French, had stormed and sacked Rome, and had kept Clement for nine months a terrified prisoner in his castle of San Angelo. Above all things, Clement feared that Charles would call another General Council to settle the matter of Luther and so ruin Papal prestige. Charles was, in fact, longing for a General Council which could discuss all the German grievances and carry out the reforms postponed by the Council of Basel. But the Popes, Clement VII and Paul III, were more interested in keeping their own power intact than in restoring the unity of the Catholic Church. It was not until 1545, when it was too late to win back the Lutherans, that the Council of Trent at last met; and by then, the Pope had made it clear that this was not a General Council like that of Constance, but one called by him, presided over by his delegates and subject to his final decisions.

Thus, though Charles was able to patch up a temporary peace with the Papacy and get Clement's outward support for his Italian federation, there was no real understanding between them. For the moment, the Pope gave way to superior force and at Bologna crowned Charles as Holy Roman Emperor with great pomp and ceremony. It was the first time for years that an Emperor had been strong enough to force the Pope to set this final seal on his authority. But it never happened again. Within a few months, Clement was once more intriguing with the French against Charles; and before long a Pope was to order public rejoicings in Rome for a Lutheran victory over the Emperor, just as Innocent IV had rejoiced at the death of Frederick II. The spiritual and temporal heads of Christendom were never again to show themselves united. The coronation at Bologna was a last splendid demonstration of an ideal which was already dead. Even though the infidel was battering at the gates of Europe and the Church was threatened by heresy from within, Pope and Emperor could not combine. The forces which were to influence the developments of the future were to be those of nationalism and independence.

HUNGARY INVADED BY THE TURKS

Charles thus had to meet the two great dangers to the unity of his Empire single-handed. In his fight against the Turks and his struggle to prevent a permanent schism within the Roman Church, he found the King of France always on the other side, the Pope only occasionally friendly, and the King of England a capricious and useless ally. Yet, even though men had ceased to think of the unity of western Europe as a living idea, Charles was able to unite a very considerable portion of Christendom for objects which were undoubtedly international. Against the Turks, at any rate, he roused one last flicker of the spirit which had once sent great armies crusading to the East.

After the fall of Constantinople there had been a pause in the main Turkish advance. But at the beginning of the sixteenth century one of the ablest of the Sultans, Solyman the Magnificent, had launched another wave of the attack. Belgrade, the last outpost in the Balkans, had been besieged and taken, and the great Hungarian plain lay at the mercy of the invaders. In 1526 the blow fell. Solyman advanced against Budapest, and the Hungarian nobles proved themselves, as usual, incapable of united action. Some resistance was organized by Charles's sister, Mary, later Regent of the Netherlands; but she was a mere girl, and the army which her young husband, Louis of Hungary, led out against Solyman was outnumbered and outgeneralled. It was annihilated in the great battle of Mohacs, a battle so decisive that its name became a byword in the folklore and songs of Europe: "No matter," ran the refrain, "more was lost at Mohacs field." King Louis was killed, Budapest fell into the enemy's hands, and Ferdinand, Charles's brother, was able to save only a corner of the Hungarian kingdom which he had inherited from his brother-in-law.

HOW CHARLES MET THE THREAT FROM ISLAM

Three years later, the attack was pushed forward yet farther, and Vienna itself was besieged. Had the city fallen, the Turks would have found a disunited Germany in front of them and no solid power to stem their advance up to the Rhine. Vienna held out, and Solyman was forced to retreat; but he returned in 1532, and Charles himself came to meet the danger. Fortunately he had secured a truce with the French; and Catholics and Protestants were induced to sink their differences in face of their common danger, and to vote the Emperor an army. Charles was able to put a splendid force of Spaniards, Italians, Germans and Flemings into the field, and the Turks, already dispirited by their failure to take the little towns of Güns and Gran, retired without risking a battle. It was not a spectacular success, but it relieved the pressure. Turkish energy was dying down. Vienna was not attacked again for a hundred and fifty years; and, though there was continuous fighting in Hungary, Ferdinand was able after 1532 to hold his own without assistance, especially after 1540, when a war with Persia distracted the Turkish efforts.

On the Mediterranean front, the situation remained critical until the end of the century. The Turks gradually captured all the Venetian possessions, first among the islands of the Levant and then on the mainland of Greece and Dalmatia, Venice put up a good fight; and occasionally the Emperor was able to form a Holy League of Italian states to help her. But such leagues were rarely effective, and though Venice held her own in most of the sea-fighting, her trading colonies had all been lost by the middle of the century. Her most important allies were the Knights of St. John of Jerusalem, who had established their headquarters on the island of Rhodes after the loss of the Holy Land. This last military order of the Church preserved its crusading character far into modern times. The great galleys equipped and officered by the Knights were the only naval force permanently available to check the depredations of Turkish pirates. When Rhodes was besieged and taken by Solyman in 1522, they fell back on Malta and Tripoli, and from these bases continued their running fight against Islam for centuries. They were not powerful enough to meet the full force of the Turkish fleet in battle; but they harried the enemy continuously in the endeavour to free the Christian slaves who were forced to man the oars of the Sultan's galleys.

The Sultans secured control of the eastern Mediterranean by the middle of the sixteenth century, but the efforts of the Venetians and of the Knights of Malta checked them there. The main Turkish fleet rarely penetrated the west of Sicily, though on occasions Turkish troops were landed in southern Italy to co-operate with the French. There was, however, a perpetual danger that they would extend their conquests westwards—a danger which was not finally removed until the great battle at Lepanto in 1571, when Don John of Austria, an illegitimate son of Charles V, led a combined fleet of Spaniards and Venetians to a decisive victory. Even after this initial advantage, the Christian powers were still not able to carry the war into enemy waters; but there was no longer any real cause for them to dread a large-scale Turkish invasion of south-western Europe.

MOSLEM PIRACY IN THE MEDITERRANEAN

The Mediterranean situation was rendered all the more difficult for the Christian powers because the Turks had an invaluable ally in the West. Early in the sixteenth century, two renegade Christians, the brothers Barbarossa, set themselves to weld the states which fringed the north coast of Africa into a single power. They established themselves at Algiers and maintained the prosperity of their subjects by piracy, and by slave raids all along the coasts of southern Italy and Spain. The government of Ferdinand and Isabella tried to check the evil by setting up strong fortified posts on the African coast; but since these depended on the Spanish fleet for supplies, and sometimes even for water, it was found impossible to maintain them. The elder Barbarossa was killed in 1518 in an attack on Tunis; but his younger brother, Kheireddin, carried on his work. He captured Tunis in 1533, and Sicily lay at his mercy. The coasts of Italy, Valencia and Catalonia were rapidly depopulated by his raids: thousands of Christians were carried off to die at the oars of the corsair galleys, among them the great Spanish writer, Cervantes, author of *Don Quixote*, who was lucky enough to escape and return to Spain. The corsair ranks were swelled by the Moors expelled from Spain, who longed for revenge on their persecutors, and by every kind of adventurer and desperado, including many Christian renegades. Algiers became a pirate stronghold, and Barbarossa's fleet an invaluable ally for the Sultan in time of war, and a permanent menace to Mediterranean commerce in time of peace.

What was needed to meet the evil was a systematic Spanish colonisation of North Africa to some distance inland. But Spanish energies and men were all needed for South America. Charles did what he could in the intervals of his French war. Thanks to the help of the Genoese fleet, he was able to score a brilliant success in 1535, recapturing Tunis and destroying two hundred of Barbarossa's galleys in harbour. But Tunis was lost again, and with it Tripoli. And when Charles in 1541 attacked Algiers, a storm wrecked his fleet

and ruined the enterprise. He did, however, check the pirate depredations to some extent, and earned thereby the heartfelt thanks of
the peasants of southern Italy and Spain who had supported his
expeditions with fervour, subscribing money and enrolling volunteers. Had France helped, the evil might have been stamped out.
But Francis I, though he enjoyed the title of "Most Christian King",
was no true descendant of St. Louis. His fleet often co-operated with
Barbarossa; his ambassador was on the Turkish flag-ship at the
capture of Tripoli; and once he even allowed the corsairs to set up
their slave-market at Toulon and sell there the prisoners taken in a
raid on Nice. Thus the evil persisted, and Algerine pirates continued
to prey on European shipping, down to the eighteenth century.

PROTESTANTS AND JESUITS

In his struggle against the Reformation, Charles was even less
successful; and here again he was handicapped by the lack of principle, both of his enemies and of those who ought to have been his
allies. The Princes of North Germany led the Reformation in their
own lands, very largely because of the wealth to be gained by appropriating Church property, and also because it was an easy way of
securing popular support and so making themselves completely
independent of the Emperor. They could count on the help of the
King of France, who, having used Turks to distract his enemy, had
no scruples about using Protestants as well. The Pope, moreover,
who ought to have been their greatest enemy, was so afraid of
Charles's growing political power in Italy that at times he actually
appeared to favour the cause of the heretics in order to make the
situation more difficult for the Emperor in Germany.

In spite of these obstacles Charles did achieve a temporary
triumph when the Peace of Crespi gave him a free hand. He persuaded the Pope to call a General Council at Trent, which began a
preliminary purification of Catholic doctrine and organization, and
so removed some of the reformers' main grievances. The Council
broke up in 1552 and did not meet again for some years. But it
marked the beginning of that movement which was later to be called
the Counter-Reformation; and the Jesuits, an order newly founded
by St. Ignatius Loyola, had already set about the re-conversion of the
heretics.

Loyola had been a Spanish officer and had been wounded in the
early stages of the French war. He organized his order on military
lines and sent his men out as missionaries, not only in Protestant
Europe, but among the heathen all over the world. In southern
Europe, in Austria and in Bavaria, the Catholics soon began to
recover the ground which they had lost. But in the north, Protestantism triumphed. Charles defeated the army of the Schmal-
kaldic League, the political union of the Protestant princes and cities,
at the battle of Mühlberg in 1547. But he found himself unable to

force Catholicism on either princes or people. In 1552 civil war broke out afresh. Henry II, son of Francis I, reopened the French attack in Italy and on the Rhine, and a Turkish threat paralyzed the Emperor's Austrian forces.

At one moment, in 1547, Charles V had seemed supreme in Europe. He had defeated the French, checked the Turks and humbled the Lutherans. Five years later, he was forced to fly from Innsbrück over the Brenner Pass at midnight, his litter carried through a blinding snowstorm by a handful of guards. The Protestant princes, with the aid of French and Turks, had beaten him; and though he fought back with characteristic obstinacy, he was a worn-out and broken old man. After a bitter civil war, Germany was at last pacified by the Religious Peace of Augsburg of 1555, which settled that in future any Prince might be allowed to choose his own religion, though his subjects were to be forced to accept his choice or go into exile. It was an unsatisfactory peace; but it lasted for sixty years because both sides in Germany were exhausted.

In 1559, the war with France drifted to the same sort of end at the Peace of Câteau Cambrésis. There was nothing new or decisive about this treaty. It left the Habsburg ring round France intact and it settled none of the old disputes. But the King of France had suddenly discovered that religious differences were threatening to divide his own country, and that, while he had been helping Protestantism abroad, the new doctrines were being rapidly spread through southern France by Calvin's missionaries from Geneva. Spain, too, needed her strength to meet a growing movement towards Protestantism and independence in the Netherlands. So both countries were concentrated on internal divisions; and forty years of almost continuous fighting came to an end with no advantage accruing to either side.

CHARLES RETIRES TO A MONASTERY

Charles was not personally responsible for Augsburg and Câteau Cambrésis. In 1555, before the deputies of the Netherlands, gathered at Brussels, he solemnly abdicated his sovereignty in Spain, the Burgundian lands and Italy to his son, Philip II. The Empire and his German lands he had already handed over to Ferdinand. So his inheritance was divided, and he himself retired to a Spanish monastery to end his life in peace among simple pleasures, making clocks and mechanical toys and later rehearsing his own funeral. He had striven consistently to preserve a framework of European life which was already decayed; and by the time of his death in 1558, it had finally perished. England, the states of North Germany, and the whole of Scandinavia had been permanently won over to Protestantism. The Church of Rome could no longer claim universal authority, even in western Europe. The last attempt to make the Holy Roman Empire something more than a high-sounding title had failed. The future lay with the nation-states.

PART X

BEGINNING OF MODERN TIMES

CHAPTER 51

GOLD AND PRIVATEERING

AT Charles V's abdication in 1556, his son, Philip II, inherited the Habsburgs' Spanish and American dominions, while Philip's uncle, Ferdinand I, received Austria and the Imperial crown. This division weakened Habsburg power in Europe; but it left French fears and ambitions unappeased. The sixteenth and seventeenth centuries were coloured by the Austrian and Spanish Habsburgs' attempt to retain their hold over Europe and by France's efforts to displace them.

Philip regarded himself as the Spanish king, divinely appointed to lead the Counter-Reformation to victory. He proved an industrious administrator, studying every plan in detail. But narrow vision and bigotry prevented him from framing a policy sufficiently comprehensive to achieve success. He remains a tragic figure in a century in which romantic adventure abounded.

Spain was too insecure economically for Philip to rely on her providing the means for effecting his religious and political aims. The Spanish Government controlled Mexico, Central America, most of the West Indian islands, the north and west coastline of South America, and the Philippines in the Pacific. Portugal held Brazil and scattered settlements along the African and Indian coasts. The Atlantic sea-routes converged on the Canary Isles, which, like the Azores, belonged to Portugal. When Portugal fell into Spanish hands in 1580, England could pretend that, in attacking Spain, she was aiding the Portuguese claimant to the throne.

The Spanish Empire provided the treasure to finance Philip's schemes. It came from two sources: plated and moulded gold, which once decorated the houses and persons of Indian rulers; ore from which Peruvian silver and Mexican gold could be extracted. The former was soon exhausted, and Spain demanded greater output from the mines. America was primarily a source of bullion; trade and colonization were subordinated to gold and silver. In Spain itself the influx of wealth upset prices, and established illusory economic standards. Money is a symbol of wealth, not wealth itself. Spanish home industries were hampered by a ten per cent. tax on sales, and the possibilities of foreign trade were ignored. Spaniards gathered treasure from the corners of the globe into Cadiz and Seville, only to pass it on to other European countries in payment of debts or else in return for the articles of merchandise which they did not produce at home or in their own colonial possessions.

Spain's wealth flowed into the pockets of rich bankers, like the Fugger group of Augsburg, who advanced Philip loans for his campaigns. The Fuggers had been the most energetic speculators of the sixteenth century, and the sovereigns of Europe granted them economic concessions in part-payment of the interests on their loans. A German had discovered that silver was extracted more easily from its ore by using quicksilver, which had to be exported from Spain to America. Fear of bankruptcy forced Philip to grant his valuable monopoly to the Fuggers, who exploited it from 1563 to 1641; they fleeced the unsuspecting Philip, who was ignorant of the theory and practice of trade.

The mother country kept tight control over her dominions. Councils at home directed West Indian affairs, appointed governors and supervised the annual loads of treasure, which were shipped according to a rigid schedule. The government in America itself was based upon a division of powers. The Law Courts, called *Audiencias*, quarrelled with the civil government. Some of the viceroys were men of enlightenment and enterprise, but local grievances, and the harsh arbitrary control exercised from Madrid, damped enthusiasm. There was no complete subordination, for the question of distance and lack of communication made Spanish America subject to periods of reasonable freedom, broken on occasions by the hasty recall of a viceroy to Madrid or else by the arrival of peremptory orders from Spain.

JESUIT INFLUENCE IN SPANISH AMERICA

The Church, especially the Jesuits and the other missionary orders, complicated the situation further. They not only demanded political power through the exercise of their Inquisition, but they frequently interfered in the government's dealings with the Indians, whose easy-going nature made them good Catholics and earned them the protection of their father confessors. In the area now known as the Argentine, the Jesuits founded missions which completely controlled the Indians in the district. Unity of government and the amicable relations between governors and governed probably gave the Argentine a stability which later compared favourably with the civil strife of other districts.

Spain did not ignore trade completely. By keeping the Pacific routes secret, she enjoyed trade with the Philippines undisturbed till the early seventeenth century, when the Dutch became rivals. Spices, perfumes and cosmetics were shipped to the Panama Isthmus, carried by mule-trains to ports on the Atlantic shore, and exported, with the bullion, to Europe. In the West Indies, a growing sugar-cultivation gradually replaced prospecting for gold.

The Spanish seldom proved good colonists or good traders. At first, permanent settlements were rare—the idea was to get rich quickly and return to Spain—but the laxity of convention, bred by adventurous life and contact with the peaceful and semi-civilized native population, stimulated intermarriage; this was little impeded by the presence of white women, for the Spaniards had generally left their own womenfolk at home. A polyglot population appeared which combined the vices and virtues of the two races. The Creoles, the pure descendants of the original Spaniards, were a minority, as intermarriage increased and gave rise to a half-Indian, half-Spanish, race called Mestizos. Thus the Spanish Empire encountered racial difficulties which the English in North America were later able to avoid by settling both men and women in newly-founded colonies.

SPAIN'S YEARS OF GLORY

The rapid rise and no less rapid fall of Spain's empire make it difficult for us to visualize the position she held in Europe. Spain set the cultural and social standards of the time, and the golden age of Spanish art and literature, from 1580 to 1680, coincided with the heyday of this world domination. The Court of Madrid patronized painters, architects, poets and travellers. Palaces and monasteries, built partly from the subscriptions of subjects and partly from the wealth of the Americas, sprang up over the Castilian countryside, exhibiting the Italian ideas of their builders. Noblemen and their ladies had their portraits painted by Velazquez, who had ousted the formalist El Greco. Spain set the fashion in matters of taste, and whilst the lower middle-classes continued their wonted habits of thought and activity, fashionable European society aped the manners of the Spanish aristocracy, just as they were, a century later, to turn to the France of Louis XIV for their standards of etiquette.

All Europe learned of the chivalry of Don Quixote through the works of Cervantes, and the amours of Don Juan through those of Alarcon. The attractive faults of Don Quixote and Don Juan probably explain the fundamental weakness in the Spanish national character, which was too heavily endowed with the spirit of adventure and the zest for personal glory. The aristocracy, who filled the posts of government and led the adventurous overseas, was sufficiently strong to prevent the rise of an able middle class.

Sea-power had been ignored by medieval statesmen and warriors, educated in the traditions of siege warfare. But in the Mediterranean, the Spanish had been forced to take to the sea in order to defeat the Moslem *corsairs* who terrorized the surrounding countries. With their long swift galleys, rowed by slaves and criminals, Spanish sailors learned to grapple and board their adversaries' ships. Such methods, successful on an inland sea, proved of little avail against English and Dutch competitors on the wind-swept Spanish Main. Though the galleons were of larger bulk and were entirely dependent on their sails for motive power, their sailors still used the tactics employed in the Mediterranean galley warfare. The Spaniard remained an expert hand-to-hand fighter; he never became an efficient navigator. The smaller English vessel, part merchantman, part privateer, of the type of Drake's *Revenge* (500 tons), could easily elude the more cumbersome galleon, sail closer to the wind, and by clever manoeuvring, pour its shot into the enemy, while the return fire generally passed harmlessly through its rigging. The huge aft- and fore-castles made the Spanish galleons unstable and the gunnery of their sailors proved to be hopelessly inaccurate.

THE PRIZE OF SEA POWER

The methods of naval warfare popularized by Drake and Hawkins on the Spanish Main were adopted by Howard, the English Admiral, when the Spanish Armada sailed against England in 1588. This invasion was Philip's most determined attempt to remove English competition for supremacy on the sea. The Spanish failure was due not to lack of strength or of numbers, but to ignorance of the laws of seamanship. The incompetent Medina Sidonia was placed in charge of the expedition, because he was an aristocrat, whose training as a soldier would prove useful if the Spaniards succeeded in making a landing in England.

A similar situation arose when the Netherlands, tired of Spanish rule under Alva (1567–73), and of Catholic attacks on the Calvinist religion, rebelled against their sovereign. Fishermen became mariners, and the Dutch buccaneers, known as "Beggars" of Brill, prevented a small country with a limited population from falling once again into the hands of a power immeasurably superior in wealth and in military strength. We shall see how, through sea-power and the trade that sea-power brought, this little corner of Europe, defended by dykes against which the sea battled in vain, took the lead for the first half of the seventeenth century. Holland did not weaken until, just at the time when she needed all her strength to repel the onslaughts of Louis XIV of France, she became subject to English attacks.

The size and wealth of the Spanish Dominions in America eventually excited the envy of other countries. England, increasingly prosperous under the peaceful Tudor rule, felt an urge to expand which appealed especially to her seafaring citizens. But the courage and personality of these sea-dogs have often clouded the fact that England owes less perhaps to them than she does to the more insignificant and less romantic traders travelling in Asia, the Levant, Russia and the western coasts of Africa. Frobisher, Drake and Hawkins were the first to realize that, though privateering on the Spanish Main was a profitable concern, religion and their own Queen had to be protected against Spanish attacks by a competent well-manned navy. The freebooter of the early part of Elizabeth's reign, like Drake, was technically a mere pirate, liable to be hanged if the Spanish managed to catch him. Yet it was these men who provided the leaders and the ships which attacked the Spanish Empire in 1585, repelled the Spanish Armada in 1588, and even raided the shores of Spain itself.

It has been said that the discoverer is soon followed by the trader, and that exploration is generally advanced by those who seek new channels of trade. John Hawkins had been taught by his father that slave-trading was a prosperous investment. Hawkins made several voyages, between 1562 and 1568, to the west or Guinea coast of Africa, where he captured negroes, and transported them to the West Indies. The Spanish rulers of America frowned on this trade; they disliked their colonists and traders dealing with foreigners. But the Carib population of Hispaniola in the West Indies had been rapidly decreasing, and the labour necessary for the sugar plantations and the gold-mines had to be drawn from Africa. Hawkins supplied the want, and with the connivance of the Spanish colonists themselves, he drove fairly lucrative bargains. So important was the slave-trade that licences to participate in it formed a valuable part of the Spanish state-revenue; in 1713, at the Peace of Utrecht, England secured the monopoly as her share after the Spanish Succession War.

Early explorers of the Atlantic found the huge American continent blocking their path to China. Many English voyagers, undismayed by this discovery, thought that there might be a way of escape from the Atlantic to the Pacific either north or south of America. The southern route, already sailed by Magellan, was chosen by Drake, despite the dangers of navigating the Straits and the fear that Spanish vessels might bar the return journey.

DRAKE AND FROBISHER

Drake was blown out of his course, and found that open sea stretched south of Cape Horn, but after plundering the west coast of South America, he pushed northwards, landing in New Albion (California), which he thought could be used by the English as a port to guard the western exit of the supposed North West Passage from the Atlantic to the Pacific. Crossing the Pacific, he called at Ternate in the East Indies hoping to strike a trade bargain with its ruler; then, sailing round the Cape of Good Hope, he reached England three years after he had set out. The *Golden Hind*, the little ship that had accomplished this great feat, was only 100 tons, and manned with but eighteen guns. She was brought to London to be placed on show, and was preserved for a while as a national monument.

The northern route round America was attempted by Frobisher, between 1576 and 1578, and later by Davis; both gave their names to straits and bays of the no-man's-land north of Canada. They failed to discover the passage, for the Arctic was colder than they at first believed it. In his first voyage, Frobisher turned back, with high hopes that further voyages would solve the riddle of the North West Passage. In London an assayer of gold declared that iron pyrites, brought home by one of the sailors, contained particles of gold. Subsequent voyages were made to obtain supplies of ore, but the search proved fruitless, and finally Frobisher gave up the idea.

It was gold which attracted these adventurers—either the crude ore which Frobisher found in the north-west or the gold which had been mined and minted by the Spaniards, and shipped in huge galleons, unprotected, to Spain. Elizabeth was prepared to take shares in these piratical robberies, and when she gave Drake a knighthood on his return in 1577, it was a reward for bringing treasure to her parsimonious purse as much as for his brilliant seamanship. In England he planned further expeditions; one in 1585, often known as Drake's Armada, was prepared on a large scale. Courtiers and merchants provided capital for the enterprise, in return for which they were to be given two-thirds of the booty acquired. Ransom money and captured treasure provided the interest on the capital. The following year, a Suffolk sea-captain, Cavendish, attempted to emulate the exploits of Drake, and left behind him a train of burnt towns and scuttled ships. His fleet was too small to bring home a fraction of the treasure he could have amassed as the result of his raids.

THE TREASURES OF THE NEW WORLD

Guiana, on the northern coast of South America ("the Magazin of all rich mettals . . . hath more quantity of gold by manifold, than the best partes of the Indies or Peru"), attracted Ralegh, one of the most enlightened characters of the age. He was a dilettante, loving new fashions and scientific novelties. Though not a sailor, his interest in colonization and the discovery of gold led him to organize expeditions to America. In 1595–6, attempts were made to discover El Dorado, the fabulous capital of the fabulous kingdom in the Amazon jungle. Despite support from grasping London speculators, these expeditions failed, but the legend has lived to this day. Somewhat naïvely, Ralegh unconsciously indicated the transitory character of these searches for treasure; "Where there is store of gold", he said, "it is in effect needlesse to remember other commodities for trade." Elsewhere, he paradoxically placed his finger on the frailty of Spanish economics when he said: "It is this Indian gold that indangereth and disturbeth all the nations of Europe."

The craze for tapping the new world of its treasures affected social life in Europe to a degree that was equalled only in the period of the Crusades. New fashions, new foods and new comforts were introduced. In an age when king and courtier took shares in voyages and townsfolk were beginning to ape, in belated manner, the behaviour of their betters, it is not surprising to discover frivolities in literature and in dress which reflected the extravagance of the time. Spain perhaps provided the best example; it was from Spain that Elizabeth's courtiers obtained their latest dress creations. Spices and cane-sugar, which had been expensive luxuries in the past, were introduced into Europe in ever larger quantities. The drinking of cocoa and chocolate later became an acquired taste among the aristocracy. Cavendish found the Mexican Indians of Aguatulco using cacaos, or cocoa-beans, as money, food and drink. Potatoes, now a humdrum vegetable, were reported by visitors to Virginia to "bee the most delicate roots that may be eaten and do far exceed our parsnips or carrots". They became the staple diet of the Irish, and a substitute for bread amongst the English lower classes.

Another discovery, perhaps more epoch-making, was that of tobacco. Hawkins, in his second voyage, returned to England by way of Florida, a route generally chosen because of the favourable current. He noticed that "the Floridans, when they travelled, have a kind of herb dried, who, with a cane and an earthen cup in the end, with fire and the dried herbs put together, do suck through the cane the smoke thereof, which smoke satisfieth their hunger, and therewith they live four or five days without meat or drink". The narrator mentions, however, that the French who had been initiated in smoking the "weed" had suffered acute indigestion. Difficulties of trade with the Spanish, and the delay of the English in growing their own tobacco overseas, forced the price higher than we should expect, considering its common use amongst the Indians. About 1580, an ounce cost 3s. in the money of that time; but, for a small sum, poorer people were able to enjoy whiffs from a communal pipe generally kept by tavern-keepers for their patrons. We may wonder how far history has been affected by the growing popularity of tobacco, soothing discontented minds and making men more tolerant of each other.

Tobacco was an article that could be produced at home, but home-growers were dissuaded by the Government, who wished to give the English colonists in America an opportunity to pay for English manufactures with colonial-grown tobacco. The suitability of the North American climate for settlement, and the freedom of that area from Spanish dominion, gave Englishmen in the early seventeenth century an opportunity to expand which was readily taken. England had curtailed the Spanish monopoly, though the Dutch were becoming serious rivals. This rivalry was to be intensified by their eventually seeking the same trade-routes and the same trade-objectives.

CHAPTER 52

TRADE AND COLONIZATION

TRADE in the Middle Ages had travelled along land-routes leading from the Baltic and the East to the plains of Germany and to Champagne in France. It was necessary for traders to work together, so as to obtain privileges and relief from the excessive tolls which rulers levied on goods passing through their territories, but the ordinary individual was free to bargain as he liked. He was a separate unit, selling and buying independently of his fellow-merchants, bound only to deal justly towards the others and to conform to the standards of price and quality that the state and business community imposed.

The opening-up of the world and the increase of ocean travel and trade raised problems which could only be settled by greater co-operation amongst individuals. There was danger from shipwreck and interference from interlopers. The equipment for a single voyage proved more expensive than its promoters dared risk. The solution was found in an organization that spread the risk without decrease in profit. The joint-stock enterprise attracted those who wished to take part in trade but were content to leave the administration to others. A company would be formed, and the venture financed from the contributions of merchants, courtiers and promoters. Each shareholder had the right to attend meetings and vote on questions of policy. The object might be to trade with a far-off country like Russia, or to colonize the Bermudas, or even to harass the Spanish fleet and plunder their American ports. Any profit acquired would be distributed amongst those shareholders who had regularly paid up their contributions.

It would be wrong to suppose that this type of company was similar to that of the present day. The amount of money to be provided by each shareholder was not fixed; the governors might, by order of the general meeting, call up further sums from those interested, so as to defray additional expenses or incidental debts. Some of the investors might actually take part in the voyage. Others would stay at home to await the result. At the end of the voyage, the concern would be wound up; if a further attempt was made, a new subscription-list would be opened. The company would be very careful to obtain a grant of monopoly from the government, to safeguard it from poaching by interlopers or the rivalry of independent traders, who might attempt to snatch some of the advantages.

THE FIRST JOINT-STOCK COMPANIES

The first English joint-stock company was formed in 1553, when a group of merchants equipped an expedition to reach the Pacific by way of the Arctic. Later, these merchants were incorporated as a company "for the discoverie of regions, dominions, islands and places unknown". Sir Hugh Willoughby, who commanded the expedition, was caught by the winter ice in the White Sea and frozen to death with the crews of two of his ships. Willoughby had recorded in his own hand the early incidents of the voyage, which was just one among the many examples of courage and fortitude described by Hakluyt and other contemporary writers.

Chancellor, commanding the third ship of Willoughby's expedition, was able to visit the Russian Tsar, who, he hoped, might lend aid and grant concessions to English traders. Ivan received the sailors favourably. The search for the North-East passage was dropped. For a period, the Russia Company enjoyed a lively trade, and one of the agents, named Jenkinson, opened up a route to Persia through Bokhara, Moscow and the White Sea; war had made the more direct route to the Levant too dangerous for regular trade. When Ivan captured Narva, on the Gulf of Finland, the Russia Company found that a great deal of trade fell into the hands of interlopers or merchants outside the Company. The Hanseatic League and the Dutch also began to compete, for Narva was nearer their sphere of interest than the former port of Archangel had been. When allegations of corruption and inefficiency were levelled at the Russia Company, the Tsar found a pretext for breaking off relations.

Companies were founded to trade with the Guinea coast of Africa. The elder Hawkins brought away a few slaves, but his son, John, was the first to reap profits from the slave trade. Working in opposition to the official Guinea Company, which had not been able to obtain a monopoly, Hawkins provided the slaves desired by the Spanish colonists, under pretext that he was trading with the African natives.

THE EAST INDIA COMPANY

The most important of the new trading companies was the East India Company, formed to tap Asia of her resources, at a time when Portugal, then united with Spain, was unable to ward off Dutch and English poaching. In 1592, English privateers brought a Portuguese carrack, the *Madre de Dios*, into Dartmouth Harbour. London merchants hurried to view these "secret trades and Indian riches, which hitherto lay strangely hidden and cunningly concealed from us". The Queen obtained the largest share out of the £150,000 realized from the sale of the cargo. In the catalogue a wonderful picture of the wealth of the East was given . . . "spices, drugges, silks, calicos, quilts, carpets and colours, etc. The spices were pepper, cloves, maces, nutmegs, cinamom, greene ginger: the drugs were benjamin, frankincense, galingale, mirabolans, aloes, zocotrina, camphire: the silks, damasks, taffatas, sarcenets, altobassos, that is, counterfeit cloth of gold, unwrought China silke, sleaved silke, white twisted silke, curled cypresse. There were also canopies, quilts of course sarcenet and of calico, carpets like those of Turky; whereunto are to be added the pearle, muske, civet, and ambergriece."

A charter was granted to the East India Company in 1600, and shares were taken in a series of voyages which proved very successful. As it sometimes happened that the interest on a former voyage was not immediately paid off, but left to be confused with the capital of a later voyage, the Company in an attempt to remedy matters decided to abolish the system of separate undertakings. In 1657 a permanent stock was created, providing an uninterrupted flow of capital. As a consequence, a market in stocks and shares sprang up in London.

The defects of the English companies were made patent by the greater success of the Dutch in the same direction. The states of Holland had a keen struggle to obtain their independence from Spain. Because of the smallness of their country and its openness to attack, they became the greatest trading nation of the day. Efficient business methods and a strong mercantile marine led them to build up an empire which could provide them with the wealth and power necessary for defence against the threats of Spain, England and France. The Dutch saw that foreign trade depended on the good graces of the rulers who dominated their routes and governed the areas neighbouring their trade-posts. It was not enough to obtain concessions; the Dutch by skilful defence and government made sure that their traders in the Spice Islands were protected from danger. The Dutch East India Company was given the right of acquiring territory on which factories and forts were built. The English East India Company, worrying more about quick returns, were not so careful to take precautions against armed attacks, and for a long while were easily surpassed by the more industrious and long-sighted Hollanders.

The French, under the paternal guidance of Cardinal Richelieu and Colbert, in the middle of the seventeenth century, attempted to compete with the Dutch and the English. Companies were formed for African, Indian and American trade. Their failure was due to the fact that the merchant community depended too much on the state. Initiative and determination were lacking; government interference sapped the strength of French business life. The French government thought that a strong navy and a fund of capital were the sole necessities for successful trading. They had not learnt that the essential factor was education in mercantile theory and practice; without this, no country could hope to compete successfully with the Dutch. The Dutch leapt to the forefront, because their economy, their religion, even their artistic life, reflected and were permeated with the trading spirit which made them such formidable rivals to the English.

PROGRESS IN FINANCIAL METHODS

When Philip II broke the Fugger bankers by repudiating his debts, the financial centre of Europe shifted to Amsterdam, where a bank was opened in 1609. Here flocked the bankers of Europe, who trafficked in the currencies of the various countries and decided the exchange-value of each denomination. An easy flow of money and a low rate of interest gave confidence to the country and allowed a small and energetic population to lead the way for a century. Financial methods elsewhere were still primitive. The extravagance of a monarch might bring a state from prosperity to bankruptcy within a few years. Taxation remained indifferent to new sources of income and its administration, medieval in its inefficiency.

England, learning slowly from the Dutch, or perhaps even more from the bad house-keeping of its own Stuart monarchs, adopted Paterson's plan for a Bank of England in 1694. This was valuable in a period of intense war against Louis XIV, when it was necessary to retain the support of the business people, and at the same time to borrow the money that the government dared not obtain by an increase of taxation. The large deposits of bullion, in a bank which was guaranteed by the state, provided an atmosphere of security and allowed England to get over the worst evils of financial crisis and distress. Another indication of the general desire for safety was the appearance of insurance companies. Though many of the policies appeared more like wagers than *bona fide* precautions taken against a possible loss, the gain to trade and industry were immeasurable. There were periods of panic and distress, but nevertheless the optimism and foresight gradually enabled the trading class to adapt themselves to the fluctuating nature of a profit-making economy.

ESSENTIALS OF MARITIME TRADE

Maritime trade required certain essentials for its success:— strength to resist nations that were attempting to dominate the sea-routes; strategic points of call on the various trade-routes; factories or forts in the countries with which trade was to be conducted. The most important trade-routes were the transatlantic. The Spanish and the Portuguese used the Azores as a half-way station to the West Indies and America. Outgoing ships would make directly for Havana in Cuba and for the Central American ports. The return voyage would be by the Floridan coast, to take advantage of the Gulf Stream. Precious metals were the chief cargo brought home, but the galleons generally carried other commodities as well; sugar was brought from the West Indian islands and Brazil, logs from Honduras. Much of the cost was eventually met by the illicit woollen and slave trade which the Dutch and English carried on.

The trade-route most frequented in the seventeenth century was the longer and more hazardous Indian route. Though traders had reached Persia overland, India itself was approached by sea from the south. The Portuguese, who had been first in the field under Albu-querque, attempted to acquire a territorial foothold. As we have seen, they failed because they antagonized the native population by a régime of religious oppression.

The Dutch, who followed in their steps, were more tolerant, and established a much stronger government in the Spice Islands. Able leaders planted stations on the route to India; the Dutch at various periods occupied the Cape of Good Hope, Mauritius and Ceylon, and in 1618 a separate administration was set up at Batavia in Java. At first, the Dutch had hoped to secure the trade with the Indian continent as well as that with the East Indies, but they were prevented by the arrival of the English. After the incident of Amboyna, when the English were driven from the East Indian islands, a tacit agreement grew up between the two powers that England should exploit the mainland and the Dutch the Eastern Archipelago.

The English, after a struggle with the Portuguese, established themselves first at Surat in 1612, but progress was slow, owing to the rapacity of the merchants at home and the growing anarchy of the Mogul empire. The French had appeared with the Dutch and English, but until the closing years of the seventeenth century they were not serious competitors. They not only wanted to participate in the trade, but constantly interfered in the affairs of the native rulers. The foundation of Calcutta heralded a new era for the English, who were becoming increasingly empire-conscious.

The Indian trade was valuable for its cheap calicoes and its spices. Calicoes competed with home-made woollens, and the woollen manufacturers protested against the frequent "dumping" of Indian cloths. There was no such difficulty with the spice trade, for there had been a constant demand for these delicacies from the early Middle Ages. The Dutch managed to keep prices at a high level, and retained almost a complete monopoly of one of the most valuable commodities of the time. Porcelain and lacquer were sent from China. The potteries at Delft and Lambeth copied Chinese motifs and set the fashion for collecting china which provided an immense stimulus.

THE FIRST AMERICAN COLONISTS

North America was not yet developed as an area for trade, because of the hostility of the Red Indians. The French had discovered the Newfoundland fisheries; and around the Hudson Bay, furs were collected by English and French hunters. In the southern English colonies, especially in Virginia and Carolina, tobacco and maize provided employment and profit for colonists and home country alike.

The newly explored areas, especially those whose climate and geography were suitable, provided ample opportunity for colonization by the European races. The first attempts were tentative, and often failed completely. Men went to new homes, not because economic conditions at home were unsatisfactory, nor because population was growing beyond the capacity of the domestic system to employ and feed it. Adventurousness brought some of the colonists. The desire for profit encouraged speculators, royal and mercantile, to paint emigration in glowing colours, but it was difficult to combine money-making with early colonization.

With the increasing rivalry between the various states, the claims of empire satisfied the desire for prestige and national strategy. French colonization was dictated purely by considerations of state policy, and Dutch colonization by considerations of economic strength. But the chief incentive, when colonization began to succeed, was religious, and most of the ablest colonists were men and women who were tired of persecution at home and were prepared to risk life and fortune in a land where they had freedom of worship. The means were provided by speculating companies, but the extent of their profits depended upon the fertility of the soil and the enterprise of the settlers.

The earliest colonists of the period were the Iberian races, but they were not farmers and depended on the native tribes for the necessaries of life. Many were exploiters occupying an alien land, rather than husbandmen striving to plant the features and habits of their mother country in fresh soil. North America was too cold for the warmer blood and temperament of the Spaniards and Portuguese. The popularity of joint-stock companies in Elizabeth's reign suggested the idea of planting colonists in Virginia and the Bermuda Islands. The promoters were to be given land according to the size of their shares, whilst the colonists, by their labour and the trade they created, were to provide the profit. The object of Ralegh's Guiana Company was that the settlers should look for the legendary gold of El Dorado. The project failed, like the earlier attempts to settle Virginia in 1584-6. Gilbert, with greater foresight, turned to the temperate climate of Newfoundland. He hoped to solve the vagrancy problem which worried Tudor statesmen. But his plan was not adopted, and many years were to pass before statesmen thought of emigration as a solution for the unemployment question.

Gilbert emphasized the value of the fishing-grounds round Newfoundland, and the possibility of discovering silver ore. He thought that the country could be made a base for discovering the North-West Passage to India and China. But after taking ceremonial possession of the island, Gilbert withdrew his crew and sailed for England, meeting his death when his frail vessel, the *Squirrel*, was sunk in a storm.

Captain John Smith, whose captive Indian princess, Pocahontas, has proved a favourite theme for literary romance, tried in 1609 to succeed where Ralegh had failed. Instead of landing at Chesapeake Bay, he chose Jamestown, a little northward, for his settlement. Difficulties arising with the Indians and amongst his own men robbed the colony of Virginia of immediate success.

THE PILGRIM FATHERS

The first effective and continuous settlement was made by the Pilgrim Fathers in 1620. They were Puritans who refused to conform to the established Church of England, and after a period of refuge in Holland, had decided to cross the Atlantic. Instead of landing the Fathers in Virginia, their original destination, the captain of the *Mayflower* unintentionally took a more northern route than preceding colonists, and brought the Pilgrim Fathers to the peninsula of Cape Cod, where a settlement was made at New Plymouth. Though the expedition was in the hands of a company in London, the purpose of the Fathers was to set up a permanent home, economically self-sufficient, where they were free from religious persecution.

As the century progressed, other refugees went out. Catholics and discontented cavaliers emigrated to Maryland, Quakers under William Penn to Pennsylvania. The people of Pennsylvania extended toleration to all sects, a policy which was condemned in other colonies and repudiated by the European states. By far the strongest and also the most independent among the colonies was Massachusetts.

T (H.W.)

Holland and even Sweden attempted to found settlements, side by side with the English, at New Amsterdam and on the Delaware river. The Dutch, who were better traders than colonists, were left defenceless by their home country. New Amsterdam was renamed New York, after the English Admiral, the Duke of York, whose ships captured the settlement in 1664. The Swedes, after the death of Gustavus Adolphus, drifted into anarchy and soon forgot their earlier aspiration to build an empire overseas.

The French, divided by quarrels between Catholics and Huguenots in the sixteenth century, were slow in settling colonies. Champlain, after discovering the St. Lawrence river, placed a settlement inland and named it Quebec in 1604. He realized that France possessed an opportunity for filling these fertile prairie lands with loyal settlers; the territory, however, remained undeveloped until the days of Richelieu. The Cardinal encouraged his business men to finance trips to Canada or New France, but he was thwarted by the lack of enthusiasm. Though a number of men went out, encouraged by the government, they were lacking in the spirit of adventure and the desire for freedom which had marked the voyages of the English.

FRENCH AND ENGLISH POLICY IN CANADA

In contrast with the independence and enterprise of the English settlements, the French in Canada were almost completely subordinate to home policy and patronage. The English government regarded America as a dump for its troublesome Puritans and Catholics, but France refused to allow her energetic Huguenot citizens to populate Canada, preferring to suppress them by force. Many Huguenots fled from France to the more tolerant Protestant states of the north; the great Elector of Brandenburg issued advertisements in the Dutch press to induce these refugees to colonize the marshy districts and unfertile fields of his country. Thus France not only lost a fund of industrial technique and inventiveness, but stultified her colonial policy from the beginning by shutting out from Canada the very type of population that would have brought prosperity there.

Another reason for the success of England in colonizing America was the close connection between commerce and emigration. An industrial or manufacturing country finds it easier to support and protect her colonies than one whose strength is largely agricultural. Spain was helped by her possession of the Flemish cloth-trade. The English trade in serge and broadcloth reached markets not only in Europe but amongst her own colonists. At first, the colonists were able by their husbandry to pay for manufactures from home, and this allowed them to devote their time to farming. The tobacco of the south increased the prosperity of Carolina and Virginia; but the northern states, which did not produce anything that England wanted, found it increasingly difficult to pay for their imports. They could offer only wheat and fish, with a certain amount of iron ore. Economic difficulties, however, were at this period of much less consequence than the fact that America was ignored by Parliament, and her people were free to worship as they themselves thought fit.

MERCANTILISM AND WEALTH

It was an age of trade—foreign trade especially. Gradually one or two notions were accepted as guides for merchants and shippers; the name "mercantilist" has been given to these broad generalizations. The rise in the standard of living during the sixteenth and seventeenth centuries was the result of commercial prosperity rather than of industrial invention. Mercantilism was the faith of statesman and trader alike until the days of the Industrial Revolution. The danger from attack by privateers at sea, and the suspicious attitude adopted by foreign rulers towards merchants from other countries, led the state to take increased interest in foreign trade.

As trade was linked with finance, it was the state's concern to see that the exchequer was full and that the country, which had to fill that exchequer, was well supplied with coin and bullion. This interference with foreign trade was in curious contrast with the growing freedom allowed to industrialists and merchants at home. In the Middle Ages, carefully regulated guilds or companies had supervised home manufactures and the traffic of goods between the various boroughs. In the Tudor period, guild restrictions broke down, and capitalism at home was allowed to progress unchecked. Merchant adventurers and profiteers, who travelled overseas and brought home foreign produce and treasure in well-laden ships, were given monopolies and privileges by the monarch.

The early mercantilists said that a country's prosperity depended upon the amount of money it possessed. Steps were taken to prevent money passing out of the country. Ordinances encouraged traders to bring back bullion in payment for the wares—especially cloth—which they had sold on the continent. This doctrine was favoured as there was a fear that money would become scarce in England. The credit idea—that is, the carrying out of business operations without the actual passing of money, by substituting notes or bills of exchange for coins—was still only imperfectly grasped by financiers.

Capital is wealth that can provide the equipment and defray the initial expenses of a new undertaking. In the event of the undertaking proving profitable, the owners of the original capital take the surplus profits, after the costs of production have been subtracted. The social consequences of the rising importance of capital in trade and industry, though gradual, were highly important. The ownership of wealth was divorced from manual and skilled labour. Instead of labour controlling the means of livelihood, the power was passing to that section of the community which had succeeded in collecting and owning surplus profits and in using them to their advantage.

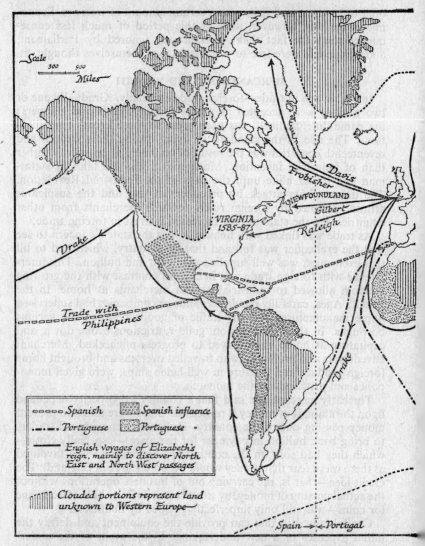

Scale
300   900
Miles

Frobisher

Davis

NEWFOUNDLAND

Gilbert
Raleigh

VIRGINIA
1585-87

Drake

Drake

Trade with
Philippines

ооооо *Spanish*   *Spanish influence*

.—.—. *Portuguese*   *Portuguese* "

——— *English voyages of Elizabeth's
reign, mainly to discover North
East and North West passages*

|||||| *Clouded portions represent land
unknown to Western Europe*

Spain → ← Portugal

TRADE ROUTES OF

From the great oversea empire possessed by Spain in the sixteenth century
flowed a seemingly inexhaustible supply of treasure, but nevertheless bureaucratic
and incompetent methods of administration, combined with lack of interest on
the part of colonial officials and unsound economic conditions within Spain
itself, made the Spanish empire rest on unsure foundations. The Portuguese,
with their brilliant seamanship and navigation, succeeded in creating an imperialism that was inferior only to that of Spain, but Portugal came under Spanish
hegemony in 1580 and her trade was systematically despoiled by the latter.

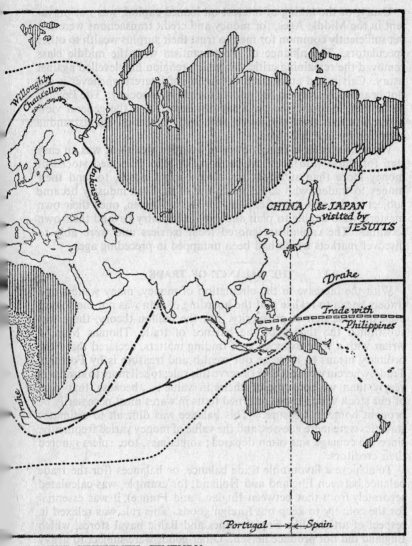

CHINA & JAPAN
visited by
JESUITS

Drake

Trade with
Philippines

Portugal →←— Spain

THE SIXTEENTH CENTURY

Unable to gain a foothold in South America, Britain turned her attention to North America, and began the exploration of that area. At the same time freebooters, encouraged by the Crown, plundered Spanish and Portuguese vessels. Willoughby and Chancellor opened up a trading route to Russia, and for a time the Russia Company was encouraged by the Tsar. Jenkinson, one of the company's agents, established a mainly overland route to Persia by way of Bokhara, Moscow and the White Sea, providing an alternative method of reaching the Levant to the more direct one, which was dangerous for traders.

Usury, or the taking of interest on loaned capital, was not prevalent in the Middle Ages, for money and credit transactions were not yet sufficiently common for men to trust their surplus wealth to other speculators. The alliance of Protestantism with the middle class removed the remaining criticisms which religion had levelled against usury. Calvin had authorized the taking of interest whenever it did not bear too heavily on the poorer members of society. The English parliament legalized the payment of interest, and the general view taken was that the State was a sufficient protection against undue extortion by moneylenders.

With the greater earning power of hoarded wealth, it was an easy step for those who acted as bankers, or who possessed stocks of money more than sufficient for their current needs, to lend their money to traders who could make use of it. Even industry became subject to the new use of capital, for the craftsmen, once their own masters, were unable to plan and exploit industry beyond their own localities. The capitalists ignored local barriers and were able to discover markets which had been untapped in preceding ages.

THE BALANCE OF TRADE

With the increase in the circulation of money, many writers and traders began to realize that the hoarding of coin was not the sole or even the best sign of prosperity. For the bullion theory, there was substituted the theory of the balance of trade. Thomas Mun, a writer with a wide experience of trading matters, declared that "the ordinary means to increase our wealth and treasure is by Forraign Trade, wherein we must ever observe this rule; to sell more to strangers yearly than we consume of theirs in value . . . because that part of our stock which is not returned to us in wares must necessarily be brought home in treasure." This balance was difficult to estimate; statistics were mere guesses, and the value of money varied frequently, since the coinage was often debased; sometimes, too, rulers ignored their creditors.

To achieve a favourable trade balance, or balances (for the trade balance between England and Holland, for example, was calculated separately from that between England and France), it was essential for the country to keep out foreign goods. This rule was relaxed in respect of articles like French wines and Baltic naval stores, which England did not produce herself. Other goods were subject to heavy tariffs, which not only gave protection for home industry and agriculture, but provided a fruitful source of revenue to the state and a favourable balance of trade. Few people realized that the amount of exports depended to a certain extent upon the amount of imported goods, since the one paid for the other.

Free trade was unknown. If it were not for the unscientific and rule-of-thumb methods of these traders of the seventeenth century, we should be able to draw an interesting comparison between that age and the present day; protection and a favourable balance of trade have once more been accepted as guides to private enterprise and public finance. Customs duties in the seventeenth century show that a great deal of wealth was flowing into the English exchequer from foreign and colonial goods imported by English and Dutch, who were prepared to get their cargoes into the country by "leaping" the tariff walls. From a miserable £127,000, customs yields had increased to nearly a million pounds sterling in 1689.

Each country liked to consider itself an isolated unit, able to provide the essentials of life and of defence. When it was necessary to buy abroad goods which could not be produced at home, the law forbade their being imported in foreign ships, and so the home mercantile marine derived the benefit. Yet shippers were ready to poach on another country's preserve. The Dutch were careful to exclude English ships from their docks, but their own vessels were found bringing goods from the Baltic and the East, even from the English colonies, to London, Bristol and Southampton.

The rivalry that sprang up between Dutch and English caused two wars, which failed to settle the issue. In 1651, the Commonwealth government, acting on the advice of London merchants, passed the Navigation Act. This was re-enacted by Charles II in 1660. Trade with the English colonies had to be carried on "in such ships as do truly belong only to the people of England, Ireland and Wales, or are of the build of and belonging to any the said lands (*i.e.*, colonies) and whereof the master and three fourths of the mariners at least are English". To prevent the Dutch from acting as intermediaries between foreign merchants and English buyers, foreign goods could be imported only in English ships or alternatively in the ships of the countries where the goods were produced or manufactured.

EFFECT OF THE BRITISH NAVIGATION ACT

The disadvantage of all systems that attempt to regulate trade is that, sooner or later, differences will arise between the economic interests involved. The Navigation Act helped English shipbuilders and the mercantile marine; but traders and capitalists grumbled at having to use English ships where it would have been more profitable to use foreign "bottoms". Tariff walls aided some manufacturers, but injured those who needed foreign raw materials at a cheap rate. The English colonists gained protection at sea and an economic alliance with the homeland; yet they were refused the benefits of trade with the Spanish colonies and denied the right of undertaking their own manufactures.

There was the idea that colonies were mere sources of raw material and markets for dumping home manufactures; and this, when the colonists refused any longer to remain under economic domination, was to deprive England of her first empire across the Atlantic. The Spanish colonies had minted money. The Dutch had preferred to trade rather than to colonize. The French were anxious about prestige and tended to ignore economic questions. The English regarded their American plantations as profitable investments and as asylums for religious refugees. In the seventeenth century, the welfare of the colonies was a minor consideration in English theory and practice. Cloth and iron were exported from England, and the colonists were forbidden to compete in the manufacture. As a recompense and a financial expedient, the English allowed Virginian tobacco to enter their ports, and made one valuable concession to the planters by refusing to allow their own Gloucestershire men to grow it in England.

STATE INTEREST IN TRADE

A study of the ordinances of the French cardinals Richelieu and Mazarin, or of the legislation of the English parliament, gives us some idea of the wide-reaching interference exerted by the state in the lives and fortunes of the people. The difficulty lay in the enforcement of these laws. Communications were poor and strong local prejudices sharpened political conflict. Many of the laws remained pious wishes on the part of governments who were incapable of effectively policing the high seas and the area under their charge. Smuggling was common; it provided employment for villages on the coast. Gradually the government woke up and created a preventive service. In some countries, the interest of the state in trade had helped the middle classes to become experienced and successful tradesmen. On the other hand, in Holland and England, whose populations seemed to take naturally to trading, the business community as a whole strove continuously to escape the attentions of the state, and their own selfish attitude prepared the way for free trade.

CHAPTER 53

THE EASTERN WORLD

WHILE Europe was in an economic and religious ferment, Asia preserved existing conventions and refused to compromise with Western ideas. Proud of their historical and cultural past, India and China were suspicious of the Western newcomers and strove to deny them access to their countries. Although the Moguls in India, and the Manchus in China, introduced new political forces, these invaders left the traditions and civilization of their subjects untouched. Religion, Hindu, Jain, Buddhist, Confucian, Taoist, Mohtist, Mohammedan or Shintoist, neither stimulated fresh spiritual activity nor developed a progressive ethical code able to combat the humanisn and the determination of Christianity.

In the Middle Ages, Europe had learnt much from association with the East. In the age of discovery and expansion, Asia had little to offer and refused to absorb what the West was prepared to give her—though individual rulers were sometimes more enlightened than their subjects. The Far East was closed until economic exploitation from the West, with its incessant perseverance, found itself strong enough to force the door open, degrading the East and providing her with facile imitations of European culture and industrialism.

AN ELIZABETHAN DESCRIPTION OF THE RUSSIANS

Russia might have remained exclusive and untouchable, if her rulers, freed from the Tartar Horde, had not pushed her into the stream of European influence. From the petty province of Muscovy, Holy Russia, the descendant of Byzantium, had grown, by the reign of Ivan the Terrible (1533–84), into a large prairie community, possessing trade connections with Persia and an outlet in the White Sea. Through Archangel, English traders came to barter their wares and to establish diplomatic relations with Ivan, who received them and showed approval by sending presents to Queen Elizabeth. When he wanted a wife, he had drawn up before him two thousand of the prettiest and most aristocratic young women of Russia, so that he would be unconfined in his choice. With the same audacity, Ivan in later years offered his hand to Lady Mary Hastings, who was a kinswoman of Queen Elizabeth; to his intense chagrin and surprise his offer was ignored.

The English were surprised at the barbarity of the court and the degraded habits of the people. Superstition took the place of religion; many of the saints of the Russian calendar were disguised pagan deities. Some of the races over whom the Tsar ruled, Tartars, Lapps and Finns, were heathen, believing in witch-doctors and sacrifices. Every Russian home had its icon, its religious image or picture, placed at the entrance, so that visitors might do obeisance to the patron saint, or the Holy Family. The higher clergy were conservative and ignorant; the visit of certain Greek prelates led to a struggle between the reactionaries and the reforming party—who wanted to bring Russian ritual into line with that used in the Greek and Jerusalem churches.

At Moscow, the ancient capital, the court delighted in bestial pleasures and ignored the arts. The secretary to Elizabeth's Ambassador wrote a poem, describing the conditions that he saw in Russia. The Russians, he said, were drunken and superstitious. Women of the upper classes were guarded from the public gaze, wearing veils over their faces when they walked abroad. At home, they were confined to an upper storey and left to their own devices, indulging in the numerous vanities and indolent gossiping that marked the life of an Eastern harem. Byzantine traditions, and contact with Moslem habits, had retarded their progress. Rich women rouged and plastered their faces so heavily that even the English, accustomed to Elizabeth's toilet, found it difficult to guess their ages. Both sexes drank much, becoming fat and ungainly—"drink is their whole desire . . . the pot is all their pride . . . the Russie men are round of bodies,

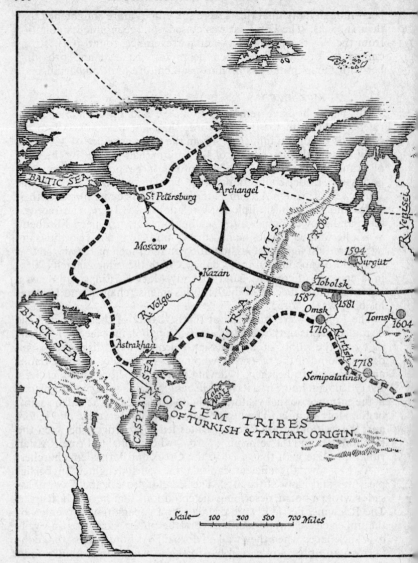

THE EXPANSION OF RUSSIA

The hardship of the peasantry during the seventeenth century caused a migratory movement which had the effect of expanding the frontiers of Russia. Not only were colonies of labourers formed among the Don and Dnieper Cossacks, but the plain of Siberia was gradually opened up by the settlements which pushed even further eastward as far as the borders of the Chinese Empire, then passing under the rule of the Manchu invaders who destroyed the weakened Ming dynasty.

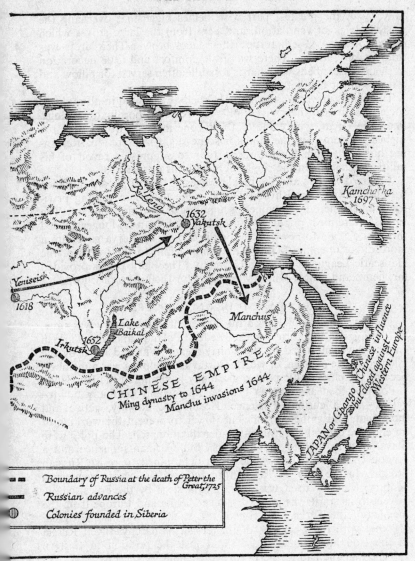

Yeniseisk
1618

Yakutsk
1632

Kamchatka
1697

Lake
Baikal

Irkutsk
1652

Manchus

CHINESE EMPIRE
Ming dynasty to 1644
Manchu invasions 1644

JAPAN or Chipango
but closed against
Chinese influence
Western Europe

━ ━ ━ Boundary of Russia at the death of Peter the Great, 1725
━━━━ Russian advances
◍ Colonies founded in Siberia

IN THE SEVENTEENTH CENTURY

Under Peter the Great (1689–1725) a new phase of development began, this taking the form of a deliberate policy of westernization. In the west, Russia was hemmed in by her powerful neighbours, Sweden, Poland, and Turkey, and her efforts to relieve this pressure constituted the series of radiating thrusts shown in the above map to the Baltic, the Black Sea, and deep into the territory held by the Poles. This process gradually brought Russia in contact with western culture.

fully fac'd, the greatest part with bellies bigge that overhang the waste". Lack of ventilation, and heat from the large stoves which every house possessed, turned their faces brown. Their dress was drab and utilitarian. There was little comfort and little decoration in their houses; beds were hard; a saddle often served for pillow and a bearskin for blanket.

The Tsar's power was absolute. Cruelty was found in all ranks of society; men beat their wives; officials treated subordinates as dogs. Peter the Great, who came to the throne in 1689, would cane the highest noblemen in the land for some slight indiscretion. Returning hurriedly from his European tour to suppress a revolt of his militia, he beheaded the ringleaders with his own hands.

The hard winters and the reckless lives of the people did not keep travellers away. English and Dutch came to obtain trading privileges, and sometimes remained, grumbling at their unhappy lot. The English were most popular at first; but soon Ivan no longer needed the White Sea–Moscow route, for his capture of Narva gave him a more direct opening to the West, linking him to the towns of the Hanseatic League in northern Germany. The Baltic coasts provided tar, hemp and timber which were used for the navies of Europe.

RUSSIA AND HER NEIGHBOURS

The development of Russia till the seventeenth century was slow. Bordering her territories were Sweden, Poland, and the Turkish empire. Sweden, aided by the Thirty Years' War and ruled by the talented house of Vasa, of which Gustavus Adolphus was a member, became the chief Baltic power, gradually hemming in the Russians.

Poland—then as large as France, Spain, and Germany put together—led a curious existence. Her feudal nobility, active and intelligent, had gathered sufficient power to prevent the working of an effective central government under the monarch. The Poles were Slavs, akin in race to the Russians, but German influence and a fanatic Catholicism had made them determined to resist Russian designs. In the years of Russian anarchy, in the early seventeenth century, Moscow itself was subject to a siege by the Poles, whose adventurous spirit was later to relieve Vienna and Europe from the menace of the Turks. The rise of the Romanov family in Russia, together with the weakness of the Polish monarchy, saved Russia in the troublous times, and Poland lost the position in Eastern Europe that she had formerly earned by military success.

To the south, the Turks had reached the limits of their power. Sultan Solyman, an enlightened statesman, succeeded in staying the progress of disintegration. But the might of western Europe and the generalship of John Sobieski of Poland thrust the Turks back from Vienna. The Austrians were able to continue the counter-attack, so that by 1715 the whole of Hungary was again in the hands of the Holy Roman Emperor.

Western Europe had been endangered by the Mohammedan pirates whose ships sailed from the ports of North Africa to molest the trading communities of Italy. These *corsairs*, backed by the might of the Turkish Sultan, were defeated by a league of Catholic naval powers at Lepanto in 1571. The battle proved the superiority of Spanish and Italian galleys and sailors over the Mohammedans who had swept the Mediterranean for so long. After Lepanto, the Turkish menace disappeared gradually in face of determined resistance. The Turks had contributed little to European civilization; their fame rested entirely on their military prestige, which had been preserved solely by the existence of a standing army. King Louis XIV accustomed Europe to this new development in the art of war.

EFFORTS OF PETER THE GREAT TO WESTERNIZE RUSSIA

A new era began with Peter the Great in 1689. The hesitating efforts of previous Tsars to make contact with the West were replaced by a vigorous and determined policy of westernization. Though Peter was sensual, gluttonous, cruel and overbearing, he had a good head, an iron will and intense devotion to his huge, sprawling, helpless country. He saw that Russia must be adapted to the civilization and the military technique of the nations that encircled and threatened her. Moscow with its incense-laden atmosphere and its quarrelsome nobles, clogged his progress; he built a new capital at St. Petersburg, and so took the first step in winning Baltic sea-power from Sweden. He drove his engineers, masons and labourers with ruthless determination to overcome the difficulties of the Neva swamps, and make his capital a rival of Venice and Versailles.

To make St. Petersburg secure and push Russian power southwards, the Tsar knew that he must create an efficient army and navy. He travelled incognito to the dockyards of Deptford in England and Zaandam in Holland, studied the habits of trading nations, and learnt the shipbuilder's art. He paid large salaries to competent German and Switzer officers to train an army, which was eventually to be led by Russians. Europe was ransacked for doctors, sailors, engineers, craftsmen and schoolmasters, and Scots, English, French, Germans and Dutchmen worked vigorously in his service.

Peter took the printing press, first introduced by Ivan, under government control. The official gazette and numerous printed ukases bore the Tsar's edicts through his broad territories, and spurred on mines, factories and warehouses, which he started and tried to control by energetic planning.

The Church, the nobility and the traders had to bow to Peter's absolute power. But it was a hard task to civilize the *boyars* or landed gentry. Peter ordered them to shave off their beards, which had been regarded as inviolable in Ivan the Terrible's reign. He remoulded clothes and customs by the fashions of the West. He brought men and women together at public assemblies and dances, and hoped that

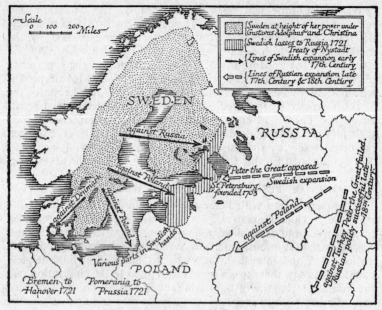

Scale
0   100   200 Miles

Sweden at height of her power under
Gustavus Adolphus and Christina
Swedish losses to Russia 1721
Treaty of Nystadt
Lines of Swedish expansion early
17th Century
Lines of Russian expansion late
17th Century & 18th Century

SWEDEN

against Russia

RUSSIA

against Denmark

against Poland

Peter the Great opposed
Swedish expansion

St Petersburg
founded 1703

against Poland

against Turkey Peter the Great failed.
Russian policy successful late
18th Century.

Various parts in Swedish hands

POLAND

Bremen to
Hanover 1721

Pomerania to
Prussia 1721

RUSSIA'S WINDOW INTO EUROPE

the *boyar* would give up drinking and fighting, to escort his wife to
these functions; but it was hard work persuading the women to conquer their shyness and learn the art of conversation. The Russian
upper classes were gradually converted into bastard editions of the
French seigneur, endowed with Prussian manners; they lost contact
and sympathy with their poorer neighbours.

But in many ways the country remained backward as ever. The
feudal relationship of peasant and landlord were unaffected by political and social changes. Peter compensated the *boyars* for their loss
of political power by leaving the serf in his old subjection. Throughout the seventeenth century, the hardships of the peasantry increased.
Many labourers migrated to found colonies among the Don and
Dnieper Cossacks; others had moved eastward, following the track
of Russian conquests in Siberia, to Irkutsk on Lake Baikal and
Yakutsk on the Lena river. By 1689 a string of colonies dotted the
Siberian plain, and the Russians had reached the borders of the
Chinese Empire. Frontier quarrels were settled by a treaty, which
made the river Amur the limit of Russian advance for many years.

Peter did not allow the migrating peasants to move freely from
place to place, but maintained the old restrictions. In Ivan's day most
serfs had been free to leave their master on St. George's Day of each
year, and find a new one. It was now enacted that runaway serfs
could be recaptured and punished; their compulsory registration

made the search for them much easier. A code had been drawn up in 1649 which denied the serfs any legal remedy against the injustice of their landlords. In 1675, serfs could be sold without their land, a condition bordering on open slavery. Disorders consequently broke out; they were ruthlessly put down. The national character, if it can be said to have existed, became marked by a defeatist and sullen spirit, and this reflected itself later in music and literature.

Ignorance and childish credulity prevented the peasantry from working out their own solution. Weather added its cruel toll to the wretched life of the mass of the people. They found some enjoyment in the village dances and singing groups, and in the spiritual comfort provided by uneducated but faithful priests. The court and government, concentrating on the huge political tasks that faced them, had no time (and perhaps no inclination) to consider the lot of the people. Peter had made Russia a European power; the social problems that he left unsolved were to prove a stumbling-block for his successors.

INDIA'S RELIGIOUS PROBLEMS

India had been invaded many times. Diversity of race and religion had added to the difficulties of orderly government. When the Moguls pierced the Afghan passes in the sixteenth century, peace and security soon appeared to be assured. Within a century they had built an empire that covered the most valuable and fertile portion of the peninsula. The Moslem warriors were granted land in return for service, but as they and their Indian subjects were in the proportion of one to two hundred, the social system of the country was very little affected by the occupation. Local government remained in the hands of village elders, elected by their neighbours; over them were placed *zemindars*, or tax collectors, who assessed the villagers according to the amount of land they farmed. This simple system was found to provide sufficient revenue and outlasted the Mogul period, being taken over by the English during the eighteenth century.

Religion remained the most difficult problem to solve. The arrival of the Moguls, full of new fervour to sweep India clean from corruption, made the problem even more complicated. Not only were there Hindus and Moslems, but the Hindus themselves were divided into a number of mutually hostile sects. Instead of accepting the situation in a spirit of tolerance, these sects felt growing suspicion and hate for each other. India's political future was to depend a great deal upon the settlement of the communal question.

To placate the devotees of these various religions, the Emperor Akbar turned prophet and philosopher himself. Akbar, who ruled from 1556 to 1605, was a man of great judgment, a lover of novelty and beauty; he was, incidentally, the first Indian to smoke a pipe. Akbar encouraged his army to use artillery in battle. A brave warrior, he tackled political problems in the same spirit as that in which he challenged opponents to fight duels on elephant-back. He studied the writings and ritual of all religions and employed his study-hours in criticizing the Koran. When a Christian missionary came before him carrying a crucifix, the emperor knelt before it and then prostrated himself in Hindu and Mohammedan fashion.

Akbar attempted to abolish the cruel practices of the Hindus and temper the fanaticism of his own Mohammedans. Suttee—the burning of the widow on her husband's funeral pyre—was restricted to those women who earnestly desired to sacrifice themselves. Akbar extracted the best tenets and rites from various religions and formed a new faith which satisfied his desire for political and religious unity. Many followers hailed him as a new Brahma or a new Buddha. This synthesis of beliefs did not outlast him; yet it was the main development at this period in Asiatic religion. More original and striking was his edict of toleration, which compared favourably with the political makeshifts and persecutions that marked European politics.

If the Moguls had been less cultured than the races they conquered, they would have become as infamous in history as the Mongol Hordes. But during the reign of Akbar and his successors, India experienced a revival of art such as she had not known for many a century. Though there was little sculpture, the Moguls were great builders. Along the Ganges valley, they built a string of royal towns, palaces, and tombs—Agra, Delhi, Ahmedabad. Akbar himself resided at Fatihpur Sikri, where he held his magnificent court. His grandson, Jehan, built the Taj Mahal at Agra, as a memorial to a much beloved wife. In this domed marble tomb, with walls inlaid with precious stones, Mogul art reaches its zenith.

Painting was especially patronized by the court, and artists were treated with as much ceremony as if they were government officials. The heightened sense of colour and the crowded activity of Mogul pictures show how deeply indebted India was to Persian inspiration.

EUROPEAN TRADERS IN INDIA

Whilst the Moguls were conquering the northern plain, Portuguese adventurers, bent on trade and empire, had appeared in the south with superior ships and armament; they had won the Persian Gulf from the Arabs, who formerly held control of the chief seaports. The natives accepted the change of rulers, as they were in no position to resist; the Portuguese could bombard their towns from the sea or from the forts that had been built near the harbours. Muscat and Hormuz were so situated that they guarded the Gulf like a gate.

The Europeans landed in that part of India which was outside Mogul control and was inhabited by races more anarchic and backward than those of the north. In the first few years of the seventeenth century, Dutch, English, and French had founded companies for the East Indian trade. By supporting the Persian ruler, Shah Abbas the Great, against the Portuguese, the English obtained the right to export Persian silk. Their Dutch rivals withdrew to the East Indies.

In 1612, Surat, on the south-west corner of the Mogul Empire, was given by Emperor Jehangir to English merchants, after a sea-fight between English and Portuguese in which the latter were worsted. Sea-power and commercial experience gave the westerners an advantage not possessed by the Moguls. Rivalry between English and French in the later seventeenth century led both to seek alliances with local native rulers, thus perpetuating divisions and encouraging treachery, which the Moguls might have prevented, if their attempt to unite the continent had not been frustrated.

Missionaries came with the Portuguese traders. St. Francis Xavier had been sent out by the Portuguese government to administer the church at Goa, their Indian capital. Akbar welcomed the missionaries to his court and interested himself in their arguments, taking part in person in the discussions which followed.

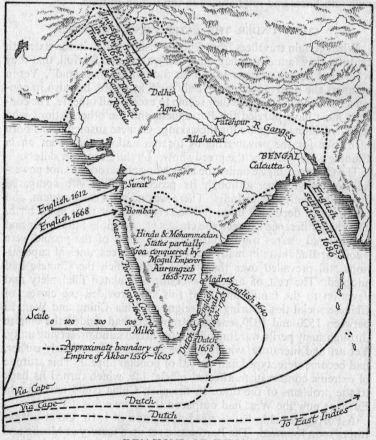

INVASIONS OF INDIA

After Akbar, degeneration set in at the Mogul court. Jehangir, a tolerant ruler, took to opium-smoking, winebibbing and the delights of the harem. But the glory and the conquest continued. Aurungzebe (1658–1707), daring soldier as he was, wasted men and money on impossible conquests and deprived India of the energy she needed in her future contests with the English and French. Toleration once again gave way to harsh persecution, encouraging many of the Hindus to rise in semi-religious, semi-military, sects—Sikhs, Rajputs and Mahrattas—whose power grew as the demands of the Mogul autocrat became more exorbitant. Many of the rebels expected help and sympathy from European merchants and adventurers, whose desire for trade blinded them to the political consequences of their interference. They eventually came to the conclusion that European occupation was the only remedy for the disorder which had arisen through their own selfishness and interference in the Indian Empire.

CHINA UNDER THE LATER MING EMPERORS

When certain travellers from Europe visited China in the sixteenth century, they found its inhabitants "so jealous and fearfull, that they would not have a stranger to put his foot within their land". Yet in manners the natives were not "only civill at meate, but also in conversation, and in courtesie they seeme to exceed all other". The contrast must have puzzled the Portuguese and the other nations who regarded China as theirs for the asking. Chinese suspicion was born of dislike for the privateering by foreign nations that went on in Chinese waters and for the greed shown by the European sailors.

The Chinese Empire under the later Ming emperors was not powerful nor progressive, although its peaceful village life compared favourably with that of India. There was no rigid caste-system, and social status depended upon public service rather than upon birth. The chief difference between the classes was religious; the upper and professional classes were Confucian; the mass of the people were Taoist or Buddhist; in many out-of-the-way areas, ancient superstitions still prevailed over the ethical faith which the Chinese had adopted. The cult of ancestor-worship stimulated filial piety and devotion to the family unit, and this still provided the closest of Chinese social ties. During the reigns of Chia Ching and Wan Li between 1520 and 1620, energetic ministers had guided the empire through many perils, warding off foreign attacks and preserving unity. Yet art and literature, which had blossomed so luxuriously earlier, had become stereotyped and devoid of popular appeal. This attitude of extreme conservatism affected official life, which turned its back to the problems of the time. In the past, China could have taught Europe; now the West had outpaced the more cultivated East.

A Portuguese ship had arrived at Canton in 1516. Other adventurers soon followed. The Portuguese set up a factory at Macao and were allowed to trade with inland China, paying the same duties as native merchants. The Dutch built a fort at Zelandia, in Formosa. The English settled at Canton as agents for the East India Company. Inevitably quarrels between the various nationalities broke out. The Ming emperors at first had no definite policy towards these "barbarians" of the West, but later they became more and more convinced that the "ocean devils" or "red heads" (as they called them) were bent on exploiting the Celestial Empire.

Since trade was recognized by the Chinese government as a profitable source of revenue, suspicion had at first to be tempered with common sense. In the past, Arabs and Malays had been welcomed; pack-trains had carried silk and porcelain across Asia to the markets of Persia and the Levant, whence they had passed to western Europe. With the arrival of European ships in the sixteenth century, the trade was partially diverted to the sea-route, which provided a more regular and lucrative traffic with the West.

Both the Mings and the Manchus despised trade and discouraged their subjects from participating in it. This did not prevent China from supplying the West with her famous porcelain wares. Factories were built where Ming designs were copied to suit European taste. Some of the work was beautiful; much of it was hastily decorated and mass-produced for the world market. While the Manchu, K'ang Hsi, reigned from 1661 to 1672, an improvement in quality took place; new shades of green and rose replaced the traditional blue and white. Heraldic, pastoral and naval scenes, which China had found to be popular abroad, were increasingly used. Pottery figures were made as ornaments and were collected by connoisseurs. The advent of tea-drinking among the western nations created a demand for teapots, of which the output grew during the second half of the seventeenth century. The Chinese had little use for woollens or for the trinkets of the West; they preferred to be paid for their exports in silver, a metal which had come into standard use for currency.

THE MANCHU DYNASTY

In the north, the warlike Manchu tribe had built up a state in the area which is known as Manchuria to-day. The Ming dynasty tried to ward off this foe, but difficulties with Japanese pirates and refractory Europeans sapped their remaining strength. Peking, the capital, fell to the Manchus in 1644, and the last of the Ming emperors committed suicide.

Under the Manchus, who, like the Turks, were magnificent soldiers but barbarians in culture, China drifted into a backwater. The Manchus had little to contribute except a fairly efficient military government—and the shaven head and pigtail which they foisted on their new subjects. The ruling Manchu class became more subservient to traditional Chinese habits of thought than even the Ming court had been. A civil service was built up, entrance into which was forbidden to those uneducated in the Confucian classics. There were no religious revivals, no new philosophies; the conservative attitude of the government prevented serious theological argument, for it frowned on originality and genius. It is true that K'ang Hsi, the most enlightened of the Manchu emperors, dabbled in art and litera-ture. He edited a dictionary, encouraged scholars to translate the classics into Manchu, and published elementary textbooks. His labours proved sterile; the mass of the people were not interested in their rulers, nor in their attempts to pose as patrons of the arts.

The novel and the drama, more popular amongst the lower classes than at court, provided a picture of ordinary life in the country villages and towns, as distinct from the conventional manners of the court. In architecture, the Manchus excelled in building huge vulgar palaces. Mechanics were unknown to the Chinese, and they wel-comed the missionaries, Ricci and Roger, who tutored them in mathematics and in the use of artillery. China afterwards expelled the Christians, as Japan had done in 1636. Europeans were prohibited from travelling in China unless they had obtained a special licence; they were forbidden to convert the people or to learn the language.

Self-reliance, and fear alike of Western traders and of missionaries, increased China's isolation. Two factors—the distance from Europe, and the military strength of the Manchus—preserved the empire until, in the nineteenth century, European industry and the growth of Japanese imperialism combined to exploit and disrupt it.

JAPAN'S SELF-ISOLATION

Cipango, or Japan, was known both to China and to Europe. Japanese pirates ravaged the Chinese coasts, and dictator Hideyoshi led an army of three hundred thousand men into Korea as a prelude to an attack on China. But the invaders had to retire from the main-land after the death of Hideyoshi in 1598. From then onwards, the Japanese became increasingly self-centred, allowing the prizes of the Far East to fall into the hands of the European nations.

The inhabitants and government of Japan, though influenced by contact with Chinese culture and institutions, developed along differ-ent lines. The Japanese were chivalrous and callous; they preferred suicide by *hara-kiri* to living in disgrace or dishonour. Their Emperor, the Mikado, was a grand priest living in seclusion, and the religion of the country was largely based on ancestor-worship. The actual ruler was the Shogun, or chief landowner, and places in the govern-ment were given always to men of property. Hideyoshi and his successors built up a social and political system akin to the feudal system of the Western Middle Ages. Each man had his lord; each lord his bodyguard of *samurai*, keen brutal soldiers who oppressed the peasantry and safeguarded the "liberties" of their masters.

Europe was allowed access to Japan until 1636, but in that year the Western intruders, merchant and missionary alike, were expelled. Those unfortunate Japanese who were caught corresponding with foreigners or trying to leave the country were punished with death. Rewards were offered for information about Christian activities, and a stern persecution removed all traces of the work of the missionaries. Japan found it easy to forget that the strength of her navy and her trade had been built up by the efforts of the Englishman, William Adams, who had once become Master of the Japanese fleet.

CHAPTER 54

RELIGIOUS FERMENT OF CHRISTENDOM

THE rapid success of Protestantism was soon checked by the determination of the Catholic world to resist further inroads. The method adopted was dogmatic and missionary. The culture of the Renaissance period, marked by increased licence in private life, and the materialist outlook of many of the Popes, had obscured the characteristic features of the Roman Church. At the Council of Trent, which dissolved in 1563, the cardinals, advised by ministers from the various Catholic sovereigns, refused to compromise over matters of doctrine. The Catholic Church once again achieved a fixity of belief, that has prevailed unquestioned to the present day. To spread the revived religion and emphasize the distinction between orthodoxy and heresy, art and music became the handmaids of the Church.

The body chosen to preach Catholic doctrine in Protestant and heathen territory was the Company or Society of Jesus. Its founder was Ignatius Loyola, a Spanish noble of combative instincts. When recovering from a wound, he renounced soldiering for religion, and hobbled off to Paris University to study theology. There he met Faber and Xavier, who were later to share his missionary labours. The ascetic Loyola, fortified by the visions which accompanied his long fasts, saw that the Catholic Church needed purpose and blind obedience from those whose mission it was to regenerate her.

INFLUENCE OF THE JESUITS

He formed a group of missionaries in Paris, and by 1540, the movement was strong enough to obtain the Papal blessing. The evils of the older monastic orders were avoided by giving the society a missionary character and organization. Its members were constantly shifted from place to place, and thus conserved their enthusiasm. Where there were Jesuit monasteries, the Society was careful to use them not as hermitages, but as centres for propaganda and schools for the young. The attempt to win Europe back to the Catholic faith is known as the Counter-Reformation.

The Jesuits earned hatred, because their fidelity to the Church overrode their obligations to the state in which they lived. Since they proclaimed the infallibility and the omnipotence of the Roman

Pontiff, they often refused obedience to heretical rulers, and even preached the duty of the ordinary Catholic to get rid of Protestant tyrants. Elizabeth of England attempted to strike a middle path between extreme Calvinist and Catholic. Encouraged by Jesuit advisers, Pope Pius V excommunicated the English Queen and aided Mary Queen of Scots, the heroine of the English Catholic community. The murders of two French monarchs, Henry III and Henry IV, and that of William the Silent, Protestant champion of the Netherlands, were committed by men filled with zeal for their own beliefs and possessed of a fanatical hatred for those who differed from them.

SUCCESSES OF THE JESUITS

In some countries the success of the Jesuits was immediate and permanent. Ireland, Hungary and the greater part of Poland were regained for the Roman faith. The dominions of the Austrian Habsburgs were riddled with Jesuit propaganda; priests penetrated into the universities, the schools, and the Court. They came disguised, ready to die for the sake of their cause, and followed a narrow path, intent only on saving souls and restoring the former Catholic unity of Europe. Persistence and burning faith captured the imagination of sovereigns as different as Henry IV of France, and Queen Christina of Sweden.

Missionary activities in the new empires of Spain and Portugal were monopolized by the Jesuits, to the disgust of other monastic orders who had opened the way. St. Francis Xavier and Nobile went to India, converting high-caste Brahmans and Untouchables alike. At the Mogul Court, the Emperor Akbar listened carefully to the arguments of his Catholic visitors, and strove to incorporate some of them in his new universal religion. The scholar Ricci visited China, and some of his followers even reached Japan, where in 1612 they suffered keen persecution from the ruling classes. The ancient and isolated Ethiopian Church sided with rebellious chiefs against their monarch, who sympathized with Catholic doctrine and ritual.

Wherever the Jesuits went, they carried their lamps of faith, refusing surrender to heathendom and convinced that their endeavours would eventually bear fruit. With religion, the Jesuits brought human sympathy; they regarded a Christian Indian or a converted Brahman as spiritually equal to any Western European. The kindness of the Catholic fathers to South Americans softened the harsh rule of Spanish imperialism. Their lot compared favourably with that of their cousins in North America.

There was less missionary activity amongst the sister Protestant Churches; the Red Indians in North America were too warlike and vigorous to accept Christianity and treat the newcomers peacefully. Some of the more progressive divines from New England visited the wigwams to preach the gospel, whilst the Quakers of Pennsylvania hoped by their example to persuade the braves to lay down their tomahawks. But for several centuries missionary ardour was damped by the habitual aloofness of the English, and by the Puritan supposition that negroes and Indians were predestined to damnation.

The division of Europe between Protestant and Catholic, and the further subdivision between the Protestant followers of Luther and those of Calvin, made religious differences a matter of major political importance in the turmoil of the sixteenth and seventeenth centuries. Religion still provided the inflammable material for war and civil strife. Resurgent Catholicism, with its agents, the Holy Inquisition, the Society of Jesus, and the reformed Papacy, gave a force and motive to Catholic rulers.

THE THIRTY YEARS' WAR

In 1555, a compromise had been arranged in Germany, by which the religion of any particular state was to be determined by that of its ruler. This solution held until Catholicism made its counter-attack. Ferdinand II, ruler of Austria and Holy Emperor, stifled Protestantism within his own borders and wanted to enforce a similar policy on his neighbours. The discontent of the Bohemians, one of Austria's subject races, led Ferdinand to crush their resistance and depose their leader, Frederick, Count Palatine of the Rhine, in 1620. Papal support and the assistance of Catholic Bavaria, whose army was commanded by the famous Tilly, made Ferdinand the arbiter of Germany for much of the Thirty Years' War. The King of Denmark, who intervened in the Protestant favour, was defeated by the Austrian Commander, Wallenstein, who was a Czech of tolerant religious views, but possessed dictatorial ambitions which were to ruin not only his own career but the Austrian power in Germany.

The War appeared to Wallenstein not as a religious crusade, but as a political plan to give Austria the key-position in central Europe. By making Ferdinand's cause a danger to other powers, both Protestant and Catholic, he broke the comparatively solid Catholic Front. Pope Urban VIII himself became afraid of a Germanized Italy; France, under Richelieu and Mazarin, was even prepared to aid the Protestant side, so that French boundaries would be secured against Ferdinand's ambitions. The year 1629 marked the height of Austrian advance. There was no further opposition from the princes of the Empire; England was at that time preoccupied with her own troubles with her king and parliament at each other's throats.

But a Protestant power was rising in the north of Europe. Sweden under the rule of Gustavus Adolphus of the energetic house of Vasa, repelled the attacks of Russia, Poland and Denmark. Protestant Europe looked to Gustavus, when Ferdinand II tore up the Augsburg Charter of 1555, and ordered the restitution of German Church lands, which had been alienated to Protestant rulers. Gustavus anticipated that a successful war in Germany would give him control of the Baltic, and reward his ambition and his piety at the same time.

"The Lion of the North" seized his opportunity, when the Emperor dismissed Wallenstein. The Protestants were seething with discontent at the Edict of Restitution. Gustavus invaded Germany, and crushed the imperialist armies, restoring Lutheranism even in areas of Catholic settlement. He fell at the battle of Lützen; but, though the Swedes were repulsed by Wallenstein, who had been received back into favour, his intervention had restored the balance between the two groups of warring states.

Gustavus's death did not bring peace, for France still supported the Protestant cause, in the interests of her traditional anti-Habsburg policy, desiring a weak Germany, so that she could advance to the Rhine, her "natural" frontier. The desultory fighting dragged on till 1648, when the Peace of Westphalia re-enacted the Augsburg decree, and made certain territorial rearrangements in favour of Sweden.

Calvinism, which had not been recognized at Augsburg in 1555, was now admitted as one of the three German sects. The republic of the United Provinces of the Netherlands, after almost a century of conflict, was declared by common consent to be independent; she had, in fact, freed herself from Spain as early as 1609. The war had given opportunities to the larger German states, like Brandenburg, Saxony, and Bavaria, to expand their frontiers at the expense of the smaller. Sweden was recognized as being the principal Baltic power.

RESULTS OF THE THIRTY YEARS' WAR

The Thirty Years' war was brutal and callous, even by contemporary standards. Mercenaries were gathered from the dregs of European society, and generals were too timid to control their soldiers when a city was surrendered to them. Magdeburg, burnt to the ground after Tilly had captured it, is said to have lost twenty thousand of its population in one night. The armies encamped on the countryside and drained it of food and resources, paying no compensation. Germany suffered such an economic setback that for a century her rulers were nearly bankrupt. They sold their youth as soldiers to other countries, in order to pay for Court extravagance and for the quarrelsome diplomacy which marked the relations of German princes after the Peace of Westphalia. The English, in their Civil War, suffered the same expropriations from both sides, and farmers in some parts of the country banded together to resist the tyrannous demands of Cavaliers and Puritans.

Neither Ferdinand the Catholic, nor Gustavus the Protestant, had prevailed. Where many soldiers were fighting for religion, others treated the war as a political game. The Jesuits failed to achieve their aim—a united Catholic Europe. France, though officially Catholic, had begun to pursue a line which led her into conflict with Catholic Austria. From Westphalia onwards, the Catholic Church becomes a spiritual entity, and religious forces no longer decide, or even expect to decide, international questions.

In the Middle Ages, the Christian world had been divided between the Orthodox Greek and the Roman Catholic Churches. The Protestant break-away from Rome in the sixteenth century ranged Western Europe into two opposing camps, each claiming to be the true religion, with the right to persecute the other. A good Catholic could logically treat the other side as heretical, for his Church had once been generally accepted in the West as the only true Church of Christ. For a Protestant, it ought to have been exceedingly difficult to deny to his opponents the same freedom of belief that he himself claimed in breaking away from the Roman Church.

A PERIOD OF RELIGIOUS INTOLERANCE

Yet Lutheran proved as intolerant towards Calvinist, and Calvinist towards Anabaptist and Quaker, as the Church of Rome had been towards all of them. Calvin at Geneva punished those who refused to recognize his government; the Dutch Calvinist Church attacked Arminius, who threw doubts on the truth of predestination. Anglican Churchmen sent Jesuits to the gallows and Dissenters to the pillory and into exile. Necessity in face of a common danger brought rival sects together, and there could be seen in certain Protestant communities the glimmerings of a mutual tolerance, which were to become generally accepted.

If the Catholic Church had allowed freedom of worship for those who preferred other communions, it would have admitted failure in its crusade to restore Catholic unity and authority. It therefore refused to make concessions, although events were to prove that European peace could only be realized by leaving untouched the existing line of religious differences.

The attitude of the Catholics was further shown in the Jansenist question. Jansen was a Flemish theologian and Bishop of Ypres; he accepted the Calvinist doctrine of predestination and preferred the simple teachings of the early Fathers to the tortuous reasonings of later theologians. His views were condemned, and attempts were made to embroil him in an argument as to whether he accepted Papal authority. Fortunately for the Jesuits, Louis XIV, under the influence of his morganatic wife, Madame de Maintenon, sided with the orthodox party against the Jansenists. The latter were forced into open heresy or into an insincere recantation. Once again, the Catholic Church had defeated differences within its own communion, probably at the expense of spiritual progress.

Political divisions and the quarrels of earthly rulers prevented the Catholic Church from acting as a harmonious whole. The Spaniards believed that they were the true sons of the Church; the Jesuits in Spain, whose power was very great, bickered with the Italian monastic and missionary orders. In such differences the Jesuits held their ground, since they were better organized than their opponents and enjoyed the powerful support of Philip of Spain and Louis of France.

A uniform Protestant faith would have been a contradiction in itself. The aim of most Protestant leaders was to establish a uniform religion in the particular community where their opinions held sway. Protestantism in opposition to a state, or to a religion that was not sympathetic, necessarily had to preach mutual toleration amongst its own supporters. When in power, devotion to a particular state system and a policy of persecution marked the illogical outlook of Protestant thinkers and leaders. The justification for such persecution could be founded only in the fervency with which they upheld their chosen faith and in the political necessities of the situation.

POLITICAL ASPECTS OF PROTESTANTISM

John Knox, the preacher and agitator of the Scotch reformation (c. 1550–70) in the sixteenth century, found himself in many an intellectual dilemma, though he never admitted that he had been mistaken or that a change of circumstances had modified his policy. When in exile at Geneva, he had described the Anglican settlement as a "mingle-mangle"; for he detested the compromise of the Tudor reformers. Knox treated the Catholic queen-dowager of Scotland and her daughter, Mary Stuart, as wicked women, deserving of assassination. Yet as a Calvinist, he was supposed to believe in the omnipotence of magistrates, even though they might be appointed by Catholic sovereigns.

After the victory of the rapacious Scots nobles over the monarchy, and of the reforming party over the Catholics, Knox had to modify his attitude. His attacks on Queen Elizabeth of England, who was the hope of all the Protestants in Europe, were resented not only by his Scottish followers but by the Calvinist Church at Geneva. These Protestants had to think in terms of political reality, and Elizabeth, holding the balance between France and Spain, aiding Huguenot rebels in France and Dutch rebels against Spain, was too important to antagonize. Knox saw a Presbyterian Church established in his Scotland. It recognized his theocratic views in theory, but gave undue weight to the power and pretensions of the Scots nobility. Nowhere, except in Geneva and in a few of the Puritan colonies in America, did pure Calvinism, with its ideas of government by priests and lay-elders, obtain full recognition.

Where the religious settlement, as in England, was the result of political considerations, the policy of the monarch was to establish uniformity with a wide sphere of comprehension. Those who refused to come in were persecuted, but not until Charles I's reign did Archbishop Laud attempt to secure complete submission to his narrow policy of unity through uniformity of ritual.

In France, the political and social power of the Protestant Huguenot minority had forced the weak government of Henry III and the sympathetic government of Henry IV to grant concessions. These included freedom of worship, and the Huguenots were given the right to control certain fortified towns and equip a private army. As the French monarchy became more powerful, these exceptional privileges of the Huguenots were withdrawn; but it was not until 1685 that Louis XIV took the final step, revocation of Henry IV's Edict of Nantes, in an effort to bring the Huguenots completely within the Catholic fold.

Progress towards religious liberty was not carried on by the Lutherans or Calvinists, who were merely trying to substitute a Protestant for a Catholic system. Real tolerance, however, was preached with sincerity by the minor Protestant sects, who had one common feature—a dislike of Church dignitaries and of centralized control. The true Church did not appear to them in the guise of Catholicism, Lutheranism or Calvinist Presbyteranism. The true Church was primarily a small and local gathering of sincere believers, under the guidance of elders and pastors elected by the congregation. These sectaries were known as Independents in England; they hoped that, by a process simplifying Church government, they would avoid the trammels of state interference and persecution.

THE DISSENTERS

Some of the earliest Independents were to be found in scattered communities in eastern Europe. They were the followers of Socinus, who believed in the efficacy of Christian doctrine, but denied divinity to Christ. In Holland, Anabaptists and Independents formed societies, and their ideas of organization spread to England. The heyday of Independency—or Congregationalism, as it later came to be called—appeared during the English Commonwealth from 1650 to 1660, when the Protector, Oliver Cromwell, gave it his sympathy and encouragement. Cromwell disliked Calvinism of the Scottish type, as much as he disliked Anglicanism with its bench of bishops.

But the country was not ripe for toleration; most people hated the Puritan habits of worship and their mournful outlook on life. In 1660, Charles II was restored and the Church of England re-assumed its former power. The sectaries, or Dissenters, were persecuted. Chancellor Clarendon produced his famous Code, which removed Dissenters from Church livings and the teaching profession. They were not allowed to build conventicles or chapels within a five-mile radius of chartered boroughs. Later they were forbidden to enter government service or sit in Parliament, unless they had taken communion according to the Anglican rite. Some Dissenters conformed; others waited for happier times, when they would be allowed to worship as they liked. They engaged in industry and commerce, where their thrift and grit helped them to amass wealth and gain business experience in a community which denied them religious and political freedom. Roger Williams, who founded the colony of Rhode Island in America, would not allow any religious barriers between his colonists; Jews were able to acquire full citizenship.

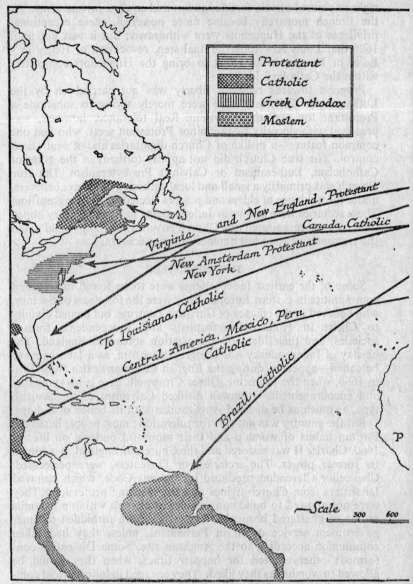

THE SPREAD OF RELIGION IN THE

The discovery of the New World opened the way for a great extension of
Christianity. The Jesuits spread Roman Catholicism among the natives of
Mexico and South America; French Canada and Louisiana were populated
by Roman Catholic settlers; Virginia and New England mainly by Protestants.

SIXTEENTH AND SEVENTEENTH CENTURIES

North-western Europe was preponderantly Protestant, with the exception of Ireland, and the Greek Orthodox Church became generally accepted in Russia. Islam, by then firmly established in Africa, penetrated into Eastern Europe and was a powerful force in Asia Minor. Mohammedan warriors invaded India.

Generally the period brought persecution to Jewish communities. The Inquisition had ousted most Jews from Spain and Italy, and they drifted to the economically backward areas of central and eastern Europe, where they were tolerated by their Polish and Turkish overlords. Elsewhere, the Ghetto system, which had originated in Venice, confined them to a narrow quarter of the city, where they lived. Outside the Ghetto, Jews were compelled to wear a distinctive badge. In Germany the system of repression was enforced with brutal harshness. Most of western Europe was closed to the Jews, until Holland and England raised the ban in the seventeenth century and profited by the energy and enterprise of the newcomers.

Towards the end of the century, Europe seemed to be returning to the dark days of repression. But the spirit of the age no longer favoured savage and unthinking persecution. New advances had been made in science and philosophy. The welfare of the state demanded expediency in religious policy, so that all sections of the community might contribute their share to the common cause. In these circumstances Protestantism and Catholicism relapsed into a lethargy, which marked the beginning of the Age of Reason.

SCIENTIFIC METHODS OF THOUGHT

Attempts were made to combine the new discoveries with current theological views, with the result that theology suffered. Political thinkers were advocating toleration, on the grounds that it would aid the state and the general welfare of the people. The Englishman Locke, the Frenchmen Bayle and Descartes, and the Dutchman Spinoza, admitted that revelation and the doctrines of religious infallibility should be tested in the light of reason, and if reason contradicted revelation, reason must prevail. Even the miracles described in the Bible were subjected to argument. In fact, the intellectual world of the West was questioning the bases of its religious beliefs; scepticism was becoming a fashion amongst the well-to-do; literature and art were being divorced from the worship and praise of God. The mass of the people, who remained outside the world of culture and learning, adhered to their ancient beliefs; for them, religion still appealed to the emotions. The first half of the seventeenth century had been a fanatical age; in the second half men became readier to study their opponents' point of view.

There had been little advance in science and mathematics since the first century A.D., until the new age of expansion stimulated man's inventiveness. Discoverers demanded new and accurate maps, and mathematical and nautical instruments. Business men wanted calculators and efficient methods of book-keeping. Unfortunately, advance was slow, for this period was primarily an age of philosophy. It was difficult to detach science, the study of fact, from philosophy, the study of theory. Inventions of a practical nature were few, and were confined to revising and developing ideas known to the Greeks.

Chemistry, the hobby of dashing Prince Rupert, the Royalist cavalry leader in the English Civil War, became a subject of great interest. Other aristocrats, like Robert Boyle, made important discoveries and enunciated new laws of matter. The old preoccupation with attempts to make gold out of baser substances no longer continued. Gases were distinguished from air and vapours. The balance was being used to check calculations. The study of mathematics and the passion for collecting facts, which especially marked this age, led to interesting developments as in clock-making. The microscope and Galileo's telescope provided the means, the one for discovering biological details, the other for understanding the relations of sun, earth and other planets. Biology, however, was completely stultified by the rarely-questioned belief in non-evolutionary creation.

GALILEO, ISAAC NEWTON, AND WILLIAM HARVEY

Modern astronomy was born in this age. Copernicus had suggested that the planets revolve round the sun and that the earth turns on its own axis. Galileo, who died in 1642, used the skill of an optician to make a telescope and prove the statements of Copernicus by direct observation. He not only tested scientific hypotheses, but by working from actual experiments, he made the path of future scientists much easier, suggesting methods of a surer character than the superstitions of the past. The dead weight of Catholic tradition and conservatism prevented Galileo from receiving the rewards due to an original thinker. He was forced by Pope Urban VIII not only to admit that he might be wrong, but to abjure in public his faith in the Copernican system. Advanced age and the threat of torture proved too strong for human frailty, and Galileo spent his remaining years in retirement—a victim of religious dogmatism, which frustrated the search for impartial knowledge. With similar stubbornness, many phenomena, such as comets, plagues and disease, were regarded as God-sent, and not as logical results of certain causes, the discovery of which would lead mankind to a more optimistic view of life.

Isaac Newton, who was born in 1642, used the discoveries of Copernicus and Galileo, and the more recent work of Kepler and Halley, to prove that the spacing and the motion of the heavens were due to a law of gravitation. His knowledge of mathematics allowed him to discover and to prove the scientific principle of gravitation, which he had noticed when an apple fell off a tree in his orchard. Galileo, trained in less exact sciences, had wondered why substances of unequal weight fell with the same rapidity from the top of the Leaning Tower of Pisa.

The development of medical knowledge was not so revolutionary as some discoveries suggested. Paracelsus tried to persuade chemists to turn from alchemy and use their talents in the dispensing of medicines. The universities still studied the old Greek and medieval doctors, and refused to adopt experimental and inductive methods.

Outside the established medical schools, a few men of talent and ingenuity gathered at Gresham College (founded in 1596 in London for
lectures of scientific interest), and established a dissecting school.
A plentiful supply of corpses from Tyburn gallows allowed these
amateurs to develop the anatomical theories of the Fleming Vesalius.

The Royal Society, founded by Charles II "for improving Natural
Knowledge", co-ordinated these early experiments, and went on to
practise vivisection of a crude nature, and attempt blood transfusion.
These scholars, who counted Wren, the architect, and Newton, the
mathematician, amongst their numbers, corresponded with continental thinkers, published treatises, and equipped a museum in
London and an observatory at Greenwich. William Harvey won a
European reputation in 1628 when he published his work on the
circulation of the blood—a tremendous discovery, which led to a
truer conception of the part played by diet and exercise in the prevention of disease. Although of general interest, researches were of
little immediate practical value in the development of medicine.

SCIENCE AND RELIGIOUS BELIEF

Most scientists were mathematicians and not practical inventors.
There was very little industrial development. The medieval ideal of a
general education was sufficiently strong to interest mathematicians
in theology and physicians in politics. Descartes emphasized the
supremacy of science, and suggested that the universe was subject to
mechanical laws. He ignored the contradictions of theological and
materialist theories about the origin of the universe, and much of his
thought was wasted and proved sterile, in an age when authority was
still superior to scientific proof. Spinoza tackled the question of
man's relation to God, exciting ridicule and opposition. Pascal, not
so daring, preferred to seek refuge in the doctrine of the helplessness
of the thinker who had no religious faith. Belief in God, which to
Pascal meant obedience to the Catholic Church, provided an anchor
for the rudderless soul.

Important as were these steps towards freedom of thought and the
recognition of science as a means to the better human understanding
of creation, they were unimportant in ordinary educational and
social life. The tendency was for the cultured to scoff rather than to
argue. The Churches defended themselves as best they could. The
mass of the people remained true to their traditional beliefs. Witch-
burning, advocated by Catholics and Protestants alike, became rarer
with the growth of a more educated and sceptical magistracy.
Religion, not yet completely freed from superstition, provided solace
to thousands, and gave them some idea of the meaning of the universe. Hell-fire, to many, betokened the punishment of sin; the
wrath and providence of God were as potent as ever. The Catholic
peasant bent his head at vespers. The Protestant read his Bible,
treasuring it as the Word of the Lord.

The ability and culture of James I's divines in their translation of the scriptures into homely English language, had provided a simple textbook of conduct and belief, understandable by gentleman and labourer alike. Conversation, especially among the more devout, was coloured by biblical phraseology; Puritan children were named after Old Testament heroes. Lack of education, and the patronage of their betters, prevented the lower classes from assimilating the scepticism and freethinking common in intellectual circles. Society remained static, and the doctrines of predestination and salvation by good works suited agricultural communities accustomed to the fatalism and the beauty of the countryside.

True belief, sincere and zealous, was found amongst the poor and humble and created a bulwark against atheism and agnosticism. The Catholic St. Teresa added a mystic touch to her Church which had so often placed doctrine before revelation. The Quietists in the Catholic world were like the Quaker followers of George Fox; they claimed direct contact with God. Among the German Protestants, hymn-writing and singing, which spread to England, gave an opportunity to the ordinary church or chapel-goer to take part in divine service. John Bunyan, the tinker and preacher of Bedford, wrote his *Pilgrim's Progress* in gaol, where he was imprisoned for his beliefs. Bunyan had read and re-read his Bible, and Christian's journey from this world to the next was described in Biblical language and illustrated by numerous texts. In an age that continued to ferment with Christian ideas and beliefs, it would be wrong to emphasize unduly the intellectual quarrels between philosophers and theologians.

CHAPTER 55

SOCIAL LIFE IN EUROPE

MANY changes divided the sixteenth and seventeenth centuries from the Middle Ages—the growth of capitalistic commerce, the foundation of colonies, the rise of sovereign states, and the break-up of the spiritual monopoly of the Catholic Church in the West. The social institutions and economy of Europe remained remarkably indifferent to these new factors in human development. Feudalism, or the theory that political and military duties arose out of land-tenure, had been broken by the Tudors, the Bourbons, and the Habsburgs.

Yet wealth still lay in land, rather than in chattels and bank accounts. Towns, the natural centres for political and commercial organization, though growing in size and opulence, retained in many ways a provincial outlook which reflected local agricultural interests. The younger sons of the aristocracy, however, were increasingly turning apprentice to merchants, whilst commercial magnates not infrequently sought to spend their retirement as country squires.

U (H.W.)

We must not exaggerate the changes that occurred in the economic habits of Europe, nor assume that Western Europe turned completely to shopkeeping. Universal trade was only in course of development, and industrial activity was the concern of the future. Mankind, looking forward and becoming more critical of the past, was still bound to many of the old accepted mercantile ideas and institutions. Only the Industrial Revolution could break the final bond with the past and introduce an epoch fully as important as that of the coming of Christianity and Islam in the development of mankind.

EVERYDAY LIFE IN WESTERN EUROPE

Western Europe had progressed so rapidly by the time of Louis XIV and Charles II that a man of the present day would have found it comparatively simple to sink himself into the life and customs of that period. He might have felt that the petty tyranny of the upper classes was unbearable, but in the company of ordinary folk he would have discovered tastes and conversation very much like the topics discussed in the living-rooms and bar-parlours of to-day. In an age not yet marked by the drabness and class disputes of the Industrial Revolution, he would have found an amazing colourfulness in dress and furniture that is not so noticeable to-day. The lack of sanitary precautions, however, might have offended his nose.

By the end of the seventeenth century, European habits were much more akin to those of the present day than at any time since the Roman Empire. This advance was unparalleled elsewhere in the world, for most of Africa remained barbarous, and the East—Turkey, Persia, India, China and Japan—kept conservatively to the path of centuries-old customs.

Elsewhere the distinct features of Spanish, French and Dutch civilization will have been noted. It remains to consider the life led by normal Englishmen of the period. Social life is complex and varied. At no single date in the history of mankind is it possible to draw a completely fair picture of man's life on the globe. Social life varies from one kingdom to another, from one province to another in the same kingdom. England perhaps had progressed further than her neighbours in this period. She was now a principal actor on the world's stage.

French culture was to receive mortal blows during the French Revolution of 1789. The Dutch bourgeois, after teaching the English the new commercial methods and morals of the age, were to sink to a minor place. Spain had already begun to drift, clinging to a social system which was suitable to the sixteenth century but worthless in face of the economic struggles of the period. Germany, laid waste by the religious struggles which culminated in the Thirty Years' War, contributed little to European culture. Russia aped the West. America provided a playground for adventurous Spaniards and Englishmen, bent on destroying native civilizations.

England alone among the stirring powers of Western Europe can claim that her civilization was inextricably woven into the history of her great expansion, both at home and abroad, during the significant events of the sixteenth and seventeenth centuries.

Outside the chief towns, London, Paris, Rome and Vienna, social life continued along grooves marked out by ancient custom. Each village possessed its squire, its seigneur, its Freiherr, the patron of village activities and the most important landlord. Where, as in England, the divine right of kings and centralized administration had been criticized by the independent country gentry, the squire, as justice of the peace, acted as local delegate of the government, executing laws that favoured his interests and ignoring those that did not. In France, the power of the monarch had been sufficiently great to make the gentry politically incapable of protest. But social prestige was a powerful weapon in the hands of the aristocracy.

The continental countries refused their peasantry the one concession which, if granted, would have marked this period clearly from that of the preceding feudal age. Emancipation would have given the serf the right to be free, to go hither and thither, to bargain for just wages, even to leave the countryside for employment elsewhere. By ignoring the just claims of the agricultural masses, the governments of Europe were providing combustible material for future revolutions. In France, many of the serfs had saved sufficient money to buy small farms from their masters, but this did not enable the peasantry to escape the old feudal claims and fines.

In England, the villein or serf had succeeded in ridding himself of many of the most degrading burdens that had marked his former status. Yet this emancipation was not as complete in practice as in theory. The conservative gentry managed to retain their hold on their tenants and labourers by a policy of paternal despotism.

IMPORTANCE OF AGRICULTURE

Agriculture remained a matter of primary concern for statesman and reformer. An Act of Elizabeth's reign, passed to maintain husbandry and tillage, began with the preamble ". . . the strength and flourishing estate of this kingdom hath been always and is greatly upheld and advanced by the maintenance of the plough and tillage". The fear of poor harvests and malnutrition among the bulk of the population was reflected in the attitude of economic pamphleteers of the period. Defence required man-power, and as the militia was recruited from those working on the land, any distress in the countryside would react upon the nation's fortunes in the time of war. Furthermore, though commerce was spreading its tentacles far and wide, the bulk of national wealth was still to be found in agriculture.

Sir W. Petty, one of the first English statisticians, estimated that the land in 1665 gave 144 millions and merchandise 31 millions to a total national weath of 250 million pounds. Land in that day was the only gilt-edged security, because speculation in trade was a risk that comparatively few attempted. The governing class, whether remnants of the feudal aristocracy, or country gentry whose former commercial success had allowed them to buy up the fat acres of the abbeys and priories in the reign of Henry VIII, were primarily interested in their rents. Good crops meant higher rents and, equally important, increased tithes.

The stimulus given to trade and industry affected agriculture, which is always slow to react to new methods and new influences. During the Middle Ages, there had been a certain amount of progress in cultivation, but this was necessarily limited whilst land was still ploughed, sown, and harvested according to timeworn formulas.

The fifteenth century, however, had seen an increased demand from Flanders and from our own English clothiers for wool. Landowners soon saw that, by decreasing costs and revolutionizing agricultural methods, they would not only be able to produce the accustomed amount of corn, but large areas formerly arable would be turned into pasture for sheep, with an increase in wool production.

LAND ENCLOSURE AND ITS RESULTS

This could only be done by reducing the wastage of time, material, and labour that was inherent in the old scattered strip system of the common fields. Enterprising farmers would urge their neighbours to possess their own enclosed crofts, properly hedged and marked off, and no longer subject to customary rules of cultivation. The common fields were first tackled, but the heaths and the meadowland which each village possessed for feeding the cattle, swine, sheep, and geese of the inhabitants, were, on the whole, left undisturbed until the eighteenth century.

The economic arguments of the would-be enclosers were difficult to contradict; the law of necessity was successfully invoked by men of foresight who saw that a primitive agriculture could not satisfy an expanding and increasingly commercial England. In an age when, socially and politically, the ordinary villager retained many of his former feudal disabilities, it was difficult for him to compete with the greater rapacity and power of the squire and other important local landlords. The best land naturally fell to the lot of the more influential. Where the enclosed land was converted into pasture, destitution appeared, as agricultural labourers were no longer wanted.

Many of the dispossessed offered themselves to their more successful neighbours as day- or year-labourers, but this proved of little avail, since the supply of labour was greater than the demand. Elizabeth and her advisers encouraged the custom, for they were alarmed at the growing numbers of vagabonds and out-of-works.

Although the amount of corn-land was reduced, there does not seem to have been any lack of food. Some years were bad, but, on the whole, England was sufficiently well fed, with a surplus that could be exported to other countries. New crops—turnips and potatoes—were raised. Marshy districts like the Fens were drained with the aid of pump-engines and windmills constructed on more efficient lines. The best breeds of sheep were sent from the Dorset downs to the Midland counties, from which their wool was despatched to the clothing districts of the south-west. The farmer who owned arable as well as pasture, fed his sheep and manured his fields by folding his flocks on ploughed and harvested land. With such marvellous opportunities, many of the gentry, no longer interested in military activities, became absorbed in rural pursuits and their estates.

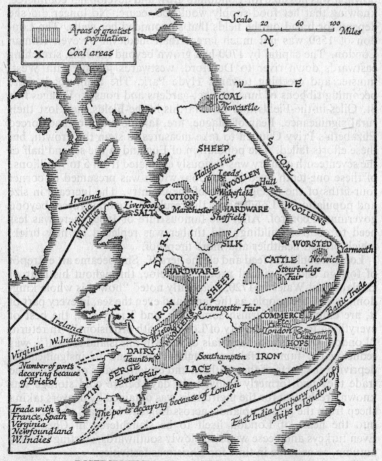

DISTRIBUTION OF TRADE IN ENGLAND

In the sixteenth and seventeenth centuries the prosperity of England and Wales rapidly increased, the main centres of trade and production being shown above.

A more remarkable development in this period was a tendency for some areas, because they possessed either a suitable climate or good communications, to concentrate on producing some one thing in sufficient quantities to allow of its being sold to other districts. This development is referred to by economists as "specialization"—it marked a break in the old medieval tradition that each village should be self-sufficient and dependent almost entirely on its own products.

LONDON BECOMES A GREAT CENTRE OF TRADE

Now that the barriers between district and district were breaking down, it was possible for London to grow and develop her commerce, knowing that her food-supply would be secure. No longer did she depend for bread on the fields that surrounded her walls. The London of 1550 was not much larger than medieval or even Roman London. The capital by 1700 had grown beyond its walls, stretching eastwards down river to Deptford, westwards joining with Westminster and creeping towards Hyde Park. The main roads were becoming ribbons of inns, market-gardens and houses. Villages like St. Giles-in-the-Fields and St. Martins-in-the-Fields, had lost their rural significance. Fear of plague, fire, famine and riot had forced Elizabeth's Privy Council to take measures to stem the growth, but these efforts failed. The population of England in the second half of the seventeenth century was variously estimated from 5 to 7 millions; of these one-tenth lived in London, which was presumed to corner four-fifths of the foreign trade of the country. The increase in size and population of London was the result of economic forces beyond government control. After the famous Fire of 1666, there was less need to control building; old timber was replaced by new brick, which proved healthier and more fireproof.

London could not feed and clothe herself. She became an entrepôt of foreign and provincial products. Defoe, throughout his tour of England and Wales in 1720, frequently noted "how this whole kingdom, as well the people, as the land, and even the sea, in every part of it, are employ'd to furnish something, and I may add, the best of everything to supply the city of London with provisions". In return, "London, which sucks the vitals of trade in this island to itself", was reducing the famous fairs throughout the land to insignificance, depriving the ports of the southern and eastern coasts of much of the trade they had formerly enjoyed. In days before cold storage was known, fresh meat for the metropolis was obtained by drovers taking sheep from the grassy uplands, across England by grass tracks, right into the heart of London itself to be slaughtered in Cheapside. Even turkeys and geese waddled slowly southwards, starting in early autumn, so as to be in time for Christmas festivities.

The most localized and specialized industry of all was the clothing manufacture. Guild restrictions in the chief towns in the Middle Ages had kept up prices to a limit which benefited master and journeyman alike, and supervised the quality of materials and workmanship in the interests of the consumer. From the social standpoint, there was little to criticize in this arrangement. Every apprentice became a journeyman; every journeyman with thrift, skill, and patience could become a master. This sunny period did not last long.

By 1550, the Guilds had fallen into the hands of commercial capitalists, interested not in the "mystery" of the craft, but in its exploitation. They weakened the Guilds, which were called Companies in the sixteenth century, by spreading their enterprises into the countryside, beyond the limits of guild regulation. Here, cheap labour and lack of organization among the workers gave the capitalist an opportunity to strengthen his control over industry and to usurp functions which had hitherto been subject to the mutual co-operation of master and workman. In the West Riding of Yorkshire, in the villages around Norwich, along the Suffolk–Essex border, and in the huge area covering Gloucestershire, Wiltshire and part of Somerset, clothing districts were already in existence. With the coming of the merchant-capitalist, these areas produced most of England's cloth, whilst the town Guilds became mere anachronisms.

"DOMESTIC" INDUSTRY

The industrial system of this period has been given the name "domestic", because articles were manufactured in the home and not in factories. The capitalist or his travelling agent would buy wool in London or at one of the fairs at Stourbridge, Cirencester or Tetbury, and pass it on to spinners, who were generally villagers trying to eke out a livelihood in addition to their own gardening and cowkeeping. Women and children did most of the spinning; they worked at the wheel whilst the men were in the fields. The yarn collected from the spinner would be redistributed to the weaver. Some of these weavers might be able to work independently of the trader, but the difficulty of acquiring machinery and a cheap and regular supply of yarn became increasingly greater as the years passed. The weavers generally worked in their own houses, although in the north there were signs of something approaching a factory system. Looms would be hired from the trader-employer who paid the weavers piece-rate wages, minus fines for waste and charges for use of the machinery.

This system was capitalist in the sense that the weaver was paid for his labour and had no share in the profits from the sale of his manufactures. The loss of self-respect and of economic independence made the existing division of classes wider than before. As finance began to play a more important part in industry, we can already see, in embryo, a society where one section possessed the power to tap markets, to control the instruments of production and to employ labour, whilst the mass of the people were unable to rise from the position of wage-earners. It was money-power, and not skill in the craft, which determined the relationship between the two classes.

The manufacture of lace, stockings, and even shoes came under the same influences. The Tudor government, fearing that social unrest would follow the enclosure of land and the break-up of the Guild system, attempted to replace the latter by state legislation. But the government proved more successful in regulating foreign commerce than in establishing just wages and conditions at home for English labourers and weavers. Some crafts remained safe from capitalist control, because they demanded such a degree of skill in their exercise that it was very difficult to exploit the craftsmen. Other industries were so localized that they seemed to escape the notice of the capitalist entrepreneur who might have been expected to exploit them.

INDUSTRY, TRADE, AND COMMUNICATIONS

At the lower end of the scale, the less skilled and most dangerous occupations were left entirely in the hands of individual employers who treated their workmen as they thought fit. Quarrymen and miners, working in conditions and for pay that indicated their servile origin, escaped the attention of legislator and humanitarian, although travellers in their diaries often remarked on the disgusting conditions that existed in the lead-mines and other underground industries.

Most of the coal areas of to-day were known in the seventeenth century and the coal trade was sufficiently brisk to serve most of the counties of England. In spite of repeated efforts no one had yet discovered how to use coal to extract iron from iron ore. Instead charcoal, burnt from the forests of the Weald, was used, and its production gave the counties of Kent, Surrey and Sussex an industrial appearance which they no longer possess. Some enterprising industrialists, realizing that England's forests were rapidly dwindling, attempted to tap the Yorkshire streams for water-power, but the real fruit of their inventiveness was not to be obtained until the middle of the eighteenth century.

A difficulty which escaped contemporary notice, except that of travellers, was the lack of rapid and efficient communications, in an age when trade was increasing and business life becoming very complex. The newspaper, which had already appeared in the early seventeenth century in the form of periodical news-summaries issued at the trading centres of Frankfurt, Antwerp and Venice, had begun to take shape in England by 1665, when the bi-weekly *Oxford Gazette* was published. Known later as the *London Gazette*, it was soon followed by a succession of reviews and advertisers which were sold in the coffee-houses of Queen Anne's reign. Some of these, like *Lloyd's News* in 1690, contained business information which aided commercial transactions. A certain number of pages of Houghton's *Collections for the Improvement of Husbandry and Trade* were devoted to quotations of share prices in the various joint-stock companies. The personal touch in business dealings was still important and in the coffee-houses, taverns and Exchanges of London, men met to clinch bargains which would have been delayed and misrepresented if done from a distance. A postal system had been established in the reign of Charles I. London was able to obtain the privilege of a local penny post in 1680.

ROADS AND RIVER-WAYS

A postal system might have been expected to stimulate the upkeep of the main roads across England, but little heed was paid by the government to travellers' complaints. The roads were in the care of the local justices of the peace, who could use compulsory parish labour for their repair. Whereas France, with its love for centralization, had appointed a surveyor for roads and bridges as early as 1599, the first concerted effort in England to keep long stretches of road in regular repair was made not by Whitehall, but by energetic gentlemen living near the roads and interested in their upkeep. In 1706, a turnpike trust was formed, composed of local notabilities who supervised the erection of toll-gates, the collection of tolls, and the use of these funds in repairing part of the Holyhead Road. Defoe gives a list of tolls for turnpiked roads in the beginning of the eighteenth century which reads as follows: "a horse a penny, a coach three pence, a cart four pence, at some six pence to eight pence, a waggon six pence, in some a shilling, and the like; cattle pay by the score, or by the head, in some places more, in some less".

Coaches had been introduced in 1572; they were very commodious, but were open at the sides. The seventeenth century saw not only the use of coaches for carrying the post and for passengers; there was also an increase in the number of privately-owned "chariots", which were frail boxes made of wood and leather perched upon a delicate chassis. The witty diarist Pepys, who held a post at the Admiralty, bought his own chariot and took his wife for airings in it; in 1660, the possession of such a vehicle was a necessary condition of gentility. Difficulties on the road were not completely overcome, for local acts of Parliament dealt only with sections of the trunk-roads, whilst the risk of coaches breaking down on the way combined with footpads who frequented lonely stretches of road to make the traveller's life one of surprise and discomfort.

Rivers were deepened here and there, as ships became larger and the volume of trade increased. Holland and France proved more enterprising than England. Holland showed how in a low-lying country an effective system of canals could set nature at bay and enrich trade and agriculture. In France, under the rule of Richelieu and Colbert, the rivers Seine, Loire, Rhône and Garonne, were connected by canals, along which the proprietors of the French vineyards transported their wines. England, with her comparatively long coastline and wide river estuaries, preferred to develop a system of coastal trade, which possessed the advantage of allowing goods to reach London without having to use internal river-ways and roads.

The enclosure movement, with the consequent conversion of much arable land into pasture, and the growing capitalist control of the clothing industry, led to an increase in unemployment and indigence which could no longer be left, as in the Middle Ages, to the care of the Church. The breaking up and secularization of monastic lands deprived England of its first unemployment fund. Unless individuals continued wholesale charity, as the Church had formerly done, the state was forced to remain the sole guardian of the landless, the workless, and in addition those persons who were intentionally idle.

EFFORTS TO ALLEVIATE POVERTY

The state was slow to realize the obligation that lay upon its shoulders to take care of the more unfortunate members of the community. In Henry VIII's reign, the bishops had ordered collections to be made in the churches; certain towns levied compulsory rates to be used to setting the able unemployed to work and in relieving the sick and aged. In 1601, a nation-wide scheme was produced by Parliament. This act compelled the local gentry as justices to appoint overseers of the poor and to make all property-owners pay contributions which were known as poor-rates. Charles I showed a humane regard for his poorer subjects, whereas Puritan harshness held unemployment to be a judgment for individual sin.

The parsimony of the local squires made the English system of poor relief a half-hearted and barely successful solution for a permanent social distress. Local rates, then as now, were regarded as evils to be lessened, rather than as means to effect a juster distribution of unequal incomes. So afraid were the justices that newcomers to their parish might, in the event of sickness or unemployment, become a charge on the poor rate, that in 1662, by Act of Parliament, each labourer was declared to have a "settlement"—that is, a parish in which he was born or apprenticed, and to which he had to return if the justices thought fit.

Another evil arising from this crude attempt to relieve the poor was the lack of classification. The aged sick received food, clothing, and fuel in their own homes. The orphan was apprenticed, and in some enlightened towns, he might even be given a smattering of schooling. But, among the unemployed, the idle were mixed up with those who were ready to find and accept work. Both types were liable to be whipped as vagabonds; both could be forced into a "house of correction" (an early form of workhouse), to labour at a "stock" or material provided for them by the overseers. Recipients of relief were marked with the letter P and treated as outcasts. The harshness of this régime became more evident later. There was little permanent unemployment, on the whole, during the seventeenth century, but there grew up among the lower classes a subterranean loathing for a system which had originally been intended to relieve their sufferings.

Sickness, orphanhood and permanent physical disability were very common in an age when medieval medicine, with its star-reading, was still the guide to remedies and treatment. A high mortality-rate, aided by frequent years of widespread plague which ravaged the whole of Europe at intervals, explained the slow increase in population, despite growing national wealth and a rising standard of living. Bleeding and quack remedies that depended on propitious seasons for their success, were the common refuge of physicians, faced with cases they could not diagnose. Pedlars at fairs sold pills to gullible countrypeople. Housewives, skilled in nursing their many children, believed in the greater efficiency of tonics and ointments made from garden herbs.

It is difficult to say whether men were becoming cleaner in habits, though shaving was usual. The water-closet, known to ancient Crete and Rome, was reintroduced by Sir John Harrington in 1596; but it was considered unnecessary and ridiculous, and was to be found only in the houses of a few enlightened aristocrats. Washing was regarded as outlandish and detrimental to health; the upper classes used rosewater and perfumed clothing. The countryfolk had their pores well opened by perspiration, and so avoided the grime of their town neighbours. Soap was supplemented by harder materials, like pumice, and ashes from the fire mixed with oil. Its manufacture increased during the Stuart period, probably to wash articles of linen and lace, which were often cleaner than the body they decked.

SANITATION AND HYGIENE

Sanitation was ignored. The habit of throwing slops into the gutter, the overcrowded alleys and tenements, the lack of fresh water, and the non-segregation of those stricken with fever and pox still gave opportunities for disease to strike high and low. One of the most successful joint-stock enterprises was the formation of the New River Company, which gave seventeenth-century London a reasonable supply of river water. The Thames in Elizabeth's time had been a mixture of natural filth and sewage which spread infection.

Fatalism and a strong religious faith made the ravages of sickness and plague less frightful than we should have expected. A plague was thought to be a visitation for sin and unbelief, and few realized that it could be prevented by medical research and personal cleanliness. Those who had delicate noses avoided some of the most noisome odours by smoking tobacco and by constantly spitting. In places of entertainment, oranges were sold, and those who could afford such delicacies sucked them, in order to ward off plague.

Some people thought that tea was a good antidote against infection; and the large amount of alcohol consumed by the average person, though it increased indigestion, flatulence and gout, may have saved many from an early death. All classes were affected by the ravages of infectious disease, though the gentry could leave town whenever plague broke out. But smallpox struck high and low, and the face of a famous beauty at Court could be permanently marred within a few weeks. Suitors, before declaring their affections to their ladies, would discreetly discover whether the beloved ones had as yet caught the smallpox.

Many ailments came from irregular habits that tapped physical energy. The existence of healing springs had been known in the past; their properties were linked with the miracles of local saints, and so they suffered a period of unpopularity after the Reformation. Doctors, however, frequently prescribed treatment at Bath and Buxton. Some of the bolder spirits of Elizabeth's Court followed their physicians' advice, though the Queen remained incredulous. In the seventeenth century the English aristocracy's slavish regard for continental ideas and fashions led to the introduction of "spa" treatment from the Continent. After 1660, the returned Cavaliers flocked to Bath and the newly discovered wells near Tonbridge. Thither went the Court; Charles II's Catherine to cure her barrenness, some of the men to reduce girth, others to seek new pleasures in an atmosphere less formal than that of Whitehall. Bath enjoyed a permanent popularity, for its well-built pools and retiring-rooms provided enough accommodation to attract regular custom, whilst the arrival of Beau Nash, the "King of Fashion", in 1705, made the town a haven of wit and beauty, as well as a sanatorium.

The poor might be able to obtain relief from pain and ill-health, if they were fortunate to live near a well, but even this benefit depended upon the attitude of the well-proprietors towards folk whose presence might lose them more profitable custom. Except in the neighbourhood of London, the inland watering-places catered exclusively for the gentry and the well-to-do. Sea-bathing, the sport of George III, had not yet become popular, although as a matter of interest it is recorded that some of the more high-spirited among Cambridge undergraduates were caught by their tutors bathing in the River Cam.

CHAPTER 56

LEISURE AND LITERATURE

MANY of the most important fashions in dress were adopted downwards through the grades of society. Only the labourer and his wife retained their distinctive smocks and petticoats. In the sixteenth century, the Spanish set the fashion and in the seventeenth century the French, though the more sober middle-class, until the Restoration, preferred the plainer clothes worn by English Puritans and by Dutchmen. In Elizabeth's reign, men endured tight-fitting "peascod belly" doublets and balloon-like breeches which extended half-way down the thigh. They found it difficult to bend forward or to sit in chairs with arms.

The extravagances worn by the women are best described in the words of a contemporary dramatist. They

> "wear curlèd Periwigs, and chalk their faces
> And still are gazing in their pocket glasses,
> Tyred with pinned ruffles, fans and partlet strips,
> With Buskes and Vertingales about their hips,
> And tread on corkèd stilts at prisnor's pace."

Busks were thick, heavily ornamented pieces of material attached to the front of the corset. A vertingale, or farthingale, consisted of a petticoat covering a hoop made of wood and metal wiring.

FASHION AND PERSONAL ATTIRE

The hair at first was worn of medium length by men, although longer hair became fashionable about 1600. Puritans went close-cropped. Charles II and his courtiers introduced the wearing of wigs, which had become fashionable at the French Court. Many of the middle class followed suit, though they found the habit somewhat inconvenient. Pepys was not sure whether to let his own hair grow long, or to cut it short and wear a wig. Women attached ringlets if they did not possess them naturally, wore low-necked dresses, dyed their hair and painted and powdered, to the genuine disgust of many of their more conservative menfolk. Gowns were more delicately coloured, and the farthingale discarded in favour of a looser shirt gathered away from the front so as to display a flowery petticoat beneath. The society lady of King Charles II's reign looked much handsomer and more natural than the gawky and over-dressed Elizabethan beauty.

Male attire, which was very expensive and decorative, became increasingly comfortable and threw off the eccentricities of the earlier period. Breeches were now worn down to the knee; wrists and neck were laced and frilled. A loose coat replaced the Elizabethan cloak. Dress, like the other arts, was adapting itself to a more cultured and pleasure-loving society. Comfort was beginning to dictate to fashion.

And yet, despite the growing evolution of manners, and the introduction of lighter foods and beverages from hotter countries, English grossness remained proverbial. The meal times reflected not only the division between the classes, but the growing emphasis on dinner as the chief meal of the day. For the upper classes, the hour was gradually moved from 11 in the morning (about 1550) to 4 and even later (about 1700). The labourers ate their dinner at the more convenient hour of 12.

In the higher ranks of society the lateness of the dinner-hour led to the introduction of breakfast, which gradually developed from a mere sip of whey or chocolate in the early morning to a meal which often had a meat course. If we ignore the magnificent meals served at the tables of the nobility, we should find that the most common dishes for ordinary people were beef and pudding. Even the humblest family on Sunday fed largely on roast beef, for the strictness of the

English Sabbath led naturally to an excess of eating, the only possible occupation for that day, apart from attendance at church. A Frenchman, in a travel book which was published in 1697, noticed among other interesting facts that "it is a common practice even among people of good substance, to have a huge piece of roast beef on Sundays, of which they stuff till they can swallow no more, and eat the rest cold, without any other victuals, the other six days of the week".

EATING, DRINKING, AND MERRY-MAKING

Butchers' meat and big puddings made the diners thirsty. English drunkenness continued to grow, despite a tentative alehouse licensing system and the harangues of religious leaders like Bunyan. The evil was accentuated by the lack of an alternative drink which would be refreshing and palatable; tea was still a luxury. The strength of alcoholic beverages was greater then than now; beers made from hops had been, since Tudor days, substituted for the old-fashioned but less potent ales. Rum was imported from the West Indies, but remained primarily a favourite amongst sailor folk. Gin, distilled from malt and juniper berries, made its appearance in the reign of William III and ushered in the worst age of drunkenness. The upper classes, too, had their novel drinks—champagne, the heavy wines of Southern Europe, and brandy. Tea-drinking, sport, and alternative amusements were eventually to alleviate a social evil that marked the life of our ancestors.

Although the rise of a Protestant state in England resulted in official denunciation of Catholic superstitions, and the growing middle class, with its emphasis on thrift, attempted to abolish many of the established pastimes, the mass of the people remained faithful to the old merrymaking, traditional feasts, fairs and games. Nor was the Court, at first, ambitious to isolate itself from its subjects, until foreign influences taught the upper classes new modes of amusement, beyond the pocket and against the inclination of ordinary Englishmen. Not until the later Industrial Revolution, with its mechanization, squalor and drabness, did the people forget how to play innocent games and entertain themselves. May Day and Hallow-e'en were losing their significance.

The chief festivals in the seventeenth century were New Year's Day, when presents were exchanged between friends and relations, and Whitsun, when the villagers betook themselves to the taverns, regardless of Puritan censure, which had attempted to suppress them. In some districts, the day of the patron saint of the parish was celebrated, often giving rise to debauchery, riot and even manslaughter. The reduction of saints' days in the Anglican Church calendar was followed by scathing Puritan attacks on the jollities of the few that remained. The Stuart kings, however, took the view that disturbances might be expected if the people were deprived of their sports; they agreed with an Earl of Newcastle who once suggested that "divertisementes will amuse the peoples' thoughts and keepe them in harmless action which will free your Majestie from faction and rebellion", and with the bishop who thought that his flock "would go either to tippling houses and there talk of matters of church and state, or else into conventicles". Politicians are rarely recruited from athletes and football fans.

The Puritan attitude reflected in their attack on the *Book of Sports* which was published by order of the king in 1618, was understandable. The strict Puritan regarded these pleasures as encouragements for lust and drunkenness; he did not condemn them merely because they were allowed on Sundays, for Sundays were no different from the other days. During the gloomy years, when England was subjected to a Puritan régime, ordinances and acts were passed not only to make the Sabbath holy but to suppress "lewde sports" on all days. The pendulum swung in 1660 to the opposite extreme, and Charles II earned his title, "The Merry Monarch", by his own licence and the freedom he allowed among his subjects.

But government, and the traditional reverence of the lower classes for those above them, could not be carried on without some restriction of the amusements which might lead to disorderly gatherings. The *Book of Sports* had allowed only innocent games; it had prohibited "all unlawfull games, as Beare- and Bull-baiting; interludes (stage plays) at all times; in the meaner sort of people, bowling". Yet a satisfactory compromise was very difficult to reach in practice.

RELAXATION AND AMUSEMENTS

Religion, in the later seventeenth century, was not as seriously regarded as it had been in the past. Mr. Pepys went to church to contrast the preaching qualities of the various ministers, and to flirt with his lady neighbours when his wife was not looking. After the Revolution of 1688, societies for "Reformation of Manners" and the official toleration extended to nonconformity made the Sunday we know to-day. Sunday, the rest-day of the week, was observed quietly by the mass of the people, who were excessive neither in their religious devotions nor in amusements that might disturb their neighbours. Heavy meals, a little church or chapel-going, and walking in the parks, became the usual Sabbath activities for most English families.

While the Court preferred the stately French dances, known by such delightful names as the Pavane, the Courante, the Sarabande and the Capriole, folk-dancing gradually died out, even among the country labourers. However, as late as 1663, there was morris dancing in Leadenhall Street in the City. The growing middle class, unable to lower themselves to the pleasures of the masses, or to associate with the entertainments at Court, had to be content with more sedate amusements, reminding one of Bank Holiday jaunts to-day. Pepys was representative of these. He took his wife to St. Bartholomew's Fair on August 24th, to see Italians dancing on ropes and women doing the same strange tumbling tricks that had delighted Crete and Rome. Puppet-shows, wrestling-matches and shooting were among the attractions, and the many side-stalls sold hot cakes and innumerable knicknacks.

Sight-seeing was another respectable amusement, and increased in popularity with the arrival of visitors from the provinces and the Continent. There were the tombs at Westminster Abbey, the Court functions at Whitehall, the beauty-parades in the gardens of Foxhall (Vauxhall), where musical parties were held in the alcoves—and the various places of public execution. Crowds of over twelve thousand would gather to watch the last moments of famous criminals and to hear their confessions or their brave orations, which were often printed and circulated as broadsides. There was a Zoo in the Tower of London, which at this time was used as a depository for the miscellaneous property belonging to members of the royal family.

SPORTS AND PASTIMES

Archery, the old pastime, went out of fashion when musketry took its place as a means of defence. The decay of strenuous open-air sports naturally encouraged the lower classes to imitate the Court in playing games that were marked by their vice and wastefulness. Even as early as Elizabeth's reign, we find the south bank of the Thames a den of courtesans, gamblers and vagabond players. Dicing and its associates—bull-baiting, prize-fighting, cock-fighting— provided opportunities for wagers. It was impossible to expect improvement in the habits of the populace when the Court itself encouraged wagering within its own confines.

Hunting remained as popular as ever among the rural gentry. Joseph Addison, an English Secretary of State who contributed articles to society periodicals, described the squire's activities in *Spectator*: "Sir Roger [de Coverley] . . . has in his youthful days taken forty coveys of partridges in a season and tired many a salmon with a line consisting but of a single hair. The constant thanks and good wishes of the neighbourhood always attended him on account of his remarkable enmity towards foxes, having destroyed more of these vermin in one year than it was thought the whole country could have produced."

The passion for horseflesh became so much a part of the habits and outlook of all classes that horse-racing gradually became as popular as the more primitive chase of stags and foxes. Banstead Downs in Surrey attracted those who could not afford the expensive luxury of attending the race-course at Newmarket, where Charles II kept his stables and visited the races.

Less exacting pursuits, like tennis and pell-mell (both from France), were played in the royal parks and courtyards. Pell-mell was played in a long alley, with hanging arches or hoops at each end, through which the ball had to be struck by a mallet. The more plebeian counterpart of this was bowls, already common in France. It started as a genteel game in the sixteenth century, but developed into a tavern pastime and its followers were soon more attracted by its more popular rival, ninepins or skittles.

Just as the labourer loved to watch prize-fighting and even to participate in it himself, so the gentlemen learned to fence, and instructors from Italy and Spain came over to give classes in duelling, laying emphasis on its detailed code of honour. A rebuke could easily lead to a challenge and a challenge to a death. Medieval chivalry committed suicide in the fifteenth century, but "honour" remained to plague the public and private life of one section of the community, too leisured to be able to ignore personal slights.

FACILITIES FOR EDUCATION

School life had tended to drop behind in the assimilation of new ideas and branches of learning. The schools of the sixteenth century, though many of them had been founded to teach the classical languages that were becoming popular amongst the learned, were conducted and disciplined in traditional fashion. Grammar schools, a peculiarly English product at a time when religion and class were in the melting-pot, could be found in most country towns. After the suppression of the monasteries, some of the old abbey and priory schools were re-endowed by King Edward VI. Tradesmen and professionals, as well as members of the squirearchy and the Church sent their sons to be educated at these schools.

In Catholic countries, the convents often undertook the education of children; the Jesuits regarded this as an important part of their missionary work and set up schools of a very high educational standard. A change for the worse occurred in the seventeenth century. The wealthy and high born chose to put their children into the charge of a private tutor, generally a young man who regarded his post as a step towards better things. The compromise between private tutor and grammar-school master was later to be found in the growth of special, or so-called public, schools for the children of the governing classes.

The poor were left to their own devices. In some towns, charities might provide cheap schooling for the brilliant son of a labourer, but this was uncommon. Generally the tradesmen saw to it that their sons took any scholarships provided by benefactors.

Wider facilities for education resulted in greater literary output and the appearance of national literatures. Political vigour, too, has generally had a beneficial influence on writing and on the arts. In progressive states, there are always men prepared to subsidize poets and extend their patronage to the drama and music. Spain, England and France in this period had their Golden Ages of literature. In Germany and Italy, rent by wars and aggressions, there was very little creative art or literature. German Protestants wrote hymns which were eventually to become part of our own religious heritage, but apart from this, Germany had to wait for her own Golden Age until the eighteenth century when the influence of French writers stimulated German consciousness in the field of thought.

LITERATURE AND THE DRAMA

The reign of Queen Elizabeth, when the English were a race of adventurers, saw much writing, and very great interest was taken in literary criticism. William Shakespeare, an Alderman's son, educated in a grammar school, escaped from the stuffy atmosphere of a country town and went up to London to see life and mix with the wits. He was attached to a theatrical company and wrote plays, probably spending odd moments in the pay box and acting small parts in the plays he helped to produce. He took his plots from exciting episodes of national history, or tales brought over from Italy, where he loved to place the scene of his comedies. Out of this material, and the life of the ordinary folk who thronged the streets of London and ruled over his own native Stratford, Shakespeare built up characters which have appealed to all nations and all classes, for all times.

Lesser dramatists there were, who, though dimmed by comparison with Shakespeare, produced a great number of plays of outstanding merit, dealing chiefly with the manners and controversies of the time. In poetry, a similar advance was shown. Spenser, who wrote the *Faerïe Queene* as a compliment to Elizabeth, built up a tradition that was to be developed by John Milton, giant among poets. *Paradise Lost* and *Paradise Regained* not only showed a mastery of classical allusion, but introduced into poetry a sublime emotion, which influenced many later poets. Milton's prose, fervent and righteous, thundered against injustice and bigotry, and gave political philosophy an interest which it has so often lacked.

Classical influences increased, and with them came a lighter and more frivolous spirit. This was partly due to French literature, which had been forced by political considerations to prefer satire and humour to direct criticism of the state. Dryden and Samuel Butler directed their shafts at political personalities and at the anarchy of the Civil War period.

The age of the "Sun King", as Louis XIV was called, saw a revival in French literature, so important as to influence the writings of all other countries and leave traditions of greater permanency than any of the military successes of Louis himself. As writers were not allowed to mention the king or discuss politics, the dramatists turned to classical themes and the story-tellers to allegories and fables. Corneille, aided by the compilers of the dictionary which standardized the language, was godfather to the literary movement in France. He simplified the plot, insisted that the play should deal with heroic sentiments, and ignored the details of character and incident which so delighted Elizabethan dramatists. There was nothing plebeian or ridiculous in Corneille's plays. Racine preferred the more feminine and emotional feelings, but even he was careful to retain unity of plot and avoid any incidents or by-play which would divert the interest of the spectator from the story. Molière wrote on lighter themes, introducing humorous characters, but his plays retain an artificiality born of the Versailles atmosphere.

La Fontaine, a would-be critic of the government, hid his meanings in the morals he attached to his re-telling of Aesop's Fables. Perhaps the most important, though the least interesting, of this school of literature, was Boileau, a poet, but more famous as author of *The Art of Poetry*—the textbook of the age—which propounded all the writer's tricks of the trade. Boileau earned the scorn of nineteenth-century romantics and of all who believed that poetic inspiration could not be made the subject of rules.

DEVELOPMENT OF THE THEATRE

Mimicry and burlesque have at all times provided popular entertainment, and even the simple, impressionable artisan of the Middle Ages loved to belittle his superiors, the local abbot or the devil himself, in sculpture and in plays on the village green. The borderline between mimicry and true drama is difficult to draw, but in Tudor England there were early glimmerings of a dramatic art. Aristocratic patronage, seeking to while away long wintry evenings, sponsored companies of actors. Writers like Marlowe, Jonson, and Shakespeare, gave their talents to play-acting, investing their money and their reputation to provide Court gallant and London apprentice with constant amusement. Outside the confines of the city, small circular play-houses were built with the stage open to the sky, the more respectable part of the audience being housed in covered galleries. The shape and arrangement of these playhouses were based upon the tavern-yards and bear-baiting houses, where the earliest plays were probably produced. Devoid of scenery, they depended chiefly upon speech and gesture; there was little opportunity for the stage settings that we associate with the modern theatre; boy actors played the female parts.

After a period of repression under the Puritans, a revival took place in Charles II's reign. The London theatres, though they continued to serve aristocrat, bourgeois and orange-girl alike, produced plays that were written and acted chiefly for the amusement of the Court. Plots were based on witty and compromising situations. Characters such as Shakespeare's Dogberry, Caliban, Falstaff and the foolish magistrates, Silence and Shallow, were disliked by the new set of Court dramatists. To suit the tastes of the king, who aimed at making his Court as far as possible a reproduction of that set up by Louis XIV of France, actresses for the first time appeared in the women's parts which in Shakespeare's day had been played by boys.

Other continental influences, including that of the masque, were shown in the lavish use of scenery, which became possible now that the stage and auditorium were covered in and theatres were no longer at the mercy of the weather. The stage was moved from its former central position to the back of the theatre, and the actors and audience were separated from each other by the proscenium arch and the curtain. Nevertheless this love for foreign fashions led to variations of lofty classic themes of a type popular in France.

MUSIC AND PAINTING

The same diversion of the English genius, which had begun to flower in Elizabeth's reign, was to be found in music. In religious music, Tallis and Byrd produced motets, or short religious pieces, that were second only to the work of Palestrina, the Italian musician who wrote masses for the reformed Catholic Church. But more important even than the tradition of English church music, which continued into the seventeenth century, was the popular art of singing madrigals and airs. Madrigals—lyrics set to music—were generally sung unaccompanied. Airs were sung either to the music of the lute (a pear-shaped stringed instrument) or to that of the virginal (a keyboard instrument).

The love for music was common among Queen Elizabeth's courtiers, and the Queen was herself a musician. The Court of James I was more interested in the masque, an elaborate kind of charade, for which Inigo Jones designed the scenery and Ben Jonson wrote the words. The simpler musical entertainment was ignored, and the great Henry Purcell, who died in 1695, though recognized as a Court musician, wasted his talents in producing Court entertainments in competition with the efforts of imported Italians, whose thin voices and excellent violin-playing were captivating London society. The masque provided the world with the beginnings of opera and oratorio, and the Italian influence, however detrimental to English madrigal art, led to the writing of vocal and instrumental solo-pieces by the greatest composers of the eighteenth century.

In painting, Italian masters inspired artists of other countries to work from nature. In Flanders, Rubens founded a school which combined religious subjects with classical treatment. The fleshy sensual figures, covering the walls and ceilings of Flemish churches, represented the opulence of the period and the high level of craftsmanship which was found among the artists of Antwerp. Rubens's portraits and huge canvases are stereotyped, and lack the individuality shown in the faces painted by Rembrandt.

In Holland, whose people were characterized by bourgeois simplicity and strict Calvinism, painters were preferring subjects taken from homely scenes and local landscape-settings. Ruysdael and Hobbema gave a true picture of the Dutch countryside. Vermeer painted "genre" pictures which dealt with ordinary human life—

domestic scenes, incidents in the market-place and in the family parlour. Steen, "the Hogarth of Holland", added a satirical touch to his work. No other school of painting has ever approached the detailed sympathetic Dutch attitude towards commonplace things. Still life often supplied the subject for the picture. Rembrandt was the greatest representative of this school; he managed to translate into his pictures the strength and determination of the Dutchman, placing the portrait against a background where light and shadow were perfectly balanced. Collections of pictures were to be found in the houses of all those who could affort to buy them. If there was anything in the seventeenth century which can be said to have approximated to popular art, it was to be found in this school.

Elsewhere, the life and fortune of the artist depended upon Court patronage. Velazquez at Madrid received a pension for supplying the Spanish grandees with their portraits and for his canvases depicting important events. Charles I of England patronized Van Dyck; later on, Lely was busily occupied in filling Hampton Court Palace with the portraits of Charles II's mistresses and courtiers. The glimmerings of a French school of painting were seen in the reigns of Louis XIII and Louis XIV. Claude and Poussin were landscape-artists of a strictly classical bent. Claude placed his figures, who were dressed as nymphs or deities, in the foreground; in the background there appeared the ruins of a classical temple or a grouping of Athenian sculpture. Watteau, who lived till 1721, made his landscapes less natural and his figures more sophisticated, frivolous, and amusing. He used lighter colours, and although his talents have been overpraised, his canvases nevertheless provide an interesting pictorial commentary on the golden age of Louis XIV.

ARCHITECTURAL INFLUENCES

The swing from Gothic to Renaissance building was more marked in Italy, in Spain, and even in France, than in England. Philip II of Spain built the Escorial Palace near Madrid, and the French monarchs the Louvre and Tuileries in Paris, at a time when English gentlemen of conservative habits were still devoted to traditional plans and materials. Yet, in Elizabethan houses, foreign influences can be seen —architects introducing a classical 'motif' here and an Ionic pillar there. This compromise between the two styles lasted into the sixteenth century; it was more marked perhaps in the colleges of the old universities of Oxford and Cambridge, than in domestic buildings.

Although some of the ugliest houses are those which try to synthesize opposite styles, nevertheless the Elizabethan or Jacobean houses, with their picturesque arrangement of gables, turrets, and square-headed windows, have become part of the traditional English landscape. The interiors of these houses were remarkable for the profuse and ingeniously-carved woodwork of hall-screen and staircase, and also for the ornate furniture which embellished them.

England could not withstand the influence of the Renaissance. Inigo Jones planned a new palace at Whitehall for Charles I; only the Banqueting Hall was finished. This is one of the earliest classical buildings we possess. The more brilliant and versatile Christopher Wren, who had visited Paris and seen the heavy soulless architecture of the royal palaces, tried to keep the peculiar charm that we associate with the Elizabethan houses, and yet to introduce proportions and ornamentation of a classical character. He was prepared to experiment, and the opportunity came when London was destroyed by fire in 1666. Though the opposition of vested property interests and the sentimentalism of the authorities prevented him from planning the entire city afresh, Wren was commissioned to re-build the city churches. The interiors were designed to suit the unobtrusive ritual of the Anglican Church and the lengthy sermons which our ancestors delighted to hear. Ornament was sparingly applied, for Wren's aim was to achieve a simple dignity. Some authorities praise him more for his red brick well-proportioned houses than for his numerous churches. After Wren, there was a slight degeneration, and foreign examples were introduced without regard for local traditions. Vanbrugh's Blenheim Palace is an example of over-weighted, straggling, ill-planned "Palladianism".

Furniture, other than the purely utilitarian stools and tables of the lower classes, lost the clumsy and heavy look it had possessed in the sixteenth century and became lighter and more delicate in appearance. The manor house was no longer the meeting-place of all grades of local society. Class-divisions were accentuated by contrasts in culture and amusement. In the past, the dining-hall had been open to all for festive occasions; the centre of activity now shifted to the drawing-room, and the hall disappeared and dwindled into an entrance-passage. English houses of the Queen Anne period were compact in plan and symmetrical in elevation; they preserved the elegance of the traditional English house, but respected the convenience and comforts which the gentlemen of that period so much desired.

CHAPTER 57

RIVAL STATE SYSTEMS

IF the break-up of an international society into smaller units can be considered a retrograde step from the point of view of human progress, then the sixteenth century produced a situation fraught with danger for human peace and security. Europe was no longer united in its religious beliefs; the Papacy was often opposed by its own Catholic princes. The Holy Roman Emperor, once the recognized leader on the Continent, had become more interested in the welfare of his own Austrian possessions than in the unity and concord of Europe. Yet certain philosophers still hoped that princes would place considerations of peace and humanity before those of state-craft and personal ambition. Hugo Grotius, a Dutch lawyer, attempted to prove, by research into the past, that the ethical rules which applied to ordinary individuals were also to be considered binding on the negotiations and dealings of sovereign rulers.

THEORIES CONCERNING THE POWER OF KINGS

The current was flowing towards a system of strong national states, independent of each other, rather than towards international-ism. Political thinkers ignored the duties owed by the state to the larger world-community. They concentrated on defining the duties of the ruler and the rights of the subject. These questions had to be worked out in an age when kings claimed to rule by divine right, and ordinary people either submitted fatalistically or attempted to hedge the powers of the ruler by constitutional checks or open rebellion.

Those who loved peace and efficiency, social comfort and unified government, turned towards the monarch as the sole arbitrator in a warring world. When sect persecuted sect, and local landowner attempted to rule as if he had the dispensation of ordinary men's lives and fortunes, the monarch generally stood out as protector of the weak. The divine attributes of the king, as, for instance, his sup-posed possession of power to heal those who were touched by the royal hand, aided the development of royal government. However unhappy were the lives of the mass of the people, their irrational and superstitious loyalty provided the king with a cloak of divinity. In England, Elizabeth and Charles II, and in France, Louis XIV—selfish and fond of pleasure as they were—ruled by popular acclaim as much as by any other title. Peter the Great of Russia, and, too, the Electors of Brandenburg, sought the affection of the mob, when they lacked the support of their own courtiers.

The doctrine that full power rested with the monarch stirred keen dispute in the sixteenth century. In the Middle Ages, Pope and Emperor had claimed to be superior to the various European poten-tates. At that time, the relations of king and subject were based on a feudal contract, consisting of mutual rights and obligations. If the contract was broken by one side, the other was free to resort to force.

Bodin, a French jurist in the sixteenth century, worked out a theory of government which was taken up, tested and criticized by other thinkers. Among these, Thomas Hobbes, a mathematician who was private tutor for the Cavendish family, was foremost. Since he lived during the English Civil War, he thought that the sole hope of security, self-preservation and happiness lay in giving full power to one man. Though Hobbes admitted that an individual had the right to resist the ruler if the latter was weak and incapable, the general trend of his book, *Leviathan*, published in 1651, was towards unqualified despotism. The ruler decided, by his own positive decision, what was lawful and what was unlawful. Justice became the handmaid of the state, and no individual was allowed to plead that his sovereign's actions were immoral and unjust. Not only could the ruler declare war and peace, make laws and judge those subjects who broke them, appoint and reward officials, but he decided the rules concerning private property. The ruler was "Judge of what Opinions and Doctrines are averse and what conducting to Peace". Even religion was subject to his interference and supervision.

Hobbes's views were not welcomed by English monarchs. They preferred to rule autocratically without theorizing about it, and saw that his system suited the English Cromwellians as much as it supported the Stuarts. James I of England claimed that kings were appointed by God, to whom alone they were responsible. Kings had power "to exalt low things and abase high things and to make of their subjects like men at chess"—in fact, to turn the social system topsy-turvy as the fancy took them. Louis XIV of France, the typical despot of the age, believed that all his actions, policies and successes were foreordained by God. In his *Historical Memoirs*, written as a textbook for his son, Louis claimed that his power was divine, a part of God's power: the ruler was God's viceroy, and to him alone did God reveal the secrets of good government. In India, Akbar had been trying to teach the same ideas, although in his case the matter was more complicated as it was necessary for him to act as an arbitrator between the religions held by his subjects.

FREEDOM OF RELIGION AND PRESS

In countries like France and Spain, traditions of constitutional government (that is, government according to fixed rule and the advice of a Parliament) had been forgotten. In England and in the Netherlands, the ideals and hopes of freedom were kept alive by thinkers, writers and statesmen. To many men, the sovereign was not irresponsible and uncontrollable, but was to be guided by laws more important than his own enactments could be. These laws, or natural rights, which were supposed to date from time immemorial, were concerned with property and with the liberty to say, write and believe what the individual preferred. Emphasis was at first placed on the freedom of worship. But, as many Protestants claimed freedom for their own particular brand of doctrine, and at the same time refused it to those who differed from them, the chief advocates for individual liberty were to be found among rationalists like Locke, and democratic pamphleteers.

Censorship of the Press was considered by most governments as a necessary step to ensure order and prevent discontent. Very few thinkers went so far as to preach complete freedom for the Press, though Milton believed that truth was more valuable than security and uniformity. "She [truth] needs no policies," he said, "nor stratagems, nor licensing to make her victorious ... give her but room, and do not bind her when she sleeps, for then she speaks not true." Governments, whether democratic or absolutist, have, during every period of history, found it sometimes necessary to place certain restrictions on the liberty of the Press.

England possessed a tradition that the chief landowners should advise the king. France and Spain had had estates, or parliaments, which attempted to control royal power. From 1614, until Louis XVI summoned an assembly in 1789, the French Estates-General did not meet. By the sixteenth century, England and the Netherlands alone retained the forms of constitutional government, in which the ruler had to consult, and even on occasion bow to, the wishes of the chief personages of the state.

When the Dutch freed themselves from the Spanish tyranny, they carefully avoided setting up a monarch or dictator in place of Philip II. Each province had an elected assembly; whilst the provinces together elected a central Parliament, or States-General, which supervised defence and foreign affairs. In time of danger, as in the early days of the rebellion, or when Louis XIV was planning to extend his frontiers on the north-east, the States-General would give sovereign power for the moment to a Stadtholder, or military dictator. This office was generally held by a member of the Orange family, from whom both William the Silent and our own Dutch William sprang. Popular consent, aided by military dictatorship, preserved the Dutch merchants from annihilation by stronger powers, in an age when small states were finding it difficult to exist.

The careful economic policy of the Tudor monarchs, their good relations with Parliament and their alliance with the middle classes and the country gentry, gave England the same advantages that were possessed by Holland. Men of wealth and ability were employed by the government; at the same time, the monarch's perspicacity and activity preserved the state from stagnation and disruption. Valued traditions, dating from the signing of the Magna Carta and the early days of Parliament, still lingered on in the country.

DIVISION BETWEEN KING AND PEOPLE

With the accession of James I, monarch and people gradually drifted away from each other. Neither James I, the first Stuart King of England, nor his successor, Charles I, understood their subjects; they did not appreciate the strength of those who were prepared to resist arbitrary interference and irregular taxation. The Stuarts alienated the middle classes, who were soaked in Puritanism, by their support of Archbishop Laud's attempts to bring back colour and ritual into the services of the Established Church. The country gentry were loyal to the monarchy until Whitehall, under Strafford's advice, tried to deprive them of their direction of local affairs.

The Civil Wars of 1642–9 were at first an attempt to make Charles abolish bishops and accept the decisions of Parliament. But, as usual, the final settlement was very different from that which had been desired by the gentlemen, lawyers and merchants who had set up the standard of rebellion. The military genius of Oliver Cromwell brought into the situation a completely new factor.

At first, neither side could get the advantage over its opponent. Parliament had more resources, since it controlled the ports of the south-east, including London, East Anglia and the Midlands. The Royalist areas—the south-west, Wales and the north—were scattered and not so fertile and populous. It was difficult for Charles to carry out a concerted attack on London, and equally difficult for the Parliamentary armies to defeat the Royalists on the battlefield. But Cromwell, a Huntingdonshire gentleman, trained a New Model Army out of raw East Anglian recruits. With this force, he defeated Charles at Marston Moor in 1644 and at Naseby in 1645. The King's execution in 1649 was the work of a Parliamentary "Rump" overawed by an exasperated army, and it was not approved by the majority of the people. Although a Parliamentary Commonwealth was proclaimed, the country was, in fact, ruled by one man possessed of dictatorial powers.

Cromwell, as firm a believer in his mission as any monarch, established the only military government England has possessed since the Rule of Rome. A cavalier described him as a blunt, awkward, country squire, ". . . very ordinarily apparelled, [with] a plain cloth-sute, which seemed to have been made by an ill country-taylor; his stature was of a good size, his countenance swoln and reddish, his voice sharp and untunable, and his eloquence full of fervor". The same observer noted that, after the establishment of the Protectorate, Cromwell was persuaded to "having better taylor, and more converse among good company". The Earl of Clarendon, who was a royalist and a severe critic of the Protector, had to admit that "he was not a man of bloode, and totally declined Machiavell's methode".

CROMWELL'S EXPERIMENT IN GOVERNMENT

Cromwell believed in the justice of his ends—the fall of the Stuarts and the rule of the godly—but his impatience, in difficult circumstances, made him adopt harsh unconstitutional measures, and involved his government in increasing unpopularity. Though he earned the gratitude and praise of free-thinker and idealist alike, he failed when he granted a small measure of religious toleration. He set major-generals over the English squires, and placed his army chaplains in country livings. On the one hand, he alienated many of those who supported traditional English institutions; on the other, he refused to make any change in the social system to gratify parties like the Levellers, who were the revolutionaries of the day. His soldiers aroused the natural civilian dislike for military government. When Cromwell died in 1658, the Englishman had forgotten the tyrannies of Charles I, and welcomed Charles's son as a happy relief from years of uncertainty and constitutional experiment.

Charles II had learned commonsense and moderation in exile. He was a cosmopolitan, hating exertion, placing pleasure before principle. He accepted many restrictions which his father would have opposed. Though Parliament was composed of royalists, thirsting for the blood of those who had supported Cromwell, it was careful to keep religion and taxation out of the hands of the monarch and legislate about those matters itself. After experience of Cromwell's rule, standing armies were hated, and Parliament carefully withstood any attempt to create a new one. The only way in which Charles could follow his own policy was by forming secret councils and dispensing with Parliament, with the help of bribes received from his fellow-monarch Louis XIV.

The bigot, James II, misread the history of his brother's reign. He opposed the Anglican Church, and chose his advisers from Catholic priests and courtiers, rather than from the country gentry. He began to build an army to overawe his subjects. Gradually intense opposition to the policy of the king grew from all ranks and parties. The Stadtholder William III of Orange was invited to take the throne from which James was finally deposed in 1688.

WILLIAM OF ORANGE

William was accepted only on certain conditions; he had to respect the Anglican Church and the powers of Parliament. The gentry had brought the monarchy to heel once again. The Act of Settlement, in 1702, finally established the English traditions of Parliamentary government, which were later to astonish visitors from Europe. The King of England had to be a Protestant in faith and his advisers were excluded from the Commons; this innovation was repealed when passing years showed that Parliament could keep a better check on the executive, if the latter was under its constant supervision. Two further steps were taken to make Parliament the strongest body in the state; the discipline of the army and the voting of supplies were subject to annual acts. To preserve order and to avoid bankruptcy, it was thus necessary for the king to summon Parliament at least once a year. Members of parliament were elected by men who owned land, leaving unenfranchised the bulk of the labouring class and most of those working in industry. Elections generally reflected the prevailing opinion of the richer classes.

Every revolutionary change of government demands a philosopher —someone who will explain lucidly the ideas and motives underlying the change. John Locke, in his *Treatise of Civil Government*, wrote a textbook which became a political gospel, first for the Whig party, finally for Englishmen in general. He laid it down that each individual possessed certain inalienable rights, which the ruler could not touch or disregard. Between the ruler and the ruled, there existed a carefully drawn-up contract, delimiting the powers which the individual had surrendered to the monarch, and carefully defining those powers which the individual retained. The origin of human society was to be found in the desire of most people to live in peace and protect the fruits of their labour. Private property could not be touched by the government; but in the interests of the community as a whole, the individual could consent to taxes being levied upon his property. But these taxes had to be voted in an assembly, freely elected by the people.

Locke and his associates claimed that the English Parliament was the best example of government carried out by consent of the governed; he ignored the fact that many people had no say in government and did not possess the vote, though they were taxed and were forced to carry out other duties. Yet Locke's dictum that laws were to "be directed to no other end but the peace, safety and public good of the people", saved England from the fear of tyranny and provided the substance for the new constitutions which were formulated in America, France, and the English Colonies.

LIBERTY AND DESPOTISM

We owe much to the doctrine of absolute government and to that of individual rights; for from them have been welded the principle that government must be strong and efficient, not interfering with the lives of individual citizens unless it is necessary for the social good. The state exists for the people, not the people for a ruling dynasty or governing class. The idea of individual liberty gave opportunities to the most humble to develop their talents and powers of criticism. The seventeenth century saw the two doctrines in opposition; later generations were to provide the synthesis, and show that there was no necessity to place absolutism and democracy in watertight compartments.

In the sixteenth century, an efficient government became necessary, owing to the increase in the number of difficult problems with which the state had to deal. A competent democracy is the fruit of education and economic development, and so the only hope of obtaining an expert government lay in the setting up of centralized despotisms. The landed gentry of England were unique in their grasp of political questions and their aptitude for affairs; but the gentry in other countries were less politically minded and probably more factious. In England, the monarchy depended on the gentry for advice; but abroad, the nobility, clinging to ancient customs and wholly lacking in constructive ideas, proved a hindrance to the development of order and the march of progress.

Philip II of Spain was the first of these European despots. Power over the Church, independence of the Cortes, and possession of the Indies gave Philip a weapon which struck at local customs and privileges. His passion for the details of government amazed his contemporaries and confounded his critics. The lack of able servants, and Philip's dislike of sharing his labours with others, resulted in an undue emphasis on the personal side of government. After Philip's death, Spain fell rapidly to a low place among the monarchies of Europe. She became the sport of other rulers who planned to divide her dominions. The success of absolute government depended upon good administration rather than upon the personality of its head.

The other Habsburg family, that of Austria, bred a line of monarchs of more vigorous ability. The Austrian dominions, polyglot in population and language, demanded unity at the head. Unfortunately for the country, its greatest emperor, Ferdinand II, followed Philip II's policy in endangering the interests of his state by indulgence in fruitless wars for the Catholic religion. During the Thirty Years' War, there appeared the first of a series of military commanders, whose ruthlessness and self-admiration, supported by men-at-arms, were to cause Europe years of bloodshed.

Wallenstein created a standing army of efficient soldiers, and his methods were adopted by others. Cromwell in England, Condé and Louis XIV in France, and later the Prussian monarchs and Napoleon, were to secure power by means of naked force. Certain radical changes in the organization and strategy of warfare were made by Wallenstein. He organized his commissariat, instead of depending upon plunder to supply his troops with food. His soldiers were chosen for fitness, irrespective of their religion or nationality. Moreover, Wallenstein carefully thought out his campaigns, and his forces did not move unless the general possessed adequate reserves.

NEW TYPES OF MILITARY TACTICS

Gustavus Adolphus, the Protestant leader of the north, also made important changes in the methods of fighting. His troops moved quickly, and the use of lightly-armed forces gave him an advantage in outflanking his opponents in battle. He revolutionized tactics and developed the art of generalship, so that the Thirty Years' War can be regarded as the first modern war. His men were cared for; medical units attended the march. Engineers prepared fortifications and communications. An interest in gunnery led Gustavus to lighten the musket and increase its firing range. Artillery was no longer subsidiary to cavalry and pikemen, but was placed at scattered posts of vantage, and moved about the field to back up advances and create diversions. Gustavus's army did not fight *en masse*, but in carefully selected battalions distributed about the field. Cavalry, which had been useless when sent against solid masses of pikemen, came once more into its own and proved effective under cover of musket fire. Similar tactics were introduced into the armies of Charles I and Oliver Cromwell; Louis XIV and his adviser Louvois popularized them in France.

Absolute monarchy and militarism advanced hand in hand. Armies grew in size and efficiency as wars became more general. Wallenstein commanded 100,000 troops, whereas Spanish and

Imperial forces in the early sixteenth century had rarely been more than 50,000. Louis XIV's army, which in 1667 numbered 70,000, increased to 270,000 in 1678, when he was planning his wars of aggression. Smaller powers were at the mercy of the greater; Cromwell overran Scotland and Ireland; Wallenstein aimed at dictatorship. Even the Duke of Marlborough, the English victor in the wars with Louis, was suspected at home of dictatorial ambitions.

The middle classes, in politically backward countries like France and Spain, had no objection to the heavy hand of the monarch if, in return for their obedience, he assured them of privileges at home and protection abroad. In countries where commercial interests were more powerful, the middle classes were generally to be found among the anti-monarchical party, because of the greater freedom enjoyed where the monarch was forced to listen to the voice of Parliament.

VALUE OF A STRONG MONARCHY

The most valuable support for a strong monarchy was usually found among the "intelligentsia" and the professional classes. Francis Bacon, lawyer, scientist and politician, preferred to work under an enlightened despot, instead of following the criss-cross policies of a parliamentary government. In France, opposed alike to Catholic and Huguenot, a group of public-spirited men who dubbed themselves *politiques*, or moderates, gathered round the vigorous Henry IV, as their sole hope against the disruption of Church and state. The great Elector, Frederick William of Brandenburg, built up a civil and military organization filled with able men who were devoted to the state. Peter the Great, assisted by German advisers, tried to instil traditions of public service among his nobles.

The success of the absolute monarchs compared strikingly with the backwardness and anarchy of states where the ruler was hedged round by restrictions. Poland, a territory of natural wealth, inhabited by a vigorous population, sank into the position of a third-rate power. The Polish king could legislate only with the unanimous support of his aristocracy. The Emperor, absolute in his own German dominions, found it difficult to curb the Magyar nobility in Hungary, and left them a certain amount of freedom.

Except in England and Holland, where economic progress, allied with political freedom, provided advantages of government as important as those to be found in despotic states, Europe preferred one-man rule to the selfishness and vagaries of aristocracy and demagogy. With Louis XIV as a pattern of what a successful despot could achieve, there was little hope for government based on the active consent of the governed, until national feeling educated populations to a realization of the important part they could play.

In 1598, Henry IV of France had established his rule over Catholic and Protestant alike. His own conversion from Protestantism to Catholicism conciliated the Roman Church. His grant to the Huguenots of certain walled towns and a restricted right of worship, though a temporary measure, brought the religious wars to an end. The difficulties facing Henry were very great and he managed through his minister, Sully, to smooth out only the most important of them. Financial reform became necessary in face of an exhausted treasury and the need for defence against Spain.

During the reign of Louis XIII, real power rested with his ministers. Cardinal Richelieu, a ruthless figure in political life, possessed a passionate and ambitious temperament. He knew what France and her monarchy wanted. Wily in diplomacy, he managed to secure England's neutrality, so as to allow him to intervene successfully in German affairs and in the Thirty Years' War, which he prolonged in order to ensure the ultimate exhaustion of the Habsburg monarchies. Richelieu's religious zeal was but skin-deep; abroad, he supported Protestant Dutch and Swedes, so as to retain the European balance, while at home he was responsible for an attack launched on La Rochelle, which was the chief Huguenot centre, and left that Protestant sect with only its religious privileges.

His desire to secure a strong French monarchy led Richelieu to deprive the nobility of the trappings of political power. In each locality he established intendants, or administrators, who were appointed by the central government and made responsible, not to the local landowner or communal assembly, but to the king. Ignoring the protests of lawyers and courtiers, he laid the foundations of power upon which Louis XIV could build.

FRANCE UNDER LOUIS XIV

Richelieu's successor, Cardinal Mazarin, was more cosmopolitan and less brilliant. He continued the active foreign policy of the preceding period; he was hated for being a foreigner, and his oppressive taxation stimulated the nobles and lawyers to revolt. In 1648, the chief law court of the kingdom claimed the right to discuss the laws passed by the government. The Paris mob joined them in a rebellion known as the Fronde, and Mazarin was forced to make concessions. In 1651, Condé, an aristocrat and a successful general, hoped to displace Mazarin and set up a tyranny of the Cromwellian type. His forces were defeated by the loyalist commander Turenne.

Louis XIV possessed many attractive qualities—ease, tact, an equable temper, punctuality and attentiveness to the details of government. His pleasures—and they were many—never interfered with his state business, and he commanded his son to keep love affairs distinct from matters of government. Yet, on occasions, he could be easily influenced by friends and favourites. Courtiers thronged his early morning receptions to gather lucrative appointments and pensions. Madame de Maintenon, his second and morganatic wife, warped his policy by backing up the suggestions made by lawyers and priests that the Huguenots, having become weaker, were ripe for persecution.

The active reign of Louis XIV began in 1661. He had tired of the Palace of St. Germain and hated the noise and smells of Paris. A passion for hunting and for seclusion in the country drew him to the Palace at Versailles, which his father had built. Mansart, the royal architect, added new wings and terraces to the old château; the park was planted with trees and shrubs and decorated with fountains and gardens. There was no general design; new additions were made in a casual and unaesthetic fashion whenever Louis' fancy took him. When Versailles in its turn began to bore him, he ordered Mansart to build two smaller palaces in the park—the Trianon and Marly. At the Trianon there were performances of ballets, set to music by Lully, elaborate dinner-parties, and performances of Molière's comedies. At Marly, Louis entertained a series of mistresses.

FRENCH POLICY AND ITS RESULTS

To be summoned to Versailles was a mark of extreme favour for the French seigneur. Those who were fortunate enough to attend Louis were subject to the tyranny of a detailed programme of daily events. In the seven hundred pages of the *State of France*, there appears a list of all the officers of the king—the various gentlemen who had to assist in his rising, toilet, travelling, eating and drinking.

Louis had a purpose behind this display of extravagance and etiquette. His nobility, busy in competing with each other for royal favour, ceased to be a potential danger to the state. Foreign countries were impressed; ambassadors wondered at such magnificence.

Louis had inherited the civil service built up by the cardinals, and during the first twenty years of his active reign, he retained the services of able men. Among them was Colbert, a financier who followed in the footsteps of Sully. A tradesman's son, he understood the feelings and aspirations of the middle class. Louis preferred his ministers to be men of humble birth, so that their devotion would prove greater than their sense of privilege. Under Colbert's management thrift became a virtue, and confidence in the national credit returned. State accounts were carefully kept and audits were regularly made. Those who had invested money in public loans received their interest punctually. Trade and colonial effort were encouraged. Colbert's policy was frustrated by the innate conservatism of the French merchants, the difficulties of providing money for an ever-growing standing army, and the arbitrary foreign policy of a monarch who thought in terms of power-politics. Louis had persuaded himself that grandiose schemes of foreign policy and aggrandizement were more valuable to his people than their social well-being.

From 1672, Louvois was war minister. Although a successful administrator, he proved a bad adviser, for he supported Louis' ambitious schemes in Europe and opposed the careful economies of Colbert. Louvois was served by Vauban, the greatest military engineer of the day. The wars of the late seventeenth century were

Oliver Cromwell, 1599–1658, the Parliamentary general who defeated Charles I, became Protector but failed to govern with a parliament.

There is in existence no authentic portrait of William Shakespeare, 1564–1616. This design (by Droeshout) appears in the First Folio.

The Central Office of the Dutch East Indies Company in Bengal in the year 1665.

Louis XIV of France and his family, by Nicolas de Largilliere. From left to right: Madame de Maintenon, Duc d'Anjou (Louis XV) the Grand Dauphin, Louis XIV, and the Duc de Bourgogne.

Marlborough at the Battle of Blenheim, 1704, from the painting by l'Eveque.

concerned chiefly with sieges, rather than with open battles in the field. Trench warfare and skilful attack on weak points in their opponents' fortifications gave the French an advantage over their less scientific adversaries. Vauban accustomed the French soldier to the handling of flint-lock muskets and socket-bayonets. Unfortunately for France, when Vauban's fortified towns fell to the enemy, Louis dismissed him in his usual arbitrary fashion. The minister had fallen under suspicion on several occasions for suggesting administrative reforms derogatory to the royal authority. France lost a valuable adviser just when she needed him.

Now that France's internal troubles were settled, Louis could embark on aggression with confidence, for the country was united behind him and the army was trained to efficiency. Careful diplomacy, backed up by bribes, succeeded in isolating the king of England, who was encouraged to turn his attentions to the Dutch, colonial rivals of the English. Whilst English and Dutch were fighting in the Channel, Louis sent Turenne into the Spanish Netherlands and Burgundy. France gained by the Peace of Aix-la-Chapelle.

Turenne's campaigns were intended as a mere preliminary to an invasion of the Dutch Republic. Louis disliked the Dutch for their republicanism and for their successful commerce, which he hoped to capture. Holland was saved by the vigour of the Prince of Orange, who had deposed the conservative oligarchy that had lately been in power. The Dutch obtained allies and the war became general. In 1678, a breathing-space was provided by the Treaty of Nimeguen.

Despite the great effort made by France, her material gains so far had been few. Instead of concentrating on the more vulnerable frontiers in the north-east, Louis turned to the Rhineland. The capture of Strasbourg added to the moral prestige of France, although, from a military point of view, it was comparatively unimportant. The European states consulted together, and the Spanish and Dutch made frantic endeavours to protect the Netherlands.

WAR OF THE SPANISH SUCCESSION

The attention of Europe was now directed to the question of the Spanish Succession. The last Habsburg, Charles II, had no heirs; the best claimants were Louis XIV and the Emperor. In an attempt to prevent war and to safeguard Dutch and English interests, William of Orange, now King of England, persuaded Louis to sign Treaties of Partition. The Emperor refused to agree to them. These Treaties were put on one side when Charles II of Spain died in 1700, leaving the whole of his dominions to Philip of Anjou, a younger grandson of Louis. Family pride, insensate ambition, and the advice of his economists, who wanted to corner the trade with the Spanish colonies, persuaded Louis to repudiate his word, thus ranging against himself most of the European powers, who naturally feared that Spain and France would now be merged into one country.

X   (H.W.)

Attempts at a coalition of powers against France had been made
in the war of 1690–7, but the bad generalship of the Allies had given
Louis undeserved opportunities. The Peace of Ryswick left the real
question undecided. In 1701, England, Holland, and the Empire
formed a Grand Alliance. These powers were too much worried
about the Bourbon danger to pay any attention to the feelings of the
Spanish people, and busied themselves with plans of compensation
that would have deprived Spain of her colonies and dependencies.
The most practical steps taken by the alliance were the creation of a
string of fortressess dividing France from Holland, and the appointment of John Churchill, later Duke of Marlborough, as English
commander. The Imperial troops were led by Prince Eugene; his
own abilities coupled with his admiration for the English commander
ensured a co-operation which was eventually to defeat Louis.

THE PEACE OF UTRECHT

Marlborough advanced rapidly into Bavaria and defeated the
French at Blenheim, in 1704. This battle saved Austria, and allowed
the Allies to invade France and Spain. They pressed southwards
through Flanders and defeated the French in a series of battles.
Meanwhile, the Whig government which supported Marlborough
was overthrown by a Tory government which was hostile to him.
This, together with the mutual exhaustion produced by the war, led
to the signing of the Peace of Utrecht in 1713. Though Philip was
recognized as king of Spain, Louis and Philip had to promise to keep
their dominions separate. France was again confined on the north-
east to her boundaries of 1691, and the Dutch were protected by
garrisons in certain Flemish towns. The Emperor came to terms in
the following year.

The Peace of Utrecht was a great European settlement more
lasting than the Peace of Westphalia. For the first time in European
history a combination of minor powers, led by England and the
Habsburgs, had withstood an aggressive state. Britain had established naval and colonial supremacy, and although in Europe she
remained on the defensive, her aggressions abroad were as clearly
marked as those of her rivals.

Louis' grandiose schemes of conquest had been defeated, and
Europe had learned the danger of placing confidence in an ambitious
and amoral monarch. Not only had Europe been dragged into
unnecessary wars, but the French king had made these wars deadlier
and more exhausting, especially to the lower classes of population
who served, suffered, and died so that his policies could be advanced.
International morality had been ignored by a monarch who placed
dictates of selfishness and vain glory before considerations of responsibility. Later ages were to follow his guidance, when military
successes and an active foreign policy appeared to most statesmen as
the real ends of all "good government".

PART XI

REASON AND REVOLUTION

CHAPTER 58

THE OPENING SCENE

SOME eighteenth-century writers criticized their own civilization, by viewing it, or trying to view it, from the standpoint of an educated oriental, such as a Persian nobleman or a Chinese mandarin. They could not at will cut their minds off from the manifold impressions and influences which had moulded them; any more than a modern critic could draw the outline of his contemporary world as it might strike the man in the moon. But the device was a witness to the new spirit at work in the Western world. The wars of religion were definitely over. Men no longer referred their lives to a divine revelation set forth in the teachings of a Catholic Church, or laid down in the words of an infallible Bible. They attempted to judge, to criticize, to assess their own inheritance and prejudices. They appealed to reason.

By reason they meant the reign of law, as opposed to arbitrary action. We still speak of things being "unreasonable" or "beyond all reason"; this use of the word may help us to understand the eighteenth-century point of view.

We can discern three influences which ran together to produce the eighteenth-century faith in reason. First, the immense power of the printing-press had created an educated public outside the hierarchy of the Church. Secondly, the astonishing progress in mathematics and the physical sciences revealed a reign of law in the world of nature, so that the mysterious heavens which had always declared the glory of God were now brought within the measurement of man's arithmetic. Thirdly, the leaven of Christianity had been working throughout the centuries, and now, freed from the ecclesiastical pretences of jarring sects, the essential underlying charity of the Christian faith was able to manifest itself in widespread feelings of toleration and humanity.

Two centuries of religious warfare had bred apathy over dogmas and creeds. The best minds were free to subject their world to the judgment of reason. Critics and reformers desired to refashion human society and human institutions upon reasonable lines. Reason had no use for despotisms, no use for ecclesiastical privilege or religious persecution, no use for national enmity, no use for overseas possessions, no use for personal ambition or inherent rights, no use for war. It appealed to the *natural rights* of man. To use the words of Priestley, the English scientist of George III's reign, govern-

ment should be " calculated for the general good ", and should leave
"all men the enjoyment of as many of their natural rights as possible".
The men who believed in reason had faith in human nature.

When Edmund Burke condemned the excesses of the French
Revolution, Priestley wrote a reply in which he said: "If time be
allowed for the discussion of differences, so great a majority will
form one opinion, that the minority will see the necessity of giving
way. Thus will *reason* be the umpire in all disputes, and extinguish
civil wars as well as foreign ones. The reign of reason will ever be the
reign of peace."

By contrast, the ordering of society and the practice of government were anything but reasonable. The simple medieval division of
mankind into the peasant who worked, the priest who interceded, the
landed baron who defended Christian society against its enemies,
and the Holy Roman Emperor and other hallowed kings who were
founts of honour and wielded the temporal swords of justice—this
division had long since been overlaid. The peasant still worked, it is
true, and most of the people of Europe were peasants and most of
them illiterate. But neither priests nor barons nor anointed rulers
were under any definite obligation. Instead, they existed as privileged
classes. Governments consisted of kings ruling not with the help and
advice of the local landowners, as had usually been the case in the
early Middle Ages, but by the paid service of skilled officials.

POLITICAL GROWTH AND SURVIVALS IN EUROPE

Except in Great Britain, the medieval Parliaments had disappeared
and despotism was unchecked. The fortunes of the civilized Western
world were in the hands of what Voltaire called " three or four
hundred persons scattered on the face of the earth under the name of
princes or ministers". These men treated Europe like a collection of
personal estates, partitioning the countries without regard to the
wishes of the inhabitants, taxing them without their consent, issuing
decrees and edicts, good or bad, without any sanction save that of
their own inherent or inherited right.

While national government had become centralized and despotic,
municipal government was a farce. The Roman Empire built up its
rule upon a network of municipalities. These had dwindled and
decayed in the Dark Ages. During the earlier Middle Ages, when they
began to revive, kings and lawyers tried to ignore them by making
them part and parcel of the feudal system. Then by the power of
their wealth, the townsmen won privileges and became self-governing
communities or corporations; by the fifteenth century the wealth,
vigour and culture of Western civilization were centred in the cities
of North Italy and the Netherlands.

But the ambition of princes and the wars of religion had played
havoc by the eighteenth century: the old medieval commune had
either disappeared, or else, where its arrangements had persisted,

they persisted in a corrupt form, the town being ruled by self-appointed cliques and closed corporations. Thus, in a century when industry was developing beyond all previous bounds, when merchants were actually ruling over vast dominions in the East, when the modern system of banking and finance first commenced to flourish, the traders and the skilled artisans were in fact politically powerless.

THE RIGHTS OF MAN

The age of reason ended in revolution. It was not a mere accident that the revolution began in France; for the French were not only the leaders of Western civilization, but the most unreasonably governed of all European peoples. Still less was it an accident that the revolution in France was in many of its phases the work of the middle-class citizens of Paris, active, intelligent people, long excluded from a share in governing themselves.

Montesquieu, Diderot, Voltaire, Rousseau, Tom Paine, Priestley —the apostles of reason—certainly reacted against their environment. Yet the first-fruits of the new harvest were gathered in the New World when, in 1783, the English colonists in North America declared their independence and set up a federal republic. "We hold", they said, "these truths to be self-evident, that all men are created equal, that they are endowed by their Creator with inalienable rights, that among these are life and liberty and the pursuit of happiness, that to secure these rights, governments are instituted among men, deriving their just powers from the consent of the governed."

Six years later, the National Assembly of France issued its Declaration of the Rights of Man. "Men are born and remain equal in rights. Social distinctions can only be founded upon the general good. . . . Law is the expression of the general will. Every citizen has a right to take part, personally or through his representative, in its formation. It must be the same for all. . . . Society has the right to require of every public agent an account of his administration." This Declaration was reissued many times down to 1848.

Neither in France nor in North America were the governments systematically oppressive. In both, the inhabitants, or those who were the most politically active, believed the conditions under which they were governed to be unreasonable, and therefore intolerable. There might be something to be said for a rigorous and effective despotism, nothing for an inefficient one. Without a doubt, the countries which were the most enlightened and the wealthiest in the eighteenth century were France, Great Britain and the American colonies. Revolutions changed the history of two of them. Great Britain was exceptional in her political history and in her legal history. It is worth while noting that by the enactment of the Bill of Rights of 1689 the king could levy no money in any way without the consent of Parliament. Much, of course, depended on the character of Parliament; but this plain and practical safeguard went to the root of the matter.

The age of reason thus became the age of revolution, and the age of revolution continued far into the nineteenth century when the "reason" of the eighteenth-century writers became the "liberalism" and the "humanitarianism" of reformers. National Parliaments based upon the consent of the governed—obtained by new voting systems—gradually filled the place of the older despotisms.

ENGLAND UNDER THE GEORGES

Upon the death of Queen Anne, her second cousin, the Elector of Hanover, became king of Great Britain, the first of the Four Georges who ruled in succession till 1830. They were the only monarchs in Europe to hold their office by the will of a Parliament and not by divine right. But the British Parliament was itself controlled by an oligarchy of Whig noblemen—a "Venetian" oligarchy, as it has been called. Talent and loyalty to the public service, however, are not monopolies of a democracy. In spite of a small and corruptible electorate, this oligarchy was one of the world's great schools of politics, even of statecraft, and produced statesmen of the calibre of Sir Robert Walpole and the two Pitts.

It was not an inspiring age. Fervour and enthusiasm were taboo. Good humour and commonsense were the cardinal virtues. Party feeling ran high, but the battles were won and lost by oratory and ink. Coarse manners and the artificial usage of wigs, powder and patches existed side by side. While the etiquette of the aristocrat became a fine art, brutality in punishment and in sports persisted. The English were a drunken nation: port-wine provided the potations of the well-to-do, while beer and spirits flowed in copious streams for the poor. The squalor of the slums was appalling, the death-rate from smallpox and fever high.

The country squire lived well, like the Franklin of Chaucer's day, in whose house it "snowed meat and drink". The immortal caricature of the Englishman as John Bull first appeared from the pen of Dr. Arbuthnot in 1712. Extremes were then, as now, often encountered. The polite man about town might fight a duel over the placing of a Greek accent, while his younger brothers roamed the streets at night in gangs and assaulted old watchmen and unprotected women, and while prejudiced mobs gave chase to any unfortunate suspected of being a foreigner. The country villages were not yet denuded of their most vigorous and alert families by migration to the towns. Country life was busy and robust: man's local interests were often his sole interests; only occasionally was he brought into the mainstream of national life.

The Peace of Utrecht had put an end to an exhausting and expensive war against France. In spite of Marlborough's victories, Britain had not prevented the French king's grandson from becoming king of Spain; but the peace had recognized her right to Gibraltar, to Nova Scotia and Newfoundland, and her destiny was already clearly marked in commerce. Her merchant-fleets carried the trade of the Indies, both East and West, and her wealth, fostered by a sound national finance and a reformed and trustworthy coinage, was growing by leaps and bounds.

Across the Atlantic, 375,000 white people acknowledged the authority of the British King in Parliament. To the plantations in Virginia and the Carolinas, Britain sent batches of criminals as indentured labourers. Her trade with the colonists, which she kept jealously to herself, was making fortunes for her merchants. Yet the ties of blood between the mother-country and the settlements were not as strong as might be expected. Emigration to New England had practically ceased by 1640. Most Americans in 1714 were colonial-born, and already looked upon native Englishmen as "strangers". They governed themselves in local affairs by the same sort of restricted franchise that obtained in Britain, and the state-assemblies controlled the pay of the state-governors sent out by the mother-country. The Parliament at Westminster, although largely ignorant of colonial life and in no way representing colonial opinion, could, and did, pass laws for the colonists to observe.

LIFE AND WEALTH IN THE COLONIES

Colonial life was free and abundant. Land was boundless—subject, of course, to the raids of the redskins. A landed nobility was unknown, its place taken by a few planters of wealth and family— descendants often of younger sons of the English nobility and squires. The only polite society was the circle about the state-governor. In the north, the chief occupations were farming, lumbering and fishing. In the south, the staple industry was tobacco-planting, run by negro slave-labour. There was a definite cleavage in sentiment and political feeling between north and south, the northerners being a puritan and independent race, the southerners tending towards a tolerant aristocracy.

Much wealth by trade came to Britain also from her West Indian sugar islands. In these, again, negro slaves formed the economic basis of society. For the rest, the British Empire was a network of factories and trading-posts. Trading companies built up their own fortunes and the fortune of their country by traffic with the shores of India and Africa, and with the great forests of northern Canada, in tea, spices, silks, muslins, slaves, gold, ivory and furs.

On the Atlantic coast of Europe, the other Powers with overseas possessions were Portugal, Spain, France and Holland. The once-opulent empire of the eastern seas which Portugal held had now shrunk to a few trading-posts, but she still retained her settlements on the east coast of Africa and a long line of ports on the west coast of the same continent. By the beginning of the century, the principal purpose of these last was to provide a constant stream of negroes for the sugar and tobacco plantations of Brazil, where they died rapidly.

The greatest effort of the Portuguese had been the colonization of Brazil. Gold had recently been discovered in the south of that land, and Rio de Janeiro was the viceregal capital. A notable viceroy, John of Lancaster, had recently administered the colony with resolution and success. Jesuit missions still assisted in dealing with the natives and the *mestizos* or half-breeds. But Brazil was still dependent on Europe for its daily food; the clothing, provisions and metal-goods needed by its settlers in their everyday life were all made in England—Portugal merely acting as England's agent.

SPAIN'S FALL FROM GREATNESS

The Spanish Empire consisted of all Central America, South America (except Brazil) and—a five-months' voyage from these, across the Pacific—the Philippines. Despite this splendid endowment, the Spaniards impoverished themselves. They governed in a jealous and cruel manner. They had only one aim—to extract precious metals from their dependencies—and they went so far as to destroy the olive-groves and vineyards of Peru for fear these should compete with their own at home. All trade must flow through Spain, where the threads of colonial government were gathered together. The wealth of two worlds came yearly to the great fair at Acapulco in Mexico: yet "the cursed hunger for gold" forbade any progress. Like the Portuguese, the Spaniards provisioned their colonies with merchandise from England, Holland and France, having no industries of their own. The result of this was smuggling on a large scale by the seamen of the northern countries, who thus sold their goods direct and cheaply to the Spanish colonists. Between them, Spain and Portugal owned a vast portion of the earth.

Such colonial ineptitude was a reflection of the decline of both countries from the greatness of the sixteenth century. Spain had lost the industrious members of her population in 1611, when she expelled the Moors—driving away a million of her most thriving peasantry through the intolerance of her Church and Inquisition. A European war had been fought mainly by France and Britain to decide whether a French or an Austrian prince should succeed to the throne of Spain: she could not decide for herself! Her peasants remained sunk in medieval dependence upon a wealthy and numerous but bigoted priesthood. Her hidalgos, charming, polite, lazy, proud, lacked the fiery enthusiasm that had projected three armadas against the heretic nations of England and Holland in the sixteenth century. But perhaps those early heroics had exhausted her; if there is anything in the idea of a "national character", we may trace in her history a continuous thread of bigotry and heroism. After all, she had been led to a task of immense magnitude by the dream of a Genoese seaman—Columbus: and if, according to our lights, she failed, we must remember that South America is to-day a Spanish-speaking, Christian continent.

The Dutch had wrested from the Portuguese the mastery of the spice trade. By 1714, England's Navigation Acts had checked the Dutch; they were no longer the "waggoners of the world", and the time had gone by when Holland still benefited from her position on the Rhine delta, from the fertility of her soil, and from the industry of her burghers and farmers. She kept, and has since kept, most of the gains made by merchants and seamen in the heyday of her triumphs over Spain and Portugal. Her most precious possession was the Spice Islands, or East Indies—those coveted lands which, to-day, yield their possessors wealth in the less romantic form of rubber and oil. The Cape settlement, a handful of Boer farmers invigorated with Huguenot stocks, she regarded merely as a revictualling station on the long and hazardous route to the Indies. The monopoly of the Royal Dutch East India Company over these places was extremely restrictive. At home, Dutch national policy remained one of constant hostility to their nearest and most powerful neighbour, France.

THE FUNDAMENTAL WEAKNESSES OF FRENCH POLICY

L'état, c'est moi ("I, myself, am the State"). Louis XIV's words epitomize the glory of the French monarchy and the weakness of France. Paris, the heart of the kingdom since the Dark Ages, had been replaced by the amazing wonderland of Versailles, where Louis XV held his Court. In England, the mercantile class took part in the government along with the aristocracy. In France, neither lords nor merchants were consulted. For official purposes, France was still composed of medieval estates—privileged lords, privileged priests, and the remainder who formed the *tiers état*, or third estate. But the conduct of affairs was in the hands of the king and his ministers alone.

The representative government of Great Britain may have been corrupt and narrow, based upon "rotten boroughs" whose handfuls of voters were bribed. In France, representative government did not exist. Even "rotten boroughs" sometimes produced statesmen—a proof that in Britain there was something that France lacked—namely, a sense of public service.

French law varied from place to place, and tolls were taken on goods in transport. Want of experience in local government had turned the towns into bear-gardens of jealous trade-guilds. Each district was under an intendant responsible to the king and appointed by him. Parish-pump politics and weighty matters of state were alike decided by him and his ministers at Versailles. Caesar himself would have found it impossible to cope with the task of governing the country in such a fashion. Under the easy-going and amiable Louis XV, the situation was tragic.

During the first half of the eighteenth century, French colonial and maritime enterprise still moved forward, under the impulse given by Colbert, the hard-working and methodical minister of Louis XIV.

Colbert had subsidized shipbuilding, and had substituted for the crude business of the press-gang a regular conscription of seamen. The result was a powerful navy and a flourishing mercantile marine. In France, as in Britain, the opportunities of exploitation offered by the New Worlds had led to a great development in the methods and range of finance; the new finance of banking and funding in its turn hastened the development of overseas trade and empire.

FRENCH COLONIAL SETTLEMENT

In the north Atlantic, a colony of 16,000 French peasants in Acadia or Nova Scotia had recently been transferred to the British flag by the Treaty of Utrecht. But in the matter of wealth, Acadia was of less moment to France than the Newfoundland fisheries, visited each year by over 25,000 Norman and Breton fishermen. The richest of the West Indian sugar-islands, Martinique and Guadeloupe, were French, while the West African trade, apart from that in slaves, was almost a French monopoly.

The one great French colony was Canada, where some 80,000 *habitants*, or peasants of north French stock, lived under conditions which were a replica of those in France. The king appointed a governor and a council. The peasants, a gay and cheerful race, held their lands on feudal tenure from *seigneurs*, who received their quit-rents and commanded them when military service was required. A lucrative fur-trade was centred in Montreal, whose factors and trappers often came into desperate conflict in the Indian wildernesses with the agents of the Hudson Bay Company: fur was the principal export, and it was obtained by exchanging a few trinkets and common utensils with the redskin Indians, who spent their winters in obtaining the pelts of animals.

French colonial ambition aimed at more than merely wealth by immediate trade. No praise can be too great for the Jesuit fathers who preached and lived in the wigwams of the Hurons, making them the allies of France, or for the French explorers who traced the long waterways that linked Canada to the Gulf of New Orleans. A small settlement at the mouth of the Mississippi, named Louisiana in honour of the king, was an earnest of the French claim to a "New France" that should stretch west of all the English colonies and, with the waterways secured by stockaded forts and the Indians converted into "friendlies", effectively shut off the English colonists from the distant interior of the continent.

In the East, the French East India Company had tried, but failed, to develop Madagascar. Their agents, however, entered upon the commerce with India and now dominated the trade of the Carnatic through their factory at Pondicherry. Hitherto, the Indian peninsula had been the prey of northern invaders coming overland from the north-west. Now, white men in splendid ships were getting a foothold on its coasts and traded in its calicoes, muslins and spices.

They brought gold and silver in exchange. They came at a time when India was rapidly becoming a no-man's-land—or any man's land. Since the middle of the sixteenth century, the Mogul emperors had ruled the plains and the peninsula from Agra and Delhi. Their palaces and mosques of marble, serpentine and lapis lazuli still stand as witnesses to their efficient and ruthless personal despotisms. They kept armies and used cannon in their wars. But the last of the great Moslem rulers, Aurungzebe, had died in 1707. His death was followed by chaos. He had antagonized the martial Hindu races of the Rajputs and Marathas. These were both inland races. The European factories were set up among the more passive Hindus of Bengal and in the south. Already, the India of independent nawabs, owing merely a nominal allegiance to Delhi, had come into being.

So the scene was set for one of the dominating themes of the eighteenth century: colonial and maritime rivalry, trade-war and naval-war, between the Powers of Great Britain and France. Linked to this theme by the diplomacy of the nations concerned was the older and purely European theme of deep-rooted family rivalry between the Bourbons and the Habsburgs of Austria.

THE ASIATIC PEOPLES

Outside the orbit of all but a few Europeans lay the Mongol and Mongoloid peoples of farther Asia. The deltas and luxuriant forests of the Indo-Chinese peninsula were scenes of dynastic and tribal warfare. Their populations—Malays, Burmese, Peguans, Cambodians, Annamites, Siamese, Chinese—lived in a civilization that was in decay. The prevailing worship of Buddha was corrupted by local superstition and devil-worship. Yet the land was rich in precious metals, spices and fruit-bearing trees. Only occasionally did European factors set foot there to see the gorgeous gilded temples and pagodas, or hear the music of the Siamese.

Beyond Indo-China were the eighteen provinces of China, comprising some 125 millions of people in an empire stretching over 25 degrees of latitude between the ocean and Tartary. The Manchus, a Tartar race from Manchuria, had recently seized the dragon-throne at Peking. They held the land by Tartar garrisons, and their rule was much resented by the southerners about Canton who set up secret political societies, such as the "White Lily", to preserve their independence. The civilization of China was ancient and static; ancestor-worship and the moral precepts of Confucius preserved family life and secular authority. At the beginning of the eighteenth century, the empire was ruled by a wise Manchu, named K'ang Hsi, who patronized literature and was a friend of the Jesuits.

Beyond China were the islands of Japan, subject to earthquakes and swept by tropical storms. The Shoguns who then ruled the Japanese had closed the country against all foreigners. To the south and south-east stretched the East Indies, covering an area of ocean

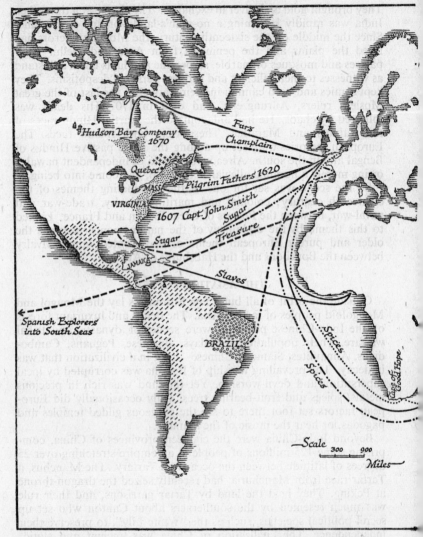

Hudson Bay Company
1670

Furs

Champlain

Quebec

Pilgrim Fathers 1620

MASS

VIRGINIA

1607 Capt. John Smith

Sugar

Sugar

Treasure

JAMAICA

Slaves

Spanish Explorers
into South Seas

BRAZIL

Spices

Spices

Cape of Good Hope

Scale
300   900
Miles

TRADE ROUTES OF

The latter half of the seventeenth century witnessed a vast development in
European trade with other countries, this being due to improved methods of
navigation and shipbuilding and the growth of European settlements and
trading stations in America, India, and the East and West Indies. This period
also marked the beginning of England's industrial and commercial supremacy
that was to be a vital feature of the eighteenth and nineteenth centuries. In
contrast the great Spanish Empire fell into decay through incompetent
administration. Spain's reliance on precious metals brought from her South
American dependencies ruined her domestic industries and agriculture.

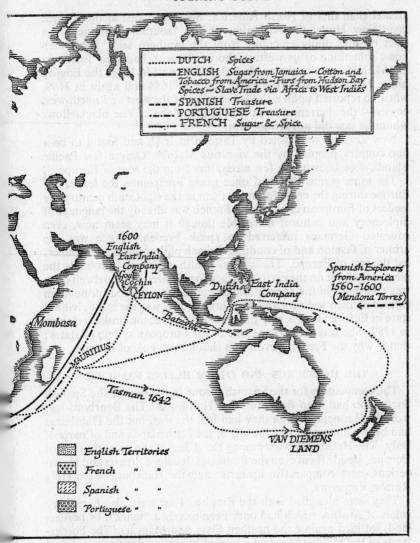

DUCH .... *Spices*
ENGLISH *Sugar from Jamaica ~ Cotton and Tobacco from America ~ Furs from Hudson Bay Spices ~ Slave Trade via Africa to West Indies*
SPANISH ---- *Treasure*
PORTUGUESE ·-·-· *Treasure*
FRENCH ····· *Sugar & Spice*

1600
English East India Company
Goa
Cochin
CEYLON
Mombasa
MAURITIUS
Batavia
Dutch East India Company
Tasman 1642
VAN DIEMENS LAND

Spanish Explorers from America 1560-1600 (Mendona Torres)

English Territories
French   "   "
Spanish   "   "
Portuguese "   "

THE SEVENTEENTH CENTURY

To Bristol, for many years the greatest port in England, came sugar from Jamaica and valuable spices; the North American settlements exported cotton and tobacco in increasing quantities; furs were shipped from the territories opened up by the Hudson Bay Company, and England's Indian trade continued to expand. Simultaneously the trade in slaves—"black ivory"—grew as colonial demand for them increased. In India the influence possessed by the English, French, and Portuguese became stronger as the Mogul Empire gradually disintegrated. Foreign trading companies were able to consolidate their foothold, among them being the East India Company, formed in 1600.

greater than that of North America. South and east again of these lay "New Holland"—Australia, or the "southern continent"—a tract of land dimly emerging from the southern seas. The Dutch knew something of its western shores. Tasman had seen Tasmania in 1642 and some of the north Australian coast in 1644: the English pirate Dampier visited the north shore in 1688 and again in 1699, when he reported upon a thousand miles of the west and north-west coasts—"the barrenest spot upon the globe". The blackfellows whom he saw did not attract him.

New Zealand was visited by Tasman in 1642, and found to be a fine country peopled by the vigorous Maoris. Only a few Pacific islands were known to a few navigators from the seas of Europe.

The same genius that had once made Frenchmen the leaders of Europe during the crusades made them in the eighteenth century the leaders of European civilization. French was already the language of diplomacy and culture; incredible though it may seem now, even educated Germans preferred to speak French. France was the arbiter of fashion and of conduct. French philosophers and thinkers led the rest of Europe. The natural wealth of France—probably the pleasantest spot on the earth's surface for civilized man to dwell on— was enormous in the agricultural age, and her numerous population thrived by their industry and frugality. France was the most civilized state in Europe; that is why the revolution of reason broke out there in 1789. She was the corner-stone of the European system of states; that is why the French Revolution shook the whole of Europe.

THE HABSBURGS AND OTHER RULING FAMILIES

The competitors for the Spanish throne in the War of the Spanish Succession had been Bourbons and Habsburgs. The Bourbons had won the throne, although they had lost the war, but the Habsburgs had been compensated by the gift of the Netherlands and of parts of Italy. The Habsburgs were among the oldest of the great families of Europe. Beside them even the Bourbons, let alone Stuarts and Hanoverians, were comparative upstarts: and the Habsburgs were Holy Roman Emperors.

They were identified with the Empire. They were also hereditary rulers of Austria, which had once been merely a "mark", or borderland, fortified against the heathen Slavs and Magyars. The borderlands of the Middle Ages had a way of becoming dominant political states. Prussia, for example, became the leader of the Germanies later in the eighteenth century; while the barons of the Welsh border and those of the Spanish "March" played decisive parts in the histories of England and Spain respectively.

The political structure of the Germanies in the eighteenth century was so complicated that a coloured map of them looks like a jigsaw puzzle, particularly in the regions between the Rhine and the Elbe. Some three hundred potentates, lay and spiritual, governed terri-

tories varying from a few square miles to kingdoms like Saxony and
Bavaria. These kingdoms, principalities, free cities, grand-duchies,
bishoprics, archbishoprics, dukedoms, margravates, and what not,
comprised the major part of the Holy Roman Empire. An Imperial
Diet met at Ratisbon, but its decisions carried little weight. An
Imperial army, made up of contingents from each separate state,
existed on paper. It it could ever be got together, its uniform was
delightfully varied, even in the same regiments, and its equipment
and drill were chaotic. Since each ruler could issue coinage, raise
taxes, impose customs, make treaties and decide the religion of his
subjects, the nominal Imperial federation was in effect merely an
attenuated phantom of the medieval Holy Roman Empire.

OPPRESSION AND MISERY IN GERMANY

Corruption, tyranny and cruelty were common in these tiny despotisms. The vigorous civic life, the flourishing trading communities
and craft-guilds of the later Middle Ages had disappeared. The wars of
religion had all but destroyed civilization itself in Germany. If music
and the arts were occasionally patronized by a few exceptional rulers,
the people at large benefited nothing. Most of them were peasants
living on a bare subsistence level, holding their plots by servile
tenure, doing so much forced labour in Prussia that some of them
could till their own land only by moonlight. They were tied to the
soil. Some princes sold their subjects as mercenaries to the greater
Powers. It was in this way that Great Britain provided herself with
Hessian soldiers, bivouacked them in England and sent them to
garrison Ireland and North America. Central and Eastern Europe
was a poverty-stricken plain.

In the Rhineland and in South Germany, the gradual slackening
of the spice trade from the East, via Venice and the Alps, had brought
about a diminution of industry and trade. A remoter and perhaps
more debatable cause of decay was the decline, all over Europe, of
the civic spirit. Civilization is primarily the life of men in cities: with
the exaltation of personal monarchy at the Renaissance, civic virtue
and enterprise was doomed. This dismal state of the people in the
German lands explains why there were no revolutions there, as in
France at the close of the century; revolution is always born of hope,
not of despair.

Of all the parts of the Holy Roman Empire, Prussia most deserves
attention, because of what she has since become. There were four
facts to notice about Prussia. Her kingdom comprised considerable
lands outside the jurisdiction of the Empire. She was the chief
Protestant state in Germany. She was a border-country built up by
warfare against the Slavs and Letts. As in England, her territory
passed undivided by primogeniture, while Saxony, which had promised during the time of the Reformation to become the leading
kingdom of Germany, suffered division upon the deaths of her kings.

Besides ruling Austria, the Habsburgs were masters of Bohemia, Hungary, the Austrian Netherlands, and parts of Italy. While in Europe they were the rivals of the Bourbons of France, their eastern territories were also the bulwark of Christendom against the Turk. Austria was happy in little but the marriage alliances of her royal and imperial house. The Emperor Charles VI directed most of his diplomatic energies towards persuading the Western powers to recognize his daughter, Maria Theresa, as his successor, and in this he was successful: yet, as his most powerful subject, the valiant Prince Eugene of Savoy, told him, a full treasury and a strong army were the best guarantees of his daughter's succession. The Habsburgs found it almost as difficult to get money and arms as rulers of Austria as they did as emperors of the Germanies. The Austrian lands lacked unity. The nobles of the component kingdoms, whose titles in some instances ran back to the heroic days of Charlemagne, were virtual kings on their own estates. Austria, Bohemia, Hungary, had their separate administrative, judicial and financial systems.

Austria's neighbours, Poland, Russia and Turkey, were all involved in the wars of Peter the Great and Charles XII of Sweden. Poland was a land of peasants ruled by nobles whose martial valour was more than balanced by their political incompetence. Russia under the Romanovs was still "Muscovy"—a vast land of huge domains, under nobles who owned their peasants as serfs—a semi-oriental despotism, centuries behind the rest of Europe. Its people were Christians of the Greek Orthodox Church, their piety profoundly simple and unquestioning. At the turn of the century, Peter the Great was still in the midst of his "regeneration" of the Russian state.

TURKISH RULE

The crescent of Islam reached in a wide sweep from Tangier in Morocco to Belgrade on the Danube. Along the north coast of Africa were the lairs of the Barbary corsairs, the merciless sailors who levied continual blackmail on the merchant fleets of the Christians. The lands of the Near East, the region whence came our own civilization, Greek and Christian, were under the rule of the Ottoman Turk. His government lay like a dead hand over the Balkans, Asia Minor, Syria, Palestine and Egypt. All the common sacred ground of the Western nations—Athens, Constantinople, the Straits, Galilee, Jerusalem—was in the power of the infidel. Yet that infidel was little else than a lazy soldier. The Turk possessed the better half of antiquity, but he was incapable of using his possession fruitfully. He never mingled with his subject peoples, but remained aloof. His indolence made him tolerant; his lack of political principle made him capricious. He recognized and supported the authority of the Greek patriarchs, and his Christian subjects worshipped without hindrance. Alone of the many European districts under his sway, Albania accepted Islam.

Although indifferent to the people's creeds, the Turkish government was swift enough to tax them, and to tax them till they sank into apathy. It was the relentless oppression of Ottoman taxation that gradually brought ruin over what were once the most prosperous provinces of Rome. Agricultural countries recover speedily from wars and even from pestilence, but not from over-taxation, which denies the farmer his just reward and his margin of profit against bad years. The Turk himself belonged to an aristocracy, comparatively few in number. His wars were fought by members of the subject-races under his leadership: his best warriors came from those same uplands in Asia Minor that had provided the Isaurian emperors of the eighth century with the cream of their troops—indeed, the pedigree of an Anatolian peasant might well surprise Turkish nationalists to-day. His administration was largely in the hands of Greeks, who also engrossed the trade of the Near East, their competitors being Armenians and Salonica Jews. His pleasures were provided by slave-girls from Circassia and Georgia. His crack troops were the Janis-saries—kidnapped Christian boys trained to serve Islam. His litera-ture was that of Persia and Arabia. He discovered nothing, and created nothing. In his capacity of sovereign of such extensive terri-tories, he proved a very unreasonable being. But the Age of Reason began with a notable series of Austrian victories that definitely confined the power of the Turk to the lands south of the Danube.

DECLINE OF VENICE AND POLAND

The defence of Christian Europe had been maintained by Venice, Poland and Hungary. Venice, ruined by the discovery of the Atlantic route to the Spice Islands, was in decline in the eighteenth century, although still outwardly a city of splendour. She could no longer protect her ships from Dalmatian pirates, or hold her own against the Turks in the Grecian islands. At the beginning of the eighteenth century, a series of Imperialist victories drove the Turks from Transylvania and Hungary, and this was the turning-point in the long contest between the Ottoman Empire and the Western Powers. Hungary, however, was very unwillingly subjected to the rule of the Austrian Emperor.

Poland, the largest kingdom in Europe outside Russia, had no good natural frontiers. Its government was in a condition of feudal anarchy, wherein swarms of nobles quarrelled in the diet or repre-sentative assembly, whose action could, on any occasion, be vetoed by any one of them. The peasants were impoverished serfs. The Jews were most numerous, their ghettos forming in some instances half the population of a town. The only really progressive energetic people in Poland were the Germans who populated West Prussia. The whole country was in the nature of a thorn in the sides of its powerful neighbours. It was destined to be divided up between Russia, Prussia and Austria at the end of the eighteenth century.

CHAPTER 59

THE FIRST MOVES

ALTHOUGH the Western Powers had made peace at Utrecht the war in the north-east was continued to satisfy the ambitions of two remarkable men, Peter the Great of Russia and Charles XII of Sweden. With demonic vigour Peter was reshaping his dominion of Muscovy into a personal monarchy, modelled on the Western kingdoms, by forcing all to his ruthless will, and by introducing Western ideas, customs and methods of industry. He broke the long sleep of the Muscovite and began that lasting conflict between oriental placidity and superstition on the one hand and Western progress on the other, which has been, since his time, the main theme of Russian history.

Russia needed sea-coasts of more utility than the frozen north at Archangel. Shipbuilding was Peter's lifelong passion. He longed to launch his fleets on the Black Sea, and the Baltic—the two seas, eight hundred miles apart and each almost landlocked, that wash the Russian shores. The Turkish Empire in the south, the Swedish Empire in the north, barred his way: the ancient kingdom of Poland, which stretched across the western land-frontier of his dominions, linked up the two.

Peter fought the Turks but his main effort was made in the Baltic lands, where he had already laid the foundations of his new "western" capital, St. Petersburg, in the swamps about the mouth of the river Neva. The Baltic sea had been a Swedish lake. By the military skill of the Vasa kings, Sweden dominated the Baltic shores from Finland to Denmark. The neighbours of this Swedish Empire were apprehensive and resentful. Denmark, Russia and Poland had conspired to attack it. Charles XII, the young and impetuous king of Sweden, checked the allies, raided Poland and even Saxony—whose king was also king of Poland—and then marched into Russia, where he sought Cossack help. He wintered in the Ukraine, but in 1709 he was overwhelmed at Poltava by Peter the Great and escaped into Turkey. Here he incited the Turks to make war on the Tsar. They did so, and regained Azov from the Russians.

Such was the position in 1714 when suddenly Charles XII crossed Europe and entered his fortress of Stralsund. His northern foes took alarm, and soon Sweden was again ringed about with enemies— Prussia, Denmark, Poland and Russia. Charles was not clever enough in diplomacy to take advantage of their jealousies; yet all the chancelleries of Europe were interested in the Great Northern War with its possible shifting of the balance of power. Whether war or diplomacy accomplishes most is a moot question. Charles was a born leader of men in battle. But we must keep in mind Voltaire's words— "three or four hundred persons scattered on the face of the earth under the name of princes or ministers". Kingdoms and empires depended so much upon so few persons. Charles XII, the matchless captain, fell with a bullet through his brain, while besieging a Norwegian fortress in 1718. A series of treaties ended the war. As the result of these Sweden lost all her Baltic lands save Pomerania and Finland. Russia received the lion's share of the spoils.

SWEDEN AND RUSSIA

The Swedish monarchy became elective again through a new constitution. The monarchs were mere figure-heads, the fortunes of the country being at the mercy of two political factions known as "Caps" and "Hats", symbolic designations abbreviated from nightcaps and cocked hats, and expressive respectively of senile timidity and manly aggression. Until 1738, under the cautious guidance of Count Horn and his "nightcap" party, the country was kept out of war. Then the Hats came into power and resumed the old French alliance. They made war on Russia, promptly lost Finland, and only recovered it by the acceptance of a Russian nominee as future king of Sweden. The four estates of the Swedish *riksdag*, or parliament, were in intention democratic, in effect a clumsy contrivance which easily became a happy hunting-ground for the ambition of parties. This miserable strife between Hats and Caps continued until, in 1772, Gustavus III completely restored the power of the crown by means of a military *coup d'état*.

The decline of Sweden in the councils of Europe was more than balanced by the participation of Russia. We have already seen how the new Tsardom had been modelled by Peter the Great, that jovial giant with a passion for doing things for himself, who delighted in buffoonery and debauchery with his cronies, and in digging and hewing and hauling with his workmen. His attempt to compass the work of centuries in one short lifetime came very near success. When he died in 1725, Russia had advanced a long way on the path of Western progress, which he had designed. His chief assistants in this advance were mainly foreigners, Dutchmen, Poles, Germans and Scots. But he had Russian favourites too; the most constant was the meat-pie seller, Menshikov, whom Peter raised to a princedom from the gutters of Moscow.

While the Tsar's foreign agents taught the Russians mathematics, geography, Latin, rhetoric, astronomy, navigation, shipbuilding, cannon-founding and printing, he himself encouraged the exploitation of minerals, timber and leather, and reformed the coinage. A new form of administration was designed on Swedish lines, and Peter devised a code of laws based on the Swedish model. But his efforts were constantly thwarted by the chronic dishonesty of his officials, which defied the most savage punishments. As long as he lived, the power of the great princes was curbed. He managed to bring the Greek Orthodox Church, whose clergy and monks had been the obstinate champions of old Muscovite ignorance, under his firm control.

Peter accomplished his reforms by terror of the torture-chamber, the searing-iron, the wheel and the scaffold. In securing the good of of his empire, he held all means to be justified. From his time onward, Russia was a member of the Western comity of states. His work was carried forward by his pupils, the Germans Osterman and Münich, in the reigns of his widow, Catherine, and the German-bred Anne. Foreigners held high commands in the Russian armies. These armies engaged successfully both Poles and French in the war of the Polish succession; for the first time in history, Russian troops bivouacked on the Rhine. In spite of victories, the war against the Turks in the Crimea proved fruitless. The War of the Polish Succession decided that Russia was to dominate the Polish monarchy; the struggle with Turkey foreshadowed Russia's destined expansion southward and eastward.

Warfare in the early eighteenth century was carried on by small professional armies. It did not absorb the energies of a whole nation, wrench trade from its normal channels, and feed itself upon irrational hatreds. Nevertheless, the states involved in the war of the Spanish Succession were heartily tired of hostilities and eager for the peace brought about by the conferences at Utrecht in 1713. The balance of power had been preserved, as between Habsburg and Bourbon. A Bourbon prince sat on the Spanish throne—that throne of an empire upon which, it was claimed, the sun never set. But Austria obtained the former Spanish Netherlands and most of the former Spanish provinces in Italy, Naples, Milan and Sardinia. France was exhausted. Under the regency of the shrewd but dissipated Duke of Orleans, it could turn its attention to the restoration of its finances. Great Britain was occupied with the possibility of a disputed succession and Jacobite invasions when Queen Anne should die. The Holy Roman Emperor, Charles VI, was thus free to begin the delicate task of persuading the powers to recognize his daughter, Maria Theresa, as the legitimate heir to the vast Habsburg possessions.

MONARCHS WHO LACKED CHARACTER

The monarchs of the early eighteenth century were not like the Plantagenets, Capetians or Hohenstaufens. As far as character and ability went, hereditary monarchy in the West had fallen upon evil days. Never were there such unkingly sovereigns. George I of Great Britain was a German prince ignorant of British speech and ways, an honest though unattractive personality with no capacity for culture, an elector of the Holy Roman Empire governing an aristocratic and commercial commonwealth, of which he knew little and for which he cared little. Louis XV of France, who succeeded to the throne in 1715, while still a boy, had some talent in mathematics and mechanics, but grew up into the perfect trifler, idling away his life with dogs, horses and mistresses. Charles VI of Austria was a mediocrity, who initiated an ambitious foreign policy that ended in disaster. Philip V of Spain was a religious maniac, irresolute and indolent, and in his later years mentally unstable. He was uxorious to an absurd excess, never letting his wife from his sight. This woman, an Italian of Parma, Elizabeth Farnese, was the most capable of all the crowned heads. She shared with many Spaniards the ambition to regain Spain's lost provinces in Italy, desiring them as inheritances for her sons. Because of her undeviating efforts to acquire them and thus upset the Treaty of Utrecht, all the ministries of Europe were kept in a flutter till the death of her demented husband in 1746.

STATESMEN OF EUROPE

The fortunes of Europe were left almost entirely to statesmen. In Great Britain, a Norfolk landowner, Sir Robert Walpole, a man with a genius for finance and a character that could manage the politicians, held the reins for twenty years. He preserved a strong navy, fostered external trade by a system of bounties, maintained tolerantly the Protestant establishment, and above all, kept peace. In Spain and France, ecclesiastics predominated. In Spain, Cardinal Alberoni, the son of an Italian gardener, a quick-tempered and sanguine man, almost raised Spain to the greatness her empire warranted. He encouraged the American trade, stimulated manufactures, put a stop to corruption in the administration and built a powerful navy. The ambitious designs of Alberoni and Elizabeth Farnese in respect of Italy brought Spain into armed conflict with Great Britain, France and Austria. The allies won, and insisted upon Alberoni's retirement. In three more years of office, he might have compassed new and lasting glories for the country of his adoption; as it was, the policy he laid down was continued by his successors, the greatest of whom, the Spanish grandee Patino, was Sir Robert Walpole's contemporary in power and opponent in policy. The Spain of this time was a land of promise, whose maritime and naval commitments carried her inevitably into overseas rivalry with Great Britain.

In France, the Abbé Dubois, son of a chemist, did his best to preserve peace and at the same time foil Alberoni's schemes. He was vain, self-seeking, immoral, persistent. It was rumoured that France paid eight million francs for his cardinal's hat. Dubois was followed by Cardinal Fleury, whose power was absolute for seventeen years. By a masterly inactivity, Fleury gave France and her colonies time to recuperate. He was misguided into engaging in the War of the Polish Succession, which brought France portions of Lorraine, but left Poland (an elective monarchy) at the mercy of Russia. Though he insisted upon honesty and economy among state servants, Fleury's lack of positive qualities allowed the French navy to rot in its harbours.

Holland, Great Britain, France and Spain were all in a position to do well abroad. Asia, Africa and the New World were like orchards with golden fruits waiting to be plucked. The art of navigation and knowledge of geography far surpassed those of the old pioneer days, and the newly-elaborated system of banking and share-holding provided rich opportunities to those merchants who were shrewd enough to exploit these new developments.

DUTCH, FRENCH AND ENGLISH COLONIAL RIVALRY

In the east, commerce was in the hands of the Dutch, French and English companies: when the Emperor Charles VI tried to found an Imperial East India Company at Ostend, he was prevented by the diplomacy of the other Powers, so great was the influence of the India merchants. The Dutch monopolized the Spice Islands. They had driven the Portuguese from their trading-stations and had acquired Malacca and Batavia, the two ancient centres of the Arab trade. They extended their power over Java, where they tolerated oriental religions, but levied tribute on the native princes and took a handsome toll in licences from the gambling dens run by Chinese immigrants. The Dutch, however, were often involved in petty wars and had to ensure protection against the pirates of Malaya. Moreover, the direction of the Company lacked breadth of vision, and was far too narrowly monopolistic.

The impetus given to French overseas enterprise by Colbert continued. The early part of the century was the heyday of French colonial and commercial activities. Their East India Company, under able governors like Dumas and Dupleix, forged ahead with ambitious schemes which aimed at political as well as mercantile supremacy, not only on the mainland of India, but as far as the East Indies. In 1720, Mauritius was taken and colonized, and in 1746, the English station at Madras was captured by La Bourdonnais.

BRITISH NORTH AMERICAN COLONIES

Similarly, in North America, where they held the two great maritime entries of the continent, the St. Lawrence and the Mississippi, the French projected great schemes of domination. Here they were in conflict not with a peaceful trading Company intent on its dividends, but with thirteen British colonies with a gross population of over a million. The British and French were both busy in the twenties and thirties building forts along the eastern lakes: both kept a jealous and intermittent watch on the lands of the Ohio valley. When Great Britain was at war with France in the forties, the men of Massachusetts stormed Louisburg at the entry of the St. Lawrence. Ten years later, while the two nations were nominally at peace, General Braddock marched on Fort Duquesne; but his regulars were ambushed in the dense forest and routed by French and Indians.

The British colonies were either crown colonies, or under royal charter, or under proprietors. All enjoyed a political freedom found nowhere else at that time. Their trade was restricted by Navigation Acts, but this helped the mother-country rather than harmed the colonist, who was, if he wished, served readily by the smugglers running sugar between the French West Indies and, say, Philadelphia. Colonial trade and population both increased phenomenally. One instance must suffice: Pennsylvania took in six thousand settlers in 1729, most of them Irishmen; while Pennsylvanian trade with Britain multiplied itself fifty-fold between 1704 and 1772. Not only Irish, but multitudes of Germans from the Palatinate and Württemberg, sailed every year for Philadelphia, attracted by the dream of a new, opulent world where their Protestantism would be welcomed. In the face of this tremendous development, the ambitions of the most brilliant French governors and generals could do little to further French policy. The French were not by nature a colonizing nation.

THE WEST INDIES AND SOUTH AMERICA

More precious, in the eyes of the European governments, than the white colonies of North America were the West Indies, where imported African negroes worked on great sugar-plantations and outnumbered the few whites to such an extent that these latter enacted harsh and cruel laws to ensure their own protection. Great Britain prospered mainly from the dreadful traffic in slaves; her merchants transported over two million negroes from Central Africa to the New World during the century following 1680. The loss of Canada in 1763 mattered little to the French government so long as they kept Martinique and Guadaloupe; but what might have been a splendid and fertile field for civilized colonies, set in the summer seas of the Caribbean—islands fit for Prospero—became debauched in a most immoral exploitation for gold. Not only were the islands the homes of pirates and outcasts and the scenes of slave revolts and slave-murder, but as sources of wealth, they became objects of attack upon the outbreak of every war between Great Britain and France. Nowhere does human history provide so terrible a record of "man's inhumanity to man".

South America, the untouched preserve of the Latin races, produced one remarkable experiment which reached its height in the forties of the century; this was the Jesuit government of Paraguay. The Society of Jesus, from its inception, took as one of its principal tasks the conversion of the heathen, and its missionary activities ranged from the islands of Japan to the forests of Canada. Early in the seventeenth century, Jesuit fathers commenced work among the natives of the Plate River. They obtained concessions from the king of Spain, and by shielding the natives most carefully from the pernicious elements of Western civilization, they built up a self-contained utopia under their own paternal direction. They supervised everything, from sowing the seed to allocating the fruits of the harvest: they educated and preached: they introduced manufactures: they allowed no accumulation of wealth, no exploitation of labour, no European language, no capital punishment. They even led their native converts with success against the regular troops of the Portuguese king. Elsewhere, also, the Jesuits converted vast numbers of natives, notably in Chili and Peru, Brazil and Canada. When the Society was proscribed in Spain and dissolved by the pope in 1773, Paraguay fell under the civil Spanish governors of Buenos Aires, and its natives reverted to the comparative barbarism of their neighbours. They had been taught everything but self-reliance.

THE PRUSSIAN ARMY

The records of the past display to the historian a manifold and multicoloured tangle of skeins. He surveys the pattern and picks out the chief strands; but he is necessarily limited by his own position in relation to the skein. Only by guesswork can he ever discern that some insignificant thread now caught up in the weaving will lead on towards a dominant motive. More usually than not, prophets are refuted by the event. To contemporaries, the outstanding *motifs* in the early eighteenth century were the clear division in Europe between the Catholic and Protestant powers, and the approaching struggle for overseas trade and colonies. To us, now, an equally important fact was the consolidation of the state of Prussia, under Frederick William I.

Other monarchs might enjoy their days, like butterflies in the sun, indulging themselves according to their natures and leaving their affairs to ministers. Frederick William I was a king who knew his own mind. During his reign, from 1713 to 1740, he lived not for himself but for his country. He lived and thought as a Puritan. He filled his treasury by the most drastic economies, cutting down salaries to mere pittances and even abolishing the Court. He raised the strength of his army to eighty thousand men, half of them foreigners recruited by kidnappers and flogged into discipline. He welcomed immigrants from other German states, whom he settled on the infertile wastes of East Prussia. Money, population, soldiers —these were the triple foundation of the Prussian state, upon which his son, Frederick the Great, built the Prussian monarchy.

Frederick William I and Peter the Great were contemporaries. Lord Acton, the English historian, writing of these men in 1906, said: "That which arose in Northern Europe about the time of our revolution settlement was a new form of practical absolutism. . . . Henceforth the State oppressed for its own sake. . . . Government so understood is the intellectual guide of the nation, the promoter of wealth, the teacher of knowledge, the guardian of morality, the mainspring of the ascending movement of man. That is the tremendous power, supported by millions of bayonets, which grew up in the days of which I have been speaking at Petersburg, and was developed, by much abler minds, chiefly at Berlin."

To contemporaries, the small scarlet strands of Russia and Prussia were negligible: Lord Acton lived nearly two centuries later.

CHAPTER 60

BACKGROUND OF LIFE AND THOUGHT

THE greater part of mankind in the eighteenth century were peasants or artisans; and the greater part of the peasants, except in England and France, were servile. They created the wealth of nations: forced labour and taxation took their strength; the profit of their strength gave luxury and ease to their lords. "Is not this an unjust and unkind public weal, which giveth great fees and rewards to gentlemen, as they call them, and to goldsmiths, and to such other, which be either idle persons, or else only flatterers and devisers of vain pleasures: and of the contrary part maketh no gentle provision for poor ploughmen, colliers, labourers, carters, ironsmiths, and carpenters, without whom no commonwealth can continue?" We can ask Sir Thomas More's question as well of the eighteenth century as he did of the sixteenth.

LIFE OF THE PEASANTS

The peasant was the basis of civilization. His method of farming was still primitive. Scythe and sickle, flail, ox-drawn wooden plough, huge lumbering wagon well matched the earth floors, daub walls and thatched roof of his dwelling. The lord's mill alone could grind his corn. The lord's wine-press could alone crush his grapes. The lord's doves were a pest to his crops. Fish and game were the lord's preserves: the peasant could not add such luxuries to his table. His marriage needed the lord's consent. His inheritance was not valid unless he paid a tax to his lord for entering into it. He could not come and go freely. He paid toll and tithe. His womenfolk worked beside him in the open field, fair weather and foul. His children were born in serfdom. Yet he carried on from year to year, and from century to century, on the land tilled by his forefathers. It has been placed on record recently that some Italian peasants still hold the farms their ancestors worked a thousand years ago.

Famine was a constant menace and a frequent reality. Peasant revolts in France were common in the seventeenth century. La Bruyère, a French satirical writer, described his countrymen in words which were an indictment of his time: "Fierce animals may be seen, male and female, scattered over the country, black, bloodless and shrivelled by the sun, bound to the soil which they cultivate with unflagging labour. They have a kind of speech, and when they stand erect, they reveal the lineaments of the human face. They are men. They go home at night to their burrows where they live on black bread, roots and water. They save others the trouble of sowing, ploughing and reaping, and they deserve therefore not to lack the bread which they have sown." It is a sad picture. Men spent their lives in unremitting toil, struggling for food, and their methods of cultivating the soil by which they gained a living hardly changed for ages.

665

In the first half of the eighteenth century, improvements in all branches of farming had begun in the rich, mercantile commonwealth of Great Britain, where a succession of enterprising landowners revolutionized the management of both arable and pasture. Jethro Tull invented a seed-drill, by which seed was sown in orderly rows, not broadcast by hand; he showed the value of continual hoeing, and both he and Lord Townshend were among the earliest to utilize the old fallowfields by growing turnips in them. This gave a root-crop from which cattle could be fed during winter months. Both these men died before the middle of the century. Then Bakewell began breeding sheep by careful selection. The record of Coke of Holkham is instructive; by using root-crops and manures, by feeding his cattle on oil-cake, by giving long leases to his farmer tenants and improving their cottages, he increased his rent-roll ninefold in forty years. He did this by spending over half a million pounds on improvements. In a reasonable world, there was hope for the peasant who cultivated the soil.

European society was still feudal, without being pious. In the ages of faith, money had been lavished on minsters and shrines, for the welfare of the soul in the life to come; now that gifts to the Church were no longer in fashion, money was lavished upon palaces and châteaux, for the delight of the senses in this world. The need for embattled castles was gone. It was Versailles that set the fashion for every petty potentate and every grand seigneur. Even the Germans were content to take their cue from France in respect of such matters.

CRAFTSMANSHIP FOSTERED BY WEALTH

One excellent result was the patronage given by noblemen to painters, sculptors, architects, craftsmen, scholars, writers and musicians. Architecture diverged at times and in places from the Renaissance severity of Versailles and Blenheim Palace: it effloresced into rococo, or else broke new and mysterious ground in the sham gothic of Fonthill in Wiltshire. At the best, it achieved a restful and graceful dignity of pilaster and pediment; at its worst, it ran into masses of stucco and endless decoration of plaster and gilt. The smaller domestic houses of brick and stone of the period are wholly delightful and reflect the saner, leisured life of the time. Furniture, though exquisitely made, lent itself to a display that easily became vulgar. Mahogany and inlay chairs and tables, great gilt-framed mirrors, ornamented timepieces, porcelain jars and figures, lacquered screens, elaborate candelabra, upholstery in figured silks and satins— these were some of the craftsman's tribute to wealth in a world rapidly growing richer.

Cottage industry provided the strong, coarse homespun of the peasant: and he went in wooden clogs hewn from underwood timber. Far otherwise were the wealthy classes clothed and shod. Velvet and gold-lace, lawn and brocade, coloured silks and sprigged satins, fine linen, muslins of almost cobweb delicacy, offered a wide variety of dress; while there was good leather for the feet, plain blue shoes with silver buckles, dainty shoes with prodigious painted heels, and stout, square-toed riding-boots for the use of the horseman.

THE LIFE OF THE ARISTOCRACY

The stately manners of Louis XIV's Court had set a pattern for the rest of Europe. In the gay world of candlelight and masks, patches and perukes, society lived and moved like actors. All the world was a stage. Artifice and formality were carried to extreme lengths. Polite society amused itself at play, and vast sums were lost at loo and other games of hazard. Whole nights were passed at cards. This was the century in which Lord Sandwich invented the convenient morsel of food named after him, in order to save the interruption of a formal meal. Drinking, of course, never checked any game: it was always an informal business. Even the ladies had their clubs where they took a hand of picquet, or tried their wits over chess and draughts. Gambling is a vice almost honourable with age, and drinking had always been a very human frailty. There never was a century when both were so prevalent. Tea and coffee were slowly gaining ground as beverages, but the tankard and the bottle were still supreme ministers to conviviality and mighty snares for the weak and improvident. Gentlemen went armed and vindicated their honour in duels over the most trifling affairs. The marriage-tie was held lightly; and, if immorality was not more widespread than usual, it was accepted in polite society with more complaisance.

A rage for landscape-gardening followed, in reaction against the formal Dutch gardens. There was a "romantic" return to Nature. Men of letters collected popular ballads, painters depicted rustic scenes, aristocrats held open-air parties at which they played such innocent games as battledore and blindman's buff. Of course, it was a return to Nature in a decorous and comfortable manner, not a Franciscan revival. Emphasis was laid on the joys of the countryside. Milkmaids might be seen in the gardens of Versailles; they took care never to milk cows. Pastoral delights were exemplified in the disporting of the Corydons and Daphnes of the Court; but they never assisted at a sheep-shearing. Insensibly, however, this artificial interest did lead on to a recognition of the needs of rural poverty, and deepened, towards the end of the century, into a real interest.

Entire villages were often the property of one landowner. But frequently the great house itself was a small world, subsisting on locally-grown food and employing scores, and even hundreds, of servants and dependants—including its own craftsmen, such as carpenters, wheelwrights, smiths, and masons. Important, too, were the verderers, foresters, falconers, and especially the grooms and farriers. Foxhunting was reckoned to be the king of sports, and game of every kind was jealously preserved on the large estates.

Roads were bad in summer and wellnigh impassable in winter except by horsemen. Goods were carried long distances on pack-horses. Carts and waggons were for village use; carriages were slow, cumbrous and uncomfortable. The horseman dominated the scene. Highway robbery and banditry were encouraged by lack of police and by the long stretches of lonely road. But for horsemen, the green trackways and bridle-paths were good enough—far better, indeed, than broken roads. In an age of tariffs, the smuggler guided his train of pack-animals across open country; the merchant drove his laden beasts along the high ground from town to town. The horse, as a topic of conversation, held the place of cars and planes to-day.

THE TOWNS AND THEIR CITIZENS

Most of the towns were small market-towns with crooked, narrow streets, cobbled and paved, and often malodorous. Half-timbered houses with thatched roofs were common, and their projecting upper storeys darkened the ways. Alleys and court-yards abounded, scarcely the width of a hand-truck—so narrow, in fact, that an ox could not turn in them. In bad weather, the filth underfoot was thick, and ladies were carried in sedan-chairs. Many towns, especially in Germany and the south of Europe, were still contained within the circuit of their medieval walls. Sanitation and ventilation were un-known. Smallpox and typhoid were endemic, and tuberculosis common. Vienna could boast its numerous professional street-cleaners and its street-lamps, but most towns were dark and dirty.

The shopkeepers—or tradesmen, to use that word in its older sense —lived in their shops and kept apprentices. The guild-system was still in being, and certain youths, instead of going to school, were bound to serve master-craftsmen for a long term of years—seven or even nine—to learn the craft. Incidentally, the apprentice was a source of profit to his master, in that he became proficient fairly quickly, but the human relationship between master and man was a better thing than the nineteenth century's formality of master and "hand". When the apprentice was out of his articles, he became a journeyman, working for a wage, again in immediate contact with a master who knew the craft himself. This system was much abused in the masters' interests, but its replacement by universal education in schools, followed by employment in factories, has not necessarily been an improvement. The German guilds were stricter than the French or English; in France, the statesman Colbert encouraged them, while in England, the justices always upheld them. The guild-system produced some excellent work, and had for its aim the pre-servation of good quality in workmanship. The jibe at the Jack-of-all-trades comes down from the days when the cobbler was required to stick to his last and the tailor to his "goose", or smoothing-iron; and if, in some trades, specialization was carried to absurd lengths, a few craftsmen were permitted a wider range. Modern progress owes much to the wheelwright and the instrument-maker of those days. In some districts barbers were still practising the cure of blood-letting, though the apothecary and the man of medicine, the "doctor", was rapidly becoming a recognized member of lay society.

LONDON AND PARIS

Two cities, London and Paris, stood pre-eminent—both with about half a million inhabitants. The boulevards of Paris were already laid out, and the city was better policed than London, which depended for its order upon old watchmen—"Charlies". London was, in great part, a newly-built city dominated by Wren's classic cathedral of St. Paul's; but while Paris had recently been deserted by the French kings, the fame of the City of London had never been dependent on the existence of a royal household within its precincts. No town has been, or is now, so jealous of its rights as the "City" : the multitudinous richness of its story is the historian's despair. Had it possessed a temple to its own particular deity, in the fashion of the old pagan Romans, the shrine, surely, would have burst with offerings. By the chances of its position and its past, London in the eighteenth century was rapidly expanding and becoming the wealthiest and most populous city in the world.

Civilization was, in a sense, a tale of these two cities: with the growth of them, the mob re-enters Western history. We cannot easily imagine those mobs—illiterate, ragged, feckless, drunken, clamorous, gregarious, rising in their thousands from hovels that were a disgrace to their rulers. In 1782, the London mob sacked and pillaged for four days at will, opening prisons, burning shops, looting breweries: King George III turned the military on them and drove them back to their mean streets. In 1789, the Paris mob took a hand in the Revolution that was beginning in France: there was no single man with enough authority or vigour to drive them to their homes in that unhappy city. Perhaps these instances illustrate, as well as any, the utter difference between the political habits and traditions of Great Britain and of France.

Daniel Defoe, the author of *Robinson Crusoe*, made a tour of Great Britain in 1724–26 and recorded what he saw. Of London he says: "Here are the South Sea Company, the East India Company, the Bank, the African Company, etc. whose Stocks support that prodigious Paper Commerce, called Stock-Jobbing; a Trade, which . . . is still a Negotiation, so vast in its Extent, that almost all the Men of Substance in England are more or less concerned in it. . . ."

What was a thing of wonder to Defoe is a commonplace to-day. That "prodigious Paper Commerce", first swelling to a flood in his day, is the financial system on which we have built our civilization—a system of values and credits, pledges to be honoured, and, through their honouring, guarantees of the future. The new stockjobbing gave rise to many "bubbles" which burst with disastrous effects. In

Britain, a South Sea Company was formed to manage part of the nation's debt, in return for monopolies of the Spanish American trade and of colonizing ventures in South America. An immense boom in stocks followed. All sorts of smaller schemes were advertised, and taken up, including one fantastic proposal for "a certain design . . . which will hereafter be promulgated". Optimism cooled with time, and many of these lesser companies became bubbles. Their bursting was the signal for a slump in the shares of the great South Sea Company which eventually brought ruin and disaster to its shareholders.

In France, an even vaster scheme was mooted by John Law, a Scotsman of genius. The country was on the verge of bankruptcy. He offered to take over the entire debt, and establish a Bank to issue paper currency, which should be so managed as to develop trade and industry at home and in the colonies. He further undertook to gather all the trading companies of India, Africa, America, into one great corporation which should co-ordinate the whole of French business. He started his Bank, and he merged the Companies into one concern. The Regent made him Superintendent of France. Society fêted him; diplomats sought his advice. But the very magnitude of his schemes, and the mad speculation of fortune-hunters involved them in ruin. By 1721, Law was an exile, and other men were trying desperately to cope with widespread disaster.

RELIGIOUS LIFE

Since the Middle Ages, Europe had been moving from feudalism to despotism. The exaltation of personal monarchy diminished the power of the Church of Rome. A universal church, governed piecemeal by secular princes, was bound to result in tangled loyalties. The Protestant rulers had cut through the knots by severing their states from the universal church. The Catholic rulers were still in conflict with the Papacy.

None of the eighteenth-century Popes was remarkable for statesmanship. Benedict XIV was, perhaps, the shrewdest of them. He was genial and witty, a talented writer, a patron of art and scholarship worthy to occupy the throne of his Renaissance predecessors. But he was no Gregory VII. Rather, he accepted the world as he found it. Voltaire praised him. Horace Walpole called him "a priest without insolence or interest, a prince without favourites, a Pope without nephews." Benedict, himself, wrote that "princes are a better support to the Papacy than prelates". No wonder, then, that he made concessions to the Catholic sovereigns. By concordats, he granted to them the right of appointing to nearly all benefices in Spain, Naples and Sardinia.

The French kings claimed likewise to appoint bishops, but there was no concordat with France. The country was divided into hostile camps, Papal and anti-Papal, Jesuit and Jansenist. The Jansenists

took their theology from S. Augustine. They differed from the orthodox Jesuits in the doctrine of grace and the matter of confession and
absolution. They stressed the need for an inflexible morality, and
opposed the casuistry of the Jesuits. Their cause, a popular one, was
strengthened by their connection with the convent of Port Royal, a
noted centre of piety and education. The dispute between Rome and
the "Gallican" or "Home-Rule" section of the French Church continued throughout the century. A fierce battle of pamphlets and
books was waged between the Jansenists and the Jesuits, until in
1773 a Franciscan Pope was persuaded to suppress the Jesuit Society.
It had, however, already been turned out of France and Spain.

THE CHURCH AND THE COMMON PEOPLE

Frederick the Great called the Jesuits "the advanced sentinels of
the Court of Rome". Unswerving fidelity to Rome was their first
principle. Of all the Orders originating in the Catholic Church, they
were certainly the most remarkable. Saints and heroes and martyrs
were numbered among them. They were unflinching, tenacious,
whole-hearted, talented; but, rightly or wrongly, they earned a
reputation for intrigue and intellectual unscrupulousness. They were
rich and powerful, and like the Templars, they were dissolved by the
Pope at the instigation of the temporal sovereigns.

Christendom, whether Catholic or Protestant, was not noted for its
piety or for its zeal in spiritual things. Louis XVI's amusing comment
on a sermon to which he listened—"If the Abbé had only said a little
about Christianity, there is no subject which he would have left untouched"—goes to the root of the matter. The Churches had become
worldly. Only a great saint or a man of tremendous personality can
mould people to his will or turn them to his convictions. Ordinarily,
the Church must be served by average men; and the Church takes on
the complexion of the society in which it exists. In the eighteenth
century, indifference to things of the spirit was the rule. Enthusiasm
was taboo in polite circles. French society was more than tinged with
atheism. Clerics were worldly; bishops stayed away from their
dioceses; priests neglected their duties. In many Catholic churches,
the music of the Mass and the Offices, given by stringed instruments
instead of the organ, became a concert: and many new churches were
in the rococo style of excessive and tasteless decoration. Fat plaster
cherubs looked down from plaster ceilings, while tinted marble
columns twisted voluptuously upward to ornate capitals, creating an
atmosphere akin to that of the gilded salons of the nobility.

The indifference of fashionable society and the laxity of the clergy
are a prominent part of the picture of the age; but they are only a
part. Most men were illiterate: most men were superstitious. Many
of the simpler folk were pious. The Catholic peasant who kneeled in
genuine devotion before a wayside calvary could be matched by the
Protestant peasant who linked up his duty towards his neighbour

with his duty towards God. The Quaker merchant in England and the Pietist of Holland or Germany maintained a Puritan rigour in their morals and a profound reverence for the Bible in their life of devotion. Moreover, there were men in all the Churches who sought to reanimate them. Junipero Serra, the Spanish Franciscan friar, apostle of California, converted the Indians and civilized them; Count Zinzendorf, a devout Lutheran who spent his first Christmas in a Pennsylvanian stable which he called Bethlehem, established the fervent Moravian sect not only in the English colonies but also in Greenland and Surinam; greatest of all, John Wesley, who organized the Methodists, spent his life prodigally in preaching to the thousands of simple people who were neglected by the apathy of the established Churches. However much Wesley and the Evangelicals relied upon emotion and even upon hysteria, their insistence on a moral and methodical life created a great body of earnest Nonconformists, especially in Great Britain, who played an important part in the immense growth of her industry and commerce later in the century.

ABSOLUTE MONARCHY CRITICIZED

Monarchy is a divine institution. The king is the Lord's Anointed and holds his office by divine right. His absolutism is justified because he is God's lieutenant on earth. Such was the dominant political theory of the seventeenth century. It did not satisfy the philosophers of the eighteenth century: it was too crude, too unreasonable, too much at variance with known facts. Whether the Popes had power to bind and to loose was, perhaps, a debatable question: it was incredible that God should have elected to govern the nations by "three or four hundred persons scattered on the face of the earth under the name of princes or ministers".

Since Englishmen had executed Charles I and exiled James II, it is not surprising that it was an Englishman who declared that kings ruled by virtue of a contract with their people. John Locke, indeed, not only declared this but carried his argument farther: kings, he said, were trustees, and as such, they were not only accountable for their actions but replaceable. "Absolute monarchy is inconsistent with civil society."

Locke appealed to the Laws of Nature and of Reason. The old-fashioned writers on politics appealed to the Bible, to the works of the Fathers of the Early Christian Church, to Aristotle, to medieval commentators. But now the ages of "reason" and rational enquiry had commenced, and it was becoming more and more clear that the universe did not behave in an arbitrary manner, but that events followed certain sequences which—for want of a better term—were named "laws". In a large and loose way, this had been recognized since Babylonian days. Day and night, the seasons, the changes of the moon and of the visible stars were accepted as recurrent and inevitable. Such regularity did not preclude divine interference:

The scene at the signing of the Declaration of Independence at Philadelphia in 1776 to create the United States of America.

The Hall of Mirrors, in the Palace of Versailles, scene of the signing by the Allies and Germany, of the Treaty of Versailles in 1919.

François-Marie Arouet Voltaire, 1694–1778, French poet, historian, wit and philosopher.

Catherine the Great, 1729–96, Empress of Russia. She extended Russian territory at the expense of the Ottomans.

The scene in the Champ de Mars, Paris, in 1790, when a demonstration and religious service were held on the first anniversary of the taking of the Bastille. The people of Paris swore loyalty to the new regime.

tempest, famine and plague were "acts of God", and much ingenuity was used in working out a scheme whereby heaven, hell and purgatory were set up as spheres of the firmament. "O Lord, how manifold are Thy works. In wisdom hast Thou made them all": the whole of Psalm 104 may be said to express man's attitude towards creation.

INVESTIGATION OF SCIENTIFIC PHENOMENA

Telescope and microscope had extended the range of man's sight, and the secret places of the universe were being revealed. The multiplication of printed books carried to the many the thoughts and observations of the few. The Hebrew psalmist sang of his God "who laid the foundation of the earth, that it should not be removed for ever". By the eighteenth century, the scientists had created a new heaven and a new earth; it was two hundred years since Copernicus enunciated his theory that the earth revolved in space round the sun, and a hundred years since Galileo brought proofs of the whirling system of planets. New observations were found to be in harmony with the Copernican theory. The Englishman Isaac Newton enunciated the law of gravitation, saying that all heavenly bodies were attracted to each other, and that their attraction or pull could be expressed precisely in mathematics. Other scientists during the century probed more deeply, more systematically, and without prejudice, into phenomena closer at hand. The Frenchman Lavoisier decomposed both air and water into their component parts, and proved that burning was the union of oxygen with other matter. Linnaeus the Swede systematized the science of biology.

Medicine likewise threw off the trammels of philosophy: Boerhaave of Leyden and his pupil, von Haller of Göttingen, brought to the service of their art the new studies of chemistry and botany. Morgagni the Italian made a systematic study of morbid anatomy, following upon the great anatomists and physiologists of seventeenth-century Italy. In France and in England, the classification of facts went steadily on, under the inspiring guidance of such men as the Scottish surgeon, John Hunter, and his brother, the anatomist, William Hunter. By the end of the century, Jenner had introduced vaccination as a preventive against the scourge of smallpox, and Avenbrugger had discovered how to detect chest disease by percussion methods. Not only the universe, but man himself, was being brought into the scope of reasonable enquiry.

Nor was this all. Theologians might condemn the scientists for their impiety and error, but they condemned in vain. The new knowledge was being secured. The Royal Society in England, and the Academies in Paris and Berlin, had been established under princely patronage for the advancement of science. Periodicals were devoted to scientific discovery. Encyclopaedias, or dictionaries of universal knowledge, were issued in England, France and Germany. The printing-press had created a lay public eager for all knowledge.

Y   (H.W.)

The Church, bemused by her age-long authority, was neglecting to learn, and therefore neglecting to teach, forgetting that an ordered universe is no less a witness to the glory of God than an arbitrary one—and forgetting, too, that the ignorant cannot lead the wise. When the first volumes of the French Encyclopaedia appeared in 1752, they aroused a storm of opposition from the clergy. Its editor, Diderot, complained that the clergy expected men to become Christians, as farmers expect cattle to enter a stable, willy-nilly. He protested that they offered men a choice between commonsense and religion. The French Government interfered with Diderot's publication, but encouraged by Voltaire, he persisted and in the end, triumphed. His Encyclopaedia was composed of articles written by experts upon philosophy, religion, art, industry and politics. It condemned intolerance, slavery, stupid forms of taxation, and harsh criminal laws. It encouraged the researches of the scientists. Above all, it formed its views upon the fundamental proposition that all ideas and institutions should be tested by reason alone.

VOLTAIRE, ROUSSEAU, SMITH AND HUME

The life of Voltaire covered most of the century. With ceaseless energy and a cruel wit, he poured out a mass of writing of all sorts—dramas, history, satirical fiction, pamphlets, philosophy and letters—ridiculing the follies of government and society. He often exaggerated, and was often unscrupulous: for in any age, authority is always liable to folly. Voltaire spared nothing. He directed the savagest of his attacks against the Church, frequently urging his correspondents to "crush the infamous thing"; so great, indeed, was his detestation of ecclesiastics that he derided Protestants as well as Catholics. Such was his animus against authority that he rejected the Bible, preferring the revelation of God within him. The excellence of his style—and the length of his life—made him a European institution. If any one man can be said to have made the French Revolution inevitable, it was this bewigged skeleton who was the companion and correspondent of Frederick the Great, who spent the autumn of his life in exile at Geneva, and who returned to Paris just before his death, to be crowned with laurel at a public performance of his play "Irene".

Voltaire was all brain. Rousseau, his younger contemporary, urged men to return to simplicity. He mistrusted the new knowledge. Civilization brings demoralization and servility: government is too elaborate: in a natural state, men are equal and have a tendency towards goodness. This sentiment was fashionable in Rousseau's day—the savage being looked upon as an innocent whose perversion by civilization was only too certain. In his book *The Social Contract*, Rousseau declared that man is born free, "yet everywhere we see him in chains": he further asserted that government is only good in so far as it expresses the "general will" of the people. What Rousseau attempted to find was a way of escape from the complexity and problems of civilization: and it is easy to sympathize with his attempt. But when a sophisticated citizen talks of the innocence and goodness of natural society, it is only because his very sophistication gives him a false picture of the "noble savage". Rousseau, therefore, hardly used reason as a criterion.

In other fields of enquiry, reason made lasting conquests. Beccaria, an Italian jurist, examined the harsh criminal laws then in vogue and proved that they accomplished nothing; he pointed out with conviction that prevention of crime, and not revenge, is the aim of society. The Scottish professor, Adam Smith, wrote the first systematic work of political economy in a style and on a scale that make even that study a pleasant one. His *Wealth of Nations* argued convincingly against governmental restrictions on trade, saying that the duty of government was done when it had secured justice and defence.

Against the passionate assertions of Rousseau, we may place the calm statement of David Hume, the sceptical Scottish philosopher: "The world is too young to fix many general truths in politics." Hume was a sober historian, and those who survey the past of mankind dispassionately are apt to eschew wild schemes and hopes for humanity: they doubt the perfectibility of human nature, which the idealists assume as a fact. The development of an historical, and therefore critical and sceptical, sense was an accompaniment of the scientific spirit of the century. It is rash to play the fool with human institutions: by historical study, we can prove their worth and hold fast to those that are good. These were the assumptions that, consciously or unconsciously, underlay all the speculations made by the English authors during the age of reason.

MASTERS OF LANGUAGE

Perhaps no nobler memorials of the age persist to-day than the prose of Dr. Johnson, Edward Gibbon and Edmund Burke. Dr. Johnson was as typical of his country as Voltaire was of France. He is chiefly known to fame as a superb conversationalist and a lexicographer, a man of shrewd commonsense and sound scholarship, a burly, kindly figure who ruled over English letters like a king. His writings offer no panacea for the ills of society: yet no man—not even in France—was more conscious of them. "At the conclusion of a ten years' war, how are we recompensed for the death of multitudes and the expense of millions, but by contemplating the sudden glories of paymasters and agents, contractors and commissaries, whose equipages shine like meteors, and whose palaces rise like exhalations?"

For Gibbon, writing was his life, and his writing was a *History of the Decline and Fall of the Roman Empire*, a monumental work of unsurpassable dignity and economy, ranging over a dozen centuries of Europe. Quotation from it on anything but a grand scale is futile, but one sentence may be given, if only to show Gibbon's affinity with his age: "The generality of princes, if they were stripped of their purple, and cast naked into the world, would immediately sink to the lowest rank of society, without a hope of emerging from their obscurity."

Edmund Burke, in his parliamentary speeches, wrought the English language into "an amplitude of comprehension and richness of imagination, superior to every orator, ancient or modern". The words quoted are Macaulay's. The richness of Burke's imagination coloured the political fabric of his speeches; emotion as well as intellect was given expression.

The emotional side of man's nature had already found vent for some men in pietism and evangelical religion. In literature, a romantic return to nature was manifest in the lyrics of such writers as Goethe and Blake: these reveal a personal reaction that comes refreshingly after the ordered couplets of Pope and the classical French dramatists. Rousseau had set the fashion of appealing to the emotions, in his *Discourses* and in *Emile*: after him, emotion, as well as reason, joined in protest against insincerity and injustice. In music—allowing much for its more direct emotional nature—a similar change is noticeable in passing from the disciplined beauty of Bach and Handel to the romantic works of Gluck and Beethoven. Men were returning with open eyes to Nature, to Religion, and, with the growth of the historic spirit, to the Past.

> "The curfew tolls the knell of parting day,
> The lowing herd wind slowly o'er the lea,
> The ploughman homeward plods his weary way,
> And leaves the world to darkness and to me."

These first lines of Gray's "Elegy" were written in 1751. They were recited—so the story goes—by the British commander, Wolfe, as he passed down the St. Lawrence at the head of his bewigged and powdered redcoats to the successful assault on Quebec. The story has considerable significance, if we remember how closely the life and happenings of the century seemed to imitate those of the stage.

CHAPTER 61

FREDERICK THE GREAT

FREDERICK WILLIAM I of Prussia, the man who dispensed with pomp and ceremony, who scraped and saved every thaler he could and turned his kingdom into a camp, drank himself to death in 1740. His son, Frederick, commonly called Frederick the Great, succeeded him and ruled for the next forty-six years. With Frederick the Great, kingship in the eighteenth century came into its own again. He was not one of Gibbon's obscure personalities born by accident in the purple, but a leader of men. But for the overshadowing of all

Europe by Napoleon at the end of the century, Frederick the Great's reputation would have stood pre-eminent. He was both soldier and statesman. He made Prussia a power to be reckoned with.

He was twenty-eight when he came to the throne. He had been a quick, sensitive child with a passion for music and the arts, but the education of the barrack-square to which his boorish father subjected him, and the cruel rigour of Prussian discipline, warped his natural geniality into cynicism. It did not impair his gifts of mind, although it restricted their development. At the age of eighteen he ran away, was retaken, compelled to watch the execution of his beloved accomplice, and forced back into the old hideous routine. Luckily for him, his mother and sister were both sane and sympathetic, and were devoted to him, and his tutors were kinder than Frederick William I intended them to be. His mother he could visit only by stealth; and both he and his sister grew up to loathe their father's memory.

FREDERICK'S POLICY OF AGGRESSION

It was not an ideal training for a prince. The discipline had a lasting effect upon him, but his was essentially a nature amenable to persuasion and enlightened education. He found escape from intolerable tyranny, as any clever man would, in hypocrisy. Deceit and insincerity were his only defences; he learnt to be self-reliant and friendless, to control his emotion, to depend wholly upon his own strong clear intellect. He became a lonely man, and all through his life he kept his own counsel, the complete autocrat. Unlike his father, who despised the French, Frederick enjoyed French literature, preferred to talk in French, and even wrote French verse. He corresponded with Voltaire and other philosophers, and imbibed the ideas then current in French literary circles, which included a disregard of religion amounting to a cynical atheism, and a stoical acceptance of both good and evil fortune—in other words, a reliance on reason rather than emotion. As a boy, he had penned a refutation of the politics of Machiavelli's book, *The Prince*, which puts considerations of state above morality: as a king, he placed the welfare and extension of his kingdom first, regardless of the means employed.

He inherited a full treasury, a large and well-drilled army, and subjects accustomed to autocratic rule. All these he used for the aggrandizement of his power. He began by claiming Silesia from Maria Theresa of Austria, and fought two wars, the first to win it, the second to keep it. This was an unscrupulous piece of robbery. France and Britain were involved in these wars, France as an ally of Frederick, Britain as a friend of Maria Theresa. But France and Britain had their own lasting quarrel over maritime and colonial affairs. From 1746 to 1756, Anglo-French rivalry was working up to war-pitch again, and Maria Theresa was scheming to recover Silesia. Austrian diplomacy managed to reverse the old alliances, so that France and Austria—Bourbon and Habsburg—became allies

THE GROWTH OF

Prussia, which eventually came to dominate the German Empire, was formed gradually. The Mark of Brandenburg, once occupied by Slavonic tribes, was reconquered by the Germans after the tenth century, and in 1415 was bestowed upon the House of Hohenzollern. East Prussia passed by marriage to the Electors of Brandenburg in 1618; they took the title of Kings of Prussia in 1701.

BALTIC

SEA

SWEDISH POMERANIA

EAST
PRUSSIA

POMERANIA

Danzig

*Remaining
from the
conquests of the Teutonic Knights*

WEST
PRUSSIA

*From 1ˢᵗ partition of the
Polish Kingdom 1772*

NBURG

*ancient "marks" of
the heathen.*

°Berlin

POSEN
1815
(Formerly Polish)

RUSSIA
(Poland)

1815
SAXO

ONY

SILESIA

*Taken from Maria Theresa
of Austria, 1745*

BOHEMIA

MORAVIA

□□□ *Acquisitions of Frederick
the Great.*

▨▨▨ *Lands assigned to Prussia
at the Congress of Vienna, 1815*

AUSTRIA   HUNGARY

°Vienna   Scale
0   100   200

Miles

PRUSSIAN POWER

In 1772 the first partition of an enfeebled Poland enabled Brandenburg and
East Prussia to be linked by the acquisition of West Prussia, and Danzig was
gained from a further partition. The Napoleonic wars, and the defeat of the
Prussians at Jena in 1806, deprived the Hohenzollerns of their gains, but the Congress of Vienna restored these, together with Westphalia and Swedish Pomerania.

against Prussia; Austrian diplomacy managed also to array Russia and Saxony against Frederick, who was now surrounded by foes. Great Britain, with interests in Hanover, concluded a treaty with him and subsidized him, while herself keeping France busy outside Europe. Frederick struck first by invading Saxony: the Seven Years' War had begun.

In Europe, this war comprised seven bloody campaigns. Frederick himself fought ten great battles, and estimated, after the war, that one-ninth of his subjects had perished in it. The net result was that he kept Silesia. The cost of keeping it was widespread devastation and poverty and the killing and maiming of millions of men—Prussians, Austrians, Frenchmen, Hungarians, Saxons, Hessians, Mecklen-burgers, Brunswickers, Hanoverians, Swedes and Russians. Frederick made himself a great reputation as a soldier, and the seven years of warfare left the map of Europe unchanged.

The end justifies the means. This taunt, often flung at the Jesuits, was an accepted maxim of conduct in international politics in the eighteenth century. Reason is a good servant, but a bad master when justice and faith make way for the worship of the state. Even in the fury of battle, Frederick's cynicism revealed itself. "Dogs! would you live for ever?" he shouted on one occasion to his men, as they were lagging back from repeated charges against the enemy's position.

FREDERICK'S DOMESTIC POLICY

Yet Frederick the Great was something more than the soldier of genius who continued his father's brutal discipline over conscripted peasants and kidnapped foreigners. He governed Prussia for twenty-three years after the war, and during those years, he worked un-ceasingly for the good of his kingdom. Although he was superior in intellect and talent to the greater number of his subjects, and knew himself to be superior, he was not vain. He dressed badly in an old grey hat, an old snuff-stained uniform of blue cloth and unpolished boots; but his demeanour showed the king. He could talk well and his voice was clear and resonant. He lived, apart from his wife, in *Sans Souci* (Carefree Castle) at Potsdam, and his long day was made up of parades, interviews, state business with secretaries, voluminous writing, inspections of household accounts and menus, and—for relaxation—flute-playing. Frederick strove hard to repeople and replenish his wasted lands. He distributed spare cavalry horses to needy farmers and remitted rents in the hard years following the wars. He repaid the towns that had been held to ransom by the enemy. He overhauled the government, tightened up the system of taxation, increased the army of clerks and inspectors to see that his will became law. He encouraged agriculture by the reclamation of swamps. He settled West Prussia, which he stole in 1773 from the unhappy kingdom of Poland. He set up state granaries and state warehouses, and protected new industries. He reformed the law.

The churches he treated with intolerant indifference. When the Lutherans complained of his blocking out the light from their church at Potsdam, he jested: "Blessed are they which have not seen and yet have believed". To a friend who had changed his religion for gain, and then asked him for a rich canonry, he said: "I have still a place of Rabbi to dispose of; turn Jew and you shall have it". He taxed the clergy, and then exhorted them to practise apostolic poverty.

The clue to Frederick's character is his clear intelligence, which saw through shams. It was his dealings with the wreckage of medieval institutions and with the wreckage of the Reformation that show him so clearly to be the supreme monarch of the age of reason. He was the true father of his country, and although he treated his ministers as mere clerks, making all decisions himself, he never shrank from the immense burdens of state. Two days before he died, he rose at five in the morning and was busy with affairs of state. His energy was not without result. He may truthfully be said to have laid the foundations of modern Germany. His reign may be summed up in the three words—intelligence, autocracy, efficiency.

RESULTS OF INDIA'S WEAKNESS

We have seen how Akbar had failed to grant toleration to his Indian subjects, and how Aurangzebe's ambitious schemes had sapped Mogul power. Moslem princes and governors still despised Hindus, Jains and Buddhists, though they respected the fighting qualities of Rajputs and Mahrattas. But the Moguls failed to drive off the invaders, who came from the north-west and from overseas.

Nadir Shah, the warrior-king of Persia, marched across the plains of Hindustan and crushed the Mogul army in 1739. His men slaughtered unnumbered multitudes and carried back with them as loot the treasures stored up during three centuries of Mogul rule. Then the Afghans raided the plains. Their chief, Ahmad Shah, routed the forces of the Maratha confederacy at Panipat in 1761.

This battle of Panipat marks the end of the Mogul domination. India, peninsula and plains, was anarchic. Within three years, the English East India Company, a group of respectable London merchants, had ousted the French from southern India and had become responsible for the government of Bengal. They were even accepted as the "protectors" of the Moguls at Delhi.

The explanation of this astonishing political transformation is simple and straightforward. The gates into India are in the north-west, and it was through them that India's conquerors came, time after time. Once in Hindustan, they had to choose, either to settle there as the reigning caste and dynasty, or else to despoil the country and return whence they came; for the gateways of the north-west passes are devious, long and vulnerable; they make a good link, but a bad highway. Just at the juncture when no warlike successors appeared to stay and supplant the miserable tail of the Mogul line, the French and English traders were established in a few footholds on the coasts. They built factories where their merchants and clerks could live in a sort of college life, protected by a few troops, and employed in accumulating wares against the periodic arrival of cargo vessels from far-off Europe. Moreover, they belonged to an entirely different civilization from the Indian, one which valued the individual, one which had behind it the experience of two thousand or more years of organized and efficient government, one which had come to believe in the reign of law and reason. These newcomers must preserve their highway—the sea; for they could not live and breed in India, let alone merge with the native races. They came for trade: they must have order. Their governors and factors at French Pondicherry and English Madras took a hand in the politics of the native states. They raised battalions of native troops—known as *sepoys*— and armed and drilled them on steady European lines. With the aid of these troops, they found it possible to establish their power.

EXPANSION OF BRITISH INFLUENCE IN INDIA

Notwithstanding the work of their governors, particularly of Dupleix, the French possessions lagged behind the English in wealth of trade. Dupleix managed to acquire for a brief space the mastery of all South India. Then his work was ruined by the military genius of a clerk in the English company's service, Robert Clive, who defeated a large native army at Arcot. Dupleix was recalled by the French company which, like its rival, the English company, deprecated these political schemes as being harmful to commerce.

With the outbreak of the Seven Years' War in Europe, hostilities began again between the rival companies in South India. Dupleix's successor was decisively beaten by Sir Eyre Coote, and the French were left with two small trading-stations only, one at Surat and the other at Calicut. Meanwhile, the Nawab of Bengal had attacked the English settlement at Calcutta, and his men had barbarously imprisoned the English in a tiny guard-room—"the Black Hole of Calcutta"—where most of them died of suffocation. Clive sailed from Madras and overthrew the Nawab's army at Plassey, pursued it for six miles and captured its camp and baggage, guns, elephants and horses. This battle gave the victors the mastery of Bengal. The English company appointed another Nawab, who massacred some 200 Europeans and was decisively defeated at Buxar by Hector Munro in 1764. Clive, then on leave in England, predicted that this battle would give his countrymen the mastery of India. Indeed, after the battle, the emperor granted the company the *diwani* of Bengal, Bihar and Orissa—that is, the right of supervising the revenues.

For the company's servants, it was a flood-tide of fortune. They made money out of Indian princes and merchants by methods only to be described as bribery and blackmail. Clive himself profited in the grand manner, although he did his best to stop petty corruption.

One man stood firm against temptation—Warren Hastings, "writer" in the company's employ, governor of Bengal in 1772, and governor-general of all the company's possessions in 1774. He was not only the first but the greatest of governor-generals, and perhaps the greatest of Anglo-Indian administrators. He created an entirely new administration and tried to keep it honest: he strove against brigandage and injustice: he held the territories entrusted to his care, in spite of native wars and French schemes, while Great Britain, during the rebellion of her American colonists, was at war with half Europe. More than all, he fostered the study of Indian languages, customs and laws, desiring, as he said, "to found the authority of the British government in Bengal on its ancient laws"; he had himself studied Persian and Bengali. Warren Hastings was neither a factor nor an adventurous soldier, but a statesman. Throughout his rule, he was bitterly opposed by members of his own council: at its termination, he was impeached before the House of Lords for cruelty, injustice and oppression. The trial, which lasted seven years and cost £70,000, ended in his acquittal.

Before his trial began it was decided to abandon the system of government under which his difficulties had arisen. From 1784, the British Government itself supervised the political activities undertaken by the East India Company, and appointed as governors-general men chosen from outside the company's service.

BRITISH SEA-POWER

The victory of the English East India merchants over their French rivals was due primarily to the sea-power of Great Britain, and it was this sea-power which decided the American issue of the Seven Years' War. In Europe, the narrow seas were held by British warships, and small forces, despatched to the aid of Hanover and of Frederick the Great, acquitted themselves valiantly. These, however, could have but little effect upon the general course of the struggle between Great Britain and France. It was across the long rollers of the Atlantic that the main British effort was put forth.

The first shots that opened the contest in the New World were a volley of musketry fired by order of a Virginian militia colonel, George Washington, who advanced with a reconnoitring force against French outposts in the Ohio valley. This was in 1752. An expedition to the same valley under the British General Braddock, three years later, came to grief in an ambush. When war was officially declared in 1756, the superiority of the British navy prejudiced the chances of the French from the outset. The traditions derived from Blake were nobly continued by Anson, Hawke and Boscawen and their captains. Moreover, in William Pitt Great Britain discovered a war-minister of singular genius. It was he who pursued relentlessly the complete humiliation of France. Under cover of a blockade of the French coast, Pitt dispatched expeditions to all parts of the world.

To America went the transports which carried the English and Highland regiments destined for the conquest of Canada itself. This conquest was to be effected by a threefold advance upon the colony, two columns moving by land and the third by water. That part which fell to the navy—the passage of the uncharted St. Lawrence—was superbly accomplished by Admiral Saunders and his officers. They landed General Wolfe's army opposite Quebec, the citadel of New France. Wolfe's redcoats forced the stronghold: the skill of the mariners made it possible for them to do so. Both Wolfe and the French General Montcalm fell mortally wounded, and their countries could ill spare either of them: nevertheless the capture of Quebec foredoomed the rest of New France to a British occupation.

BRITAIN AND HER COLONIES

In 1763, at the peace of Paris, Great Britain "bestrode the world like a colossus"; her fleets were unchallenged and unchallengeable, her arms crowned with victories in the four quarters of the globe. Yet even this did not represent her utmost effort. William Pitt had been displaced by the machinations of the new sovereign George III, and peace was concluded without Pitt's approval. To end for ever the domination of France in Europe—that had been the great war-minister's object, as indeed it had been Marlborough's object. Pitt, like Marlborough, was frustrated by small-minded men. France survived as a military power, to produce the Napoleonic nightmare which was to cost Great Britain and all Europe so much blood and treasure.

But to all appearances Great Britain was supreme among nations in 1763. She now ruled all North America east of the Mississippi: she had gained West Indian islands and trading-posts in West Africa: she had ensured the domination of India by her merchants: she had even restored her superfluous conquests—Havana and Manila to Spain, St. Lucia, Martinique, Belleisle and Goree to France. Within sixteen years, she was fighting against her rebellious colonists in North America, against France, against Spain and against Holland, and she was hard put to it to hold her own.

The thirteen colonies of Great Britain in America were strung out along some 2000 miles of coast from the St. Croix river to the borders of Florida. They had been built up diversely—the northern colonies as refuges for Puritans, the southern colonies as deliberate "plantations". New York and New Jersey had been taken by force of arms from the Dutch. Their populations showed a rich variety of race, religion, occupation, temperament and mode of living. The New Englanders were mainly of English stocks—self-reliant, hardworking members of independent Christian congregations. They farmed a sterile soil intelligently, and exported their corn, timber, tar and salt-fish in Boston-built keels: their sailors were hardy and skilful, their trade largely with the West Indies. The more cosmopolitan populace

of New York and New Jersey included Dutch and Swedes who profited by the fur-trade from the Hudson valley; their opulent merchants kept great domestic establishments staffed by negro-slaves.
In Pennsylvania were the English Quakers and the German Evangelical sects—the "Pennsylvanian Dutch", tolerant, vigorous, but not
always practical in things political. The iron-fields of this state were
already being worked in the eighteenth century.

Maryland, which contained a considerable Catholic population,
and Virginia, the "Old Dominion", both lived on the tobacco-crop,
estimated all values in terms of tobacco, and enjoyed the social
amenities of a leisured life, at the expense of a great servile black
population who tilled their plantations. North Carolina was the
poorest of all the colonies, peopled by a motley collection of small
farmers who lived on their own scanty produce: they were chiefly of
Swiss, German, Scots or Irish stocks. South Carolina raised rice as
its chief crop, negro slaves doing the work. In Georgia, the latest
colony to be founded, were English Westcountrymen, Moravians,
Salzburgers, and a strong group of Highlanders—all useful people in
a country whose climate made big demands on the stamina and
resolution of Europeans.

A traveller through the colonies would have noted the differences
of race and social organization: he would have observed, as an outstanding fact, the great divergence in temperament and outlook
between the northern and the southern colonies: but he would also
have noted the general well-being and outspokenness of the colonists.
He would have scorned as fantastic the notion that they were
oppressed by the mother-country. Yet these colonists rebelled against
the mother-country in 1775, and after a few years, they proved powerful enough to gain their independence from the mother-country.

GRIEVANCES OF THE AMERICAN COLONISTS

Great Britain, like all colonial powers, regulated colonial trade.
Regulation meant restriction. Restriction led to smuggling, and like
the English at home, the colonists proved themselves most competent
smugglers. The loss of revenue alarmed the British Parliament, and,
of course, defeated the object of its trade regulations. So the British
Parliament took steps to raise colonial revenues in other ways, *e.g.*,
by passing a Stamp Act requiring all legal documents to bear stamps
of prescribed value. This was obviously not trade regulation but
actual taxation. The Americans fiercely objected to being taxed by a
body in which they had no representation.

But, long before the Stamp Act of 1765, the issues were clearly
marked. The Act was a consequence, not a cause. The colonials
acknowledged Great Britain's right to regulate trade, but not to
regulate it in such a manner as to benefit herself only: if the advantage was mutual, smuggling would not happen. Boston merchants
properly objected to the issue of "general" writs of search to the

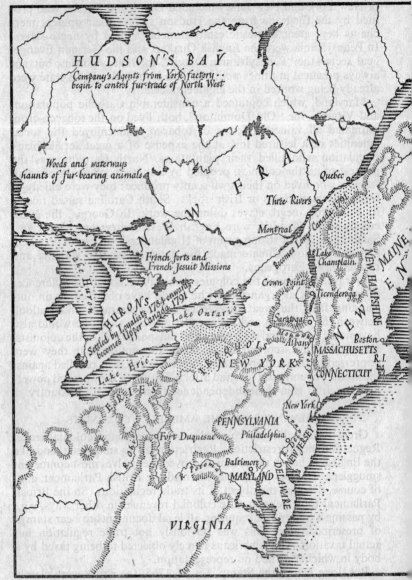

NEW ENGLAND

The English settlement in New Hampshire began in 1623, at Massachusetts Bay in 1629, in Maine in 1632, in Connecticut in 1635, and at New Haven in 1638. Maine and Massachusetts, and Connecticut and New Haven became joined, and New Jersey was founded in 1665. The French landed at Acadia (afterwards known as Nova Scotia) in 1605. Quebec was founded in 1608 and Montreal in 1642.

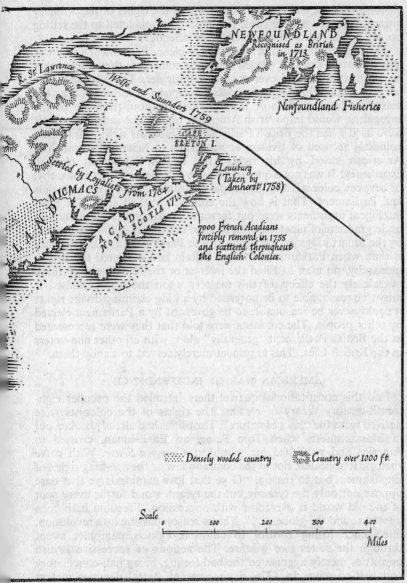

NEWFOUNDLAND
Recognised as British
in 1713.

R. St. Lawrence

Wolfe and Saunders 1759

Newfoundland Fisheries

CAPE
BRETON I.

Settled by Loyalists from 1784

Louisburg
(Taken by
Amherst 1758)

MICMACS

ACADIA
NOVA SCOTIA 1713

7000 French Acadians
forcibly removed in 1755
and scattered throughout
the English Colonies.

⦂⦂⦂ Densely wooded country   ⧓⧓⧓ Country over 1000 ft.

Scale
0   100   200   300   400

Miles

AND NEW FRANCE

The freedom and prosperity of the English settlements on the east coast of
North America were in marked contrast to the poverty-stricken and badly
administered French possessions of New France. Two foreign settlements in
New England, the Dutch colony of New Netherlands (renamed New York in
1664) and the Swedish settlement on the River Delaware, were incorporated.

customs-officers, as being infringements of the rights of the ordinary citizen. Such writs were liable to abuse. They objected to the setting up of special Admiralty courts to try offenders without juries.

The logic of the position was only too clear. Parliament's case was that desperate diseases needed desperate remedies: they argued that no Boston jury would ever convict a smuggler. The Massachusetts lawyers argued that smuggling was a symptom of a disease, viz., the biased trade regulations of Britain which, without the work of the smugglers, would impoverish American trade. The same arguments were used when the British Parliament asserted its right to transport colonials accused of treason or misprision to Britain for trial. The American stood by his rights: the British Parliament claimed expediency. It was not a quarrel between colonials and the monarchy, or between colonials and the people of Britain, but between colonials and Parliament. That is how the colonials looked at it. The most intelligent arguments were put forward by Alexander Hamilton, an undergraduate of nineteen, who pointed out that the charters granted by the Stuart kings gave no authority to Parliament at all. The truth is that, when Parliament in Great Britain had mastered the British monarchy, no man had had the interest or the intelligence to think out clearly the effects of this mastery upon the free colonists. It might be reasonable to be governed by a king claiming divine right: it could never be reasonable to be governed by a Parliament elected by other people. The colonists were told that they were represented in the British Parliament "generally" along with all other non-voters in the British Isles. This argument merely served to annoy them.

AMERICAN WAR OF INDEPENDENCE

Into this constitutional quarrel there intruded the peculiar eighteenth-century theory of reason. The rights of the colonists were derived from the "laws of nature". Hostilities had already broken out in Massachusetts when Tom Paine, an Englishman, crossed to America and published his pamphlet *Common Sense*. With naïve rhetoric it appealed, not to the common law or the age-long rights of Englishmen, but to reason. "O ye that love mankind; ye that dare oppose not only the tyranny but the tyrant, stand forth; every spot of the old world is overcome with oppression. Freedom hath been hunted round the globe. . . ." This is reason passing into revolution, intelligence losing control to emotion. Paine's pamphlet swept through the states like wildfire. The actions of successive British ministries merely aggravated the bad feeling, being half-conciliatory and half-coercive. In 1776, a congress of states' deputies met at Philadelphia and issued the famous Declaration of Independence which asserted the natural rights of man.

The attempt by Great Britain to retain her colonies by military force failed. The war was not popular in Britain. The soldiers were handicapped by the novelty of the terrain—woods, swamps, immense distances of inhospitable country—and also by the elusiveness of a citizen-militia fighting in its own land. In George Washington, the states had a capable, wise, if not brilliant, commander. The British generals were of indifferent talent. Worst of all, Britain was opposed by France, Spain and Holland: she lost command of the seas at a fatal moment, with the result that Cornwallis was forced to surrender at Yorktown in 1781. No censure can be too heavy for the incompetence of Great Britain's corrupt politicians; they could neither prevent war nor conduct it successfully. Yet the traditions and environment of the colonists were so divergent from those of the mother-country as to make some sort of separation in authority inevitable. The unwisdom of the British governments decided the time of the separation and the form it took.

Disputes feed on themselves: once started, the American revolt grew with every misunderstanding. But, throughout, the lead was taken by a clamorous "secession" party; there were thousands of Americans, especially in the southern states, who remained loyal to Britain, and who, rather than live under the new American government, migrated into Nova Scotia, New Brunswick and the West Indies, and also founded the state of Ontario in Canada. Many, too, returned to the mother-country: all of them had suffered intense hardship because of their persistent loyalty to the British cause.

THE CONSTITUTION OF THE UNITED STATES

A general peace in 1783 recognized the United States as a sovereign power among nations. It was to begin with a clumsy confederation of jealous communities. In 1787, deputies discussed and framed the resolutions which compose the federal constitution. Their task was complex; they had to resolve the several interests of thirteen independent democratic states into harmony with the urgent need for an overriding authority. They could not, of course, foresee the time when their constitution would have to serve the needs of a federal government comprising forty-eight separate states. They had much the same task as the politicians of Britain had faced when the quarrel with the colonies first arose. They did their work efficiently. The constitution of the United States has stood the test of time remarkably well. The man behind it was Alexander Hamilton, who would have been the first to admit that his fellow-countrymen began their labours with the inestimable advantage of having their societies based upon the fundamental commonsense and justice of the English common law. Washington became the first president of the new Federal Republic, and after a period of bickering and recrimination, the component states fell to working together in a practical way.

For many years a depression afflicted American trade. The public debts were large and there was no machinery to discharge them. The great wars in Europe, caused by the French Revolution, and the war between America and Great Britain, caused by Britain's insistence upon her right to search neutral vessels, almost wiped out American commerce between 1812 and 1815. The energies of her citizens turned towards the new lands of the west. Ohio, Kentucky and Tennessee received thousands of immigrants from the east. These settled on their 160-acre allotments (granted by the federal government), cleared the undergrowth, ringed or felled the trees, sowed the crop, and lived in a rough log-shelter until harvest. The shelter gave place to a decent log-cabin, the log-cabin to a two-storeyed house. By 1815, immigration and expansion had raised the population to eight millions, and there were eighteen states in the union. This quiet period of self-development saw the beginning of the prosperity of the union based upon the exploitation of the Middle West. It also saw the beginning of the ominous dispute over negro slavery. Congress disallowed slavery in the new states, and there came into being the distinction, only dimly outlined previously, between states which countenanced slavery and those which did not. The true, tragic import of this, however, lay in the future: the new republic had established itself and was, in Paine's words, "an asylum for mankind".

CHAPTER 62

ENLIGHTENMENT AND MACHINES

"EVERY spot of the old world is overcome with oppression." So wrote Tom Paine to the citizens of the new world. In the endless adventure of politics, there are few periods so interesting as the later eighteenth century. The states of Europe were despotisms. By their efforts to make their countries prosperous and powerful, the despots gave benefits to their subjects. One benefit they withheld: freedom.

Freedom is a much-abused word and a much-abused thing. The masses of men were then still illiterate; the merchants looked only to their own profit, the noblemen to their own privileges. Gustavus III of Sweden by a *coup d'état* made himself master of his country, which for half a century had suffered miserable misrule under rival factions. Gustavus was talented and shrewd: he had energy and patriotism and could manage men. He reformed the administration, the judiciary, the currency, the army, the navy; he freed the Press; he abolished torture; he won the admiration of the peasants, and with them drove out the Danish invaders. He remodelled the constitution so that the monarchy, although strengthened, was still limited by Parliament. Yet he was murdered by a group of nobles.

Who did most for mankind, Caesar or Brutus? The question still stands to-day. In the eighteenth century, reason was leading by two divergent paths to a conflict: it was reasonable that men should be well-governed and orderly if they were to live together in amity; it was also clearly reasonable that men should be free. What was reasonable in the eyes of enlightened monarchs was unreasonable in the eyes of the champions of freedom. Monarchs might think that they existed to do good to their people. Disciples of freedom thought that monarchs should exist only by the will of their people. We have the paradox of revolution in a world of enlightened despots.

UNFETTERED POWER OF THE DESPOTS

Europe had a bad political heritage. The dual control of mankind by Church and State had finally broken down at the Reformation. There had always been a conflict between the spiritual and secular powers. Now the secular powers were supreme. Of old, their divine sanction came from the Popes, who could excommunicate and outlaw them; now, they claimed a divine right as part of their own nature. Charles III of Spain told the Pope that he was responsible to God alone. The secular powers were now unchecked and untrammelled, save in Britain, Holland and Sweden. Only the revolution of their own subjects could limit them.

The Church could still boast its saints, but they were not its leaders. It had persecuted when it should have persuaded, asserted when it should have argued, and ignored when it should have learned. It feared knowledge and stood upon privilege. The despots dealt hardly with it. Frederick the Great was impartial: "I stand neutral", he said, "between Geneva and Rome." To him religion mattered nothing, patriotism everything. Joseph II of Austria appointed his own bishops and made marriage a civil contract. He abolished nearly six hundred monasteries and devoted their wealth to the service of education, on the ground that "the principles of monasticism contradict human reason". In Spain, Charles III taxed the church lands, which were estimated to form one-fifth of the total area of the country, and put a check upon any further acquisition of land by the ecclesiastics. During his father's reign, eight hundred people had been burned at the stake by order of the Inquisition. Charles kept the Inquisition, but under his rule only four persons suffered such a death. Charles further insisted on being judge of the expediency of the Pope's actions in regard to the Church in Spain. He expelled the Jesuits. These "papal soldiers" were also suppressed in Portugal, France and the Bourbon states in Italy. The universal dislike of the Jesuit Order even resulted in its dissolution by the Pope, who acted under Bourbon persuasion. Thus did the authority of the Catholic Church suffer, even at the hands of the "Most Catholic King" of Spain, while in Russia, the Empress Catherine II appropriated the lands of the Greek Orthodox Church.

Apart from Frederick the Great, who may be said to have been creating both a state and a nation in Prussia, the outstanding despots were Charles III of Spain, Catherine II of Russia and Joseph II of Austria. Indeed, it is one of the outstanding facts of the eighteenth century that an undistinguished group of monarchs in the first half was followed by such a vigorous group in the second half.

In Spain, a country with immense potential resources in her over-seas colonies, there was plenty of scope for enlightenment. Charles III was called to its throne in 1759. He had had experience as Bourbon king of the Two Sicilies, where he had attempted to reform an outworn feudal system which had been imposed upon a medley of stocks descended from Greek, Carthaginian, Roman, Arab, Lombard and Norman. Charles was a man of strong character, if not of exceptional ability. His life was that of an honest and methodical man of business. His common sense kept him a robust sportsman. His sincere piety did not forbid his interest in the advancement of knowledge. In his twenty-nine years of rule he worked wonders. Aided by such talented ministers as Pedro Rodriguez, he reorganized the national finances, stabilizing them upon a national bank. Irksome duties on manufactures and commodities were reduced or abolished, and their place taken by a graduated income-tax. Restrictions upon colonial trade were swept away. The response to this was astonishing: the volume of colonial trade increased fivefold. New industries, such as glass-making and leather-working, were set up with the help of foreign experts, and the needs of the farmer were recognized by the establishment of a school for agriculture. Attempts were made to afforest the barren regions. Old canals were completed, new canals begun. Miles of new roads were built. Hospitals, infirmaries, workhouses, schools and colleges were founded with the money taken from the Jesuits. Towns were policed effectively and vagabondage checked, the laws revised and justice made speedy.

Such an achievement was all the more creditable in view of the losses Spain bore during the Seven Years' War. Yet Charles III's work is a warning of the insecurity of despotic benevolence. The despot dies; another takes his place. In Spain, all the labours undertaken by Charles III were undone by his successor Charles IV.

CATHERINE THE GREAT OF RUSSIA

Russia, if she fared less badly than Spain, yet gained nothing tangible from the Seven Years' War. Within two years of its close, the worthless young Tsar Peter III was deposed and murdered—probably with the connivance of his wife, a German princess, who succeeded him as the Empress Catherine II. This remarkable woman ruled Russia for thirty-four years. She lacked perseverance, but had courage, good humour and an understanding of human nature. She was a true daughter of her age, being widely read in French authors, who, for her, included not only the romancers, but Diderot the encyclopaedist and Montesquieu the writer of *L'Esprit des lois* (The nature of laws). She even staged a grand assembly of representatives of all races and classes at Moscow. It was an elaborate farce ending in much talk after the Muscovite fashion. Catherine was also a disciple of the Italian Beccaria: she lessened the severity of punishments and stopped the use of torture.

On the whole, however, her personal enlightenment did little to ameliorate the lot of her people. She was a sensible woman and liked to see her subjects happy, but she accepted serfdom as the basis of society. When she made a grand tour of her provinces in 1787, accompanied by the Emperor Joseph II of Austria and a swarm of foreign diplomats, charming villages sprang up in her path—sham pleasaunces devised by the ingenuity of Prince Potemkin, her favourite. Catherine dispensed largess to the Ukrainian and Crimean peasants, and entertained her entourage with sparkling conversation. She squandered great sums of money founding a new city to be called Ekaterinoslav after her: within ten years, the site was almost desolate. Her Court was extravagant; and under her rule, taxation was burdensome. Yet, if Catherine's internal policy cannot compare with that of Charles III of Spain, it must be remembered that her empire was vast and backward, that the ingrained Muscovite sloth and corruption of that period made any reforms a herculean task. Her despotism was a tremendous improvement upon her ill-fated husband's misguided imitation of the methods employed by Frederick the Great. Imported political devices seldom give satisfaction.

POLICY OF REFORM IN THE AUSTRIAN EMPIRE

Of all the despotisms, that of Joseph II of Austria had, at the same time, the most reason and the least prospect of success. Some sort of racial and traditional unity gave a stimulus to reform in Spain and Russia, while Great Britain and France were homogeneous states. Joseph II was the Holy Roman Emperor. His subjects—Germans, Italians, Slavs, Czechs, Croats, Magyars, Roumanians, Belgians—had no bond save that of their common emperor. His dominions had no unity save that vaguely afforded by the mighty river Danube and its tributaries which traversed them. Belgium, indeed—or the Austrian Netherlands, as it was then called—had not even a physical contact with the rest of the empire. The Holy Roman Empire was the very pinnacle of unreason: yet its variety of races could hardly be expected, in reason, to co-operate loyally in the work of reform.

Maria Theresa of Austria had won the love of all her subjects, whether Austrians or not, by sheer force of character. Although not clever, she set an example of kindness and virtue, and was honest and most courageous, a welcome contrast to the unscrupulous and shifty politicians of the time. Joseph II was cultured, well-informed, unprejudiced, unpretentious and hard-working. He travelled far and wide without pomp, but with observing eyes. He was passionately convinced of the blessings of religious toleration. He reformed the chaos of justice, making one comprehensive system of courts leading up to the High Court at Vienna. He abolished servitude (*robot*) in the Slav lands, and took steps to check the local powers of the feudal lords. He made the provincial "estates" of representatives dependent on his will, and planned a rational division of his empire into administrative "circles". Although his government was run economically, taxes were heavy. The greatest charge upon the emperor was one he could not diminish; the army must be maintained to guard such heterogeneous and wide-spreading territories. He imposed prohibitive import duties and rearranged the land-taxes. Like other monarchs of his time, he tried to foster new industries.

In Belgium, the citizens revolted because Joseph's reforms threatened their local "rights" or "liberties", which had survived from medieval days. In Hungary, the nobles objected because his reforms threatened their privileges. They showed their sense of nationality by demurring to his substitution of German for Latin as the official language. When he attempted to abolish serfdom in Hungary, he was unable to prevent a savage war breaking out between the Hungarian peasants and the resentful Hungarian nobles.

THE TANGLE OF EUROPEAN DIPLOMACY

The foreign policy of Joseph was, of course, linked up with that of Russia, Prussia and Turkey. Both Catherine II and Joseph II feared Frederick the Great, and they both made war upon the Turk—Joseph because the Turk was the traditional enemy of the empire, Catherine because she dreamed of a new "Greek" empire under Russian tutelage. She supported a revolt of the Greeks. In spite of French diplomacy, Russia and Austria took Turkish lands—Russia the Crimea, Austria the Bukovina. More important than any advantage of territory, however, was the recognition, at the treaty of Kainardji, of Catherine's special interest in the Christian subjects of the Turk. Thus began the claim of Russia to be the champion of the Christian races of the Balkans and the mentor of the Turk in his treatment of them.

It was amidst the tangle of diplomacy and war against Turkey that the ancient kingdom of Poland disappeared from the map. Her lack of decent government did not justify the action of her neighbours in partitioning the land between 1764 and 1795. Even in the eighteenth century, when scant respect was paid to nationality, the partition stood out as an indefensible crime. Poland had once saved western Europe from a horde of Turkish invaders. She deserved better than to be absorbed into the Prussian kingdom and the Austrian and Russian empires.

Three of the enlightened despots died within a short span of four years, Frederick the Great in 1786, Charles III in 1788, and Joseph II in 1790. Catherine the Great of Russia lasted till 1796. There was no despot in Great Britain: that island was governed by an aristocracy which had just blundered very badly over the American War of Independence. But even the British government was toying with the idea of a rational reform of the parliamentary voting system: and the government of Great Britain had contained a great deal of reason in its workings and conventions for centuries.

Scale
0   100   200
Miles

BALTIC SEA

RUSSIA
(Catherine the Great 1761-96)

Riga

R. Dvina

1772

Frederick the Great 1740-86
Frederick Wm. II 1786-1797

R. Niemen

PRUSSIA

Danzig

1793

Königsberg
EAST PRUSSIA
Remaining
1772 front
the conquests
of the Teutonic
Order

To

Dnieper

1772

To PRUSSIA

R. Vistula

1795

Third partition resisted
arms of Kosciusko
the Polish part

Warsaw

1793

RUSSIA

1795   1793

R. Pripet

1772

R. Bug

AUSTRIA

1795

R. Dniester

SILESIA
(Taken from Austria
in 1745 by
Frederick
the Great)

1772

HUNGARY
(Joseph II 1765-90
Leopold II 1790-92
Francis II 1792-1835
Emperors of the Holy Roman Empire
and Kings of Hungary)

R. Pruth

OTTOMAN EMPIRE

Mustapha III, Abdul Hamid and Selim III in turn

Danube Mouths

BLACK SEA

N
W   E
S

To Russia
To Prussia
To Austria

THE PARTITIONS OF POLAND

The first Partition of Poland occurred in 1772, Russia seizing the provinces along her own frontier and Austria and Prussia annexing large territories, reducing Polish sovereignty by roughly one-third. In 1793 Russia obtained all the eastern provinces of Poland with further gains to Prussia. Poland was now one-third of her original size. She still managed to retain the capital of Warsaw, but in 1795 Russia, Austria and Prussia combined to make the final division.

One monarchical power showed no signs of enlightenment. France, where the philosophy of reason had been born and elaborated, was untouched by any reasonable reform. Louis XIV had squandered wealth on his dynastic ambitions. Although a "grand monarch", he was but an average man, certainly no Frederick the Great or Charles III. Louis XV was a trifler, an amiable cynic who reigned too long. His mistress is reported to have said, "*Après nous, le déluge*"— "Ourselves . . . and then the Flood!" Yet Louis was the author of the flood. His years were, in the words of the Hebrew prophet, the years which the locust had eaten. His successor was well-meaning, but had no strength of character. France had men with ability, men with ideas, men with ideals, a large middle class excluded from political power; her noblemen and her clergy were helpless. Such was the passion for intelligent reconstruction that the royal intendants, the bishops and the nobles, all tried to do what they could in their very restricted spheres—at least, the better sort of them did. It was in vain. The Bourbon monarchy was spent: it could produce no man to give rein to the pent-up desire for reform in the hearts of all sensible Frenchmen, and not only give rein, but later guide, curb and control. The French monarchy, besides being unreasonable, was actually bankrupt. An empty treasury and a mountain of debt forced the king to the expedient of calling together a medieval assembly called the "States-General". Reason had been dammed up too long: it became revolution.

ACCUMULATION OF WEALTH

The age of reason fulfilled itself not only in politics, but in the arts. Craftsmanship reached a level unknown before: individual craftsmen had always excelled both in design and execution, but in the eighteenth century, knowledge, gained alowly through the past by toiling hands and observing eyes, became available in printed books. Diderot's great Encyclopaedia devoted much of its space to arts and crafts—pottery, spinning, weaving and the rest of the ancient activities of mankind. Moreover, there was wealth accumulated in individual hands to engage and to reward the craftsman. France and Britain had for a long time been unscathed by war; Britain, indeed, thanks to her encircling seas, had been remarkably free from serious upheaval or widespread devastation. This fact is the cardinal one of her history—namely, the continuity of her social structure—not, indeed, rigid, but capable of slow growth and change. Britain, again, was a mercantile nation abounding with riches drawn from the East and West by sailing-ships. Peace and commerce had heaped up riches: puritanism and evangelical piety had fostered a habit of saving among the middle classes; from these riches, employed by vigorous men, came the power that changed the world's industry.

The Romans had made good straight roads. Between the passing of their power and the eighteenth century, no central authority took up the task, and local selfishness brought chaos. It was an era of the horseman, the knight, the pack-animal and the bridle-path. Eighteenth-century prosperity needed better roads. At first, sections of the old ways and many stretches of new ways were enclosed between toll-gates or pikes—the sort of obstacle so often leaped (in romantic tales) by daring highwaymen. But haphazard repair by private companies did not do more than mitigate the hardships of travelling. A Scotsman named Macadam invented a good road-surface of broken granite, close-packed and rolled well into the foundation, which would stand wear and tear. It was a great success. Reason, applied to the problem, soon discovered the importance of road drainage. The most celebrated of all road builders, Telford, showed how to take advantage of the lie of the land. He also specialized in bridge-building. The general reconstruction of roads led to the building of light coaches and carriages worthy, in their adaptation to function, to stand beside the solid beautifully-made farm-waggons. In 1784, mail-coaches were established between London and Bath; the coaching era had begun. With a rational organization of relays of horses on a good road, the mail soon travelled at ten miles an hour. In Britain, at least, transport was now approaching the excellence it had once reached in the days of the Antonine emperors of Rome.

Roads were supplemented by an entirely new form of transport—canals. In this, the Earl of Bridgewater was the capitalist patron and a simple millwright the pioneer. Brindley, the millwright, learnt how to build canals by constructing the Bridgewater Canal. He discovered how to carry the canal through and over obstacles, so as to provide the maximum of ease in transit for the barges. Again shrewd commonsense triumphed—backed by capital. By the end of the century, over 5000 miles of these inland waterways were finished, and it looked as though Britain might work out a civilization based upon water transport. Needless to say, the experience gained in all this work by the gangs of "navigators" who were employed in the task was of untold service to the railway companies later.

SCIENTIFIC DISCOVERIES

Roads, bridges, canals, in their turn produced an acceleration in trade that engendered new wealth. Nor were improvements in transport confined to land. Sea-travel was made safer by Harrison's invention of the chronometer in 1773, and by the publication of the Nautical Almanac by the British government from 1767 onwards. Progress in lighthouse-building was marked by Smeaton's erection of the famous third Eddystone light in 1756-9. The science of navigation and the art of cartography were encouraged by many European governments, particularly by the French. In 1769 when it became known that the planet Venus would that year cross the face of the sun, no fewer than four governments—the Danish, the Russian, the French and the British—despatched expeditions of scientists to the ends of the earth to observe the phenomenon. It was upon the return

journey of the British expedition that Captain Cook saw the shores
of New South Wales; he was the first white man to discover the
fertile lands of south-east Australia which, during unknown ages
of her existence, had been the home of the primitive blackfellows.

PRACTICAL APPLICATION OF SCIENCE

Mechanical devices were known to the peoples of antiquity and of
the Middle Ages, but they were mere toys. In the eighteenth century,
they became the adjuncts of industry. Stocking-frames had been in
use in the days of Queen Elizabeth; water-wheels were ancient con-
traptions; clocks and watches had for centuries been made with
remarkable ingenuity. The ordinary mechanical principles involved
in wheels, pulleys and levers were all well established. Now, these
principles were applied and adapted by a succession of inventors to
the cotton-spinning industry, where, owing to the size of the imported
crop, the masters had considerable sums of money at their command.
The work of Paul, Hargreaves, Arkwright and Crompton, from 1732
to 1789, produced the spinning-mule which was set up in mills near
the Lancashire coalfield. There, steam-engines could supply the
motive power. The cottage spinning-jenny soon became a thing of
the past. The housewife ceased to eke out the family income by her
labour.

> "Yarn is an income, and the Huswive's thread
> The larder fills with meat, the bin with bread."

Herrick's lines lost their meaning when the spinners were operatives
gathered in large mills.

It was the application of steam-power that ultimately changed the
structure of society, making factory life the rule and home industry
the exception, abolishing the human relationship between master
and apprentice for the industrial relationship between employer and
employee.

The craft of the smith is the most famous in the world. The smith
produced the millwright, and the millwright produced the engineer,
upon whose work the world rests to-day. The principle of the steam-
engine was known to ancient Greek scientists. Italian physicists
toyed with the idea of steam-power in the seventeenth century. The
Marquess of Worcester worked a 2-horse-power engine at Vauxhall
in 1656. In 1677, a Frenchman suggested using gunpowder to drive
a "heat" engine. The first practical steam-engine was made on a
coalfield when Newcomen in 1711 introduced a steam-pump to
clear water from the coal-mines by the Tyne. Thenceforward the
development of coal and iron and steam-power went side by side.
Iron-founding was revolutionized by the substitution of coke for
charcoal, and it soon became possible to work iron on a large scale.
By the end of the century, over a hundred Newcomen engines were
in use. Other engineers—the Cornishman Trevithick and the Scotsman Watt—also perfected types of steam-engines, and experiments

were made to get a satisfactory locomotive. Success in this direction did not come, on land, for some time; but in 1807, the Americans could see a small steamboat plying on the Hudson, and in 1812, Bell ran a successful passenger steamboat on the Clyde.

Chemistry also had begun to play its part in this revolution in the world's work. Calico-bleaching by chloride of lime and the use of coal-gas as an illuminant were both established before 1815. Once the engineers and chemists had started, changes and improvements in industrial processes took place continually in most branches of human activity.

Thus, at a time when the application of reason to human arts and crafts had promised a steady amelioration of the economic condition of mankind in the West, a series of inventions—themselves the outcome of unfettered human reason—transformed human society in a short span of time. Exploitation of the whole earth was speeded up: power was in the hands of the scientists and inventors; society was in the hands of the masters of capital. Good and evil were strangely mixed: the old order of centuries was disappearing, but disappearing too fast for government to evolve a suitable control. Law and custom are not made in a day or a year. The swiftness of the mechanical revolution precluded any period of stability in which custom could be established or law perfected. "The empire of reason will ever be the reign of peace", wrote Priestley the scientist in 1791. He did not foresee the strange adventures into which reason was to plunge creation, or the natural helplessness of the politician to cope with a continually changing scene. Moreover, the outburst of human reason in French politics gave the politicians enough to do to maintain the integrity of their own lands and inheritances.

CHAPTER 63

THE MAN OF DESTINY

IN 1789, the French monarchy was bankrupt. As a last hope, Louis XVI called together the medieval States-General. The outlook and temper of France was anything but medieval: its peasants were comparatively well-to-do, though resentful of feudal tolls and impositions; its townsmen (*bourgeoisie*) and its lawyers were energetic and quick-witted folk, though absurdly jealous of their local and sectional rights; its intellectuals were the vanguard of all Europe. Still everyone hoped for big things from this meeting of representatives. The monarchy had a splendid opportunity of re-creating itself upon popular support gained by wise reforms.

The States-General was made up of the three estates of the realm— Nobles, Clergy and the Third Estate (*tiers état*). Its task was to end the bankruptcy; and since, under existing conditions, bankruptcy was inevitable, it was necessary to introduce reforms. But the States-General had not met for a hundred and seventy-five years. What was its procedure? Should its members vote as individuals or as estates? It was this matter that first revealed the shocking inefficiency of the monarchy and the lack of decision in the king. As long as his courtiers opposed any concession to popular opinion, Louis XVI was helpless; for they had no politicians, let alone statesmen, among them. After much bickering and bitter argument, the Third Estate, in defiance of the king and court, proclaimed itself a National Assembly; and then spent valuable time in formulating a Declaration of the Rights of Man. After this, it began to enact a new constitution piece-meal. It seemed that the age of reason had dawned, even in France.

The Paris mob took a hand. It rioted and seized the old Bastille fortress, murdering innocent persons. There was nothing exceptional or alarming about the riot. The exceptional and alarming thing was

FRANCE BEFORE 1789

Before the Revolution the local unit in France corresponded to the old provinces, with the executive power resting in the hands of the King and the ministers appointed by him. Considerable local rivalries arose from the system.

that it went unchecked. A detailed history of France shows that a few score determined men, under resolute leaders, could at any time have mastered the city: it is a witness to the inefficiency of all parties in France that such men and such leaders were lacking. Neither the courtiers nor the Third Estate could control affairs. The exclusion of her nobles from a share in the government had long since deprived France of her natural leaders. The country drifted towards anarchy and violence. In the towns, men everywhere looked to their own government and their own defence. In the countryside, the peasants rose against their seigneurs, in many places burning the châteaux and murdering the landowners, and everywhere taking possession of the land.

The intrusion of the Paris mob marked the Revolution in all its phases. A great mob, carefully organized so that the women marched in front, went out to Versailles and brought the royal family back to the Tuileries Palace by force. Later, it attacked and looted the Tuileries. In the frenzy that followed upon the outbreak of war with Austria, it massacred the political prisoners. Finally, moved by unscrupulous agitators, it tried to overthrow the Republican government in 1795: but by that year, the mob had found its master in the army. A young artillery officer, Napoleon Bonaparte by name, turned his guns on it and blew it out of the Revolution for good.

THE COURSE OF THE FRENCH REVOLUTION

Revolutionaries are seldom statesmen. Yet nothing is more remarkable than the lack in Revolutionary France of men of good character and common sense at the head of affairs. There were men deeply moved by ideas, men who toiled like ants in their country's service, men who sought their country's welfare—provided, of course, that this was consonant with their own political doctrines. But there was no firm control at the centre. The new constitution swept away all feudal arrangements; it made the law uniform throughout the land—thus reaching the point which England had reached in the thirteenth century; it devised a jury-system; it ordered all officials, even judges, to be elected. All was done by reason, nothing by experience. The constitution was flawed by inexperience and shackled the executive. In vain did Count Mirabeau, the finest orator and the only statesman in the Assembly, plead for a strong executive. He wanted a limited monarchy at peace with Europe. Had Louis XVI been a man of decision instead of a good-natured man whose weakness appeared to be duplicity, this might have come about. Mirabeau died in 1791, and his death was a grave blow to France.

No attempt was made to secure the allegiance of the nobles, many of whom were as eager for reform as the Third Estate. Thousands of loyal subjects fled from France into the Rhineland and elsewhere to live in exile as *emigrés*. France became, as she has since remained, a land of political parties. The Girondists wished to rally the nation

FRANCE AFTER 1789

One of the most important results of the Revolution was the sweeping away of the former cumbersome methods of civil administration, and the substitution of departments which roughly corresponded to the English system of counties.

round the monarchy; the Jacobins, well organized in a chain of revolutionary clubs all over the country, advocated the formation of a republic; besides these two main political groups, there existed a multitude of shifting cliques and contradictory policies.

The question of peace or war pivoted, like so much else, on the unhappy king and queen. The first welcome given to the Revolution by the democrats and reformers in Europe had been considerably modified by the wildness of the peasants and the excesses of the mob. The monarchs of Europe disliked the virtual imprisonment of the French royal family. The Rhineland princes objected to the spread of revolutionary doctrines in their own territories. The *emigrés* thirsted to lead foreign armies into their native land; there is no hatred so strong as that of the dispossessed exile against his own countrymen. Moreover, Leopold II of Austria was naturally anxious for the safety of his sister, Marie Antoinette, the French queen. Leopold did his best to keep the peace. When he died, hopes for peace died. Catherine of Russia and Frederick William III of Prussia were both very hostile in their attitude towards the Revolutionaries, whose attempts to ride successfully the whirlwind of passion that their Revolution had evoked were far from triumphal.

THE SPIRIT OF REVOLUTIONARY FRANCE

France declared war on Austria in 1792. Her raw levies, though valorous, were repulsed, and the enemy entered upon French territory, coming to the rescue of Louis XVI and Marie Antoinette. There was still plenty of royalist sentiment in France, but Louis was not the man to inspire it. Now his cause had brought foreign armies into the fatherland. The revolution became military and so saved itself. Here was a task simpler than governing civilians—a direct business of training and equipping armies who do what they are told. The men of Marseilles had marched into Paris singing a new song, the Marseillaise. It was a marching song for soldiers. All was patriotic fervour and bustle. Recruits hurried to defend the frontiers, learning the use of arms on the way. Reason was giving way to an emotion older than itself. By a seeming miracle, the French army checked the enemy in the Cannonade of Valmy. On the same day, a National Convention met in Paris and declared France a republic. Fresh successes in the north, and the conquest of Savoy in the south, intoxicated the Revolutionaries, who announced themselves the allies of all peoples against all kings. This sounds a piece of unnecessary impertinence. Actually, it was a manifestation of the intensity of the democratic faith that moved its authors. Other manifestations included the guillotining of the king early in 1793, and the declaration of war against Spain, Holland and Great Britain. Britain was concerned, as always, with the territorial integrity of Flanders, which was now threatened by the French revolutionaries. From now on, there was more of the passion of nationality than of reason in revolutionary France.

The military danger created a strong executive known as the Committee of Public Safety. Men were conscripted. When the people of La Vendée resisted, they were dragooned ruthlessly in civil war. A reign of terror sought to dispose of all enemies of the republic, actual or potential; the footpad, the aristocrat, the unsuccessful general, the half-starved street-girl, alike expiated their misfortune on the guillotine. The unhappy queen was executed towards the end of 1793. In the provinces, agents of the Committee administered the "terror" according to their discretion. Some were merciful. Others, as at Nantes, where they drowned prisoners in batches, took their cue from Paris. Meanwhile, the revolutionary armies stood their ground against the invaders, and by a great victory over the Austrians at Fleurus, 1794, secured the French frontier for twenty years. So the Committee held control, and saved the Revolution, partly by the energy of its war measures, partly by pandering to the butcher's instinct in the mob. Its most notorious member, Robespierre—Rousseau's "man of action"—was a fanatic and a puritan, who sent to the guillotine all who disagreed with either his political or his religious views, including men like Danton and Desmoulins. When Robespierre himself fell a victim to plotters, who broke his jaw and carried him off to the scaffold in 1794, the Terror abated.

ITALY IN 1789

In the south a Spanish Bourbon line had reigned in Naples from 1735, while in the north of Italy the influence of Austria was supreme. The kingdom of Sardinia had expanded and Venice still maintained her Adriatic and mainland territory. Genoa had recognized French sovereignty over Corsica in 1768.

Viscount Horatio Nelson, 1758–1805 (*left*), the British admiral whose command of the sea did much to break Napoleon's hold on the Continent, and David's portrait (*right*) of Napoleon Bonaparte, Emperor of the French, painted while he commanded the armies of the French Republic.

The Battle of Copenhagen, 1801, after Serres. A British naval force under Admirals Hyde Parker and Horatio Nelson inflicted a crushing defeat on the Danes which ended their policy of "armed neutrality."

The Post Office, St. Martin's le Grand, in the reign of George IV. Horse transport was still the fastest means of communication.

The Canterbury and Whitstable Railway on the opening day in 1830. In the early nineteenth century many independent railways were built in England, and from them unified railway systems were developed.

Since 1789, France had been governed in turn by the National Assembly, the Legislative Assembly, and the National Convention for which the Committee of Public Safety had acted. Reforms had been made in accordance with the dictates of reason: even the calendar—that relic of despotic Caesars and Popes—was abolished, and its place taken by another. From now on, Frenchmen lived in Rainy months, Hot months, Foggy months, Fruitful months, and since they had created the world anew, they dated from the First Year of the Revolution. Good citizens wore the Phrygian cap, the red cotton nightcap of liberty, and this sacred symbol was even sent to Tippoo Sahib of Mysore, a ruler of ferocious cruelty, to honour him as a fellow-worker with France in the cause of freedom. Christianity was never in any real peril, although the Church suffered confiscation. But among extremists, the worship of Reason was carried to sacramental lengths. On one notorious occasion they went so far as to celebrate its worship in Notre Dame, Reason on this occasion being exemplified in the person of an attractive young woman.

THE DIRECTORY

After the fall of Robespierre, a fourth government was devised, a Directory of five members, which entered upon a calmer period following the Terror, and which saw in Paris a rebirth of social life, with styles and fashions since known by its name. The Committee of Public Safety and the Directory were responsible for the defence of France, and they both worked wonders. The Austrians, the Italians, the Spaniards, the Prussians had all been defeated. Belgium was annexed to France, and Holland had become a "Batavian" republic under French protection. In 1795 all her enemies, except Austria and Great Britain, made peace with France. They accepted her government as legitimate and stable, and they feared her great military power. That power was now the dominant fact in Europe. The army was the soul of France, and among its officers were many men of outstanding ability and experience, who knew well how to govern both men and affairs.

The young French republic was still at war with Austria and Britain, so there was plenty of work for her soldiers. They crossed the Rhine and marched to the Danube. They moved into Italy through Savoy. They came back from the Danube, driven for forty days through the woods and mountains of south Germany, by the Austrian archduke, Charles. Moreau, their commander, handled his men well on the retreat, which enhanced his military reputation. Yet it was a retreat, and the men who ruled France expected and demanded victories.

Not so did the army of Italy return to France. There, on the Lombardy plain, it drove the Austrians, in battle after battle, back into Austria. The French commander brought Sardinia, Parma, Modena and the Pope into submission. He disposed of the Italian states like

z   (H.W.)

a conqueror of some heroic age, organizing north Italy into a number
of republics on the French model. He sent to Paris waggon-loads of
loot—money to replenish the emptying treasury, and works of art
to adorn the capital. He was a Corsican commissioned in the old
royalist army in 1785 and now about twenty-seven years old, a
regular officer devoted body and soul to his profession of arms. A
product not of revolutionary enthusiasm but of the old régime, he
descended not from French ancestry but from Tuscan stock. His
name was Napoleon Bonaparte. It was not long before all Europe
was ringing with the news of his masterly victories in Italy. The
man of destiny had arrived at the beginning of his power.

NAPOLEON BECOMES MASTER OF FRANCE

Meanwhile, the admirals of Britain had destroyed the Spanish and
Dutch navies, which were acting in concert with the French republic.
While Great Britain held the seas, the French could not assail her.
General Bonaparte, the hero of the hour, when ordered to prepare
an invasion of England, demurred, and suggested an attack upon
Egypt, with some ulterior notion of mastering India or Turkey. He
was, consequently, appointed to command an overseas expedition to
the East. When he sailed for Egypt, he restored France's military
contact with the Levant, broken since the days of St. Louis; when he
landed in Egypt and conquered the Mamelukes, he established an
intercourse which has not since been broken. His savants began the
study of Egyptology. His countrymen began their cultural and
commercial dealings, which still persist, with Egypt and the Levant.
Although he came to grief on the Syrian coast, which has seen the
failures of races and empires since remote antiquity, he made a lasting
impression in Egypt. British seamen checked his advance at Acre
and Admiral Nelson destroyed his fleet in Aboukir Bay. British naval
victories were becoming a habit—but naval power needs an army to
supplement its actions. Bonaparte was still the conqueror.

Then he heard bad news of France. Its armies were being defeated
and its politics were in a turmoil. The Russians had joined in the
war, and Russian armies were campaigning in Italy and the Alps.
Bonaparte left his army to fend for itself and slipped back to France
with a few officers. Again he was the hero of the hour, the man who
could win victories. A *coup d'état* took place which made him the
chief of three consuls who were to govern France. The appointment
of three preserved republican appearances. "Gentlemen," said one
of the three to his friends, "we now have a master. He knows everything: he can do everything: and what is more, he wants to do everything." The mad Tsar, Paul I of Russia, had such an admiration for
Bonaparte that he made peace and even advised the general and First
Consul to style himself king of France! Within fourteen months
from the end of the eighteenth century, a victorious general was
master of the French republic.

ITALY IN 1810

The Kingdom of Italy was consolidated at the expense of Austria, the Duchy of Modena, and part of the Papal States. In 1806 the Kingdom of Naples came under French domination; while the Kingdom of Sardinia, the other duchies, and the remainder of the Papal States, were subject to the direct rule of the French.

For fourteen years, Napoleon filled Europe with the noise of his wars. Thrones and dynasties were his playthings. Yet he was no mere conqueror, but the greatest of the benevolent despots. He forced his will on kings and princes by the power of his bayonets and guns; but he had at his back the tremendous momentum of a great people, released from a restrictive and artificial bondage by a doctrine that invigorated all—the doctrine of liberty. France had become a nation, instead of a mere monarchy. She was a nation with Napoleon as her embodiment. In his work, he summed up and preserved the Revolution, which was itself the climax of the Age of Reason. His cavalier treatment of the old Europe was an harmonious finale to the themes sounded earlier by Voltaire and the Encyclopaedists.

In June 1807, Napoleon and the then Tsar of Russia, Alexander, met on a raft moored in the waters of the river Niemen at Tilsit. Napoleon unfolded his plan, and the Tsar was flattered by the confidence of the world's greatest soldier. They would divide the world between them : [there should be two vast empires, an Eastern one for Alexander and a Western one for Napoleon. Nor was this a mere roseate vision, for before the Tsar lay the untamed tribes of Asia, awaiting a master, and the faltering empire of the Turk; behind Napoleon lay a Europe subjugated by his amazing genius. He had succeeded in completely overwhelming the Austrians at Marengo and re-won north Italy : he had overthrown both Austrians and Russians at Austerlitz and entered Vienna in triumph: he had overthrown the Prussians at Jena and entered Berlin in triumph: he had but recently decisively defeated the Russian Army at Friedland. Now he was playing at being a Caesar with Tsar Alexander for an associate.

NAPOLEON'S DOMINATION OF EUROPE

Europe was more than subjugated: it was transformed. France extended to the Rhine and included Savoy. Holland, Switzerland, Naples and Italy were republics dependent upon France. Napoleon's brothers were kings of Holland and of Naples, his step-son was viceroy of Italy, his kinswomen were married to German princes of the first rank. The ancient republic of Venice was absorbed into Italy. The Holy Roman Empire was gone for good. Its last emperor, Francis II, abdicated at Napoleon's bidding in 1806. For nearly four hundred years, not one of its emperors had been crowned in Rome. For nearly four hundred years, it had been practically a Habsburg patrimony. But its traditions ran back to the emperors of ancient Rome, and its web of feudal government, stretching across the Germanies and Italy, preserved a medieval texture woven through many centuries of splendour. In its place stood Napoleon's own empire. For he had brought the Pope from Rome in 1804 to crown him Emperor at Paris: the Pope conducted the solemn rite and had the privilege of watching Napoleon crown himself. Afterwards, Napoleon travelled to Milan—like any mailed Hohenstaufen in the Ages of Faith—to receive the iron crown of Lombardy. He created a nobility and surrounded himself with courtiers—marshals, chamberlains, equerries, huntsmen and almoners—like a second Charlemagne. And like Charlemagne's, his rule extended to the Elbe; for he re-organized the west German states, and grouped them into a confederation of the Rhine under his own protection.

Unfortunately for his ambition, the naval and commercial power of Great Britain stood in the way. He had already spent time and

THE HOLY ROMAN EMPIRE (WEST OF THE ELBE) IN 1789

treasure upon a projected invasion of England, whose fishermen
could often see his troops practising embarkation in their flat-
bottomed transports off Boulogne. But the warning beacons were
never fired across England for the French army: instead, the fleets
of Britain held the narrow seas, and in 1805, Admiral Nelson destroyed both the French and the Spanish navies off Cape Trafalgar,
the great sailor meeting his death during the battle.

This continued hostility on the part of Great Britain was gall and
wormwood to the French Emperor, who could improvise armies but
not fleets. He never understood the true nature of sea-power, and,
while he was subduing the Continent, the ships of Britain stripped
France and her European dependencies of their overseas possessions.
Napoleon therefore tightened up the "Continental System", which

had been taking effect since 1793: he ordered Europe to blockade British ships and goods. Great Britain retaliated by blockading all the European coasts, and by seizing the Danish navy rather than let it fall into Napoleon's hands. It was the severity of Britain's blockade that led to a costly and futile war between Britain and the United States of America a few years later, since the Americans, as neutrals, objected to British interference with their shipping. Portugal and Sweden suffered for not enforcing the blockade: the French occupied Portugal, while Alexander took Finland from Sweden.

British diplomacy and British subsidies of money were constantly used to build up fresh alliances in Europe against the Emperor. Austria again made war upon him. He manifested his imperial power by leading Bavarians, Rhinelanders and Italians into battle behind the eagles of France, and forced Austria to make peace. He gave strips of territory to Italy, to Bavaria and to the new Polish state (the "Grand Duchy of Warsaw") which he had created, and later he married the Archduchess Marie Louise, daughter of Francis II.

IMPORTANT REFORMS ACCOMPLISHED

Napoleon organized his empire along simple lines. He was the supreme power, and all civil officials owed their duty to him, in the same way that his military officers did. He allowed no freedom of printing, nor right of petition. In fact, the Rights of Man went by the board. Yet, as a true benevolent despot, he did much good for the peoples under him. Serfdom was abolished in Switzerland, Belgium, North Italy and Germany. Religious toleration was extended throughout the German lands under his control. Privilege disappeared and in its place came the principle of all careers being open to men with talents to achieve them. Justice was simplified and cheapened. In France, great codes of law, which aimed at simplification and a speeding up of justice, were drawn up by jurists at his direction. In education and in finance, the same spirit of simplification and expedition was at work. In Prussia, similar reforms were carried out, but by the Prussian statesmen themselves—Stein seeing to civil affairs and Scharnhorst to the army. A national sentiment grew up in Prussia, fostered by poets and thinkers, which accepted Prussia as the leading state of Germany: in fact, Germans from other states served Prussia in the hope of opposing French domination. Napoleon's conquests aroused national feeling throughout Europe.

THE NATIONS TURN AGAINST NAPOLEON

Like all ambitious conquerors, Napoleon overreached himself. He tried to annex Spain in order to perfect his Continental System. He proclaimed his brother Joseph king of Spain, and when the Spaniards resisted—to the extent of capturing a French army—he marched to Madrid himself to inaugurate his brothers' reign. An English army interfered. It should have warned him. Instead, he

ITALY IN 1815

After Napoleon's overthrow the old order was restored as far as possible.
Venice and Lombardy came within Austria's sphere of influence, the Papal
States were restored to the Holy See, and the Kingdom of the Two Sicilies reverted
to the Bourbon King Ferdinand IV, who had been dispossessed by Napoleon.

defeated it, and then left Spain to his marshals, who were kept busy
till 1813. For again the sea-power of Great Britain, used this time in
conjunction with a land force, proved its worth. A small British
army of regulars was maintained in the Peninsula, based on the
magnificent harbour of Lisbon, and well supplied from Britain. By
a happy chance, its commander, Sir Arthur Wellesley, later Duke of
Wellington, was a military genius who never took risks which could
be lessened in any way by his own care. From 1809, he kept the

marshals of Napoleon on the alert. From 1811 to 1814, he drove the Frenchmen through the Peninsula, across the Pyrenees and into France, all the while helped by a savage and incessant guerrilla war, maintained by the Spaniards against their invaders. When Wellington was able to enter France from the south, a great concourse of Russians, Prussians, Austrians and Swedes were advancing from the north and east.

This uprising of Europe, like the Spanish war, was a vindication of the rights of nationality. It was also, in its way, the revolt of the eighteenth century against its own offspring, Napoleon; for the rights of men are determined ultimately by the right of each community to look after its own affairs and decide upon matters affecting its own national life and institutions.

THE RUSSIAN DISASTER AND ITS RESULTS

The prelude to this discordant chorus of war was an invasion of Russia by Napoleon who had found that the Tsar was not faithful to the Continental System. At the head of half a million men, most of them drawn from his dependent nations, he crossed Europe, and with the majority of them, marched to Moscow in 1812. One sanguinary battle sufficed the Russians. They retreated before his advance, and left him to return from Moscow over devastated, wintry plains. His grand army was shattered. He hurried to France and raised more troops. Prussia rose in arms behind him and joined with the slowly advancing Russians. Austria declared war. Sweden declared war. Again and again, Napoleon collected men and opposed the nations. By sheer weight of numbers, they bore him back, from Dresden, from the terrible field of Leipzig, across Germany into France. He was still the incomparable general. He defeated them again and again when they were divided. But the masses of men moved onwards relentlessly, impelled by a sense of national wrongs and sustained by British gold. The flower of Napoleon's armies lay beneath the soil of Russia, of Spain, of Germany. Garrisons of veterans were locked up in the German towns, besieged by national militias. Napoleon could not replace the horses flung recklessly away on his tragic march across Russia in 1812. He was still more than a match for any leader the Allies could bring against him: but the trumpets of France blew in vain—they had blown too often in the past. The best of the men were dead in strange lands. The boys who rallied to the eagles could not defend them. By the 20th of April, 1814, Napoleon was on his way to honourable confinement in the island of Elba. The Bourbon prince, Louis XVIII, was on his way to Paris, where the Allies waited to install him as king of France.

Six months after Napoleon sailed for Elba, the diplomats gathered in congress at Vienna to re-shape Europe. The four leading powers were Great Britain, Russia, Austria and Prussia. But the French bishop and prince, Talleyrand, upset their intentions. He had been one of Napoleon's right-hand men. Now, as representative of France, he played his part with consummate skill, making himself the champion of the smaller states, and thus establishing his own country as a fifth power in the negotiations. The Austrian representative at the congress was Prince Metternich.

It was impossible to return to the feudal Europe of pre-Revolutionary days. The spoils, of course, went to the victors. Great Britain acquired Malta, Heligoland, Mauritius, Tobago, St. Lucia, Ceylon, Trinidad and the Cape, all of which had fallen to her arms. Poland—or that part of it which Napoleon had resurrected as the Grand Duchy of Warsaw—was again engulfed by Russia, Prussia and Austria. To Prussia also went Pomerania and part of Saxony. Austria received all north Italy, outside Piedmont and Savoy. There was little or no vindictiveness towards France, who retained her old boundaries with trivial adjustments. The diplomats perpetuated Napoleon's policy in western Germany, where the German states, apart from Prussian territory, were diminished to thirty-eight in number and formed into a Germanic federation, ruled by a diet under the aegis of Austria, and sworn to preserve peace. Italy remained a geographical expression. A new kingdom of the Netherlands comprised both Belgium and Holland, Norway was ceded to Sweden.

ABOLITION OF THE SLAVE TRADE

By the efforts of the British representative, Lord Castlereagh, it was agreed to abolish the trade in negro slaves within a fixed term of years. The navigation of international rivers, like the Rhine and Danube, was placed upon a reasonable basis, not to be impeded by arbitrary tolls and dues. These two resolutions did not concern Britain overmuch; she had already abolished the slave trade among her own nationals, and her interests lay not in the traffic of continental rivers but on the high seas. For many years, she had been warden of those seas: and her empire had grown enormously. In India, her soldiers, under capable officers, not only defeated French intrigues but extended her power over the native states in the south and centre. In Canada, she had received from the revolted American provinces many thousands of loyalist settlers. In Australia, she possessed a convict settlement at Sydney, New South Wales, and, what was more important, a nucleus of free settlers who had already begun to squat with their merino sheep on the grasslands. The voyages of Cook, La Pérouse, Bougainville and Dentrecasteaux had revealed also the nature and extent of New Zealand and Polynesia. European curiosity began to speculate upon the origin of the Pacific races, the intelligent attractive cannibals of the island groups, the fierce and chivalrous Maoris of New Zealand and the squalid ignorant blackfellows of Australia.

Notwithstanding the drain upon her gold caused by the great wars, Britain was the wealthiest country in the world, and thanks to her inventors and capitalists, was rapidly becoming the workshop of the

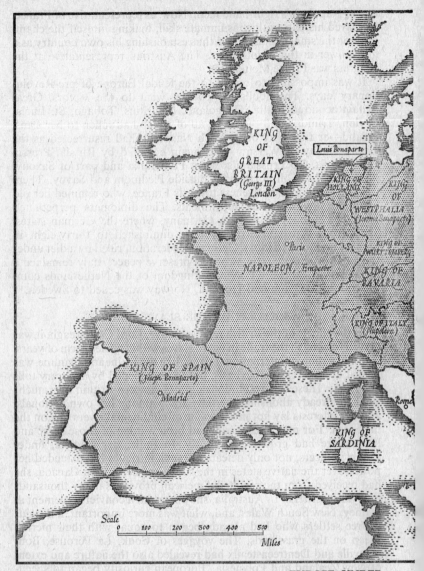

EUROPE UNDER

The shaded areas in the above map illustrate the territories ruled directly, or indirectly, by Napoleon at the zenith of his career. The keystone of the political system was a France which stretched from the Baltic to the Mediterranean and Atlantic, and which commanded the German North Sea and the Adriatic. The German States were organized into the Confederacy of the Rhine, and the Kingdoms of Prussia and Austria at the same time considerably reduced in size.

NAPOLEON

The Grand Duchy of Warsaw was revived as a puppet " buffer state", and Italy existed completely under French influence. Spain, upon whose throne Napoleon placed his brother, Joseph, involved France in a costly struggle against a people driven to arms. Portuguese independence was not suppressed, and Sweden maintained her foothold on the German mainland. Against this French continental domination, Britain opposed command of the seas and commercial wealth.

world. She was the only country in Europe that had not been, at one time or another, a theatre of the war. Even the Turks had been implicated by an alliance with the French Emperor, and had had their Danubian provinces of Bessarabia and Moldavia wrested from them by the Tsar.

From the States-General at Versailles in 1789 to the Congress of Vienna in 1814, there elapsed a period of time that cannot be measured merely in years: for statesmen and soldiers, it had been a lifetime of tumult and disaster, with the eagles of imperial France overshadowing Europe and the world. Even the peasant had been stirred from his age-long groove of servile labour. Now, at last, men could settle down to a peace where reason and not arms should dictate the arrangements of mankind.

A year after his accession Louis XVIII fled from Paris. Napoleon with eight hundred Guards had escaped from Elba, had landed in France, had been received with acclamations, had marched north-wards in triumph. Marshal Ney, "the bravest of the brave", had gone over to him with the army which recognized him as its destined leader. Napoleon promised liberty of speech and a democratic constitution. He made overtures to the Allies. The Allies feared him too much to treat with him. Their armies began marching and assembling. Wellington with a composite force of British, Dutch, Belgians and Hanoverians, and Blücher with his Prussians were both near the French frontier. Reinforcements were set in motion. All Europe was stirring to throw its multitudes against the forces of the Corsican.

THE BATTLE OF WATERLOO

Napoleon's hope was to strike swiftly and to cleave the alliances. He drove back Blücher's Prussians at Ligny. He drove back the advanced regiments of Wellington's force at Quatre Bras. Wellington prepared to stand his ground on a ridge near Waterloo, and await both the onset of the French and the return to the field of the Prussians. On Sunday the 18th of June, 1815, the battle of Waterloo took place. While Wellington's men withstood the great charges of the French cavalry and the French Guards, the Prussian guns came into action on Napoleon's right front. When the momentum of the French attacks had died down, Wellington ordered a general advance, and simultaneously Blücher's Prussians joined in. The French retreat was turned to a rout. Napoleon, after wandering about for some days, surrendered to H.M.S. *Bellerophon* off Rochefort.

On the 8th of August, H.M.S. *Northumberland* sailed down Channel. On board was Napoleon, the man of destiny, a prisoner, at last, of the British navy to which, more than to all else, he owed his downfall. He was going to St. Helena, a lonely island in the South Atlantic, his last exile, where there would be no sound of guns, but only the noise of the breakers.

PART XII

FIFTY YEARS OF PROGRESS

CHAPTER 64

MACHINE CIVILIZATION

WITH Napoleon's banishment to St. Helena, the first great problem of Europe appeared to be solved. But many of the gravest problems which were to confront statesmen were not political, but social and moral. The battlefield was no longer Austerlitz or Waterloo, but the smoking chimneys and filthy slums of Glasgow or Lyons. The thousands who lost their lives in the Napoleonic wars were nothing in comparison with the millions who died young or existed as physical wrecks—the victims of the new industrial civilization which had not yet learned humanitarianism.

Napoleon's career had shown that the egotism of one man, by exploiting the newly-developed forces of patriotism, could cause bloodshed in warfare on a gigantic scale. Similarly, the new industrial technique, exploited by the ambition and acquisitiveness of employers, led to unparalleled wastage and thwarting of human life in the new industrial towns. The materialism and greed of the men who were in control of the new machine-technique were the most destructive forces which had yet appeared in world history.

Men needed to grow up morally if they were to make a success of the technical advance of their civilization. It was not enough for there to be a few enlightened employers and a few enthusiastic reformers. A new public opinion was needed to realize with shame the festering sores that had grown on civilization as a result of previous apathy. The investing public needed to learn that their responsibilities did not end with subscribing capital and ensuring the payment of interest.

NEW CONCEPTIONS OF POLITICS AND SOCIETY

New materialist philosophies of politics and society were the outcome of the new industrial civilization. At the same time, there was an increase in the forces of goodwill, which aimed at correcting the evils of the new civilization. Materialism and idealism, religion and selfishness, warred with each other; out of this ferment emerged the historical tendencies of the century.

During the Napoleonic wars, the industrial towns of Western Europe and America had begun to spread to quiet valleys and farmland. Factory chimneys belched out soot for miles around. Streams and rivers became choked with rubbish and defiled by the waste-matter of the factories. Steam-power was superseding water-power as the source of energy for the Industrial Revolution. Cotton-mills by the side of streams might be crowded and dirty, but they often possessed the advantage of an elevated and fairly isolated position.

STEAM-POWER AND INDUSTRIAL OUTPUT

But steam-power made far larger factories possible, with the accompanying hideous congestion of life in the workers' hovels which surrounded them. The sites of these factories were dictated no longer by the presence of rapid water, but by the convenience of transport, favourable climatic conditions, and the availability of coal. The North-West of England was the seat of the important cotton-industry, and Lancashire became, to some extent, the hub of the industrial life of the world. Steam-power caused a vast growth in the demand for iron and coal. Sometimes the rate of output increased extraordinarily rapidly; between 1830 and 1833, the output of iron in England rose from 680,000 tons to three million. This was nothing to the expansion which occurred in the middle of the century, after Henry Bessemer invented a process for making steel almost as cheaply as iron.

In France and America industry developed at a much slower rate than in England. Not till the 'thirties had factory methods in America entirely superseded the "domestic system" for the manufacture of woollen and cotton textiles.

This development was dependent on improvement in communications. The countries of North-Western Europe were fairly well equipped with canals, and these continued to be built till the coming of the railway. The first large canal of North America, from New York to Lake Erie, was completed in 1825; in England, the age of canal-building did not extend more than ten years after this date.

The development of road communication was also checked by the coming of railways, but not until the stage-coach had had its period of glory. New standards of speed were made possible by the discoveries of Telford and Macadam. Macadam, a Scot from Ayrshire, devoted the fortune he had won in business to his passion for experimenting in the making of hard metalled road-surfaces. His discoveries were given publicity by a committee of the House of Commons in 1819, and were applied on all the main roads throughout England. There resulted the "palmy days" of coaching, from 1820 to 1840, when there were several daily services between most of the important towns. During the last years of this period, many famous records were set up, such as three hours forty minutes for the fifty-two miles from London to Brighton.

Hedley's "Puffing Billy" of 1813 is the father of the railway engines which, by the middle of the century, had sent the coaching companies out of business. It worked for the colliery at Wylam, near Newcastle, where George Stephenson was born. Stephenson's origins were of the humblest; he was one of a family of six for whose support his father earned only 12s. a week, by tending a colliery engine. Stephenson began by herding cows for 2d. a day, and went on to hoeing turnips for 4d.; he later obtained work as fireman at a colliery, and was able to save enough to take night-classes. He first became known by inventing a miners' safety-lamp, in the same year as Sir Humphry Davy did so. In 1814, he built his first locomotive; further inventions made possible the running of the Stockton and Darlington line (opened in 1825), of which he was the engineer. He then built the Liverpool and Manchester line, in spite of enormous opposition, and won the competition for deciding its form of traction by making the "Rocket", which ran at the unheard-of speed of 35 m.p.h. As chief engineer of a number of railways he directed much of the early railway building in England. The first locomotive used on the Continent was also built by an Englishman, John Cockerill, in the works which he and his brother established at Seraing in Belgium.

THE RISE AND FALL OF INDUSTRIAL PROSPERITY

In all countries there came a period when the production of manufactured goods increased with astonishing rapidity. For manufacturers and investors, the main object was the increase of profits and the expansion of business. Of the money accruing through profits, a large proportion was re-invested in business; it was not till the middle of the century that some of this surplus began to go towards raising the wages of the workers. In France, till the middle of the century, wages continued to fall. During the 'thirties in Paris, the average worker's wage was between 2s. 6d. and 4s. for a twelve-hour working-day. Elsewhere in France, wages for textile workers were as low as 9d. for men, $7\frac{1}{2}d$. for women, and $5\frac{1}{2}d$. for children.

Manufacturers had constantly to expand their sales, in order to make full use of their equipment; the settlement of America and of the British colonies, and the opening up of the East, supplied new fields for expansion. In spite of this, goods were produced more rapidly than they could be sold. Every time new machinery was set up, there was an increase of production; after a time, the markets were glutted and there was a slump. When accumulated stock had been sold off, there was another boom. The earliest years of the Machine Age in England saw the beginning of this alternation of boom and slump, which was to be a chronic feature of the new civilization. Every slump threw thousands of already needy workers out of employment and caused a social and political crisis. Legislation which limited the exploitation of labour, did something to modify the catastrophic effect of this violent economic oscillation.

The rise and fall of industrial prosperity was made more uncertain owing to the increasing dependence of industry on distant countries. The world was growing into a single economic unit. Raw materials for Lancashire came from the ends of the earth; cheap clothing from Manchester was sold to Chinese coolies who had never heard the name of England. The demand for raw cotton was met by the enormous development of cotton-growing in the U.S.A., India, and Egypt. Wool came mainly from Australia; the greatest advance of the wool-manufacturing industry became possible with increased supplies from there in the middle of the century. England before long found it impossible to live on home-produced corn, and began to import largely from Canada and the U.S.A. But increased resources meant less security. The holding-up of supplies of cotton from America could throw half the Manchester operatives out of work, while wars in the Orient were also capable of creating a slump by hampering the sale of the finished article in the Eastern markets.

INCREASE IN POPULATION

The working population was therefore at the mercy of situations over which it had no control. Just as the interference with the wheat supplies to Imperial Rome had thrown the population into want, so the holding-up of overseas supplies of raw materials for the English market produced a terrible situation in the industrial towns.

Suffering increased as the towns grew larger. The working population in England was increasing rapidly. This was due partly to the bad conditions existing in agriculture, which made the labourers escape to the towns; for the same reason, swarms of Irish poured in through the western ports of England and Scotland, and offered to work for wages still lower than the already inadequate rates which the English were prepared to accept. In response to the demands of industry, the population of England increased from fourteen million in 1801 to thirty-one million in 1870. Although industry came later to Germany, her population grew almost as rapidly as England's, and in other countries the rate of increase more or less corresponded with the speed of industrialization; France's population increased in the years between 1800 and 1870 by a third. In all European countries, it is noticeable that the growth of population was to be found almost entirely in the towns.

Population grew, not so much on account of any great increase in the birth-rate as of a considerable decrease in the death-rate. This was in spite of the overcrowding and the terrible sanitary conditions of the slums, and the unhealthy character of much of the work in factories. The death-rate in England, during the centuries when she was primarily an agricultural country, had been still higher. In the nineteenth century, the death-rate for the upper classes fell rapidly; and in other families, it fell in proportion as they shared in the advantages of the new civilization. With the introduction of machine-processes for textiles, clothing became cheaper: it could be changed more frequently and washed more easily. With Jenner's discovery of vaccination, smallpox rapidly decreased, especially after vaccination became compulsory—as happened in England in the middle of the century. In this period, too, the Board of Health was set up, with local boards in the various towns.

Conditions of employment were an incentive for the workers to have large families. There was a great demand for children to do mechanical work at rates which no man would accept, and instead of working long hours for low rates of pay, men sometimes preferred to depend on their wives and children for their livelihood. The Poor Law in England was also, till the 'thirties, an incentive to large families, for a man with low wages, or no employment, could draw extra amounts as relief according to the size of his family.

In the poorest classes in England, the death-rate increased till the middle of the century. For Glasgow, the figure of twenty-eight deaths per thousand in 1821 had increased to forty per thousand in 1841. In another town, the lease of life for workers in textile factories was, on the average, eighteen years; for the well-to-do, it was almost three times as long. The lower classes suffered most from the cholera epidemics which swept the world four times in the first three-quarters of the century; the loss of life among the poorer of the town-populations of Europe was almost as great as among the Indian peasants.

Overcrowding in industrial towns was terrible. One-tenth of the population of Manchester lived in cellars. According to a Commission's report of 1842, "in Manchester 12,000 families were supported by charity, 2000 families were without a bed . . . and it was calculated that there were 8666 persons whose weekly income did not exceed 1s. 2d. each".

Conditions in London were equally bad. One slum was described by the Report of a Parliamentary Commission, appointed in 1840, as "ruinous buildings, streets without sewers, overflowing privies and cesspools, and open ditches filled with a black putrefying mass of corruption infecting the air for miles".

In the industrial districts in France, conditions were similar, and the standard of health was correspondingly low. Out of the thousands of recruits from the industrial districts who were called up, a disturbingly large proportion were unfit for service.

EXPLOITATION IN THE FACTORIES

The conditions of the old home industry, though unhealthy enough, were infinitely preferable to the grinding routine, the rigid discipline, the heat and noise of nineteenth-century factories. In the old days, a man could take an hour off when he wished, or devote a day to cultivating his garden. Now the workers had to be in the factory punctually, usually at six in the morning, and stay there, except for a nominal hour for lunch, till six or seven in the evening. At one factory near Manchester, according to a pamphlet, "they work fourteen hours per day . . .; the door is locked in working-hours, except for half an hour at tea-time; the work-people are not allowed to send for water to drink in the hot factory". The machines set the pace, thereby subjecting the workers to a nervous strain and tension that had never been known in previous conditions.

The most horrible feature of the system was that children were condemned to grow up in these over-heated, ill-ventilated prisons, where
even whistling was an offence. Their labour was often described as
light, but it was calculated in one factory that children walked 20
miles during a twelve-hours day, in attending to the machines. The
fatigue was so great and the hours so long that they could be kept
awake only by terror, and the sound of beating and cries went on all
day long. The children would beg anyone who came near to tell them
how many more hours they still had before them.

In French factories, discipline—at first, at any rate—was not so
strict. In one factory where an Englishman was appointed as over-
seer, he found the workmen had the habit of leaving work when they
felt they had done enough for the day, and his efforts to introduce
English standards of discipline led to a serious strike which was
quelled only by the intervention of the military authorities.

OVERCROWDING AND PHYSICAL DETERIORATION

The conditions in coal-mines, revealed by a Parliamentary Commission's report in 1842, were a great shock for middle-class opinion.
Children were working from the earliest age, often sitting for twelve
hours at a time in complete darkness, opening and shutting the trapdoors for the miners to go by with their loads. On the correct working of these doors depended the circulation of air, and therefore the
safety of the mine. Children were employed to draw the loaded
trucks through galleries where grown persons could not go—sometimes these galleries were not more than 18 inches high. Women,
especially in Scotland, did much of this work of hauling, being
harnessed like dogs in go-carts. Sometimes they were employed to
carry heavy loads on their backs up the long ladders to the surface.
But perhaps the worst offence against humanity was making children
do the pumping operations at the bottom of the mines, where they
sometimes worked ankle-deep in water for twelve hours a day.

Physical deterioration, in the manufacturing districts of England,
became so widespread as to be a danger to the race. This was due to
poor food as much as to conditions of labour—bread and tea formed
the staple diet of factory "hands" in Lancashire. The women had
neither time nor money to prepare adequate meals—cooking had
become a lost art. Men and women who had spent their childhood
in the overheated and unnatural conditions of factory work became
increasingly unfitted to propagate a healthy race.

Because of the long hours of work, home became little more than
a place for eating hurried meals and for sleeping. There was a
noticeable decline of family affection. The necessity of forcing their
children to work often produced a brutal attitude in the parents; and
children, as a result of paying part of their wages to their parents,
soon came to regard their parents' house not as their home, but as a
lodging-house.

To compensate for lack of adequate food and relaxation, many of the working population, both men and women, were becoming slaves to dram-drinking in the numerous gin-vaults and beer-houses which sprang up in every industrial town. Drunkenness was widespread as a result of this.

Conditions in the United States were quite different; owing to shortage of labour, poverty was practically unknown. Men were not prepared to work in factories when there was plenty of unoccupied land, where they could set up as independent farmers. Employers had to ensure good living conditions in order to attract workers for the cotton-mills, which for some time continued to have their healthy situations by the side of streams in otherwise almost virgin country. Labour was provided for the most part by girls from hard-working farming families. Cotton-manufacturing settlements, with their well-organized lodging-house system, were model communities compared with the slums of Manchester or Lille. Not till the 'twenties was there the beginning of any considerable movement into the towns; as late as 1840, only one-fifth of the population lived in cities of over eight thousand inhabitants.

In England and France, and before long in America, the new industrial methods brought about a large increase in the number of the employing class, besides making new possibilities of accumulating fortunes quickly. In France, the employers grew almost as quickly as the workers, since many industrial establishments employed only one or two hands. London remained, till the twentieth century, a city of small businesses. For an able and determined man, it was far easier than before to rise from humble circumstances to be the owner, at any rate, of a small business; others were as successful as the humanitarian and socialistic Robert Owen, who became owner of one of the largest cotton-mills then to be found in England.

RAILWAYS REVOLUTIONIZE TRANSPORT

The revolution in transport made possible the spectacular career of George Hudson, the "Railway King", who was born in 1800. His father was a farmer and village constable of Howsham, near York. Hudson went as an apprentice to some drapers at York; later he became a partner in the business, and at the age of twenty-seven was already a rich man. Then a relative left him £30,000, which he invested in North Midland Railway shares. He strongly supported a projected Yorkshire railway scheme, and subscribed five hundred of the shares, becoming the company's chairman. For a new line from York to Edinburgh, he subscribed five times as much as any other director. He bought up three lines which were competing to come to Derby, collecting £5,000,000 capital for the purpose, and became director of the new company, henceforward known as the Midland Railway. At the zenith of the railway boom in 1844, Hudson controlled 1,016 miles of track and became an M.P. the following year.

Then dishonesty corrupted his transactions. On the amalgamation of two of his companies, he increased the issue of shares from forty-two thousand to fifty-six thousand, and made no entry of this on the books, appropriating almost ten thousand of them, and making about £145,000. Two years after he had bought the great North England Railway, on ruinous terms, the railway bubble burst (1847). The shares of ten of the leading railway companies depreciated to the extent of £78,000,000. Actions were brought against him, in which he was found personally indebted to several companies for enormous sums. Hudson then went abroad, and tried operating on the Continental exchanges, though with little success. On returning to England, he was imprisoned for failing to pay a debt, and was saved from ruin only by an annuity provided by his friends.

As the new industrial classes gained political power in England and the U.S.A., they were able to pass laws which made it safer and easier to invest. In England, companies in which money was invested, unless authorized by royal charter or an Act of Parliament, were legally partnerships; if the company failed each individual was responsible for paying the company's creditors. But by an Act of 1856, "limited liability" became possible for all companies; in the event of a company's failure, an investor was responsible only for any part of the capital he had not yet paid up.

New banks sprang up rapidly, doing brisk business when times were good, but the small banks were liable to fail as soon as a depression came. Legislation in England, France and America was passed, in order to prevent this danger. In France investment companies were formed with a state-guarantee for part of the interest. This legislation was made possible principally as a result of the investing public's stronger influence upon the Government's policy.

BRITAIN'S FOREIGN INVESTMENTS

England was the only country to invest money in large quantities abroad, and as a result, London was the undisputed financial centre of the world. France and the United States were favourite fields of investment, but at first the largest investments were in the new South American states. Investments in these countries were made in years when they were still fighting for their independence, and partly explain the strongly favourable attitude which England took up on their behalf. Safer fields were found in railway development, especially in France. Between 1833 and 1845, £50,000,000 of British capital was invested in foreign railways.

The larger bankers had enormous power in influencing the policy of governments. In this connection, the House of Rothschild is most famous. The business was begun by Mayer Anselm Bauer (later Rothschild), a Frankfort Jew, in the eighteenth century. Branches were established at Vienna, London, Paris and Naples, each being under the management of one of his five sons, of whom the eldest, in charge of the Frankfort bank, co-ordinated the activities of all. Solomon Rothschild of the Vienna house was a friend of Metternich, Chancellor of Austria. Jacob, the youngest, was in charge of the Paris branch, where the Monarchy, restored after Napoleon's defeat, depended on him very largely for loans. Later, he did much to finance railway development, and made enormous profits. The third son, Nathan, settled in London, and assured the future international greatness of the house by purchasing some drafts which Wellington had issued but was unable to meet. He made use of carrier pigeons and fast ships of his own, in order to get early information. The centralized system of the whole house, with agents and sub-agents everywhere, gave it world-wide power.

More important was the part they played in enabling European capital to develop industry and transport at home, and to open up the New World. Nathan Rothschild, especially, did much in popularizing loans in England for foreign countries. The family influence was perpetuated by bringing sons and relatives into the business, and in addition by intermarriage between the various branches.

CONTRASTING WEALTH AND POVERTY

Everywhere the industrial revolution was sharpening the contrast between rich and poor. The well-to-do were growing in numbers and had more wealth at their disposal—so much that they had to find a use for their money in large-scale investments. They lived well, but the comforts of life were not much greater than in the eighteenth century, until the railway began to make travelling less of a hardship than before; road improvements in the first half of the century had already begun to have this effect. Wealthy middle-class families often bought country estates where, like the eighteenth-century "Nabobs" who had piled up huge fortunes in India, they took up the traditional country-house style of living, with house-parties and hunting. In their social and political outlook, they often began to have much in common with the older landed families.

Many industrialists were eager, through political reforms and their own private work, to do something towards improving the workers' conditions. Such men were John Fielden, the owner of the largest cotton business in England, who was mainly responsible for the Ten Hours Act, limiting work for women and children. Others were strongly opposed to any change which they thought might lessen their profits. In a matter like shortening workers' hours, they argued that more leisure would be demoralizing; there was much legislation for bettering the workers' condition, but there was also strong opposition.

One example of successful opposition was against a measure for preventing the worst type of slums, by forbidding the building of back-to-back houses. Even in the most disgraceful slums, there were large rents for the proprietors: it was calculated that quite a small slum district in Westminster produced an annual rent of £40,000.

That low wages and bad conditions were not essential to prosperity and rapid development was proved by the United States. The comparative absence of working-class discontent is one reason for America's success in working out, during this period, a democratic civilization which was in many ways more harmonious in its nature and operation than that of the other industrial nations of the West.

HOW AGRICULTURE WAS AFFECTED

In England, industry before long became more important than agriculture, but she was the only country in the world in which this state of affairs obtained.

In France, the large peasant population which the Revolution had established in possession of their own small farms was a moderate conservative element. The peasantry felt little community of interest with the working-class of the towns, who were only a small minority of the total population. At the same time, they were not reactionary in politics, like those of the landowning aristocracy who still remained in possession of their lands.

During the period of the wars, serfdom had disappeared in Germany and Spain. But in the three most autocratic states of Europe—Austria, Russia and Turkey—the social system was feudalism. The middle class was small in Austria and smaller still in Russia. The mass of the population were peasants, for the most part serfs in Russia and practically serfs in Austria, entirely under the control of those members of the aristocracy on whose lands they lived. Meanwhile, the aristocratic families drew their rents and continued to enjoy their privileges, among these being exemption from compulsory military service and the right of a special code of justice.

CONDITION OF THE PEASANTRY

The disappearance of feudalism in Germany had partly the same result as in France—the establishment of a free peasantry owning their land. But there also existed large estates—especially those owned by the *Junker*, or Squire, class in Prussia—which were worked by landless labourers.

England was the country in which there was the sharpest division between great landlords and wage-earning labourers. This took a form of agricultural capitalism, in which the work of management was done mainly by tenant-farmers, while the owners took a large and directing interest in their estates. The condition of the labourers, like that of the wage-earners in the cities, was, in the first half of the century, very bad. Wages remained extremely low; workers' cottages were insanitary; prices were high and food often difficult to obtain. In Ireland, conditions were even worse, except for the independent farmers, descendants of Scottish colonists in the north. In the rest of the country, the landowners, for the most part, took no interest in the development of the land. Many of them were absentees and lived in

England. The tenant-farmer system had not developed in Ireland, and the peasantry had to pay ruinous rents to the landowners, who had less compunction in evicting them since the land was much over-populated and another tenant could easily be found. The peasants had no motive for improving their holdings, since high rents or eviction were likely to deprive them of any advantage. These conditions, together with religious and political grievances, made Ireland a land of discontent and underground agitation.

The agricultural population of the Continent remained, as for the most part throughout the centuries, in unthinking acceptance of their circumstances. Only now and then in France, or in Eastern Europe, when racial or national questions arose, did the peasantry become an important political factor. Discontent in Prussia and other districts of Germany, where big estates left little room for an expanding population, was lessened, as in England and Ireland, by numbers of labourers moving to the towns or emigrating.

In the world as a whole, methods of agriculture remained traditional. Only in England and America, and among individual landowners on the European continent, was there real advance. In America especially, the new machine technique was applied to agriculture, and there was a fertile crop of inventions, such as the mechanical reaper, which helped to make possible the feeding of the growing industrial population of Europe. In their willingness to adopt these new methods, the independent farming population of America showed their innovating and practical outlook, which was manifest also in the sphere of politics. In contrast, the cotton-plantation owners in the South of the United States were as conservative and unprogressive in politics as they were in their agricultural methods. Slave labour in the plantations did not lend itself to up-to-date methods; cultivation by slaves was notoriously slow and wasteful, but the planters' attachment to an old system, which they gave up only after four years of civil war, became a dogma and a point of honour. The desire to maintain this system intact led to their having a somewhat stereotyped and uncreative outlook.

CHAPTER 65

SPIRITUAL MOTIVE-FORCES

PROGRESS and freedom—these words are stamped across the pages of nineteenth-century history. Progress may often have been an illusion, freedom often a sham, but faith in progress was a tenet of almost all, and the desire for freedom was a motive-force of men and nations.

Belief in the perfectibility of man, and in the right of individuals to realize their capacities, were ideas which writers such as Rousseau had made popular in the last part of the eighteenth century. The extraordinary fertility and creativeness of the nineteenth century in the realms of literature, politics and mechanical inventions were due partly to a great sense of new possibilities. The overthrow by France of her ancient order and of her long line of kings, the building by Napoleon of an empire such as Europe had not seen since the time of Charlemagne, made people think that in the political realm nothing was impossible—just as, once the period of inventions had begun, material progress seemed unlimited. This outlook, together with a new analytical and scientific attitude of mind and in many countries an increased religious fervour, led to the unloosing of creative forces which the static character of the eighteenth century had dammed up.

These were similar forces to those which had made the Renaissance. There was a new interest in Man and a new conception of his place in the world. Together these brought about a new desire for freedom: the sense of new possibilities for the human personality, and the demand that these possibilities must be fulfilled. There was a great movement for freeing the human personality from shackles in the realms of religion, politics, society and culture. This showed itself destructively in the political sphere in removing laws and regulations which had become restrictions, and in abolishing political boundaries and foreign dominations. It showed itself in the realms of thought and art by abolishing out-of-date theories and formulae. Constructively it established a new framework in thought and society wherein the freed personality could better express itself.

These spiritual forces are closely connected with material progress, which, besides helping to liberate them, gave them a strongly materialist stamp. Utilitarianism was content to judge all things by the material satisfaction they gave to men. The rationalism of the age was materialist in so far as it denied previously-held spiritual values, and was forced by this to attempt purely scientific explanations.

INFLUENCE OF THE MIDDLE CLASS

The wealth which the mechanical inventions and factory organization brought, opened new horizons, especially to its possessors—for the most part members of the rapidly increasing middle classes. The shackles which they felt most keenly were political—exclusion from political power, and government interference with trade, such as was caused by high tariff policies. At the same time, the new middle class, as a whole, wished to construct a new civilization which had more than the good of their particular class as its aim. When the Middle Class had practically obtained a monopoly of power, it was the turn of the class below them, the working-class, to struggle for the advantages which material progress had made possible.

The spiritual forces of the age were, therefore, primarily, though not exclusively, those of the middle class, and were the outcome of their new material conditions. Their outlook was sometimes imaginative, emotional, idealistic, adventurous—this is the Romantic tendency. Sometimes it was intellectual, analytical, materialistic and scientific. These two tendencies were reflected in every spiritual activity of the age—in religion, thought, politics, art, and literature —so that in everything there occurred inevitable contradictions, together with blendings of apparent opposites.

THE RELIGIOUS REVIVAL

It is impossible to explain on material grounds the great development of religion which took place during this period. In England, the movement begun by Wesley continued to spread in the growth of Methodism, as well as in the revivals in all the Protestant churches, including the Church of England. In the latter, it took the form of the Evangelical Movement, whose adherents believed in the duty of Christians to effect conversions, and to work in a practical way for the betterment of humanity. This religious outlook, no less than the rationalist tendencies of the time, made the nineteenth century the age of humanitarianism; men and women were enthusiastic for good causes, which ranged from the protection of animals to the abolition of slavery.

In the frontier districts of America, vast crowds listened to itinerant preachers with the same enthusiasm Whitefield and Wesley had evoked. In France and Germany, Protestantism remained strong in the sections where it had already existed, although it did not increase. Everywhere, however, the Catholic Church showed a revival—in France, through the efforts of the Congregation, a religious society numbering many well-known men among its members; in Ireland, under the leadership of Bishop Doyle; in America, to some extent through Catholic immigrants, though the increase there cannot be entirely explained on those grounds.

The revival in the churches is partly shown by the number of political leaders who were influenced by it; at one time, a French Prime Minister and his Foreign Minister were both members of the Congregation. For the Italian patriot, Gioberti, the Papacy was the keystone of the new Italy as he saw it. It was his religion which made Abraham Lincoln perhaps the greatest president America has ever had, Gladstone one of the greatest of English statesmen.

More important was its effect on vast masses of the population. In England, very large numbers of the working-class became convinced Christians. This was one reason why there were so few violent attempts at bettering their lot during the years of falling wages and unemployment—attempts which would have been disastrous, because premature.

William Wilberforce, chiefly known in connection with the abolition of the Slave Trade, was one of the leading Evangelicals. A Member of Parliament before the age of twenty-one, and one of the most popular figures of London society, he was converted by a Cambridge tutor during a Continental tour. From that date, his outlook changed; he became known as a rigid Sabbatarian—and though succeeding generations had to endure the Victorian Sunday, it was partly owing to his efforts that working-people throughout the world were ensured one day's rest in seven. In spite of his new seriousness of purpose, such was Wilberforce's charm and simplicity that he was always one of the most welcome guests in London.

NEW HUMANITARIAN IDEALS

The missionary spirit which was the foundation of Evangelicalism found perhaps its best statement in Wilberforce's tract, *A Practical View of the Prevailing Religious System of Professed Christians in the Higher and Middle Classes in this Country contrasted with Real Christianity*. He defined the starting-point of practical Christianity as "an absolute surrender of soul and body to the will and service of God". He appealed to all "true Christians" of England to "consider as devolved on them the important duty of serving, it may be of saving their country . . . by that sure and radical benefit of restoring the influence of religion".

"We bear upon us but too plainly the marks of a declining empire. . . . To the decline of Religion and Morality our national difficulties must, both directly and indirectly, be chiefly ascribed; my only solid hopes for the well-being of my country depend, not so much on her fleets and armies, not so much on the wisdom of her rulers or the spirit of her people, as on the persuasion that she still contains many who love and obey the gospel of Christ."

Such convictions as these made the circle of Wilberforce and other like-minded friends—there was quite a colony of them at Clapham—one of the most influential social and political forces. Wilberforce himself lived to see Parliament vote £20,000,000 for making possible the freeing of the eight hundred thousand slaves which existed in the British Empire.

The anti-slavery movement in America was also supported on religious grounds. Lundy, who inspired W. L. Garrison to become the most famous champion of the slaves, was a Quaker, as was Whittier, the poet of the anti-slavery movement.

Humanitarianism showed itself in many ways. One of the most practical reformers was Florence Nightingale, who began the scientific training of hospital nurses and complete reorganization of hospital methods and conditions. She astonished public opinion by going out to the British hospital-base during the Crimean War. Apart from reducing the terrible rate of mortality among the casualties, this action roused a great interest in the question of hospitals as a whole.

The religious and humanitarian tendencies of the age are shown particularly in education. There was an enthusiasm for education comparable with that of the Renaissance, but it was more democratic. Here the effect of social and political advance is most noticeable. The progress of education is mainly due to the middle class—

it was among them that the forces of humanitarianism and the demand for culture were strongest. The national idea, and the increasing importance of the state, gave a further impulse to the movement for providing education more widely among the mass of citizens. Prussia, where the state-idea was strongest, had a system of compulsory education from the middle of the eighteenth century. The movement for national regeneration, after the *débâcle* of Jena, caused Prussia's statesmen to put educational reform in the forefront of their programme. Seventeen schoolmasters were sent by the Prussian Government to learn at first-hand the new principles which were being expounded by Johann Pestalozzi in Switzerland.

EDUCATION AS AN INSTRUMENT OF REGENERATION

The German–Swiss Pestalozzi is the central figure in the revolution in teaching aims and methods. His inspiration came originally from Rousseau, whose primary canon was that the child's sense-impressions were the natural medium of learning, not the memorizing of words, facts and phrases. Nature, not man, should be the teacher—a dogma which was whole-heartedly accepted by Pestalozzi. It was necessary only to draw out the developing capacities of the child, not pump things in. It was far less important that a child could read and write than that it could observe accurately, and draw its own conclusions. On the moral side, Pestalozzi's teaching was based on the great Christian truths.

It was not till the founding of his school at Yverdun in 1804 that his work received world-wide recognition. From there, his ideas spread throughout Europe and America, gradually transforming curriculum and method. The elementary schools of Germany, and particularly of Prussia and Saxony, led the way.

In all countries, this new education, by developing faculties of criticism and a consciousness of power, gave strength to the growing labour movements. These movements, and the propaganda accompanying them, had an effect which would not have been possible without the ability of large masses of people to understand reasoned economic and political arguments.

Not till the middle class was in power did the great period of educational advance take place. In England and France, the old aristocracy and the biggest industrialists (both representing a social system which was increasingly threatened), successfully opposed an extension of public education. In both countries, education had been in the hands of the established Churches, Catholic and Protestant respectively; in England, the dissenting Churches also did much in organizing education. In 1832, the English Parliament voted £20,000 towards education: this small sum increased to £663,000 in 1858. In France, the law of 1833 made it compulsory for every commune to have a primary school. The financial support necessary, in addition to the fees, was provided by a communal tax and a state subsidy.

America was already democratic in the northern states, where public education first appeared in the world. In New England and New York primary education was compulsory. As democracy developed, so public education expanded: in newly settled districts one square mile out of every block of land settled was reserved to provide a site and rent for public education. It was due to Horace Mann and other champions of education that by 1860 most towns had free common schools, some teachers' training-colleges had been set up, and there were the beginnings of an organized nation-wide university system. The democratic tendencies of Scandinavia showed themselves when Sweden, as early as 1852, made primary education compulsory, while Denmark developed a magnificent system of state-aided adult schools, under the inspiration of Bishop Grundvig.

Russia, with its almost complete absence of schools and very few universities, was a great contrast. To the liberal outlook of Alexander I, it owed such educational institutions as it had, but educational progress was completely checked under the autocratic Nicholas I. Similarly, when a reactionary government came into power in France in 1850, the law of 1833 was rescinded; though public education was not abolished, it was largely in the hands of the Roman Church.

THE PUBLIC SCHOOLS IN ENGLAND

Middle-class school education also developed, but along its own lines. Here England led the way, inspired by Thomas Arnold, who became head-master of Rugby in 1828. He aimed at producing a generation of men who should lead the world through the difficult social and political problems which he saw on all sides. For him, the great object of education was to fit the sons of the now powerful middle class to take up a leadership worthy of their responsibilities. He was a great Christian as well as a great scholar, and believed in a religious education, not merely one based on religion. He developed the prefect system by which boys could early learn responsibilities.

These principles, and the new spirit he brought, revolutionized the "public schools" (as the expensive, privately-organized schools in England are called) at a time when new schools were being founded in large numbers to supplement the older foundations, whose history went back to the Middle Ages. Many of these schools, such as Winchester and Harrow, which had been low in numbers, grew rapidly after the middle of the century. The new middle-class education was one main reason for the stability of England in the latter half of the century, because of the new quality of personnel provided for government, business, educational, and Church positions.

Progressive principles, such as those Arnold applied, can be traced back to the late eighteenth- and early nineteenth-century reformers. Pestalozzi, the Germans Froebel and Goethe, the Englishman Lancaster, had initiated a movement scientific in its study of child psychology, and emphasizing simplicity and a return to naturalness.

Rationalism, which in the eighteenth century had helped to free the forces which made the French Revolution, continued to affect the outlook of men. In the New England states of America, men could no longer accept the old Calvinist theology, with its doctrines of election, damnation, and the judgments of God. The resulting liberation of the religious life, and the new conception of the relation of God to man, led to a burst of militant humanitarianism and political progress. Thus rationalism contributed to the abolition of slavery, while the forces of political democracy in the northern United States became stronger than those existing anywhere else in the world.

RATIONALISM AND RELIGIOUS REVIVAL

Rationalism also led to a new critical spirit in regard to religion. This partly showed itself in a minute examination of the texts of the Bible to see how far they fulfilled the canons demanded by the new scientific historical criticism. This critical approach was adopted particularly by German theologians; the Frenchman Renan was also a great exponent of it, publishing his *Life of Jesus* in 1863. Such work was largely, though by no means entirely, destructive of generally accepted views of religion: it tended to undermine religion by making it a matter of common sense rather than of real spiritual significance.

The revival of worship in the churches did not always signify an increase of religion. It was sometimes due to a tendency which showed itself most fully in literature and art—the romantic tendency. One of the characteristics of romanticism is its exaltation of feeling as one of the highest values of life; and in religion, feeling was placed more and more above moral purpose and power. Men tried to find in religion the fullest satisfaction for the imagination and the desire of beauty. The religion richest in tradition and historical appeal, which emphasized the awe and majesty of God, and which made much of colour and ceremonial, would most fully satisfy the romantically minded. Such was the religion of the Roman Catholic Church, and this partly explains its growth in numbers and influence during this period. Partly, also, this was due to a reaction from rationalism, which was doing so much to destroy the foundations of belief; men went to the church which put forward the strongest claim to settle disputed points by its authority. The French writer and statesman Chateaubriand was among the most famous of those who set the Roman Church in the light which appealed to the romanticism of the age. In the Church of England, the Oxford Movement represented the same tendency, stressing the principles of authority, historical tradition and ceremonial. Its leader, Newman, eventually joined the Roman Church.

As a political force, the Roman Church regained power during this period. The French Revolution and Napoleon had shaken its position throughout Europe. The governments who returned after Napoleon's defeat restored it inside their states, without allowing it all its previous privileges. The Church became, in most countries, subordinate by law to the state, though at the same time it became the strongest supporter of the restored conservative régimes. This weakening of the Church's position, in regard to the governments, was counteracted by the immense strengthening of the power of the Pope over the Catholics themselves. A sign of this was the restoration of the Jesuits in 1814. Pius IX took action which led up to the declaration of Papal Infallibility in 1870.

Before the French Revolution, it had been fashionable for the French aristocracy to be cynical about religion. After the Revolution had broken out, and throughout the century, as democratic forces increased in power, the aristocracy of France, and of the other Catholic countries of Europe, came to lean more and more for support on the Roman Church. Later, when the *bourgeoisie* also began to find their positions threatened, Catholicism became fashionable for them, too. The Catholic revival is far from being entirely explained by such political factors, but the result for the Church, by the middle of the century, was that it was being given a far more privileged position in all the European Catholic countries.

GREAT THINKERS OF THE AGE

The great thinkers express the tendencies of the age, while their variations of outlook correspond in the main to differences of nationality. Hegel, who, for some years before his death in 1831, had been the philosophical dictator of Germany, expressed the new interest in Man. Nature existed for man, and man supplied the key to understanding the hiden things of nature. He explained nature as the revelation of God; material objects were only the counterpart and the basis of things spiritual. The spiritual world was the more important; contemplation and the practice of religion were the main purpose of life. In this outlook, Hegel represented a majority of educated Germans, who were not deeply concerned with politics, since they were satisfied with the pursuit of philosophy and literature.

The Frenchman Auguste Comte, on the other hand, expressed the materialist outlook. With the intensely logical attitude typical of his countrymen, he tried to analyse history in the same way as scientists analysed chemical and physiological processes. After sketching out a science of social development, he concluded that further progress would be possible only as men brought their moral sense increasingly to control the other elements of human nature. To this end, a religion was necessary, and Comte elaborated a religion of humanity to take the place of Christianity, which he regarded as having fulfilled its historical rôle.

Emerson had an American's optimism in the possibilities of every individual, believing that "God was in every man". Favourable circumstances would ensure each individual his full development.

This was an expression of American democracy—faith in the equality of every man; it was an expression of American nationalism—the belief that America could and should provide the ideal conditions for the free development of its citizens.

The philosophy of the Scotsman Carlyle is exceptional, and not typical of his democratic nation. He believed that it is the great men, such as Cromwell, Frederick the Great, and Luther, who make history. Such an outlook represents the reaction to authoritarian and dictatorial government, which began to appear in the latter half of the nineteenth century, and may be regarded as in many ways a prelude to the dictatorial régimes of the twentieth.

ECONOMIC THEORIES OF THE MIDDLE CLASS

The mind of the middle class showed its materialist bias by concerning itself particularly with economic thought. The great prophet of the middle class was the eighteenth-century thinker, Adam Smith. His followers, J. B. Say in France and Ricardo in England, explained how necessary it was that all restrictions on trade and industry should be removed. This expressed the attitude of the new industrial and commercial classes, in so far as they wished to be free from all government regulations that were a restraint on the development of their businesses. Many regulations had come down from the Middle Ages—guild laws in France, apprentice laws in England. Above all, the English industrialists and merchants wanted the abolition of all restrictions on trade, such as high tariffs.

This doctrine of freedom from government interference in all economic matters should have led, in France and England, to a removal of the laws against workmen associating in unions and similar organizations. But the application of this doctrine, which the government thought would be dangerous to the safety of the state and the ability to secure cheap labour, did not come about till the middle of the century—and then it was due to the increased sense of security.

In opposition to the raising of wages or the shortening of hours, the employers often used an argument which was a popular version of one of Ricardo's theories. Wealth resulting from the application of capital to labour went in part to the capitalist, as interest on the money he had invested, in part as payment of salaries and wages, and in part as accumulation for further investment. It was understood that the part available for wages, the "wages fund", was limited, increasing only as total wealth increased. Any attempt to increase the proportion which went as wages would lead to an insufficient amount for the other parties—if, for instance, there was too little for capitalist accumulation, it would be disastrous for the economic system as a whole, and the workers would be the first to suffer. This "Iron Law of Wages" was one of the firmest props of employers who wished to oppose possible government interference on behalf of the workers.

The gloomiest of the economists was Malthus, who believed that population would always increase to the limit at which it could be supported. Judging from the rate at which population was growing during the first phase of industrial development in England, Malthus concluded that in time there would not be enough even for the bare subsistence of all the human race. He argued that to better the working-class conditions would only aggravate the problem.

DARWINISM AND UTILITARIANISM

One of the most surprising results of Malthus' writing was in natural science. Charles Darwin, after reading Malthus' *Essay on Population*, suddenly realized that in the idea of the elimination of part of the human race lay the key to the development of nature. In the struggle for existence, favourable types were preserved, unfavourable ones disappeared. Independently, Wallace came to the same conclusions, also after reading Malthus. The two naturalists exchanged their ideas before Darwin published their common conclusion in the *Origin of Species*.

Social thought shows the same scientific critical outlook and the same preoccupation with the problem of historical development. One of the greatest social thinkers was the Englishman Jeremy Bentham. The test he applied to every social and political institution was its usefulness in advancing the greatest happiness of the greatest number; he and his followers were called Utilitarians. By this test of Utility he condemned the penal, educational and Poor Law Institutions, and he made practical suggestions for reforms, which had the greatest influence on the legislation of the times. In political questions, his tests led him to take up a far more extreme standpoint than that of the middle class as a whole. Not only did he consider the House of Lords as altogether useless, but he did not see sufficient justification for the continuance of the monarchy either. He was a republican, a democrat and a staunch believer in universal suffrage. As for colonies, he was at one with most of the early nineteenth-century economists; he thought them more trouble than they were worth, and that they would be more profitable financially and more likely to be profitable to Britain if separated from her. Bentham gave the philosophical basis for the English Radical party.

Later English political philosophers followed, in the main, in Bentham's footsteps. James Mill presented a more typical middle-class outlook, believing it, as he said, "the chief source of all that has exalted and refined human nature". His son, J. S. Mill, was more concerned with finding guarantees for the individual's freedom. When he wrote his essay on *Liberty* in 1859, the state had already begun to have a vast new power, through legislation that gave it control, especially in the sphere of industry. Mill was also a believer in the equality of women with men, and one of the first to advocate that women should have the vote.

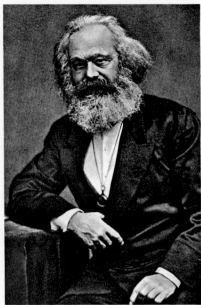

Charles Robert Darwin, 1809–82, British naturalist who established the theory of the origin of species.

Heinrich Karl Marx, 1818–83. His work, *Das Kapital* encouraged Socialist activities throughout the world.

Carding, drawing and roving in a woollen mill of 1835. The development of machinery for spinning and weaving started swift development of the cotton and woollen industries in England.

Giuseppe Garibaldi, 1807–82, Italian patriot who helped the statesman Cavour to free Italian territory from Austrian occupation.

Abraham Lincoln, 1809–69, President of the United States of America, maintained the Union against the Confederate States.

The procession at the celebration in 1897 of Queen Victoria's Diamond Jubilee passing down Poultry after leaving St. Paul's Cathedral.

There was a great development in socialist thought, beginning with Saint-Simon, a representative of the idealistic section of the aristocracy that was to be found everywhere in Europe and America at this time. In some ways he belonged to a past epoch; he based his thinking not so much on a scientific study of facts as on principles laid down by himself, of which the most novel was that every man had the right to work. He showed the faith of an aristocrat in his demands that the monarchs and nobility, who had been restored to power after the defeat of Napoleon, should begin the reforms. These were to bring in the new era, in which the basis of society was to be formed by self-supporting communities, in which the control would be in the hands of the industrial and scientific experts.

This idea of self-supporting communities, whose members lived together in freedom and equality, is a feature of all romantic socialist thinking, with its suggestion of forming an ideal society by means of an almost monastic escape from the world. His successor, Fourier, drew up a detailed scheme as to the type of organization such communities should adopt. These were to a large extent taken over by Louis Blanc, who at one time seemed to have a chance of putting them into effect, aided by a revolutionary government in France.

ROBERT OWEN'S INFLUENCE ON SOCIALISM

The first man to work out the community idea in practice was the Welshman Robert Owen. He started life as a draper's apprentice and went on to a cotton factory in Manchester, where, owing to his supreme organizing ability, he became general manager at the age of nineteen. Later, he bought some mills in New Lanark, which he managed successfully, making a profit, besides carrying out socialist experiments there. He reduced hours of work, paid good wages, rebuilt workers' dwellings, made no dismissals during a time of stagnation, and provided schools for the workers' children. His view was that factories, instead of representing a system of exploitation, should be centres of progress and enlightenment. But his ideas were too far advanced even for such partners as Bentham, and as a result he resigned the management, and devoted himself to establishing self-supporting communities.

In 1825, two such experiments were begun—one in America—but neither was successful, owing to the ill-assorted and often poor type of people who composed them. Later experiments had no better result, with the exception of one in Ireland, which did well for several years. With what little money he had left, Owen tried organizing a co-operative bazaar, where workers could exchange their products—but this too was a failure. So was the grandiose attempt in 1834 to organize all the Trade Unions in the country into one body, the Grand National Consolidated Trades Union, of which Owen was President. In the height of his fame at New Lanark, Owen attracted the attention of governments throughout Europe, and received visits from

A A   (H.W.)

such men as the future Tsar Nicholas I of Russia. His anti-Christian attitude alienated public opinion in England, and, after the failure of his magnificent experiments, he ended his days in dreamy spiritualism.

KARL MARX AND HIS TEACHING

Karl Marx, the father of modern communism, was born three years after Waterloo. Owing to his unorthodox views as a newspaper editor, he was driven from Germany, and in Paris met another German, Friedrich Engels, who was in business in Manchester. Settling in England, he worked long hours in the British Museum, and with Engels' aid he produced *Das Kapital* and other works which expounded the new creed. The economic basis of Marxism was borrowed from Ricardo and the "classical" school. Land, capital and labour in combination produced wealth over and above these elements separately. Hence it was argued that the worker was not getting his rightful share of this "surplus value", which his labour was responsible for creating.

Marx developed his theory into a revolutionary creed, and an ideology. He appealed to the greed of the worker to oppose the greed of the employer. "Dialectical materialism", in part borrowed from Hegel, was the theory he advanced to show that each historical situation was transformed by the conflict of opposing factors within it, and that the outcome was the creation of an entirely new historical phase. Capitalism tended to cause fewer people to own more and more of the means of production and therefore of the total wealth; this clashed with the tendency of more and more workers to own less and less. The result of this conflict would be a revolutionary rising by the workers to cast off their wage-slavery, and so create a new phase of society, the opposite of capitalism, in which everyone would own everything. "The workers have nothing to lose but their chains", proclaimed the *Communist Manifesto* in 1848. "They have a world to win", "Proletarians of all lands, unite!" Marx burned with resentment against the authorities who had closed his country's press against him, and he appealed to the hatred which workers felt, or might be induced to feel, against their capitalist "oppressors". The worker must rise and smash the enemy class and its system.

Though a confessed atheist and materialist, Marx had in a strangely perverted form something of the prophetic qualities of his Hebrew ancestors. He believed that the world was destined to move to a new era, where the poor would inherit the earth, but only in a materialist form; he opposed violently all spiritual and Christian ideas. The tyranny of the state and the capitalist class which controlled it was destined to be broken, and the "dictatorship of the proletariat" would usher in a man-made paradise, where the state would "wither away". Hatred and idealism were the twin appeals, supported by a plausible, but defective, philosophy whereby Marx and his collaborators mobilized the spearhead of their revolutionary striking force, the Communist Party. Though Marxist appeal is international, working-class movements during this period developed mainly on national lines, British socialism, with its roots in the Christian tradition, grew quite independently of Marxism. Conditions in the United States were unfavourable to class-war doctrines.

MAZZINI'S REPUBLICANISM

Another great internationalist was the fervent Italian patriot, Mazzini. After a term of political imprisonment, he went to Marseilles to spin his endless web of intrigue. With inexhaustible energy he wrote letters, newspaper articles, directions for "Young Italy", "Young France" and the other societies he founded. Mazzini taught that the countries of Europe, inspired by the spirit of nationalism and free, though republican, institutions, should work together in a new era of mutual sympathy and peace. But these ideals were compromised by the violence which societies, such as the Carbonari in Italy, sometimes used as a political weapon. Though their direct effort was small, these societies helped to stimulate the nationalist spirit, while the Continental Freemasons attacked the Roman Catholic Church.

GROWTH OF GERMAN NATIONALISM

Napoleon had unwittingly aroused the nationalist spirit in many lands. To resist France's aggressive nationalism, many writers returned to the sources of national life, and harked back to medieval ideals, medieval themes, and the medieval religion of Rome. The modern form of nationalism was first expressed by the German philosopher, Fichte. Like the Prussian military class, he endowed the state with a personality of its own and claimed unconditional obedience from its citizens. He translated these theories into terms of economics, saying that the state should be, as far as possible, self-supporting and independent of foreign trade—the doctrine of economic nationalism.

Nationalism, however, usually went hand in hand with liberalism, or the movement for free political institutions. The German middle class, in fact, loved liberalism more than nationalism. The philosopher, Hegel, went even farther. For the Germans, free institutions were not necessary, nor were union and independence: all these things they had already, in the realm of culture. Germans could rejoice in their republic of letters, which overstepped the bounds of their petty states. For the cultured middle class, this was a true democracy of the spirit, and it was a democracy which spread beyond Germany, throughout the whole of Europe.

It was Goethe, poet, philosopher, novelist and dramatist, who, in the eighteenth century, had made German literature international; he continued his great work till his death in 1832. Other German writers, like Schneckenburger—the author of *The Watch on the Rhine* —and the poet Arndt, were strongly nationalist in their appeal. But, on the whole, the German middle class followed the outlook of Goethe. And though the liberals almost succeeded in their determined bid to make a political empire as well as their empire of the spirit, this political empire was eventually achieved only through the ambitious plans and under the leadership of Prussian militarists.

THE INFLUENCE OF ROMANTIC LITERATURE

Italy was the country in which literature had the strongest influence on the national struggle for freedom. Alfieri escaped from the sense of being cramped and thwarted in his own life by directing an attack against the narrowness of life in Italy as a whole. He painted the greatness of Italy's past, and raised the cry for liberty to remake that greatness anew. Manzoni's historical novel, *I Promessi Sposi*, dealing with a betrothed couple who were persecuted by one of Italy's foreign rulers, was among the most powerful works of national propaganda. A more moving appeal was made by the autobiography of Silvio Pellico, for ten years imprisoned in an Austrian fortress for taking part in the abortive rising of 1820.

A fully-fledged romantic is often a morally unhealthy creature. With feeling in all its forms as the main object of life, he tends to demand the breaking of moral barriers in order to achieve freedom for his self-gratification. Absorbed in his own feelings and emotions, the romantic poet was usually introspective, unhappy, exacting a morbid satisfaction from his gloom and from the tragedy of life as he saw it. Feeling, indeed, could be raised above the ordinary things of this world, as Shelley raised it; it could be transformed, so that poetic impulse could be a force to regenerate the world. But often, as in the American Edgar Allan Poe, morbidity and melancholy were the dominant note.

Byron is one of those who escaped for a time from the chains of a morbid personality. He had a title and a fair amount of money, was intelligent and handsome, yet (partly on account of having a club-foot) was acutely self-conscious, besides being morbidly dissatisfied. His poems, in which he dramatized himself as the adventurous wanderer through the eastern Levant, or as the mysterious Oriental hero, took London society by storm. He was idolized by society, only to be ostracized by it on his separation from Lady Byron. He went to the Continent and spent most of his time in Italy, sometimes in a life of pleasure at Venice, sometimes in the plottings of the revolutionary Carbonari. Finally, after the outbreak of the Greek War of Independence, he went to Greece, and died at Missolonghi, while defending the town against the Turks.

Wordsworth, in some ways a contrast to Byron, is one of the simplest, as well as one of the most patriotic, of English poets. He believed profoundly that the sources of spiritual life were to be found in community with Nature and in the quiet pursuits of country life. This philosophy he expresses in poems full of power like *Tintern Abbey*, though at other times he falls into bathos. Wordsworth's admiration for the life of simple people was linked with his interest in humanity and with the advance of freedom.

> "Two voices are there, one is of the sea,
> One of the mountains; each a mighty voice;
> In both from age to age thou didst rejoice,
> They were thy chosen music, Liberty!"

Victor Hugo sums up many of the tendencies of the age, while his genius stands above them. As the son of an officer who, though he had served under Napoleon, was a loyal supporter of the restored Bourbons, Hugo gave vent in his earlier poems to the extremest forms of royalist adulation. On the change of dynasty, he became a supporter of the new ruler, but when Louis Napoleon began his dictatorial rule, Hugo opposed it and went into exile. In the vigorous unreality of his plays and poems, he appealed to the rising middle-class public by providing them with an escape from the dull everyday world. In his later days, he became a republican and a champion of humanity; of this period his great humanitarian novel *Les Misérables* is the finest expression of his work and opinions.

The spiritual forces of the age, as they were expressed in literature, are too manifold to admit of classification under a few simple headings. Most novelists—Dickens, the Brontës, Balzac, Dostoevsky in particular—have the study of character as their main interest. But further tendencies constantly show themselves: a sense of futility in Flaubert, the imaginative painting of the past in Scott and de Vigny, sympathy with the oppressed masses in Turgeniev, and to some extent in Dickens, and the representation of peasant life in the works of the Frenchwoman George Sand.

MUSICAL AND ARTISTIC MOVEMENTS

Similar tendencies are revealed by art and music. A Byronic turbulence in the paintings of Delacroix represents the new forces of romanticism, as the classicism of Ingres stands for the old eighteenth-century values restored in the political realm in 1814. In the paintings of Corot's later days, romanticism has become sentimental, while the return to medievalism is dominant in the works of the English Pre-Raphaelites. Sometimes the themes are fantastic and whimsical, as in the works of the German von Schwindt; at others, calm and peaceful, as when J. M. W. Turner, a Wordsworth in painting, seeks God in sunsets and in distant views.

It is in architecture that the return to the Middle Ages, fostered in England by the writings of the Pugins and, after them, of John Ruskin, is most clearly shown. It is marked by the usually sentimental and barren productions of the Gothic Revival—though this too produced fine works in such buildings as the Houses of Parliament, the Law Courts in London and in the Rathaus at Munich.

The powerful music of Beethoven breaks through old forms in its effort to express the very spirit of man—his new possibilities, his wrestling with new problems, his struggle to be free. Those who came after him were vigorous or sentimental or nationalist, but the works composed by Ludwig van Beethoven, particularly his nine great symphonies, embody most fully those spiritual forces which were striving during his lifetime to mould the world into new forms.

CHAPTER 66

NEW NATIONS APPEAR ; NEW CLASSES
SEIZE POWER

THE wars of Napoleon did not end at Waterloo. They still continued on the other side of the Atlantic in the Spanish colonies of South America. Napoleon had lit the flame by making his brother, Joseph, King of Spain. The rebellions began with the object of restoring Ferdinand VII, but the governments which had been formed in his name made declarations that the territories they ruled were free and independent republics.

The strength of this movement came from a feeling of distinct nationality, which had been largely inspired by the success of the United States in winning independence. As the United States grew and flourished, the desire for freedom and for republican institutions spread southwards. National consciousness appeared first in the Spanish colonies; the movement for independence came later in the Portuguese colony of Brazil. Nationalism was stimulated by the hatred between the Creoles (American-born Spaniards), and the Spaniards from Europe. The chief official positions almost invariably went to the European-born Spaniards, who despised the Creoles. The full extent of this hatred is shown by the remarkable fact that every important revolutionary leader who arose was a Creole.

THE SOUTH AMERICAN REPUBLICS

But there was no national consciousness, in the fullest sense. The desire for independence was almost entirely a local affair. South America was such a gigantic continent that it was impossible for a sense of community to grow up among all its Latin inhabitants. Colombia was twice as large as the Austrian Empire, while not only Austria, but also European Russia, France and Germany could be fitted into Brazil.

Except for two great leaders, the risings might have remained largely isolated. José de San Martin was one of the most generous and unselfish leaders that the revolutionary movements of the nineteenth century produced. He was American-born, the son of a Spanish official, and had been sent to Spain for a military education.

There he had served with the Loyalists during the Napoleonic wars, but hearing of the risings in South America, he sailed to Argentina. He secretly trained a small army until it was more than a match for any other troops in the continent. In 1817, like another Hannibal, he crossed the Andes by what was supposed an impassable route and completely surprised the Spanish forces in Chile. With the help of a fleet of English and Irish volunteers, he transported his army to Peru and seized the capital, Lima.

There his troops were not far from those of the second of the Liberators, Simon Bolivar, who had been fighting in the north for some years previous to San Martin's campaign in the south. Except for his inherited position as owner of large estates in Venezuela, he appeared completely unsuited to be a leader. He was puny, narrow-faced, and, though vain, entirely unattractive; his moral character was not good; he was domineering and ambitious.

In his first campaigns against the Royalists, Bolivar lost no fewer than three armies. But his skill as a general improved, and he always kept his burning enthusiasm for the cause, which was his greatest asset. One of the most important steps towards independence was taken when he defeated the Spaniards decisively at Boyaca in 1819; this was partly due to a stiffening of British volunteers, useful when there was an increasing danger of intervention from Europe against the revolutionaries.

It was four years later when San Martin and Bolivar met. San Martin quickly realized that he could not work successfully with such a domineering colleague as Bolivar. Entirely unselfishly, he resigned his leadership into Bolivar's hands and left for Europe, where he spent the remainder of his life in peaceful retirement.

AUSTRIA AND RUSSIA DOMINATE THE CONTINENT

After the subsidence of the Napoleonic flood, the map of Europe emerged largely in its eighteenth-century form. The degenerate Ferdinand returned to Spain. A Bourbon was restored to France. Petty princes went back to their Courts in Germany or Italy. In Germany their numbers were considerably diminished, as the larger Powers among the victors had taken the opportunity of helping themselves to additional territory. Most of the overseas Empire of France was considered by England a suitable reward for having borne the heat of the day against the Revolution and Napoleon. France herself, after Waterloo, was reduced to her pre-revolutionary frontiers.

The two great autocracies of Eastern Europe, Austria and Russia, once more dominated the Continent. The political life of these countries depended on the landowning caste, who were, from the nature of their position, the greatest enemies of revolutionary movements among the masses. After Europe had been re-arranged according to the old monarchic and aristocratic pattern, it was considered important that this arrangement should be solidified.

It was at the Congress of Vienna, from 1814 to 1815, that the final arrangements as to the frontiers of Europe were made, and a system was devised for solidifying not only her frontiers but her social structure. Outwardly, fashionable entertainments appeared to be the business of a large number of those who had come to the Congress. The old eighteenth-century society reappeared to strut before the world in receptions and balls, while in secret conversations the real work went on, often apparently unnoticed. "The Congress does not *go*, it dances", wrote an observer. "There is literally a royal mob here. . . . With the exception of a few Englishmen (easily distinguished by the richness of their clothes), I do not see anyone without a title to his name."

But the work was finished in the end, and the restored system was crowned by an alliance between the four victorious Great Powers— Austria, Russia, Prussia and England—for the purpose of seeing that the peace treaties were observed. The British delegate, Castlereagh, who had proposed this, also brought about the inclusion in the treaty of an agreement that the Powers should consult together from time to time. By this means, it was considered that appropriate steps could be taken in time to allow for any new political developments that arose inside Europe.

Prince Metternich, Chancellor of Austria, was not interested in new developments but in maintaining the *status quo*, and he began to turn the alliance into an instrument for this end. He had a peculiar hatred of revolutions. The son of a noble house, he had been brought up as a page at the Austrian Court. His university days had been passed at towns on the frontier of France, where he was near enough to the Revolution to have his horror of such upheavals considerably strengthened. During the wars, he had done much of the work of organizing coalitions against Napoleon.

As Chancellor of Austria, he had particular dangers to guard against, since the subject nationalities of the Empire might rise against the German minority who ruled them from Vienna. All these circumstances made him the arch-enemy of popular movements; pompous, though genial in his manner, a master of diplomacy, and with a constant and comprehensive stream of information from spies and informers at his disposal, he watched over a political system which it was impossible that any human power could preserve.

REPRESSION IN SPAIN

The first revolution with which the Great Powers had to deal was in Spain. The army, which had been waiting four years to be transported to South America in order to suppress the revolution there, itself rebelled. Ferdinand was forced to grant the Constitution of 1812, which he had abolished on his restoration, but which he now swore loyally to uphold. France, which had become a member of the alliance of Great Powers, was called upon to subdue the revolution.

She agreed to do so, and after a campaign which was little more than a military parade, Ferdinand was restored to absolute power and the constitution was suppressed. In its place, Ferdinand established what was, in effect, the Inquisition in a modernized form. By this means he was able to suppress doctrines dangerous to his regime.

THE U.S.A. FORBIDS FOREIGN INTERVENTION IN AMERICA

At the same congress which decided on French intervention in Spain, Chateaubriand, one of the delegates for France, suggested that when the revolution in Spain had been "pacified", the Great Powers should undertake to restore order in the South American colonies as well. But England did not intend to lose the large trade which had grown up between herself and the revolted colonies; under Spanish rule, foreign trade, except such as went on by smuggling, was almost entirely excluded. The English Foreign Minister, Canning, negotiated with the United States. The outcome was President Monroe's declaration in 1823, the "Monroe Doctrine". The United States, it said, would consider any attempt on the part of the European Powers "to extend their systems to any portion of this hemisphere as dangerous to our peace and safety. With the existing colonies or dependencies of any European power we have not interfered and shall not interfere. But with the governments who have declared their independence and maintained it, and whose independence we have, on great consideration and just principles, acknowledged, we could not view any interposition for the purpose of oppressing them, or controlling in any other manner their destiny, by any European power, in any other light than as a manifestation of an unfriendly disposition towards the United States."

This attitude of the United States, which would be backed if necessary by the British fleet, decided the independence of the South American states. A year later, the last Spanish force in the continent was defeated by Bolivar at the Battle of Ayacucho. Mexico and Brazil had already declared their independence, the latter as an Empire under the rule of one of the Portuguese royal house. The attempt of Bolivar to bring about some system of federal government, such as that achieved by the United States, was a failure, and South America, except for Brazil, remained a continent of independent republics. For the most part, they were to have a disturbed internal history, but in spite of this lack of political unity and a fixed policy they nevertheless became increasingly important as a source of food and raw materials for Europe and North America, and as a market for manufactured goods.

It was in Eastern Europe that Metternich's system was to suffer its next failure. The submerged peoples of the Balkans were, for the most part, of Slav stock: such were the Serbs, Bulgarians and Albanians. Racially distinct were the Greeks and the Macedonians, and there was also one Romance-speaking people—the Rumanians.

Like the other states of Europe in 1815, the Ottoman Empire was based on an aristocracy—not of birth, but of religion. All Mohammedans were members of the ruling caste; only a minority of them were pure-blooded Turks. The subject-peoples were Christians and Jews, who already formed a state within the state; the finances of the empire had long been in their hands, and Greeks manned the civil service of the Porte. Their religious organizations, especially the Greek Orthodox Church, were very strong. Altogether, the subject-populations of the Turks were practically self-governing communities. The Sultans favoured this development, since they themselves had failed to establish any sound principles of central government.

THE MOVE TOWARDS FREEDOM IN EUROPE AND SOUTH AMERICA

The first of the submerged races to gain freedom were the Serbs. The Principality of Belgrade came into existence in 1815, under the leadership of the former pig-raiser, Obrenovich. His rule of the new nation was a disturbed one, but after bringing about the assassination of a rival, Obrenovich was able to keep his position for many years.

The cause of the Greeks made a wider appeal to public opinion in Europe, though the fisher-folk and bandits, who rose in 1827, were almost as brutal as their Turkish masters. The Greeks began the series of massacres which characterized the war, and the Turks retaliated by murdering the Patriarch of Constantinople. Enthusiasm for the Greeks, however, rose to a high pitch when Byron and other volunteers, such as the Piedmontese revolutionary Santa Rosa, and the French Colonel Fabvier, went out to help the patriots.

Metternich urged the Powers to suppress the rebellion, but the excited state of public opinion made this impossible, even had the governments been willing. Another terrible massacre, and a rumour that the Sultan's vassal, Ibrahim Pasha of Egypt, intended to exterminate part of the population, led England and France to intervene in order to enforce an armistice. An attempt to do this led to a naval battle at Navarino, where the whole Turkish fleet was destroyed. Meanwhile Russia, under her new Tsar, Nicholas, had broken away from Metternich's system, and entered the war on the side of Greece. After the capture of Adrianople by the Russians, the Turks came to terms, and the new independent Greece came into existence.

On the two major issues of Greece and South America, Metternich's international conservative system had been defeated. In the same way, in matters of internal government, aristocratic systems found it increasingly difficult to maintain their existence. In France and England, the old order was overthrown by the rising power of the middle class, and in the United States and the Scandinavian countries, there was a parallel development.

In Europe, the farther north, or the higher above sea-level, one goes, the more democratic the countries become. This is mainly because the poverty of the land is unable to support a nobility.

Scandinavia is well in the van of democratic progress, and in this respect, the northernmost and most mountainous of the three Scandinavian countries, Norway, comes first. Till 1814, she was part of the Kingdom of Denmark: almost the only aristocracy she possessed were the Danish officials. For the rest, the population were mainly peasants and sailors, besides a small business community. The Congress of Vienna decided that she should belong to Sweden; the Danish officials were dismissed, and the new government tried to replace them by Swedes. But the Norwegians were determined to achieve both national and democratic freedom. They had established a constitution in 1814, and they refused to accept their new ruler until he had ratified it.

Sweden's constitution consisted of a Council of State and a legislative assembly. This assembly was, in form, democratic, though, as in England, it represented only a minority. Another resemblance to England was that the power of the monarchy was strictly limited. There was still a considerable nobility, but of the landed proprietors as a whole, about 95 per cent. were peasants, owning an average of 240 acres each.

Denmark, in contrast with its neighbours, remained a country of the old order. The low-lying, fertile soil made it possible for the nobility to maintain their privileges far into the nineteenth century. The King had absolute power, and Denmark had to wait till 1849 for the democratic constitution of which it was later so proud.

PARLIAMENTARIANISM IN FRANCE

In France, after 1815, the old order had not been fully restored. The landed aristocracy had returned, but they found the peasants in full possession of much of their old lands, and there was little possibility of recovering them. The monarchy could no longer rule unfettered, for a parliament had come into existence, and the King was responsible to it. The right to elect the deputies depended on wealth, not landed property, so that the nobility had to share the power with the richer bourgeoisie.

Where purely economic matters were concerned, the two groups in Parliament made an alliance. Both wanted heavy protection. The industrialists wanted the exclusion of English goods, which began flooding in as soon as the war was ended, while the landowners wanted the monopoly in corn and home-grown raw materials, such as wool and flax. Although the industrialists liked cheap corn for the sake of cheap bread and low wages, and the cheapest raw materials, they consented to the landowners' tariffs; in return, the landowners made little effective opposition to the tariffs which were introduced against manufactured goods.

But the dominance of the upper bourgeoisie, and the alliance of the rich, were both threatened by Louis XVIII's successor, Charles X. In younger days a charming and dissipated cavalier, he was a devout upholder of the divine right of the Bourbons. He relied upon the priests and Roman Catholic opinion in order to bring his policy of re-establishing autocratic rule to a successful conclusion. But public opinion, as a whole, was against him. When, in July 1830, he suspended the liberties of the constitution and announced that he would rule by decree, a revolution broke out: bourgeois and workers together manned the Paris barricades in the cause of liberty. Charles decided that his best course of action was to leave the French capital altogether, and before long was on his way to exile in England.

REVOLUTION IN FRANCE AND THE NETHERLANDS

A small force of workers and students had made the revolution, but the bourgeois party seized the power. They offered the crown to Louis-Philippe, Duke of Orleans, of the younger branch of the Bourbons. He was to be a citizen-king. He conciliated republican sentiment by walking about with an umbrella, shaking hands with the National Guard (middle-class militia), and allowing workmen to stand him drinks. The laws of the new régime gave the preponderance definitely to the upper bourgeoisie, who consolidated their position against the unrepresented classes by an enormous tax on newspapers, which it made it possible for only the most expensive to be published, and for only the wealthiest people to read them. Thus it was hoped to stem revolutionary propaganda.

The revolution had been the signal for a rising in the Southern provinces of the Kingdom of the Netherlands, on the other side of the French frontier. These provinces, whose languages were partly French and partly Flemish, had belonged to Austria, till overrun by the French early in the revolutionary wars. Although they were entirely Catholic in religion, they were united by the Congress of Vienna to Holland with its Protestant traditions.

The rising middle class of these provinces objected to the union, since it largely excluded them from political power. They disliked being under Dutch officials and they had little influence on the government at Amsterdam. They wanted protection for their growing industries, instead of the free-trade policy which suited the seafaring and trading character of Holland's traditional economy.

BELGIUM BECOMES A SEPARATE STATE

But the country was prosperous, and except for the example of the French revolution of 1830, Dutch and Belgians might have remained longer united. On hearing the news from France, some Belgians began planning their own revolution and took advantage of a rising started by the audience at a Brussels theatre, who were inspired by the revolutionary theme of the play they had just seen. The Dutch forces could not keep order in Brussels, and reinforcements which they sent were driven off with considerable loss. After this Metternich could no longer press a policy of intervention on the

Powers, as there was a danger of this leading to a general European war. In a conference which was sitting at London, England and France showed themselves ready to support the revolution. The new government in France did not feel strong enough, however, to attempt any close union with Belgium, although a National Assembly offered the crown to one of Louis Philippe's sons. He thought it best to refuse, and Prince Leopold of Saxe-Coburg accepted it instead. The independence and neutrality of Belgium was recognized and guaranteed by the Great Powers, including Prussia.

PARLIAMENTARY REFORM IN BRITAIN

England's development during these years is similar to that of France. In 1815, the landed aristocracy had the power, but the richer of the middle class shared in it. Wealthy manufacturers bought land, and with land went sometimes pocket-boroughs and always electoral "influence" of different descriptions. The old aristocratic landed families were still dominant in the Commons and impregnable in the Lords. The franchise remained as it had been in the eighteenth century, the electorate consisting of only four hundred and thirty-five thousand, of a population of nineteen million.

Except for abolishing restrictions on public office-holding for dissenters and Roman Catholics, most social legislation of this period was repressive. The Combination Act of 1799 was the parallel of the French laws of the Revolution period against workers' associations and strikes. In both countries, these laws still held good, and though rescinded in England in 1824, were re-imposed the following year with some modifications. Repressive legislation was demanded by the propertied classes because they were alarmed at the rioting, burning and machine-breaking which accompanied every economic crisis—1816, 1819, 1826, 1829. The unemployed, already almost one and a half million in 1811—an appalling number, considering the much smaller population of those days—had increased by another half million in 1827.

Monster meetings and demonstrations were organized by the Radicals—a partly lower middle-class, partly workers', party, whose object was Parliamentary Reform: its leaders were Place, a tailor, and Cobbett, a yeoman farmer and political journalist. The Whigs, representing in Parliament the progressive section of the upper landed and industrial interests, also favoured Reform. It had been a tradition of the party: now, under the leadership of Earl Grey and Lord John Russell, it seemed as if this tradition might be realized through an alliance with the Radicals. The riots and demonstrations accompanying the slump of 1827–1829, and the comparatively peaceful French revolution of 1830, were a great impetus to their cause.

The elections of 1830 gave the Whigs a majority, but, even so, the Reform crisis continued for two more years, owing to the opposition of the Lords. The Political Union, a powerful middle-class organization centred at Birmingham, threatened not to pay taxes till it was passed. Doherty, an Irish cotton worker from Lancashire, organized a National Association of working men in co-operation with them. Finally, terrible rioting throughout England helped to make the Lords give way, in order to avoid revolution. It was fortunate that the warm-hearted but muddleheaded King, William IV, sided with the reformers, and promised if necessary to swamp the House of Lords with Whig Peers. The Duke of Wellington, who realized that, once defeat had become inevitable, there was no point in prolonging a war, advised his followers to abstain from voting.

The Reform Act abolished "rotten boroughs" and redistributed the seats. Although the franchise was widened, it was still reserved for the rich, though the landowners' predominance had gone. The electorate was increased, but only to six hundred and fifty-six thousand—barely half as much again as the old figure; whereas the total population had increased by some three million since 1815. As in France, the upper middle class had captured power by making use of the revolutionary lower middle-class and workers.

AMERICAN ECONOMIC DEVELOPMENTS

Even in the democratic United States, there was a ruling minority which had to be dislodged from power. This minority had no titles like the European nobility, but they often had more money. Many of them were descendants of English gentry who had come to America more than a century before. Most of them, in the land south of Virginia, had invested their money in cotton-growing when the boom came in 1810. But during the 'twenties, the price of cotton fell. The smaller men were ruined: the richer bought them out, and the "poor whites" went off to settle elsewhere. The gentry who were left became less numerous and wealthier. One other section had much in common with them—the old-established New England families.

This aristocracy, dominant in the government, had as its object the development of the country's resources. The first step towards this, as in England and France, was financial reform, and to this end, the second Bank of the United States was founded in 1816 with five government directors. All sections, as in France, had felt the effect of the restoration of free trade after the war to their considerable disadvantage. The manufacturers of New England wanted to have the home market exclusively for their products; the agriculturalists of the centre and South feared the competition of European wool and grain. So in 1816 heavily protectionist measures were voted.

But during the "Era of Good Feeling", as it was called, a regrouping of parties had been taking place. New democratic forces were coming into the field, due partly to the growth of population in previously unsettled areas west of the Appalachians.

The split which, a generation later, led to civil war was already beginning to appear between North and South. The Southerners were dissatisfied with the tariff. They wanted to get cotton-working machinery cheaply; they also wanted the benefit to their export trade which might result from a free trade policy towards other countries. So acute was the conflict that their leader, John Calhoun, from being an ardent nationalist, became an advocate of the right of states to secede from the Union in certain circumstances. The slavery question divided the South more sharply from the North. In 1820, when Missouri was admitted to the Union as a slave state, there was strong opposition from the Northerners. All parties were dissatisfied because of the slump. This widespread trade depression, as was also the case in England, sharpened opposition to the régime and correspondingly accelerated democratic advance.

The presidential candidate of the dissatisfied voters was General Andrew Jackson, a bluff frontiersman, the son of a farmer from Carrickfergus, Scotland. He received the largest number of votes in 1824, though a vagary of the constitution enabled his opponent to become President. But four years later, with the aid of a powerful Press campaign, he was elected. At his inaugural reception at Washington, early in the following year, the city was invaded by an army of his supporters—rough-mannered frontiersmen, farmers, editors, politicians. They celebrated the occasion with tubs of punch from the White House. The people had taken over power.

POLITICAL INNOVATIONS IN THE U.S.A.

Since the people were now in power, and not merely a minority, as in most other countries, America's history in the next thirty years is unique. A new era had begun, in her attempt to build a fully democratic civilization. Progress in working this out, in a political system, was along two lines: in ensuring, as far as possible, that the will of every individual should have its full weight in the government, and in preventing the growth of a special class of officials.

Inside the separate states, many appointments to offices, previously made by the legislatures, now became elective. The system of "rotation of office" was also made general, whereby office-holders could only come up for re-election once or twice. In the elections themselves, universal suffrage had already, in the past few years, largely superseded the property franchise. The most important case in which election took the place of nomination by the state legislatures, was in the appointment of the President. The members of the Electoral College, instead of having the real choice of the next President, as was originally intended by the Constitution, simply voted as their states had previously directed.

The organization of the electorate, so that each voter could make his wishes felt as effectively as possible, developed in two ways. There were political clubs like Tammany Hall in New York, which decided the policy of its members and brought local electors to the polls; such clubs often had considerable funds at their disposal. In most states, these were not a very important factor, with the result that the convention system developed. For Presidential elections, one delegate was sent by conventions in every county to a state convention, which nominated the state's candidates for the Presidency and other Federal offices.

When Jackson was President, he went a step farther, and called a national convention, representing his supporters, from the various states. Before long, his opponents had adopted this scheme: by 1840, both parties selected their candidates according to the votes of the majority of the delegates who had assembled in party conventions, and at the same time drew up a platform of party principles.

PRESIDENT ANDREW JACKSON'S POLICY

This work of organizing the parties was expensive. Partly in payment for this, partly because of his objection to professional officials, Jackson turned out a large number of office-holders and gave their positions to his supporters. Thus the "Spoils System", which had existed previously in the separate states, was brought into the Federal Government, and the vicious system became established by which the winning party in the elections considered the state offices as the fruits of victory and filled them with their own men. Since there was no impartial civil service, ambitious place-seeking became an integral part of America's political life.

Freedom was also an essential part of the Jacksonians' ideas of democracy—freedom to let every state and every individual manage their own affairs in their own way. One of the national institutions, in particular, was singled out by certain states as placing unnecessary restrictions on this freedom—the Bank of the United States, which was considered to have refused to advance money sufficiently freely for speculative land- and building-development. Jackson fought the Bank as if it had been a personal enemy. When its charter expired in 1832, he refused to renew it. The Eastern industrialists, who had come to regard the Bank as an essential part of the country's economic system, raised a storm of protest. The Bank's future became the main issue when Jackson stood for re-election at the end of his first term of office. He won even more decisively than before, and the Bank ceased to be a national institution. Jackson insisted on breaking it entirely by the simple process of withdrawing the Federal funds deposited there.

At a time when the central bank of England was about to be strengthened, the central bank of the United States was abolished. But the government soon found it necessary to strengthen the national credit system. On the disappearance of the bank and its state branches, independent state-banks began to issue paper money freely on insufficient credit, and an unhealthy boom resulted. Jackson himself precipitated the crash by issuing a regulation that only gold or silver would be taken in payment for public lands. Eventually, this "hard-money" policy and the new treasury system established in 1839 led to better financial stability, but the immediate effect was a wholesale panic. Prices fell disastrously; farmers were ruined, or heavily burdened with debt; a large number of businesses closed down.

Many people had foreseen the crash, and the candidate of the Democrats (as Jackson's party came to be called) only just secured election in 1836. In 1840, the so-called "Whigs" (who were later to be merged with the Republican Party) were again, though only temporarily, in power.

During the period of Democratic rule, considerable advance had been made towards free trade, in accordance with Democratic theory. The tariff of 1828, just before Jackson took office, had been the highest in American history. Laws were now passed to lower the tariffs till they reached the level of 20 per cent. on all articles taxed, which actually happened a few years later. This aimed at satisfying the Southerners; under the previous high tariff, South Carolina had even threatened not to enforce the payment of duties at her ports.

GROWTH OF INDUSTRY IN THE U.S.A.

The wealth of the United States was increasing during this period as rapidly as that of Europe, although America was a long way behind England in the development of the factory system. For cotton goods between 1840 and 1850, although the price was gradually falling, the value rose by twenty million dollars. In 1850, the year's value of industrial and agricultural products was estimated as being about $1,000,000,000 for each.

The age of the small manufacturer with a single establishment was passing; large-scale industry, with its concentration of firms and processes under the control of a relatively few capitalists, was beginning to appear. But industrialization did not bring with it the horrors which disgraced England and France. Though there were the beginnings of the Labour movement, it did not spring, as in Europe, from the evils of factory conditions. In branches of industry organized on eighteenth-century lines, the journeymen and master-mechanics began organizing to prevent themselves falling to the same common level as wage-earners, a tendency which was a normal accompaniment of capitalist development. For this end, the *Mechanics' Union of Trade Associations* was organized in Philadelphia in 1827. An attempt was made to form a union of the different trades throughout the country, but this was given its death-blow by the panic of 1837. The socialistic ideas of Fourier had been introduced into the country, and after 1840, America seemed ideal soil for them. Communities for productive association sprang up; the failure of Robert Owen's experiment in "new harmony", some years before, had not inoculated the idealists against a desire to repeat this experiment upon similar lines. But in a short time, these had all failed.

CHAPTER 67

THE AGE OF REVOLUTIONS

IN Europe after 1830, the uneven nature of progress in political, social and economic matters became more evident. In England and France, where industry was furthest developed, the wealthier of the middle class had gained political power. In the next year, each of these countries in different ways proceeded to build up a middle-class civilization. But Conservative influences remained supreme in most other countries, though revolutionary forces were silently growing. In 1848, these broke out in an attempt to overturn the old order in all parts of Europe.

The English working-classes, during the 'thirties and 'forties, were in an even worse state than before. There was considerable unemployment, overcrowding in the slums grew worse, the death-rate for poorer people increased. But the minds of those who were represented in Parliament, and especially of members of the middle class who had gained votes as a result of the Reform Act, were becoming enlightened. The increasing influence of religion and humanitarian sentiment inspired them to alleviate considerably the evils which working-class unrest and rioting brought forcibly to their notice.

IMPROVEMENT IN WORKING-CLASS CONDITIONS

Though the relief of poverty was left to a great extent to private charity, the Whig Government, which had passed the Reform Act, turned its attention to reforming the state's system of relief.

In 1795 began the practice of making allowances to unemployed or insufficiently paid workers and their dependents; this was the Speenhamland system. As a result, employers (in many cases, farmers) tended to pay low wages and employ labour only casually. The average cost of Poor Relief from 1813 to 1834 was above £7 million a year. Whole parishes were living on this form of dole. By the Act of 1834, no able-bodied person could obtain relief except by entering a workhouse. Though a bad system was thus ended and the amount spent on Poor Relief greatly decreased, the result, for the time being, was additional hardship for the needy.

The greatest champion of legislation for improving working-class conditions was Lord Ashley, later Earl of Shaftesbury. The descendant of a long line of peers, he was aristocratic in outlook and a Puritan in religion; in him the religious spirit of the age showed itself most clearly. His deep religious convictions made him give his whole time and energy to charitable work, and particularly to bringing about reforms through Parliament.

In 1833, came the Factory Act which abolished night-work for children and further limited working-hours, which remained however appallingly long. Henceforward it was impossible to employy children under eighteen for more than eleven and a half hours a day and children under twelve for more than eight hours. This only applied to textile factories. Ashley also had a commission appointed to inquire into coal-mines. Conditions were discovered to be so disgraceful that in 1842 an Act was passed which prohibited in the future employment of females in mines, and of boys under ten years old.

LANDOWNERS *VERSUS* INDUSTRIALISTS

In England Sir Robert Peel, Prime Minister from 1841 to 1846, was in many ways typical of the new governing class. His grandfather, originally a yeoman, had established a cotton-printing factory. His father carried this on, took up cotton-spinning as well, and built up the family fortune; like others who rose into the upper ranks of society, he bought land and became a baronet. The great Peel himself went to Harrow and Oxford; he entered Parliament for a pocket-borough at the age of twenty-one and became a Cabinet Minister at twenty-four. He converted the Tories, after their defeat over the Reform Bill, from a mainly reactionary into a moderately progressive party, with the name of Conservatives.

The first essential for further middle-class development was a strengthening of the country's economic system. To this end, Peel passed the Bank Charter Act, by which the Bank of England, the keystone of the country's financial structure, was given a dominant position. Limitations were put on the note-issuing powers of other banks, and legislation prevented the danger of inflation.

The Reform Act had not made the industrialists more powerful politically than the landowners. The struggle began again. Free trade, strongly advocated by the industrialists, was the issue. From the first year of his ministry, Peel had steadily reduced duties; by the end of it, he had reduced 1,035, and abolished 605. But the Corn Laws still remained. They had the effect of making the average price of a quartern loaf only a little less than a shilling.

Again, popular agitation, especially as a result of the founding of the Anti-Corn Law League in 1831, helped the industrialists' party. Peel himself wanted to continue the laws, but his hand was forced by the famine in Ireland in 1845, resulting from the failure of the potato crop, and he was obliged to "open the ports" for the time being. Once opened, they could not easily be closed. In 1846, the Corn Laws were repealed. Peel's Conservative Party was composed partly of industrialists, but mainly of landowners. His action split the party into roughly these two elements. This meant the definite predominance of the industrial element in Parliament.

Such reforms accelerated industrial progress: from 1832 onwards, development was particularly rapid. The cotton industry far outstripped its expansion of the years 1813–1820, when its two thousand power-looms had grown to fourteen thousand: by 1835, another one hundred thousand had been added. In 1800, the value of foreign trade had been £62 million; in 1850, it was £175 million. This was the great era of railway building: by 1850, there were over five thousand miles of railway built and under construction.

Parliamentary reforms were a beginning, though progress resulting from the action of the possessing classes was lamentably slow, compared with the evils that had been attacked. The workers began to rely more on efforts to help themselves. They had expected great things from the Reform Act. When they and the lower middle class, whose combined agitation had been so largely the cause of its being passed, found they had gained no more political power than before the passing of the Reform Act, they came into alliance again.

THE CHARTIST MOVEMENT

There developed a great movement for the next step in Parliamentary reform. Lovett, a joiner who was a member of the London Working Men's Association, in co-operation with the old Radical, Place, drew up the People's Charter in 1838.

Its six demands were universal suffrage, equal electoral districts, abolition of property qualifications for parliamentary candidates, annual parliaments, the ballot, and payment of M.P.s. Next year, these were presented to Parliament in the form of a petition with signatures, set out in a roll four feet in diameter. Parliament, composed of representatives of the industrialists and landowners who thought reform had gone far enough, refused to consider it. Riots broke out and there was a threat of a general strike. The movement was weakened, however, by the division of its members into "moral force" and "physical force" Chartists.

The French Revolution of 1848 led to a last effort to have the Charter considered by Parliament. A monster meeting was arranged, under the leadership of the enormous and eloquent Irish lawyer, O'Connor, to escort another petition to Parliament. The Government forbade it, and enrolled one hundred and seventy thousand special constables from the London middle class. In face of this, O'Connor called off the procession. Ridicule fell on the movement when it was found that instead of the five million seven hundred thousand signatures claimed by the Chartists, the petition contained under two million, many of which were forgeries. This *débâcle*, and the prosperity of the succeeding years, sounded the death-knell of Chartism, though it lingered for some years.

Louis-Philippe, whose umbrella was the symbol of his boasted middle-class outlook, was a king who made the upper bourgeosie of France confident of their position. The government, too, represented their interests. The first two Prime Ministers of the new régime were both bankers.

There was hardly any legislation for the benefit of the working classes. Industrialists and financiers had no intention of allowing advanced theories to interfere with their private interests, and the protective system of the previous régime, which made prices far too high, was rigidly continued. Financially the government was sound : the annual trade deficit, almost a chronic recurrence with every French régime, was only slight. In these circumstances, prosperity increased. The value of French foreign trade doubled between 1831 and 1847; production in the cotton industry almost trebled.

Railway building was the most important economic development of the period. It had been foreshadowed in the previous reign, but its era really began with the opening of the Paris–Rouen line. But there were difficulties, due to the heavy cost (iron was approximately three times more expensive in France than in England, owing to prohibitive tariffs), together with the relatively small amounts of capital owned by individuals.

The industrialists therefore made use of the resources of the state. Their private companies undertook the contracts while the government subsidized them, and became owner of the road bed. With state aid came state planning, and eventually France held an advantage over England by having a more unified system. In actual length of line, France had much leeway to make up before she equalled the achievements of other countries.

Not enough was done to improve factory conditions, though the children's lot was lightened. But in other ways the spread of education secured some progress. Penal reform followed Peel's lines in England. Medieval relics, like branding and the pillory, were abolished and the death-penalty laws were modified, with the result that executions fell by a half.

But such laws were inadequate in the face of working-class distress. In 1831, when the employers in the cotton industry refused to employ men at the rates fixed by the Prefect, the working men of Lyons rose with the battle-cry of "Live working or die fighting". For ten days they were masters of the town. The laws of the Napoleonic Code against associations of working men for the purpose of raising wages still held good. For the workless, there was no government provision. Here humanitarian sentiment acted. During this period, hospitals and welfare institutions were helping about 1,125,000 people per annum, or one out of every twenty-nine of the population.

POPULARIZATION OF SOCIALIST DOCTRINES

In these circumstances, the doctrines of the Socialists attracted increasing attention. In 1840, Proudhon published his pamphlet *What is Property?*—to which the answer was "Property is Theft". A year before, another influential book had appeared—*The Organization of Labour*, by Louis Blanc. Blanc had begun as a teacher, gone on to journalism, and ended with communism. Like the English Radicals, he believed that political reform was the essential preliminary to social reform. There must be universal suffrage and an increasingly higher standard of education for the masses. The truly

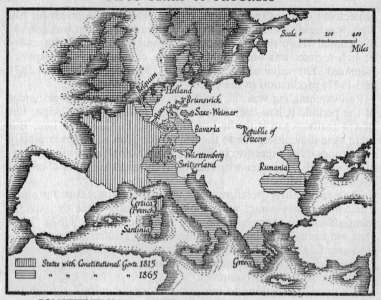

CONSTITUTIONAL GOVERNMENT IN EUROPE, 1815–65
Great Britain, Switzerland, and Scandinavia preserved their constitutionalism
during these fifty years. France, under Napoleon III, drifted to autocracy, but
other nations, notably Italy and the Netherlands, achieved a measure of political
freedom. Within Spain the attempt to establish a constitution had been defeated.

democratic state would be the "banker of the poor", supplying the
working-classes with the instruments which they lacked. A huge
loan should be made to finance the "social workshops", and directors
should be appointed by the government till such time as the workers
could take them over entirely for themselves. Part of the profit should
go to the workers, part to a fund for pension and sickness benefit,
part to running expenses and capital development. These workshops
would compete with those of private enterprise, and eventually
extinguish them.

The revolution of 1848 seemed to be an opportunity of putting these
ideas into practice. This revolution was by no means solely due to the
working-class socialists, but also to the lower bourgeoisie, who were
disgusted at having no representation in Parliament. There was
widespread dissatisfaction, both inside and outside Parliament, with
the methods of corruption whereby the Right, representing the big
industrialists, maintained power. It was a system of distributing
lucrative offices and the business of government contracts and loans.

The Paris mob came into the streets, and there was a skirmish with
some soldiers. The government found that they could not rely on
the National Guard or even on the regular troops. Louis-Philippe
abdicated and was permitted to seek refuge in England, and a
provisional Republican government was proclaimed.

The provisional government was half Republican, half Socialist: Louis Blanc and two other Socialists were members of the Ministry. At first, by marching in enormous processions on the Town Hall where the government sat, the Socialist workers got their demands accepted. To undertake the "organization of work", a Government Labour Commission was set up, with Louis Blanc as President. It issued decrees limiting working-hours and abolishing piece-work, but the government, which passed more and more under Moderate control, was content to take no steps towards ratifying them.

DEFEAT OF FRENCH SOCIALISM

One more momentous step was, however, taken. In the middle of a cabinet meeting, while the mob was surging outside, a workman rushed in, gun in hand, and demanded the "right to work". Louis Blanc seized the moment to pass a government decree establishing National Workshops.

The unemployed, whose number was increased by the trade-paralysis which accompanied the revolution, flocked to these workshops from all parts of Paris and the provinces: by May, they numbered one hundred and twenty thousand. But there were no workshops. Instead, navvy work was provided in the shape of levelling operations, road-building and heaping up an embankment along the Seine. There was too little work to go round, and the workless were paid a franc and a half as a dole. When the government found it was spending twenty thousand francs a day, it reduced payments.

The elections, on a basis of universal suffrage, returned a large majority for the moderates. These decided to bring the Socialistic experiments to an end, after no more than three genuine workshops had been opened. Their main plan for the workshops was to make them so ridiculous that socialism itself would become discredited. Before long, they declared the workshops closed.

The workmen decided on one last stand and raised the barricades. The government was ready with General Cavaignac, trained in colonial warfare in North Africa; he had one hundred thousand men (including the loyalist National Guards) under his command. The street fighting of "the Four June Days" was terrible. Nine thousand soldiers, among them four generals, were killed. The number of workers killed is not known; it was far higher than that of the soldiers. What was new and strange about this rising was that, for the first time, the working-class were fighting by themselves for a system of government in their own interest. They were decisively defeated.

The constitution established by the victorious middle class was adopted from the United States. It was to have, besides an Assembly, a President elected by universal suffrage: but since France had a strong army and civil service, the President would be far stronger than in America and would wield enormous power. One of the candidates for the office was Louis Napoleon Bonaparte, nephew of the Emperor, and son of the one-time King of Holland. A man in whom the romantic outlook of the age was strong, he had a mystical belief in his own mission and in that of France. But he was weak in character, and his large conceptions and his enthusiasm were no substitutes for moral purpose. By temperament, he was an adventurer : he had already taken part with revolutionaries in Italy and had twice made fantastic raids into France, both of which proved laughable failures.

AUTOCRACY IN FRANCE AND GERMANY

He had more success through his propaganda. Especially since the death of the great Napoleon in 1821, there had grown up in France a strong sentimental interest around his name. Louis Napoleon exploited this Napoleonic legend in writings which appealed to the egotism and vanity of the French.

He also stood as the champion of order. The desire for stability, caused by the troubles of the Second Republic, brought about a great increase in the Bonapartist party. To it rallied the old Legitimist landowners, and also the peasants, who were attracted by the glamour of the name and alienated from the government by a tax which fell especially heavily on them ; in fact, Louis Napoleon had the support of all who disliked the government but were dissatisfied with definite alternatives. The will of the Paris mob no longer counted ; it had had half Paris and all France against it, except during the earliest days of the revolution. Louis Napoleon was elected President by an enormous majority, and began steadily to prepare the way for his autocratic rule.

Napoleon had been the inspirer of the National movement in Germany: the War of Liberation which freed Germany from his rule had been a war of the people. But after 1814, the old order had returned. Germany was still split up into a number of states, though now there were only thirty-nine, instead of the three hundred or so existing before the Napoleonic wars. The constitution of the German Confederation gave Austria all the power, and Metternich fastened his system rigidly on the country. Almost the sole function of the Confederation was to carry out Metternich's repressive policy ; as a means of giving the country any real unity or expressing popular feeling, it was useless.

Most Germans were apathetic about political conditions. The middle class and the aristocracy were cosmopolitan in outlook ; among the aristocracy, French was still commonly spoken. But there were already two movements in Germany, for constitutional freedom and national independence. Almost all the states were autocratic, but in the south demands were growing for constitutional government. Before long the three large states of Baden, Bavaria and Württemburg had achieved this, together with Saxe-Weimar in the north.

It was the students throughout Germany who mainly fostered the desire for national unity. Students who had fought in the Wars of Liberation kept the spirit of those days alive. *The Universal German Student Society* was founded, to unite all German youth, "in view of the coming unity of the Fatherland". For many young Germans, the nation of the future was personified by Jahn, who began a cult of physical training. All over Germany, gymnasiums were opened. Jahn was a big rough-mannered peasant's son, and always wore a coarse grey shirt, open at the neck. He was a strong nationalist, fierce in his denunciations of everything foreign, especially connected with France. He thought Germany needed a war as the best way of bringing her unity.

These were extreme views. For the time being, the majority of those wanting unity hoped to achieve it by peaceful means. Metternich was alarmed by the behaviour of the German students, for some of their noisier celebrations seemed to herald revolution. After a student had assassinated Kotzebue, a writer who was known to be paid by the Tsar to send him news-bulletins, Metternich made the governments dissolve the student-societies, close the gymnasiums, and set up a strict censorship.

But economic interests beyond Metternich's control were preparing the way for the unity of Germany. Soon after Prussia had revised her tariff in 1818, other states asked to come into a customs-union with her. This was found to bring so great an increase of prosperity that, by 1844, most of the other states, who in economic isolation could hardly balance their budgets, had joined the Prussian customs-union, and in the next years the progress of railway-building, which began in 1835, greatly assisted in linking the country together.

THE GERMAN LIBERAL MOVEMENT

The national movement grew silently, apart from occasional outbreaks, especially after the French Revolution of 1830. The German states had for a long time been looking increasingly to Prussia for leadership, especially since the accession of Frederick William IV. But the Liberals had mistaken their man. In Frederick William, sentimental piety reinforced a mystical belief in the divine right of kings to govern in their own way, and he was determined that he would maintain intact the privileges of the Hohenzollern crown. Although he occasionally allowed reforms, and thereby gave an impression of having Liberal tendencies, he departed from his principles only because of weakness of will. In reality, he detested anything which savoured of the ideas of the French Revolution, although forced to compromise with them for a time.

No other course than revolution seemed possible after the news of the Paris Revolution reached Berlin in 1848. The whole city was in a state of wild excitement. Business was almost at a standstill; the Press, disregarding the censorship, burst its shackles in encouraging the popular demand for a constitution. Shots were fired, and soon the barricades were up in the streets. To stop the bloodshed, the King ordered the military to leave Berlin, and with considerable bravery rode round the city, promising rather wildly that he would put himself at the head of the national movement. A proclamation assured the citizens that Prussia would be given a constitution.

Meanwhile, a number of prominent Liberals, mainly from South Germany, had come together at Frankfurt-am-Main. Without authority or commission, they decided to call a National Assembly of representatives elected from all the states, in order to work out a constitution for the new Germany.

The governments which were already Liberal authorized this procedure; the others were forced by public opinion to follow their example. Elections were held by universal suffrage in all the German states, including Austria, and the deputies assembled at Frankfurt. Apparently one of the most amazing revolutions by consent was about to be achieved.

There was much talking but little result. For eight months the various parties deliberated: the main difficulty was to decide whether Austria, with all her dominions, should belong to the new Germany. Austria refused to join unless with her complete empire, for without the support of her non-German provinces, she would soon lose the leadership of Germany to Prussia. Finally it was decided to exclude these non-German dominions: it naturally followed that the King of Prussia was offered the crown of the new Empire.

DEFEAT OF GERMAN REPUBLICANISM

It seemed as if the dream of a united democratic Germany was about to be realized. But Frederick William hesitated, and finally refused. He could not bring himself to soil his conscience by accepting a crown offered by an assembly of revolutionary upstarts. An equally weighty point was that Austria's opposition might lead to war, for which the Prussian military system was not yet prepared.

Frederick William could refuse more easily since he himself had been saved from the revolution in Prussia. A reactionary clique in the Court had taken over the direction of the royal policy. The national assembly which had come together to debate a constitution was at first sent out of Berlin and finally broken up by force. Another constitution was indeed granted, but in it the responsible power still remained in the hands of the King and his ministers.

The government then felt itself strong enough to suppress risings elsewhere in Germany. On the failure of the movement for a Germany united under a constitutional monarchy, republican risings in some of the states became formidable. It cost the Prussian army two days' fighting before it defeated the rebels in Saxony; in Baden, there was a regular battle. As a result, the Republican party in Germany entirely disappeared.

In Austria, during the period of Metternich's rule, revolutionary forces were silently developing. The nationalism of the different peoples was growing in a way that threatened the break-up of the Empire. In German Austria itself, especially in Vienna, the growing middle class was becoming more and more impatient under the repressive rule of Metternich, with its censorship, spies and secret police. They were dissatisfied with his financial policy, which led to an ever-increasing burden of debt and did nothing towards developing the country.

In Vienna, the working-class made its appearance in the 'forties and grew steadily: owing to the bad conditions prevalent there as elsewhere, it was a potential revolutionary force. The introduction of machinery had not led to the prosperity of the factory-hands. There was over-production combined with unemployment, while the hand-workers found their occupations steadily disappearing.

DISCONTENT WITHIN THE AUSTRIAN EMPIRE

In the patchwork of races which formed the ramshackle empire of Austria, the spirit of nationalism was beginning to stir. In the case of Hungary, this was nothing new. The Magyars, a proud and racially self-conscious minority, had always been sensitive concerning the free institutions of their country. Although willing to remain under Habsburg rule, it was only on condition that they should be largely self-governing. On the point of allowing as little freedom as possible to the subject-races of Hungary, all Magyars were united, but they were divided among themselves. The middle-class Magyars saw no reason why the nobles, by having almost all the seats in the Hungarian assembly and all the important positions, should control the country. But the nobility, not wishing to lose their privileges, such as freedom from taxation, were determined to maintain their power.

Of Hungary's subject-peoples, the Croats, though half-independent, were in the difficult position of being ruled by two masters: mainly governed from Budapest, they were, in certain important matters, subject to the Imperial Government at Vienna.

Just as the Hungarians were the aristocrats among the subject Slav peoples of Austria, so were the Czechs the intelligentsia. Gifted with considerable administrative talents, they filled the lower positions in the Imperial civil service. Their reviving nationalism, largely stimulated by historical and literary works, took a strongly intellectual line, and they saw themselves as leading all the Slav peoples to a position of cultural supremacy in Europe.

Uneasiness among Austria's Slavonic populations was increased by the terrible fate that had befallen Poland. After the Napoleonic Wars, the lion's share of Poland had gone to Russia, and the idealistic Tsar Alexander had made it a semi-independent kingdom. But the Poles would not be satisfied till complete independence for their country was recovered, and they followed the example of France in

1830 by making a revolution. Against the huge power and resources of Russia, this rising had no chance of success: the Tsar was no longer the sentimental and vacillating Alexander, but the ruthless Nicholas I. For eight months the Poles, with unbelievable bravery, continued the futile struggle in spite of enormous losses. They were finally crushed and every vestige of their former freedom taken away.

SLAVS AND MAGYARS REVOLT

Since then, the refugees had been tirelessly agitating among the Poles, who were subjects of Prussia and Austria, till they caused the rising of 1846. Too weak to suppress it, the Austrian government called on the peasantry, who, being Ruthenians, regarded their Polish landlords as foreigners. The appeal resulted in one of the most horrible massacres ever perpetrated by class and racial hatred. The one reminder of Poland's past freedom, the tiny independent Republic of Cracow, was suppressed and annexed by Austria.

The revolutions of 1848 in the Austrian Empire did not at first begin among the subject-races, but in the capital itself. The mob was in the streets, smashing windows and shouting for a constitution. The aged Metternich, apparently as calm as ever, counselled measures of repression; the Court thought it better to sacrifice him to the popular wrath, and he set out, like other fallen great ones, for England. The government further agreed to a national assembly, elected from all the provinces of the Empire, except Italy, which was already in revolt, in order to determine a constitution. In this motley assembly, an especially picturesque touch was contributed by the representatives of the peasants—who, however, departed as soon as an important law abolishing feudal burdens had been passed.

Meanwhile, revolutions broke out in all parts of the Empire. In Prague, the soldiers had to fire on the mob in front of the house of the Governor, Prince Windischgrätz, who had to bombard the city before order was restored. After this success, which was the beginning of the army's victory over the revolution, Windischgrätz marched on to Vienna. There a renewed rising had taken place, this time under the leadership of a revolutionary working-class committee, who seized control of the city.

The revolution in Hungary was made at first by the middle classes, led by Louis Kossuth. They were able to deprive the nobles of their old privileged position by abolishing feudal services and establishing taxation for all without distinction. At the same time, the Hungarians were united in their determination to allow no further freedom to their Croat subjects, who had risen under Baron Jellachich.

After some hesitation, the Imperial Government recognized Jellachich as Governor, thereby virtually establishing Croatia's independence of Hungary. Hungary, more and more in the hands of the extremists, was before long at war with both the Croats and the Imperial Government. A Hungarian army marched to the help of the insurgents in Vienna, but had to turn back before the combined forces of Jellachich and Windischgrätz. Windischgrätz then reduced Vienna, which surrendered after a short bombardment. Before the Hungarians, with good generals and a vigorous Defence Committee, could be defeated, the Imperial Government had to ask for help from Nicholas of Russia. He willingly sent an army, and after much hard fighting, as bloody as that of the Polish rebellion, order was restored by the end of 1849.

The defeat of the Slav revolutions was a great triumph for the imperial government, especially as it was hampered by the terrible war in Italy which was going on simultaneously. Its success was due largely to lack of unity among its opponents: in the ranks of the revolutionaries, nation was divided against nation, and class against class, in a way which made it impossible for them to succeed against the discipline of the regular military forces brought against them.

CHAPTER 68
THE EXPANSION OF EUROPE

IN the third decade of the nineteenth century, there began a movement of the peoples of Europe which can be compared only with the great migrations of the fifth century A.D. It is an era of rapid progress in colonizing the continents of North America, Australia and Africa. In the East, there were signs of conflict between European Powers, and the increasing European influence began to alter its ancient civilizations.

Emigration was the safety-valve of nineteenth-century Europe, as it had been of ancient Greece. The pressure of unemployment at home was diminished, and markets began expanding abroad. A large number of those who emigrated were the more energetic characters—the type of men who, had they stayed at home, might have become revolutionary leaders as a result of economic suffering. This is one reason for the dying down of revolutionary movements after the outbreaks of 1848.

Bad conditions in industry and agriculture were the main cause of the movement. The heaviest emigration, especially in the earlier years, was from the British Isles, where low wages, unemployment and a rapidly increasing population existed together. Of these emigrants, a large proportion came from Ireland, where the density of population was almost as great as in England, but where there was practically no industry and little fertile land to support them. Their condition was aggravated by the terrible system of sub-letting and absentee landlords. After the starvation-year beginning in 1846, emigration was very rapid: largely for this reason, the population dropped from eight million to under six million in 1861.

Discontent at the failure of the Liberals to bring about an improvement in social and political conditions was one reason for the emigration from Germany which began in the 'fifties.

The voyages of the emigrants were formidable owing to their length, though the increased speed of vessels lightened hardships to some extent. Even before the age of steam in ocean transport, voyages had become much shorter, since in the middle of the century, sailing-ships had reached their perfection. The average length of the Australian passage was one hundred and twenty days, but records of sixty-eight and sixty-three were set up. The Atlantic crossing in the old days had taken anything from five to eight weeks, or even more; but by the 'forties, the best ships were taking only three weeks, and considerably less for the return journey to England. These were the great days of the American clippers, especially the famous schooners from Baltimore, long, narrow vessels which were constructed from the soft-wood trees that American forests produced in abundance.

EUROPEAN EMIGRATION TO THE NEW WORLD

After 1860, sailing-ships, however fast, began to be displaced by steamers. The first steam-vessel was floated on the Seine in 1803 by the Irish-American Fulton. Steamers proved their success in the United States, where they came into general use on the rivers, but it was some time before they won their way for ocean transport. At first, steam was used merely as an auxiliary to sail, and it was not till 1833 that the Atlantic crossing was made entirely under steam. A few years later, the paddle-boat the *Great Western* crossed from Bristol to New York in a fortnight, and in 1839, Samuel Cunard established the first regular line of steamships crossing the Atlantic between England and America.

For a large majority of the emigrants, the promised land was the United States. There was plenty of land there; in the 'thirties, settlement of the vast and fertile Mississippi Valley area had only just begun. It became more and more easy to acquire land. The settler was allowed to buy his land outright, and in small quantities. As time went on, the purchase price was lowered. No discrimination was made against a man who had settled without a legal title on the land; in fact, he was given a preference when the land eventually came up for sale.

The political status of the settler was equally ideal. After a short time in the country, he was a full citizen, with the same rights as the original inhabitants. A newly settled area, as soon as it had six thousand free inhabitants, could become a state on equal terms with the others. It could make its own constitution, which the Federal Government ratified; it had its own state laws. Nor could these laws conflict with certain guarantees of freedom laid down in the constitution of the United States, such as complete freedom in religion. As there was no mother country to exploit the settler in her own interests, he was assured of a market for his produce. The demands of Europe, and especially of England, were rapidly increasing. The abolition of the Corn Laws in England led to a great increase in imports, and wars and revolutions in Europe, by dislocating the ordinary sources of supply, swelled Europe's demand for supplies from America.

The results of the demand for cotton contrasted with the results of the demand for wheat. The development of cotton-growing made slavery once more profitable in the South, while the wheat-growing North, with its population of independent proprietors, became one of the areas most remarkable for every kind of freedom in the world, except industrial.

The opening-up of the interior by the development of water transport, and still more by the building of railways, made it possible for the new settlers to market their produce. Without the trans-continental railways, rapid development of the West would have been impossible. The cost of transporting wheat from Chicago to New York had been prohibitive; it now cost only fifty cents a bushel for the whole one thousand five hundred miles. Morse's invention of the telegraph, first successfully applied in 1844, was of the greatest importance to the farmers, by giving them weather-forecasts and news of market conditions. Capital for these developments was available, owing to the flourishing state of American industry and trade, and the flow of foreign—especially British—capital.

OPENING-UP OF NEW TERRITORIES

The vast district of the North-west, the Oregon territory, had been claimed by Russia, Spain and England. Russia and Spain renounced their claims. For England, the deciding point in drawing the boundary was the large majority of American citizens who had settled in the territory that went to the United States.

From the Southern States, there had been considerable migration into Mexican territory, where land was much cheaper than in the United States. Annoyed at the Mexican demand that they should free their slaves, these settlers revolted, and with the assistance of American volunteers, established the Republic of Texas, which, a few years later, was admitted as a state into the Union. This provoked a war in 1848, since Texas claimed certain areas as being within her boundaries, which were, in fact, occupied by Mexicans, and Mexico refused to sell California and New Mexico. The United States won, and annexed these territories, as well as the disputed parts of Texas. Within three years, the territory of the United States had increased nearly fifty per cent; "Manifest Destiny" drew them to the Pacific.

Almost immediately after California had been annexed, gold was discovered there, and a rush of miners resulted, which quickly brought up the population figures. A trans-continental railway seemed to be essential. More territory was purchased from Mexico in order to provide the best route, and the railway was eventually opened in 1869.

British colonies also offered lands suitable for settlement, though they were not so ideal as the United States. Australia was twelve thousand miles from England. The general opinion about Canada was put forward by Cobbett, who described it as "wretchedly poor; heaps of rocks, covered chiefly with fir-trees"—and it was thought to be overrun with bears and almost constantly cold. There was another reason; settlement was connected in the popular mind with transportation. In fact, transportation was the method whereby Australia had been colonized in the beginning. Transportation to Western Australia did not stop till 1867.

The long voyage was, however, perhaps the strongest reason why emigration to Australia and New Zealand was, at first, small. The voyage, before the days of steam, often took four and a half months. In the worst ships, conditions were terrible. The space between the berths was sometimes so small that it was almost impossible to creep in. Furthermore, the ships had to pass through the tropics. Epidemics were liable to break out, and usually considerable numbers died during the crossing. The voyage to Canada was almost as bad, although it took the comparatively short time of sixty to seventy days. There was the same danger of epidemics: on one occasion, a ship arrived at Nova Scotia with everyone on board, including the crew, suffering from typhus. These conditions were, however, no worse than those which had to be faced by emigrants to the U.S.A.

PARLIAMENT'S ATTITUDE TOWARDS EMIGRATION

The overcrowding on ships was due largely to the emigrants' poverty. Legislation was passed through the British Parliament specifying the number of passengers to be carried and other regulations; but rather than pay, for instance, the £10 charged by boats which fulfilled the requirements, an emigrant might choose to go for £3 on certain fishing-boats where the regulations did not apply. In any case the Acts were frequently disregarded; and one of them, owing to a mistake in the drafting, legalized the most terrible conditions. By the 'sixties, such regulations had been improved and were being more strictly enforced, while the development of steam was making the voyages much shorter.

One reason why Parliament did little to control emigration, apart from a few comparatively small schemes, was the outlook of a majority of those in government circles. They took their lead from the "Manchester School" of economists: it did not matter where the emigrants settled—it was equally good for British trade. According to this outlook, it was the world supply of raw materials, and the world demand for British goods, that was the important point. In fact, emigration to the U.S.A. was, if anything, to be preferred to emigration to the Empire, since it was to the U.S.A. that the largest part of British investments had gone, and further settlement would increase America's wealth, and swell British dividends.

The Empire was not regarded as a favourable field for investment, because business men had little faith in its future. There was a general opinion that the colonies might separate from the mother country, following the example of North and South America. By some, this dropping-off of colonies, like ripe fruit, was considered a necessary phase of historical development, and considerable dissatisfaction and the expressed opinions of political movements in Canada and South Africa seemed to support this contention.

ECONOMIC PROBLEMS OF THE COLONIES

Discontent in the colonies had been largely due to an economic policy which was the reverse of that advocated by the Manchester School. It was realized, though only by a small number of people, that England's economic policy had been largely the cause of the loss of the American colonies. Nevertheless this policy persisted. Transport of goods between the colonies and England, and between the colonies and the rest of the world, was still reserved as far as possible to British or colonial ships. This gave rise to irritation on all sides, and these monopolistic laws began to be repealed. In 1822, three hundred statutes, some dating to the Middle Ages, were swept away.

Huskisson, Colonial Secretary in the 'twenties, while going much farther in abolishing the old restrictions, tried to keep the Empire, as far as possible, a closed economic unit. Inter-imperial trade was to be limited to British and Colonial ships, though direct trade with the Colonies could be carried on by foreign countries. A preference was given to British goods by higher duties on foreign imports; the most important preference was the lowering of the tariff on Canadian wheat, which gave it an enormous advantage in the British market.

In 1846, the abolition of the Corn Laws in England meant the end of this system of imperial preference. Canada was the hardest hit. Suffering from an intense economic depression, she led the Colonies in demanding the right to manage their own affairs.

The two provinces of Upper and Lower Canada had representative assemblies, but the Lieutenant-Governors had all the real power, since they were not responsible to these assemblies. This constitution did not work smoothly. It was partly the racialism of the French Canadians, and the privileges of the Protestant Churches, that were the immediate causes of the rebellion of 1837, which was suppressed in Northern Canada only after considerable fighting.

In South Africa, there was fighting with the Boers, who had *trekked* northwards to escape British rule; but in spite of these ominous signs, the British Empire did not break up. Loyalty was increased by the gain of economic and political independence. While the old links which were supposed to bind the Empire together were being removed, a new and enlightened interest in the Empire began to grow among the English public, and this was correspondingly strengthened by the rapid increase which took place in imperial trade.

B B   (H.W.)

During the days of the imperial preference policy, Canada had tripled her export of wheat to England. Though the abolition of the Corn Laws meant a disastrous depression, by 1870 she had more than recovered her previous trade, and was even exporting more than twice the amount of her best year. The importance of Australia to England had become apparent by the middle of the century, by which time she had surpassed all her other rivals in the world as a producer of wool. After the middle of the century, South Africa, too, was enabled to embark upon a period of rapid trade expansion.

BRITAIN, THE COLONIES AND INDIA

Instead of countering grievances by oppression, Great Britain adopted the principle of giving responsibility to the Colonies themselves. The constitution which was granted to Canada after the rebellion of 1836 was an advance towards complete self-government. This came in 1867 through the British North America Act, by which all the provinces were formed into the Dominion of Canada, with its own parliament to which the Governor-General was responsible. Already in 1859 Canada had shown her economic independence by setting up a protective tariff, against British as well as against foreign goods. Some years earlier, the Australian colonies had been given similar economic powers; and from 1854 onwards, the states had their own self-governing constitutions.

While such measures of independence were being granted, the links between England and the colonies were strengthened in other ways. Enthusiasm for the Empire was aroused by a group of men, among them Lord Durham, whose Report prepared the way for the Canadian Constitution of 1840, and Gibbon Wakefield, who devised a Government scheme for settling Australia. Money was granted to finance the bringing-out of workers to man the industries which were being started in Australia. Land was to be sold at a fairly high price, as a means of keeping the workers in industry for some years before they could save enough to start farming. Wakefield thought that a balanced colonial economy would lead to harmonious development.

He also did much for New Zealand, which the British Government ordered to be annexed in 1839. Settlement went on, too, under the auspices of church societies: there were settlements of German Lutherans, Anglican High Churchmen, and Scotch Presbyterians, each with their own community. By 1852, the colony was large enough to receive a grant of self-government, though not till 1860 did immigration become rapid.

Government aid was only a small factor in advancing colonization. One of the biggest waves of emigration to Australia was the result of the discovery of gold in Victoria in 1851.

India differed from most other British possessions in that she was a country where colonization was almost impossible. The English officials and soldiers formed a minute percentage of the total population. Trade had originally been the sole concern of British interests in India; political aims came later. India was important both as a market and as a source of raw materials. In the twenty years before 1859, India's exports had doubled, and her imports from England had increased by 100 per cent. Of both exports and imports, the most valuable item was cotton, England depending to a large extent on India for supplies of the raw materials, while India was her best market for manufactured goods. In the 'sixties, India's trade was almost solely with England.

India was governed through the East India Company, over which the British Government's control had been gradually increasing. In 1833, the Company was no longer allowed to engage in trade, and became almost entirely a governmental agency. As this happened, England could more easily pursue the policy of expansion and westernization which she thought necessary for the safety of her rule. Much of this expansion was peaceful. Numerous treaties were made with native princes, by which Residents, and sometimes garrisons, were established. Some provinces of Burma were annexed; the Punjab was secured after two years; three other states were taken over, on the claim of the Governor-General that, since the later rulers had no children, their lands "lapsed" to the British Crown. Oude was annexed because of misgovernment.

The Europeanization and economic development of the country was encouraged by the Governors-General. Bentinck introduced a scheme of Higher Education, with European, instead of Asiatic, sciences and literature as the subjects. Lord Dalhousie began railway building and in addition was able to introduce a telegraph and postal system. At the same time steps had been taken towards admitting Indians as government officials.

THE INDIAN MUTINY

Unrest at the speed of westernization formed a background to the growing discontent among the Indian soldiers, which was mainly caused by questions of pay. Agitators made much of the rumour that the fat of pigs and cows was used for greasing the cartridges of the newly-introduced rifle—for the cow was sacred to the Hindu and the pig an abomination to the Mohammedan; the discontent was exploited by the disappointed claimants of the "lapsed" states. The situation was particularly dangerous at a time when rumours of defeats in the Crimea had lowered British prestige, and when there was only one British soldier to every eight sepoys.

The Mutiny broke out early in 1857. A party of the mutineers seized Delhi, where there were only a handful of British troops; these were massacred, together with their wives and children—not, however, before the telegraph office had sent out messages for help. In the ancient capital of Delhi an aged descendant of the Great Mogul in Bahadur Shah was once again set up as the titular emperor.

At Cawnpore, in the "lapsed" province of Oude, still worse massacres were perpetrated. After a heroic defence, the general surrendered to save the women and children, but later the whole of the white population was shot down. At Lucknow, the capital, Sir Henry Lawrence put up a heroic defence in the Residency for nearly three months, while shot and shell were rained upon the building and its enclosure. Lawrence himself was killed before a relieving force could fight its way through; the relief column was in its turn besieged. It was another two months before the Residency was finally relieved.

By this time, Delhi had been re-captured, after months of hard fighting, made famous by the heroic leadership of John Nicholson, who was mortally wounded during the siege of the city. An extraordinarily skilful campaign by General Sir Hugh Rose, who on one occasion defeated twenty thousand mutineers with one thousand five hundred men, cleared Central India, and by the middle of 1858, order was completely restored.

The acceptance of British rule by the population as a whole is shown by the fact that there was no general rising, and the resulting isolation of the mutineers simplified the task of reducing them. Public opinion in England was roused to a new sense of responsibility for India, with the result that the East India Company was brought to an end and the British Government took over direct administration. The pace of westernization was slowed up, and the succeeding years of sound administration did something to clear away the bitter memories and racial antagonisms which the Mutiny had aroused.

BRITISH FEAR OF RUSSIAN ENCROACHMENT

India was secured, but there was always one power which was feared by British opinion as a possible rival for dominion there; this was Russia. A duel went on between the two countries for the control of the States lying between Russian territory and the Indian North-West frontier, of which Persia and Afghanistan were the most important. To prevent Afghanistan from falling under Russian influence, a ruler favourable to Britain was installed at Kabul, with a British force of eight thousand men to support him. He was forced to flee, however, and the British force was cut up as it tried to march to the nearest garrison town some eighty miles away. To restore British prestige, a second war had to be fought and an example made of the hostile Afghans.

In Europe, fear of Russia's encroachments, and in particular, the fear that she would dominate the increasingly important route to India, the Eastern Mediterranean (the Suez Canal was to be opened in 1869), eventually led to war. The immediate cause of hostility was a Russian attempt to gain control over Turkey, by securing a position as protector of the Greek Orthodox Church. France also had interests in the Eastern Mediterranean, especially in Syria and Egypt, and she no more wished to see Russia in control of Constantinople—

the key to the Eastern Mediterranean—than did Britain. She therefore joined with England in opposing Russia's designs: both countries declared war after Russia had occupied Turkey's North-eastern provinces, in 1854.

Having defeated Russia in Turkey, the two allies decided to continue the war in the Crimea. Their objective was the capture of Sevastopol, Russia's Black Sea naval base. This cost a terrible winter campaign. The British troops, especially, were not equipped for such extreme cold; apart from the losses in fighting, hundreds were carried off by cholera. Balaclava, Alma and Inkerman were battles where the troops on both sides showed heroic fighting qualities, without much being achieved. The charge of the Light Brigade, in which four hundred out of the Brigade's six hundred lost their lives, was glorious but futile. The mortality among the wounded was appalling, owing to the inefficiency of the hospital work and equipment, and would have been far heavier but for the devoted efforts of Florence Nightingale. Eventually Sevastopol was captured, and after the death of the grim and inflexible Tsar Nicholas, his successor, Alexander II, came to terms.

England and France now felt themselves to be secure in the Mediterranean. Meanwhile, the clash of rival powers on the other side of the world was beginning to shatter the stillness of the Far East.

POWER POLITICS IN THE FAR EAST

China and Japan had long followed a policy of excluding European influences. In doing this, China was in a weaker position than Japan, being far less under strong control from the central government.

England turned greedy eyes towards China because of the value of the opium trade. Opium had been introduced in the seventeenth century, but because of its harmful effects, the government had declared its use illegal. The main supplies came from India: there was a large trade by smuggling. It was to the interest of the East India Company, who had a monopoly of the trade, that there should be a good market for opium in China, but the Chinese government tried to stop the smuggling by force.

In reply, England sent a military expedition. The extraordinary weakness of China immediately became apparent. Though she had brought the arts of peace during the long ages of her history to an enviable pitch of perfection, she had no fighting strength. Without difficulty, the British advanced up the Yangtse and China was forced to make the Treaty of Nanking (1842), by which Hong Kong was opened to British trade.

It was the first step towards the complete opening of China. England as first-comer had the main advantage. Gradually she gained more privileges and secured the opening of more ports. After another war between England and China in 1860, this process went one stage farther, and diplomatic ministers were established at Peking.

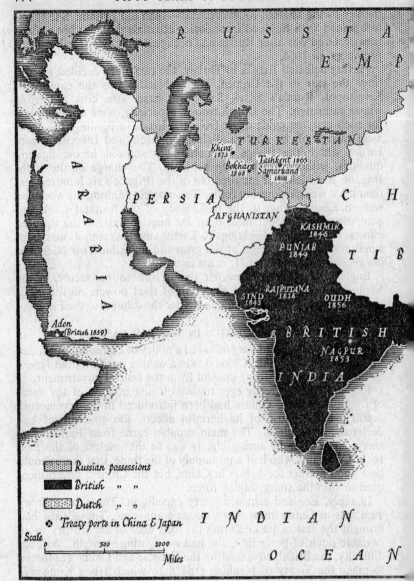

EUROPEAN EXPANSION

The nineteenth century saw the nations of the West turning towards the Far East for an extension of trade. In India, Britain secured her hold by abolishing the East India Company after the Mutiny and substituting direct rule. She was also able to annex Assam and the Burmese seaboard, as is shown on the above map. The Arabian seaport of Aden provided a useful coaling station for ships.

IN ASIA, 1815–1865

In China, Hong Kong and other treaty ports grew up. Following American pressure, Japan was opened to European and American merchants. The Dutch exploited the fertile and wealthy East Indies, and the British established settlements in Australia which soon became a valuable asset. Russia's population immensely increased through the occupation of great Asiatic territories.

Japan had been able to go much farther than the Chinese in a policy of exclusion. As has been told in an earlier part, the openness of the Japanese to new influences had, in the seventeenth century, given way to a rigid policy of isolation—the exclusion of foreigners, their commerce and their creeds. The Dutch alone were allowed the use of one port for trading purposes, under certain conditions and after performing humiliating ceremonies. The Christian missionary effort had been stamped out, and the national customs, Buddhist and Shintoist, alone remained. This was the work of the Shoguns, the real rulers. In the background, the Emperors maintained the succession of their immemorial dynasty. Though powerless, they were venerated as mystical personages, linking their people with Heaven.

During the two hundred years of peace which followed the closing of the country, modern civilization had begun to develop. The social system remained aristocratic, being based on privilege and birth, but a new class, that of the wealthy capitalists, came into existence; by the nineteenth century, there was a nationalist party that wished for the overthrow of the ruling family and the return of power to the Emperor, as the first step towards modernizing the country. The demands made by the Western Powers in China indicated what would happen to Japan if she did not at least improve her defences.

RUSSIAN AND AMERICAN AGGRESSION

In 1853, like a portent from another planet, four warships of the United States Navy steamed into Uraga harbour. In command was Commodore Perry, with a mandate from his government to gain, if possible, the opening of trade relations. Playing for time, the government opened two ports. English, French and Russian ships soon appeared, and more ports were opened. In 1865, the British Minister entered into relations with the nationalist party; with this support, it was able to restore power to the Mikado. The next half-century carried out the Europeanization of Japan.

Besides forcing the opening of trade-relations, European expansion threatened territorial conquests. China had already felt very directly the effect of this European expansion, by the loss of her northern provinces to Russia.

Russian expansion was never the result of pressure of population. The already vast territories which she controlled in 1815 were very thinly populated. In Russia, unlike the other countries of Europe, it had never been necessary to introduce the law of primogeniture for the sake of maintaining the wealth of noble families: each portion of an estate divided among the sons could often, by more intensive methods of cultivation, be made to produce as much as the whole estate had previously yielded. If there was any desire for emigration, there was a huge area of Siberia, where much of the soil was highly fertile, to satisfy it. There had already been voluntary colonization, though settlement was mainly by those who had been banished.

The main motive of Russian expansion was the need of better outlets for trade. By annexing Chinese territory which lay north of the Amur River, Count Muraviev, Governor of Eastern Siberia after 1847, carried the Russian Empire to the China Sea. Here he founded Vladivostok, marking the new outlet of Russia to the Pacific. This outlet was made more valuable by the extensive trade-privileges gained from China.

In Central Asia and the East Caucasus, a more spectacular struggle went on with the object of securing lands ceded by independent princes. The consolidation of this territory was prevented by the mountain-tribes of the East Caucasus, one of whose chiefs held up the Russian advance for thirty years. When he was overcome in 1859, the way lay open for Russia to secure almost all the territory between the Black Sea and the Caspian, bringing her to the borders of Persia.

The conquest of Turkestan was particularly difficult owing to the vast distances and enormous desert areas. Breaking an agreement signed with England concerning the neutrality of Turkestan, the Russians gradually conquered it, the final stroke being the capture, in 1868, of Samarkand, the ancient capital of Tamerlane. The moral effect of this was such that other resistance was quickly overcome. Khiva, the worst centre of raids into Russian territory, was captured, and soon the advance brought Russia to Afghanistan, which was a British sphere of influence. The only other independent state between Russian and British territory in this area was Persia—soon to become so dominated by the Russians that it was practically a vassal state.

FRANCE'S SECOND COLONIAL EMPIRE

The founding of the second French colonial empire had no deep-laid material causes; it was an accident. France had lost almost her entire first Empire. The last of her American territory had gone when Napoleon sold the Louisiana territory to the United States; there remained only a few West Indian islands and some trading-stations in India. It seemed unlikely that France would ever again be an important colonial power. She had little excess population for emigration, for the peasantry limited the size of their families to prevent too great subdivision of their lands, and the growing industries were able to absorb the increasing population of the towns.

The motive behind the foundation of the new colonial empire of France was Charles X's need of prestige to strengthen an already tottering throne. For this reason he decided on an expedition to Algiers. Algeria had been a vassal state of the Ottoman Empire, but the decline of Turkey removed all danger of opposition from that quarter. Moreover, it was the home of the Barbary Pirates, and a constant menace to the shipping of the Mediterranean. Even the bombardment of Algiers that was undertaken by a combined British and Dutch fleet in 1816 had failed to check the ravages of its pirates.

In spite of the law and order which a French occupation would undoubtedly bring, the British Government, jealous of the extension of French power, opposed it. But Charles X was determined on a policy of conquest and glory. An insult to the French consul, following on a financial quarrel, gave the excuse for intervention, and the resulting expedition had no difficulty in capturing the town which for three centuries had terrified the commerce of Europe. The news of this was scarcely noticed in France during the excitement of the revolution of 1830, but the new government had to decide what to do with this legacy of the old order. To hold it meant still further expansion: there would be no security from constant raids on the city unless the surrounding belt of territory was conquered too.

Thus the second phase of building up this empire was due to the same causes as decided the Russian advance towards India—the necessity for security against constant raids. The French accordingly began a series of wars with neighbouring chiefs; the Moslem hero Abd-el-Kader was conquered only after the greatest difficulty.

FRENCH COLONIAL SYSTEM

The French found themselves in possession of new territory, much of it highly fertile and particularly suitable for grain and vines. The difficulty was to find settlers. Under the Second Republic, some of the workers who had risen during the June Days were transported to Algeria; but this attempt at settlement was not successful. A number of soldiers, however, who had fought in the long Algerian wars, settled there with government assistance. The shortage was partly made up by immigration of Italians to the eastern districts and of Spaniards to the western; the newcomers found little difficulty in adopting French nationality.

Under Louis Napoleon, the colony was divided into departments and communes, and came into the same administrative system as France. Its local affairs were in the charge of Prefects, while control over the Prefects, and the administration of important departments, was vested in the central authority at Paris. The inhabitants were given the right of citizenship, and with it the right to elect deputies for the French chamber, but only on condition that they accepted the French legal code. The Jews accepted, but the Moslems refused to renounce such customs as polygamy: separatist aims among the Moslem population remained. In spite of this, France had considerable success in the policy of treating Algeria as part of the mother country—a policy made more practicable, when modern means of communication brought it closer to France.

In thus making African territory again a part of Europe, the French, as befitted the most logical nation in the world, carried the principle of European expansion to its furthest possible conclusion, and revived the civilization of Rome on the southern shores of the Mediterranean.

French rule brought many benefits to the native population of Algeria, just as English rule in India brought the inhabitants entirely new standards of health and new opportunities for a favoured few in business careers. Although westernization certainly brought advantages, it tended to thwart the natural development of peoples.

EUROPEAN INFLUENCE ON NATIVE PEOPLES

The coming of Europeans to America had tragic results for the aborigines both in the Northern and Southern continents. In the South, such tribes as were brought into close contact with the Spanish and survived the early period of colonization—as did those of Mexico —accepted the position of a subordinate race, and have increased considerably since then. In North America, the Redskins, being a more vigorous and a prouder people, fought bitter wars against the constant encroachments of the Europeans. Even when, in the nineteenth century, the policy of reservations was adopted the position of the Redskins was not much improved. Deprived of their usual activities, they tended to become aimless and pauperized, losing their attractive characteristics of courage, dignity and hospitality. Idleness and the coming of alcohol introduced them to the white man's vices and diseases. In Canada, the excellent policy of the French settlers, continued by the British, made the condition of the Indians there far better. Towards the end of the century, the number of Redskins in North America seemed to be increasing.

In Australia, the aborigines presented less of a problem to European settlers than anywhere else, owing to the smallness of their numbers; probably they did not exceed one hundred and fifty thousand, and during the era of colonization, this figure was reduced to half. The most primitive people in the world except the African pygmies, with almost no organization beyond the unit of the family, these aborigines could offer no concerted resistance to the Europeans, apart from occasional murders provoked by the atrocities of the newcomers.

The Maoris of New Zealand were of a different race, with finer physique and a higher culture, being passionately devoted to singing and poetry. By the Treaty of Waitangi of 1840, the Maoris were guaranteed their possession of the soil, and every acre since acquired by settlers was paid for. In spite of this, war broke out between them and the settlers, which lasted in a desultory manner for ten years. But the tradition of good government established by Sir George Grey, and the efforts of missionaries, did much to improve the position of the natives. A large majority accepted Christianity; the constant fighting, with its accompanying cannibalism, besides other institutions such as infanticide and slavery, became things of the past.

European influence brought about the abolition of slavery, after the Slave Trade had been ended in the years following the British government's lead of 1808, which made it illegal for British subjects to own slaves. The emancipation of slaves in the British Colonies in 1834, and in the colonies of France and Holland in 1848 and 1864, did much to redress that greatest of all crimes committed by Europeans on the native inhabitants of the lands which came, for good and evil, under their influence. Nevertheless, it still needed four years of very bitter fighting in the United States before this ancient wrong could in some measure be redressed in the New World also.

CHAPTER 69

FREEDOM AND PROSPERITY

AFTER the upheavals of 1848, "reaction was restored" on the Continent. But old systems could not remain immune from the influence of new principles, and even autocratic governments borrowed constitutional forms. Parliamentary government was established in many countries, and had in England one of its most splendid periods. The desire for freedom and unity brought about the independence of two more nations. Increasing wealth and industrialization prepared the way for further change.

In England, even though prosperity had been rapidly increasing, the speed of increase became truly amazing. In 1865, Gladstone, who was Chancellor of the Exchequer, speaking of the excellent returns from taxation, called it an "intoxicating augmentation of wealth and power", though he noted that it was "entirely confined to classes of property". Industry was making huge profits, and paid 50 per cent. more in taxes than ten years before. Germany, especially Prussia, where development had been slow, now entered on its first great phase of industrial expansion. Before long, she was almost rivalling England in cotton manufacture; the output of her mines increased by 600 per cent.; her towns grew rapidly. This new prosperity was accompanied by lower tariffs. In the Anglo-French agreement of 1860, England gained a considerable reduction of duties on her goods; the process of lowering tariffs in England itself was completed by leaving only a few duties for revenue. The Great Exhibition which was held in Hyde Park in 1851 seemed to the minds of many people to symbolize the beginning of a new era of plenty and progress.

POLITICAL AWAKENING OF THE WORKING-CLASS

But, although the working-class as a whole was growing better off, they only very slowly received a share of this rapidly increasing wealth, and many of them were even worse off than before. In England the number of paupers increased for a time during the years after 1856. This was partly due to a further introduction of machines.

The conditions of the worse-off workers, most glaring perhaps in England, but reproduced in France, and beginning to appear in Germany, Russia, and the United States, provided a fertile soil for the extremer forms of socialism and communism. Internationally, under the leadership of Marx, the working-class movement began to be organized. Marx's writings, especially the Communist Manifesto, had a considerable circulation, and workers in different countries were becoming conscious of the solidarity of their interests. In 1864, under the chairmanship of a London University professor, a meeting was held in London which led to the establishment of the International Association of Working-men.

But the English working-class movement was far from being identified with Marxian Communism. The workers began a new development, in organizing themselves into unions of the same trade throughout the country, while forming affiliations of the various unions in the same localities. Their next step, as in previous years, was a further extension of the vote. Their leaders were the permanent paid officials of the new Trade Unions—workers who had risen to form a bureaucracy of the working-class, which, like all bureaucracies, had a conservative tendency. Their allies were the lower middle-class, who were also excluded from the right to vote. There was, as formerly, a small idealistic section of the Lords ready to support a progressive movement, besides a considerable number of intelligent and conscientious industrialists. As in the days before 1830, to such people the next step seemed to be a further measure of parliamentary reform, which would give the vote at least to the lower middle-class and some of the workers.

The reform was finally carried in 1867 by the Conservative ministry of Disraeli and the Earl of Derby. Its passing was partly due to the reappearance of mass-meetings and demonstrations. Although the new Bill had the result of extending the vote to every householder, this was still some way from universal suffrage.

QUEEN VICTORIA'S INFLUENCE ON NATIONAL LIFE

One cause of the new stability of England, which enabled the next step to be peacefully achieved, was the influence of Queen Victoria and the Prince Consort. The Crown became a far stronger centre of loyalty for all classes and sections. Victoria, whose natural ability was only moderate, grew, under the direction of her husband, to have a statesmanlike view of English affairs. She influenced policy by protesting against measures which she disapproved, but she made clear the Crown's position in never thwarting the determined will of the Commons. She had all the dignity of a queen, with a strong conception of the duties of her office. But she was simple in her tastes, and aristocratic society and interests meant little to her. The ordinary people regarded her far more as one of themselves; her religion, her careful upbringing of her family, and the complete absence of scandals such as had marred previous reigns, besides the apparently personal interest which the Queen never failed to take in their well-being, all helped to win for the Crown new affection and prestige.

Lord Palmerston dominated the period in England. Robust, a lover of sport, jaunty and self-confident, he was one of the most popular statesmen in English history. As Foreign Secretary during the revolutions of 1830, he had helped to support the throne of Louis Philippe and had used all the influence of England on the side of an independent Belgium. His vigorous handling of policy greatly increased British prestige, though he was sometimes too hasty in his decisions—as when he recognized the *coup d'état* of Louis Napoleon without consulting the cabinet or the Queen. Dismissed because of this, he was called back to become Prime Minister at the age of seventy-one, as the one man capable of bringing the Crimean War to a speedy conclusion. Palmerston remained in office as Prime Minister, with two short intervals, until his death, which took place in 1865.

THE FOUR GREAT CONTINENTAL POWERS

The four Great Powers of the Continent, Russia, France, Austria, Prussia, were all autocracies. They differed from each other, however, in important respects. In France the dictatorial power which Louis Napoleon had seized by the *coup d'état* of 1851 was based on the bourgeois fear of a social revolution, and the sentimental attachment of the peasantry to his name. The old aristocracy went into retirement, which became permanent. Louis Napoleon did not associate the bourgeois fully in the government, since the majority of them gave him no more than passive support. The only possible form of government was therefore through a civil service directed by the Prince President, who became Emperor in 1852, and his personal friends. At the same time, he made certain liberal elements a part of the new constitution. In order to ratify some of his decisions, he appealed to plebiscites held under universal male suffrage. He formed an assembly of two houses, of which the *Legislative Body* was elected. But its functions were only those of a debating society, and the government was able to bring about the return of all but a handful of the official candidates. The real power, apart from the Emperor, lay with the Council of State, some fifty men who were the cream of the civil service. Members of the legislative body were mainly landed proprietors or industrialists, representing the more conservative element of the middle class who were the pillars of the régime.

Napoleon III's highly centralized government largely depended on the recent invention of the telegraph. Suspicious movements in the provinces could be watched, distant officials could be more easily controlled. He tried to strengthen his alliance with the bourgeoisie by giving them government assistance, chiefly through public utility companies, founded with government subsidies. Of these the Société de Crédit Foncier was used chiefly by large landowners for developing their estates, and it also partly financed the rebuilding of Paris. The Société de Crédit Mobilier was slightly more speculative and financed railways, mines, and other industries. The government took special care for the development of railways, by means of concessionary companies, whose interest it guaranteed. As a result, the length of lines in France more than tripled during the first six years of Napoleon's rule: even so, they amounted to less than half the English mileage covered.

His schemes of public works were partly due to his socialistic sympathies, for the Emperor had been influenced by Saint-Simon's doctrines. Public Works helped to some extent in making these years the height of the Industrial Revolution in France. The first great industrial exhibition of the reign, though it took place in the middle of the Crimean War, was a complete success.

The new prosperity quieted working-class discontent, and Napoleon improved the workers' position by abolishing the old laws against association, though his government controlled, while encouraging, the growth of Trade Unions. The socialist movement was little heard of: its only leader not in exile was Proudhon. But the workers grew in their sense of solidarity, though they gradually learned to exploit more peaceful tactics.

Other sections, too, who were doubtful in their allegiance began to support the new régime. As time went on and it did not appear that Napoleon's throne would be upset by violence, he began to allow more headway to the democratic forces of the country. These re-asserted themselves increasingly as the bourgeoisie lost their fear of a socialist rising. The veiled, sometimes flippant, criticism of some of the papers, under strict government censorship, showed this movement in public opinion. Gradually reforms in parliamentary procedure were decreed: for the *Corps Législatif*, certain powers of criticism and of financial control, and of initiating measures, were allowed. Parliamentary debates were published. More opposition members were elected to Parliament. It seemed as though the transition was gradually being made to a fully constitutional régime.

AUTOCRACY IN RUSSIA

Since the accession of Nicholas I, Russia had been the most autocratic country of all. History had placed supreme power in the hands of the Tsar; and the nobles, while providing a firm support for his rule, had little influence on his government. He ruled with the aid of a civil service which became more powerful as the century went on.

Industry in the middle of the century was just beginning; but idealism, as much as economic forces, was the spur to the reforms of Alexander II, who succeeded the reactionary Nicholas in 1855. He had as his supporters idealistic members of the nobility. He sympathized with the socialists, and the discontent of the new working-class was a stimulus to action.

In 1861, he decreed that the serfs should be freed and given guarantees of ownership of their houses and farm-buildings; they had the right of working on certain lands, and the possibility of buying more. In practice, most of them had only enough land to keep them occupied for three days a week; the result was to extend the capitalist method of farming with landless labourers, who, owing to their need of extra employment, had to accept very low wages. The peasants tended to fall easily into debt, and thousands were forced to sell their holdings; this provided a propertyless labour army for supplying the growing industries.

In Austria and Prussia, the autocracies rested on the nobility and the upper landed proprietors. The civil service of both these countries was also of the utmost importance: the higher members continued to belong to the aristocracy, who, in Austria in particular, dominated the government. There the problem was one of setting up a form of government which would represent not the people, but the peoples. The constitutions of the years 1848–1849 had disappeared. One attempted reform was baulked, like earlier ones, by the refusal of Hungary to co-operate. A policy was then originated to bind the racial groups of the Empire together by a common loyalty to the emperor, the young Francis Joseph. A constitution was made for a parliament which representatives from all districts were to attend. Had this constitution succeeded, control over the hotch-potch of races would have been secured to the civil service—or rather to the German-Austrian aristocracy who filled the highest positions in that service. But the attempt broke down, again owing to strong nationalist opposition—this time from Croats and Venetians, as well as Hungarians, all of whom refused even to send representatives.

JUNKER INFLUENCE IN PRUSSIA

In Prussia, the struggle was between the Liberal, mainly middle-class, section of society, and the military aristocratic *Junkers*. The second constitution of 1848, decreed by the king, had not set up constitutional government: the king was not obliged to choose his ministers according to the majority of the chambers, and he kept the power of veto. But it seemed as though constitutional government would soon be achieved by the Liberals. The parliamentary majority of Liberals (aristocrats and middle class) were ready to go slowly.

The struggle became critical when the question of the unity of Germany as a whole was involved. The Junkers believed that Prussia, backed by a strong army, could defeat outside enemies and impose unity from above; the Liberals believed that public opinion without the use of force would be enough. The issue was whether or not the army should be increased and re-equipped. The parliament voted the money as a provisional measure, but in the following year, supported by an overwhelming electoral majority, it refused to re-new the credits. The war minister, von Roon, saw that it was necessary to defy the parliament, but was prepared to do this only with the support of the strongest and ablest of the Junkers, Bismarck, at that time ambassador in Paris.

The apparent difficulty of proceeding with his cherished plan of army reform brought the king, William I, to the verge of abdication. The accession of the liberal-minded Crown Prince Frederick would have secured the triumph of the constitutionalists. But when summoned by his father, Frederick refused to read the abdication document. Roon immediately wired for Bismarck. It was the turning-point. Constitutionalism had failed in Prussia; henceforth Germany was destined to be united under the leadership of an autocratic Prussia, which in turn was dominated by the Junker military class.

ITALY'S STRUGGLE FOR FREEDOM

In Italy, during the 'thirties and 'forties, the new forces of Liberalism and nationalism had begun to grow rapidly. This was due largely to the coming of the Industrial Revolution and the rise of the middle class. After Napoleon's defeat, the old order had once more frozen its grip over Italy. The King of Sardinia put the clock back to 1798, the date when he was driven away—no one was ever allowed to mention anything that had happened between then and his restoration. But even he could not blot out the memory of Napoleon's Kingdom of Italy, which gave fire to men's longing for unity.

There was a growing impatience with the divisions that split Italy into a number of states, with Austria firmly established in the north in Lombardy and Venetia. Austria, with Metternich directing her policy, dominated the peninsula: three of the central states were ruled by Habsburgs.

Up to the 'thirties, the movement for unity was led by army officers; it was romantic and imaginative, an affair of poets, novelists, and secret socities. Of these the Carbonari were the most widespread, mysterious through its ritual and dreaded owing to its assassinations. The risings which it supported were fruitless, but the imagination of the Italians was stirred.

The real period of development came with the appearance of industry in the north, and the improvement of communications. Good roads were made in some of the states; the first railway was built in 1837. Commerce began to flourish with the reopening of the Mediterranean as a route to the East. In 1835, a British shipping service was started from London to Alexandria, to connect up with the East India Company's line from Suez to Bombay. The Eastern commerce, which Italy had largely lost with the discovery of the route round the Cape at the end of the Middle Ages, began to enrich her again.

A school of economic thinkers taught that if economic progress continued, national unity would follow. Railways, even if begun only inside states, would soon link up the peninsula. They would "stitch Italy's boot", as the writer d'Azeglio put it. Business interests were nation-wide. Already the conferences of scientists and economists, and the meetings of agricultural societies, were reaching beyond state boundaries. These views were put forward in newspapers, in the form of technical articles full of statistics, and in spite of being a powerful form of revolutionary propaganda, they escaped censorship. At the same time, there was more direct propaganda, especially from Mazzini, advocating unity. Although relatively few Italians agreed with Mazzini's republican doctrines and his advocacy of violent measures, his enthusiasm and his organization roused the feeling of nationalism throughout Italy.

In spite of middle-class development, Italy remained predominantly an agricultural country, with a Catholic and credulous peasantry who were strongly conservative, especially since they had come into ownership of their land. It was therefore of the utmost importance that some of the nobility should give them a lead. This happened when men such as Count Cavour in Sardinia and Baron Ricasoli in Tuscany came forward, as did some of the sovereigns— Charles Albert, the King of Sardinia, and—for a short time—Pope Pius IX. The blessing which the Pope gave the movement, though later withdrawn, enabled the bulk of the population to follow the national leaders with a clear conscience.

So the way was prepared when the French Revolution of 1848 gave the signal. The refusal of the Milanese to smoke, in order to prevent the Austrian government making money out of the tobacco duty, led to riots in Milan. The Austrian general thought it best to retire to his fortresses. A republic was proclaimed at Rome, under the leadership of Mazzini and Garibaldi, and another at Venice. Now seemed the moment for Charles Albert to lead the Italians against the Austrians and expel them. Idealistic and pious, he was indecisive and hesitated too long, allowing the Austrians to be reinforced. He was defeated, but a year later he made a second attempt. A second time defeated, he abdicated in favour of his son, who, he thought, might succeed where he had failed. The Republics at Rome and Venice were crushed.

But this was not the end of the movement for unity. Stimulated by the Press, by societies and by the new economic forces constantly striving to break through the petty state boundaries, it could not be smothered much longer. This situation explains how a relatively few strokes of statesmanship by Cavour brought about national unity in so short a time and with comparatively little bloodshed.

CAVOUR AND GARIBALDI

Count Camillo Cavour was one of the finest examples of an enlightened nineteenth-century aristocrat. He had been an officer in the Sardinian army, but found it best to leave it, owing to his advanced views. On his inherited estates he adopted the most up-to-date ideas of land-development, and soon made them a model. He was often to be seen inspecting the work, being recognizable from afar by his short figure and bespectacled face underneath an enormous sun-hat. After fifteen years of the life of a country squire, he

UNIFICATION OF ITALY

From the above map may be seen the stages of Italian unification, with the years in which the component states accepted union with Sardinia, whose King, Victor Emmanuel, was made King of Italy in 1861 by the first parliament.

came into public notice in 1848, when it was his initiative which led to the granting of a constitution by the King of Sardinia. In 1852, Count Cavour became Prime Minister of the new king, Victor Emmanuel II. He began to enlarge the Sardinian army, but he realized that it could never be strong enough by itself to defeat the power of Austria. By bringing Sardinia into the Crimean War on the side of

France and England, he gave her a place among the powers at the Peace Conference that followed it, and gained for her the diplomatic friendship of her two allies. Three years later, Cavour met Napoleon III at Plombières, a Riviera watering-place, where the statesman gained the acquiescence of the romantic-minded emperor in a plot for the deliverance of Italy. It only remained for a quarrel to begin between Sardinia and Austria. This soon happened: the French army came to Sardinia's aid, and the Austrians were decisively defeated in 1859. At this point, Napoleon went back on his agreement, which was to continue the war till Sardinia had possession of Venetia as well as Lombardy. This war was unpopular in France, and Napoleon withdrew, gaining only Lombardy for Sardinia.

Victor Emmanuel had called on all Italians who wished to help him with their arms in the war of liberation. Revolutions broke out in the central provinces of Italy. But Sardinia would not accept the annexation of these territories till public opinion had definitely spoken through plebiscites; there were enormous majorities in favour of union with Sardinia.

Garibaldi with his thousand Red Shirts took the next step. With the secret approval of Cavour and Victor Emmanuel, he set sail for Sicily, where, backed by the inhabitants, he seized the fortresses of the Neapolitan king. Crossing to the mainland, he began to march on Naples: the king abdicated and the population welcomed Garibaldi with wild enthusiasm. He next marched against the Papal States, where a strong army, with volunteers from many nations, was gathering to oppose him. It seemed impossible that Garibaldi's handful of troops would have any chance against them.

CONSTITUTIONAL GOVERNMENT TRIUMPHS IN ITALY

Cavour saw that, to save Garibaldi, he would have to intervene. Although Napoleon still kept a French garrison in Rome to secure it for the Pope, he made no objection to Sardinia's conquest of the rest of the Papal territory. Sardinian troops thereupon defeated the Papal army, and the remainder of the Papal States, excepting Rome, voted by plebiscite for union with Sardinia. Shortly afterwards, Garibaldi held a plebiscite in Naples and Sicily, with the same result. A parliament with deputies from all Victor Emmanuel's new provinces met, and declared him King of Italy in 1861.

Because Sardinia had been, since 1848, the sole constitutional state of Italy, and because Cavour himself was a convinced parliamentarian, the new Italy was also constitutional—a triumph in nation-building for the democratic forces of nineteenth-century Europe.

One other new country came into existence at this time—Rumania. At the Peace of Paris which followed the Crimean War, two former Turkish provinces, Moldavia and Wallachia, were made independent, though separate. Plebiscites in each, however, elected the same noble as prince, and proceeded to make a single constitution.

In America the same national, economic and social forces as were disturbing Europe combined to bring about a struggle. In conflict with the independent attitude of the Southerners was the nationalism of those who believed in the United States as one great, free nation. The industrial and business classes of the North clashed with the Southern landowners. The working-classes of the North disliked the slave-labour of the South, which, they thought, prevented a betterment of their own conditions. It was a conflict between two civilizations, that of the North, democratic and progressive, and of the South, slave-ridden, aristocratic, conservative.

CAUSES OF THE AMERICAN CIVIL WAR

Further, it was a conflict between two ways of life. The ideal of a Southern gentleman was to do his duty in ruling his dependents like the father of a family, and to practise a way of living whose standards and values were strange to the Northern States. It had little in common with the bustle and commercialism of the American businessman, or with the primitive life of the pioneer.

The persistence of this aristocratic, slave-holding civilization was almost entirely due to the vast increase in the demand for cotton. Cotton-growers had produced 160 million pounds of cotton in 1820; by 1860, they were able to sell 230 million. Since there had been no improvement in the methods of growing cotton, the cotton kingdom had constantly to be taking in new lands; expansion in any case was necessary, because the wasteful methods of cultivation exhausted the soil.

As was proved later, slavery was not essential for growing cotton, nor for the civilization of the South. A leading patriot of the South and her greatest general, Robert E. Lee—one of the finest characters in American history—abhorred slavery, and had freed the few slaves which he had inherited. Yet he thought the freedom of the South to choose its own course so essential that he fought for it.

But with most Southerners, it had become a point of honour to uphold the slave system. From thinking it an inevitable evil, they had come to consider it the essential condition of an ideal social system—as their leader Calhoun had put it, "the most safe and stable basis for free institutions in the world". It was necessary and right for the cultivated section of society to exist on the labour of others, so that they might have time to exercise their higher faculties of mind and soul. It was the philosophy of ancient Athens applied to a section of nineteenth-century American society.

In spite of loudly proclaiming these principles, the South felt itself on the defensive against the humanitarianism that was equally loudly proclaimed in the North. In the course of the century, strong opposition had developed against slavery. The cause of abolition was preached especially by Garrison in his paper *The Liberator*. He never spared his efforts to rouse the churches, societies, organizations of every kind, and people everywhere, to realize the wickedness of slavery. Writers like Harriet Beecher Stowe the authoress of *Uncle Tom's Cabin*, the poet Whittier, the philosopher Emerson, all helped to stir the conscience of the North. Public opinion became determined to get rid of the evil which dishonoured the freest country in the world. The Republican Party was founded to fight slavery.

In the face of this movement the South felt almost in a state of siege. The upper-class Southerners became conscious of their interests as a community; even the "poor whites", who had been the people to suffer most from the slave system, shared this sentiment. The South was developing a national consciousness of its own.

During the 'fifties, there were continual quarrels between North and South on the question of the extension of slavery. Where the organization of new states was concerned, the dispute raged as to whether they should be free or slave. It was decided, owing to Southern influence, that the old method of settling this question, whether they lay north or south of a line drawn through the centre of the United States, should no longer hold good. Instead, it should be decided by the inhabitants on the spot. In Kansas, this led to what was almost a civil war in miniature between rival factions.

ABRAHAM LINCOLN'S EVENTFUL PRESIDENCY

Abraham Lincoln came from a poor farming family in Kentucky. He had educated himself, and then gone into local and State politics, without being particularly successful. After much thinking and meditating, he became convinced that the existence of slavery was "a moral, a social, and a political wrong" for which the whole American nation was responsible. He felt it was God's will that he should rouse the nation to bring about its abolition. He began to speak like a prophet: his eloquence, his simplicity, his appeal to everything that was best in the people, his obvious and complete altruism, made him in four years the best-known figure in the country. At the Presidential Election of 1860 the issue of slavery divided the country into two opposing camps; the old Democratic party was split by rival candidates and Lincoln, the candidate of the Republican party, was elected by a large majority.

Immediately South Carolina seceded, and was followed by six other Southern states. These formed themselves into the Confederate States of America, and elected their own president. Still no war broke out. The immediate cause was the question of the Federal forts remaining in the government's hands. One of these, Fort Sumter, was bombarded and captured. This meant war.

In spite of the enormous preponderance of the North in man-power and industries, the balance was more even than appeared. The personnel of the South was better. Most Southerners were used to handling a gun, and both gentry and "poor whites" were always excellent riders. A large number from the upper-class families had been trained as regular officers, and all were used to the command of men. Owing to its aristocratic structure, the people of the South easily accepted military organization, and capable leaders were chosen. Of these men it was Lee and Stonewall Jackson who most of all made it possible for the South to continue the war so long.

THE WAR BETWEEN THE STATES

Although the South had practically no industries to balance against those of the North, it was never seriously short of munitions. Partly this was due to the trade which it carried on with Europe, in spite of the Northerners' blockade. The Navy was one of the great assets of the North. Its blockade became increasingly effective, and it was able to give the most valuable support to the land forces. This was especially seen when a naval expedition seized the mouth of the Mississippi, and worked its way up the river, while a land column under General Grant advanced downstream from the North. With Grant's capture of Vicksburg, the Northerners were in control of the whole length of the river: the Southern territory was cut in half and the Southern forces seriously threatened in the flank.

Anything short of a defeat, any terms which gave them freedom to continue their own form of society, would be a victory for the Southerners. Defeat meant for them the greatest of humiliations. But the North, fighting not for their way of life but for a principle, could make peace at almost any moment, and after four years of war, there was a strong movement for peace without victory. The North was fighting for freedom for all in a free country.

Business interests in Europe almost universally supported the South. A free-trade, independent South, supplying their need for cotton and taking their goods in exchange, would have suited them admirably. Conservatives in Europe also supported the South. They saw it as a war between the principle of rule by a hereditary, privileged class, and that of rule by the people as a whole. Reactionaries in Europe had long regarded the democratic institutions of America with horror, and would have liked to see the country's power broken by a permanent division. On the other hand, particularly in France, where democracy remained one of the greatest ideals of the age, there was a strong sympathy with the North. The working-class, in England especially, were at one with the working-class of the North.

In the face of such sympathies, it was impossible to bring about intervention. But the English industrialists gained what was next best, a decree of neutrality; English shipbuilders fitted out privateers such as the famous *Alabama*, which did considerable damage to the United States Navy; engineering companies helped to keep the South supplied with arms. Relations between the United States and the British Government became so strained that at one moment it seemed certain that it would lead to war. Two agents of the South had been arrested on board the British steamer *Trent*. British

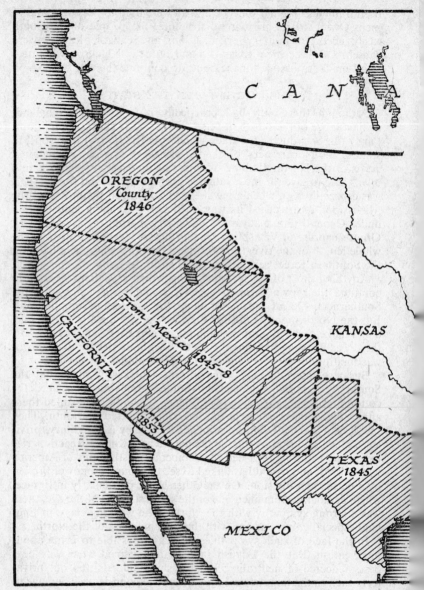

CANA

OREGON
County
1846

CALIFORNIA

From Mexico 1845–8

1853

KANSAS

TEXAS
1845

MEXICO

DEVELOPMENT OF THE

The shaded portions of the above map indicate the new territories taken over by the U.S.A. between 1819 and 1865, with the dates of their annexation. The greater part were to the west of states already in existence then and their acquisition indicates the progress of the American expansion towards the Pacific coast.

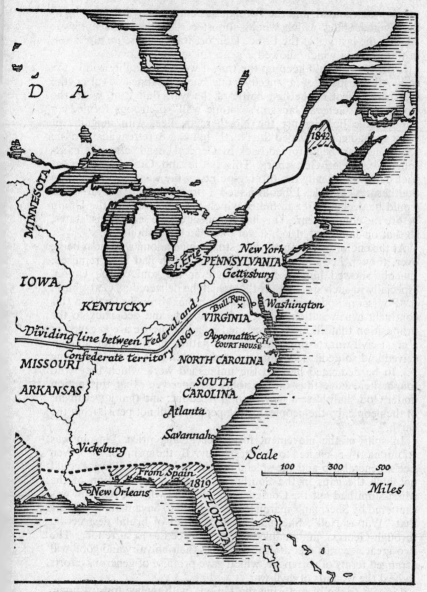

UNITED STATES OF AMERICA, 1861–65

The Civil War (1861–65) between the North (Federal) and South (Confederate)
was precipitated by the secession of the latter from the union as the result of the
opposition by the Southern land-owners to the proposed abolition of slavery. The
struggle, fought with great bitterness, resulted in the final victory of the North.

opinion was roused, and the Foreign Secretary wrote a sharp note to the United States which would almost certainly have meant war. Almost the last act of the Prince Consort was to cause an alteration in the wording which allowed a peaceful settlement.

If the North could keep up the war, it would inevitably win in the end. All prospect of a speedy conclusion disappeared after the Northern defeat in the first battle of the war, Bull Run, when the Confederate General Jackson's "stone wall" of troops formed an unbreakable line against the Northerners. Lee, with magnificent strategy, had early invaded the North, but had to retreat again in the following year, being forced back by General Meade after the hard-fought battle of Gettysburg. This battle and Grant's victory at Vicksburg were really the turning-points of the war. To weaken the Southerners' morale, Lincoln issued a proclamation that all slaves would be declared free in States which did not return to the Union before the coming year. This had no effect on the secessionist states, so that on January 1, 1863, slavery was declared abolished.

At the end of that year, the war still seemed a long way from being over, though Lee's latest thrust into the North had been repulsed. Lincoln showed himself more than ever the soul of the Union, especially in such speeches as that which he delivered at Gettysburg.

"Fourscore and seven years ago our fathers brought forth on this continent a new nation, conceived in liberty, and dedicated to the proposition that all men are created equal. Now we are engaged in a great civil war, testing whether that nation, or any nation so conceived and so dedicated, can long endure. . . . It is for us, the living . . . to be dedicated here to the unfinished work which they who fought here have thus far so nobly advanced . . . that this nation under God shall have a new birth of freedom; and that government of the people, by the people, for the people, shall not perish from the earth."

In spite of the movement for peace at any price, Lincoln was triumphantly re-elected to the Presidency. By the spring of 1865, even Lee's generalship and the splendid fortitude of his followers could not hide the gaps in the Southern shield. The occupation of the Mississippi had cut the Confederate states in two. The remnant was shattered by Sherman's march from Atalanta to Savannah. Believing that "War is Hell", Sherman blasted a trail of brutal destruction through Georgia, and enabled Grant to force Lee to surrender. The two great generals met at Appomattox; their chivalry and good will arranged terms of surrender, which gave promise of generous efforts to heal the wounds of civil war.

Lincoln spoke of restoring the Union "with malice toward none, with charity for all". But he was not fated to carry out his great design. As he sat with his wife at the theatre in Washington, watching *Our American Cousin*, he was shot by a fanatical Southerner. With him died all hope of a statesmanlike rebuilding of the South.

PART XIII

NATIONALISM
AND INTERNATIONALISM

CHAPTER 70

THE UNITED STATES AND AMERICA

MUCH of what was valuable in the abolition of slavery was lost by Lincoln's death. Had he lived, reconstruction might have meant reconciliation, for he was big enough to help white and coloured folk rebuild the South and capable of controlling the North. So long as Lincoln was alive, the ideals of the old America lived in all their piety and simplicity; after his death, selfishness and materialism came quickly to the fore.

The South was the first to suffer. It was easy to accuse the beaten foe of the assassination of Lincoln, though this was only the act of a crazy fanatic. A period of oppression made life intolerable for whites south of the Potomac. Government passed into the hands of corrupt "carpet-baggers" and "scallywags" (Northern immigrant adventurers owning no more than the contents of a carpet bag), under whom negroes and half-breeds formed black-and-tan legislatures which spent all too little money on education or on other measures to better the lot of the emancipated slave, but plenty on themselves. In South Carolina, the new coloured rulers ate off gold plate and furnished themselves with champagne, gold watches and elaborate spittoons at the public expense. Broken by the costs of the war and collapse of Confederate bonds, the squires and the farmers of the South were prevented by crushing taxation from making what economic recovery could be made without slave labour.

The poor whites growled still more over the excesses of the negroes they had despised. It was unfortunate that the President, Andrew Johnson, was one of their narrow-minded breed, though opposed to their politics—a tailor from the Tennessee mountains who had been pushed forward in war days, as the instrument of Northern politicians wishing to parade themselves as the "poor whites'" friends. Johnson disliked the Southern squires and had old grudges against them; he took pleasure in seeing them suffer.

So the whites of the South took affairs into their own hands. Secret societies were formed, of which the most notorious was the Ku Klux Klan. Robed in white sheets and riding by night, they seemed to the simple negro to be the ghosts of the armies which had died for the Confederacy. Strong-armed ghosts they were, as "bad niggers" found. For the most, however, they had only to threaten. Especially did they scare the negro from the ballot-box, and so

796   NATIONALISM AND INTERNATIONALISM

knock away whatever foundations of popular support "carpet-bag" rule possessed. Northern Radicals made some attempts to rule the South autocratically and to renew military occupation, but they tired of their effort; when President Hayes took office, in 1877, carpet-bag rule had been overthrown in every state except South Carolina and Louisiana, where it existed only with the aid of Federal troops. The former was really governed by bluff and aristocratic General Wade Hampton, who carried on his régime with voluntary contributions, while good South Carolinians ignored the Governor and his "black-and-tans" who still occupied the State House. Hayes saw the ridiculous side of this state of affairs, withdrew the Federal troops and allowed the Southern whites to take control of their affairs.

THE NEW SOUTH AND THE NEW WEST

The South in 1877 was no longer the proud rival of the middle-class, commercial Puritan North. Proud still, she had become politically a backwater, inferior in importance to the North, and later to the West. Economic change was represented by the rapid industrialization of these districts. The Southern poet, Lanier, had written during the period of reconstruction that "Pretty much the whole of life has been merely not dying". Existence was miserable enough both for the impoverished squires and the ill-paid slaves, lucky enough to find work, who were now treated with a new loathing and suspicion. There had been plenty of loyalty and friendship on the plantation of pre-Civil-War days; but households now were small. The blacks lived mostly in hovels little better than their old cabins, and were treated like pariahs by the white "trash", who would not travel in the same coaches, live in the same streets, or even worship in the same churches as negroes. Political terrorism and an exacting interpretation of the federal constitution enabled the whites to keep the blacks away from the polling-booths at elections. Lynch-law, backward education and racial bitterness remained characteristic of the South. The abolition of slavery did not solve the negro problem, but merely brought it to a new phase. One benefit the Civil War did bring: after its conclusion there was no more serious talk of secession from the Union.

Nature and the machine made up for whatever slow-down of progress there was during the Civil War. The mileage of railway-line in the country increased sixfold between 1865 and 1900, with the result that what had been an unknown continent became a conscious nation. Railways opened up first the Great Plains and then the Far West. Metals which had hitherto travelled from the western states to Europe by way of San Francisco and Cape Horn could now be sent more quickly by railroad for transhipment from New York.

The Indians disappeared from the Great Plains of the Middle West into the reservations. The land they had once owned became more populous than ever before; the population of the three western states of Washington, Oregon and Idaho increased from 280,000 in 1880 to over two millions in 1910. Improved machinery and methods of farming and the development of steamer traffic on the Great Lakes, together with immigration and the prolific families reared by the pioneer settlers in a rich new land, accounted for most of this.

IMMIGRATION AND AMERICAN EXPANSION

Cowboys drove cattle from Texas to the Plains, where they could winter, and from there to the nearest railroad-head. The refrigerator enabled them to freight the beasts dead as well as alive. Hard winters and the development of the trusts caused the cow-puncher to lose his independent status and become the employee of the individual capitalist or the combine.

In the Middle West, population was chiefly European—British, German and Scandinavian. Towards the end of the century, Slavs and Lithuanians began to arrive in the East, and gradually they fitted into the population of more westerly states. As the percentage figure of these new immigrants rose, those of the British and Irish fell, and America of the famine became as unlike the United States of 1900 as was the America of Independence days. Meantime, the number of immigrants rose, reaching eight hundred thousand in 1882. The country ceased to be predominantly agricultural, and the majority of the population was to be found in the cities. From producing one-fifth of the amount of iron produced by Great Britain, as they did at the close of the Civil War, the United States at the end of the century almost equalled the combined totals of Germany and Great Britain, and had become the greatest iron- and steel-producing nation of the world. Even the South shared in this era of industrial development, Arizona becoming the second copper-smelting state in the Union. Better farming methods, especially the use of fertilizers, and the brains of white landowners, helped to revive the States of the Confederacy.

Charleston still manages to preserve the graceful mien and the classical ease of architecture which she acquired in the eighteenth century. The new America had little of this spirit. The chance of quick riches and the thrustfulness of life, in a new country which was growing too quickly, made public life selfish and corrupt to an extent hitherto unknown. City-councils, politics and big business worked hand in hand. Bosses, often more ruthless and less feudal than the slave-owners, had less interest than they in the welfare of their wage-slaves. Mr. Upton Sinclair's novels have portrayed the type, as those of Mr. Sinclair Lewis have shown us the complacent middle-class Babbitt who was to America what Bagehot's bald-headed man on the top of a 'bus was to Victorian England.

While dollar-chasing and greed for power facilitated the acquisition by magnates of large sums of money voted by city-councils for the development of public health and welfare, labour was slow to organize. Many of the new immigrants had been bred on a soil less democratic than that of Northern Europe, and racial conflicts and a rampant individualism hindered the growth of Trade Unions. The ease with which many of the workers rose to wealth hindered a speedy development in the status of the working-class. The wage-earners of the 'forties had become the small capitalists of the 'seventies, so that the Labour movement was continually passing through the same early stages and there was little chance of development. Some attempt to organize American Labour along the craft Trade Union lines of Great Britain was made by Terence Powderly with his Knights of Labour, but these faded before Sam Gompers' American Federation of Labour, organized on a national basis. Not wishing to be suspected of dangerous radicalism, Gompers strove to keep his movement away from politics and to confine it to industrial issues. Membership stood at only half a million by 1900.

Art and Literature were in a transitional or undeveloped condition. A new phase began in architecture with the skyscraper, which rose first in Chicago, the city of the Great Exhibition of 1893. Washington remained the capital and New York the greatest city of the country; but many felt that Chicago was the real Metropolis of the United States. Meanwhile, the dignified, if rather staid, literary tradition of New England had passed away; instead, there was Mark Twain. Education developed; well-equipped high schools and universities were founded, with perhaps a tendency to put more money into the bricks and mortar of the buildings than into the flesh and blood of the staff. By the '80's, Massachusetts and Connecticut possessed what the British call public and the Americans private schools.

Religion could scarcely flourish side by side with the worship of money, though the native Puritanism succeeded in finding the same sort of compromise as in sixteenth-century England and Holland. Immigration enormously increased the Catholic element in the population, while America's Mormonism grew rich and Christian Science was born.

WAR BETWEEN THE U.S.A. AND SPAIN

The nation which had bestridden a continent was likely soon to reach beyond it. Towards the end of the century, a revival of the Monroe Doctrine, with regard to a dispute between Great Britain and Venezuela, created conditions which could easily have made war possible between the United States and a great European Power.

Mutual tact saved the situation. It was otherwise in the following year, when Spanish activities in suppressing a Cuban rebellion aroused popular feeling throughout America and prompted the United States to a war of cheap glory and speedy conquest. In February 1898, the U.S. battleship *Maine* was blown up in Havana harbour. The act was attributed to Spanish sabotage, but it is hard to believe this theory, and perhaps the Cubans had a hand in it.

War came in April, and was over by July, after a series of cheap and glorious victories for young democracy against a tyrant who was frankly very poor game. Anglo-Saxon readers are inclined to associate Spain with defeat in naval affairs—they forget Lepanto and the period of maritime discovery—but few victories can have been more overwhelming than Dewey's destruction of the Spanish Pacific fleet in Manila Bay, without the loss of a single man, and the defeat of the Cuban squadron with the loss of only one life. The Spaniards had more troops available than the Americans, but some they could not get to Cuba and others they could not get out of the island, where, harried by Theodore Roosevelt, who afterwards became President, and his Rough Riders, and handicapped by their own incompetent tactics, they lost the remnants of an American Empire.

AMERICAN IMPERIALISM

Cuba, Puerto Rico, the Philippines and one of the Ladrone Islands were handed over to the United States; a nation which had been born as a pioneer for the rights of colonies had acquired dominions of her own. Outside the Philippines, there was little difficulty; the territories were small and backward. The Filipinos wanted the freedom for which the American had ostensibly been fighting, and they submitted to Washington only after an unsuccessful rebellion in 1898. Cuba became nominally independent, but was continually under the threat of American battleships and marines; economically, too, the power of American business interests was considerable.

The Empire grew. The Hawaiian Islands were annexed in 1898 at the request of the American business community, and a share in the Samoan Islands was secured the following year. An attempt to obtain a first-class naval base in the Caribbean by purchasing the Danish West Indies was frustrated. Denmark refused the offer, which was increased fivefold during the War of 1914–18 and led to the sale of the islands to the United States in 1917. Meantime, public health and education were well cared for by the Americans in their new territories; the removal of the yellow-fever menace was an immense service to the islanders.

In 1901, the assassination of McKinley brought Theodore Roosevelt to the Presidency. It was an epic date in the chapter of America's imperial development. Roosevelt was the greatest figure in the list of American Presidents since Lincoln; and he knew more of world-politics than either Lincoln or Washington. Bluff and genial in manner, forceful as a statesman, with his Rough-Rider tradition to help him, he had friends everywhere, and he soon acquired his own legend and a great reputation.

It was of value to Roosevelt that he inherited, as Secretary of State, John Hay, who had been Ambassador at St. James's, a man who knew Europe and loved England. Rapidly—with Roosevelt things had a way of moving so—an understanding developed between Great

Britain and the United States by means of which the former did not interfere in American affairs and the latter did not trouble the British Empire. The appointment of James Bryce to Britain's Washington embassy showed that both countries were eager to promote good feelings and had set the best men to bridge the gulf.

At the same time, Roosevelt made it clear that any infringement of the Monroe Doctrine would meet with immediate and formidable resistance. Such an interference in American affairs was suggested by a German threat to invade Venezuela in order to collect debts. The lessons of Napoleon III's Mexican adventure in the 'sixties had suggested that such a bailiff's expedition might lead to conquest. However, the Kaiser heeded Roosevelt's threat and had the good sense to respect the President for his downright methods. In 1903, within a year of the Venezuelan affair, at the request of the Dominican Republic American fiscal officers took charge of the Dominican customs-houses in order to save that state from bankruptcy. Washington's responsibilities had come inevitably to cover the continent; realization of the fact was announced by Roosevelt's declaration that, while the United States had no wish to interfere with any American state keeping her house in order, they might in other circumstances play the rôle of an international police force.

THEODORE ROOSEVELT'S VIGOROUS POLICY

Vast developments, both in the extent of trade and the scope of engineering, had long made it evident that a canal must be driven through the narrow isthmus which separated the two Americas. In June 1902, Congress gave the President power to acquire a strip across Panama from the Colombian Republic. By January of the next year, that republic had consented to lease such a strip on a hundred-year agreement to the United States. But the dilatory methods of the eighteenth century are the heritage of Latin America. Roosevelt did not wish his prize to escape, and without giving any official help, allowed American officers and business men to encourage a revolt by which, in November 1903, Panama proclaimed herself an independent republic. The U.S. fleet kept Colombian troops from landing and induced their admiral to sail away; within a fortnight the Panamanian Republic had leased the canal zone to the United States. In 1921, to help reassure their position in post-war America, the United States paid twenty-five million dollars from their ample Treasury to appease Colombia.

Roosevelt's activity in foreign affairs was chiefly concerned with the promotion of peace outside America. He played a prominent part in the Treaty of Portsmouth, which put an end to the Russo-Japanese War. At the Algeciras Conference over Moroccan affairs in 1906, he helped to calm a Europe riven already into two hostile alliances. Assuredly he deserved the Nobel Prize for Peace, and the world should probably regret that precedent dissuaded him from standing again for office: completion of his term in 1909 deprived mankind of the services of a powerful friend of peace during a critical period. The year 1912 found the United States engrossed in their own affairs, a pre-occupation from which it took the First World War to awaken them.

CONDITIONS IN LATIN AMERICA

By 1865, Latin America had freed itself from Spain and Portugal. On the mainland, only the Guianas remained in foreign hands. The close of the Civil War at last enabled the United States to give attention to Napoleon III's luckless and ill-considered attempt to found a French Empire in Mexico; the French avoided the encounter by evacuating Bazaine's troops, and so abandoned the country to another period of haphazard and fluctuating government.

This succeeding period was one of establishment of the new states. There was a great development of railways, canals and steamship-lines; some of the railway-tracks, especially in the wilds of Brazil and the Andes, surmount amazing natural obstacles and count among the finest feats of engineering in the world. The project of a Pan-American railway connecting the continent from end to end has not, however, been fulfilled.

Latin America is immense. Brazil is larger than the United States, and the whole continent is three times their size. In Central America, every state, and in South America all but Bolivia and Paraguay, touch the sea; while this last is watered by the great river whose name it bears. There are some curious boundaries—Chile is three thousand miles long, but only seventy in width. Many cities on the continent stand at a height of little less than ten thousand feet above sea-level. Fantastic beauties of nature exist—the Amazon, Rio Harbour and the strangely beautiful volcanoes above Mexico City.

There is a reverse side to the picture. It is to be found in the disease-ridden, illiterate, underpaid masses of the people. Too frequently miserable are the *rotos*, or poor labourers, in the mines and nitrate fields of Chile and the *peons* or peasants elsewhere. At the time of the Conquest, Spanish invaders were accustomed to demand labour from the native population. This state of affairs in many parts of the continent has changed very little; often the wages of the *peon* are little more than food and drink. Their families tend to be large, and they may be evicted from their holdings, if they are lucky enough to have any; the lot of the *peon* is indeed wretched. In Mexico, risings have from time to time been made against a wealthy, talented, pleasure-loving upper class, between whom and the *peons* a chasm of social difference is fixed. The poorer classes are either Indian, *mestizo* (mixed European and Indian), or, in Brazil, negroid. By the end of the nineteenth century, few pure-blooded Indians were left in Chile; there were many in Peru, Bolivia and Guatemala, where Indians or *mestizos* predominate, though the white men rule.

C C   (H.W.)

THE UNITED STATES AND

Early European settlements in North America were formed along the coastline east of the dotted line between the Great Lakes and the Gulf of Mexico. With the development of the United States, territories west of the pioneer states acquired statehood, their dates and boundaries being shown on the above map.

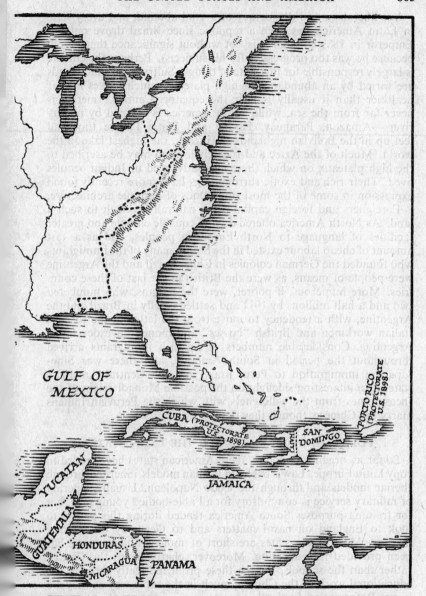

CENTRAL AMERICA

Mexico had shaken off the rule of Spain and formed a republic, in 1867, which endured in spite of the lack of continuity in her administration. She had lost California, Utah, New Mexico, Arizona and Texas to the United States, who secured a protectorate over the formerly Spanish islands, Porto Rica and Cuba.

Yet liberalism and democracy of a kind abound, and every state in Latin America has been a republic since Brazil drove out her Emperor in 1889 (though it is not without significance that he fell because he was too progressive for his subjects). Perhaps the climate is largely responsible for this state of things. Sultry tropical lowlands are varied by an abundance of high plateaux which makes life far healthier than it usually is near the equator. Central America is never far from the sea, while South America is drained by mighty rivers—Amazon, Paraguay, Parana and Plate. Twelve thousand feet up in the Bolivian highlands is Titicaca, the highest lake in the world. Much of the Aztec and Inca civilization may be ascribed to the high plateaux on which these most advanced of Indian peoples lived. Their rich and exotic surroundings have more recently found expression in some of the most sumptuous of baroque architecture.

Foreigners and foreign capital came naturally enough to such a land. As North America offered a more equable climate and greater facilities of language to North European peoples, and as a vast amount of cheap labour existed in the South, many of the immigrants who founded the German colonies in Chile, Brazil and the Argentine were people of means, as were the British in the last of these countries. More numerous, if poorer, were the Italians, who numbered two and a half millions by 1911 and settled chiefly in Brazil and the Argentine, with a tendency to move from the latter to the former. Italian workmen and British "bosses" and money have developed Argentina. Considerable numbers of Spanish immigrants arrived throughout the period in South America, and there was Sino-Japanese immigration to Peru, Brazil and the Central American states. An interesting sidelight on the possible Mongol origin of the Incas comes from the willingness with which the Peruvian Indians marry the Chinese, though they despise the negroes.

POLITICAL ORGANIZATION OF THE LATIN STATES

So far as organization goes, these American states have tended to copy Latin Europe. Law is based on Roman models, inherited through Iberian models and through the Code Napoléon. Usually, a period of military service is compulsory for all able-bodied young men, but for training purposes South America tended during this period to look to England on naval matters and to Germany on military matters. Most of the states are short of money, and too little has been provided for education. Moreover, charity helps the Church rather than the schools, though these profit indirectly through the educational work of the Church, much in the same way as they did in pre-Reformation England.

Reforms and material development were the order of the day. In Brazil, the most important of the states, this was retarded somewhat by the chaos which followed the emancipation of the slaves. As a result of the consequent disaffection among the capitalist classes, the Emperor Pedro II lost the throne which he had occupied for nearly fifty years, and Brazil the guidance of a shrewd and experienced ruler. With time, however, the wealth of the coastal districts developed, though the interior still remained largely jungle.

DEVELOPMENT AND DISPUTES

Mexico and Brazil are both United States. The "Americans" of the United States itself are "North Americans" or "gringoes" to the South. In Mexico, the period was one of comparative prosperity, especially during the stern rule of Porfirio Diaz, who, with the exception of the years 1880–4, occupied the Presidency from 1876 to 1911. Discontent grew among the *peons*, who demanded the restoration of land which had passed into big estates in the sixteenth century. With this came anti-clericalism, for the Church owned much land, and a growing dislike of foreigners for the same reason. Eventually, in 1911, the Madero revolution broke out, which overthrew Diaz, but which opened up a long period of unrest.

More fortunate was the lot of the Argentine. Immigration on a large scale, considerable British moneyed interest and the vast possibilities of a fertile land, made Argentine cattle famous and Buenos Ayres the first city in Latin America, and second only to Paris in the Latin world. At the beginning of this period, the country along the Paraguay River was not so well developed as it had been before. The Jesuit missions were expelled in the eighteenth century; the first passenger dock at Buenos Ayres was opened only in 1855, and the population of a country almost one-third the size of Europe was no more than two million. By the early years of the twentieth century, it had reached the eight-million mark.

Lack of good natural frontiers, and an abundance of sparsely populated districts, have led to many disputes, the inevitable growing-pains of the period. On one occasion, these resulted in a war during which Chile's naval superiority enabled her, in a region where land is desert and where sea is the highway, to deprive Peru of the nitrate deposits of Tarapaca and of the Tacna-Arica region, and Bolivia of the province of Antofagasta. Until a few years ago Bolivia still demanded an outlet to the sea, and Peru the return of what was still a district mainly populated by Peruvians. Bolivia also became involved in a dispute with Paraguay over the Gran Chaco, an unwholesome jungle which reaches to the Paraguay River, another outlet to the sea. The quarrel between Argentina and Uruguay over the La Plata estuary and boundary, disputes between Guatemala and Honduras, Panama and Costa Rica and Peru, Columbia and Ecuador were unsettled until the First World War. The existence of such dissident factors helped to develop tendencies of disunion provided by nature, which has made Latin America mostly long and narrow, and by man, whose railways run east and west to the sea, rather than north and south as a connecting-link.

CHAPTER 71

THE EUROPEAN NATIONS

In the eighteen-sixties the world was new: new countries were settled, new industries started and new ideas came into fashion. But if the philosophers still dreamed of Utopias, they were beginning to give way as leaders of thought and action to a more realist policy. The age of revolution had bred cynicism and disillusion. Instead, the new men, from Socialist leaders to Nicholas I, Tsar of All the Russias, who welcomed a Polish delegation with "No dreams, gentlemen, no dreams", all tended to regard violent rather than parliamentary measures as decisive in the world of politics.

Yet England was the model of many. Her parliamentary system seemed to have solved a horde of problems. Italy copied her, and so did Greece and Mexico, but new countries were to find it hard to graft a plant which had grown before Magna Carta. In France, the Second Empire was proving more autocratic than liberal; in Russia the Duma had little hope after the assassination of the progressive Alexander II; in Germany, the country in which the main theme of the age is best exemplified, Bismarck was building a totalitarian state.

PRUSSIA EXTENDS HER INFLUENCE

Nationalism was at its most intense in Prussia. Its new prophets were the Frenchman Gobineau and the Englishman Houston Stewart Chamberlain; but their belief in the superiority of German culture was readily absorbed by the German people, whose Emperor presented a copy of Chamberlain's *Foundations of the Nineteenth Century* to every officer in the army. So the main theme in political history of this period is the rise of Germany and its challenge to the world. The state which was to unify Germany, and which is supposed to represent all that is most efficient in the German character, is by no means purely German in race. The name of the state itself is taken from its primitive inhabitants, the Borussians, whose blood, with that of Slav races, has gone to form the modern Prussian and give him a dash of liveliness which is particularly noticeable east of the River Vistula, and which is quite unlike the typical North German phlegm.

The early 1860's found King William I and his Chancellor, Bismarck, emerging successfully from a constitutional struggle with the Prussian Chamber, which had refused to make the money grants necessary to the War Minister, Roon, and the Chief of Staff, Moltke, in their work of reorganizing effectively the Prussian "Army". Bismarck persuaded the simple, sensible William to govern without Parliament and reassured him that nineteenth-century Prussia was not seventeenth-century England, and that their fate would not be that of Charles I and Strafford.

In 1863 came up the extremely complicated problem of Schleswig-Holstein, which, according to Palmerston, was only understood by three men, of whom one, the Prince Consort, was dead, another, a German professor, was mad, and the third (himself) had forgotten it. The Duchies of Schleswig and Holstein form the bottle-neck of the peninsula which joins Denmark to Germany. Holstein is chiefly German in race, the race and language barrier running through Schleswig roughly along the line of the frontier delimited in 1919.

Since the fifteenth century, the Kingdom of Denmark and these Duchies had been ruled by the same royal house. The tie was solely personal, and appeared likely to cease when the Danish King Frederick VII should die, as he possessed no male heir and the Salic Law held good in Schleswig-Holstein. During the period of political impotence through which Prussia passed after the Olmütz Convention and before the accession of William I, the Danes had persuaded the Powers, by the Treaty of London in 1852, to recognize the right of Prince Christian of Glücksberg, the heir to their throne, as heir to the Duchies. This agreement was ignored by the German Diet, and Bismarck challenged the claims of Prince Christian and backed his rival, Prince Frederick of Augustenberg.

He asked for Austria's help; Prussia was not yet ready to act without or against the leading German state. Austria assented; the task in alliance with Prussia looked easy enough, for Vienna was eager to recover prestige after the recent Austrian defeats in Italy. The Danes had hopes of help from England; Palmerston had suggested that this might be forthcoming, and so many praises had been lavished on the new Danish Princess of Wales that her fellow-countrymen were led to over-estimate her political importance, which was actually negligible in comparison with that of the Queen. Victoria had German connections, and was on occasions quite ready to snub the boisterous, popular, overbearing Palmerston.

AUSTRIA AND PRUSSIA

Denmark had to fight alone, and the Duchies were quickly overrun. By the Treaty of Vienna in 1864, Prussia received Schleswig to administer and Austria Holstein, a small territory sandwiched between Prussian lands. Berlin lawyers found that the claims of Prince Frederick were illegal, and that luckless man turned for aid to Vienna, only to become again a *casus belli*. Despite the fact that many observers thought the Austrian troops had done better than the Prussian in the Danish War, Moltke and Roon seem to have had little doubt of the outcome of a struggle with Austria. War was necessary, before Prussian hegemony could be secured even in North Germany.

In 1866, unlike 1914, there was no opposition on the part of the Great Powers at this critical period of Prussian history. Actually, the victory of Prussia was not foreseen: the Berlin Government had not only Austria but the South German states, Saxony and Hanover, as enemies. Bismarck's brilliant diplomacy had mastered the European stage. Russia was his friend since the suppression of a Polish rising in 1863, Italy stood to gain Venetia by Austria's defeat, and England's bluff had been called over Schleswig-Holstein. There remained France. Bismarck visited the French Emperor at Biarritz, flattered him with vague promises of territorial compensation, and so misled Napoleon as to his ultimate sinister intentions that the Emperor unwisely said of him, *"Ce n'est pas un homme sérieux"*.

REWARDS OF BISMARCK'S POLICY

The war of 1866 lasted only seven weeks. Prussia at once occupied Saxony, in two weeks knocked out the Hanoverian army, and within another week decisively defeated the Austrians at Sadowa in the Bohemian plain. The victory was due to the superiority of Prussian organization and armaments, especially the needle-gun, and to the military genius of Moltke. Then came the advance on Vienna. Threatened by a rising in Hungary, the Austrians sued for peace. Bismarck was wisely merciful, and against the wishes of the fire-eaters, refused to annex South Germany—sooner or later, that would come voluntarily into a Prussian Empire. Instead, he contented himself with consolidating the north; and Hanover, Hesse and Frankfurt-on-the-Main became Prussian. The rest of the South grew to admire the unexpected mildness as much as the unforeseen military skill of the north.

Racked by the stone and disappointed at the ill-success of his plans, Napoleon floundered and blundered from one scheme to another. He looked for compensation, economic and political, in Belgium, in Luxembourg and in Germany. The first irritated England with her fears lest the further shore of the narrow seas fall under another Power, the latter provided Bismarck with the trump he needed to win the South German trick. He did not even offer Napoleon vague promises now, but spoke of his policy as one of asking for tips.

North Germany became efficient, centralized, Prussian. Then arrived the question of the Hohenzollern candidature for the Spanish throne. The worthless Isabella of Spain had been deposed in 1868 and her subjects were looking round for a successor. The Spanish throne was refused by the Duke of Genoa. Bismarck succeeded in getting it offered to Prince Leopold of Hohenzollern-Sigmaringen, a Catholic relative of the Prussian royal house, by whom it was eventually accepted. This was in July 1870. Within a month, the French Emperor, reasonably alarmed at the prospect of the rule of the same powerful German house across both Rhine and Pyrenees, protested and persuaded the amiable William of Prussia to withdraw support from his kinsman. Unwisely elated by his easy success, Napoleon went further, and requested William to give his word that the candidature would never be renewed. This was excessive, and William informed Benedetti, the French ambassador, to that effect. Bismarck received the news when he was dining with Moltke and Roon: they altered the famous Ems telegram, and gave to the Press a message which suggested that the King of Prussia had affronted the Ambassador of France.

War followed before the month was out. The story of French inefficiency is told later. All the German states participated in the victory over the traditional enemy, which was followed by the proclamation of the King of Prussia as Emperor of Germany. The invitation was brought by the King of Bavaria, ruler of the most powerful South German state, who had been suspected of being for some time in receipt of a pension from the Prussian secret service. William disliked imperial pomp and consented only unwillingly to accept the crown, the ceremony taking place in the same Gallery at Versailles where Louis XIV had proclaimed his grandson King of Spain.

BLUNDERS OF NAPOLEON III

The year 1860 marks a turning-point in the history of the Second Empire. Until that time a progressive home policy and a not inglorious foreign policy had made comparatively popular the nephew of the Great Napoleon, whose name and adventurous disposition had won France nine years before. But 1860 brought the withdrawal from the War of Italian Liberation. Napoleon III pleased his wife and the clergy, but forfeited the goodwill of the mass of Liberal opinion in France. Memories of the Revolution and of the White Terror had naturally embittered French politics to a degree unknown in Britain: "Your fathers were at Quiberon, ours at Waterloo," said the radical Jules Favre to a royalist opponent.

The commercial treaty bringing freer trade with England, in 1862, was a mere flash in the pan; a foreign policy increasingly adventurous and disastrous combined with growing unrest in France to make the Empire unpopular. First came the Mexican affair. That country had been in a state of political unrest since the breach with Spain, forty years before. In 1863, it was more or less ruled by a remarkable Indian, Benito Juarez, whose popularity with his people was matched by the hostility of the Church, whose vast wealth and power in Mexico he had attempted to curtail. Juarez decided that his country could not at once pay the debt owed to foreign creditors, mostly to England, France and Spain. Napoleon felt that what had been conquered by Spain should be easy game for French arms, and determined on military intervention, a step which the British and Spaniards were unwilling to take. The United States were fighting one another and could therefore be ignored.

To Napoleon, ideas came too easily. It has been said that "His mind was as full of schemes as a warren is full of rabbits". He pictured easy victory, the gratitude of the Church and a way of

FRONTIERS OF

In 1865 Europe was on the threshold of events which were to make Prussia the leader of the German states. Under Bismarck, Prussia had combined with Austria to seize Schleswig-Holstein in 1864, and gained Russian goodwill by helping the latter to suppress a Polish rising which had occurred in 1863.

EUROPE IN 1865

Guided by Palmerston, Britain viewed with great suspicion Russia's aspirations in the Balkans and her desire to win Constantinople from the Turkish Empire. Napoleon still ruled in France, although after a success in Algeria, he was embroiled in an ill-fated attempt to place a Habsburg on the throne of Mexico.

approach to friendship with Austria; he offered the crown of an Imperial Mexico to Maximilian, brother of the Emperor Francis Joseph. His nominee accepted, against the wishes of the Emperor and Great Britain. Napoleon had failed to take into account the Mexican climate, the patriotic wishes of the inhabitants, and the fact that their powers of resistance in the nineteenth century were more formidable than they had been in the sixteenth. The conquest of the country proved difficult. Napoleon disliked the absence of so many good troops and in 1867 recalled them: before the summer was out, Maximilian, who, as a stubborn Habsburg, had refused to leave with his French guard, was captured by insurgents and shot in a courtyard at Queretaro.

The shot resounded through France. Catholics, Austrians, and fair-minded people throughout Europe felt that Maximilian's death lay at Napoleon's door. Contempt was heightened by the fact that the French regiments had left shortly after a notice to quit had been served by the United States, whose Civil War had now come to an end. Napoleon had always the gambler's instinct. He was confronted with the sudden gains of Prussia after her victories over Denmark in 1864 and Austria in 1866. Had he decided to intervene to save the latter, he might have averted his own disaster: "After Sadowa, Sedan" became a catch-phrase in France.

FRANCE'S OVERWHELMING DEFEAT

Europe was surprised at the ease and suddenness of the German victory—it was a German and not only a Prussian Army which Napoleon had to face: the revelation of his indiscreet claims for compensation in the Rhineland and South Germany had seen to that, just as the publication in *The Times* (Bismarck gave a special correspondent the draft) of his designs on Belgium prevented any chance of British intervention on the French side. In mobilization, the French system showed the defects of its organization; commanders could not find their units, soldiers crossed to Algiers to join their regiments for a war fought in France, and the French were so confident of victory that they were insufficiently supplied with maps of their own country, which speedily became the theatre of war.

Man for man, the French "poilu" was as good as the German, but his officers, equipment and organization were inferior. By the beginning of September 1870, the Germans had routed one big French army at Gravelotte, shut it up in Metz, the fortress-capital of Lorraine, and captured another led by the Emperor in person at Sedan. There followed a series of gallant but mostly unsuccessful attempts by the French to recover from a knock-out blow in the first round. Paris surrendered, and an armistice was signed on January 28th, 1871; ten days earlier, the German Empire had been proclaimed at Versailles.

With enemy forces encamped outside Paris, the French had to face the civil outbreak known as the Commune, an abortive Socialist rising in Paris, during which large sections of the capital were destroyed. Railways facilitated the rapid mobilization of soldiers from country regiments. Town and country have never been over-fond of one another in France, and the power of the mob was completely broken in the fierce and bloody suppression of the movement, as it never had been during the Great Revolution.

FRANCE'S THIRD REPUBLIC

There remained the Republic. At first, it was adopted only as a temporary measure, and plenty of monarchist sentiment remained in the country. There were three claimants to the throne—the Legitimist Comte de Chambord, grandson of Charles X; the Orleanist Comte de Paris, grandson of Louis Philippe, and the House of Bonaparte. "There is only one throne, and three people cannot sit on it at the same time," said Thiers. Public opinion, for lack of anything better, veered towards a republic, and the Comte de Chambord, who had the best claim, refused to change the white flag of the Bourbons for the tricolor which had waved beside the guillotine of Louis XVI. It had also waved at Austerlitz; even MacMahon had to confess that if it were supplanted by the lilies, the "chassepôts would go off of themselves". So, in January, 1875, a majority of one vote in the Assembly precariously established the Third Republic in France. The Royalist MacMahon was its first head. Chambord sank into insignificance outside Vienna; the exiled Comte de Paris lavished half-crowns on the yokels of Buckinghamshire; the Prince Imperial fell fighting for the British flag against black men. With its constitution resembling that of Great Britain— a place was left for a king, who would have been popular if obtainable —the Republic set out to restore the fortunes of France.

By the end of 1860, Italy, south of the Alps, with the exception of Venetia and Rome, had become a kingdom under Victor Emmanuel of Sardinia and Piedmont. It was a humane liberation and unaccompanied immediately by such serious consequences to Europe as followed the unification of Germany; the Italians, whilst freeing their compatriots, did not annex foreigners.

Cavour, the greatest architect of Italian unity, died in the following year. He was survived by the King and the soldier Garibaldi. The latter's part in the final act of unification was inglorious: he commanded a brigade of skirmishers in the Tyrol against the Austrians during the Seven Weeks' War, but it was Moltke's victories which added Venetia to Italy. Meantime, Garibaldi's ill-timed and unsuccessful free-lance attempts to capture Rome might have provoked war with France had they not been speedy failures: he was wounded and captured at Aspromonte by Italian troops when on such a mission in 1862, and defeated by the French garrison of Rome at Mentana, some dozen miles from that city in 1867. Again, however, German victories helped the Italian cause, for the advance on Paris of the victorious invaders caused Napoleon III to need in France all available French troops. So the "chasse-pôts" were recalled and the Holy City became the capital of the Kingdom of Italy. An overwhelming majority by plebiscite showed the popularity of the annexation: it was distinctly unpopular with the Pope, who looked on the Italian army as successful bandits, refused to recognize the new kingdom, and continued to remain on bad terms with the reigning House of Savoy until 1929.

PROBLEMS FACED BY ITALY

Liberation did not prove to be the end of domestic evils, as had been hoped; the first period in the history of the New Italy was disappointing to many. For more than a thousand years, the country had been divided, and its peoples were in very different stages of civilization; ignorance, ill-health and corruption increased as one went southwards. Good Italians were not so easy to make as Italy. The parliamentary government, carefully developed in England over many centuries, was scarcely likely to make a ready-made fit for a new Italy which had known nothing of the kind. That same prevalence of bribery which existed in the early days of the party system in this country was only too frequent at the similar stage of Italian development. This political immorality was all the more dangerous because the powerful ecclesiastical authorities, hostile as they were to the state, did little to check it.

The people of Italy were ill-informed about what was going on. Most of them were illiterate, and they were handicapped by a long period of misgovernment from any real sense of values or capacity for organization along genuine democratic lines. The Government became unpopular when it tried to raise by taxation the sums necessary to provide reasonable standards of public health and education. National defence was also an expensive item in a country which had small industrial resources and no colonies. Yet it had to be adequately maintained, for Austria still ruled, in the Trentino and Trieste, territories predominantly Italian in race, and France was increasingly regarded as a treacherous friend who had blocked the just way of Italian expansion in North Africa and the Levant.

RUSSIAN INFLUENCE IN THE BALKANS

Behind her interest in the health of moribund Turkey and in the development of the vigorous young Balkan nations, Great Britain concealed a distrust of Russia which dated from the eighteenth century, when the empire of the Tsars reached the Black Sea. The younger Pitt was the first important British statesman to feel that a Russian occupation of Constantinople menaced British interests in the Levant and in India.

This fear had not decreased with the outbreak of revolts among the subject-peoples of the Ottoman Empire, early in the nineteenth century. Many of the rebels were Slavs in race, and more still were akin to the Russians in their Orthodox religion. The fact that, when the Serbs and Bulgarians had established their independence, they might dislike their Russian cousins does not seem to have often entered the heads of British politicians; Russia already counted millions of non-Russian people in her population, and Palmerston and Disraeli were of the opinion that, when the time came, the Tsar would pay little heed to the wishes of the smaller Slav nations if they showed themselves unwilling to support his imperial policy.

Foiled in their advance southwards by the Crimean War, the rulers of Russia carried through a vast and encouraging reform by the emancipation of the serfs in 1861. Thirty-five million of these people were freed, and the reform was largely the work of the Tsar Alexander II himself. There seemed a chance that the vast awakening conscience of the people of Russia, a land in which primitive communism had never altogether died, might inspire an enlightened monarchy to make a happy country. Emancipation was followed by liberal grants of land, by judicial and educational reforms, and by grants of local self-government. Unfortunately, the lack of an educated middle class, of an efficient civil service or body of lawyers, and of enough roads and railways, combined to hinder the efficient working of reforms which were inevitably hampered by the traditions of the Russians and the low state of civilization of the masses.

Meantime, the Little Father legend revived and the peasants became more ready to back the Tsar in his crusades against the Turks on behalf of their fellow-Slavs and co-religionists. A vigorous and popular foreign policy became increasingly advantageous and necessary in a country where wide-spread famines were frequent, epidemics prevalent and attempts made to achieve reform a failure.

MINORITIES WITHIN THE AUSTRIAN EMPIRE

In the neighbouring empire of Austria, too, changes had been taking place. The revolutions of 1848 had apparently failed, and Hungary was, for a time reduced to the level of an Austrian province. A new development, however, occurred after the defeats of the Italian Campaign of 1859, and was carried farther in 1867 after the defeat of Sadowa, Hungary had been united by the moderate and constitutionalist Deak, who wished, not for separation from the Government of Vienna, but for federation and equal rights with Austria. This was effected by the *Ausgleich* or Compromise which made Hungary self-governing, so far as internal matters were concerned, and a partner with Austria in the ministries of war, finance and foreign affairs. "Take care of your barbarians; we will take care of ours," said the Austrian Foreign Minister to a Hungarian colleague. There lay the snag. If the Dual Monarchy had broadened its basis by admitting Croats, Rumanians and Czechs on equal terms, it might have endured, but the Hungarians proved harsher masters than the Austrians had been. In the meantime their interest in the Balkans and Austria's elimination from Germany brought the Eastern Question increasingly to the fore.

DECAY OF THE OTTOMAN EMPIRE

Russia coveted Constantinople; Austria, Salonika. Prussia was the friend of Russia, for both had a common interest in suppressing Polish nationalism, and after 1870, the new Prussia-Germany was on increasingly good terms with Austria. Great Britain and France were averse to either Russia or Austria gobbling the Balkans. Their sympathies lay with the subject Christian races, but, as has already been said, they were afraid lest independence of the Slavs should become a Tsarist catspaw. Politically, therefore, they stood— intermittently—for the preservation of the Ottoman Empire.

In 1861, the year of the emancipation of the Russian serfs, the union of the principalities of Moldavia and Wallachia was proclaimed, with a native Rumanian noble, Colonel Alexander Couza, as prince. This appearance of Rumania as a new state on the map of Europe was important for a variety of reasons. It placed a buffer between Russia and Turkey in Europe; it marked the independence of a state with millions of kinsmen still under Austrian rule—a new threat, therefore, to the Balkan aspirations of that Power—and it witnessed the resurgence of a Latin island in the Slav sea, a potential ally for France—Bucarest admires Paris.

The course of history was to bring yet another powerful political interest to the Balkans. For Prince Couza reformed so quickly— his abolition of monasteries and feudal dues may have seemed archaic to anyone with a western education, but it was modernist in Rumania—that his subjects deposed him in 1866. The not too-attractive crown was declined by a Belgian prince, but was accepted by Prince Carol of Hohenzollern. Bismarck favoured the chance of increasing German influence in the Balkans and overcame the doubts of King William, who was as dubious about the scheme as the honest, stupid Francis Joseph had been over his brother's Mexican adventure. Under Carol and his talented wife, Rumania prospered; the Court party was mostly pro-German, and the democrats pro-French.

It was time for Russia to strengthen her hold. In 1867, under the guise of a scientific meeting, a Pan-Slav congress was held at Moscow. Young Slavs went in numbers to Russian universities; the Tsar appointed Pan-Slav consuls throughout the Peninsula, and this policy began to breed more secret societies than ever. An outbreak might have come sooner but for the untimely murder in 1868 of Michael of Serbia, an able prince who seemed on the verge of bringing a Balkan League into war with the Turks. Rebellion smouldered.

It broke out eight years later in Bosnia and Herzegovina, provinces largely Moslem in religion, but Serb in race and full of economic grievances. The Turks ruined their cause by murdering the French and German consuls at Salonika, and by carrying out that massacre of the Bulgarians which led Gladstone to demand their expulsion from Europe, "bag and baggage". Serbia, Montenegro, Rumania and Russia went to war with Turkey, whose armies—save for the gallant defence of Plevna—put up little resistance, lost Kars in Asia and everything but Constantinople in Europe.

The Turkish Empire west of the Straits was saved by the arrival of the British fleet in the Bosporus. Even then, by the Treaty of San Stefano of 1877, Russia secured for the new Principality of Bulgaria not only the purely Bulgarian lands but also Thrace and Macedonia. Britain was still haunted by the "catspaw" spectre, and she had with her Austria, who saw in this Treaty the end of her Balkan ambitions. Bismarck could do no more than play the "honest broker" with two such Powers hostile to Russia. A new Treaty, signed at Berlin on 13th July, 1878, restricted Bulgaria to a narrow strip between the Danube and the Balkan Mountains, and saved Thrace and Macedonia for Turkey, who owed a debt of gratitude to Britain and Germany. The next phase of the Eastern Question showed the rivalry of these two Powers and the rivalry of Austria and Russia for the friendship of the Balkan States which were a long way from attaining political maturity.

THE POLITICAL SCENE IN BRITAIN

In Great Britain, the years between 1865 and 1878 were alive with great names. The period opens with the death of Palmerston, the last of the Whigs, who had dominated British political life for over thirty years. The rival giant figures of Disraeli and Gladstone were evidence that personalities still existed in politics. Prominent, too, were the events of these thirteen years; Palmerston's death was followed by the very modest Reform Bill which the Lord Derby of the time called a "leap in the dark", and the period closed with the Treaty of Berlin

The great leaders of the two major English political parties were anomalous. The Conservatives, the party of country squires and established clergy, were led by the adventurous exotic Jew, Disraeli. Gladstone, a High Churchman with an Eton-cum-Oxford education, made himself famous as leader of the Liberal nonconformist middle classes. As usual, the Conservative Party had the more ambitious foreign policy. Disraeli bought the Suez Canal shares from the bankrupt Khedive of Egypt. He had the Queen proclaimed Empress of India. He got Cyprus without firing a shot, and was hailed by Bismarck as the "man" of the Berlin Conference. Gladstone's Second Ministry closed in 1885 discredited by the death of General Charles Gordon at Khartoum in the January of that year.

In domestic reforms both parties had a worthy record. Between 1874 and 1880, the Conservatives, inspired by the progressive Toryism of Disraeli, passed a Public Health Act, an Artisans' Dwelling Act and the measure which introduced the Plimsoll Line. Before this, in 1867, the Second Reform Bill, a Conservative measure, had extended the middle-class limits of the First Reform Bill and given the vote to the artisans. It is curious that the Conservatives enfranchised a class which has often voted largely against them, while it was left to the Liberals to enfranchise, by the Third Reform Bill of 1884, the agricultural labourer, who has helped to keep rural England solidly Tory. The reforms of Gladstone's Ministry of 1868–74 were many and important. Education was made compulsory, trade unions were legalized; secret voting was established, religious tests for Members of Parliament were abolished. Meantime, Cardwell reorganized the Army. He abolished the sale of commissions, divided the country into territorial districts for military purposes, and introduced the short-service system which had contributed to Prussia's easy victory over Austria in the war of 1866, since it provided adequate and systematic training for far more men than had been possible under the old system.

THE IRISH QUESTION

The Second Gladstone Ministry was too much hampered by its unhappy foreign policy and the Irish Question to be able to accomplish much in the way of domestic reform, except the Reform Bill of 1867. Gladstone himself was ahead of his own party in realizing that a major operation, Home Rule, would alone solve the Irish Question. But, like many other Englishmen, he failed to see that no amount of material betterment would make up for the refusal to grant that degree of independence which alone would satisfy the spiritual side of Irish nationalism. Land Purchase Acts were but sops to the Irish, who looked on the land as their own and most of the landowners as robbers.

The Dissolution of the Monasteries was forgotten so soon in England because the monks had no children; the Irish are prolific, and the tradition of hatred was handed down to the children. The reply to the execution of the Manchester Martyrs came in the shooting of Lord Frederick Cavendish in the Phoenix Park. The Protestant Church was disestablished and schools reformed, but the Irish of all denominations opposed Gladstone's scheme to found an undenominational university, and a Connaught peasant supposed that "the Famine and the National Schools took the heart out of the people". It was not efficient government but self-government that the Irish wanted. British politicians have rarely realized this, and have in their own generation made concessions which would have satisfied the past but not the present, and the future asks for more. Pitt realized that Catholic Emancipation might have made the

Union acceptable; Gladstone might have satisfied the Irish with his Home Rule Bill, which left military, naval and excise control in English hands. When the O'Shea divorce case wrecked the career of Parnell, Ireland was left without a constructive statesman who combined ability and popularity to a degree helpful to a solution of the Irish question.

SCANDINAVIA AND SPAIN

The majority of smaller nations in Europe were happy in that they had little history. The most important of those not already considered, Sweden and Spain, followed very different courses. In Sweden, the period marks a passive foreign, but a progressive home policy. With little desire or means to rebuild their empire, the Swedes succeeded in making their country one of the happiest in Europe. The population, for long too scanty for so extensive a territory, reached four millions. Marshes were drained and forests felled to bring more land into cultivation. The surplus population migrated to the scanty Swedish towns, which increased in size, trade and industry. These careful Scandinavians did not allow urban dirt-rashes to develop. Education, public health and decent housing conditions were many years in advance of England. Nonconformity and temperance-leagues helped to give the country a sound, unambitious middle-class outlook.

Spain was different. No longer had the Bourbon dynasty French cousins to follow. The people were poor, undeveloped and discontented. Provincial differences were accentuated by a geography which divided the country and a varied regional history which made unification difficult. The Spanish crown was bandied about Europe and made the excuse of a war between France and Prussia. With a feeble Cortes and a dissolute Queen, Spain could take little pride except in her score of daughter American nations and the national spirit of self-confidence which has always been her most obvious characteristic and her principal cause for hope.

CHAPTER 72

THE FAR EAST

THE rise of Japan and the decline of China were largely dictated by the enormous growth and proximity of the European Powers and the United States, due to the Industrial Revolution and the speeding-up of transport. In a quick-thinking age, China and Japan had to jump from feudalism to the twentieth century. Among much which spells difference and failure, perhaps the most surprising feature is the degree to which both have succeeded.

In 1865, the twenty-two dynasties of China were moving towards their close. The country was as tolerant and as unmilitary as ever, though the recent Taiping Rebellion and the inauguration of a foreign inspection of customs wrote new unfavourable tidings on the wall. The Chinese turned to Russia. By the Treaty of Aigun, the left bank of the Amur was ceded by the former country to the latter; Muraview, who signed the treaty, was made Count Amursky, founded a military port called Blagovestchensk or "Good-tidings", and the Pacific port of Vladivostok or "Dominion of the East".

Meantime, French control had been established over Annam, Cambodia and Cochin-China, and in 1886, the British completed the conquest of Burma; China had even to allow her nominal observance of sovereignty over the last of these regions to lapse in 1895. In the same year, too, all the Malay states except Johore were federated; this last was already under the protection of Great Britain.

REACTION IN CHINA : PROGRESS IN JAPAN

China had to contend with rebellions in her north-easterly provinces. Threatened within and without her empire, she adopted a more tractable attitude towards the hitherto despised Western Powers. The dominant figure was the Empress Dowager Yehonala, more popularly known as the Old Buddha. She had the same forcefulness and will to live as Queen Elizabeth and Catherine the Great. Even after her son's death in 1875, she continued to be the most powerful political factor in China, though her nephew assumed the reins of government in 1889. Yehonala took the name Tzu Hsi (Motherly and Auspicious): its interpretation was reactionary and anti-foreign, until the ignominious failure of the Boxer Rebellion persuaded the Empress Dowager that the old system was dead.

Had Tzu Hsi put herself at the head of the party of reform, the history of Modern China might well have been happier. A Foreign Office was established, but its value was summed up by the British Minister at Peking, who said that its decisions were as difficult to get as "water from a well with a bottomless bucket". Elsewhere, the old corruption and inefficiency flourished; in the civil service examinations of 1889 at Foo-chow, nine candidates were over eighty and two over ninety years of age. A disagreeable development was the beginning of attacks on Christian missionaries, which were often tolerated by local officials and welcomed by the anti-foreign mob because converts and their clergy were inclined to criticize the less Christian ways of Chinese life. In 1870 came a rising in Tientsin, during which not only the cathedral but the French consulate was destroyed and many French nationals killed: France might well have taken military action but for the outbreak of war with Germany.

French and American shelling of Shimonoseki and the more disastrous British bombardment of Kagoshima broke down the self-imposed isolation which had separated Japan from the outside world for two centuries. The nation which had retired into obscurity at the time when the British Empire was being founded proceeded to set its house in Western order with thoroughness and rapidity.

Two deaths helped the metamorphosis. In 1866 died the Shogun, and in the following year, the Emperor. The latter was succeeded by the young Mutsuhito, a person of first-class ability who departed from the traditional anti-foreign policy of Japanese emperors and became the champion of reform. He was helped by the powerful *daimyo*, or Lord, of Tosa, by a band of other liberal nobles, and by the patriotic unselfishness of the new Shogun, who handed over his power to the Emperor. The period of dual control had ended, though civil war lasted for two years before the diehards finally surrendered: the period of Meiji, or "enlightened government", had begun.

JAPAN ABANDONS FEUDALISM

In 1868, British, French and Dutch ministers arrived at Tokyo (the new name for Yedo, formerly the capital of the Shoguns). Foreigners were no longer to be described as "foul beasts" or "red-haired barbarians", epithets previously applied to them even in Imperial Edicts. Feudalism was abolished; indeed, out of loyalty, the Japanese nobles voluntarily abandoned their feudal rights and settled down to enjoy a pension amounting to one-tenth of their former wealth. A uniform national law and currency were introduced. Foreign experts were brought to Japan, and in general, they served the country's interests well. French instructors trained the new army and British the navy—both considerably increased by the introduction of conscription. Britain, too, became the model for telegraph and railway services, while Americans trained the Japanese farmer and teacher, and Germans the Japanese doctor. Permission, too, was given to Japanese to visit foreign countries for purposes of study, and to take their wives with them. After the Franco-Prussian war, the Japanese were not slow to change their French for German military instructors. There was one sad side. Many of the samurai lost, in unwise investments or business ventures, what little material wealth remained to them and became servants, or even burglars.

In several ways, Japan grew, as Britain has grown, from the common-sense adaptability and courage of her people. To this was added the essential Japanese sense of self-shame, a feeling which spurred on every citizen to remove the slur of inferiority from the country. Toleration grew, and foreign missionaries went unmolested. The years 1876 and 1877 provided examples of the startling progress made by the reformers. In the former year, an attack by Koreans on a Japanese ship was countered by a peaceful demonstration, instead of by the active use of armed strength. Consequently the schoolboys and samurai of Satsuma organized a revolt which led to a brief civil war, ending with the defeat of the rebels, the suicide of their leader and the very lenient treatment of the insurgent rank and file who—representing the last challenge of feudal Japan—pleaded that they had rebelled not against the Emperor but against the evil counsellors who surrounded him.

In the development of parliamentary government, there was a wise spirit of cautious progress. Twenty-one years elapsed between the Emperor's promise and its fulfilment in the issue of a constitution. Sixty years were to pass until, in 1927, manhood suffrage was introduced. The Emperor intervened rarely, but his consultation with the Elder Statesmen produced an effect more worthy of a family council than of representative government. Japanese constitutionalism moved along lines more German than British. The Emperor became the guiding force, a position to which he was well suited, as he was the most able and long-lived of Japanese men-of-state; his subjects were devoted to him, and most grateful for the success of his new experiment in Westernization. Modern civil and commercial codes were put into force, with the result that Japan negotiated in 1894 a treaty with Great Britain, which was followed by treaties with the other Great Powers.

KOREA, JAPAN AND CHINA

In the sixteenth century Korea had repulsed the invasion which Japan had launched across the intervening hundred and twenty miles of water. Her traditions made her oppose Japanese plans of expansion. Tokyo had learnt from her European mentors, and used the velvet glove. To punish a Korean attack on their nationals, and to secure a commercial treaty, the Japanese gave ample warning and adopted only such mild measures as the Americans had used against them in their own period of emancipation. However, besides paying an indemnity and granting privileges, the Koreans were compelled to maintain a Japanese garrison. All this happened in 1882, only fourteen years after the opening of the country to foreigners.

China was jealous. In 1894, her Korean agents murdered a Korean leader friendly to Japan. Peking was reactionary, Tokyo on the side of Western progress. The Japanese people felt that it was a national duty to make their country's influence paramount in Korea. Better equipped and better soldiers than the Chinese—whose generals were often corrupt and their guns wooden dummies—the Japanese gained an easy victory. Typical of the feudal courtesy still prevalent at Tokyo was the fact that, because a Japanese fanatic attempted to assassinate the leading Chinese delegate to the peace conference, China got better terms than she otherwise would have done. The peninsula of Liao-Tung, with its great fortress of Port Arthur, Formosa and the Pescadores were ceded to Japan. China recognized the independence of Korea, paid an indemnity and opened four additional treaty ports to the Japanese, who waived their claim to Manchuria.

Chinese diplomacy regained part of what Chinese arms had lost. The goodwill of Russia, France and Germany was secured: Russia disliked the Japanese occupation of Port Arthur, and the other

Powers were courting Russian friendship. At the time, Japan was unable to meet such powerful opposition, and so had to evacuate Liao-Tung. Enmity from Russia was understood, and France was the Tsar's ally; but the Japanese generally resented Germany's attitude, which they repaid in like coin during the First World War.

CONFLICT OF JAPANESE AND RUSSIAN POLICIES

The Sino-Japanese War was followed by three developments in the political situation of the Far East. Japan had her first and least fortunate experience in attempting to direct the affairs of a smaller state. Japanese influence in Korea was soon endangered by too sudden reforms, affecting cherished habits. Thus at the advice of Count Inouye, they interfered with the pipe and top-knot of the Korean. The most powerful conservative force in opposition to the Japanese came from the Queen, who so angered Inouye's soldier successor that he instigated a horrid massacre in which she and her ladies were hacked to death and their bodies burnt. In consequence, the King took refuge in the Russian consulate, and the Tsarist Government supplanted whatever chances Tokyo had of maintaining popularity in Korea.

The clash of Russian and Japanese interests was accompanied by increasingly successful pressure put by Russia and other European states on China, subsequent to the latter's defeat in the Sino-Japanese War, and her partial rescue by the Three-Power Intervention. France was the first to secure her reward—the exploitation of certain lines and the extension of the Annamese railways into Southern China. Russia followed, and scored a major success by the permission to construct a railway across Manchuria, which gave her considerable influence over that province, and the means of shortening the distance between Vladivostok and the towns of Central Siberia. Germany made the murder of two of her missionaries by a Chinese mob the excuse to enforce the lease of the fine harbour of Kiaochow. Britain then leased Kowloon and Wei-hai-Wei; France, Kwangchow-wan; and Russia, that very fortress of Port Arthur which the Japanese had been compelled to surrender in 1895. China had lost more than she secured by the Three-Power Intervention.

The third development in this period which followed the Sino-Japanese War resulted in the annexation of the Philippines by the United States after their own successful struggle with Spain. At the time, Japan made no objection; she was fully occupied with Korea and the Russian advance

Meantime, at Peking itself, the Emperor and a pro-Japanese party wished to promote reforms, but were opposed by the Empress Dowager and by Li Hung Chang, the minister responsible for the Three-Power Intervention, and a strong Russophile. An attempt by the Emperor to have the Empress Dowager arrested was betrayed, and resulted in his own arrest. Henceforward Tzu Hsi was supreme

The change in front made itself soon apparent: the Powers were told that they need expect no further concessions, and Italy's belated requests for these were refused. An anti-foreign movement swept the country. It was directed principally against the missionaries; they were regarded as the apostles of an alien civilization and their converts as the "secondary foreign devils". The construction of railways increased the feeling of unrest, as it led often to a disturbance of the sacred graves of ancestors, a situation which was considerably worsened by the rapacity of Chinese officials in frequently withholding the compensation paid by the railway companies.

THE BOXERS AND MANCHURIA

Secret military organizations, such as the "Plum Blossom Fists" and the "Fists of Public Harmony", appeared. They were anti-foreign, and the foreigners fixed on these bands the name of Boxers because the Fists of Public Harmony were ostensibly a gymnastic and boxing club. Raids on the property of Christians began in Southern China in 1899. The Powers demanded that the imperial government should denounce these bands, whose organization it had actually encouraged. Reinforcements were sent to the legations at Peking, whereupon, convinced that an invasion of China had begun, the Boxers began an attack on foreign buildings and railways.

Events followed in rapid succession. Landing parties from foreign warships seized the Taku Forts, at Peking's outlet to the sea. The Chinese military party got control of the government, declared a state of war, and ordered foreign diplomats to leave the country. On his way to protest, the German minister was shot dead. Over two hundred missionaries were murdered, but the Boxer rising was confined to the northern provinces. Meantime, an international relief force was raised, largely owing to the insistence of Germany, who had her representative's death to avenge. Neither Russia nor Japan wished to compromise their position in China. Great Britain was busy with the Boer War and could spare hardly any but Indian troops, and the United States was engaged in suppressing a Filipino revolt. To the force which relieved the Peking Legations, the Japanese contributed the largest contingent, and there were no Germans, though these last made an evil name for themselves in the subsequent punitive expeditions; the Kaiser had told his expeditionary force to remember Attila's Huns and act "so that a Chinaman would never dare to look a German again in the face".

As a result of the war, Russia was able to occupy Manchuria without protest from the Powers, the Empress Dowager realized the hopelessness of her anti-foreign attitude, and the Japanese came to regard themselves as the equals of European troops. China suffered no loss of territory, but her hatred of foreigners grew as a result of the compulsion to execute Boxer leaders, who were generally regarded as patriots, and to pay an indemnity out of customs dues.

Russia was slow to evacuate Manchuria, which, she claimed, lay outside the Powers' sphere of influence. By a certain amount of opposition to them, she came to be regarded as China's friend. Meantime, Britain and Japan found in one another the ally each required, and a treaty, signed in January 1902, provided that the contracting Powers, while maintaining neutrality if either was attacked by one other Power, would help one another if attacked by two; so far as the Far East was concerned, this meant that, if France came to the help of Russia, the Anglo-Japanese *bloc* would fight.

The stage had been set for a struggle between Russia and Japan to decide the future of Manchuria and Korea. Russia was chiefly to blame for the outbreak of hostilities. Isvolsky's rapacious instincts were as disastrous in the East as they were to be in the West on the eve of the World War. Alexeiev, the Russian Commander at Port Arthur, had a long experience of the East and a hearty contempt for the Japanese. The Schleswig-Holstein desertion, and an incident in 1898 when British warships left Port Arthur at Russian dictation, led the Russian Government to believe that they had little to fear from Britain. The Russian military party won control, and Japan's efforts for peace were ignored with a stupid callousness typified by the Tsar's remark "What insolence!" when, in February, 1904, the Japanese Ambassador asked for his passport.

RUSSIA DEFEATED BY JAPAN

Elsewhere in Europe, it was felt that, although the Japanese had made great strides and acquitted themselves well in the China War and Boxer rebellion, they were foolhardy to pit themselves against a great Power. But both Russia and Europe under-estimated the preparedness of the Japanese and the knowledge which an army of spies, from high officials to barbers and prostitutes, had contributed about the positions and resources of the Tsarist armies. Many factors favoured the Japanese. They were fighting near their own homes, and the whole nation stood behind a struggle which was looked on as one for self-preservation. The Russian peasant was inspired by neither of these motives in defending distant Manchuria, which was already eating up money required for reform at home. Actually, the Japanese had offered Russia a free hand in Manchuria in return for the same right in Korea, but this was turned down.

In order to transport troops freely to Manchuria and Korea, the Japanese had to gain command of the sea. They were helped here by the fact that war was declared suddenly, in winter-time, before the Russians could move a large section of their Pacific squadron which was ice-bound in Vladivostok. The destruction of two Russian ships outside the Korean port of Chemulpo, and the crippling of part of the Port Arthur force which was then blockaded, enabled the Japanese to move troops as they wished. An attempt by the Russophile King of Korea to proclaim neutrality was disregarded.

Within three months of the outbreak of war, Korea had been occupied and Manchuria invaded from that side. There was severe fighting near Mukden, the forces employed being as big as any combatant forces until the First World War. The Russians fought stubbornly, but were compelled to retreat northwards, and Port Arthur, isolated, fell into Japanese hands in January, 1905.

Before the war finished, the Russians suffered another and more humiliating reverse in the destruction of their Baltic fleet, which had made the long journey to the China Sea—after almost precipitating a war with Britain by firing on East Coast trawlers off the Dogger Bank—only to be more utterly destroyed than the Spanish Armada; one Russian vessel escaped from the Battle of Tsushima. Three days later, the Japanese Minister at Washington asked President Roosevelt to act as mediator. Both sides were ready for peace. Russia, defeated in Asia, was faced with revolution in Europe, while Japan, almost bankrupt, was conscious of the fact that Russian communications were improving, though trains on the single-track Trans-Siberian Railway could still only pass at sidings.

Under the Treaty of Portsmouth (New Hampshire), Russia ceded the Liao-Tung lease and the South Manchurian Railway lease, with the southern half of Sakhalin; she ceded fishing rights off the Siberian coast and paid the generous sum of four million pounds to cover the upkeep of Russian prisoners of war. Japan's interests in Korea were recognized, and the Russian Government evacuated Manchuria.

JAPAN'S GROWING EMPIRE

Japan's prestige was necessarily increased by her victory. European Powers accredited her Court with ambassadors instead of ministers, while the Asiatic peoples looked with respect on a yellow people which had defeated a white; Indian and Javanese nationalist movements took courage, and reform became popular from Turkey to Peking. At home, the Tokyo Government conformed to the historic Japanese maxim "After victory, tighten your helmet-strings". The army and navy were strengthened, so that the defence forces of the nation amounted to two and a half million men, and many ships, dockyards and arsenals were built by native experts without the aid of foreign technicians.

In Korea, the appointment of the brilliant and humane Prince Ito as Resident-General was token of Japan's goodwill to a country where her alternate reforms and repressive measures were as lacking in fortune as those of England have been in Ireland. Ito was developing the public services of one of the worst-governed countries in the world when struck down by a Korean assassin's bullet on Harbin railway station in 1919. His successor, a general, dealt roughly with his charge. The Koreans rebelled, were savagely repressed, and finally, because of their "unrest and disquietude", annexed to Japan. While Meiji had transformed out of all knowledge the might of Japan, the

Korean royal house, four thousand years old, perished and its last representative became a Japanese pensioner. A territory of over eighty thousand square miles and a population of over thirteen millions were added to the Japanese Empire.

REVOLUTION IN CHINA

Meantime, the Chinese showed themselves more and more ready to learn from Japan. Forty thousand students came to Japanese schools. The Empress Dowager showed her capability in old age by backing the reformers. With the friendly co-operation of Great Britain, the opium trade with India was greatly diminished, Chinese cultivation restricted, and civil servants, teachers and officers forbidden to consume the drug.

It was unfortunate that Tzu Hsi became a convert to reform so late in life and that she died before the programme had been carried out. She died in November 1908, having bequeathed the succession to her infant great-nephew, Pu Yi, under the regency of his father, Prince Chun, who had married a daughter of one of her most loyal advisers. Chun was an admirer of Western ideas, but ineffective as a ruler and the personal enemy of Yuan Shih-kai, the reformist leader, who was the only man powerful enough to hold the existing order together after the Empress's death.

The revolutionary movement grew quickly. It was inspired by the desire for Westernization, especially noticeable since Japan's victory over Russia, by Chun's incompetence, by his delay in summoning a national parliament and giving it due powers, and by the anger of the capitalists against the government's attempt to nationalize the projected railways. The leader of the reform party was Dr. Sun Yat-sen; in his native city of Canton, open revolt broke out in April, 1911, and spread throughout China in a manner characterized by very small loss of life and by the speedy collapse of the Manchu régime. In February, 1912, the boy Emperor abdicated, and in the following month, the old Conservative statesman Yuan Shih-kai became president of the new republic.

Hopes that China might settle down speedily to ordered government proved premature. Her republicans were divided and their task immense. Foreigners took advantage of the somewhat chaotic state. Russian troops occupied Urga, the capital of Outer Mongolia, ostensibly to protect their consul, and the British encouraged Tibet to declare its independence of China. Japanese immigration to California had grown to formidable proportions and was estranging Japan from the United States, which had so long been her benevolent governess. The situation began to take on its modern shape.

Japan was ready to imitate the West: China despised soldiers and materialism and wished to be left alone. The former had become a Great Power, eager to copy Britain and Germany; the latter had to face a long domestic struggle embittered by anti-European feeling.

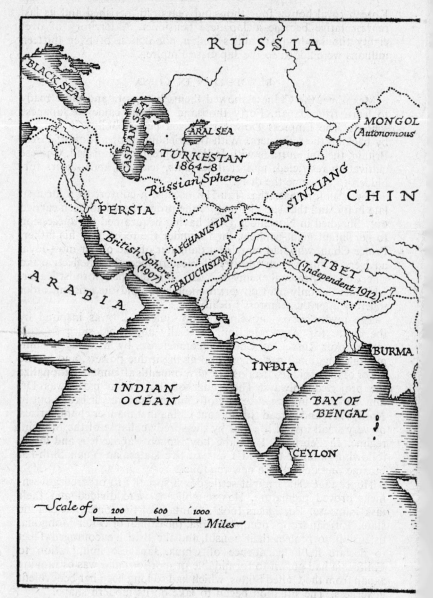

THE POWERS

In the years that preceded the First World War the western powers steadily increased their influence in the Far East. At the same time Japan emerged, after she had defeated Russia in 1905, as a formidable rival, although she still pursued a policy of ostensible friendship towards the U.S.A. and Great Britain.

IN THE FAR EAST

Great Britain's interests clashed with those of Russia in Persia and Afghanistan, while Russian expansion eastwards was checked by the Japanese in Manchuria. China, reduced to impotence, was forced to make concessions to the principal powers. Meanwhile the U.S.A. established control over the Philippine Islands.

Civil war and famine have provided again and again a hard old remedy for China's problem of population. Japan's case was more difficult. Growth of population coupled with industrial expansion made her no longer self-sufficing in foodstuffs and produced the same social and political dangers which have troubled Europe. By 1912, Japan needed colonies and a new social order: the old order seemed strong enough to grab colonies and postpone reform.

CHAPTER 73

THE BRITISH EMPIRE

WHILE the map of Europe was undergoing small important changes and while Abraham Lincoln saved the North American Union, the face of the globe was painted red. This phase in the latter half of the nineteenth century signified British Imperialism. It is the "Second British Empire" which succeeded the lost thirteen colonies and lasted until the First World War bequeathed a heritage of mandates and colony-owning dominions.

British common sense learnt a lesson from the loss of her North American colonies. On the morrow of the war, Englishmen were inclined to blame France rather than the colonists for defeat, and George III hoped that "Religion, Language, Interest and Affections" might still unite the two countries. Already, before the eighteenth century was out, a new empire was being extended in Canada and India; the French wars provided an excuse to seize the Cape.

BRITISH COLONIAL POLICY

By 1865, the losses were already made good, before German or Italian unity had been achieved and without serious foreign rivalry. The conference which met at Quebec in 1864 discussed proposals for union between that province, Ontario and the seaboard districts, with the result that, in 1867, the Dominion of Canada came into existence. Far away, New Zealand had secured a considerable measure of control over her own affairs; the Maori wars did not finish until 1870, but two years before that date Maori representatives had seats in the General Assembly.

The British "Second Empire" was founded, to a degree remarkable in those times, on goodwill, mutual understanding and self-government in local affairs. There were still plenty of people who looked on colonies as a tiresome, unnecessary burden and expense; they merely echoed the sentiments of men like Lord Glenelg and Lord John Russell, who had been Colonial Secretary as late as the eighteen thirties. Even Disraeli at this time had little use for colonies, and Granville, the Liberal expert on such matters, appears to have hoped that Canada would separate from Great Britain. It was in that very country that the tide most decisively turned; Lord Durham and his successor as Governor-General, Lord Elgin, justified their progressive policy when the French and British elements united to form the Dominion of 1867; mutual distrust between Canada and the United States had been fostered by the Civil War and by the opportunities and dangers provided by the development of the Canadian West.

THE SCRAMBLE FOR AFRICA

A discovery of diamonds at Kimberley in 1871 helped to awaken British imperialism. The find was north of the Orange River, in Boer territory; but powerful commercial interests were involved, and the tenacity of the Dutch settlers made war and eventual annexation inevitable. With tact, British sovereignty might have been established without resort to arms; the Boer farmer republics, almost bankrupt and harassed by native tribes, contained a party ready to accept British rule so long as their local governmental rights were protected.

In general, the natives were more humanely treated by the British than by the Dutch, who had far fewer native resources and little native policy apart from the gun and the whip. Great Britain annexed the Transvaal, and then had to fight the militant Zulus, who were menacing it. Though ultimately vanquished, the Zulus won victories which lessened British prestige.

Although Disraeli had become a convinced imperialist, his Liberal opponents maintained the old contemptuous view of colonies. Disliking annexation, and freed from the Zulu menace, the Boers took up arms and inflicted on a tiny British force at Majuba a defeat whose psychological and international proportions far outweighed its military significance. Gladstone made a speedy peace which gave the Boers back their country and made a second war certain.

A picturesque streak coloured the dingy record of British imperialism in this corner of the globe. Cecil Rhodes' bold settlement in the Matabele land lent the flavour of romance to international greed, which became more rapacious after the discovery of Transvaal gold in 1885; the wealth of the country, though not its flag, was ensured. Stubborn and adverse from progress, the Boers opposed schemes of co-operation; victory had affected their narrow international vision and apparently perpetuated that bullying treatment of the natives which led these latter mostly to prefer the British.

The "scramble for Africa" had begun. Besides the ventures in what is now known as Rhodesia, due to the great imperialist whose name that state bears, Britain secured territory in Uganda, in what is now called Kenya and on the Niger. France, Portugal and Germany made strides at the expense of native rulers, but they were none of them able to challenge the banks and navy of Britain, whose interests in colonial affairs was stimulated by the Second Reform Bill, enfranchising the artisan (who had plenty of relations abroad), and by the opening of the Suez Canal, two years later (1869).

The extravagance of the Egyptian Khedive, and Disraeli's brilliant purchase of the former's half-share in the control of the Canal, gave Great Britain very great influence over the new quick route to India, a main artery of Eastern trade. France was angry; she had built and largely financed the Canal; Louis IX had invaded Egypt and Napoleon I had conquered her; Mehemet Ali and his Khedival line were Francophile. However, she allowed Britain to clinch her hold over this part of Africa when she left that country to deal alone with a patriotic revolt under Arabi Pasha in 1882 against the Dual Control exercised by France and England since the Khedive's bankruptcy six years before. For the immediate future, France had plenty to occupy her at the other end of the North African coast, where she carved out her own empire, spreading from Algiers to Morocco and from Tunis into the Great Sahara.

THE SUDAN AND BRITISH WEST AFRICA

Britain also had to push south, in order to safeguard Egypt from the warlike tribes of the Sudan. A successful sword-and-Koran rising under the Mahdi made control of this great region temporarily impossible and cost the life of a popular hero, the brave, if rash, General Gordon. Episodes like this and Majuba provided martyrs for the new Imperialism and provoked British pride. Disraeli persuaded the Queen to adopt the imposing title of Empress of India. Meantime, a rapid success was gained in the West, where the husky negroes liked British rule, and flourished under it, thanks to the admirable administration of Lugard and a series of capable governors. There was no immigration of Indians to create in West Africa the problems which troubled British East Africa; there the fertile highlands provided good farm-land for settlers from the Mother Country, whose aims were somewhat naturally selfish and who were often incapable of considering the welfare of the African.

DEVELOPMENT OF AUSTRALIA

More peaceful was the development of distant Australia, where no foreign European rival threatened and Japanese immigration did not become a menace until the twentieth century. Perhaps the remoteness of the sixth continent helped to keep down population; it is significant that in no set of circumstances has any British colony advanced at the speed of the United States, though development may be none the less healthy. Four of the five Australian states were already self-governing, in local affairs, at the beginning of this period; the fifth, Western Australia, reached the same status in 1870, as soon as the convict element sank into insignificance. But federal self-government did not follow as quickly as in Canada. The states were small—Western Australia's population was still under fifty thousand when that state got control of her own affairs—and there were great differences between them. Victoria was a land of mines and high tariffs, while the other considerable state, New South Wales, stood for free-trade, sheep-farms and industry; Queensland, South Australia and the island Tasmania were largely self-sufficient units whose particular interests were jealous of the creation of a strong central power. Only when the extravagance of independent existence and the growing shadows of Japanese and German power in the Antipodes became evident, did Australia unite in 1900; then her Commonwealth possessed local powers, and limited the right of interference from the British crown in a way comparable with the limitation of the Federal authority in the United States.

NEW ZEALAND, NEW GUINEA AND INDIA

To the east lay New Zealand, the most British—part English, part Scots—of all the Dominions. Here self-government had been achieved as early as 1862, and something of the inherent tolerance of the people was shown by the readiness to admit Maori representatives to the State Assembly as early as 1868, though that fine warlike people were not pacified until 1870. It should be added that, although with a total population of one hundred thousand they outnumbered the British colonists by two to one, they were allowed only four representatives. However, the heart was in the right place. New Zealand early showed a keen sense of nationality. The British were blamed for inadequate support in the Maori wars and for allowing Germany to get a footing in Samoa; New Zealanders received the support of their Australian neighbours on this point, for Queenslanders were angry at German annexations in neighbouring New Guinea, and at the refusal of their request for British annexation on the grounds that "the Queen has already black subjects enough".

Subsequently the Queenslanders hoisted the British flag in eastern New Guinea: Gladstone blundered in persuading them to withdraw on the grounds that Germany had no intention of annexing that part of the country, which she did in the next year. Finally in 1886, a settlement was made by which the Germans took the northern and the British the southern part of New Guinea and the Solomon Islands; but for long, New Zealand and part of Australia were almost as full of separatist talk as the American colonies had been in earlier days. Development of imperial trade and the common struggle against the German menace, together with the ever-growing popularity in the Dominions of the British royal house, enormously improved the position of the Empire in Australia and New Zealand.

More populous, and with a far older civilization than any other part of the Empire, India is in a class by itself. A vast class-cleavage allowed a few thousand British soldiers and civil servants to administer this huge country with its population of three hundred millions. The Mutiny was succeeded by twenty years of comparative quiet, and then by the ever-increasing unpopularity of the British Raj, but most Indians realized that their lot would be worse under

Indian capitalists or freebooters and hostile religionists. The apparent "hauteur" of the English made itself often as distasteful in the older civilization of India as in Ireland, but the tale of achievement and unselfish public service was, on the whole, magnificent.

THE GOVERNMENT OF INDIA

The Mutiny was succeeded, on the one hand, by a development of railways and irrigation which helped to diminish the terrible famines rife in the country, and on the other, by a rectification of the frontier, by means of which Burma was annexed and Afghanistan turned into a buffer-state. Three significant events characterized the period. The first was the proclamation in 1879 of the Queen as Empress of India. The second was the period of Lord Curzon's term as Viceroy from 1899 to 1905. His measures of reform were as useful and able as his methods were arrogant and unpopular. Higher education, but not elementary, was characteristically improved; the North-West Frontier Province was competently established as a bulwark on one side and Assam with Eastern Bengal on the other. The nationalist intelligentsia disliked this last measure, which was rescinded to grace the third ceremony, King George V's Durbar, in 1911.

Self-government in an Asiatic country would obviously be a plant of slow and careful growth so far as Whitehall was concerned. The councils of the Viceroy and the leading provincial governors contained Indian members—though without any but debating power— soon after the Crown took over the government of territory from the East India Company following the Mutiny. Towards the end of the century, Lord Dufferin favoured an extension of this native membership and welcomed the first National Congress in 1885. A very limited system of representative, but not responsible, government was introduced by the Indian Councils Act of 1909. The unsuccessful attempt to murder the Viceroy, Lord Hardinge, in 1912, showed that events were not moving fast enough for some nationalists. The Durbar ceremonies of 1911 and countless reports showed that the Raj was popular enough, the usual grumbles excepted, among the vast masses of a nation awakening from illiteracy, plague and the dead weight of a myriad effete ideas.

The term "crown colony" denotes a group of mostly small and undeveloped communities. They vary immensely; Nigeria is large, and the Barbados have a representative, if not self-governing, assembly which dates from the time when wealth, as well as seniority, among British possessions gave the West Indies a prestige scarcely maintained in these days, when their economic decline has resulted from an increase of beet-sugar production in other parts of the world. Malta has some degree of control over her own affairs. The Mother Country fostered a degree of nationalism as a remedy against Italianization. The variety, which is typical of the second British

Empire, is also well illustrated by the history of Sarawak, an East Indian state ruled by the English dynasty of Brooke, and under British protection, though by law independent.

It was not until after the First World War that the Dominions became colony-owning states, though, in 1912, Australia was to some extent responsible for Papua, and New Zealand for Cook Island. The first Colonial Conference was held in 1887 in London; it re-assembled at regular intervals, and developed into the Imperial Conference. The new sense of Empire spread, largely through the skill and enthusiasm of Joseph Chamberlain, who became Colonial Secretary in 1895. This product of the biggest of Midland industrial towns typified a movement at the same time materialist and spiritual of the kind which comes so easily to Anglo-Saxon peoples. Chamberlain did much to develop the resources of the colonies, especially by improving health and communications; the remarkable advance of the Sudan after its conquest by Kitchener was largely due to his methods. But, despite his success, the country was not convinced of the advantages of imperial as opposed to free trade.

SOUTH AFRICA AFTER THE DEFEAT OF THE BOERS

Significant of the transition in Imperialist politics was the history of the South African question during the last twenty years of this period. Britain's surrender after Majuba had given the Boers a false sense of their rivals' military incapacity, and Kruger's suspicion of British designs on the Boer republics was confirmed by Jameson's raid to free the Uitlanders, or foreign settlers on the Rand, from bullying by the Boers—an ill-conceived and unsuccessful move condemned by Rhodes himself too late to prevent its being attempted. Milner's effort to negotiate with Kruger in 1899 broke down; war was declared in the same year. The initial defeats of the British troops were unexpected at home, but the Boers, with their superiority in men and in knowledge of the country, did not take full advantage of them. They made the mistake of wasting time and men in besieging the garrisons of Ladysmith, Kimberley and Mafeking, instead of making swiftly for the Cape. The arrival of Roberts with a considerable army, in which contingents from the Empire served, turned the tide, and though the Boers kept up guerrilla resistance until 1902, their ultimate defeat was ensured.

The important part of the episode began. Not only was the Peace of Vereeniging generous in granting loans and credits for the repair of damage to sufferers on both sides, but equality of justice and language was recognized when the Boer republics were merged into the British Empire. Six years later, delegates from the four provinces of Cape Colony, Natal, Transvaal and the Orange River Colony met to draft a South African constitution. In 1909, the last of these was allowed to revert to its old, pre-war name of Orange Free State, and in the following year the Union of South Africa came into being, the finest fruit of the eight-year period of Liberal administration in Great Britain. Gone, indeed, were the days not only of Lord North, but of an early Victorian England which considered Guadeloupe to be more important than Canada. Disraeli had eaten his own words and helped to found the second British Empire; by 1912 Rhodes had lived and died; the Third Empire was about to be born.

The demand for raw materials and colonial foodstuffs greatly enhanced the value of colonies and intensified this period of imperialism. High tariffs made it advantageous to possess colonies of one's own. But these were nearly all in the hands of the countries

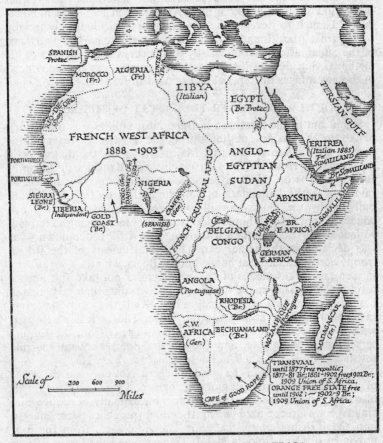

EUROPEAN ANNEXATIONS IN AFRICA

The imperialist rivalries of the European nations before the First World War were revealed in the struggle to acquire territory in Africa shown in this map.

which had up to now, at one time or other, been great maritime Powers. England, France, Holland and Portugal had large empires overseas: Russia and the United States were vast territories of continental dimensions, but Germany and Italy owned little of value, and Germany had come to feel that she merited a more considerable "place in the sun".

Colonial ambitions meant possession of important trade-routes— for England, the Suez Canal and the Mediterranean; for Russia, a way into the Mediterranean and an ice-free port in the Orient; for both Britain and Germany, some control over the communications of the Ottoman Empire, a most important bridge between East and West. The Powers clashed, too, in countries like China, independent but unsettled and torn by civil strife, which often weakened the security of foreign investments.

Increased speed in communications had made the world shrink without making it less dangerous. Much of the direction of diplomatic affairs was in the hands of autocrats and aristocratic statesmen whose tempers often outdid their abilities, as is made evident by the "Willy-Nicky" letters, the correspondence which passed between the Kaiser and his cousin the Tsar. In such circumstances, and in the absence of any powerful or experienced international control, the dangers of war on a very large scale were considerable.

CHAPTER 74

MIND AND MATTER

THE great contrary forces of romanticism and realism were still in conflict. Each gained strength in its citadels, Catholicism and atheism. The Roman Church could set, against ground lost along its pious backwaters in the Iberian Peninsula and Mexico, successes, not only among the intelligentsia in England, Holland and Switzerland, but also in the New World.

During an age of doubt, the Papacy gained more than it lost from its steadfast tenure of an orthodox position. Modernist ideas failed to secure any real footing in the Roman Church, but obtained a firmer hold in the Protestant Churches. In England, an Anglo-Catholic movement came into being through the efforts of Newman and others. It owed much to Oxford. Later religious movements, which strongly interested themselves in all questions concerning social welfare, were the Salvation Army and the non-sectarian but Protestant Y.M.C.A.

Meantime, the development of materialism threatened not only the Christian Powers; defeats at the hands of Italy and the Balkan peoples lost territory and prestige to the Caliphate and many Jews drifted away from their creed, while others joined the fervent Zionist movement as the result of this decline and Russian persecution. Probably, the Orthodox Church in the latter country was the most effete and threatened religious body in Europe, and the attitude of its leaders was complacent and opposed to any idea of progress.

TRENDS IN ART, PHILOSOPHY AND LITERATURE

Philosophy in this age was mostly materialist and anti-Christian. Typical of its great figures was Renan, who had abandoned his youthful vocation for the priesthood to attack the Church in the superior manner of middle-class Liberals of the epoch. After a brief stay in Palestine, he published his *Vie de Jésus*, in which Christ appears as a disappointed and unconvincing figure.

In England, Huxley believed in the evolutionist theories of his friend Darwin. Herbert Spencer, with his Methodist and school-teacher upbringing, evolved a brilliant self-made bourgeois gospel of the survival of the fittest. This theory devolved into that of the superman in the harsher German hands of Schopenhauer and Nietzsche; both of them died mad and the latter by his own hand, though both perpetuated a creed which did much to break up German democracy. At the same time grew up the philosophy of the Liberal Comte who justified Capitalism under the guise of Positivism.

In the art and literature of the nineteenth century there was the same struggle as in religion: the trend of their evolution being from romance to realism. Thus the great Victorian literature culminated in the concern with social and political problems of H. G. Wells and George Bernard Shaw; the great Russian literature in the proletarian writings of Gorky. In France, Flaubert, Zola and Anatole France, in their various ways, dealt realistically with the problems of society, this also constituting the importance of the plays written by the Norwegian, Ibsen.

The visual arts, too, discarded romantic subject-matter. In France the realism of Courbet was followed by a new and quasi-scientific interest in colour and light with the paintings of Monet, Manet and Pissarro. Impressionism, as this was called, became the most important movement of the century. Its offshoot was Post-Impressionism, a loose term descriptive of the work of Cézanne, Gauguin and Van Gogh, whose influence on the twentieth century has been very great. Music ran a parallel course. The development of a social consciousness in architecture and craftsmanship was late in showing itself and has not even yet reached a conclusive stage.

Meanwhile, education was developing, and played an increasingly important part in moulding the citizen of the future. It was compulsory and free in Switzerland by the eighteen-seventies; and Gambetta ascribed Germany's success in her war with France to the Prussian schoolmaster. By the early 'eighties, education was compulsory in France; it was free and compulsory in Great Britain by 1891, and in Holland by 1900. When Spain made elementary education compulsory in 1909, the only large countries in Europe to remain mostly illiterate were Russia and the Ottoman Empire. The development of secondary education has continued to make steady progress with the twentieth century.

An increased number of readers swelled newspaper circulation. The Press was helped, too, by the decrease in taxes on newspapers, the growth of advertisements, and improvements in printing-office machinery. News technique developed with more funds available. The Press Association was founded in 1865 and the now famous agency started by Reuter fourteen years before in London. As Editor of the *Pall Mall Gazette*, Stead popularized interviews, but perhaps the first successful piece of popular journalism was T. P. O'Connor's *Star*, with its sections devoted to arts and crafts, its criminal news and its sensational serials: Shaw wrote and Pennell drew for T.P.'s paper. Alfred Harmsworth's halfpenny morning paper achieved unprecedented figures for circulation in England, and the *Daily Mail* became a force in national politics. Elsewhere, France had the first newspapers to reach a daily circulation of one million, and Germany probably had the best-informed newspapers on the Continent.

Mankind increased at a prolific rate. Such figures as those of the United States, swollen by emigration from seven million in 1810 to ninety-two million in 1910, could scarcely be equalled in Europe, but Italy increased from twenty-seven to thirty-six million in the forty years ending in 1910, and the birth-rate rose considerably throughout Western and Central Europe. This was very marked in Germany, which far outstripped France, where peasant properties and radical middle-class conventions kept families small.

THE INVENTIVE GENIUS OF THE MACHINE AGE

With the growth of population, came increased machine activity and greater comfort, particularly for the moneyed classes. Much of this was built on coal, the production of which between 1870 and 1910 went up from one hundred and ten to two hundred and sixty-five million tons in Great Britain, thirty-seven to two hundred and twenty-two million tons in Germany, and still bigger proportions in the U.S.A. Europe and the world were knit by new railways and steamship lines. Telegraphs, invented in the 'thirties, first linked England and America in 1866. The following year saw the introduction of dynamite, while 1875 was notable for the launch of the first practical submarine. In 1876 Bell, who had built a school for teachers of the deaf, invented the telephone. Edison invented the phonograph and patented the incandescent filament lamp. Trams, bicycles, sewing-machines were innovations which eased the life of millions; Marconi's wireless telegraphy and J. J. Thomson's wireless telephony prepared the way for still more surprising possibilities. Leisure and amusement found new outlets in the Eastman company's roll-film camera, the cinema and the automobile. Four cars were produced in the United States in 1895, and nearly two hundred thousand in 1910, by which year that country controlled both cinema and automobile industries. The development of the internal-combustion engine marks a new phase of social and industrial progress.

Life had become fuller. The greater facilities for travel, together with such inventions as the cinema, the bicycle and the motor-car, brought new interests and amusements into the lives of rich and poor. Meantime, an improved medical science and hygiene were prolonging the life of man beyond the psalmist's three score years and ten. In highly-civilized countries like France, the birth-rate had already begun to shrink, but the population of Europe trebled in the nineteenth century; by the end of it there were more people in the world than ever before. Old men lasted longer and promotion became slower for the young, many of whom turned in disappointment to Socialist plans for a reorganization of society. Such changes were made more likely by the enormous growth of the labouring class, consequent on industrial development. In Western Europe the movement proceeded mostly along constitutional lines, but in Russia it was closely connected with nihilism and the doctrine that the existing order should at any cost be overthrown.

There was great advance in the heavens above and the earth beneath. In the newer continents, it was marked in both directions; in England, more pronounced in the air than in the fields. The turn of the century saw the construction of the first Zeppelin, an airship lighter than air. Blériot flew across the Channel in a heavier-than-air machine in 1909. Petrol and rubber industries developed immensely and with them the prosperity of Central and South America and the East Indies.

Drills, harvesters and cultivators became household words: agriculture—oldest, most likeable and most backward of industries—was at last moving forward. The lot of the agricultural worker in Europe, except perhaps in France, was poor; but the fortunes which were being made in the great fields of the New World encouraged men to think that there were new opportunities for all.

CAPITAL AND LABOUR

Ideas of toleration and liberty grew, especially in Western Europe, in the British Dominions and—to some extent—in the United States; both capitalists and socialists were realist in outlook. Lighting, housing and sanitary conditions improved; often not very quickly, and not quickly enough for Left-Wing leaders and slum-dwellers. Progress was made in regulation of hours and conditions of work, especially where women and children were concerned. Earlier nineteenth-century ideals, such as Freedom of Contract, were dropped, as, outside Great Britain, was Free Trade: Britain's older and more established industries, her large mercantile marine, and her much greater regard for industry than agriculture, made her case and symptoms different from those of other nations. Germany favoured high tariffs. Despite her Prussianism and rigidity, this latter country was ahead of other Powers in the matter of pensions and insurance: Bismarck hoped to wean the working-class from socialism by bread and circuses brought up to date.

Both Capital and Labour worked in combines rather than individually: trusts were typical of one side, trade unions of the other. Founded in 1864, the First International, an association of working-men from many lands, was a small and not very powerful body: the Franco-German War and the failure of the Paris Commune disappointed it, and no meetings were held after 1873. Karl Marx had expelled the Anarchist members who criticized him; the First International dissolved in '76. The continued life of international socialism, especially in Germany, where it was most powerful, was due to the energy of middle-class admirers like Liebknecht, Lassalle, and Jaurès; in Germany, fervent oratory was contributed by a man of artisan stock, August Bebel.

The Social Democratic Party of solid progressive Germany was founded in 1875 on the lines of Marxian Socialism. In Southern Europe and Russia, backward conditions led to extremism and a distrust of new-fangled Westernizing Parliamentary government. Bakunin, violent and agnostic as ex-officers are likely to be when they go Left, was typical of this reaction: he was expelled from the First International. Meanwhile, socialist delegates from many countries had met in Paris in 1889 and founded a Second International, a somewhat ineffective body which talked a great deal, held congresses and naturally failed to prevent the War of 1914–18.

PROGRESS IN SCIENCE AND MEDICINE

The part played by electricity can scarcely be exaggerated. Electric light, of a kind, existed in 1876, but the first adequate electric lamp was that patented by Edison in 1879. In the more purely scientific world, there followed the experiments of Hertz and Maxwell in electromagnetism and of Thomson in the conduction of electricity through gases. Stupendous discoveries were made by Röntgen with his X-rays at Würzburg and by the Curies with radium at Paris.

Through electro-chemistry developed the study of thermodynamics. Yet more important for the average man-in-the-street and student was the progress of biology. Partly it came through Pasteur's experiments in bacteriology; partly through the works of Darwin. *The Origin of Species* was followed in 1871 by *The Descent of Man*, which developed Lamarck's theory that characteristics are hereditarily transmitted. A dispute followed. Weismann of Freiburg opposed Darwin, and the Augustinian monk, Mendel, suggested that certain characteristics might be transmitted as unchangeable units. Archaeology and palaeontology helped this study of the origin of man. Schliemann's excavations at Troy and at Mycenae showed that intelligent civilizations existed at dates earlier than those deduced from the Authorized Version for the Creation, and the discovery of the Cro-Magnon skeletons in 1868 confirmed the theory, based on the Neanderthal excavations, as to the vast length of man's life upon the earth.

But it was in the sphere of medicine that the greatest progress was made. Two great landmarks were Lister's work on antiseptics, and Pasteur's discovery of the germs that caused disease. The German Koch developed Jenner's practice of inoculation, and discovered the germs of anthrax and cholera. Lock-jaw and malaria were conquered in turn. Apart from cancer, septicaemia, infantile paralysis and the more intense attacks of influenza, the road to health seemed clear. The psychologists attacked the problem from another angle, and, in diagnosing nervous troubles, combined the rôles of doctor and schoolmaster. By 1912 it was clear that humanity had the knowledge to build a remarkable age, if it were unhampered by war.

CHAPTER 75

THE ROAD TO WORLD WAR

THE Treaty of Berlin had little chance of long life. Russia could not abandon her march towards Constantinople, whose importance, since the spread of industrialization, had become not only strategic and sentimental, but also economic. Threatened with disintegration from Balkan rebellions, the Turkish Empire was more sick than ever, despite the new lease of life provided by the Berlin Treaty. The Eastern Question grew increasingly acute, until it finally blazed into the World War.

A *rapprochement* between Russia and France grew from the tendency at St. Petersburg to feel that Germany had failed her Russian friends. France was eager to find an ally, and especially to have one on the German eastern frontier. The friendship between Germany and Austria–Hungary grew stronger, and further estranged Germany from Russia, Austria's rival in the Balkans. However, for ten years after the Treaty of Berlin, Bismarck managed to preserve that understanding between the three great continental nations of Europe which went by the grandiloquent name of the League of the Three Emperors and lasted until 1888, when it disappeared before the close alliance between Germany and Austria, broadened to include Italy in 1882. In case of a French attack, Italy was assured of her allies' support, and she pledged hers in case of a French attack on Germany. If one or two of the allies were attacked by two other Powers, all three members of the Triple Alliance promised to act together. In view of later events, it is interesting to note that Italy specified that she would in no case fight Great Britain: gratitude existed in Italy for Britain's sympathy during the War of Liberation, and the guns of the British fleet increased the unpopularity, in a country with a long and exposed coast-line, of war with the greatest naval power. The unnatural alliance of Italy with her old tyrant Austria, still ruling over three-quarters of a million Italians, was due to the tact and skill of Bismarck, who exploited Italian hatred of France, which revived when the latter country established a protectorate over Tunis: the Italian Government had looked on this as a desirable nucleus for her own second empire in Africa.

GERMANY AND THE QUEST FOR COLONIES

England remained for twenty-five years outside the orbit of alliances. Her sympathies lay mostly with the Middle European *bloc*. Such a state of affairs was made likely by dynastic ties with Germany; by traditional friendship with Austria and Italy, who interfered nowhere with British aspirations; and by traditional hostility towards France and Russia, who competed in most quarters of the globe. Expecially was there no quarrel with Bismarckian Germany. Busy with his struggles against the Church and the Social Democrats, the Chancellor had little time or patience for interests outside Europe, and he keenly desired to maintain British friendship, though he seems to have despised British men and women as individuals. With regard to the nascent, colonial ambitions of some of his fellow-countrymen, Bismarck said that "It was as foolish for a young Germany to chase after colonies as for the nobles of old Poland to cover themselves with finery when they lacked shirts". So the German government had no hesitation in acquiescing readily in the establishment of British control over Cyprus and Egypt, and in the considerable extension of the British Empire that occurred during the "Grab for Africa" period.

However, Germany took her share. The colonial enthusiasts were powerful enough for that. In 1884, Togo, the Cameroons and German South-West Africa were annexed, while in the following year the valuable territory between Lake Tanganyika and the sea was taken over by the German East African Company; it passed to the Reich in 1890. Hamburg and the seaports particularly welcomed a new commercial outlet, while Joseph Chamberlain spoke of Anglo-Saxon brotherhood and held out a hand to the United States. On the other hand, the British Government countered a disagreeable proposal to build a railway from German South-West Africa to the Transvaal by annexing the intervening Bechuanaland. There was friction, but on the whole Germany and Great Britain showed mutual readiness to settle minor colonial disputes; the position appeared brighter than ever when, in 1890, after Bismarck's fall, Britain exchanged Heligoland and recognized the German rights on the African East coast in return for Uganda, four million marks and the Zanzibar protectorate. Further, Whitehall showed no objection to Italy's then modest designs in the Mediterranean, and countenanced the Obrenovich dynasty in Serbia and the rule of Ferdinand of Bulgaria, both of them satellites of the Triple Alliance.

There were, however, many clashes with France and Russia. After their unsuccessful war with Germany, the French turned with renewed interest to the task of building an empire overseas. Bismarck encouraged them in this; he hoped that they would forget Alsace-Lorraine and spoil their chances of friendship with England. Perhaps the stormiest centre was Egypt. Here a Dual Control of Britain and France had existed from 1876, the year after Disraeli's purchase of the Suez Canal shares, until 1882, when the French backed out of the suppression of Arabi Pasha. Tel-el-Kebir was the decisive battle: the restored Khedive was now the puppet of Britain. France was very angry. Dr. Lesseps had built the Suez Canal, Frenchmen had introduced the cotton plant and pioneered in the construction of Egyptian dams, Mehemet Ali and his successors had been lovers of French civilization and proclaimed their will to "franciser l'Egypte". Russia and Turkey, too, condemned British policy in Egypt, which Bismarck was wise enough to support. Britain remained dominant and, although temporarily rebuffed by the Mahdi's success and Gordon's death in the Sudan, arrived at an understanding with Italy over the possibility of an eventual partition of Abyssinia, and finally reconquered the Sudan as Egypt's friend and champion. At the other end of the North African coast, France was laying the foundations of a great Empire and a dusky army in Algiers, Tunis and Senegal.

Meantime the French suspected British missionaries in Madagascar, scrambled with British imperialists in West Africa, and argued over the right to catch, as well as to fish, in Newfoundland, and to claim the remote New Hebrides. In Asia, France annexed Annam and Tonkin, and Britain subsequently annexed Burma. Elsewhere British and Russian interests clashed all around the Indian frontier, in Persia, Afghanistan, Tibet and China.

Undoubtedly British sympathies were rather with the Triple than with the Dual Alliance, though the country held itself aloof in a position of self-imposed isolation. Bismarck's successor, the soldier Caprivi, was friendly to Great Britain, and when he fell before agrarian attacks in 1894, the new Chancellor, the seventy-five-year-old Prince Hohenlohe, was not unfriendly. An agreement was reached over the Fiji Islands; England acquiesced in the German seizure of Kaiochow, and there seems to have been some agreement over the partition of the Portuguese colonies. In 1898, Lord Salisbury sounded the Berlin Government over a possible Anglo-German alliance; the scheme fell through, partly because the German demands were excessive and partly because Germany was unwilling to oust Russia as much as England wished. Some *entente* between the two nations was again attempted by both Governments in the following year; but Great Britain was unwilling to join the Triple Alliance, and the Kaiser unwilling to accept Joseph Chamberlain's policy. It is significant that Cecil Rhodes favoured an Anglo-German agreement: he desired to promote what Chamberlain somewhat inaccurately termed the reunion of the "two Anglo-Saxon branches", and wanted Portuguese rather than German colonies to round off his South African scheme.

Change came with the Boer War. Public opinion on the Continent regarded England as a greedy bully and ignored her claims to protect British nationals, among the Uitlanders on the Rand mines, who were being shabbily treated by the obscurantist Boer government. Rude French caricatures of Queen Victoria were unpopular in London, but not so widely criticized as the telegram of congratulation sent to President Kruger by the Kaiser on the former's suppression of the Jameson Raid. Austria and Italy remained friendly to Britain, while Russia seems twice to have attempted to draw Germany into an alliance, if not a revised Armed Neutrality, against this country.

However, it was Germany's unexpected hostility which particularly disappointed Englishmen, as in 1895 it had made Japan resentful. Reports from consuls began to show that the more ingratiating manners and cheaper wares of German commercial travellers were beginning to oust British goods from certain continental markets; the Kaiser meanwhile talked of a policy of encirclement on the part of his foes, into whose camp his ambitious policy of naval and colonial development threatened to drive the Government of Great Britain.

ACCORD BETWEEN FRANCE AND BRITAIN

The accession of Edward VII marked a change. The new King had many pleasant memories of Paris and disliked his braggart, unbalanced nephew, William II. The appointment of Delcassé as Foreign Minister and Cambon as French Ambassador to London in 1898 brought to the front two diplomats extremely keen to promote an understanding with England. Lansdowne, the British Foreign Minister, was ready for a settlement; the Germanophil views of Chamberlain and others had grown milder since the Boer War. In 1903, the King visited Paris, and his visit was speedily returned by Loubet, the first French President to come to England. A committee was set up to discuss points in dispute between the two countries; this was a step towards the convention signed in April 1904, whereby France recognized British claims in Egypt and Britain those of France in Morocco, while boundary disputes were settled in West Africa and along the Indo-Chinese frontier; agreement was also reached over proprietary rights in Madagascar and the New Hebrides and over the Newfoundland fisheries. The Anglo-French *entente* had become an accomplished fact. For the moment, Britain, as ally of Japan, could scarcely agree with their common enemy Russia, the ally of France. However, the Far Eastern air was soon to be cleared by war, and did not hinder the rapid improvement which was taking place in Anglo-French relations.

Despite the growth of foreign competition, British wealth increased and Britain remained the banker, the workshop and the carrier of the world. British wealth, estimated at six thousand million pounds sterling in 1865, rose to nearly eleven thousand million in 1895, and reached the fourteen thousand million mark in 1910. Population had increased, but not so rapidly as the national wealth. Expenditure and revenue developed enormously; that the state accepted other duties in addition to providing for the protection of the citizen is shown by the great increase of the amount spent in the civil service.

POLITICAL CHANGES IN BRITAIN

Forty years of mostly Liberal rule came to an end in 1886, to be succeeded by a period of twenty years during which the Conservatives were supreme. The Liberals who seceded over the Irish question gave a new and progressive fillip to the Conservative party, which was still alive with Disraeli's Tory Democracy. Gladstone's unwillingness to acquire colonies—one of the few traits he shared with Bismarck—seemed unpatriotic in the light of the new England overseas for which Rhodes and Chamberlain had laboured and whose ideologist was Kipling. The importance of Joseph Chamberlain can scarcely be sufficiently stressed. Typical of middle-class businessmen who found Gladstone old-fashioned and doctrinaire, he was a keen reformer, and, as Mayor of Birmingham, was responsible for clearing away slums and for giving his city a decent supply of gas and water. Meantime, Socialism grew with the desire for more thorough reforms; John Burns was much more extreme than John Bright, and largely responsible for the great dock strike; in 1893 Keir Hardie initiated a conference at Bradford which originated the Independent Labour Party on Marxist lines.

In other ways, the Boer War showed that Britain was changing. The unpopularity which this country had then to experience made Englishmen face the danger of a hostile world-coalition of less wealthy Powers: the alliances with France and Japan were foreshadowed. Again, a series of defeats convinced a large section of the population that the country was in a state of military unpreparedness, and ultimate victory led to a newly-confident imperialism. The counterblast was David Lloyd George. Like more than one candidate for the Presidency of the United States, he claimed to be cottage-bred; he was actually the son of a typical elementary school head-teacher. Ready even as a boy to attack the squirearchy, he was careful to speak of Welsh nationalism as "home-rule all round", and his power over Wales was unexampled in modern history. Great gifts of oratory, ardour and charm, which were combined with a mastery of detail, pushed him rapidly to the forefront.

To Lloyd George, the duke was "more of a danger than the Death's Head Hussar". His common-sense and proletarian contacts enabled him to realize the great steps made by the Germans in social reform; while his limited knowledge of European history kept him from a full realization of the German menace. In a series of speeches, he celebrated his appointment as Chancellor of the Exchequer by announcing that he meant to spend public money on social reform, rather than on supposed military needs, and to tax the "very shabby rich men". Limehouse heard this last epithet, and Birmingham witnessed his escape in policeman's uniform after an attack on imperialism and all that the local idol, Chamberlain, stood for.

In 1906, the Liberals began their period of power, which was to last into the First World War. The chief cause of the Conservative downfall was Chamberlain's policy of protective tariffs, not readily understood in a country whose commerce had become supreme during an era of free trade. An ambitious programme of social reform introduced health insurance for workers, more humane conditions for child-welfare, and old-age pensions, while reversing the Taff Vale decision, which had made trade-union funds responsible for strike damages. Conservatives, at any rate in the Commons, voted frequently for these reforms. A change came when, to provide for the ambitious policy of social reform and the increased needs of the Services, Lloyd George brought in his Budget of 1909, which upset the tempers and threatened to ruin the pockets of the middle classes. On a party vote, the House of Lords threw out the Budget. In the general election of 1910, the Conservatives gained seats and equalled the Liberals, who were kept in power by the new Labour Party and by the Irish Nationalists.

Henceforward, restriction of the House of Lords' veto, disestablishment of the Welsh Church, and Irish Home Rule were the main planks in the Liberal programme. The first two measures succeeded, though Home Rule proved to be as much of a stumbling-block as it was in Gladstone's time. The year 1911 showed British citizens their soldiers guarding British railways in a great strike, Winston Churchill at the Admiralty and the threat of Civil War in Ireland. European enemies might well conjecture that the moment for attack was near. It says much for the political honesty of Britain that her statesmen did not seek for the solution of her domestic troubles in war.

FRANCE'S MATERIAL PROSPERITY

The spirit of revenge for Alsace-Lorraine was tempered by the growth of a French empire overseas. Under the premiership of Jules Ferry in the early 'eighties, France acquired Tunisia, Indo-China, Madagascar and part of Somaliland. By 1912, the Empire was fourteen times the size of France. Much of it was desert, but its population amounted to thirty millions; treated on equal terms by the French authorities, these people adopted the French régime.

Meantime, the country grew immensely in both agricultural and industrial wealth. French capital increased from two to three hundred billion francs between 1872 and 1913; the peasant was relatively happy, not only because farming improved, but also because the government skilfully kept down direct and imposed on him indirect taxes. An intellectual swing towards Catholicism was accompanied by the threat of dictatorship on the part of a popular, supposedly Radical, general called Boulanger. His triumph would probably have meant war with the Germans, who might have taken advantage of his chauvinist speeches to declare war on France. However, his courage failed before a threat of arrest, and he fled to Brussels—to pass swiftly from history and die two years later.

FRENCH POLITICAL QUESTIONS

A revival on the Right was accompanied by development on the Left. Leaders of first-class calibre, Briand, Jaurès and Millerand, began to appear. France was backward in educational and social reform; first steps had to be taken as regards pensions, insurance, working-hours and elementary education. Two great scandals embittered the French world. The first concerned a scheme to dig a Panama canal, which went bankrupt, largely as the result of corruption on the part of politicians, bankers and journalists. Many of them were Jews and the anti-Semitic drive increased. In France, it was associated with growing mistrust of the banking system, and the irritation caused by commercial failure. This hatred brought Alfred Dreyfus, a Jewish captain of artillery, to trial for espionage on behalf of Germany. He was convicted on doubtful evidence and sent to Devil's Island. Though pardoned in 1899, he was not reinstated till 1906. Meanwhile the injustice he had suffered weakened the Conservatives, and the Radicals won the elections of 1902.

Unfortunately, the consequence was a display of anti-Christian intolerance as stupid as anything in the preceding régime. The part played by monks and nuns in education was countered by a law prohibiting them from teaching at all, and even compelling them to emigrate. The excessive property of the Church became the pretext for a confiscation all the more unjust because it repudiated the obligation to compensate the clergy undertaken by the Government during the Great Revolution in return for a then partial seizure of ecclesiastical lands. Combes was responsible for the measure; he had behind him Clemenceau, a French Lloyd George. For two years, there was a bitter struggle before the success of the more politic Briand, whose efforts left the clergy the right to use their churches for worship.

The era of Liberal reform was accompanied by strikes, as in England, and by a development of the Socialist party, as in that country and Germany. Movements of revolt took place; wine-growers went on strike during the vintage, farm-labourers during the harvest; even the soldiers mutinied. Yet Jean Jaurès, the Socialist leader, was probably the sanest influence in French politics. Labour troubles and anti-clericalism played their parts. To console Germany for French hegemony in Morocco, she was given part of French West Africa. But the tide turned again, and the drift to war grew greater, when the logical, middle-class, chauvinist Poincaré became Prime Minister. His military reforms strengthened the French army, but played into the hands of the Russian war-party. As armaments grew on all sides, lovers of peace began correspondingly to despair.

GERMANY'S FOREIGN AND DOMESTIC DEVELOPMENT

The eighteen-eighties found Germany with a competent bureaucracy, well ahead with social reforms and possessed of an educational system which was excellent in a rather narrow way. The country's head had been turned by rapid success and was caricatured by the outlook of the clever, unstable, megalomaniac Emperor. Any doubt as to whether the House of Bismarck or that of Hohenzollern should dominate was determined by the Kaiser's dramatic gesture in "dropping the pilot" in 1890. Germany's course was scarcely changed; but the steersmanship was inferior; neither the Emperor nor the four chancellors who succeeded Bismarck were of first-class ability; the chancellors were appointed, controlled and dismissed by the Emperor.

Domestic politics became increasingly difficult with the rise of the Socialist party under Bebel. William II had at first hoped to win them by a mild flirtation with Left-Wing principles; one of the causes of his quarrel with Bismarck was the latter's refusal to drop his anti-Socialist policy. But the Emperor could not forgive the Socialists their republicanism; indeed, he went so far as to say that they were "unworthy to be called Germans".

Meantime the country developed in population from forty to sixty-five millions, and in coal production and export trade threefold, between 1878 and 1912. Emigration fell to the low figure of twenty-five thousand a year, though even colonial enthusiasts repeatedly urged the necessity of preventing German talent from leaving German soil. Nevertheless colonial development increased rapidly, and it was accompanied by naval expansion, both policies being promoted by Tirpitz and other new men, who had been appointed at the Emperor's instigation after Bismarck's fall.

A more suave and clever influence came to the Chancellery with the accession of Bülow in 1900. Like the Kaiser, more interested in foreign than in domestic affairs, he tried to keep the home front quiet and actually succeeded in materially reducing the strength of the Social-Democratic party in the Reichstag. But Bülow's effort to improve Germany's place in the sun was not lightened by the exposure of moral scandals concerning some of the Emperor's closest friends, or by some indiscreet utterances of William's published by

FRONTIERS OF

In 1912 the nations of Europe were divided into two antagonistic groups. Of the major powers, France, afraid of the German menace that had robbed her of Alsace and Lorraine in 1871, sought security in closer ties with Great Britain and Russia. Germany was building up her fleet and expanding her large army.

EUROPE IN 1912

The Austro-Hungarian Empire, ridden with unsolved minority questions and estranged from Russia, was allied to Germany. The Turkish Empire, whose weakness was apparent in her war of 1912 against Italy and the Balkan League (Bulgaria, Greece, Serbia, and Montenegro), supported Germany against Russia.

the *Daily Telegraph*, which united against him the Social-Democrats, the Pan-German League and English public opinion. He seems to have lost his nerve after this crisis. A section of Conservatives, abetted by the Crown Prince, censured Bülow for not having checked French designs in Morocco; the Chancellor thus lost his majority in the Reichstag at the instance of the class he was trying to protect, and resigned in 1909.

Bülow's successor was the honest, slow, high-principled Bethmann-Hollweg. His mild liberalism was in accord with the policy of the Kaiser and the majority of the Reichstag, but failed to reform the franchise or to placate the Poles and Alsace-Lorraine. In the latter, a series of clashes with the Prussian officer-caste inflamed an already grave situation, while the prolific birth-rate of the Catholic Poles increased their numerical superiority in many districts of Prussian Poland. Yet another omen of discord came with the Reichstag elections of 1912, which made the Social-Democrats the largest single party, with one hundred and twelve seats and four and a quarter million votes. Germany, like France and England, was faced with a serious domestic situation; in Germany, as in France, powerful groups began to feel that a foreign war would provide the most adequate solution of the problem in their own interests.

PARLIAMENTARY GOVERNMENT IN ITALY

A short period of prosperity which followed the capture of Rome ended in the financial crash of 1873. Three years later, the rôle of those men of the Right who had united Italy came to an end, and the Left began a period of supremacy which lasted, with minor interruptions, until the First World War. There was talk of reform, but little was accomplished, owing to the prevalent system of corruption under which votes, seats and members were bought and sold. Parliamentary government, associated with bribery, neglect and political mendacity, had few friends, except among the professional politicians. There was, however, a considerable amount of material development along familiar lines; there were plenty of new harbours, roads and railways; Milan surpassed Lyons as the chief silk market of the world, though Genoa continued to lag behind Marseilles as the chief port of the Mediterranean. Most of the advance was in the North; the South continued to be the prey of brigands, disease and illiteracy. Unlike Germany, Italy's tide of emigration swelled to the huge figure of half a million in the year 1910.

The political leaders—Depretis, Crispi and Giolitti—were not great men, though the last was an adept demagogue, whose promises at election-time were fulsome enough to keep him in almost dictatorial power between 1903 and 1914. The accession of Victor Emmanuel III in 1900 gave the country a King who must be credited with the effort to remove the harsh conditions of life which had led to the death of ninety Milanese in the riots of 1898 and his own father's assassination, two years later. But Victor Emmanuel could not prevent the increasing bitterness between chauvinism and socialism, which distracted Italy and most of Europe. The new nationalism grew with economic prosperity. There were demands for colonies. The Irredentist party demanded the redemption of Italian territory still under foreign rule, and found its poet in d'Annunzio, with his memories of pagan Rome, his Latin style and imperial manner. The Abyssinian campaign of the 'nineties had ended in humiliating defeat; but a war with Turkey in 1911–12, secured Tripolitania and Cyrenaica for Italy. The outbreak of war between Greece and Turkey facilitated Italian retention of the Islands of the Dodecanese. But taxation had to be increased, with the result that Giolitti's ministry was violently attacked. To placate the Left, he brought in various reforms, some—like universal suffrage—long overdue. Nevertheless, he was defeated, in the general elections, by the Conservative, chauvinist, Anti-Austrian party of Salandra, which was to guide Italian destinies during the First World War.

THE PROBLEMS OF THE HABSBURG EMPIRE

Austria had been expelled from Italy and from the German Empire. The rise of Russia and of the Balkan States prevented her from seeking her traditional compensation in the east for reverses in the west, while within the Dual Monarchy nationalism threatened the end of the oldest Empire in Europe. The Emperor grew old along with his Empire. Well-meaning but of limited ability, he had the misfortune to find no first-class brain among his statesmen, once Metternich was gone.

In 1879 began the ministry of Taaffe, which lasted fourteen years. Taaffe justified his theory that all the subject-nations of the polyglot Empire should be equal by playing one off against the other. He persuaded the Czechs to return to Parliament, at the risk of embittering the Bohemian-Germans; he kept the support of the Polish landowners of Galicia by letting them do what they would with the Ruthenian peasantry; and he was liked by the most civilized of South Slav races, the Slovenes, who found themselves much better treated by Austria than were their Serb and Croat kinsmen by Hungary. These friendly subject-peoples he united in a quaint alliance with nobles and clericals, and pursued a mild policy of reform, hoping thus to wean the poorer classes from subversive nationalism, which he not unjustly diagnosed as primarily a middle-class movement.

This revival of the traditional Austrian policy of "divide and rule" was defeated by the rise of a democratic Czech party under Thomas Masaryk. The brilliant son of an Imperial coachman, he was professor at the Czech University at Prague, which became the intellectual focus of national movements within the Austrian Empire. The Czech democrats disturbed the sittings of the Reichsrat with a series of scenes of successful rowdyism. In consequence, the Austrian

Ministry lost faith in Parliamentary Government, until it found a strange ally in Dr. Lueger. Lueger was for ten years Mayor of Vienna, where he did much towards giving that city its reputation for fine and humane public services. He also scotched the Liberal Catholic "Away from Rome" movement, which, with nationalism, was gaining ground in Bohemia. Lueger was a very Christian Socialist; his reforms and democratic speeches cut the ground from what remained, for the time, a purely intellectual movement with little popular teaching and a comparatively small following.

CROATS AND MAGYARS

Among the subject-peoples of Hungary the conditions were far worse than among those of Austria; the soldierly Magyar had little use for democracy and education, and he certainly felt them to be unsuited to Slavs and Rumanians. Many of these were very backward; among the Hungarians there is a proverb "The Slovene is not a man". But the Croats had a civilization intellectually often more developed than that of the Magyars; and the Serbs are a proud race. The Croats were granted some kind of control over their own affairs in 1868, twenty years after the same rights had been granted to the Hungarians; mindful of their loyalty to the Habsburgs during the revolutions of 1848, they said that they had received, as a reward for their loyalty, what the Magyars had received as a punishment for their disloyalty. The Viennese authorities were very stupid. Instead of welcoming the activities of the Croat Bishop Strossmayer, they turned against him, and Strossmayer's soul went into his Yugo-Slav Academy and the University of Agram, from both of which Masaryk learnt much. The situation in the South Slav provinces became much worse after the Dual Monarchy's purchase, in 1908, of Bosnia and Herzegovina, which Serbia had hoped to snatch.

Francis Ferdinand, heir to the throne, who, however, contracted a morganatic marriage, might have healed the wounds by his introduction of a triune monarchy, to embrace Croats as well as Austrians and Hungarians. He had studied events in the U.S.A., which country he persisted in supposing to have the same nationalist problems as his own. Francis Ferdinand, too, shared Taaffe's belief that the promotion of reform and improvement in the economic position of the poorer classes provided the best antidote to nationalism, which he regarded as a middle-class movement not so interesting to the worker as daily bread. It was his friend Beck who carried through the Reichsrath a measure giving the vote to every literate man over the age of twenty-four. Over the question of deputies, the various nations of the Empire were split; for the Italians, Poles, Germans, Slovenes and Rumanians received more favourable representation than the backward Ruthenes and the hostile Serbs, Croats and Czechs. In the General Election, the Socialists polled more than a million votes and became a new problem to the Central

Government, which earned their immediate dislike by gerrymandering constituencies at their expense before the elections held in 1911. Meantime, two energetic men, eager to assert Austrian prestige and initiative, rose to high positions—Aehrenthal, a Balkan specialist, to the Foreign Office, and Conrad von Hotzendorf, a fire-eating soldier, to be Chief of Staff. The former arranged the annexation of Bosnia and Herzegovina, succeeded in dominating the Balkan policy of the Triple Alliance, and enraged Russians and Serbs.

The Magyars opposed the measures of increased suffrage introduced by Beck. However, they feared the designs of Russia also, and in 1911 sent Count Tisza with a Liberal majority to the Budapest Chamber. Discontent grew in the Serb and Croat provinces. Returned Americans spread it; they found Magyar rule unbearable after acquaintance with trans-Atlantic ways.

Racial ill-feeling was intensified by the Agram trial of 1909, when, under pressure from Aehrenthal, Serb subjects were condemned in the Croatian capital on a charge of treason. His attempts to justify the sentence by the publication of Foreign Office documents brought Masaryk into the field with charges of forgery, and the Austrian Government lost caste badly in the eyes of the public.

Internal troubles increased in 1912. The Czechs were restless; the Poles, usually loyal, resented Bülow's expropriation of their kinsmen's land; to keep them quiet, Vienna stirred up the Ruthenes; Lemberg University was closed. Italy's Irredentist movement stirred Italians in Austria; they rioted at Graz, and forced the dissolution of the Tyrolese Diet. Two attempts were made to assassinate the new Governor of Croatia. The shadow of Sarajevo was creeping over the "ramshackle empire" which was ruled by the Habsburgs.

THE RUSSIAN EMPIRE

The Russian Empire was the largest after the British Empire. One-sixth of the world's surface and one-twelfth of its inhabitants were under Russia's flag. Her solid territory was dominated by the Great Russians, who numbered sixty millions out of a population which, at the first census in 1897, proved to be nearly 130 millions. Kindred racial and linguistic groups, the "Little Russians" (of the Ukraine) and "White Russians," supplied nearly thirty of the remaining millions. Advance was rapid. Population grew by one and a half million a year, a figure which would have been vastly increased had the infant mortality rate not been so high, and the people so backward and ignorant. Territorially, progress was swift; Bokhara and Samarcand were occupied in 1868, Khiva in 1873, and the Pamir ranges, near the Indian frontier, twenty years later.

Russia became the bogey of Western Europe. Backward and incompetent though the nation then was, its numbers and size, with the fear that they might soon be enormously increased, created the scare. The Tsar was more autocratic than other emperors, and his people used to refer to him as the "Little Father". The bureau-cracy was inefficient and the Court corrupt, but so long as Alexander II lived, there were prospects of improvement. He had freed the serfs and created the *zemstvos* (or provincial councils), which were followed in 1870 by the *dumas*, or town councils. But reform from above seemed hopeless and unreal. The live movements of the late nineteenth century were that of the Pan-Slavs and that of the Anarchists; the latter, after various unsuccessful attempts to assassinate the Tsar, Alexander II, succeeded most inopportunely in 1881, on the eve of his intended promulgation of a constitution.

REACTION AND WEAKNESS WITHIN RUSSIA

Alexander III succeeded to the throne. Stupid, well-intentioned and clumsy, his reactionary policy made the fall of the Romanovs certain, just as the similar policy of Louis XV had ended in disaster for the Bourbon dynasty in France. The most important ministers were Plehve, Chief of Police, of Lithuanian extraction, and Pobedo-nostsev, who, as Procurator of the Holy Synod, was lay head of the Orthodox Church. Both were reactionary and largely responsible for the fact that, by the end of Alexander's reign, the percentage of illiterates was higher in Russia than elsewhere in Europe. The appointment of Witte to be Minister of Communications in 1892 and Minister of Finance in the following year brought to the front the ablest Russian statesman of the period. A native of the Caucasus, where his father was an important civil servant, Witte had much of the bluntness, industry and business capacity of his Dutch ancestors. Though a supporter of autocracy, he was a greater champion of Westernization than Russia had had since Peter the Great. Witte put the country on the gold standard, was largely responsible for the building of the Trans-Siberian railway, and secured the vodka monopoly for the Government.

The accession of Nicholas II in 1894 made little difference. The new Emperor was weaker, but as reactionary and absolutist as his predecessor. Plehve and Pobedonostsev continued in office, as did Witte, though the last was dropped in 1903; Nicholas did not like him as Alexander had done, and listened to the Russian landowners who loathed Witte's development of industrial, as opposed to agri-cultural interests. After the Russo-Japanese War, the Tsar brought back Witte to put some order into Russian finances; but he was soon dropped again.

Socialism was growing. A split in 1903 brought the Bolshevik (Majority) and Menshevik (Minority) parties into existence, with Lenin as a leader of the former. After securing Witte's fall, Plehve and the reactionaries tried to crush Socialism. They failed, and the Socialist movement was swelled by patriots of the minority nations suffering from the Russification policy, and by propaganda in workshops and at the Universities. Defeat in the war with Japan and the brutal shooting of an orderly mob on "Bloody Sunday" in St. Petersburg in 1905 was followed by the assassination of the Grand Duke Serge, naval mutiny and a revolt which was suppressed partly by armed force and partly by concessions, granted all the more easily because Plehve had been killed during the revolution. Religious toleration alleviated the grievances of the Protestants; the use of the Polish language in private schools was permitted.

For a time, the future looked a little brighter. A loan was floated in Paris and the *entente* with England secured financial help from London. In the elections for the new Duma, the moderate Left triumphed, but the Government continued to be interested in the Assembly so long as hope remained of a loyal peasant party; the Duma was little more than a debating society in which protests could be registered. Meantime a Liberal middle-class party, known as the "Cadets", or Constitutional Democrats, arose under Miliukov, and secret societies drawn from the ranks of the middle-class, known as the Black Hundred, beat up Socialists in the villages.

STOLYPIN'S POLICY

Reaction triumphed again. Witte's skilful persuasion secured for Tsardom loans from France and England which gave the Government a new lease of life. Then Witte was dropped, to be replaced by Goremykin, an old man who was a mere tool in the hands of the reactionary forces. The foreign loan had made the Central Government independent of the Duma, which was dissolved on the ground that it had failed to co-operate with the Emperor. The Cadets withdrew to Viborg in Finland, where they opposed the reactionary measures and urged the people to refuse to pay taxes or render military service. When the vigorous reactionary Stolypin succeeded Goremykin, they found their clubs suppressed.

Stolypin proposed to "pacify" the country and then reform it. Apart from his policy towards the Cadets, his energies first devoted themselves to the disfranchisement of Central Asia; henceforth, Asiatic Russia returned only fifteen representatives, of whom half were the nominees of the Cossack Armies. Elsewhere, an electoral redistribution gave more power to the middle classes at the expense of the poorer classes.

The economic development of the country was rapid. If the people's well-being was neglected, the enormous and speedy increase in national wealth should not be overlooked. Railways and banks developed very considerably between 1905 and 1914; though economically behind Britain and Germany, Russia was on a par with France and Italy. Cheap labour helped this industrialization: the miserable conditions under which the people worked encouraged Chauvinists to another anti-foreign bout directed especially against Germans and Jews. This led to a further estrangement from the Central Powers, and plunged the dagger of a revolutionary into

Stolypin's heart. But this murder at the Kiev Opera House in 1911 came too late to mend the situation. Reaction continued in a less efficient way under the unwholesome neurotic influence of the Tsarina and Rasputin. The Minister of Agriculture said in 1912, "We want thirty years of peace", but the business men wanted Constantinople. In Russia, perhaps more than anywhere else, the propertied classes saw in war relief from the dangers of Socialism.

BACKWARDNESS OF THE BALKAN STATES

These little countries which had been the chief interest of the settlement of 1878 were to be the occasion of the war of 1914. Rulers counted more in the Balkans than elsewhere; parliaments were new toys and the people as yet counted for little.

Rumania was, in a way, the senior state. She was the nearest to Western Europe, she was vaguely Latin, and she had the most important cohesive minority in Austria-Hungary. With a Hohenzollern dynasty, it was natural that her political institutions and army should be modelled on those of Prussia. But her morals were Byzantine and her rulers had for long been Greeks. Bucarest hovered between being a second-rate Paris and a second-rate Berlin, the people preferring the former alternative and the King the latter. After 1883, Rumania was in secret alliance with Austria-Hungary and attached herself to the Triple Alliance. There had been a considerable agricultural development, due to a black earth as rich as that of the Ukraine: oil and some industries had developed, to the advantage of native and foreign capitalists.

Domestic issues played a small part in Balkan history during this period. In Bulgaria—the Scotland or Prussia of the Balkans—progress was most marked. The first German prince did not last long there, but he was succeeded by the cunning Ferdinand, the Balkan "fox", who soon proved himself to be both a good German and a good Bulgarian: he was friendly to the Triple Alliance and had only five per cent. of illiterates among his recruits. Until 1892, he depended largely upon the peasant demagogic politician Stambulov; but after the latter's assassination in 1895, Ferdinand was in control of Bulgarian government.

Serbia was backward. The murder of King Alexander and Queen Draga in 1903 did, however, end the feud between two rival dynasties for the Serbian throne. The new King Peter and his minister Pasitch had both much of the democrat, as well as the chauvinist, in them. Education scarcely existed in Serbia, but her wheat and pigs prospered; as a source of food supply, she became increasingly useful to the Central Powers.

The most prosperous of the Balkan States—she scarcely regarded herself as Balkan—was Greece where, despite corrupt politicians and a neglected people, national prosperity increased with surprising rapidity. Athens bristled with a hundred factories; a thousand miles of railway were built and the merchant service developed, especially in the Levant. The Cretan Venizelos became prominent when he refused to lower the Greek flag at Canea in 1897. Warships of the Great Powers had to shoot it down.

Venizelos entered the Greek Government in the following year, and immediately began his feud with the royal house. In and out of office, he succeeded in uniting Crete with Greece and in pushing through reforms which promoted education and the fight against malaria, suppressed brigandage, and attempted to lay the foundations of an honest civil service. Of different race from her Slav neighbours, Greece might well have found recompense for the modification of territorial aspirations, so far as Turkey was concerned, in return for commercial and financial agreements; but the Porte pursued a stupid policy of opposition to Greek aspirations.

The inevitability of war was made more certain by Italy's entry into the Eastern Mediterranean, when she seized the Dodecanese during the war with Turkey. King George's assassination brought to the Greek throne the chauvinist and military hero Constantine. While Serbs were thinking of war with Austria, Greeks meditated a second war with Turkey to complete the work of the first.

In Turkey there was, for long, talk of reform, but little else, while the Empire slowly disintegrated. Railways developed and spread Western ideas to remote parts of the Empire. The names of Enver Bey and Mustafa Kemal became prominent in the Young Turk movement, which had as its aim a revived Turkey.

THE MINOR POWERS OF WESTERN EUROPE.

Here, at last, with one exception, the record is one of steady, peaceful progress. The wisdom of the ruling classes released Norway from Sweden peacefully and gave home rule to the Danish possessions of Iceland and the Faroë Islands; the wisdom of great socialists like Branting and Vandervelde governed the path of reform.

Norway had a merchant marine surpassed only by that of Britain, Germany and the United States. Sweden possessed more shipping tonnage than its larger neighbour, Russia, and was a comfortable land of big estates and increasing prosperity. Emigration to America was considerable, but that seems to have been due to love of adventure as much as to unpromising conditions for the poor man at home. Overshadowed though Sweden was by Russia, her people were always capable of holding some stronghold for liberty of thought, as they had done in the seventeenth century. Sweden was aristocratic, a lowland country of big estates; Norway had an ancient democratic constitution, mountains and small farms. The Norwegian constitution limited the power of the Crown more than did that of Sweden, so that the nineteenth-century monarch tended to prefer the Swedes, and find in Stockholm a mellow, attractive place in which to live.

Oscar II refused to allow the Norwegians to appoint their own consular officials. They already complained, as had the Belgians of the Dutch, that the Swedes kept for themselves far too large a control over the civil service. A plebiscite confirmed the Norwegian Parliament's demand for independence in 1905, and Sweden sensibly agreed. A feeling of Scandinavian unity grew, when a Danish prince became King of Norway.

Rich in her colonial empire, whose value increased with the development of world-trade, Holland prospered. So did Belgium, despite bickerings between the Flemish and the Walloon or French-speaking section of the community; her development of the Congo Free State gave her many valuable raw materials. Switzerland became probably the most democratic state in Europe; she also made admirable cheap watches and milk chocolate. Portugal overthrew the monarchy and broke with Rome.

Spain had no revolution; yet one seemed always imminent. Although the Conservative and Liberal parties stood for much the same *status quo*, Socialism grew and found strong supporters among the Catalans and Basques, whose demand for home rule was ignored by the Spanish Government. In the background lurked always the menace of the Carlists, clerical and conservative, but ready to work with agnostic Socialists against the Madrid Government. The Philippines and Cuba were lost in 1898—to attacks by the United States—but Spain began to find compensation in Morocco. A Liberal Government broke off relations with the Pope and expelled the religious orders. In 1912 warfare became very likely. But Count Romanones' *coup d'état* restored relations with Rome, and Spain settled down to a conservative régime.

While historic prestige still perhaps made Spain and Sweden the most considerable of these countries, Holland, Belgium and Portugal had colonial empires more extensive than those possessed by Germany and Italy. These empires, too, had the added advantage of being especially rich in the important raw materials.

EUROPE DIVIDES INTO TWO ARMED CAMPS

Germany was not slow in testing the *Entente*. During the spring of 1905, the Kaiser's yacht anchored at Tangier. William landed, visited the Sultan's uncle, and informed him that he regarded the Sultan as the "independent sovereign of Morocco". This was a direct challenge to the French, who looked on that country as their rightful sphere of influence. France was not altogether sorry to let England see the German mailed fist: she wanted confirmation that the *Entente* was not merely an agreement over colonies, but a defensive alliance. However, England did nothing at the time of the Tangier incident, and William II won the appearance of a diplomatic triumph. The time for Germany's trial of strength was well chosen, for Russia had just suffered a crushing defeat at Mukden.

In 1906, a Conference met at Algeciras to discuss the Moroccan question. Britain loyally backed France, who had also the sympathy of Russia, Italy, Spain and the United States. The Conference accepted the majority of the reforms recommended by the French to the Sultan in the previous year: Tardieu declared that the Anglo-French *entente* had passed from the static to the dynamic stage, and French statesmen did their best to persuade Sir Edward Grey that Lord Lansdowne had promised them military help in case of war.

RUSSIA SWINGS TOWARDS BRITAIN AND FRANCE

Before long, the Dual developed into a Triple *Entente*. The Japanese defeat of Russia did much to allay England's fear of her in the East. Both countries had a mutual friend in France. In Russia, it was felt that Britain had helped to secure the mild terms of the Portsmouth Treaty, and the new Foreign Minister, Isyolsky, was pro-English. The Treaty of Algeciras gave Russian diplomats a chance of many talks with the British representatives. In 1907, the fleets of the two countries exchanged visits and a treaty was signed by which Persia was divided into two spheres of influence, Afghanistan passed largely under British influence, and Tibet was to some extent neutralized. The Treaty had violent opponents in Witte and Curzon, but its worth seemed proven by the fact that two such doughty patriots could agree in opposite senses that it did not give enough. It was followed by a *rapprochement* between Russia and Britain's ally, Japan.

The year 1908 brought a crisis in Europe which worsened Russia's relations with Austria. Isyolsky, anxious to preserve his plan of making Europe the main sphere of Russia's interest in foreign policy, wrote to Aehrenthal, the Austrian Foreign Minister, that he would be willing to recognize an Austrian annexation of Bosnia, Herzegovina and the Sanjak of Novibazar, in return for support in the opening of the Straits to Russian ships of war. Surprised and pleased, Aehrenthal agreed. Taking advantage of the Young Turk revolution and of Bulgaria's declaration of independence in 1908, he occupied Bosnia and Herzegovina. Europe was aghast. Even the Kaiser was angry; he felt that his ally should have consulted him first. Indeed, he could not but look with disfavour on a move bound to enrage Italy and to further the split with Russia.

Isyolsky found that Aehrenthal's move had made such a commotion that his own was impossible. For the time being, violent opposition from the Pan-Slavists occupied him; he was accused of betraying Russian interests and being the tool of Austria. He developed a hatred of the Central Powers which he displayed both during the remainder of his term as Foreign Minister, and after his transfer as Ambassador to Paris in 1910.

Serbia also became henceforward much more hostile to Austria, who had deprived her of the chance of winning from moribund

Turkey provinces populated by her kinsmen. Only King Peter's moderation prevented the Serbs from taking a rash step in 1908 instead of in 1914. The bellicose Crown Prince George became a national hero; he was Saint George and Austria the dragon, and the windows of the Russian Embassy in Belgrade were broken by patriots angry at what they took to be Isyolsky's weakness. As a result there followed a bitter series of recriminating trials. For the time being, Serbia could only content herself with the fact that Austrian troops had not cut her communication with her kinsmen in Montenegro by annexing Novibazar; Turkey was compensated for the loss of two provinces, long beyond her effective control, by the payment of two and a half million pounds.

GROWING INTERNATIONAL TENSION

The storm-centre shifted to Morocco again. In 1911, a French occupation of Fez raised shrill protests in Germany against French imperialism in North Africa. The German gunboat *Panther* was sent to Agadir. At the time, neither Russia nor England were eager to risk war for the sake of French aggression; the former had recently come to an agreement with Germany over Persia, and the latter had no particular wish to help France progress in Morocco, though she did not want the German flag hoisted at Agadir. Isolated, France's inferiority became evident. In return for German recognition of her rights in Morocco, she ceded part of the Congo. England became alive to the gravity of the situation. Bosnia and Agadir were defeats to the *Entente*, whereas Algeciras had been a victory.

War was not far off in 1911, for part of the British fleet was mobilized and the British Chief of Staff, Wilson, sent to France to discuss the possibility of joint military action with the French authorities. As yet, however, the Kiel Canal was not finished, nor were Russian plans. There followed a last attempt at reconciliation—Lord Haldane's mission to Germany in 1912. He speedily made friends with Bethmann-Hollweg whom he called a "high-minded, sincere gentleman", but he could only promise British neutrality in case of an "unprovoked" attack on Germany. This was not enough for a country in which Admiral Tirpitz was strong, and the Berlin Government refused to modify its programme of naval development. In the same year, the chauvinist Poincaré came to the head of the government in France, and Turkey, who had just lost Libya and the Dodecanese to Italy, was routed by the Balkan League—pro-Russian and, at least in Serbia's case, anti-Austrian. The encirclement of the Central Empires was threatened and a dangerous foreign situation was complicated by the domestic difficulties already mentioned. War was near, and Bosnia seemed a likely spark for the powder-magazine.

PART XIV

THE LATEST AGE

CHAPTER 76

THE EUROPEAN UPHEAVAL

IN the first decade of the twentieth century the advance of science had seemed to promise almost limitless benefits to the progressive nations of Europe, America and Asia. Minor wars had ruffled the surface of peaceful progress, but there was a general feeling that the Foreign Offices of the Great Powers could adjust their differences and prevent the troubles of the smaller nations from destroying the Concert of Europe. Whatever difficulties there might be in the Balkans or North Africa, it seemed incredible to most civilized men and women in the splendid summer of 1914 that mankind would jeopardize its material gains by recourse to war.

On a sunny morning in June, the Archduke Francis Ferdinand of Austria-Hungary and his wife were shot by a student, Princip, in the streets of Sarajevo, a Bosnian town near the Serbian frontier. Princip hated the Habsburg Dual Monarchy, because his dreams of a kingdom of all the Serbs could not be realized while thousands of his fellow-countrymen lived, as he would have said, in captivity in a strange land. In particular, he hated the Archduke for his efforts to reconcile these Serbs to their "captivity" by giving them Home Rule: the Archduke wanted to turn the Dual Monarchy of Austrian-Germans and Hungarians over the Slavonic Serbs, Czechs and Slovaks into a Triple Monarchy of Germans, Hungarians and Slavs. So Princip killed Franz Ferdinand. He struck to bring down the Habsburg Empire, and with it he brought down Europe. Under the semi-collective security of twentieth-century alliances, an injury to one ally was an injury to all. And so, in the fullness of time, men from Manchester and Chipping Sodbury, from Capetown and San Francisco, from Amritsar and Melbourne, came to France to die.

There were two great problems in Europe before the War: a western and an eastern problem. The system of alliances linked up these two distinct controversies, and turned what might have been another local war into a World War. The first problem was that of France, Germany and England. For three centuries France had gradually pushed her frontier eastward, biting off little pieces of German-speaking territory. She assimilated them so thoroughly that there was no one more French and less German than the ordinary Lorrainer, although Lorraine became French for the first time in 1766. Poincaré, the incarnation of unyielding French nationalism, came from Lorraine. French expansion had been checked in 1870, when Bismarck founded the German Empire and annexed Alsace and Lorraine. From that time onward France and Germany had stood eyeing each other suspiciously—Germany afraid that France would try once again to make the Rhine her frontier, France terrified lest 1870 should be only the first of a series of wars of reconquest.

North of the Alps, France had a land frontier of about five hundred miles, most of it protected from invasion by hills. There were three possible routes of invasion, two of them closed by French fortifications; and the international guarantee-treaty was supposed to have closed the third by making Belgium into a neutral state.

WESTERN AND EASTERN PROBLEMS

If the Germans had not violated Belgian neutrality, the British peoples might not have been persuaded to fight; if Belgium had not been opposite the mouth of the Thames, the British Government would not have wanted to fight. England fought Germany in 1914 for the same reason that she fought Spain in 1600 and France in 1700 and 1800. It has always been an axiom of British foreign policy that the predominance in Europe of one great Power, particularly if that Power holds the coast and the ports opposite the mouth of the Thames, is a menace to Britain's safety.

By 1900, it was clear that Germany had replaced France as the the supreme military Power on the Continent. Britain might at one time have agreed that Germany should be supreme on land while she herself was supreme at sea, but the German demand for colonies— it was difficult to see how they were to be acquired except at Britain's expense—and the building of a great German navy destroyed any hope of compromise, and Britain found herself in Edward VII's reign driven into a friendly understanding with France. By 1914, that understanding had developed into something very like an alliance—l'Entente Cordiale—although only the inner circle of the British Cabinet knew how far France could count on their help in war. These men could not in honour have allowed Britain to remain neutral in 1914; but the obligation was to France, not Belgium. Britain guaranteed to respect Belgian neutrality; she did not guarantee to go to war with other countries which did not respect it.

The parties to the eastern problem were Austria, Russia and Turkey. Less than 250 years before, the Turkish armies had besieged Vienna; Turkey in Europe was now confined to a small strip of land to the north and west of Constantinople. The problem was how the country abandoned by the Turks was to be divided and governed. The earlier reconquests had been added either to Austria-Hungary or to Russia; the later reconquests, from the middle of the nineteenth century onwards, were made into more or less independent and largely barbarous little Balkan kingdoms. Serbia, for instance, had a record of political assassination almost unequalled in any country or century. Out of the relation of these poor and brutal states to the two large eastern Christian empires, the war of 1914 arose. Nine-teenth-century Englishmen laughed at Turkey, as the "sick man of Europe", but the two empires competing for his former possessions were only a little less sick. It was because of their fear lest any blow to their prestige should prove fatal, that the war started.

The weakness of Austria-Hungary was that it was built on a prin-ciple that no modern European could possibly approve. There could be no Austrian patriotism. Austria was the negation of nationalism: her peoples spoke German, Hungarian, Italian and half a dozen Slavonic languages. The people of the United States represent many nationalities, but they are bound together by a strong democratic sentiment—after nationalism, the strongest emotional force in the modern world. Austria-Hungary was not a democracy. The only bond of union was the person of the aged emperor, and only the officers of the army and the higher civil servants felt any great loyalty to him. The sort of feudal political organization he repre-sented had been out of date when he came to the throne, more than sixty years before. The French Revolution had killed it. In 1914, Austria-Hungary had been spiritually dead 125 years. There was, of course, plenty of patriotism in the Empire. There was German patriotism, Italian patriotism, Rumanian patriotism and Serbian patriotism, all looking outwards across the frontiers. In addition, there was Hungarian, Czech, Slovak and Polish patriotism. But there existed very little Austro-Hungarian patriotism as such.

RUSSIA'S ASSETS AND LIABILITIES

The weakness of Russia was her backwardness, her inefficiency and her tyranny. Russia was the most complete despotism of all the Great Powers, but hers was a despotism strictly limited by incom-petence. The only part of the Government which was really efficient was the police force. The Tsar's Government had somehow sur-vived the disastrous war with Japan in 1904, and had even managed to suppress, with great brutality, an attempted revolution in 1905. Its position, however, was precarious. A defeat in war was bound to be fatal, and a victorious war was almost impossible, so disorganized was the army and so poor the means of supplying it with food and munitions. At the same time, a severe blow to the national prestige abroad might equally well be fatal because of the almost universal disaffection at home. Russia, then, might find herself almost forced to go to war to save her "honour".

The Tsar's Government had only one asset—the spirit of Pan-Slavism, the belief that Russia was the big brother and protector of all the little Slav states of the Balkans against Habsburg imperialism. And so Serbia became the cause of war between Austria and Russia. Russia dared not allow Serbia to be destroyed by Austria, because if she did so, she could no longer claim to be the protector of all the Slav states and thus a crucial decision was forced on her.

E E   (H.W.)

The eastern and western European problems were linked up through the action of Germany. When Kaiser William came to the throne, he abandoned Bismarck's policy of a friendly understanding with the Emperors of both Austria and Russia (the Three Emperors' League), and of encouraging France to seek compensation for the loss of Alsace-Lorraine by expanding her colonial empire. Under the Three Emperors' League, Germany promised to keep the peace between Austria and Russia by undertaking the same sort of guarantor position which England, under the Locarno treaties, held later to France and Germany. The new Kaiser substituted for this an exclusive alliance with Austria. In this way, he hoped that the Austrian empire—and beyond it, the Turkish empire in Asia—would become attached to Germany's colonial empire. He did not, of course, propose to take over the government of these territories, but only to provide a field for the investment of German capital and the marketing of German goods. The disadvantage of this plan was that it alienated Russia and turned her into an enemy of Germany.

The same demand for imperial economic expansion led the Kaiser to give up Bismarck's policy on the west. The French and the British between them had either colonized, or were colonizing, nearly all the backward parts of the world. The new German competition scared them both and threw them into each other's arms. Looking for allies, they turned towards Russia, while Germany and Austria turned to Italy, which had also been left behind in the race for colonies. By 1914, the Triple Entente of England, France and Russia, the possessors of colonies, stood opposed to the Triple Alliance of Germany, Austria and Italy. Both sides were piling up armaments, and the actual outbreak of war was a matter of time.

NATIONALISM PREVENTS PEACEFUL NEGOTIATION

The growth of industry in western Europe—in Britain, France, Germany, and to a less extent, Italy—had created a need for bigger markets, more raw materials, and new fields for investment. The west European states were no longer self-sufficient economically, but they had become more self-sufficient politically than before. Sentimental rivalry between the peoples of different countries had been produced by universal education. History was taught from a strictly nationalist angle. Even the poorest people became acutely conscious that they were, for instance, Germans and not Frenchmen, and they thanked God that they were not as the Frenchmen.

In this way, nationalism replaced religion, as a cause for which it was worth while to die or to kill. People, therefore, naturally thought of German industry as opposed to French industry, and the industrialists' simple demand for bigger markets and more raw materials became translated into a demand for bigger German markets, as opposed to French. Instead of being peaceably arranged by international co-operation, trade became a source of international competition leading to war. There was nothing inherent in the search for raw materials or markets which need have brought international, as opposed to colonial, wars. International war came because the search was conducted by nations who were old political enemies.

THE FAILURE OF THE GENERAL STAFFS

For a generation, the general staffs of Europe had been preparing for the war, but when it came, it took them by surprise. It did not develop in a way they understood. In 1909, Blériot had flown across the Channel, and it might have been expected that, in the next five years, the military experts of Europe would have developed the aeroplane as an efficient fighting-machine. Yet in the early stages of the war, military aviation played only an insignificant part. Under war conditions, however, the aeroplane developed faster in months than it had in years of peace. Similarly the internal-combustion engine, the armoured car and the caterpillar tractor were all known before the war. All the components of the tank were already in existence, but it took years of war before they were put together. The general staffs of all the belligerent nations had failed to apply contemporary inventions to the requirements of the war. When war came, technicians produced the new machines, and the machines fought their way to the front without an invitation from the generals. A battle in which the higher command is at fault and everything is left to the ordinary soldiers is called a soldiers' battle. In this sense, we may describe the war of 1914 as a machines' war.

It was not only the weapons, but the type of campaign, which took the staffs by surprise. They had expected a war of movement, of manoeuvres and battles in the summer, followed by a lull in the winter. In the west, apart from a few months of open fighting in 1914 and 1918, the war was confined to siege operations on a front of about four hundred miles, lasting summer and winter, without relaxation, for three and a half years. This siege warfare of the trenches was punctuated by a series of extremely costly battles at Arras, Ypres, the Somme and Verdun, in which the attacking side might truthfully have said: "This hurts me more than it hurts you". The front was so long, the masses of men so vast, and the staffs so remote from actual fighting, that the war was out of control. It became a monstrous machine of death, moving onwards of its own impetus.

In earlier wars, an able general could visualize his problems, calculate the means to achieve his ends, and execute successfully a well-thought-out plan of campaign. Marlborough, Napoleon and Wellington had imposed their will on the military situation: the military situation dictated the actions of Haig and Cadorna and Ludendorff; only Ferdinand Foch rose to real greatness. The generals were defeated not by the enemy, but by the colossal and intractable problem which confronted them; so it is not they who are remembered by posterity, but the unknown soldiers of every nation.

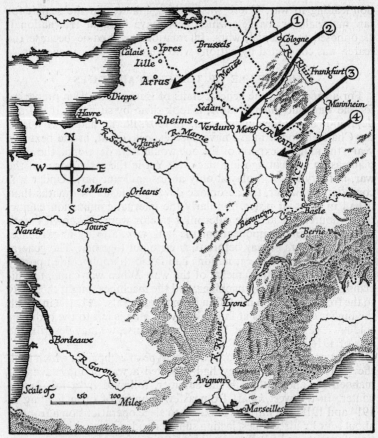

THE FRANCO-GERMAN FRONTIER PROBLEM

The routes numbered 2, 3 and 4, indicated above by arrows, consist of relatively narrow valleys between mountains, and are thus capable of being defended
by fortifications at either end.   This makes route 1, viâ Belgium, the obvious
and easiest path for an invading army to take as has been often demonstrated.

For a month after Francis Ferdinand's murder, Englishmen were
more concerned with the threat of civil war in Ireland than with the
Balkan situation. "Ulster will fight, and Ulster will be right", was the
cry of the Conservative party. Germany listened to that cry, decided
England was too disunited to fight, and failed to restrain her Austrian
ally's indignation against Serbia. On July 28, Sir Edward Grey
announced that Austria had rejected the Serbian reply to her ultimatum, although this was satisfactory on most points. On August 1,
Britain learned that Russia's mobilization had brought Germany
into the war; next day she knew that France was involved.   Two days
later, Germany invaded Belgium and Britain too was at war.

The German plan, which aimed at a quick victory over France, to be followed by a full-scale attack on Russia, very nearly succeeded. The Germans swept on through Belgium. When the British Expeditionary Force, prepared by Lord Haldane long before the war, hurried north over the Belgian frontier, it was forced to share at once in a long and difficult retreat. In September the German advance was stopped by the Franco-British troops under Joffre at the battle of the Marne; they had come so close to Paris that last-moment reinforcements were sent out in hastily commandeered taxis.

The German failure in 1914 really lost them the war. That failure was due not so much to the Entente commanders and the magnificent tenacity of their troops, as to the fatal hesitation of the German leaders, and particularly of Von Kluck. After the Marne the Germans were pushed back to a line running from the sea just south of Ostend, roughly through Ypres, Arras, Lille, Verdun, Rheims and across the Vosges. For the next three years that remained " the front " in the west. Each side made slight advances from time to time; but the territorial gains were small, and the losses in men enormous. Substantially there was no significant change in the military situation on the west until the great events of 1918.

THE SEA BLOCKADES

The empires of Germany and Austria-Hungary were in the position of a beleaguered fortress. There were gaps in the encircling chain; supplies could be obtained through neutral Powers, such as Holland and the Scandinavian countries; when Turkey and, later, Bulgaria came into the war on their side, there seemed strong hopes for the success of William II's policy of pushing German influence down to Baghdad. But the British Navy, whose civilian head, Winston Churchill, had kept the fleet mobilized in the critical days of August, 1914, was a constant threat to the encircled empires.

While the armies on the western front settled down to trench warfare, and Russia fought with varying success in the east, the real strategic interest of the struggle lay on the seas. There were two simultaneous blockades: the surface blockade of Germany by England, and the submarine blockade of England by Germany. The first was one of the main factors that caused the collapse of the Central Powers; the second was defeated by the British Navy, after an anxious period during which out of every four ships that left British ports one never returned. Had this blockade continued unchecked for a few more months, food stocks would have been dangerously depleted and England, rather than Germany, might have experienced internal collapse in 1918.

The possibility of an offensive blockade was almost new in 1914. Formerly a blockade was designed to prevent an enemy invasion; European countries could feed themselves, and, though the supply of luxuries might be cut off, they would not starve. Now it was possible for either side to starve the other, if the armies of one could prevent the other from winning a quick victory. The surface blockade was helped greatly by Japan's action in declaring war on Germany. The Japanese captured Tsing-Tau in November, 1914, and cleared the German flag from the Pacific. A few weeks later Sturdee's squadron defeated von Spee at the battle of the Falkland Islands, and German surface craft were confined to the North Sea and the Baltic.

Henceforward the English blockade of Germany was only challenged once. In the summer of 1915, von Scheer led his High Seas Fleet into battle with Jellicoe and Beatty off Jutland. As far as the actual fighting went, the battle was drawn, but the results were decisive. Never again was the German Fleet allowed to risk a battle. By the winter of 1917–18 food was very scarce in Germany, and during the next winter there was a real famine among the civilians.

U-BOAT WARFARE AND AMERICAN INTERVENTION

The Germans operated their submarine blockade from the conquered port of Zeebrugge and from their own North Sea bases. At first it seemed impossible to stop these invisible enemies, but the submarine had a number of weaknesses. It had to come to the surface every twenty hours to recharge its batteries; while it was moving, its position could be detected by delicate apparatus; although it could take refuge at the bottom of the sea, it could do so for only forty-eight hours at a time, a period defined by the capacity of its air storage, and it could lie only in comparatively shallow water. Moreover, it was slow-moving, and could not be absent from its base for more than a month. Gradually, working on these weaknesses, the Admiralty was able to defeat the submarine blockade entirely. Mines and depth-charges, submerged nets across the Straits of Dover, naval decoy-boats disguised as innocent merchantmen, the arming of every sea-going ship and the use of a convoy system for the principal trade-routes, all proved to be effective measures. Finally, Sir Roger Keyes, by his raids on Zeebrugge and Ostend in the spring of 1918, helped to drive the German submarines away from their Flemish base to the more distant German home-ports.

The two blockades had indirect effects which were almost as great as their direct influence. By the end of 1915, the United States was the only great Power which was not a belligerent. If she had remained neutral, the war might have ended in a stalemate, so equally matched were the rival Powers. American intervention was bound to be decisive. Both sides had devoted great attention to securing American favour and had organized elaborate propaganda campaigns.

The British blockade naturally annoyed neutrals. Disputes about what was contraband and about the right to search neutral ships were inevitable, and Germany relied on these disputes to keep America on bad terms with Britain. There was a large and influential German community in the United States, and its policy was likely to be supported by the Irish-Americans, who nursed bitter grievances against England. But the submarine blockade altered the position entirely. The Germans could not prevent ships leaving port and could not take prizes; therefore they sank them at sight and generally left their crews to drown. As early as 1915 the sinking of the British liner *Lusitania*, which was carrying many American passengers, had enraged American opinion. Later the German policy of "unrestricted" submarine warfare finally alienated it, and by the end of 1917 the United States, with their great resources, were at war with Germany.

THE BRITISH EMPIRE RALLIES HER MILITARY STRENGTH

Except for the British Expeditionary Force and the small Belgian army, which continued the struggle under its heroic King Albert, the brunt of the fighting on the western front fell on France. Britain was slow to cast off her traditional dread of conscription, and it was only in January, 1916 that Asquith carried the National Service Act, in the face of opposition. Gradually a formidable army was built up, which, besides holding a considerable part of the western front, fought in the Balkans, Egypt, Syria and Mesopotamia. India and the four Dominions, Australia, New Zealand, South Africa and Canada, had supported the "old country" from the outbreak of war. The British Empire was slow in developing its full strength, but it never wavered in its determination to smash Prussian militarism.

Meanwhile there were signs that Russia, once regarded as the "steam-roller" which would flatten out Germany and Austria by sheer weight, was losing strength. She had never really recovered from the overwhelming blow which Hindenburg and Ludendorff dealt her at Tannenberg in 1914. Against Austria she won some successes, particularly in the capture of Przemysl, but the loss of Warsaw in the summer of 1915 was a severe blow to her prestige. When her old enemy Turkey joined the Central Powers, co-operation with her Western allies became more difficult, and they determined to strike at Constantinople; its capture would restore communications through the Mediterranean and Black Seas, in place of the long sea-route round Norway. British and Dominion troops were landed at the Dardanelles in 1915, and a great effort was made to force the Straits. But the Turks strengthened their fortifications in time, and the campaign proved a glorious failure.

The Turkish peasants were stubborn fighters, and it was not easy to dislodge them from their hold on the ancient centres of civilization, Mesopotamia, Syria, Palestine, Arabia and Asia Minor. The British advance up the Euphrates valley was checked by the Turkish recapture of Kut in April, 1916. Defeated in their attack on the Suez Canal and Egypt, the Turks held a strong defensive line in southern Palestine. Their Arab subjects were stirred into revolt by liberal English subsidies and the genius of T. E. Lawrence, an Oxford archaeologist who knew the eastern mind. In the Balkans the Turks found themselves, under German pressure, in alliance with their traditional enemies, the Bulgarians. Against them stood Greece, Rumania and the remnants of the hard-fighting Serbians, whose country had been overrun in the winter of 1915–16 by Bulgarians, Germans and Austrians under von Mackensen. The landing of French and British forces at Salonika was too late to save the Serbian crown for King Peter; but he and his son, Alexander, continued to inspire Serbian resistance. Rumania's ill-equipped army was badly battered by Mackensen and Falkenhayn in 1916, in spite of some help from Russia and France. The opposing groups of confederate armies faced one another on a line running from the river Struma past Monastir to the Adriatic north of Valona. The attempt of Sarrail, the French commander, to push northward in April, 1917, failed.

ITALY JOINS THE ALLIES : THE SOMME AND PASSCHENDAELE

The chief effect of Italy's entrance into the war had been to secure the Mediterranean for her allies, and to divert Austrian divisions from the Russian front. Fighting went on over the most difficult terrain of the war, the Trentino and the Isonzo plain. After checking the Austrian threat to the Venetian plain, Cadorna pushed his troops slowly forward across the barren plateaux south of the Julian Alps till the news of the Russian revolution in 1917 halted his offensive, and enabled the Austrians to receive German reinforcements.

Meanwhile, the slow ebb and flow of trench warfare on the western front had been marked by great battles, which brought heavy losses to France, Germany and Britain alike. The British suffered severely in the battles of Ypres and at Neuve Chapelle. Ammunition and equipment were needed in far greater supplies, and there was a general feeling that the direction of the war called for greater vigour. At the end of 1916, Lloyd George displaced Asquith as Prime Minister. Pétain had held the furious German attacks at Verdun. The great battles of the Somme had weakened the Kaiser's armies, but had brought little advance to the French and British forces. Nivelle's costly failure to break the enemy positions on the Aisne led to mutinies in the French armies. These were ended by Pétain's resourcefulness, while Haig fought the third battle of Ypres to draw the German armies to the defence of Flanders. The object was achieved at the cost of dreadful casualties in the mud of Passchendaele.

With the coming of winter in 1917, the war moved to its climax. The German and Austrian empires were heartened by the collapse of Russia; but the intervention of the United States forced them to risk everything before the raw American troops could be trained and could pour their overwhelming numbers into France. Once Russia's allies had failed to break through the Dardanelles, her ultimate collapse was inevitable. Corruption and incompetence sapped the resolution of the Tsar's armies, and Nicholas II abdicated. Germany was free to transfer large forces to the western front, when she made peace with the new rulers of Russia at Brest-Litovsk in March, 1918. The two central empires struck hard at Italy, where poor equipment and indifferent organization had sapped the spirit of her soldiers. The spread of the new Russian doctrines led to riots in Turin, the greatest munition centre. Cadorna misjudged the danger, and, when his enemies attacked at Caporetto in the winter of 1917–18, the Italians lost heavily and were forced back to the Piave. France and Britain came to their ally's rescue, and, when Diaz took over from Cadorna, he had the help of Plumer's and Fayolle's men in holding the north-eastern gate of Italy.

In the Asiatic theatres of war, fortune turned against Germany's Turkish allies. Maude restored British prestige in Mesopotamia and pressed on towards Mosul, after having captured Baghdad. Allenby broke the Beersheba-Gaza line in November, 1917, and next month captured Jerusalem. Everywhere Arab partisans rallied to the victorious prophet (Al Nebi), who brought with him the waters of the Nile to Palestine. The German grip was loosened, and the vision of a victorious advance as far as Baghdad gradually faded away.

GERMANY'S SUPREME EFFORT FAILS

In France, Haig's initial breakthrough with tanks to Cambrai at the end of 1917 could not be followed up owing to the exhaustion of his troops. In the following spring Ludendorff launched an overwhelming attack, which forced the line of the Somme, and threatened to split the French and British armies. The danger brought about unity of command, and both armies were placed under Foch. Though forced back to the line of the Marne, Foch held on against Ludendorff's shock-troops. As the summer went on, the American army grew to impressive size. By the middle of July, Foch was ready for his counter-offensive.

Though its defenders had come desperately near victory, the besieged fortress was beginning to crumble. Its eastern outposts were the first to collapse. In September, Allenby smashed the Turkish armies and went on to capture Damascus and Aleppo. In October, Turkey sued for peace. The long stalemate in the Balkans was broken when, in September, the Serbians broke through the Bulgarian lines and captured Prilep. French, British, Greeks and Italians pressed forward with them, and by the end of the month Bulgaria had surrendered. In Italy, Diaz and his allies crossed the Piave in October, and began the break-up of the Austro-Hungarian army. The racial components of the Habsburg empire fell apart with astonishing rapidity after the battle of Vittorio Veneto. In October, the rulers of Vienna sued for an armistice.

The sudden change of fortune left Germany bewildered. Short commons and disappointed hopes broke the morale of her home front. But her western army was still strong and its positions heavily fortified. Foch's strategy made full use of the British, French

and American troops at his disposal. Arras was relieved, and the
great Hindenburg Line was breached by Haig. The allied forces
swept forward into open country, and Ludendorff insisted on peace
negotiations. The German navy mutinied when ordered to put to
sea. The land and sea dangers were increased by the new menace of
the Royal Air Force, which had been unified and strengthened—
largely owing to Lloyd George, Smuts and Churchill. Its fighting
chief, Hugh Trenchard, was ready to bomb Berlin. By the end of
October, it was clear that Germany was decisively beaten, and
William II abdicated. The Armistice was granted on November 11,
the day that English troops re-entered Mons, the Belgian town where
the expeditionary force had fought its first battle four years before.

THE TREATY OF VERSAILLES

At the end of the war, Europe fell under the spell of Woodrow
Wilson, the thin precisely-dressed university professor, with rimless
pince-nez, who was President of the United States of America.
Wilson brought to the problems of Europe the detachment of an
American and an ingrained liberalism of thought. He expressed the
passionate desire for a lasting peace which had seized the front-line
soldiers of all countries. President Wilson offered them the sort of
peace they wanted : a peace without indemnities and without annexations ; a peace made openly in the light of day, not secretly by intrigues
among diplomatists ; a peace in which all countries should live side
by side as equal partners in a League of Nations ; and a peace which
would allow men to choose freely their government.

The President's peace aims, summarized in the Fourteen Points in
1918, seemed to offer a new start for a better Europe. When, therefore, the old imperial Germany withered away, it was to America that
the leaders of the new Liberal Germany turned for peace. They
believed that the final peace treaty would follow the lines of the
Fourteen Points, and they had to accept the severe conditions
demanded for an immediate armistice, conditions designed to make it
absolutely impossible for Germany to re-start the war. The German
army was disarmed, the German Rhineland occupied by Entente
troops. The new start was symbolized by the arrival in Europe of
President Wilson. Never before had a President of the United States
left his country, never before had a foreign visitor to England
received so rapturous a welcome.

But the passions nourished by four years of bitter war left many
difficulties. Unrestricted submarine warfare had diminished the
world's shipping, and the blockade of Germany was continued.
Though they had now a Liberal constitution, her people went hungry.
Generosity and revenge were strangely mixed among the victors.
They liked the President's vision of a brave new world, guided by a
League of Nations. But they remembered Germany's use of poison-
gas, her rape of Belgium and her submarine atrocities ; it was hard to

EUROPE AFTER VERSAILLES

Above may be seen how the Treaty of Versailles affected the boundaries of Europe as they existed before the First World War. Germany lost Alsace-Lorraine and the Austro-Hungarian Empire split up. The new state of Czecho-Slovakia was formed, and Poland reconstituted with territory taken from Russia and Germany. Russia lost Bessarabia to Rumania and control of the Baltic.

believe that the leopard had changed his spots. When the peace conference met in Paris, the Germans were excluded from the discussions. As at Brest-Litovsk, peace was to be by dictation. But no one proposed to rob Germany as she had robbed Russia, whose Soviet rulers had been forced to yield a quarter of her population, railways and farming land and three-quarters of her coalfields.

The peace treaties were drawn up largely by the representatives of the United States, Britain, France and Italy. Clemenceau, the French premier, who was nicknamed The Tiger, wanted security for France, and he interpreted security as a permanent stranglehold on Germany. Orlando devoted himself to extracting payment of the promises made to Italy when she joined the Entente Powers. Lloyd George had a Welshman's affection for small and distressed nations, and supported the claims of Poles, Czechs, Lithuanians and the rest; he also tried to fulfil his promise of making Germany pay. Wilson's detachment from the quarrels of Europe was joined to a considerable ignorance of their nature. Between them, "the Big Four" produced the Versailles Treaty.

Six countries—Finland, Esthonia, Latvia, Lithuania, Poland and Czecho-Slovakia—were established at the expense of the defeated Powers, among whom Communist Russia was included. Germany lost some territory to Lithuania, Poland, Denmark, Belgium and France. The occupation of the Rhineland by Entente troops was continued. The Habsburg Empire disappeared. Serbia (now called Yugo-Slavia) and Rumania doubled their territories at its expense; Czecho-Slovakia was cut bodily out of it; Italy annexed large districts; Austria and Hungary were left as two small, separate, disarmed countries. On the ruins of the vanished Turkish Empire were set several Arab states, under the control of France or Britain. Greece received a footing in Turkey-in-Asia. The German colonies were divided between Japan, France and the British Empire.

The new theory of "self-determination" dictated most of these changes. But the races of Europe are mixed inextricably, and the new states contained many reluctant foreigners. The rights of minorities were to be protected by the new League of Nations, which was also made trustee for backward peoples in Asia and Africa. These reforms were only applied to the new or the defeated states. The Germans felt that the victors were making a peace of revenge rather than of justice.

The war had been fought on borrowed money. Every government had borrowed from its own people; the continental Entente powers had borrowed from Britain; Britain had borrowed from the United States. The victors naturally intended to make Germany pay for the war and make reparation for the destruction she had wrought. "Reparations" were framed to include personal as well as material damage, pensions as well as buildings. This brought the bill up to the enormous figure of £6,600,000,000.

Germany felt that this decision reduced her to a state in which, though she might promise everything, she could pay nothing. She was as much embittered by reparations as by territorial losses. Many economists believed that European economy must suffer as long as Germany was crippled. England began to realize that the whole system of reparations and war-debts could lead only to world economic disaster. She failed to persuade France to relax her demands for reparations or the United States to relax war-debt payments.

CHAPTER 77

NEW WORLDS: THE U.S.S.R. AND THE U.S.A.

THE last stages of the war were marked by the withdrawal of Russia and the entrance of the United States. In this chapter their experiences will be traced through the post-war world. Both are new and united countries—almost continents. Europe, excluding Russia, is divided into about thirty different countries, each with an average population of about 13,000,000. Russia and the United States have populations ten to twelve times as great.

Russia emerged late into history because she has few of the "natural frontiers" which divide Europe into small, more or less self-contained, states. She was too large to be civilized in the days when only small areas at a time could be won from the surrounding jungle of political anarchy, but her size helped her in the modern world of huge manufacturing output. She shared this advantage with the United States. Both countries possessed great fertile plains, much more suited to the economics of mechanized farming on a very large scale than is the undulating surface of England or France.

THE MELTING POTS OF RUSSIA AND AMERICA

The absence of history helps these new worlds. Lancashire was an industrial centre when Pittsburgh was still a fort in a forest clearing, and English and European industry is still governed by the habits of the small-scale factories of the past. In Lancashire, for instance, cotton is handled by four or five different parts of the county before it is marketed. American and Russian industry, being of more recent growth, are free to benefit by the economies of rationalization.

Russia and the United States are both melting-pots for numberless nationalities. All the races of Europe are reproduced in the United States. In Europe, they are segregated behind frontiers, eyeing each other suspiciously; in America, they are intermingled, sharing the same towns, moving towards a common nationality. This took place even more rapidly than before, when the stream of immigration was almost stopped by law in 1926. In 1931, for the first time, the emigrants from the United States exceeded the number of immigrants.

Russia's problem was similar; her people speak sixty-two different languages and have nearly as many religions. Her rulers tried to solve their problem by allowing these different peoples to grow up, each with their own language and culture, but with a common political tradition. To be a Frenchman means to be French not only in culture but also in politics, and therefore to be anti-German. But the Government of Russia believed that a Ruthenian by language need not be a Ruthenian in politics. Tartars and Ruthenians may differ in language provided that they agree in politics—Communist politics. By taking politics out of nationality, Russia tried to remove one cause of war, but her communist system introduced another.

All the peoples of America are taught to read the same things in the same language—the cult of the machine and the gospel of self-help and individual charity—for the American tradition is the tradition of lonely pioneers. The peoples of Russia are taught to read the same things but in their own different languages—the cult of the machine and the gospel of social or state help—for the Communist background is not the backwoods clearing but the slum and factory.

TACTICS OF LENIN

In March, 1917, a squat little man, with a trim beard and piercing eyes, waited in Switzerland, eating his heart out to be back in Russia. Lenin was convinced that he could make a Socialist revolution out of what was, at the moment, no more than a breakdown of government. The Entente Powers saw in him a man who might rob them of an ally by making peace with Germany, or by plunging Russia into civil war. He turned from Russia's allies to Russia's enemies. Germany, like the rest of Europe, hated Communism, but in her desperation, she was ready for any risk. She allowed Lenin to travel through Germany to Russia. An enthusiastic crowd met him at the Petrograd railway station. Personal friends and unknown workers pushed eagerly round him, somebody thrust a bouquet into his hands, all stood on tiptoe, eager to catch his congratulations on the Revolution which they had brought about in his absence. They felt they deserved congratulations, and they could hardly believe their ears when he spoke. He was not praising them. He was scolding them. They had not made the Revolution, he said. It had just happened; the Tsar's Government had fallen because it was rotten, not because they had cut it off. And now, while they celebrated the victory they had not won, their enemies, backed by the Entente Governments, were building in Russia a new capitalist society, all the healthier because the worn-out Tsarist Government had been removed. The real Revolution had not yet begun.

Such words were not popular. Lenin found himself first neglected, then hunted. He left Petrograd to avoid arrest. Gradually the course of events convinced the factory-workers that Lenin had been right and they wrong. By November, the second revolution was ready.

From their headquarters in the Smolny Institute, a hitherto fashionable girls' school, the soviets, or councils of working-class organizations, announced that they had taken over the Government. The Petrograd garrison joined them, and Kerensky, the Prime Minister, fled. This was the second Russian Revolution—the Revolution that did not just "happen" but was planned. It was the fulfilment of a lifetime of apparently hopeless dreaming. At the university, in Siberian exile, in riots at Kronstadt, in the British Museum Reading Room, in a bare lodging in Zürich, in a haystack near Petrograd, Lenin had waited patiently for the day of deliverance for the workers in fields and factories. Now it had dawned.

Factory-workers were few—Russia was only just beginning to be industrialized—they were badly treated and they were politically educated. By 1917, the wage-earners of the towns were united in desiring a Socialist revolution. They had no use for political democracy, unless it was accompanied by economic democracy; if they had to choose, they preferred the latter. By economic democracy, they understood a society in which they would not be dependent for their living on the caprice of a privileged employer. They knew that the sort of independence a peasant or a shoemaker may possess, by owning his own holding or shop, was impossible for a factory-worker, and they sought the equivalent in common ownership by the workers. Of course, like everybody else, they wanted better conditions; what principally distinguished them from other groups was their theories concerning the private ownership of property.

BREAKDOWN OF TSARIST GOVERNMENT

By 1917, the Russian Government had broken down. Her armies had three enemies to face—the Germans, the weather, and the Russian Government. The troops were starved of food and munitions, and far more concerned with what was happening in their homes than with the war-aims of the Tsar's Government. They showed where their interests lay by wholesale desertions. Russia was a medieval country trying to fight a modern war. She could not produce munitions in sufficient quantities; and even if she had had enough at the base, her transport system was so overburdened that she could not have distributed them. The mismanagement of the war brought with it the inevitable end of the monarchy.

A nation almost entirely of peasants was ruled by the Tsar, whose lightest word was law. Nicholas II, a well-meaning but feeble-minded gentleman, was under the thumb of his superstitious wife, who in turn was controlled by an ignorant, disreputable, crafty and half-crazy monk, Rasputin. The fate of governments depended on this trio. Russia had many devoted men of intelligence, and a small rising class of able business men, but they were powerless unless they gained the ear of the Court clique. A revolution of some sort was as necessary for the upper classes as for the lower classes. The first step was taken in December, 1916, when a group of patriotic nobles murdered Rasputin. The second step followed in March, 1917, when demonstrations led to the abdication of the Tsar.

The real revolutionary struggle, which decided the future government and social organization of Russia, took place between March and November, 1917. The upper class and the manufacturers, backed by the Entente Governments, wanted Russia to be governed either like England, as a constitutional monarchy, or like France, as a constitutional republic. The Government must be made politically competent, the social system left unchanged. The weakness of this group was that their numbers were insignificant and scattered. They had little middle-class backing, because there was only a small Russian middle class. Many of the shareholders in Russian industries were foreigners; the shopkeepers, who in most countries are supporters of the existing social order, were largely Jews. In Russia, the Jews were always despised and sometimes massacred. They might not be supporters of Socialism, but in the circumstances they could not be enthusiastic supporters of things as they were.

RUSSIAN WORKERS DEMAND SOCIALISM

Although their numbers were small, the wage-earners of the towns were united in desiring a Socialist Revolution. Their most trusted leaders in the early days were middle-class Socialists who were willing to co-operate with the Entente Powers and with the people who wanted a political revolution only. When the workers saw that this co-operation was not leading to Socialism, they accepted Lenin's leadership. It was they who made the November Revolution.

Lenin held that the industrial working-class, the proletariat, could not be justly treated except under Socialism, and that the possessors of power would never voluntarily surrender their privileges. He would have held that this doctrine applied to any country, whether the proletariat was in a numerical majority or not. But Socialism by democratic means was impossible in Russia because the industrial proletariat was only a small fraction of the population. The "dictatorship of the proletariat" was the only way to Socialism in Russia. If the workers of Petrograd were right in desiring Socialism above all things, they were right in rejecting the leadership of Kerensky, Prime Minister between March and November, 1917, for the leadership of Lenin.

The Russian workers would not have been successful if either the peasants or the army had actively defended the existing social order. The army was composed of factory-workers and peasants rather than of professional soldiers. The officers were a class apart, and the harshness of military discipline had reproduced in the army the characteristic bitterness of Russian social divisions. The military breakdown had robbed the private soldiers of all *esprit de corps*. Increasingly they thought of themselves not as soldiers but as civilians in uniform. And, above all, they wanted peace. The words of a soldier delegate to the Petrograd Soviet reflect their opinion: "Comrades," he said, "I bring you greeting from the place where men are digging their graves and call them trenches."

The peasants were suffering from land-hunger. Fifty years before they had been serfs, as people in England had been in the Middle Ages. Now they were free, but they were still bitterly poor. They had no desire to waste their energies on affairs of state when they might be seizing land in their own villages. Thus the Communists under Lenin were able to seize power in November, 1917, almost without bloodshed.

In one of the innumerable debates in the Smolny Institute, whilst the November Revolution was in progress, Trotsky summed up the position in these words: "There are only two alternatives: either the Russian Revolution will create a revolutionary movement in Europe, or the European Powers will destroy the Russian Revolution". The leaders of other European states agreed, and for three years they devoted all the energy they could spare from their own quarrels to crushing the new Russian Government. For two years more western Europe continued confidently to expect the inevitable overthrow of the Soviets, and it was not until 1923 that the capitalist countries understood that they both could and would have to live side by side with a Socialist great power.

THE SOVIETS SURVIVE CIVIL WAR AND FAMINE

In March, 1918, Russia made peace with Germany, and the Communists were free to turn their attention to the civil wars in progress all over the country. In the Far East, Admiral Kolchak attacked the Communists with Japanese help; in the south, General Denikin pushed forward with French and English help; in the Ukraine, the Germans had helped to establish a reactionary government under Skoropadsky; in the north, an English army was helping General Yudenich against Petrograd. The Communists had no allies and no advantages, except the possession of the capital, an indomitable crusading courage, and in Trotsky a great military organizer. The White armies had external support, but they were riddled by corruption and lacked unity. Some were fighting for the Tsar, some for a constitutional republic, all were fighting for foreign countries. Reasons of patriotism brought many Russians who had no love for Communism as such to the side of the Russian government.

The Russian civil war was marked on both sides by gross brutality and inspiring heroism. It left the country exhausted, ruined, dismembered. When peace finally came in 1920, Russia had lost her Baltic provinces, which became the new states of Finland, Esthonia, Latvia and Lithuania, and also Poland. The remainder of the country was firmly under Communist rule: the Russian Revolution had failed to turn Europe Communist, but equally Europe had failed to suppress

Communism in Russia. The Union of Soviet Socialist Republics was by then firmly established in the saddle of government.

No sooner was the civil war over than there was a terrible famine, which killed men by millions where the war had killed them by thousands. An occasional crop failure is inevitable in any agricultural country. It was the utter paralysis of transport and the general disorganization of the country which turned this shortage into one of the greatest famines in modern times. It nearly succeeded where the expeditionary forces of 1919–1920 had failed. The survival of Communist Russia was due to the change of plan introduced by Lenin in the year before his death.

From 1917 until 1922, the Soviet Union had been organized on a completely Socialist basis. Private trading and private property—except personal possessions—were strictly forbidden. Socialism had not brought with it the promised prosperity. Food was less plentiful, the conditions of life considerably harder than before the formation of the U.S.S.R. The peasants in particular grumbled. Why, they asked, should they feed the cities for nothing? It seemed probable that the natural famine of 1921–22 would be succeeded by an artificial famine in 1922–23, for the peasants threatened not to sow the fields.

ECONOMIC POLICIES OF LENIN AND STALIN

Lenin met this danger by introducing the New Economic Policy. Strict Socialism was abandoned; whole areas of economic life were set free for private exploitation; individual traders once more appeared in the towns; the peasants were again allowed to sell their crops for their private profit. Lenin thus turned aside the blow which had seemed likely to destroy him; but his victory had been gained by giving in to private enterprise, the enemy of Socialism. Foreigners naturally thought that, before long, Socialism would be only a name in Russia, and that her vast undeveloped areas would again be open to capitalist exploitation. They had not realized the extent to which Lenin had kept in Communist hands the key-positions of economic power. Individuals were allowed to trade on their own, but only under licence from a Socialist government; every precaution was taken to see that no new vested interests grew up. The outside world had underestimated the Soviet Government's tenacity of purpose.

Lenin did not live to see the return to Socialism. In January, 1924 he died, worn out by his labours. They buried him in a plain red granite tomb in the Red Square at Moscow, under the walls of the Kremlin, over which the Red Flag now flies night and day. His body still lies there embalmed in a glass coffin.

Most people expected Trotsky, who had been Lenin's right-hand man since 1917, would succeed him. But Stalin ousted Trotsky and drove him into exile. Stalin had been understudy to Lenin, as secretary of the Communist party, which dominates every part of the machinery of government in Russia, from the smallest factory committee to the Cabinet—the Council of People's Commissars—itself. The Russian Government was not so much a dictatorship of the proletariat, as a dictatorship over the proletariat by the disciplined, devoted Communist party.

Even Trotsky, the preacher of world revolution, could not succeed against the Communist party machine. To him Socialism was an international movement for all workers everywhere; he believed that it must conquer the world, or the world would destroy Russian Socialism. Stalin did not agree, and Stalin prevailed. Although Stalin was prepared to postpone international revolution, he returned at home to a stronger Socialist policy with the First Five-Year Plan.

The New Economic Policy was abandoned; private enterprise was again forbidden, and a plan was made to double, or more than double, the country's industrial output within five years. In 1922 the peasants had held the Revolution up to ransom. To prevent this recurring, the small peasant-holdings were merged into co-operative farms, ranging in size from areas as big as Yorkshire down to farms no bigger than a large English holding. Through the use of tractors and mechaniza-tion, the output of Russian agriculture would increase, removing the fear of starvation from town and village alike. Further, it would introduce the mechanic into country life, and thus break up the village worship of tradition; the smallholder would acquire the mentality of the factory-worker, there would be a new environment in which Communism would flourish, and the Socialist towns would be freed from the spectre of a conservative peasant rising. The peasants must be persuaded to come in; if they could not be persuaded, they must be forced. After a struggle they were forced. The old system was ruth-lessly destroyed, and after another severe famine, agriculture, like industry, was organized on a comprehensive Socialist basis.

DEVELOPMENT OF SOVIET INDUSTRY AND AGRICULTURE

Side by side with the agricultural revolution went a great develop-ment in industry. The safety of Socialism in Russia was menaced by foreign capitalist countries as well as by peasants at home. To meet this danger, Russia must become self-supporting in industry. Her mineral resources must be developed, her manufacturing plants extended. Machinery, above all machines to make machines, had to be bought from abroad, and to pay for them, Russian agricultural produce must be exported, and people at home must go short. The revolution in agriculture was carried through largely by force, against the wishes of most of the people concerned; the industrial revolution was carried through with the enthusiastic co-operation of the factory-workers, secured by a tremendous advertising campaign. As a result of this planned and rushed development, Russia has become an industrial country; and so great are her raw-material resources that she may claim in peace time to be more nearly self-supporting than any other great power, with the exception of the United States.

The success of the First Five-Year Plan was seen in the revival of the Franco-Russian alliance. The Franco-Soviet pact of 1935 was made by a conservative French Government with the approval of the General Staff. The pre-war alliance between republican France and feudal Russia sprang from their common fear of Germany. The post-war understanding between capitalist France and Socialist Russia rested on the fact that the U.S.S.R. had succeeded in her task and, on a Socialist basis, had made herself sufficiently strong, both militarily and economically, to be well worth having as an ally.

LIFE IN SOVIET RUSSIA

The old Socialist formula had demanded that each citizen should work according to his ability and each receive according to his need. In Russia the workers still work for wages, fixed not by the worker's need, but by the value of his output.   But no one is in a position to build up a private fortune and become the employer of others with all the power over their happiness which that implies. The workers need not fear that their energy is directed to increasing their employer's wealth; they believe what every device of publicity insistently drums into them—that they are working solely for their own and their children's benefit. This belief may even have been fortified by the knowledge of the recurrent "purges" which have appeared to outsiders such a mysterious feature of life in Russia since the beginning of the Revolution and removed many Revolutionary leaders.

INDIVIDUALISM OF THE UNITED STATES

In contrast with the State control exemplified in the U.S.S.R. there is, in the United States, little interference by public authorities with the conduct of life. This is a result of the blending of the original Puritan tradition with that of later political refugees from Europe. Both brought with them a hatred of government, because both had suffered from persecuting governments. The United States constitution, therefore, not only proclaims the right of the individual to "life, liberty and the pursuit of happiness", but tries to secure it by limiting the powers of government, by weakening them through a division between the Federal authority and the states, and by setting up a supreme law court to see that they are not exceeded. Consequently, competitive capitalism has been free to develop, almost unchecked by such European restrictions as unemployment insurance and minimum wage-rates. This "hands off" business policy is popular, not only because of the traditional hatred of state control, but because of the traditional Puritan pride in self-help and individual prudence and restraint.

The only public interference in private life which the American Puritan tradition encouraged was interference in morals. In 1917, the Eighteenth Amendment of the Constitution came into force, and it became illegal to sell or to purchase any sort of alcohol. This was the outcome of a long and bitter fight by the churches and by the women of America to put down the drunkenness which was common throughout the country. It had been difficult to pass the law making America "dry"; it was impossible to carry it out; and finally, after sixteen years of effort, the experiment was abandoned in 1933.

In the cause of good morals, Americans had permitted the government to make encroachments on individual liberty which they would never otherwise have tolerated; but a very large minority always regarded Prohibition as an unwarrantable interference with their private lives, and defied the law. Illegal wine-merchants, known as "bootleggers", were established in every town, and the supply of prohibited drinks became an important nation-wide industry; but because the trade was illegal, it could not, except corruptly, get the protection of the law, and it became the prey of highly organized gangs of armed thieves.

"Racketeering", the levying by criminal gangs of a toll on the turn-over of a business, spread from the illegal bootlegging trade to perfectly legal trades such as laundering. In some big towns, the official administration fell under the influence of gangsters who bribed and bullied their way to power. Rival gangs of criminals carried on open vendettas, and innocent men, women and even children who happened to come into the line of fire were sometimes killed. Most Americans probably never saw a gangster, but they heard a great deal about them. The whole system of law was brought into contempt. Eventually Prohibition was abandoned, not because men were convinced that it was wrong to enforce morals by laws, but because of the social evils it had either intensified or created.

AMERICAN MASTERY OF INDUSTRIAL TECHNIQUE

Corruption was widespread. The Presidency of Calvin Coolidge from 1923 to 1929 was marked by investigations into charges of corruption against two cabinet ministers who, during President Harding's previous administration, had been concerned in the lease of government oilfields at Teapot Dome, Wyoming, to private companies. Large and unexplained sums of money were shown to have been paid to the ministers, who were forced to resign. As long as America remained prosperous, however, the Republican party might be discredited, but it could not be dislodged from the power which it had won when, in 1920, Woodrow Wilson, the Democratic party, and the policy of intervention in Europe were irately rejected by the electors. The prosperity of the war and post-war years, and with it the ascendancy of the Republican Party, continued until 1929.

During the golden years of wealth, many Europeans looked to the United States as the land which had solved the problem of prosperity. It was significant that, while the most famous men of the Old World were politicians, the most famous American was a business man, Henry Ford, whose life was widely read in England and still more in

Germany. America's secret seemed to lie not only in her jealously guarded home market of over 100,000,000 customers and in her industry's freedom from government control, but also in her high-wages policy, which encouraged efficiency; in her extensive use of labour-saving machinery, and in the great demand for goods, stimulated both by high wages and by the almost universal use of hire-purchase systems. In 1925, wages in London, measured in terms of power to buy food, were not much more than half what they were in Philadelphia. In Vienna and in Milan, they were only a quarter of the Philadelphia level. The use of machinery enormously increased production per worker in the United States. In coal-mining in 1923, the American worker's output was 693 tons compared with the Englishman's 229 tons, the Frenchman's 134, and the German's 103. At about the same time, there were roughly as many steel-workers in the United States as in Great Britain, but the American output was more than twice the British.

In 1920, the United States had abandoned any idea of political intervention in Europe, but could not give up economic intervention. As a result of the war, European governments owed the United States, mainly on account of American goods supplied, well over £2,000,000,000. But the United States could not be paid unless her debtors received payments from Germany as reparations. How interested America was in European finance is shown by the fact that the three main stages in the resettlement of reparations were each popularly known by the name of an American: the Dawes plan of 1924, the Young plan of 1929, and the Hoover moratorium of 1931, which suspended payments for a year, and in practice ended them.

THE SLUMP OF 1929

There were two sides to the resettlement: an official and a private side. Officially Germany's liabilities were reduced to sums which she might be able to pay; privately she was put in a position to pay them through large commercial investments by American and English financial houses. Individual Americans were lending Europe the money with which to pay the American government. At the same time, nearly all nations, and not least the United States, were making it impossible for international debts to be paid at all by refusing to accept goods from the debtors. Payment, therefore, could be made only in gold, and gradually the limited amount of gold in the world was collected more and more in New York, until three-fifths or more of the world supply lay idle there. Before this happened, there had been a panic in New York. In October, 1929, American investors suddenly took fright and the value of shares fell. Bankruptcies soon became common; weaknesses in the American banking system were discovered, and one bank after another closed its doors. American farmers, whose holdings were mortgaged to the banks, were sold up and whole areas of the Middle West were ruined.

The crisis spread throughout the world. In less than two years, the price at which goods could be sold was halved, but debts remained at their old level. Crops were destroyed in a vain effort to keep up prices, although, in the cities, the ever-increasing army of unemployed went hungry. The governor of Texas declared martial law in his state in an effort to keep up oil prices by reducing production. The crisis could not be checked. In the United States, no one knew how many were unemployed; as there was no unemployment insurance there was no record of their number. But there were at least 6,000,000; there may have been 15,000,000.

The panic-stricken country demanded new and vigorous leadership. They found both in the Democrat Franklin D. Roosevelt, who in 1932 was elected President by an overwhelming majority over President Hoover. The situation was so serious that his first act was to declare a general holiday for all banks. The depression had taught the United States two things: firstly, their unparalleled industrial prosperity had been won not by economic planning but by salesmanship—and salesmanship cannot control a financial crisis; secondly, America had suffered more than England from the crisis because she was unprotected by social legislation. Roosevelt determined to remove both these disabilities, and he propounded a series of far-reaching reforms. Congress gladly gave him emergency powers.

FRANKLIN D. ROOSEVELT'S NEW DEAL

First, aid was given to the farmers to save them from being sold up as bankrupts, while by controlling output, better prices for their goods were assured. Gigantic public works were undertaken to relieve unemployment. Among these were large afforestation schemes, which were urgently needed if enormous areas of the Middle West were not to become uncultivable desert as a result of soil erosion and drought. Within a month, a quarter of a million young unemployed men volunteered for this forest work. Industrial organization was remodelled by the introduction of "codes", regulations for industry, which were binding both on employers and employed. These codes fixed wages, hours, and conditions of employment. Schemes for unemployment insurance were suggested for the future. The carrying out of this social legislation was entrusted to the National Recovery Administration, a new body set up to popularize the "New Deal", as President Roosevelt christened his programme. The President's infectious confidence did much to remove the psychological obstacles to recovery, and his legislation stopped the terrifying progress of economic impoverishment.

Renewed prosperity brought a vigorous attack on Roosevelt's reforms. His opponents had not dared to move in the dark days of 1933; but by 1936 almost every employer and newspaper was assailing him bitterly. They had their answer in the presidential elections of that year, which Roosevelt won by an overwhelming majority.

The most venomously attacked provisions of the "New Deal" were those which recognized trade-unions and collective bargaining; American employers, as a class, had always hated the unions. Their dislike was shown vigorously; it was not uncommon to use firearms against strikers. The assault on the New Deal was carried out in the Supreme Court, which in America is charged with seeing that neither the Executive nor Congress takes powers which are not expressly granted to it by the Constitution. A long series of judgments declared that Congress had no authority to grant the President most of the special powers by which the New Deal had been carried out.

Gradually the scheme had to be abandoned; almost the only exception was the Tennessee Valley Administration, which brought prosperity to a derelict part of the United States, by compulsorily planning the economic life of the district. Roosevelt believed that the real obstacle to his plans was the Supreme Court. When he proposed to change the conditions under which the judges were appointed, violent opposition arose. Many previous supporters felt that he was destroying the independence of the judges, and turned against him. Political bickering and economic warfare absorbed energies in 1938: few citizens, except the President and his inner circle, had eyes for the shadow of German militarism which had fallen over Europe.

CHAPTER 78

EUROPE : THE RISE OF DICTATORSHIPS

FOR every European country, the peace was one of ambition unsatisfied. The French wanted security; the Germans wanted to establish a Liberal republic; both had their way, but not for long. Italy did not obtain the colonies which she passionately desired. East of the Rhine and the Rhône, where the new poverty was greatest, an acute class struggle led to the establishment of Fascist dictatorships. Liberal Italy went down before Benito Mussolini; Poland exchanged the gentle rule of the pianist Paderewski for the dictatorship of Marshal Pilsudski; the Austrian republic disappeared before Dollfuss, and the German before Adolf Hitler in 1933. Of the new or reconstructed states of Europe, only Czechoslovakia remained true to the democratic vision, and that despite the many races within her borders. She owed her immunity from dictatorship to her relative prosperity, her people's unusual instinct for orderly administration, and her fortunate possession of a great democratic prophet—the eighty-year-old President Masaryk, and a great democratic politician —Edward Benes.

The explanation of Europe's retreat from democracy lies in the changing experiences and attitude of the middle classes. After the war, lawyers, doctors, civil servants, soldiers and business men were exposed to the risk of unemployment, which had long been familiar to the working-classes. Poverty and unemployment had made the working-class revolutionary; they had the same effect upon the middle class. Before the war, the middle class had prospered in a capitalist society. No need, therefore, to attack capitalism; it was sufficient to attack the changes in capitalism since the war. Members of this class admired the small independent business man and denounced big trusts, Socialist agitators, bankers, and especially the Jewish bankers. They were strongly nationalist because they had received a good education and had entered fully into the literary, political and sentimental tradition of their various countries.

AFTER VERSAILLES—CENTRAL EUROPE : ITALY

The first two years after the war were a time of indecision. The old rulers had been utterly discredited, and the middle-class parties, which had shared their ideals, suffered from the same loss of prestige. For a time, authority throughout Central Europe passed to the Socialists, because they had had the least to do with the old order. Thus, in Germany, a working saddler, Fritz Ebert, became the first president of the German republic.

The fate of Central Europe throughout 1919 was as uncertain as that of Russia between March and November, 1917. In Hungary, a Communist dictatorship was established under Bela Kun, and was only overthrown after an invasion by Rumanian troops. In Germany, a Soviet government was set up in Munich, and there was a serious Communist rising in Berlin. In Italy, where disappointment with the peace had produced the outlook of a defeated power, there was the same chaos. Big strikes were frequent, and workers' soviets seized control of many northern factories.

In each country these movements failed. The middle class realized that its continued existence on a higher plane was threatened by the workers. It acted energetically, in alliance with the old discredited Conservatives, and it won unexpected support from the moderate Socialists, who believed in democracy and opposed the Communists on grounds of their constitutional principles. In Germany, the Communist movement was suppressed with considerable brutality by the middle-class parties and the old guard of imperialist Conservatives, under the leadership of the Socialist, Noske. Though a Liberal constitution was drawn up, the Republic was always in danger.

The defeat of Soviet Russia by Poland finally ended the prospect of a Communist revolution in Central Europe. In 1920 Marshal Pilsudski drove back the Soviet armies, which, after their victory in the civil wars, had been concentrated under Voroshilov against Poland. When peace was made, the Polish frontier was pushed about 150 miles eastward. With Russia's defeat, European Communism lost all hope of outside support.

It was Italy, under Mussolini's leadership, that set the fashion in middle-class dictatorships. Before the war, Mussolini had been an advanced Socialist, so advanced that he was driven into exile in Switzerland. The war turned him into a nationalist, who hated German oppression, but he did not become a Conservative.

As a political nation, Italy in 1919 was only sixty years old. She had achieved unity of Government, but still lacked unity of spirit. Above all, her political leaders were inadequate. The successors of the heroes of Italian liberation were no more than adroit politicians. England can live, in times of political dullness and self-seeking, on the inherited capital of a long, noble and continuous history. Italy had no such reserves of heroic emotion.

THE ECLIPSE OF ITALIAN LIBERALISM

The first stage in the Italian national uprising was associated not with Mussolini but with D'Annunzio, the best-known writer of pre-war Italy, a flamboyant personality whose name captured the imagination of young middle-class intellectuals. In the war, his exploits as an airman won for him a second reputation and a second following, this time of young middle-class men of action. Half artist, half soldier, he was a sort of Italian T. E. Lawrence. Italy wanted Dalmatia, the eastern shore of the Adriatic, whose little towns had been Italian in the days of the Venetian Empire, and earlier still, had been the home of Roman emperors, although the majority of the people were Slavs. The peace conference gave the whole coast-line south of Trieste to Yugo-Slavia. Italian politicians protested; D'Annunzio acted. In September, 1919, he seized the port of Fiume and there he established himself at the head of a state which was a strange mixture of musical comedy and high adventure. At Christmas, his reign was forcibly ended, when the Liberal prime minister Giolitti sent an Italian battleship to bombard Fiume.

The bombardment killed Liberal Italy, as well as D'Annunzio's political career. Parliamentary Italy, already dull, had now become anti-patriotic in the eyes of the nationalist middle-class. The future of Italy lay between a Socialist dictatorship and a middle-class dictatorship. The decision was not made until the end of 1922. In north Italy, Mussolini was building the Fascist party. They took their title from the Fasces, or bundles of rods surrounding an axe, carried before the magistrates of old Rome. In this badge are symbolized three of the main Fascist doctrines: the importance of unity, the authoritarian state, and the tradition of ancient Rome.

Mussolini's party was made up of young men who believed in direct action. They wore uniform—the black shirt; their marching song was called "Giovinezza", or "Youth", and was full of talk about the spring and the re-building of Italy. They carried on a vigorous street war with the young Socialists and Communists. They seemed the one alternative to Socialism; in October, 1922, a cabinet crisis showed that no government could be formed without their approval. Mussolini had won power, but he was determined not to take it in the ordinary parliamentary way. Instead of going quietly to Rome to take part in negotiations for a new government, he organized a March on Rome by thirty thousand Fascists from Milan. It was unnecessary, but it was good advertisement; from that march dated the Fascist revolution.

During the next two years, the Socialist and Liberal opposition to Fascism was suppressed. Communist and Socialist leaders were murdered; parliamentary opposition was extinguished by a new electoral law which limited the voters' choice to Fascist candidates; some politicians went into exile and others were interned on small Mediterranean islands. The most obvious feature of Fascism, as of Communism, was the dictatorship of one political party. Just as in Russia the only lawful party was the Communist party, so in Italy the only lawful party was the Fascist party. But while membership of the Russian Communist party was a carefully restricted privilege, the Fascist party sought a mass membership. Teachers in schools and universities, civil servants and business men were all, in practice, members. Such a party was not a government but a propaganda instrument. From the beginning, the dictatorship in Italy was personal. It was always Mussolini's dictatorship. Italy remained a kingdom, but the King, Victor Emmanuel III, had less power and less position than any other constitutional ruler.

WHY FASCISM PREVAILED

Fascism had its origin, in part, in the economic discontent of the middle class. It succeeded because Mussolini was able to lessen that discontent, through the creation of the Corporate State. He defended private property, but emphasized the social purpose of industry. Industries, he taught, existed for the good of the state and the good of the worker. If private owners were inefficient, the state itself undertook either to run their business or to see that it was run properly. The interests of the workers were protected by the new Fascist Corporations. Every worker and every employer had to belong to a trade union. Each industry was placed under a Corporation composed of representatives of employers and employed. The corporations fixed hours and conditions of work, and saw that they were kept. Labour courts took the place of strikes and lock-outs. A Ministry of Corporations formed a sort of industrial parliament. Old-age pensions, holiday and spare-time organizations were provided by the state—of course, like the corporations, in the name of Fascism, and for Fascists only. This economic settlement satisfied the middle classes; it exorcised their two bogeys, the profiteer and the striker.

Fascism meant also the nation in arms. Originally the Fascist militia was the body of enthusiasts who won the party's civil war against the Communists. It soon became the normal end of an Italian's education. As small children, as "boy scouts", and as young men, the male was educated to believe in the manliness of war, and to worship the example of the soldiers of Old Rome. Italian girls were brought up to be the mothers of soldiers.

Warlike opportunities were soon found for the new Italy. The bombardment of the helpless island of Corfu broke the recent alliance of Greeks and Italians, and emphasized Mussolini's claim that the Mediterranean was an Italian sea. In 1935, with the aid of poison-gas, de Bono and Badoglio overran Abyssinia, which had checked earlier Italian colonial aspirations at the battle of Adowa in 1896. In 1936, Mussolini's soldiers and airmen gave substantial help to the Spanish military rebellion, which overthrew the Liberal-Socialist government, supported by Russia. In Spain, Mussolini was the defender of Catholicism; across the Mediterranean he declared himself the Defender of Islam. The Fascists began to talk of "redeeming" Nice, Corsica and Tunisia, and to weaken the ties with France and Britain. Mussolini showed plainly that he regarded Fascist Italy as the heir of the old Roman Empire.

GERMANY'S ECONOMIC WEAKNESS

The Fascist revolution was the product of middle-class irritation; the Nazi revolution was partly the result of economic forces. The post-war history of Germany falls into two deep depressions separated by a high plateau of precarious prosperity. The first depression lasted from 1918 to 1923 and was the period in which the Nazi movement was born. There followed seven years of reprieve for Liberal Europe, and then in 1930 came the second depression which paved the way for the conquest of power by the Nazis in 1933.

In May, 1919, Germany was told the terms of the Treaty of Versailles. If she had refused to sign, the Entente occupation would have been extended from the Rhineland to Berlin. Every politician knew that acceptance was inevitable, but so great was the stampede from responsibility that only the Socialists were left to sign. They signed, reluctantly and with bitterness, to save the country from anarchy and foreign occupation; and because they signed, they were execrated by those of less political courage.

The treaty gave France the iron of Lorraine and the coal of the Saar to compensate her for the destruction of her northern coalfields; two years later, the mines of Upper Silesia were handed over to Poland. Germany was deprived of important sources of wealth but was expected both to keep her 60,000,000 people and to find £6,600,000,000 for reparations—the amount was not fixed until 1921. She fell behind with her payments, and in January, 1923, France invaded the Ruhr valley, the one large remaining German coalfield. She was met with a universal refusal to work. Eventually the Germans called off passive resistance, and European experts, under the chairmanship of the Chicago banker, Dawes, sat down to devise a scheme by which Germany could pay something.

Meanwhile, a social revolution had taken place inside Germany as a result of the inflation of the currency. The inflation was caused partly by the one-way traffic in foreign exchange—foreign currencies having to be bought for reparation payments with no corresponding purchases of German currency to offset them—and partly by the German government's frantic need for money, which could only be met by the printing-presses. There was complete ruin for everyone with a fixed income—such as pensioners and those living on savings. In the later stages of the inflation the purchasing power of wages fell before the worker could bring them home; the price of a restaurant meal increased between the time it was ordered and the time it was eaten. The only possible safeguard against this inflation was the immediate purchase of foreign currency.

Prudent middle-class people found themselves reduced to beggary and starvation. Many became violent and hated those who had caused, or were thought to have caused, their distress, or were profiting by it. They hated the Entente governments, who had carried the war into the peace. They hated the Socialists, who had signed the treaty. They hated the profiteers, who were making fortunes and spending them ostentatiously. They looked askance at debtors, who gained by the inflation, paying off in worthless paper marks money which had been lent and spent when marks were valuable. The vast debts which the German Government had accumulated during the war were wiped out in this way.

THE BEGINNINGS OF NAZISM

A great deal of German business and finance was in the hands of Jews, who provided another scapegoat to keep the Socialists company. Since the opening of the ghettos they had achieved eminence in Germany, not only as financiers, but also as doctors, lawyers, artists, musicians and writers. Now their brief enjoyment of toleration was abruptly ended, and the German people returned to its medieval hatred of these intrusive and persistent Semites. The young German, debarred from a military, naval or colonial career, turned to the professions, only to find them already crowded with intelligent Jews, who had won little scope for their abilities in the old imperial army. The men of Prussia, Saxony, Bavaria and the Rhineland, in their own distress, envied the apparent prosperity of men of an alien race and faith.

The condition of Germany led to a number of revolutionary movements. In 1920, the army attempted to overthrow the Republic, and was frustrated only by a general strike. Political assassinations became frequent. Rathenau, the Liberal Jew who controlled the great Electricity Trust, was murdered. Violence increased, and men who believed in democratic government began to despair.

Among the revolutionary movements was one which started in Bavaria under the leadership of Adolf Hitler, an Austrian-born ex-corporal in the German army. He called his party the National Socialist (Nazi) German Workers' Party. It had a programme and an appeal similar to Mussolini's Fascists. It stood for the middle classes and against big business, Jews, Socialists and friendship with foreign nations. It believed in force, and in 1923, Hitler, who had allied himself with Ludendorff, tried to copy Mussolini's march on Rome by a march from Munich to Berlin. The attempt was a failure; the military turned the marchers back a few miles outside Munich; Hitler himself was imprisoned, but he was released after a few months. The German republic not only believed in liberty—it practised it.

At the next general election, Hitler's party, already profiting from Dr. Goebbels' talent for advertising, gained over thirty seats; but by the end of 1924, when another election was held, the approach of prosperity made Hitler seem a tawdry and unnecessary revivalist. He lost half his followers and was condemned to an obscurity from which he did not escape until the return of the depression. There was nothing as yet to mark out Hitler's party from the mass of flamboyant and high-handed nationalist groups competing for the favour of students and ex-servicemen who were without work or prospects.

The next seven years are the years of Gustav Stresemann's ascendancy. Stresemann, a fat good-humoured member of the upper middle-class, was a fervent German patriot. He had been a militant nationalist in his youth, but the peace had convinced him that his country's prosperity depended on loyally carrying out her treaty obligations; if Germany continued to act as though she believed that France and England would treat her decently, in time they would come to do so. The conservative Prussian squires regarded such a policy as dishonourable; the Communists denounced it as opportunist capitalism; but the nation as a whole supported the policy of Stresemann while the fat years of prosperity continued to last.

FAILURE OF THE GERMAN REPUBLIC

In the end, his patience was rewarded when in France Poincaré's policy of vigorous realism was replaced by Briand's policy of reconciliation. In July, 1925, the French withdrew from the Ruhr; in October, the Locarno treaties were signed, by which Britain guaranteed Germany against a French invasion as well as France against a German one. In 1926, Germany was admitted to the League of Nations and given a permanent seat as a great power on its Council. In 1929, reparation payments were revised once more in Germany's favour, and in 1930, the last foreign troops left the Rhineland. This result was largely due to the fact that the countries who had won the war felt that Stresemann was a man who could be trusted.

Unhappily Stresemann died in 1929, while still in early middle age; the Liberal Briand was replaced by Tardieu, a determined enemy of Germany; and there was a slump in Wall Street, which gradually overwhelmed most of Europe. The slump brought down the flimsy structure of German prosperity, financed entirely on foreign borrowing. Prices fell, and the number of unemployed rose rapidly. The German Government had a paralysing fear of a return of the horrors of inflation. Its policy, therefore, was financially orthodox—at all cost, bankruptcy must be avoided, because bankruptcy would mean a new fall of the mark. Taxes were increased, social services reduced, wages and salaries cut and staffs decreased. By 1932 the distress caused by avoiding bankruptcy was almost as great as that which had been caused ten years earlier by courting it.

The return of distress brought with it the return of revolution. The extreme parties on either side had always maintained private armies: now these armies were put on a war footing, and street fighting between Hitler's Brown Shirts and the men of the Communist Red Front became an almost nightly occurrence in Berlin and other big towns. Only the Communists and the Nazis had survived the years of prosperity, and they alone profited by the new depression. The Republicans did nothing to put down the armed menace.

HITLER ACHIEVES POWER

The survivors of the old imperial Germany thought that their time had come again. They were entrenched in the small professional army allowed by the Versailles Treaty and in the presidency to which Field-Marshal von Hindenburg—the perfect Prussian squire in his obstinacy, his rigid conservatism and his narrow uprightness—had been elected in 1925. These men hated the Communists as natural enemies of their country, despised the Republicans as ineffectual degenerates, and disliked the vulgarity of Hitler's revolutionary party. They saw an opportunity to re-establish the old disciplined Prussian state. They abolished parliamentary government, and ruled by emergency decrees, with Brüning, von Papen and von Schleicher as their successive Chancellors. They built up the army, in spite of the Versailles Treaty, and persuaded the Lausanne Conference to abolish reparations in 1932; but they failed to suppress National Socialism, because patriotic Germans had gone over to that creed.

Hitler provided the emotional outlet of mob oratory, while the Conservatives were inarticulate. A man of the people himself, he held out to the people the bait of wider opportunities and a revolutionary settlement of the economic problem. Against this the Conservatives had nothing to offer, except an impossible return to the past, in which four quarterings of nobility had been the best passport to position and employment. The German middle class, thirsting for an outlet for their patriotism, supported Hitler, and at the beginning of 1933, Hindenburg reluctantly appointed him Chancellor. The Communists' defeat, which began at the polling-booth, was consummated in the fire which destroyed the Reichstag early in 1933.

Once he had won power, Hitler began to establish a Nazi state, which would reserve all authority to his party, and block any possi-

bility of a change of government. He had secured Germany's
gratitude by buttressing her confidence and self-esteem, and a succession of plebiscites confirmed his aims. In foreign affairs he completed
his predecessors' task. They had freed the Rhineland; he refortified
it, and repudiated the armaments clauses of the Versailles Treaty.
They had secured Germany's admission to the League as a great
power; he left the League, but won from it the return of the Saar to
Germany. His people gave him the credit they had refused to his
predecessors, because, where Republican Germany had asked, Nazi
Germany took. German propaganda had been used skilfully. Hitler
could take without asking, because the rest of Europe no longer
approved wholeheartedly of the Versailles peace terms, and was in no
position to enforce them against a rearmed Germany.

The German military staff was rapidly rebuilding the military
machine which had devastated Europe twenty years earlier. Hitler,
who ruled as *der Führer*, or The Leader, after Hindenburg's death,
went almost too fast for them in his audacious foreign policy. But
France and Britain did not combine to enforce the Versailles terms.
The former was distracted by struggles between Capital and Labour;
Britain's wish for "Peace in our time" moulded the policy of successive premiers, MacDonald, Baldwin and Neville Chamberlain.

Even in these favourable circumstances Hitler's sudden annexation
of Austria, in March, 1938, was a dangerous stroke. Vienna was one
of the great European capitals; Austria had been a sovereign state
since the Middle Ages. Since 1919 she had maintained a precarious
independence, largely under the protection of Italy. Now Italian *Duce*
and German *Führer* were drawing closer together. No power did
anything to help the Austrian Chancellor, Schuschnigg, when his
capital was occupied by the Austrian-born dictator of Germany.

THE THREE GREAT DICTATORSHIPS

Meanwhile the National Socialist dreams of Hitler's followers were
fading. Goering, the chief of the rapidly expanding Luftwaffe, which
overshadowed the British and French Air Forces, bluntly gave his
countrymen the choice of "Guns or Butter". Plain living and hard
work were accepted loyally by the nation. The big employers who
supplied Hitler with funds were right in trusting him not to destroy
Capitalism. On June 30, 1934, many of the more radical Nazis were
butchered, and the Brownshirt Army ceased to be a semi-independent
force. Those who hated capitalists were encouraged to bait the Jews,
and that persecuted race became a lightning-conductor to protect
"Aryan" capitalists.

Like other dictatorships, the Nazi state secured itself by terror and
propaganda. The terror crushed all opposition to the government;
critics were sent to concentration camps, and the Gestapo under
Himmler's rule proved as ruthless and efficient a secret police as the
Ogpu in Russia. Gestapo agents operated among all classes. Chil-

dren were encouraged to denounce their parents for criticizing Hitler and the other Nazi leaders. The old sanctities of friendship and family life disappeared. No one who failed to give total obedience to the Nazi creed was safe against betrayal to the Gestapo. Goebbels dictated propaganda to prevent Germans from learning anything that damaged Nazi credit. Broadcasting, newspapers, letters, telephone conversations, books, schools, boy scouts and churches were strictly controlled; no one could hear news or views distasteful to the government. By these means the German people, and particularly the young, were schooled to believe that Hitler was right.

Nazis, Communists and Fascists were consequently all opposed to the Christian claim to a loyalty separate from and higher than that due to the state. In Russia the Communist hatred of religion was at the beginning quite open and every possible difficulty was put in the way of its teaching and practice, though with the passage of time freedom of worship and the use of churches was resumed. The Church, however, continued to be separated from the State.

The Communist persecution was not altogether surprising since in Russia the leaders of the Church had been the close allies of the Tsars and supporters of the existing social order. The same alliance between the leaders of the Church and the leaders of society characterized the greater part of Europe—in Great Britain and America, on the other hand, there were influential non-conformist bodies, which broke the general union of Church and capital by drawing the leaders as well as their members from working-class people.

Since the Nazi and Fascist dictatorships drew support from the comfortable classes they could not afford to quarrel with the Church as openly as the Communists had done. They even had to pose as allies of religion, while securing that control of opinion to which the Church could never consent. Mussolini even found it worth while to conciliate Roman Catholic opinion by recognizing in 1929 the Pope as sovereign ruler of the tiny Vatican State—the palace to which Pius IX retired when in 1870 the Kingdom of Italy deprived him of the last part of the Temporal Power and made Rome its capital.

But the quarrels over education were serious and far more important in the long run than the surface friendliness between the Church and Vatican State.

In Germany conflict was more open. Hitler faced serious opposition from both Lutherans and Roman Catholics. Persecution of the Jews is an integral part of the Nazi creed. Christianity repudiates this activity, and the position was made worse when many of the anti-Semitic Nazi leaders attacked Christianity because of its Jewish origin. Lutheran pastors were imprisoned, Catholic monasteries persecuted. It seemed impossible to reconcile Christian ideals with those who claimed total obedience to *der Führer* and talked of his subjects as a *Herrenvolk*, by which he meant they were destined to impose their "Aryan" will on all "inferior" peoples.

F F   (H.W.)

CHAPTER 79

THE STORY OF THE FAR EAST

THE ten years between Queen Victoria's first and second jubilees were the heyday of the British Empire. Never had England been so powerful. London was crowded with young men from distant dependencies who came to learn the secret of her strength that they might share it. Among them was Mohandas Karamchand Gandhi. He dressed elaborately in English clothes, he learned ballroom dancing, he took lessons in French, he was called to the Bar. In short, he turned himself into a copy of an English gentleman.

Forty years later, Gandhi was once again in London. He had grown old and frail, but the greatest change was the change of spirit. His carefully chosen West End clothes, the symbol of British prestige, had been replaced by the simplest native dress, of plain "khaddar" homespun cloth—the symbol of revolt from Western materialism. He lived in a settlement among the London slums, but by day he made his way to St. James's Palace, to the Round Table Conference.

In the United States of America, there are twice as many people as in the largest of the disunited states of Europe, excluding Russia; in India, there are three times as many people as in the United States. In Europe, there are twenty-seven nations and forty languages; in India, there are two hundred languages and two thousand caste divisions. Europe has one religion, Christianity; India is split by the deep hatred between Hindus and Moslems. Except under the reigns of Asoka and Akbar, India has never known political union.

GANDHI AND INDIAN NATIONALISM

The English are the parents of modern Indian nationalism. They brought India under one government, so that peace was secured; they built her roads and railways, alleviated famines and gave every villager impartial justice. Schools and universities were built—there are about eighty thousand students in Indian colleges to-day. Her sons from the north and the south learnt a common language, the language of their conquerors. They studied English books. Shelley fired them with a passion for liberty, Burke inspired them with his faith in representative government.

Unlike India's previous conquerors, the English in India refused to be assimilated. They remained aloof. They could direct India, they could not lead her. And so Indians came to think of self-government and nationality as something to be taken from England, and not as something to be achieved with English help.

In the war years, promises were easily given, and in 1917, England offered India self-government as soon as she was capable of it. In 1919, a first instalment of reforms was introduced. A central assembly was set up, but it was a debating society rather than a parliament. In the provinces, real Indian parliaments were established, but they were given control only over certain social services, and the money they could spend on them was limited. Indian disappointment was reflected in an outbreak of terrorism, to which the Government replied by allowing the police to arrest suspects without a warrant and imprison them without a trial. The Indian leaders proclaimed a one-day strike of protest. In Amritsar, the military were called in, for fear of rioting; their commander ordered his men to fire. Four hundred unarmed Indians were killed and over a thousand wounded. The Amritsar "massacre" turned Gandhi from a friend of England to the prophet of Indian nationalism.

European rule had brought with it European industry. The Indian villager—and almost every Indian is a villager—used to spin his own cotton. The English connection brought Lancashire cotton goods to India; later, Japanese factories competed with Lancashire; and by the end of the war, India herself had a large manufacturing industry. Machinery made cotton cloth more cheaply than the village spinning-wheel and handloom could do; and throughout India, the peasant became merely a farmer and gave up his subsidiary occupations. For six months in the year, he was condemned to idleness; for twelve months, to a devastating poverty which has no European parallel. To Gandhi, this was "the problem of problems". The solution he found was the revival of the village cloth industry. He preached and practised the wearing of nothing but home-made khaddar cloth. The spinning-wheel became the emblem of Indian nationalism side by side with the hammer and sickle of Soviet Russia, the crooked cross of Germany and the Fascist lictor's rods.

Gandhi found India rotten with drug-taking and drink, so he imposed a complete abstinence on himself and his followers. The revival of khaddar hit the Lancashire cotton trade; the preaching of prohibition also injured Britain, for opium was a Government monopoly and spirits were extensively imported by British merchants. Purdah (the seclusion of women), child-marriage and widespread prostitution were common features of Indian life. Gandhi persuaded the Nationalist Party Congress to oppose these time-honoured customs.

GANDHI'S METHOD OF MORAL REVOLUTION

Even more important was the campaign of atonement to the untouchable outcasts. Hindus are rigidly divided into castes, which roughly correspond to social position and occupation. Each caste is a watertight compartment. Men are born into a caste and die in it; they may not marry outside it. Below the lowest caste, even, are the untouchables or outcasts. Two Indians out of every three are Hindus; out of every four, one is an untouchable, who may not enter a temple or use the common village-well. Orthodox Christianity, believing in immortality, had preached a hell in which, after this life, sinners would be punished; orthodox Hinduism, believing in reincarnation, imposed a hell in this life on millions of their fellow-men, who were supposed to have sinned grievously in some previous existence. Gandhi set his face against this doctrine. To the shame and horror of the orthodox, he, a high-caste Hindu, ate and drank and lived with outcasts. After a struggle, he was able to persuade the members of Congress to accept his teaching and his personal authority.

GANDHI'S POLICY

So important did Gandhi consider this question that, in 1933, he virtually retired from political politics, in order to devote himself to what might be called moral politics. By instinct, Gandhi was a conservative, eager to preserve and restore the traditions and practices of India's past. In his advocacy of khaddar against machine-made cloth, he seemed to Europeans little better than a sentimental and impractical reactionary. But in moral questions, he was a violent revolutionary.

To Hindus, Gandhi became Mahatma Gandhi, a religious teacher, not a politician. His religion is Hinduism, but Hinduism transformed by contact with Christian ethics. The means he uses to attain his ends is called Satyagraha, a practice which he first undertook in a successful struggle for Indian rights in South Africa before 1914. It is a difficult word to translate. It means something like "the force of spiritual love". Englishmen found Gandhi's non-co-operation, passive resistance and civil disobedience particularly tiresome forms of insubordination. To Gandhi's followers they were expressions of a pure and loving spirit, leading to the compelling self-sacrifice which sent Jesus to the Cross and established Christianity. In 1920 and 1930 Gandhi called all India to Satyagraha; on both occasions some of his followers turned passive resistance into violence. Gandhi did not then blame police provocation, as other leaders would have done, but the lack of single-minded purity in himself and his followers.

Many Indians did not accept the Mahatma's leadership. In particular the Moslems stood apart. They had ruled most of India for eight centuries, and they despised most Hindus as a conquered people, who worshipped innumerable idols instead of the one god, Allah. They respected fighting Hindus like the Sikhs and the Rajputs; but they had no liking for the prospect of a Congress-ridden India.

DISUNITY BETWEEN HINDUS AND MOSLEMS

In 1930 Gandhi proclaimed the second campaign of his religious warfare, when the Indian Government refused the Hindu demand for certain immediate reforms and ultimate independence. He opened hostilities by picking up a handful of salt on the sea-shore, and thus broke the Government ban on a tax-free salt. He was arrested, and by the end of the year fifty-four thousand men and women had joined him in gaol. The Viceroy, the present Viscount Halifax, was fitted by his deep personal religion to understand Gandhi and win his respect. A truce was agreed upon so that an attempt might be made to find a form of government for India agreeable to all parties.

Gandhi went to London to join the Round Table Conference which was studying the problem. The differences of Moslems and Hindus, princes and lawyers, had to be reconciled by political methods. The Mahatma could not work with such instruments; in a conference of politicians he was lost. He returned to India a disappointed man, to find a new Viceroy and a truce which had been broken on both sides. He was put back into prison, and a rigorous attempt was made to repress the nationalist disorders which arose as the result of the failure of the Conference.

Meanwhile in London British ministers proposed an All-India Federation, in which it was hoped that the native princes, as well as British India, would be represented. Though many Britons looked on Gandhi as a disastrous obstructionist, the central Government was given considerable powers. The Congress party hesitated to work the new constitution; and its refusal would have made the whole scheme a failure.

Eventually Congress decided to take part in the elections; it won victories in a majority of the provinces, and formed provincial ministries. This decision seemed to indicate a growth of political common sense in India. There were many difficulties. Provincial governors were faced by recalcitrant ministries when they exercised their "reserved" powers. Moslem–Hindu jealousy still continued, and Jinnah, the Moslem leader, put forward his scheme of *Pakistan*, to protect the predominantly Moslem provinces from Hindu domination. The responsibility for the defence of India rested with the British Government and the Viceroy; there was little sign that they would receive the whole-hearted support of Indian politicians, though the Indian princes maintained their traditional loyalties. Gandhi's non-resistance seemed out-of-date in a world darkened by the growing shadow of militarism. In spite of much good will in all quarters, no solution had yet been found of India's problems of races, castes and creeds.

SUN YAT-SEN LEADS THE CHINESE REVOLUTION

When Dr. Sun Yat-sen died, in 1925, the congregation at his funeral service sang his favourite hymns, "Jesus, Lover of my Soul", and "Peace, perfect peace", for Sun was a Christian. His body was laid in a great shrine at Nanking, where each year thousands came to reverence the leader whose teachings are the new commandments of Chinese life. His metal coffin with its crystal lid was sent as a gift from Moscow, whose rulers had aided him, though they did not share his faith.

Sun Yat-sen was born into a China which had been exposed against her will to Western influence. Her humiliating defeat in the Japanese War, in 1894, made Sun an implacable rebel against the

Manchu dynasty. For seventeen years, he lived the precarious life of a hunted outlaw. The Government set a price of £100,000 on his head, but he travelled throughout China in disguise. He gained the confidence of the great secret societies which, for hundreds of years, had united the Chinese in a patient struggle against the Manchus.

He made two world-tours, inspiring the Chinese everywhere with his passion for a national renaissance. Once, in broad daylight, he was kidnapped in the streets of London and taken to the Chinese Legation, but his life was saved by an English servant, who carried a message to Sir James Cantlie, under whom Sun had studied medicine. When, at last, in 1911, the emperor was deposed, power fell not to Sun, who had inspired the revolution, but to Yuan Shih-kai, an old Manchu official who ruled by the power of the sword.

JAPANESE IMPERIALISM IN CHINA

The Manchu empire had been overthrown because it had not protected the country from foreign pressure. Even less successful was the nominal republic which followed. With a population even bigger than India's—out of every four men living, one is a Chinese—China was the world's richest prospective market and a fertile source of raw materials. Plainly, it would be difficult to regain her lost independence, the right to run her own economic life in her own way for her own profit. In the nineteenth century, the danger had come from the European countries which had established settlements at the mouths of the three great rivers along which the life of China flows. Their special privileges were still a grievance, but the chief difficulty now came from Japan. The imperialism of the Western Powers was stationary, that of Japan was advancing.

While Europe was at war, Japan forced Yuan Shih-kai to agree to the "Twenty-One Demands", which, if they had been fully carried out, would have made China a Japanese protectorate. Yuan died in 1916, and Sun Yat-sen came into power—but only in South China. As often in Chinese history, the north was divided from the south.

At the peace conference, China trusted in President Wilson's promises of self-determination. At the very least, she hoped to regain Germany's settlements in China, but Japan having conquered these possessions in the course of the war, refused to surrender them. Europe and America would not, or could not, help China to become a free and united nation, so she looked elsewhere for help. In exile, Sun had met many Russian Communist leaders. Since the Liberal powers had failed him, he turned to Soviet Russia. Lenin agreed to help to free China and not to raise the issue of Communism. That agreement was loyally carried out, but in 1927, Chinese Communists attempted to make a revolution. The Kuomintang, Sun Yat-sen's national party, was split. The majority followed the anti-communist, Chiang Kai-shek. The minority collected a Red Army, which, at different times, controlled various parts of China.

The civil war with the Communists, complicated by further divisions in the Kuomintang, paralysed the central Government and gave Japan an excuse for more interference. She first conquered Manchuria and turned it into the protectorate of Manchukuo under the Manchu ex-emperor. Later she seized control of Jehol and the other northern provinces of China from the disunited Chinese war-lords. In 1937 Japanese armies attacked Central China. They anticipated little resistance from their disunited and ill-equipped enemies, and omitted the old formality of declaring war. They treated their opponents as Communists or guerillas, who obstructed Tokio's plans for the "Greater Asia Prosperity Sphere". Shanghai and Nanking were captured, and no consideration was paid to the commercial interests of Japan's old allies.

Chinese spirit remained unbroken. Civil wars were forgotten in a widespread rally to protect the old Chinese way of life. Chiang Kai-shek proved himself a wise and vigorous leader of the national resistance. He managed to secure a small supply of modern equipment, much of which came along the Burma road, as the invaders overran the Chinese seaboard. Russia and America were sympathetic with China, but neither country intervened actively against the Mikado's army, air-force and fleet. Chiang Kai-shek fought on, and was prepared to retire far inland to Chung-king rather than be absorbed into the fast-growing Japanese empire. The Chinese "incident" refused to be liquidated. Chinese men and women endured stubbornly all the savage penalties of modern warfare, rather than abandon the new rights they had won and the old traditions they still held dear.

When the Chinese Republic was founded, men cut off their pigtails and women ceased to bind their feet. The pigtail was the badge of obedience to the foreign Manchu dynasty. Its disappearance was the proclamation of an independence which has been achieved in spirit, though it has not yet been realized completely in politics.

BUILDING A NEW CHINA

Independence meant not only the liberation of old China from foreign rule, but the building of a new China, free from the tremendous tyranny of the past. The giving up of foot-binding was a demonstration of that renewal. In the old China, young girls had their feet painfully bound, in submission to the customs of family life. The family was the centre of all loyalties, greater than patriotism or personal attachment. Men, and, still more, women, were not regarded as individuals, precious to God for themselves, but simply as sons or grandsons, wives or daughters-in-law. Marriages were arranged between young children by their respective families, and unwanted girls were strangled at birth. The Chinese family was dominated by the dead: ancestor-worship, the essential Chinese religion, was its supreme purpose. It was a miniature patriarchal state—a clan, not a family.

The bonds which held it together were those of moral obligation, not of love: if a man's duty as a son or a brother cut across his duty as a husband, it was the former which prevailed.

The new China adopted the Western Christian ideal of the small family, based on personal affection, in place of the old clan, based on official relationship. The equality of women and men, which Sun taught and the new China practises, was a reform in Europe; it is a revolution in Asia. Typical of the new position of women were the Soong sisters, one of whom married Chiang Kai-shek and shared with him the glory of reviving and protecting Chinese life.

DIFFICULTIES OF CHINESE REFORM

The old China honoured learning above all things. In the order of social classes, the scholar came first, the soldier last. Entrance to Government service was controlled by a strenuously competitive examination, and to prevent "cribbing", the candidates were shut up in separate cells for several days on end. But boys were taught only the Chinese classics, and taught them unintelligently.

Education was confined to the few, for the written language of China was almost as different from the spoken language as French is from Latin, and there was not one spoken language, but many. Further, it took years of hard study to learn to read and write Chinese correctly, for instead of the twenty-six letters of our alphabet, there were thousands of Chinese characters. The new China modernized the subject-matter of education and simplified the written language so drastically that anyone could learn it. The country remained illiterate as a whole, but it was only a question of time before everyone would be able to read. China was always a land which honoured scholars; it aimed at becoming a land of scholars.

Besides national independence and democratic government, Sun Yat-sen was determined to secure for all Chinese a decent standard of living. The undertaking was tremendous. Englishmen were alarmed by the competition of Japanese workers with their low standard of living; the Chinese are accustomed to a still lower standard.

The rice-farming of China was carried on by methods which were old before Britain was invaded by Rome. The peasants had no machinery and little manure. Their tiny farms were divided into strips which were sometimes as much as a mile apart. The fields themselves depended on an irrigation-system which had not greatly changed for three thousand years.

Everywhere the peasants were harassed by heavy rents, if they were tenant-farmers, and by intolerable loan interest. In Kiangsi, tenant farmers had to surrender between 50% and 80% of the produce of their farms, for rent and interest charges. Then taxes had to be paid, and taxes in China grew larger to meet the needs of the rival warlords whose armies had to be fed. In good years, there was just enough for peasants and soldiers. In bad years, there was only enough for the soldiers, and sometimes not even enough for them. The one crop which flourished was the poppy, from which the opium was made, the sale of which enriched the generals but impoverished the people. Constant famine was the Chinese farmer's reward.

Into this world of poverty came modern industry. Here employers found marvellously cheap labour: in 1926, a cotton operative in Shanghai earned 24s. a month, although the cost of living was said to be 32s. a month for a man and wife and 42s. 8d. for a family of five. The long hours and low returns which the peasant suffered were now experienced by an ever-growing army of factory workers. But there was a difference. The farmer was poor because he produced little. The factory worker was poor although he produced much.

Sun's solution to this problem, similar to that of India but even more intense, was the opposite of Gandhi's. The poverty of the peasant, the root of China's troubles, was to be cured not by the return of the spinning-wheel, but by the introduction of artificial manure. Floods, such as that which, five years after Sun's death, killed millions of Chinese in the Yang-tse valley, could, he saw, only be cured by costly works of river-improvement; efficient relief work depended on the improvement of communications and the building of roads and railways. Many thousands died in 1931 and 1932 simply because the food, which America would willingly have provided, could not be transported to the starving. Sun was ready to welcome foreign capital, foreign experts and foreign machinery; but only if they came as the guests of a strong government, to be used to raise the people's standard of living, and not to exploit a land which promised immense profits from low wages. But China failed to achieve political independence, and she had to receive "capitalism" as a master and not as a servant controlled by the Chinese people.

RELIGION IN THE CHANGING EAST

China's religion, from the time of Confucius, always laid more stress on conduct than on the supernatural, although Buddhism and Taoism still influenced the minds of millions. The ethics of Christianity made an enormous appeal to China. Not only Sun but many other Chinese leaders became Christians. They believed that their programme for the renaissance of China was a necessary implication of the social teaching of Jesus. They did not find the Christian Powers quite of their opinion, and the help given towards its fulfilment was insufficient for the purpose. The future of China was to be fought out between those who believe in Christianity, in spite of the Christian Powers, and those who believe that the salvation of China can only come from using the un-Christian methods employed by the Christian Powers in the past, and in the present by Japan.

In China, the soldier's has been the least honourable of occupations; in Japan, it is the noblest. China, the peace-loving, had to surrender before Western imperialism; Japan, the warlike, successfully overrode those Western nations with whom she came into conflict. Throughout Asia, men began to think that Japanese militarism was something to be imitated as well as feared.

The officers of the imperial Japanese army are the heirs of the Samurai, the knightly class of old Japan. They inherit the highly developed military code of honour, called Bushido, which exalts the soldier's qualities to a general ideal of behaviour. The good soldier is the good man. Courage, honour, discipline, physical fitness, chivalry are the most prized virtues. These qualities are devoted entirely to the service of the Emperor, whose family has ruled in Japan since before the birth of Christ. The Emperor is the Mikado, the son of Heaven, a god on earth. His service is religion.

Shintoism, the national religion, teaches worship of the natural forces of the homeland. The word "Japan" means the Rising Sun, which is depicted on every Japanese flag; the country is still under the special protection of the sun-goddess, Amaterasu-O-Mi-Kami, from whom Jimmu Tenno and every subsequent Mikado is descended. To the Japanese, religion and patriotism were not separate forces; religion was patriotism. Every Japanese is the son of God: his national inheritance is a complete and unthinking devotion to his country, which Hitler and Mussolini could never quite command, because of the European Christian tradition that "our citizenship is in heaven".

JAPAN'S INDUSTRIAL POLICY

The period of Meiji, or enlightened government, lasted from 1867 until the world economic crisis. To meet the threat of Western imperialism, the Samurai had surrendered their feudal privileges, stopped quarrelling among themselves, and helped to build up their country as a first-rate power on Western lines. Japan adopted, with conspicuous success, the methods of modern industry. During the European war of 1914 to 1918, she doubled her industrial output.

Although Japan escaped the horrors and destruction of the war, she suffered a paralysing disaster of her own. In 1923, an earthquake destroyed the cities of Tokio and Yokohama. At one stroke, 160,000 people were killed and over £500,000,000 worth of damage done. The immediate horror of an earthquake and its lasting moral effects are greater than those of any other calamity. Yet Japan's industrial advance was not broken. Less than ten years later, she had become the greatest cotton-exporting country in the world. For a hundred years, Lancashire had clothed the world; now Japan drew level. Low wages and long hours (though not so low or so long as China's) gave her an advantage, but her success was due still more to modern equipment and sensible organization.

Japan had to become the workshop of the East, if she was to live. Her population was increasing at the rate of nearly a million a year. In two generations, it had doubled. The extra mouths had to be fed, but every scrap of cultivable land was already worked. In 1924, there were 2,000,000 farmers in Japan with holdings of less than $1\frac{1}{4}$ acres, and two-thirds of all the farmers cultivated less than $2\frac{1}{2}$ acres apiece. The Japanese are a home-loving nation, but even if they had been willing to emigrate, there was nowhere for them to go. The relatively empty lands of Manchuria were too cold for Japanese farmers; the empty spaces of Australia, New Zealand, and America's Pacific coast were closed to them. Japan had to sell goods abroad if her people were to be fed; she had to sell vast quantities if they were to be well fed. But Japan, whose geographical position and industrial achievements are similar to England's, had not England's advantage of raw materials. Japan must import and pay for her raw materials in vast quantities of manufactured goods or in banking and shipping services. Until these payments are made, Japan's industry cannot raise her standard of living. She had every motive to secure colonies which could supply her with raw materials.

In her search for the secret of European power, Japan had adopted parliamentary government, as well as capitalist industry. A gradually widening electorate (in 1925 working-class men were given the vote) chose members of parliament to whom the cabinet ministers were nominally responsible. Two great parties, very roughly corresponding to the English pre-war Conservative and Liberal parties, took turns in governing the country. The industrial workers of the towns began to organize trade-unions and a Socialist party. The two great capitalist banks, which stood behind the two leading political parties, disapproved, and drastic laws were passed to suppress "dangerous thoughts", which is the Japanese euphemism for Communism.

JAPANESE IMPERIALISM AND MILITARISM

For ten years after the war, Japan, under its parliamentary government, followed a conciliatory policy abroad. Four crises were met with great restraint. The peace conference gave Japan all Germany's Pacific colonies—not only those in China, but the island colonies which stood between the United States and her Philippine dependency and were the cable stations of the American system. The United States were alarmed by Japanese imperialism, and in 1921 a war in the Pacific seemed possible. Instead, a conference was held in Washington, at which Japan not only agreed to limit her navy to three-fifths of the American, but also gave back Shantung to China. In 1924, the United States passed a law forbidding Japanese to settle in America. She genuinely feared that her standard of living would be lowered by Asiatic competition. But to the Japanese the new immigration act was an insult; they accepted it with their national power of hiding their feelings. In 1927, for a short time, the militants in Japan gained power and reoccupied Shantung, but very soon a Liberal government was back in power and ordered a fresh evacuation of the province. Finally in 1930, at the London Naval Conference, Ramsay MacDonald appealed over the heads of the Japanese delegation to the Japanese Prime Minister—a most unusual breach of diplomatic etiquette. The Prime Minister agreed to the limitation of Japanese auxiliary naval craft, which Britain wanted to secure. But it was the last victory of conciliation: two weeks later, the Japanese Prime Minister was assassinated, and a new period of Japanese history opened.

The Japanese army had long been restless. In 1931, the world economic crisis gave it the opportunity it needed, if it was again to take control. All countries suffered, but Japan was less able than most to bear the loss, because, even in prosperity, her people were only just able to keep themselves alive. The prices obtainable for all products fell disastrously, but most serious was the fall in the price of silk. Japanese farmers had just been able to exist by cultivating mulberry leaves and raising silkworms, to supplement the staple crop of rice. The silk was sold mainly to the United States. The growing use of artificial silk was a long-term threat to this vital industry, but it was the sudden poverty of America which brought ruin to Japan. In its desperation, the country welcomed an aggressive foreign policy, just as the people of Germany did under rather similar circumstances. Japan did this the more gladly because the Chinese met her aggression by destroying her export trade by a widely-observed boycott, and because Manchuria was showing signs of restlessness.

THE INVASION OF MANCHURIA

Manchuria had been part of the Chinese Empire for centuries, but it was an empty and unwanted territory until recent years. In the twentieth century, however, it was coveted by the Japanese for the sake of its coal and iron, and also for its wheat-growing possibilities—since the Japanese are beginning, though reluctantly, to eat corn as well as rice. It was being developed by Japanese, but peopled by Chinese. Each year, a million men and women moved north from the overcrowded lands of China proper to the open spaces of Manchuria. It seemed as if, in time, China would, by mere weight of numbers, rob Japan of the economic monopoly in Manchuria. To prevent this, the Japanese army decided on annexation.

The unsettlement of Manchuria, under the rule of a Chinese war-lord, seemed sufficient reason, and an excuse was soon found in a bomb outrage on the South Manchurian railway in 1931. Within a year, the Chinese armies and officials had been driven from the country. Manchuria became Manchukuo and a new government was installed, under the complete control of the Japanese army-chiefs. All this was carried out despite protests from the League of Nations; of which the only result was that Japan promptly resigned from the League. Subsequent Japanese penetration inside China proper, which made Peking and the three northern provinces a virtual Japanese protectorate, was carried out with even less resistance from Europe and the League.

The significant fact behind this rapid extension of the Japanese empire was that it was the work of the army, acting independently of the political Government. The official Cabinet and parliamentary system were not rejected, as in Germany; they were put on one side, largely by the judicious use of assassination. Japan adopted representative government as part of the secret of European success. She came to the conclusion that she was mistaken in this belief, and therefore put it aside in favour of a system more suited to her own ideas. This was easy, because the heads of the army and navy were always responsible personally to the Emperor, and not to the parliament.

THE ARMED FORCES DICTATE JAPANESE POLICY

The army placed itself at the head of the nation, seeking to lead it in every way to a kind of national socialism. The officers pointed out that their ancestors in 1867 had surrendered their privileges to secure the good of the country: similar sacrifices, they maintained, should be made by the wealthy manufacturers of the day. The widespread corruption of parliamentary politics must be replaced by soldierly obedience and frugality. Thousands of pamphlets preaching these doctrines were distributed each year by the army authorities. The ideal preached was a family state under the divine emperor.

Japan had the fanatical desire and the cold courage to realize this ideal. In 1933 some young officers were being tried because they had assassinated for "patriotic" reasons a former Prime Minister. A number of sympathizers petitioned for clemency, sending as proof of their sincerity their severed little fingers. Japan had also the discipline to achieve it. In February, 1936, a group of young officers mutinied and murdered a number of high civil and military officials who, they felt, were standing in the way of their ideal state. When it was made clear to them that the Mikado disapproved, the leaders committed suicide and the troops surrendered the positions they had seized.

It was a bitter blow to Japanese pride, when, to conciliate American opinion, the British Government ended their alliance with the Mikado's empire. Japan had modelled herself on Britain in many ways, particularly in her naval and parliamentary development; she had helped to hold the Pacific against Germany in the war. Now she felt herself rebuffed by the two great English-speaking Powers, and the war-lords of Tokio drew closer to the dictators of Berlin and Rome. Though Japan was still denied control of many of the vital necessities for war, she could prove a formidable enemy. Her nationals swarmed through Asia and South America, and used their great powers of industry, observation, guile and self-control to build up a far-reaching system of espionage. From the distant days of Kublai Khan her army and her navy had never known defeat. Both scientists and manufacturers had learnt the lessons of the West. Her man-power increased yearly with astonishing speed, and furnished her with soldiers, sailors and airmen, all devoted to the Mikado.

CHAPTER 80

THE PEACEFUL DEMOCRACIES

THE ancients believed that somewhere beyond Europe in the western ocean lay the Islands of the Blest, the paradise to which the happy dead were carried. Many Europeans in the 1920's must have been tempted to share that faith, and to believe that, in the British Isles, they had discovered an earthly paradise where politics were a game and sometimes a bore, but never a matter of life and death.

Between 1918 and 1930 the one dramatic movement was the General Strike of 1926; to Englishmen this seemed dangerously near revolution, while continental observers regarded it as typical of English moderation. For a few days in May, railwaymen and bus drivers tried to support the miners' demand for a tolerable standard of living by the same strike methods by which, quite legitimately, Scottish miners supported the miners of South Wales. It was, from their point of view, a purely industrial dispute. But its size and its paralysing effect on the life of the country, made it something more.

Without meaning to do so, trade unionists were bringing unconstitutional pressure to bear on the Government. Their defeat left little real bitterness behind it; many of them realized that, with the best will in the world, they had imperilled the English system of representative government, which they valued at least as highly as their opponents. They were convinced that their action had been perfectly legal; but they were more than half persuaded that it had been inexpedient.

Three other political changes marked the post-war years in England. The once-famous Liberal Party almost disappeared; but it was not, like the continental parties, the innocent victim of Communist and Fascist blood-feuds. It was not murdered, but simply ousted by the Labour Party, which sapped its strength when, in 1918, it welcomed farm-workers as well as manual workers, and accepted individuals as well as trade unions as Party members. The two Labour Governments, in 1924 and 1929–31, if they did nothing else, proved that a Labour Government was now the only possible party alternative to a Conservative one. The disappearance of the continental Liberal parties left the greater part of Europe devoid of Liberalism; the virtual extinction of the English Liberal Party made England more Liberal than it had ever been before. Its followers, in separating to become Conservatives and Labour Party supporters, carried with them that care for individual liberty which was the chief contribution of their Party to human well-being.

With the Liberal Party, there disappeared also the system of Free Trade, under which the foreign trade of Britain had been conducted since the middle of the nineteenth century. The continuity of English political life is illustrated by the circumstances surrounding the introduction and the desertion of Free Trade. It was Sir Robert Peel, born and brought up a Protectionist, and not Cobden, the Free Trader, who removed the taxes on foreign food and foreign goods. It was Walter Runciman, a lifelong opponent of Protection, and not Neville Chamberlain, its hereditary advocate, who re-imposed them in 1931. Both cases illustrate the incurable English habit of securing that those who have opposed, and not those who have advocated changes, are the ones to introduce them. The knowledge that, in England, great alterations are not likely to be made until at least some of the opposition have been won over is an important safeguard of government by consent.

At the outbreak of war in 1914 the suffragette agitation stopped, and the very women who had been most bitter in attacking the Government by every means, lawful and unlawful, became foremost in war service. At first nursing was the only war work thought suitable for women; in the lifetime of many then living, even the nursing of soldiers had been reserved for men. Soon, however, women appeared on the farms and in munition factories, doing men's work. Women's auxiliary detachments were formed to help as far as possible in the regular non-combatant work of the army, navy and air force. By the Armistice, their war service, crowning their pre-war political vendetta, had won women the right to vote for and to sit in Parliament. Either consideration alone might have been ineffective in securing their demands; together, they were irresistible.

EMANCIPATION OF WOMEN

In 1918, all married women and unmarried women over thirty were enfranchised. A few years later, the vote was given to women on the same terms as to men; since then, women have held ministerial and even Cabinet positions. Almost the only public appointments forbidden to them were membership of the diplomatic services and the priesthood. Women doctors became common, and women lawyers, though much rarer, have ceased to be of great news interest; for many trades, women clerks almost entirely replaced men. Women, however, are still, as a rule, paid less than men for similar work, and, no doubt, this is partly the reason why their invasion of industrial life has been so successful.

This emancipation of women, brought about, in the end, quietly and almost unnoticed, is very nearly a revolution in itself. When it is remembered that it has been accompanied by other changes almost as important, it is clear that, since the end of war years in 1918, there has been a social revolution which is all the more likely to be lasting because it has been brought about silently and without opposition. This social revolution, however, has not been accompanied by an economic settlement. Britain escaped from a world of poverty to a world of plenty; she did not discover how to distribute that plenty.

Until this is done, the gains of this silent social revolution can be described as provisional. These social changes took place throughout the civilized world, but they can more easily be discerned in those democratic countries where there were no political revolutions to distract the observer's attention.

A generation ago, the mill-girls of Lancashire, the pioneers of modern women in industry, were known by their clogs and shawls, which took the place of the hats and coats worn by their "betters". It was not only in Lancashire, but everywhere in England, that working women could be distinguished from leisured women by their dress. Cheap cottons and ugly heavy woollens were the uniform of the poor. The coming of artificial silk and "permanent waves" had a great levelling effect. Mass-production and mass-salesmanship enabled the poor to buy clothes which, in appearance if not in durability, were closely modelled on those of the rich.

The gulf between the classes was bridged in other ways. Broadcasting, the cinema, secondary education and public libraries, all helped the factory-worker to think herself as good as a duchess. Perhaps for the first time since civilization began, everybody, irrespective of class or income, shared the same entertainments, and often the same dreams. The rich continued to pay more for their amusements, but it was doubtful whether they got value for their extra expenditure, whether it was incurred in the cinema, the theatre, the surgical ward or the classroom.

In housing too there were revolutionary changes. A famous pre-1914 story tells how the head of an Oxford College, which contented itself with hip-baths, declared that large baths were unnecessary since "the young men are only here for eight weeks at a time". In working-class houses large baths were, of course, unknown. After 1918 the municipalities, building with help from taxes and rates, saw that every new house had a bathroom. The lay-out of great housing estates and the design of municipal houses and flats secured excellent living conditions for increasing numbers of workers.

ART AND SCIENCE IN THE TWENTIETH CENTURY

These various social changes have brought bad consequences, as well as good. If films are to repay the enormous cost of their preparation, they must be shown to many million people without offence. If newspapers are to attract advertising revenue, they must develop gigantic circulations and avoid, at all costs, boring or antagonizing their public. There has been a great amount of literary and artistic experiment and innovation, whose range and variety is a measure of the unsettled and yet active nature of the period. The work of the Irishman James Joyce in literature and of the Spaniard Picasso in painting, may be cited as representing this phase. Surrealism, the last European movement of note in art before war broke out in 1939, was in some ways an outburst of extreme individualism shadowed by the foreboding of war. The final reconciliation of such experiments with the constructive efforts that were at the same time being made towards an improved social order was left in abeyance under war conditions.

In contrast to the attitude of the Victorian scientists, who considered the limits to human knowledge to be within sight, Twentieth Century science has opened immense vistas for further exploration. Physics, in which the name of Albert Einstein is perhaps most widely known to the general public, has become highly specialized, while medicine and its contributory channels of research have advanced at an extraordinary rate. New operational techniques, of which plastic and brain surgery deserve special mention, together with improved methods of diagnosis, have been responsible for saving thousands of lives each year. New drugs and serums, with almost miraculous power of reducing mortality and speeding recovery in certain diseases, have been produced by the great modern laboratories. Dietetics have aided doctors to stamp out diseases caused by malnutrition, such as beri-beri and rickets, while applied psychology has become an accepted and valued branch of medical science.

DEVELOPMENT OF THE BRITISH EMPIRE

The nineteenth century saw the birth of new Anglo-Saxon nations in every corner of the globe. In the twentieth century, they won their complete political independence, and were welcomed by Great Britain as equal partners in an association which is so unlike any previous empire that many prefer to speak simply of the British Commonwealth of Nations. But the new nations were hardly born before their future was threatened, not by foreign enemies, but by that fall in the birth-rate which is the most important, though the least discussed, of all our social revolutions. Canada and Australia each have room enough and riches enough to support a population greater than the mother country's; New Zealand is larger in area than Great Britain. The builders of the empire looked forward to a time when the new nations would grow, as the United States have grown, to be the equals and perhaps even the superiors in importance of the mother country. The Dominions have gained equality in status; the trend of population seems to condemn them to a perpetual inferiority in importance. The white population of all the British Dominions outside Europe is only half that of England and Wales, and the population of Greater London alone is four-fifths that of Canada, the largest of the new nations.

It was the great increase in population which caused the planting of Europe overseas and the growth of tiny settlements into new nations. In less than a hundred years, the population of the world has almost doubled. There were three times as many people alive in England and Wales in 1921 as in 1821; while the white population of North America, where immigration helped the natural growth of numbers, multiplied by five between 1850 and 1933. This enormous increase made necessary the expansion of industry. The wheatlands of North America, the grazing lands of the Argentine, of Australia and of New Zealand, had to be pressed into service to feed the new millions who populated the earth.

There seemed no end to this process, but already it is at an end. The birth-rate in England first began to fall in 1876; for fifty years, people paid little attention to its continued decline, because the population went on growing until 1935. In order to maintain a stable population, each generation of women must give birth to at least a similar number of girls to be the mothers of the next generation. Actually, the number of girls born must be larger than this to guarantee stability, because some will die in childhood or early womanhood. In England, roughly speaking, every ten women bear only seven girls between them. In Europe, the only countries in which more than ten girls are born to each ten women are Russia, Bulgaria and Italy.

The National Health Insurance scheme, the school medical service, and the provision of ante-natal and maternity clinics in big cities, has helped to reduce the death-rate.

Thus the swift and continuous advance of medicine long concealed the fact that the population of England and of Europe had begun to decline. For social and economic reasons parents cut down the size of their families. By 1930 in almost every European country the fall of the birth-rate had stopped the momentum of an increasing population; even Germany and Italy could only retard, not avert, the decline. Each fall in the birth-rate meant a smaller number of potential mothers; there is a limit beyond which the death-rate cannot fall.

The falling birth-rate may be due entirely to the increasing practice of birth-control, or it may be due partly to a natural decline in fertility. Whatever the reasons, the white peoples were faced with a future in which they will be less numerous than at present, and have a far bigger proportion of old people. Careful statisticians think that the population of Great Britain may fall to less than half its present size in the next century, and that France and Germany will suffer similar, but not such extensive decreases in populations. Against this background the young Dominions appeared as the last adventures of an expanding Europe. But their numbers failed to expand rapidly, and the sparsely inhabited territories of Australia and New Zealand naturally attracted covetous eyes from Japan's crowded millions.

THE STATUTE OF WESTMINSTER

The self-governing Dominions won their right to full nationhood by their services during the war of 1914–18. Their equality of status was recognized when General Smuts, who had crushed rebellion in South Africa, was given a seat in the Imperial War Cabinet. The conduct of the war made it necessary to provide some central body in London which could speak in the name of the Empire as well as of

Great Britain. The Imperial War Cabinet might have been the beginning of some form of federal organization for the self-governing parts of the Empire. After the war, however, the various Dominions became less, not more, closely linked.

At the Peace Conference, there was not one British delegation but half a dozen, and when the treaties were signed, it was not thought right that the signatures of the United Kingdom delegation should bind Canada, Australia and the other Dominions, which joined the new League of Nations as separate nations. The process then begun has since been carried much farther. The Canadian Government has its own diplomatic representatives in the United States, who take their instructions from Ottawa, and who are entirely independent of the British Ambassador; in Dublin there are many foreign ministers, including a Papal nuncio, accredited to Eire.

The Statute of Westminster, passed by the British Parliament at the request of the Dominion Governments, legally recognized the complete independence of the Dominions. England has no longer any right to make laws or decisions to bind the new nations. The person of the King is now the only formal link between the new nations and the mother country, and there is nothing except the will of the Dominions to preserve even this shadow of unity. This complete emancipation of old colonies has been carried out willingly at their request. The wish for political separation has been at least as strong in "loyal" countries, such as Canada, Australia and New Zealand, as in "rebellious" South Africa and Eire, both of which fought wars with Great Britain in this century. The substitution of a British Commonwealth of Nations for a British Empire was necessary to satisfy Canada and Australia; the change made it possible to retain in the group South Africa and Eire. Most of the nations in the Commonwealth have agreed on a common policy in world affairs; the absence of a single directing will did not prove disastrous, and the widely scattered communities were bound together by the strong, but simple tie of a common loyalty to King George V, who won their confidence by his single-hearted devotion to duty.

CO-OPERATION BETWEEN BRITAIN AND THE DOMINIONS

Under his successor, Edward VIII, the new constitution of the British Empire was tested in unexpected fashion. As Prince of Wales, he had won great popularity both in the mother country and the Dominions. But his desire to make a woman who had passed through the divorce court his Queen shocked the deeper feelings of many, and stirred Stanley Baldwin's Ministry into reluctant action. The Dominion premiers were consulted, and with surprising unanimity they agreed to Edward's abdication.

When the great depression of 1929–31 suddenly brought the world to the edge of ruin, the Dominions suffered even more severely than the mother country. They were largely dependent on the sale of agricultural goods, and the fall in prices was greater for agricultural products than for manufactured goods. Bankruptcies became frequent. Neither prudence nor ability nor industry could save the farmer, whose calculations were upset because, between sowing and reaping, the expected value of his crop was halved.

The Dominions and the mother country soon became ready to believe that in closer co-operation lay the only possibility of escape from the crisis. The first Imperial Economic Conference met at Ottawa, the Canadian capital, in 1932. Much was expected of it. England had adopted Protection because she had found that, with the surrounding tariff walls rising rapidly, her traditional policy of Free Trade was no longer a highroad to prosperity, but a gloomy blind alley. The paramount importance of agriculture in the Dominions seemed to promise a profitable agreement, under which Canadian farmers and English manufacturers might buy almost exclusively from each other.

These dreams soon faded. The Conservative Government in England could not sacrifice the English farmer to the English manufacturer, and the Conservative Government in Canada could not sacrifice the Canadian manufacturer to the Canadian farmer. The result of the Ottawa Conference was merely the building of still higher tariff walls between the Empire and foreign countries, with no corresponding reduction of the tariff walls between the Dominions and the mother country. In fact, more satisfactory bargains were concluded between Great Britain and such countries as Denmark than between Great Britain and her own Dominions.

The natural outlet of Canadian trade was the United States, and not Great Britain. Since 1914, the United States and Canada had grown increasingly interdependent. In 1914, Canada's purchases from the United States were three times as great as her purchases from Great Britain; in 1930, they were nearly four and a half times as great. In 1914, Great Britain spent a third more money than the United States in buying goods from Canada; in 1930, the positions were reversed, and the United States spent more than one-and-three-quarter times as much money in Canada as Great Britain did.

THE IRISH QUESTION

The history of the British Empire, since the war, seems to show that its vitality depends on the complete absence of formal unity: attempts at political and economic unity have been fruitless, but the English-speaking Dominions grew more united in feeling than before. Ireland is an exception only because England has been slower there than elsewhere to admit that friendship and compulsion are incompatible ideals.

To most Irishmen to-day outside Ulster, the Easter rising of 1916, when the Republic was proclaimed on the steps of the General Post Office, is the birthday of freedom. They did not think so then. The strange group of poets and dreamers, professors and trade-union leaders, who led that hopeless rebellion had little right to represent the Irish people. The English Government was entitled to execute the leaders; but the death of fifteen of them turned an insignificant rebellion into an irresistible revolution. In 1918, the English Parliament committed a further blunder, when it tried to impose conscription on Ireland. The end of the war should have meant the end of the Irish Question and the coming into force of that Home Rule Bill for which the Irish Nationalist party had fought so long. Instead, the general election of 1918 saw the extinction of the Nationalist party and the return, for every seat in southern Ireland, of Sinn Feiners, men pledged to serve an Irish Republic, and nothing else.

Then began what Irish children are taught to regard as the war of independence. It was a war without battles, a struggle of midnight raids, of arson and assassination. The excesses of the English "Black and Tans" matched the excesses of the Irish Republican Army; what one side termed murder, the other labelled execution. The horror and the pathos of those days are mirrored in the plays of Sean O'Casey, who ranks with Sheridan and Shaw as one of the three great dramatists Ireland has given to England. At last, at the end of 1921, peace was made, when the English Government signed a treaty with the Irish rebels. Protestant Northern Ireland was allowed to keep its cherished connection with England; the rest of Ireland was given Dominion status, under the title of the Irish Free State.

Southern Ireland had the substance of independence, but the hated British Government had refused it the title. While the Irish negotiators in London felt that they had gained a triumph, many of their colleagues in the rebel Government in Dublin felt they had suffered a defeat. Civil war broke out between the unrepentant Republicans, led by De Valera, and the compromising Free Staters, led by Arthur Griffith and Michael Collins. After two further years of atrocities, the Free State faction won. But the Government had not convinced its enemies, and in 1932 the Republican De Valera was returned to power at a general election. He set himself to remove all the remaining signs of the English connection.

He refused to make certain annual payments due to England under the treaty, and the troublesome dispute dragged on. For some years there was economic war between the two countries; in 1938 a final agreement was reached. De Valera could not overcome the stubborn resistance of Ulster, which guarded her ties with England tenaciously, and Ireland remained divided between the Protestant North and the Catholic South. He was more successful with the British Government over the naval bases which it still retained in Ireland. Winston Churchill protested strongly that these ports would be of vital significance in any future European war; but in 1939 Neville Chamberlain handed them over to the Free State. It was clear that the British Government meant what it said, when it promised independence.

A community which uses the labour of native peoples seems to derive from the position which is thus created an uncommonly strong regard for its own privileges. It is perhaps for this reason that the Union of South Africa has insisted more strongly than any other dominion, except Eire, on its own full nationhood and independence.

POSITION OF THE AFRICAN NATIVES

South Africa is a country in which 5,000,000 natives do most of the heavy manual work for a population of about 1,750,000 white people. The European settlers had long been divided by the bitter hostility of the conservative Dutch farmers and the commercial English. After the war, the two white peoples drew much closer together. The colour question so dominated life that even the Labour Party, an organization of class-conscious white workers, opposed the competition of Bantu workers.

In the years after 1918, South African policy had two main objectives: the withdrawal of the native vote in the Cape of Good Hope, and the absorption of the three great native protectorates into the Union. Basutoland, Bechuanaland and Swaziland are inhabited almost entirely by natives, for whom the British Government is still responsible. In 1934, for the third time, the South African Government formally asked for their inclusion in the Union, but after long negotiations, it was agreed that the natives must first be consulted, and so once again the realization of South Africa's hopes was postponed. The Cape native franchise, however, was a matter entirely for the South African Government. In three of the four South African provinces, the natives had never had the right to vote, but in the Cape a limited number could vote on equal terms with the white population. In 1936, this right was limited to voting for two European "caretakers" for native interests.

White settlement in a tropical or semi-tropical country is only possible on a basis of native labour. Though slavery is forbidden, the European population could rely upon a plentiful supply of sufficiently cheap native labour. Both in the Union of South Africa and in Kenya, farther north, development resulted in the reservation of the best and most healthy land for the European settlers. A consequence of this was that the land allotted to natives was not sufficiently large and fertile to maintain them all, and thus there was a supply of labour to work the white settlers' farms. In South Africa, the European settlers were supreme through their possession of Dominion status, and native labour helped to support the resident Boer and British population in a state of considerable comfort. In Kenya, the white population were not self-governing; the Governor and his officials were appointed by and responsible to the Colonial Office in London. There was constant friction between the Government and the missionaries, who wished to protect the natives, and the settlers, who regarded the Union of South Africa as their model.

In Nigeria, the British Government under Lord Lugard had already, before the war, adopted a policy of developing and encouraging native rule. This worked so well that, by 1918, not only were the people more prosperous than they had ever been before, but the country was self-supporting. Nigeria, under British rule, made progress which it could not have made without it. The interests of the natives were not in any way sacrificed to the interests of the colonizing power, and native institutions were helped to develop, in such a way that not only individual natives but whole tribes could benefit. In Nigeria, indirect British rule proved itself superior to the direct European rule which other colonizing nations, such as the Germans, adopted during the pre-1914 period of African colonization.

THE MANDATES SYSTEM

The doctrine of "trusteeship" for native peoples is not new. It may indeed be traced back a hundred and fifty years, to the speeches in which Edmund Burke impeached Warren Hastings for misgovernment in India. At the end of the war, it was laid down as a general principle, to regulate the conduct of European governments in control of backward peoples. The best traditions of British colonial administration were to be applied to the former German colonies, which were assigned to various Western powers as mandated territories, not as colonies. The mandates laid down that in areas "which are inhabited by peoples not yet able to stand by themselves under the strenuous conditions of the modern world, there should be applied the principle that the well-being and development of such peoples form a sacred trust of civilization". France, Belgium, Great Britain and the Union of South Africa all administer portions of the former German colonial empire on these terms.

The mandates system was also applied to those portions of the Turkish empire in Asia in which new Arab states were established. Since 1900, the race for the Middle East had replaced the scramble for Africa as the great preoccupation of the colonizing Powers. Before the First World War, Germany prepared a scheme for a railway from Berlin to Baghdad, which thoroughly scared British officials concerned with the safety of the Indian Empire. Tsarist Russia's designs on Constantinople were sufficient to bring Turkey into the war on the side of the Central Powers.

The Sultan was still looked up to by all Moslems as the Caliph, the Commander of the Faithful, a sort of lay pope with power to launch a Jehad or holy war against the idolatrous Europeans. His power as Caliph depended on his being the greatest independent Mohammedan ruler; it was balanced by the power of the Sherif of Mecca, the guardian of the Holy Places, who claimed direct descent from the Prophet. Encouraged by Britain's promise of an independent Arab Empire, the Sherif Hussein started an Arab war of independence. In the early days of this rising, his son, the Emir Feisal, with the help of Colonel T. E. Lawrence, saved the Arab cause. Later, in 1918, in co-operation with the main English army under Allenby, they helped to clear Syria of Turkish troops from Gaza to Damascus.

Peace-making was difficult, because Britain had made three inconsistent promises. The Irishman MacMahon had promised the Arab Hussein that all Arabia, Mesopotamia and Syria should be Arab; the Englishman Sykes had promised the Frenchman Picot that northern Syria should be French; and the Scotsman Balfour had promised the Jew Weizmann that there should be a Jewish National Home in southern Syria. The second and third promises were kept in full. This meant that the first could be kept only in part. The French drove Feisal from Damascus, which he had made the capital of his new kingdom, and northern Syria was placed under French mandate. Palestine west of Jordan (southern Syria) was placed under direct British rule, as a mandated territory in which Jews and Arabs were to live side by side. The remaining Arab provinces were to be ruled by Hussein and his sons, Abdullah and Feisal, who was compensated for the loss of Damascus by the gift of Baghdad. The Turks were confined to Asia Minor, and even there, they had to surrender the fertile Smyrna countryside to the Greeks.

MOSLEMS, JEWS AND ABYSSINIANS

The unquestioned authority of the Western Powers was destroyed by two men as dissimilar as contemporaries could be. Mustapha Kemal Pasha, later known as Kemal Ataturk, was the great iconoclast of Islam. As soon as he was in power, he began to destroy the most cherished traditions of his people. Women left the harem; the Mohammedan fez was replaced by the infidel hat; Western handwriting and the Western calendar were introduced; in the mosques, the sacred Arabic was replaced by the vernacular Turkish; and the Caliphate, the sign of Turkey's triumphant military past, was abolished. Railways were extended, schools built, tractors replaced oxen in the fields. Other Eastern rulers tried in vain to introduce much smaller changes. Mustapha Kemal succeeded, among a people who for centuries had been the most stubbornly conservative in the world. He was able to do this because he had first won the heart of his people by his courage in adversity. Between 1920 and 1922, he drove the Greeks out of Asia Minor, and tore up the Treaty of Sèvres which the Western Powers had dictated. In 1923, at Lausanne, his minister, Ismet Pasha, negotiated with Europe a treaty which awarded Turkey all she had won by Kemal's generalship.

Kemal's destruction of the peace settlement in Asia Minor was followed at once by Ibn Saud's destruction of the treaty position in Arabia. In 1924, Ibn Saud left his desert home, where he ruled over the Wahabis (the Puritans of the Mohammedan world), and drove Hussein from his kingdom. He entered the Holy City of Mecca as a pilgrim, not as a conqueror. He overthrew the will of the Allies not by abandoning Islam, as Mustapha Kemal did, but by stressing it. Britain gradually resigned all pretensions to bearing the whole of the White Man's Burden in the Middle East. She has confined herself to the protection of her essential interests—oil and her communications with India. In 1933, the mandate for Iraq or Mesopotamia was surrendered, and the Iraqis were left free to do whatever they liked, except to cut the pipe-line from the oil-fields to Palestine or to imperil the British air-route to India. They celebrated their independence by a massacre of Assyrian Christians. No one stopped them. In 1936, Egypt was given a similar measure of independence; the British minister at Cairo retained considerable influence, and British troops were left to safeguard the Suez Canal.

In Palestine the new order of 1919 survived, though with attendant problems. There the Jews steadily developed a national home, which set an admirable example in its co-operative colonies, where university graduates were proud to work as farm labourers. But the nationalist home of the "Zionist" Jews depended on the British army and police; the Arabs remained unreconciled to Jewish settlement. There was an outbreak of serious unrest in 1937. The British Government reluctantly decided that the original terms of the mandate could no longer be observed; instead, it proposed to divide the country territorially between the Arab and the Jew.

The French made some attempt to follow the English example. But they roused the racial and religious antipathies of the Moslem heretics of the Djebel Druse. A small war broke out, and was only ended by rigorous military action, which robbed Djebel Druse of the bulk of its fighting men. The struggle produced unfavourable reactions on the French territories in North Africa. Moslem sympathies lay with the Druses, and Mussolini, self-styled Defender of Islam, encouraged the Moslems of Tunisia, Algeria and Morocco in their grievances against the French administration. The Moslems had long felt that they had been reduced to political inferiority compared with the Jews, and they emphasized their claims to full suffrage.

In marked contrast with the conciliatory policy of Britain and France was the Italian attack on Abyssinia. After long and careful preparation Mussolini sent his soldiers and airmen against the last independent African kingdom. The Abyssinian ruler, Haile Selassie, had made a real effort to introduce Western civilization into his medieval realm, and to unite his powerful chieftains against the Italian aggression. But Italian gold had been used skilfully, and a few months of modern warfare were sufficient to crush the brave, but ill-equipped Abyssinians and to drive Haile Selassie into exile.

THE LOW COUNTRIES AND SCANDINAVIA

Germany, Austria and Hungary had lost their monarchs, but kingship survived to the north and west, where rulers had accepted democratic and parliamentary government. King Albert's chivalrous re-

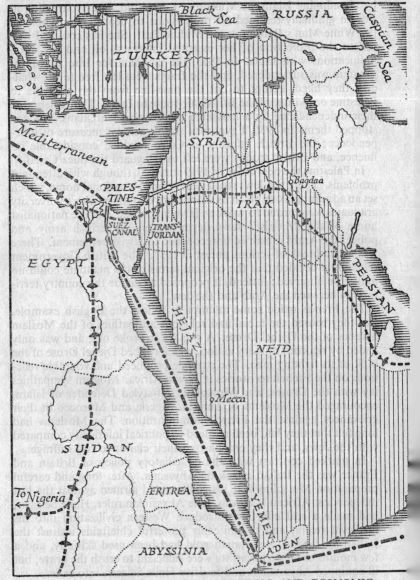

THE STRATEGIC AND ECONOMIC

The end of the First World War brought about many important changes in the Middle East. The old Turkish Empire, indicated in the above map by shading, was split up, and mandatory and Arab states were created. As a result a new spirit of Arab nationalism arose, and redistribution of land created many problems.

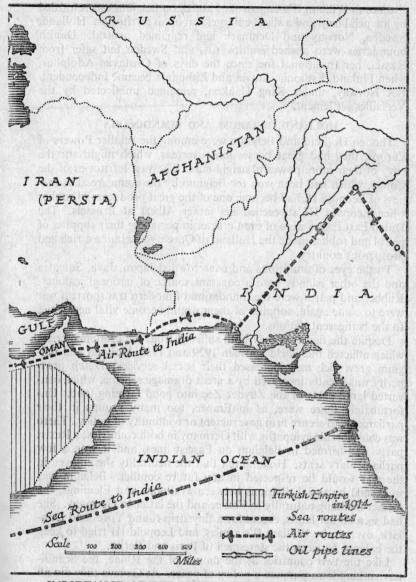

IMPORTANCE OF THE MIDDLE EAST

The safeguarding of the sea route to India, through the Suez Canal, remained a vital interest to Great Britain, and the steady development of civil aviation created another line of communication—the air route to India. At the same time the exploitation of oil deposits gave increased importance to Iraq and Iran.

sistance to William II's unprovoked attack on Belgium was rewarded by financial help and a slight enlargement of his territories. Holland, Sweden, Norway and Denmark had remained neutral. Danish boundaries were pushed southwards, and Sweden felt safer from Russia, her traditional foe since the days of Gustavus Adolphus, when Finland, Esthonia, Latvia and Lithuania became independent. But Norway, under King Haakon, remained unaffected by the Versailles settlement.

HOLLAND, BELGIUM AND SCANDINAVIA

Though Holland and Belgium were among the smaller Powers of Europe, they had great possessions overseas, which might stir the envy of their more powerful neighbours. The vast territories of the Congo, which had been won for Belgium by the commercial astuteness of Leopold II, had become one of the great producers of rubber when Leopold III succeeded his father Albert at Brussels. The Dutch East Indies were of even greater importance; their supplies of petrol and rubber made the Holland of Queen Wilhelmina a rich and prosperous country.

To the eyes of ambitious and overcrowded Japan, Java, Sumatra and the other islands were a constant source of national jealousy. Rubber and petrol were the foundation of modern transport; if war were to come again, supplies of them would become vital necessities to the belligerent nations.

Despite the fact that they both suffered from the economic crises which afflicted the world between 1929 and 1933, Holland and Belgium grew rich and increased their social services; Dutch prosperity was greatly increased by a great drainage scheme, which converted large parts of the Zuyder Zee into good farming land. Unfortunately there were, as in France, too many groups in their parliaments to secure firm government or continuity of policy. There was considerable sympathy with Germany in both countries; a Rexist party was formed in Belgium on Fascist lines, and it won a few parliamentary seats. Holland felt that the neutrality she enjoyed in the war would be respected in any future conflict. Belgium was weakened by racial divisions between Walloons and Flemings, the former inclining naturally to France and the latter to Germany. She had seen all her lands, except for a tiny strip round Ypres and Dunkirk, overrun by William II's armies, and Leopold III tried to keep the balance between the statesmen of Paris and Berlin.

Like the two countries at the mouth of the Rhine, the Scandinavian kingdoms pursued a policy of peace. At Geneva they did all they could to discourage aggression; but they had small military or naval strength to support their ideals. They devoted the money that might have been spent on armaments to building up their own economic and social progress. Education was improved, and Norway shared with Czecho-Slovakia the honours of developing physical training for both children and adults. The old Norse tradition of seamanship built up a successful mercantile marine, and land communications were greatly improved. Agriculture flourished, particularly in Denmark, where co-operative farming led to a high standard of comfort in all classes. In all three countries the ordinary man and woman felt themselves part of a peaceful community, where industry and good will brought freedom and content for all.

CHAPTER 81

THE TANGLED SKEIN

IN 1920, President Wilson attended the formal opening of the Panama Canal. The Canal itself had been used for traffic for several years, and the opening ceremony had originally been fixed for that month of August, 1914, which saw the European nations drawn into war. The building of the Canal was an even greater triumph for medicine than for engineering, for the greatest obstacles the promoters had to face were mosquitoes and the yellow fever which they carried. By joining the Atlantic and Pacific oceans, distances by sea between east and west were enormously reduced. Thus Yokohama in Japan was brought some 3750 nautical miles nearer New York, a saving equal to the total distance from New York to Hamburg.

The greatest advances in speed of transport have been due to faster travel rather than to short cuts. The internal-combustion engine had before 1914 replaced the horse, as far as passenger transport in England and the U.S.A. were concerned; after the war, it captured also the greater part of road-borne goods traffic. But it was by making possible the development of the aeroplane that the internal combustion engine most decisively narrowed the world.

CONQUEST OF THE AIR

The quickened tempo at which the world now moves was well illustrated in the history of flying. It took mankind more than thirty centuries to conquer the ocean; thirty years have been sufficient for the conquest of the air. Sir John Alcock and Sir Arthur Whitten Brown flew the Atlantic from Newfoundland to Ireland in June 1919, only ten years after Louis Blériot made the first air-crossing of the English Channel. The same year saw the founding of the first regular commercial air-line, when a London–Paris service was started. Ten years later, India was brought for the first time into weekly communication by air with England. The time necessary for a journey from London to Delhi was by 1936 only a third of what it had been in 1929.

For the most part, the story of air-transport has been the story of the aeroplane. But Germany retained confidence in the airship, in spite of its poor showing in the war, and the *Graf Zeppelin* and the

Hindenburg provided an occasional passenger-service across the Atlantic. The Pacific Ocean was crossed by American air-lines, and no one doubted that in less than thirty years from that first cross-channel flight, the whole world would be bound together by a regular air-service. It is easy to see what this may mean in time-saving. In 1872, Jules Verne, the novelist who pleased his public by making the impossible seem almost credible, wrote a best-seller called *Round the World in Eighty Days*. Before his book was sixty years old, the aeroplane had made his hero's journey seem tame and tedious, for in 1931 two American aviators, Post and Gatty, accomplished a flight round the world in a tenth of the time.

SPANNING THE WORLD BY WIRELESS AND TELEPHONE

Even the aeroplane is slow when compared with the speed with which the human voice now travels by telephone and wireless. We accept long-distance telephone calls now as a matter of course; but elderly journalists still remember the days when pigeons were the quickest means of carrying news. The development of these long-distance telephones grew enormously after the outbreak of the First World War. The human voice was first heard across the Atlantic in 1915. Twenty years later, there was hardly a place in the civilized world with which communication by telephone was not available from any private house in England, since the ordinary tele-phone systems of the various countries had been linked together across the oceans by wireless. In 1938, it was possible for the English-man to ring up not only New York or Moscow, but places as remote and little known as Naivasha in Kenya or Pnom-Penh in French Indo-China.

The telephone brings two private individuals together. Whole nations were linked together by broadcasting, across thousands of miles of land and sea; Englishmen could share in the excitement of an American presidential election, of May Day in Moscow, of Hitler at a German Nazi conference; or they could listen on Christmas afternoon to the pealing of the bells of Bethlehem. The United States, with its thousands of isolated farmhouses, was the first country to develop broadcasting on a large scale. There private enterprise was allowed to control the provision of programmes, and broadcasting became a branch of the highly-developed advertising industry. In England, from its beginning in 1922, broadcasting was treated as a public monopoly, not to be exploited for advertising. The British Broadcasting Corporation was free from day-to-day political control, but in times of national emergency—such as the general strike of 1926—it was strictly controlled by the Government. In the various dictatorships of Europe, broadcasting showed no benevolent neu-trality towards dissident politicians as in Britain; nor did it become the instrument of commercial propaganda as in America. It was simply a means of political propaganda. The unanimity, the intimacy and the persuasiveness of wireless gives broadcast propaganda an authority which neither newspapers nor public meetings can exert. An efficient broadcasting organization became one of the surest supports of every European dictatorship.

In 1938, the world stood on the verge of a further great development of wireless services. Television was introduced as a regular daily broadcast feature, and, though the first experiments were crude and expensive, it was clear that, before long, human sight would be mechanically extended as far as human hearing already was.

Speed in communications has brought dangers as well as benefits to mankind. The last year of the First World War was marked by an epidemic of influenza even more destructive than the war itself. Its simultaneous appearance in a dozen different countries was due to swift and frequent intercommunication which the war made possible and necessary. The epidemic came in three great waves; the first in the early summer, the second in the autumn of 1918, and the third in the spring of 1919. Its outbreak coincided with the arrival of the first American troops in France; it spread within a few weeks to all the countries of the Entente, striking in the trenches, the troopships and the munition factories. This first wave was "like a mild attack of measles, without the rash".

The second wave was much more serious and much more widespread. It was the relatively young who provided most of the victims. Thousands of soldiers, to whom the Armistice had made a long life seem a reasonable expectation rather than a forlorn hope, returned home only to find death. In Australia, quarantine measures half repelled the attack; and St. Helena and Mauritius escaped altogether. The rest of the world had no defence. In India alone, that winter, influenza killed more men than had fallen fighting in the whole four years of calculated slaughter. Rapidity in transport has made it impossible any longer for one country to live safely to itself in health matters. Just as the existence of slums is a menace to the health of a wealthy suburb, so the existence of unhealthy parts of the world is now a danger to Europe.

THE LEAGUE OF NATIONS

The war, which started in 1914 as a purely European affair, had within four years involved nations as remote and unimportant as Guatemala and Siam. It seemed certain that, in a world which machinery had made one, mere remoteness from a quarrel could never again be a guarantee of peace. It was only common sense, therefore, that an attempt should be made to organize the world for a better future in which the shadow of war would not be present.

The peace treaties of 1919 contained among their provisions the Covenant of a League of Nations which from its headquarters at Geneva would provide, it was hoped, not only opportunities to avoid wars by consultation and arbitration, but also machinery to stop them. The Covenant set up a Council, an Assembly and a Secretariat; these three organizations might have been the forerunners of an international government, an international parliament and an international civil service. In the Assembly equal voting-rights were given to every state which was a member of the League; in the Council, the Great Powers were given a predominant position. France, Britain and the other stronger nations became permanent members; the weaker countries had to be content with occasional representation, sharing four seats between fifty nations.

DISABILITIES OF THE LEAGUE

From the beginning the League suffered from three great disabilities. First, it was composed of representatives of governments not of peoples. The governments had surrendered none of their sovereignty. The only real obligation the various nations had undertaken was to submit disputes to some form of peaceful settlement, though not necessarily to accept the result. A loop-hole was left for any country to persevere in its determination to fight.

The Covenant bore other traces of the reluctance of nations to surrender real power to the League. Many types of decisions had to be unanimous before they could become effective, and others were mere recommendations. At the end of June, 1930, there were thirty-three agreements and conventions, more than a year old, made under the auspices of the League. Nearly a thousand signatures had been obtained at Geneva for these various documents, but well over a third of these signatures were never ratified by the respective governments. Great Britain and her Dominions and the European states which had been neutral in the war had the best records for ratification. Among the South American republics, though signatures were fairly common, ratifications were extremely rare. The League was an organization for making international treaties, not international laws.

Although the Covenant had promised a reduction in armaments, it was not until 1932 that the Disarmament Conference met under the presidency of Arthur Henderson. An economic crisis in Great Britain had driven him and the Labour Party from office. The same crisis brought Hitler into power in Germany. Ramsay MacDonald united some of his Labour followers with the Conservative party and a few Liberals to form a National Government, which persisted in the hopeless policy of unilateral or one-sided disarmament. Meanwhile Hitler was rebuilding German militarism on the basis preserved by Streseman, and hopes of disarmament by common agreement dwindled rapidly.

The second great disability of the Covenant was that it made the League a guarantee of the state of affairs in 1919. The Assembly was given power of advising the reconsideration of the treaties; it could not compel the victorious Powers to act on its advice. There was no provision for meeting new conditions in a rapidly changing world.

Assembly line at a modern car factory. Methods of mass production have increased output but have to some extent lowered the standards of skill required by the individual worker.

The waterfront at San Francisco, showing the bridge over the Bay. The skyscraper buildings and the bridge are both achievements in building with steel and reinforced concrete.

One of the giant air liners the invention of which has increased the speed and
ease of communication to an almost incredible extent.

A session of the League of Nations in progress at Geneva. Eventually the League
failed but it paved the way for the United Nations Organization.

The third and fatal weakness of the League was that it never included all the Great Powers. The United States refused membership; Soviet Russia remained at enmity with France and Britain for several years and did not become a member till 1934. Under Stresemann's guidance Germany secured admission to a permanent seat on the Council in 1926, and the Locarno treaties gave some hope that the Great Powers of Europe might yet work together to preserve peace. But by 1933 Germany and Japan had resigned; the former complained that she was not given equality of armaments with her old enemies; the latter resented the League's ineffectual protests against her aggression in Manchuria. In 1936, Italy ceased to take any part in the work of the League, and was free to ignore its half-hearted attempt to check her invasion of Abyssinia by an economic boycott.

Though the statesmen who planned and guided the League failed to provide the guarantee of peace which the world needed, the League had many notable achievements to its credit. Europe abounded in refugees when the war ended. Under the League's auspices, the Norwegian Dr. Nansen, who had won world-wide reputation as an explorer, gained even greater fame by the success of his heroic work for these unfortunate folk. Russians and Greeks were the greatest sufferers; the administration at Geneva strengthened and extended Nansen's careful plans for them and their fellow-refugees. The League also did good humanitarian work, especially in checking the international traffics in women and noxious drugs. It also helped in the settlement of many disputes between the smaller Powers, which might have led to wars in earlier days.

AMERICAN ISOLATIONISM

President Wilson's advocacy was the driving-force in Europe's embarkation on the adventure of a League of Nations. He failed utterly to persuade his fellow-countrymen to share that adventure. His Republican opponents refused to support the scheme, and their refusal was confirmed decisively by the electors. America's traditional hatred of foreign commitments led her to seek peace in the future, as she had found it in the past, through isolation and not through association. Successive Republican presidents, Harding, Coolidge and Hoover, made isolationism the cardinal point in their foreign policy.

It was not so easy for the United States to retreat from Asia as from Europe. Their comfortable and prosperous seclusion was troubled by the thought of their interests in the Pacific. The fate of China interested America as much as it interested Japan, Russia and England. American missionaries and merchants both played an active part in Chinese life. She was suspicious of Japanese aggression, and her sympathies lay entirely with the older civilization of the mainland and not with the unscrupulous and intrusive islanders. Renunciation of her interests was difficult, but it was apparently made by President Roosevelt in 1934, when he promised the Philippine Islands their independence. Though the United States retained Hawaii and Pearl Harbor, they had no effective naval base in the Far East, and Japan felt she had little to fear from America in the pursuit of her military ambitions.

If the United States had less to do with the Old World, they had a great deal more to do with the other half of the New World. Before 1914, they had shared almost equally with England in the profitable work of supplying South America with manufactured goods. By 1927, they were providing a good deal more than twice as much as England. Thirty-eight per cent of the total imports into South American countries that year came from North America. This commercial conquest was largely made possible by the opening of the Panama Canal, which brought the Pacific ports of South America many thousands of miles nearer to the great manufacturing districts of the Atlantic seaboard of the United States. The economic friendship between the two American continents was fostered by the "Good Neighbour" policy of Cordell Hull, who became Foreign Secretary at Washington in 1932; he worked unceasingly to dispel any suspicions the "Latin" nations of Central and Southern America might harbour of the peaceable intentions of the United States.

WEAKNESS AT GENEVA

Politically America succeeded in her decision to avoid European entanglements. Economically she could not reach the same isolation. In 1929 the economic crisis in the United States brought disaster on all Europe and a revolution in Germany. A future economic crisis in Europe could hardly fail to involve America in disaster, and possibly in revolution. Washington could not contract out of revolutions, which might spring from the quarrels or misfortunes of Europe. Isolation guaranteed America temporary peace, but not security.

America thought that her refusal to join the League increased her chances of peace; it lessened those of the rest of the world. In each major dispute which came, or should have come, before the League for settlement, there were too few important states which were disinterested.

The terms on which the League was founded, the inviolability of the 1919 treaties, always gave the formal victory to the possessor nations. But the dissatisfied Powers, the "have nots", got as much of their own way as they were strong enough to extort, either by leaving the League or by defying it. The loss between 1933 and 1936 of Germany, Japan and Italy as effective members made a vital change in the nature of the League. From being an association of all sorts and conditions of nations, it came more and more to resemble an alliance of like-minded nations ranged against another alliance of nations, which were united at least in two respects: they were all dissatisfied both with the League and with their present position in the world.

The conflicts between the two groups became sharper. Crisis succeeded crisis. Each might have produced a war, but each in turn subsided peacefully. This, however, was not due to any statesmanlike removal of the cause of trouble; but simply to the fact that neither side yet felt that it had a sufficient preponderance of force to risk a war. The "haves" felt they were too strong to be attacked; the "have-nots" built up their strength and bided their time.

The first of the two centres which threatened peace lay in Eastern Asia. A strong China might have kept the balance between Japan and Russia. But she was split by the quarrels of those who claimed to inherit Sun Yat-sen's programme. The minority followed the peasant-scholar, Mao Tse-tung, who preached the doctrines of Marx. He found an excellent general for his peasants in Chuh-teh. Chiang Kai-shek held the allegiance of the majority; he venerated Confucius, not Marx. Japan's hold was weakened by Russia's grip on Vladivostock and Outer Mongolia. There were frontier incidents over many years; in nearly all Russia gave way. Her experience in the Russo-Japanese war had taught her the impossibility of fighting a modern war when the army is separated from its base by thousands of miles of barren country with poor communications.

After 1934 Russia became firmer in her attitude towards Japan. The country had settled down under Stalin's rule, and unreliable elements had been "eliminated". The two Five-Year Plans had enormously developed Siberian industries, communications and agriculture. Soviet armies were in a position to fight from a Siberian as well as from a European base, if Russia decided to attempt to stop the advancing Japanese troops from occupying more of China.

FRENCH EFFORTS TO ACHIEVE SECURITY

The second storm-centre was in Europe. From 1933 onwards, the antagonism between Germany and Russia grew ever sharper. Communist Russia was Nazi Germany's "natural" enemy. Hitler resented her entrance into the League of Nations, which he left; he resented still more the Franco-Soviet Pact, which seemed to revive the old danger of "the war on two fronts", in opposition to his forward policy. French leaders saw their traditional enemy across the Rhine building up her military strength to its old level. The politicians of the Right could not bring themselves to co-operate wholeheartedly with a Communist ally, and the politicians of the Left were too deeply involved in satisfying the demands of Labour to spare much time for armaments. When Britain and America refused to guarantee her safety, France built the Maginot line, an elaborate system of static defence running from the Alps to the Belgian frontier. She had already sought to secure herself by reviving her historic alliance with the restored Poland and by treaties with Czecho-Slovakia and the Balkan kingdoms of Yugoslavia and Rumania.

THE PACIFIC

The gradual extension of Japanese imperialism after the First World War raised problems for Britain, America, Russia and Holland. The situation was worsened by Japan's seizure of Manchuria in 1931 and her invasion of China in 1937. Territories which were controlled by Japan, Great Britain and her Dominions, the United States, and Holland in 1941 are indicated on the above map.

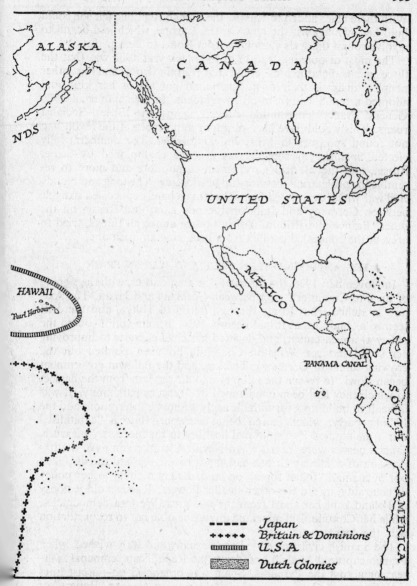

ALASKA

CANADA

NDS

UNITED STATES

HAWAII
Pearl Harbour

MEXICO

PANAMA CANAL

SOUTH AMERICA

- - - - - Japan
+ + + + + Britain & Dominions
▨▨▨▨▨ U.S.A.
▨▨▨▨▨ Dutch Colonies

PROBLEM

Australia, the Dutch East Indies, Burma, and French Indo-China became potential objects of Japanese aggression, while even the Pacific seaboard of America came within the zone of danger. The United States possessed inadequate bases, and the strategy of Britain hinged on Singapore, whose impregnability was to prove illusory when confronted by enemy power on land and sea.

With these allies added to Russia, the French Republic felt she could hold her own against the new Central Europe, which had begun to revolve round the Axis stretching from Rome to Berlin.

The most disquieting feature of the black year 1936 was that the three great dictatorships could not refrain from making other peoples' quarrels their own. Spain had got rid of her king and adopted a republican form of government. In the summer of 1936 General Franco led a military revolt against the Liberal-Socialist rulers. This would have been of minor importance, if the revolt had not found sponsors in Mussolini and Hitler. The democratically elected Spanish government was at once championed by Soviet Russia, and the Madrid government came more and more to resemble the proletarian dictatorship of Moscow. The long and bloody civil war which devastated Spain, became a barely concealed struggle between Germany and Italy on the one hand and Russia on the other. France and Britain, desiring peace above all things, tried to prevent the concealed conflict from becoming an open one.

THE ANTI-COMINTERN PACT AND WAR IN SPAIN

In November, 1936, the threat of war grew darker, with the signing of an anti-Comintern pact between Germany and Japan. The Axis now stretched from Rome through Berlin to Tokyo, and the drift seemed as ominous as it had been in 1914. Britain still favoured the policy of appeasement, and devoted her chief energies to improving her social services. Winston Churchill, however, pointed out the growing threat of German militarism, and the Baldwin government began slowly to rescue the military and air services from the neglect to which they had been condemned by Treasury parsimony. It was difficult to build up a formidable army without conscription, and the Labour party, which feared being entrapped into a "capitalists' war", maintained its traditional hostility to that necessary measure. French nerves were frayed when Neville Chamberlain gave the impression of confining British assistance to the sea and the air, eked out by a small "token force" on land. Belgium clung to her policy of neutrality, as did the other smaller Powers. Russia's old jealousy of Poland kept her apart from the two great Western democracies, while her Communism appeared an insuperable bar to reconciliation with the Axis powers.

The Spanish civil war ended as Germany and Italy wished, when Franco captured Madrid and drove the Republican remnants overseas or across the Pyrenees. Spain was organized on Fascist lines with Franco as *Caudillo*, deeply indebted to his brother "leaders" of Berlin and Rome. The absorption of Austria into the German *Reich* was another strong challenge to the democracies, although the appeasers in France, Britain and America justified it as an example of racial "self-determination". This was cold comfort to democratic Czecho-Slovakia, whose frontier now marched with Hitler's. Italy stirred French anger, when the more enthusiastic Fascists began to clamour for the annexation of Tunisia, Corsica and Nice. Europe split into two hostile camps. The two Axis Powers tightened their totalitarian systems, and pushed on with the work of weakening the free nations by corrupting venal politicians; they formed "Fifth Columns" to disrupt the democratic governments, just as Franco's four columns in the field had been helped by what he called his Fifth Column in Madrid. Russia and America, for widely different reasons, stood apart from the two hostile groups. The smaller European Powers still hoped that neutrality might save them.

In 1938 even the most ardent appeasers and anti-conscriptionists began to incline to rearmament. Hitler openly challenged France by demanding the virtual dismemberment of her ally, Czecho-Slovakia. As in his previous forward moves, he declared that this was his last demand to satisfy the just claims of Germany. Most of the inhabitants of the Sudetenland were of German origin, though they had never been part of the German Reich. Hitler's Fifth Column worked up a furious agitation under Henlein, and the democratic Czech president, Benes, was placed in a dilemma. Russia was ready to play her traditional role as protector of the Slav peoples; France was bound by military agreement to stand by the Czechs; Britain resented Hitler's perpetual bullying of the weak; even in the United States men were beginning to think it "was about time someone called that fellow Hitler's bluff". Benes had the splendid Skoda armament-works and a vigorously patriotic army with which to defend his country; but that country was honeycombed with small racial minorities, who were not enthusiastic supporters of the government.

THE MUNICH COMPROMISE

After hurried negotiations, Benes decided to rely on British friendship and the French treaty. He consented to the question of the Sudetenland being settled by direct negotiations between Britain, France, Germany and Italy. The civilized world felt that war was very near, when Chamberlain, Daladier, Hitler and Mussolini met at Munich, the ancient German city which had been the cradle of the Nazi party. It was that feeling that led to the policy of appeasement making its last supreme effort in the autumn of 1938.

The four negotiators at Munich decided that this was really Hitler's last demand for territorial adjustment and that his racial claims were just. The Czechs were deprived of all effective control over the Sudetenland, and the Nazi, Henlein, became the real ruler of the district. Guarantees were, of course, given to Benes for the integrity of his country; but Hitler, with Mussolini's faithful support, had won all he needed, and the French and British premiers felt that they had silenced the threat of war. Chamberlain flew back to England and told his countrymen that, like Disraeli on his return after the treaty of Berlin, he had brought to them "Peace with Honour".

The peaceful respite was brief. Benes and the Czechs were helpless to check Henlein's unscrupulous intrigues. Hitler broke his pledges as easily as he had given them. In March, 1939, the Wehrmacht occupied Prague, and the deserted Czechs re-entered their German prison. Italy redoubled her clamour for the annexation of French territory. Even the Socialist parties in the two great Western democracies began to realize the vital necessity of rearmament. As hopes of maintaining peace dwindled, the British parliament adopted conscription; a British military mission went to Russia to seek from Stalin the help which had been rejected before Munich.

THE SUCCESS OF HITLER'S DIPLOMACY

In the late spring of 1939 Hitler seemed to have won his duel with the Western democracies without firing a shot. It was an astonishing result to have achieved by six years of resolute and unscrupulous diplomacy. When Hitler rose to power, the strength of France and Britain appeared overwhelming, and Italy, if not a friend, seemed prepared to co-operate with them. The Fuehrer could have been stopped by force, but no country was prepared to take the necessary action. He found that the same tactics, which gave him power in a distracted Germany, were equally effective in a disunited Europe.

Hitler proceeded piecemeal in tackling both problems. From 1930 to 1933 under Hindenburg's nominal rule the Nazis carried on street warfare against their opponents. From 1936 to 1939 the Wehrmacht, under the direction of the General Staff, was almost continually, though unofficially, active in Spain, in Austria, in Bohemia and in Lithuania. In each case the balance of force was demonstrably against the Fuehrer at the start of the period; yet in each case his opponents allowed him to carry his gangster methods from success to success. The indecision of Dr. Bruening gave him his chance to bludgeon his way to the Chancellorship; the indecision of Blum and Baldwin gave the German Reich the chance of becoming the best-armed instead of the worst-armed country in Europe, of seizing Vienna and Prague without a blow, and of establishing something very like an economic sovereignty over the Balkan peoples.

Hitler and his foreign minister, Ribbentrop, had formed definite estimates of the three great democratic powers, whom Mussolini had contemptuously labelled "pluto-democracies". They judged all three so wedded to a peaceful life and so intent on winning for their citizens material comforts and social well-being as to be incapable of serious military effort. Each was denied a vigorous foreign policy by its devotion to "liberty and the pursuit of happiness". England had apparently carried her national foible of inconsistency to a point where she could be safely disregarded. The foreign policy of successive British governments of varying political composition was one of "collective security". Ideally, collective security should have given each country the luxury of a strictly limited expenditure on armaments. But this was true only if all countries agreed to share in this collective security. If certain countries contracted out; if, in fact, collective security meant not a co-operative insurance amongst all countries, but a grand alliance against certain "aggressive countries", then collective security must be accompanied by a rapid and thorough rearmament. The traditional armaments policy of the Right must be combined with the traditional foreign policy of the Left. But British politicians never really faced the fact that the Axis had contracted out. They continued to practise collective security with a limited liability for armaments at a time when this could only mean collective insecurity. Only here and there a few leaders, more far-sighted than the rest, notable among them Winston Churchill, advocated a strong Army, Navy, and Air Force.

Nearer the Rhine stood France, a land of emptying cradles and place-seekers, sheltering behind a Maginot line which ended where, as past history showed, real danger began. French politics repeated the indecision of the British and added a corruption all their own. But if Hitler was to be opposed the first step must obviously be taken by France, his only neighbour among the great non-Fascist powers. It is not surprising that no step was taken. Hitler could probably count with confidence on Fifth Column intervention to hamper French action against him. The conflict between Labour and Capital was probably more acute than elsewhere in Europe and the armed forces were certainly not armed by Nazi standards, being short of tanks and aeroplanes.

POLITICS WITHOUT CONSCIENCE

Hitler had used to his own advantage the incompatibility between his Communist and non-Communist opponents in his rise to power in Germany. He repeated his tactics in his rise to power in Europe. The Spanish Civil War was used by him as a reconnaissance of the possibilities. Both Communist Russia and the Western Democracies ran true to form. The one intervened, the others preached "non-intervention". The non-intervention of the Western allies enabled Hitler and Mussolini to secure complete victory for General Franco over the Republicans and their Russian allies. After this experience nobody should have been surprised, though everybody was, when Stalin in his turn decided to practise "non-intervention" in 1939.

One of Hitler's greatest assets in the years from 1936 to 1939 was the fact that he had no conscience. His acts of aggression were directed to ends which large sections of opinion in Britain at least were not prepared to say were indefensible. The annexation of Austria was a thing which in pre-Hitler days a majority of Austrians had desired; the Sudeten Germans of Czecho-Slovakia were known to be not altogether happy under Czech rule; Danzig and Memel were undeniably German cities. It is difficult to fight a war for a cause which you half believe to be unjust. Hitler calculated that

France and Britain would not go to war to oppose something which they were inclined to think was only wrong because Hitler was behind it. He was right. He calculated that consequently they would be too weak to go to war by the time he had exhausted all the plausible issues and come to something plainly indefensible by any standard like the invasion of Poland. He was very nearly right.

Hitler also counted on American neutrality. He remembered that intervention of the United States in 1917 had led to Germany's defeat in 1918. Similar intervention might again bring disaster. But American eyes were fixed on Hirohito rather than on Hitler. The vast growth of the "America First" movement, the strength of the isolationists and the passage of neutrality laws seemed to make it impossible for the United States to help the European democracies effectively.

THE APPROACH TO WAR

The failure of the Munich settlement compelled the French and British governments to hurry forward belated attempts to rebuild their fighting forces. They were hampered by the spirit of the French army, which, under the gloomy tradition of Pétain, had lost the spirit of attack. Their weakness was increased by the corrosive influence of Fifth Columnists, whose underground activities sapped the strength not only of France but also of Holland, Belgium and Scandinavia. Allied difficulties encouraged Hitler to attack Poland under the feeble government of Smigly-Ridz and Beck; the status of Danzig gave him the pretext for yet one more final demand. He knew that the Italian forces had no great fighting value; but their mere existence weakened France. Italy had been the first and the least expensive of Hitler's conquests, though Mussolini had matched Germany's predatory policy by similar aggression. Together the two dictators had helped the Caudillo to victory in Spain; but, though the Duce had Abyssinia and Albania to match the Fuehrer's Austria and Czecho-Slovakia, he had been bound to Hitler's chariot wheels since the sacrifice of Austria.

The only power that Hitler feared was Soviet Russia, which hated Poland as much as he did. But her huge resources were not yet organized for war, and her military leaders seemed inferior to the German General Staff. Though Blomberg and Fritsch had lost the Fuehrer's favour, he had at his disposal the services of such men as Brauchitsch, Milch, Keitel, Bock, Manstein and Rundstedt. Soviet divisions had to police the eastern frontier, where Stalin felt that no more concessions must be made to Japan; though they had pushed as far south as Swatow and Hainan, the Japanese might still strike westward towards Lake Baikal or eastward against Vladivostock. Swift victory in western Europe would leave Hitler free to break Stalin's forces before they reached their full strength.

Meanwhile, to secure his eastern frontier, the Fuehrer bid against

Britain and France for Russia's support, and a non-aggression pact was signed between Berlin and Moscow. Hitler staged a brief farce of negotiating with Beck over the Danzig question; then, ignoring the declaration of the Western Powers that they would honour their pledge to stand by Poland, he accused the Warsaw government of rejecting his ultimatum which it had not received. On September 1st, 1939, Goering and Milch sent the Luftwaffe to bomb the Polish capital. Two days later France and England declared war on Germany.

CHAPTER 82

THE SECOND WORLD WAR

DURING twenty years of troubled peace mankind had changed its conception of the scope of war and sharpened the weapons designed for its own destruction. The cinema, the Press and the wireless had given everyone everywhere an idea of some of the horrors to be expected, once the world's peace was shattered. The age of total war had arrived. Women and children had become targets for destruction in face of military necessity; conventions laboriously erected at Geneva by earnest humanitarians went by the board; every weapon designed by scientists and technicians and mass-produced in the factories was to be used ruthlessly by the combatants to break the enemy's resistance. Bitter experience had already taught China, Spain and Abyssinia how indiscriminately death came from a clear sky.

There were only six powers fighting in the autumn of 1939, but there was every prospect that the flames of war would spread. Hirohito and Hitler had started the conflagration; against them stood China, France, Poland and the British Commonwealth of Nations. The rest of the world at that time was neutral.

THE STRENGTH OF THE AGGRESSORS

Each of the two great aggressor states promised a new way of life to its destined victims. Both were convinced that the old liberal ideals were worn out, that democracy was a dismal failure, and that the free peoples were too soft, too self-indulgent and too divided to withstand well-disciplined nations under resolute and far-sighted leaders. Hirohito's ministers offered to "Greater Asia" a wide "co-prosperity sphere" under the banner of the Rising Sun. Hitler proclaimed for Europe under the swastika a New Order, which should last a thousand years.

Japan and Germany possessed two advantages in the struggle they had started—they were united internally, and they held the initiative. In the vast empires they were striving to create, the rule of a Domi-

nant Race underlay every branch of government. For Asia this race
was to be the Japanese, descendants of the gods; over Europe the
glories of the New Order were to be enforced by the Master Race of
pure "Aryan" blood, the *Herrenvolk*. The Mikado held the unquestioned obedience and devotion of the Japanese. Rich and poor,
sailor and fisherman, soldier and farmer, airman and artisan, all
put their lives at Hirohito's disposal and served as their leaders
directed. There was none of the fumbling and incoherence which
seemed inseparable from the operations of a democracy. The unity
that Hitler had inspired in Germany lacked the sanction, which lay
behind the Mikado's semi-divine power. There was, in consequence,
some wishful thinking among his enemies, and they hoped that
gangster feuds would disrupt Nazi solidarity. But Hitler's curiously
magnetic personality exercised a boundless fascination over the
leaders of Germany, and his hoarse, grating voice had the power of
whipping millions to frenzied enthusiasm. Elaborate Nazi propaganda, backed by Gestapo terrorism, had moulded the national inferiority complex of the Germans into a sturdy belief in their destiny
as the *Herrenvolk*. There was passionate devotion, especially among
the younger age-groups, to the leader who had rescued the nation

GERMAN OCCUPIED TERRITORY: SEPTEMBER 1939

from the indignities of Versailles. Traditional docility and trained aptitude for laborious and detailed planning placed in Nazi hands a formidable weapon, with which to beat down men and women who cherished the traditions of free loyalties and individual liberty.

Naturally in a world which, only twenty years before, had been "made safe for democracy", the balance of numbers was heavily against the attacking powers. But those superior numbers could certainly not be rallied immediately; possibly they would never be given the chance to organize themselves. Germany's geographical position isolated Poland, and the policy of piecemeal absorption could be continued in war. Though Spain and Italy remained at peace, they menaced Britain's communications in the Mediterranean and immobilized French forces. The distracted neutrals could be weakened still further by the underground work of Fifth Columnists. The building of the Siegfried Line would check any offensive by the French generals, who had massed the bulk of their troops behind the Maginot fortification. Meanwhile the *Luftwaffe* and the *Wehrmacht* could be prepared for a smashing blow in the west; submarines would roam the seas; Japanese generals would push their troops southward, while their navy and air force prepared for the next spring forward.

THE RESOURCES OF DEMOCRACY

Only on the seas were the immediate resources of Britain and France superior to those of Germany. The British Navy had made up some leeway from the years of parsimony, but there was a dangerous shortage of cruisers and destroyers. The efforts of Admiral Darlan and other French sailors had raised their country's maritime strength. In the other two services the outlook was bleak. Though Baldwin's government had begun the re-equipment of the Royal Air Force, it was still pitifully inadequate for its task. Years of dreary mismanagement had left French air-power in far worse shape. The immediate burden of land fighting fell inevitably on the French Army. It lagged far behind the *Wehrmacht* in equipment, especially in tanks and guns. Generals and officers were wedded to an unsound theory of static defence, approved by the septuagenarian Pétain. It was hard to see what practical help Poland could expect from her Western Allies, when she faced the determined offensive of a General Staff, which practised the *blitzkreig*, the lightning war.

Politically too, democratic prospects were disheartening. Chamberlain and Daladier were not the men to secure unity among rival parties or to plan the strategy of a continental war. The Socialist leaders refused to join Chamberlain's government, and the main hope lay in Churchill who was back at the Admiralty, where he had served a quarter of a century earlier. Daladier's grip on Senate and Chamber was limp, and, while the factions bickered, the sinister figure of Laval loomed larger in the shadows of political life. The

Communists hampered the industrial effort, and gave their loyalty to Stalin in the Kremlin rather than to the capitalist cabinet in Paris. Yet the union between French and British leaders seemed firm. They began to develop the latent resources of the two empires, and to build up the fighting services. But time was needed for the task. Total war could be waged only if the free democracies were prepared to follow their enemies' example—prefer guns to butter, restrict the citizen's individual freedom, and adopt many other unwelcome totalitarian practices.

Time was needed also for the two democracies to adapt their industrial strength to war. Some years earlier their leaders had realized the necessity of co-ordinating not merely the three fighting services, but of planning and protecting the enormous and varied output of armament and equipment necessary for modern warfare, so that management, labour and scientists could co-operate with the service chiefs. The growing strength of the *Luftwaffe* had made it prudent to disperse factories over a wide area and so prevent output being stopped by the destruction of one or two large industrial centres. Greater progress had been made in Britain than France with this intricate planning. If it could be perfected, the naval resources of the two powers and their access to almost inexhaustible supplies of raw material from overseas would eventually give them superiority over Germany.

To secure this result wise and courageous leadership was essential. But the most brilliant statesmen, admirals, generals and air-marshalls could not win victory without the fortitude of the common folk. In the end the war would be decided by the abilities and the staunchness of the ordinary man and woman. If the free peoples were to be saved, there must be no limit to their endurance.

THE NEUTRALS

Britain and France could hope for some support from one of the two great powers which stood outside the conflict. In spite of neutrality laws, Nazi-fostered intrigue, and the traditional hostility of the descendants of Irish immigrants, there were millions in the United States of America who hated all that Hitler and, still more Hirohito, stood for. The great country had grown to be the world's workshop and was eager to become the " arsenal of Democracy". But, while pro-Britons asserted that they stood behind the Old Country, the Briton reflected grimly that the nearest stood three thousand miles behind.

American sympathy might grow into a valuable asset. From Russia the democracies had more to fear than hope. Stalin disliked the Poles for their Catholic and anti-Russian traditions; he resented the presence of Finnish troops on Lake Ladoga; he had not forgotten Munich; for the time he had close trading relations with Germany. He and his advisers, Voroshilov and Molotov, felt that the Soviets must build up their armed forces to overwhelming strength. Memories of Munich had weakened French influence with the Balkan peoples and with Hungary. Dutch and Belgians were torn between fears for their homelands and their possessions overseas; Germany might overrun the former, but the latter were at the mercy of the British and French fleets. The Scandinavian countries were important for the supply of food and raw materials, and the Norwegian coastline would be a valuable base for naval operations.

Franco and Mussolini, though nominally neutral, gave support to Hitler. At the other end of the Mediterranean, Turkey sympathized with Britain, as did many Arab states. Greece never allowed her internal quarrels to weaken her faith in Britain's cause. Most of the South American governments, except that of the Argentine, were inclined to look to Washington for a lead. Brazil, like the Mother Country, Portugal, maintained her traditional friendship with England. But all over the southern continent there were Axis sympathisers. Busy Japanese agents were to be found in every walk of life, and the tentacles of German business were widely spread.

The Dominions, the Princes of India and the Crown Colonies rallied at once to the Mother Country. Only Eire stood apart, controlling the Atlantic ports which Chamberlain had handed back, and causing anxiety by retaining the German and Japanese embassies in Dublin. De Valera gave little sign of sympathy with his co-religionists in Poland, who were the destined victims of the first demonstration of the *blitzkreig*.

POLAND'S COLLAPSE

The Polish Air Force was soon driven out of the skies, and Polish cavalry were of little value against the rapid advance of Germany's mechanized divisions. In sixteen days Hitler's men were at the gates of Warsaw, and Stalin had sent his troops across the eastern frontier. The Germans captured Gdynia and Premsyl, Lwow fell to the Russians, and the Polish Government fled to Rumania. The full fury of the German onslaught fell on Warsaw; continuous bombing from the air, supplemented by heavy artillery fire, broke the heroic defence. The invading armies met near Brest Litovsk, and it was decided by the rulers of Germany and Russia that, as in the eighteenth century, Poland should suffer the cruelty of partition. After barely thirty years of troubled freedom, the unhappy country found herself divided and enslaved by her two totalitarian neighbours.

A month had been sufficient to destroy the balance of military power in Europe. The Western Allies had been robbed of Poland's armed strength almost as easily as they had lost Czecho-Slovakia's in the spring of 1939. While Polish airmen and soldiers crossed the Rumanian frontier on the long journey to join their fellow-countrymen in France, Germany enjoyed a fresh recruiting ground, and Russia held a new frontier which made Moscow more secure.

For the next six months hostilities on land seemed to dwindle into insignificance. While the Russians attacked Finland unsuccessfully, the small British Expeditionary Force took its station at the northern end of the French line. Gamelin, the French Generalissimo, carried on minor operations in the Saarbrücken district, and some German divisions were brought to the Siegfried Line from conquered Poland. Strong French forces were kept on the Alpine frontier; others protected Morocco, Algeria and Tunisia. An effort was made to prolong the uncompleted Maginot Line.

Once again Germany experienced the effect of maritime blockade; in the first week of the war the British Navy captured 76,000 tons of cargo, destined for her use, and she was cut off from much that was essential to her war economy. Following the pattern of the First World War, Germany countered the allied effort with the U-boat. The *Luftwaffe* hampered the blockade by sowing magnetic mines from the air, and helped the U-boat by supplying vital information of British and French naval movements. Britain lost no time in employing the convoy system; but she had neither enough warships nor sufficient swift merchant tonnage to avoid losses. It was not till December that the British victory of the River Plate and the scuttling of the *Graf Spee* gave a much-needed fillip to the Allies' morale.

THE WAR IN EUROPE

Both on land and sea the two Western democracies were handicapped by the smallness of their combined air forces. But in the second month of the war Chamberlain announced that the British Commonwealth would build up a large air potential by the well-planned scheme which was operating in Canada. After the decisive bombing of Warsaw most land and air activity died down, except for reconnaissance and leaflet propaganda. There were still warm-hearted democrats who believed that Hitler might be overthrown by his own countrymen, and the R.A.F. flew to Berlin to encourage these hypothetical freedom-loving Germans by dropping leaflets.

The Far Eastern struggle continued, though China's supplies were running low. The United States, prevented by her isolationists from fortifying a strong forward base in the Pacific, looked on uneasily, while Japan pushed her forces westward and occupied more of the Chinese coast. Though her citizens showed great generosity in sending gifts across the Atlantic, public opinion grew impatient at the inability of the democracies to strike hard at Hitler. They repudiated Molotov's view that Germany was striving for peace and England was now the aggressor; but they found little that was spectacular in the operations on the Rhine or on the high seas, and Yankee wit christened the struggle "the phoney war". English, French, Scots, Poles and Welsh were being killed or drowned; but no British civilian was killed by a bomb until March, 1940, and Gamelin seemed content to hold his hand indefinitely. The average American began to think that the whole thing was bogus, though he was cheered by the temporary success of the Finns in checking Stalin's aggression.

By the end of April, Hitler had shaken this belief in the phoney war; by the end of June it was dead, and the overwhelming menace to democracy was desperately clear. The *Wehrmacht* occupied Copenhagen and the rest of King Christian's territory without serious resistance. Crossing the Skagerrak to Norway involved some naval losses, but the Germans seized Oslo, and began at once to reap the reward of their tireless propaganda and their brilliant nursing of the Fifth Columnists in Europe. Quisling, a politician who believed in a Master Nordic Race, came forward to betray King Haakon and his constitutional ministers, and to hand his country over to the invaders. In spite of the resistance of Norway's scanty armed forces, the Germans found their advance made easy by Quisling's followers. The British Navy fought two vigorous actions off Narvik, and a British Expeditionary Force was landed; but Quisling's efforts hamstrung its intelligence service, it could not secure the air-bases necessary to counteract the ubiquitous *Luftwaffe*, and after stiff fighting round Namsos and Stavanger the troops were forced to withdraw.

Quisling's successful treachery stamped his name on all the other pro-Nazi politicians and gangsters in Europe, who worked to win power and place for themselves by bringing their countries under Hitler's heel. But the great majority of Norwegians remained faithful to their democratic constitution and its emblem, King Haakon. Many soldiers, sailors and airmen followed him to England, under the shield of the British Navy. The remainder settled down to the dreary life enforced on them by Quisling and his Nazi overlords.

As time passed, the old Viking energy began to revive; in the north fearless men probed the weakness of the invaders, who were scattered over a wide and trackless area; in the southern towns men and women formed groups, which kept alive the flame of patriotism in spite of Nazi threats and punishments. For the moment Hitler's victory was absolute. The western coastline gave passage for his warships and provided bases for his U-boats and a far wider field for the *Luftwaffe* offensive.

The shock of these swift disasters drove Chamberlain and Daladier from power. Reynaud succeeded the latter, and on May 10, 1940, Churchill became Britain's premier. He formed a coalition government, which united Conservatives, Socialists and Liberals in the common resolve to accept their leader's promise of "blood and toil, tears and sweat" and to sacrifice everything to the war effort. That same day Hitler attacked the Low Countries and occupied Luxembourg. Glider-borne troops were dropped near Rotterdam, and part of the city was destroyed from the air. Despite French and British reinforcements the Dutch were in a desperate position; with airborne troops and Quislings behind them they could not hold the frontal thrust of German tanks and motorized infantry. Five days of the

new warfare drove the Dutch Army to surrender and Queen Wilhelmina to a refuge in England.

Belgian resistance began to crumble as Degrelle and his followers
copied Quisling's example. The Germans struck at the hinge of the
Allied advance and isolated the forces in the north. Before the end
of this amazing May King Leopold had capitulated. The German
thrust over the Meuse seemed to doom to destruction the Anglo-
French armies, which had gone to the rescue of Belgium.

Evacuation was hastily organized from the beaches of Dunkirk.
The outnumbered R.A.F. proved their individual superiority over
the *Luftwaffe*, while from every corner of Britain merchant ships and
small craft of all shapes and sizes came to help the Navy in its
momentous task. More than 650 little boats worked with the 220
light naval vessels through the sunny days and the windless nights.
Eventually more than 330,000 men were brought back to England.
By this epic of improvization Britain gathered behind the cliffs of
Dover fighting men, who could be rearmed and regrouped to form
the core of forces destined for the task of liberating Europe.

THE BREAKING OF FRANCE

The two democracies had suffered a grievous disaster. Though
more than a quarter of a million British soldiers had achieved a
miraculous escape from capture, they had lost all their arms, artillery,
transport and equipment. Gamelin's northern defences had been
pierced at a vital point, and he was superseded by Weygand. But
tanks and motorized troops continued to pour through the Sedan
gap, and Rundstedt and Bock broke Weygand's resistance on the
lines of the Somme and the Aisne. Every day brought "hard and
heavy tidings" of the fall of French towns—Amiens, Abbeville, Brest,
Strasbourg, Toul. These disasters encouraged Mussolini to declare
war and invade south-eastern France. Four days after the last
British troops had been evacuated from Norway, the Germans
entered Paris, and Reynaud's government retired to Bordeaux. There
Churchill offered his allies common citizenship and a union of the
two states, but the offer was rejected. Reynaud's last despairing
appeal to the United States for all help short of war was ineffectual.
While French Quislings worked for Hitler in Paris and the north,
Laval emerged from the shadows, and Pétain formed a government,
with first Weygand and then Laval as vice-premier. Pétain asked
for an armistice, and the French laid down their arms. Germany
took over north, west and south-west France, leaving the centre and
the south-east to Pétain and his cabinet at Vichy. By the end of June
all France lay at Hitler's mercy. The bulk of the population was
forced to acquiesce in the submission of its rulers.

But many Frenchmen did not agree with Pétain, Weygand and
Laval that all was lost. The tank general, de Gaulle, rallied this unbroken spirit and founded the Free French Movement. Churchill

recognized his leadership, and he was welcomed to Britain with his followers. The French nation was split into three groups—those who collaborated actively with the Germans, those who obeyed the Vichy cabinet, and those who believed that France could endure till she regained her freedom.

The most pressing question for Britain was the problem of the French fleet; if this fell to Hitler, Britain could no longer depend on "the solid assurances of sea-power". Churchill decided to put out of action the warships lying at Oran and other African ports. This unhappy but necessary operation decided Pétain to break off relations with Britain, leaving the country which had offered France equal citizenship without an ally in the world.

HITLER TRIUMPHANT

Three swift and brilliant campaigns had shown that the German commanders could not only train and equip armies, but could lead them to overwhelming victory with the minimum of loss. The triumph which Hitler, the ex-corporal, had promised exceeded their expectations, and compelled even the Junkers to believe in the Fuehrer's genius. Their enemies had been "poisoned by intrigue before they were struck down by violence". Four months' actual land-fighting following five years' war of nerves, had added to the Reich Austria, western Poland, Czecho-Slovakia, Norway, Denmark, Holland, Belgium, Luxembourg and France, and the English Crown had lost the Channel Islands, the last remnant of its old inheritance from the Dukes of Normandy.

When Hitler went to Paris in June 1940 and visited the tomb of the other "Little Corporal" he could boast of triumphs comparable to those of Chenghiz Khan and Alexander of Macedon, and far surpassing those of Cyrus, Attila, Charlemagne, or even of Napoleon himself. Hitler's dominions stretched from the Vistula to the Atlantic, and from the North Cape to the Pyrenees. The willing support of Spain and Italy extended his influence to the Mediterranean. Sweden and Finland regarded him as their natural protector against Soviet Russia, which seemed content with such modest territorial gains as eastern Poland, Bessarabia and the Bukovina. There was no firm obstacle in the disunited Balkans to any thrust he might plan southeastward to crush Turkey and absorb Vichy-controlled Syria and turbulent Iran. With these countries in his hands, Hitler would be free to co-operate with Mussolini. The pincers would close on Egypt from Libya and from Syria. Victory might spread her wings still farther, and the Swastika and the Fasces might link forces with the Rising Sun of Japan to dominate the world. With pluck and luck the New Order could be established for a millennium.

Only one obstacle threw a shadow over these dreams of universal empire—the British Commonwealth of Nations. Across the Channel lay the shores of England, towards which Napoleon had cast covetous eyes a hundred and thirty-five years earlier. Like the Corsican conqueror, Hitler lacked command of the seas; but in the *Luftwaffe* he had an apparently irresistible weapon. The Fuehrer had seen state after state disrupted by internal treachery and the threat from the air; he might well believe that among the nation of shopkeepers, the lovers of appeasement, he could find men content to co-operate with him, if he promised them an era of peace and commercial prosperity.

Hitler was wrong. He had often told his victims that his patience was exhausted; now he was to find that, though there was no limit to British patience, there were limits to British credulity.

The nation had found a leader, who could express its resolution and direct its skill and fortitude. Parliament and people alike endorsed the pledge Churchill gave after Dunkirk: "We shall not flag or fail. We shall go on to the end; we shall fight in France, we shall fight on the seas and oceans, we shall fight with growing confidence and growing strength in the air, we shall defend our island, whatever the cost may be; we shall fight on the beaches, we shall fight on the landing-grounds, we shall fight in the fields and in the streets, we shall fight in the hills. We shall never surrender".

Once more, as in the struggles with Philip of Spain and Napoleon, danger brought the temper of the islanders to its finest edge. The Navy and the Merchant Marine faced vastly increased difficulties and dangers; the western ports of the Continent from Narvik to Bayonne were in the enemy's grip; hostile Italy cut Mediterranean communications in two. Only a single division of the army was fully equipped for war; yet it was vital, while manning the island defences and arming the Free French, to send reinforcements abroad to check Italian aggression. The Home Guard was formed; its ranks were quickly filled from those above and below military age, armed mainly with shot-guns and equipped with home-made grenades.

The expansion of the fighting services necessitated swift and vast expansion of industry to equip them. This was made possible by the skill and endurance of the women, of whom many thousands flocked into factories and the farms, while more joined the army, navy and air force, taking over clerical and other duties to release men for foreign service. Nowhere else were women utilized so extensively as in Britain, but the British example was followed later by Russia and Germany, and to a smaller degree by the Americans, when they in turn were drawn into the fighting. Home life became increasingly difficult, as food grew scarce, rationing increased and housing accommodation diminished; British housewives not only tackled these problems, but many gave part-time war-service as well. The older children too used their out-of-school hours to help the national effort, both in farm and factory and in the Civil Defence organizations.

Britain stood four-square to meet the greatest peril that had ever threatened her freedom. There was even a curious feeling of relief that henceforward no allied defection could harm, and her safety lay in her own hands. The burden of self-protection was great; she added to it by hospitality, extended to all those who had been bruised by Hitler's blows. Poles, Norwegians, French, Belgians, Austrians, Czechs, Dutch, Danes and anti-Nazi Germans—all alike found a refuge in the island-fortress, and added their quota to the war effort against Germany.

THE BATTLE OF BRITAIN

While Mussolini sent his Italian and African troops to attack Egypt, the Sudan and British Somaliland, Hitler began the so-called Battle of Britain, which might more properly be described as the Battle of England. He assembled large forces in north France and the Low Countries, and collected an armada of self-propelled barges in the ports and estuaries facing the east and south coasts of England. As the Royal Navy denied him the command of the Narrow Seas, he sent the *Luftwaffe* to soften resistance. Milch's air-squadrons began their task in July, attacking firstly channel convoys and coastal towns, and then fighter-bases and aircraft factories. September saw night and daylight raids on London, carried out by heavy bombers and fighter-bombers. The Civil Defence services worked indefatigably to cope with the ever-mounting damage. A considerable portion of the civilian population slept fitfully underground during the night, and carried on their work as usual during the day. Men, women and children became siren-trained. London, Coventry and the other bombed cities felt that they could "take it", and looked forward to the day when their aggressors would have to take it too. The struggle in the air was prolonged and bitter; but the fighter-squadrons of the R.A.F., under Dowding's command, proved more than a match for the *Luftwaffe*, though the margin was desperately narrow. The Germans broke off the action at the end of October, when more than seventeen hundred of their aircraft had been put out of action.

Hitler had expected that the fall of France would force Britain into a negotiated peace. His intelligence service gave him an entirely false estimate of her military strength after Dunkirk, and he dared not risk the invasion he had begun to plan under Rundstedt's leadership. By the turn of the year he knew that he had suffered his first definite check, and that the Battle of Britain was lost. Had it gone the other way, or had Britain negotiated peace on the favourable terms he was prepared to offer, his grip on Western and Central Europe would have been complete, and he might have driven the Soviet armies at least as far back as the Urals. Instead of this British factories developed the bomber strength of the R.A.F. and British raids were made on a small scale. As the months slid by, steadily growing forces attacked manufacturing and communication centres, and went as far afield as Berlin and Naples.

In the Mediterranean, enemy air attacks did great damage in Malta, but failed to break the island's resistance. From its bases in

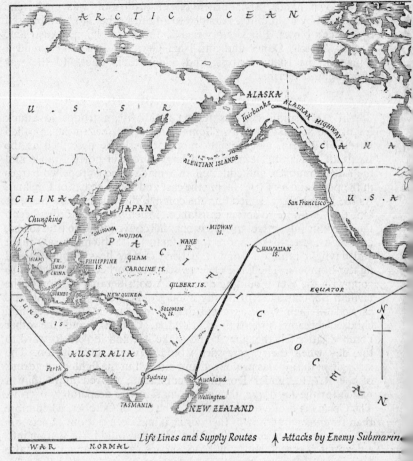

Life Lines and Supply Routes ⚓ Attacks by Enemy Submarine

WAR   NORMAL

PRINCIPAL ALLIED SUPPLY ROUTE

Egypt Andrew Cunningham's fleet protected the Suez Canal Zone. By the beginning of 1941 Wavell had driven the numerically superior Italian forces deep into Libya. Troops from British Africa and India took the field, and pushed the Italians back in Eritrea and Somaliland.

Britain had gained a small but courageous ally when the Greek Government rejected Italy's ultimatum in 1940. Greece renewed her ancient claim to be the stubborn enemy of totalitarian aggression. Fighting in Albania exposed the hollowness of Mussolini's military pretensions. Badoglio was superseded, and Hitler was drawn reluctantly into the Balkan fighting. The connivance of the Bulgarians allowed the *Wehrmacht* to occupy strategic points, from which to

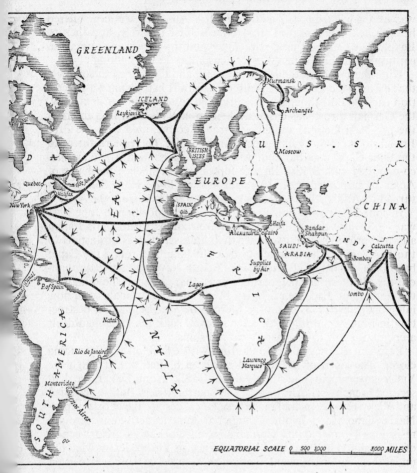

EQUATORIAL SCALE 0 500 1000 3000 MILES

OF THE SECOND WORLD WAR

attack not only Greece, but also Yugo-Slavia which had been crippled by its pro-Nazi rulers.

Though every available man was needed for the African campaigns, Churchill answered the Greeks' appeal for aid. Wavell's handling of British forces was securing brilliant results both in Libya and Abyssinia. But many of the troops had to be sent to Greece, and Britain's gains in Libya, except Tobruk, were lost, when Hitler reinforced his Afrika Korps. Italy found herself playing second fiddle to her aggressive ally in Libya, and she suffered another blow when Cunningham hammered her fleet in the clear-cut victory off Cape Matapan.

But the *blitzkreig* won another success in the Balkans. Greece and Yugo-Slavia were overrun, and a third British expeditionary force was evacuated from a friendly country. All three services suffered heavily in the withdrawal from Greece, first to Crete, and then to Egypt. The Germans used parachutes and troop-carrying aircraft to capture Crete, and suffered severe casualties in the fighting.

Hitler had reached the Mediterranean, and threatened to complete that drive to the East which Kaiser William II had planned a generation earlier. But, though Turkey refused to abandon her neutrality, the German thrust was checked. Britain intervened in Iraq to crush the pro-Nazi faction, and British troops co-operated with the Free French to expel the Vichy general from Syria. The eastern threat to the Suez Canal was blocked. Meanwhile Abyssinian irregulars had co-operated with British Empire forces, and compelled the Duke of Aosta to surrender at Amba Alagi in May 1941. Haile Selassie returned to Addis Ababa, and one nation was freed from the Axis.

In spite of his swift Balkan victories Hitler's position in June 1941 was less secure than it had been twelve months earlier. His Italian ally had proved a liability rather than an asset. English transport to the Far East had been driven to take the long haul round the Cape; but Malta still defied all attacks; the British Navy was active throughout the Mediterranean. Goering's boast that no bomb should fall on the Fatherland had been falsified by the R.A.F. U-boats were now inflicting grievous losses on the Mercantile Marine; but the destruction in May of the *Bismarck* after she had sunk the *Hood* had dealt a crippling blow to Germany's capital ships.

President Roosevelt's co-operation with Churchill was becoming closer. The spirit of France had not been blotted out. Though the Vichy government had repulsed de Gaulle from Dakar, he had secured French territories in West and Central Africa. Both in occupied and Vichy France, men planned resistance, despite the efforts of pro-Nazi collaborators. In other conquered countries active underground resistance hampered the Germans. Even Goebbels's great weapon of propaganda had lost its early brilliance, as Europe learnt what life under the New Order meant in practice. Men risked their lives to listen to British broadcasts, which revived their hopes of freedom restored.

HITLER INVADES RUSSIA

The *Wehrmacht's* record of victory was still unbroken, though some small detachments in Western Europe were disturbed unpleasantly by occasional pinpricks from raiding British and Canadian commandos. Hitler moved the bulk of his armies to his eastern frontiers, and on June 22, 1941, attacked Russia, with the active support of Italy, Finland and Rumania, who were joined later by Hungary and Czecho-Slovakia. In spite of earlier differences, Churchill immediately hailed Stalin as an ally; Eden and Molotov signed an Anglo-Russian pact; Britain and the United States began to send aid to the government of the Kremlin. The Germans' plan of a threefold attack, striking towards Leningrad, Moscow and the Ukraine, started brilliantly, especially in the north where Stalin lost Latvia, Lithuania and Esthonia, which he had just annexed. There was ferocious fighting round Smolensk, but the Germans made good progress both in the central sector and in the south. Berlin began to anticipate the fall of Moscow.

Much of this first success was due to the *Luftwaffe's* superiority over the Russian Air Force. But on the ground the Germans soon knew that they were encountering a far stiffer opposition than they had yet met. The Russian soldier was well equipped and showed all his old tenacity. The Germans gained ground rapidly, but the lengthening lines of communication were attacked savagely by well-organized bands of partisans. Though thousands of captured soldiers and civilians were forced to work for the invaders, thousands more withdrew eastward. Russia began to use her greatest asset—space. Her railway system had been re-organized, and there was no repetition of the 1916 breakdown. Stalin adopted the "scorched earth" policy, and directed his retreating countrymen to destroy everything which might assist the enemy's advance.

The Balkan and African fighting had disorganized Hitler's time-table, and he needed a decisive victory quickly. His armies pressed on to encircle Leningrad, to thrust hard at Moscow, and to overrun the Ukraine. Of these glittering prizes Moscow seemed the most valuable, and a huge force of tanks was devoted to the attack on the capital. Stalin prudently withdrew several government departments to Quibishev on the Volga, and ordered the wrecking of the great power-station at Dniepropetrovsk. Voroshilov took over the task of training fresh levies in the interior; Zhdanov inspired Leningrad's heroic resistance; Timoshenko and Zhukov directed the long defensive line from Moscow to the Black Sea.

After staggering losses on both sides, Bock's attack on Moscow failed. But in the south Rundstedt overran the Ukraine. Aided by their Balkan satellites, the *Wehrmacht* advanced from the Dnieper to overwhelm the industrial towns of the Donetz Basin, and then pressed forward to the Don, where Rostov was captured in November. Rumanian troops occupied Odessa, the Caucasian oilfields were threatened, and all the Crimea with the exception of Sevastopol was captured. Then the Russian winter began to control operations, as it had in Napoleon's day; the German advance was halted before Leningrad and Moscow, and Rostov was recaptured.

HIROHITO'S HUNDRED DAYS

In that same December the smouldering Asiatic war blazed out over an immense area. Japan had captured Shanghai and Nanking at the end of 1937. Next year, in spite of China's "scorched earth" policy, she overran the provinces of Honan and Amwhei, and captured Canton and Kwantung. The Yangtze fell into her hands as far as Ichang. But the invaders failed to make their conquests secure, in

JAPANESE PENETRATION IN CHINA

The Japanese had invested much capital in Manchuria to develop the iron, coal and timber, of all of which supplies in Japan are inadequate to requirements. When in 1931 the Chinese attempted to restrict the special privileges enjoyed by Japanese nationals, Japan seized control of the region. So began the China "incident" which ended only with the surrender of Japan in 1945. The successive Japanese incursions into Chinese territory between 1931 and 1945 are shown above.

spite of the weaknesses caused by the opposition of Mao and his communists and the traditional corruption of Chinese government. The Koumintang purged itself of disloyal members, such as Wang-Chin-Wei. Administration, education and medical services were organized from Chung-King; troops were trained for both regular and guerilla warfare. The Japanese occupied city after city, but the most savage brutalities failed to hold down the intervening country-side. Hirohito's men were beaten in the battles of Changsha, in spite of their air superiority and the help given by Fifth Columnists to their parachute troops. Chiang's airmen were trained in the U.S.A., and in October, 1941, an American volunteer group, "the Flying Tigers", was sent to reinforce the Chinese. Welcome financial help came from Washington and hard-pressed London; the two democracies hampered the Tokio government by stopping the transit of war-material to Japanese territories. But Chiang's difficulties had been increased by the loss of Hainan Island and by the opening of Indo-China by Vichy sympathizers to Japanese occupation. The European partners in the Axis recognized Wang-Ching-Wei's puppet government at Nanking. China retorted by declaring war on Germany and Italy.

JAPAN'S OFFENSIVE IN THE PACIFIC

On December 7, 1941, while the Japanese envoy discussed the maintenance of peace with the American Secretary of State, Cordell Hull, Tokio sent planes to bomb Pearl Harbour. A formidable blow was struck at American naval strength, and the balance of sea-power in the Pacific was changed entirely. Advanced American bases at Guam and Wake Island were battered into submission. To achieve her long-planned expansion into "the southern seas", Japan sent out five expeditions. One captured Hong-Kong after seventeen days' fighting. A second sailed against Borneo and Indonesia. Two others attacked Mindinao and Luzon. The fifth thrust was directed towards Malaya. Fortunately for the Anglo-American cause the Philippine President had invited MacArthur back to Manila. This able American general had a sympathetic understanding of the islanders; he had trained Philippine troops, who helped the U.S.A. forces to oppose a stiff resistance to the aggressors. But command of the seas enabled the Japanese to seize the airfields, capture Manila and squeeze out opposition in the Philippine archipelago. The Dutch secured little support from the Indonesians, and Java and Sumatra fell to the Japanese.

It was in Malaya that the invaders won their most spectacular triumphs. Pushing on from Hainan and Indo-China, the Japanese Army and Navy won Siam after a four hours' token resistance. From conquered Bangkok they sent air-raiders against Burma and pressed southward to secure Malaya's rubber and tin. Australian, Indian and British reinforcements came out to Singapore piecemeal; there were few native levies to support them. British naval strength had been weakened fatally, when torpedo-carrying planes sank two battleships just after Pearl Harbour. Japanese troops thrust their way swiftly to Singapore. In February the great port and 100,000 men surrendered—the most humiliating disaster the British Empire had suffered for a century and a half.

Adversity spurred the three defending nations into closer union. American and British military leaders met Chiang-Kai-shek in Chung-King to co-ordinate operations. The American veteran, Stilwell, who had served in the Philippines, led Chinese troops into north Burma to help the British. But the Japanese swept on. Aung San recruited Burmese levies to help them. Rangoon was captured. The heavy task of evacuating the defending forces over the jungle ranges into Manipur and India was organized, while the Chinese troops in Burma withdrew into Yunnan. The fall of Lashio blocked China's southern supply-line. American resistance in the Philippines ended with the fall of Corregidor. Japanese warships and aircraft carriers moved across the Bay of Bengal and seized the Andaman Islands. Japanese submarines hampered supply routes across the Indian Ocean. The attack was pushed south to Timor and New Guinea, and Australia was threatened. Hirohito's "lightning war" had been even more spectacular than Hitler's, and his conquests swifter and more widely flung.

THE IMPACT OF AMERICA

In the spring of 1942 the Axis Powers might well believe that a' victorious peace was within their grasp. With the passing of the Russian winter, Hitler, who had assumed complete military responsibility, planned another offensive against the Russians. There had been advance and retreat along the Libyan coast; but May would see a determined German thrust against the British forces in Egypt, and Mussolini prepared to ride his white charger into Alexandria. Japan was sweeping forward to break American power in the Pacific, and was planning fresh offensives in China as well as the closing of the Burma road. The rulers of the Axis made ready for their final triumph.

Against the improved Axis prospects there was little to set for the moment, except the building-up of British air-power, the unbroken morale of the Russians led by new generals, and the undeveloped resources of America. Under President Roosevelt's wise guidance the Americans threw their unrivalled industrial capacity into the war effort. Huge new factories sprang up and were filled with workers, drafted from their homes in distant states. Mass-production of guns, planes, tanks and munitions was organized on a stupendous scale. New camps and airfields helped the expansion of the army and the air force. Kaiser's genius built hundreds of "Liberty Ships", which carried American help across the Atlantic and the Pacific. Though the policy of the miners' leader, Lewis, sometimes threatened this rapidly expanding production, the combined energies of politicians, scientists, manufacturers and labourers achieved astonishing results in the next four years in a country untroubled by enemy bombing.

Even more astonishing was the co-operation which Roosevelt and Churchill fostered in their naval, military and air staffs. History is studded with the disastrous quarrels of jealous allies. The President and the Premier made combined team-work their policy from the beginning, and it became stronger as the war spread over the world. Naval, military and air leaders were found to match the men who had carried out Hitler's and Hirohito's *blitzkreigs*. They had to plan combined operations in every quarter of the globe, and to work in unison with the Russian commanders. Their loyal co-operation stood the test of every strain and surmounted every difficulty. The credit for it belongs not only to the genius of the Supreme Commander in Europe, the American Eisenhower, but to the singleness of purpose which inspired all ranks of the British and American forces.

Against Japan the main task of the Anglo-American leaders was to build up air and naval strength, while they held the land offensives planned by the aggressive Tojo. Britain had to be guarded against the possibility of invasion and the damage of attacks from the air. New transport lines had to be developed, not only to deny the control of the Mediterranean and its shores to Germany and Italy, but also to help Russia with supplies in her bitter struggle against the *Wehrmacht*. Fresh air-routes were developed; a railway was built in Iran; convoys carried munitions to Stalin over the bleak sea-route to Murmansk. Casualties were more frequent than thanks, but the route was maintained through the unrelenting work of the Royal Navy and the unflinching fortitude of the British merchant seaman.

British and Russian troops met in Iran to block Hitler's drive to the East. The Allied air forces grew steadily stronger, as science and industry supplied them with faster planes and such devices as radar, air-cannon, precision sights, jet propulsion and bombs which increased in size and destructive power until 12,000-pound "block busters" were used against industrial targets.

THE EBB AND FLOW OF WAR

Many months were bound to pass before America could pull her full weight. Meanwhile, the first winter of Russian warfare had inflicted terrible suffering on the inadequately equipped *Wehrmacht* and exposed the blunders of Hitler's planning. The German line was pushed back from Moscow; Rostov and Kerch were re-captured. But the spring mud checked operations, and in May Hitler launched another offensive, with Finnish support in the north, Hungarian in the centre, and Rumanian and Italian in the south. Heavy pressure was exerted against the Leningrad and Moscow sectors. Rostov changed hands again: the Maikop oilfield was seized: the great port of Sevastopol was captured after six months' siege: the Black Sea fleet was driven to the east, where its bases were threatened by the

TERRITORY OCCUPIED BY THE AXIS BY AUTUMN 1942

thrust towards the Grozni oilfields. By September the invaders were fighting in the streets of Stalingrad, and the Fuehrer proclaimed the certainty of its fall before the coming of another Russian winter.

Commandos raided the French coast, and Hitler erected strong coastal defences with conscripted French labour, recruited by Laval and directed by the Todt organization. Helped by Norwegian seamen, British sailors and commandos raided the Lofoten Islands and Vaagso. The French resistance movement assisted the attack on St. Nazaire. In August Canadian troops landed in Dieppe in a raid designed to probe the possibilities of a successful breaching of the Western Wall. The scale of air raids increased. Harris sent a thousand British bombers against Cologne in May, and similar attacks on Essen and the Ruhr followed. The U.S.A. Air Force came into action in Europe in July.

In the Mediterranean, aircraft and submarines waged continual war on the two great opposing supply-lines, north–south and west–east. On the Libyan coast British troops had won and lost Benghazi twice. The defence of Tobruk had hampered the Axis advance towards the Nile. But the new Nazi commander, Rommel, had built up the Afrika Korps into a formidable weapon, especially strong in armour. In May 1942 he swept the British back to El Alamein within sixty miles of Alexandria.

Japanese naval activity west of Ceylon was checked by the British occupation of Madagascar. Tojo did not attempt a sea-borne landing in India; but there was heavy fighting in Burma before the Japanese advance on the Arakan front was checked. Gradually British troops learnt the art of jungle fighting and became physically acclimatized. The Chinese continued their dour struggle, in spite of supply difficulties and the clash between Chiang and Mao-Tse-Tung.

The American admiral, Nimitz, struck the first great blow at Japan's expanding "Co-prosperity Sphere" by the victories of the Coral Sea in May, 1942, and off Midway Island in July. The Japanese Navy was weakened, and their transport tonnage was seriously diminished. The threat to Australia and New Zealand lifted.

DEGRADATION OF HUMAN LIFE

War developments in two hemispheres drew increasing numbers of civilians into the manufacture of weapons of defence and destruction. Women worked in addition to men, and home life was disrupted. Children grew up with little help from parents and teachers. As food and clothing became scarcer, rationing was made increasingly stringent: to counteract these discomforts, "black markets" sprang up. Dishonesty spread throughout Europe as rapidly as government regulations. Loot from conquered lands enriched the leaders of the two *blitzkreigs* and their followers: in the rest of Europe and Asia the material conditions of life grew steadily worse, with the mounting destruction of public and private buildings. Drab monotony became the lot of the more fortunate. Terror was the daily portion of the countries ruled from Berlin and Tokio, and the terror grew with the mounting spirit of resistance.

For nine years the Chinese had accepted death and devastation with their traditional fortitude. Now it was Europe's turn to show that human nature was tougher than the intellectuals had taught. Nazi practice had always used the concentration camp as the normal instrument for crushing opposition. War increased its torments and expanded its range. Torture became a fine art, and science was called in to perfect new ways of breaking down the human body and the human spirit. Murder was mass-produced: the Auschwitz camp disposed of many hundreds of thousands of men and women by the gas-chamber, execution or mere ill-usage. The Nazi persecution of the Jews developed into a policy of extermination, and Poles, Czechs

and Russians suffered only a little less severely at the hands of
Himmler and his trained sadists. Japan did not lag behind her ally
in inflicting physical and moral degradation on her enemies.

SCIENTIFIC PROGRESS

By his great work in his Cambridge laboratory Rutherford had
shown men how the atom could be split. On either side of the
Atlantic physicists had carried forward his discoveries. When war
came, the immediate task of the scientists, "the backroom boys",
was to devise annihilating implements of war. But not all scientific
discovery was sheerly destructive. The brains which had learnt from
Rutherford aimed primarily at producing the atom-bomb; yet their
labours in that field gave promise of developments which later would
provide a vast increase of power for industrial and other uses.
Mepacrine, a drug which suppressed malarial fever, was of immense
value in reducing the sickness rate among the many thousands whose
duty exposed them to the ravages of the mosquito in malarial
regions. Victims of tuberculosis and septicaemia were saved by those
who worked out treatment by penicillin and the sulphonamide de-
rivatives. In the operating theatres surgery made great strides, especially in prophylactic method. Saline baths helped to heal bodies,
scarred by the flames of aerial bombardment. Perhaps the greatest
advance was made in the different branches of radiotherapy.

Largely owing to the demands of the air force, engineering achieved
gratifying progress in the expanding output of plastics and light
alloys. Peace could release these discoveries for domestic and social
purposes. Peace too could find useful developments of such wartime
achievements as radar, jet propulsion, the gas turbine and the electron
microscope. Despite the strain of war, Britain never abandoned her
plans for social reform. Her Coalition government passed an ambitious Education Act in 1944, and laid down the broad lines of
"social security".

EL ALAMEIN, NORTH AFRICA AND STALINGRAD

Meanwhile Hitler's chief objectives in the autumn of 1942 were the
Volga Line and the Caucasian oilfields. But he did not neglect
Rommel, who was preparing for his final drive into Egypt, and a
heavy attack was made on Malta to secure Mediterranean communications. With Alexander in command at Cairo, vigorous preparations had been made for the battle of Egypt; quantities of guns
and tanks were sent forward to strengthen Montgomery's Eighth
Army. On October 25 a concentrated artillery bombardment opened
the attack at El Alamein; British paratroops went into action, and
desert forces harassed Rommel's communications. Tedder's air force
outfought the *Regia Aeronautica* and the *Luftwaffe*. The Afrika Korps
was driven westward, abandoning the Italian divisions on the south of

The meeting of Winston Churchill, F. D. Roosevelt and Marshal Stalin at the Yalta Conference in 1945.

Madame Marie Curie, 1867–1934, the Polish scientist who carried on her husband's work and developed the use of radium in curative treatment.

Ernest Rutherford, 1871–1937, the New Zealand physicist whose work in the Cavendish laboratory at Cambridge led to the splitting of the atom.

Torch bearer entering the Stadium at Wembley for the opening ceremony of the Olympic Games held in 1948. The flame he bears has been brought from Athens by relays of runners. The revival of the Olympic Games was due to Baron Pierre de Coubertin who aimed at fostering international goodwill between the nations through these peaceful athletic contests.

the line. Tobruk and Benghazi were recaptured. Montgomery pressed on through Tripoli, and, with Leclerc's Free French troops coming up from Lake Chad on his left, reached the Mareth Line in March, 1943.

While Alexander's command had carried out this advance of 1,350 miles mainly over inhospitable desert, an Anglo-American expeditionary force had been safely convoyed in November to French North Africa over 3,000 miles of sea. Allied strategy surprised the Axis, and Andrew Cunningham's naval dispositions enabled Eisenhower's troops to make a safe landing.

The Germans reacted vigorously. Rundstedt occupied Vichy France and its ports. Paratroops and commandos were rushed across the Mediterranean. Eisenhower failed to overwhelm Tunisia by a swift advance, and Axis troops, which had occupied Tunis and Bizerta, pushed southward to link with Rommel on the Mareth Line. Patton's command was beaten backwards towards Tebessa, and there was some desperately hard fighting before Montgomery drove Rommel from the Mareth Line and made contact with the other British and American troops in North Africa. Alexander co-ordinated the final operations, and the Axis troops were pressed into a narrowing circle and driven into the Cap Bon Peninsula. Though Messe's Italian divisions fought well, all resistance had collapsed by May, and a quarter of a million prisoners were taken.

On the eastern front the thrust to the Caucasian oilfields was no longer pressed heavily. Stalingrad was the magnet that drew Hitler's main attack. In November he renewed his offensive on the battered Volga town, where German air-superiority had little influence on the close-quarter fighting in the ruined streets. For the winter campaign the Russians had trained their infantry on skis, and had prepared an all-white kit, "snow-shod" lorries and sleigh transport. While Stalin pinned the invaders down in the centre by an offensive in the Rzhev sector, his "pincers" began to cut into the Stalingrad salient. The attacking *Wehrmacht* was forced on to the defensive, and, though supplies were dropped to them by air, the Russians closed in remorselessly. In February Paullus surrendered with 25,000 men. Many other towns were recaptured, including Mozdok, Kursk, Rostov and Rzhev; but it was Stalingrad that symbolized and inspired Russia's unconquerable spirit.

The seven months since El Alamein had altered entirely the prospects of Hitler's war. North, south, east and west the shadow of Allied strategy fell on his Fortress of Europe. Germany itself suffered from the ever-growing air raids of the Anglo-American bombers—Berlin, Wilhelmshaven and the Moehne and Eder dams being among places attacked. Zhukov, Malinowski, Koniev and other Russian generals were breaking down the German "hedgehogs" and forcing withdrawals over large areas, and Hitler was faced with the old nightmare of a Slav advance on a 2,000 mile front. North and west he might be attacked by Anglo-American

H H

soldiers trained in the battle schools of Britain to deal with every new development in the business of fighting. To the south across the Mediterranean stood a victorious Allied Army.

The Western Allies decided to strike first at the weaker Axis partner. The French fleet at Toulon had been scuttled, when the Germans had sent their troops into Vichy France. Malta's defenders had passed to the offensive: the Allies had secured superiority on sea and in the air. By July the invading armies in Tunisia had been regrouped: preceded by airborne troops and carried by two thousand ships, the Anglo-American forces were safely landed on the beaches of south-east Sicily in July, 1943. There was stiff fighting, especially at Catania, but most Italians had lost heart for the war.

THE FASCIST COLLAPSE

Mussolini's Fascist state disintegrated rapidly. The Duce resigned and was arrested. Badoglio prepared to make terms with the invaders, and dissolved the Fascist party. In September Montgomery led the Eighth Army into southern Italy and seized the port of Taranto. The Italian fleet surrendered at Malta. American and British troops made good their landing at Salerno and other points on the Italian mainland in September after a critical struggle. But again the Germans reacted vigorously. Though the Italians had surrendered unconditionally, the Germans drove Badoglio from Rome, rescued Mussolini and set up a puppet government of Republican Fascists. They also utilized the material difficulties of the terrain and established skilful defensive "lines"; the Allied advance was difficult. But Alexander pushed steadily northward. There was bitter winter fighting at the Anzio beach-head and Monte Cassino. Veteran allied divisions were withdrawn to England to be prepared for the invasion of Western Europe, and the Germans defended the river crossings and successive "lines" tenaciously. But in June, 1944, the Allies entered Rome and resistance groups became active in northern Italy. Eleven months' hard fighting lay ahead before the whole country could be cleared. Without undue losses Alexander pinned down large German forces in Lombardy and Provence, and so depleted the reserves available for the defence of the Western Wall.

The Allied progress in Italy helped to increase German difficulties across the Adriatic. Mihailovitch and his Chetniks had kept alive resistance to the Axis when the royal government left Yugo-Slavia. Later Tito attacked the invaders in the north: but there was no goodwill between his Communist partisans and the Chetniks, who stood for the tradition of Serbian supremacy. Eventually, Britain transferred her help from Mihailovitch to Tito. On Mussolini's fall the Germans had disarmed the Italian garrisons, and their grip on the Balkans weakened as British help strengthened the resistance movement in Greece as well as Yugo-Slavia. The Royal Navy began to

THE RUSSIAN FRONT

The map shows the vast area over which the German and Russian armies were engaged against one another during the Second World War.

find bases on both sides of the Adriatic as it worked northward in co-operation with Allied land and air forces.

The German General Staff was faced with the threat from the Mediterranean and the probability of an Anglo-American landing in France or the Low Countries. Before either danger could mature, they decided that Russia must be dealt a knock-out blow. They had rebuilt their eastern armies after the Stalingrad disaster, and had found a powerful weapon in the Tiger tank. By July, 1943, they had effected a heavy concentration of armour, air-power and infantry, stretching from Byelgorod round the Kursk bulge to Orel. But Stalin's intelligence service and the guerillas denied them the element of surprise. Great improvements had been made in Russian artillery: Stalin had created a new and effective air force, while the *Luftwaffe* had to detach many of its best fighters for home defence against the growing Anglo-American air raids, which were crippling Germany's industry. The Germans made some progress near Byelgorod, but three weeks' terrible fighting proved that the Russians had the measure of the Tiger tank and the dive-bomber. The great gamble failed. Henceforward, though there were to be many fierce counter-attacks, the initiative lay with the Russians.

GREAT RUSSIAN ADVANCE

They went over to the attack at once, capturing Orel, Byelgorod and Kharkov, forcing their way to the Pripet marshes, and pushing the enemy steadily out of the Ukraine. No time was given for the formation of a solid defensive line, and the Germans were pressed back all along their eastern front. Advantage in numbers enabled the Russians to add a third force to their previous summer and winter formations. These troops were designed for autumn and spring service, when Cossack cavalry and horsed vehicles could cope with the mud that bogged down tanks and motorized transport. German infantry fought as stubbornly as ever, and their sappers were skilled in demolitions. But civilians and women joined Stalin's soldiers in keeping the roads in repair in all weathers and rivalled in their voluntary work the conscripts of the Todt organization.

By the end of September the Russians were in Dniepropetrovsk, and had forced their enemies back from the Caucasian oilfields to defend the southern Ukraine. Next month Manstein was fighting to hold the Dnieper bend. The mud of a fickle winter helped his resistance, but a crossing of the broad river was effected, and Russian communications were improved. In February, 1944, the siege of Leningrad was raised after lasting two years. The Baltic coast was cleared up to Narva, and the Novgorod area recovered. In March a hundred thousand Germans surrendered to Koniev at Korsun; Nikopol and Krivoi Rog were recaptured; the lines of the Dniester and the Bug were crossed, and Zhukov, Koniev and Malinowski, cleared the southern Ukraine. The six months' battle of the Dnieper Bend had cost Hitler three-quarters of a million casualties, and the spring saw Zhukov in the Carpathian foothills.

Hitler still insisted recklessly on defending his forward positions in the east, while he prepared to use in the west the flying bombs which his "backroom boys" had produced for the devastation of London and southern England. But, with Rumania invaded, Odessa and Tarnopol had to be evacuated, and the Crimea was cleared of Germans. Three days' sustained attack recaptured Sevastopol, and the Black Sea fleet moved westward again.

In June the Finnish and German fronts round the Baltic were broken. White Russia was attacked and its defensive line smashed; the "hedgehogs" proved no match for the new mobility of Stalin's artillery. Defeat in the east, combined with disastrous news from France, brought the discontent of the Junker generals to a head; but in July they failed in their attempt to assassinate Hitler. Strategical unity and morale on the eastern front were shattered, as city after city fell again into Russian hands. The bold Russian thrusts between the Dwina and Pripet rivers went swiftly forward, helped by the indomitable guerillas. Koniev recaptured Lwow, and Russian tanks crossed the Vistula. In August the Polish Home Army rose in Warsaw; but Stalin withheld support, and the Germans retained their hold on the Polish capital. Next month the Russians overran Esthonia; though there was stubborn resistance round Riga, Kronstadt harbour was cleared and East Prussia was invaded.

By the autumn of 1944 the satellite nations had lost their faith in Hitler's star. Germany's supplies of wheat and oil suffered seriously when King Michael brought Rumania over to the Russian side. Zhdanov signed armistice terms with Finland in September. Esthonians and Lithuanians escaped from German rule. Bulgaria followed Rumania's example, and deserted the Nazi cause.

THE FAR EASTERN STRUGGLE

The heavy task of holding and breaking the bulk of the *Wehrmacht* forbade Stalin shouldering any additional burden on his eastern frontier. The struggle with Japan's "Co-prosperity Sphere" was carried on by the U.S.A. aided by the British Commonwealth and the Indian forces. MacArthur and Nimitz had the assistance of Australia in the Pacific theatre of war. America continued to send help to Chiang-Kai-Shek, who failed to establish union with Mao and the Chinese Communists and his own lack of tanks, transport and heavy artillery; but he managed to repulse a strong Japanese thrust towards Chungking. Fighting India built up its military strength gradually. Air warfare began to reveal the essential dangers of Tojo's strategical position, with its overlong communications by land and sea. But Hirohito's generals could still rely on their infantry's fanatical courage and superb marching-powers.

Though the Japanese continued their air-attacks on Darwin and

JAPANESE CONQUESTS AT

In 1942 the Far Eastern possessions of Britain, France, the U.S.A., the Netherlands and Portugal, as well as the independent Kingdom of Siam and great tracts of China had been captured by the Japanese. The enormous task of re-

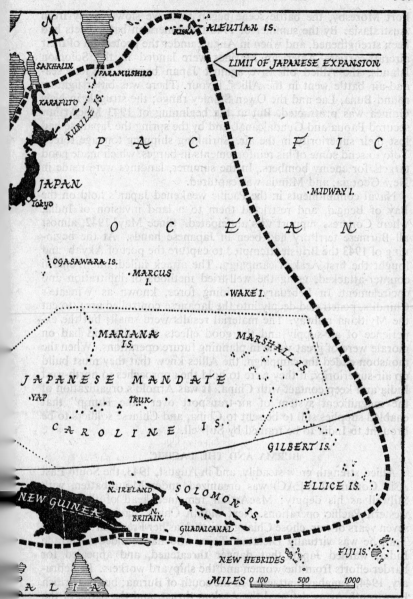

LIMIT OF JAPANESE EXPANSION

ALEUTIAN IS.

KISKA

SAKHALIN

PARAMUSHIRO

KARAFUTO

KURILE IS.

PACIFIC

JAPAN

Tokyo

OCEAN

MIDWAY I.

OGASAWARA IS.

MARCUS I.

WAKE I.

MARIANA IS.

MARSHALL IS.

JAPANESE MANDATE

YAP

TRUK

CAROLINE IS.

GILBERT IS.

ELLICE IS.

N. IRELAND

SOLOMON IS.

NEW GUINEA

N. BRITAIN

GUADALCANAL

FIJI IS.

NEW HEBRIDES

ALIA

MILES 0 100   500   1,000

THEIR GREATEST EXTENT

conquest successfully undertaken by the Allies can readily be appreciated from
the immense distances revealed by the scale of the maps.

Port Moresby, the battle scene began to move slowly away from Australasia. By the summer of 1942 the American battle-fleets had been strengthened, and when in August under the protection of their aircraft-carriers American Marines were landed in the Solomon Islands, the Allied offensive against Japan began. The long sea-and-air battle went in the Allies' favour. There was bitter fighting round Buna, Lae and the Owen Stanley range; the struggle in New Guinea was protracted. But at the beginning of 1943 MacArthur secured Papua and Guadalcanal, and by the spring the Japanese had lost their superiority in the air. Shrinking shipping tonnage forced Tojo to send some of his reinforcements in barges, which made good targets for enemy bombers. In the summer, landings were made in New Georgia, and Munda was captured.

Naval commitments in the Pacific weakened Japan's hold on the Bay of Bengal, and restricted them to a land invasion of India, where Congress support was anticipated. Since May, 1942, almost all Burmese territory had been in Japanese hands. At the beginning of 1943 the British attempted to capture the port of Akyab, and fought the first Arakan campaign. The attack failed, and Tunashi counter-attacked, using the well-tried methods of infiltration and encirclement. In February a raiding force, known as Wingate's Chindits, penetrated deeply into the Japanese controlled area, to cut the Myitkina railway. The material results were small; but the experience of air-supply and the good effects that the raid had on morale were of great value in planning future operations. When the monsoon ended the campaign, the Allies knew that they must build up air-superiority, if they were to hold the approaches to north-west India and keep contact with China. It was Arnold's organization of the magnificent system of air-transport over "the Hump" that enabled supplies still to be sent to China, and Chinese soldiers to be brought to India to be trained by Stilwell.

BURMA AND THE PACIFIC

Allied strength grew steadily, and in August, 1943, the South East Asia Command (SEAC) was organized under Mountbatten, with Stilwell as his deputy; MacArthur remained head of the South-western Pacific operations. Next month China, having completed seven years of war, chose Chiang Kai-shek as her President; as Tsung Tsai, he was virtually Dictator. Tojo, who had decided to invade India, warned Japan that danger threatened, and appealed for harder efforts from the women and the shipyard workers. In February, 1944, Tanahashi attacked in the south of Burma; but the British Fourteenth Army defeated the Arakan thrust, and the battle of the "Admin box" showed how air-transport could supply encircled troops. Then the British went over to the offensive, fighting even during the monsoon and, with the aid of mepacrine, in malarial regions, which both sides had avoided earlier in the campaign. In the north Wingate and his Chindits, British, Gurkhas and West Africans, struck across the Irawaddy to support Stilwell, who was fighting his way down the Ledo road, which was designed to re-open communications with China. The road was driven over trackless, wooded ranges by white, yellow, bronze and black labour, directed by American engineers. The Chindits were landed in gliders behind the Japanese lines, and were then supplied from the air. They hacked their way through the jungle, and disrupted the Mandalay–Myitkina railway, while the Chinese attacked from the east.

But the main struggle was on the central front, where Mutaguchi led three crack divisions across the Indian frontier. His aim was to force the British back by cutting Slim's communications, and so stop China's supplies over "the Hump"; then the Japanese would secure the Assam oilfields and march on Delhi. Slim withdrew his troops into defensive "boxes" at Kohima and Imphal. The beleaguered garrisons were supplied from the air, and after savage fighting they were relieved. Slim's troops struck heavily at the invaders, as they recrossed the Chindwin.

In its jungle and mountain-warfare SEAC had learnt to endure tropical rains, malaria, dysentery, insects and snakes. South-western Pacific Command faced many of these difficulties, and had also to adapt itself to life on the numerous atolls it seized, as it edged northward. In the winter fighting of 1943–44 Americans and Australians broke the Japanese strength on the east of the island of New Guinea. In the summer the Dutch joined in clearing the west. On the Allies' right wing the stubborn fanaticism of the enemy was smashed by a series of skilful amphibious operations, covered by growing strength in the air. Advances were made in the Gilberts, the Solomons and New Britain. A heavy naval and air attack on the great harbour of Truk repaid in part the Pearl Harbour "debt". The numerous American aircraft-carriers proved too much for the Japanese navy, which suffered another heavy defeat in the Carolinas. Two Japanese admirals, Yamamato and Kogo, fell in battle and their successor was driven back to Luzon. Guam was recaptured in July; the loss of Saipan in the Marianas led to the fall of Tojo.

THE LIBERATION OF EUROPE

Hitler's case in the summer of 1944 was worse than Hirohito's. Invading forces were marshalled in southern England under Eisenhower's command with Tedder as his deputy. Months of intricate preparations had produced the "Mulberry", an artificial harbour, designed to enable a flow of supplies to be maintained without the need for capturing and clearing a major port. Security precautions left the Germans ignorant of the weight and direction of the attack.

On June 6, 1944, the blow fell. Air-borne troops landed during the previous night, while Ramsey's vast armada was escorting Montgomery's Anglo-American divisions across the Channel. The Western Wall was breached on a 60-mile front between Cherbourg and Caen. The British and Canadians met desperate resistance at Caen, drawing on themselves the main German counter-attack and allowing Bradley's Americans on the right flank to smash through and capture Cherbourg. Patton led his tanks into Brittany, and then, wheeling westward, swept towards the Loire, and liberated Tours, Orleans and Chartres. His astonishing onslaught ended only at Verdun. Neither Runstedt nor Rommel could check the building up of the Allied forces to a million within two months. The French Resistance Movement hampered the march of German reinforcements. While the Allies attacked from the Mediterranean and cleared southern France, the remnants of thirty divisions were sucked into "the Falaise sack", and there smashed. The forward rush outran supplies, and Eisenhower determined on a methodical progress toward the Siegfried Line.

An attempt was made in September to turn the German northern flank, by dropping air-borne troops at Arnhem. The gallant venture failed. There was bitter fighting on the Scheldt estuary to secure the transport of supplies to Antwerp. German morale recovered, and in December Rundstedt thrust towards Liege and pierced the American lines in the Ardennes. He was held by the stubborn "soldiers' battle" fought by the Americans at Bastogne, and Bradley and Montgomery closed the gap. Transport problems were eased when petrol was brought from Liverpool to the front by "Pluto", the under-sea pipeline. Stubborn fighting continued through the winter till March, when the Allies were ready to cross the Rhine.

Bombing of Germany by the Allied air forces had continued relentlessly, crippling munition-works, blocking transport and weakening morale. There were insufficient reserves behind the Rhine defences, and when, after intensive preparation, the Allied armies fought their way across the great river, resistance began to crumble. Six weeks later Germany had collapsed.

The Canadians freed Holland. The British moved north-east to the Baltic, capturing Bremen and Hamburg. Two American armies isolated and overran the shattered Ruhr, seized Brunswick and Magdeburg, and reached the Elbe. Patton's "last great romp in Europe" took him past Frankfort and Nuremberg towards the Czecho-Slovakian frontier. The French captured Stuttgart and crossed the Danube. Mussolini's body was hanged in Milan. New Zealand troops joined hands with Tito's army on the Isonzo. A million Germans surrendered in northern Italy. Everywhere the Allies liberated the Nazis' slave-workers, and multitudes of "displaced persons" began to move through the victorious armies towards their old homes. Emaciated victims from concentration camps showed the world the essential foundations of Hitler's creed.

The headlong advance from the west owed much to Hitler's preoccupation with Russia. But, stubbornly, as the *Wehrmacht* struggled against Stalin's forces, they were beaten in the south, the centre and the north. Two months' ruthless fighting at Budapest led to Hungary's capitulation. Warsaw, Lodz and Cracow fell. Tilsit, Memel and the Masurian Lakes were cleared. Zhukov penetrated into Pomerania and Brandenberg. At Yalta, where the last of the many inter-Allied conferences was held in February, 1945, Churchill, Roosevelt and Stalin re-affirmed their policy of unconditional surrender. By April Silesia had been overrun, Koenigsberg isolated and Vienna freed. When Russian armies encircled and bombarded Berlin, Hitler committed suicide. Nazidom collapsed.

Denmark, Norway, Austria and Czecho-Slovakia were rid of their German masters. The British Navy received the surrender of such surface-ships and U-boats as it had not destroyed on the high and narrow seas. Keitel made the final surrender of the whole *Wehrmacht* to Eisenhower at Rheims. By May 8, 1945, the European war was ended.

THE COLLAPSE OF JAPAN

Japan still carried on the struggle in China, Burma and the Pacific. Russia delayed declaring war on her, but her position in Manchukuo and the north was seriously threatened by the Communist government at Yenan; Mao's general, Chuh-teh, attacked her strong points with increasing success. In the south Chiang Kai-shek passed to the offensive, and pushed down to the coast. Mountbatten decided to continue the Burman campaign through the monsoon. Air superiority helped Slim to push Kimura southward. The Japanese infantryman began to starve. By 1945 the road-link with Chungking had been reforged. Chinese troops trained by Stilwell came down the Salween gorges, and the veteran Wei-Li-Huang co-operated for a brief period with Slim. With naval help the British drove eastward through Arakan to secure the oil-fields. The brilliant capture of the road and rail junction of Meiktila forced Kimura's dogged infantrymen out of Mandalay. Aung San's Burmese guerrillas changed sides, and harassed the Japanese retreat. As the Fourteenth Army poured down the Irrawaddy towards Rangoon, seaborne troops closed in from the south. In May the Japanese evacuated the port, and a seaborne invasion of Malaya was planned. But September found the enemy incapable of further resistance, and 650,000 Japanese surrendered to Mountbatten in Singapore.

The peaceful occupation of the great port was due to the abrupt collapse of Japan's Pacific front. In repeated engagements the American Navy, reinforced by British ships, broke enemy resistance. American air forces bombed Tokio, Osaka, Kobe and the great industrial towns. Though the New Guinea struggle dragged on, the Marines progressed steadily northward from island to island. MacArthur recaptured Manila: Iwojima and Okinawa fell.

Then applied science dealt the final blow. America had produced an atom-bomb, which had explosive force equal to 20,000 tons of T.N.T. This was dropped on Hiroshima, and obliterated four square miles of the city. On August 9 a bigger atom-bomb struck Nagasaki. Compared with these annihilating blows the Russian attack on Manchuria was only a minor setback for Japan. Hirohito commanded the capitulation of his people and divested himself of his " divinity".

The Americans ended their long "island-hopping" Odyssey by steaming peacefully into Tokio Bay. On September 2, 1945, MacArthur received Japan's unconditional surrender on the deck of the American battleship *Missouri*. A week later the formal surrender of about one million Japanese troops was signed at Nanking, and Chiang Kai-shek closed "the China incident".

CHAPTER 83

DIVISION AND FRUSTRATION

THE horrid obliteration of Hiroshima and Nagasaki proclaimed the end of the Second World War and the arrival of the Atomic Age. The power of science and technology to shape human life seemed limitless. Mankind needed to make good the devastation of the last six years and to use recent discoveries for the common benefit. Sanity demanded priority for economic problems. But it is not easy for men and women to be sane, when they have been exhausted physically and spiritually by a long and sombre war, and when power seems the only thing that matters. International co-operation was essential; it was hoped that the United Nations might be organized to carry their victories into the field of peace.

"DEMOCRACY" IN THE NEW WORLD

The Axis had been smashed by powers who claimed to be "democratic"; but there was a sharp contrast in the meaning of the word to the East and the West. Russia and her satellites believed in a one-party system, enforcing rigorous and uncritical loyalty to the ruler, who claimed total power over all his nationals, and exercised it through a small oligarchy. Moscow considered Communism, based on the teaching of Marx, to be the inevitable development of Socialist democracy. America and the British Commonwealth practised parliamentary government, which depended on the interplay of parties and a nation-wide suffrage. This same tradition, deriving from Elizabethan England, held good in France, Poland, Scandinavia, the Low Countries and many of the Balkan states. The bleak contrast between the "democratic" groups began to emerge as soon as the United Nations met in London in 1946. It was accentuated when the delegates crossed the Atlantic to Lake Success.

The rulers of the nations faced a new world, from which the Axis had disappeared. The United States, untouched by enemy action and replete with material wealth, stood out as the greatest power. If

America could plan the future with her European allies, peaceful progress would be assured. But the debates at Lake Success showed that it was impossible to resolve the difference between the two types of "democracy". Another problem was the new spirit in Asia. Hirohito's career fostered a strong spirit of independence in the Asian peoples. They were anxious to "take up the White Man's burden" and shape their destinies unaided.

THE RESURRECTION OF CHINA

Nowhere was this spirit stronger than in China. For the first two years of Japanese aggression there had been a united front against the invaders. Then the old differences reasserted themselves. In spite of the mediation of Stilwell and Marshall, the end of hostilities found Chiang Kai-shek's Kuomintang at bitter enmity with Mao Tse-tung's Communists at Yenan. Three-quarters of the population acknowledged the generalissimo, and he claimed the complete submission of Red China. America helped him lavishly with arms and equipment. But his generals and bureaucrats proved corrupt and inefficient. The Chinese peasantry repudiated them, and Chuh-teh captured American supplies to equip Mao's growing armies. By 1949 the Kuomintang was discredited, and Chiang withdrew to Formosa, held by MacArthur after seventy-six years of Japanese domination. Washington remained loyal to her old ally, and Chiang's nominee held China's seat on the United Nations.

Mao shared his countrymen's ingrained suspicions of Russia; he was a Communist, not a Stalinist, and he adapted Marxist theory to Chinese life. He looked on MacArthur as his chief danger. The great general ruled Japan like the old Shoguns, with the Emperor in the background. He used the disciplined toughness of the Japanese to make good the devastation of war. He improved the health services, crushed the dangerous secret societies in the cities, and weakened the feudal powers of the landowners. From Tokio he controlled the naval and military forces of the Pacific with little interference from Washington.

The Yenan Government aimed at satisfying the peasant's land-hunger and at keeping close contact with the worker. Landowners were tolerated for a time, but the small man was given sufficient land for a decent livelihood. Both in town and country there was frank discussion on the moulding of the New China. Officials were paid adequately but economically. Chinese and foreign traders acknowledged that they practised the new slogan of "no graft, no squeeze". Mao broke with the old Confucian tradition of rigid family organization. Sun Yat-sen's widow held high place in the new government. Women acquired a surprising degree of freedom. Without destroying home life, they worked in factories and spoke in village councils. But, as obstacles grew, earlier tolerance disappeared. Purges re-

INDIA, CHINA, AND

SOUTH-WEST ASIA

placed persuasion. Critics became "counter-revolutionaries". By
1951 full publicity was given to trials and executions; listeners to the
Canton radio could hear the mob in the Memorial Square howling
for the blood of accused prisoners.

For a century China had been the prey of foreign powers. The
new Democratic Front rejected "European Imperlialism" and substituted an imperialism of its own. Mao reasserted suzerainties once
exercised over Korea, Tibet and Indo-China. Guerillas drifted
south to terrorize British settlers in Malaya. France and Holland
were faced with similar Communist attacks in Indo-China and Indonesia. The Dutch created an Indonesian Federation, united by
treaty with Holland. To the Western Powers all the Asiatic fighting
seemed part of the Cold War, which Russia had begun to wage
against her former allies.

INDIA AND PAKISTAN

Communism played no part in the political changes which transformed the Indian sub-continent. Britain had pledged herself to
end her rule, though few administrative or judicial bodies have done
better work than the Indian Civil Service. Maintaining a high level
of personal integrity, it had raised the standard of public health,
encouraged transport and communications, fought famine and
plague, and preserved the peace with impartial efficiency. The antagonism between Hindu and Moslem went far back into history;
frequent communal disturbances still showed its baneful power. The
Sikhs and the fanatical Hindu Mahasaba pursued divergent aims.
But all parties demanded the speedy granting of self-government and
the end of the British *Raj*, which had been supreme for nearly two
centuries. Congress wanted an undivided self-governing India,
which the Moslem League rejected. When Mountbatten succeeded
Wavell as Viceroy, he announced that the British *Raj* would end in a
few months, and that the administration would be handed over to
representative bodies, who would undertake control. To Jinnah and
the Moslems went Sind, the North-west Frontier Province, part of
the Punjab and the western half of Bengal, to form the state of
Pakistan with Karachi as its capital. In the rest of the sub-continent
Pandit Nehru became Prime Minister; he ruled from Delhi, with
Mahatma Gandhi as counsellor in the background.

Nominally the native Rajahs, whose territory covered nearly half
the sub-continent, had the choice of acceding either to Delhi or
Karachi, or of remaining independent. But though Junaghad opted
for Pakistan and Hyderabad for independence, Nehru brought both
into the new Dominion of India. In Kashmir there was a deadlock,
the Moslem population opposing their Hindu ruler's wish to acknowledge Delhi. Sporadic fighting between Pakistan and Indian troops
was followed by an uneasy truce.

In both states well-tried officials were replaced by less experienced men. But the worst results of partition were rioting and massacres in the frontier areas. About four million Moslems fled from India, and six million Sikhs and Hindus from Pakistan. Many thousands perished, and the two governments had the task of giving the refugees homes, food and work.

Nehru and Jinnah showed themselves capable rulers. Both took vigorous action against the small Communist party, though Nehru's championship of Asian independence led him to maintain friendly contacts with Mao. Progress was threatened by the assassination of the Mahatma and the death of Jinnah. Fortunately Liaquat Ali Khan proved his worth at Karachi. The two dominions inherited large standing credits, which Britain repaid in yearly instalments for war indebtedness; these strengthened the finances of the sub-continent.

Unhappily political quarrels, especially about Kashmir, increased the tension between Karachi and Delhi, and led to the erection of trade barriers. India needed wheat, jute, cotton and other raw materials from Pakistan, and should have supplied her neighbour with manufactured goods in return. Famines broke out, and exposed the weak points in Nehru's administration. Some progress was made with public works, and European firms continued to increase the wealth of the two dominions. But too much money was devoted to their armed forces, and economic progress slackened.

Nehru's eastern neighbours suffered from Communist aggression. Burma had been granted her freedom, and chose to leave the Commonwealth. Her government suffered from rioting and rebellion, but began to achieve stability by 1950. Siam remained friendly; but farther east Chinese support kept the Communist danger alive, while to the north Tibet was under the shadow of Mao's troops.

PROBLEMS OF THE NEAR AND MIDDLE EAST

In Persia the small pro-Communist *Tudeh* party exercised little influence, though poverty weighed heavily on peasants and artisans. The young Shah favoured a policy of land-reform, but his progressive premier was assassinated. Much of Persia's revenue came from the British enterprise which controlled the great oil-fields and the Abadan refinery. Increased demand for heavy fuel-oil and paraffin had caused a world shortage of refining capacity, and the Persians claimed a larger share of profits from the industry. Independent American companies offered technical help, and Russia followed their example. When Moussadeq became premier he found it easy to direct nationalist aspirations against the Anglo-Iranian Oil Company. He repudiated his country's agreement with British capitalists, and persuaded the *Majlis* to nationalize the industry. The company was attacked, and work at the refinery came to a standstill. Attlee's domestic policy made it difficult for

I I

(H. W.)

him to disavow the principle of nationalization; but he obtained a verdict favourable to British interests from the International Court at the Hague. Helped by Truman's intervention he opened negotiations with Moussadeq.

Turkey remained a steadying influence in the changing world of Asia. She accepted the transfer of power from the People's to the Democratic party by a general election in the best tradition of parliamentary government. She welcomed United States aid in equipping her excellent fighting men and building up her industries. As she no longer had a Caliph, she could keep clear of Moslem quarrels, whether with Hindus or Jews.

Palestine presented an intractable problem. The need for a National Home for the Jews had been emphasized by Hitler's massacres and the flight of thousands from Europe. Industrious Jewish immigrants were settled as farmers and artisans. Homes for Jews inevitably meant the displacement of some local Moslems. The Mandatory Power, Britain, kept the peace between the rival factions, and protected the Holy Places of the Jewish, Moslem and Christian faiths. The Arab League was formed in 1945, and, when Britain laid down her mandate three years later, hostilities broke out between the League and Israel. Farouk of Egypt and Abdulla of Transjordan joined with Syria, Lebanon, Iraq, Saudi Arabia and the Yemen against the new state. But Israel held the Moslems at bay, and won an armistice. The League lost some of its cohesion, and Abdulla annexed Arab Palestine.

Checked to the north-east, Farouk might still extend his influence to south and west. The slogan of "Unity of the Nile Valley" revived Egyptian claims to rule the Sudan. Good progress had been made in the education and technical training of the Mahdi's old subjects. There was little enthusiasm for reunion with Egypt. Westward the late Italian colony of Libya attracted the Cairo Government; but a free election gave control to the native Emir, Idris. Farouk felt that his country's sovereignty was incomplete while British troops remained in Cairo. Westminster was slow in moving them out of the citadel, and ruffled national aspirations. Protracted negotiations continued on the protection of the Suez Canal by British forces.

AFRICANS AND THE COLOUR BAR

The spirit of native independence spread in Africa. In the north France kept her Empire, though Tunisia had its Bey and Morocco its Sultan. After their Spanish victories the Moors resented subjection to European rule. France found herself opposed by the Sultan and his *Ulemas*. In the British colonies Westminster proceeded steadily with its policy of training the native populations for self-government. It was a most difficult matter to reconcile the claims and the needs of European settlers not only with African and Arab labourers, but also with Asiatic immigrants. These varying interests complicated the question of the union of Kenya, Nyassaland and Uganda and their relations with the two Rhodesias. In Nigeria considerable progress was made with the training of many districts in managing their local affairs. Education sharpened the political appetites of the coloured populations, before they had reached European standards in maintaining the public services. A form of self-government was given to the Gold Coast; the elections of 1951 placed power in the hands of the one-time prisoner, Kwame Nkrumah.

These egalitarian ideas were bitterly resented in South Africa, where Jan Smuts lost office. The Afrikaans premier, Malan, proceeded with his policy of *apartheid*, designed to secure supremacy for men of European descent. In matter of residence, education and voting the various races were to be segregated. Though the coloured labourer and the Indian trader were needed economically, they were kept on a lower plane than "white folk". The new franchise laws raised the constitutional question of the powers of the South African Parliament under the Statute of Westminster. Malan objected that Britain had no constitutional right to plan Dominion status for colonies without the consent of other Dominions. He also claimed that the South African Union should annex the native reserves, where Swazis, Bechuanas and Bantus lived under the control of the Colonial Office. The Four Freedoms, which Franklin Roosevelt had proclaimed as the objective for his country and her allies, came into sharp conflict with practical politics, and racial feelings were embittered.

The colour bar was also resented by the descendants of the Africans who had been taken as slaves to the West Indies and the Southern States of the American Union. In Jamaica the native vote kept Bustamente in power. In other Caribbean Islands there were sporadic rioting and unrest. Truman's efforts to extend educational and voting privileges to "coloured folk" were frustrated by the traditional convictions of the "Deep South". Only in hospitals and the Air Force were their claims considered favourably. In Latin America the men and women of Indian blood remained generally apathetic to politics. But elsewhere it was clear that rule by the white races was no longer accepted as an axiom.

WORK OF THE UNITED NATIONS

The diplomats at Geneva had dealt mainly with European problems. The United Nations at Lake Success were faced with the new spirit in Asia and Africa, as well as the restoration of Europe. The Washington Government had stood apart from the League; it was the most prominent power in the United Nations from the start. The Norwegian, Trygve Lie, became the first Secretary of the new body.

Most decisions were made in the small Security Council, on which each of the Great Powers served, with the right of veto. As deadlocks became more frequent, the General Assembly was employed to register a solution of the problems involved. The veto was designed to prevent the secession of powerful states, which had nullified policies adopted by the majority at Geneva.

Russia had never played a big part at the League's meetings. She was one of the Big Five at Lake Success from the start. Her sufferings had been far greater than her allies', and her political outlook was very different. Her ingrained suspicion of the West led her to reject the economic help offered by America. She showed how progress towards union and peace could be blocked by her veto. Her aggressive delegates, Molotov, Vishinsky and Gromyko, accused the United States and the British Commonwealth of imperialism, though they had demobilized their forces, while Stalin kept a huge standing army in being. Russia claimed to be the true representatives of "democracy" against states which denied full freedom to the "coloured" inhabitants of their territories. But the bulk of the United Nations followed American leadership against Russia and her Communist neighbours.

In non-political matters some progress was made by international co-operation in food supplies and agricultural science, where the pooling of knowledge helped many nations. When UNESCO was set up in Paris with the object of diffusing education, science and culture, the Kremlin refused membership; Czecho-Slovakia and Hungary joined, but their participation in UNESCO activities dwindled. What was welcome to the West was anathema to Russia and her satellites, especially when the state began to control scientific inquiry. It was natural for Stalin to stand aloof from the World Health Organization at Geneva, which concentrated its chief efforts against malaria and tuberculosis. It helped to fight cholera in Egypt, distributed urgently needed drugs and other supplies by air, and aided many backward countries.

THE STALINIST STATE

Old Russia had not disappeared with the Romanovs. The Soviets inherited the Tsars' land-hunger, and they copied their forerunners by making the secret police the mainstay of their internal rule. For a period after the war there was an easing of controls, and the death penalty was abolished; but in 1947 discipline was tightened, and concentration camps spread. Undesirable citizens were herded into the silence of Siberia. Members of the secret police infiltrated into all organizations, and freedom of speech withered. Powers of arrest and imprisonment without trial multiplied. But public trials were still held; police methods of examining defendants out of court produced sensational confessions, which seemed inexplicable to the western world. The example was copied by the Communist rulers of frontier countries.

The police secured unhesitating loyalty to Stalin. His cult was encourged by every possible device. His control spread over literature, art, music and science. One writer put Socrates by Stalin's side on the summit of human intelligence; the majority hailed the Comrade-Leader as the greatest man of all time. A poet wrote of the morning stars obeying his will.

In Russia the Orthodox Church was traditionally subservient to the civil power. Open persecution had ceased, and during the closing stages of the war it enjoyed a brief spell of the Kremlin's favour. Then metropolitans and archbishops relapsed again to the level of state functionaries, useful for strengthening the loyalty to the state of the religious-minded. Poland's long record of devotion to the Vatican created some difficulty; but the new Communist rulers of Warsaw, like those at Prague, worked steadily to weaken the tie. Many Poles preserved their freedom of worship by settling in the western democracies. In Bulgaria there was persecution of Protestants as well as Roman Catholics. In Hungary Cardinal Mindzenty disappeared after a sensational treason-trial, and a little later the same fate befell the Archbishop who succeeded him. Behind the Iron Curtain the state sequestrated endowments, imprisoned religious dignitaries, extracted confessions of treason in law courts, and strangled religious development by controlling the schools and the youth movements. The cult of Stalin could brook no rival loyalty.

RUSSIA'S FOREIGN POLICY

Stalin had seen a great deal of war since 1914, and he felt it vital not only to maintain an overwhelming army and air force and to build up his navy, but also to be cushioned on every frontier by friendly or subservient states. He held that the best criterion of friendship was a common political creed. It would have been wiser perhaps to use the economic resources of America to build up his sorely devastated country; but he was suspicious of his subjects being infected with capitalist heresies from their would-be benefactor.

In Asia, where Japan's collapse had strengthened his long eastern frontier, his foreign policy was marked by wise caution. He continued to recognize Chiang's Government after Tokio's surrender. But naturally he welcomed Mao's establishment at Pekin, and displayed a sympathetic consideration of China's needs, which was not shown by the western powers. He was rewarded by Mao's growing confidence, emphasized by the visit of the new ruler to Moscow to negotiate a friendly treaty. Farther west neither India, Pakistan, Persia, nor Turkey was acceptable politically. Stalin confined himself to the formation of Communist cells and the encouragement of national prejudices against the intrusive capitalism of the West.

In the Balkans the war had made the Slav predominant over the German. The Kremlin hoped to spread Communism to the Mediterranean, following Russia's traditional quest of a warm-water port. Great success followed the policy of helping forceful Communist minorities, after a brief alliance with the "historic parties", to assume control of police and army, and then establish themselves as the recognized government. Without fighting himself, Stalin secured one-party rule in Bulgaria, Albania, Hungary, Roumania, where King Michael lost his throne, and Czecho-Slovakia, where Benes's overthrow roused Western Europe to fear a Third World War.

His failures were in Yugo-Slavia and Greece. At Belgrade Tito wiped out the Chetniks, freed other subjects from Serbian domination, and established a Communist economy. But he rejected full control by Moscow, and accepted western help for his civil and military needs, using it to develop a vigorous programme of economic reconstruction. In Greece the Communists attacked the restored King Paul as a Fascist reactionary; but they had the bulk of the nation against them. The Liberals and their political allies were supported by British and American assistance in rebuilding the national army. The rebels were driven to the northern mountains and, despite help from Albania and Bulgaria, were gradually worn down. Greece returned to parliamentary democracy under a constitutional king. As with Spain, her chief troubles came from poverty and the need of foreign capital for development. Fortunately Truman's policy helped her to recover her economic balance.

On his north-western frontier Stalin had established friendly relations with Finland, after reabsorbing Esthonia, Latvia and Lithuania. Farther south he had deprived Poland of her lands in the Ukraine. But he had compensated her with the industrial area of Silesia, and, with Rokossovsky placed in control of her army, he could rely on her new government to serve as a protecting bastion, thrust far into the shrunken countryside of East Germany. This advance to the Oder may have gratified Polish ambitions, but it did not reconcile the opponents of Communism, many of whom settled in Britain or found a new citizenship across the Atlantic.

THE DIVISION OF GERMANY

Stalin strengthened his western safety-belt by organizing a Communist administration in Eastern Germany, though its inhabitants must have resented their loss of what had so long been Prussian territory. Western Germany was controlled by America, Britain and France. In both parts the policy of "denazification" was enforced, though with different degrees of severity. An international court was set up at Nuremberg under Lord Oaksey, to try leading war-criminals. Himmler had committed suicide earlier, and, when the case went against him, Goering followed his example. But Schacht, Ribbentrop, and other generals and politicians were duly sentenced and punished. Nuremberg was followed by smaller courts who tried lesser men for many years.

Except on the punishment of war-crimes, the occupying powers were sharply divided. All four were established in Berlin, which lay inside the Russian zone. Financial trouble soon arose from the low value of the East Berlin currency, compared with that of the three allies in the west of the city. Moscow controlled the roads, railways and canals round the Prussian capital, and she tried to squeeze the westerners out by an economic blockade. This was met by the Berlin air-lift; British and American planes contrived to supply their dependent Germans with food and necessities. In spite of flying casualties the blockade was broken, and Stalin's prestige suffered, even though he employed a heavily-armed police force to support the puppet premier he installed. His German subjects had lost much of their territory to the despised Poles and had gained nothing except a standard of living lower than their western compatriots. Their one-party rule was in sharp contrast with the parliamentary democracy which the three allies encouraged under Adenauer. Freely elected delegates met at Bonn, and the Socialists under Schumacher criticized Adenauer forcibly, even though he persuaded the allies to transfer more and more power to Germans. Nazism had been checked effectually for a time, but it began to regain some power in Saxony.

Austria suffered from the inability of the victorious powers to proceed from armistice to peace. Six years after the end of hostilities she was still occupied by the Armed Forces of four nations. In spite of this she enjoyed a limited economic recovery. Vienna escaped the squalid and vicious quarrels which distracted Berlin. But the future of the country was not easy to foresee.

PROSPERITY OF THE UNITED STATES

After the breathless demobilization of the bulk of her forces, Washington feared a business depression and inflationary troubles. But she possessed large corporation reserves and family savings, which soon filled the gaps made by war in machinery, consumer goods, railways, houses and supplies. The threat of inflation was more serious. But the roots of American prosperity were deep in the ground. Confidence was quickly re-established. In spite of Republican hopes Truman's personal hold on the electorate was strong enough to secure his re-election to the Presidency in 1948. Losses due to war and disease were made good. Population increased in the industrial centres, and their manufactures enabled fewer farms to keep more acres under cultivation and to produce more food. By 1950 mechanization had reduced the horse and mule population to a quarter of what it had been in 1915. Industrious and well-paid labour, working under skilled direction, made American manufacturing pre-eminence more marked than ever. More articles could be purchased from the proceeds of fewer hours of work than ten years ago. More individuals shared the abundance of goods than ever before.

Increased prosperity gave the workers not only better wages under the "escalator system", but also hospital benefits and holidays with pay, in which they had lagged behind Britain. An attempt to establish a universal health service failed to win the support of the medical profession. The Federal Government administered Old Age and Survivors' pensions without strangling individual enterprise. These benefits, growing steadily till 1970, could be enjoyed by the citizen both from the state and from private assurance companies.

"The American way of life" had produced thirty million family cars to carry the worker to his factory, while his women had refrigerators and many other domestic fitments to ease household work, and countless cinemas to amuse their leisure. Now fifteen million television sets bring pictures to the home, familiarize citizens with political personalities, and grip the attention of the future citizen from his (or her) earliest years. American trade unions, unlike the British, aim at economic rather than political power. "Labour Barons", such as Lewis of the miners, and Reuther of the automobile and associated workers, influence industrial policy without assuming political responsibility. They resented the Taft–Hartley Act, which shackled their energies, but failed to repeal it, or to drive its author, the Republican, Robert Taft, from the Senate.

A dark shadow was thrown across this scene of abounding prosperity by disclosures that legitimate business had been invaded by hordes of racketeers and gamblers. Communism might have been expected to profit from these repulsive scandals; but it had played no part in the nation's progress, and it alienated the majority by its Fifth Column activities. Atomic secrets were betrayed to Moscow. Hiss and other leaders were condemned for planning the violent overthrow of the Government; arrests on similar charges took place a few months later. Washington's foreign policy based itself on opposition to Communism; in this Republicans joined hands with Democrats; but the two parties diverged gradually on the choice of Asia or Europe as the main field of American effort.

In opposing Stalin's encroachments Truman was supported by Mexico and South America, which shared the rising prosperity of the western hemisphere. Latin America had nearly rid herself of the political instability which had checked her economic progress. Population increased in Rio, Buenos Aires and the other large towns; but over vast spaces the primitive way of life prevailed. Urban existence took on the forms created and embellished in the United States. Some attempt was made to construct a balanced economy, especially by Peron, who ruled the Argentine with the support of the Army and the organized workers. He shared his nation's traditional suspicion of the "Yankee dollar", but he used it to break the old dependence on British capital, and widened the breach by exacting a high price for his exported meat from the bulk-buyers of Whitehall.

Uruguay remained friendly to Britain, while joining Chile and Peru in forming economic ties with Peron; in foreign affairs the three republics followed the lead of Washington and Westminster, and regarded Moscow as the enemy. In Brazil Vargas, who had introduced far-reaching labour legislation during his fifteen years of power, was driven from his dictatorship in 1945. Five years later he was elected President constitutionally, and he continued to protect workers' rights, even at the cost of inflation. Considerable manufacturing development took place in Santos, Rio and other towns, and immigrants helped to push the population to fifty-two millions. If she can check the wasteful use of her vast natural resources, a great future lies before Brazil, the largest of the Latin states both in acreage and population.

THE BRITISH COMMONWEALTH OF NATIONS

At the general election of 1945 Churchill suffered the fate of many other victorious war-leaders and fell from power; but he remained the most popular figure in Western Europe and North America, where he was overwhelmed with personal honours. The Socialists under Attlee took office with a large majority in the Commons. Britain's "finest hour" had left her materially weaker; but Attlee decided to implement the Welfare State, which had begun with the National Government's Education Act. Full employment was the overriding consideration. Regulations and increased taxation were used to redistribute the national income in favour of the lower paid. Holidays with pay were increased. Attlee applied the principles of nationalization to public health, coal, gas, electricity, transport and the steel industry. The country suffered from inflation, as the pound lost its value; higher nominal wages were paid for shorter hours of work, and unofficial strikes lessened production and increased costs. Rising prices slowed up the housing programme, and kept meat on the ration. To ensure raw materials and food, the Chancellor, Cripps, organized a vigorous export drive, which depleted the home market. Household articles became scarcer, and too much paper money chased too few goods to too high price-levels.

Westminster like Washington was disturbed by the betrayal of atomic secrets to the Kremlin, but Fifth Columnists were still treated as citizens. Though the national effort was continually lessened by subversive action, the Socialists were content to keep the whip hand over the Communists politically. They claimed that the moral leadership of the world lay not with the Kremlin, but with the Welfare State established in Britain. The nation itself was sharply divided on the problem of nationalization. The 1950 election gave a precarious majority to the Socialists, who had abolished the representation of the Universities. But Attlee's parliamentary skill kept his Government in office, in spite of occasional minor defeats in the Commons. There was a pause in nationalization plans, as attention was diverted to financial and defence problems.

The Socialist Governments of Australia and New Zealand both lost power in 1949. At Canberra Menzies took office with a coalition of the Liberal and Country parties, and Holland's National party governed New Zealand after fourteen years of Socialist rule. Both Dominions continued to help the Mother Country with raw materials, and both were hampered by Communist violence in fomenting industrial troubles. Strikes and sabotage impelled Menzies to propose the outlawry of those who gave their allegiance to Moscow. The bill was contested in the courts. When Menzies appealed again to the electorate, he won control of the Senate as well as the Lower House. The electors of Australasia refused to admit that liberty gave an aggressive minority the right to hold up the economic life of their countries.

Canada did not encounter the troubles of her Australian cousins. She continued to show the same activity in the United Nations and the British Commonwealth as she had displayed in war. In 1948 Newfoundland voted for union with the Federation, which it entered as its twelfth province. In the same year Mackenzie King laid down his long premiership, and was succeeded by St. Laurent; the Liberal party retained control of the Government. Canadian capital helped the Caribbean colonies to develop their fruit trade. Her ministers played an important part in negotiating the necessary economic adjustments between the dollar and sterling areas. Though manufacture and trade bound her to her great southern neighbour, she maintained her allegiance to her King, as she grew in population and material resources.

South Africa ranged herself with the Australasian Dominions against Communism. Malan improved his parliamentary position by the election of members from the former German colony of South-west Africa. But his *apartheid* policy involved him in differences with Delhi and Karachi. Though Nehru made India a Republic, she remained within the Commonwealth. Ceylon and Pakistan retained their allegiance to the Crown. Eire proclaimed herself an independent Republic, and broke her last link with the Commonwealth. But Britain refused to implement the legal consequences of this unilateral action, and continued to treat her as a part of the family group.

In spite of financial losses, economic lapses and family quarrels between some of its members, the British Commonwealth remained a world power of immense possibilities. Its structure was complex and illogical but flexible. It was capable of united action, and there was hope that disputes between its members could be settled by reasonable discussion. Britain continued to spend money on developing backward colonies, though some of her plans went astray financially; she also pursued the political aim of extending self-government so that the colonies could reach Dominion status eventually. Spread widely over both hemispheres, the Commonwealth had great opportunities of influencing other countries. Perhaps this influence was most powerful in the spheres of education and social welfare.

THE WESTERN DEMOCRACIES

When war ended, de Gaulle was the strongest man in France. His old chief, Pétain, was tried and imprisoned, and France had to devise a new constitution for her Fourth Republic. De Gaulle wanted greater power for the executive and less party intrigue. The Resistance had bound him to the Communists; the numerous middle parties and the Socialists combined successfully against him, and he withdrew from political life for a time. A constitution like that of the Third Republic was established, and France was governed by a series of short-lived Cabinets, with Schumann, Bidault and Queuille as the leading figures. The Communists under Thorez strengthened their allegiance to Stalin, and strikes delayed recovery. But her natural resources and her industry carried France through, though she was slow to mechanize her agriculture. Her man-power was hardly strong enough to protect all her African and Asian territories.

Italy recovered gradually under the sagacious rule of the Vatican-trained de Gasperi. He survived frequent strikes, weakened the Communists and the extreme Socialists, and improved the economic position. Though he failed to recover Libya, he worked for closer relations with France and Britain, and he tried to establish better feelings with Yugo-Slavia, in spite of the Trieste quarrel. When Eisenhower returned to Europe as supreme commander, de Gasperi's forces were placed at his disposal.

All the peoples of Western Europe hoped to restore their peaceful, Christian way of life after 1945. That they could meet in healthy rivalry was proved by the international gatherings in England to see the Olympic Games of 1950. Men and women felt that they could rejoice in happier things, as the damage of war was gradually made good. Norway and Denmark, Holland, Belgium and Luxemburg renewed their parliamentary systems under constitutional monarchies. Each made good the damage of war vigorously. Holland had the hardest task in reclaiming her submerged lands from the sea. Belgium, comparatively unscathed by hostilities, achieved great economic success. She rejected Leopold as king, and kept his brother, Charles, as regent for Prince Baudouin.

Spain and Portugal were still totalitarian, but their dislike of Stalin made them friendly to the western democracies. Salazar con-

THE LATEST AGE

tinued his efficient rule at Lisbon, and increased Portuguese resources. Franco stood as a bulwark of Roman Catholicism, relying on a strong army. As time went on, Washington gave him financial aid, and Westminister acquiesced reluctantly in his rule.

THE COLD WAR

British Socialists had claimed that the Kremlin would co-operate with them. But, confronted by Stalin's encroachments, their Foreign Minister, Bevin, was driven to pursue much the same policy as that advocated by the Conservative Eden. The first result of close co-operation with Washington was the breaking of the Berlin blockade. For Czecho-Slovakia nothing could be done, except to give asylum to Benes's followers. Practical help was given to Greece, and to Tito, when he rejected Stalinist domination. What the Kremlin feared most was America's supply of atomic bombs and the threat of the hydrogen bomb with its wider area of devastation. Truman felt that he must give economic help to Western Europe; this was organized by his Secretary of State, Marshall, who had given great service against Hirohito and Hitler. Marshall Aid invigorated the economic life of the democracies; it also gradually laid foundations upon which to build armed forces to withstand Stalin's hordes.

The Christian civilization of the West felt that its humane and tolerant way of life was threatened by Stalin, as it had been by Hitler. Peaceful citizens realized that they must support their governments, and take up the military burden again, if life was to be worth living. They had seen one European country after another drawn behind the Iron Curtain. Their nationals were attacked by terrorists in Malaya and Indo-China. Tibet and Persia were threatened. Stalin's troops moved through Roumania, Hungary and Bulgaria to line up on the Turkish frontier. To meet the danger closer union was established between the smaller powers. Denmark and Norway joined with the Benelux states, Belgium, the Netherlands and Luxemburg. France proposed an overall economic union, which Britain did not feel able to join. The Atlantic Pact bound all seven powers and Italy together with the United States, within the framework of the United Nations. The parliamentary machines moved cumbrously, but equipment and recruiting went on. With the return of Eisenhower to Europe as supreme commander the West felt some degree of confidence, as it shouldered the financial burden of rearmament.

WAR IN KOREA

It was doubtful how far China played a deliberate part in Stalin's Cold War. She did not respond to Bevin's offer of recognition. MacArthur looked on her as Russia's cat's-paw. As time went on, Mao seemed to discard his earlier toleration, to control his subjects with fiercer brutality, and to threaten all western interests in Asia.

Pekin resented the policy of the South Korean government, which adopted the American way of life and chose a parliament by free election. She supported the North Korean Communists, when they crossed the 38th parallel. In the spring of 1950 the Northerners captured Seoul and pushed forward towards the south coast. The United Nations denounced this act of aggression, and MacArthur took command of their forces. The great bulk of the troops was American; the Americans were supported by contingents from the British Commonwealth, France, Belgium, Ethiopia, Turkey, Greece and a dozen other states. MacArthur held the invaders, and then drove them across the parallel. China intervened, sending "volunteer" forces into action. Though the United Nations had naval and air superiority, the struggle swayed backward and forward. MacArthur wished to bomb supply bases and to invade the mainland with Chiang's troops from Formosa. This strategy was rejected, and Truman relieved the general of his command. His successor, Ridgway, once more pushed his troops north of the parallel. The Korean peninsula had been terribly devastated, and had lost a considerable part of its population. Ridgway decided that an attempt should be made to negotiate a cease-fire.

SCIENTIFIC ADVANCE AND FRUSTRATED IDEALS

With its radio-active dust and its scorching fires the hydrogen bomb would be thirty times more devastating than the atom bomb had proved itself. Without these formidable missiles air superiority effected little in the Korean war, though Delta-winged fighters had a speed of 700 m.p.h. The developments of light alloys gave stronger machines without increasing weight. Civil aviation improved, and politicians and business executives could cover the globe rapidly. Rocket propulsion developed, and the problem of getting away from the earth's gravitational pull became a practical proposition. New theories were expounded on the solar system. Radio telescopes and new optical telescopes were built to aid investigation. Increasing study of electronics stimulated the improvement of radar devices.

Ordinary folk, especially women, were more interested in the production of artificial yarns, new dyes and healing drugs. Nylons not only revolutionized dress, and gave a fresh yard-stick to social life, but also improved and cheapened many industrial materials. Developments in elastic nylons may carry this revolution even further. There were renewed hopes of extirpating malaria, which infects a quarter of mankind. Though penicillin did not prove a universal panacea, the list of antibiotic drugs grew rapidly, largely through the brilliant efforts of Fleming and his fellow-workers, who developed Florieg's teaching. Aureomycin, chloromycetin and terramycin have been termed all-purpose antibiotics, because of the many disease-producing micro-organisms they can combat. Advances in surgery foreshadow victory over certain types of valvular disease of the heart. The discovery and commercial production of active hormones from the adrenal and pituitary glands promise relief from symptoms in rheumatism, asthma and many other disorders. The electron microscope has aided biology greatly. The general health of the world seems to have improved, giving a longer expectation of life.

Longer lives and the fecundity of the Asian peoples expand the population beyond the nourishment available. Shortage of supplies enriches the food-producing countries; agricultural improvements become more and more necessary. Perhaps the solution of the problem lies in improved fertilizers, selective weed-killers and a wiser conservation of the land. Atomic fission' has not yet improved material supplies. Plastics have proved invaluable, especially in mitigating the timber and metal shortage. If it chooses, the human brain can improve living conditions immeasurably.

Until the last few years money has served as a useful standard of value. War damage, political experiments and America's gold hoarding have almost destroyed its old use. Pound, franc, lira and other currencies have been devalued. Prices have risen, as the world-wide and catastrophic increase in the cost of raw materials has checked the flow of trade. By creating a needless time-lag between demand and supply planning has slowed down production. Power must be centralized in a planned economy, which acts through the multiplication of regulations that are only enforceable through decoys and informers. Economic records do not substantiate the claim that nationalized industries are capable of efficient and economic working.

International indebtedness has been replaced by Lend-Lease and Marshall Aid. This has been rejected by Russia and China as a capitalist device for destroying Communist economy, and as a clear proof of America's ever-growing financial despotism in both hemispheres. Britain adopted a cheap money policy; the Bank of England was nationalized, and restrictions were imposed on bank credits. Something beneficial may be accomplished by international organizations, if they can make suitable grants to undeveloped countries, and can remove obstacles that check the freedom of trade.

Peace on earth is promised to men of goodwill. The last six years have not seen that goodwill spread through the world. The lesson of the two great wars has not been learnt sufficiently for mankind to have security against a third. The advance of the Four Freedoms has been disappointing. Freedom from want has only been secured in small parts of the globe. Freedom from fear is barely as widespread as it was during hostilities. Freedom of belief and of speech is denied by the very nature of the police state. The material means for establishing the Freedoms grow more and more plentiful. Humanity can only enjoy them when goodwill comes to a divided world.

EPILOGUE

SUCH, in outline, is the story of man's development from the distant past, when he made tools for himself, learnt the use of speech, and began to work with his fellows. We have seen how prosperous communities arose round the shores of the Mediterranean, and in the valleys of the Yellow River, the Indus, the Euphrates and the Nile; how they built cities, fashioned beautiful objects, traded and grew prosperous; how they were ruled by kings and priests; and how the heavy and disagreeable work was done by slaves. Beyond these rich countries, bands of nomad hunters and herdsmen roamed over the wide spaces of Arabia and the great Northern Flatland. From time to time, through long centuries, warfare or severe changes of climate drove these free and fierce tribes into the civilized lands, to break their peace and waste their wealth. Great kingdoms were destroyed so utterly that they passed from human memory; only within the last century have science and the archaeologist's spade brought to light their shattered records. In other lands the invaders were merged with the mass of conquered men and women, and learned to carry on their art, religion and way of life.

The three civilizations which showed the greatest tenacity were the Egyptian, the Sumerian and the Chinese; the two latter absorbed their nomad enemies. On the Iranian tableland and in the valley of the Indus, the invaders gradually built up strong states: it is hard to determine their actual debt to the older cities they destroyed. From early days, Syria linked the civilizations of the Euphrates and the Nile, and handed on their culture to the Hebrew tribes, who settled within her borders and became the ancestors of the Jews.

The great sixth century B.C. saw an immense stirring of religious and moral ideas through Greece, Judaea, Persia, India and China. The old gross nature-worships, which had held the loyalty of priests and people for centuries, lost their grip. New religions began which are the faiths of millions to-day. In the cities and isles of Greece, men learnt to regard reason as the guide of belief and conduct. When Alexander of Macedon carried the Greek standard to victory over Persia and the old kingdoms of the Nile, Euphrates and Indus valleys, the idea of the brotherhood of man cast a wavering shadow over the western world. Men were ready for the Roman Peace.

Greeks and Romans preserved their civilizations for shorter periods than their eastern forerunners. The prosperity of their cities and their countryside rested on the shoulders of their slaves, "living tools" who could be bartered as easily as wood or iron. In spite of slavery, wars and plagues, the peoples of the civilized parts of the world grew closer to each other. Caravans carried the goods of east and west over the land trade-routes, and seamen linked all parts of the Mediterranean together and brought the wares of China to Malayan, Indian and Roman ports. The missionary was as active as the merchant; while Christianity overflowed the Roman frontiers, Buddhism spread north and east, reached the followers of Confucius and Lao Tse, and disputed with Jainism and Brahmanism in India. In the fourth century the four great empires of Rome, Persia, India and China were bound together by ties of trade. Though war threatened from time to time, the life of the citizen seemed secured as the type to which the rest of the eastern hemisphere would gradually conform.

From the beginning of the fifth century, invaders began to break down the old slave-based civilizations. In Europe, the wanderings of German-speaking tribes first shattered and then slowly transformed the Roman Empire; in the middle of the century the fighting nomads of Central Asia threatened ruin over a wider area, and made the name of Hun the symbol of destruction. In the seventh century, Arabia boiled over once more; the fighting men from her deserts carried against the weakened cities of the old civilizations a new religious creed, the last that was destined to win the hearts of millions. Islam threatened, in turn, Zoroastrianism, Christianity, Buddhism, Hinduism and Jainism. In the Far East China preserved her agelong way of life, but on the old civilizations of Rome, Persia and India the Dark Ages descended.

The cities got the better of the wandering tribes in the end. The Moslem forgot his desert origins, and built his mosques in the cities of Spain, North Africa, Syria, Persia and North India. To guard Christendom from his attacks the German chieftains made the Holy Roman Empire, and the Byzantines preserved Constantinople. Gradually the gloom of the Dark Ages lightened. The life of the citizen took on new forms. Slavery persisted; but in western and central Europe it became less oppressive. Religion remained the vital test of men's loyalties; in a world of force, its claims became harsh and intolerant. The champions of the great faiths fought against one another with a ferocity which was exceeded only when their many sects fought against each other. The revival of commerce did something to break down religious barriers; great buildings and rich courts recalled the material glories of vanished empires. But the spirit of reason, which had been fostered in the old Greek cities, seemed dead, and the sciences, which it had created, survived only among a few inquiring Moslem minds.

The last two attacks which the nomad launched on the citizen were the fiercest and most dangerous of all in the long duel between the two ways of life. Early in the thirteenth century, Chenghiz Khan led his devil-worshipping horsemen with superb generalship against China, India and the rival powers of Islam and Christendom. So huge were his conquests that for a moment he seemed destined to bring almost the whole eastern hemisphere together. Though his dominions were divided later between his descendants, Europeans could travel across the breadth of Asia to the court of his grandson, Kublai Khan. Christendom was distracted by the feuds of emperor and pope, kings and nobles, and the Caliph, the titular head of

Islam, fell an easy prey to the Mongols. Then Christendom grew stronger, and the bulk of the raiders from Central Asia adopted the Islamic faith. When Timur launched the last great desert foray, about the beginning of the fifteenth century, his Tartar cavalry made his name as dreadful as Chenghiz's had been. But the nations of Europe were beginning to find themselves, and a new spirit was growing amid a welter of war and religious disputes. The world was not destined to be ruled by the lords of Karakorum and Samarkand.

In the middle of the fifteenth century, the Turk carried forward the threat of the Mongol and the Tartar. He won Constantinople for Islam, but his victory strengthened the Renaissance or new birth of the European spirit, and sent Christian sailors across the ocean on voyages of discovery. Columbus and Vasco da Gama were apostles both of religion and commerce. With them, the balance of trade began to swing from the Mediterranean to the Atlantic; the seaman replaced the soldier as the builder of empires; the world's unknown lands were linked with the fortunes of Europe. Of the three civilizations which had grown up in America, the Mayan had perished during the Dark Ages; the Aztec and the Inca survived, only to collapse before the attack of Catholic Spain. In the duel between Christendom and Islam, the New World more than redressed the balance of the Old. While China and Japan preserved their isolation and the Moslems tightened their grip on India, the busy genius of Europe brought North and South America under her sway, settled her traders on the Indian coast, and went on to discover Australasia.

The reawakening of the scientific spirit and the growth of the capitalist system widened the gap between the two great fighting religions still further. In the empires of the Ancient World both had played a minor part. From the end of the seventeenth century, they exerted an increasing influence in Europe. They brought material prosperity to large classes, and turned men's minds away from the quarrels of royal families and the bitter feuds between the Catholic, Orthodox and Protestant divisions of Christendom. They strengthened England and France greatly; while Spain grew feebler, in spite of her control of the precious metals of America, the two great nations of Western Europe fought out their traditional quarrel of the Middle Ages on a vaster stage. England had long been free from the shackles of serfdom, and she had a vigorous and ambitious middle class, which gave her victory over a France hampered by class privilege and aristocratic inefficiency. She drove French rule from North America, whose savage inhabitants were no match for the white man's gunpowder, and from India, where the Mogul power had decayed. The loss of the American Colonies shattered the first British Empire, but it left the western hemisphere open to the ideas and the enterprise of men and women of the same stock as those whose energies maintained the Mother Country in the position of the most prosperous state in Europe.

When the age of revolution followed the age of reason, British wealth and policy proved too strong for the genius of Napoleon. But enthusiasm for Liberty, Fraternity and Equality was not extinguished, though the monarchs of Europe regained their dominions. Science moved forward with ever-increasing momentum. Manufacture, commerce and war alike demanded more and better-paid workers, to increase prosperity, or to destroy it. Education ceased to be the luxury of the nobleman, the gentleman and the priest. It was claimed as a right by one class after another in Western and Central Europe and North America; in the end, it was even recognized that the female brain might repay education as well as the male. The progress of science and the spread of schools were accompanied by a great wave of humane feeling, which refused to regard the sufferings of the poor as a necessary evil in a world growing materially richer.

In the main, the Second British Empire may claim to have led the way in the progress of the first seventy years of the nineteenth century. England's triumphs were won under the parliamentary institutions she had created slowly through the centuries. Liberal thinkers in all the countries of Christendom urged their adoption as the obvious panacea for all human ills, and looked forward to the time when they could be given to the "backward" races, which still cherished their old belief in obedience to king or priest. The most dramatic witness to the growing love of freedom came from the United States of America. When parliamentary methods failed to solve the problem of negro slavery, it was settled by a civil war, waged between armies drawn from the same English-speaking stock.

Half a century ago the world seemed destined to become the inheritance of the "white man". His scientific and mechanical progress gave him the promise of enjoying world dominion in ever-growing security and prosperity. There were quarrels between governments and armaments grew; but there seemed no reason why the statesmen controlling the Great Powers should not find a way of adjusting grievances and so preserve the normal prosperous life which their different peoples shared in common. Nationalism and socialism appeared to be the greatest dangers to the existing order. The nineteenth century had seen the submerged nations of the Balkan peninsula win their freedom from Turkish rule, and the scattered parts of Germany and Italy achieve national unity. There were still peoples, such as the Poles, the Irish and the Czechs, who wanted independence. Their aspirations were a threat to the maintenance of peace; but a greater threat came from the rivalry of the nations already free.

Socialism cut across national divisions, and in its advanced form, as Communism, it aimed at uniting the working-classes against capitalist governments, whether monarchical or republican. Both Socialism and Communism were particularly distasteful to emperors and kings, who felt they governed their peoples by divine right, and grudged the concessions they made to their parliaments. There were picturesque survivals in both Europe and Asia; the three Emperors of Germany, Austria and Russia still had something of the romantic glitter and the religious veneration which surrounded the Son of Heaven in China, the Shah in Persia and the Mikado in Japan. The "white" man, under the shelter of parliamentary government, seemed to be moving forward steadily to a fuller life of ordered freedom and material happiness. Liberal thinkers planned hopefully for "the parliament of Man, the federation of the World".

These high hopes were shattered by the ravages of the First World War and the plagues that followed it. Yet to many the League of Nations seemed to be the ideal instrument designed to secure peace for mankind in a world made safe for democracy. But the beaten and the discontented nations, failing to win satisfaction from the League, put their trust in dictators, who promised them the rewards which parliamentary leaders had failed to deliver. The bitter lessons of the war were swiftly forgotten. Nations clung to their traditional ideals and ambitions, and rejected the teaching that "peace is indivisible". In the 1920s thinkers could claim that the dominating feature of the world situation was "a new sanity". In the 1930s they began to talk of mankind perfecting "elaborate methods for its own suicide".

However brightly political thinkers outline a reasoned Utopia, man does not easily forget his irrational past. The past played a vital part in shaping the Second World War. Fascist Italy dreamed of restoring the Roman Empire. Germany remembered the many peoples the German Kaiser had ruled. The long traditions of Christendom fostered distrust of Russia, whose Soviet rulers gave no official recognition to organized Christianity till the war was nearing its close. Japan believed her Mikado was the lineal descendant of the Sun Goddess, and cherished her record of invincibility since she had defied Kublai Khan. Chinese records stretched centuries further back than those of upstart Japan; neither cajolery nor cruelty could force her to accept the leadership of Tokio.

The democratic nations honoured the old conventions of neutrality, signed agreements and formal declaration of war. The totalitarian states believed in ruthless aggression. It paid handsome dividends till 1942. Germany's first year of war and Japan's Hundred Days after Pearl Harbour proved the terrible efficiency of the *blitzkrieg*. When its edge was blunted, the Axis surpassed the ancient horrors inflicted on mankind by Sargon and Esarhaddon, Chenghiz and Timur. To the cruelties of Old Asia modern science added a sharper efficiency in torture. Human beings were used like guinea-pigs for medical experiments. "Useless mouths" disappeared by tens of thousands. When the victorious allies tore Germany apart they found in the concentration camps nauseating proof of the depths to which scientific cruelty could drag humanity. But few of their conquered enemies felt any personal responsibility for what had been done in the name of the totalitarian state.

Resistance to the Axis had been encouraged by visions of "Utopia round the corner". Wonderful results had been promised from the future development of atomic energy. But first of all it was vital to restore an exhausted and impoverished world. Mankind was faced by its earliest problem, how to feed itself. The difficulty was accentuated by the rapid increase in the population, especially in many Asian countries, and the cleavage between the policies of Washington and the Kremlin. The war had left the United States of America incontestably the strongest power the world had ever known. She offered help to devastated countries; but those behind the Iron Curtain rejected it for political reasons. The Cold War froze essential activities. When the "shooting war" enveloped Korea, America and her friends decided they must rearm, if they were to hold their own against Russia, which had never disarmed.

On both sides of the Iron Curtain scientific progress helped to make planning a part of state development. Even in traditionally-minded China the family lost its old importance. Individual initiative crumbled as the "state-servant" relieved parents of the care of children, and parents were controlled by ever-growing masses of regulations enforced by officials armed with ever-growing powers. As their eyes and ears were assaulted by continuous and concentrated publicity, men and women began to accept propaganda as truth. They acquired insensibly the mass-mind, which is the surest support of the totalitarian ruler.

A "brave new world" may bear a race whose disciplined organization exceeds the monotonous efficiency of the ant-heap. But possibly mankind, looking back to the ways of life once preached in the little countries of Greece and Palestine and the wide spaces of India, China and Arabia, will still prize above all the liberty of the mind and the worth of the individual soul.

ACKNOWLEDGMENTS

In producing the Second Edition of this *History of the World* the Editor and the Publishers wish to record again their sincere thanks to all those mentioned in the First Edition. This applies not only to such standard works as the three Cambridge Histories, the *Encyclopaedia Britannica* and the *Dictionary of National Biography*, but to all those friends here and overseas who have helped in the work. Gratitude is also due to the many publishers who have given permission for publication of extracts from works of which they hold the copyright. The Editor owes a particular debt to his old tutors, Sir Charles Oman and H. A. L. Fisher, not only for their written works, but also for their inspiring training.

The changes in Chapter 18 call for no acknowledgments. For Part XIV the authors had continuous recourse to the files of *The Times* and its "Review of the Year", *The Manchester Guardian* and *The Annual Register*. Apart from the Editor's personal obligation to Mr. Philip Graves and Professor Mallowan acknowledgments are also due to Sir R. Storrs and P. Graves, *A Record of the War* (Hamish Hamilton); A. Brady, *Democracy in the Dominions* (University of Toronto Press); W. S. Churchill, *The Second World War* (Cassell); General Eisenhower, *Crusade in Europe* (Heinemann); W. Eberhard, *A History of China* (Routledge and Kegan Paul); S. Labin, *Stalin's Russia* (Gollancz); G. S. Fraser, *News from South America* (Harvill Press); P. Winterton, *Report on Russia* (Cresset Press); A. Moorehead, *The End in Africa*, and *Mediterranean Front* (Hutchinson); E. Crankshaw, *Russia by Daylight* (Michael Joseph); O. B. Van Sprekel, *New China*, and *Three Views* (Turnstile Press). Considerable help has also been derived from G. Stein, *The Challenge of Red China*; E. W. Shanahan, *South America*; A. K. Wu, *China and the Soviet Union* ; and A. Falcomer, *New China, Friend or Foe?* (Naldrett Press).

The quotation from the broadcast after the capitulation of France in 1940 by the Rt. Hon. Winston S. Churchill is included by permission of the author.

War-time difficulties prevented illustrations appearing in the First Edition, They were included in the Norwegian translation, published in Oslo in 1949. For the illustrations in the Second British edition the Editor and the Publishers wish to express their thanks for permission to publish to: The British Museum; the Victoria and Albert Museum; the National Gallery; the Science Museum; the National Maritime Museum, Greenwich; H.M. Stationery Office; Messrs. Forres, Ltd.; Picture Post Library; the British School of Archaeology in Iraq.

Copyright T.152.1R.Q.
Made and printed in Great Britain by Richard Clay & Company, Ltd., Bungay, Suffolk.